# Congress and the Nation

## Volume VII
## 1985-1988

*A Review of Government and Politics*

Congressional Quarterly
Washington, D.C.

# Congressional Quarterly

Congressional Quarterly, an editorial research service and publishing company, serves clients in the fields of news, education, business and government. It combines Congressional Quarterly's specific coverage of Congress, government and politics with the more general subject range of an affiliated service, Editorial Research Reports.

Congressional Quarterly publishes the *Congressional Quarterly Weekly Report* and a variety of books, including college political science textbooks under the CQ Press imprint and public affairs paperbacks on developing issues and events. CQ also publishes information directories and reference books on the federal government, national elections and politics, including the *Guide to the Presidency,* the *Guide to Congress,* the *Guide to the U.S. Supreme Court,* the *Guide to U.S. Elections, Politics in America* and *Congress A to Z: CQ's Ready Reference Encyclopedia.* The *CQ Almanac,* a compendium of legislation for one session of Congress, is published each year. *Congress and the Nation,* a record of government for a presidential term, is published every four years.

CQ publishes the *Congressional Monitor,* a daily report on current and future activities of congressional committees, and several newsletters including *Congressional Insight,* a weekly analysis of congressional action, and *Campaign Practices Reports,* a semimonthly update on campaign laws.

An electronic online information system, Washington Alert, provides immediate access to CQ's databases of legislative action, votes, schedules, profiles and analyses.

Library of Congress Catalog Number: 65-22351

ISBN: 0-87187-532-2
ISSN: 1047-1324

Second Printing

# Editor's Note

*Congress and the Nation Vol. VII* continues a series launched by Congressional Quarterly in 1965 with the publication of *Congress and the Nation Vol. I*, a 2,000-page reference book covering national government and politics from 1945 through 1964. Each of the succeeding volumes has covered governmental action during a four-year presidential term: *Congress and the Nation Vol. II*, 1965-68; *Congress and the Nation Vol. III*, 1969-72; *Congress and the Nation Vol. IV*, 1973-76; *Congress and the Nation Vol. V*, 1977-80; and *Congress and the Nation Vol. VI*, 1981-84.

With the publication of this volume, librarians, historians, political scientists, journalists and students now have seven volumes spanning nearly 45 years of Congressional Quarterly's reporting on public policy.

In compiling *Congress and the Nation Vol. VII*, Congressional Quarterly has condensed its legislative, presidential and political coverage during the 1985-88 period into a 1,200-page volume. Readers are given both an overview of the four-year period and detailed chronologies of governmental action in every major subject area.

This volume chronicles the second, and last, term of Ronald Reagan, one of the most popular presidents to occupy the White House. The Reagan legacy could claim to its credit that the president restored America's self-esteem, brought a new prosperity to its citizens and eased international tensions with a more conciliatory attitude toward the Soviet Union.

It was during Reagan's watch, however, that the federal budget deficits set records, the national debt nearly tripled, the United States was transformed from the world's biggest creditor nation to the world's biggest debtor nation, the trade deficit skyrocketed, the bank and savings and loan industries suffered massive failures and the stock market witnessed its largest one-day fall in history.

Disputes with Congress over aid to the Nicaraguan contras and continued White House frustration with its inability to gain release of American hostages held in Lebanon culminated in a major scandal that rocked the Reagan administration in 1986-87. The Iran-contra affair triggered multiple investigations both within and outside Congress.

Reagan faced a changing political climate in the Soviet Union and a bold new Soviet leader, Mikhail S. Gorbachev. Reagan met several times with Gorbachev and traveled to Moscow to sign a treaty banning intermediate-range nuclear-force (INF) missiles. It was the first treaty to eliminate an entire class of nuclear weapons.

Congress, which followed Reagan's lead during his first term, reasserted itself during his second. Its actions, however, were hamstrung by the huge budget deficits. Cost was a major and persistent consideration to members in debate over policy. Nevertheless, notable legislation was passed, including a tax-overhaul measure, a trade bill, an immigration reform bill and a welfare reform measure.

*Congress and the Nation Vol. VII* is a record of these and other congressional activities — from momentous events to routine extensions of programs. Researchers can find the pertinent facts on issues and legislation; descriptions of proposals and bills; succinct accounts of legislative, executive and lobbying action; key votes; and provisions of legislation.

## How to Use This Book

The **Summary Table of Contents** following this editor's note shows the overall organization of the volume. The detailed **Table of Contents** *(p. ix)* provides an outline of each chapter, as well as a listing of all the stories contained in a particular chapter. For a specific topic within a story, the reader should consult the **Index** *(p. 1145)*. For example, a reader who is interested in congressional action on foreign aid would find in the Table of Contents that there are stories on this issue in the Foreign Policy chapter. A reader who needs more specific information, such as details of executive and legislative action on aid to a specific country or region, could consult the Index and find specific page references under each separate listing of a geographic area.

The first chapter, Politics and National Issues, gives a legislative summary of each session of the 99th and 100th Congresses and a discussion of the 1986 and 1988 elections. The chapter forms a framework for the legislative chapters that follow.

Note the organization of the legislative chapters — Economic Policy, Foreign Policy, Defense Policy, and so on. Each opens with an introduction providing the reader with an overview. That is followed by a chronology of legislative action, divided by Congress, from 1985 through 1988.

The final chapter assesses the Reagan administration and the impact Reagan had on the presidency as an institution.

The **Appendix** *(p. 911)* contains a variety of supplementary material, including Senate and House key votes (identified in boldface in the legislative chapters) during the four-year period, with charts showing how each member voted; a glossary of congressional terms and an explanation of how a bill becomes law; lists of committee and subcommittee chairmen; biographical data on members of Congress in 1985-88; profiles of Cabinet members and other senior officials; controversial nominations; presidential vetoes; major presidential speeches and messages to Congress; and political charts, including presidential election returns for 1984 and 1988 and House, Senate and gubernatorial election returns for 1986 and 1988.

Colleen McGuiness
February 1990

# Summary Table of Contents

# Table of Contents

## Chapter 1 — Politics and National Issues

## Chapter 2 — Economic Policy

# Chapter 3 — Trade Policy

# Chapter 4 — Foreign Policy

# Chapter 5 — Defense Policy

# Chapter 6 — Transportation and Commerce

# Chapter 7 — Energy and Environment

# Chapter 8 — Agricultural Policy

# Chapter 9 — Health and Human Services

# Chapter 10 — Education Policy

# Chapter 11 — Housing and Urban Aid

# Chapter 12 — Labor and Pension Policy

## Introduction ...................... 687

# Chapter 13 — Law and Justice

## Law and Law Enforcement

### Introduction ...................... 713

## The Supreme Court

### Introduction ...................... 785

# Chapter 14 — General Government

# Chapter 15 — Inside Congress

# Chapter 16 — The Reagan Presidency

# Appendix

## Key Votes

## Congress and Its Members

## The Presidency

## Political Charts

technologies and other practice-pattern changes.

● Required the secretary to establish separate methods for making payments to urban and rural hospitals for so-called "outliers"; cases that were far more expensive to treat than most others within that DRG.

● Changed the formula by which hospital payments were calculated to reflect the average cost per patient, instead of the average cost per hospital.

● Extended a program that paid certain rural and suburban "regional referral centers" at (higher) urban rates for three years, and stipulated that existing regional referral centers continue receiving the urban rate. The bill also created new criteria for hospitals to qualify as regional referral centers.

● Reduced payments for capital-related costs (construction and equipment, for example) by 3.5 percent for fiscal 1987, by 7 percent for fiscal 1988 and by 10 percent for fiscal 1989. Hospitals that were the sole providers for their communities were exempted from the reductions. The HHS secretary was authorized, in the absence of further congressional action, to incorporate capital costs into the prospective payment system beginning Oct. 1, 1987, but only if the total capital payments would have been the same as under the existing system.

● Required that hospitals in Puerto Rico be included in the prospective payment system beginning Oct. 1, 1987.

● Required the HHS secretary, within two years, to submit to Congress proposed legislation to refine the prospective payment system to take into account severity of illness and case complexity.

● Required hospitals serving Medicare patients, as a condition of eligibility, to provide patients with a written notice of their right to appeal what they considered a premature discharge from the hospital. Hospitals also were required to have in place a discharge planning program to help ensure that Medicare patients received appropriate and needed care after leaving the hospital.

● Extended the so-called "waiver of liability" under Medicare to hospices and home health services providing homebound and intermittent care. The waiver allowed non-hospital health agencies to be reimbursed by Medicare for non-covered services if the providers reasonably thought they were providing covered services.

● Established a new category for rural hospitals to qualify for increased PPS payments if they served a "disproportionate share" of low-income patients and extended for one year, until Oct. 1, 1989, disproportionate-share payments to qualifying hospitals. The payments were to end Oct. 1, 1988.

● Changed the method of payments for hospital outpatient departments for ambulatory surgical procedures.

● **Periodic Payments.** Discontinued the Periodic Interim Payment (PIP) system for PPS hospitals, except those serving rural areas or a high proportion of low-income patients. PIP allowed hospitals to receive biweekly payments based not on actual claims submitted, but on the average of all claims over a full year. At the end of the year, payments and claims were reconciled.

The measure also required that hospitals and physicians receive payment on 95 percent of their "clean" claims (those requiring no further information or documentation) within 30 calendar days in fiscal 1988, 25 days in fiscal 1989 and 24 days in fiscal 1990 and thereafter.

HHS also was required to pay so-called "participating physicians" (those who accepted Medicare payments as full fees for services) on 95 percent of their clean claims within

19 days in fiscal 1988, 18 days in fiscal 1989 and 17 days in fiscal 1990 and thereafter.

● **HMOs and CMPs.** Required HMOs and competitive medical plans (CMPs) to provide their Medicare beneficiaries with an annual explanation of their rights to services under the plan.

HMOs and CMPs provided all medical services for a single monthly fee, instead of charging for each service provided. Medicare beneficiaries were allowed to disenroll from an HMO or CMP at any local Social Security office, and civil penalties of up to $10,000 were imposed for HMOs that "fail substantially" to provide necessary services to Medicare patients.

● **Hospital Stay Incentives.** Prohibited hospitals from making incentive payments to physicians for shortening hospital stays or otherwise reducing services to Medicare (or Medicaid) beneficiaries. HMOs and CMPs also were prohibited from making such payments beginning April 1, 1989.

● **Graduate Medical Training.** Clarified circumstances under which hospitals could be reimbursed under Medicare for the costs of graduate medical training when medical residents performed duties outside a hospital setting.

● **Home Health Providers.** Required that Medicare calculate what it would pay providers of home health services on an aggregate basis for all services instead of on a discipline-specific (skilled nurse or physical therapist, for example) basis.

● **Effectiveness Study.** Required the HHS secretary to provide for a research program on patient outcomes of selected medical treatments and surgical procedures, to assess their appropriateness, necessity and effectiveness, and authorized $21 million for the study for fiscal 1987-89.

● **Organ Donation.** Required hospitals, as a condition for participation in the Medicare and Medicaid programs, to establish procedures for encouraging the donation of organs and tissue. Such procedures had to include "routine requests" for donations from a deceased person's next of kin, and notifying the local organ procurement agency when a potential organ donor was identified.

Hospitals performing organ transplants were required to be members of the national organ transplant network established under the National Organ Transplant Act of 1984 (PL 98-507). Organ procurement agencies were required to meet certain criteria to be eligible to receive Medicare or Medicaid reimbursement for the costs of organ procurement. (*Organ transplants, p. 558*)

● **Disabled Persons.** Made Medicare the secondary payer for disabled persons who elected to be covered by employer-based health insurance of an employer with 100 or more employees. This provision was scheduled to terminate in 1991.

● **Nurse-Anesthetists.** Extended through Oct. 1, 1988, procedures by which hospitals were reimbursed for the costs of nurse-anesthetists on staff, and authorized direct reimbursement for anesthesia services and related care furnished by a nurse-anesthetist who was legally authorized to perform such services. Required nurse-anesthetists to accept Medicare reimbursement as payment in full and provided civil penalties for violations.

● **Physician Payments.** Granted to all physicians a 3.2 percent increase in prevailing charges effective Jan. 1, 1987. The amount equaled the medical inflation rate for physician services as determined by the Medicare Economic Index (MEI).

The measure stipulated that in future years all physicians were to receive increases equal to the percentage increase in the MEI, and made permanent the existing 4.15 percent differential between payments participating physicians received over non-participating physicians.

The HHS secretary was prohibited from changing the way the MEI was calculated until completion of a study to ensure that the index reflected medical economic changes in a fair and equitable way.

● **Cataract Surgery.** Required participating and non-participating cataract surgeons to reduce their charges by 10 percent, effective Jan. 1, 1987, and by an additional 2 percent, effective Jan. 1, 1988. Non-participating physicians were not permitted to make up the reduction by charging patients more, with civil penalties for violators. The HHS secretary was required to reduce payments for cataract surgery anesthesia.

● **Kidney Dialysis.** Required the HHS secretary to reduce the per-treatment rate for facilities providing kidney dialysis services to Medicare patients in the End Stage Renal Disease (ESRD) program by $2, effective Oct. 1, 1986. The rate could not be altered for two years.

Medicare was authorized to pay for up to one year of immunosuppressive drugs, which helped prevent rejection of transplanted organs. The HHS secretary was required to impose standards and conditions under which Medicare would make payments to ESRD facilities that reused dialysis filters. *(Immunosuppressive drugs, p. 558)*

● Required the HHS secretary to consolidate the existing 32 ESRD networks, charged with ensuring quality of care for ESRD patients, into 17 networks. Increased the role and responsibilities of the networks, including requiring that networks set up grievance procedures for ESRD patients, conduct on-site review of ESRD facilities and gather and analyze data. Stipulated that the networks' activities be funded by reducing the per-treatment payment to facilities by 50 cents.

● **Vision Care.** Authorized Medicare to pay for optometrist services if the services were among those for which Medicare would pay if performed by a physician and if the optometrist was licensed to provide such services.

● **Occupational Therapy.** Extended Medicare Part B coverage of occupational therapy services to include those provided in nursing homes (when Part A Medicare coverage had lapsed), clinics, rehabilitation agencies and other locations. The measure extended coverage, on a different reimbursement basis, to services performed in a therapist's office or the patient's home, if a physician had certified the need for such services.

● **Physician Assistants.** Authorized Medicare coverage of services performed by physician assistants under the supervision of a physician in hospitals, nursing homes or as an assistant at surgery.

● **Claim Appeals.** Permitted Medicare beneficiaries who were dissatisfied with reimbursement of claims submitted under Part B of Medicare to obtain a hearing by an administrative-law judge if the amount in controversy was $500 or more, and judicial review if the amount was more than $1,000. Stipulated that national coverage determinations could not be overturned solely on the basis of not having met the notice and comment requirements under the Administrative Procedures Act.

● **Alzheimer's Disease.** Required the HHS secretary to conduct up to 10 demonstration projects to determine the effectiveness, cost and impact of providing comprehensive services to Medicare beneficiaries with Alzheimer's disease. Services could include home- and community-based services, outpatient drug therapy, respite care, mental health services and supportive services and counseling for family members. The measure limited spending for the projects to $40 million over three years.

● **PROs.** Expanded the role of peer review organizations (PROs) in ensuring that Medicare beneficiaries received quality medical care and required a consumer representative to be placed on each PRO governing board. PROs were required to share certain confidential information with state licensing boards and national accreditation organizations.

● **Continued Health Insurance.** Amended the continuing access to health insurance provisions instituted in the fiscal 1986 reconciliation law (PL 99-272) to require that any retiree or dependent who lost employer-based health insurance coverage because the employer filed for Chapter 11 bankruptcy would be entitled to remain in the employer's health insurance plan by paying up to 102 percent of the applicable premium. The retiree, his or her spouse and dependent children were allowed to remain in the plan until the retiree's death, with the spouse and children allowed to continue for three years following such death.

## Pensions

● **Retirement Age Limits.** Prevented employers from cutting off an employee's right to continue accruing pension rights simply because he had reached the normal retirement age under his pension plan, usually age 65. Under the new law, if an employee needed to work 30 years before getting a full pension but reached the age of 65 after only 27 years of work, his pension rights could continue to accrue so long as he continued to work after age 65.

Under existing law, an employer could cut off the worker's pension rights simply because he reached retirement age, even though he was still working.

Anticipated savings to the government of at least $1 million would result because employees remaining in the work force after age 65 would be less likely to draw Social Security benefits and would continue to pay income tax on earnings.

## Revenues

● **Conrail Tax Treatment.** Stipulated the tax treatment of the sale of the government's 85 percent share of Conrail. Conrail was to be treated as a new corporation that purchased its assets the day after the public sale. No carryover of net operating losses or other benefits, such as unused investment tax credits, was to be allowed for tax purposes. *(Conrail sale, p. 359)*

With one major exception, the public sales price was to be allocated among all of Conrail's assets, both depreciable assets, such as equipment and buildings, and non-depreciable assets, such as land. After the sale, Conrail's depreciable assets were expected to be worth considerably less than before the sale. As a result, Conrail was likely to suffer a loss in its tax deductions for depreciation.

The sales price was not to be allocated among Conrail's existing assets — its inventory and accounts receivable. Without this exemption, Conrail conceivably would have had to pay taxes on the difference between the existing value of its accounts receivable — the money owed to it for transportation services — and its reduced value after the sale.

● **Customs Fee.** Imposed a fee on the value of commercial merchandise imports of 0.22 percent, beginning Dec. 1, 1986. The fee was to go into a fund to pay for the costs of U.S. Customs Service commercial activities.

The fee was to decrease to 0.17 percent in fiscal 1988, and expire after fiscal 1989. The fee could be reduced below 0.17 percent if it would otherwise raise more than needed to pay for the commercial activities of the U.S. Customs Service.

Exempted from the fee were Schedule 8 imports (those not otherwise subject to duty) and products of least-developed countries, U.S. insular possessions and countries included in the Caribbean Basin Initiative.

Fees could be lowered for small airports where existing user fees already supported the entire cost of customs activities.

● Authorized fiscal 1987 appropriations for the U.S. Customs Service of $1.0 billion.

● **Tax Collections.** Increased the penalty for employers and other taxpayers who failed to make timely deposits of withheld Social Security, income or other taxes from the existing 5 percent of the amount of under-deposit to 10 percent. The provision applied to penalties assessed after the date of enactment.

● Increased the penalty for substantial understatement of income tax liability on tax returns from the existing 10 percent of the amount understated to 25 percent. The provision applied to penalties assessed after the date of enactment. (The 1986 tax-overhaul bill had increased the penalty to 20 percent, but the need for revenue prompted Congress to increase it even further.)

● Increased the frequency with which state and local governments had to make deposits of Social Security tax contributions by putting them on the same footing as private businesses.

● Relieved state governments from responsibility for collecting Social Security contributions from local governments.

● Speeded up collection of excise taxes on beer, wine, distilled spirits and tobacco.

● **Foreign Tax Credits.** Denied tax credits usually given to companies for taxes paid to foreign governments if the other country was designated by the secretary of state as one that supported terrorism or was one with which the United States did not have diplomatic relations. Such taxes could be counted as deductions, however.

● **Oil-Spill Liability.** Established procedures to collect funds for a new oil-spill liability trust fund, to pay for the costs of cleaning up offshore oil spills. The fund was to be financed by a tax of 1.3 cents per barrel on domestic crude oil and imported petroleum products. It was not to become effective, however, unless separate authorizing legislation was enacted by Sept. 1, 1987.

Both chambers passed enacting legislation (S 2799, HR 2005), the House as part of its "superfund" toxic waste cleanup bill. But differences centering on whether federal law on oil-spill liability should pre-empt state laws could not be resolved before adjournment, and the provisions died. *(Oil-spill liability, p. 421)*

The fund provisionally established in the reconciliation bill was to have a limit of $300 million. No more than $500 million could be paid for any single incident; if more than $300 million had to be paid, the fund could borrow from the general Treasury.

● **Tax Bill Changes.** Provided a "transition rule" for a Des Moines, Iowa, trucking company permitting it to take a 10 percent investment tax credit on purchases of new equipment, even though the company did not meet the requirement of the new tax law (PL 99-514) of having had a binding contract to make such purchases as of Jan. 1, 1986. The provision was similar to those given to scores of other companies in the tax bill. *(Tax bill, p. 79)*

● Expanded, for rural low-income housing, protection from the full effects of the new tax law on real estate tax shelters for those who had multi-year commitments to invest in such shelters in rural areas.

Under the new tax law, investors still were permitted to take deductions for their paper losses in such shelters provided they had made the investment commitment before Aug. 16, 1986, the date of the conference agreement on the tax bill, and providing they still owed 50 percent or more of the total they had agreed to invest. Under the reconciliation bill provision, the 50 percent requirement was reduced to 35 percent for some rural housing funded in part by the Farmers Home Administration.

● Liberalized the rule in the new tax law under which investors in low-income housing projects could claim credit for investing in such projects even if they were using borrowed funds. Under the provision, if the loan was made by a disinterested third party, such as a bank, instead of by the developer of the housing project, it would qualify as money the investor had "at risk" and thus would become part of the basis for the credit.

## Social Security

● **Cost-of-Living Increases.** Eliminated the 3 percent trigger for Social Security COLAs. Previously, COLAs were not provided in years following one in which the Consumer Price Index rose by less than 3 percent. Under the new law, COLAs would be provided in any year in which inflation was greater than zero.

Eliminating the trigger for Social Security COLAs also eliminated it for several programs tied by law to the Social Security increase, including insurance premiums under Part B of Medicare, railroad retirement, Supplemental Security Income and veterans' pension benefits, and eligibility standards for Medicaid, food stamps, housing assistance and AFDC.

## Transportation

● **Conrail.** Required the transportation secretary, in consultation with the Treasury secretary and chairman of the board of Conrail, within 30 days after enactment, to retain the services of investment bankers to manage the sale to the public of the federal government's 85 percent share of the Conrail freight railroad.

● Directed the transportation secretary to choose four to six investment banking firms as "co-lead managers" of the public offering. One was to be designated to coordinate and administer the offering, but all had to be compensated equally. Selection criteria had to include a firm's financial strength, knowledge of the railroad industry and past contributions in promoting the long-term viability of Conrail. Firms not in existence before Sept. 1, 1986, were ineligible, and fees were to be paid from the proceeds of the stock sale.

● Required an opportunity for minority-owned or -controlled firms to participate in the stock sale.

● Permitted the General Accounting Office to audit the accounts of Conrail and the co-lead managers.

● Required Conrail to make a $200 million cash payment to the federal government, within 30 days after enactment. An additional $100 million payment could be required by the transportation secretary, taking into account Conrail's long-term viability.

● Canceled, in consideration for the $200 million cash payment, Conrail's debts to the federal government.

● Directed Conrail to file with the Securities and Exchange Commission (SEC) a registration statement with respect to the securities to be offered. The transportation secretary could require Conrail to declare a stock split before the filing.

● Directed the transportation secretary to schedule a public offering after the registration statement was declared effective. The transportation secretary, in consultation with the Treasury secretary, Conrail's chairman of the board and the investment bankers, could decide to conduct the sale in stages.

● Required a finding by the transportation secretary, before proceeding with the sale, that the gross proceeds would be "an adequate amount." A $2 billion non-binding goal was set. The secretary's finding was not subject to judicial or administrative review.

● Required Conrail to make minimum capital expenditures of the greater of its financial depreciation or $500 million in each fiscal year over a five-year period following enactment. However, expenditures could be reduced to an average of $350 million per year by Conrail's board of directors.

● Barred dividend payments if Conrail was out of compliance with the capital expenditure requirement. After such payments Conrail also had to have on hand $400 million in cash. Subject to certain restrictions, Conrail could borrow to meet the minimum cash-balance requirement. Common stock dividends could not exceed 45 percent of cumulative net income less the cumulative amount of any preferred stock dividends.

● Required Conrail over the five-year period following enactment to continue its existing affirmative action and minority vendor programs; to continue to offer to sell lines that the Interstate Commerce Commission (ICC) had approved for abandonment for 75 percent of net liquidation value; not to permit deferral of normal and prudent maintenance on its properties; and not to permit a takeover of all or any substantial part of its assets.

● Required annual certification by Conrail of compliance with all five-year covenants, except for the dividend covenant, for which certification had to be provided to the transportation secretary after the declaration of any payments.

● Authorized the transportation secretary to bring legal actions against Conrail or others to require compliance with the five-year covenants and ownership limitations.

● Prohibited ownership of more than 10 percent of Conrail's voting stock over a three-year period beginning on the sale date by anyone except for the employee stock ownership plan, the transportation secretary, a railroad or certain others.

● Limited major railroads to ownership of 10 percent of voting stock for one year beginning on the sale date. No merger applications could be filed with the ICC during this period. Except if a merger application was approved, railroad stock had to be voted during the three years after a sale in the same proportion as all other common stock.

● Provided for the transition from Conrail's existing board of directors to a board elected by Conrail's public shareholders. After the initial sale date, one director was to be elected by shareholders for each 12.5 percent increment of the government's share of Conrail that had been sold. Interim arrangements were provided for in the event that less than 50 percent of the corporation had been sold by June 1, 1987.

● Required Conrail to assume financial liability for the existing supplemental unemployment benefits plan, which had been federally funded, until the sale date.

● Required Conrail to provide labor protection to its employees after the sale date, pursuant to a previous agreement with union representatives of the workers. The federal government would have no liability for benefits due workers.

● Directed Conrail to pay $200 million to present and former workers in compensation for deferred wages.

● Provided for the distribution of the 15 percent of Conrail stock vested in the employee stock ownership plan to participants and beneficiaries. Individual shares in the plan could not be sold for at least 180 days from the date on which 100 percent of the federal government's shares were sold.

● Abolished the United States Railway Association, effective April 1, 1987. Congress created the association, a government corporation, in 1973 to finance and monitor Conrail.

● Provided that the Regional Rail Reorganization Act of 1973 should not apply to Conrail after the sale date, with certain exceptions. For example, existing law was retained requiring Conrail to keep its headquarters in Philadelphia. (*Congress and the Nation Vol. IV, p. 513*)

● Exempted Conrail's directors and others from lawsuits by stockholders, employees and others, with certain exceptions. For example, a director would not be exempted if he made a false statement on the registration form filed with the SEC.

● Protected the federal government from any and all liabilities resulting from the implementation of Conrail sale legislation, except for actions brought to require the transportation secretary to proceed with a public offering.

● **Rail Competition.** Required greater public disclosure of the terms of rail contracts between shippers of agricultural goods and rail carriers. The provision was intended to make it easier for small shippers to receive the same favorable contract terms as large shippers.

● Confirmed the legal authority of the ICC to issue a rule to require compensation by major railroads to small railroads for the use of the latter's boxcars.

## Welfare

● **Eligibility.** Eliminated the requirement that states use income and eligibility verification systems to check the eligibility of all recipients of public assistance in an effort to make better use of limited resources and make the system more productive.

● **AFDC.** Restored, for fiscal 1987 only, the biennial calculation of the federal share of Aid to Families with Dependent Children benefits for the 13 states that lost funds as a result of a shift to an annual calculation mandated by fiscal 1986 reconciliation law (PL 99-272).

● **Child Support.** Required states that participated in the federal child support enforcement program to change their laws to bar retroactive changes in child support court orders and provide that child support payments be modified only from the date that notice was given by the parent desiring the change to the other parent.

# Appropriations, Fiscal 1987

Congress on Oct. 17, 1986, gave final approval to the conference agreement on a half-trillion-dollar continuing appropriations resolution for fiscal 1987. The measure (H J Res 738 — PL 99-591) funded about half the government; the remainder was sustained by permanent appropriations bills. The resolution combined all 13 regular annual appropriations bills, none of which had been enacted by the start of the fiscal year Oct. 1. Four successive stopgap funding measures kept the government going as Congress struggled with the yearlong bill.

The trend toward huge, comprehensive continuing appropriations bills was an unhappy one for many members of Congress. The unpopularity of H J Res 738 was reflected in the narrow **201-200 (R 15-157; D 186-43) key vote** by which it passed the House. *(1986 key votes, p. 949)*

H J Res 738 appropriated $575.9 billion in fiscal 1987 budget authority, the amount that could be obligated under programs and activities covered in the bill. That, according to estimates at the time of enactment, would yield $560 billion in outlays. It was the largest spending bill in the nation's history.

The comprehensive measure departed significantly from President Reagan's budget priorities, giving $30 billion less to defense and $2 billion less to foreign aid than he had requested and more to the domestic side of the ledger.

Early in the 100th Congress, lawmakers approved a supplemental appropriations bill (HR 1827 — PL 100-71) providing an additional $9.4 billion for fiscal 1987, including $5.6 billion for several farm programs. The bill cleared July 1, 1987, after House Democrats agreed to drop arms control provisions that could have provoked a presidential veto.

# Other Legislation

## Line-Item Veto

Despite a personal lobbying campaign by President Reagan, a filibuster blocked Senate floor consideration in 1985 of a bill (S 43) that would give the president authority to veto spending for individual programs in appropriations bills. Under existing procedures enumerated in the Constitution, a president had to veto an entire appropriations bill, sometimes containing hundreds of funding items, to block spending for an individual program.

Sponsor Mack Mattingly, R-Ga., said the line-item veto power was needed to bring government spending under control. His bill would be similar in effect to a constitutional amendment Reagan had requested in 1984. *(Congress and the Nation Vol. VI, p. 52)*

S 43 was opposed by most Democrats and several moderate Republicans who charged it would have only a limited effect on federal spending and would result in an unnecessary and dangerous shift of power from Congress to the president.

The bill was reported unfavorably (S Rept 99-92) by the Senate Rules Committee June 27, 1985. Opponents, led by Senate Appropriations Committee Chairman Mark O. Hatfield, R-Ore., refused to let the Senate vote on a motion to bring the bill to the floor. During a weeklong filibuster, the Senate voted three times on motions to invoke cloture — a procedure to shut off debate. The bill was withdrawn after the third cloture motion failed July 24 on a **key vote of 58-40 (R 46-7; D 12-33)**. *(1985 key votes, p. 933)*

## Balanced Budget Amendment

A proposed constitutional amendment to require a balanced federal budget failed in the Senate by a single vote in 1986. The Senate killed the measure (S J Res 225) March 25 on a **key vote of 66-34 (R 43-10; D 23-24)** — one short of the two-thirds majority required. *(1986 key votes, p. 949)*

The proposal was a compromise version of resolutions reported by the Senate Judiciary Committee in 1985 (S J Res 225 — S Rept 99-163; S J Res 13 — S Rept 99-162). It would require a balanced budget unless three-fifths of the House and Senate agreed to deficit spending or in case of a declared war. A tax hike would be allowed to balance the budget if a majority of both houses agreed to the increase.

President Reagan had long championed a balanced budget constitutional amendment that would restrict Congress' ability to raise taxes to avoid deficit spending. An amendment of this type was approved by the Senate in 1982 but was rejected by the House. *(Congress and the Nation Vol. VI, p. 52)*

The Constitution provides two amendment procedures, only one of which had ever been used. That procedure permitted Congress to propose amendments to the Constitution by a two-thirds majority vote in each chamber. Under the untried alternative procedure, Congress had to call a constitutional convention to consider an amendment if two-thirds of the states (34) request one. In either case, proposed constitutional amendments would take effect only if ratified by three-fourths (38) of the states.

By 1984, 32 states had called on Congress to assemble a constitutional convention to consider a balanced budget amendment. The convention drive stalled, however, and pressure for congressional action eased following enactment of the Gramm-Rudman anti-deficit law in 1985. *(Gramm-Rudman, p. 44)*

## President's Deferral Authority

The Reagan administration and Congress clashed in 1986 over a White House decision to defer the spending of some $5 billion in appropriated fiscal 1986 funds. The deferrals, or spending delays, became controversial because they imposed funding freezes or cuts that President Reagan had proposed a year earlier and that Congress had rejected. The controversy centered principally on cuts in housing and community development programs.

Congress overturned the deferrals — forcing the administration to spend the money — in a fiscal 1986 supplemental appropriations bill (HR 4515 — PL 99-349) cleared June 26.

The U.S. Court of Appeals for the District of Columbia on Jan. 20, 1987, upheld a lower court ruling that Reagan had been wrong to defer the spending. The three-judge panel held unanimously that the president could not halt spending of appropriated funds for policy reasons. The ruling left intact presidential authority to delay appropriated funds for routine management reasons, such as unanticipated delays in federal construction projects.

# 1987-88

The 100th Congress saw the most dramatic budget action since President Reagan's first year in office, when he was able to use a Republican majority in the Senate and a infusion of conservative Democrats to enact his agenda of tax cuts, defense spending increases and domestic spending cuts.

Since that first year, however, most congressional-presidential budget talks had failed to secure significant compromises.

Two things made a difference in 1987 and 1988. First, Democrats regained control of the Senate and pressed their plans to force a tax increase to aid the cause of deficit reduction. Second, the stock market took a severe tumble in October 1987, as budget negotiations were again failing.

The upshot of the crash was a White House-congressional budget "summit" that yielded a two-year budget agreement and more than $75 billion in reductions in the deficit. A sidelight was the fact that 1988 was the least controversial budget year of the Reagan presidency, since most of the decisions had been made the previous year. *(Stock market crash, p. 28; budget summit, p. 33)*

## Fiscal 1988 Budget

Congress' consideration of the fiscal 1988 budget resolution was a typical partisan exercise. Each party had a political strategy for the annual budget fight: The Democrats wanted to force President Reagan into negotiations they hoped would lead to a tax increase or a cut in defense spending or both; the GOP wanted Democrats to take full responsibility for a spending plan they hoped to convince voters was extravagant.

By year's end, a budget "summit" meeting had occurred, producing a deficit reduction agreement that superseded the congressional budget resolution and set spending and revenue limits for fiscal years 1988 and 1989. But some congressional Democrats were upset that it neither raised taxes as much as the budget resolution would have allowed nor cut defense spending as deeply.

The budget resolution (H Con Res 93) won final approval June 24, 1987, when the Senate voted 53-46 to accept the conference report (H Rept 100-175). The House had approved it, 215-201, on the previous day.

The final plan recommended a fiscal 1988 tax increase of $19.3 billion and $23 billion in three-year cuts from anticipated increases in spending. The chairman of the Senate Budget Committee, Lawton Chiles, D-Fla., said that the budget called for an increase in overall federal spending in fiscal 1988 of 0.3 percent, after the effects of inflation and growth in programs — such as Social Security — which resulted in more people becoming eligible for benefits, were factored out. The fiscal 1987 budget had promised a 1.1 percent growth rate. *(Fiscal 1987 budget, p. 47)*

The budget contained a novel provision that made the level of fiscal 1988 military spending contingent on Reagan's approval of a $64.3 billion, three-year tax increase. Very few observers thought he would reverse his longstanding opposition to new taxes. Nevertheless, the stipulation was that if the tax increase were enacted, military expendi-

tures would be increased enough to offset inflation; if not, they would be frozen at current spending levels.

In the House, three Republicans voted for the measure and 34 Democrats, from the most liberal and conservative ranks of the party, voted against it. Liberals thought that too much of the tax increase would be consumed by defense spending; conservatives said military spending would be too low and tax and domestic spending levels would be excessive.

Three Northeastern Senate Republicans voted for the measure. Two conservative Southern Democrats joined Republicans in voting against it, as did Wisconsin Democrat William Proxmire.

The resolution was designed to result in a budget deficit for fiscal 1988 of $133.9 billion, down from what would have been an estimated $171 billion with no changes in tax and spending policy. However, a technical maneuver enabled both Congress and the president to meet in their respective budgets the $108 billion deficit target mandated by the 1985 Gramm-Rudman-Hollings deficit reduction law.

The resolution, which did not need the president's signature, established spending ceilings for some 20 broad categories of government activity. It also set out minimum revenue requirements and the total federal debt limit for the upcoming fiscal year. The resolution itself did not make the changes in law that would yield budgetary savings assumed in the spending and revenue totals. That was to be done using other legislative vehicles: a budget reconciliation measure that made changes in authorizing laws and appropriation bills that were supposed to conform to spending limits derived from the resolution. *(Fiscal 1988 reconciliation, p. 61; appropriations, p. 66)*

### President's Proposals

In what was a familiar ritual, Reagan Jan. 5 sent Congress a budget that helped the military, harnessed the bureaucracy, held the line on taxes and put Congress in the hot seat. *(Budget message, p. 1079)*

The president's budget met the requirements of Gramm-Rudman, which directed the president to submit his budget a month earlier than usual, with a fiscal 1988 deficit no greater than $108 billion.

The 1988 Reagan budget called for a deficit of $107.8 billion, based on outlays (money actually spent, as opposed to legally obligated) of $1.02 trillion and revenues of $916.6 billion. New spending authority was $1.14 trillion, 6.4 percent greater than fiscal 1987.

The fiscal 1988 deficit targeted in the president's budget was less than half the record $221.2 billion posted in fiscal 1986, which ended Sept. 30, 1986.

The centerpiece of the president's budget was a $42.4 billion deficit reduction program, divided roughly equally between spending cuts and revenue increases.

Most of the spending reductions were vintage Reagan proposals to slash or eliminate domestic programs that dated back to Lyndon B. Johnson's Great Society or even to Franklin D. Roosevelt's New Deal.

According to the Senate Budget Committee, the budget proposed terminating 46 federal programs. Further, the budget sharply reduced federal support of education, mass transit, community development, public housing and agriculture.

On the revenue side, Reagan was careful to avoid anything that sounded like a general tax increase, although

Treasury Secretary James A. Baker III conceded that $6.1 billion could be described as additional taxes. The bulk of new revenues was to come from sales of government assets such as Amtrak, oil reserves and loan portfolios and from fees for government loans and services.

Reagan asked for the smallest increase in defense spending of his presidency, 3 percent in addition to inflation. New defense spending authority of $312 billion still constituted 27 percent of his budget.

Another major category, Social Security, was unchanged by the president's budget. It accounted for 21 percent of federal spending.

While the budget focused on the 41 percent of federal spending that was governed by annual congressional action, it did not steer entirely clear of "entitlements" — ongoing programs whose spending was determined by the level of participation.

The president proposed to save approximately $10 billion from revisions in Medicare, Medicaid, and student-loan and agriculture programs. But few specifics were new. The health proposals, which would have saved $7.2 billion in fiscal 1986, would compound to $65.8 billion through fiscal 1992, according to the Office of Management and Budget (OMB).

## Budget Resolution

Reaction in Congress to Reagan's budget request, while generally negative, was muted in comparison with prior years. This was traced to several factors: the familiarity of the proposals, submission of the budget even before Congress convened and the overhanging shadow of the Iran-contra affair. *(Iran-contra, p. 253)*

This muted response also showed how difficult it was for Congress to produce its own plan. Defense, for instance, had in the past presented a fat target in Reagan budgets, but in the fiscal 1988 budget, a freeze in military spending was expected to save only about $9 billion.

And even if Congress ignored many specifics of the budget, its overall numbers and its line-by-line totals for most agencies set the parameters for federal spending.

Congressional Democrats, who controlled both the House and Senate for the first time since 1981, decided early in the year they would attempt to beat an April 15 Gramm-Rudman deadline for completion of budget resolutions by both chambers.

Aides and members said that the chairmen of the Budget committees — Sen. Chiles and Rep. William H. Gray III, D-Pa. — would try to work out a broad budget that could pass in both chambers, with a few issues to be ironed out in a conference. Speaker Jim Wright, D-Texas, and Senate Majority Leader Robert C. Byrd, D-W.Va., would play a major hand in crafting the budget, they said.

And Budget panel members hoped for high-level discussions with the White House to consider revenue and defense compromises, even though administration officials were wary of a summit meeting where the word "taxes" would even be mentioned.

**House Action.** The House Budget Committee on April 1, by a 21-14 party-line vote, approved a budget resolution (H Con Res 95 — H Rept 100-41) for fiscal 1988 that called for $21.9 billion in new revenues and $8.8 billion in what Gray termed "real, permanent substantial reductions" in domestic spending compared with current levels.

The House Democrats' resolution would hold defense spending to $288.7 billion, compared with Reagan's $312

billion request. That meant about $2.1 billion more in actual expenditures — outlays — than in fiscal 1987, but not enough to offset inflation, according to Pentagon officials.

The Democratic measure also allotted $1.45 billion in new fiscal 1988 spending to combat AIDS (acquired immune deficiency syndrome), overhaul welfare, enhance U.S. trade, start catastrophic medical insurance for the elderly and improve long-term care for the aged poor, and assist impoverished children and the homeless.

By using Reagan's economic assumptions, the House resolution claimed a fiscal 1988 deficit of $107.6 billion, less than the $108 billion target set by the Gramm-Rudman-Hollings anti-deficit law and less than the administration budget's deficit of $107.8 billion.

Republicans on the House Budget Committee complained strenuously that they were shut out of the budget process and given no information about the resolution on which they were to vote. Gray declared that GOP members dealt themselves out when they rejected his earlier invitations to join budget negotiations.

House Democrats adopted the committee version of the budget resolution April 9 on a **key vote of 230-192 (R 0-173; D 230-19)**. *(1987 key votes, p. 965)*

Though no Republicans voted for the Democrats' budget, few GOP members chose instead to vote for either Reagan's budget or one put together by conservative Republican Rep. William E. Dannemeyer of California. By large margins, the House rejected these two budgets and a third formulated by the Congressional Black Caucus.

The House debate demonstrated the Democrats' determination to portray a tax increase as fiscally responsible and the Republicans as fiscal cowards.

"When the going gets tough, the Republicans quit," scoffed liberal Barney Frank, D-Mass. Democrats cheered when conservative colleague Marvin Leath of Texas declared, "I don't like this budget," but added that compromise, and shouldering the imperfections of compromise, was better than inaction.

The vote in the House was to accept the committee resolution as a substitute for a "sequester" budget (H Con Res 93) requiring 20 percent reductions from fiscal 1987 levels in military programs and 14 percent cuts in non-defense programs. Sequester was the technical term for the across-the-board spending cuts under Gramm-Rudman.

Budget Chairman Gray put this stark budget before the House because Gramm-Rudman-Hollings would require spending cuts of about that size to reach its fiscal 1988 deficit target of $108 billion if Congress did not reduce the deficit by legislative means.

Gray said members should have to vote on these cuts if they rejected all other budgets put before them.

There was no vote on the sequester budget because, after accepting the committee resolution as a substitute, the House adopted the amended H Con Res 93 by voice vote.

**Senate Action.** The Senate Budget Committee agreed April 8, on a 13-11 vote, to report a fiscal 1988 budget resolution (S Con Res 48 — S Rept 100-40) that matched new taxes with reductions in spending growth, divided between defense and non-military accounts. As in the House version, the new taxes were to go into a special deficit reduction reserve fund.

When it approved the plan proposed by Senate Budget Chairman Chiles, the committee took the unusual step of agreeing also to report, without recommendation, Reagan's budget (S Con Res 50), a sequester budget (S Con Res 49), a budget (S Con Res 51) by Ernest F. Hollings, D-S.C., and an amendment to Chiles' budget. The amendment, by Kent Conrad, D-N.D., was intended to raise about $1 billion in revenues through a federal tax amnesty program and apply the extra money to agriculture. Chiles said the Senate should have a chance to vote on the other budgets inasmuch as so many members faulted his.

A slightly different version of Chiles' plan had failed April 1, on a 12-12 vote, to win committee approval when Hollings voted against it. Before that vote, Chiles had removed two controversial features: administration economic assumptions that brought his plan into compliance with the Gramm-Rudman target and language barring amendments to debt limit bills. *(Debt limit, box, p. 42)*

Without the OMB economic assumptions, Chiles' plan exceeded the Gramm-Rudman target and so was subject to a Gramm-Rudman objection — known as a point of order — against floor consideration. The objection, which Phil Gramm, R-Texas, promised to raise, could be overturned only by a 60-vote majority of the Senate.

Chiles presented his budget to the committee on March 26, saying it would end deficit spending by fiscal 1991, as required by Gramm-Rudman. Chiles' budget, like the House plan, called for savings of about $36 billion, the amount of annual reductions required by Gramm-Rudman. That was not enough, under Congressional Budget Office (CBO) economic assumptions, to get to the deficit target of $108 billion. But if calculated by OMB economic assumptions, it hit the mark.

Chiles' budget called for about $18.5 billion in new revenues and an equivalent amount in spending cuts. It assumed defense cuts of $6.9 billion and domestic cuts of $13.8 billion in 1988. It also included a $3.4 billion package for education and research.

The plan set defense spending at $290.5 billion for fiscal 1988, a level permitting no program growth and, according to the Pentagon, not enough to offset inflation. In years after 1988, Chiles' budget assumed 1 percent annual defense spending growth, with inflation adjustments.

Unpublished provisions in Chiles' proposal, creating powerful new budgeting procedures, were a factor in the Senate committee's original rejection of the plan. The section barring amendments on debt limit bills in both chambers would thwart plans to amend the high-priority debt bill, due for action in mid-May, to restore the automatic spending-cut device of Gramm-Rudman. The original sponsors of Gramm-Rudman, two of whom sat on the Senate Budget Committee, were determined to revive the device. *(Gramm-Rudman "fix," p. 67)*

Most Senate Budget Committee members were unaware of the budget process proposals until they were given them, in draft form, a short time before the April 1 vote on the Chiles plan. The disputed changes went down with the rest of his resolution.

Senate Democrats unanimously approved the budget resolution May 7, while Republicans and the White House blasted the budget as a reprise of Democratic "tax and spend" policies.

The Senate approved the Democrat-drafted budget by a **key vote of 56-42 (R 3-42; D 53-0)** several minutes after midnight in a session that began nearly 12 hours earlier on May 6. *(1987 key votes, p. 965)*

In a first for the party, all Senate Democrats voted for the budget resolution, except for an absent Albert Gore Jr. of Tennessee. Gore had supported the budget earlier in the day, in a preliminary 57-42 vote.

The final vote was on the text of a Senate Democratic compromise. For procedural reasons, the final vote occurred on the Senate compromise as substituted for the text of the budget resolution adopted by the House.

Before the final vote, the Senate rejected Reagan's budget by an 18-81 vote and a budget prepared by Pete V. Domenici, R-N.M., by a 29-70 vote.

Senate floor action on the fiscal 1988 budget began the last week in April. After very little progress on the floor, Democrats and Republicans met separately to try to decide what to do next.

Senate Democrats were unable to agree on a combination of taxes and defense and domestic spending that would attract the 51 votes needed for passage. Republicans debated whether to sit out the fight. After inconclusive votes, senators opted to try resolving their problems off the floor, leaving behind a complicated parliamentary situation involving a "tree" of amendments designed to let Chiles and the Democratic leadership control the order of votes and the offering of additional amendments.

Just as had been the case in the House, had no amendments been adopted, the Senate would have had to vote on the sequester budget.

Chiles also fashioned a complicated parliamentary maneuver to avoid the 60-vote majority needed to waive the Gramm-Rudman point of order against the committee's budget resolution. Ranking Budget Committee Republican Domenici formally objected to the procedure, but his objection was not upheld by the Senate parliamentarian.

Domenici, Gramm and Hollings lashed out against Chiles' move, saying it violated the basic tenet of Gramm-Rudman — that it should be very difficult to breach the deficit target.

The final budget altered several key aspects of Chiles' original proposal. In four private meetings, Democrats agreed on a series of adjustments to the committee version. The final compromise added $7 billion more for defense — tied to $7 billion in additional, unspecified new taxes — and about $2 billion more for domestic programs.

The additional domestic spending in the compromise was offset by an added $1.8 billion in revenues from improved enforcement of tax laws. Reagan's budget included a similar revenue increase.

Apart from defense, the biggest addition to the budget was an extra $870 million in budget authority for education programs, one of the few areas of the committee budget that already had allowed for inflation-adjusted growth in fiscal 1988.

**Conference, Final Action.** Democratic leaders in Congress negotiated a budget agreement June 17, ending a five-week House-Senate budget conference that was distinguished by the absence of public debate or votes. The Democrats had hoped for speedy resolution of their differences but spent a long period of time wrestling with the interlocked issues of defense spending and taxes.

The next day, House and Senate conferees approved the agreement on a party-line vote. Fifteen of 16 Democrats signed the conference report. House Democrat George Miller of California and all 11 GOP conferees refused to sign it. Miller said the budget allotted too much money to military activities at the expense of social programs. Republicans reversed that complaint and also condemned the budget's call for tax increases. And Republicans denounced the budget's claim that it met the Gramm-Rudman deficit target.

The conferees met May 12 and 13 for preliminary speeches and once more, on June 18, for final comment. In the intervening weeks, the agreement was forged in private by Budget chairmen Chiles and Gray, with input from House Speaker Wright, Senate Majority Leader Byrd and other party leaders.

As the talks continued there were reports of fierce disagreement and misunderstanding between a handful of Democratic conservatives in the Senate and more liberal members in the House on defense spending. Wright, Byrd, Chiles and Gray warned that the dispute would destroy Democratic aspirations to govern the nation. Republicans crowed over the Democrats' troubles.

By the June 18 conference session, Democrats were finally together. The hardest issue for them was how much to provide for military programs. The final agreement included something for all sides by providing high and low defense spending amounts, and making the higher figure contingent on the president's approval of the tax increase. The arrangement was lifted in a slightly altered form from the Senate version of the budget resolution.

The resolution showed the higher defense numbers of $296 billion in budget authority, $289.5 billion in outlays. However, it specified that part of this total would be withheld until enactment of a reconciliation bill. Defense spending would drop to $289 billion in budget authority and $283.6 billion in outlays if that bill failed.

Only part of the spending reductions assumed in the budget resolution, plus the tax increase, was required to be accomplished through the reconciliation process. The resolution's total fiscal 1988 reductions, from what would be spent if current programs continued unchanged, totaled $6.3 billion in domestic programs and $950 million in defense. Among domestic programs, the largest reductions were to come from agriculture, which faced a $1.2 billion cut; Medicare, a $1.5 billion reduction; foreign assistance; and physical resource programs, such as water projects.

# Reconciliation, Fiscal 1988

The first session of the 100th Congress adjourned Dec. 22, 1987, after lawmakers enacted two unwieldy budget measures bearing the weight of a year's worth of legislative work.

The two bills marked the end of a political odyssey that began Oct. 19 when the stock market crash drove Congress and the White House out of their partisan trenches and on the road to a budget "summit" agreement. There were, however, long detours in the path to enactment of the summit's Nov. 20 compromise plan to reduce the deficit by $76 billion over two years. (*Stock market crash, p. 28; budget summit, p. 33*)

The real job of writing the budget pact into law was carried out in House-Senate conference committees on a governmentwide appropriations bill (H J Res 395 — PL 100-202) and deficit-reducing reconciliation bill (HR 3545 — PL 100-203). Together the two bills would cut the anticipated budget deficit by $33.4 billion in fiscal 1988 and $42.7 billion in fiscal 1989. (*Appropriations, p. 66*)

The two bills also repealed $23 billion in Gramm-Rudman-Hollings spending cuts that had been formally in effect since Nov. 20.

HR 3545, the reconciliation measure, originally was designed to make savings required by the congressional budget resolution (H Con Res 93) adopted in June. But the

## OMB Leadership

David A. Stockman stepped down as director of the Office of Management and Budget (OMB) Aug. 1, 1985, and was succeeded by James C. Miller III.

Stockman, architect of the Reagan administration's budget-cutting efforts since 1981, left office the day Congress completed action on the fiscal 1986 budget resolution (S Con Res 32). He previously had served two terms (1977-81) as a Republican representative from Michigan. (*Background, Congress and the Nation Vol. VI, pp. 35, 1025*)

Miller, who easily won Senate confirmation Oct. 4, 1985, was chairman of the Federal Trade Commission (FTC) at the time of his appointment to head OMB. Before going to the FTC in 1981, he had served briefly as administrator of OMB's Office of Information and Regulatory Affairs. (*Cabinet profiles, p. 1043*)

When Miller resigned Oct. 15, 1987, he was succeeded by the agency's deputy director, Joseph R. Wright Jr., who held the post for the remaining months of the Reagan administration.

deficit reduction targets set in the budget resolution had been changed twice by the time the reconciliation bill was cleared — first, by new targets set in a revised Gramm-Rudman measure signed into law (PL 100-119) in September and, second, by the budget summit accord reached by White House and congressional negotiators. (*Fiscal 1988 budget, p. 58; Gramm-Rudman "fix," p. 67*)

The reconciliation conference agreement, hammered out in eight days of marathon negotiations, included a $9.1 billion fiscal 1988 tax increase, aimed primarily at corporations, plus $2.1 billion in restraints on the growth of Medicare (the federal health-care program for the elderly), $1 billion in curbs on farm subsidy increases and other changes in permanent spending programs, all mandated by the economic summit. It was designed to cut the anticipated federal deficit by an estimated $17.6 billion in fiscal 1988 and $22 billion in fiscal 1989. (*Tax action and provisions, p. 96; Medicare action and provisions, p. 585*)

In an unprecedented step, the reconciliation bill wrote into law aggregate spending levels for appropriations for the 1988 fiscal year that began Oct. 1 and for fiscal 1989.

The levels were, for fiscal 1988: defense, $292 billion in spending authority and $285.4 billion in actual expenditures; non-defense, $162.9 billion and $176.8 billion, respectively. For fiscal 1989: defense, $299.5 billion in budget authority, $294 billion in outlays; non-defense, $166.2 billion and $185.3 billion. The president's fiscal 1989 budget, Congress' fiscal 1989 budget resolution and subsequent legislation, all were supposed to observe these levels.

To keep a key aspect of the summit pact in force in the next budget cycle, Reagan signed the two budget bills in reverse order, making the reconciliation measure the last to become law. Thus, a reconciliation provision meant to discourage "supplemental appropriations" that exceeded the budget overrode a conflicting provision in the omnibus spending bill.

The reconciliation measure provided for an "indefinite," open-ended authorization for funding the Commodity Credit Corporation (CCC), which operated farm price-support programs. In effect, the CCC would get appropriations "as needed." *(CCC, p. 524)*

The change was meant to end an annual rite of spring known as supplemental appropriations bills. The summit negotiators promised no supplementals in 1988, except in a "dire emergency." Supplementals had been driven in recent years by predictable crises, one of which was recurring exhaustion of CCC appropriations.

The House approved the reconciliation agreement late Dec. 21, by a 237-181 vote. The Senate cleared the measure early the following morning, by a 61-28 vote. President Reagan signed the bill Dec. 22.

## Legislative History

**House Action.** HR 3545 was reported from the House Budget Committee (H Rept 100-391) Oct. 26. House and Senate committees first started the deficit reduction process in July to take aim at savings targets set under the budget resolution. Oct. 15 was the deadline for House committees to report their recommendations for the fiscal 1988 reconciliation bill. The Budget Committee met the week of Oct. 19 to package the recommendations into one bill.

The key elements of the deficit reduction package dropped into place when the House Ways and Means Committee, on Oct. 15, and the Senate Finance Committee, on Oct. 16, approved close to $12 billion in new taxes, in somewhat different forms.

The tax provisions were the centerpiece of a wide-ranging package including spending-reduction provisions and other proposals that had little to do with the budget. The action provoked a fresh, sharply worded veto threat from Reagan. The House version also brought strong objections from House Republicans and from some of the most conservative members of the Democratic Party.

Partisan divisions were reflected in the straight party-line 23-13 vote by which the Ways and Means Committee approved its tax package. But several Republicans on the Senate Finance Committee said they would work with Democrats if Reagan was involved in negotiations, and two GOP members voted for that panel's reconciliation package.

Next to the tax provisions, in terms of its controversial nature, was a major overhaul of welfare (HR 1720) that Ways and Means recommended be included in the reconciliation bill. The committee had previously adopted provisions to make money-saving changes in Medicare and the federal pension guarantee program. *(Welfare, p. 616; pension guarantees, p. 696)*

The Democratic strategy was to paint votes against the deficit reduction legislation as votes in favor of the automatic cuts, which were known as a "sequester." Because the Gramm-Rudman automatic cuts had been re-enacted, these cuts were to occur if the deficit was not reduced $23 billion by ordinary legislative means.

In addition to the revenue sections, the fiscal 1988 reconciliation bills, as was customary, combined thrift measures with major policy changes.

In trying to meet savings requirements of the budget resolution, committees also added ephemeral savings schemes dubbed "smoke and mirrors" by critics. Perhaps the most creative proposal was adopted by the House Merchant Marine and Fisheries Committee, to charge "cruiser fees" to foreign ships protected by U.S. Navy escorts in the troubled Persian Gulf.

By the time the reconciliation bill reached the House floor Oct. 29, the market had crashed and Reagan had agreed to negotiations with Congress; included in that agreement was an implicit understanding that a tax increase would be considered.

To keep pressure on the negotiators, Speaker Jim Wright, D-Texas, decided to bring the reconciliation bill to the floor and pass it with its $11.9 billion tax increase intact. It was a risky strategy that nearly failed.

The House passed HR 3545 Oct. 29 on a much-disputed **key vote of 206-205 (R 1-164; D 205-41)**, after House Democratic budget strategy nearly exploded in Wright's face. *(1987 key votes, p. 965)*

Wright eked out his controversial victory by delaying announcement of the vote's outcome for several minutes until fellow Texas Democrat Jim Chapman switched his vote — and the results. Chapman said he first opposed the bill because of doubts about many of its specifics. But when he returned to his office and saw, frozen on a television screen, the losing 205-206 vote, he rushed back to the floor. "I could not sit and watch it go down," he said.

After Wright declared the bill passed, Republicans shouted that he had cheated them of victory and booed the Speaker with rare ferocity.

Earlier in the day, conservative Democrats had joined with a unanimous Republican vote at first to defeat the rule for floor consideration of HR 3545, apparently stalling the bill. But Democratic leaders, resorting to unusual parliamentary maneuvering, managed to bring the bill back up after stripping out welfare provisions that had helped defeat the rule.

Before final passage, the House rejected 182-229 an amendment by Minority Leader Robert H. Michel, R-Ill. It would drop most of the taxes from the bill and substitute a freeze on discretionary government programs at fiscal 1987 levels.

**Senate Action.** After the budget summit negotiators reached agreement Nov. 20, five Senate committees spent the week of Nov. 30 revising sections of their pending reconciliation bill (S 1920). By the end of the week, key sections raising business taxes and pruning Medicare spending were completed, as were provisions trimming college students' and veterans' loans and farm programs.

The Finance Committee finished the core of the legislation Dec. 3. In a formal vote, after several days of private talks with Treasury Secretary James A. Baker III, members unanimously approved a tax package targeted almost entirely at businesses and new restraints on Medicare spending.

The tax provisions, details of which were drawn from a pre-summit reconciliation bill, yielded the required $9 billion in new taxes in fiscal 1988 and $14 billion in fiscal 1989.

The pre-summit measure was approved by the Senate Budget Committee Dec. 3 by a 15-6 vote, and the summit provisions were attached as a partial amendment to that bill.

The Senate then passed the two-year, $52 billion deficit reduction bill (HR 3545), after emphatically rejecting a more ambitious budget "freeze" plan offered by Kansas Republican Nancy Landon Kassebaum. The action seemed to vindicate the judgment of summit negotiators that Congress had less appetite for politically risky budget options than critics had thought. The measure was intended to slow the growth of federal spending by a little less than $30 billion over the two years. HR 3545 passed by voice vote, after the text of S 1920 was substituted for the House-passed language, shortly after midnight Dec. 10 in a session that began the previous morning.

Kassebaum, whose freeze proposal was killed in a 71-25 vote, said Treasury Secretary Baker, Senate Majority Leader Robert C. Byrd, D-W.Va., and Finance Committee Chairman Lloyd Bentsen, D-Texas, all lobbied against her.

The Kassebaum amendment would freeze most federal spending and nearly all the federal tax code for a year, delaying scheduled tax-rate reductions. It also would limit inflation adjustments for Social Security benefits to 2 percent for a year. For fiscal 1988 and 1989, this combination would yield $87.5 billion in deficit reduction, compared with about $75 billion in the leadership package.

**Conference, Final Action.** The broad shape of the reconciliation bill and most of its details had been settled in the summit, by leaders of both parties in both chambers and by the White House. That was an extraordinary circumstance, perhaps unparalleled for a legislative conference.

The Senate-passed bill, with certain exceptions, conformed to the summit. The House did not rework its version following the summit agreement, preferring to fight out the substantial differences in conference.

Conferees eliminated most of the major barriers to final action on HR 3545 during the week of Dec. 14. But bitter fights over a few key issues delayed efforts to finish the work of Congress until Dec. 22.

Negotiators working on the reconciliation bill forged compromises on a two-year, $23 billion package of tax increases, new limits on the growth of farm subsidies, special treatment of federal loans to rural utilities and a site for dumping the nation's nuclear waste. Still unresolved by late in the day on Dec. 18 were Medicare savings and congressional demands for more spending for Medicaid.

In the final days of the session, fatigue began to wear down resistance, and members who were willing to hold out for controversial funding provisions gained extra clout.

But with Congress eager to leave town for the holidays, the White House also gained extra leverage. Reagan indicated Dec. 18 that he would forgo his Christmas vacation if necessary to rid the bill of provisions that he strongly opposed. After a closed-door meeting at the White House, Republican congressional leaders warned that Reagan would veto any bill that breached the summit agreement on deficit reduction and taxes.

The conference report for the budget reconciliation measure (H Rept 100-495) was filed in the House Dec. 21. The House agreed to it that day and the Senate agreed the following day.

Reagan did not support the measure before he signed it; White House officials withheld the president's imprimatur in the final hours of negotiations while they scanned the thousands of pages of legislation.

A last-minute administration effort to get an extra $1 billion in cuts from Medicare, based on a "scoring" dispute over the amount saved by Medicare cuts already made in conference, failed. But, in a process in which negotiations on the reconciliation bill became intermingled with negotiations on the massive continuing appropriations resolution (H J Res 395) that incorporated parts of the summit agreement, the administration succeeded in scuttling most of the extra money for Medicaid expansion sought by Rep. Henry A. Waxman of California and other House Democratic liberals.

The administration swallowed some tax provisions that it had objected to up until the end, including a new tax on vaccines and an end to tax breaks for businesses operating in South Africa.

While the bills satisfied most of the requirements of the summit pact, they fell considerably short of the $8.5 billion in government asset sales that had been anticipated in 1988 and 1989. Most members expressed displeasure with the final summit legislation, many complaining that it did not go far enough in reducing the deficit.

## Major Provisions

The reconciliation bill was intended to raise $23 billion in taxes over two years. The bill also was intended to reduce the budget deficit through a host of changes in federal spending programs, including Medicare and Medicaid. *(Tax action and provisions, p. 96; Medicare and Medicaid action and provisions, p. 585)*

In addition to its tax law and major health program changes, HR 3545 (PL 100-203), as signed by the president:

### Agriculture

● **Target Prices.** Reduced target prices for the 1988 and 1989 crops of wheat, feed grains, cotton and rice by about 1.4 percent below levels established for those years by the 1985 farm bill (PL 99-198). Target prices for wheat were set at $4.23 a bushel in 1988 and $4.10 in 1989; corn was set at $2.93 a bushel in 1988 and $2.84 in 1989; cotton was set at 75.9 cents a pound in 1988 and 73.4 cents in 1989; rice was set at $11.13 per hundredweight in 1988 and $10.79 in 1989.

● **Loan Rates.** Limited declines in price-support loan rates for wheat, feed grains, cotton and rice to a maximum of 3 percent in 1988, instead of 5 percent as allowed in the 1985 farm bill. In 1989, the loan rates could decline by 5 percent, plus an additional 2 percent if necessary to maintain a competitive market position for the commodity.

● **Price Supports.** Required reductions in price-support levels or increases in producer assessments for the 1988 and 1989 crops of tobacco, peanuts, sugar, honey, wool and mohair to achieve a 1.4 percent annual reduction in program outlays for those commodities. Dairy producers would be assessed an additional 2.5 cents per hundred pounds of milk products marketed during 1988.

● **Paid Land Diversion.** Offered feed grain producers the option of diverting an additional 10 percent of their acreage base in 1988 and 1989, at a payment rate of $1.75 per bushel (corn) of the established program yield.

● **Optional Land Diversion.** Allowed wheat and feed grain producers to enroll in a "0-92" program in 1988 and 1989, giving them 92 percent of projected income subsidies on land taken out of production.

● **Payment Limitation.** Limited farm program income-support payments beginning in the 1989 crop year to no more than $100,000 per person by limiting an individual farmer who received payments under the current $50,000 payment cap to receiving payments on no more than two farm entities.

A new definition of a "person" eligible for payments included individuals, corporations, joint stock companies, associations, limited partnerships and charitable organizations that were "actively engaged" in farming. Foreign landowners who were not actively engaged in farm operations were made ineligible for program payments. States and state agencies were made eligible to receive payments in conformance with the $50,000 payment limitation; lands owned by public school districts were exempted from the limitations.

● **Commodity Credit Corporation.** Established a new funding mechanism for the Commodity Credit Corporation, called a current, indefinite appropriation, which would supply the CCC with unlimited funding throughout the fiscal year to reimburse its net realized losses.

● **Advance Payments.** Required the Agriculture Department to make advance deficiency payments on the 1988 through 1990 crops of wheat, feed grains, cotton and rice of not less than 40 percent or more than 50 percent for wheat and feed grains, and not less than 30 percent or more than 50 percent for cotton and rice. Advance deficiency payments were currently made at the agriculture secretary's discretion. In addition, 75 percent of the portion of wheat producers' final deficiency payments that were projected to be made in July must be accelerated to the previous December at the producer's option.

● **Yield Adjustments.** Required the secretary to compensate producers if the calculation of farm-program payment yields under current law caused a producer's yield payments to fall more than 10 percent below the 1985 farm-program payment yield.

● **Loan Rate Differentials.** Limited the secretary's discretion to adjust county loan rates from year to year to no more than the percentage change allowed in the national average loan rate plus or minus 2 percentage points.

● **Storage Costs.** Required the Agriculture Department to adjust storage, handling or transportation costs as necessary to reduce CCC expenditures by a total of $230 million in fiscal 1988 and 1989. This would be done by lowering the rates for commercial handlers.

● **Farmer-Owned Reserve.** Changed the trigger mechanism requiring the secretary to provide incentives to producers to place grain in the three-year, long-term storage program, revising the minimum storage requirement from 17 percent of wheat use and 7 percent of corn use to 300 million bushels for wheat and 450 million bushels for feed grains.

● **Oat Acreage Reductions.** Limited the acreage-reduction requirement for producers of oats to a maximum of 5 percent in the 1988 and 1989 crop years to encourage increased production.

● **Tobacco.** Authorized the lease or transfer of tobacco quotas, in certain cases.

● **Honey Payment Limitation.** Eliminated the current $250,000 limit on the price-support loan that an individual honey producer could receive; reduced the honey loan rates for the 1987 through 1990 crops to cover any resulting costs.

● **Rural Telephone Bank.** Required the Rural Telephone Bank to apply its most current cost-of-money rate at the time of each advance on future loans.

● **Rural Electrification Administration.** Allowed a utility borrower to invest its own funds or to make loans or guarantees not in excess of 15 percent of its total utility plant.

## Asset Sales

● **Rural Electrification Administration.** Authorized up to $2 billion in penalty-free prepayment of Rural Electrification Administration loans to rural utilities in fiscal 1988.

Provided that eight borrowers whose applications for prepayment were previously approved would have first priority; other borrowers seeking to prepay would be treated on a first-come, first-served basis.

● **Rural Telephone Bank.** Authorized penalty-free prepayment of Rural Telephone Bank loans, if the prepayment was made before Oct. 1, 1988.

● **Reclamation Loan Sales.** Authorized the sale of Bureau of Reclamation loans to raise at least $130 million in fiscal 1988. The loans were debts owed to the federal government by beneficiaries of federal water projects in the West. The rights of borrowers under reclamation law would be the same as if the government still held the loan.

## Budget Policy

● **Spending Levels.** Set aggregate levels for defense and domestic discretionary spending for fiscal 1988 and 1989. The 1988 levels for defense were $292 billion in spending authority and $285.4 billion in actual expenditures; non-defense levels were $162.9 billion and $176.8 billion. The 1989 levels for defense were $299.5 billion in budget authority and $294 billion in outlays; for non-defense, $166.2 billion and $185.3 billion. Required that fiscal 1989 levels be observed in the congressional budget resolution for that year and subsequent legislation. (The Nov. 20 budget summit pact also assumed that the president's fiscal 1989 budget would observe these levels.)

● **Gramm-Rudman Cuts.** Canceled Oct. 20 and Nov. 20, 1987, orders invoking automatic spending cuts in fiscal 1988 under the Gramm-Rudman-Hollings law and restored amounts already reduced or cut under those orders, except where cuts were explicitly retained elsewhere in the law.

● **National Economic Commission.** Established a 12-member National Economic Commission to examine methods of reducing the federal budget deficit while promoting economic growth, encouraging savings and capital formation and ensuring that the burden of achieving deficit reduction was equitably distributed. The commission's final report was due March 1, 1989.

## Civil Service, Postal Service Programs

● **Federal Retirement.** Deferred a portion of lump-sum retirement payments for federal workers, including postal workers, who retired after Jan. 4, 1988; these workers would receive 60 percent of their retirement benefits in 1988 and 40 percent in 1989. Workers retiring by Jan. 3, 1988, were still eligible for a full lump-sum payment under the old rules.

● **Postal Service.** Required the Postal Service to pay $350 million into the Civil Service Retirement and Disability Fund in fiscal 1988 and $465 million into a newly established Postal Service Escrow Fund in fiscal 1989.

Required the Postal Service to pay into the Federal Employees Health Benefits Fund $160 million in 1988 and $270 million in 1989; specified that the funds must come from savings in the operating budget, not from increased borrowing or increased postal rates.

Capped Postal Service capital costs at $625 million in 1988 and $2 billion in 1989.

## Education

● **Guaranteed Student Loan Program.** Required limits for cash reserves held by state guarantee agencies of no more than 40 percent of the total amount paid by an agency on insurance claims during the previous year, 0.3 percent of original principal amount of outstanding loans insured by an agency or $500,000, whichever was greater. Agencies with excess cash reserves in fiscal 1986 must use up to a total of $250 million in fiscal 1988 to pay off claims against defaulted student loans before the agencies could be reimbursed with federal funds.

## Energy and Environment

● **Nuclear Regulatory Commission License Fees.** Authorized an increase in the fees that the Nuclear Regulatory Commission charged the electric utilities it regulated to recover at least 45 percent of the agency's costs — up from 33 percent.

● **Oil, Gas Leasing.** Overhauled the system of leasing federal lands, other than those offshore, for oil and gas drilling and production. The conference bill blended House and Senate provisions to set a national minimum bid of $2 per acre (up from 50 cents per acre) with authority for the energy secretary to increase the minimum later. It also prohibited the federal government from deducting its administrative costs before it shared drilling revenues with the states.

● **Park Land Acquisition.** Extended the authorization for the Land and Water Conservation Fund, set aside for purchase of federal and state park land, until the year 2015. The primary source of revenue for the fund was federal offshore oil and gas leasing.

● **Park User Fees.** Authorized higher fees for users of certain national parks, especially major parks attracting the most users. Levels are similar to those set in fiscal 1987 appropriations legislation (PL 99-591). The bill set a maximum fee of $10 at Yellowstone and Grand Teton national parks, $5 at Glacier National Park and, beginning Oct. 1, 1991, $10 at Grand Canyon National Park. Fees would be prohibited at urban parks with many access points. Fee revenues would be subject to appropriation until 1991. Ten percent of the revenue would go to a discretionary fund to be allocated by the director of the National Park Service among various park units on the basis of need.

● **Tongass Timber Fund.** Repealed for fiscal 1988-89 the permanent appropriation of at least $40 million annually for the Tongass Timber Supply Fund. The fund subsidized logging operations in the Tongass National Forest as part of a 1980 compromise that set much of that forest aside as wilderness that was off-limits for logging. Making the fund subject to annual appropriations allowed it to be counted as savings in the budget reconciliation process. Those savings were largely theoretical, however, because after enacting them Congress appropriated about $56 million for the fund in the 1988 continuing resolution — roughly the same spending level as in fiscal 1987.

● **Reclamation Reform.** Required the interior secretary to audit certain large landholders within three years to make sure they qualified for federal irrigation subsidies. The Reclamation Reform Act of 1982 set a maximum size of 960 acres on farms that could receive federal irrigation

water at less than full cost. The provision was a response to charges that some landholders were using devices such as trusts and management agreements to evade the limits.

● **Wyoming Mine Fund.** Authorized Wyoming to spend up to $2 million from its 1987 allocation under the Abandoned Mine Reclamation Fund (PL 95-87) for aid to citizens evacuated from their homes in Campbell County because of danger from methane and hydrogen sulfide gases.

## Miscellaneous Health

● **National Commission on Children.** Established a 36-member, bipartisan National Commission on Children. The commission was charged with studying and making recommendations to the president and Congress by Sept. 30, 1988, regarding children's health, social and support services, income security, tax policy and education, and ways to ensure that the needs of families and children were met.

● **'Boarder Babies' Demonstrations.** Authorized $4 million per year for three years for demonstration projects to provide residential care for newborn babies who were abandoned by their parents in hospitals. Such "boarder babies" often were the offspring of drug addicts but were generally healthy and did not require hospitalization.

● **Study of Children with AIDS in Foster Care.** Authorized the Department of Health and Human Services (HHS) to conduct a study to determine the number of infants and children in the United States with AIDS (acquired immune deficiency syndrome) who had been placed in foster care, the problems social service agencies encountered finding foster families for such children and the potential growth in the number of such children requiring foster care over the following five years. Required the department to complete the study and make recommendations to Congress by Dec. 22, 1988.

## Unemployment Compensation

● **Extended Benefit Deadline.** Granted six extra months to states that failed to enact laws requiring job search activities for recipients of unemployment compensation. States had been given three months to comply with the provision.

● **Self-Employment Demonstration Program.** Authorized three state demonstration programs to test temporary continuation of unemployment compensation benefits for unemployed people who tried to set up their own businesses.

## Veterans' Programs

● **Veterans' Home Loans.** Extended the 1 percent fee generally imposed on veterans who obtained a home loan that was guaranteed, insured or made by the Veterans Administration (VA) through Sept. 30, 1989.

● **Veterans Administration Foreclosures.** Increased for fiscal years 1988, 1989 and 1990 the proportion of acquired foreclosure properties that the VA was required to sell on a cash, instead of a vendee-loan, basis, from a minimum of 25 percent and a maximum of 40 percent to a minimum of 35 percent and a maximum of 50 percent.

## Welfare

● **Extension of 'Disregard' for In-Kind Assistance.** Permanently extended provisions that expired

Sept. 30, 1987, disregarding in-kind assistance such as home heating for purposes of calculating eligibility and benefits under Supplemental Security Income (SSI) and Aid to Families with Dependent Children (AFDC). The disregard was mandatory for SSI and optional for AFDC.

● **AFDC, Fraud Control.** Raised federal matching funds from 50 percent to 75 percent for state administration of the welfare program, including fraud-control activities. Temporarily disqualified from AFDC eligibility, people who had intentionally violated the program; required written notice to applicants of fraud penalties.

● **Exclusion of Real Property.** Excluded real property from SSI eligibility calculations if the property could not be sold because it was jointly owned and the sale would cause a hardship to other owners, its sale was legally prevented or reasonable efforts to sell it had been unsuccessful.

● **Transfer of Assets Rule.** Allowed the secretary of HHS to waive the transfer of assets rule — which counted the value of assets sold at less than market value for 24 months after the transaction in computing benefit eligibility — if the absence of such a waiver would cause undue hardship.

● **Nursing Home Couples.** Allowed a husband and wife in a nursing home to be treated as a couple with regard to Medicaid benefits.

● **Extension of Deadline for Applications.** Extended to July 1, 1988, the period during which widows and widowers who would have lost eligibility for SSI could apply for Medicaid as SSI recipients.

● **Increased Emergency Payments.** Increased from $100 per month to $340 per month the amount of immediate emergency payment that could be made to an SSI recipient.

● **Interim Assistance Reimbursement.** Allowed reimbursement to states that paid cash benefits to people whose eligibility was terminated or suspended but who later were found to be eligible. Reimbursements also could be made to states for interim assistance to people whose SSI checks were lost or stolen.

● **Blind Recipients.** Required the Social Security Administration to inform blind SSI recipients about their benefits by telephone, certified letter or some other process. Continued SSI benefits to people whose blindness had ceased, as long as they were attending a vocational rehabilitation program.

● **Benefits to People in Shelters.** Provided that a person in an emergency shelter could receive SSI benefits for six months in a nine-month period.

● **Disregard of Retroactive Payments.** Extended from six months to nine months the period during which retroactive benefit payments must be disregarded as an income resource. The provision ran for two years starting Jan. 1, 1987.

● **Benefits to Hospitalized People.** Continued full SSI benefits to people in hospitals or nursing homes if a doctor certified they were not likely to stay more than three months.

● **Widows and Widowers.** Continued SSI eligibility for blind or disabled widows or widowers who must apply for Social Security benefits at age 60.

● **Homeless People.** Authorized several kinds of demonstration projects designed to assist homeless people who could qualify for SSI benefits. Prohibited the secretary of HHS, until Oct. 1, 1988, from counting funds received for shelter in an AFDC family's standard of need.

● **Needs Benefits.** Increased the personal-needs allowance for SSI recipients in nursing homes from $25 per month to $30 for an individual and from $50 per month to $60 for a couple.

● **Exclusion of Death Benefits.** Excluded from calculation of an individual's SSI eligibility death benefits, gifts and inheritances from a family member if the benefits were used to pay for the deceased person's last illness and burial.

● **Demonstration Programs.** Authorized the state of Washington to conduct its Family Independence Program, a work and training program for welfare recipients.

Authorized New York state to conduct a child-support supplement demonstration program to test it as an alternative to Aid to Families with Dependent Children.

● **Extension of Voluntary Foster Care Placements.** Permanently extended federal matching funds to states for voluntary placements of AFDC-eligible children in foster homes.

● **Mother/Infant Foster Care.** Required that, where a child in foster care was a parent of a child in the same home or institution, foster care maintenance payments included amounts needed to cover the costs of items for the son or daughter.

● **State Entitlement Cap.** Increased the state block-grant entitlement cap by $50 million, to $2.75 billion.

● **American Samoa.** Made American Samoa entitled to block grant funding starting Oct. 1, 1988.

# Appropriations, Fiscal 1988

As its last significant act before adjourning for the year Dec. 22, 1987, Congress cleared an omnibus spending bill (H J Res 395 — PL 100-202) that combined all 13 regular appropriations bills for fiscal 1988.

It was the third time since 1950 that all spending bills were rolled together; it happened in 1986 for fiscal 1987 as well.

And, although President Reagan objected to the monstrous measure that paid for roughly half of all government activities (the rest being covered through permanent appropriations, such as those for Social Security and interest payments on the national debt), he should have expected it. The White House-congressional budget "summit" that concluded a two-year spending deal in November 1987 left Congress with little choice other than to package all appropriations measures together, if for no reason other than to avoid political games-playing with the 13 individual measures.

The bill, known as a continuing appropriations resolution, contained $603.9 billion in new budget authority and was calculated to result in fiscal 1988 outlays of $593.2 billion. It was the largest continuing resolution ever enacted.

Together with the deficit-reducing reconciliation bill for fiscal 1987 (HR 3545 — PL 100-203), which also grew out of the budget summit, the continuing resolution promised to reduce spending by $33.4 billion in fiscal 1988 and $76.2 billion over two years. *(Fiscal 1988 reconciliation, p. 61)*

Reagan won two major victories during negotiations on the bill: It contained money for the Nicaraguan contras that Congress otherwise might not have provided, and it did not contain a provision that some in Congress badly wanted to write into law — the so-called fairness doctrine, which required broadcasters to air all sides of controversial issues. (Contras, p. 209; fairness doctrine, p. 405)

Because the big continuing resolution was not enacted before the Oct. 1 start of the fiscal year, four short-term continuing resolutions were needed to keep the government functioning (PL 100-120, PL 100-162, PL 100-193, PL 100-197). The last expired at midnight Dec. 21, and Congress cleared H J Res 395 in the early morning of Dec. 22. Reagan signed the bill the same day.

Congress also enacted a supplemental appropriations measure for fiscal 1987 during the year (HR 1827 — PL 100-71). The bill, which cleared July 1 after three bumpy months in the legislative mill, provided $9.4 billion, much of which went for farm price- and income-support payments from the Commodity Credit Corporation. Money also was earmarked for federal pay and pension benefits, homeless aid and economic aid to Central America.

House efforts to include arms control provisions threatened to derail the measure, as did an effort by Sen. John Melcher, D-Mont., to require the Labor Department to study a new consumer price index for the elderly. (CPI for the elderly, p. 74)

The bill was noteworthy for another reason: It was an early battleground to test Congress' mettle in the deficit reduction war. During House floor action on the bill April 23, Buddy MacKay, D-Fla., offered an amendment to cut $2.2 billion from the measure, almost 21 percent, in an across-the-board sweep that touched nearly every account. The amendment was adopted on a **key vote of 263-123 (R 121-39; D 142-84)**. (1987 key votes, p. 965)

# Gramm-Rudman 'Fix'

Congress took advantage in 1987 of its perennial obligation to increase the federal government's borrowing authority to enact major changes in the 1985 Gramm-Rudman-Hollings deficit reduction law. Members also, as some did with the fiscal 1988 budget resolution, tried to use the debt limit bill to force President Reagan to a budget "summit" meeting. This effort failed, and it took the Oct. 19 stock market crash to convene high-level White House-Capitol Hill negotiations. (Gramm-Rudman, p. 44; stock market crash, p. 28; budget summit, p. 33)

Reagan Sept. 29 signed the bill (H J Res 324 — PL 100-119) extending the limit on the government's debt from $2.1 trillion to $2.8 trillion, enough to cover federal borrowing through May 1989.

Amendments to H J Res 324 eased the deficit targets of Gramm-Rudman and pushed the original law's deadline for a balanced budget back two years to 1993. They also modified and re-enacted the automatic spending-cut provisions of Gramm-Rudman that were to be triggered if Congress and the president failed to reduce the deficit to the law's targets. The Supreme Court had declared the automatic procedure unconstitutional in 1986. (Supreme Court ruling, p. 834)

Lengthy negotiations over budget procedures and what became known as the Gramm-Rudman "fix" caused Congress to enact three short-term debt increases before finishing work on H J Res 324. The first (HR 2360 — PL 100-40), which cleared May 14, lasted through the end of July. The second (HR 3022 — PL 100-80) was signed by the president July 30 and lasted through Aug. 6. The final short-term bill (HR 3190 — PL 100-84) was signed Aug. 10. It ran through Sept. 23.

Few people relished the idea of reviving the automatic Gramm-Rudman cuts. Some in Congress who had been enthusiastic supporters of the original law — Sen. Pete V. Domenici, R-N.M., for example — said flatly that the deficit-cutting measure would not work.

Reagan, who had favored the original measure then had gone to court to have its automatic mechanism nullified, never fully supported revitalizing the automatic procedure. The threat of serious harm to the military budget was a constant refrain from the White House, which was equally unnerved by the prospect of higher taxes.

There were those, such as Treasury Secretary James A. Baker III, who warned that failure to enact this bill would be a political embarrassment and a fiscal disaster, because it would be difficult to extract another debt measure from a roiled Congress. The bill's sponsors insisted that the renewed threat of harsh cuts would force the White House and Congress to compromise.

Still, most who voted for the bill were less convinced than in 1985, when Gramm-Rudman was swept into law on a tide of anger against the budget deficit and against the failure of Congress and the president to come to grips with it. Then many said that the threat of automatic spending cuts would surely end the Congress-White House impasse.

But by 1987 there was a pervasive belief that the deadlock would continue until Reagan left office, because the president would block the tax increases that many influential members believed were critical to balance the budget. The widespread certainty that Reagan would never bend to new taxes fed fears that he would let automatic cuts occur instead and blame Congress for the resulting harm.

The final version of the bill represented a significant step back from the promises of the original law and from the more modest expectations of the budget resolution (H Con Res 93) Congress had adopted earlier in the year. It not only relaxed the deficit targets in Gramm-Rudman, but also set an easier deficit reduction target for fiscal 1988 than had the budget resolution. (Fiscal 1988 budget, p. 58)

## Background

Enacting a long-term debt increase was a chore left over from 1986. The "must-pass" debt hikes had become a target for legislators who needed a vehicle for measures that might not pass on their own. The debt increase had to pass because, without it, the government would suffer an unprecedented default.

In 1986, proponents of a Gramm-Rudman fix blocked a long-term debt increase by threatening to offer Gramm-Rudman amendments. They finally agreed to adoption of a short-term debt limit increase — until May 1987 — after congressional leaders promised to allow them to offer their amendments then.

By May, another group of lawmakers had laid plans to hold the debt bill hostage until the White House and Congress agreed to a budget summit meeting to negotiate a compromise on budget process and spending and tax issues. This group, led by Rep. Buddy MacKay, D-Fla., wanted to force congressional and White House negotiators to face politically difficult deficit-related options, such as tax increases or reduced spending for Social Security.

The MacKay group was in competition with the architects of Gramm-Rudman-Hollings — Sens. Phil Gramm, R-Texas; Warren B. Rudman, R-N.H.; and Ernest F. Hollings, D-S.C. — who wanted to attach amendments to fix their bill. The original Gramm-Rudman gave authority to ratify the amount and scope of across-the-board spending cuts to the General Accounting Office (GAO), an arm of Congress. The Supreme Court in 1986 ruled that this arrangement violated the Constitution's separation-of-powers doctrine because the president was bound to impose the cuts as ratified by the GAO. The Gramm-Rudman repairs envisioned by its creators would give the ratification power to the executive branch Office of Management and Budget (OMB).

The predicted crisis in May passed after Reagan agreed to bargain on budget matters. In return, Congress enacted the first of the short-term debt limit increases of the year (HR 2360 — H Rept 100-88).

Procedural changes were to be the sole subject of the promised budget talks between the White House and Congress. Administration officials said Reagan would not discuss the more difficult specifics of deficit reduction, such as new taxes proposed by Democrats.

By July, however, the White House was no longer interested in plans to reinstate Gramm-Rudman because administration officials feared its effect on defense spending. Congress, though, was intent on making changes to the deficit reduction bill, including raising its annual deficit targets.

Congressional Democrats had announced in late February that they could not reach the Gramm-Rudman target of $108 billion in their fiscal 1988 budget. Instead, House Budget Committee Chairman William H. Gray III, D-Pa., and Senate Budget Committee Chairman Lawton Chiles, D-Fla., said their goal was to reduce the federal budget deficit by $36 billion to $40 billion. That would leave a fiscal 1988 deficit of $131 billion to $135 billion, under Congressional Budget Office (CBO) estimates.

The decision to miss the 1988 Gramm-Rudman target was a clear signal that law's targets were no longer considered realistic on Capitol Hill and would have to be altered.

## Legislative History

**House Action.** Raising the debt ceiling was always politically difficult. But the House adopted a procedure to make it less so. Whenever the House adopted the conference report on a budget resolution, it was deemed to have passed and sent to the Senate a separate bill raising the debt ceiling sufficiently to support borrowing specified in the budget resolution. *(Debt limit, box, p. 42)*

So, when the House adopted the fiscal 1988 budget resolution June 23, it sent on to the Senate H J Res 324, which also raised the debt ceiling to $2.565 trillion.

**Senate Action.** The Senate did not have a similar rule to avoid debt limit votes. After amending H J Res 324 with the Gramm-Rudman modifications and extending the government's borrowing authority to $2.8 trillion through May 1989, the Senate passed the measure July 31 on a 54-31 vote.

Long negotiations among a handful of House and Senate leaders followed, and a compromise was not enacted until late September.

Senate action began, however, on the floor, where a Democratic version of the Gramm-Rudman fix was rejected July 23. Republicans voted against the Democrats' plan because they favored a GOP version, which would give more authority to the administration's OMB in determining the size and shape of automatic cuts. Many Democrats

voted with the Republicans because they believed the strategy behind the scheme, to force Reagan to accept a tax increase, could not work.

By a 25-71 vote, the Senate rejected the Democrats' anti-deficit amendment. Twenty-five Democrats joined with Republicans in voting against the amendment, put forth by Budget Chairman Chiles.

Fearing the Republican alternative could pick up enough Democratic votes to pass, Chiles and his allies twice blocked Republican efforts to clear away a procedural objection to consideration of the GOP plan sponsored by Domenici and Gramm. After these votes, Chiles resumed private talks with Domenici and Gramm.

The Republican plan stuck close to the original Gramm-Rudman, except it gave OMB a more prominent role. Chiles' elaborate rewrite of the automatic-cut device gave greater authority to CBO. Both also would relax existing deficit targets. Gramm, Domenici and Chiles all agreed the targets were unrealistic.

As Congress struggled with the Gramm-Rudman amendments, lawmakers approved another short-term debt increase (HR 3022 — H Rept 100-244), through Aug. 6. The measure, raising the debt limit from $2.111 trillion to $2.320 trillion, passed both chambers July 29.

Two days later, the Senate adopted its version of the long-term debt limit increase, amended with the Gramm-Rudman modifications.

J. Bennett Johnston, D-La., and his allies complained that the plan spared Reagan and nervous Democrats from politically difficult decisions until after the 1988 elections. By raising deficit targets, thus reducing the savings required for fiscal 1988, all parties could put off considering the tax increase that congressional leaders of both parties thought essential.

Sponsors Gramm, Chiles and Domenici rejected Johnston's claim, and the Senate approved the Gramm-Rudman fix amendment by a strong 71-21 vote on July 31.

Johnston tried to make the deficit targets less lenient, to prevent Congress and the president from escaping meaningful deficit reduction in 1988. But his amendment split a frail alliance between Republicans and Democrats, and it failed on a **key vote of 41-52 (R 0-45; D 41-7)**. *(1987 key votes, p. 965)*

Late the same day, the Senate rejected, 41-48, an amendment by Daniel J. Evans, R-Wash., that would give the president authority to veto single appropriations bills that had been combined into an omnibus continuing appropriations resolution.

**Conference, Final Action.** Lawmakers had hoped to finish work on the combined debt limit and Gramm-Rudman fix quickly and leave for their August recess. The conference began Aug. 4, but members were unable to settle their differences before the Aug. 8 start of the vacation. Despite protests from various quarters, yet another short-term debt increase (HR 3190), through Sept. 23, was enacted Aug. 7.

Negotiations among a small group of House and Senate conferees resumed after Congress reconvened Sept. 9. And an agreement was reached Sept. 17 that pushed the target of a balanced budget back to 1993, from 1991 in the original Gramm-Rudman and 1992 in the Senate fix amendment. At the same time, deficit targets for the intervening years were relaxed even more than in the Senate bill. But conferees more or less followed the Senate version on giving authority to determine the cuts to OMB.

The House approved the conference report (H Rept

100-313) on Sept. 22, by a 230-176 vote, and the Senate voted 64-34 in favor of the conference agreement Sept. 23.

## Major Provisions

As signed by the president Sept. 29, 1987, H J Res 324 (PL 100-119):

● **Debt Limit.** Raised the permanent federal debt limit to $2.8 trillion, from $2.1 trillion, which was expected to be enough to last through May 1989.

● **Automatic Spending Cuts.** Established, for fiscal years 1988-93, an automatic spending-cut procedure to reduce the estimated deficit to specified targets. The automatic-cut procedure was called a "sequester" in budget jargon.

Each year, the Congressional Budget Office and, five days later, the Office of Management and Budget were required to issue reports on the size of the estimated deficit for the coming fiscal year, the amount that federal spending had to be reduced to reach the deficit target for the year and the uniform percentage by which program accounts had to be reduced to achieve the required reduction.

OMB was required to "give due regard" to the CBO report and to explain differences between its report and CBO's. The two agencies had to observe specific restrictions on economic and technical assumptions used in making deficit estimates and on distribution of the percentage cuts.

The president was required to issue the OMB report twice as an order making the spending cuts. The first time the order would temporarily halt spending. If legislation was not enacted after the first order to meet the deficit target by other means, CBO and OMB would again report and the second OMB report, issued by the president, would make the spending cuts permanent. The second version would reflect savings made in the interim. The legislation explicitly authorized changes or cancellation of the final order by joint resolution under a special, expedited procedure.

● Revised schedules for the automatic-cut procedure, as follows: for fiscal 1988 only, Oct. 10, the "snapshot" date by which spending and revenue laws and final regulations had to be in effect to be counted by OMB and CBO in making the deficit and automatic-cut estimates; also the date by which the president had to notify Congress if he intended to adjust military spending in the automatic-cut order, as permitted by the bill; Oct. 15, CBO report; Oct. 20, OMB report to the president and to Congress and the date the report went into effect, withholding funds retroactive to Oct. 1; Nov. 15, second CBO report, showing any changes in spending and revenues that had become final; Nov. 20, final OMB report to the president and to Congress and the date the reported spending cuts became permanent cancellations in spending authority. Within five days after the cuts went into effect, any joint resolution affirming the defense spending modifications as proposed by the president had to be introduced. Within 10 days after the cuts went into effect, any joint resolution revising the final order had to be introduced.

For years after fiscal 1988, the schedule was: Aug. 15, presidential notification on military accounts and "snapshot" date; Aug. 20, CBO report; Aug. 25, OMB report, and president issues order, to become effective Oct. 1; Oct. 10, second CBO report; Oct. 15, final OMB report, effective immediately.

The timing of joint resolutions following the final order was the same for all years.

● Retained the overall composition of the automatic cuts, with half from defense and half from non-military programs, and exempted Social Security, interest payments on the federal debt and certain poverty programs. Reductions in Medicare, as in the original law, were limited to 2 percent. The bill also restated various exemptions enacted in other legislation and clarified an exemption for the Commodity Supplemental Food Program.

● **Deficit Targets.** Established federal budget deficit targets as follows: for fiscal 1988, $144 billion; fiscal 1989, $136 billion; fiscal 1990, $100 billion; fiscal 1991, $64 billion; fiscal 1992, $28 billion; fiscal 1993, zero.

A $10 billion margin of error was allowed for all years except fiscal 1993, meaning that the automatic spending-cut provision was supposed to be triggered only if a deficit estimate exceeded the target by more than $10 billion. Thus, the real targets were $154 billion, $146 billion, $110 billion, $74 billion, $38 billion and zero.

The automatic process was designed to reduce the estimated deficit to the target, but there were exceptions for fiscal years 1988 and 1989.

For 1988, the automatic cuts could be avoided with a total of $23 billion in budgetary savings, subtracted from total spending for programs as provided by current law, with adjustments for inflation and for changes in program participation. Cuts under the automatic procedure were to be limited to $23 billion, even if they failed to get the deficit down to the target.

For 1989, the automatic cuts would be triggered by a deficit estimate exceeding the target by more than $10 billion, but the cuts would be either the amount needed to reach the target or $36 billion from current spending (adjusted for inflation and program participation) — but no more than $36 billion.

Original Gramm-Rudman targets were, for fiscal 1986, $171.9 billion; 1987, $144 billion; 1988, $108 billion; 1989, $72 billion; 1990, $36 billion; 1991, zero, with a $10 billion margin of error for all years except the last.

● Revised the method of calculating the spending total ("baseline") used to estimate the deficit and from which the cuts were to be subtracted in the automatic process. The effect of the change was to ease the impact of the automatic cuts by enlarging the base to be cut.

Under the original law, the baseline was supposed to reflect spending and revenues resulting from laws and final regulations in effect at specific dates. For appropriations that were not finished for the coming fiscal year, the spending level was to be the amount appropriated for the previous fiscal year, with no allowance for costs of inflation in the coming year or for changes in rates of participation in federal programs.

In the new version, allowances for inflation (specified in the bill) and for changes in participation rates could be added to the previous year's appropriated levels.

Also, if a continuing appropriations resolution covering less than a full year was in effect at the time of an automatic-cut order, the baseline would reflect spending levels of the resolution, prorated for the duration of the spending-cut order. A continuing resolution that provided appropriations for part of a year usually reflected amounts set by the previous year's appropriation or by partially completed bills for the fiscal year in question, or combinations of both.

The bill also specified that certain expenditures, including advanced price-support ("deficiency") payments to farmers, were to be assumed in the baseline.

● **Military Spending-Cut Alternatives.** Permitted

the president, in the spending-cut order, to deviate from uniform percentage reductions in military accounts. For personnel expenditures, the president could exempt all or part from cuts if an equivalent amount were subtracted from other defense programs, and if he notified Congress of this change.

For non-personnel accounts, the president could cut less from some accounts and more from others, but only if Congress approved under special expedited procedures. None of these accounts could be increased above the appropriated level, however, and the aggregate defense reduction could not change.

● **Limits on Budget Gimmicks.** Imposed new restrictions on what could be counted as budgetary savings for purposes of complying with Gramm-Rudman. Receipts from the sale of federal assets such as loans and from early "prepayment" of loans, including those of the Rural Electrification Administration, could not be counted. Also ineligible were temporary savings from shifting government actions, such as a military payday, from one fiscal year to the next.

● Prohibited Senate consideration of a budget resolution that utilized more than one set of economic and technical assumptions; both the House and Senate in 1987 used two sets of assumptions, one to calculate spending and another to calculate compliance with Gramm-Rudman targets.

● **Extraneous Provisions on Reconciliation Bills.** Continued for the duration of the bill a Senate rule that barred extraneous provisions from the Senate version of budget reconciliation legislation. Also barred from Senate reconciliation bills provisions increasing federal spending in future years even if they were within budget limits for the year covered by reconciliation. Reconciliation bills enacted deficit-reducing changes in program authorizations and revenue laws, as assumed in the budget resolution.

● **Deferrals.** Affirmed court decisions that the president could defer spending appropriated funds only for reasons of management, not policy. A three-judge panel of the U.S. Court of Appeals for the District of Columbia had ruled Jan. 20, 1987, that Reagan had improperly delayed spending money appropriated to the Department of Housing and Urban Development. The court left intact deferrals for management reasons. Critics of the president's deferral efforts called them merely another form of unilateral impoundments, which the courts had rejected in 1974 and which were abolished by the 1974 Congressional Budget and Impoundment Control Act (PL 93-344). *(Congress and the Nation Vol. IV, p. 73)*

● **Points of Order.** Specified that a 60-vote majority was required to overturn Senate rulings on Gramm-Rudman points of order that could be waived only by a 60-vote majority. Existing practice permitted the rulings to be overturned with a simple majority.

● **Two-Year Appropriations.** Recommended development of a plan for experimental two-year appropriations for certain agencies; directed CBO, in consultation with the General Accounting Office, to report on certain aspects of federal credit programs.

## Fiscal 1989 Budget

After two months of conference negotiations and other delays, the Senate's June 6, 1988, action cleared a largely symbolic, $1.1 trillion budget resolution (H Con Res 268 — H Rept 100-658) for fiscal 1989. The Senate voted 58-29 for

the budget. The House had adopted the conference report May 26 in a surprisingly close, 201-181, vote.

The comprehensive federal spending blueprint allowed for no new taxes and was projected to leave a deficit of $135.6 billion, just under the $136 billion deficit target set by the Gramm-Rudman-Hollings anti-deficit law.

The accord came five months after most of the big decisions on defense and domestic spending had been sealed in a two-year, $76 billion deficit reduction plan, an outgrowth of the October-November 1987 budget "summit."

The plan was enacted into law in the fiscal 1988 deficit-reducing reconciliation bill (HR 3545 — PL 100-203). It included spending levels for fiscal 1989 for three broad categories of government that were financed on a year-to-year basis through the appropriations process: $299.5 billion for defense, $18.1 billion for foreign aid and $148.1 billion for domestic programs. *(Fiscal 1988 reconciliation, p. 61)*

President Reagan reaffirmed those limits in his February 1988 budget request.

House and Senate Budget Committee leaders were left with the relatively inconsequential task of setting priorities among the various discretionary domestic spending programs. Even those recommendations had no legal force. The powerful Appropriations committees could take them or leave them as they chose, so long as the caps on broad functional categories were not breached.

Indeed, even before the budget resolution was adopted, the Appropriations panels had made several key decisions on fiscal 1989 spending levels for their subcommittees. In many cases those decisions varied significantly from the corresponding allocations for domestic programs that were eventually incorporated into the budget resolution.

Nonetheless, the process of crafting a budget resolution was important to the House Democratic leadership, which wanted to show it could produce a bipartisan agreement early in the year. And final action on the resolution allowed the House to begin floor consideration of individual appropriations bills. Congress ultimately cleared all 13 regular appropriations bills before the beginning of the fiscal year, Oct. 1, a feat not accomplished since 1976. *(Fiscal 1989 appropriations, p. 74)*

Fiscal 1989 was unique during the Reagan presidency for another reason: there was no specific deficit reduction bill enacted, nor was one called for in the budget resolution.

The two-year deficit reduction deal cut in the summit and enacted in late 1987 allowed Congress and the president to meet their Gramm-Rudman target without having to endure the pain of a reconciliation bill. It was the only time since reconciliation was first used in 1980 (for fiscal 1981) that there was no congressional action on a deficit reduction measure.

### President's Proposals

The fiscal 1989 budget submitted by Reagan on Feb. 18 was a relatively passive document — a sharp contrast to 1981 and 1982 when White House fiscal strategists, led by Office of Management and Budget Director David A. Stockman, used the budget process to ram Reagan's agenda through Congress. *(Background, Congress and the Nation Vol. VI, p. 37; budget message, p. 1101)*

The main outlines of Reagans $1.094 trillion budget

request followed the summit accord.

He met the cap set by the 1987 budget summit precisely in defense, requesting $299.5 billion in new spending authority, or money obligated during the fiscal year, and $294 billion in outlays, or money actually spent during the fiscal year.

That was the smallest defense increase requested during his tenure. It raised defense spending from fiscal 1988 by only 3 percent, lower than the administration's forecast of a 3.8 percent increase in inflation — a sharp departure for a president who had made the size of the military a barometer of its strength.

In international affairs, Reagan's request for $18.1 billion in new budget authority also met the summit cap. Because of the way that money and previous appropriations were spent, however, the projected outlays of $15.6 billion in fiscal 1989 came in $500 million under the summit ceiling.

Reagan requested $147.6 billion in new spending authority for domestic programs, $500 million less than allowed under the summit agreement. White House budget officials said the figure was limited by a summit ceiling of $169.2 billion on outlays for domestic programs.

Reagan included hefty increases for certain of those programs — particularly federal aid to education and funding to combat AIDS (acquired immune deficiency syndrome) — that were the type of congressional largess he once reviled. He sought $5 billion for so-called Pell higher education grants for low-income students, twice what he requested for fiscal 1988. He wanted to increase AIDS research by 38 percent to $2 billion, which included $1.3 billion in funding for the Public Health Service.

Reagan estimated a need for $511.5 billion in 1989 for entitlements and other mandatory programs controlled by eligibility criteria and benefit formulas. That was up from $459.6 billion in fiscal 1987 and an estimated $491.6 billion in fiscal 1988.

And while Reagan kept and even expanded on previous ideas for turning over several government functions to private enterprise — his so-called "privatization" agenda — gone were the radical and sweeping government-cutting propositions that used to characterize his annual budget messages to Congress. *(Prior cuts rejected, box, p. 34)*

The president's $129.5 billion deficit projection appeared to fall below the target of the revised Gramm-Rudman-Hollings anti-deficit law (PL 100-119), which directed the president to submit his fiscal 1989 budget with a deficit no greater than $136 billion. The projected deficit was smaller than the $200 billion-plus deficits that occurred in three of the previous five years. But it was still nearly twice as large as the $73.8 billion deficit recorded in fiscal 1980, when Reagan was elected on a pledge to balance the budget by 1984. *(Gramm-Rudman, pp. 44, 67)*

However, that deficit projection assumed the government would reap about $14 billion in new revenues from the proposed sale of various government assets. Congress was not allowed to count those revenues when squaring its final deficit estimate with the Gramm-Rudman targets later in the year.

The proposed asset sales were part of a revived privatization package, in which Reagan once again asked Congress to sell some of the government's physical assets, including Amtrak, the national passenger railroad; the Naval Petroleum Reserves in Elk Hills, Calif., and Teapot Dome, Wyo.; and the Alaska Power Administration.

But the president backed off from earlier, highly controversial ideas to privatize the Postal Service and the in-house research laboratories of the National Institutes of Health.

The administration also planned to raise up to $4 billion by selling portfolios of government-sponsored loans for education, housing and development, and by allowing rural electric and telephone cooperatives to refinance government loans through private lenders without prepayment penalties.

The third largest item in Reagan's budget request, behind defense and Social Security, was $151.8 billion for interest on the national debt. A natural product of deficit spending, which forced the government to borrow money to pay its bills, net interest was expected to be larger than the deficit itself in fiscal 1989, according to White House calculations, and to keep rising well into the 1990s.

## Budget Resolution

For the first time since 1981, when the newly elected president won control of the congressional budget process — thanks to an infusion of Republicans and conservative Democrats — Congress moved relatively quickly to adopt a budget, and to do so in a fairly bipartisan way.

The reason for the speed and comity was that decisions made six months earlier during the budget summit negotiations took away much of the discretion of the Budget committees.

There were still disagreements over the specific levels of allowed spending for the 20 or so "functional" categories into which the budget was divided for accounting purposes. And House and Senate negotiators on a compromise budget between the differing versions adopted by each chamber managed to bicker for a protracted period. But there was little of the ideological battling that usually characterized the budget process.

**House Action.** After two weeks of unusual working harmony, the House Budget Committee March 17 approved its version of the budget resolution (H Con Res 268 — H Rept 100-523). The panel, better known in previous years for its partisan division and rancor, climaxed two weeks of closed-door bargaining with a quick voice vote ratifying the measure.

The committee provided more money for education, and certain health and welfare programs than was appropriated in 1988. It also included more for space and science initiatives and for drug interdiction and law enforcement.

At the same time, it called for no new taxes, and, other than a prearranged deal with Reagan on defense slowdowns, no important constituency was forced to take big cuts in spending.

Yet the measure appeared to conform with the tight restrictions on discretionary spending imposed by the budget summit accord, and with the $136 billion deficit target set by Gramm-Rudman.

That paradox was possible because the committee adopted the administration's more optimistic economic forecasts and tinkered with other budgetary "scorekeeping" interpretations. The upshot was more money to spread around than first appeared possible.

The decision to go with the administration's rosier outlook had been a foregone conclusion from the day Reagan submitted his relatively non-controversial budget for fiscal 1989. Neither Congress nor the White House wanted to deal with major spending decisions so soon after the prolonged budget battles of the previous year and so far into a major presidential election year. Reagan's economic forecast was expected to allow both sides to delay major budget-cutting decisions until the following year.

The committee also found a way to pump more money into pet projects than at first appeared possible under the summit caps by reclassifying a number of budget accounts — mainly the revolving loan accounts in the Farmers Home Administration and the Federal Housing Administration — as mandatory instead of discretionary spending.

The president's budget had devoted nearly $11 billion in budget authority for reimbursing those revolving funds and other accounts. The committee earmarked only about $7 billion to those accounts, on the assumption that the rest should be considered mandatory spending. That "freed up" almost $4 billion in discretionary budget authority to allocate to other domestic programs.

Committee Chairman William H. Gray III, D-Pa., said Democrats and Republicans went out of their way to work out compromises on virtually every dispute. "There was no acrimony about it," he said. "I can't even remember a vote we had that wasn't bipartisan."

The apogee of committee harmony occurred when two longtime nemeses, Democrat Barbara Boxer of California and Republican Dick Armey of Texas, joined to cosponsor a recommendation to give another $220 million to the Coast Guard for drug interdiction. Startled committee members could not stand in the way of such a "historic" alliance, Gray said.

Even conservative Democrats who often opposed the House leadership on budget issues were brought into the fold with new spending recommendations catered to their local interests. Budget panel member Buddy MacKay of Florida, home of Cape Canaveral, fought hard for a committee recommendation for a $1.25 billion increase for the National Aeronautics and Space Administration (NASA) — about half of what Reagan requested but more than others on the committee were willing to support.

A final roadblock to an agreement surfaced March 22, several days after the resolution was approved by the committee and only a day before it was scheduled to go to the House floor. House Democratic liberals, led by Henry A. Waxman of California, had gotten the committee to set aside a $100 million "pot" of money in the function for undistributed receipts, to be used for Democratic proposals to expand entitlement programs.

Waxman wanted the money earmarked specifically for Medicaid expansions to cover infants and pregnant women below the poverty line, spouses of nursing home residents and other low-income relief. But the panel's Republicans, under pressure from their own party members to limit entitlement spending, insisted on wording that was not so partial to Waxman's own legislative proposals.

Daylong negotiations finally produced a compromise that committed the money only generally to new education, health or welfare programs, but only if those programs were enacted separately.

The full House gave overwhelming, bipartisan support to H Con Res 268, approving it March 23 by a **key vote of 319-102 (R 92-78; D 227-24)**. *(1988 key votes, p. 981)*

"This budget shows the process can work," said Gray, who hailed the measure as a direct byproduct of the two-year summit agreement. "It was important to send a message to the American people — and to the marketplace — that Congress, or at least the House, was going to act differently on the budget this year," Gray said.

The unusually quiet floor action saw only mild rebukes

from conservative Republicans and very little support for three alternative budgets offered by William E. Dannemeyer, R-Calif.; John Edward Porter, R-Ill.; and Timothy J. Penny, D-Minn.

**Senate Action.** The Senate Budget Committee followed suit on March 30, giving quick approval in an 18-3 vote to its own spending plan (S Con Res 113 — S Rept 100-311). Like the House version, the Senate committee's budget resolution stuck closely to the restrictions on taxes and overall discretionary spending imposed by the budget summit.

The Senate budget met the $136 billion deficit target required under Gramm-Rudman, with the help of $3.5 billion in loan asset sales and other savings. Discounting the asset sales — which could not be used to avoid Gramm-Rudman automatic cuts — the committee's deficit was estimated to be $143.2 billion, still within the $10 billion margin-of-error range allowed by the law.

The Senate panel also followed the House lead in adopting the administration's optimistic economic forecast for the economy.

However, the Senate budget provided more for science and space than did the House version, with the increases coming mainly at the expense of community and regional development programs and, to a lesser extent, programs in energy and natural resources.

Chief among the few new spending proposals in the resolution was a $2.2 billion increase in budget authority over the 1988 level for NASA, which wanted to add a new space shuttle as well as a manned space station to its ongoing space exploration programs.

That was about twice the amount recommended for space programs in the companion House budget.

The Senate plan also channeled about $200 million in new spending for the Energy Department's proposed superconducting supercollider, twice as much as provided by the House. The total of $13.4 billion for space and science programs was $1 billion more than recommended by the House, though still $500 million less than the $13.9 billion level requested by the president.

The Senate panel's particular focus on space programs could be traced to the regional and political interests of its chairman, Democrat Lawton Chiles of Florida, and ranking Republican, Pete V. Domenici of New Mexico.

In addition, four of the seven states still in the running to host the $4 billion supercollider project were represented on the committee, including both senators from Colorado, Democrat Timothy E. Wirth and Republican William L. Armstrong. *(Supercollider, p. 863)*

Reagan added his own voice to the call for increased science and space spending, summoning leaders of the Budget and Appropriations committees to the White House March 29 for a "pep talk" on the subject.

Although the panel did not go as far as the president, who wanted to eliminate programs such as Urban Development Action Grants, the Senate resolution reduced funding for community development by $400 million, or 7.5 percent less than the $5.4 billion that would have been spent if the program were frozen at its 1988 level.

The $2.5 billion Community Development Block Grants program bore the brunt of those cuts. Particular commerce and housing programs received even deeper reductions, with small business and housing for the elderly facing cuts of nearly 9 percent.

These urban-oriented programs were the biggest losers in the Senate plan, prompting a last-minute lobbying effort by the U.S. Conference of Mayors. The group persuaded committee leaders to add $200 million to their original proposal for community development programs, cutting science and space by the same amount.

Further tinkering with the scorekeeping interpretations of certain revolving-loan accounts gave the committee another $2.7 billion in budget authority to allocate to discretionary domestic programs. (The House had found a total of $4.3 billion in much the same way simply by redesignating budget authority for those and other accounts as "mandatory" instead of "discretionary.")

In one other significant departure from the House, the Senate panel agreed to issue "reconciliation instructions" directing four committees with jurisdiction over asset sales to come up with a total of $3.5 billion in net "contributions" to deficit reduction. The House did not issue formal reconciliation instructions when it recommended a similar amount of new asset sales.

The Senate adopted H Con Res 268 by a 69-26 vote April 14, after amending it to conform to its own budget plan. The Senate ratified the Budget Committee's recommendations for big increases in space, science and, to a lesser extent, education programs and anti-drug law enforcement.

In the only significant floor amendment, senators agreed 93-0 to pump an additional $2.6 billion in new spending authority into an expanded anti-drug campaign. The money was slated to pay for a pending bill sponsored by Dennis DeConcini, D-Ariz., and Alfonse M. D'Amato, R-N.Y., to increase spending for drug-treatment programs, law enforcement and interdiction efforts.

Since no offsetting revenues or savings were included to cover the expense, the amendment appeared to bust budget summit caps on domestic spending.

But Senate Budget Committee leaders came up with a way to get around the limits by keeping the money in a "reserve fund" to be released only after three conditions had been met: enactment of the pending bill, provision by Congress of offsetting revenues or savings to pay for it and a declaration by Reagan and leaders of Congress that a "dire emergency" existed to justify such a clear violation of the summit spending caps.

Once those hurdles were cleared, $2.6 billion in new budget authority and $1.4 billion in outlays were to be added to the Appropriations committees' budget allocations, allowing them to provide nearly twice as much to anti-drug initiatives as was appropriated in fiscal 1988.

The Senate budget resolution already contained a $550 million increase in federal anti-drug spending, which received $3.47 billion in fiscal 1988, according to committee aides.

Budget Committee leaders insisted the reserve allocation for an anti-drug bill would not breach the budget summit agreement. "We'll be raising it in a deficit-neutral way," said Chiles. The amendment's sponsors believed it could be paid for with increased tax enforcement and public debt collections.

**Conference, Final Action.** The bipartisan spirit that had swept the resolutions through both chambers quickly gave way to fundamental House-Senate disagreements over domestic spending priorities in conference.

Conferees struggled to marry the Senate's overwhelming support for space and science initiatives with the House's equally strong predilection for anti-poverty programs and urban-oriented grants to state and local governments.

At one point, Budget committee leaders angrily halted negotiations as the debate deteriorated into an exchange of insults and accusations of refusing to negotiate in good faith.

Finally, after six weeks of negotiations, House and Senate budget leaders finally agreed May 26 on a compromise $1.1 trillion budget resolution (H Rept 100-658). The plan's $135.3 billion deficit was just under the $136 billion Gramm-Rudman target.

By that point, it was becoming apparent that the Budget panels were on the verge of being eclipsed in both word and deed by the real spending arms of Congress, the Appropriations committees.

Both the House and Senate Appropriations panels had moved quickly to reassert their primacy in the budget process. The House committee began reporting out individual spending bills the week of May 9 and scheduled floor action on three of the measures the week of May 16.

The Senate Appropriations Committee was proceeding with its own spending blueprint, allocating money to its subcommittees without waiting for a completed budget resolution.

J. Bennett Johnston, D-La., acting on behalf of Appropriations Chairman John C. Stennis, D-Miss., worked aggressively to get a plan that would supersede any agreement that Chiles and Gray might work out.

"What the Budget Committee decides is advisory only," Johnston said. "It's an endless wrangle over endless assumptions that are not binding. It's a waste of time."

The discrepancy in their definitions of discretionary programs — which amounted to $1.7 billion — was a crucial sticking point. That was the amount in new spending authority that the House had freed up for other discretionary programs by deciding that certain revolving loan funds and other accounts should be considered mandatory spending.

Senate leaders questioned those scorekeeping interpretations and said the White House could eventually veto spending bills on the premise that the scoring violated the summit agreement.

In the final compromise, the Senate prevailed on most of the scorekeeping differences. A $525 million advance appropriation for clean-coal technology passed in 1988 was ruled a discretionary item in fiscal 1989.

House Budget conferees caved in to Senate demands to provide at least $13 billion in new budget authority for science and space programs, while Senate leaders agreed to increase their spending recommendations for education and job-training programs by $600 million, to $37.2 billion.

The House also accepted a Senate plan to set aside $2.6 billion for a major anti-drug initiative if offsetting revenues were found to pay for it.

But the Senate call for instructing authorizing committees to produce needed asset sales through the reconciliation process was abandoned; there were no reconciliation instructions in the final budget resolution. And conferees agreed on a House demand to accommodate tariff reductions and other revenue losses that would result from enactment of the omnibus trade bill (HR 3) and a Canada-U.S. free-trade agreement. (Trade bill, p. 148; free-trade agreement, p. 159)

Bipartisan support for the budget faded when the conference report reached the House floor. Republicans, who had provided rare consensus on the original House-passed budget measure, voted in droves against the conference compromise. Many were opposed to a $400 million allowance for new "entitlement" spending in fiscal 1989, including a $275 million Senate provision to expand an Agriculture Department program that provided cheese and butter to the poor.

## Appropriations, Fiscal 1989

Congress once again in 1988 failed to get all 13 regular appropriations bills enacted before the fiscal year began. But largely as a result of the budget "summit" agreement, which kept tough decisions and partisan conflicts to a minimum, Congress did complete action on all 13 with seconds to spare before the new fiscal year began at midnight, Sept. 30.

It was the first time since 1976 that Congress acted on all 13 measures in a timely way. The feat also broke a two-year trend of rolling all 13 measures into one, giant spending bill, called a continuing appropriations resolution.

The lateness of congressional action on the last bills forced Reagan to cancel a scheduled signing ceremony. The event was intended to take note of the fact that for the first time since 1948 all required appropriations bills were enacted by the start of the fiscal year. Instead, the remaining bills were signed by Reagan on Oct. 1.

Congress and the president were both able to claim political credit for their ability to avoid enacting a sweeping continuing resolution for fiscal 1989. Reagan had promised in his Jan. 25, 1988, State of the Union address never to sign another "behemoth" continuing resolution into law. *(Text of address, p. 1095)*

Congressional Democrats, embarrassed by the episode and wanting to prove during an election year in which they hoped to retake the White House, also promised to enact separate appropriations bills.

Congress also enacted two "dire emergency" supplemental appropriations measures during 1988 for fiscal 1988. Only such emergency supplemental spending measures were permitted under the terms of the November 1987 budget summit agreement.

The first (H J Res 552 — PL 100-304) provided $709 million for a veterans' housing program that was scheduled to run out of cash in early May, and for other education, training assistance and rehabilitation programs. The House passed the joint resolution on April 27 by voice vote; the Senate followed suit the next day. The money had been requested by the White House and the measure was kept free of unasked-for encumberances by Congress.

A second emergency measure (HR 5026 — PL 100-393) was cleared by the Senate Aug. 11. The House had first passed the bill July 27, and the Senate did so Aug. 10, after amending it. The Senate dropped most of its amendments, enabling the two chambers to agree to it the next day.

The bill provided $672 million for a wide variety of programs, including Soviet and other political refugees, disaster relief, drought relief and drug-interdiction efforts of the Coast Guard.

## CPI for the Elderly

Congress, against the protests of the Reagan administration, ordered the Labor Department in 1987 to develop a consumer price index (CPI) to reflect the higher-than-average living expenditures of Americans aged 62 and over. The department was given 180 days to carry out the directive. No action was taken, however, to enact a revised index into law. The order was included in a bill (HR 1451 — PL 100-175) reauthorizing the Older Americans Act; it cleared Nov. 17. *(Older Americans Act, p. 629)*

Each year, recipients of Social Security and federal civilian, military and railroad retirement pensions received a cost-of-living adjustment (COLA) based on the increase in the CPI over the previous year. But critics said the COLAs were not enough to keep pace with the actual increase in the cost of living experienced by older Americans. The rate of inflation in 1986 was just over 1 percent and resulted in an additional $6 per month for the average Social Security recipient or federal retiree who got COLAs based on the CPI. For the one-third of all senior citizens who depended upon Social Security for 90 percent or more of their annual income, it was not much of an increase.

The problem, said Sen. John Melcher, D-Mont., and other critics, was the way the CPI was calculated. The index used in setting Social Security and other COLAs was based on a survey of the spending patterns of urban wage-earners and clerical workers, who made up 32 percent of the population. The elderly — whose spending patterns were quite different — were not included in the survey.

Melcher and lobbyists for senior citizens argued that because the elderly spend far more on health care than the rest of the population, the CPI understated the inflation they experienced. For years, health costs had risen faster than prices in most other sectors of the economy.

But the Labor Department's Bureau of Labor Statistics (BLS), which calculated the CPI, insisted that a new index would be costly to develop and would probably not result in a significant difference in the overall inflation measurement for older Americans. BLS officials argued that the elderly's patterns of purchasing — they spent considerably more than the general population on health care, groceries and household fuels, but less on education, gasoline, new cars and new clothes — compensated for any disadvantages caused by the existing CPI.

### Legislative History

A consumer price index for the elderly — a CPI-E — was not a new idea. Over the past decade, more than 20 bills on the subject had been introduced, but none had made it out of subcommittee.

Melcher tried often in 1987 to persuade the federal government to develop one. He originally offered his proposal as a floor amendment to the fiscal 1987 supplemental appropriations bill (HR 1827 — PL 100-71). On May 27, his amendment was adopted by the Senate 95-0, but it ran into strong opposition from BLS during the House-Senate conference on HR 1827 and was dropped. *(Supplemental appropriations, p. 57)*

Melcher July 1 tried to reattach his measure to the conference report on HR 1827, but he was rebuffed by colleagues who wanted to pass the supplemental spending bill and begin their July 4th recess.

On Aug. 6, the Senate added Melcher's amendment to the Older Americans Act reauthorization by voice vote.

# Tax Policy

Revisions to federal tax law, most of them relatively small, come around like clockwork. Even for a president like Ronald Reagan, who was so averse to increasing taxes, the chance to alter the tax code was not to be missed. And he made the most of his opportunity.

Reagan presided over two of the most significant experiments in the nation's tax policy in 1981 and 1985-86. Both were his ideas; and both were premised on a key notion of income tax policy — markedly lower rates.

But in some respects the two tax plans were radically different, and the bill enacted in 1986 undid much of what the administration achieved in 1981.

The Tax Reform Act of 1986 was a dramatic departure from previous tax bills for several reasons. Chief among them was because Congress was willing to act against the special interests that over the years were responsible for the tax code's tapestry of favors. Although the 1986 law had its critics, it was hailed by a broad spectrum of economists and politicians as "real reform" of a tax system gone haywire.

Reagan, the top tax-basher in the country, called it "the best anti-poverty bill, the best pro-family measure and the best job-creation program ever to come out of the Congress of the United States."

Economist Henry J. Aaron of the liberal-leaning Brookings Institution, a think tank in Washington, D.C., called the legislation "the most important improvement in the broad-based taxes on individual and corporate income in at least two decades."

Reagan's point and Aaron's were not necessarily the same, but they were not far apart either. There was much to like in the new law: It greatly reduced tax rates, long the aim of those who, like Reagan, adhered to supply-side economic beliefs; it eliminated many corporate and individual tax breaks that were opposed by more liberal economists on the grounds that they mostly benefited upper-income taxpayers; and it shifted the individual tax burden up the economic ladder, limiting or eliminating taxes for poorer people, and reversing a 40-year trend of declining corporate tax liability.

Moreover, the bill did not violate Reagan's 1984 reelection pledge of no new taxes. The 1981 tax cut was the biggest in the nation's history, but Congress — with Reagan's cooperation and occasionally his insistence — had rolled back some of its giveaways in 1982 and 1984. Combined with a Social Security tax increase enacted in 1983, about a third of the 1981 tax cut had been reversed in the following three years.

But Reagan did not want to be known as the president who raised taxes — only the one who made the tax system more fair.

So, in first suggesting a "reform" of the tax code in his 1984 State of the Union address, he insisted that such a change neither increase taxes nor reduce them. This "revenue-neutral" approach, as it was called, guaranteed a united front from conservatives and liberals who favored the low rates and fewer tax breaks the measure promised. And it protected the measure from amendments that would have been its undoing.

But the law's supposed revenue-neutral behavior was among the major complaints about it; liberal Democrats and even some conservative Republicans had favored a tax increase that would help to reduce the budget deficit. Against Reagan's opposition, the notion of increasing taxes attracted few supporters.

In fact, the law eventually proved to be anything but revenue-neutral. Because many of its provisions were to be phased in over five years, and because taxpayers reacted to changes in the code by significantly altering their economic activity — such as selling off appreciated assets in 1986 to avoid higher capital gains taxes in 1987 — the act produced increased revenues in its first year and was expected to produce decreased revenues in later years. And those fluctuations, while predicted in part before the law was enacted, turned out to be much greater than expected. In 1988 the administration estimated that the law would result in a $23.2 billion revenue loss over its first five years.

## Roots in 1981

The 1986 law began life in the minds of Rep. Jack Kemp, R-N.Y., and his supply-side allies. Kemp and Sen. William V. Roth Jr., R-Del., first began pushing a low-rate

## References

Discussion of tax policy for the years 1945-64 may be found in *Congress and the Nation Vol. I*, pp. 397-442; for the years 1965-68, *Congress and the Nation Vol. II*, pp. 141-182; for the years 1969-72, *Congress and the Nation Vol. III*, pp. 77-96; for the years 1973-76, *Congress and the Nation Vol. IV*, pp. 83-106; for the years 1977-80, *Congress and the Nation Vol. V*, pp. 231-251; for the years 1981-84, *Congress and the Nation Vol. VI*, pp. 63-82.

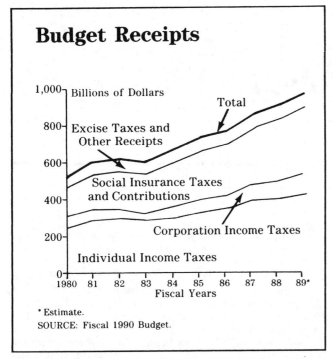

## Budget Receipts

Billions of Dollars

Total

Excise Taxes and
Other Receipts

Social Insurance Taxes
and Contributions

Corporation Income Taxes

Individual Income Taxes

1,000 — 800 — 600 — 400 — 200 — 0

1980 81 82 83 84 85 86 87 88 89*
Fiscal Years

* Estimate.
SOURCE: Fiscal 1990 Budget.

tax code in 1977 as an economic stimulus, but without the offsetting effects of reduced or eliminated tax breaks.

Some of what they advocated wound up in the president's 1981 tax proposal that was for the most part enacted into law. In 1982, two Democrats — Sen. Bill Bradley of New Jersey and Rep. Richard A. Gephardt of Missouri — embraced the idea of a few very low rates, not to pay for a tax cut but to eliminate the incentive for massive adjustments to taxable income in the form of exclusions, deductions and credits.

The plan then was adopted by Reagan, who in January 1984 called for a wholesale simplification of the tax code. Kemp joined with Sen. Bob Kasten, R-Wis., to offer in April 1984 a new tax simplification bill based on a single, flat rate. And the race was on.

Treasury Secretary Donald T. Regan proposed a three-rate income tax system in November 1984 that would curtail many tax breaks and eliminate accelerated depreciation for business equipment, the centerpiece of the 1981 tax cut. Businesses reacted warily — and in some cases angrily — to the plan, which became known as Treasury I. Reagan, himself, was lukewarm and said he would have his own proposal later and would like to hear suggestions from others in the meantime.

Bradley, Gephardt, Kasten and Kemp reintroduced their bills in January 1985, sharing the stage at a joint press conference where they played down their disagreements and promised to work together to "reform" the tax code. It was clear that, with White House support, Congress would be in a unique position to challenge the special interests that had derailed prior reform efforts, including some dating to the early 1960s.

Also in January 1985, Regan switched jobs with White House Chief of Staff James A. Baker III, who eventually produced a new plan, known as Treasury II, more appealing to some business interests. This proposal was embraced by the president, and it was Baker who, with his key aide and tactician Richard G. Darman, led administration negotiators for the next two years in dealing with Congress.

## Fairness and Simplicity

Reagan's announced goals of a fairer and simpler tax code proved more difficult to achieve than he wished. One taxpayer's fairness was another's higher tax bill, after all. So a key battle that was waged throughout the debate in 1985 and 1986 was whether the proposed changes were more "fair."

General agreement was reached that a substantial elimination of tax breaks — deductions, exemptions and credits — would put more taxpayers on a "level playing field," where financial decisions would be based not on tax considerations, but on pure economics.

Certainly the 1986 law's restrictions on sheltering income were expected to eliminate large amounts of uneconomic investment. For example, previously taxpayers with sufficient income could buy into businesses — often limited partnerships — set up strictly for the purpose of taking advantage of tax breaks and without any regard for the profitability of the enterprises.

Investment tax credits, accelerated depreciation schedules, particularly for real estate, and other benefits were used by these partnerships to create paper losses in excess of actual income. Since partnership income and losses were passed through to the partners, the paper losses could — before 1987 — be deducted against an individual's wage income, thereby reducing tax liability. Often before a tax shelter used up its tax benefits and began earning real profits, the partners would sell their interests and move on to a newly formed shelter.

The 1986 law made it impossible to deduct paper or so-called "passive" losses against anything but "passive" income — in other words, real income from the same kind of investments that generated the paper losses.

But the tax-rate reduction that was designed to accompany the elimination of tax breaks posed another "fairness" problem. By definition fewer, lower rates jeopardized a prominent feature of the income tax code: "progressive" or graduated rates that increase for higher income taxpayers.

The concept of a progressive rate structure means that each taxpayer's first dollar earned is taxed at one rate and, as more is earned, the rate on higher earnings is taxed at higher rates. The so-called marginal rate is that paid on the last dollar earned.

The marginal rate had declined from the end of World War II to 28 percent in the 1986 law (except some very-high-income taxpayers were subject to a 33 percent rate, but not the wealthiest).

Liberal critics of the 1986 law argued that it was abandoning the historic progressive aim of the income tax code. But supporters of the law countered that many wealthy taxpayers escaped most tax liability through tax breaks that did not benefit poorer persons. By eliminating those tax breaks, the argument went, the aim of progressivity could still be maintained.

And, significantly, the new law stiffened requirements that individuals and corporations pay at least a minimum amount of tax; one of the driving forces behind the reform effort was the seeming unfairness that many large — and seemingly profitable — U.S. businesses were able to escape paying taxes altogether just by exploiting legal loopholes. One intent of the 1986 law was to put an end to that.

In fact, the corporate minimum tax and other changes affecting taxes on businesses were designed to reverse a long-running trend of corporations to pay a smaller and smaller share of the total tax collected. And some businesses were guaranteed to pay more, while others, which had been more heavily taxed in the past, would fair better.

One study from the Congressional Research Service, an arm of the Library of Congress, found that overall the effective tax rate on corporations would increase under the 1986 law from 38 percent to 41 percent. But for industry the change was more dramatic: Agriculture, manufacturing and trade, which paid the highest effective rates under the previous law, would see no change or a slight reduction in their tax liabilities. But oil and mining, utilities, construction, communication, transportation and service industries would see their effective rates climb from as low as 23 percent to as high as 41 percent.

It was no wonder that many U.S. businesses strongly favored the bill, while others opposed it.

If the 1986 law was challenged on grounds of fairness, few believed that it achieved Reagan's initial call for simplicity.

Nothing about it was simpler, except that the law reduced the number of persons eligible to itemize their deductions. The tax code was still thousands of pages long, with countless provisions affecting all manner of activities in different ways. But persons with average incomes were expected to benefit from efforts to make the law less complex for them: Individuals had fewer items with costs that were tax-deductible; therefore, record-keeping for them should be simpler. For high-income persons and corporations, the stiffer minimum tax was expected to make record-keeping and tax calculations more complex, but the trade-off was considered necessary to ensure that those taxpayers with the most income paid their share.

## Ending Some Tax Breaks, Keeping Others

In the course of eliminating tax breaks, Congress allowed individual taxpayers to continue to deduct interest paid on money borrowed to purchase a house: It is perhaps the most important concession in federal law to the American Dream of home ownership.

But if that tax break survived largely unscathed (albeit there were a few changes for very wealthy taxpayers), many other seemingly sacred tax breaks went down the drain in the 1986 law. Before their repeal, most of these tax breaks were calculated by the Congressional Budget Office (CBO) to be major revenue losers for the Treasury.

The foremost change may have been ending the special tax rate on capital gains income.

A central tenet of the code since 1921 had been a reduced tax on capital gains — income derived from the sale of an asset that had increased in value, such as real estate or artwork or stocks. As long as maximum effective tax rates were quite high, individuals and businesses were allowed to exclude from their reported income part of the gain from the sale of a capital investment.

But in 1986, when marginal rates were cut back severely, Congress eliminated the so-called differential. Prior to 1986, a person taxed at the maximum 50 percent rate would have paid tax on only 40 percent of a capital gain; the result was an effective 20 percent tax rate on capital gains. That effective rate rose to 28 percent (or 33 percent for some taxpayers) in the 1986 law, which taxes capital gains as regular income.

The effect of the 1986 change was to eliminate entirely what CBO had projected to be a $56.1 billion revenue loss in 1991 due to the capital gains exclusion.

## Taxes as Percentage of GNP

|  | Individual Income | Corporate Income | Social Insurance | Excise |
|---|---|---|---|---|
| 1935 | 0.8% | 0.8% | — | 2.1% |
| 1940 | 0.9 | 1.2 | 1.9% | 2.1 |
| 1945 | 8.6 | 7.5 | 1.6 | 2.9 |
| 1950 | 5.9 | 3.9 | 1.6 | 2.8 |
| 1955 | 7.4 | 4.6 | 2.0 | 2.4 |
| 1960 | 8.0 | 4.2 | 2.9 | 2.3 |
| 1965 | 7.3 | 3.8 | 3.3 | 2.2 |
| 1970 | 9.1 | 3.3 | 4.5 | 1.6 |
| 1975 | 8.0 | 2.7 | 5.6 | 1.1 |
| 1980 | 9.1 | 2.4 | 5.9 | 0.9 |
| 1981 | 9.6 | 2.0 | 6.1 | 1.4 |
| 1982 | 9.5 | 1.6 | 6.4 | 1.2 |
| 1983 | 8.7 | 1.1 | 6.3 | 1.1 |
| 1984 | 8.1 | 1.5 | 6.5 | 1.0 |
| 1985 | 8.5 | 1.6 | 6.7 | 0.9 |
| 1986 | 8.3 | 1.5 | 6.8 | 0.8 |
| 1987 | 8.9 | 1.9 | 6.8 | 0.7 |
| 1988 | 8.4 | 2.0 | 7.0 | 0.7 |

NOTE: Social Insurance includes Social Security, railroad and other retirement programs and unemployment insurance.

SOURCE: Office of Management and Budget.

The 1986 law also dramatically altered the way in which businesses were allowed to deduct from income the declining value of their purchased assets.

So-called depreciation allowances had been altered over the years through formulas designed to give taxpayers sooner more of the tax benefit of the cost of their equipment, factories and other buildings, and other assets. The intent was to grant a higher tax value to the asset through some method of accelerating the depreciation.

The 1981 tax law, for instance, assigned artificially short depreciation periods for most assets, so they would still be functional long after their owners had recovered their worth through tax deductions. The 1981 depreciation schedules were completely rewritten, although for many kinds of equipment, the effective deduction was little changed.

Beyond depreciation, from time to time, the tax code granted an investment tax credit for spending on equipment that was often in addition to available depreciation.

Such tax incentives have been controversial. The investment credit, first proposed by President John F. Kennedy, was enacted in 1962, repealed in 1966 and reinstated and repealed twice more, the last time in 1986.

Repeal of the investment tax credit was an obvious target of the "reformers" in 1985 and 1986. It had previously been increased to 10 percent, and many economists thought it had skewed investment benefits, especially when combined with the very generous depreciation schedule enacted in 1981.

Before the 1986 law repealed the investment tax credit, it had been projected to cost the Treasury $38.6 billion in 1991, according to CBO. After the provision was repealed, the 1991 revenue loss was set at $1.6 billion,

# Revenue Losses Since 1982

*(Dollar amounts in billions; totals may not add due to rounding)*

| | 1982 | 1983 | 1984 | 1985 | 1986 | 1987 | 1988 | Total 1982-88 |
|---|---|---|---|---|---|---|---|---|
| Economic Recovery Tax Act of 1981 | −35.6 | −91.1 | −136.8 | −170.3 | −209.8 | −241.7 | −264.4 | −1,149.7 |
| Tax Equity and Fiscal Responsibility Act of 1982 | — | 16.6 | 36.0 | 39.2 | 46.7 | 56.9 | 57.3 | 252.7 |
| Highway Revenue Act of 1982 | — | 1.5 | 4.2 | 4.2 | 4.5 | 4.7 | 4.9 | 24.0 |
| Social Security Amendments of 1983 | — | — | 5.7 | 8.7 | 10.2 | 12.1 | 24.6 | 61.3 |
| Interest and Dividends Tax Compliance Act of 1983 | — | −0.1 | −2.6 | −2.4 | −2.1 | −1.7 | −1.8 | −10.7 |
| Railroad Retirement Revenue Act of 1983 | — | — | 0.2 | 0.7 | 1.1 | 1.2 | 1.2 | 4.4 |
| Deficit Reduction Act of 1984 | — | — | 0.9 | 9.3 | 16.1 | 22.0 | 25.4 | 73.7 |
| Consolidated Omnibus Reconciliation Act of 1985 | — | — | — | — | 0.9 | 2.7 | 2.9 | 6.5 |
| Federal Employees' Retirement System Act of 1986 | — | — | — | — | — | −0.1 | −0.2 | −0.3 |
| Omnibus Reconciliation Act of 1986 | — | — | — | — | — | 2.7 | 2.4 | 5.1 |
| Superfund Amendments and Reauthorization Act of 1986 | — | — | — | — | — | 0.4 | 0.6 | 1.0 |
| Fiscal 1987 Continuing Resolution | — | — | — | — | — | 1.9 | 2.8 | 4.7 |
| Tax Reform Act of 1986 | — | — | — | — | — | 21.5 | −8.9 | 12.6 |
| Omnibus Reconciliation Act of 1987 | — | — | — | — | — | — | 8.6 | 8.6 |
| Fiscal 1988 Continuing Resolution | — | — | — | — | — | — | 2.0 | 2.0 |
| Annual Total | −35.6 | −73.1 | −92.4 | −110.6 | −132.4 | −117.4 | −142.6 | −704.1 |

SOURCE: Office of Management and Budget.

resulting from unused credits that businesses were eligible to carry forward to future years.

Just as depreciation and investment credits were designed to stimulate business investment, various elements of the tax code were intended to spur savings and investment by individuals: a $100 per taxpayer exclusion from taxable income of dividends earned from stock holdings and Individual Retirement Accounts (IRAs), to name two. The 1986 law repealed the dividend exclusion and the availability of all taxpayers to invest tax-free in IRAs.

From 1981 to 1986, all taxpayers with earned income could put $2,000 into an IRA, whether they were covered by pension plans or not, and they could put another $250 a year into an account for a non-working spouse. During that time, revenue losses from the IRA provision skyrocketed, however, and the individual savings rate fell from 7.5 percent to 4.3 percent. It appeared that most taxpayers were merely transferring their existing savings into tax-deferred accounts and not increasing their savings as was intended.

So, in 1986, Congress rolled back the IRA deduction to allow only lower-income taxpayers, or those with no pension plan, to deposit tax-exempt dollars in an account. Other taxpayers, however, were allowed to deposit money on which they had already paid taxes into an account where the interest would be tax-exempt until retirement.

The IRA change was expected to be a net gain of $10 billion to the Treasury in 1991, according to CBO.

# Chronology
# Of Action
# On Taxes

# 1985-86

As the 99th Congress wound down in 1986, members put the finishing touches on the most extensive overhaul of the nation's tax laws since World War II. The bill, President Reagan's No. 1 legislative goal for his second term, had been more than two years in the making. Its progress through Congress had been tumultuous, and at times the bill had appeared doomed. The final legislation was hailed as an extraordinary accomplishment even by those who criticized its dramatic cuts in individual and business tax rates and its elimination of preferential tax treatment in many areas. "I feel like we just played the World Series of tax reform," Reagan said when he signed the bill into law.

## Tax Law Overhaul

Congress in 1986 enacted the first complete rewrite of the Internal Revenue Code since 1954. The bill (HR 3838 — PL 99-514) was the product of more than two years of work by Congress, the Treasury Department and the White House. It sharply reduced income tax rates for corporations and individuals and curtailed or eliminated dozens of special tax benefits.

Over the five years from 1987 through 1991, the bill was expected to shift an estimated $120 billion of the total income tax burden from individuals to corporations. The corporate share of total income tax collections, however, still was projected to remain below the proportion that prevailed during the entire period 1940 through 1979.

The new law reduced the top individual tax rate from 50 percent to 28 percent and taxed 85 percent of all individuals at the bottom rate of 15 percent. Its dual origins were a Democratic tax "reform" plan first advanced in 1982 by Sen. Bill Bradley, D-N.J., and Rep. Richard A. Gephardt, D-Mo., and President Reagan's 1984 call for a "historic reform" of the tax laws, aimed at "fairness, simplicity and incentives for growth."

On the one hand, as enacted, the legislation cut individual tax rates more than either the Reagan plan or the Bradley-Gephardt bill envisioned. The president proposed a top individual tax rate of 35 percent and Bradley-Gephardt put it at 30 percent. On the other hand, corporate taxes were cut slightly less than either proposal envisioned. The new law reduced the top corporate rate from 46 percent to 34 percent. The president proposed 33 percent and Bradley-Gephardt 30 percent.

Enactment of the measure was accomplished through the perseverance of its chief backers in Congress and over the objections of many special interests who stood to lose their favored status under the tax code. There was never a groundswell of support from the public at large. If anything, the public perception was that record-high federal budget deficits were a more critical concern for Congress than tax reform. The deficit, and the understanding that the tax bill must not contribute to it, set the framework for action on the legislation. (*Deficit reduction, p. 96*)

Reagan stood fast against a tax increase and insisted that the tax bill be revenue-neutral. The result was adherence in the House, in the Senate and in conference to the principle of revenue neutrality — defined for this purpose as neither raising nor reducing total federal tax collections over a five-year period following enactment. Ultimately, that principle allowed the bill's supporters to turn back costly amendments to restore special tax benefits because their sponsors could not produce offsetting revenues.

## Background

As early as August 1982, Bradley and Gephardt jointly had proposed revising the tax system to curtail sharply most preferential tax treatment and to reduce individual and corporate rates. Reagan joined the call for tax reform in his 1984 State of the Union message, in which he charged the Treasury Department with drafting a plan to simplify the tax code "so all taxpayers, big and small, are treated more fairly."

During the 1984 presidential campaign, Democratic candidate Walter F. Mondale also called for a "fairer" tax code. Mondale asked for higher taxes on middle- and upper-income taxpayers to help reduce the deficit — and he predicted that Reagan would seek tax increases as well. Reagan, however, promised he would not raise taxes, and he cautioned that no tax increase would be acceptable in the guise of tax reform. (*Congress and the Nation Vol. VI, p. 78*)

The Treasury Department released its proposal Nov. 27, 1984, but the plan received a lukewarm response from Congress and the White House. Major elements of the plan would cut individual and corporate tax rates, curtail many special tax benefits and repeal accelerated depreciation, the centerpiece of Reagan's 1981 tax cut. The White House was besieged with complaints about specific features of the plan, particularly from businesses, which stood to lose considerably, and Reagan declined to embrace it.

The president did not reveal his own blueprint for a new tax system until May 28, 1985. Under Reagan's plan, most taxpayers would pay taxes below or at the same level they paid under existing law. About one in five individuals and many corporations would pay more. The plan held to the rate structure of the Treasury proposal: three individual tax rates of 15, 25 and 35 percent and a top corporate tax rate of 33 percent.

Reagan proposed retaining deductions for charitable contributions and interest payments on primary residences but eliminating many other benefits, including the deduction for state and local tax payments. Deductions for some other interest payments, including those for second homes, would be limited or repealed, and a portion of employer-paid health insurance premiums would be taxed. (*Evolution of bill, box, p. 82*)

Reagan's plan called for limits on the use of some investment tax incentives, but he sought more generous treatment of capital gains income to encourage investment in new industries.

# Prior 'Reforms' Sometimes Have Gone Awry

For as long as it had been in existence, the income tax was the target of schemes to "reform" it.

The first tax on income, a Civil War-era emergency measure, lasted from 1862 to 1871. The existing income tax was established after the ratification of the 16th Amendment to the Constitution.

The amendment, ratified on Feb. 25, 1913, states, "The Congress shall have power to lay and collect taxes on incomes, from whatever source derived, without apportionment among the several states and without regard to any census or enumeration."

That power was exercised often. Prior to the comprehensive rewrite of federal income tax law in 1985-86 (HR 3838 — PL 99-514), the tax code itself was last overhauled in 1954. But it was often modified. *(Congress and the Nation Vol. I, p. 416)*

Beginning in the mid-1960s efforts were made to bring order and fairness to a tax system that had become increasingly unwieldy. Often, however, changes made in the name of reform led to more of the confusion and perceived inequity that were the target of congressional and White House reform efforts in 1985 and 1986.

Even the changes enacted in 1986 failed to live up to the billing given the measure by President Reagan. Although it succeeded in reducing the number of taxpayers who would need to file comprehensive itemized returns, and it swept a great many poor persons off the tax rolls, the code was in most ways not "simplified." And for moderate- and high-income individuals, and those whose dependent children had more than modest amounts of income, the 1986 code became, if anything, more complex.

Previous reform attempts included:

● **Revenue Act of 1964 (PL 88-272).** President John F. Kennedy in 1963 proposed massive cuts in tax rates to help stimulate economic growth. They were to be financed by placing restrictions on several existing tax breaks. His plan included a limit on total itemized deductions and reductions in tax breaks for the oil and gas industry.

Congress enacted the tax cuts, but many of Kennedy's "reform" proposals fell by the wayside.

Kennedy made initial proposals to close tax loopholes in 1961. But they also were rejected by Congress when it passed the Revenue Act of 1962 (PL 87-834), which created a new tax credit for business investment. *(Congress and the Nation Vol. I, pp. 429, 437)*

● **Tax Reform Act of 1969 (PL 91-172).** Spurred by widespread discontent with inequities in the federal tax system, Congress passed legislation eliminating or restricting a number of tax breaks, such as the investment tax credit, and allowing the poorest American to avoid paying income taxes.

Nonetheless, loopholes remained and some of the provisions in the original legislation, such as a proposed reduction in the oil depletion allowance, were watered down before the bill was enacted. *(Congress and the Nation Vol. III, p. 79)*

● **Tax Reform Act of 1976 (PL 94-455).** After two years of turbulent tax debate, Congress agreed to legislation restricting oil and gas, real estate and other tax shelters, increasing minimum taxes on corporations and individuals and setting limits on business expense deductions. The legislation also expanded investment incentives, raised the standard deduction and created a number of miscellaneous special-interest tax breaks. *(Congress and the Nation Vol. IV, p. 99)*

● **Revenue Act of 1978 (PL 95-600).** President Jimmy Carter proposed an ambitious tax program that included many changes similar to those considered in 1985-86. He recommended a 2 percent cut in tax rates, restrictions on preferential capital gains treatment and elimination of a number of widely used tax breaks. He urged limits on business expense deductions for entertainment, meals and travel.

But the time and politics were not ripe for Carter, and his proposals were rejected. Congress instead enacted a wide range of tax cuts, many of which benefited middle- and upper-income taxpayers. *(Congress and the Nation Vol. V, p. 238)*

● **Tax Equity and Fiscal Responsibility Act of 1982 (PL 97-248).** Although not advertised as tax reform, this bill went a long way toward reducing existing tax loopholes and improving tax collections and compliance with existing law. It included provisions to limit generous business tax breaks enacted in 1981, require withholding of interest and dividend income (later repealed) and impose a more comprehensive minimum tax on wealthy individuals. But the legislation, aimed primarily at raising revenues to reduce the deficit, also added hundreds of provisions to the tax code and further complicated the law. *(Congress and the Nation Vol. VI, p. 72)*

● **Deficit Reduction Act of 1984 (PL 98-369).** This legislation also was designed to raise revenue to help reduce an ever-growing budget deficit. It attempted to close additional loopholes, including restricting tax breaks for expensive automobiles and placing limits on tax-exempt industrial development bonds. But, as in 1982, the legislation added greatly to the complexity of the law. *(Congress and the Nation Vol. VI, p. 79)*

Widespread dissatisfaction with the confusion caused by these two bills, and the shifting of the tax burden from corporations onto individuals in a major tax-cut bill enacted in 1981, helped to fuel the sentiment for a clean sweep of the tax code.

## House Action, 1985

The tax measure had a bumpy and unpredictable voyage through the House. The legislation, opposed by a wide range of interest groups, was thought to be near death several times during a two-month markup in the Ways and Means Committee. But Chairman Dan Rostenkowski, D-Ill., managed to negotiate enough changes to Reagan's original plan to keep the effort alive. The Ways and Means Committee reported HR 3838 Dec. 7, 1985 (H Rept 99-426).

A bigger threat awaited on the House floor, however. In an unexpected defeat for the president, House Republicans banded together in opposition to the legislation; a rule to bring the measure to the floor was defeated Dec. 11 by a **key vote of 202-223 (R 14-164; D 188-59)**. Many Republicans said they were annoyed they had not been consulted by the administration, which had worked closely with Rostenkowski on the bill. They also charged the final product did not live up to Reagan's goals of simplicity, fairness and economic growth. *(1985 key votes, p. 933)*

But the White House stepped up its lobbying efforts — which included a rare trip by Reagan to Capitol Hill to stump for his No. 1 domestic priority — and the vote was turned around. On a second try Dec. 17, 70 Republicans supported the rule, which was approved on a **key vote of 258-168 (R 70-110; D 188-58)**.

Eight hours later the House passed the bill by voice vote, having agreed to two relatively minor amendments. House passage of the tax bill was one of the last major legislative actions of 1985.

The House-passed bill boosted the top individual and business tax rates to 38 and 36 percent, respectively. It increased the top effective rate on capital gains to 22 percent, from 17.5 percent under the Reagan plan. Among other changes, the bill retained deductions for state and local tax payments and interest payments on second homes, which Reagan had proposed to eliminate. *(House bill provisions, p. 82)*

## Senate Action, 1986

The Senate Finance Committee took up the tax bill in 1986 in an atmosphere of growing pressure to reduce the deficit first and to find sources of revenue to pay for retaining tax benefits lost in the House bill.

Committee members rejected the idea of working from the House version of HR 3838, which was opposed by almost every member of the panel. Their starting point was a markup draft prepared by Finance Chairman Bob Packwood, R-Ore.

The committee initially began writing a bill that would expand the list of special tax benefits. In early May, however, Packwood junked that version and pushed through his committee a measure that radically cut both rates and special benefits. The Finance version of HR 3838, approved May 7 by a 20-0 vote, established two individual tax rates — 15 percent and 25 percent — and a top corporate rate of 33 percent. *(House and Senate bills compared, box, p. 82)*

The Finance Committee bill, which was formally reported May 29 (S Rept 99-313), survived almost intact on the Senate floor and became the basis for the measure drafted in conference.

A crucial test for the Finance Committee provisions came June 11, when the Senate upheld a committee decision severely limiting tax-free contributions to Individual Retirement Accounts (IRAs). By a **key vote of 51-48 (R 35-17; D 16-31)** senators tabled an amendment to preserve at least part of the popular retirement benefit. Packwood and others had warned that a vote to restore even one special tax advantage would lead to a flood of amendments that could jeopardize the bill. *(1986 key votes, p. 949)*

The Senate passed its version of HR 3838 on a 97-3 roll call June 24.

## Conference, Final Action, 1986

Senate-House conferees filed their report Sept. 18, 1986 (H Rept 99-841). All 12 Democrats and five of the 10 Republican conferees supported the conference agreement.

The compromise measure, which conferees had agreed to Aug. 16, essentially followed the Senate version of the bill in its adherence to two, dramatically reduced tax rates for individuals. The final bill reduced the top individual rate to 28 percent and the top corporate rate to 34 percent, each 1 percentage point above the rates in the Senate bill and well below what many had believed possible. The bill also curtailed or eliminated more business benefits than the Senate version and more individual benefits than the House measure.

Those who had supported simplification of the tax code and an end to special tax benefits were disappointed. Many tax benefits were kept and many new ones added, even though most new ones were rather narrow. And many of the new provisions were expected to complicate, not simplify, the preparation of tax returns.

The House adopted the conference report Sept. 25 on a **key vote of 292-136 (R 116-62; D 176-74)**. Senate approval of the conference report two days later, 74-23, completed action on the bill. *(1986 key votes, p. 949)*

There followed a final dispute over what was expected to be a routine resolution (H Con Res 395) correcting typographical and drafting errors in the bill. Both chambers attempted to include substantive changes to HR 3838, however, and members were never able to resolve their disagreements over these provisions. The tax bill thus went to the president for his signature full of acknowledged errors. Legislation to correct the technical flaws in the 1986 law did not clear Congress until 1988. *(Story, p. 100)*

## Major Provisions

As signed into law Oct. 22, 1986, the Tax Reform Act of 1986 (HR 3838 — PL 99-514) was expected to reduce the taxes paid by individuals by $121.9 billion over the five years 1987-91 while increasing the taxes of corporations by $120.3 billion and miscellaneous taxes by $1.4 billion.

The full tax-rate reduction for individuals was to take effect for tax year 1988, but even in 1987, four out of five individual taxpayers were expected to receive tax cuts, despite the curtailment or elimination of many existing deductions, exclusions and credits.

At least 682 so-called "transition rules," which would reduce the taxes of a great variety of businesses and institutions by about $10.6 billion over the five years 1987-91, were included in the bill. Most were written to benefit a single taxpaying entity, although some were designed to aid broader groups of taxpayers. Most were aimed at easing the transition from old law to new for those unfairly affected by the change, but not all met this test.

# Evolution of Proposals to Overhaul the Tax Code . . .

| | Existing Law | Reagan Plan [a] |
|---|---|---|
| **Individual Tax Rates** | 11-50 percent (14 brackets) | 15, 25 and 35 percent |
| **Corporate Tax Rates** | 15-40 percent on first $100,000 of income; 46 percent thereafter | 15-25 percent up to $75,000; 33 percent above $75,000 |
| **Capital Gains** | 60 percent exclusion; top effective rate of 20 percent | 50 percent exclusion; top effective rate of 17.5 percent, but limits on eligible assets |
| **Minimum Tax** | 20 percent "alternative" minimum tax imposed on individuals who greatly limit their tax liability through tax breaks; 15 percent "add-on" minimum tax for corporations that use tax breaks to reduce greatly their liability | Revise the way of computing the individual minimum tax to include more taxpayers; redesign the corporate minimum tax as an "alternative" to tax the value of some so-called preferences, but not depreciation |
| **Personal Exemption** | $1,080 (1986) | $2,000 |
| **State and Local Taxes** | Deductible | Deduction eliminated |
| **Charitable Donations** | Deductible | Full deductions for itemizers; none for non-itemizers |
| **Interest Deductions** | Deductions for home mortgage and non-business interest | Unlimited deduction for mortgages on primary residences; additional interest deductions capped at $5,000 |
| **Retirement Benefits** | Tax-deductible Individual Retirement Account (IRA) contributions of $2,000 for each worker and $200 for each non-working spouse; employer-sponsored 401(k) tax-exempt savings plans with maximum contributions of $30,000 annually | Allow non-working spouse IRA contributions of $2,000; limit 401(k) contributions to $8,000 annually, less amounts contributed to IRAs |
| **Investment Tax Credit** | 6-10 percent | Repealed |
| **Depreciation** | Recovery periods of 3-19 years with accelerated write-off | More generous write-off over 4-28 years; value adjusted for inflation |
| **Business Expenses** | Deductible | Deduction for entertainment repealed; limit on meals |
| **Tax-Exempt Bonds** | Bonds earning tax-free interest allowed for governmental and many non-governmental purposes, such as sports arenas and mortgages | Effectively eliminate use of bonds for non-governmental purposes |

SOURCES: Treasury Department, House Ways and Means Committee, Senate Finance Committee, Joint Committee on Taxation.

# ...From Existing Law Through HR 3838 as Cleared

| House Bill [b] | Senate Bill [c] | HR 3838 [d] |
|---|---|---|
| 15, 25, 35 and 38 percent | 15 and 27 percent (lower rate phased out for high-income taxpayers) | 15 and 28 percent (lower rate phased out for high-income taxpayers) |
| 15-30 percent up to $75,000; 36 percent above $75,000 | 15-30 percent up to $75,000; 33 percent above $75,000 | 15-30 percent up to $75,000; 34 percent above $75,000 |
| 42 percent exclusion; top effective rate of 22 percent | Special exclusion repealed; taxed at same rates as regular income | Special exclusion repealed; taxed at same rates as regular income |
| Increase the rate on the individual and corporate minimum tax to 25 percent and revise it to tax more so-called preferences | Retain the individual minimum tax rate of 20 percent but revise it to tax more so-called preferences; retain the 20 percent corporate minimum tax but redesign it to include more preferences, basing the tax on "book income" to include many corporations that escape taxation | Increase the rate on the individual minimum tax to 21 percent and revise it to tax more so-called preferences; retain the 20 percent corporate minimum tax and redesign it to include more preferences, basing the tax on "book income" to include many firms that escape taxation |
| $2,000 for non-itemizers; $1,500 for itemizers | $2,000 for low- and middle-income taxpayers (exemption phased out for high-income taxpayers) | $2,000 by 1989 for most taxpayers (exemption phased out for high-income taxpayers) |
| No change from existing law | Income, real estate and personal property taxes deductible; sales tax deduction limited to 60 percent of the amount in excess of state income taxes | Income, real estate and personal property taxes deductible; sales taxes not deductible |
| Full deduction for itemizers; non-itemizers could deduct amount above $100; appreciated value of charitable gifts subject to minimum tax | Full deductions for itemizers; none for non-itemizers | Full deductions for itemizers; none for non-itemizers; appreciated value of charitable gifts subject to minimum tax |
| Unlimited deduction for mortgages on first and second residences; additional deduction of $10,000 ($20,000 for joint returns) plus the value of a taxpayer's investment income | Unlimited deduction for mortgages on first and second residences; no consumer interest deduction; interest paid on borrowing to produce investment income deductible equal to the value of the investment earnings | Unlimited deduction for mortgages on first and second residences; limits on mortgage borrowing for unrelated purposes; no consumer interest deduction; interest paid on borrowing to produce investment income deductible equal to the value of the earnings |
| Continue existing law on tax-exempt IRA contributions; restrict 401(k) contributions to $7,000 annually; limit to $2,000 the total exemption for contributions by an individual to both an IRA and a 401(k) plan, to encourage 401(k) and discourage IRA contributions | Limit tax-exempt IRA contributions to persons not covered by pension plans; restrict 401(k) contributions to $7,000 annually; make sweeping changes in private pension plans to improve coverage and restrict benefits for high-income persons | Limit tax-exempt IRA contributions to persons not covered by pension plans or those below specified income levels; restrict 401(k) contributions to $7,000 annually; make sweeping changes in private pensions to improve coverage and restrict benefits for high-income persons |
| Repealed | Repealed retroactively to Jan. 1, 1986 | Repealed retroactively to Jan. 1, 1986 |
| Recovery periods of 3-30 years; partially indexed for inflation | Retain existing system of rapid write-offs, permitting larger write-offs for most property over longer periods | Retain system of rapid write-offs similar to existing law; permit larger write-offs for most property, but over longer periods |
| Deduction of 80 percent of business meals and 80 percent of entertainment costs | Similar to House for meals and entertainment; most miscellaneous deductions eliminated | Deduction of 80 percent of business meals and entertainment costs; miscellaneous employee business expenses limited |
| Cap use of non-governmental bonds; reserve a portion for charitable organizations; some interest subject to minimum tax | Cap use of non-governmental bonds, exclude multifamily rental housing and charitable organizations from the cap | Cap use of non-governmental bonds, exclude charitable organizations from the cap; some interest subject to minimum tax |

[a] Proposed May 28, 1985.   [b] Passed Dec. 17, 1985.   [c] Passed June 24, 1986.   [d] Cleared Sept. 27, 1986 (PL 99-514).

Most provisions in the bill were to take effect Jan. 1, 1987; provisions with different effective dates are indicated below, as are provisions that were to be phased in.

The final version of HR 3838 included provisions to:

## Individuals

● **Rates.** Replace the existing 14 tax brackets (15 for single taxpayers), which ranged from 11 to 50 percent, with a two-bracket system, with rates of 15 and 28 percent, for 1988 and later years.

Under the two-bracket system, the use of the 15 percent rate would be phased out — that is, gradually eliminated — for taxpayers with relatively high incomes. For those with the highest incomes, it would be completely eliminated.

Within the range of incomes affected by the phase-out, the benefits of the 15 percent bottom rate would be eliminated by imposing a 5 percent surtax on income above the starting point for the phase-out. Taxpayers in this phase-out range would thus be subject to a marginal tax rate (on their top dollars of income) of 33 percent, though their overall tax rate would never quite reach 28 percent. For those with the highest incomes, beyond the phase-out range, all taxable income would be subject to the 28 percent top rate.

To eliminate the possibility that high-income married couples would try to avoid the phase-out of the 15 percent rate, couples filing separate returns would be required to calculate the phase-out based on their joint income.

For joint returns, taxable income up to $29,750 (the "break-point") would be taxed at 15 percent, and income above that at 28 percent. The 15 percent bracket would be phased out on taxable incomes of between $71,900 and $149,250; couples with income above that would pay 28 percent on all taxable income.

For single individuals, the break-point at which the 28 percent rate would start to apply would be $17,850 of taxable income and use of the 15 percent rate would be phased out between $43,150 and $89,560 of taxable income.

For single heads of households, the 28 percent rate would begin to apply at $23,900 of taxable income and use of the 15 percent rate would be phased out between $61,650 and $123,790 of taxable income.

The 15 and 28 percent rates would go into effect Jan. 1, 1988, and the various break-points would be indexed annually thereafter to reflect inflation.

For 1987 only, the bill provided a temporary five-bracket system, with rates ranging from 11 percent to 38.5 percent.

● **Personal Exemption.** Increase the personal exemption for taxpayers and their dependents from the existing $1,080 to $1,900 in 1987, $1,950 in 1988 and $2,000 in 1989. The exemption would be indexed to reflect inflation beginning in 1990.

Use of the personal exemption would be phased out, through use of a 5 percent surtax, on taxable income above the level at which the phase-out of the 15 percent tax bracket is completed. The start of the phase-out of the personal exemption would thus be $149,250 for married couples, $89,560 for single individuals and $123,790 for single heads of households. The end of the phase-out range would depend on the number of exemptions. For a couple with no children, it would be $171,090; for a couple with two children, it would be $192,930.

The phase-out of the personal exemption would begin in 1988; there would be no phase-out in 1987.

● Eliminate the use of the personal exemption by any individual (usually a child) who must file a tax return but also would be eligible to be claimed as a dependent on another person's tax return.

● Repeal the additional personal exemption for elderly and blind persons and replace it with an extra standard deduction, intended to ensure that elderly or blind non-itemizers pay no more tax than under existing law.

● **Standard Deduction.** Reinstate for those who did not itemize deductions — the majority of taxpayers — the standard deduction in place of the existing zero bracket amount in the tax tables. The new standard deduction, effective in 1988 and thereafter, would be $5,000 on joint returns, $3,000 for single individuals and $4,400 for single heads of households.

The standard deduction would be indexed for inflation beginning in 1989.

For 1987 only, the standard deduction would be $3,760 on joint returns, $1,880 for single individuals and $2,540 for single heads of households.

● Provide an additional standard deduction for elderly or blind persons of $750 for single taxpayers and $600 for each partner on a joint return. A person who was both elderly and blind would be allowed both additional deductions.

These additional standard deductions would be indexed for inflation beginning in 1989.

● Permit an individual who was claimed as a dependent on another person's tax return to use only $500 of the standard deduction to offset unearned income. The deduction could be used in full against earned income.

● **State and Local Taxes.** Retain the deduction for state and local property and income taxes but eliminate it for sales taxes, effective Jan. 1, 1987.

● **Charitable Contributions.** Allow the deduction permitted those who did not itemize deductions to expire at the end of 1986. Itemizers would continue to be allowed to deduct all charitable contributions.

● **Medical Costs.** Require medical expenses to exceed 7.5 percent of a taxpayer's adjusted gross income, instead of 5 percent as under existing law, before such expenses could be deducted. As under existing law, capital expenditures incurred to accommodate a residence to the needs of a physically handicapped person would be deductible as a medical expense.

● **Business and Investment Expenses and Miscellaneous Deductions.** Allow deductions only to the extent that they exceeded 2 percent of a taxpayer's adjusted gross income. Among the deductions subject to this "floor" were business expenses borne by employees, such as union dues and safety equipment; expenses for producing income, such as commissions on stock purchases and investment advice; and miscellaneous deductions, such as subscriptions to professional publications. Expenses of moving, for employment purposes, would continue to be subject to all existing limitations but would not be subject to the 2 percent floor. Gambling losses, deductible to the extent that they did not exceed gambling winnings, also would be exempt from the floor. An exception to the floor for performing artists would cover such expenses as fees paid to agents.

● **Unemployment Compensation.** Tax all unemployment benefits as income.

● **Dividends.** Repeal the existing exclusion from income of up to $100 in dividends received by an individual

# Who Pays What Share of Income Tax and How Much They Pay

| Income Class | Percentage of Total Tax Collections, 1988 | | Average Income Tax Payment by Taxpayer, 1988 | | |
|---|---|---|---|---|---|
| | Current Law | HR 3838 | Current Law | HR 3838 | Tax Cut |
| Less than $10,000 | 0.6 % | 0.2 % | $ 60 | $ 21 | $ 39 |
| $10,000 - $20,000 | 6.4 | 5.3 | 895 | 695 | 200 |
| $20,000 - $30,000 | 11.8 | 11.3 | 2,238 | 2,018 | 220 |
| $30,000 - $40,000 | 12.0 | 11.8 | 3,527 | 3,254 | 273 |
| $40,000 - $50,000 | 10.9 | 10.6 | 5,335 | 4,849 | 486 |
| $50,000 - $75,000 | 16.2 | 16.9 | 8,538 | 8,388 | 150 |
| $75,000 - $100,000 | 6.7 | 7.1 | 14,469 | 14,293 | 176 |
| $100,000 - $200,000 | 11.9 | 12.4 | 27,965 | 27,353 | 612 |
| $200,000 and above | 23.4 | 24.3 | 138,463 | 135,101 | 3,362 |
| **Total** | 100 % | 100 % | **Average** $ 3,176 | $ 2,982 | $ 194 |

NOTE: Totals may not add due to rounding.

SOURCE: Joint Committee on Taxation (as of Oct. 1, 1986).

($200 for a married couple).

● **Marriage Penalty.** Repeal the deduction for two-earner couples. Changes in the rates, personal exemption and standard deduction were designed to ensure a tax cut for most married taxpayers, but their taxes would be higher than those of two single individuals with the same total income as theirs.

● **Mortgage and Consumer Interest.** Allow taxpayers to take an unlimited mortgage interest deduction for first and second residences.

Phase out, over five years, deductions for interest on consumer purchases, credit cards, charge accounts and other forms of consumer interest. Among existing interest deductions that would be disallowed in the future were interest payments on delinquent taxes.

The potential loophole that would be opened by the combination of the continuing deductibility of mortgage interest combined with the ban on deductions for consumer interest would be partially closed by a complex provision limiting the deductibility of interest on new loans secured by a taxpayer's first or second residence. Loans for any purpose other than educational or medical expenses could not exceed the cost of the residence, plus improvements. That limitation would not apply to borrowings against a residence for certain educational or medical purposes.

Loans using a first or second residence as security that were made on or before Aug. 16, 1986, would be exempt from the new restrictions.

● **Investment Interest.** Allow taxpayers with investment income to deduct interest paid on borrowings used to make the investments, but limit such deductions to the amount of net investment income. Interest deductions disallowed in one year could be carried forward and deducted in subsequent years against net investment income.

● **Meals, Travel and Entertainment.** Limit deductions for business meals and entertainment to 80 percent of the amount spent, except that when an employer bore the cost (and was, thereby, subject to the 80 percent limit) the employee could be reimbursed for the full cost of meals and entertainment.

A few types of entertainment, such as employer-provided holiday parties and tickets for charitable sporting events would remain fully deductible.

Most hotel and transportation costs would remain deductible, but no deduction would be allowed for attending investment seminars or conventions. Deductions for business travel on cruise ships or other luxury liners would be limited. Deductions for travel taken for educational purposes would be disallowed, as would travel to engage in charitable activities, unless there was no significant element of recreation or vacation.

Deductions for rentals of "skyboxes" at sports arenas would be disallowed, after a three-year phase-out.

● **Income Averaging.** Repeal income averaging, which allowed taxpayers with dramatic fluctuations in income to reduce their tax liabilities. Such fluctuations would have much less impact under the new two-bracket tax system than under existing law.

● **Earned Income Credit.** Increase the existing earned income tax credit for working poor families to 14 percent of the first $5,714 of income, to a maximum of $800. The credit would be phased out between $9,000 and $17,000. The change would be effective Jan. 1, 1988, and the credit would be indexed to reflect all inflation since August 1984.

Employers would be required to notify persons whose incomes were so low that they had no tax withheld that they might be eligible for the credit. Such persons would be informed that they must file a tax return to claim the credit, which was paid in cash to some persons who owed no tax against which to deduct it. The timing and form of the notices would be spelled out in Treasury regulations.

● **Rounding.** Adjust downward to the nearest $50 the

standard deduction, personal exemption and rate brackets, when indexed for inflation in future years. The earned income tax credit would be rounded down to the nearest $10, making that adjustment relatively more generous.

● **Adoption Expense.** Abolish the existing deduction for up to $1,500 in expenses related to adoption of hard-to-place children and expand a direct spending program to compensate for the change.

● **Scholarships and Fellowships.** Tax as income scholarships and fellowships that were not used for tuition or equipment required for courses, or were received by students who were not degree candidates. Scholarships and fellowships granted before Aug. 17, 1986, would be exempt from this provision.

● **Prizes and Awards.** Repeal the existing exemption from taxable income for awards won for charitable, educational, religious and similar achievements, unless the award was transferred by a taxpayer to a charitable or governmental organization. Certain employee achievement awards for length of service or safety achievements would continue to be tax-exempt, providing they met certain limitations, but had to be in the form of property, not cash.

● **Handicapped.** Permit a severely handicapped employee to deduct the cost of attendant care and other services necessary to enable the employee to work.

● **Ministers and Military Personnel.** Allow ministers and military personnel receiving tax-free housing allowances to deduct mortgage interest or real property tax payments.

● **Home Offices.** Limit deductions for home offices to a taxpayer's net income from the business, except that excess deductions could be carried forward and taken against income in future years. Under existing law, the deduction could not exceed gross income. The limitations also would apply in cases where a taxpayer leased a home office to his employer.

● **Hobbies.** Expand the definition of "hobbies" for which expense deductions were more limited than for regular businesses. A business activity would be a hobby if it was not profitable in at least three out of five consecutive years, instead of two out of five years as under existing law. Horse breeding or racing would be exempt from the tightened restrictions.

● **Political Contributions.** Repeal the existing $50 credit ($100 for joint returns) for contributions to political campaigns and certain political campaign organizations. The existing presidential campaign "checkoff" of $1 for individuals and $2 for joint returns would be retained.

## Corporate Taxes

● **Corporate Tax Rate.** Reduce the top corporate rate from 46 percent on taxable income over $75,000 to 34 percent.

The four lower corporate tax brackets under existing law would be collapsed into two: Income up to $50,000 would be taxed at a rate of 15 percent and income from $50,000 to $75,000 would be taxed at 25 percent. The graduated rates would be phased out on taxable incomes between $100,000 and $335,000 so that corporations with taxable income above $335,000 would pay a flat rate of 34 percent on all income.

These rates would be effective for taxable years beginning on or after July 1, 1987. Corporations with taxable years beginning earlier than July 1, 1987, would be subject to a blended rate for 1987, reflecting the portion of the

taxable year that falls before July 1, 1987. Calendar year corporations, for example, would have a top rate of 40 percent for 1987.

● **Dividends.** Reduce from 85 percent to 80 percent the percentage of dividends received that could be deducted by a corporation.

● **Business Tax Credits.** Reduce from 85 percent to 75 percent the amount by which businesses could use business tax credits to reduce the amount of their tax liability in excess of $25,000. Firms would still be allowed to use business tax credits to reduce all of their regular tax liability up to $25,000.

● **Targeted Jobs Credit.** Extend for three years the existing credit for those who hire economically disadvantaged youths, welfare recipients and other hard-to-place workers.

The so-called targeted jobs tax credit would be reduced from the existing level of 50 percent of the first $6,000 of wages in the first year and 25 percent in the second year to 40 percent in the first year only. The first-year credit could not be taken unless the worker is employed for at least 90 days.

● **Corporate Liquidations.** Repeal what is known as the General Utilities doctrine, thus taxing corporations on the gains from liquidation of their assets, which under existing law were taxed only when distributed as dividends to shareholders. Existing law provided an incentive for corporate mergers and acquisitions, in the view of many who opposed it.

The change would not apply to small, closely held corporations.

● **Corporate Takeovers.** Deny deductions for expenses relating to repurchase of a corporation's own stock, whether to fend off a hostile takeover, or for any other reason. The denial was made effective for repurchases on or after March 1, 1986.

● **Net Operating Losses.** Impose a variety of restrictions on the use of net operating loss carryovers following a change in ownership of a corporation, in an effort to remove a tax incentive for corporate acquisitions.

● **REMICs.** Create a new entity, known as a real estate mortgage investment company (REMIC), which, like mutual funds, would be allowed to pass along taxable gains to its investors. It would not, itself, be taxable.

## Capital Gains

● **Individuals.** Tax capital gains at the same rates as ordinary income: 15 percent and 28 percent, beginning in 1987. The higher rates in effect on ordinary income for 1987 would not apply to capital gains. Under existing law, capital gains were taxed at 40 percent of the ordinary income rate, which put the top effective rate at 20 percent.

● **Corporations.** Tax capital gains at the same rates as ordinary income, or 34 percent for the top bracket, beginning in 1987.

For both individuals and corporations, the existing, separate statutory structure setting capital gains rates would be retained to facilitate reinstatement of a reduced capital gains rate if there is a future increase in tax rates on ordinary income.

## Minimum Tax

● Revise the minimum tax to make it more difficult for individuals with high incomes and corporations with sub-

# Chronology of Tax-Overhaul Efforts

● **August 1982.** Sen. Bill Bradley, D-N.J., and Rep. Richard A. Gephardt, D-Mo., introduce their "Fair Tax" plan (S 2817, HR 6944) to set individual tax rates at 14, 26 and 30 percent.

● **January 1984.** President Reagan calls in his State of the Union address for simplification of the federal tax system. He directs Treasury Secretary Donald T. Regan to draw up a plan by December 1984, one month after the next presidential election.

● **April 1984.** Rep. Jack F. Kemp, R-N.Y., and Sen. Bob Kasten, R-Wis., introduce the "Fair and Simple Tax" (HR 2222, S 1006) to impose a flat 24 percent tax rate.

● **Fall 1984.** Democratic presidential candidate Walter F. Mondale accuses Reagan of having a "secret plan" to raise taxes after the election and releases his own proposal to raise taxes to reduce the federal deficit.

● **November 1984.** The Treasury Department releases its blueprint for overhauling the federal tax system. Reagan's reaction is lukewarm, and he says he is open to suggestions before submitting his own plan.

● **May 1985.** Reagan announces his tax-overhaul plan, which lowers individual and corporate tax rates, limits numerous special tax breaks and raises the same amount of revenue as the current tax system. House Ways and Means Committee Chairman Dan Rostenkowski, D-Ill., says Democrats will work with the president to draw up a bill. A summer of hearings begins in both the Ways and Means and Senate Finance committees.

● **September 1985.** Ways and Means staff draws up a draft tax plan, similar to Reagan's proposal, and the committee begins to mark up a bill.

● **October 1985.** Markup bogs down when Ways and Means Committee members vote to give banks a costly new advantage. Rostenkowski breaks the deadlock with backroom negotiations, including informal agreement that the state and local tax deduction will be retained.

● **Nov. 23, 1985.** Committee completes its markup amid growing partisanship. Republicans complain they were shut out of decision making in final hours and talk of offering a substitute bill.

● **Dec. 4, 1985.** Reagan expresses lukewarm support for the Ways and Means bill (HR 3838) and asks Congress to vote for either it or the GOP plan to keep the tax-rewrite effort alive.

● **Dec. 11, 1985.** Tax bill is dealt a severe blow when the House votes 202-223 to reject the rule allowing the measure to come to the floor. Of 178 Republicans voting, only 14 voted for the rule.

● **Dec. 17, 1985.** After intense lobbying by the White House, the House reverses its vote on the rule and the Ways and Means tax bill is approved by voice vote with only minor changes.

● **March 13, 1986.** His committee having rejected using the Ways and Means bill as its markup document, Senate Finance Chairman Bob Packwood, R-Ore., puts his own plan on the table. Full of wish-list items, the bill uses controversial revenue-raisers, including restriction or elimination of individual deductions for most state and local taxes.

● **March 19, 1986.** The municipal bond market shuts down over a provision in Packwood's plan to subject all previously tax-free municipal bond income to the minimum tax. Some Finance members immediately object to the bond provision.

● **March 24, 1986.** Finance begins markup and in a 19-0 vote limits application of the minimum tax to municipal bond interest to newly issued bonds.

● **April 18, 1986.** During three weeks of work, Finance members endorse additional tax breaks for Packwood's draft that would cost $29 billion in lost revenue over five years. Packwood suspends the markup and over lunch with committee staff chief Bill Diefenderfer decides to offer a radical bill with a top individual rate of 25 percent and virtually no deductions.

● **May 7, 1986.** Committee votes 20-0 in favor of a bill with top rates of 27 percent for individuals and 33 percent for corporations after a day of open markup and a week of closed-door sessions.

● **June 24, 1986.** Senate votes 97-3 in favor of a bill largely unchanged from that reported by Finance. The key vote comes June 11, when proponents of a provision severely limiting Individual Retirement Accounts (IRAs) beat back 51-48 an effort to restore the tax break.

● **July 17, 1986.** Conferees begin work, but the conference bogs down over individual rates and the tax "hit" on corporations. Most of the work is done in one-house conferences, with offers passed back and forth. As negotiations drag into the second week of August, Rostenkowski and Packwood negotiate privately, taking agreements back to their colleagues for ratification.

● **Aug. 16, 1986.** Conference, by voice vote, endorses a bill that strongly resembles the Senate version. Of the 22 conferees, every Democrat is in favor and only five Republicans are opposed.

● **Sept. 25, 1986.** House votes 292-136 in favor of the conference report. It adopts at the same time a resolution making "technical corrections" in the conference bill and sends both measures to the Senate.

● **Sept. 27, 1986.** Senate clears conference report 74-23. Disagreements over provisions in the corrections resolution prevent its adoption, however, and the cleared tax bill is kept from the White House.

● **Oct. 22, 1986.** Reagan signs tax bill into law (PL 99-514); the technical corrections measure dies.

stantial profits to combine various tax benefits — known as preferences — elsewhere in the tax code in ways that would permit them to escape all, or nearly all, tax.

● **Individuals.** Retain the basic structure of the tax, by which certain preference items were added back into taxable income. The rate of the tax would be raised from the existing 20 percent to 21 percent. Some new preferences would be added to the list that went into the calculation of the tax and others eliminated.

The amount of tax-exempt income that could be earned by Americans who work abroad (cut to $70,000 by the bill) would no longer be a preference subject to the minimum tax.

The interest on newly issued, tax-exempt industrial development bonds, except for those issued by charitable, or 501(c)(3), organizations, would become a preference, subject to the tax. This marked the first time that interest on any form of tax-exempt bonds was made subject to the individual income tax.

Other additions to the list of preferences subject to the tax included the benefits of investing in most tax shelters, which would be eliminated entirely over five years by other sections of the bill, but would become fully subject to the minimum tax in 1987, without any phase-in; deductions for the appreciated value of property donated to charitable organizations; and most of the preferences contained in the corporate minimum tax, such as those for excess depreciation, when used by owners of unincorporated businesses filing as individuals.

● **Corporations.** Redesign the corporate minimum tax with the objective of making it close to airtight. The heart of the new tax was its use of reported "book income" as a separate new test of taxability, in addition to a list of "preference" items given favorable treatment under regular provisions of the tax law that would be subject to the minimum tax.

● Interest on all tax-exempt securities, outstanding and new, public or private purpose, would be included in book income for corporations subject to that test of taxability. Interest on non-governmental purpose bonds issued on or after Aug. 8, 1986 (except for those issued by 501(c)(3) organizations), would become a tax preference for corporations.

Other major new preferences included: accelerated depreciation, insofar as it exceeded what could be deducted using what is called Asset Depreciation Range (ADR) depreciable lives and the 150 percent declining balance method; the so-called completed contract method of tax payment for government and construction contractors; the installment method used by retailers and other sellers; and intangible drilling costs for oil and gas wells.

● A two-level method of figuring the tax would be used. A company would, first, calculate its taxable income under existing law, including all the various deductions, exemptions and exclusions. Then, starting with taxable income, it would add these preferences back and make other adjustments, and from this calculate minimum taxable income. Next it would compare this minimum taxable income total with book income, as reported to shareholders or a regulatory agency or a bank for purposes of obtaining a loan. If book income was more than the minimum taxable income, one-half of the difference would be added to the minimum taxable income and the tax would be calculated on this total amount at a 20 percent rate. A few existing preferences would remain untouched, even with the use of the book income concept. One of the largest was the expensing,

or writing off in one year, of research and development costs.

● The book income basis for calculating the corporate minimum tax would remain in effect for three years, starting in 1987, after which the basis would shift to the "earnings and profits" concept.

## Tax Shelters

● **Real Estate.** Eliminate, over a five-year phase-out period, provisions allowing so-called "passive losses" generated by investments in limited partnerships in real estate and most other types of tax shelters, in which the investor took no active management role. Such losses could, under existing law, be used to reduce wage or portfolio income for tax purposes.

Passive losses arose principally from depreciation deductions, and investment tax and other credits, which were large in the early years of investments. A typical shelter investor sold out of the partnership when income from the real estate started to exceed the deductions. Depreciation deductions then started all over again for the new buyer.

An exception to the ban on deducting passive losses would be provided to individuals who had at least a 10 percent interest in rental property and actively participated in its management. Such persons could deduct up to $25,000 in passive losses annually.

● Apply to some real estate transactions existing, so-called "at risk" rules preventing investors from deducting losses greater than the amount actually invested.

● **Oil Shelters.** Create a new class of passive losses in cases in which an investor in an oil or gas drilling enterprise had a working interest in the partnership, defined as some liability beyond the original investment. Passive losses created by such deductions as the expensing of intangible drilling costs would still be permitted for working-interest partners.

● **Effective Date.** As for most provisions of the bill, the effective date for the passive loss sections would be Jan. 1, 1987. However, to take advantage of the five-year phase-out, rather than losing passive-loss deductions immediately, investments in these tax shelters had to be made no later than the date of enactment of the bill.

## Tax-Exempt Bonds

● **Public Use.** Continue to exempt from regular federal income taxes the interest earned on bonds issued by state and local governments for public purposes, such as the construction of schools or roads.

● **Industrial Development Bonds.** Define as non-public purpose bonds those in which more than 10 percent of the money raised (or $15 million, for some public utilities) was used for other than a public purpose. The existing maximum was 25 percent. Bonds that exceeded this limit would be designated industrial development bonds (IDBs) and subject to various limitations.

The bill imposed a new and generally lower ceiling on the volume of IDBs that could be issued annually in each state, and placed more types of non-government purpose bonds under the caps. Under existing law, the cap was $150 per resident, or $200 million, whichever was greater. For 1987, the cap would be set at $75 per person or $250 million; and for 1988 and thereafter, the cap would be $50 per person or $150 million. Bonds issued to fund multifamily housing and single-family mortgage revenue bonds would come under the cap for the first time.

● **Section 501(c)(3) Organizations.** Bonds issued by charitable, educational and other organizations whose own operations were tax-exempt under section 501(c)(3) of the Internal Revenue Code would not come under the cap. However, private universities could have no more than $150 million in tax-exempt bonds outstanding at one time, a cap that would keep 20 or 30 large private universities from issuing any new tax-exempt bonds for the foreseeable future.

● **Minimum Tax.** For corporations subject to the minimum tax, the interest on both outstanding and new tax-exempt bonds, including those issued by governmental entities, would be included in the book income calculation of the tax. For both individuals and corporations, interest on IDBs issued after Aug. 8, 1986, except for those issued by 501(c)(3) organizations, would become a preference under the minimum tax.

● **Prohibited Uses.** Tax-exempt financing could no longer be used for privately owned air or water pollution control facilities; sports, convention or trade show facilities; parking garages; industrial parks; or facilities such as restaurants and office buildings adjacent to an airport that were in excess of the size needed to serve airport passengers and employees. This would be effective Aug. 15, 1986.

● **Bank Interest Deductions.** Repeal the existing provision that permitted banks, unlike other investors in tax-exempt bonds, to deduct some of the interest on loans used to purchase the bonds. The existing 80 percent deduction would be continued only for public purpose bonds or those issued by 501(c)(3) organizations that did not issue more than $10 million of such bonds a year.

● **Arbitrage and Advance Refunding.** Permit the Treasury to recapture the excessive profits from, and thus discourage, the practice known as arbitrage, which involves using funds raised from the sale of tax-exempt securities to buy taxable securities carrying a higher interest rate. Advance refundings, use of which can raise tax-exempt money several times for the same purpose, without repayment of the old indebtedness, would be limited to government-purpose bonds and those issued by 501(c)(3) organizations.

● **Costs of Issuance.** Payments for services of architects, engineers, lawyers and underwriters, and other costs of issuing IDBs, may not exceed 2 percent of the amount being raised by the bond issue.

## Depreciation

● **Investment Tax Credit.** Repeal, effective Jan. 1, 1986, the existing 10 percent tax credit (6 percent for certain short-lived assets) allowed for a taxpayer's investment in machinery and equipment.

Permit businesses with investment tax credits they could not use in the past — because their profits were too small — to use up to 82.5 percent of their unused investment tax credits to offset taxes owed in 1987, and up to 65 percent in later years. Currently, firms could carry the full amount of unused credits forward 15 years or back three.

A variety of both generic and special transitional rules were provided to determine whether a specific piece of property was eligible for the investment tax credit despite not having been acquired by a binding, written contract by the cutoff date of Dec. 31, 1985.

● **Accelerated Depreciation.** Lengthen the periods of time over which many categories of business equipment and machinery would be depreciated, but permit these

assets to be written off under a 200 percent declining balance system, instead of the existing 150 percent, in most cases. The net result would be somewhat smaller depreciation deductions for most businesses.

Automobiles and light trucks would be depreciated over five years, instead of three years, as under existing law, as would equipment used in research and development. Users of these assets would, however, gain the benefit of 200 percent declining balance depreciation. Other assets whose costs could, under existing law, be recovered over three years would remain in the three-year class. Some assets with an existing five-year cost-recovery period would remain in the five-year class, but others would be shifted to a seven-year class, with 200 percent declining balance depreciation. Assets in the 15- and 20-year classes would be depreciated at a 150 percent declining balance rate.

The shifts in and out of various cost-recovery classes were based on type of asset, instead of the industry that used them, for the most part. However, there were some specific industry provisions, essentially favorable to the industries involved. Among them were telephone central office switching equipment, which would be given a depreciable life of five years, as other computers; railroad tracks, given a depreciable life of seven years; and single-purpose agricultural structures, such as henhouses, given a life of 15 years.

Real estate would be among the hardest-hit areas. Residential rental property would be depreciated, using the straight-line system, over 27.5 years and non-residential over 31.5 years. Under existing law, both were depreciated over 19 years.

● **Effective Date.** Businesses for which the new depreciation rules would be advantageous could elect to use them for any equipment put into service on or after Aug. 1, 1986. Use of the new rules would be required of all businesses as of Jan. 1, 1987, covering property constructed or acquired under a binding, written contract by March 1, 1986. A number of exceptions to this date were provided.

● **Expensing for Small Businesses.** Allow taxpayers to write off in one year, or expense, up to $10,000 in personal property used in a trade or business, providing their total investment in such property did not exceed $200,000. The existing expensing limit was $5,000.

● **Handicapped Barriers.** Extend permanently a deduction for up to $35,000 in expenses for removing architectural and transportation barriers for the handicapped and elderly, instead of writing them off over a long period.

## Financial Institutions

● **Bad-Debt Reserves.** Limit the deduction commercial banks with assets of $500 million or more — about 450 of the nation's largest banks — could take to cover bad loans, allowing deductions only when actual losses were incurred.

Banks with assets of less than $500 million would be able to take the more generous deduction allowed under existing law, which was based on a percentage of the bank's outstanding loans or on its past record of bad debts.

The balance of existing reserves would be recaptured through taxation over five years: 10 percent in 1987; 20 percent in 1988; 30 percent in 1989; and 40 percent in 1990. There would be an exemption from the recapture provision for a bank in years when it was "troubled," defined as having non-performing loans exceeding 75 percent of its capital.

● Allow some thrift institutions to take bad-debt deductions equal to 8 percent of their taxable income or an amount based on their past experience with bad loans, in contrast with the more generous 40 percent deduction allowed under existing law.

● **Investment Interest Deduction.** Eliminate a deduction financial institutions could take under existing law for 80 percent of the interest payments they made on debt used to invest in tax-exempt obligations.

Banks that invested in tax-exempt bonds issued by small jurisdictions for governmental purposes or by charitable organizations could continue to deduct the interest they paid on money used to purchase the bonds, so long as the jurisdiction limited its qualified bond issues to $10 million in a calendar year. The provision would apply to interest earned after Dec. 31, 1986, on bonds purchased after Aug. 7, 1986.

● **Thrift Reorganization.** Repeal special tax advantages for the reorganization of troubled "thrift" institutions, including a provision that allowed troubled savings and loans to be acquired tax-free. This provision would be effective for reorganizations after Dec. 31, 1988.

● **Bankruptcy.** Make it easier for individuals to claim losses when their financial institution became bankrupt or insolvent.

● **Net Operating Losses.** Change special rules allowing commercial banks and thrift institutions to deduct their net operating losses against income from the preceding 10 taxable years or the succeeding five taxable years. The 10-year carry-back deduction for commercial banks would be retained for bad-debt losses incurred before 1994; otherwise, the 10-year carry-back would be repealed. Thrift institutions would be allowed to carry forward for eight years losses incurred after 1981 and before 1986.

## Accounting

● **Installment Sales.** Eliminate for some taxpayers and restrict for others the tax benefits realized by so-called installment sale contracts, which under existing law allowed deferral of taxes on the proceeds from such sales spread over two or more years.

Deferral of taxes under the installment method would be disallowed for sales pursuant to revolving credit accounts, and for sales of certain publicly traded property, such as stocks and bonds, effective for sales after Dec. 31, 1986.

For other installment sales, including those involving real estate, deferral of taxes would be limited by use of new accounting methods that measure the ratio of a taxpayer's total debts to assets. Sales of crops, livestock for slaughter and certain farm property would not be subject to this limit, and sales of certain residential lots and timeshares (such as those commonly used by vacation resort developers) could be counted as installment sales, except the taxpayer would have to pay interest on the tax deferred. The new limitations on installment sales would be effective for tax years after Dec. 31, 1986, and for sales effective after Feb. 28, 1986.

● **Long-Term Contracts.** Restrict a special accounting method that allowed defense and construction contractors to delay tax payments until work on a project had been completed, thus often dramatically reducing or permanently postponing their tax liabilities. The ability of some defense contractors, in particular, to avoid all taxes, despite large profits, through use of the "completed contract method" of accounting was one of the major sources of public complaint about the tax law.

Basically, the provision would require contractors to calculate each year what proportion of the contract they had completed and pay taxes on an amount equal to 40 percent of that proportion of the total payments expected from the contract. Taxes on the other 60 percent would be deferred until the contract was completed, as under existing law. Some stricter capitalization requirements also were imposed.

● **Cash Method.** Prevent the use of the so-called "cash method" of accounting for businesses with gross receipts exceeding $5 million a year. But professionals, such as lawyers and accountants, farm and timber businesses, partnerships and certain personal service companies, would be exempt. Tax shelters also would be prohibited from using the cash method.

Critics charged that cash accounting — where income is declared at the time cash is received and deductions are taken when an expense is actually paid — does not accurately reflect a company's economic circumstances and allowed some firms to delay tax payments unduly.

Instead, companies exceeding the $5 million limit would be required to use accrual accounting, where income and expenses are reported at the time they are earned or incurred, but not necessarily paid.

● **Bad-Debt Reserves.** Prevent businesses and large banks from taking deductions for reserves held to cover bad debts. Instead, deductions would be allowed when specific loans become partially or wholly worthless.

Smaller financial institutions and finance companies would retain a partial benefit from the bad-debt reserve deduction, but it would be severely limited for thrifts.

● **Capitalization.** Adopt a uniform set of rules for most costs incurred in manufacturing or construction of property, or in purchase and holding of property for resale. The rules also would apply to some interest costs, but not to research expenses, oil, gas and mineral properties, or some farming operations.

Wholesalers and retailers with sales of $10 million or more a year would have to capitalize over a period of time certain inventory costs instead of deducting the costs in one year.

● **Small Businesses.** Allow certain firms with incomes of less than $5 million to use an inventory accounting practice known as simplified LIFO (last in, first out). The practice benefits businesses at times of rising costs because it effectively raises the value of older, less-expensive inventory when it is sold.

● **Utilities.** Require utilities using the accrual method of accounting to report income as of the time utility services were provided to customers, instead of when billed.

● **Taxable Years.** Require all partnerships, so-called "subchapter S" corporations and "personal service" corporations to conform their taxable years to the taxable years of their owners. The provision was intended to prevent deferral of taxes.

## Low-Income Housing

● **Tax Credit.** Provide a new tax credit to owners of low-income rental housing projects, which would apply only to units occupied by low-income persons. At least 20 percent of the units and space in a project would have to be occupied by persons whose incomes were below 50 percent of the median income for the area or 40 percent would have to be occupied by persons whose incomes were below 60

## Winners and Losers: How Many Pay More, How Many Less

| Income Class | Computed for 1987 (In Thousands of Tax Returns) | | Computed for 1988 (In Thousands of Tax Returns) | |
|---|---|---|---|---|
| | Returns Showing a Tax Increase | Returns Showing a Tax Decrease | Returns Showing a Tax Increase | Returns Showing a Tax Decrease |
| Less than $10,000 | 1,666 | 11,997 | 1,692 | 12,315 |
| $10,000 - $20,000 | 3,368 | 22,072 | 4,198 | 22,463 |
| $20,000 - $30,000 | 3,095 | 16,982 | 4,677 | 16,547 |
| $30,000 - $40,000 | 2,580 | 11,334 | 3,519 | 10,537 |
| $40,000 - $50,000 | 1,445 | 7,078 | 1,697 | 6,797 |
| $50,000 - $75,000 | 3,100 | 4,817 | 2,947 | 4,927 |
| $75,000 - $100,000 | 989 | 854 | 722 | 1,186 |
| $100,000 - $200,000 | 791 | 880 | 655 | 1,126 |
| $200,000 and above | 319 | 326 | 311 | 393 |
| **Total** | 17,353 | 76,338 | 20,419 | 76,291 |
| **Percent of Total** | 18.5 % | 81.5 % | 21.1 % | 78.9 % |

NOTE: Totals may not add due to rounding.

SOURCE: Joint Committee on Taxation (as of Sept. 25, 1986).

percent of the area median. Both income figures would be adjusted to take family size into account for the first time under any of the various tax-incentive programs for low-income housing.

The credit would be 9 percent a year of the value of the units occupied by the low-income tenants, and not otherwise benefited by federal subsidies. It would be used over a period of 10 years, and adjusted for inflation. For buildings receiving other federal subsidies, the credit would be 4 percent. The credit would be subject to recapture, with penalties, if the units were converted to any other use for a period of 15 years.

Newly constructed, acquired or rehabilitated buildings would be eligible.

There would be exceptions to the restrictions on deductions of passive losses, contained in the tax shelter section of the bill, for low-income housing.

The low-income housing credit would, with some exceptions, apply only to buildings placed in service before Jan. 1, 1990.

### Historic Rehabilitation

● **Tax Credit.** Replace existing-law credits of 15 percent for the rehabilitation of buildings at least 30 years old and 20 percent for buildings at least 40 years old with a 10 percent credit that could be used only for buildings constructed before 1936.

● Reduce from 25 percent to 20 percent the tax credit allowed for rehabilitation of certified historic buildings.

● **'Passive Losses.'** Permit limited exceptions to the general ban on deduction of tax-shelter "passive losses" for investments in historic rehabilitation.

### Agriculture, Timber, Energy and Minerals

● **Agriculture.** Allow farmers to continue writing off in one year the cost of soil and water conservation measures, instead of depreciating the costs over several years, provided the improvements were consistent with Agriculture Department-approved plans. The deduction would be limited to 25 percent of gross farm income.

● Retain one-year write-offs for certain fertilizer and soil conditioning costs, but repeal retroactively to Jan. 1, 1986, the write-off for land-clearing expenses.

● Exempt certain farmers from accounting rules to which they would otherwise be subject, as under existing law. Generally, farmers using the cash method of accounting could not deduct the prepaid costs of seed, fertilizer or other expenses, if they were used in the year following prepayment, and if more than 50 percent of the farmer's costs were prepaid.

● Exclude from taxable income a discharge of indebtedness granted farmers. The provision was designed to permit marginally solvent farmers to take advantage of federal farm credit programs guaranteeing loans in exchange for debt forgiveness.

● **Timber.** Repeal special capital gains treatment for corporations and individuals on the proceeds from timber sales; capital gains would be taxed at the same rates as regular income.

● Allow taxpayers a 10 percent tax credit for reforestation costs, and allow up to $10,000 annually of such costs to be written off over seven years, as under existing law.

● Allow most costs for timber production to be written off in the year paid or incurred, as under existing law.

● **Oil and Gas.** Retain nearly all existing-law provisions granting favorable tax treatment for exploration and development of oil and gas property by domestic producers.

Upon sale of oil, gas or geothermal property, expensed intangible drilling costs and percentage depletion deductions that reduced a taxpayer's basis in the property would be recaptured as ordinary income for tax purposes. The provision would apply to property acquired after Dec. 31, 1986, unless acquired pursuant to a contract binding on Sept. 25, 1985.

Intangible drilling expenses and exploration and development costs incurred outside the United States would have to be written off over 10 years or under a cost-depletion system; 30 percent of domestic intangible drilling costs incurred by some producers would be written off over five years.

● **Coal, Iron and Hard Minerals.** Retain nearly all existing-law provisions granting favorable tax treatment for exploration and development of mineral property by domestic producers.

Upon sale of mineral property, expensed exploration and development costs and percentage depletion deductions that reduced a taxpayer's basis in the property would be recaptured as ordinary income for tax purposes. The provision would apply to property acquired after Dec. 31, 1986, unless acquired pursuant to a contract binding on Sept. 25, 1985.

Intangible drilling expenses and exploration and development costs incurred outside the United States would have to be written off over 10 years or under a cost-depletion system; 30 percent of domestic corporate exploration and development costs would have to be written off over five years.

● **Energy Credits.** Allow all residential credits to expire, as under existing law.

● Extend business credits for innovative energy sources: for solar energy at 15 percent in 1986, 12 percent in 1987 and 10 percent in 1988; for geothermal energy at 15 percent in 1986, and 10 percent in 1987 and 1988; for ocean thermal energy at 15 percent through 1988; and for other new energy sources at lower rates for shorter periods of time.

● **Alcohol Fuels.** Retain the 6-cents-per-gallon exemption from federal fuel excise taxes for fuels containing 10 percent alcohol. The existing 9-cents-per-gallon excise tax exemption for fuels that were at least 85 percent alcohol would be reduced to 6 cents.

## Research and Development

● **Existing Tax Credit.** Extend through 1988, but reduce from 25 percent to 20 percent, the tax credit for new research and development expenses. The bill would tighten the definition of research and development to focus it exclusively on "research that is technological in nature." Research in economics or marketing, for example, would not qualify.

The bill would apply the general limitation on use of business credits to offset tax liability to the research and development credit.

● **University and Non-Profit Research.** Allow a new 20 percent tax credit for three years for corporate contributions to or contracts with universities or non-profit organizations to conduct new research and development. The provision would take effect Jan. 1, 1987.

● **Charitable Deduction.** Expand an existing charitable deduction allowed businesses for donations of newly manufactured scientific equipment to colleges and universities for physical or biological science research. The bill

would allow deductions for donations to organizations primarily involved in research that qualified as charitable under section 501(c)(3) of the Internal Revenue Code. Private foundations would not qualify.

● **'Orphan' Drugs.** Extend through 1990 an existing 50 percent tax credit for clinical testing of certain drugs, called "orphan" drugs, for rare diseases and conditions. The credit was due to expire at the end of 1987.

## Insurance

● **Life.** Repeal an existing-law percentage deduction that life insurance firms used to cap their top tax rate at 36.8 percent, instead of the 46 percent top rate paid by other corporations under existing law. The deduction, 20 percent of certain income, would be eliminated because the bill would reduce tax rates substantially. But the effect for 1987, because of the higher blended top corporate tax rate of 40 percent for that year, would be a one-year tax-rate increase for some life insurance firms.

● Continue the existing tax-exempt treatment of the increased value of life insurance policies, called "inside buildup."

● Eliminate business deductions for interest on large life insurance policy loans that, in effect, provided tax-deferred retirement savings.

● Repeal a $1,000 exclusion survivors claimed under existing law for interest they received on the unpaid proceeds of their spouses' life insurance policies. The provision would be effective for deaths after the date of enactment and tax years beginning after Dec. 31, 1986.

● **Property and Casualty.** Restrict deductions for loss reserves, by requiring a discount for part of the financial advantage to the company of retaining the money for other uses until claims were actually paid.

● Require property and casualty firms to count as income 20 percent of any increases in the value of special reserves used for soliciting premium income in advance of providing insurance coverage.

● **Blue Cross.** Repeal an existing tax exemption for Blue Cross and Blue Shield insurers, which critics argued gave them an unfair advantage over competitors. Blue Cross and Blue Shield insurers would be treated as stock property and casualty firms, with certain exceptions, including a "fresh start" for accounting purposes and loss reserves. Some YMCA, church-sponsored and other similar insurers would retain their tax-free status.

## Foreign

● **Income Exclusion.** Reduce the existing $80,000 exclusion of income earned by U.S. citizens working abroad to $70,000. The bill also would add Libya to the list of countries to which the exclusion did not apply.

● **Foreign Tax Credits.** Revise a complex system of tax credits allowed U.S. corporations, which reduced their U.S. tax liability by the amount of foreign taxes they paid on income earned overseas. The provisions would alter the existing overall limitation on the extent to which taxes on foreign income could be used as credits against U.S. taxes, replacing the overall limit with a variety of separate limitations, which would restrict their usefulness in reducing U.S. tax liabilities.

● **Sourcing.** Impose new sourcing rules for interest expenses and research and development costs with the aim of restricting the ability of multinational companies to claim

# Halting Shrinkage of Corporate Tax Share

A key, intended result of the tax bill (PL 99-514) was to reverse the decline in the corporate share of total tax payments, which had persisted almost without interruption in the post-World War II period.

Many economists and business executives expressed fears that the additional corporate tax burden would prove harmful to economic growth. The law was projected to shift about $120 billion in taxes from individuals to corporations over the five years 1987-91.

But despite the increased importance of corporate taxes, their share of federal tax collections was still expected to be lower than it was at any time between the end of World War II and 1979.

## From Some Paying Nothing ...

From the tax debate's beginnings, attention was repeatedly focused on the corporate sector's tax burden. Two separate and somewhat different studies, published during July 1986 — in the midst of the tax bill conference — showed that one out of six of the largest, profitable corporations paid no federal income tax in 1985.

The surveys, updates of earlier work in both cases, were aimed at influencing conferees who were considering which of a large number of existing corporate tax breaks to repeal or restrict.

In one analysis, Citizens for Tax Justice, largely funded by organized labor, found that 42 of 250 corporations paid no federal income tax in 1985, and 130 — more than half — paid none in at least one of the five years, 1981-85, surveyed. The group was responsible for a widely publicized 1984 study of no-tax and low-tax companies that helped create public pressure for reform.

Tax Analysts, an organization supported solely by income from sales of its publications to corporations, tax lawyers and accountants, found that 95 of the 604 corporations it studied paid no tax in 1985.

Citizens for Tax Justice based its study on data from corporate annual reports and filings with the Securities and Exchange Commission (SEC). Tax Analysts used the SEC filings but also attempted to get additional information from the companies themselves to make more detailed analyses.

"For most of America's largest corporations, no-tax years are now commonplace," said Robert S. McIntyre, head of Citizens for Tax Justice. Thomas F. Field, executive director of Tax Analysts, said, "It is fair to conclude on the basis of our figures that the U.S. corporate income tax is seriously flawed. In particular, the finding that effective corporate tax rates continue to vary widely from industry to industry means that our tax system promotes misallocation of capital and losses of economic efficiency."

Tax Analysts identified apparel, newspaper, tobacco and non-durable goods wholesalers as the highest tax industries, with rates of tax paid ranging from 34 to 46 percent. Construction, railroad, motion picture and large oil companies had the lowest tax rates, ranging from net tax rebates to 8 percent.

## ... To Paying More

Treasury Secretary James A. Baker III, in response to complaints from the business community, repeatedly argued during the yearlong tax debate that the corporate share had greatly declined. He noted that in 1967 corporate taxes represented 22.8 percent of total federal receipts, whereas they had been estimated to equal only 10.2 percent in 1987, under existing law.

Baker also cited the proportion of all income taxes represented by corporate income taxes, which many analysts considered more valid because it left out of the calculation taxes whose rise in recent decades had dwarfed the changes in all others. These funded "social insurance" programs, principally Social Security.

Counting only income taxes, and leaving out social insurance, excise, estate and miscellaneous taxes, corporate taxes showed the same declining pattern displayed when their share of all tax payments was calculated. Under the new law, the corporate share of income taxes reverted to where it was before 1980.

## Share of Income Tax Payments

| Fiscal Year | Individuals | Corporations |
|---|---|---|
| 1957 | 62.7% | 37.3% |
| 1967 | 64.4 | 35.6 |
| 1977 | 74.2 | 25.8 |
| 1978 | 75.2 | 24.8 |
| 1979 | 76.8 | 23.2 |
| 1980 | 79.1 | 20.9 |
| 1981 | 82.4 | 17.6 |
| 1982 | 85.8 | 14.2 |
| 1983 | 88.6 | 11.4 |
| 1984 | 84.0 | 16.0 |
| 1985 | 84.5 | 15.5 |
| 1986 | 84.7 | 15.3 |
| 1987 | 82.4 | 17.6 |
| 1988 [a] | 78.8 | 21.2 |

[a] Estimate.

SOURCE: Office of Management and Budget.

that expenditures were made in the United States and thus were deductible against U.S.-source income.

● **Financial Services.** Terminate the ability of multinational companies to defer U.S. tax on income from overseas banking operations, unless the interest was earned in connection with export activities. Impose a separate limit on foreign tax credits against income from overseas financial services so that credits arising from other types of foreign activities could not be used to offset income from financial services.

● **Space and the High Seas.** Discard the general rule that the United States asserted primary tax jurisdiction only over income generated within its borders and territorial waters. Most income derived from space or ocean activities would be treated as if produced in the country of residence of the person generating the income.

● **Foreign Taxpayers.** Enact a number of new provisions taxing more of the income earned in the United States by foreign individuals and businesses, including earnings by foreign government corporations.

● **Tax-Haven Income.** Make extensive revisions in subpart F of the Internal Revenue Code to limit tax avoidance through investments in "tax-haven" countries.

● **U.S. Possessions.** Impose a variety of new restrictions on the use of tax credits to eliminate virtually all U.S. tax on income earned by corporations in Puerto Rico, the Virgin Islands and other possessions.

● **Copyrights and Patents.** Require adequate royalty payments back to the United States, where they would be taxable, for patents and copyrights transferred to subsidiaries operating overseas, including those in U.S. possessions.

● **Transportation Income.** Eliminate the deferral of U.S. tax on reinvested income from foreign-flag shipping.

● **Foreign Investment Companies.** Restrict deferrals of tax and conversion of ordinary income into capital gains by U.S. shareholders in foreign investment companies.

## Trusts and Estates

● **Child's Income.** Tax the unearned income in excess of $1,000 of a child under 14 years of age at the parent's tax rate, instead of at the child's rate, regardless of the source of the assets from which the income was derived. The first $500 of a child's unearned income would be offset by the standard deduction and the second $500 taxed at the child's rate. The $500 figures would be indexed to increase with inflation after 1988.

Use of so-called Clifford Trusts, another method used by parents to transfer income to their children to avoid taxes, would be effectively repealed for transfers of income-producing assets after March 1, 1986.

● **Estimated Tax.** Require both new and existing trusts and estates to pay estimated tax in the same manner as individuals, except that new estates would be exempted for their first two years.

● **Taxable Years.** Require all trusts, except charitable trusts, to adopt calendar years as taxable years to prohibit unwarranted deferral of tax.

● **'Generation-Skipping Tax.'** Revise the so-called "generation-skipping tax" imposed on those who tried to avoid paying estate taxes by passing wealth on to their grandchildren, instead of to their children. The changes would allow a couple to pass on $4 million to a grandchild without paying the generation-skipping tax.

The existing-law tax was more stringent, but it also was considered so complex that few taxpayers complied and the Internal Revenue Service never enforced it. It would be repealed retroactively to June 11, 1976, but earlier transfers would still be subject to estate taxes.

## Pensions

● **Individual Retirement Accounts.** Continue the existing tax-deductible contribution to Individual Retirement Accounts (IRAs) for individuals with incomes up to $25,000 and married couples up to $40,000 or those at any income level not covered by employer-provided pension plans, including 401(k) plans. If one spouse was covered by a pension plan, both would be considered covered. Persons not yet vested in a pension plan would be considered covered. Those with incomes between $25,000 and $35,000, if single, or $40,000 and $50,000, if married, would be subject to a phase-down of the amount of the tax-free contribution they would be allowed.

Taxpayers ineligible to make tax-deductible contributions could continue to add to IRAs, although the contributions would be taxable. The interest earned by IRAs held by taxpayers ineligible for tax-deductible contributions would continue to be tax-deferred, however.

The basic deduction limits, without reference to the phase-down, would remain unchanged at $2,000 (or total earned income, whichever is lower) per employed person and $2,250 for joint returns where one spouse has no earned income.

Taxpayers would have until April 15, 1987, to make their 1986 tax-free contributions to IRAs under the old rules.

● **401(k) Plans.** Reduce the maximum tax-exempt employee contribution to a 401(k) savings plan from $30,000 a year to $7,000 annually, a figure that would be indexed for inflation beginning in 1988.

Tighten the non-discrimination rules governing employer contributions to these plans, which could still be as much as $30,000 annually per employee.

● **Government Retirees.** Eliminate a provision in existing law allowing public employees to receive tax-free pension benefits until the benefit payments exceeded the total contributions made by the individual to a pension plan. Instead, the tax-free portion of the benefits would be spread out over the retiree's life expectancy. The new rule would apply to pensions received beginning July 1, 1986.

● **Other Pension Changes.** Make sweeping changes in tax laws governing private pension plans in an attempt to encourage firms to provide greater coverage for their lower- and middle-income employees, to shut off a variety of avenues for favoring highly compensated employees and to discourage employers from shifting a greater share of the cost of retirement savings to employees. Generally, the changes would be effective for pension plan years beginning after Dec. 31, 1988.

● Require that for an employer's pension plan to qualify for special tax treatment, the plan must cover 70 percent of the firm's employees. Under existing law, employers were required to cover only 56 percent or "a fair cross-section" of workers as the test of whether a pension plan treated employees fairly. Employers could still use the fair cross-section standard, but then would be required to provide all employees with at least 70 percent of the benefits received by those fully covered by the pension plan.

● Provide full vesting of employees in pension plans

# Foreign Policy

The Reagan administration's foreign policy was marked by zeal and pragmatism. When it was zealous, as in trying to rid Nicaragua of communism or to save Lebanon from its warring factions, the administration overextended U.S. power and influence, and it failed. When it was pragmatic, as in negotiating over conflicts in Afghanistan and Southern Africa, it set realistic goals and cooperated with its allies, and it achieved a greater degree of success.

While seemingly contradictory, zeal and pragmatism were central features of President Reagan's personality, and so they became hallmarks of his administration's approach to the world. Reagan took office in 1981 with a few unshakable ideas about foreign affairs. The most important of these was that the Soviet Union was bent on world domination and that only an aggressive response by the United States could stop Soviet expansionism.

But in putting his ideas into practice, Reagan often demonstrated a remarkable flexibility. A Reagan who had long disdained arms control negotiations with the Soviet Union would, over the long run, negotiate the first treaty actually banning an entire class of nuclear weapons. And a Reagan who had made ousting the Sandinista leaders of Nicaragua one of his highest priorities would, at the end of his tenure, quietly drop the issue to avoid creating election-year troubles for his chosen successor.

Reagan's ability to accommodate himself to reality frequently confounded and confused both his supporters and adversaries. The president engaged in long-running battles with Congress over the entire range of defense and foreign policy issues, but many of his victories resulted from his adaptability.

Critics charged that Reagan was successful only when he was lucky. In many cases, Reagan did benefit from developments that were beyond his control, most importantly the launching of fundamental change in the Soviet Union under the leadership of Mikhail S. Gorbachev. But supporters contended that Reagan's determination and consistency helped create fortunate circumstances and that he knew what to do once they appeared.

Supporters and critics alike agreed that Reagan did succeed in re-establishing American self-confidence at a crucial moment. Reagan took office at the end of an era of frustration and bitterness for Americans that began with the defeat in Vietnam and culminated with the imprisonment of hostages in Iran for 444 days. The United States of January 1981 was unsure of its role in the world and hesitant to use its military might overseas.

With his can-do attitude that brushed aside worrisome details, Reagan largely succeeded in bolstering Americans' confidence and nationalistic pride in their country.

Reagan was unable to erase memories of Vietnam, however. In spite of his interventionist rhetoric, Americans remained reluctant to employ armed forces overseas, especially when the goals were unclear or victory was uncertain.

Opposition to his policies in Central America was fostered as much as anything by a widespread fear that the president ultimately would send U.S. soldiers to fight communists in El Salvador and Nicaragua. While he chafed at congressional restrictions on his foreign policy powers, Reagan appeared to recognize the limits to public support for direct intervention abroad; for example, he accepted with only a little grumbling a cap on the number of U.S. military advisers in El Salvador.

For the most part, Reagan's use of American military power was for specific, narrowly defined purposes: invading Grenada to oust a Marxist regime; striking at Libya to protest its sponsorship of terrorism; and protecting shipping in the Persian Gulf to strengthen U.S. relations with Gulf allies, ensure the flow of oil through the Strait of Hormuz and exert pressure on Iran to end its war with Iraq. His one ill-considered deployment of troops was a disaster: the assignment of Marines to a hopeless peace-keeping mission in Lebanon.

Reagan also sought on several occasions to use foreign paramilitary forces to roll back the Soviets' presence in the Third World. An informal concept called the Reagan doctrine was based on the premise that it was easier and more prudent politically to equip and train guerrilla forces to battle Soviet-supported Third World regimes than to send in thousands of American soldiers.

## Dealing With Gorbachev

At the beginning of the 1980s, the West had real fears of an expanding Soviet empire. Moscow's military buildup

## References

Discussion of foreign policy for the years 1945-64 may be found in *Congress and the Nation Vol. I*, pp. 91-232; for the years 1965-68, *Congress and the Nation Vol. II*, pp. 49-116; for the years 1969-72, *Congress and the Nation Vol. III*, pp. 853-948; for the years 1973-76, *Congress and the Nation Vol. IV*, pp. 847-912; for the years 1977-80, *Congress and the Nation Vol. V*, pp. 31-95; for the years 1981-84, *Congress and the Nation Vol. VI*, pp. 123-197.

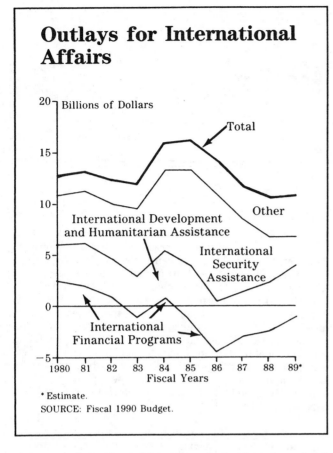

## Outlays for International Affairs

20 — Billions of Dollars

Total

15 —

International Development and Humanitarian Assistance

Other

10 —

5 —

International Security Assistance

0 —

International Financial Programs

-5 —

1980  81  82  83  84  85  86  87  88  89*
Fiscal Years

* Estimate.
SOURCE: Fiscal 1990 Budget.

that started in the mid-1960s and the invasion of Afghanistan in November 1979 signalled a renewed aggressiveness, one that ultimately could be aimed at the Western world's vital oil lifeline in the Persian Gulf.

By the end of the decade, however, the Kremlin was in retreat internationally and was concentrating on its formidable domestic problems. The Soviet leaders had negotiated a face-saving withdrawal from Afghanistan, had set limits on their willingess to subsidize fumbling Third World client regimes and were tolerating — even encouraging — the dismantlement of communist governments in Eastern Europe.

Ironically, the new Soviet posture posed new challenges for the West, especially in maintaining the cohesion of NATO. Ever since World War II, the greatest unifying force for the Atlantic alliance had been the perceived threat from the Soviet empire. But with Gorbachev declaring an end to the arms race, offering significant unilateral reductions in Soviet military forces and allowing Warsaw Pact countries to turn to the West, NATO was put in the uncomfortable position of appearing to be a conservative force resisting positive change.

During his first term, Reagan was the dominant personality in world politics, using the force of his convictions and the strength of his personality to shape events. By the time he left office, however, Reagan was overshadowed by Gorbachev. As a bold figure struggling to reverse history, Gorbachev excited the world as Reagan never could. Among the enthralled was Ronald Reagan, who strolled through Red Square in May 1988 and declared that the Soviet empire no longer looked as evil as it did when he took office eight years earlier.

## Central America

For historical reasons, Central America emerged as the region of the world that received the most attention from the U.S. government during the Reagan years. The Sandinista revolution in Nicaragua in 1979 and the overthrow later that year of a dictatorship in El Salvador set in motion a series of events that led Reagan to spend more energy, American tax dollars and political capital on Central America than any of his predecessors.

The results of U.S. efforts were mixed, at best. Both of Reagan's policies toward Nicaragua failed: his stated policy of pressuring the leftist Sandinistas to accept democracy and stop threatening their neighbors, and his unstated goal of ousting the Managua regime from power. Reagan also failed, during his last year in office, to force out the military dictator of Panama, Gen. Manuel Antonio Noriega.

More uncertain, at the end of the Reagan years, was the outcome of Washington's attempt to promote democracy elsewhere in the region. El Salvador, Honduras and Guatemala emerged as fledgling democracies in the 1980s, complete with competitive political parties and relatively peaceful elections. In all three countries, however, the military continued to wield the ultimate power.

Nicaragua proved to be the single most contentious foreign policy question for Reagan throughout his two terms in office. The president and his congressional opponents fought more than a dozen battles between 1983 and 1988 over providing aid to the contra guerrillas, who hoped to foment a revolution against the Sandinistas just as the Sandinistas had revolted against the Somoza regime. The balance of power on that issue swung back and forth in Washington, sometimes from month-to-month, in reaction either to the political climate in the United States or to internal developments in Nicaragua.

Once opposition to the contra aid policy surfaced in the House in 1983, Reagan won only one complete victory: in 1986, when he capitalized on Sandinista fumbling and election-year jitters among Southern Democrats to force Congress into appropriating $100 million for military and non-military aid to the contras. With that money, contra leaders and their CIA advisers managed to recruit some 15,000 fighters to the anti-Sandinista cause. The contras carried their guerrilla war deep into Nicaragua. They never seriously threatened the Sandinistas' grip on power but did shake their confidence and provoked a harsh reaction that undermined public support for the regime.

In the end, the anti-contra Democrats on Capitol Hill got their way. The Iran-contra affair in 1987 doomed any prospects for a renewal of military aid to the guerrillas, and even Reagan seemed to lose interest in the matter toward the end of his time in office. Seeking to avoid further political battles on the issue, the Bush administration in 1989 negotiated a deal that allowed another year's worth of non-military aid to the contras but pinned U.S. hopes for Nicaragua on elections rather than military force.

In retrospect, some of Reagan's aides and his critics agreed that the president made a mistake in trying to carry out his policy first in secrecy and then, once it was revealed, with only a narrow base of public support. But the two sides disagreed about what Reagan should have done instead. Some supporters, such as former national security adviser Robert C. McFarlane, said Reagan should have confronted Congress on the Nicaragua question early in his administration, declaring that a policy of ousting the Sandinistas was vital to U.S. national security. Of course, such an approach was not what Reagan's opponents had in mind. They said the president should have avoided a militaristic policy and instead applied more sustained political and diplomatic pressure on the Sandinistas to open up their political system and to curtail their military buildup.

While his Nicaragua policy was faltering, Reagan did succeed in averting a victory by the leftist guerrillas in El Salvador who had been so threatening when he took office. Reagan armed the Salvadoran military with millions of dollars worth of weapons and sent advisers to professionalize what had been, at best, a part-time fighting force. At the insistence of Congress, the administration applied pressure on a succession of Salvadoran regimes to curtail the terrorism of right-wing death squads that had operated from within the security forces.

After eight years of war, the guerrillas still held large chunks of territory in El Salvador but had failed to spark a full-scale public uprising on their behalf. The guerrillas resorted increasingly to urban terrorism — a tactic that kept the military off balance but did little to generate public support for their cause.

Results also were mixed on the other aspects of U.S. policy toward El Salvador: building a democratic political system and stabilizing the economy. A centrist government headed by José Napoleón Duarte ensured the continued flow of U.S. aid dollars but was unable to cope with the country's economic problems or to rule effectively.

The right-wing ARENA Party gained control of the National Assembly in 1988 and consolidated its hold on government by winning the presidency in April 1989. Although somewhat reluctant to embrace a party that in earlier years was associated with death squads, the Bush administration declared the elections to be a victory for democracy. To some liberals on Capitol Hill, however, El Salvador appeared to be slipping back into the polarization that U.S. policy had sought to overcome.

The one unqualified disaster for Reagan in Central America was the desperate gamble to force Noriega out of Panama. Using sanctions and then negotiations, Washington instead bolstered Noriega's determination to hang onto power. After Reagan was out of office, Noriega consolidated his grip by rigging elections in May 1989.

By creating a U.S. vs. Noriega confrontation, the Reagan and Bush administrations revived old questions about Washington's relations with Latin America, and especially about the future of the Panama Canal treaties. In one of his last statements as president, Reagan reverted to his role as opponent of the treaties, saying whoever was president in 1999 should reconsider turning the canal over to Panama.

## Iran-Contra Affair

The Iran-contra affair, which engulfed Reagan at the mid-point of his second term, could be viewed in one of two ways: as an unfortunate, and possibly overblown, aberration that marred an otherwise successful presidency or as a political and foreign policy disaster that was an inevitable outcome of Reagan's philosophy and style of governing.

The president and his supporters chose the former interpretation, arguing that the Iran-contra affair was an isolated incident that said nothing profound about the overall course of the Reagan administration. As a defense, Reagan's backers borrowed a position that long had been one of the principle criticisms of the president — that he was "disengaged" from the daily routine of government. According to this argument, Reagan's detached man-

agement style caused him to be unaware of secret activities in the White House: the secret supply network organized by Lt. Col. Oliver L. North to skirt a congressional ban on aid to the contras and the diversion of funds to the contras from the sale of weapons to Iran. Moreover, Reagan said he never believed that the main purpose of selling weapons to Iran was to gain the release of American hostages. The White House public relations apparatus embraced this view shortly after the scandal broke in November 1986.

Many of Reagan's critics — including the select congressional committees that investigated the affair — developed another view. They argued that Reagan, by allowing free rein to a small group of ideological zealots, in effect condoned an abuse of power. In their strongly worded majority report of November 1987, the committees said that "secrecy, deception and disdain for the rule of law" were the ingredients of the Iran-contra affair.

The committees' report, and evidence presented at North's trial in 1989, challenged the standard picture of a president who was kept in the dark by scheming assistants. Although there was no evidence that Reagan approved the illegal diversion of funds to the contras, the facts showed that he attended many of the meetings at which key Iran-contra decisions were made and approved some of the steps that later stirred controversy.

A parallel line of criticism was that the Iran-contra affair was a natural outgrowth of the way the Reagan administration did business. Excessive secrecy, disregard for standard procedures, deception of Congress and the public and an eagerness to employ military solutions to diplomatic problems were characteristic flaws of the Reagan administration and were not confined to the Iran-contra affair, according to critics.

The administration's actions in the Iran-contra affair arose out of frustration with the failure of conventional approaches to foreign policy problems.

In the Iran case, Reagan and his aides were stymied by the inability of routine diplomacy either to secure the release of U.S. hostages in Lebanon or to moderate the behavior and rhetoric of the extremist rulers in Tehran. Covert arms sales, first suggested by Israel, seemed to offer hope for progress on both counts. With little assessment of the potential risks, the administration gambled on this policy, which sharply departed from its official position of not negotiating with terrorists or nations that supported terrorism. Ultimately, the arms sales bought freedom for three hostages, but at a cost of substantial damage to overall U.S. foreign policy interests in the Middle East.

White House frustration over Nicaragua stemmed from the refusal of House Democratic leaders to support a policy of trying to oust the leftist regime in Managua. Reagan launched this policy secretly in late 1981, resorted to shifting justifications when opposition arose and directed aides to find other means of sustaining the contras when Congress suspended official aid in 1984.

The decision by some White House staff members in early 1986 to fund the contras with some of the profits from the Iran arms sales had the effect of merging policies toward the two countries that were at the center of Washington's international agenda during much of the Carter and Reagan administrations. Revolutions in Iran and Nicaragua in 1979 contributed to the public perception of Carter's weakness — a major factor in his loss of the presidency. Reagan himself kept Iran and Nicaragua at the forefront of American political debate during the 1980s, calling the former "Murder Inc." because of its support for terrorism and the latter a communist "dungeon."

The mixing of the Iran and contra policies was therefore an explosive one. First, Reagan was shown to have betrayed his tough-guy posture of refusing to deal with terrorists — and not just any terrorists, but the government that had held 52 Americans hostage for more than a year. Then it was revealed that Reagan had allowed, possibly even encouraged, his aides to skirt the legal prohibition on official U.S. support for the contras.

Reagan repeatedly insisted that he never approved, much less knew about, the diversion of Iranian funds to the contras — the action that put the two secret policies in tandem. Aides all stood by him on that count, and no documentary evidence to the contrary emerged.

Largely because of the "what did the president know?" standard established in the Watergate scandal, the question of whether Reagan approved the diversion scheme became the overriding issue before the House and Senate investigating committees in 1987. Even before the committees began their work, congressional leaders concluded that Reagan probably was telling the truth, and so there would be neither legal nor political grounds for impeaching him.

## Reagan and Congress

On foreign policy, as on many other issues, mutual confrontation was the hallmark of relations between Congress and the Reagan administration.

Reagan's standard approach was to demand either that Congress approve his proposals intact or that it stand aside while he carried out the policy of his choice. The president often seemed to view Congress more as a bothersome obstacle than as a co-equal branch of government with a legitimate role in foreign affairs.

Many in Congress, especially liberal Democrats, reciprocated that attitude. While impressed by the president's personal popularity, a substantial bloc of Democrats tended almost automatically to oppose his foreign policy initiatives on partisan or ideological grounds. They saw little to be gained by cooperating with a president who referred to them as part of the problem that the voters had elected him to fix. Reagan never succeeded in allaying fears among Democrats about his motives, in part because they tended to view his harsh denunciations of them as thinly veiled challenges to their patriotism.

Not surprisingly, given this combative atmosphere, Reagan's dealings with Congress often turned into unpleasant battles for both sides. Some of the contests — particularly that over aid to the Nicaraguan contras — lasted for years with neither side able to gain an unalloyed victory. Other conflicts between were short but intense, lasting only as long as the issue at hand commanded attention.

On most foreign policy matters, Reagan tried for quick political victories. He rarely worked to build sustained congressional and public support for his policies. On Nicaragua, for example, conservatives and liberals both faulted him for failing to outline his goals or to make his case against the Sandinistas in a compelling enough manner.

Reagan's success was most limited when the public was divided or was in opposition to his policies. In one such case, Congress took the extraordinary step in 1986 of overriding Reagan's veto of sanctions against South Africa; whatever its merits, the president's position was not politi-

cally sustainable in an election year.

Reagan occasionally settled for compromises in his dealings with Congress. But those deals often came only after he initiated battles he could not fully win. In his early years, Reagan perfected the technique of accepting compromises at the most propitious moment, enabling him to declare victory. He later seemed to lose that touch, at times carrying disputes with Congress past the point when he could have gained any real advantage.

## The Middle East

With the exception of Lebanon in 1982-83, Reagan managed to get through his two terms without becoming mired in a major crisis in the Middle East.

At the beginning of the Reagan administration, the Persian Gulf seemed the most dangerous part of the world. The war between Iran and Iraq was escalating, causing fears about the safety of the industrialized world's oil lifeline. The United States had just ended its yearlong dispute with Iran over the embassy hostages. And the Soviet Union's move into Afghanistan provoked worry about its long-term intentions in the region.

The Iran-Iraq war dragged on until late 1988, costing hundreds of thousands of lives, but the oil supply never was seriously endangered. The United States and some of its European allies sent naval forces into the Gulf in 1987-88 to protect neutral shipping from attacks by both belligerents. The latter move also was intended to improve relations with U.S. allies in the Gulf region and to exert pressure on Iran to end the war.

After the collapse in 1981 of negotiations spawned by the Camp David agreements, the Middle East peace process stagnated. Washington and Arab leaders offered competing proposals, but until the end of the Reagan years none of the central actors appeared ready to make the necessary concessions to get negotiations going again.

The peace process was given a new urgency by an unexpected source: the Palestinians who had lived for 21 years under Israeli occupation in the West Bank and Gaza Strip. In December 1987 a widespread and sustained uprising against Israeli control erupted in the occupied territories. The Palestinian revolt, or *intifada*, reinvigorated the Palestinian cause and spawned a new wave of self-doubt and uncertainty within Israel. Israel's harsh crackdown on the Palestinians also began to weaken public support for the Jewish state in the United States.

An indirect outcome of the *intifada* was Reagan's decision in December 1988 to begin a "dialogue" with the Palestine Liberation Organization (PLO). That action, in response to PLO Chairman Yasir Arafat's tacit recognition of Israel and stated renunciation of terrorism, created the best chance for peace in the Middle East since the Camp David agreements 10 years earlier.

Reagan's decision caught many by surprise, given his closeness to Israel and his repeated denunciations of PLO "terrorism." But in a broader sense, Reagan's last major move in foreign policy was typical of his pragmatic, rather than his zealous, side. It was a concession to reality that had the advantage of making the United States seem bold and magnanimous. It also was a step that Reagan could take at the end of his tenure but, given the same set of circumstances, might not have been willing to consider at the beginning.

# Chronology
# Of Action
# On Foreign Policy

# 1985-86

The 99th Congress ended a decade of reluctance to intervene in foreign conflicts when it backed President Reagan's policy of aiding anti-communist insurgencies around the world. Congressional support for assistance to guerrilla forces in Nicaragua, Afghanistan, Cambodia and Angola was a major victory for the Reagan administration.

But Reagan had his losses, too. Congress handed the president a major legislative defeat when it enacted over his veto a bill imposing economic sanctions against South Africa. Not since 1973, during the reaction against U.S. intervention in Vietnam, had Congress overridden a president so decisively on foreign policy. Congress also forced Reagan to cut back a major arms deal with Saudi Arabia and to shelve a similar sale to Jordan.

The White House and Congress worked closely on U.S. policy toward the Philippines, an ally of historic and strategic importance to the United States. Together they pressured Ferdinand E. Marcos to undertake meaningful political and economic reforms and finally, in the wake of a fraud-ridden election, to step down from the Philippine presidency.

Congress in 1985 took a big step toward restoring its process for considering foreign assistance programs when — for the first time since 1981 — it passed a full-scale authorization bill for foreign aid. But Congress failed in 1985 and again in 1986 to produce a separate appropriations bill and the foreign aid programs were folded into omnibus funding bills.

As 1986 ended, a major foreign policy scandal emerged. Reports that the Reagan administration, despite its anti-terrorism policy, had sold U.S. arms to Iran and that some of the money from the sales had been diverted illegally to the contra guerrillas in Nicaragua caused an uproar on Capitol Hill and triggered major investigations. *(Iran-contra affair, p. 253)*

## Contra 'Humanitarian' Aid

After two years of sustained battles, President Reagan in 1985 won congressional approval — if not full-hearted support — for U.S. involvement in the war against the leftist government of Nicaragua.

Congress authorized and appropriated $27 million for non-military aid to some 15,000 contras in 1985. That action represented a dramatic turnaround from a previous-year cutoff of assistance to the rebels in their fight against the Sandinista regime in Managua. *(Box, p. 175)*

But with the aid to the anti-government rebels due to expire on March 31, 1986, the stage was set for a renewed confrontation over the issue. President Reagan returned to Congress early in 1986 to ask for additional support for the Nicaraguan guerrillas. *(Details, p. 177)*

The contra funding was included in supplemental appropriations legislation (HR 2577 — PL 99-88) for fiscal 1985. Voting in April, the House rejected a joint resolution (H J Res 239) that would grant Reagan's request to resume aid to the contras. Nicaraguan President Daniel Ortega's trip to Moscow helped shift the political climate in favor of the rebels and the House reversed itself when it took up the appropriations bill in June.

It was a major victory for Reagan, who had thrown the weight of his presidency behind the contras' battle against the Sandinistas. Reagan had called the issue "one of the greatest moral challenges" to the United States and described the contras as "freedom fighters."

The shift by the House had many causes, the most important of which appeared to be a new receptiveness by many Democrats to Reagan's argument that Nicaragua was a test of American will to fight communism.

Nevertheless, to gain victory, Reagan accepted two conditions of enormous political importance imposed by Congress.

The first was the insistence by most congressional leaders that U.S. aid be spent for food, clothing and other "humanitarian" purposes, not for guns, ammunition and other military items. Reagan accepted that demand but retained the right to ask for military aid later.

The second condition was Congress' rejection of an administration request that either the CIA or the Defense Department be allowed to administer the aid. The CIA had administered the original military aid program to the rebels begun in December 1981.

Authorization for the $27 million in aid was contained in the fiscal 1986-87 foreign aid bill (S 960 — PL 99-83), which also prohibited the CIA or the Pentagon from administering the assistance.

In November, however, Congress loosened some of its restrictions. Adopting the fiscal 1986 authorization bill for the CIA and other intelligence agencies (HR 2419 — PL 99-169), members allowed the CIA to give the contras advice and intelligence information. The measure also broadened previous congressional definitions of humanitarian aid.

Those provisions were reaffirmed in defense-related provisions of the fiscal 1986 continuing appropriations resolution (H J Res 465 — PL 99-190). And the defense authorization bill (S 1160 — PL 99-145), cleared in October, contained a sense-of-Congress declaration that no combat forces should be sent into Nicaragua.

### Reagan Proposal

Officially, the United States halted its involvement in the Nicaraguan war in mid-1984.

In October 1984, Congress set aside $14 million for the rebels for fiscal 1985. But to get use of the money, Reagan was required to submit a report to Congress, after Feb. 28, 1985, and convince both houses to approve the aid by joint resolution.

At the beginning of 1985, that prospect looked unlikely. The Democratic-controlled House already had voted four times since 1983 against U.S. aid to the contras. Support for the contras weakened in the Senate in 1984 after the administration committed a series of political blunders, including its failure to inform the Intelligence Committee about CIA involvement in the mining of Nicaraguan harbors.

The contra cause was not helped by press reports that several countries had used U.S. foreign aid to support the contras, but investigations by the intelligence panels launched in early 1985 had stalled by year's end for lack of evidence.

In the weeks before renewing his request for military aid to the contras, Reagan mounted what administration officials called a "public education" campaign, making some of his harshest attacks ever on the policies of the Sandinistas and acknowledging publicly for the first time that he was seeking to overthrow the Managua regime. Reagan and his aides for three years had given several purposes for aiding the anti-government guerrillas, but the ousting of the Sandinistas had not been among Washington's official aims.

Reagan shifted his tactics when he asked Congress on April 3 for $14 million in renewed U.S. military aid to the contras. He put his Capitol Hill critics on the defensive by coupling his request with a proposal for a 60-day cease-fire during which negotiations would be held under the mediation of Nicaraguan church officials. The $14 million initially would be used for food, clothing, medicine and "other support for survival" of the contras, but, if the Sandinistas did not accept the cease-fire by June 1, the plan called for using what was left of the $14 million to resume contra arms aid.

## Aid Rejected

Two weeks after making his request for $14 million in military aid to the contras, Reagan backed down. Confronted by opposition in both houses of Congress, Reagan on April 18 tentatively agreed to a compromise, advocated by Republicans and conservative Democratic senators, restricting contra aid to non-military purposes — at least through the end of the 1985 fiscal year.

Reagan had hoped for a narrow victory in both houses on his original request, but the option in his peace plan to resume military aid generated deep opposition on Capitol Hill. After years of appearing to push for military solutions to conflicts in Central America, the president's sudden eagerness for peace talks struck many in Congress as having been contrived merely to win votes in Congress.

Both the Senate and House acted on the Nicaragua issue in a highly partisan, pressure-cooker atmosphere.

The Senate on April 23 narrowly approved S J Res 106, which would provide $14 million in aid to the contras. That 53-46 vote was made possible only by Reagan's promise not to use the money for military purposes.

But Reagan's compromise was not enough to win over the House. Handing Reagan one of the most serious foreign policy defeats of his presidency, the House on April 23-24 voted against the resumption of U.S. aid to the contras. An hour after the Senate had acted, the House overwhelmingly — 180-248 — rejected Reagan's request (H J Res 239).

The House ratified its action on April 24 with a series of votes on a substitute resolution (H J Res 247) that would bar further military aid to the contras and instead provide $4 million for fostering peace talks and $10 million for humanitarian aid to Nicaraguan refugees, to be administered through the Red Cross or United Nations.

The House tentatively adopted the proposal, 219-206, and rejected a GOP plan for non-military aid by a two-vote margin — 213-215. But then H J Res 247 was defeated on a 123-303 vote.

## Humanitarian Aid Approved

Within weeks of the votes rejecting contra aid, many critics of the program were having doubts, second thoughts that ultimately led to the congressional turnaround in favor of $27 million in non-lethal assistance for the contras.

A major reason for the change in climate on Capitol Hill was Nicaraguan President Ortega's aid-seeking trip to Moscow less than a week after the congressional votes against the contra aid.

Several moderate and conservative House Democrats, many of whom had voted against the $14 million in contra aid in April, soon began trying to revive proposals for humanitarian aid to the rebels.

And Reagan, acting on advice from many in Congress, on May 1 imposed a trade embargo and other economic sanctions on Nicaragua. Administration officials acknowledged that the action was largely symbolic, because Nicaragua's trade with the United States had dropped sharply and because other nations could make up for whatever trade was lost.

But the sanctions filled in what many in Congress saw as an inconsistent gap in the Reagan administration's policy toward Nicaragua. The United States was maintaining full economic and diplomatic relations with Nicaragua, while waging rhetorical and military warfare against the Sandinista government. Most members reacted favorably to the sanctions.

On June 12, the House reversed itself and agreed to supply $27 million for the guerrillas. Although called humanitarian aid, most of the money was set aside for uniforms and other logistical support for the contras. The money was authorized by the fiscal 1986 foreign aid bill (S 960 — PL 99-83) and included in a fiscal 1985 supplemental appropriations bill (HR 2577 — PL 99-88). A related provision established a procedure for rapid congressional consideration of Reagan's expected request for follow-up aid to the contras in 1986.

**Appropriation.** The Nicaragua issue returned to the Senate floor June 6-7, as amendments to a routine bill (S 1003) making authorizations for the State Department and related agencies. The Senate, which consistently supported the contra aid, reaffirmed that position by approving, 55-42, $38 million for non-military aid in fiscal years 1985-86. (State Department authorization, p. 199)

Although the money voted by the Senate was called humanitarian aid, there was little doubt among most senators that the actual result of the funding would be to increase the effectiveness of the contras' paramilitary operations.

Much of the Senate debate centered on the question of whether resumed support for the contras would increase the prospect of U.S. military intervention in Nicaragua. The Senate rejected several Democratic-sponsored proposals to restrict the nature of the contra aid and to limit Reagan's freedom to send U.S. troops to Central America.

The climax of the House's stunning turnaround on contra aid occurred June 12, when members voted to attach $27 million in non-military contra aid to HR 2577, the supplemental appropriations bill.

Reagan's victory came after he yielded to congressional insistence that the aid be spent for humanitarian purposes, not for military items. On a broader level, Reagan also gave assurances that he was not seeking to overthrow the Nicaraguan government.

The House voted directly on the contra issue four

# Earlier Restrictions on Contra Aid

Almost from the beginning of U.S. aid to anti-government guerrillas in Nicaragua, Congress sought to set limits on both the tactics and goals of that aid.

Administration officials first told the House and Senate Intelligence committees in December 1981 about President Reagan's secret decision to channel money and arms through the CIA to Nicaraguan exiles. Members of both committees said they expressed concern at the time about the covert program. In a letter to CIA Director William J. Casey from Chairman Edward P. Boland, D-Mass., the House committee said it was worried about such things as the number of guerrillas to be supported and whether the United States would have any control over their actions.

Casey early in 1982 assured the committees that the CIA would support no more than a few thousand guerrillas and would monitor their actions closely. However, the number of the Honduran-based guerrillas, formally called the Nicaraguan Democratic Force and informally called contras or counterrevolutionaries, expanded rapidly to more than 10,000 by 1983.

## 1982: Boland's Curbs

To head off a move by some Democratic members to cut off the covert aid to the contras, Congress in 1982 placed several restrictions on the aid.

The classified portion of the fiscal 1983 intelligence authorization bill (PL 97-269) required that the aid be used solely to interdict arms shipments from Nicaragua to leftist guerrillas in El Salvador and stipulated that it was not to be used to overthrow the Nicaraguan government or to provoke a military exchange between Nicaragua and Honduras, where most of the contras were based.

The defense portion of the fiscal 1983 continuing appropriations resolution (PL 97-377) contained similar restrictions, offered by Boland. The so-called Boland amendment said: "None of the funds provided in this act may be used by the Central Intelligence Agency or the Department of Defense to furnish military equipment, military training or advice, or other support for military activities, to any group or individual, not part of a country's armed forces, for the purpose of overthrowing the government of Nicaragua or provoking a military exchange between Nicaragua and Honduras."

## 1983: The Boland Cap

Early in 1983, publicity about the supposedly covert operation mushroomed, with the media carrying detailed reports on the war in Nicaragua. The contras and some officials in the Reagan administration sought the publicity, which, ironically, helped undermine public and congressional support for the war.

Congress included, at Boland's insistence, in the fiscal 1984 defense appropriations bill (PL 98-212) a $24 million cap on funding the contras in fiscal 1984.

## 1984: The Boland Cutoff

In March 1984, Reagan asked Congress to approve $21 million for the contras, in addition to the $24 million limit then in the law.

As Congress was considering that request in early April, Reagan's Nicaraguan policy was shaken by the revelation that the CIA had provided the logistics and supervision for the mining of several Nicaraguan harbors.

The mines had little explosive power, but they damaged several ships and caused a furor in Congress. Barry Goldwater, R-Ariz., chairman of the Senate Intelligence Committee, was particularly infuriated by the CIA's failure to give his committee advance notice of the mining. Both chambers overwhelmingly condemned the mining.

After several attempts to win congressional approval of the aid failed, Reagan made no further effort to get the $21 million for fiscal 1984, but he did press Congress to approve $28 million in renewed aid to the contras for fiscal year 1985.

Conferees on the fiscal 1985 continuing appropriations resolution (PL 98-473) rejected Reagan's request and barred any U.S. agency from spending money "for the purpose of or which would have the effect of supporting, directly or indirectly, military or paramilitary operations in Nicaragua by any nation, group, organization or individual."

But, in a complicated provision, the legislation gave the president the opportunity to return to Congress in 1985 to seek approval to spend $14 million in aid for military or paramilitary operations in Nicaragua. (Details, Congress and the Nation Vol. VI, pp. 162, 175, 181)

times and supported the president by comfortable margins each time.

The first, closest and most important vote came on the issue of whether to extend indefinitely a legal ban on any U.S. aid for "military or paramilitary operations in Nicaragua." That prohibition, which the House had supported consistently since 1983, had been U.S. law since October 1984 and was to expire on Oct. 1, 1985; it was called the Boland amendment, after Rep. Edward P. Boland, D-Mass., former chairman of the Intelligence Committee.

Boland on June 12 offered his provision as an amendment to an underlying amendment that provided the aid for the contras. The House rejected Boland's amendment by a **key vote of 196-232 (R 7-174; D 189-58)**. The basic amendment providing the $27 million was approved 248-184. *(1985 key votes, p. 933)*

The two chambers' contra aid differences contributed to a delay in appointment of House-Senate conferees on the supplemental appropriations bill. The question of who would handle the funding was the most controversial point. The Senate plan would allow the National Security Council — an arm of the White House — to designate what agency would administer the aid, while the House bill would allow the president to use any agency except the CIA or the Defense Department.

Conferees accepted the House method of distribution, as well as the House-passed amount of $27 million. The conference agreement on the supplemental appropriations bill (H Rept 99-236) exempted the $27 million from the Boland amendment bar against aiding military operations in Nicaragua but did not repeal the amendment, as the Senate had wanted.

Conferees also accepted House conditions on the timing of the aid and defined it as "food, clothing, medicine and other humanitarian assistance," not to include "weapons, weapons systems, ammunition or other equipment, vehicles or material which can be used to inflict serious bodily harm or death."

The conference report also included $2 million in the House bill to help implement a regional peace accord resulting from talks led by the "Contadora" countries: Colombia, Mexico, Panama and Venezuela.

Congress cleared the measure Aug. 1.

**Authorization, Final Provisions.** Authorization of the $27 million in non-lethal aid for the contras was contained in the fiscal 1986-87 foreign assistance authorization act (S 960 — PL 99-83), which cleared Congress July 31. *(Foreign aid authorization, p. 186)*

Earlier action on the legislation produced several ironies. The Senate, usually more supportive of contra aid, did not include money for rebels because Senate leaders were trying to keep the foreign aid authorization bill free of controversy. And the Democratic-controlled House, in spite of its past disputes over the program, followed up its June pro-contra vote by adding the provisions to the foreign aid bill on July 10.

House-Senate conferees on S 960 authorized the $27 million in non-military contra aid through March 31, 1986 (H Rept 99-237). But even in agreeing to allow Reagan to resume U.S. involvement in Nicaragua, the conferees kept some restrictions on the president. Most important was the bar on CIA or Defense Department involvement in distributing the aid.

Conferees deleted a House-passed provision extending the Boland amendment into fiscal 1986; that issue was to be resolved in the fiscal 1986 intelligence authorization bill.

Other contra provisions in the foreign aid bill:

● Barred the administration from entering into an agreement that forced a country receiving U.S. foreign aid or weapons to help the contras.

● Divided the $27 million into three parts, to be provided every 90 days upon the president's submission to Congress of reports on Nicaragua.

● Allowed the provision to the contras of food, clothing, medicine or other humanitarian aid, but expressly barred weapons, arms systems, ammunition, vehicles or "material which can be used to inflict serious bodily harm or death."

● Required the president to establish procedures to prevent the humanitarian aid from being diverted to military purposes.

● Required the president to suspend aid to the contras if he determined that they were engaged in a consistent pattern of human rights abuses.

● Authorized $2 million in fiscal 1986 to help implement a Contadora regional peace accord.

● Established a procedure for expedited congressional consideration of any future request by the president for additional aid to the contras.

## U.S. Troops Ban

An effort to bar the introduction of U.S. combat troops into Nicaragua produced debate and amendments to the fiscal 1986 defense authorization bill (S 1160 — PL 99-145) in the House. In a series of votes June 27, the House adopted a combat-troops ban.

In conference, as had been done in the fiscal 1985 defense authorization conference report, the provision was transformed into a sense-of-Congress declaration that no combat forces should be sent into Nicaragua.

## CIA Role

Congress in November expanded U.S. backing of the contras by approving an intelligence authorization bill (HR 2419 — PL 99-169) that allowed the CIA to give them advice and intelligence information, a function barred under existing law. The bill also broadened previous congressional definitions of humanitarian aid. *(1986 intelligence authorization, p. 203)*

The House approved HR 2419 on July 18 by voice vote and with little debate. The Senate adopted its version (S 1271) by voice vote Sept. 26.

The House Nov. 19 approved, 387-21, the conference report (H Rept 99-373), and the Senate adopted it by voice vote Nov. 21.

**Contingency Fund.** Both chambers expressly denied Reagan's request for renewed CIA funding of the contras in fiscal 1986; the conferees said that meant the agency could not dip into its multimillion-dollar contingency reserve to provide aid to the guerrillas.

Congress authorized only one role for the CIA in the Nicaraguan war: the provision of intelligence information and advice to the contras. There was no clear definition of what that meant; however, conferees said the CIA could not provide training or advice that would "amount to participation in the planning or execution of military or paramilitary operations" or participation in "logistics activities integral to such operations."

**Radios, Trucks.** The conferees consented to an administration request for a broadened definition of humanitarian aid — thus increasing the scope of U.S. involvement in the contras' war against Nicaragua.

First, the conferees authorized a secret amount to buy radios to allow contra leaders at their base camps along the Nicaraguan-Honduran border to receive intelligence information from the United States and to pass that information along to units stationed deep within Managua.

Second, the conferees accepted the administration's contention that the $27 million aid law allowed the provision of "transportation equipment" (trucks and possibly helicopters) to the contras, "so long as no modifications are made to the equipment designed to be used to inflict serious bodily harm or death."

Third, the conferees said the State Department was allowed to solicit other sources, including other countries, for humanitarian aid to the contras, but such aid had to come from those countries' own resources and could not be a condition of foreign aid.

## Contra Arms Aid

After a battle of more than two years, President Reagan in 1986 persuaded Congress to renew military aid to the contra guerrillas who were seeking to overthrow the leftist government of Nicaragua.

The fiscal 1987 appropriation marked the first time since mid-1984 that the United States legally would be allowed to give weapons, ammunition and other military supplies to the 10,000-15,000 contras, who were in camps along the Nicaraguan-Honduran border.

However, the future of the program was put in doubt late in 1986 by the administration's disclosure that high-ranking officials had skimmed some of the profits from secret arms sales to Iran to provide funds for the purpose of arming the contras. *(Iran-contra scandal, p. 253)*

The fiscal 1987 omnibus spending bill (H J Res 738 — PL 99-591) included $70 million in military aid and $30 million in non-military aid for the rebels. It also included $300 million in economic aid for Central American nations other than Nicaragua.

The money resumed the flow of U.S. assistance to the contras. The previous dose, $27 million in non-military aid voted by Congress after a bruising battle in 1985, ran out March 31, 1986.

The deadlock over contra aid was broken June 25, 1986, when the House voted for the $100 million.

Perhaps more important than providing the money, Congress agreed to lift most of the restrictions that it had imposed in 1984-85 on direct U.S. involvement with the contras. Among other things, the bill allowed the CIA to resume management of the contra aid program. However, the separate fiscal 1987 intelligence authorization bill (HR 4759 — PL 99-569) barred the CIA from tapping into its multimillion-dollar contingency fund to give aid to the contras above $100 million. *(Intelligence authorization, p. 203)*

Contra aid took a tortuous path through Congress in 1986. Reagan unveiled his $100 million aid plan in February, and Congress took it up as a pair of resolutions (H J Res 540, S J Res 283). The House voted the bill down on March 20. The Senate passed its resolution March 27.

The next legislative vehicle in the House was a supplemental appropriations measure for fiscal 1986 (HR 4515). In a complicated legislative ploy, Republicans on April 16 scuttled the contra program rather than see it married to the omnibus spending measure.

Contra aid next was taken up during consideration of the fiscal 1987 military construction appropriations bill (HR 5052). The deadlock over contra aid was broken June 25, when the House voted for the $100 million aid as part of HR 5052. The Senate approved the same contra aid provisions Aug. 13. The underlying bill was one of many to be folded into the continuing appropriations resolution, which cleared Oct. 17.

Reagan Oct. 24 signed legal papers to resume the flow of military aid. In a report to Congress that day, he said the contras had taken several reform steps required by the aid legislation. In addition to military hardware such as rifles and anti-aircraft and anti-tank weapons, the United States would give the contras military training and guidance.

## Handling of Aid Questioned

While Congress debated whether to continue aiding the Nicaraguan contras, investigations were conducted into charges of wrongdoing by some of the rebels and their American supporters.

At issue was the $27 million in "humanitarian" aid that Congress had approved for the rebels in fiscal 1986 (PL 99-83). The House Foreign Affairs Committee on May 8, 1986, subpoenaed bank records to determine what happened to $13 million-$15 million of the aid. That panel's Subcommittee on Western Hemisphere Affairs held hearings in June on allegations of corruption, drug smuggling, gunrunning, assassination plots and other misdeeds.

During House consideration of contra aid June 25, the subcommittee's chairman, Michael D. Barnes, D-Md., charged that the subpoenaed records showed that some of the $27 million may have been diverted to improper uses. But Republicans brandished a State Department report that denied some allegations of misused aid. By a surprisingly wide margin of 198-225, the House rejected an amendment to bar distribution of aid to the contras until Reagan fully accounted for the $27 million.

The General Accounting Office Dec. 5 issued a final report on its probe into how the money was spent. It found that some funds were diverted to buy military items and noted discrepancies in record-keeping. The State Department attributed most of the discrepancies to "poor bookkeeping" by agents, time lags between suppliers' statements and payment records and misinterpretations of what the statements were to include.

The United States had backed the contras since late 1981, and through that period there had been charges that individuals or groups of the rebels had engaged in questionable practices. Most allegations had involved human rights abuses, such as attacks on innocent civilians.

But in late 1985, a handful of Americans and former contras who once worked with them began airing charges involving corruption, drug smuggling and other activities. Sen. John Kerry, D-Mass., a member of the Foreign Relations Committee, began investigating those charges in December 1985, and others followed suit.

Several news organizations also pursued the charges, raising questions about the activities of contra groups, particularly the Nicaraguan Democratic Force, the largest unit supported officially by the United States.

Contra spokesmen and Reagan administration officials denied most of the charges, saying they were inspired to sway Congress against Reagan's request.

## House Rejects Aid

Reagan submitted his contra aid request on Feb. 25. He asked for $100 million, $30 million of which would be used for non-military aid. He also called for the elimination of previously imposed restrictions on contra aid — primarily on direct involvement by the Pentagon and the CIA and other intelligence agencies. In return for congressional approval, Reagan pledged, among other things, to begin direct "discussions" (not negotiations) with the Nicaraguan government — if Managua simultaneously agreed to church-mediated negotiations with the contras.

Shortly after Reagan made his request, he made remarks that Democrats saw as red-baiting and even some Republicans called extreme. In two separate statements on March 5, the president seemed to imply that his critics on Capitol Hill were doing a favor for Sandinista leaders in Nicaragua.

In a column in *The Washington Post* that same day, Reagan's communications director, Patrick J. Buchanan, wrote: "With the contra vote, the Democratic Party will reveal whether it stands with Ronald Reagan and the resistance or [Nicaraguan President] Daniel Ortega and the communists." Publicly, the administration and its conservative supporters never repudiated Buchanan's statement.

Democrats reacted angrily to the rhetoric, and several moderate Republicans said they shared the Democrats' unhappiness. The bitterly partisan tactics employed by the White House and conservative members and groups that lobbied for contra aid may have cost Reagan important swing votes.

In an effort to win a handful of votes in the House, Reagan on March 19 offered cosmetic changes in his request. But he balked at substantial compromises, such as agreeing to unconditional negotiations with the Sandinistas, that might have guaranteed him an immediate legislative victory.

The House firmly rejected Reagan's request for $100 million in contra aid (H J Res 540) on March 20 by a 210-222 vote, after two days of acrimonious and partisan debate.

## Narrow Win in Senate

The Senate on March 27 approved the $100 million in aid (S J Res 283) but deprived Reagan of the sweeping bipartisan majority he wanted for the rebel assistance. By a **key vote of 53-47 (R 42-11; D 11-36),** the Senate helped ensure that Reagan would get most of what he sought, including military aid. *(1986 key votes, p. 949)*

In private negotiations leading up to the Senate vote, the White House and its GOP allies had hoped to fashion a bipartisan compromise that would capture the votes of an overwhelming majority and put to rest charges that Reagan did not have broad support on Capitol Hill for his policy toward Nicaragua. But the compromise negotiations foundered on the issues of mandating Reagan to hold direct talks with the Nicaraguans, regardless of whether the Sandinistas had agreed to simultaneous negotiations with the contras, and of requiring a second vote after 90 days on whether to release the remaining $75 million of the aid program.

During the March 27 debate, the Senate defeated a series of amendments that offered stark choices on the contra aid issues before approving the $100 million aid program. The administration won its narrow victory by agreeing to pressure the contras into making reforms.

The White House-approved plan adopted by the Senate would delay until July 1 the release of most military aid. At that point, the remaining $75 million was to be released according to a schedule if the president reported to Congress that a peace agreement had not been reached, that the Sandinistas were not engaged in "serious dialogue" with the contras and that the contras had begun to implement reforms. The major reforms advocated by the Senate bill, and accepted by Reagan, were aimed at establishing civilian control of the military, curbing human rights abuses and improving contra unity. Congress could reject Reagan's report and block further aid only by passing a joint resolution over the president's certain veto.

The bill also barred U.S. personnel who trained or advised the contras from entering Nicaragua, and it explicitly forbade U.S. forces from engaging in armed combat against Nicaragua.

## Second Defeat in House

The second phase of the contra battle in the House also produced a defeat for Reagan, but with a curious procedural twist. In a complicated legislative scenario, Reagan's aid request was attached to a bill (HR 4515) to make supplemental appropriations for fiscal 1986.

The linking of assistance for the rebels to the $1.7 billion supplemental, which was considered veto bait because of unrelated spending items that Reagan did not want, prompted House Republicans on April 16 to scuttle the contra aid. That move set off more than two months of jockeying to revive the package.

The surprise vote came on April 16, when Republicans voted for a Democrat-sponsored amendment to the supplemental, withholding aid for the contras. That enabled the amendment, which everyone had expected to lose, to pass handily, 361-66.

With the GOP parliamentary tactic taking the House to the brink of anarchy, Democrats abruptly halted action on the bill, effectively killing the just-passed amendment.

The immediate purpose of the GOP strategy was to prevent the House from considering yet another Democrat-sponsored amendment that Republicans feared might pass. Offered by conservative and moderate Democrats, that amendment would require a second vote by Congress in the summer of 1986 to release most of the contra aid. Under the procedure approved by the House Rules Committee, the second amendment could not be offered if the first amendment withholding aid passed, as it had.

The Republican maneuver succeeded in separating the contra issue from the administration-opposed supplemental. Republicans said they feared contra aid would be delayed for months if tied to the supplemental, and they insisted that the contras urgently needed weapons and other supplies.

Contra aid supporters then tried to get enough signatures — 218 — on a discharge petition to bring up S J Res 283. But by the April 30 deadline, they had garnered only 159 signatures. A factor was the House leadership's agreement to allow a vote on contra aid on a new bill, one appropriating funds for military construction in fiscal 1987 (HR 5052).

## House Approves Aid

The House on June 25 approved Reagan's contra aid proposal, giving the president a major foreign policy victory.

By a **key vote of 221-209 (R 170-11; D 51-198)**, the House agreed to a Republican-sponsored proposal allowing Reagan to provide $100 million to the contras, including up to $70 million in guns, ammunition and other military supplies. *(1986 key votes, p. 949)*

Reagan prevailed over the Democratic leadership, which since 1983 had opposed direct military aid to the contras. In personal meetings at the White House, in telephone calls and in an unusually conciliatory television speech, Reagan successfully lobbied about two dozen undecided members of both parties.

The president was working from a strong position, since a clear majority of House members supported aid to the contras, as was evident in a 183-245 vote taken June 25 against an amendment that would bar direct aid to the contras. The only issue was whether aid would include military hardware. Leaders of both parties said Reagan convinced enough members that giving military assistance to the contras offered the best hope of convincing the Nicaraguan regime to negotiate seriously with its non-communist opposition and with other countries in the region.

The House attached contra aid to an otherwise unrelated fiscal 1987 military construction appropriations bill (HR 5052), which was passed by a 249-174 vote.

In addition to military aid, the bill provided $30 million for non-military aid to the contras. It also allowed the CIA to administer the aid and to help the contras militarily, a provision that caused surprisingly little controversy. Earlier CIA backing of the contras, especially the mining of Nicaraguan harbors, led to the cutoff of aid to the contras in 1984 and to a June 27 decision by the World Court that the United States had violated international law in seeking to oust the Sandinistas.

The bill also provided a total of $300 million in economic aid to Costa Rica, El Salvador, Guatemala and Honduras, on top of about $900 million already allocated for fiscal 1986.

In other action, the House voted, 215-212, to bar U.S. personnel from aiding the contras in Honduras or Costa Rica within 20 miles of the Nicaraguan border.

## Back to the Senate

The House's June 25 acceptance of the modified contra aid package sent the issue back to the Senate, which had approved Reagan's original proposal on March 27. Because it was part of a new bill, military construction appropriations, contra aid became fair game for senators' efforts to kill it by delay or filibuster.

Ultimately, the Senate approved the $100 million contra package by a narrow margin and after an intensely partisan debate. The Aug. 12-13 action came as part of an elaborate arrangement by which the Senate also dealt with another highly controversial foreign policy issue: South Africa sanctions. *(South Africa, p. 180)*

Under a complicated unanimous consent agreement that had taken more than two weeks to negotiate, Senate leaders agreed to a plan to invoke cloture, or limit debate, on both the contra and South Africa issues; if cloture had failed on either one, the Senate would have had to devote as much of its August recess as necessary to resolving those matters. That meant Democrats who opposed contra aid would have to give up a filibuster against it if they wanted to pass the South Africa sanctions.

The strategy worked. The Senate approved contra aid on two key votes: on Aug. 12, a 54-46 tabling of an amend-

ment that would kill the entire aid program; and on Aug. 13, approval by 62-37 of a motion to invoke cloture on the bill. A cloture attempt earlier Aug. 13 had failed.

Those votes were ratified Aug. 13 with formal approval of the contra aid and economic aid titles of the military construction bill by a 53-47 vote and with final passage of the entire bill, 59-41.

Because they feared reopening the contra issue in conference committee with the House, Senate Republican leaders had pulled out all the stops to ensure that the bill passed with no amendments to the contra aid provisions.

Democrats tried 15 times to amend those provisions — first with major changes such as putting strict limits on CIA involvement in the program, then with relatively minor proposals that under other circumstances would have provoked little controversy. The Democrats sought to amend the contra aid section of the bill so that it would be subject to negotiations by a House-Senate conference — and thus possibly to a watering down or further delay of Reagan's request. But each time, a nearly united Republican Party staved off the Democrats.

## Final Provisions

The military construction bill, along with its contra aid provisions, was incorporated into the fiscal 1987 continuing appropriations resolution. As signed into law, H J Res 738 (PL 99-591):

● Provided $100 million in aid to the contras, of which $30 million was earmarked for "humanitarian" or non-military aid. Of the total, $60 million could be spent at any time and the remaining $40 million could be spent only after Feb. 15, 1987. Until Feb. 15, military aid was restricted to small arms, such as rifles, and "air-defense" equipment, presumably anti-aircraft missiles. After Feb. 15, the United States could provide the contras artillery and other "heavy" weapons.

Of the $30 million in non-military aid, $27 million was for humanitarian supplies such as food and clothing; the remaining $3 million would have to be used to monitor the contras' observance of human rights standards.

● Expanded involvement with the contras by U.S. intelligence agencies, essentially by allowing the CIA to work with the contras in planning military strategy and by administering the U.S. program. But U.S. military and civilian employees were barred from providing advice, training or logistical support to the contras inside Nicaragua. All U.S. personnel also were barred from providing any training or other services to the contras within 20 miles of the Nicaraguan border in either Honduras or Costa Rica.

● Committed the United States to conducting direct "discussions" — not "negotiations" — with the Sandinista government of Nicaragua if that government engaged in "serious dialogue" with the contras.

● Demanded contra reforms as a condition of U.S. aid, including broadening and coordinating contra leadership, eliminating human rights abuses and putting military forces under civilian control.

● A special congressional commission was to monitor the aid program during the first four months. The commission was to issue its report in connection with a presidential certification due Feb. 15. After then, Reagan would be able to continue aiding the contras only if he certified to Congress that no Central American peace agreement had been reached and that the Nicaraguan government had not begun "serious dialogue" with its opposition.

● Congress could block expenditure of the final $40 million in fiscal 1987 money by passing a joint resolution of disapproval. Since the president would veto such a resolution, a two-thirds vote in both chambers would be needed to override the veto and thus block the aid.

● Provided $300 million for economic aid to Costa Rica, El Salvador, Guatemala and Honduras. The bill also allocated $2 million to help those countries participate in regional peace talks.

# South Africa Sanctions

Congress in 1986 enacted into law over President Reagan's veto legislation imposing economic sanctions against the white minority regime in South Africa. Reagan insisted the bill would hurt the South African blacks it was intended to help, but both houses voted overwhelmingly to override the veto, handing the president a major foreign policy defeat.

The bill (HR 4868 — PL 99-440) barred imports of South African iron, steel, textiles, agricultural goods and other products and ordered the suspension of direct air travel between the United States and South Africa. It also called for further sanctions in a year if the government in Pretoria failed to move to dismantle the system of racial discrimination called apartheid. Proponents acknowledged that the bill would not, by itself, force an end to apartheid. But they said the bill would demonstrate to South African blacks that the United States actively opposed apartheid.

Congress in 1985 had forced Reagan to impose limited economic and political sanctions against South Africa. Spurred by demonstrations at the South African Embassy in Washington, D.C., and by growing racial violence in South Africa, both the House and Senate passed versions of a bill (HR 1460) to impose sanctions and, implicitly, reject Reagan's policy of "constructive engagement" of South Africa. Yielding to the political pressure created by that legislation, Reagan in September 1985 signed an executive order imposing sanctions and headed off final congressional action on HR 1460.

Reagan's failure to follow up his executive order with new diplomatic pressure on South Africa for real changes in apartheid, coupled with a renewed government crackdown in South Africa, contributed to the momentum for more stringent sanctions in 1986. In June 1986, anticipating demonstrations marking the 10th anniversary of the 1976 black riots in Soweto, Pretoria imposed strict press censorship and a sweeping state of emergency.

The press rules — effectively banning any reporting not sanctioned by the government — got Washington's attention as had few other events in South Africa, causing members of Congress to question why Reagan tolerated that repressive regime while he castigated others.

The House in June passed a strong version of HR 4868 that would force all U.S. companies to leave South Africa and end virtually all trade between the two countries. The milder Senate version was the one enacted over Reagan's veto.

The congressional action was the first override of a presidential veto on a major foreign policy issue since 1973, when Congress enacted into law the War Powers Resolution (PL 93-148), which was designed to limit the authority of the president to introduce U.S. forces into hostilities and keep them there without congressional approval. *(Congress and the Nation Vol. IV, p. 849)*

Congress had modified or stalled Reagan's policies on several foreign issues, most often involving Central America. But until the sanctions veto override, Congress had never repudiated Reagan so decisively.

Reagan readily accepted the congressional action and promised to implement the law. In a statement issued by the White House after the vote, Reagan said the debate between himself and Congress "was not whether to oppose apartheid but, instead, how best to oppose it and how best to bring freedom to that troubled country." The president insisted he had been correct in opposing sanctions because "they hurt the very people they are intended to help."

## Background

The United States traditionally had followed a two-pronged approach to South Africa: expressing concern about apartheid while recognizing the strategic value of having a pro-Western, anti-communist government in place.

The goal of every administration since President Truman had been to encourage gradual change in South Africa as a way of avoiding a civil war that could lead to a takeover by a pro-Soviet regime. The United States had never supported or encouraged groups that took up arms against the government.

The Kennedy administration took the first step toward a clear repudiation of apartheid, voting for the first time for U.N. resolutions condemning it and supporting the U.N. voluntary arms embargo against South Africa in 1963.

The Carter administration, as part of its human rights campaign, escalated U.S. criticism of apartheid and, in 1978, imposed an embargo on sales of U.S. goods to South African military and police forces.

Within months of taking office, the Reagan administration substantially relaxed U.S. pressure on the South African government. In 1981 and 1982, the Commerce Department eased the embargo on sales to South African security forces of non-military industrial equipment, computers and other items.

Under the leadership of Chester A. Crocker, Reagan's assistant secretary of state for African affairs, the administration implemented an overall policy of constructive engagement, or maintaining good relations with South Africa while quietly pressing for reform. The Reagan administration firmly opposed actions that would amount to punishing South Africa.

In addition to relaxing Carter's arms embargo restrictions, Reagan's policy resulted in a lowered tone of criticism of apartheid and in U.S. mediation of negotiations between South Africa and its neighbors, especially Mozambique and Angola.

Reagan maintained near silence on apartheid until December 1984, when the demonstrations in Washington, New York and other cities heightened public concern about the issue. On Dec. 10, 1984, in his annual speech commemorating International Human Rights Day, Reagan said he felt a "moral responsibility" to speak out, "to emphasize our concerns and our grief over the human and spiritual cost of apartheid in South Africa."

## 1985 Legislative Action

The Senate April 3, 1985, approved by an overwhelming 89-4 vote a resolution (S J Res 96) condemning apartheid. The resolution was approved by the House Foreign

Affairs Committee May 2 but never reached the House floor.

The House on June 5 by a **key vote of 295-127 (R 56-121; D 239-6)** passed legislation (HR 1460) imposing immediate economic sanctions on South Africa. The bill had been reported by the House Foreign Affairs Committee May 9 (H Rept 99-76, Part I). *(1985 key votes, p. 933)*

The House bill imposed modest sanctions on South Africa, such as banning bank loans to the government and businesses, barring new business investment there and prohibiting importation of South African gold coins called Krugerrands. Before final passage of HR 1460, the House defeated, by margins of at least 2-to-1, seven attempts by Republicans to water down or postpone implementation of the sanctions. The House also turned back two attempts to toughen the sanctions, including one to withdraw all U.S. business investment from South Africa immediately.

The Senate followed suit in July with an even more limited version (S 995) banning bank loans to the Pretoria government and prohibiting most nuclear and computer sales to South Africa, among other things. The bill was reported by the Foreign Relations Committee June 28 (S Rept 99-99). The Senate passed HR 1460 July 11 by an 80-12 vote after substituting the text of S 995 for the House-passed version of HR 1460.

The only vocal opposition to S 995 on the floor came from a group of GOP conservatives led by Jesse Helms of North Carolina. Helms and his allies were unable to change the bill and a last-minute flurry of amendments seeking to extend the South Africa sanctions to the Soviet Union and other communist countries was turned back easily. But Helms said he was satisfied that he was able to block toughening amendments pushed by liberals, particularly a proposal to follow the House's lead in banning importation of Krugerrands.

In an attempt to force the House to accept the Senate bill, the Senate inserted its provisions into HR 1460 and returned it to the House. That meant the House would have had to decide whether to demand a conference committee. A key issue was the timetable for blocking new investment and Krugerrands; the House would have done so immediately unless South Africa undertook major reforms. The Senate called for similar sanctions 18 months from enactment but would have implemented them only after further congressional action. Senate Republicans opposed tougher sanctions as probably leading to a presidential veto.

During a House-Senate conference, the Senate conferees accepted the Krugerrand ban in exchange for an agreement by House members to withdraw their immediate ban on new investments.

The House Aug. 1 adopted the conference report (H Rept 99-242) on a 380-48 vote.

The Senate had been expected to vote on HR 1460 Aug. 1, but a threat from opponents to filibuster the conference report delayed action until after Congress' August recess. When the Senate returned to the bill Sept. 9, Reagan, facing near certain approval of the final bill, announced his own set of sanctions.

The Senate Republican leadership Sept. 12 prevented further consideration of the bill by taking the extraordinary step of removing the official copy of HR 1460 from the Senate chamber. Under the rules, the Senate cannot consider a bill that is not physically present. The bill was returned to the Senate Sept. 25, but there was no further action.

## Reagan's Executive Order

Reagan Sept. 9 signed an executive order (No. 12532) imposing limited economic and political sanctions against South Africa just five hours before the Senate was scheduled to vote on ending debate on the sanctions bill.

The executive order included several, but not all, of the economic sanctions and other measures that were contained in the final version of HR 1460. Reagan copied the exact language of the bill on some sanctions, but on other sanctions he made major changes that weakened the legislation.

One major provision of the conference bill was an immediate ban on the importation of Krugerrands. The executive order would allow Reagan to waive such a ban if the president determined that the South African government had made at least one of eight reforms, such as releasing all political prisoners or negotiating in "good faith" with representative black leaders. The waiver would have to be approved by Congress. The president Oct. 1 ordered the ban on importing Krugerrands into the United States.

The bill banned new loans by U.S. banks or other agencies to the South African government, with certain exceptions, as did Reagan's order.

The president's order barred all exports of computers and related technology to the South African police and military, among others. HR 1460 would mandate identical limits.

Reagan's order and the conference bill barred the export to South Africa of goods or technology that were intended for, or could be used for, nuclear production facilities.

The conference bill would require all U.S. firms employing more than 25 persons in South Africa to adhere to principles of non-discriminatory employment and living conditions developed by Philadelphia minister Leon Sullivan. Reagan's executive order encouraged, but did not require, adherence to the Sullivan principles.

Reagan imposed one sanction not included in HR 1460: a ban on importation into the United States of arms, ammunition or military vehicles produced in South Africa.

## 1986 Legislative Action

Racial violence continued in South Africa in 1986, adding fuel to the pro-sanctions movement in the United States.

The House in June 1986 took up a bill (HR 4868) strengthening the sanctions Reagan had ordered in 1985 and adding new ones. As reported by the Foreign Affairs Committee June 13 (H Rept 99-638, Part I) and the Ways and Means Committee June 16 (Part II), the measure contained provisions to bar new U.S. investments and loans in South Africa and cut off imports of South African coal, uranium and steel. In addition, it would stop U.S. participation in South Africa energy development and threaten to halt American computer company sales to South African government agencies and private firms unless the Pretoria government began good-faith negotiations with black leaders and freed political prisoners.

When the bill reached the House floor, Republicans, in a calculated gamble, stepped aside and allowed the House to pass by voice vote an amendment sponsored by Ronald V. Dellums, D-Calif., suspending virtually all trade with South Africa and forcing U.S. businesses to leave that country within 180 days of enactment.

The Republicans thought the Dellums measure was so extreme that its passage by the House would kill any chance for sanctions legislation in the Senate. Passage of the milder original version, they reasoned, would have put more pressure on the Senate to follow suit.

But they were wrong. Instead, the House action shifted the entire political balance on South Africa, establishing a new set of limits for what Congress could consider and making any other set of sanctions seem moderate by comparison. As Dellums said later, the House had moved back the political "fear barrier" for members. The House passed HR 4868, as amended by the Dellums substitute, by voice vote June 18.

Reagan apparently failed to recognize the changed circumstances. In a July 22 nationally televised speech, timed to affect Senate Foreign Relations Committee action, the president came out against apartheid, but that message was lost in his condemnation of sanctions and his sharp attack on the African National Congress (ANC). The speech was a political and public relations disaster; instead of calming the furor in Congress, it generated more controversy by seeming to show that the president was unyielding on his policy and more sympathetic toward the government of President P. W. Botha than toward South African blacks.

On Aug. 1, little more than a week after Reagan's speech, the Foreign Relations Committee approved strict sanctions against the white minority government in Pretoria. The report on the bill (S 2701 — S Rept 99-370) was filed Aug. 6. Under the leadership of committee chairman Richard G. Lugar, R-Ind., the Foreign Relations panel rejected all major amendments offered by members on the opposite extremes of the issue: Sen. Helms, who opposed any sanctions bill, and liberal Democrats, who wanted the much tougher House version cutting off all trade with South Africa.

In the eyes of some senators, the South African government had thrown away its last chance to avoid sanctions on July 29, when Botha rejected a plea by the European Community for changes.

The Senate on Aug. 15 passed HR 4868 by an 84-14 vote after substituting the text of its own measure for that of the House-passed bill.

Senators loaded the measure with single-issue provisions but retained a core of sanctions ranging from a ban on new U.S. business investment in South Africa to prohibitions on trade in agricultural products, steel and nuclear supplies. The bill also threatened additional sanctions in a year if South Africa failed to make "substantial progress" toward eliminating apartheid.

In a move to avert delaying tactics by conservatives who opposed any sanctions, the Senate accepted a modified amendment by Helms, calling on both the South African government and the outlawed ANC — the most prominent black opposition group in South Africa — to renounce violence. The vote was 67-31, and with it, Helms refrained from offering any of his remaining amendments, as did most of his allies. One conservative effort to add the Soviet Union as a target for sanctions was rejected 41-57.

The Senate also turned back an attempt by liberals to sever nearly all economic ties between the United States and South Africa. By a 65-33 tabling vote, the Senate rejected a move to attach to the bill the text of the House-passed version calling for a near-total trade embargo and requiring U.S. businesses to leave South Africa within six months.

The Senate did accept several amendments adding new sanctions or toughening existing ones in the bill.

The House on Sept. 12 overwhelmingly accepted the Senate version of HR 4868, thereby eliminating the need for a Senate-House conference on the issue. The 308-77 vote was more than enough to override a threatened White House veto.

Lugar had played a high-stakes game of hardball to force the House to accept the Senate's sanctions bill. First, he warned that there was not enough time in the short September session for a conference committee to meet and resolve the Senate- and House-passed measures, and then for Congress to thwart a presidential veto. If Congress failed to act before the very end of its session, Reagan could kill the bill with a pocket veto.

When House leaders — especially leaders of the Congressional Black Caucus — continued to resist, Lugar played his ace, appointing only two senators other than himself to serve on a potential conference committee: Helms and Claiborne Pell, D-R.I. Lugar and Helms said they would refuse to accept any changes in the Senate bill, thus making a conference useless.

House leaders, including the Black Caucus, gave in to Lugar's pressure. Black leaders expressed disappointment that they were unable to press for a somewhat tougher measure. Nevertheless, they hailed passage of the bill as a victory for the anti-apartheid movement and as an important moral statement.

Disagreement with the Senate view that the bill would pre-empt state and local anti-apartheid laws led the House, in a highly unusual move, to include a statement rejecting that interpretation in the rule (H Res 548) governing House consideration of the bill.

## Veto Overridden

Reagan vetoed HR 4868 on Sept. 26, the last of 10 days he had to act. The president said sanctions would be counterproductive, hurting the black majority in South Africa rather than the white-minority government.

Reagan decided not to accompany his veto with an executive order imposing his own sanctions. Such a course had been under consideration to help swing votes in the Senate to sustain a veto. But the president's veto message instead contained veiled "hints" that Reagan might be willing to issue such an executive order if Congress sustained his veto.

The House voted to override the president's veto Sept. 29 by a **key vote of 313-83 (R 81-79; D 232-4)** — 49 more than the two-thirds majority required to pass the bill over the president's veto. *(1986 key votes, p. 949)*

The Senate followed suit Oct. 2, thus enacting the bill into law. The Senate voted to override by a **key vote of 78-21 (R 31-21; D 47-0)** — 12 more than the required two-thirds.

In spite of the seriousness of the issue, the administration never pulled out all the stops to support the veto in the Senate. Reagan telephoned and met with several senators, and the State Department dispatched its senior black official — Alan L. Keyes, assistant secretary of state for international organizations — to the Capitol.

Reagan also took two steps to demonstrate his concern about South Africa: On Sept. 29 he sent congressional leaders a letter promising to sign an executive order with limited sanctions if the veto was sustained, and the next day he named Edward Perkins, a senior black Foreign

Service officer, as the new U.S. ambassador to Pretoria. Perkins replaced Herman W. Nickel, who had served in South Africa since 1982.

In spite of those symbolic steps, one lobbyist said the vote was "never winnable" for the president, and so the administration decided not to use up political capital on it.

Some senators and White House officials said the Senate's vote was determined by the calendar: It came just a month before the Nov. 4 elections that would decide which party controlled the Senate in the 100th Congress.

Democrats were eager to exploit Reagan's political weakness on the issue, and some attempted to portray his attitude toward South Africa as a Republican policy. Nervous Republicans did not want to risk antagonizing black voters for whom South Africa was especially important.

## Major Provisions

As enacted into law Oct. 2 over President Reagan's veto, HR 4868 (PL 99-440):

**Policy Goals.** Set two kinds of policy goals for South Africa: immediate objectives, such as the government's lifting of the existing state of emergency and opposition groups' suspension of terrorist activities so negotiations would be possible, and long-term, broader objectives, including the creation of a "non-racial democratic form of government."

**Sanctions.** Imposed several new sanctions and directed the president to take other steps. It:

● Required the president, within 10 days of enactment, to direct the Transportation Department to prohibit any South African-owned airline (South African Airways) from operating in the United States, and required the secretary of state to terminate a 1947 air travel agreement between the two countries. It also prohibited U.S. airliners from taking off and landing in South Africa.

● Prohibited importation into the United States of articles produced by South African government-owned or government-controlled organizations, called "parastatals." Strategic minerals were exempt from the import ban, however, if the president certified to Congress that the amounts of those minerals produced in the United States were inadequate for military needs.

● Banned the importation of these specific items from South Africa: textiles, uranium and uranium ore, iron and steel, coal and agricultural products.

● Barred new U.S. loans to South African businesses, the Pretoria government or any entity it controlled, and forbade U.S. firms to make any new investments in South Africa. The ban on new investments, however, did not apply to firms owned by black South Africans. The ban also did not apply to renewals of existing loans, to short-term financings such as letters of credit or to reinvestments by U.S. firms of profits earned in South Africa on their existing investments.

● Prohibited U.S. banks from accepting deposits by any South African government agency, except for one account maintained in the United States for diplomatic and consular purposes.

● Prohibited exports to South Africa of crude oil and petroleum products.

● Barred the export to South Africa of any items on the official U.S. list of munitions (primarily weapons and military items), except for items that the president certified would be used solely for commercial purposes and not for use by the South African armed forces, police or other security forces. The president was required to notify Congress 30 days before allowing such sales, giving Congress time to pass a joint resolution rejecting them.

● Prohibited U.S. government agencies from engaging in any form of cooperation, directly or indirectly, with the South African armed forces. The only exception was for activities "reasonably designed to facilitate the necessary collection of intelligence" — and those activities had to be reported in advance to Congress, which had no formal power to stop them.

● Prohibited importation of sugar and sugar-related products from South Africa, and transferred South Africa's portion of the U.S. sugar import quota to the Philippines.

● Terminated immediately a 1946 U.S.-South African treaty intended to prevent businesses from paying taxes on the same income to both countries. Other U.S. laws, however, would continue tax deductions or credits to American individuals or companies in South Africa.

● Prohibited U.S. government agencies from contracting with or buying items from South African government-owned firms, except for those necessary for diplomatic purposes. U.S. agencies were urged to buy from black-owned businesses in South Africa instead.

● Prohibited use of U.S. government funds to promote tourism in South Africa or to promote or subsidize trade with that country. However, another provision authorized the secretary of agriculture to use U.S. subsidy and loan programs to encourage agricultural exports to South Africa.

● Stated that U.S. policy would be to impose more sanctions if South Africa did not make "substantial progress" toward ending apartheid in a year.

If the president determined, after a year, that substantial progress had not been made, he was required to recommend additional sanctions, such as: barring all South Africans from holding U.S. bank accounts, banning importation of South African diamonds and strategic minerals and halting military aid to any country that supplied arms to South Africa. The last provision could affect Israel, which reportedly had sold weapons to Pretoria in the past. Israel had denied selling arms to South Africa in recent years, but to determine the facts, the bill required the president to report to Congress within 180 days on which countries were violating a U.N. arms embargo against South Africa.

● Established the following penalties for violations of the sanctions: a fine of up to $1 million for businesses and a fine of up to $50,000 or imprisonment of up to five years or both for individuals. Anyone guilty of importing the South African gold coins called Krugerrands could be fined up to five times the value of the coins involved.

The bill also declared that any action by foreign companies to take advantage of the U.S. sanctions would be considered an "unfair trade practice," potentially triggering retaliation by the administration.

The bill included two provisions encouraging other nations to act against South Africa. The most important required the president to begin negotiations with other countries toward an international agreement on sanctions and to report to Congress within 180 days on the results of his efforts. If the president reached such an agreement, he could modify the sanctions imposed by the bill to reflect the agreement — but only if he reported the agreement to Congress and Congress within 30 days passed a joint resolution approving his action.

Many of the sanctions in the bill were similar to those adopted by the British Commonwealth in early August 1986.

The bill stated the sense of Congress that the U.N. Security Council should impose the same sanctions as the United States.

The bill also might have the effect of overturning state and local anti-apartheid laws, such as those barring contracts to companies doing business in South Africa.

**Lifting Sanctions.** Stipulated that all sanctions imposed by the bill would be ended if the president reported to Congress that the South African government had done five things: released from prison Nelson Mandela, leader of the outlawed ANC, and all persons persecuted for their political beliefs or detained without trial; repealed the state of emergency and released all persons detained under it; legalized democratic political parties and permitted all South Africans to join political parties, to express political opinions and to participate in the political process; repealed the Group Areas Act and the Population Registration Act, which restricted where non-whites lived and worked, and did not institute other measures with the same purposes; and agreed to enter into good-faith negotiations with "truly representative" black leaders without preconditions.

The president also could suspend or modify any of the sanctions in the bill 30 days after reporting to Congress that Pretoria had released Mandela and the political prisoners, had taken three of the other four actions and had made "substantial progress" toward dismantling apartheid and establishing a non-racial democracy. Congress could overturn the president's decision by passing a joint resolution — over his likely veto — within the 30 days.

Another provision allowed the president, acting on his own, to lift any of the sanctions against South Africa after six months if he reported to Congress that the sanctions would increase U.S. dependence for coal and strategic minerals on communist countries belonging to the Council for Mutual Economic Assistance, which included the Soviet Union, its Eastern European allies and Cuba. The president could act if he found that U.S. dependence on communist countries for any of those materials would increase over the average annual imports during 1981-85.

**Reagan's Executive Order.** Put into permanent law all of the sanctions that President Reagan imposed on South Africa in his Sept. 9, 1985, executive order. Those were bans on:

● The importation of Krugerrands.

● The importation into the United States of arms, ammunition or military vehicles made in South Africa.

● The export of computers, computer software and related items to South Africa for use by government agencies, such as the police, and the government's weapons industries.

● Loans by U.S. banks or companies to the government of South Africa or any organization it controlled. Exempted were loans for educational, housing or health facilities that were accessible to persons of all races.

● The export to South Africa of nuclear power equipment and supplies, except those needed for "humanitarian" purposes or, if South Africa committed itself to international standards, to reduce the spread of nuclear arms.

**Aid to Blacks.** Reaffirmed the U.S. commitment to help "the victims of apartheid" through direct financial aid and other efforts.

It authorized $40 million annually, beginning in fiscal 1987, for economic aid to disadvantaged South Africans, regardless of race. Of that amount, up to $3 million each year would be provided for training of trade unionists in organizing and other union-related skills. None of the funds could be provided to organizations financed or controlled by the South African government.

Another section of the bill authorized $4 million annually for scholarships for victims of apartheid. The bill also authorized $10 million for the purchase of housing for black South African employees of the U.S. government.

An additional $1.5 million annually was allocated for the State Department's human rights fund, which supported activities by rights groups in South Africa. Individuals or groups involved in "necklacing" could not receive aid. Necklacing was a practice in which black militants placed burning, gasoline-filled tires around the necks and legs of blacks suspected of cooperating with the government.

U.S. firms employing more than 25 persons in South Africa would be required to adhere to the Sullivan principles. Under the labor code, companies were obliged to practice non-discrimination and to provide housing, education and other benefits for disadvantaged workers.

**Other Provisions.** Banned the importation of Soviet gold coins.

● Required the attorney general to report to Congress, within 180 days, on actual and alleged violations of the Foreign Agents Registration Act by representatives of governments or opposition groups in southern Africa, including the ANC. The foreign agents act required those lobbying in Washington on behalf of foreign governments or groups to register with the Justice Department. The attorney general also was to report on the status of any investigations into such violations.

# Philippine Policy

Many members of Congress felt they had a personal stake in the almost-bloodless revolution that ousted Philippine President Ferdinand E. Marcos and brought in the new government of Corazon Aquino in February 1986.

For two decades Washington had overlooked Marcos' many failings because he was a friendly and strategically placed ally. But in the 1980s U.S. officials became increasingly troubled by a growing communist insurgency in the islands and feared the potential loss of two crucial military bases located in the Philippines.

Congress and the Reagan administration worked together in 1985 to pressure Marcos to make reforms. Congress took the lead, voting in two separate bills to reduce Reagan's request for military aid to the Marcos regime in fiscal 1986. First, in a foreign aid authorization bill (S 960 — PL 99-83), Congress set a $70 million ceiling on that aid, $30 million less than Reagan wanted. At the end of the session, in the continuing appropriations resolution (H J Res 465 — PL 99-190), Congress reduced the aid further, to $55 million. *(Authorization bill, p. 186; appropriations bill, p. 191)*

The administration exerted its own pressure with a series of tough statements warning that the communist insurgency could overwhelm Marcos if he did not reform his country's economic, political and military systems. Reagan also sent Sen. Paul Laxalt, R-Nev., one of his closest congressional advisers, to Manila with a similar warning. Possibly in response to those urgings, Marcos called presidential elections for Feb. 7, 1986.

Both Congress and Reagan pushed Marcos to guarantee honest voting procedures. On Nov. 14, 1985, the House and Senate approved a resolution (H Con Res 232) calling on Marcos to honor his pledge for honest elections. At

Marcos' request, Reagan sent a delegation of official U.S. observers to the elections, headed by Sen. Richard G. Lugar, R-Ind., and Rep. John P. Murtha, D-Pa.

The Lugar-Murtha observer group played a major role in Marcos' downfall. In addition to revealing to the American public the electoral fraud it observed, the group apparently helped convince top Reagan administration officials that Aquino really had won the election and that Marcos had stolen it.

The Senate on Feb. 19, 1986, passed a resolution (S Res 345), 85-9, declaring that the elections were marked by fraud and the House Foreign Affairs Subcommittee on Asian and Pacific Affairs approved a bill (HR 4198) suspending arms aid to the Philippines.

The next week, after key Philippine military officials defected to the Aquino camp and the Reagan administration issued a series of statements associating the United States with the mutiny, Marcos stepped down. Laxalt again played an important role. In his final hours as president, Marcos telephoned Laxalt for advice; the Nevadan said he suggested that Marcos "cut and cut cleanly."

Marcos fled the Philippines Feb. 26, bringing to an end his 20-year regime. Aquino, the widow of assassinated Marcos foe Benigno S. Aquino Jr., immediately took power, proclaiming that she had won the disputed election.

To encourage the new government and to bolster an economy that had suffered under years of Marcos-inspired "crony capitalism," Congress twice voted aid increases for the Philippines. First, in a fiscal 1986 supplemental appropriations bill (HR 4515 — PL 99-349), Congress voted a bonus for the Philippines of $100 million in economic aid and $50 million in military aid. That aid was in addition to about $230 million that already was allocated in 1986.

Several attempts to provide additional aid failed before Congress approved $200 million in economic aid for the Philippines, as part of the omnibus 1987 spending bill (H J Res 738 — PL 99-591). H J Res 738 also repealed the existing $50 million annual limitation on military aid to the Philippines. Aquino had visited Washington in mid-September and addressed a joint session of Congress to press for help in easing her country's financial problems.

### Background

Because of its strategic and political importance — along with memories of its status as the only former U.S. colony — the Philippines long had been a major concern for the United States. In the 1980s that concern grew in direct proportion to the rising success of the communist insurgency.

At the heart of U.S. interest in the archipelago were Clark Air Base and Subic Bay Naval Station, the two largest U.S. military installations outside the United States. Situated on Luzon, the largest Philippine island, the bases were uniquely capable of giving the United States control of vital Pacific Ocean sea lanes through which passed much of the world's commerce, including about half of all Persian Gulf oil.

Subic Bay was the main supply base for the U.S. Seventh Fleet, and it included a major naval air station and ship repair center. Clark was headquarters for the 13th U.S. Air Force; from its runways, American planes could patrol the skies west of Hawaii and east of the Persian Gulf.

In 1947, a year after gaining independence from the United States, the Philippines agreed to allow the United States to retain the two bases. Under the accord, the United States kept sovereignty over the bases and was to have use of them until 2046.

The expiration date was later changed to 1991 and the Philippines assumed sovereignty; modifications were agreed to in 1979 and 1983. The 1983 agreement called for $900 million in aid during fiscal years 1985-89, with $475 million of that in economic aid and $425 million in military aid.

All of that would have changed, however, if the guerrilla New People's Army and the Philippine Communist Party came to power. By 1985, the guerrilla force was expanding rapidly and was active in all 73 provinces. According to U.S. intelligence estimates, the guerrillas had some 15,000 armed, full-time troops, aided by an equal number of part-time irregulars.

A Nov. 1, 1985, report by the Senate Intelligence Committee estimated that Marcos had only three years to implement major reforms to save his government. The committee report painted a bleak picture of the prospects for effective reform, however.

That assessment was only slightly more pessimistic than the official Reagan administration position. Richard L. Armitage, assistant secretary of defense for international security affairs, repeatedly had told congressional committees that the guerrillas could force a "strategic stalemate" in three to five years.

## Reagan-Gorbachev Meetings

President Reagan held a summit meeting with Soviet leader Mikhail S. Gorbachev in Geneva, Switzerland, on Nov. 19-21, 1985. It was the first such encounter of Reagan's presidency.

The meeting did not produce any accords on arms control or other major issues between the two superpowers. However, it was viewed by many in Congress as helping to put U.S.-Soviet relations back on a businesslike basis, after the preceding five years, which were marked by confrontational rhetoric and by extreme intransigence on major issues.

Addressing a joint session of Congress the evening of Nov. 21, Reagan said that the 15 hours of discussions — five of them involving the two leaders accompanied only by translators — marked a "fresh start" for the two countries. Reagan's speech, which was devoid of harsh denunciations of Soviet policy, received a warm reception on Capitol Hill.

At their summit, Reagan and Gorbachev reached agreement on academic and cultural exchanges and other routine issues. However, the meeting apparently did little to settle one of the biggest arms control issues — Reagan's strategic defense initiative (SDI) for a space-based antimissile defense system. The Soviets had insisted that SDI be stringently limited as part of any far-reaching arms reduction agreement. *(Details, p. 342)*

### Reykjavik Meeting

Talks between the two leaders foundered again in 1986 over the SDI issue.

At a hastily arranged summit Oct. 11-12, 1986, in Reykjavik, Iceland, Reagan and Gorbachev discussed making sweeping reductions in their countries' nuclear arsenals.

The talks broke down, however, over the Soviet leader's demand for a 10-year moratorium on field tests of SDI components. Reagan adamantly refused to agree to limit SDI development, even in return for major cuts in Soviet nuclear weapons. *(Details, p. 343)*

# 1986-87 Aid Authorization

For the first time in four years, Congress in 1985 cleared for the president a foreign aid authorization bill.

The bill (S 960 — PL 99-83) gave President Reagan most of the economic, military and development aid he had requested and lifted several major foreign policy restrictions Congress had imposed in recent years. It authorized $12.77 billion in each of fiscal years 1986 and 1987, nearly $500 million below Reagan's request. In addition, it authorized a $2 billion emergency economic aid package to Israel and Egypt in fiscal 1985-86.

Congress is supposed to enact a separate aid measure annually, or at least every other year, but both chambers had not done so since 1981. Instead, the politically unpopular foreign aid authorizations had been incorporated into omnibus continuing appropriations resolutions.

In passing S 960, Congress signaled a renewed willingness to intervene in foreign wars by giving help to anticommunist insurgencies in Nicaragua, Cambodia and Afghanistan.

The measure also moderated, but did not entirely lift, controversial House-passed provisions that had limited Reagan's flexibility in dealing with Jordan and the Philippines. And it implemented the heart of the once-controversial recommendations of the National Bipartisan Commission on Central America, headed by former Secretary of State Henry A. Kissinger, by allowing a multi-year authorization of economic and development aid to Central America.

Reagan signed the bill into law on Aug. 8, although the administration had opposed from the outset some of its provisions — notably curbs on sales of weapons to Jordan and restrictions on his Central America policies.

The administration also had complained that House- and Senate-passed cutbacks in military and economic aid would force the United States to eliminate or reduce substantially programs in nearly 20 countries. Most of the bill's overall reduction from Reagan's request came from military assistance, always the most controversial section of the bill.

## House Committee Action

The House Foreign Affairs Committee on April 11 reported HR 1555 (H Rept 99-39), authorizing $14.5 billion for foreign aid programs.

Even as the committee was taking its final vote, a senior State Department official pronounced the bill "unacceptable." The administration objected most to a provision banning sales of warplanes and other advanced weapons to Jordan unless that country recognized and agreed to negotiate with Israel. The fiscal 1985 foreign aid law (PL 98-473) had included a sense-of-Congress statement opposing advanced arms sales to Jordan.

The administration also opposed the panel's restrictions on policy options in Central America. The bill included provisions barring any foreign aid funds from being used to support the Nicaraguan contras and prohibiting the president from sending U.S. troops into combat in El Salvador or Nicaragua unless Congress had declared war or

otherwise given its approval.

The bill imposed human rights and other conditions on El Salvador's aid similar to requirements that had been in effect at various times since 1981. Reagan had proposed eliminating all strings on aid to El Salvador. But several subcommittee proposals for additional conditions on aid were watered down by the full committee in a sign of continued congressional backing for President José Napoleón Duarte.

The committee approved $5 million to help arm and equip Cambodian guerrillas, triggering debate on whether the United States should get involved in trying to force Vietnam to end its occupation of Cambodia. The administration did not take a position on the provision, although previously it had rejected all requests for military support, insisting that U.S. involvement in the war could complicate negotiations aimed at convincing Vietnam to pull out.

Vietnam occupied Cambodia beginning in January 1979, when it ousted the communist Khmer Rouge government, led by Pol Pot, which had ruled since 1975. The Khmer Rouge was waging guerrilla war against the Vietnamese, as were two non-communist groups: the Khmer People's National Liberation Front, headed by former Prime Minister Son Sann, and a group led by Prince Norodom Sihanouk, Cambodia's leader in the 1950s and 1960s.

In early 1984, Vietnam launched massive assaults against the rebels. Thailand and other non-communist governments in the region sought international aid, expressing concern that Vietnam could wipe out the Cambodian guerrillas.

In other action, the panel approved $1.5 billion in emergency economic aid for Israel over fiscal 1985-86, aimed at easing Israel's severe economic crisis. Secretary of State George P. Shultz had sought to delay the extra funds, saying that they would do little good unless Israel committed itself to long-term economic and budget reforms.

Congress also reduced military aid to the Philippines to signal its unhappiness with the authoritarian rule of President Ferdinand E. Marcos. *(Philippines, p. 184)*

## Senate Committee Action

Working with extraordinary speed and harmony, the Senate Foreign Relations Committee on March 26-27 approved a $12.8 billion foreign aid authorization bill for fiscal 1986. The bill (S Rept 99-34) was reported April 19.

The panel's new chairman, Richard G. Lugar, R-Ind., was determined to keep out of the bill controversial amendments that could spark administration opposition; he wielded a firm gavel and made effective use of his paper-thin 9-8 Republican majority.

Democrats, also anxious to see a foreign aid bill enacted, offered to compromise on most of the politically sensitive issues they raised.

The committee's markup also was smoothed by a relative lack of controversy over support for El Salvador. In 1984, the panel was so torn over El Salvador that it was unable to muster a majority for any Central America provisions.

An example of the panel's ability to skirt sensitive issues was its decision not to include administration-opposed proposals for U.S. sanctions against the white minority government in South Africa. The panel dealt with the issue in separate legislation. *(South Africa, p. 180)*

It also accepted a bipartisan proposal to freeze foreign

# Israel, Egypt Get Aid Boosts

Responding to a severe economic crisis in Israel, and to a belated Israeli government plan to deal with it, Congress in 1985 approved an extraordinary $1.5 billion economic aid supplemental for Israel. For political "balance," Congress also approved $500 million in extra economic aid for Egypt.

Both amounts were included in the fiscal 1986-87 foreign aid authorization bill (S 960 — PL 99-83) and a supplemental appropriations bill (HR 2577 — PL 99-88). The money was to be spent over fiscal 1985-86.

Also included in the measures was $8 million for economic development programs to aid residents of the Israeli-occupied West Bank and Gaza Strip areas.

The supplemental aid was in addition to $3 billion in regular economic and military aid the United States provided each year for Israel, the biggest single recipient of U.S. aid. The assistance for Egypt — Israel's partner in the 1978-79 Camp David accords and peace treaty — topped a regular $2.3 billion annual program. Although there was no legal or official tie between U.S. aid to Israel and Egypt, both the Carter and Reagan administrations informally had linked the aid since the 1979 peace treaty.

President Reagan's request and congressional approval of the politically popular aid increase were a foregone conclusion. But Secretary of State George P. Shultz asked Capitol Hill to wait until Israel had put in place economic reforms before boosting funding. Eager House Foreign Affairs Committee members went ahead in early April and added it to the foreign aid authorization. In late April, Shultz informally told Congress he was ready to support the aid.

Administration and congressional sources said Shultz agreed to proceed with the aid request for two reasons: Leaders on Capitol Hill warned him that Congress would approve the aid anyway, and Shultz on April 22 received a letter from Israeli Prime Minister Shimon Peres offering a positive response to most economic reforms the United States had suggested.

Among Israel's economic problems were an inflation rate that exceeded 1,000 percent in 1984, rising unemployment and huge government budgets that absorbed nearly all the country's gross national product, the total value of the nation's production of goods and services.

In voting for the emergency aid boost, Congress instructed the administration to spend it before all of Israel's reforms were in place.

But early in 1986, Israel agreed to return $51.6 million of the aid, to help the United States meet fiscal 1986 budget cuts mandated by the Gramm-Rudman-Hollings law (H J Res 372 — PL 99-177). Israel's projected $1.8 billion in military aid also was to be pared by $77.4 million.

Sources said that Israel and its lobbyists in Washington rejected the prospect of an exemption because it might have caused resentment among advocates of domestic programs that would face sharp budget cuts under the Gramm-Rudman legislation.

At the end of 1985, some Senate supporters tried to get another $500 million military aid bonus for Israel. That move failed because of the overall budget crunch and because of strong administration opposition. *(Foreign aid appropriations, p. 191)*

aid spending in fiscal 1986 at the 1985 amounts. Although committee members were anxious to give extra aid to Israel, they agreed to delay the aid at the behest of Shultz.

In its only action that directly opposed the administration on a major issue, the committee voted 9-8 to restrict aid to the anti-government contras in Nicaragua. But panel members immediately disputed what they had done.

Lugar said the panel had voted only to bar the use of U.S. foreign aid to support the contras. However, the sponsor of the Nicaragua provision, Claiborne Pell, D-R.I., insisted that the committee also had voted to bar the administration from conspiring with foreign aid recipients to channel money to the guerrillas.

Pell's language ultimately was put into the committee report, but Lugar reserved the right to move to delete it on the Senate floor.

The panel rejected several other amendments that would restrict Reagan's policies in Central America.

The Senate panel, like its House counterpart, had tough criticism for Greece's outspoken socialist prime minister, Andreas Papandreou. Panel members said they were distressed by Papandreou's repeated political attacks on

the United States, by his attempts to curry favor with the Soviets and by his refusal to take part in routine NATO military exercises.

### Senate Floor Action

Breaking a four-year dry spell, the Senate on May 15 approved a foreign aid authorization bill that gave Reagan nearly everything he wanted and placed few restraints on his foreign policies. The Senate passed the measure 75-19 after only two days of debate and amendments.

Lugar steered the always-unpopular bill through the Senate with remarkable ease, prevailing upon his colleagues not to offer controversial amendments. To advocates of tough economic sanctions against the white minority government in South Africa, Lugar gave assurances of committee action on separate sanctions legislation — if they would keep the issue off the aid bill.

Lugar joined in the Senatewide exercise in self-restraint. He had wanted to offer an amendment that would repeal the committee-passed provision barring the administration from giving any U.S. foreign aid to anti-government guerrillas in Nicaragua. But to pacify Democrats who wanted that aid ban, Lugar withheld his amendment.

S 960 authorized $12.8 billion for foreign aid programs in each of fiscal years 1986 and 1987 — about $400 million less each year than Reagan had sought. An additional $2 billion for emergency economic aid to Israel and Egypt in fiscal 1985-86 had been approved by the Senate by voice vote and with little debate.

The Senate accelerated the move in Congress to provide aid to non-communist guerrillas battling the Vietnamese occupation of Cambodia, when it approved by voice vote $5 million for military and economic aid to the rebels. Although House liberals had warned that the Cambodia aid could lead to renewed U.S. intervention in Southeast Asia, no such qualms were expressed on the Senate floor. No senator spoke against the aid or raised questions about it. And the administration dropped its earlier opposition to the aid.

The Senate turned back two efforts to dismantle major portions of the Reagan administration's economic and development aid programs in Central America, when it defeated amendments to delete a multi-year authorization of non-military aid to Central America and to bar the use of U.S. foreign aid to reimburse property owners in Central America whose land was confiscated for land reform.

Also rejected were several attempts to curtail loans under the Foreign Military Sales (FMS) program.

In a sign of growing congressional anger about narcotics abuse, the Senate adopted, by voice votes, amendments restricting foreign aid to countries that were major sources of illegal drugs in the United States, especially Bolivia and Peru.

An effort by conservatives to impose the same style of conditions on aid to leftist governments as Congress imposed on rightist regimes succeeded when the Senate adopted an amendment restricting aid to Mozambique's Marxist government. The administration, which had moved to improve ties with Mozambique, opposed the restrictions.

The Senate approved $15 million in aid for "the Afghan people." The United States for several years secretly had provided military and non-military aid through the CIA to Afghan guerrillas battling the Soviet occupation of their country.

## House Floor Action

The House passed its version of the bill (HR 1555) on July 11, authorizing $12.6 billion annually in foreign aid for fiscal 1986-87. In addition, the bill authorized $1.5 billion in emergency economic aid to Israel in fiscal 1985-86.

Passage came on a highly unusual voice vote, and over the opposition of the administration, which objected to several items in the bill.

A consequence of the House action was to rescue the Foreign Affairs panel from a political graveyard. That committee had lost much of its stature and influence because Congress had not approved an aid bill.

Committee Chairman Dante B. Fascell, D-Fla., attributed the bill's success to "a very strong effort by members of the committee from both parties."

The House attached more than 60 amendments to the bill during three days of debate; ironically, adoption of controversial amendments backed by conservatives seemed to have helped the bill win passage.

Within the space of several hours on July 10, the House dismantled several foreign policy pillars that had been erected over the years by liberals. First, the House, in a series of three votes, endorsed a Reagan administration policy of withdrawing or restricting U.S. support for the two largest international family planning agencies — the U.N. Fund for Population Activities and the International Planned Parenthood Federation — because of charges that they were linked to abortions overseas. The House action was a key test of strength in Congress of anti-abortion groups, which had lobbied hard to retain the administration position.

Then, in a stunning reversal, the House voted to repeal a 1976 ban on U.S. military or paramilitary aid to anti-government rebels in Angola.

Enacted into law in 1976, the so-called Clark amendment — named after its sponsor, Sen. Dick Clark, D-Iowa (1973-79) — originally barred any U.S. support for military or paramilitary operations in Angola. The amendment effectively stopped CIA aid to a pro-Western guerrilla group that was battling for control in Angola. Congress in 1980 modified the amendment to allow such aid only if the president openly requested it and Congress approved.

The Clark amendment long had stood as a major symbol of congressional reaction to the Vietnam War. To liberals, it signaled that the United States would not intervene recklessly in regional wars where its own security was not at stake. To conservatives, the amendment was a demonstration that the United States had lost its nerve to oppose communism wherever it reared its head. *(1986 action, box, p. 204)*

The amendment to repeal the Clark amendment was adopted by a **key vote of 236-185 (R 176-6; D 60-179)**. *(1985 key votes, p. 933)*

The inclusion of aid to anti-communist rebels in Cambodia, Afghanistan and Nicaragua also gave conservatives, many of whom normally opposed foreign aid, a stake in the bill and signaled what both liberals and conservatives saw as a new mood in the House on foreign policy and defense issues.

Rejecting warnings that the United States was on the verge of re-entering the wars of Southeast Asia, the House approved 288-122 a symbolic authorization of $5 million for aid to guerrillas battling the Vietnamese occupiers in Cambodia. The wide margin by which the House approved the aid masked the deep political controversy on the issue, especially among liberal Democrats.

In spite of the past dispute over Nicaragua, the House, with no debate, added to the bill a provision authorizing $27 million in "humanitarian" or non-military aid to the guerrillas fighting the Nicaraguan government. *(Contra aid, p. 173)*

While the House's willingness to intervene around the world on behalf of forces opposed to communism was the most visible manifestation of the new mood in the House, the chamber also reversed course on several secondary matters.

For example, in one little-noticed action, the House adopted an amendment exempting El Salvador and Honduras from a longstanding ban on U.S. aid for police forces overseas. Until recently that amendment would have provoked an outcry from liberals because of the long history of U.S. collusion with repressive security forces in Latin America. But there was no dissent because proponents said the police aid was needed in the wake of a June 19, 1985, guerrilla killing of six Americans, including four Marines, in El Salvador. *(Police aid, p. 196)*

In other action, the House first rejected a proposal to end military aid to Mozambique but later reversed itself by voting to cut off all arms aid to that country. Members also voted to end non-food economic aid to Mozambique.

By a 2-1 margin — a vote of 125-279 — the House rejected a Republican-backed effort to restore $60 million in military aid for the Philippines. The Foreign Affairs Committee had deleted all but $25 million of Reagan's military aid request and made a comparable increase in economic aid.

## Conference, Final Action

The most contentious issue during the House-Senate conference on S 960 was whether the CIA could be involved in the new program of non-military aid to anti-government guerrillas in Nicaragua.

Foreign Relations Chairman Lugar staunchly held out for the Senate's position that the president should be given the freedom to decide which U.S. agency would administer aid to the contras. But House conferees of both parties said the House would reject the entire bill rather than allow renewed CIA involvement in Nicaragua. The impasse was broken when the Senate accepted the House position.

The agreement on the aid bill also helped break an impasse on a fiscal 1985 supplemental spending bill (HR 2577 — PL 99-88) that had a similar conflict on Nicaragua. *(Supplemental, p. 173)*

Hours after the foreign aid conference finished, administration officials sought to reopen the bill to delete a provision barring Reagan from making a deal with a foreign country to aid the contras. Lugar and Fascell at first rejected that appeal but, with the administration threatening a veto, later agreed to a modification that merely barred the United States from forcing foreign aid recipients to help the contras.

The Senate on July 30 adopted the conference report (H Rept 99-237) by voice vote. On July 31, the House cleared the bill for the president on a 262-161 vote, an unusually wide margin for a foreign aid bill.

## Major Provisions

Total foreign aid in the bill was set at $12.77 billion for each of fiscal years 1986-87, $500 million less than Reagan's request. Not included in that figure was an additional $1.5 billion in the bill for emergency aid to Israel and $500 million for Egypt in fiscal years 1985-86.

The final bill represented a compromise between the two chambers on priorities. The House had boosted funding for development aid programs above Reagan's request while cutting back sharply on military programs. The Senate trimmed both categories but voted to give Reagan substantially more military aid than the House. In the conference committee, the Senate agreed to the higher development aid figures while the House accepted the higher military aid figures.

The final bill included approximately $6.3 billion for military aid; $3.8 billion for the Economic Support Fund, which provided aid to bolster the economies of key allies and was, along with the Military Assistance Program (MAP) and the FMS program, part of what the administration called "security assistance"; $1.8 billion for developmental aid; and $946 million for other programs.

**Military Aid.** Reagan had requested $6.7 billion for military aid programs in fiscal 1986, a 13 percent increase

over the $5.9 billion appropriated for fiscal 1985. Conferees approved slightly under $6.3 billion, a 5 percent increase.

The bulk of the cuts came in the FMS loan program, which subsidized arms purchases by foreign countries. But the bill also froze spending at 1985 levels for the grant MAP used by the administration to provide weapons and military services to economically hard-pressed countries.

Other military aid provisions:

● Retained the traditional 7-10 ratio of military aid between Greece and Turkey. The bill earmarked $500 million in military loans for Greece and $714.28 in military aid for Turkey (of which $215 million was in grants and the rest in loans).

● Established a 5 percent minimum on interest rates charged for "concessional" loans under the FMS program (the standard rate for military loans was about 10 percent) and allowed the administration to determine what portion of military loans would be made at concessional rates.

● Allowed military aid to Paraguay only if that government had instituted reform measures in the handling of prisoners. (Military training aid was exempted from this prohibition.)

● Authorized on a permanent basis 30-year arms loans for Greece, South Korea, Portugal, Spain, Thailand, the Philippines and Turkey. Those countries had been receiving the special loans on a year-to-year basis. Standard loans had to be repaid in 12 years.

● Earmarked $15 million in MAP grants for Tunisia.

● Made several changes in the president's special authority (under section 614 of the foreign aid law) to waive congressionally imposed restrictions on foreign aid and arms sales.

● Required the president to return to Congress for approval of any decision to upgrade the level of technology to be included in a foreign arms sale after Congress had approved the original sale. This provision was spawned by the Reagan administration's decision to add sensitive radar equipment to F-16 warplanes sold to Pakistan.

**Philippines Aid.** Authorized $70 million in military aid to the Philippines in each fiscal year ($50 million in MAP grants and $20 million in FMS loans) to be used to buy only "non-lethal" equipment, such as trucks, communications gear and uniforms. The administration had said it was planning to provide only non-lethal military aid, but conferees wrote the requirement into law.

● Authorized $100 million in economic aid to the Philippines.

● Called for political and human rights reforms in the Philippines.

**Middle East.** Authorized for each fiscal year $1.8 billion in military aid and $1.2 billion in economic aid for Israel, and $1.3 billion in military aid and $815 million in economic aid for Egypt. All aid to the two countries was to be in the form of grants. Israel was to receive all of its economic aid as a direct cash transfer, meaning that the money did not have to be linked to specific programs. Up to $115 million of Egypt's economic aid was to be a cash transfer.

● Set aside $400 million a year of Israel's military aid for development of that country's new warplane, the Lavi. At least $250 million of that had to be spent in Israel. *(Lavi jet cancellation, box, p. 227)*

● Authorized in fiscal years 1985 and 1986 supplemental economic aid of $1.5 billion to Israel, $500 million to Egypt and $8 million for Mideast regional programs.

● Stated congressional opposition to the sale of advanced weapons to Jordan and required that any notification to Congress of a proposed sale include presidential certification of Jordan's public commitment to recognize and negotiate with Israel.

● Allowed the transfer of Airborne Warning and Control System (AWACS) radar planes to Saudi Arabia, as scheduled in 1986, only if the president certified to Congress that Saudi Arabia had signed agreements protecting their technology and allowing U.S. access to information obtained by the planes and that Middle East peace initiatives "either have been successfully completed or that significant progress toward that goal has been accomplished with the substantial assistance of Saudi Arabia." This provision put into law several promises made by Reagan in 1981 when he was seeking congressional approval of the AWACS sale. *(Congress and the Nation Vol. VI, p. 129)*

● Barred the administration from conducting any negotiations with the Palestine Liberation Organization (PLO). It had been a declared U.S. policy since 1975 not to negotiate with or recognize the PLO; this provision put the policy into law, with an exemption for talks for emergency or humanitarian reasons. *(PLO mission controversy, p. 243)*

**Contra Aid.** Authorized $27 million for humanitarian or non-military aid through March 31, 1986, for the anti-government guerrillas in Nicaragua. But in a major rebuke to the administration, barred the CIA or the Defense Department from administering the aid. Conferees said in their report that the ban on CIA and Defense Department involvement did not prevent those agencies from giving the contras advice or intelligence information.

● Barred the administration from entering into an agreement that forced a country receiving U.S. foreign aid or weapons to provide aid to the Nicaraguan contras.

● Required the president to suspend aid to the contras if he determined that they were engaged in a consistent pattern of human rights abuses.

● Authorized $2 million in fiscal 1986 to help implement a regional peace accord resulting from talks led by the "Contadora" countries — Colombia, Mexico, Panama and Venezuela.

● Established a procedure for expedited congressional consideration of any future request by the president for additional aid to the contras.

**Other Insurgencies.** Repealed a 1976 law, known as the Clark amendment, that barred U.S. aid to South African-backed guerrillas who were fighting the Marxist government of Angola.

● Authorized a new $5 million-a-year program of military or economic aid to non-communist guerrillas in Cambodia.

● Authorized a new $15 million-a-year relief program for "the Afghan people." Although not stated publicly by members, the purpose of that money was to support the Moslem rebels who were battling the Soviet occupation of Afghanistan. The United States also had provided hundreds of millions of dollars in military aid to the rebels through the CIA.

**Central America.** Provided for long-term authorization of economic and development aid to Central America, including, as part of the regular aid programs, authorizations for nearly $1 billion annually for the region in fiscal 1986-87, and $1.2 billion annually in fiscal 1988-89. That four-year authorization was highly unusual for foreign aid programs, normally authorized one or two years at a time, and was the heart of the once-controversial recommendations by the Kissinger commission on Central America. The

panel issued a report in January 1984 recommending long-term economic, development and military aid to the region. (House conferees, who had opposed the multi-year authorization, went along with it in return for Senate agreement to a two-year, instead of a one-year, authorization for the entire foreign aid bill.) *(Kissinger commission, Congress and the Nation Vol. VI, pp. 177, 188)*

● Authorized the president to negotiate with other countries for the creation of a Central American Development Organization — another Kissinger commission recommendation — to make recommendations for U.S. and other aid programs.

● In a major departure from longstanding congressional policy, exempted El Salvador and Honduras from a prohibition against U.S. aid to foreign police forces. Also exempted were countries that were longtime democracies, that had no standing armed forces and that did not violate human rights — a provision intended to allow police aid to Costa Rica.

Reagan had requested a blanket exemption from the police aid ban for all Central American countries. Congress had imposed the ban in 1974 in response to reports that U.S. aid was being used by repressive police forces in several Latin American nations.

● Authorized the president to provide up to $20 million each year in aid to strengthen the administration of justice in Latin American and Caribbean countries.

● Dropped a requirement, in effect under various guises since 1981, that the president could aid El Salvador only if he certified to Congress that various conditions had been met. Instead, the bill stated that the United States was providing aid to El Salvador "in the expectation that" several conditions would be met, including a willingness by the government to conduct a dialogue with the opposition, and progress in curtailing death squads, reforming the judicial system and implementing land reform programs. *(Congress and the Nation Vol. VI, p. 135)*

In another departure from past practice, the bill did not specify the amount of aid for El Salvador.

● Retained a fiscal 1985 appropriations provision barring any U.S. aid to El Salvador in the event of a military coup, making it clear that congressional willingness to loosen specific conditions on El Salvador's aid stemmed from support of President Duarte, who was elected in 1984 with U.S. backing.

● Required the president to notify Congress 15 days before providing El Salvador with any helicopters or other aircraft. Several human rights groups had charged the Salvadoran military with indiscriminately bombing the countryside in its campaign to wipe out leftist guerrillas.

● Barred military aid to Guatemala until an elected civilian government was in power and had made demonstrated progress in controlling the military and eliminating kidnappings and other human rights abuses, particularly against Guatemalan Indians. Then Guatemala could receive up to $10 million per year in military aid, to be used only for construction equipment and mobile medical facilities. Aid would be suspended in the event of a military coup. Military training aid was exempted from the pre-elections ban.

**Anti-Narcotics Provisions.** Prohibited aid to any country found by the president to have failed to take "adequate steps" to prevent production of or trafficking in narcotics.

● Restricted economic and military aid to Bolivia and Peru, until those countries curtailed illicit narcotics production, and sent a direct warning to Jamaica to curtail marijuana production, in the toughest provisions ever voted by Congress against countries that failed to limit narcotics production.

● Repealed, on a case-by-case basis, the so-called Mansfield amendment, which barred U.S. government officials from participating in drug-related arrests overseas. Under the new provision, U.S. officials could be present at such arrests if the U.S. ambassador and the country involved agreed, and if the incident was reported to Congress.

**Foreign Airport Security.** Included a series of provisions expanding the administration's authority to prohibit service between the United States and foreign airports found to have inadequate security against hijacking and other terrorist acts. The provisions were prompted by the June 14, 1985, hijacking of a Trans World Airlines (TWA) airliner outside Athens, Greece, which resulted in 39 Americans being held hostage for 17 days and one American being killed.

**Anti-Terrorism.** Authorized $9.84 million in each fiscal year for the State Department's anti-terrorism program, which provided training to help other countries.

● Authorized the president to prohibit trade with Libya and to prohibit imports from countries found by the State Department to be supporting terrorism.

● Prohibited aid to countries that harbored terrorists or that otherwise supported international terrorism. The president could waive this ban for national security or humanitarian reasons.

**Mozambique.** Barred any arms aid to Mozambique (Reagan had requested $3 million) unless the president certified to Congress that the government was making a concerted effort to comply with international human rights standards, was making progress in implementing economic and political reforms, had implemented a plan by Sept. 30, 1986, to reduce the number of foreign military personnel to 55 and was committed to holding free elections by Sept. 30, 1986.

● Allowed economic and development aid for Mozambique through non-governmental agencies.

**Population Programs.** Authorized $290 million for family planning programs. (Conflicting and complicated House and Senate provisions restricting U.S. contributions to international agencies that conducted family planning programs were dropped by conferees.)

**Pakistan.** Authorized military and economic aid to Pakistan only if the president certified to Congress that Pakistan did not possess a nuclear weapon and that the aid would "reduce significantly" the risk that Pakistan would acquire such weapons.

**Peace Corps.** Stated the sense of Congress in favor of increasing the number of Peace Crops volunteers to 10,000 by 1989; in 1985 the figure was about 5,000. The bill also allowed a limited number of Peace Corps staff members to serve for seven and one-half years, instead of the previous limit of five years.

# 1986 Aid Appropriations

The budget-cutting mood in Congress in 1985 halted President Reagan's steady four-year buildup of military assistance to friendly countries overseas.

Congress held the line on all foreign aid spending, including military aid, in the fiscal 1986 continuing appropriations resolution (H J Res 465 — PL 99-190) passed in 1985.

The bill included $15.025 billion for foreign economic, military and development aid programs. Nearly matching Reagan's overall request, the amount was about $2.7 billion below the comparable amount for fiscal 1985. Almost all the difference was accounted for by a cut in funding for the Export-Import Bank; all other programs were to get the same or slightly less money in 1986 as in 1985.

This was the fourth year in a row that Congress included foreign aid in an omnibus continuing resolution, instead of passing separate appropriations legislation for those programs. Congress last had enacted a separate aid appropriations bill in 1981.

With foreign aid one of the most unpopular issues that Congress faced each year, the main advantage of dealing with foreign aid spending in an omnibus continuing resolution was that neither chamber of Congress had to vote directly on a regular foreign aid bill. House leaders had said foreign aid would suffer major cuts if there were an up-or-down vote on a separate appropriations bill.

Congress had cleared a companion $12.8 billion foreign aid authorization bill (S 960 — PL 99-83), but it was politically less controversial because it did not actually appropriate money. (The appropriations bill included several programs — particularly U.S. contributions to international development banks — that were not part of the authorization legislation.) *(Authorization, p. 186)*

Since the beginning of the Reagan administration, foreign aid legislation had been subject to political battling between two groups on Capitol Hill: moderates and liberals whose primary interests were international development programs and conservatives whose primary interest was military aid to U.S. allies. Each year, the two sides tried to strike a balance in the aid bill.

The fiscal 1986 bill satisfied neither side, but it appeared to give a slight advantage to those who sought to slow down the growth of military aid programs.

In Reagan's first term, military aid was one of the fastest growing parts of the entire federal budget. At the president's request, Congress boosted the three military aid programs an annual average of 20 percent between 1981-85, and Reagan had sought another 15 percent increase in fiscal 1986. The continuing resolution allowed only a 3.9 percent military aid boost.

## House, Senate Action

A divided House Appropriations Committee reported a $14.5 billion foreign aid funding bill (HR 3228 — H Rept 99-252) on Aug. 1. It was reported by voice vote without much apparent opposition, but the debate before the vote showed that there were deep differences between Democrats and Republicans over the bill's spending priorities.

Democrats lined up behind efforts to hold down spending chiefly by making reductions in arms aid to other countries. By contrast, some Republicans charged that the bill favored development programs at the expense of military aid.

Republicans made two major attempts to reverse the priorities in HR 3228 during full committee action, but both were rejected. Their first proposal would expand funding for country-to-country aid at the expense of contributions to multilateral development programs.

That amendment was seen by backers as a wedge to open up the bill to another change that would increase security assistance at the expense of the Export-Import Bank's program of direct loans to foreign purchasers of

## Salvador Aid Curb Waived

President Reagan on March 14, 1985, used his executive authority to waive a limit on military aid to El Salvador that Congress had imposed in 1984.

Reagan notified Congress that he was sending El Salvador an additional $10 million in fiscal 1984 funds for training of military officers and troops. The money was on top of a $70 million 1984 supplemental appropriation for El Salvador that Congress voted in August 1984.

Although Congress appropriated the money in 1984, it gave Reagan until the end of March 1985 to spend it.

Reagan avoided the $70 million limit that Congress imposed on that supplemental aid (PL 98-396) by invoking a little-used power enabling a president to waive nearly any restriction on the use of foreign aid funds by stating that it was "important to the security interests of the United States" to do so. That power was in section 614(a) of the general foreign aid laws.

U.S. goods. That amendment also was turned down by the committee.

Aside from the argument over funding levels, the bill included a ban on aid to countries that were not enforcing security standards at their airports and a deferment of all aid for family planning programs overseas. The House bill also included only $25 million of the $100 million Reagan had requested for military aid to the Philippines.

House consideration of HR 3228 was delayed past the Oct. 1 start of the 1986 fiscal year by disputes between the Foreign Affairs and Appropriations committees. Leaders of the Foreign Affairs panel had objected to several foreign policy provisions in HR 3228, which was supposed to be limited to setting amounts of foreign aid spending.

Those disputes were resolved, but the bill was delayed further in October and the foreign aid appropriations were folded into the omnibus continuing appropriations legislation for the fourth straight year.

When the Senate Appropriations Committee completed its fiscal 1986 foreign aid spending bill (S 1816 — S Rept 99-167) on Oct. 31, it found itself in turf fights of its own — with the Budget and Foreign Relations committees.

At issue was an extra $500 million grant for Israel that was included with the committee bill. The proposed grant — which was to be on top of $3 billion annually in regular aid to Israel and another $1.5 billion in supplemental economic aid over fiscal 1985-86 — was aimed at reducing Israel's interest payments to the United States on past foreign military loans.

The Budget Committee objected that the addition of the Israel money helped make the measure a "budget buster."

The Foreign Relations Committee also objected to the extra Israel money and to another provision that would

repeal several items that Congress had enacted into law in the foreign aid authorization bill (PL 99-83).

From 1982 through 1984, when Congress failed to enact foreign aid authorization bills, the House and Senate Appropriations committees had wielded most of the congressional power over the foreign aid program, which was one of the primary foreign policy tools of the United States. But after Congress broke that cycle in 1985, the clout of the Senate Foreign Relations and House Foreign Affairs committees was restored.

The Senate Appropriations Committee's inclusion of a provision that would have the effect of repealing the authorization bill's earmarks and prohibitions that set minimum or maximum amounts of aid that could be given individual countries and groups was seen by the Foreign Relations Committee as an attack on its authority.

Both the Israel and authorizations provisions were dropped when the Appropriations Committee met to mark up the continuing appropriations resolution (H J Res 465).

Key provisions of the Senate bill included a $95 million limit on military loans to Jordan, a move aimed at forcing Reagan to return to Congress for supplemental appropriations if he wanted to give Jordan U.S. financing for a pending $1.5 billion-$2 billion arms sale.

The Senate bill also included a $70 million limit on military aid to the Philippines.

The bill, overturning a Reagan administration decision to aid groups that advocated only "natural" family planning methods overseas, allowed aid only for groups that offered "a broad range" of family planning methods.

### Final Action, Provisions

Foreign aid appropriations for fiscal 1986 were included in the fiscal 1986 continuing appropriations resolution (H J Res 465 — PL 99-190) cleared by both houses of Congress Dec. 19. President Reagan signed it into law that same day.

Funding levels in the $15.025 billion foreign aid portion of the continuing resolution included $1.47 billion for multilateral aid, $6.41 billion for bilateral aid, $6.02 billion for military aid and $1.11 billion for Export-Import Bank direct loans.

Major provisions of H J Res 465:

**Security Assistance.** Appropriated slightly more than $6 billion for the three major foreign military aid programs: the Foreign Military Sales (FMS) financing program ($5.2 billion), which made loans to help foreign governments buy U.S. weapons and military services; the Military Assistance Program (MAP, $782 million), which made grants for the same purpose; and the International Military Education and Training program ($54.5 million), which trained foreign military officers at U.S. academies and bases.

● Set the Economic Support Fund (ESF) at $3.7 billion. Along with the FMS and MAP programs, the ESF was a major part of what the administration called "security assistance": aid intended to bolster the economies and military structures of friendly countries.

**Philippines.** Set a $55 million limit on military aid to the Philippines and appropriated $125 million in economic aid, thus allowing a total of $180 million in aid related to U.S. use of two major military bases in the Philippines.

**Middle East.** Appropriated $3 billion for Israel, including $1.8 billion in military aid and $1.2 billion in economic aid, all in the form of grants. Earmarked for production of a new jet fighter, the Lavi, $300 million to be spent in Israel and $150 million to be spent in the United States. *(Supplemental aid for Israel and Egypt, box, p. 187)*

● Appropriated $1.3 billion in military aid and $815 million in economic aid for Egypt, all in the form of grants. Egypt also was to get about $220 million per year in food aid.

● Required quick Senate action on any resolution to block the sale of arms to Jordan. Another Senate-passed amendment that would set a $95 million limit in fiscal 1986 on military loans to Jordan was dropped by conferees.

● Included language from the foreign aid authorization law (PL 99-83) stating congressional opposition to a Jordan arms sale until Middle East peace talks were under way.

**Central America.** Retained House-passed human rights conditions on $10 million in military aid to Guatemala but dropped House-passed restrictions on economic aid following Guatemala's election of moderate leader Vinicio Cerezo as president.

● Set a $250 million limit on development aid for Central America.

● Required congressional notification of El Salvador's purchase with U.S. foreign aid of helicopters or other aircraft for that country's armed forces, the only condition on aid to El Salvador.

**Greece, Turkey.** Set military aid limits of $450 million for Greece and $642.8 million for Turkey, thus retaining, although it was not explicitly specified, the traditional 7-10 ratio for military aid to the two countries — Greece was given $7 for every $10 Turkey got.

**Cambodia.** Directed the president to provide at least $1.5 million, but no more than $5 million, in economic or military aid for the "non-communist resistance" forces in Cambodia, which was occupied by Vietnam.

**Population Aid.** Appropriated $250 million for family planning programs overseas, accepting for the first time in several years Reagan's recommendation for funding.

● Included a Senate provision allowing aid only for groups that offered "a broad range" of family planning methods, thus requiring changes in a new Reagan administration policy of giving money to overseas groups that advocated only "natural" family planning methods.

● Barred U.S. contributions to any international agency that "supports or participates in the management of a program of coercive abortion or involuntary sterilization."

**Export-Import Bank.** Appropriated $1.11 billion for the Export-Import Bank's direct loan program. *(Box, p. 145)*

**Development Banks.** Appropriated $700 million for the World Bank's International Development Association (IDA), provider of no-interest, long-term loans to the world's poorest countries and one of the most unpopular on Capitol Hill of all foreign aid agencies; $109.7 million for the World Bank's International Bank for Reconstruction and Development; $78 million to the Inter-American Development Bank.

● Authorized (because the House never took up the authorizing legislation) increased contributions to several international development banks: $131 million over two years for a selected capital stock increase in the World Bank; $225 million over three years for the African Development Fund; $175.2 million over five years for the World Bank's International Finance Corporation, which boosted private

## Population Control

The Reagan administration in 1985 continued its efforts to change longstanding U.S. policies toward family planning programs overseas.

Under pressure from anti-abortion groups, the administration sought to shift U.S. aid away from population control programs that included abortion and contraceptive techniques and toward programs that advocated only "natural" birth control methods.

The most controversial population control issue involved U.S. support for U.N. programs in China. Anti-abortion groups charged that the U.N. Fund for Population Activities (UNFPA) had helped the Chinese government carry out forced abortions and sterilizations and other involuntary family planning activities, and sought to reduce funding for the agency.

Although the fiscal 1985 foreign aid appropriations bill (PL 98-473) had directed the administration to provide not less than $46 million to UNFPA, the administration in 1985 announced that it would provide only $36 million to the agency, pending a review of its activities in China. The $10 million was equal to the agency's annual program in China.

The administration found support for its stance in an amendment included in the fiscal 1985 supplemental appropriations bill (HR 2577 — PL 99-88). The provision, sponsored by Rep. Jack F. Kemp, R-N.Y., said that no U.S. funds could be given to any organization that "supports or participates in the management of a program of coercive abortion or involuntary sterilization."

In another move, the administration announced in July 1985 that for the first time the United States would provide funds to agencies that advocated only natural or non-contraceptive methods of family planning, such as abstinence.

The new policy was modified in Congress, however. The fiscal 1986 continuing appropriations resolution (H J Res 465 — PL 99-190) included a Senate amendment, sponsored by Dennis DeConcini, D-Ariz., to ensure that funds be given only to agencies that offered access to a "broad range" of family planning methods. PL 99-190 also included the Kemp amendment on coercive control methods.

The resolution provided $250 million for family planning programs overseas, the same amount requested by the administration.

investment overseas; and $225 million for a new, three-year pledge to IDA's "Special Facility for Sub-Saharan Africa." The bill also appropriated the first-year installments for those contributions.

**Other Issues.** Curtailed aid to Bolivia, Peru and

Jamaica until they made progress in controlling narcotics production (conferees dropped Colombia from the list of countries whose aid was to be curtailed).

● Appropriated $15 million for "humanitarian" aid to "the Afghan people."

● Appropriated $277.9 million for international organizations, most of which were associated with the United Nations.

● Required — for the third year in a row — the president to report to Congress on the voting practices in the United Nations of countries that received U.S. aid, and barred aid to those countries consistently opposing U.S. foreign policy.

● Earmarked $250 million for economic aid to Pakistan but took no position on Reagan's request for $325 million in military aid to that country.

● Earmarked $67 million for military aid to Tunisia.

● Cut off aid to any country where the military ousted the elected government.

### Fiscal 1986 Supplemental

Congress cleared a fiscal 1986 supplemental appropriations bill (HR 4515 — PL 99-349) on June 26, 1986. Major funding items in the bill included $702 million to improve security at U.S. diplomatic posts abroad and $150 million in aid to the Philippines. *(Embassy security, p. 202; Philippine aid, p. 184)*

# 1987 Aid Appropriations

In spite of election-year politics, Congress in 1986 approved a surprisingly large foreign program for fiscal 1987, as part of an omnibus appropriations bill.

The foreign aid appropriations portion of the bill (H J Res 738 — PL 99-591) totaled $13.4 billion — $2 billion below President Reagan's request and $1 billion below the fiscal 1986 level. As a result, nearly all foreign aid programs faced cuts — but not of the meat-ax variety that had been predicted earlier in the year by many members of Congress and the administration.

As in the past, foreign aid was spared even deeper cuts partly because Congress acted on it behind closed doors. With a handful of members from the House and Senate Appropriations committees seeking to protect their favored programs, foreign aid benefited from old-fashioned horse-trading.

In addition, the House, where opposition to foreign aid traditionally was strongest, never took separate votes on those programs.

The final product was an uneasy balance among the kinds of programs favored by various members for ideological and other reasons. At the Senate's insistence, the bill provided more generous terms for foreign military-related aid programs than House conferees had wanted. And pressure by House members resulted in substantially greater contributions to the international development banks than the Senate had proposed.

For political reasons, a few programs escaped any cuts. Most important were U.S. donations to Israel and Egypt — linked together in the aid program since those countries signed a peace treaty in 1979. Their combined total of $5.1 billion was nearly half of all direct U.S. aid to foreign governments.

Because Congress earmarked minimum aid for some

countries — such as Israel and Egypt — while cutting back on the overall total, the Reagan administration was forced to make extra-deep cuts in aid to countries not protected by Congress. In the three military aid programs, for example, Congress cut Reagan's total request by 26 percent; once money was set aside for earmarked countries, military aid to all other countries had to be cut an average of nearly 50 percent.

For the second year in a row, foreign aid was the center of a dispute between the Appropriations and authorizing committees. The Appropriations conferees included in their bill several provisions that conflicted with the existing 1986-87 foreign aid authorization bill (PL 99-83) approved by Congress in 1985. Despite complaints from some members and staff aides of the two authorizing committees — House Foreign Affairs and Senate Foreign Relations — the appropriations bill simply declared that its earmarks, ceilings and limitations on funding overrode previous laws. *(1985 dispute, p. 191)*

### House, Senate Action

The House Appropriations Committee approved a $12.9 billion fiscal 1987 foreign aid spending bill. The committee reported the measure (HR 5339 — H Rept 99-747) Aug. 5, but the full House never considered it. Instead, the foreign aid bill was folded into the House version of the omnibus spending bill, passed Sept. 25.

The committee made deep slashes in all types of programs, although several countries and programs heavily favored in Congress escaped some or all of the pain. Four countries — Israel, Egypt, Pakistan and Northern Ireland — were exempted from any cut, thus ensuring that other countries and programs would face even sharper cuts than the overall 13 percent reduction in the measure.

The bill included several provisions to combat narcotics production overseas. Also approved by the committee were provisions aimed at individual countries that received U.S. aid; most focused on promoting political and economic reforms.

Once the major focus of attention, El Salvador received only secondary notice in the 1987 foreign aid measure. The Foreign Operations Subcommittee rejected amendments to put stiff conditions on that country's aid, but the full committee vented concerns about El Salvador's deteriorating economy, the ongoing war against leftist guerrillas and continuing human rights abuses.

The Senate Appropriations Committee Sept. 16 reported a $13 billion foreign aid bill (S 2824 — S Rept 99-443) that shared the cost-cutting emphasis of the House version. As in the House, the foreign aid bill was included in the omnibus spending bill, passed by the Senate Oct. 3.

Even though the House and Senate funding totals were nearly the same, the Senate bill took a huge swipe out of various programs that escaped such treatment in the House measure. At the same time, Senate drafters included much more money for bilateral economic aid than did their House counterparts.

As a way of stretching out the available dollars, the Senate committee proposed to change existing foreign aid procedures. Chief among these proposals was the elimination of the Military Assistance Program (MAP) in favor of funneling all military aid through the Foreign Military Sales (FMS) program. Because of the varying budget accounting procedures in the two programs, the change was designed to save on federal outlays — money that the government actually spent in a given year.

The Senate bill also would convert the military sales program from a loan program to grants. Senate Foreign Operations Subcommittee Chairman Bob Kasten, R-Wis., argued that the United States had been forcing foreign nations to take out massive loans so they could modernize their armies. Egypt, Turkey and several other financially strapped countries were struggling to repay past loans. The solution, Kasten said, was to give, rather than lend, those countries the money to buy military goods from the United States.

The Senate committee slashed funds for multilateral banks. No funds were included in the bill for direct U.S. contributions to the World Bank's lending resources, nor for the Inter-American Development Bank and the African Development Bank. Besides citing budget constraints, the panel also noted various policy disagreements with the international banks. For example, the committee report complained about the bank's alleged lack of concern over the environmental effects of various projects they financed.

The Senate bill cited budget pressures in rejecting the administration's centerpiece request for boosting U.S. exports: a $300 million "war chest" to subsidize the sale of U.S. goods overseas. The administration had tried for several years to end the Export-Import Bank's most popular program, which directly lent money to foreign purchasers of American goods.

The administration's alternative would encourage foreign countries to buy U.S. products by giving them a combination of subsidized loans and grants. The Ex-Im Bank had been giving highly subsidized loans in recent years but had been unable to offer outright grants. The Senate panel rejected this approach and recommended $900 million for the Export-Import Bank's direct loan program but permitted the bank to use up to $150 million of that for export financing offers.

## Final Action, Provisions

The most difficult issue in conference was the total for the Economic Support Fund (ESF), which boosted the economies of Israel, Egypt and other key allies. After extensive negotiations, conferees just about split their $700 million difference ($3.2 billion in the House bill and $3.9 billion in the Senate measure) and settled on $3.55 billion, thus permitting agreement on other issues.

House conferees refused to accept the Senate plan to convert military aid loans into grants but did agree to increase substantially the MAP grant and to mandate that all loans would carry below-market rates.

The House approved the conference report (H Rept 99-1005) Oct. 15. The Senate adopted it on Oct. 16 but because of disagreements over several unresolved items the continuing resolution did not clear until Oct. 17.

Funding levels in the $13.4 billion foreign aid portion of the continuing resolution included $1.18 billion for multilateral aid, $6.34 billion for bilateral aid, $4.99 billion for military aid and $900 million for Export-Import Bank direct loans.

Major provisions of H J Res 738:

**Security Assistance Totals.** Appropriated $4.99 billion for three military aid programs: MAP grants, FMS loans and grants and the International Military Education and Training program. Conferees boosted the MAP program to $900 million and required that all of the $4 billion FMS program would have to be either grants or low-inter-

est loans. That compromise reduced the interest rate on about $666 million worth of loans from 8 percent to 5 percent.

● Appropriated $3.55 billion for the ESF, which provided loans and grants to bolster the economies of key allies. In a move to reduce the impact of actual budget outlays during 1987, the bill allowed the administration to spend the money during both fiscal years 1987 and 1988.

**Israel, Egypt.** Earmarked $1.8 billion in military aid and $1.2 billion in economic aid for Israel — all in grants.

● Set aside $450 million of the military aid for development of Israel's new Lavi fighter plane. *(Lavi jet cancellation, box, p. 227)*

● Earmarked $1.3 billion in military aid and $815 million in economic aid for Egypt.

**Pakistan.** Earmarked $312.5 million in arms aid and $250 million in economic aid.

**Greece, Turkey.** Earmarked $343 million in military aid for Greece and $490 million in military aid for Turkey, in keeping with the traditional 7-10 ratio in military aid to the two countries.

**Central America.** $300 million in ESF aid was earmarked in the military construction part of PL 99-591 for Central American countries other than Nicaragua.

**Philippines.** Earmarked a minimum of $200 million in ESF aid.

● Repealed a provision of the 1986-87 foreign aid authorization law (PL 99-83) that limited military aid to the Philippines to $50 million annually. Aid conferees said the provision was no longer needed since the coming to power of a new government headed by Corazon Aquino. *(Philippine aid, pp. 184, 189)*

**Ireland.** Earmarked $35 million in ESF aid for both Northern Ireland (a part of the United Kingdom) and the Republic of Ireland.

**Development Banks.** Appropriated $949 million for cash payments to the World Bank and other international development banks. This included $622 million for the International Development Association, the most controversial arm of the World Bank; $55.8 million for the International Bank for Reconstruction and Development, the largest arm of the World Bank; $33.6 million for the Inter-American Development Bank; $64.8 million for the Special Facility for Sub-Saharan Africa; and $13.9 million for the African Development Bank.

**Population Aid.** Barred aid to any group involved in a program of coercive abortion or involuntary sterilization.

● Allowed funding of only groups that offered a broad range of family planning methods and services, but — in what appeared to be conflicting guidelines — said no group should be discriminated against because of its "religious or conscientious commitment to offer only natural family planning."

**Export-Import Bank.** Appropriated $900 million for the Export-Import Bank's direct loan program. Of the $900 million, up to $100 million could be used for a "tied-aid" program — a program that would encourage foreign countries to buy U.S. goods by giving them a combination of subsidized loans and grants — if the chairman of the bank certified to Congress that the money was not needed for direct loans. *(Export-Import Bank, p. 145)*

**Afghanistan, Cambodia.** Appropriated "humanitarian" aid to two guerrilla movements widely favored by members of Congress: Afghan resistance fighters battling the Soviet occupation of Afghanistan ($30 million) and Cambodian guerrillas opposing the Vietnamese occupation of Cambodia (not less than $1.5 million and not more than $5 million).

**Other Issues.** Barred any aid to the Sudan or Liberia unless the administration notified Congress of the aid in advance. (In 1985, there had been a military coup in the Sudan and controversial elections in Liberia.)

● Barred economic aid to Chile and called on the administration to oppose loans to that country by international development banks, until Chile ended human rights abuses and took "significant steps" toward restoring democracy.

● Included several new programs to encourage foreign countries to reduce illegal production of narcotics, including a $20 million bonus fund to be divided among countries making "substantial progress" in that area and a special authority for the administration to transfer extra aid to those countries.

● Barred aid to any country where the military ousted an elected government.

● Prohibited use of U.S. foreign aid to promote development of manufactured or agricultural items that would compete with American products.

### Fiscal 1987 Supplemental

Congress cleared a fiscal 1987 supplemental appropriations bill (HR 1827 — PL 100-71) on July 1, 1987. Foreign aid items in the bill included, among others, $258 million for multilateral economic assistance, the transfer of $300 million from the Defense Department for Reagan's request for aid to Central America and $50 million in military aid grants to the Philippines. The bill also reduced funding for Export-Import Bank loans from $900 million to $680 million.

## Sub-Saharan Africa Aid

Congress in 1985 appropriated a total of $784 million for emergency African relief (HR 1239 — PL 99-10). The money, which included both food and non-food aid, was in response to continuing famine caused by drought and civil strife in Ethiopia, the Sudan and some 20 other countries in sub-Saharan Africa.

Congress cleared a separate bill (S 689 — PL 99-8) authorizing $175 million for non-food aid to Africa. The other funds contained in HR 1239, for food assistance, did not require an authorization bill in 1985.

President Reagan had asked Congress to appropriate $235 million for Africa by early March. But HR 1239, which provided more than three times as much money as requested, cleared a month later, partly because of a dispute between the administration and some members of Congress over how much food would be needed to meet the U.S. goal of supplying half of Africa's emergency food needs.

Moreover, the authorization bill got entangled with an unrelated controversy over assistance to American farmers. The House passed an authorization bill (HR 1096 — H Rept 99-3) Feb. 26 by a 391-25 vote. The Senate attached three amendments providing emergency credit aid to American farmers before passing HR 1096, with the language of its own version of the bill (S 457 — S Rept 99-4), by a 62-35 vote Feb. 27. The House voted 255-168 on March 5 to accept the Senate amendments and clear the bill.

Reagan quickly vetoed the measure, claiming March 6

that its farm-loan provisions were "a massive new bailout that would add billions to the deficit." There was no attempt to override the veto and a new non-food authorization (S 689) that had been stripped of the farm-credit provisions passed the Senate on March 19 and the House March 21 by voice votes.

The House by voice vote Feb. 28 passed HR 1239 (H Rept 99-2) appropriating $880 million for emergency African relief. The Senate by a 98-1 vote March 20 passed its version of HR 1239 (S Rept 99-8) appropriating $669 million.

House-Senate conferees March 27 agreed to a compromise bill (H Rept 99-29) providing $784 million, which was approved by the House by a 400-19 vote April 2 and by the Senate by voice vote the same day.

In addition to providing $609 million for food aid, the bill gave the administration authority to use another $16 million carried over from fiscal 1984. It also included $175 million for non-food aid.

The bill authorized the Agriculture Department to give African countries up to 200,000 tons of surplus food owned by the Commodity Credit Corporation but required certification that none of it would be given to the Ethiopian government. Members were disturbed by reports that the Marxist government of Ethiopia had blocked food shipments to rebel-controlled provinces.

By the end of 1985, there were reports that the emergency food shipments, better-than-usual rainfalls and unexpectedly good harvests had sharply curtailed starvation in Africa — eliminating the need for another emergency relief bill.

## Central American Police Aid

Reviving a controversy more than a decade old, President Reagan tried in vain to win congressional approval in 1985 for police aid and supplemental military assistance for El Salvador and four other Central American countries.

Reagan called the program a "counterterrorism" effort, in response to the June 19 killing in El Salvador of four U.S. Marines and several others.

But Democrats feared the plan risked getting the United States back into the business of supporting brutal Latin American police forces. And some Republican leaders said the administration could overload the tiny countries of Central America with military aid.

In September 1985, Reagan requested $54 million for the police and supplemental military aid package. It would have been the first such assistance since Congress barred U.S. involvement with foreign police in 1974. That congressional action came after the "public safety" program the United States conducted in Latin America in the 1960s and early 1970s had created a widespread impression in the region that the United States was contributing to police torture and brutality.

In July 1985, responding to the killing of the Marines in San Salvador, the House voted, with little debate, to exempt El Salvador and Honduras from the police aid ban. That marked the first significant change in the ban since 1974. The exemption was enacted into law in the fiscal 1986-87 foreign aid authorization bill (PL 99-83), along with a similar exemption for Costa Rica. *(Story, p. 186)*

Reagan's request sought to take advantage of the new exception and add Guatemala and Panama to the list of countries exempted from the police aid ban.

After long debate, the Senate Foreign Relations Committee on Dec. 5 approved a stripped-down version (S 1915 — S Rept 99-213), allowing only $22 million in police aid for the region but under conditions designed to guard against U.S. association with repressive security forces. The measure never reached the floor for procedural reasons and because of a threatened filibuster.

The measure (HR 3463) got nowhere in the House. The House and Senate Appropriations committees, which would have initiated legislation actually funding the aid, also delayed taking any action.

Meanwhile, the State Department on Oct. 29 notified Congress that the United States would take money from other foreign aid accounts to provide $9 million worth of training and equipment — including weapons — to help the Salvadoran police combat terrorism.

# Jordan Arms Sale Postponement

To head off a legislative defeat, the Reagan administration in early 1986 indefinitely postponed a major arms sale to Jordan.

President Reagan had notified Congress in 1985 of his intent to sell Jordan advanced warplanes, missiles and other weapons — in spite of congressional warnings against such a sale until there was more progress in Middle East peace talks.

When about two-thirds of all members of Congress endorsed bills rejecting the $1.5 billion-$2 billion sale, Reagan in October 1985 agreed to compromise legislation (S J Res 228 — PL 99-162) that delayed the package at least until March 1, 1986, unless "direct and meaningful" peace talks between Jordan and Israel were under way.

But prospects for the sale had not improved by 1986. With a strong majority of members still opposed to it, Secretary of State George P. Shultz notified Congress that the Reagan administration was postponing indefinitely the sale.

## Background

The Jordan arms proposal was a replay of a familiar scenario: an American president agrees to sell sophisticated weapons to an Arab country, stirring concerns in Congress about the security of Israel.

At the heart of the debate was whether selling weapons would promote peace in the Middle East. The Reagan administration, like its predecessors, argued that military cooperation would encourage political cooperation by moderate Arab regimes. That position helped sway Congress to approve controversial sales to Jordan in 1975-76, to Saudi Arabia and Egypt in 1978 and to Saudi Arabia again in 1981. *(Congress and the Nation Vol. IV, p. 872; Congress and the Nation Vol. V, p. 63; Congress and the Nation Vol. VI, p. 129)*

In 1983, however, Congress held up funding for a "rapid deployment force" of Jordanians, and in 1984, Capitol Hill opposition to a sale of Stinger anti-aircraft missiles mounted so rapidly that Reagan was forced to withdraw it. *(Congress and the Nation Vol. VI, p. 196)*

In 1985, Reagan proposed selling to Jordan 40 advanced warplanes — either F-16s or F-20s — as well as air-to-air and anti-aircraft missiles and infantry combat vehicles. He argued that Jordan's King Hussein would feel more secure in negotiating peace with Israel if he had U.S.

backing against potential threats by Syria and other nations that rejected any dealings with the Jewish state. Proponents of the sale also argued that if the sale were blocked, Hussein could obtain similar weapons from alternative suppliers who would do less to ensure that the weapons were not used against Israel.

But these arguments swayed few in Congress, in spite of Hussein's sustained effort to open peace talks with Israel. Hussein promoted a plan for jump-starting the peace process that advocated an international conference on Middle East peace. The plan called for the participation of the five permanent members of the U.N. Security Council, including the Soviet Union, and all parties to the conflict, including the Palestine Liberation Organization (PLO).

The United States and Israel both rejected Hussein's proposals for Soviet and PLO involvement. Israel's supporters on Capitol Hill argued that Hussein had not shown that he was ready to engage Israel in serious peace talks and that he had given veto power over his participation in negotiations to Yasir Arafat, chairman of the PLO. U.S. arms sales to Jordan, they argued, would reduce Hussein's incentives to enter peace talks.

An escalation of Middle East violence in October further clouded the climate for peace talks. Arab leaders were upset in early October when Reagan endorsed an Israeli aerial bombardment of a PLO headquarters in Tunisia. And U.S. ties with Egypt — the only Arab country openly backing Hussein's peace moves — were severely strained in the aftermath of the hijacking of the Italian cruise ship *Achille Lauro* and the murder of a wheelchair-bound American passenger by Palestinian terrorists.

## 1985 Legislative Action

Reagan officially informed Congress of the Jordan arms sale on Oct. 21, 1985, but three days later the Senate overwhelmingly voted to delay the sale at least until March 1, 1986 — unless Jordan and Israel had begun "direct and meaningful" peace talks. The vote on S J Res 228 was 97-1.

The Senate's action was the sharpest rebuke the Republican-led chamber had administered to Reagan on a major foreign policy issue since June 1984, when it denied funds for anti-government contras in Nicaragua.

On Nov. 12, after little debate, the full House approved the resolution, clearing it for the president, who signed it into law Nov. 25.

The fiscal 1986 continuing appropriations resolution (H J Res 465 — PL 99-190) established a procedure for averting a Senate filibuster of any resolution to block the arms sale. Both the continuing resolution and the foreign aid authorization law (S 960 — PL 99-83) also contained language stating congressional opposition to a Jordan arms sale until Middle East peace talks were under way. *(Authorization bill, p. 186)*

Earlier in 1985, the administration had won congressional approval of $250 million in economic aid for Jordan, but not without controversy or conditions. As included in the fiscal 1985 supplemental appropriations bill (HR 2577 — PL 99-88), the $250 million was spread out over 1985-87 and was to be in commodity credits and aid for public works projects, not cash.

## 1986 Postponement

The administration in 1986 shelved the controversial arms sale to Jordan as part of an agreement with congressional leaders.

Secretary Shultz's Feb. 3 letter formally notified Congress of the decision. With it in hand, the House Foreign Affairs Committee Feb. 4 dropped plans to act on a widely supported resolution (H J Res 428) that would prevent the sale.

## Saudi Arms Sale

President Reagan barely averted a major foreign policy defeat in 1986, when the Senate upheld a White House plan to sell $265 million worth of weapons to Saudi Arabia. But, because of congressional criticism, the final arms package was much smaller than originally proposed.

By a **key vote of 66-34 (R 24-29; D 42-5)**, the Senate June 5 sustained Reagan's May 21 veto of a measure (S J Res 316) that would have blocked the sale. *(1986 key votes, p. 949)*

A two-thirds majority of those present and voting was required to pass the bill over the president's veto. With all members voting, the 34 "nay" votes — one-third plus one of the Senate's 100 members — were the absolute minimum Reagan needed to prevent a Senate override. Since action by a single chamber was sufficient to sustain the veto, no override vote occurred in the House.

A vigorous White House lobbying effort had succeeded in winning enough votes to turn around the Senate's 73-22 approval May 6 of the measure blocking the Saudi sale (S Rept 99-288). The House had adopted its disapproval resolution (H J Res 589 — H Rept 99-569) May 7, 356-62.

Opponents of the sale claimed that Saudi Arabia, despite its moderate image, had continued to provide financial support to the radical Syrian government and the Palestine Liberation Organization. Also frequently mentioned was the Saudis' condemnation of the United States' April 14, 1986, attack against Libya. *(Clashes with Libya, p. 199)*

Major Jewish organizations, led by the American Israel Public Affairs Committee (AIPAC), opposed selling arms to the Saudis, though most agreed not to lobby actively against the sale.

Supporters of the sale contended that only by agreeing to sell a fresh supply of missiles to the Saudis could the United States demonstrate its commitment to moderate Arab states and continue to exercise influence in the region.

By voting to sustain the president's veto of S J Res 316, the Senate maintained Congress' record of never having formally blocked a president from selling arms to a foreign country. The Saudi case, however, marked the first time that both chambers had passed resolutions to disapprove an arms sale. Congress in 1985 forced Reagan to delay indefinitely an arms sale to Jordan, but neither chamber reached the point of passing legislation rejecting it outright. *(Jordan sale, p. 197)*

### Weapons Package

The Senate action cleared the way for the administration to sell nearly 1,700 Sidewinder air-to-air missiles and 100 Harpoon air-to-sea missiles. Reagan aides said the Saudis needed the weapons package to bolster their defensive forces, particularly to fend off possible Iranian advances stemming from the Persian Gulf war between Iran and Iraq.

---

## AWACS Transfer to Saudis

President Reagan on June 18, 1986, notified Congress that the United States would transfer to Saudi Arabia by late June or early July the first of five AWACS radar planes the Saudis bought in 1981. Reagan's notice prompted objections from some members of Congress, but there was no serious effort to block the transfer of the planes.

Officially known as the Airborne Warning and Control System, the AWACS planes were modified Boeing 707s that were capable of detecting and tracking hundreds of airplanes simultaneously. Israel and its supporters in Congress objected to the sale of the planes to the Saudis, saying they could be used to thwart Israeli air superiority during a future Arab-Israeli war.

The United States had stationed a fleet of AWACS planes in Saudi Arabia for nearly five years, primarily to help protect Saudi oil fields from potential attacks by Iran. The new Saudi-owned planes were to replace the U.S. planes.

The total value of the AWACS sale was put at $3.5 billion, which included $1.2 billion for the AWACS planes themselves and the rest for KC-135 refueling tankers, spare parts, training, facilities to handle the planes and maintenance by U.S. contract employees.

Congress allowed the AWACS sale in October 1981, after Reagan gave assurances that several conditions would be met, including continued Saudi support for Middle East peace negotiations and Saudi agreement to protect sensitive technology in the planes. *(Congress and the Nation Vol. VI, p. 129)*

In 1985 Congress put those assurances into the law by requiring the president to certify that several conditions had been met before the planes were transferred to Saudi Arabia. The latter requirement was included in the fiscal 1986-87 foreign aid authorization bill (PL 99-83). *(Foreign aid authorization, p. 186)*

In a letter to Congress on June 18, Reagan said that the conditions and assurances "have now been met."

---

Stripped from the final package, however, were controversial Stinger missiles requested by the Saudis. The Stinger, a shoulder-fired, anti-aircraft weapon, had been singled out for criticism by foes of the arms deal on the grounds that it might fall into the hands of terrorists. Elimination of the Stingers, which cut $89 million from the $354 million package, had been suggested by the Saudis to blunt congressional opposition to the weapons sale.

The Saudis originally also had asked to buy F-15 fighter jets, M-1 tanks and other equipment. But the administration had scaled down the proposal in an effort to mollify members of Congress who opposed sales to Arab countries that had not come to peace terms with Israel.

Less than two weeks after the final Senate vote on the Saudi weapons package, Reagan announced that the United States was about to start delivering five sophisticated radar planes the Saudis had purchased in 1981. *(Box, p. 198)*

## Arms Sale Veto Procedures

Legislation to revise procedures used by Congress to block major arms sales to foreign countries was enacted in 1986.

The main purpose of the bill (S 1831 — PL 99-247) was to make existing law on congressional review of arms sales conform to the Supreme Court's 1983 *Chadha* decision, which ruled legislative vetoes unconstitutional unless the president had a chance to participate in them. Under existing law, Congress could block a major foreign arms sale by passing a concurrent resolution, which did not have to be signed by the president. *(Congress and the Nation Vol. VI, p. 833)*

S 1831 required Congress to pass a joint resolution if it wanted to block an arms sale. Such a resolution must be presented to the president for his signature or veto.

S 1831 also provided for a system of expedited consideration in both the House and Senate of any resolution to block an arms sale.

The Senate passed the measure on Dec. 19, 1985, and the House cleared it on Feb. 3, 1986.

## Clashes With Libya

Frustrated by his inability to punish terrorists who had stalked the Middle East and Europe, President Reagan in 1986 lashed out at Libya, the country he charged with giving the greatest aid and support to terrorists.

The president's military actions against Libya renewed debate about the role of Congress in initiating armed conflict. However, lawmakers took no action on legislation to alter existing war powers restrictions.

Reagan began the year by tightening economic sanctions against Libya in retaliation for the Dec. 27, 1985, terrorist attacks at the Rome and Vienna airports. Making good on his threat to back up the economic sanctions with further action, the president subsequently employed military force against Libya twice in less than a month.

In late March, the president sent massive air and naval forces to challenge Libya's claim to sovereignty over the Gulf of Sidra, provoking a shooting match during which U.S. planes destroyed several Libyan missile sites and ships.

Then on April 14, Reagan ordered a bombardment of Libyan military targets in retaliation for that country's alleged backing of terrorism. Announcing the April 14 raid, Reagan said he would "do it again" if necessary.

Later in the year, it was reported that the administration had conducted a "disinformation" campaign aimed at destabilizing the Libyan government by feeding false information to the press.

### Economic Sanctions

The president Jan. 7 ordered a total ban on U.S. trade with Libya and directed all Americans there to leave —

tightening several sanctions that he and President Carter had imposed since 1978.

The following day, in an effort to protect U.S. corporations in Libya against retaliation, Reagan ordered a freeze on all Libyan government assets located in the United States or held by U.S. banks.

Congress had signaled in July 1985 that it was ready for full-scale sanctions against Libya. In the fiscal 1986-87 foreign aid authorization bill (PL 99-83), Congress authorized the president to ban all trade with Libya or any other country that supported terrorism. Reagan cited that provision as one legal justification for his action.

Reagan also acted under a 1977 law (PL 95-223) allowing him to bar economic activity with other countries by declaring a national emergency, which he did on Jan. 7. *(PL 95-223, Congress and the Nation Vol. V, p. 139)*

### Military Clashes

Libyan missile attacks on U.S. naval forces in the Gulf of Sidra prompted U.S. military retaliation against that nation on March 24-25. Navy warplanes attacked a Libyan missile installation and several Libyan ships.

The clashes were triggered by U.S. naval exercises in the area, which Libya claimed as its own but nearly all other nations regarded as international waters.

After several anti-aircraft missiles were fired from near the Libyan town of Sirte, U.S. ships and planes in the Gulf of Sidra attacked the missile battery and several missile-armed Libyan patrol boats. U.S. officials reported no American casualties.

The United States launched massive air strikes against Libya on April 14. The U.S. attack, in which two American fliers were killed, was in response to the April 5 bombing of a discothèque in West Berlin frequented by U.S. military personnel. One U.S. soldier and a Turkish woman were killed and more than 200 persons, including some 60 Americans, were injured.

President Reagan later claimed that unequivocal evidence demonstrated that Libyan leader Muammar el-Qaddafi had sponsored the bombing, evidently in retaliation for the U.S. Navy attacks on Libyan forces March 24-25.

Both military actions against Libya generated strong support in Congress. But some members, especially Democrats, said Reagan failed to meet the 1973 War Powers Resolution's requirements for consulting with Congress in advance.

Although Reagan sent reports to Congress after both incidents, in neither report did he say he was acting in accordance with the War Powers Resolution.

The president did not consult with Congress before the Gulf of Sidra operation, and he called in top congressional leaders only three hours before the April 14 bombing got under way. Justifying Reagan's use of force against Libya, the administration contended that the War Powers act did not apply to some military steps directed against terrorists. Under that view, the president also was not required to keep Congress informed about military exercises.

## State Department Authorization

Congress effectively froze spending by the State Department and related agencies in legislation passed during 1985.

# Hill Crackdown on Soviet Spying

A series of revelations about spying activity on behalf of the Soviet Union spurred Congress to include in the State Department authorization bill (HR 2068 — PL 99-93) new restrictions on Soviet diplomats.

Early in 1985, the administration discovered that some typewriters at the U.S. Embassy in Moscow had been fitted in 1982 with electronic devices that enabled Soviet officials to monitor what was being typed. Later in 1985, a storm of diplomatic protest arose after it was revealed that Soviet agents had exposed U.S. Embassy workers to a potentially dangerous chemical.

In May and June, the FBI arrested four members of a spy ring led by John Anthony Walker Jr., a retired U.S. Navy communications specialist, on charges of selling secrets to the Soviets.

The incidents gave new impetus to congressional efforts to combat Soviet espionage both against the U.S. Embassy in Moscow and from the Soviet Embassy in Washington.

The United States employed more than 200 Soviet citizens at its embassy in Moscow and consulate in Leningrad, nearly all in service positions such as janitors. At the same time, the Soviet Union refused to hire U.S. citizens for its diplomatic offices in the United States. As a result, there were about 200 more Russian diplomatic personnel in the United States than there were U.S. diplomats in the Soviet Union. Intelligence officials told congressional committees that many Soviet diplomats and embassy employees were active espionage agents.

The final version of HR 2068 contained provisions aimed at reversing the imbalance. One barred, to the extent practicable, Soviet citizens from working at U.S. missions. Another provision established a policy that the number of Soviet diplomatic and consular personnel in the United States should be roughly equivalent to the corresponding number of U.S. representatives in the Soviet Union.

Concern over spying also was directed toward the large number of Soviet citizens employed by the United Nations. A report released June 5 by the Senate Intelligence Committee found that about one-fourth of the 800 Soviets working for the United Nations were intelligence agents.

After release of the report, the Intelligence Committee moved to close a legal loophole under which Soviets working for the United Nations had total freedom to travel in the United States. All other Soviet diplomats were required to get permission from the State Department before they could travel away from their assigned posts — thus making it easier for the FBI to keep track of them. Such permission was rarely granted, because of the Soviets' tight curbs on travel by U.S. diplomats.

The final version of the State Department authorization bill contained a provision applying existing travel restrictions on foreign diplomats to foreign employees of the United Nations.

---

The authorization bill (HR 2068 — PL 99-93) allowed $7.6 billion over fiscal 1986-87 for the State Department's operations and for the United States Information Agency (USIA), the Arms Control and Disarmament Agency (ACDA) and the Board for International Broadcasting (BIB), overseer of Radio Free Europe and Radio Liberty.

HR 2068 had the potential of leading to a major change in American policy toward the United Nations. The bill provided for a limitation on U.S. contributions to the world body unless it agreed to shift to a system under which voting strength on budget matters was proportional to each member state's financial contributions.

Critics of the United Nations charged that the United States was supplying a substantial share of funding for the organization while allowing a large number of poor countries with very small contributions to determine how the money was spent.

That system encouraged the U.N. budget to triple in the preceding decade, critics said. Passage of the U.N. amendment, which was opposed by President Reagan and the State Department, also reflected congressional frustration with the anti-American stance frequently taken by the world forum's communist and Third World majority.

HR 2068 also contained provisions on two national security issues that attracted considerable attention during 1985. The bill set aside $311 million in State Department administrative funds for improvements in embassy security. Those funds were just the precursor, however, to a major new embassy security program enacted in 1986. *(Embassy security, p. 202)*

In addition, the bill called for limits on the number of Soviet nationals who could serve as diplomats in the United States, or be employed in U.S. diplomatic or consular missions in the Soviet Union. The provisions were in response to a number of reports of Soviet spy activities that surfaced during the year. *(Spies, box, this page)*

During the course of its passage through Congress, the bill also picked up a number of provisions relating to hotly debated foreign policy issues, including Senate-passed provisions repealing a 1976 law against aid to anti-government rebels in Angola and authorizing non-military aid for contra forces battling the leftist government of Nicaragua. These provisions were dropped from the conference version because they were contained in other legislation cleared by Congress. *(Angola aid, p. 188; contra aid, p. 173)*

Overall, funding levels in the bill adhered to a spending "freeze" approved by the House. The conference version's total authorization for fiscal 1986 was $72 million less than the 1985 authorization and $131 million less than the amount sought by the Reagan administration.

## Legislative Action

The House passed HR 2068 by voice vote May 9. The major change made by the House in the bill reported by the Foreign Affairs Committee (HR 1931 — H Rept 99-40) came on an amendment, adopted 398-1, to fix fiscal 1986 spending authority at the fiscal 1985 appropriations level of $3.84 billion, after adjustment for inflation. For fiscal 1987, the amendment provided $3.97 billion.

The Senate approved its version of HR 2068 by an 80-17 vote June 11. There was lengthy debate on the Senate bill (S 1003 — S Rept 99-39), as senators argued over aid to anti-communist rebels in Nicaragua and Angola, as well as amendments restricting contributions to the United Nations and international family planning agencies.

The Senate approved an amendment to provide $38 million in non-military aid to the contra guerrillas by a **key vote of 55-42 (R 41-10; D 14-32)** June 6. It provided $14 million in fiscal 1985 and $24 million in 1986 for "food, clothing, medicine or other 'humanitarian' assistance" for the contras. It also would repeal an existing bar on military or paramilitary aid and specifically authorize the CIA to provide intelligence information to the contras. *(1985 key votes, p. 933)*

The Senate also rejected several Democratic-sponsored proposals to restrict the nature of the contra aid and to limit Reagan's freedom to send U.S. troops to Central America.

The Senate took a major policy step June 11, when it voted overwhelmingly to repeal a 1976 law that had thwarted U.S. support for anti-government rebels in Angola. Although not taken at the official request of Reagan, the Senate's action was welcomed by the administration, which had chafed at the legal curb on Reagan's authority.

By a 63-34 vote, the Senate voted to repeal the Clark amendment on Angola. Originally passed by Congress in 1976 under the sponsorship of Sen. Dick Clark, D-Iowa (1973-79), the amendment banned any U.S. "covert" aid to factions then fighting in Angola.

Other than Nicaragua, the most controversial issue dealt with by the Senate on the State Department bill was family planning overseas. By 53-45, the Senate on June 11 tabled an amendment that sought to give the president a free hand in determining what agencies could get U.S. family planning funds. The core issue was whether Congress would intervene in Reagan's decision to withhold some or all U.S. funds from the U.N. Fund for Population Activities and the International Planned Parenthood Federation. *(Population programs, box, p. 193)*

The amendment limiting U.S. contributions to the United Nations was adopted by the Senate June 7 by a **key vote of 71-13 (R 41-4; D 30-9)**. Nancy Landon Kassebaum, R-Kan., said she offered the amendment because "the United Nations can no longer be a sacred cow."

Since both the Angola and Nicaragua provisions also were contained in the foreign aid authorization bill (S 960) that cleared Congress July 31, they were dropped from the conference version of the State Department bill without opposition. With those contentious issues out of the measure, conferees were able to settle their differences informally, without a conference meeting.

The House approved the conference report (H Rept 99-240) by a 350-74 vote Aug. 1. The Senate had accepted the agreement by voice vote July 31.

## Major Provisions

As signed into law Aug. 16, 1985, HR 2068 (PL 99-93):

● Authorized $3,765,796,000 in fiscal 1986 and $3,808,818,000 in fiscal 1987 for operations of the State Department, USIA and BIB. Included in those totals were the following authorizations for major programs: $1.8 billion in 1986 and $1.9 billion in 1987 for basic State Department operations; $534 million annually for aid to international organizations; $345 million annually for refugee assistance; $888 million annually for USIA; and $125 million annually for the BIB.

Included in the fiscal 1986-87 authorization total was $90.5 million for educational and exchange programs in Latin America and the Caribbean. The legislation also called for establishment of a new college scholarship program for students from developing nations.

● Earmarked $311 million in State Department administration funds for capital spending and salaries to improve security at U.S. embassies.

● Repealed the permanent authorization, enacted in 1975 (PL 94-37), for the U.S. contribution to the U.N. peacekeeping force in the Mideast.

● Provided that travel restrictions imposed by existing law on foreign diplomats in the United States also apply to foreign employees of the United Nations; authorized the president to waive the restriction.

● Limited the U.S. contribution to U.N. organizations to 20 percent of their budgets, unless the United Nations moved toward a system under which voting strength in each organization was proportionate to each member state's financial contribution; also prohibited U.S. contributions to certain U.N. organizations.

● Required that, to the extent practicable, Soviet nationals not be employed in U.S. diplomatic or consular missions in the Soviet Union after Sept. 30, 1986; established a policy that the number of Soviet nationals serving in diplomatic or consular posts in the United States be roughly equivalent to the number of U.S. nationals serving in similar positions in the Soviet Union; and called for expulsion of at least one senior Soviet military attaché from the United States in retaliation for the March 1985 killing of U.S. Army Major Arthur D. Nicholson Jr. by Soviet forces in East Germany.

● Directed the United States to support a flexible pricing policy for some routes of the International Telecommunications Satellite Organization (INTELSAT), instead of the uniform rate required under existing law.

● Established an independent Office of Inspector General at the State Department.

● Made the National Endowment for Democracy, which made grants to private organizations abroad that promoted democracy, subject to the provisions of the Freedom of Information Act; required that the quasi-governmental agency submit to audits conducted by USIA; and barred use of endowment funds for partisan activities by the Republican or Democratic national committees.

● Required the president to submit an annual report on the compliance of other nations with arms control agreements.

● Established a new "Radio Free Afghanistan" to broadcast to that country as long as it was occupied by Soviet forces.

● Set up an International Narcotics Control Commission to monitor compliance with narcotics control treaties.

● Expressed the sense of Congress that Japan should

undertake efforts to expand its defense capabilities.

● Called on the Treasury Department and Federal Reserve Board to take steps to lower the value of the dollar relative to other currencies.

● Expressed the sense of Congress that the United States should continue seeking an accord with the Soviet Union to ban chemical weapons.

# Embassy Security

Congress approved in 1986 a five-year, $2.4 billion program aimed at strengthening U.S. overseas diplomatic posts against terrorist attacks.

The authorization fell well short of the $4.4 billion that the Reagan administration had requested to rebuild or refurbish more than 250 U.S. diplomatic posts.

The final legislation (HR 4151 — PL 99-399) contained an array of terrorism-related initiatives, ranging from anti-terrorist research and development to cash payments to U.S. hostages who had been held in Iran in 1979-81.

But the heart of the measure was an ambitious embassy construction program originally recommended in June 1985 by a special presidential commission formed after the terrorist attacks in 1983 and 1984 on the U.S. Marine headquarters and embassy compound in Lebanon. That commission, headed by former CIA Deputy Director Bobby R. Inman, reported serious security problems at U.S. diplomatic missions.

The White House responded in President Reagan's fiscal 1987 budget with a proposal for a five-year diplomatic security program.

The funds authorized by HR 4151 would allow the State Department to proceed with such high-priority projects as facilities in Cyprus, Jordan and Honduras. Other priority missions were in Moscow, Cairo, London, Athens and Pretoria.

In passing its version (H Rept 99-494) on March 18 by a 389-7 vote, the House went along with the administration's full-funding request for the embassy program. But the Senate, concerned with spending restraints and the State Department's difficulty in justifying the full amount, approved on June 25 by voice vote a two-year program costing $1.1 billion (S Rept 99-304).

The final version authorized five-year funding for capital projects, but only two-year funding for salaries and expenses. Conferees said further funding for salaries and expenses should be considered as part of regular State Department authorizations for fiscal 1988-90. The conference report (H Rept 99-783) was approved by both chambers Aug. 12 by voice votes.

Congress already had provided $702.1 million for the embassy security program in a fiscal 1986 supplemental appropriations bill (HR 4515 — PL 99-349) signed by Reagan July 2. The State Department also received $343.4 million in fiscal 1985 supplemental funds that were prompted by the Beirut bombings.

## Major Provisions

As signed into law Aug. 27, 1986, HR 4151 (PL 99-399):

● **Diplomatic Security.** Consolidated the security functions of the State Department under a Bureau of Diplomatic Security to be headed by a new assistant secretary of state for diplomatic security.

● Established within the bureau a Diplomatic Security Service.

● Authorized fiscal 1986-87 funding for the diplomatic security program as follows: $308.1 million for salaries and expenses; $857.8 million for acquisition, construction and maintenance at U.S. diplomatic missions abroad; and $15 million for anti-terrorism research and development.

● Increased the fiscal 1987 authorization for anti-terrorism training assistance to $14.7 million from $9.8 million.

● Authorized $418 million annually in fiscal 1988-90 for acquisition and maintenance of buildings abroad.

● Prohibited use of any of the authorized funds for constructing any diplomatic facilities in Israel. (The original Senate amendment would have barred construction in Tel Aviv to force relocation of the U.S. Embassy from Tel Aviv to Jerusalem. While Israel claimed Jerusalem as its capital, the United States and other countries refused to relocate their embassies there because of Arab disputes over Jerusalem's status.)

● **Anti-Terrorism Program.** Authorized the secretary of state to offer rewards for information on major narcotics trafficking and narcotics-related terrorist acts committed primarily outside the United States.

● Earmarked $2 million for the awards program from existing funding and authorized an additional $10 million in fiscal 1987.

● Authorized the secretary to impose controls on certain services to military, police or intelligence agencies of countries that supported terrorism, as determined under the Export Administration Act. Five countries were so classified as of 1986: Libya, Iran, South Yemen, Syria and Cuba.

● Amended the Arms Export Control Act to prohibit exports of munitions that were subject to control to any country designated as a supporter of international terrorism under the Export Administration Act.

● **Nuclear Terrorism.** Authorized the president to suspend nuclear cooperation with nations that had not ratified the Convention on the Physical Protection of Nuclear Materials.

● Established a uniform procedure for criminal history checks of certain employees of nuclear power plants.

● **Victims Compensation.** Provided about $22,200 — $50 per day — for the U.S. hostages held in Iran for 444 days, from November 1979 until January 1981. Subsequent hostages also would receive compensation at a lower amount, along with health and educational benefits provided to them and their families.

● **Maritime Security.** Authorized $62.5 million during fiscal years 1987-91 to boost security at U.S. and foreign seaports.

● Authorized the president to suspend passenger services to any foreign port if he determined the country concerned had aided a terrorist organization that illegally seized or threatened to seize passenger vessels.

● **Extraterritorial Criminal Jurisdiction.** Established U.S. legal jurisdiction over crimes involving violent attacks by terrorists against all U.S. nationals abroad. Existing federal law covered murder and assault only against high-ranking U.S. officials.

● **Peace Corps.** Authorized $130 million for the Peace Corps in fiscal 1986 and $137.2 million in fiscal 1987.

● **Waldheim Allowance.** Called on the administration to propose eliminating an $81,650 annual "retirement allowance" in the U.N. budget for former U.N. Secretary-General Kurt Waldheim, the new president of Austria. Waldheim had been accused of Nazi activities during World War II.

# 1986 Intelligence Authorization

For the first time since 1981, Congress in 1985 made substantial cuts in President Reagan's request for spending by the CIA and other intelligence agencies. Members said the fiscal 1986 intelligence authorization bill (HR 2419 — PL 99-169) allowed only modest spending boosts for the intelligence agencies, compared with Reagan's request for increases averaging about 10 percent.

Nearly all the major funding items in the bill were classified secret, as in previous years. However, sources said the bill authorized at least $10 billion for the intelligence agencies, which included the Defense Intelligence Agency, National Security Agency and others. Less than $2 billion of the total was for the CIA.

A key provision of the bill eased some, but not all, of the conditions Congress earlier in 1985 had placed on resumed U.S. aid to the insurgents, called contras, battling the leftist government of Nicaragua. Under the terms of HR 2419, the CIA was permitted to give the contras advice and intelligence information. The measure also broadened previously approved congressional definitions of "humanitarian" aid for the rebels to include radios, trucks and other gear. Congress had voted $27 million for the Nicaraguan rebels in July, but the bill expressly had prohibited expenditures for military items. *(Story, p. 173)*

## Legislative Action

The House Intelligence Committee reported HR 2419 (H Rept 99-106, Part I) May 15. The action marked the first time in three years that the panel voted to allow the CIA to provide information and advice to the anti-government rebels in Nicaragua. But the committee remained opposed to outright U.S. aid for the contras.

The bill was reported May 23 (Part II) by the House Armed Services Committee, which shared jurisdiction with the Intelligence Committee and reviewed spending for most intelligence programs.

With little debate, the House July 18 passed HR 2419 by voice vote.

The Senate Intelligence Committee reported its version of the bill June 11 (S 1271 — S Rept 99-79). The committee allowed the CIA to collect intelligence in Nicaragua and to share that information with the contras.

The bill was reported jointly from the Senate Governmental Affairs and Armed Services committees (S Rept 99-136) on Sept. 11.

The Senate Sept. 26 passed its version of HR 2419 by voice vote.

The House Nov. 19 approved the conference report on the bill (H Rept 99-373) by a 387-21 vote. The Senate adopted the report by voice vote Nov. 21.

## Major Provisions

As signed into law Dec. 4, 1985, major provisions of HR 2419 (PL 99-169) that were made public:

● Authorized the CIA to provide intelligence information and advice to the contras.

● Accepted an administration request to enlarge the definition of humanitarian aid to the contras to include radios and transportation equipment.

● Barred the CIA from using its contingency fund to resume "covert" military aid to the contras.

● Permitted the State Department to solicit other sources, including other countries, for humanitarian aid to the contras. The only restrictions were that any aid provided by another country as a result of U.S. solicitations had to come from its own resources, and that the United States could not condition its foreign aid on another country's willingness to back the rebels.

● Authorized $50.6 million for the FBI's domestic and international counterterrorism programs, including $500,000 to reimburse state and local law enforcement agencies for their cooperation.

● Authorized $75 million over three years ($21.4 million in fiscal 1986) for design and construction of a new research and engineering building for the National Security Agency, monitor of electronic communications around the world.

● Authorized $22.1 million for operations of the 233-member Intelligence Community Staff, which served the CIA director in his role as coordinator of all the intelligence agencies. That was an increase of $1.1 million and 26 employees over fiscal 1985.

● Authorized $101.4 million for the CIA's retirement and disability system.

● Required the president to report to Congress on U.S. counterintelligence capabilities and policies, along with recommendations for improvements. Counterintelligence was the term for operations designed to combat espionage by other countries against the United States. Among other things, it included FBI monitoring of Soviet agents stationed in the United States.

● Authorized Defense Department, Office of Personnel Management and CIA access to state and local criminal history records for information used in determining whether federal employees and contractors should have access to classified information or should be assigned to sensitive national security duties. Most states and localities already provided such access. Conferees said juvenile records, investigatory files or records that had been sealed by law or court action were exempt from the requirement.

● Required the president to notify Congress whenever an intelligence agency gave weapons or other military items valued at $1 million or more to a foreign government, group or individual. This would not apply if the arms transfer was authorized under the foreign aid laws or was not connected to an intelligence activity.

● Put into permanent law a series of provisions aimed at ensuring that the intelligence agencies spent money only on activities approved by Congress, and that they notified Congress at least 15 days in advance whenever they shifted money between accounts.

# 1987 Intelligence Authorization

After a one-year hiatus, Congress in 1986 approved legislation (HR 4759 — PL 99-569) giving the CIA and other intelligence agencies a real, after-inflation budget increase for fiscal 1987.

Spending for the intelligence agencies had increased annually from 1978 to 1985 but dipped slightly in 1986 once inflation was taken into account. The increase in 1987 was made possible by exempting the agencies from some of the budget cuts that were imposed on overall Defense Department spending. Actual appropriations for the intelligence agencies, hidden within the Pentagon budget, were made in the defense portion of the omnibus spending bill for fiscal 1987 (H J Res 738 — PL 99-591).

# Angola Aid

With little fanfare, Congress in 1986 gave the go-ahead for the Reagan administration to support a guerrilla war against the Marxist government of Angola.

President Reagan in February 1986 approved a CIA "covert" operation to provide up to $15 million worth of weapons, ammunition and other supplies to a guerrilla faction called the National Union for Total Independence of Angola (UNITA, in the Portuguese acronym).

The Democratic members of the House Intelligence Committee failed in their attempts to kill the aid plan. When separate legislation (HR 4276 — H Rept 99-508, Parts I and II) failed to reach the floor, committee Democrats attached an amendment to the fiscal 1987 intelligence authorization bill (HR 4759) barring further aid to UNITA unless the aid was publicly debated and approved by Congress. In a major victory for Reagan, the full House deleted that amendment Sept. 17 by a **key vote of 229-186 (R 166-7; D 63-179)**. *(1986 key votes, p. 949)*

The House vote completed a transformation of congressional sentiment on the issue. In 1976, Congress cut off a CIA aid program to UNITA; it weakened the ban in 1980 and repealed it in 1985. *(1985 action, p. 188)*

Congress in 1986 also went on record as opposing continued U.S. business dealings with the Angolan government. It included a provision in an Export-Import Bank authorization bill (HR 5548 — PL 99-472) deploring business support for the Angolan government and requesting the president to use his power under the 1979 Export Administration Act (PL 96-72) to restrict business dealings that were in conflict with U.S. security interests. *(Ex-Im, p. 145; PL 96-72, Congress and the Nation Vol. V, p. 274)*

As in the past, most of the bill was kept secret. The most important non-secret provision barred the CIA from using its contingency fund to give aid to the contra guerrillas who were battling to overthrow the leftist government of Nicaragua. *(Contra aid, p. 177)*

During House action on HR 4759, a similar ban on aid to a guerrilla group that was battling the Marxist government of Angola was defeated.

## Legislative Action

The House Intelligence Committee reported HR 4759 (H Rept 99-690, Part I) on July 17. Supplemental reports (Parts II and III) were filed July 28 by the House Post Office and Civil Service and Armed Services committees.

The House Sept. 17 passed HR 4759 by voice vote after rejecting an effort to limit President Reagan's program of covert aid to Angolan guerrillas. *(Box, this page)*

The Senate Intelligence Committee had reported its version of the intelligence bill (S 2477 — S Rept 99-307) on May 21. The Senate passed HR 4759 Sept. 24 by voice vote, after substituting the provisions of its version for those of the House-passed bill.

While acting on the intelligence bill, the Senate approved two amendments by Sen. Jesse Helms, R-N.C., demanding reports from the CIA. The more controversial amendment, adopted 53-46, required the agency to report to Congress on human rights violations, government involvement in drug trafficking and other matters in Panama. The other amendment called for reports to Congress by the CIA and other agencies on a variety of subjects, most dealing with alleged CIA failures to analyze Soviet military capabilities.

The conference report on the bill was filed Oct. 1 (H Rept 99-952). The House approved the report Oct. 2 and the Senate gave its approval Oct. 6, completing congressional action.

**Contingency Funds for Contras.** Aside from spending differences, the major conflict between the House and Senate bills concerned the CIA's right to dip into its secret contingency fund to aid the Nicaraguan contras.

Siding with the House, conferees agreed to bar the CIA from using the contingency fund for that purpose. The issue was important because a limitation on the contingency fund would be the only major congressional stricture on contra aid once Congress approved Reagan's pending request for $100 million in military and non-military support for the Nicaraguan guerrillas. The money was included in an omnibus appropriations bill (H J Res 738) cleared Oct. 17.

Under the intelligence bill's provision, Reagan could use CIA money to aid the contras only if Congress passed another bill allowing him to do so, or if he reprogrammed money to the contras from other programs.

Under normal circumstances, the contingency fund was used to begin "covert action" programs such as aiding anti-communist guerrillas and supporting pro-Western political movements abroad. Reagan used the fund in 1981 and 1982 to launch CIA backing of the contras and again early in 1986 to supply arms and equipment to anti-government guerrillas in Angola.

The amount of money in the fund was one of the government's best-kept secrets, but there had been reports that it was between $50 million and $500 million at any given time. Since 1983, the House Intelligence Committee had tried to bar use of the contingency fund for aid to the contras, and the annual intelligence bills had included such a provision since fiscal 1984.

**Other Issues.** Conferees approved a House-passed provision barring cooperation by U.S. intelligence agencies with the South African government, with some exceptions. The provision was a response to reports in early 1986 that U.S. agencies had shared information with South Africa on the African National Congress and other black opposition groups.

Conferees deleted the two Helms amendments requiring reports from the CIA but the Senate requested in the conference report that the CIA provide the information.

## Major Provisions

As signed into law Oct. 27, 1986, major provisions of HR 4759 (PL 99-569) that were made public:

• Put into permanent law a requirement that intelligence agencies notify Congress in advance of "covert" arms transfers to foreign governments or groups valued at $1 million or more.

• Barred the CIA from using its secret contingency fund to aid the contras. The agency could provide contra aid only if Congress specifically authorized it or if money was reprogrammed or diverted from other CIA programs.

• Barred U.S. intelligence agencies from cooperating "in any fashion" with the government of South Africa, except for activities "reasonably designed to facilitate the collection of necessary intelligence." Neither the public portion of the bill nor the conference report gave a definition of the exception.

The bill also stated U.S. policy that no intelligence agency could provide information to the South African government that pertained to a South African internal opposition group or individual. In their report, conferees said intelligence agencies could provide information to South Africa only if the information "credibly indicates the imminent likelihood of violent action calculated to threaten human life" and providing that information to South Africa "could be expected to contribute to avoidance of that violent action."

• Stated the policy of Congress that the number of personnel permitted at the Soviet Union's mission to the United Nations in New York City could not "substantially exceed" the number of personnel at the U.S. mission. The bill also required reports to Congress on the number of Soviet personnel admitted to the United States for service at the United Nations.

• Authorized $22 million and a personnel limit of 237 for the Intelligence Community Staff, which served the CIA director in his capacity as coordinator of the intelligence agencies.

• Authorized $125.8 million for the CIA retirement and disability fund.

• Gave the FBI mandatory access to state and local criminal records as part of its background investigations for security clearances for government personnel and contract employees. The Defense Department, the CIA and the Office of Personnel Management already had this authority.

• Amended 1978 banking privacy legislation (PL 95-630) to give the FBI, in counterintelligence investigations, authority to subpoena bank records of individuals, companies or other entities suspected of being a foreign power or an agent of a foreign power. The provision pre-empted state and local laws and state constitutional provisions that set stricter privacy protection standards than did the 1978 federal law.

# Genocide Treaty

After almost 37 years of intermittent debate, the Senate in 1986 overcame opposition by conservatives and approved a treaty declaring genocide to be a crime.

The Senate approved ratification of the treaty (Exec. O, 81st Cong., 1st sess.) on Feb. 19 by an 83-11 vote, after a filibuster threat was dropped. But the action was largely symbolic, because "reservations" limiting the treaty's application had been attached in 1985 to defuse opposition by conservatives, who saw the treaty as a threat to American sovereignty and who worried that the Soviet Union — already a signatory — could use it against the United States.

Drafted in response to the Nazi Holocaust, the genocide pact was approved by the United Nations Dec. 9, 1948, and signed by the United States. On June 16, 1949, President Truman first submitted it to the Senate for approval. The Senate failed to approve it, but all subsequent presidents except Dwight D. Eisenhower urged its adoption. President Reagan, however, did not signal his support until shortly before the 1984 elections. After that, the Justice and State departments lobbied in a low-key way for its approval. *(1988 action, p. 250)*

## Controversial Reservations

By most accounts, a confluence of events led to final approval: Reagan's support and the effort by Senate Foreign Relations Chairman Richard G. Lugar, R-Ind., to assuage conservatives' concerns through reservations within the treaty.

These reservations were unilateral declarations that excluded or modified the terms of the treaty and affected only the party entering the reservation. However, other signers would have to acquiesce in the U.S. actions. According to the 1985 Foreign Relations Committee report on the treaty (Exec Rept 99-2), the practice of reservations was widespread, and the document noted that a number of signatories had entered reservations to the genocide pact.

The most important reservation was one giving the United States the right to exempt itself from compulsory jurisdiction in genocide treaty cases before the World Court, formally known as the International Court of Justice.

The administration opposed such a reservation in 1984, but it changed course in 1985, apparently because the World Court asserted jurisdiction in a suit filed by Nicaragua against the United States over the CIA's mining of Nicaraguan harbors.

The Foreign Relations Committee said the reservation would allow the United States to protect itself if World Court jurisdiction were sought for a case that was "brought solely for the propaganda value that might result."

Supporters of the treaty had strenuously opposed the provision, contending that it would weaken U.S. efforts to bring genocide charges before the court. They said another nation could resist the World Court's jurisdiction by noting that the United States, itself, was not compelled to come before the court.

The other controversial reservation attached by the committee stated that nothing in the treaty required the United States to take any action that might be prohibited by the U.S. Constitution.

The committee majority said the language was intended to "avoid placing the United States in a position of having to choose between its obligations under the Constitution and those under the [treaty]."

Opponents said the reservation was not needed because the genocide treaty did not conflict with the Constitution.

Despite supporters' concerns about the additional language, they conceded that the reservations were necessary to get final action on the treaty. And it was Lugar's willingness in 1985 to deal with Jesse Helms, R-N.C., long the treaty's staunchest opponent, that broke the committee logjam. But when leaders tried to take the treaty to the Senate floor in 1985, Helms objected and threatened a filibuster — thus killing it for another year.

## Major Provisions

As approved by the Senate Feb. 19, 1986, the genocide treaty:

● Declared genocide to be a crime under international law and instructed treaty signers to prevent and punish the crime.

● Defined genocide as the intentional destruction of national, ethnic, racial or religious groups and covered attempts to kill members of these groups, cause serious bodily or mental harm to members of the groups, deliberately inflict conditions upon these groups designed to physically destroy them, impose measures intended to prevent births within the groups and forcibly transfer children of a protected group to another group.

● Specified that the crimes covered included genocide, conspiracy to commit genocide, direct and public incitement to commit genocide, attempt to commit genocide and complicity in genocide.

● Provided that persons who committed genocide should be punished, whether they were "constitutionally responsible rulers, public officials or private individuals."

● Specified that genocide would not be considered a "political" crime for purposes of extradition, and provided that parties to the treaty would "pledge" to grant extradition to the requesting country in accordance with existing extradition treaties.

The Senate added a "proviso" making clear that extradition would be granted only in cases in which the activity was a crime in the United States as well as in the requesting country.

● Provided for trial within the territory in which the act was committed or by an international tribunal with jurisdiction over the person charged.

● Provided that disputes between parties to the treaty be submitted to the World Court. The Senate reservation declared that the United States had the right to refuse jurisdiction when it determined that going before the international tribunal would not be in the national interest.

# Micronesia Compact

Congress in 1985 passed the Compact of Free Association with Micronesia, a measure to bestow limited autonomy on the sole remaining U.S. trust territory in the Pacific.

The compact (H J Res 187 — PL 99-239) provided about $2.4 billion over 15 years in aid and tax and trade benefits in return for exclusive and permanent U.S. military rights to the island region.

Congress' action came after an Oct. 1 deadline to approve the compact; that was the expiration date for the U.S. lease on the Kwajalein missile range in the Marshall Islands. Kwajalein was the Pentagon's most important facility for testing the MX missile and parts of the administration's proposed anti-missile defense program. As a result of the delay in Congress, some missile tests at Kwajalein were postponed.

Of larger significance was the islands' strategic importance in the region. Pentagon officials wanted to maintain good U.S.-Micronesia relations in light of a growing communist insurgency in the Philippines, the site of two huge U.S. military bases serving the Pacific. (Philippines, p. 184)

Both houses of Congress made numerous changes in the compact to tighten up trade and tariff concessions negotiated by the administration. Lawmakers feared original terms of the compact would create a new tax haven for wealthy Americans and a major trade loophole for Asian imports.

The House passed its version of the compact (H Rept 99-188, Parts I-IV) on July 25 by a vote of 360-12. The Senate approved H J Res 187 by voice vote Nov. 14 after amending it to conform to its version (S J Res 77 — S Rept 99-16).

The House Dec. 11 approved a substitute text that incorporated numerous changes agreed to by the administration; the Senate accepted the changes Dec. 13.

President Reagan signed PL 99-239 Jan. 14, 1986. The compact still had to be reviewed by the island governments and endorsed by the United Nations before it took effect.

## Background

Largely undeveloped, Micronesia encompassed about 130,000 residents and 2,000 islands spread over three million square miles. The nearest islands to Hawaii were about 2,000 miles to the west. The territory consisted of four governments: Northern Mariana Islands, the Federated States of Micronesia, the Marshall Islands and Palau.

The United States became the administrator of the Micronesian islands in 1947 under a trusteeship arranged by the United Nations. Bikini and Enewetok atolls subsequently were used by the Pentagon as nuclear target ranges.

A 1976 accord granted commonwealth status to the Northern Mariana Islands. (Congress and the Nation Vol. IV, p. 887)

In 1982-83, the United States agreed, after negotiations with each of the other three governments, to set up a new relationship that was detailed in the Compact of Free Association.

The compact was approved by the voters of all three units, but the 67 percent majority it received in Palau did not satisfy requirements of the Palau Constitution. In 1979, Palau had adopted a constitution banning all nuclear ships or weapons from their territory, unless 75 percent of the voters in Palau agreed to overturn the ban. The Reagan administration had opposed the ban and included provisions in the compact allowing a limited U.S. nuclear presence if needed. The result was a stalemate. (1988 action, p. 249)

## Major Provisions

As cleared, H J Res 187:

● Granted sovereign status as "freely associated states" (FAS) to the Federated States of Micronesia and the Marshall Islands, with self-government under their own constitutions and authority to conduct their own foreign policy in consultation with the United States.

● Committed the United States to defend the FAS for at least 15 years.

● Required the United States to provide $2.39 billion in aid, primarily economic assistance, to the FAS over the 15 years.

● Gave the United States a 30-year lease on the Kwajalein missile range.

● Granted the United States the right in perpetuity to deny other nations a military presence in the region.

● Established a $150 million trust fund to settle all claims against the United States resulting from nuclear weapons tests in the region in the 1940s and 1950s. (About $5 billion worth of lawsuits were pending.)

● Provided duty-free treatment for goods from Micronesia, except watches, clocks, certain timing devices, buttons, textile and apparel articles, footwear, handbags, luggage, work gloves and leather apparel.

● Exempted from tariff Micronesian canned, water-packed tuna, up to 10 percent of total U.S. consumption, or about 80 million pounds a year. Tuna was the region's chief export.

● Established a $30 million aid package to compensate for other tax and trade benefits cut by Congress.

● Included the government of Palau on a contingency basis, to expedite congressional approval if Palau's residents endorsed the compact.

## Chinese Nuclear Accord

Congress in 1985 approved a 30-year agreement providing for the sale of nuclear fuel, equipment or technology to China, in spite of widespread concern on Capitol Hill that the agreement did not contain tough enough provisions to ensure Chinese cooperation in halting the spread of nuclear weapons. Congress adopted a resolution (S J Res 238 — PL 99-183) approving the agreement but imposing conditions on nuclear exports to China.

The agreement was the first nuclear agreement between the United States and a communist country, and the first bilateral nuclear accord with another country that acknowledged possessing nuclear weapons.

The formal agreement between the United States and China was signed July 23. Final approval of the accord followed months of negotiations between officials of the two countries, as the United States sought to allay its concerns about China's role in providing nuclear materials and technology to countries seeking to develop their own nuclear weapons. According to press reports, China had provided Pakistan with plans for construction of a nuclear bomb. It also was a major supplier of nuclear power equipment to other countries, such as Argentina and Brazil.

The 1978 nuclear non-proliferation act (PL 95-242) barred the United States from selling nuclear supplies to any country that had "assisted, encouraged or induced" any other country to obtain nuclear weapons and that had failed to make "sufficient progress" toward ending such a relationship. Eventually, U.S. officials proclaimed themselves satisfied with public and private assurances from the Chinese that they would not help other countries acquire nuclear weapons capabilities. *(PL 95-242, Congress and the Nation Vol. V, p. 147)*

U.S. officials said the agreement prohibited China from using American-supplied equipment or technology for building weapons. In addition, the agreement allowed the United States to inspect facilities where any U.S.-supplied equipment was located.

The Senate approved S J Res 238 by voice vote Nov. 21 and the House cleared it for the president Dec. 11 by a 307-112 vote. There was considerable opposition to the resolution from both liberals and conservatives. However, the measure cleared because members realized the agreement would go into effect without any conditions if Congress failed to act.

Under non-proliferation and export control laws (PL

## China Arms Sale

The Senate Foreign Relations Committee on May 1, 1986, rejected a resolution (S J Res 331) that sought to block a sale of $550 million worth of electronic gear for China's F-8 warplanes — Chinese-built versions of the Soviet MiG-23.

The resolution, sponsored by Jesse Helms, R-N.C., was rejected on a 1-14 vote. At Helms' request, the committee then unanimously reported the resolution to the Senate floor with an unfavorable recommendation (S Rept 99-293). There was no further action before the May 7 deadline for Congress to act on the deal.

The sale was the largest ever to the People's Republic of China, and Helms argued that it would upset the balance of power in the region, posing a particular threat to Taiwan.

Congress in 1985 raised no objection to the first major arms sale to China: $98 million worth of equipment and designs for plants to produce ammunition and explosives.

95-242, PL 99-64), the agreement was to go into effect in 90 legislative days unless Congress passed, and the president signed, a joint resolution blocking it.

A subsequent attempt to impose tougher conditions on nuclear exports to China failed in December, when conferees on the fiscal 1986 continuing appropriations resolution (H J Res 465 — PL 99-190) deleted a Senate-passed amendment that would require China to accept international standards for ensuring the peaceful use of all its nuclear power facilities.

### Major Provisions

As cleared by Congress, S J Res 238 stated that Congress favored the agreement. It also stated that no transfer to China of nuclear materials, facilities or components could take place until 30 days of continuous congressional session after the president had certified to Congress:

● That the United States and China had made arrangements that were "designed to be effective" in ensuring that any nuclear supplies provided China would be used solely for "intended peaceful purposes." Such arrangements normally included exchanges of information, inspections of nuclear plants by the supplying country or by the International Atomic Energy Agency (IAEA) and standards for keeping track of nuclear materials. However, neither the agreement nor the resolution specifically required IAEA inspections or adherence to other IAEA arrangements, as some critics had wanted.

● That the Chinese government had provided "additional information" about its nuclear non-proliferation policies and that, based on this and all other information available to the U.S. government, China was not in violation of provisions in the 1978 non-proliferation law that would require termination of the nuclear supply agreement.

• That a clause in the agreement obligating the United States to "consider favorably" a Chinese request for permission to enrich or reprocess U.S.-supplied nuclear fuel would not prejudice the U.S. decision on whether to approve or deny such a request. Enriching uranium and reprocessing fuel were two ways of obtaining the necessary ingredients for nuclear weapons.

The resolution further barred nuclear licenses or transfers to China until the president sent Congress a report detailing the history and current developments of China's nuclear non-proliferation policies.

# Extradition Treaty, Irish Aid

The Senate in 1986 approved a long-stalled treaty setting new standards for extraditions between the United States and the United Kingdom. The impasse on the treaty was broken after it became linked with legislation (HR 4329 — PL 99-415) that authorized $120 million in economic aid in fiscal 1986-88 for Northern Ireland and parts of the Republic of Ireland.

The main purpose of the treaty (Treaty Doc 99-8) was to make it easier for Great Britain to extradite from the United States members of the outlawed Irish Republican Army (IRA), which sought to end British rule in Northern Ireland. President Reagan had asked for quick Senate approval of the treaty as a sign of gratitude to Prime Minister Margaret Thatcher for her support of the April 14 U.S. bombing raid against Libya. *(Libya attack, p. 199)*

Senate action on the treaty had been thwarted by a variety of factors. These included vigorous lobbying against the pact by Irish-American groups and charges that Britain's courts were prejudiced against those accused of anti-British acts in the longstanding conflict in Northern Ireland.

Foreign Relations Committee Chairman Richard G. Lugar, R-Ind., finally was able to press action on the treaty by delaying Senate action on an Irish aid bill until a deal was struck with Democratic opponents of the treaty.

## Treaty

Signed by U.S. and British officials on June 25, 1985, the treaty was sought by the British government, which had been unable to extradite members of the IRA who had sought refuge in the United States. Some had been accused of violent crimes, including murder.

Under an existing treaty between the two countries, such persons could avoid extradition by convincing a U.S. court that their crimes were political. Known as the political offense exception, this provision was included in U.S. extradition agreements with a number of countries.

As sent to the Senate, the treaty removed violent crimes, such as murder, kidnapping and bombing, from the list of offenses that could be claimed as politically protected. That would have taken away the authority of U.S. judges to refuse extradition of persons accused of such crimes.

The Senate Foreign Relations Committee approved the extradition treaty (Exec Rept 99-17) June 12 after delicate negotiations to resolve major Democratic objections while preserving the treaty's intent.

At the insistence of some Democrats, the panel included a section that would allow U.S. courts to deny extradition if the accused would "be prejudiced at his trial or punished, detained or restricted in his personal liberty by reason of his race, religion, nationality or political opinions." The original treaty had given the president the authority to deny extradition on such grounds, but critics insisted that U.S. courts retain a role in handling extradition cases.

The Senate on July 17 approved the extradition treaty by an 87-10 vote, far above the two-thirds majority required for consent to ratification of a treaty.

The Senate amendments were subject to approval by the British Parliament. A British diplomatic source said his government did not object to the new language.

## Irish Aid

Sponsors of the Irish aid package said the aid would demonstrate U.S. support for a landmark accord on the future of Northern Ireland that was reached in November 1985 between Great Britain and the Republic of Ireland. That accord gave Ireland a say in governing Northern Ireland, which had been under British rule for 64 years. Ulster, the traditional name for Northern Ireland, had been caught for many years in a cycle of violence between the pro-British Protestant majority and the region's Irish Catholic minority, which wanted to end British rule. Aid supporters said the United States could help promote peace and reconciliation in Northern Ireland by assisting the economically depressed Ulster get on its feet while the accord took effect.

The administration had proposed $20 million in aid annually for five years. The House passed a $250 million, five-year version (HR 4329) on March 11 by voice vote.

The Senate passed a compromise version of HR 4329 by voice vote Aug. 13. The House accepted the Senate version Aug. 14.

The compromise, which had been developed without a formal Senate-House conference, authorized $50 million for fiscal 1986 and $35 million annually for fiscal 1987-88 for an international fund to support and promote economic and social reconstruction and development in Northern Ireland and parts of the Republic of Ireland affected by the sectarian strife. The higher authorization for fiscal 1986 reflected the fact that Congress already had appropriated that amount in a supplemental appropriations bill (HR 4515 — PL 99-349) signed July 2.

HR 4329 authorized additional aid under certain foreign aid loan and loan guarantee programs.

# U.S.-Iceland Treaty

Acting with unaccustomed speed, the Senate Oct. 8, 1986, approved a treaty (Treaty Doc 99-31) between the United States and Iceland. The Senate acted just eight days after getting the measure from the White House so that President Reagan could carry it with him to a "presummit" meeting in Iceland with Soviet leader Mikhail S. Gorbachev. *(Story, p. 343)*

Approved by voice vote with no debate, the treaty allowed both U.S. and Icelandic shipping firms to compete for the business of carrying huge quantities of U.S. military cargo to a major NATO air base at Keflavik, Iceland.

Under U.S. cargo preference laws, an American company had gotten most of the shipping business since 1984, angering Iceland. In a Sept. 30 letter to the Senate, Reagan said the dispute "could impair the critical U.S.-Icelandic defense relationship."

The Senate floor action came less than two hours after the treaty had been reported by the Foreign Relations Committee.

# 1987-88

After seven years in office, President Reagan achieved what many observers believed was his most significant foreign policy accomplishment — the signing of a U.S.-Soviet treaty eliminating intermediate-range nuclear-force (INF) missiles. But it came at the end of a year dominated by a scandal that was regarded as the low point of his administration.

Reagan and his aides spent most of 1987 battling the damage caused by the Iran-contra affair, particularly the congressional hearings that exposed the deceit and fumbling at the White House that the president was unable or unwilling to control. The revelations seriously undermined Reagan's credibility and highlighted the difficulty he had in carrying out an agenda that did not have broad public support. *(Iran-contra affair, p. 253)*

Reagan failed to get renewed congressional support for one of his highest priorities: backing the contra guerrillas in Nicaragua. In 1987, he had to settle for stopgap infusions of aid, while the pro-U.S. countries of Central America tried diplomacy as a means of convincing the Nicaraguan regime to reform. In 1988, Reagan essentially washed his hands of the issue, after the House handed him a major defeat by refusing to renew military aid to the contras.

The 100th Congress continued to wrest from the president power over key foreign policy tools such as foreign aid and arms sales.

By 1988, Congress was earmarking spending on more than 90 percent of key foreign aid accounts, and pro-Israel senators were forcing the administration to negotiate the tiniest details of proposed arms sales to Arab countries. Major arms sales to Saudi Arabia and Kuwait went through only after the administration yielded to congressional pressure and modified the arms packages.

The normally routine State Department authorization measure in 1987 became a magnet for amendments stating positions on U.S.-Soviet relations, the United Nations, the Palestine Liberation Organization and other issues.

Congress in 1987 sidestepped one its most ticklish foreign aid issues, that of expressing unhappiness with Pakistan's refusal to drop its reported development of nuclear weapons. The administration essentially won its case for the first installment of a new aid program for Pakistan.

Some efforts in Congress to set out an independent foreign policy course failed, especially moves to impose sanctions against Iraq and South Africa. However, those initiatives were blocked for partisan or procedural reasons, not because of Reagan's political clout.

## Short-Term Contra Aid

For the first time in the Reagan presidency, the United States in 1987 found itself little more than a bystander in Central America. Buffeted for years by political battles

---

## CIA Leadership

In 1987, William H. Webster, FBI chief since 1978 and a former U.S. district court judge, succeeded William J. Casey as director of central intelligence. Casey had resigned Feb. 2, 1987, and died on May 6. *(Webster background, p. 1049; Casey background, Congress and the Nation Vol. VI, p. 1025)*

Webster was enormously popular on Capitol Hill, and the Senate May 19 overwhelmingly confirmed his nomination, 94-1, despite some questions about his failure as FBI director to act on evidence of Lt. Col. Oliver L. North's dealings on behalf of the Nicaraguan contra rebels. *(Iran-contra affair, p. 253)*

Webster was succeeded at the FBI by U.S. District Judge William S. Sessions. *(Sessions background, p. 1049)*

---

between Congress and President Reagan, leaders in the troubled region took the initiative to settle their own disputes. They made halting progress in carrying out an unprecedented peace agreement intended, in large part, to resolve the U.S.-backed contra war against Nicaragua's leftist Sandinista regime.

The rush of diplomatic maneuvering in Central America affected not only the geopolitics of the region, but also the politics of Washington. The prospect of peace killed for 1987 the chance that Congress would grant Reagan's wish for a major infusion of new military aid to the Nicaraguan rebels, as it had the year before. And it set the stage for the Democratic leadership of the House to take charge of the contra issue, at least temporarily, in early 1988.

In the final moments of the year's session, Capitol Hill gave Reagan a short-term victory on the hard-fought issue. Passing an omnibus continuing appropriations resolution (H J Res 395 — PL 100-202) for fiscal 1988, Congress allowed the president to spend more than $14 million in "humanitarian" and logistical aid for supplies and services for the contras through February 1988. But Congress also set procedures for votes early in 1988 on the issue, paving the way for House Democrats to defeat on Feb. 3, 1988, a Reagan request for $36.25 million in new military and nonmilitary aid. *(1988 action, p. 213)*

The stopgap $14 million approved at the end of 1987 was on top of smaller chunks of non-military aid Capitol Hill gave the contras through short-term continuing appropriations resolutions. Congress in September had approved $3.5 million in humanitarian aid as part of one catchall bill (H J Res 362 — PL 100-120). In November, Congress had cleared H J Res 394 (PL 100-162), containing about $3.2 million more to give the rebels food, clothing, medicine and other non-military items through mid-December.

In his January 1987 budget, Reagan had asked for $105 million for renewed military and non-military aid to the contras — far less than the $300 million to $400 million that contra leaders and some administration officials had wanted.

Contra aid for years had been one of the most closely divided issues in Congress, usually decided by a handful of votes in the House. In 1986, Reagan won congressional support for a resumption of the program, to the tune of $100 million. *(1986 action, p. 177)*

Revelations that White House officials had approved the diversion to the contras of money from arms sales to Iran and helped resupply the rebels when Congress had prohibited aid reinforced the determination of congressional opponents to cut off contra aid.

But the revelations also reinforced the convictions of many contra supporters. *(Iran-contra affair, p. 253)*

Liberals tried in March 1987 to block release of the last installment of the fiscal 1987 contra money. The House voted to impose a moratorium on spending the final $40 million, but a similar move was blocked in the Senate.

**Peace Accord.** Reagan wanted to press ahead and ask Congress for a dose of $270 million in new contra assistance. He backed off that plan, however, in the wake of a key development: the unveiling of the regional peace plan by five Central American presidents in Guatemala City on Aug. 7.

The regional pact was reached two days after the White House published its own peace plan, written with the cooperation of House Speaker Jim Wright, D-Texas. *(Wright's role, box, p. 211)*

The Guatemala City plan called for an end to civil wars in the region, a cutoff of aid to insurgencies and establishment of full-scale democracies. The chief architect of the pact, Costa Rican President Oscar Arias, later won the 1987 Nobel Peace Prize for his work on the agreement.

On a broad policy level, the Aug. 7 peace agreement undercut U.S. influence by putting important decisions in the hands of leaders in the region. At the same time, it jeopardized the central tenet of Reagan policy toward the region: that the United States would not tolerate a pro-Soviet regime on the mainland of the Western Hemisphere.

Although the accord called for peace and democracy in every Central American country, the practical result was to focus attention on ending the contra war in Nicaragua, with lesser emphasis on leftist insurgencies in El Salvador and Guatemala.

The accord allowed no active U.S. role other than to cut off aid to the contras. The administration insisted that it was not bound to do so until after the Sandinistas met all their obligations. But that position won little support in the region; even the presidents who were most dependent on backing from the United States, José Napoleón Duarte of El Salvador and José Azcona of Honduras, wanted contra aid halted until January 1988.

**Stopgap Aid.** The Aug. 7 peace agreement strongly increased pressure on Congress to stop aiding the contras.

But by year's end, the mood on Capitol Hill shifted again, prompting Congress to approve some assistance to the anti-Sandinista rebels. The reason for this change was the publication of revelations by Maj. Roger Miranda, a defecting top Nicaraguan military official. Miranda told U.S. officials and reporters that the Sandinistas planned to build up their military forces, including reserves, to 500,000 by the mid-1990s. He also claimed that the Sandinistas wanted to subvert the regional peace process, using the prospect of negotiations to undermine support for the contras.

By approving the $14 million in stopgap money, Congress showed its reluctance to end all support of the Nica-

raguan rebels. And it created a test of whether the Sandinista regime would respond to continued military pressure exerted by the contras. Congress elected not to take further action on the contra aid issue until after the five Central American presidents discussed the peace process at a meeting in mid-January 1988.

After the Central American presidents signed the Aug. 7, 1987, peace accord, the Sandinistas agreed to hold indirect talks with and made limited concessions to their political foes. But the peace process, mediated by Cardinal Miguel Obando y Bravo, Nicaragua's Roman Catholic leader, made uneven progress.

Reagan and his aides argued that the Sandinistas would make additional political concessions only if they remained threatened by the contras. The short-term contra aid agreement approved by Congress Dec. 22 was crafted, in large part, to keep military pressure on Managua.

## Moratorium Attempt Failed

Before debate began on Reagan's fiscal 1988 request, liberals in Congress tried unsuccessfully to block release of the final installment of contra aid that had been approved in 1986 for fiscal 1987.

Under the fiscal 1987 spending law (H J Res 738 — PL 99-591), Congress could block expenditure of the final $40 million of the $100 million approved by passing a joint resolution, which would be subject to a presidential veto. Even staunch opponents of contra aid conceded they did not have the two-thirds' vote necessary to override Reagan's certain veto. So the effort to block the money was widely seen as a symbolic one, with the real fight to come later on Reagan's new contra aid request. Congress' failure to block the $40 million allowed Reagan to give the contras "heavy" weapons such as artillery. Since the fall of 1986, U.S. aid had been limited to rifles and other "light" armaments.

**House Action.** On March 5, Reagan formally certified to Congress that the remaining $40 million in fiscal 1987 funding should be sent to the contras.

On March 11, the House approved legislation (H J Res 175) freezing the $40 million for up to six months while money previously given the contras was accounted for. This included $27 million in humanitarian aid approved by Congress in 1985, any funds that might have been diverted to the contras from the sale of U.S. arms to Iran in 1985-86 and any other contra aid from private donors or third countries that U.S. officials might have helped arrange. *(Humanitarian aid, p. 173)*

After the president reported on how the money was spent, Congress would have to pass a joint resolution lifting the moratorium before the $40 million could go to the rebels.

Financial records for the contras made public March 5 showed that the rebels received about $32 million from non-American sources from July 1984 to March 1985 and that $18 million was spent on weapons and other equipment. During much of that time, direct U.S. aid was banned. Sources said most of the money came from Saudi Arabia's royal family.

The financial documents were released by Adolfo Calero, head of the Nicaraguan Democratic Force (FDN), the rebels' main military faction. The FDN also reportedly received $200,000 in October 1985 from a Swiss bank account controlled by former National Security Council

(NSC) aide Lt. Col. Oliver L. North. The money came from Lake Resources Inc., which was set up by North and retired Air Force Maj. Gen. Richard V. Secord, who assisted North in the Iran-contra dealings.

H J Res 175 was approved 230-196; contra aid opponents did not have enough votes to override a veto. Although the moratorium had no chance of becoming law, the 34-vote margin by which it passed pointed to substantial erosion of contra support. The House voted 221-209 in June 1986 for the $100 million package.

A Republican attempt to pre-empt the moratorium issue by introducing a resolution disapproving the $40 million and seeking a vote on that measure got swept aside by the Democrats' plan.

The House debate featured familiar arguments that both sides of the contra issue had raised before.

Contra supporters insisted that the United States should maintain support for the rebels to block the spread of communism and Soviet influence in Central America.

Opponents, however, faulted the contras' inability to sustain a successful military campaign against the Sandinistas. These members said the Reagan administration instead should have thrown its weight behind attempts to reach a peaceful settlement.

In addition, the Iran-contra scandal and a shakeup of the Nicaraguan rebels' political leadership — which signaled sharp conflicts among the contra leaders — raised questions in Congress about continuing support for the contras.

Supporters of the moratorium said the United States had an obligation to track the money already provided to the contras before it released additional funds. Many also charged that millions of dollars could not be traced, raising questions about misuse.

Opponents, however, said the accounting issue was offered only as a thin excuse to cut off aid.

**Senate Action.** Administration supporters in the Senate filibustered the House moratorium measure that required a presidential accounting of contra aid. But on March 18 the Senate voted on a resolution (S J Res 81) barring release of the $40 million. And as expected, the Senate rejected it, 48-52.

Senate opponents of contra aid tried a week later to enact the House-passed aid moratorium but lacked the strength to prevail. Supporters of contra aid easily defeated three attempts to shut off a Republican filibuster against the moratorium legislation (H J Res 175).

By failing to invoke cloture, the Democratic-controlled Senate shelved the proposal and paved the way for Reagan to spend the remaining $40 million in fiscal 1987 contra aid.

Advocates of a moratorium cited the administration's Iran-contra scandal as proof that no one was sure what had happened to funds destined for the contras.

But supporters of the contras said the moratorium would violate U.S. promises to deliver previously approved aid.

### Iran-Contra Hearings

By May, the focus of attention on the Nicaraguan issue had shifted from contra aid to the House-Senate Iran-contra hearings and the revelations of the administration's support of efforts to keep the rebels supplied at a time when Congress had prohibited aid.

Throughout the nationally televised hearings, some of

# Wright Moves to Limelight

While 1987 was the year that influence over events in Central America slipped from the grasp of President Reagan to political leaders in the region, it also marked the emergence of a dominant player on the issue on Capitol Hill: the new House Speaker, Jim Wright, D-Texas.

As cosigner with Reagan of an Aug. 5 peace plan that helped spark a peace agreement between Central American presidents two days later, Wright put his considerable legislative muscle behind a policy of letting Central Americans work out their problems.

But Wright's ensuing intervention in the Nicaraguan peace talks stirred up a round of controversy in Washington: The Reagan administration and some members of Congress accused him of infringing on the president's diplomatic prerogatives.

Some of the concern focused on the fact that Wright met with Nicaraguan President Daniel Ortega and other Nicaraguan officials privately in Washington and said nothing about his activities for two days, until holding a press conference Nov. 13.

The Reagan administration had refused for more than two years to meet officially with representatives of the leftist Nicaraguan government.

Sen. John McCain, R-Ariz., called the Speaker's activities "at best unseemly and at worst unconstitutional."

The administration-Wright feud featured caustic comments from both sides before it was patched up publicly on Nov. 17, with Secretary of State George P. Shultz and the Speaker reading a six-point rhetorical cease-fire.

All the points either restated existing administration policy or advocated non-controversial positions. Their rapprochement helped the administration's campaign to continue non-lethal aid to the contras in the short term. Continued bickering between the two camps would have derailed the aid.

Over the long haul, the declaration of peace between Shultz and Wright had the potential to restore the Reagan administration's position as an important actor in Central America policy. Wright had pursued discussions with the Nicaraguans largely because the administration — disliking many elements of the peace plan — had refused to help the countries of Central America implement it.

By mending fences with Wright after such a public disagreement, Shultz was attempting to demonstrate that the administration really was interested in the peace process that Wright so actively embraced.

Reagan's allies seized upon the opportunity to promote contra aid, but opponents of such aid refused to respond in kind. Key Democrats on the House and Senate committees investigating the Iran-contra affair generally declined to debate the merits of U.S. policy in Central America. Instead, they focused on constitutional and legal questions.

Democrats' reticence was most conspicuous while Lt. Col. North, the former NSC aide who played a pivotal role in the Iran-contra affair, was before the panels in July. North's six days of testimony included lengthy discourses in defense of the contras. *(Details, pp. 253, 265)*

## Peace Process Effects

The political calculations about Reagan's battle for Capitol Hill support of contra aid were upset a month later by the renewed efforts for a Central America peace settlement.

On Aug. 5, the White House unveiled a peace plan for Central America, largely drafted by House Speaker Wright, which drew strongly skeptical reactions from critics as well as supporters of contra aid.

First, the plan called for a cease-fire between the leftist Sandinista government and the rebels, to be accompanied by political freedoms.

Simultaneously, U.S. military aid to the contras would be halted and Nicaragua would stop accepting arms aid from the Soviet Union or its allies.

While loath to break publicly with Wright, stunned opponents of contra aid — including most leading House Democrats — worried at first that the proposal was a political trap. As the Reagan team fleshed out the details, they feared the package would be unacceptable to the Sandinistas, setting the stage for a failure that the administration would exploit later in seeking more contra aid.

But two days later, Wright dropped a second bombshell that changed the political climate: Officials of Nicaragua and four other Central American states meeting in Guatemala City had agreed on a peace plan of their own, which Wright warmly endorsed.

The Guatemala City package, based on a plan proposed in February by Costa Rican President Arias, was similar to Wright's plan in that both called for a cease-fire simultaneously with agreement that no country would assist an insurgency against another.

But unlike Wright's plan, the Guatemala deal did not require Nicaragua to forswear Soviet bloc military aid.

At Wright's insistence, Reagan agreed to hold off campaigning for new contra aid up to Sept. 30, while the peace plan was being put into effect.

In deciding how to respond to the Aug. 7 agreement, the administration faced a fundamental question about the direction of one of its most controversial policies. In spite of its rhetoric about wanting merely to force negotiations between the contras and the Sandinistas, the administration's clear aim was to use the contras to oust the Nicaraguan government. But the Aug. 7 agreement was widely interpreted as allowing the Sandinistas to retain power, although with greater freedom allowed to the internal opposition.

**Temporary Aid.** Seeking to soothe both sides of the contra aid dispute, Wright in mid-September fashioned a plan to continue humanitarian aid temporarily; $3.5 million would be funneled to the contras for 40 days beginning Oct. 1, 1987, when the existing $100 million appropriation expired.

In drafting the plan, Wright and other Democratic leaders sought to avoid charges of abandoning the contras, even though they said they opposed further military aid to the rebels.

The new money was included in a catchall continuing resolution (H J Res 362 — PL 100-120) that funded government programs from Oct. 1 until Nov. 10. The stopgap measure was approved by the House Sept. 23 on a 270-138 vote, after a short debate. Two days later, the Senate cleared the measure, 70-27.

**Aid Request Postponed.** On Sept. 22, Nicaraguan President Daniel Ortega announced steps to demonstrate his country's compliance with the peace accord. The steps included a partial cease-fire and easing of restrictions on news media.

But in a hard-line speech Oct. 7, Reagan set standards virtually impossible for Nicaragua to meet by the peace agreement's Nov. 7 deadline. And the White House served notice that regardless of what Nicaragua did, Reagan would ask Congress for $270 million in new aid to the contras.

Administration officials insisted that Reagan's statement proposing more contra aid was intended to keep "pressure" on the Sandinistas to implement the peace agreement.

But Reagan's aid plans were dealt a blow when the Nov. 7 compliance deadline slipped until mid-January 1988. Warned by Capitol Hill leaders that any aid request in the fall of 1987 would be rejected, the White House on Oct. 28 reversed course and decided to delay the request until January 1988. The Sandinista government's Nov. 5 agreement to indirect negotiations with the contra guerrillas breathed new life into the troubled peace plan and further undermined Reagan's hopes of sustaining the contras as a fighting force.

**Additional Aid.** Members of Congress, however, continued to support small doses of contra aid pending the outcome of the peace accord.

At the request of the Reagan administration, Congress on Nov. 6 approved about $3.2 million to supply the contras with food, clothing, medicine and other non-military items through mid-December. The money was in a short-term continuing appropriations resolution (H J Res 394 — PL 100-162) that ran from Nov. 10 to Dec. 16.

**Reagan Backs Regional Talks.** After weeks of sniping at the Central American peace agreement, the Reagan administration moved Nov. 9 to embrace it — apparently to counter any possibility that it could be blamed if the talks collapsed.

Reagan announced that the United States was willing to negotiate security issues with Nicaragua, but only in the presence of representatives from four other Central American countries. That announcement, made to a meeting of foreign ministers at the Organization of American States (OAS), amounted to a major concession by the administration, which had refused since 1984 to negotiate anything directly with the Sandinistas.

Ortega, however, blasted Reagan for refusing to hold direct, bilateral talks with his government.

## Short-Term Aid Compromise

With the Central American peace process still unresolved by year's end, Congress decided to postpone sweeping action on the issue until 1988. As part of the omnibus fiscal 1988 appropriations bill (H J Res 395 — PL 100-202), Congress approved at least $14 million worth of continued supplies and services through February 1988 for the contras and mandated votes in Congress in February on additional funding.

H J Res 395, as approved by the House Dec. 3, contained no contra funds.

But during the weekend of Dec. 12-13 the State Department dropped a bombshell that radically altered the political picture in Washington: It allowed news organizations to interview the high-ranking Sandinista defector, Maj. Roger Miranda, who disclosed Nicaraguan plans for an enormous military buildup and who maintained that the government was seeking to subvert the peace process.

Congressional leaders said Miranda's statements — while not surprising because they echoed many previous reports — gave the administration a strong argument to use with members wavering on the issue. House votes on contra aid always had been settled by razor-thin margins, and both sides assumed that Miranda could sway the necessary handful of members toward Reagan's side.

Less than a week after the Miranda disclosures, the Democratic-run Senate adopted an amendment to the continuing resolution providing some $15 million in aid and logistical services for the contras. The same day, Dec. 11, the Senate defeated two attempts to restrict contra aid.

The Senate's approval of a new package put House leaders in a difficult position, forcing them to negotiate a compromise with the Senate that had to include some contra aid.

After three days of negotiations, congressional leaders and White House representatives on Dec. 20 worked out a complicated agreement to continue aid from the United States to the Nicaraguan contra guerrillas through February 1988.

The agreement also established a procedure by which Reagan could request additional contra aid, and Congress would be obligated to act on that request.

Congress adopted the contra aid agreement on Dec. 22 as part of an omnibus continuing appropriations resolution.

Major provisions of H J Res 395:

**Aid Provisions.** Provided at least $14 million for aid and transportation expenses on behalf of the contras, through Feb. 29, 1988: $3.6 million for humanitarian supplies; $4.5 million to transport the non-military aid, as well as previously purchased military aid; and about $6 million to give the CIA equipment to jam the Sandinistas' anti-aircraft radar. In addition, the bill authorized an unspecified amount — said to be about $2.8 million — to indemnify the government against the possible loss of or damage to planes transporting the aid.

● Placed restrictions on the transport of military aid during regional peace talks and in the event of a cease-fire.

**Congressional Procedures.** Allowed the president to ask Congress for additional aid to the contras no earlier than Jan. 25, 1988, and no later than Jan. 27. The bill set procedures for a House vote on a joint resolution to approve the president's request on Feb. 3 and a Senate vote on Feb. 4.

If Congress had approved the request in February — which it did not — the bill would have allowed the president to submit another request in the third quarter of 1988 and both houses would have had to act by Sept. 30.

● Repealed a provision of the fiscal 1987 continuing appropriations resolution (PL 99-591) that established, in permanent law, the expedited congressional procedures for action on a presidential request for contra aid. That provision was replaced with the requirement for one, or two, votes during 1988.

**Other Restrictions.** Extended through fiscal 1988 several other restrictions on U.S. actions in Central America. Congress originally imposed the restrictions in 1986 when it approved $100 million in aid to the contras. The most important of those conditions:

● Prohibited U.S. military and civilian personnel from providing advice or training to the contras inside Nicaragua;

● Prohibited U.S. government personnel from providing any services to the contras within 20 miles of the Nicaraguan border with Honduras or Costa Rica;

● Barred aid to any contra group found to have engaged in human rights abuses or drug smuggling;

● Required detailed procedures to account for the spending of contra aid funds; and

● Barred the CIA from tapping its contingency fund to aid the contras without the approval of the Intelligence and Appropriations committees.

## Non-Lethal Contra Aid

In the face of sustained opposition on Capitol Hill, and with his overall influence in Congress lagging, President Reagan's bid to arm Nicaragua's contra guerrillas ran out of steam in 1988.

The president in January 1988 sent Congress a request for renewed military aid to the anti-government guerrillas. The House defeated that request, in one of the most important congressional rebuffs to a Reagan foreign policy proposal. Although Reagan continued to denounce Congress, he never again asked officially for more arms money and instead allowed Congress to take the lead on the issue.

Congress provided two doses of "humanitarian" aid for the contras in 1988. The money for food, clothing, medicine and other supplies was enough to sustain the rebels, but not enough to rejuvenate them as a fighting force. By the time Congress finished its business, nearly all contras had fled to refugee camps in Honduras, where they survived on U.S.-supplied food and shelter, and waited for the next administration in Washington to decide on its Central America policy.

The first 1988 installment of non-lethal aid came in the wake of a March 23 cease-fire agreement between the contras and Nicaragua's Sandinista regime. At the end of March, Congress enacted a $47.9 million aid package (H J Res 523 — PL 100-276) for the contras and victims of the Nicaraguan civil war. When peace talks collapsed, both houses in July passed resolutions denouncing the leftist Sandinistas for their crackdown on the internal opposition.

Senate Republicans and Democrats in early August sought to craft a bipartisan contra aid package, but the Reagan administration balked at the last minute. The White House and staunch contra aid backers complained that it did nothing to give the contras immediate military aid, and they insisted that Democrats were merely trying to sweep aside contra aid as an embarrassing political issue.

The Senate attached a new contra aid plan to the fiscal 1989 defense appropriations bill. That package included $27.14 million in non-military aid and established a procedure for Reagan to ask Congress for permission to give the contras up to $16.5 million worth of military supplies warehoused in Honduras. Under the bill, the money had to be spent by March 31, 1989.

House leaders accepted that provision, and it remained in the defense bill that Reagan signed into law on Oct. 1 (HR 4781 — PL 100-463).

Contra supporters in Congress tried in early September and again in October to persuade Reagan to ask Congress to release the military aid. But the White House refused to press the issue.

Instead, the conservatives settled for a resolution, attached to an unrelated Montana wilderness bill (S 2751), warning that Congress would "very likely" renew military aid if the Sandinistas continued to violate the 1987 Central American peace plan. The underlying bill, however, was pocket-vetoed. *(Wilderness bill, p. 473)*

## Background

For Reagan, the Nicaraguan contras were "freedom fighters" and the "moral equivalent of the Founding Fathers." But while some conservatives adopted the president's heated rhetoric, most members of Congress never really warmed to the contra cause.

It was Reagan's stubbornness that kept the contra issue alive in Washington, forcing more than a dozen major political battles in Congress and leading to the expenditure of some $250 million in U.S. aid to the contras during his presidency. *(Box, p. 215)*

The president's determination was so great that, when Congress cut off contra funding in 1984, he ordered White House operatives to keep the guerrillas alive "body and soul"; they took that order as permission to establish a secret network of private aid.

All but the most adamant opponents of Reagan's policy acknowledged that the United States, having armed and encouraged the contras, had a moral commitment to them. Supporters said it was a duty to see the contras through to victory.

Others said that the United States should only feed and clothe the guerrillas until some arrangements could be made for them to return to Nicaragua, relocate elsewhere in Central America or move to the United States.

In providing non-military aid, congressional leaders and the Reagan administration chose the safest course. Contra aid opponents said that step fulfilled the U.S. commitment. The Reagan administration and its allies argued that the contras should be kept intact as a unit so Reagan's successor would have the option of trying to resume military aid.

## Reagan Request Defeated

The Reagan administration began the year hoping for a compromise on the contra aid question. Under the fiscal 1988 continuing appropriations resolution (H J Res 395 — PL 100-202), Reagan was guaranteed votes in Congress on a new request for military and non-military aid. *(1987 action, p. 209)*

To continue transporting previously purchased military aid to the contras, Reagan was required by PL 100-202 to certify to Congress that a cease-fire was not in place in Nicaragua. Reagan made such a certification on Jan. 19.

The provision also required Reagan to submit his aid request between Jan. 25-27 and mandated up-and-down votes on it in the House and Senate on Feb. 3-4.

With Congress expected to approve at least some limited non-military aid, the major battle was over military hardware.

The Sandinistas moved quickly to try to avert ap-

proval of more contra aid. Nicaraguan President Daniel Ortega, at the end of a two-day summit meeting of the five Central American presidents, agreed Jan. 16 to negotiate directly with the contras. Ortega also agreed to lift an emergency decree — ostensibly aimed at helping the government cope with the aftermath of a hurricane in late October 1987 — that had sharply curtailed civil liberties in Nicaragua.

Ortega's concessions breathed new life into a peace process that was widely viewed as near collapse. They also enabled Costa Rican President Oscar Arias, the widely respected chief architect of the accord, to call on Congress to reject further contra aid.

On Jan. 27, Reagan formally sent to the Hill a $36.25 million request for military and non-military contra aid. The request contained hidden costs that brought its actual price tag closer to $60 million.

The makeup of the aid request was a major concession by Reagan, scaling back his hoped-for $270 million in contra aid over 18 months and curtailing the portion devoted to military aid.

The $36.25 million would last until about mid-July 1988. About $3.6 million was earmarked for "lethal" supplies, including guns and ammunition. But Reagan agreed not to spend any of that money until after March 31 — and then only if there was no cease-fire in Nicaragua, and the Sandinistas had not made "good-faith" efforts to carry out the Central American peace plan.

Reagan refused to accept a demand by some undecided members that Congress be given another chance in late March or early April to decide on the release of the military aid.

Democratic leaders complained that Reagan had made fewer concessions than the White House claimed. They noted, for example, that the request also included at least $23 million, which the president failed to mention in his speeches, to provide insurance and sophisticated electronic-defense equipment for the planes carrying supplies to contra bases inside Nicaragua.

The Democrats said the administration structured the request in a way to make the military aid portion appear smaller. The administration counted as "non-lethal" aid such items as planes, jeeps and radios, which could be used for civil purposes but also were necessary to keep a guerrilla army fighting.

In a harsh rebuke to Reagan, the House on Feb. 3 killed his high-priority effort (H J Res 444) to continue U.S. military aid to the contras by a **key vote of 211-219 (R 164-12; D 47-207)**. *(1988 key votes, p. 981)*

The political impact of the action was muted only slightly the next day, when the Senate voted 51-48 in favor of Reagan's request (S J Res 243). The Senate vote was entirely symbolic, since approval by both chambers was necessary for the president's request to become law.

Two of the key factors in Reagan's loss could have been that he had little control over events in Central America, and that he refused to volunteer more control over policy to Congress.

Most members who voted against contra aid said they did so because of the "peace process," the negotiations and political concessions in Central America since the Aug. 7, 1987, signing of the peace accord.

In a last-minute attempt to counter that sentiment, Reagan offered to give Congress the final say over spending $3.6 million in what he called "lethal aid," such as guns and bullets.

Reagan said he was making a major concession of his own political power in hopes of keeping the contras alive. But he added a condition that substantially weakened his offer: Congress would have to pass its resolution within 10 days of the president's determination that military aid should be resumed. Even if the House passed such a resolution quickly, a simple filibuster in the Senate would block it, thus freeing the president to send the arms.

### Democratic Alternative Rejected

The House Democratic leadership on Feb. 24 produced an alternative proposal that would give the contras about $16 million worth of food, clothing and medicine through June. The Democrats also proposed $14.6 million for aid to children injured or displaced by the Nicaraguan civil war.

House Republicans countered with their own plan for $22.3 million in non-military contra aid, and they borrowed the proposal for assistance to children.

Both plans prohibited use of the money for arms aid. But the GOP plan would have forced congressional votes in the spring on Reagan's likely request for more military supplies. The Democrats' package posed greater hurdles to follow-up votes on military aid.

The March 3 House vote on the contra aid proposals brought out the full range of partisan emotions, as leaders of the two parties accused each other of misrepresentation and acting in bad faith. The contra debate appeared to mark a new low between House Speaker Jim Wright, D-Texas, and Minority Leader Robert H. Michel, R-Ill.

The House voted twice. First, by 215-210, the House adopted the Democratic contra aid plan as an amendment to H J Res 484, which contained the GOP-sponsored proposal.

The vast majority of the 212 Democrats who supported the aid plan had never before voted for contra aid. They did so for tactical reasons: Approval of the Democratic plan was seen as rejection of the GOP proposal, which most Democrats saw as setting the stage for yet another vote on military aid. But some liberals said they could not vote for the Democratic proposal on final passage, since that was more clearly a vote in favor of contra aid.

On the second vote, the underlying bill failed 208-216, carrying with it the Democratic plan. Among the 45 Democrats who voted against final passage were 15 — most of them liberals — who had supported the Democratic proposal on the earlier vote.

### Cease-Fire Agreement

A week before long-delayed peace talks were scheduled to resume, the Sandinistas in mid-March launched a military offensive apparently aimed at driving a key contra contingent out of Nicaragua. Pursuing some 2,000 contras, Sandinista troops crossed the border into Honduras, giving the Reagan administration an opening to denounce a Nicaraguan "invasion" and the failure of congressional Democrats to support the contras.

Reagan immediately sent 3,150 airborne troops to Honduras as a gesture of U.S. determination to fight communism. The arrival of those forces on March 16 doubled the American presence in Honduras but had no immediate military impact, since the troops were ordered to stay away from the fighting.

But the Sandinista invasion and Reagan's response created a new upheaval in Washington over contra aid.

## More Wright Controversy

The long-simmering political battle between Republicans and Democrats over Nicaragua erupted again in 1988. And again, the man at the vortex of events was House Speaker Jim Wright.

The Texas Democrat alleged on Sept. 20 that the CIA had attempted to foment disturbances in Nicaragua for the purpose of undermining the Central American peace plan. He said he based his statement on "clear testimony from CIA people."

President Reagan and GOP leaders denounced the statements as irresponsible. They said Wright had handed a propaganda bonus to the leftist Sandinista government and might have violated House rules against disclosure of classified information, although they insisted the CIA had not engaged in the activities cited by Wright.

Wright replied that he had not divulged secret information and that his information had come from press reports.

The dispute was the latest conflict featuring Nicaragua as the underlying issue and Wright as the principal political figure. Almost since his first days as Speaker in January 1987, Wright had inserted himself into the center of the hot debate on Nicaragua. And for the same period, administration officials and supporters had accused the Speaker of meddling in U.S. policy toward Nicaragua with his vigorous opposition to Reagan's backing of the contras. *(Box, p. 211)*

But the September 1988 controversy centered on a different part of the administration's Nicaragua policy. Several congressional sources said the CIA — with tacit approval of the Intelligence committees — had continued to operate in Nicaragua in spite of the legal ban on agency backing of the contras. But those operations were supposed to involve logistical and "propaganda-generating" support for political opposition forces, rather than actions aimed at fomenting violent dissent, said the sources, among whom were Republicans and Democrats.

Thus, the controversy unleashed by Wright focused on two questions — whether the administration had engaged in the activities described by Wright and whether the Speaker, in discussing the matter, breached congressional security standards.

The House ethics committee had not decided by year's end whether to open a preliminary inquiry into Wright's comments.

The controversy contributed to the demise of legislation requiring the president to notify Congress within 48 hours of all CIA covert operations he had approved. Democrats feared that the House debate on the bill would turn into an attack on Wright. *(Bill, p. 244)*

Republicans and Democrats traded charges of bad faith, with each insisting that the other was to blame for what had happened.

The Nicaraguan move into Honduras was the latest in a string of Sandinista actions that undermined the position of those who opposed contra aid. In 1985, Ortega embarrassed House Democrats by flying to Moscow immediately after they had killed a Reagan contra aid proposal. And in 1986, Nicaragua sent troops into Honduras in pursuit of contras, shortly after the House rejected another Reagan contra aid plan.

The 1988 incursion prompted Hill moderates to introduce in both chambers a package of $48 million in new non-military aid to the contras. But the aid plans were displaced less than a week later when a cease-fire agreement was reached.

At a customs house in Sapoa, Nicaragua, after three days of intense negotiations, the Sandinista government and contra leaders on March 23 signed a 60-day cease-fire agreement aimed at concluding a war that had been under way since 1981. Just as important, the agreement reaffirmed the Sandinista regime's pledges to open the political system to opposition parties, including the contras.

If fully carried out, the agreement would meet most of the demands that the contras and the Reagan administration had made. However, it would allow the Sandinistas to remain in power for the immediate future, voiding a major Reagan foreign policy goal.

The Sapoa agreement injected new life into the regional peace plan, at least for Nicaragua. As with any successful negotiation, the cease-fire accord enabled both sides to claim victory.

The Sandinistas were close to achieving their overriding goal of ending the war, which had cost some 40,000 lives since 1981 and battered the Nicaraguan economy. The government also won agreement by the contras not to accept further arms aid. Instead, the contras vowed to receive only humanitarian aid from "neutral organizations."

The contras won several significant concessions that earlier had seemed inconceivable: They received formal recognition by the government, which had agreed only reluctantly to negotiate directly with them; their leaders would be able to return to Managua, without conditions, to participate in further cease-fire talks and in a newly revived political "dialogue"; they successfully rebuffed a government demand that they lay down their arms during the initial cease-fire period; and they won the most explicit Sandinista promises ever to open the political process and release thousands of political prisoners.

The Reagan administration, which had been less than enthusiastic about the entire course of the Central American peace talks, reacted coolly to the cease-fire accord. Reagan said March 25 that "there is reason to have caution" about the Sandinista promises. His aides said they would draw attention to any backsliding by the Nicaraguans.

## Humanitarian Aid Approved

The cease-fire pact gave impetus for Congress to reach agreement on a new humanitarian aid package for the contras and get it passed in time for the congressional recess at the end of March.

The accord had eliminated most of the contentious issues that had dominated debates about contra aid. For years the major fight had been over Reagan's insistence that the United States give the contras weapons and other supplies to continue their war. The cease-fire accord seemed to settle that matter, with the contras agreeing not to accept further military aid.

After solemn debate and by overwhelming votes, Congress on March 30-31 approved a $47.9 million program that included $17.7 million in aid to the contras.

The bill (H J Res 523) had the support of an unusual coalition: the Reagan administration and its supporters, the Democratic leadership, the contras and even the leftist Sandinista government in Managua.

The House passed it 345-70 on March 30, and the Senate followed suit the next day, 87-7. Reagan signed the bill into law April 1 (PL 100-276), clearing the way for new supplies of food, clothing and other items to be shipped to contras in their camps soon after Easter.

Both the House and Senate leadership agreed to quick consideration of any future contra aid requests from the administration, although expedited procedures were not written into the law. Ever since the House on Feb. 3 rejected Reagan's aid request, the major legislative and political issue had been the procedural question of whether the president should have the right to an immediate vote on any new request for military aid to the contras. Democrats had resisted the Republicans' demand for expedited procedures because they hoped to avoid further votes on the issue in an election year and the leadership saw such procedures as excessive presidential trampling on legislative prerogatives.

Major provisions of H J Res 523 (PL 100-276):

**Contra Aid.** Authorized the president to use $17.7 million in unspent Pentagon funds to provide aid to the contras through Sept. 30, 1988. However, that total would be reduced by the value of any deliveries to the contras from stockpiled goods that had been purchased before aid was cut off on Feb. 29. The aid was to include only food, clothing, shelter and medical services and supplies.

None of the money could be used to provide the contras with weapons, ammunition, aircraft or any other non-humanitarian supplies. And the administration was barred from sending the contras military items bought with previously appropriated money.

**Management, Delivery.** Put the Agency for International Development (AID) in charge of the contra aid program, effectively removing the CIA from the direct control of the contra effort that it had exercised since 1986.

AID could spend up to $2.5 million to manage the contra aid program. However, transportation costs would be in addition to the amounts earmarked in the bill, and they would be taken from unspent Pentagon funds.

**Aid to Children.** Authorized $17.7 million in unspent Pentagon funds to provide medical care and other aid to children "who are victims of the Nicaraguan civil strife."

**Verification.** Earmarked $10 million in unspent Pentagon funds for support of the Verification Commission that would monitor the March 23 cease-fire agreement.

**Restrictions.** Reinstituted in law several restrictions on U.S. involvement in Central America that Congress originally enacted in 1986. The restrictions expired on Feb. 29, 1988, when the previous contra aid program lapsed. Among the restrictions were a ban on U.S. military personnel operating inside Nicaragua and a prohibition on providing aid to contras accused of drug smuggling or human rights violations. Another major restriction was modified: In the past, all U.S. government personnel were barred from aiding the contras in Honduras or Costa Rica within 20 miles of the Nicaraguan border. This bill exempted AID and State Department personnel from that prohibition.

## Renewed Bickering

The early weeks of April saw remarkable harmony as AID moved to start the new contra aid program in PL 100-276, in close consultation with Capitol Hill leaders and staff. But in less than two months, the Reagan administration and some Hill Democrats again were battling over the issue.

The Democrats challenged major aspects of how the administration carried out the $47.9 million program. They condemned the direct delivery of supplies to contras living in Honduras and a plan for cash payments to contras encamped in Nicaragua. They also criticized the continuation of a program that had been one of the CIA's best-kept secrets: cash payments to contras' families living in Honduras and Florida.

More important differences between the administration and its critics, however, persisted over fundamental policy toward Nicaragua. The Democrats emphasized the need to end the war, while the administration wanted to pressure the Sandinistas into making further political concessions.

The renewed debate in Washington occurred as peace talks between the contras and the Sandinistas hit a stalemate. One of the major hurdles was dissension among the contra forces, with military and civilian factions competing for power. Administration officials and other observers said the infighting was making it difficult for the guerrillas to present a united front against the Sandinistas.

Some conservatives had threatened to introduce legislation resuming direct military aid to the contras if the cease-fire talks failed. During debate on the fiscal 1989 intelligence authorization bill (HR 4387), an amendment allowing the CIA to resume covert aid to the contras was offered, but rejected, 190-214.

Contra and Sandinista negotiators on June 9 broke off their talks in Managua after failing to reach agreement on political issues or an extension of the cease-fire accord that had been in effect since March 23. Each side accused the other of bargaining in bad faith.

With Nicaragua's peace process stalemated and its economy sliding toward disaster, the Sandinistas began moving against their principal enemies: the domestic political opposition and the United States. The government broke up a political demonstration on July 10, jailed dozens of opposition leaders and closed anti-Sandinista media outlets.

Alleging that Washington was fomenting opposition political activity, the Sandinistas expelled U.S. Ambassador Richard Melton and seven of his colleagues. The United States denied the charge and responded in kind, ousting Nicaraguan Ambassador Carlos Tunnermann and seven of his aides.

Congress landed a strong rhetorical punch on July 13-14, when both chambers overwhelmingly passed resolutions condemning Managua's crackdown on internal political opponents and its expulsion of the U.S. diplomats.

## More Contra Aid

Congressional Democrats found themselves under a newly energized GOP attack for their alleged failure to recognize a communist threat. Their divided stand on the contra issue — symbolized by a disagreement between the party's presidential and vice presidential candidates (Michael S. Dukakis was against aid and Sen. Lloyd Bentsen, D-Texas, supported it) — threatened to become a political liability.

The potential for embarrassment led the Senate Democrats to negotiate an extraordinary agreement on the contra issue. For the first time in the five years of controversy over the issue, liberal and conservative Democrats united behind a contra proposal that involved the possibility of renewed military aid.

The proposal, offered as an amendment to the fiscal 1989 defense appropriations bill (HR 4781), allowed $27.14 million in humanitarian aid for the contras and gave Reagan an opportunity in late September or early October to seek release of $16.5 million worth of military supplies intended for the contras. Originally approved by Congress in 1986, those weapons were in warehouses in Central America.

The plan had been developed by leading Democrats and Republicans, with the active participation of White House officials. But at the last minute the White House refused to support the plan and the effort toward bipartisan support of the contras collapsed in an angry outburst of partisan recriminations in the Senate on Aug. 10.

The plan was approved by a **key vote of 49-47 (R 0-43; D 49-4)**. Shortly before adopting the Democrats' proposal, the Senate rejected, on a 57-39 tabling vote, a GOP plan to allow Reagan to supply the military aid without a second vote. *(1988 key votes, p. 981)*

House conferees on the appropriations bill accepted the Senate package, with one minor change, on Sept. 23. The bill cleared Congress Sept. 30.

Major provisions of the new aid plan signed into law Oct. 1 (PL 100-463):

**Humanitarian Aid.** Provided $27.14 million in new aid from Oct. 1, 1988, to March 31, 1989. This included food, clothing, shelter and medical supplies, non-military training on human rights issues and new batteries for communications gear. This provision also allowed continued cash payments to the families of contra leaders, most of whom lived in Honduras and Miami.

AID was authorized $4 million for administrative expenses, plus whatever sums were necessary to ship non-military supplies.

The bill also authorized $5 million for medical aid to Nicaragua's "civilian victims."

**Military Aid.** Provided up to $16.5 million worth of previously purchased military supplies, or comparable new supplies, once Congress passed a joint resolution approving a request by the president.

The president had to report to Congress that the Sandinistas had caused an "emergency" that was having "a critical impact on peace and stability" in the region. He also had to provide evidence of at least two of three circumstances: an unprovoked attack on the contras by Nicaragua's government; "blatant violation" by the Sandinistas of the Aug. 7, 1987, Central American peace accord; and a "continued unacceptable level" of Soviet bloc arms shipments to Nicaragua.

The joint resolution was subject to expedited procedures in the Senate, averting a filibuster. However, the House had to pass it first.

**CIA Role.** Stated that the military aid was to be administered by the secretary of state "or his designee," a phrase meant to allow a return of the CIA to the contra program — if Congress approved the president's request for release of the military aid. However, the bill prohibited any intelligence agency, including the CIA, from using its own funds to aid the contras, and it barred any other form of U.S. aid to the guerrillas unless Congress specifically authorized it.

**Incentives to Sandinistas.** Required the president to lift a trade embargo imposed in 1985, if the Sandinistas and the contras signed a "comprehensive agreement for peace and democracy." He also could spend $10 million to help contras and other exiles return to civilian life there.

After a full peace had been in effect for 180 days, and if Nicaragua was "continuing to comply," the president could make Nicaragua eligible for trade concessions and for Export-Import Bank loans.

## Warning to Sandinistas

Conservative Senate Republicans pressed Reagan to request formally that Congress authorize the release of the military equipment stockpiled in Honduras for the contras. But Reagan refused to mount yet another legislative campaign on behalf of the contras and congressional conservatives had to settle for a resolution threatening a renewal of military aid.

The Senate Oct. 18 attached to an unrelated Montana wilderness bill (S 2751) a resolution warning that continued Sandinista violations of the peace plan "will very likely" cause Congress to renew military aid to the contras. The House accepted it Oct. 20, sending the measure to the president. Reagan pocket-vetoed the underlying bill.

# Reagan-Gorbachev Meetings

The third summit meeting between President Reagan and Soviet leader Mikhail S. Gorbachev, held in Washington in December 1987, appeared to mark a turn in the style of U.S.-Soviet relations from unwavering suspicion and hostile competition, toward hard-nosed but practical dealings between longtime adversaries who had agreed to solve contentious issues through negotiations.

The 1987 summit centerpiece was the Dec. 8 signing of a treaty banning intermediate-range nuclear-force (INF) missiles. In signing the agreement, a pragmatic Reagan broke with some conservatives in his party who argued that the United States should not conclude an arms agreement until the Soviets had further liberalized their domestic politics and demilitarized their foreign policy. *(INF treaty, p. 346)*

Relations between the two superpowers advanced further in 1988. Reagan and Gorbachev met twice, first to ratify formally the INF treaty and then to set the stage for further military cutbacks.

But during their meetings the two leaders made only limited progress toward their primary goal — a strategic arms reduction treaty (START) — or toward resolving world conflicts on which the two superpowers differed.

## Washington Summit

During their three-day meeting in Washington Dec. 8-10, 1987, neither Reagan nor Gorbachev shied away from taking on the other over the merits of their respective political systems.

Reagan, among others, publicly challenged the Soviet leader on human rights, particularly the right of emigration, and the occupation of Afghanistan.

Gorbachev flared at the persistent criticism. He staunchly asserted the superiority of the Soviet definition of human rights, which he said included a right of economic security ignored by the capitalist West and a right of immigration that the United States denied by not opening its borders to all comers.

But those frank exchanges did not interfere with the signing of the INF treaty nor with the modest but solid progress on several disputes in the START negotiations. The delegations resolved some strategic arms issues outright and adopted guidelines for resolving others in future negotiations. The two leaders finessed the biggest stumbling block in the arms talks — the U.S. strategic defense initiative (SDI), Reagan's plan to develop a nationwide anti-missile defense — by agreeing to disagree. *(Details, arms control, p. 341)*

While Reagan and Gorbachev made progress on the arms control front during the December summit, they were unable to resolve any major regional or human rights issues.

Prior to the meeting, both sides hinted that Gorbachev might use the meetings at the White House to announce a timetable for the Soviet withdrawal from Afghanistan. U.S. officials also expressed hope that Gorbachev would agree to support a U.N. arms embargo against Iran.

The summit failed on both counts. Gorbachev restated a willingness to pull his troops out of Afghanistan within a year or "maybe less" but refused to set specific dates, and Reagan repeated his insistence on continuing to aid anti-Soviet guerrillas in Afghanistan. Gorbachev also rebuffed the suggested arms embargo against Iran. *(Afghanistan, box, p. 221)*

The eight-page-long Reagan-Gorbachev communiqué issued Dec. 10 devoted two and a half lines to human rights, noting only that the two leaders "held a thorough and candid discussion" of the issues and their place in the U.S.-Soviet relationship.

Reagan said Gorbachev gave him "assurance of future, more substantial movement" on human rights. But congressional leaders said Gorbachev insisted on continuing to handle human rights issues case by case. The approach represented a rebuff to the Reagan administration, which had sought to get the Kremlin to establish blanket procedures to grant freedom to Jews and political dissidents.

Although they made little headway on weighty international affairs, the U.S. and Soviet negotiators did report some progress on issues directly affecting relations between the two countries. Agreements were reached on joint air service between the two countries, oceanographic research and monitoring of underground nuclear tests.

## Moscow Summit

A little more than five years after he called the Soviet Union an "evil empire," Reagan took his unique brand of politicking to Moscow May 29-June 2, 1988, for an upbeat summit meeting with Gorbachev. When Reagan visited the Kremlin and declared that the Soviet empire no longer was "evil," he undercut his own political allies who had argued that the United States could afford no accommodation with Moscow.

During his trip to Moscow, Reagan berated the Soviet Union for human rights violations, preached the virtues of

# U.S.-Soviet Summit Meetings, 1945-88

| Participants | Location | Date | Main Issue |
|---|---|---|---|
| President Franklin D. Roosevelt<br>Soviet leader Josef Stalin<br>British Prime Minister Winston Churchill | Yalta, USSR | February 1945 | Composition of postwar world |
| President Harry S Truman<br>Soviet leader Josef Stalin<br>British Prime Minister Winston Churchill<br>British Prime Minister Clement R. Atlee | Potsdam, East Germany | July-August 1945 | Partition and control of Germany |
| President Dwight D. Eisenhower<br>Soviet leader Nikolai A. Bulganin<br>British Prime Minister Anthony Eden<br>French Premier Edgar Faure | Geneva, Switzerland | July 1955 | Reunification of Germany, disarmament, European security |
| President Dwight D. Eisenhower<br>Soviet leader Nikita S. Khrushchev | Camp David, Md. | September 1959 | Berlin problem |
| President Dwight D. Eisenhower<br>Soviet leader Nikita S. Khrushchev<br>French President Charles de Gaulle<br>British Prime Minister Harold Macmillan | Paris, France | May 1960 | U-2 incident |
| President John F. Kennedy<br>Soviet leader Nikita S. Khrushchev | Vienna, Austria | June 1961 | Berlin problem |
| President Lyndon B. Johnson<br>Soviet leader Aleksei N. Kosygin | Glassboro, N.J. | June 1967 | Middle East |
| President Richard Nixon<br>Soviet leader Leonid I. Brezhnev | Moscow, USSR | May 1972 | SALT I, anti-ballistic limitations |
| President Richard Nixon<br>Soviet leader Leonid I. Brezhnev | Washington, D.C. | June 1973 | Detente |
| President Richard Nixon<br>Soviet leader Leonid I. Brezhnev | Moscow and Yalta, USSR | June-July 1974 | Arms control |
| President Gerald R. Ford<br>Soviet leader Leonid I. Brezhnev | Vladivostok, USSR | November 1974 | Arms control |
| President Jimmy Carter<br>Soviet leader Leonid I. Brezhnev | Vienna, Austria | June 1979 | SALT II |
| President Ronald Reagan<br>Soviet leader Mikhail S. Gorbachev | Geneva, Switzerland | November 1985 | Arms control |
| President Ronald Reagan<br>Soviet leader Mikhail S. Gorbachev | Reykjavik, Iceland | October 1986 | Arms control |
| President Ronald Reagan<br>Soviet leader Mikhail S. Gorbachev | Washington, D.C. | December 1987 | Arms control |
| President Ronald Reagan<br>Soviet leader Mikhail S. Gorbachev | Moscow, USSR | May-June 1988 | Arms control |
| President Ronald Reagan<br>Soviet leader Mikhail S. Gorbachev | New York, N.Y. | December 1988 | Soviet troop cutbacks |

# Gorbachev Speech

A plan to invite Soviet leader Mikhail S. Gorbachev to address Congress during his Dec. 8-10, 1987, summit meeting with President Reagan was quickly shot down after generating animosity and confusion in equal measure.

The animosity came from lawmakers, mostly conservative Republicans but also top party leaders and some Democrats, who objected to the symbolism of such an appearance and said they wanted congressional visits reserved for world leaders who clearly were friends of democracy.

The confusion stemmed from conflicting reports on just who pushed for a Gorbachev appearance during the Soviet leader's summit meeting with the president.

The House Democratic leadership said administration officials had asked Hill leaders to schedule a joint congressional meeting for a Gorbachev appearance. But the White House account held that administration officials had passed along to Hill leaders a Soviet request, along with suggestions that they did not consider it a good idea.

According to the Congressional Research Service of the Library of Congress, 132 foreign dignitaries had addressed Congress in some forum. Of these, 66 had spoken to joint meetings, beginning in 1824 with the Marquis de Lafayette, the French hero of the American Revolution.

More recent congressional guests had included British Prime Minister Margaret Thatcher, Philippine President Corazon Aquino and Indian Prime Minister Rajiv Gandhi.

No communist leader had ever addressed a joint meeting. In 1959, the Senate blocked a request by Soviet leader Nikita S. Khrushchev to address such a meeting.

democracy and praised Gorbachev's political and economic reforms.

Both men declared that the summit, building on the work of three previous meetings, had helped improve U.S.-Soviet relations. Gorbachev said the meetings had "dealt a blow at the foundations of the Cold War."

The most concrete symbol was the INF treaty, banning short-range and medium-range nuclear missiles. The two leaders exchanged the documents of ratification for the treaty June 1. *(Senate action, p. 346)*

But the INF treaty exchange merely formalized an agreement that already had been achieved. The real challenge of the summit was whether Reagan and Gorbachev could make progress toward a START agreement that would reduce the number of strategic weapons in the U.S. and Soviet nuclear arsenals.

U.S. officials had discounted the prospect of serious movement in Moscow toward a START accord, and they proved right. As in previous summits, Reagan and Gorbachev effectively agreed to disagree on the testing of SDI or "star wars" systems, thereby postponing the tough decisions that must be made before a new treaty could be signed.

In lieu of a START pact, Secretary of State George P. Shultz and Foreign Minister Eduard A. Shevardnadze signed on May 31 two minor arms accords on nuclear testing. *(Arms control details, p. 344)*

Before the summit, Reagan had pledged to make human rights in the Soviet Union the most important topic of conversation. In his first two days in Moscow, Reagan used practically every occasion to chastise the Soviets for human rights violations, and even met with well-known "refuseniks" who wanted to leave the Soviet Union. But after Gorbachev expressed irritation, the president eased up on his high-profile criticism and blamed the Soviet "bureaucracy" for rights abuses. By the end of his visit, the president was citing a "sizable improvement" in the human rights observance in the Soviet Union.

Aside from arms control, the most substantive aspect of the Reagan-Gorbachev summit, as at their previous summits, was discussion of regional issues — conflicts throughout the world in which the two superpowers participated directly or indirectly. In their communiqué, the two leaders acknowledged "serious differences" over most such issues. But Gorbachev expressed optimism, saying "opportunities have now appeared for political solutions for all of these conflicts."

The most important regional issue in previous summits was Afghanistan, with the United States pressing for Soviet withdrawal and the Soviet Union demanding an end to U.S. backing of the Mujahedeen guerrillas. An April 14 international agreement providing for Soviet withdrawal effectively resolved that issue. However, the two sides disputed the details of how that agreement would be carried out. *(Box, p. 221)*

Specialists from the two sides appeared to make some progress on resolving the civil war in Angola, where the Soviet Union and Cuba supported the government and the United States gave aid to a guerrilla movement led by Jonas Savimbi.

A U.S. official said the two sides set a deadline of Sept. 29 for concluding an international agreement providing for the withdrawal of Cuban forces from Angola in return for a South African pullout from neighboring Namibia. Negotiators did not make that deadline, but they did produce an agreement in Geneva on Nov. 15. Angola, Cuba and South Africa accepted the pact on Dec. 13. *(Details, p. 238)*

As in the past, the Middle East was a major subject at the Moscow summit, but the Palestinian uprising in Israeli-occupied territories added a new sense of urgency. Gorbachev said he and Reagan agreed that an international conference should be the starting point for talks between Israel and its Arab neighbors. But Gorbachev made it clear that differences remained over the role of that conference. *(Middle East, p. 234)*

The two sides also remained apart on the U.S. demand for a mandatory arms embargo against Iran.

Reagan and Gorbachev also made no headway on Central America, an issue that had arisen during the Washington summit. Gorbachev in Washington offered tantalizing hints that the Soviets would be willing to stop arms shipments to Nicaragua under certain conditions — but in later talks Reagan's aides found that those conditions involved the suspension of all U.S. aid to other Central American

# Afghan Agreement Leaves Key Questions

A United Nations-brokered agreement providing for the Soviet withdrawal from Afghanistan was reached in Geneva on April 14, 1988. But it did not end the war in that troubled country, and it threatened Washington's unusual bipartisan consensus on the Afghan issue.

The agreement called for the Soviets to begin pulling their estimated 100,000-plus troops out of Afghanistan on May 15, 1988, with a stated goal of a complete troop withdrawal by Feb. 15, 1989. Soviet troops had invaded Afghanistan in December 1979.

But key questions remained, among them: how the United States and Soviet Union would keep aiding their Afghan clients, and what kind of government they would accept in Kabul.

In Washington, the accord sparked an unusual degree of dissension among the broad coalition that for years had backed U.S. aid to the Afghan guerrillas battling Soviet troops and a communist government.

Some conservatives denounced the accord as a "sell-out" of the guerrillas, who opposed it. The conservatives also worried that their liberal colleagues on Capitol Hill might weaken their support for the rebels once it was clear that the Soviets were on their way out of Afghanistan.

## Congressional Pressure

Afghanistan had been the subject of rare harmony among Washington's politicians. Ever since President Jimmy Carter stepped up U.S. backing of the Afghan guerrillas in 1980, there never had been audible dissent.

Support for the guerrillas was a natural position for conservatives, who sought opportunities to oppose the Soviet Union overseas. But the issue also was an easy one for liberals, who since the Vietnam War had hesitated to engage U.S. power in questionable causes. They had no trouble justifying support for anti-communist guerrillas in Afghanistan.

Congress at times had been more aggressive than the administration in pushing the rebel Mujahedeen (holy warriors) cause. Congress on several occasions voted more money for the rebels than the administration sought. By 1987, Congress pushed direct U.S. aid to an annual level of about $600 million, matched by contributions from Saudi Arabia.

Congress took the lead in 1983-84 in demanding that the rebels receive "effective" aid. In practice, that eventually meant supplying anti-aircraft missiles, over the objections of some Reagan officials. Those weapons, including the shoulder-fired Stinger missiles, by late 1986 played a major role in convincing Moscow it never could subdue the resistance.

At the concluding stages of the Geneva talks, Congress also intervened to stiffen Reagan's position.

In late 1985, the State Department had agreed that the United States would stop aiding the Afghan rebels once the Soviets began their withdrawal. That pledge drew little attention then, but pro-rebel forces in Washington began attacking it once it became clear that the long-stalled U.N. talks might produce an agreement.

Under pressure from members of Congress, the administration in late 1987 and early 1988 added a new condition to its backing of an Afghan accord: There had to be "symmetry" between U.S. and Soviet actions in Afghanistan. In other words, the United States would continue supplying arms to the rebels as long as the Soviets gave arms to Kabul.

The Senate went even further. By a 77-0 vote Feb. 29, 1988, the Senate approved a non-binding resolution (S Res 386) demanding that U.S. aid to the rebels continue until it was "absolutely clear" that the Soviets had withdrawn and that the guerrillas were "well enough equipped" to defend themselves.

On the House side, however, squabbling between liberal Democrats and conservative Republicans derailed a similar resolution.

## Maneuvers Toward Agreement

The continuing hard-line pressure from Capitol Hill apparently affected the administration and, ultimately, the Soviets.

In March 1988 the United States told the Soviets that it would refuse to sign an accord unless agreement had been reached allowing symmetry on the aid issue. A letter was sent to the Soviets outlining the symmetry proposal. In April the Soviets sent a response outlining their understanding of what symmetry meant. The two letters apparently constituted the U.S.-Soviet understanding that made signing of the Geneva accord possible.

During a Dec. 7 visit to address the United Nations in New York, Gorbachev included a series of last-minute proposals for a cease-fire, coupled with a suspension of outside aid. Gorbachev did not say directly whether the Soviet Union would adhere to the Feb. 15 withdrawal date.

Secretary of State George P. Shultz appeared to reject the proposals, insisting that the Soviets keep their commitment to remove all remaining troops from Afghanistan "as they are scheduled to do."

Shultz said the rebels — and by extension the United States — would reject Gorbachev's proposals. The Afghan people, Shultz said, "do not accept the fact that the puppet regime is entitled to hold certain areas of that country."

A Mujahedeen spokesman was quoted Dec. 8 as saying a cease-fire was "meaningless" as long as there were "invading forces" — the Soviets.

countries, as well as aid to the Nicaraguan contra guerrillas. *(Contra aid, p. 213)*

U.S. officials said the Soviets stuck to that position in Moscow, a position they said was not worthy of negotiation.

But there was progress on certain bilateral issues. During the summit, officials from the two governments signed several agreements providing for cultural, scientific, technical, transportation and maritime cooperation.

## New York Meeting

Gorbachev returned to the United States in December 1988 to address the U.N. General Assembly in New York. In a bold, historic speech, the Soviet leader Dec. 7 belittled the role of military force and ideological struggle in world affairs and announced plans to cut 500,000 of the Soviet Union's 5.1 million troops by 1991. *(Details, p. 345)*

His U.N. speech also called for a cease-fire in Afghanistan as of Jan. 1, 1989, and announced human rights reforms at home.

Only a few hours after extolling to the General Assembly the importance of individual liberty as the keystone of world peace, Gorbachev provided the trip's most stunning image — posing with Reagan and President-elect George Bush against the backdrop of the Statue of Liberty. But the next day Gorbachev cut short his visit and returned home to supervise relief efforts in the wake of a devastating Dec. 7 earthquake in Soviet Armenia.

Reagan, Bush and other NATO leaders lauded the Soviet troop cutback announcement. "If it is carried out speedily and in full," Reagan told a Washington audience later that day, "history will regard it as important — significant."

But he warned against taking the Soviet reductions as a cue for similar U.S. cutbacks. "This still leaves them with superiority in the amount of conventional arms," Reagan said Dec. 8 at a televised press conference. "We're still way below them."

# U.S.-Panama Relations

There was a rare degree of consensus between the White House and Capitol Hill in 1988 on the need to oust the leader of an important ally — Gen. Manuel Antonio Noriega of Panama. But the United States rapidly lost its leverage trying to accomplish that goal.

Despite a drug-smuggling indictment against Noriega, political pressure from Washington and full-scale economic sanctions against his country, the strongman — through his army cronies — maintained a tight grip on power in Panama.

Ultimately red-faced Reagan administration officials came to realize they would be unable to force Noriega from power under the prevailing circumstances. The sanctions remained in effect, causing enormous inconvenience for Panamanian citizens and U.S. businesses, but the high-profile campaign against Noriega was allowed to lapse.

As he left office, President Reagan loosed a final attack against Noriega, saying the United States should reconsider its adherence to the 1978 Panama Canal treaties if Noriega remained in power.

The two countries were nearing one of the most delicate stages of the canal treaties: the transition from near-total U.S. control of canal operations to an increased Panamanian role.

By January 1989, Panama was to submit to the United States the name of the Panamanian citizen who would take over in 1990 as canal administrator. Under the treaties and follow-up legislation approved by Congress in 1979, that person had to be confirmed by the Senate. The canal itself was due to fall under full Panamanian control on Jan. 1, 2000. *(Congress and the Nation Vol. V, p. 52)*

With its canal, huge U.S. military installations and facilities for intelligence-gathering, Panama was one of the most important countries in the Western Hemisphere, from the United States' perspective. Some 50,000 U.S. citizens lived in Panama, among whom were 10,400 troops guarding the canal and manning the headquarters for the Southern Command, which supervised U.S. military operations in Latin America.

## The Canal's Importance

The issue of the Panama Canal was always in the background, as the administration and members of Congress struggled to formulate a policy to deal with Noriega.

Nearly three-quarters of a century after the first ship passed through the canal, the prevailing view among U.S. policy makers was that smooth operation of the 51-mile-long waterway remained a key U.S. military and commercial interest. While the canal no longer was vital to U.S. trade and defense, it still remained extremely important by virtue of slicing more than 6,000 miles and two to three weeks from a voyage between the Atlantic and Pacific oceans.

The traditional view of the canal's military significance was borne out during World War II, when there were more than 15,000 transits of the waterway by U.S. warships or supply vessels. More recently, the canal carried a large proportion of supplies shipped to U.S. forces in Korea and Vietnam.

Some experts suggested that the canal might take on added military significance in the 1990s as long-range ship-launched cruise missiles proliferated. If the cruise missile revolution continued, the short-cut through the isthmus would again trim weeks off the time needed to shift significant military forces around the globe.

The canal also was of major commercial importance to the United States. Toward the end of the 1980s shipments to or from U.S. ports accounted for the bulk of commercial cargo transported through the canal. Of the 149 million tons shipped through in fiscal 1987, nearly 70 percent (104 million tons) was bound to or from U.S. ports. Trade between Asia and ports on the Atlantic and Gulf coasts accounted for most of that U.S.-oriented share of the traffic.

## Steps Against Noriega

Since mid-1987, the Reagan administration and Congress had cooperated in pressuring Noriega to step down.

A career officer who rose through the intelligence services, Noriega for years was rumored to be both an agent of the CIA and a conspirator with international drug traffickers. Since 1983, he had exercised the real power in Panama, with a succession of civilian presidents serving as figureheads.

In June 1987, Col. Roberto Diaz Herrera, after being forced to retire as Noriega's second-in-command, went public with several charges. The most sensational were that Noriega had engineered the 1984 presidential elections and had directed the 1985 slaying of opposition leader Hugo Spadafora.

The Diaz charges sparked a series of public demonstrations against Noriega and the military that were crushed by thousands of arrests and tight restrictions on the opposition, all under a state-of-emergency decree.

Congress responded quickly. The Senate on June 26, 1987, adopted, 84-2, a resolution (S Res 239) calling on Noriega to relinquish power.

The Reagan administration then suspended military and economic aid to Panama — a step it had been reluctant to take against other authoritarian regimes in similar circumstances.

With administration support, Congress December 1987 also put into the fiscal 1988 omnibus spending bill (H J Res 395 — PL 100-202) a sweeping ban on U.S. support for Panama. That provision barred all economic and military aid, suspended Panama's quota for sugar imports to the United States and ordered U.S. representatives to the World Bank and other international agencies to vote against loans to Panama. (Foreign aid bill, p. 224)

After months of hesitating about further action, the administration accompanied the congressional steps with several direct challenges to Noriega. A senior Pentagon official traveled to Panama and urged Noriega to step aside, a move publicly endorsed by Secretary of State George P. Shultz. The Pentagon also "postponed" annual military exercises between the two countries.

And on Feb. 4, 1988, a federal grand jury in Miami returned an indictment against Noriega that included racketeering, conspiracy and cocaine trafficking charges.

Noriega denied all the charges as "lies" and hired three Florida attorneys to defend him. Law enforcement officials acknowledged that Noriega probably would never face trial, since he could not be extradited to the United States under Panamanian law.

On Feb. 8 Noriega demanded that the U.S. withdraw its troops from Panama and close the Southern Command. The White House rejected that demand.

## Senate Hearings

Noriega's indictment was followed by a week of Senate Foreign Relations subcommittee hearings that focused on alleged corruption at the highest levels of the Panamanian government.

Allegations about Noriega's improprieties embarrassed Washington because of the general's close ties to U.S. agencies, especially the CIA.

The hearings produced evidence that U.S. officials were so anxious for Noriega's cooperation that they overlooked his involvement in drug activities and periodic alliances with anti-U.S. leaders such as Cuba's Fidel Castro.

Former Panamanian Consul General José I. Blandon, once one of Noriega's closest aides, testified, among other things, that he and Noriega had met with former White House aide Marine Lt. Col. Oliver L. North in 1985 and agreed to allow the training of Nicaraguan contra guerrillas in Panama. At the time, U.S. law forbade any official support of the contras. (Iran-contra affair, p. 253)

## Economic Sanctions

The State Department on March 2 moved to freeze Panamanian government funds held by U.S. banks and on March 4 advised U.S. citizens not to travel to Panama.

The Senate Foreign Relations Committee on March 4 unanimously approved a measure (S J Res 267) calling on the administration to sever all ties with Noriega and to consider economic sanctions against Panama. And on March 10 the House voted 367-2 (H Res 399) to seek Noriega's ouster and to ask Reagan to consider additional economic and political sanctions.

The White House March 11 announced a package of economic sanctions designed to cripple Panama's economy and force out Noriega. The sanctions included:

● Placing into an escrow account the monthly U.S. payments, ranging from $6.5 million to $7 million, to Panama from canal revenues.

● Placing all other U.S. government payments to Panama into an escrow account "for the Delvalle government on behalf of the Panamanian people." Panama's President Eric Arturo Delvalle remained in hiding after his unsuccessful Feb. 26 attempt to oust Noriega.

● Suspending preferences that allowed Panama reduced duty trade with the United States.

Noriega survived a March 16 coup attempt and on March 18 declared a national "state of urgency" that suspended individual liberties. Civil unrest was widespread, and Panama was critically short of cash because of the steps taken by the United States. Despite a nationwide general strike that paralyzed the Panamanian economy, Noriega maintained his grip on Panama's leadership and refused to leave.

The Senate March 25 unanimously passed a resolution (S Con Res 108) urging, among other things, additional diplomatic, political and economic pressure against the Panamanian government.

## Sanctions Tightened, Then Eased

Invoking his authority under the International Emergency Economic Powers Act (IEEPA), Reagan imposed tougher economic sanctions on Panama April 8. He signed an executive order declaring a national emergency, freezing assets in the United States owned by Panama and barring U.S. citizens and U.S.-owned firms and their subsidiaries from making any payments to the Noriega regime. The order prohibited the companies from making tax payments to Panama. Each violation of the order could result in criminal penalties of $50,000 and 10 years' imprisonment and civil penalties of $10,000. Tax payments by U.S. firms in Panama were credited with enabling Noriega to survive the March general strike.

However, the Reagan administration also appeared to be negotiating a deal allowing Noriega to stay in power — and in Panama — at least for several more weeks.

The attempt to strike a bargain with Noriega came as Washington's bipartisan consensus about Panama began to fray. Key congressional leaders accused the administration of bungling the anti-Noriega drive by turning it into a United States vs. Panama showdown and damaging Panama's economy too much.

Senate Majority Leader Robert C. Byrd, D-W.Va., and others charged that the administration undermined its policy by failing to coordinate with other Latin nations. "We need not give Gen. Noriega a Yankee devil to blame for all the evil he has unleashed upon the Panamanian people," Byrd said.

The Democrats also joined senior Pentagon officials in denouncing proposals for direct U.S. military action. Senior officials in the State Department's Bureau of Inter-American Affairs reportedly circulated proposals early in April for a military strike against Noriega. But those suggestions were rebuffed by the Defense Department.

As Noriega clung to power in the face of the sanctions, the administration began reassessing its policy.

The Treasury Department on April 30 eased a few of the restrictions on payments that Americans could make to the Panamanian government. U.S. citizens were allowed to pay for utilities, travel-related taxes and excise taxes.

### Negotiations Collapse

Administration efforts against Noriega were set back by the May 25 collapse of negotiations to remove him from power. Noriega's last-minute refusal to accept a negotiated solution left the administration with no clear options for ending an embarrassing test of wills.

The failure of negotiations brought expressions of relief from members of Congress opposed to the administration's plan to drop narcotics trafficking charges in return for Noriega's resignation.

The proposal to drop the indictments became the most controversial aspect of administration policy. The Senate on May 17 opposed the plan, as an amendment to the defense authorization bill (S 2355), by an 86-10 vote, and even Vice President George Bush spoke out publicly against it, saying he would not negotiate with drug dealers.

### Panama Covert Action Flap

Reagan reportedly in mid-July signed a "finding," or official directive, for a CIA covert operation to support Panamanian opposition groups and to promote internal unrest against the Noriega regime.

The leaking of information about the supposedly secret plan stirred a furor on Capitol Hill.

Word of the finding leaked out on July 26 — the day that CIA, State Department and other officials were briefing the Senate Intelligence Committee about it. That prompted a round of recriminations between the administration and Congress over the leak and revived old questions about Reagan's failed efforts to oust Noriega.

While refusing to comment on the specifics of the covert operation, congressional leaders made clear that they were not impressed by the latest anti-Noriega moves.

# 1988-89 Aid Authorization

Attempts to pass a foreign aid authorization bill failed in 1987 and again in 1988.

Congress in 1985 had passed the first foreign aid authorization since 1981. That legislation (PL 99-83) authorized foreign assistance for fiscal 1986-87, and when it expired on Sept. 30, 1987, Congress had not yet enacted a new authorization. *(1985 action, p. 186)*

Even as it was being drafted, the fiscal 1988-89 foreign aid bill (HR 1630) was widely viewed as being dead politically. Rarely eager to vote for unpopular foreign aid programs, members of Congress were particularly reluctant when domestic spending was being squeezed.

House Foreign Affairs Chairman Dante B. Fascell, D-Fla., and other panel members struggled to find a compromise that could be signed into law. They feared that if the panel again failed to produce a successful bill, the preponderance of influence over the foreign aid programs would

pass to the Appropriations Committee.

The House Foreign Affairs Committee April 9, 1987, approved HR 1630, which basically froze funding at the fiscal 1987 level, roughly $11.07 billion. The measure stalled, however, because of objections by President Reagan and Republicans. The administration complained that it fell below Reagan's $12 billion request and that it imposed too many restrictions on executive branch flexibility in allocating foreign assistance.

After months of deadlock, the committee approved a second bill (HR 3100 — H Rept 100-294) that made several concessions to GOP complaints, including authorizing additional funds for countries that allowed U.S. military bases on their territory: Greece, Turkey, Spain and Portugal. In a further effort to win Republican support, the new bill dropped several provisions that would have restricted the administration's discretion to shift money among foreign aid programs.

After lengthy debate and under threat of a White House veto, HR 3100 passed the House Dec. 10, 1987, on a vote of 286-122. A Republican substitute for the entire bill had been defeated on essentially a party-line vote of 173-234.

The legislation went nowhere in the Senate, however. An $11.1 billion version (S 1274 — S Rept 100-60) was reported by the Foreign Relations Committee May 22, 1987, but, because of objections by Republicans and administration officials, no further action was taken by year's end.

The governmentwide continuing appropriations resolution (H J Res 395 — PL 100-202) included $13.6 billion for foreign aid in fiscal 1988. *(Details, below)*

### 1988 Effort

Leaders of the House Foreign Affairs Committee searched for a way to get Senate action on a bill in 1988. They settled on the strategy of attaching the complex legislation to a relatively non-controversial measure, one making routine authorizations for the Overseas Private Investment Corporation (OPIC) and the Board for International Broadcasting. The House voted to pass the OPIC/foreign aid measure (HR 4471 — H Rept 100-594) by a 267-112 vote on May 12, 1988.

The OPIC bill had some political advantages, because it authorized funds for construction of a Radio Free Europe/Radio Liberty relay station in Israel — a project long sought by the Israeli government. Bills benefiting Israel normally received favorable treatment in Congress.

But, ultimately, the tactic did not work. Senate leaders refused to allow action on either the original foreign aid bill or the OPIC bill with the foreign aid provisions added.

The foreign aid authorization was attached to the fiscal 1989 foreign aid appropriations bill (HR 4637 — PL 100-461).

# 1988 Aid Appropriations

As it had every year since 1982, Congress in 1987 failed to pass a stand-alone appropriations bill for foreign aid programs — and instead put those unpopular items into a governmentwide continuing appropriations resolution, thus protecting them from potentially damaging amendments and votes.

The fiscal 1988 spending bill (H J Res 395 — PL 100-

# Pakistan Aid Raises Non-Proliferation Issue

At the outset, 1987 was to be the year when Congress confronted Pakistan over its reported development of a nuclear weapon. President Reagan asked Congress to approve the first installment — $540 million — on a six-year, $4 billion aid program for Pakistan.

To get the aid, Pakistan had to be exempted from U.S. laws barring aid to nations that tried to build nuclear bombs. Its previous exemption from U.S. non-proliferation laws had expired at the end of fiscal 1987.

Proponents of a tough non-proliferation policy tried all year to devise legislation that would force Pakistan to choose between the aid or its bomb program. But those efforts were undermined politically by the fact that Pakistan was the staging point for covert U.S. aid to anti-Soviet guerrillas in neighboring Afghanistan.

In the end, Congress accepted a compromise that allowed Pakistan's aid program to continue without significant restrictions until April 1, 1990, instead of a full six years as Reagan wanted. Congress included $480 million for Pakistan in the fiscal 1988 continuing appropriations resolution (H J Res 395).

Conferees on H J Res 395 eliminated complex Senate-passed language that linked U.S. policy toward India and Pakistan. That language would bar U.S. aid or exports of advanced technology to India or Pakistan if the president determined that either country possessed material to make nuclear weapons. It also would permit the aid or exports if the president determined that both countries possessed the material.

Senate sponsors had said the provision was meant to establish a non-proliferation policy taking into account the "regional" nature of the issue.

According to that argument, Pakistan was developing nuclear weapons because India, its traditional rival, exploded a nuclear device in 1974.

But India strongly protested being linked with Pakistan. And members of Congress who had sought to focus attention on Pakistan's bomb program objected that the Senate provision was an attempt to shift the issue away from that country.

**Seesaw Policy.** The Pakistan aid debate represented the latest chapter in Washington's struggle to balance nuclear non-proliferation policy with an anti-Soviet stance in Afghanistan.

In April 1979, President Jimmy Carter cut off aid to Pakistan under the 1976 Symington amendment (PL 94-329), which banned aid to countries trying to build nuclear arsenals. Carter reversed himself eight months later, after Soviet troops invaded Afghanistan. He offered $400 million in aid, but Pakistani President Mohammed Zia ul-Haq, angered by the previous cutoff, dismissed it as "peanuts."

In mid-1981, the new Reagan administration proposed a six-year aid package. Also included in the package was the sale of 40 sophisticated F-16 fighter jets, some of which since were delivered.

Exempting Pakistan from the Symington amendment, Congress added a provision (PL 97-113) to prohibit aid if that country conducted a nuclear test, something it had never done.

Three years later, in September 1984, Reagan wrote Zia warning Pakistan not to enrich any uranium beyond a 5 percent level at its Kahuta nuclear processing plant. Reagan's letter came in the wake of the June 1984 arrest of three Pakistani nationals in Houston for trying to smuggle atomic weapons parts out of the United States.

The Pakistani government denied involvement. But evidence taken from two of the defendants revealed that the parts had been ordered by an official at the Pakistani Atomic Energy Commission.

In 1985, Congress required the president (PL 99-83) to certify annually that Pakistan did not possess a nuclear bomb and that U.S. aid would reduce the risk of that country obtaining one. PL 99-83 also prevented aid to any country that illegally tried to get nuclear equipment from the United States.

Fears that Pakistan was building a bomb were heightened in May 1987 by the arrest of a Pakistani native on charges of conspiring with a retired Pakistani brigadier general to export from the United States restricted metals needed to produce nuclear weapons. Arshad Z. Pervez, a resident of Canada, was convicted Dec. 17, 1987.

202) included $13.6 billion for foreign assistance and related programs, an amount some $2.2 billion less than President Reagan's request and nearly identical to what Congress had approved for the previous year.

Because it was one of the most politically unpopular items on Capitol Hill, foreign aid could have been expected to suffer disproportionate cuts as Congress and the Reagan administration wrestled with reducing the budget deficit.

But the congressional leaders and Reagan administration officials who negotiated a budget "summit" agreement in November 1987 struck a deal that freed up several hundred million dollars for foreign aid — thus enabling the House and Senate Appropriations committees to restore some money for those programs even as they were struggling to make cuts in the more popular domestic programs.

H J Res 395 made significant cuts in the Reagan administration's highest priority: military aid that helped friendly countries buy U.S. weapons. By contrast, it made only modest cuts — or added money — for overseas economic and development aid programs favored by many moderates and liberals in Congress.

Early in 1988, the Reagan administration appealed to

Congress to reverse some of the cuts in foreign aid programs. In a letter to congressional leaders Jan. 28, 1988, Secretary of State George P. Shultz said the United States was facing a "foreign policy crisis" because of budget cutbacks.

Almost as serious as the cutbacks, Shultz said, was the fact that Congress virtually eliminated the administration's flexibility to decide how to spend money in several key programs. The practice of earmarking substantial portions of the foreign aid program perhaps had reached a high point in the fiscal 1988 spending bill, with 96.8 percent of the Economic Support Fund (ESF), 99.3 percent of the Foreign Military Sales (FMS) loan program and 60.4 percent of the Military Assistance Program (MAP) grants earmarked for specific countries.

Shultz said that the combination of cutbacks and earmarking meant that the administration had to eliminate aid programs for some 30 countries, most of them in Africa and Latin America. But Shultz gave no hint as to solutions. In the past the foreign aid budget had been bolstered by supplemental appropriations bills, but the November 1987 budget summit agreement promised to avoid supplementals except for emergencies.

**Pakistan.** The key compromise during the conference on foreign aid provisions centered around aid to Pakistan. Proponents of a tough non-proliferation policy hoped to make continued aid to Pakistan contingent on that country's abandoning its reported nuclear weapons program. But in the final bill, Congress agreed to allow Pakistan's aid program to go forward without significant restrictions for two and a half years. *(Box, p. 225)*

**Debt 'Reform.'** After years of talking about it, Congress acted in 1987 to ease the debt burden on countries that over the years borrowed billions of dollars to buy weapons from the United States. Some countries, especially in the Middle East, were paying the United States nearly as much each year on old loans as they received in new foreign aid.

The debt "reform" proposal was originally drafted by a Senate subcommittee primarily to benefit Israel. At the insistence of the House, the plan was broadened in the final bill to be of potential benefit to several dozen countries.

## House, Senate Action

The House Dec. 3 approved a $13.19 billion foreign aid program for fiscal 1988, as part of the omnibus continuing appropriations resolution.

The House Appropriations Committee had reported its version of the foreign aid spending bill (HR 3186 — H Rept 100-283) on Aug. 6. The panel — led by some of the staunchest proponents of foreign aid on Capitol Hill — said budget limits had forced its nearly 17 percent cut in Reagan's foreign aid request.

The House bill stipulated that certain funds would be available to some countries only if they upheld civil or political rights. It also included provisions intended to ensure that U.S. aid did not hurt the environment.

Despite its longtime support of channeling development aid through multilateral agencies, the House panel made proportionally very large cuts in the request for these programs because of the overall budget limits. But it approved 90 percent of the amount requested for direct aid to improve the living conditions of poor people in developing countries — the most politically palatable part of the unpopular aid program.

The impact of cuts in the military assistance program and the ESF, which was used to aid countries bearing especially heavy defense costs, was greater than it appeared because large amounts were earmarked for specific countries, such as Israel, Egypt and Pakistan.

Under the House bill, aid to Pakistan would be temporarily halted between Oct. 1, 1987 — the start of fiscal 1988 — and Jan. 15, 1988, and then resumed once Reagan sent Congress a report on that country's nuclear program.

By the time the Senate Appropriations Committee marked up its version of the foreign aid money bill, anticipated funding cuts were lessened by the Nov. 20 Congress-White House budget summit.

Under heavy lobbying by the administration for its high-priority foreign aid program, summit negotiators quietly accepted procedures that enabled congressional committees to preserve some of the money they had planned to cut.

The full Senate approved a $13.59 billion aid program as part of the continuing resolution.

The Senate-passed measure included an extraordinarily complex provision on the issue of aid to Pakistan that attempted to link U.S. policy toward Pakistan and India.

After several years of generally endorsing Reagan administration requests, the Senate Appropriations panel joined its House counterpart in calling for a reassessment of major aspects of the U.S. military aid program. In one of its most important actions, the committee slashed Reagan's request for the MAP grants and called for a return to the original purpose of the program: aiding a few "key nations that have severe financial problems."

Similarly, the Senate committee challenged the administration's heavy use of FMS aid to bolster friendly countries for political reasons. In its report, the panel said the program originally was intended to help countries rebuild their military forces on their own, but instead had added to the debt burdens of U.S. allies and encouraged many nations to make purchases and create military force structures they could not support on their own.

The Senate bill included a provision to help ease the debt burden of these arms purchasers, although it would primarily have benefited Israel.

In one of its most controversial actions, the committee adopted an amendment barring the sale of Stinger anti-aircraft missiles during 1988 to any country in the Persian Gulf region. The immediate impact would be to block a proposed $7 million sale of the sophisticated missiles to Bahrain. The committee provision was modified during Senate floor action to allow the sale to Bahrain, under the condition that any unused missiles would be returned in 18 months. By that time, under the floor amendment, the United States would agree to supply Bahrain with an alternative air defense system.

The Senate bill set conditions for aid to certain countries, including the socialist government of Mozambique.

## Final Action, Provisions

Foreign aid appropriations for fiscal 1988 were included in the fiscal 1988 continuing appropriations resolution (H J Res 395 — PL 100-202) cleared by Congress Dec. 22. President Reagan signed it into law that same day.

Funding levels in the $13.59 billion foreign aid portion of the resolution included $1.45 billion for multilateral aid, $6.11 billion for bilateral aid, $5.32 billion for military aid and $690 million for Export-Import Bank direct loans.

Major provisions of H J Res 395:

**Pakistan.** Gave the president authority to exempt Pakistan from nuclear non-proliferation laws until April 1, 1990 — approximately two and a half years. It also included $480 million in aid for Pakistan during fiscal 1988. Of that amount, $260 million would be military aid (including $30 million in grants) and $220 million would be economic aid.

**Debt Reform.** Allowed countries with good credit records (such as Israel and Spain) to pay off their old loans for U.S. weapons purchases — many of which carried interest rates of 11-12 percent — and obtain U.S. guarantees for 90 percent of any private loans they took out to make the prepayments. To qualify, any country that was behind on its past payments to the FMS program would have to bring them to within 90 days of being on time. The bill authorized up to $6 billion in refinancings during fiscal 1988.

● Allowed countries with poorer credit records (such as Turkey) to ask the United States to reduce the interest rate on their outstanding loans to 10 percent. To reduce the budget impact in fiscal 1987, the new rates would not be available until Oct. 1, 1988 — the beginning of the next fiscal year. The final bill established a $270 million limit on what could be spent to "buy down" the interest rates; that effectively limited the number of countries that could benefit from the program. To qualify for this program, any country behind on its past FMS payments would be given two years to start making its payments within 90 days of being on time.

**Security Assistance.** Appropriated $700.8 million for the MAP program, which made outright grants to foreign countries so they could buy U.S. weapons. The amount was just over half of the $1.3 billion request.

● Appropriated $4 billion for the FMS loan program, a cut of nearly $400 million from Reagan's request.

● Appropriated $3.2 billion for the ESF. Reagan requested $3.6 billion.

**Greece, Turkey.** Retained the 7-10 ratio for aid to Greece and Turkey, allocating $343 million in military aid for Greece and $490 million for Turkey.

● Required that U.S. military sales agreements with Turkey stipulate that arms would not be transferred to Cyprus "or otherwise used to further the severance or division of Cyprus." Turkey since 1974 had occupied the southern third of Cyprus.

**Middle East.** Appropriated $1.8 billion in military aid and $1.2 billion in economic aid for Israel, and $1.3 billion in military aid and $815 million in economic aid for Egypt.

● Included several other bonuses for Israel in return for that country's agreement to cancel its Lavi fighter plane project. *(Box, this page)*

● Allowed the sale of some 70 Stinger anti-aircraft missiles to Bahrain, an island nation in the Persian Gulf. Any unused missiles would be returned in 18 months, by which time the United States would agree to supply Bahrain with an alternative air defense system.

**Western Hemisphere.** Barred most forms of U.S. aid to Haiti and Panama until the president reported that democratically elected civilian governments were in office. The bill also suspended Panama's quota for sugar exports to the United States and ordered U.S. representatives to the international development banks to vote against any new loans for Panama.

● Allowed the CIA to continue working with the regime

# Israeli Lavi Canceled

Under enormous pressure from the United States, Israel in 1987 agreed to cancel production of a new jet fighter, the Lavi. But the United States ended up granting sizable economic concessions to Israel in exchange.

The Lavi program was a major source of jobs in Israel and in recent years had become an important symbol of Israeli nationalism. As a result, its cancellation was highly controversial.

In pressuring Israel to scrap the plan, the Reagan administration argued that the Lavi was too expensive and not substantially different from aircraft Israel could buy elsewhere. The administration also argued that the $550 million spent on it each year could be better used in other parts of the Israeli military budget.

As of the 1987 fiscal year, which ended Sept. 30, Israel had devoted more than $1.5 billion in U.S. foreign aid to developing and beginning production of the plane. Canceling contracts and taking other steps to shut down production reportedly would cost another $400 million to $500 million.

Congress had played a major role in U.S. financing of the Lavi. Beginning in 1984, Congress had required that $450 million annually in U.S. foreign aid be spent on the plane, most of it for work in Israel. Since then, Congress had earmarked $1.8 billion for the plane, some of which had not yet been spent.

Incentives offered to Israel to encourage cancellation of the program were included in the fiscal 1988 continuing appropriations resolution (H J Res 395 — PL 100-202) cleared by Congress Dec. 22, 1987.

In addition to the administration's requests of $1.8 billion in military aid and $1.2 billion in economic aid, the bill included several bonuses for Israel:

● Authority to spend $400 million of U.S. aid to buy military services and equipment in Israel. Normally, all U.S. aid had been used to buy goods and services from the United States. Israel could use as much of that aid as it wanted to subsidize the cost of closing down production of the Lavi fighter.

The bill also allocated $150 million for Lavi-related expenses in the United States. Several large U.S. defense contractors had been major participants in the Lavi project.

● Continued permission to require U.S. defense contractors to buy goods in Israel in return for the sale of their products to Israel, even when the sales were financed by U.S. foreign aid. This privilege, available only to Israel, generated about $150 million annually in sales for Israeli firms.

of Gen. Manuel Antonio Noriega in Panama for "the collection of necessary intelligence." There were reports that Noriega was a major source of intelligence information for the United States on developments in Central and South America.

● Earmarked the following amounts of economic aid: Costa Rica, $90 million; El Salvador, $185 million; Guatemala, $80 million; and Honduras, $85 million.

● Imposed several restrictions on aid to El Salvador, but none was as severe as the detailed human rights conditions that Congress imposed in the early 1980s.

● Included $7 million in military grants for Guatemala, the highest amount of military aid to that country since the mid-1970s. Since the election in 1985 of President Vinicio Cerezo, Congress gradually had been restoring military aid and lifting conditions on how it could be spent.

**International Banks.** Enacted into law the text of HR 3750, which provided statutory authority for U.S. contributions to several international development banks. It included authority for the administration to pledge $2.875 billion over three years as the U.S. share of the eighth replenishment of resources for the International Development Association (IDA), an arm of the World Bank.

HR 3750 also authorized U.S. participation in the new Multilateral Investment Guarantee Agency (MIGA), which would insure private investment in Third World countries against extraordinary losses, such as those resulting from war and civil disturbances.

● Appropriated $915 million for IDA — more than either chamber had approved.

● Appropriated the full $44.4 million request for the initial U.S. contribution to MIGA — the administration's highest priority among development banks.

**Afghanistan.** Appropriated $45 million for aid to Afghan refugees living in Pakistan. This money was in addition to the reported $500 million to $600 million in covert military aid that the United States supplied annually to guerrillas battling the Soviet occupation of Afghanistan.

**Other Issues.** Appropriated $35 million for the latest U.S. contribution to an international fund for development in Northern Ireland and the Republic of Ireland.

● Banned aid to Liberia unless political and economic reforms were made.

● Provided up to $5 million in economic and military aid for non-communist guerrilla forces in Cambodia.

● Provided $125 million in military aid, $40 million in development aid and $124 million in economic aid for the Philippines. An additional $50 million was earmarked for agrarian reform programs.

● Banned any U.S. aid to countries that supported international terrorism.

● Modified a longtime ban on any aid to Argentina and Brazil because of their alleged efforts to produce nuclear weapons, by allowing training aid to those countries' military forces.

● Permitted the administration to spend some $1 million to promote peace negotiations in Central America.

● Continued a ban on all military aid to Mozambique, but modified restrictions in previous law on economic and development aid.

● Earmarked $8 million for construction of a school for North African Jews who had resettled in France, but, after an avalanche of criticism, Congress rescinded the money in 1988. Sponsor Sen. Daniel K. Inouye, D-Hawaii, called the aid an "error in judgment." (*Rescission, p. 889*)

**Fiscal 1988 Supplemental**

Congress cleared a fiscal 1988 supplemental appropriations bill (HR 5026 — PL 100-393) on Aug. 11, 1988. The bill included $24 million for emergency assistance to Soviet and other political refugees.

# 1989 Aid Appropriations

For the first time since 1981, Congress in 1988 approved a free-standing appropriations bill for foreign aid. The measure (HR 4637 — PL 100-461) appropriating $14.3 billion for foreign aid in fiscal 1989 cleared Congress with less than a minute to spare before the Oct. 1 start of the fiscal year.

Each earlier year of the Reagan administration had seen contentious battles over foreign aid priorities and specifics such as aid to El Salvador. As a result, seven straight aid bills were folded into omnibus continuing resolution appropriations measures.

President Reagan and congressional leaders had pledged in 1988 to avoid putting all 13 appropriations bills into another continuing resolution. That meant that both chambers of Congress had to vote on a separate foreign aid bill. Administration officials and leaders of both parties realized that such a bill would escape devastating cuts in the House and Senate only if it had broad support.

That support in both chambers was made possible by the 1987 budget "summit" between Reagan and Capitol Hill leaders. The summit established the overall level of foreign aid spending for fiscal years 1988-89. That resolved the basic issue of how much to spend on foreign aid and eased the way for the Appropriations panels to craft a widely accepted bill. The administration worked with Congress at every stage of the process and wound up having relatively minor complaints about the bill.

The bill took the latest in a series of steps toward shifting the military aid program to an all-grant basis. All but $410 million of the $4.7 billion of the amount set aside to help foreign countries buy U.S. weapons was in the form of grants.

### House Action

With an extraordinary outpouring of bipartisan support, the House on May 25 passed a $14.3 billion foreign aid appropriations bill for fiscal 1989.

The 328-90 vote for HR 4637 put to rest, for the time, the conventional wisdom that foreign aid bills were too politically unpopular to be passed in election years. An overwhelming majority of members of both parties — 209 Democrats and 119 Republicans — supported the measure, giving it the widest margin of any foreign aid spending bill in the House since before 1965.

Members and administration officials credited the two leaders of the Appropriations Subcommittee on Foreign Operations with getting the aid bill through the House. Chairman David R. Obey, D-Wis., and ranking Republican Mickey Edwards, Okla., worked to reach agreement on normally contentious issues and to head off divisive amendments.

Their work paid off in two ways: members proposed only a handful of floor amendments to the bill, none of which proved especially controversial; and members apparently realized that they could safely vote for a foreign aid

# World Bank Funding

To the surprise of many, Congress in 1988 authorized paying the U.S. share of a $75 billion increase in the World Bank's capital. The money would be paid over six years. Only $70.9 million would be paid each year out of the Treasury; an additional $2.3 billion in "callable capital" would be used as collateral by the bank to borrow on the open market and would be "called" only if the bank were near bankruptcy.

The annual payments were still subject to appropriations, and $50 million for fiscal 1989 was included in the regular foreign aid spending bill (HR 4637 — PL 100-461). The reduced appropriation, and threats in the conference report on the bill to make cuts in future-year appropriations, were intended as a signal to the administration and the bank that more progress was needed on the Third World debt problem, according to conferees.

The World Bank's capital increase was widely regarded as necessary to permit increased lending to developing countries. World Bank lending would climb from about $14 billion annually to $20 billion once the increase was fully in place.

## Legislative Action

Congress was unable to clear a separate authorization for the first U.S. installment of the World Bank capital increase. The House Banking Committee had approved an authorization bill (HR 4645 — H Rept 100-994), but the measure went no further. Opposition from two fronts tied up the bill: Conservatives opposed the no-strings-attached contributions to multilateral lending institutions, and some liberals objected to the administration policy on Third World debt.

The House Appropriations Committee refused to include the first installment in its version of the foreign aid spending bill.

Underlying the World Bank impasse were disagreements over how to handle Third World debt. Congressional supporters of the development banks were unhappy that approximately 25 percent of the World Bank's loans went not for specific development projects but for "structural adjustment" — loans premised on changes in a country's economic policies.

That money, critics complained, was merely being recycled to large U.S. and European commercial banks whose loans to the Third World in the 1970s and early 1980s were not being repaid. They said it did little to benefit the countries and was not too unlike a taxpayer bailout of banks that had made bad loans to the Third World.

Taking an opposite tack from its House counterpart, the Senate Appropriations Committee approved the $70.9 million payment, but the committee attached one major condition to the money: It first had to be approved in authorizing legislation. Bills to authorize U.S. participation in the general capital increase were stalled in committee.

During floor action on the foreign aid appropriations bill July 7, the Senate took contradictory positions on the new U.S. contribution to the World Bank. On a 48-41 vote, the Senate voted to table an amendment that would have killed the contribution. The Senate then accepted an amendment requiring that U.S. contributions to the bank be the first to be cut in any sequestering of funds under the Gramm-Rudman-Hollings deficit-control act. (An across-the-board budget cut under that law generally was considered to be unlikely.) The Senate also agreed to table, 70-19, an amendment to delete the annual contribution to the International Development Association, a World Bank agency that made loans to the world's poorest countries.

House-Senate conferees on the foreign aid appropriations bill settled on a $50 million contribution and agreed to include the House committee version of the authorization bill in the appropriations measure. Opponents tried and failed in both chambers to use procedural motions to block the contribution before the bill cleared Sept. 30.

bill that was endorsed by the leaders of both parties and the Reagan administration.

Until the Reagan administration, House Democrats typically supported foreign aid and Republicans opposed it. But in the Reagan years, many Democrats had resisted the administration's emphasis on military aid to anti-communist regimes, while Republicans increasingly supported foreign aid because of that emphasis.

A major provision of the House version of the spending bill barred expenditure of any fiscal 1989 foreign aid funds unless Congress had enacted an authorization bill. Authorizations normally were required for appropriations, but Congress in recent years had avoided that requirement by folding foreign aid into omnibus governmentwide spending bills.

The House did pass a foreign aid authorization bill (HR 3100) in late 1987, but the Senate did not debate its version of the legislation (S 1274). *(Foreign aid authorization, p. 224)*

HR 4637 had been reported by the full Appropriations Committee on May 19 (H Rept 100-641). The committee had endorsed the subcommittee bill after only a 12-minute markup session. Although the bill's total nearly matched Reagan's requests for fiscal 1989, the bill shifted millions of dollars among accounts.

A key element of the bill was bipartisan support in Obey's subcommittee for rejecting two administration requests.

One of the rejected requests was for the first $70.9 million installment on a new U.S. contribution to the general capital of the World Bank. That request had only lukewarm backing from the administration and key Democrats, and it was opposed by most Republicans. *(World Bank, box, p. 229)*

The subcommittee rejected an important administration request to convert the $4 billion Foreign Military Sales (FMS) loan program to an all-grant basis. The FMS program was the last major foreign aid category that relied heavily on a combination of loans and grants. In previous years Congress and the administration had converted most other programs to grants, in hopes of easing the debt burden on developing countries.

For fiscal 1989, the administration had proposed eliminating FMS loans and replacing them with grants. It would pay for the increased budget outlays by reducing the size of the FMS program by some $400 million and by slicing another $233 million from a companion account, the Military Assistance Program (MAP).

Obey, while supporting the idea of easing foreign-debt burdens, objected to the Reagan proposal on budgetary grounds. At his insistence, the subcommittee voted to retain the overall mix of the two aid programs. However, it made a major concession to the administration by boosting the MAP to $876 million, nearly double Reagan's request and a hefty $176 million increase over the current level.

HR 4637 gave the administration the aid requested for Israel, Egypt and Pakistan, as well as some flexibility — but not much — in setting aid levels for the "base rights" countries. Those were nations that hosted U.S. military installations and received large doses of foreign aid in return. In recent years, Congress had chopped substantially the administration's requests for those countries, angering the governments, many of which were under domestic political pressure to oust U.S. military installations.

In spite of renewed concern on Capitol Hill about political developments in El Salvador, the subcommittee continued a modest loosening of the strings on aid to that country.

## Senate Action

The Senate passed its version of the foreign aid spending bill July 7 with remarkable ease. The 76-15 vote masked the customary opposition to spending on foreign aid. As in the House, Senate action was eased by the bipartisan harmony prevailing on most budget issues since the 1987 budget summit.

The Senate sidestepped nearly all controversies that could slow or threaten the bill. For example, proponents of renewed restrictions on aid to El Salvador decided not to press the issue as a floor amendment, which would face certain defeat.

Supporters of a new package of aid to the Nicaraguan contras also chose not to offer that as a proposal to the foreign aid bill, saying they would wait until the Senate considered the Defense Department appropriations bill. Wanting to avoid a vote on the contra issue prior to the Democratic convention, Senate leaders had pulled the defense bill from the schedule until after then. *(Contra aid, p. 213)*

As reported by the Senate Appropriations Committee June 22 (S Rept 100-395) and passed by the Senate, the foreign aid bill nearly matched Reagan's $14.3 billion request for economic, military and overseas development aid

programs. The bill also included funds for "export assistance," primarily operations of the Export-Import Bank.

One major difference between the Senate and House versions was a matter of congressional procedure. The House bill barred expenditure of any aid funds that were not authorized by separate legislation; in effect, that bill sought to force the Senate to act on S 1274, the stalled foreign aid authorization bill.

The Senate appropriations bill waived the requirement for a separate authorization, except for contributions to international development banks, such as the World Bank.

In considering the aid bill, the Senate devoted most of its attention to an effort by an absent member — Jesse Helms, R-N.C., who was ill — to pressure Costa Rica into negotiating with an American citizen who had a claim against that government. The issue carried political ramifications well beyond the usual disputes over international claims, because some members accused Helms of attempting to punish Costa Rican President Oscar Arias for opposing U.S. policy toward Nicaragua. The outcome was a compromise that could increase the pressure on Costa Rica while offering the possibility for a speeded-up resolution of the dispute.

The Senate adopted — on a voice vote with no debate — an amendment barring the sale of any Maverick missiles to Kuwait and barring delivery of the Mavericks even if the sale went through. The vote came just hours after the administration announced a proposed arms sale to Kuwait. *(Arms sales, p. 233)*

The Senate also considered several amendments dealing with World Bank funding, including a disputed proposal for a new U.S. donation to the World Bank that had been rejected in the House but included in the Senate measure.

The Senate bill approved one of the administration's most important aid initiatives — shifting the military aid program to an all-grant basis. Under the Senate bill, all U.S. military aid would be in the form of FMS loans, on which payment would be forgiven. In effect, those loans would be grants.

The Senate bill contained the president's full requests for aid to Israel and Egypt but made a relatively substantial cut in aid to Pakistan in light of the impending Soviet departure from Afghanistan.

As passed by the Senate, HR 4637 extended an existing ban on sales of Stinger anti-aircraft missiles to countries in the Persian Gulf region, with the exception of Bahrain. Congress objected to such sales on the grounds that the portable weapons could full into the hands of terrorists.

The Senate bill included the full $185 million requested for economic aid to El Salvador but did not earmark specific funds for military aid (the administration had requested $95 million). A close vote rejecting an attempt by liberals to impose limited but symbolically important restrictions on U.S. military aid to El Salvador had highlighted Senate Appropriations Committee markup of the bill. The committee had responded, primarily, to an appeal from the ailing Salvador president, José Napoleón Duarte, who, in spite of his political troubles, remained one of the most popular foreign leaders among members of Congress.

## Conference, Final Action

House-Senate conferees hammered out a compromise bill (H Rept 100-983) Sept. 22-23. But last-minute amendments and political battles snarled the measure up to the

Oct. 1 start of the new fiscal year.

Conferees had been unable to reach agreement on a Senate provision barring the sale of Maverick missiles to Kuwait. Although the administration and House members had worked out an agreement that involved shifting the types of Mavericks to be provided, Sen. Dennis DeConcini, D-Ariz., sponsor of the Senate amendment, insisted that the compromise was inadequate. The issue was finally resolved when Senate conferees, by a close vote Sept. 26, agreed to drop the amendment.

The House initially adopted the conference report Sept. 28 by a remarkably strong 327-92 vote. The Senate acted by voice vote on Sept. 30. But there were still battles to be fought.

On Sept. 29 the House resolved one procedural dispute when it accepted the conferees' decision to add provisions enacting authorizations for OPIC, the Overseas Private Investment Corporation (HR 5263 — H Rept 100-922) and the World Bank and African Development Fund (HR 4645 — H Rept 100-994), and waiving an authorization requirement for all other foreign aid programs.

The Senate on Sept. 30 agreed to table, 57-34, an effort to delete the World Bank provisions but then added a sweeping amendment based on its own OPIC bill (S 2757 — S Rept 100-500), with unrelated provisions. The Senate next added a series of amendments on topics ranging from diplomatic immunity to a China satellite deal to Iraq's alleged use of chemical weapons.

The House accepted the non-controversial provisions of the OPIC bill but rejected the others. The Senate agreed to drop the amendments and cleared the bill at 11:59 p.m. on Sept. 30, a minute shy of the new fiscal year.

## Major Provisions

The final version of the foreign aid appropriations bill (PL 100-461) provided $14.3 billion in fiscal 1989 for foreign aid and related programs. This included $1.54 billion for multilateral aid, $6.3 billion for bilateral aid, $5.72 billion for military aid and $695 million for the Export-Import Bank direct loan program.

Major provisions of HR 4637:

**Security Assistance.** Established a three-part military aid program: $467 million in MAP grants; $3.862 billion in FMS grants; and $410 million in FMS loans. The loans were to be at "concessional" interest rates of 5 percent or more.

● Required that at least $876.75 million of the entire military aid program ($467 million MAP grants and $409.75 million of the FMS program) be in the form of sales between the U.S. government and foreign countries. This provision was to reduce the portion of FMS aid that could be used to finance commercial arms sales overseas.

● Approved $47.4 million for the International Military Education and Training program, which provided training in the United States for officers from foreign countries.

● Appropriated $3.3 billion for the Economic Support Fund (ESF).

**Middle East.** Earmarked $1.8 billion in military aid and $1.2 billion in economic aid for Israel, and $1.3 billion in military aid and $815 million in economic aid for Egypt.

● Deleted the Pentagon's administrative and research-development expenses from the price of F-16s sold to both Israel and Egypt. Conferees set limits on the savings: $90 million for Israel's 60 planes and $49.7 million for Egypt's 40 planes.

● Extended for another year a provision allowing Israel to spend military aid in ways that no other country could. Israel could spend up to $400 million of its aid to support its own defense industry. Israel also could spend another $150 million to buy research and development services in the United States for weapons produced in Israel. *(Background, Lavi cancellation, box, p. 227)*

● Banned arms sales to Qatar unless it turned over to the United States about a dozen U.S.-made Stinger anti-aircraft missiles that it somehow obtained without Washington's permission. The ban was effective April 1, 1989.

● Earmarked $15 million for development programs in Jordan and $15 million for private development efforts in the West Bank and Gaza Strip.

**Central America.** Required that at least 25 percent of economic aid to El Salvador be used for education, health and other development programs instead of to bolster the Salvadoran government's overall budget.

● Earmarked $9 million in military aid for Guatemala and linked the money to continued support of the government by the armed forces. There had been an unsuccessful military coup attempt in Guatemala in May.

● Earmarked $85 million for economic aid to Honduras.

● Allocated $2 million for operations in Nicaragua by the National Endowment for Democracy, a quasi-government agency that provided money for opposition groups in Nicaragua, including political parties, labor unions and the newspaper *La Prensa*.

● Banned aid to the Panamanian regime of Gen. Manuel Antonio Noriega, or any successor regime in Panama that was not under civilian control and did not allow political freedoms.

**Anti-Drug Programs.** Earmarked money for several narcotics-producing countries that had taken steps to meet U.S. concerns on the issue, including the following combined amounts: $61 million in economic aid for Bolivia, Ecuador, Jamaica and Peru; $16.5 million in military aid for Bolivia, Colombia, Ecuador and Jamaica, plus an additional $3.5 million for equipment to be used in anti-narcotics efforts; $15 million under the U.S. anti-narcotics program for Bolivia; and $7 million for a Latin American regional program.

**International Banks.** Included $1.3 billion in new budget authority to cover U.S. contributions to six multilateral development banks: $50 million for the first U.S. contribution to a major increase in funding for the World Bank; $995 million for the International Development Association and $4.9 million for the International Finance Corporation, both arms of the World Bank; $152.4 million for the Asian Development Bank and Fund; $7.3 million for the African Development Bank; and $105 million for the African Development Fund. Conferees earmarked some of the funds for "arrearages," unpaid commitments to the banks.

**Congressional Prerogatives.** Barred the administration from transferring funds from one account to another, thus depriving the White House of a major degree of flexibility in spending foreign aid money. When the administration raised constitutional objections to a standard provision carried for years in foreign aid appropriations bills, requiring the administration to go to the Appropriations committees for permission to transfer money from one account to another, conferees approved more restrictive language eliminating administration flexibility entirely.

● Barred the administration from spending any money in the bill until it fully obligated the $60.4 million earmarked for UNICEF, the U.N. Children's Fund. UNICEF easily was one of the most popular items in the entire bill, but each year Reagan had proposed budget cuts and delayed making the U.S. contribution that Congress mandated.

● Required advance notice of any potential sales of ground-to-air missiles, such as Stingers, and air-to-ground missiles, such as Mavericks, regardless of price. Previously, Congress was given advance notice only of sales valued at $14 million or more.

**Pakistan.** Earmarked $230 million in military aid and $215 million in economic assistance, a move to reassure Pakistan of continued U.S. support in the wake of the death of Pakistani President Mohammed Zia ul-Haq and in the weeks leading up to that country's parliamentary elections.

**Afghanistan.** Earmarked $23 million for aid to Afghan refugees inside Afghanistan and neighboring Pakistan. The refugees also were to get $65 million in other aid programs.

**Greece, Turkey.** Earmarked $350 million in military aid for Greece and $500 million for Turkey, in keeping with the 7-10 ratio for military aid to those countries followed by Congress since the late 1970s.

**Philippines.** Earmarked $125 million in MAP grants and $40 million in development aid for the Philippines, but took no position on Reagan's request for $124 million in ESF aid for that country.

**Base Rights.** Allowed the president to shift foreign aid funds away from any nation that "significantly reduced" its military or economic cooperation with Washington — a warning to countries hosting U.S. military installations. The provision did not specify particular countries, but it clearly was aimed at Greece and the Philippines, both of which were making tough demands in negotiations over extending U.S. access to bases there.

**Third-Country Sales.** Established a new procedure giving Congress a specific right to reject so-called "third-party transfers": sales of U.S.-made arms between other countries.

**Other Issues.** Appropriated $35 million for the American Schools and Hospitals Abroad (ASHA), a small program that for years had been the focal point of intense politicking among members of Congress. The program hit the headlines early in 1988 during a controversy over an $8 million appropriation on behalf of a school in France for Jewish refugees from North Africa. That appropriation was eventually rescinded. *(Rescission, p. 889)*

● Allowed $15 million in military aid for Kenya but no economic aid, a compromise reached after one of the conference's most heated arguments because of recent political restrictions in that country.

● Released $5 million of $20 million in economic aid to Honduras that had been withheld by a fiscal 1987 supplemental appropriations bill (HR 1827 — PL 100-71) in order to force that country to settle a claim by a private U.S. citizen.

● Required the State Department to report to Congress on a claim by a private U.S. citizen against Costa Rica.

● Earmarked $35 million for Jamaican relief and reconstruction efforts required in the wake of Hurricane Gilbert.

● Mandated at least $10 million and encouraged the administration to spend at least another $10 million in aid to Northern Ireland and the Republic of Ireland. The administration had planned to end U.S. participation in an international fund that was financing Irish economic development.

● Expanded the categories of non-military aid that the United States could provide to Haiti, but conferees expressed distress at the continuing "cycle of violence and repression" in that country.

● Earmarked $50 million in economic aid to Portugal and allowed the administration to set the amount of military aid.

● Extended an existing provision allowing the administration to spend up to $5 million to aid non-communist guerrilla forces in Cambodia, despite reports of corruption in the program.

● Included a $5 million program to provide artificial limbs for civilians wounded in conflicts in countries such as El Salvador, Mozambique and Vietnam. The Senate panel had encouraged the administration to give private agencies $1 million to provide medical devices in Vietnam. Although unlikely in the immediate future, such a program would represent the first official U.S. aid to that country since the Vietnam War ended in 1975.

# 1987 Saudi Arms Sales

President Reagan in 1987 won congressional approval of a major arms sale to Saudi Arabia — but only after resorting to his practice of making compromises to overcome opposition, this time by the pro-Israel lobby.

The White House in October 1987 worked out a deal with senators allowing approval of a $1 billion arms package, including 12 new F-15 warplanes, upgraded electronics for F-15s the Saudis already owned, upgraded parts for tanks and other equipment.

At the insistence of senators, Reagan withdrew his proposal to sell the Saudis 1,600 Maverick air-to-ground missiles. The withdrawal of the Maverick sale amounted to a rerun: Reagan had sought to make the sale earlier in the year but had backed down in June in the face of congressional pressure.

One of those participating in the October negotiations, Senate Minority Leader Robert Dole, R-Kan., said the revised weapons sale "helps a friend" while not threatening Israel.

Dole also said that 68 senators had indicated disapproval of the weapons proposal that included the Mavericks, which would have made it virtually impossible for the White House to have secured congressional approval. In addition, a majority of House members also had signaled their opposition to selling the missiles to Saudi Arabia.

The Saudis had purchased 2,500 earlier models of the Maverick since 1976. The more sophisticated version sought in 1987 could lock onto a target more quickly and, in many circumstances, farther away than had been possible with earlier versions.

The administration had wanted to provide additional weapons to Saudi Arabia in part to acknowledge that country's support of the United States in the volatile Persian Gulf region. *(Persian Gulf events, p. 315)*

But critics said that Saudi Arabia did not face any kind of land threat to its security, ruling out the need for the Maverick air-to-ground missiles.

Sen. Howard M. Metzenbaum, D-Ohio, said Saudi Arabia had been "somewhat helpful" toward U.S. interests in the Persian Gulf but not as helpful as it could have been. He and others also said the Maverick missiles posed a threat to Israel's security. Metzenbaum was one of the congressional negotiators who worked out the compromise deal with the White House.

The compromise package would allow Reagan to send Mavericks to Saudi Arabia in an emergency. But lawmakers said only a drastic action such as war between the Saudis and Iran would constitute such an emergency.

The Arms Export Control Act required the administration to notify Congress of arms sales exceeding certain dollar amounts and provided lawmakers with an opportunity to disapprove such sales. Congress could block an arms sale by passing a joint resolution, which had to be presented to the president for his signature or veto.

Congress had never formally prevented a president from selling arms to a foreign country, although it had come close to breaking that record in 1986. That year, Reagan barely won approval for another Saudi weapons package after stripping from it controversial Stinger antiaircraft missiles. *(1986 Saudi arms sale, p. 198)*

### Stingers for Bahrain

Under the October compromise on Saudi arms, the White House also agreed not to provide $7 million for 60-70 Stinger missiles to Bahrain, an island nation in the Persian Gulf. Opponents said the shoulder-fired weapons could wind up in the hands of terrorists.

In December, however, Congress retreated somewhat on the Bahrain Stinger ban. The Senate, in considering an omnibus continuing appropriations resolution for fiscal 1988 (H J Res 395 — PL 100-202), agreed to allow the sale to Bahrain under the condition that any unused missiles be returned in 18 months. By that time the United States would agree to supply Bahrain with an alternative air defense system.

After intense lobbying by Defense Secretary Frank C. Carlucci, conferees on the measure let the sale of the Stingers go through.

# 1988 Middle East Arms Sales

President Reagan in 1988 again sparked some controversy on Capitol Hill when he informed Congress of several proposed arms sales to Middle East and Persian Gulf states.

The most controversial of these was a proposed $1.9 billion sale of 40 F/A-18 Navy warplanes and associated missiles to Kuwait. Pro-Israel members of Congress criticized the sale as a potential threat to Israel and as an unnecessary escalation of sophisticated weaponry in the region. But the sale went through after the administration and House members agreed to alter the types of Maverick air-to-surface missiles that would be provided to Kuwait.

In spite of that deal, several members of the Senate Appropriations Committee tried to kill the Kuwait sale by stripping all Maverick missiles from the package. But that effort failed after intense lobbying by the administration.

Another arms sale, of $825 million in ground support forces for Airborne Warning and Control System (AWACS) planes, as well as other military items to Saudi Arabia, prompted some Capitol Hill complaints but no organized opposition.

Congress also received notice from the Reagan administration of its intention to sell arms to Egypt and Israel. Each sale was worth $2 billion.

Later in the year, during the House-Senate conference on the foreign aid appropriations bill (PL 100-461), both Israel and Egypt got pricing breaks on their purchases of F-16s. *(Foreign aid bill, p. 228)*

### Kuwait Arms Sale

The Reagan administration in June informally notified Congress of its intent to sell 40 F/A-18 fighter-bombers to Kuwait — the first sale of those sophisticated Navy planes to a country other than a formal ally. The $1.9 billion proposed package also included 200 Maverick-D air-to-surface missiles and 100 Maverick-G anti-ship missiles, as well as other air-to-air and anti-ship missiles and munitions including cluster bombs.

Capitol Hill critics warned that the planes could be used to attack Israel, either by basing them in neighboring countries or by obtaining extra-large fuel tanks that would extend their range. Others complained that the United States was contributing to the Middle East arms race.

Sen. Dennis DeConcini, D-Ariz., suggested that the administration consider dropping the Maverick missiles from the proposed sale. Congressional opposition in 1987 had forced the administration to withdraw Mavericks from a proposed arms sale to Saudi Arabia.

On July 7, hours after the administration formally notified Congress of the proposed sale, the Senate voted its opposition to inclusion of the controversial Mavericks in the package. On a voice vote with no debate, the Senate adopted a DeConcini amendment to the fiscal 1989 foreign aid appropriations bill (HR 4637) barring the sale of any Mavericks to Kuwait, as well as the delivery of the Mavericks even if the sale went through.

The administration defended the decision to include Mavericks in the package, saying that not supplying the missiles to Kuwait would leave a "gap" in the ability of the F/A-18 to hit land- or sea-based targets. Officials insisted that the missile-equipped F/A-18s would not threaten Israel because they could not reach that country. They also argued that the United States was losing sales and influence when it rejected requests by Arab countries to buy U.S weapons.

Efforts continued in both houses to block the entire sale — primarily as a negotiating tactic with the administration.

The administration and pro-Israel House members on Aug. 3 announced they had reached a compromise allowing the administration to sell Kuwait nearly all the weapons it wanted, but under terms meant to reduce the potential threat to Israel. The major change from the original proposal was the deletion of the 100 Maverick-D air-to-surface missiles. Instead, Kuwait would get 100 more Maverick-G anti-ship missiles than first planned, for a total of 300.

The Maverick-D missile generally was used against tanks and other ground-based targets and could threaten Israel in an all-out Middle East war, critics insisted. But the Maverick-G, while containing more sophisticated electronic devices than the model D, would pose less of a menace to Israel.

The administration also agreed, among other things, to stipulate that the F/A-18s had to be based in the country to which they were sold, that they could not be outfitted with special fuel tanks that would allow them to attack Israel and that Kuwait must return to the United States one of its aging A-4 warplanes for each of the new F/A-18s to ensure that these were replacement planes, not an expansion of Kuwait's air force.

DeConcini insisted the House agreement with the administration was not adequate and pressed for inclusion of his amendment barring the sale and transfer of Mavericks to Kuwait in the conference version of the foreign aid spending bill. The issue became one of a handful that threatened to derail the legislation.

It was finally resolved when Senate conferees, by a one-vote margin, agreed to drop their insistence on DeConcini's amendment. Opponents of the sale settled for a Senate resolution asking the president to work with other countries to curb arms sales to the Middle East.

### Saudi Arms Sale

The Reagan administration formally notified Congress in April of a proposed sale of $825 million worth of weapons and military equipment to Saudi Arabia. The package included ground support services for the AWACS radar planes that Saudi Arabia was buying from the United States, along with armored troop carriers, anti-tank missiles and other equipment, ammunition and spare parts.

The proposed sale generated Hill complaints but no sustained opposition. Some members worried that the Saudis' acquisition of Chinese medium-range missiles posed a threat to Israel, but the administration said the Saudis had provided assurances that Hill fears were unfounded. The Saudis in late April also agreed to sign the 1968 international nuclear non-proliferation treaty — a step that would legally bar them from obtaining nuclear weapons.

Congress, in the final version of the fiscal 1989 defense authorization bill (S 2355), banned during fiscal 1989 any U.S. arms sales to any countries that had obtained Chinese-made intermediate-range missiles, unless the president certified to Congress that the country had no chemical, biological or nuclear warheads for the missiles.

Battles over Saudi arms sales had occurred regularly during the Reagan administration. Congress in the past had forced Reagan to postpone, modify or drop several proposed sales to the Saudis. The most recent case was in 1987. *(1987 Saudi sale, p. 232)*

### Egypt Arms Sale

The formal notification of the arms sale to Egypt was sent to Congress in April. The sale included 555 M-1/M-1A1 "Abrams" tanks, top-of-the line U.S.-developed equipment. The Egyptian sale was unusual in that it also involved co-production of 540 of these tanks. Under the plan, the tanks would be partly constructed in the United States and then shipped to Egypt for final assembly.

Egypt would become the first foreign country to receive M-1 tanks, and also the first to join the United States in an M-1 coproduction effort.

The administration said Egypt needed an advanced tank "to ensure the stability of the existing regional military balance, especially vis-à-vis Libya." Defense Department officials said that the United States would gain additional economic benefits from the sale because it would mean that U.S.-supplied tank components would continue to be built, despite U.S. military plans to phase out the M-1 and its more advanced model, the M-1A1. In response to the concerns of members of the United Auto Workers union, officials said this would mean U.S. jobs would be protected and eventually increased as the worldwide market for M-1 tanks grew.

### Israel Arms Sale

The administration notified Congress in April of a proposed arms sale to Israel that included 75 F-16C/D aircraft with associated support equipment. Israel already had similar weapons systems in its inventory.

Arms sales to Israel never were controversial in Congress. This one also was seen as fulfillment of a commitment that the United States made in 1987 when it pressured Israel into canceling plans to build a new fighter plan, the Lavi, which Washington said was too expensive. *(Lavi cancellation, box, p. 227)*

The administration in June committed the United States to pay the bulk of the cost of developing a new Israeli defensive missile, the Arrow. The missile was intended to help Israel cope with the threat of ballistic missiles being acquired by its Arab neighbors.

# U.S.-PLO Dialogue

In one bold stroke in late 1988, the outgoing Reagan administration restored the United States to a central role in Middle East peacemaking efforts and revived hopes for Arab-Israeli peace talks.

Responding to conciliatory statements by Palestine Liberation Organization (PLO) Chairman Yasir Arafat, Secretary of State George P. Shultz on Dec. 14 announced a willingness to begin a "substantive dialogue" with the PLO.

The talks, which opened Dec. 16 in Tunisia, represented the first officially authorized contact between Washington and the PLO since at least 1975.

Congressional reaction was remarkably mild, considering the anti-PLO rhetoric heard on Capitol Hill during the year. Pro-Israel members expressed skepticism that much would come of the talks or that Arafat really meant what he said. But across the board, members of Congress appeared willing to give the PLO dialogue a chance, despite Israel's immediate condemnation of the U.S.-PLO opening.

### Shultz Announcement

In his Dec. 14 announcement, Shultz said that Arafat, at a press conference in Geneva, Switzerland, earlier in the day, finally had met Washington's longstanding conditions for direct talks with the PLO: an acceptance of U.N. Security Council resolutions on Middle East peace, a recognition of Israel's right to exist and a renunciation of terrorism.

With the approval of President Reagan and President-elect George Bush, Shultz authorized Robert H. Pelletreau Jr., the U.S. ambassador to Tunisia, to open a dialogue — not negotiations — with the PLO.

Shultz said the talks could be "one more step toward the beginning of direct negotiations between the parties, which alone can lead" to peace in the Middle East.

Shultz and other officials resisted calling the move a change of policy, noting that the United States merely was responding to changes by the PLO. But the action potentially represented one of the most significant foreign policy moves of the Reagan era, putting the United States in the unique position of having direct access to all major parties to the Middle East conflict: Israel, its Arab neighbors and, in the PLO, the generally recognized leadership of Palestinians.

# Shultz' Middle East Peace Plan

Secretary of State George P. Shultz outlined a Middle East peace plan in a March 3, 1988, letter to Israeli Prime Minister Yitzhak Shamir and Jordan's King Hussein. An Israeli newspaper published it in full three days later.

The proposal called for several negotiating phases, with "interlocking" steps in each phase. To prevent participants from accepting some parts of the proposal and rejecting others, Shultz said his plan was "an integral whole" that should not be changed.

The overall objective, Shultz said, was "a comprehensive peace providing for the security of all the states in the region and for the legitimate rights of the Palestinian people." Shultz outlined this timetable:

● In early to mid-April, the secretary general of the United Nations would convene an international conference under the auspices of the five permanent members of the Security Council: the United States, the Soviet Union, Great Britain, France and China. Middle East participants would include Israel, Egypt, Syria and a delegation composed of Jordanians and Palestinians. The Palestinians likely would have to be approved by the Palestine Liberation Organization but also would have to be acceptable to Israel.

Shultz said the Security Council members "will not be able to impose solutions or veto agreements reached" by the negotiating parties. All participants, Shultz said, "must state their willingness to negotiate with one another," must accept Security Council Resolutions 242 and 338 and must "renounce violence and terrorism."

● At an "early date," possibly by May 1, Israel and the Jordanian-Palestinian delegates would begin direct talks toward a "transitional" plan for Palestinian residents to run local functions in the West Bank and Gaza Strip. The United States would submit a draft agreement as a basis for negotiation.

These talks would last for no more than six months. Any interim arrangements would not go into effect until negotiations began on the "final status" of the occupied territories; they would remain in place for three years.

● By December, Israel and the Jordanian-Palestinian delegation would begin talks on the permanent status of the West Bank and Gaza, based on the "land for peace" formula of Security Council Resolutions 242 and 338. The talks should end in one year, but any agreed-upon solution would not go into effect until the end of the three-year period for the interim accord.

A major uncertainty was how the talks would affect two of the occupied territories that Israel had officially annexed: the Golan Heights, captured from Syria, and East Jerusalem. Each area had a significance that would prevent any Israeli government from surrendering it. The Golan Heights overlooked the strategic approaches from Syria and was of immense military importance. Israel had united East and West Jerusalem into its capital city.

Shultz acknowledged the political and practical difficulties facing the plan but stressed that most key actors in the Middle East accepted the need for change. "The big thing that we have going right now . . . is a sense that the status quo is not going to last," he told Cable News Network on March 2. "And the question is, what are they going to change to and how's it going to happen. And we think, and people there think they should change through negotiations."

Deadlines were a key part of the process, Shultz told reporters March 4. And the situation in the Middle East "carries inherent in it a certain sense of deadlines," he said, apparently referring to the Palestinian riots and planned Israeli elections. He added: "I don't mind trying to make use of that, although you can't push people if they don't want to be pushed."

Prime Minister Shamir, during a visit to Washington in mid-March, made it clear that he was opposed to the proposal for an international conference, a key part of Shultz' peace plan.

---

Reagan officials insisted that the decision to open talks with the PLO did not represent a shift in U.S. support for Israel. Shultz said that U.S. support for Israeli security "remains unflinching." Reagan said on Dec. 15: "We have made it very plain that we have not retreated one inch from the position of guaranteeing the safety of Israel."

Even so, the U.S. action created the potential for the most important dispute in years between Washington and Jerusalem. The Israeli Embassy in Washington responded to the Shultz announcement with a statement of regret. Israeli Foreign Minister Shimon Peres said the action represented "a sad day for all of us."

Perhaps in recognition of the advantage gained by Washington, the Soviet Union on Dec. 15 expressed willingness to consider recognizing Israel once efforts got under way to hold an international conference on peace in the Middle East. The Reagan administration earlier in 1988 supported an international conference, but with a substantially lesser role than the one advocated by the Soviets.

The U.N. General Assembly, apparently seeking to add pressure on Israel, voted Dec. 15 to call for an international peace conference. The resolution also demanded that Israel withdraw from the West Bank and Gaza Strip and endorsed an Arafat proposal to put the occupied territories under temporary U.N. jurisdiction.

## Pressuring Israel

Earlier in 1988, the Reagan administration had launched its first sustained effort since 1982 to achieve peace between the Arabs and Israelis. The 1988 U.S. peace proposals, however, came up short when a divided Israeli government could not accept them.

Shultz spent the last week of February and the first four days of March jetting between Middle East capitals. In March he gave Israeli and Arab leaders a detailed "land for peace" plan for negotiations aimed at resolving the status of the territories Israel had occupied since the 1967 war.

The Shultz mission was sparked by a sustained Palestinian uprising on the West Bank and Gaza Strip that had begun in December 1987. Israeli security forces had killed scores of Palestinians who confronted them in the streets with rocks and molotov cocktails. The riots forced the administration to abandon its contention that the Middle East was not ready for another U.S.-sponsored peace mission.

The uprising, or *intifada*, also sharpened the divisions within Israel about the future of the occupied territories. And the harshness of the government's handling of the disturbances caused anguish among Israel's supporters in the United States.

Jewish leaders and members of Congress expressed concern that public support of Israel eventually could be endangered by nightly television news reports showing Israeli soldiers beating defiant Arab youths.

In the midst of the diplomatic maneuvering, reaction to the violence in the occupied territories helped spur leading members of Congress to criticize Israeli policy openly. Thirty senators, including many of Israel's staunchest congressional backers, on March 3 sent Shultz a highly unusual letter challenging Israeli Prime Minister Yitzhak Shamir's refusal to accept the longstanding "land for peace" formula of Middle East negotiations — returning some of the occupied territories in exchange for peace with and recognition by Arab countries.

Members of Congress routinely wrote letters, made speeches and introduced resolutions faulting other countries, especially ones run by dictatorships. But members rarely criticized Israel, at least in public.

The Senate letter sparked debate on the Hill. Most members concurred with the thrust of the senators' message, but some questioned the use of public pressure.

But there was no significant erosion of Capitol Hill backing of Israel. Members of Congress said differences with individual Israeli leaders about specific policies would not affect the underlying relationship between the two countries. And congressional leaders did not retaliate by cutting Israel's $3 billion-a-year military and economic aid program, in spite of the need for major reductions in overall U.S. foreign aid.

Foreign Minister Peres, prime minister from 1984 to 1986 and leader of the Labor Party alignment that shared control of the government with Prime Minister Shamir's Likud coalition, embraced the Shultz initiative and challenged Shamir to do likewise. Because of the split in government, however, Peres was not able to force a decision; the 10-member Inner Cabinet divided evenly on March 9 when Peres attempted to force a vote on endorsing the peace plan.

Shamir visited Washington on March 14-16 and bluntly rejected a key component of Shultz' plan: the international conference, in which five U.N. Security Council members, among them the Soviet Union, would oversee direct talks between Israel and a Jordanian-Palestinian delegation.

## New Pressures, Reassurances

The Dec. 14 statements put new pressure on virtually everyone involved in the Arab-Israeli dispute.

Israel, having denounced the move, was isolated in its adamant refusal to deal with the PLO under any circumstances. The sudden shift in dynamics could hardly have come at a more critical time for Israel. The country would need to present a unified front in the face of growing pressure for an international conference, and its political leaders were still trying to form a new government. Shamir's Likud coalition had edged Peres' Labor alignment in the Nov. 1 election but did not win a majority.

The U.S.-PLO opening contributed to Shamir's decision to form another coalition with Peres. Under the new coalition, announced Dec. 19, Shamir would remain as prime minister, but Labor would get as many Cabinet posts as Likud. Peres would be finance minister, and his ministry could block future settlements in the occupied territories.

Israel's Arab neighbors, who lobbied hard to bring the United States and the PLO together, also faced new pressures from the United States and the Soviet Union to moderate their conditions for peace talks with Israel. In particular, King Hussein of Jordan could be forced into a new negotiating role despite his renunciation of sovereignty over the West Bank in July 1988.

The Reagan administration served notice that Washington would apply continuing pressure on the PLO to prove its good intentions. Shultz said, for example, that the first item in any U.S.-PLO talks would be terrorism. "We'll make it clear that our position about the importance of the renunciation of terrorism is central," he said.

# South Africa Sanctions

Lack of support in the Senate — coupled with a White House veto threat — stalled legislation to impose new sanctions against the white-minority government in South Africa, and the measure failed to become law during the 100th Congress.

The House passed a bill (HR 1580) in 1988 that would halt nearly all trade between the United States and South Africa and force U.S. firms to pull out of that country. The bill was supported by only 24 Republicans, in contrast to the broad GOP support in 1986 for much milder sanctions legislation that Congress enacted into law over Reagan's veto. *(1986 action, p. 180)*

The Senate Foreign Relations Committee approved the sanctions bill but with significant weakening amendments. The likelihood of a filibuster, and the certainty of a veto, prevented the bill from reaching the Senate floor.

Both supporters and opponents of new sanctions against South Africa agreed that existing sanctions had done little to encourage Pretoria to allow the 25 million black majority more rights and political power.

## Background

Sanctions supporters asserted that the 1986 sanctions package had little impact because of loopholes in the legislation and inadequate enforcement by the administration.

For example, the 1986 law prohibited imports of South African and Namibian uranium and uranium ore. But the administration interpreted the law as allowing imports of uranium hexafluoride, which was then enriched and converted back to uranium oxide.

The law also prohibited bank loans to South Africa but exempted "short-term credits," or credits of up to 180 days provided by a financial institution for a trade transaction.

Rep. Ronald V. Dellums, D-Calif., author of the original version of HR 1580, cited Federal Reserve figures showing that, as of September 1987, nearly $3 billion in loans were given to South Africa by U.S. banks. About $2 billion of those loans were short-term credits, Dellums said.

In a March 23 report to the panel, Richard W. Leonard, a corporate research consultant specializing in South Africa, said several overseas firms and some U.S. corporations had undermined U.S. sanctions efforts by providing banned technology and goods to the South African government. Several companies cited by Leonard denied U.S. restrictions were being undermined.

Central to the argument against economic sanctions in South Africa was the belief that such measures would harm blacks more than help them.

Merle Lipton, an economist for the Investor Responsibility Research Center, a Washington-based corporate research group, told two House Foreign Affairs subcommittees March 23 of a study estimating that sanctions could give blacks a reduced share of total income from 29 percent in 1985 to 20 percent by the year 2000. Without sanctions, Lipton said, that share would increase to 36 percent by 2000.

The Reagan administration argued that South African blacks needed to gain political power through economic strength, which meant a hands-on U.S. policy of diplomatic dialogue and corporate development, not sanctions that punished working people.

Members on both sides of the issue cited, as evidence for their position, the fact that the 1986 sanctions had done little to end apartheid.

Instead, the South African government had cracked down: tightening restrictions on news coverage of protests, banning activities of 17 anti-apartheid groups and continuing a state of emergency imposed in June 1986.

President P. W. Botha on April 21 proposed giving blacks a role in selecting the president. But he did not endorse full voting rights or ending apartheid. Instead, the government stiffened its position, apparently in response to far-right political forces.

Advocates of sanctions said they never expected the 1986 legislation to end apartheid. Rather, they said, it was a repudiation of the administration's policy of "constructive engagement" and a demonstration to South African blacks and whites alike that the United States was demanding change.

Experts said the consistent departure from South Africa of U.S. firms, either in response to unrest or in anticipation of future sanctions, had been more important than the 1986 sanctions bill.

From 1984 to 1988 more than half of all U.S. firms with facilities in South Africa had left. However, most plants and other installations built by those companies continued to operate, often through franchise arrangements.

U.S. firms also had responded to a provision enacted into law by Congress in December 1987 as part of an omnibus budget reconciliation bill (HR 3545 — PL 100-203). That provision ended foreign tax credits for income derived from South African holdings.

## House Action

HR 1580 had to clear a tortuous series of hurdles before reaching the House floor.

Committee Democrats drafted a comprehensive substitute to the original Dellums version. Changes — aimed at picking up support in Congress — included a phased-in instead of immediate end to trade and investment and broader exemptions for imports of strategic minerals.

The House Foreign Affairs Committee on May 20 reported the South Africa sanctions measure (H Rept 100-642, Part I) after adopting amendments that opened small loopholes in an otherwise tight ban on U.S. trade with South Africa.

The bill then went to six other House committees for consideration: Armed Services, Banking, Energy and Commerce, Intelligence, Interior, and Ways and Means. The Public Works and Transportation Committee also had jurisdiction but did not formally debate the bill.

The last obstacle was the Rules Committee, which set the terms of floor debate and sorted out conflicting provisions added by other committees.

The full House approved HR 1580 on Aug. 11 by a vote of 244-132, after rejecting three Republican attempts to amend the bill. Unlike in 1986 — when 81 House Republicans broke ranks to help override Reagan's veto of a weaker sanctions bill — the party line generally held with only 24 Republicans voting for the bill. The margin in 1988 fell well short of the two-thirds needed to override a threatened White House veto.

Reiterating its veto threat, the White House said it feared new sanctions would jeopardize U.S.-mediated negotiations among South Africa, Angola and Cuba to end hostilities in Angola and grant independence to Namibia. A cease-fire was put into effect Aug. 8, and South Africa was to begin withdrawing troops from southern Angola within the week. *(Angola, p. 238)*

In attacking the bill, Republicans noted it would take jobs from South African blacks and American workers — points the Democrats conceded. The sanctions would eliminate U.S. exports to South Africa, worth $1.13 billion in 1987, while forcing American companies to sell nearly $1 billion in assets at "fire-sale prices," according to the administration.

"Sanctions hurt, but apartheid kills — and it kills violently," countered Dellums, adding, "Do not underestimate the power of this issue" in domestic politics. House Democrats, and many Republicans, rose to applaud Dellums at the end of his speech.

As passed by the House, major provisions of HR 1580:

● Prohibited all U.S. exports to South Africa, except for: publications; food, clothing and medicine needed to "relieve human suffering"; and commercial sales of agricultural goods. The bill explicitly banned any nuclear cooperation with South Africa.

● Prohibited all imports from South Africa, except for: publications; items produced by firms owned by persons "economically or politically disadvantaged by apartheid"; and strategic materials certified by the president to be essential for the U.S. economy or defense. (The Banking Committee had added a controversial provision barring importation of any item — from any country — if any part of it originated in South Africa, but this was stripped from the bill by the Rules Committee.)

• Prohibited U.S. citizens or firms from holding investments in South Africa. This ban was to take effect 180 days after the bill was enacted; however, individual firms could appeal to the president for a one-time 180-day extension to wind up their affairs in South Africa.

• Prohibited foreign oil companies from obtaining new U.S. energy leases if they continued to do business in South Africa. This controversial provision — which inspired international protests and inflamed political concerns in oil-producing states — would affect at least two major firms: British Petroleum, which owned BP America (formerly Standard Oil of Ohio) and Royal Dutch Shell, which owned the Shell Oil Co. Those firms launched a major lobbying campaign against the provision, but it remained in the House bill.

• Required the president to retaliate against foreign companies that took significant commercial advantage of U.S. sanctions.

• Prohibited U.S. intelligence and military agencies from cooperating with the South African government, except for exchanging information about Angola. The president could waive the ban on military cooperation with South Africa if it was in the "best interest of the United States."

• Provided $40 million in U.S. aid for disadvantaged South Africans.

• Required the president to try to reach agreement with other countries on international sanctions.

• Allowed the president to lift the sanctions if Pretoria took several steps, such as releasing political prisoners and repealing laws that discriminated against non-whites.

### Senate Action

The Senate Foreign Relations Committee in early September went through the motions of debating a companion South Africa sanctions bill (S 2756), setting the stage for a party-line vote. Members of both parties acknowledged that once approved by the committee, the bill could reach the Senate floor by late September but stood no chance of becoming law.

Senate Democrats clearly wanted the sanctions bill as an election-year issue. Republicans, for their part, hoped the issue would attract as little public attention as possible. To that end, the Republicans dropped plans to offer amendments that would weaken the bill.

Sponsors of the Senate bill made a major concession to opponents in hopes of shoring up support. Minutes before the committee was to act on S 2756, one of its most controversial features — the provision banning grants of new U.S. oil and mineral leases to foreign-owned companies that did business in South Africa — was stripped from the bill. That provision was staunchly opposed by oil-state senators of both parties.

Sponsors of the bill modified several other provisions of the House bill in hopes of undercutting the arguments of opponents. Most of the changes had the effect of weakening the bill slightly; others merely clarified provisions that critics said were vague.

As approved by Foreign Relations, the Senate measure, unlike the House bill, would allow U.S. banks to continue rescheduling, or renewing, existing loans to South African businesses, as long as doing so did not provide new money. The Senate change had been sought by several major banks, led by Citicorp.

Other differences between the House and Senate bills included a Senate provision allowing greater cooperation between U.S. and South African intelligence agencies if the goal was to obtain "necessary intelligence" information.

Senate Foreign Relations reported S 2756 (S Rept 100-545) on Sept. 23, but the measure never made it to the Senate floor.

# Angola Peace Accord

Diplomacy at the end of 1988 helped to make possible an end to twin conflicts in Angola and Namibia — but only after a military solution proved elusive.

Angola, Cuba and South Africa on Dec. 13 accepted a U.S.-sponsored peace settlement for the two countries in southern Africa. Under it, South Africa was to give up its control over Namibia (also known as South West Africa) and to allow free elections there in 1989. Within 27 months Cuba would withdraw the 40,000 to 50,000 troops that had been protecting the leftist government of neighboring Angola against South African-backed insurgents.

In addition to mediating negotiations that led to the peace accord, the United States was a major actor in one of the two conflicts: Since 1986 it had joined Pretoria in supplying weapons and military hardware to the anti-government guerrilla group in Angola called the National Union for the Total Independence of Angola (UNITA, in the Portuguese acronym), led by Jonas Savimbi.

The launching of aid to UNITA was perhaps a great political victory for advocates of the Reagan doctrine. Congress in early 1976 barred U.S. involvement in the Angolan civil war, but Reagan successfully fought to get that restriction lifted in 1985 and began supplying weapons to the guerrillas a year later. *(1985 action, p. 188; 1986 action, box, p. 204)*

Details of the U.S. aid program were classified secret, but supporters said the aid started at about $13 million per year, rising to about $20 million. Estimates of South African aid to UNITA ranged from $100 million to $200 million, while the Soviet Union provided the Angolan government with more than $1 billion per year in military and non-military support, according to the Reagan administration.

Although it had broad support, the aid to UNITA was controversial in Congress because of Savimbi's heavy reliance on South Africa, which sent troops to southern Angola for a direct confrontation with Cuban forces in 1987.

Savimbi countered liberal criticism of his South African ties by saying that he was forced to turn to Pretoria in the 1970s when Congress barred aid to him.

UNITA gained control over substantial portions of Angola, but after 13 years of warfare it was a long way from ousting the Luanda government.

### Renewed Fight on Hill

Angola re-emerged as an issue on Capitol Hill in October 1988. Backers of UNITA worried about the direction of the U.S.-sponsored talks. They were concerned that the agreement would not resolve Angola's internal political problems.

Hill leaders pressured the administration to toughen the U.S. stance in the Angola talks. Conservatives demanded "national reconciliation" in Angola — free elections and direct talks between UNITA and the leftist ruling party in Luanda.

To express their views, those members held up legislation (HR 5551) authorizing the transfer of up to $150 million from Defense Department or foreign military aid accounts for the U.S. share of new peacekeeping efforts by the United Nations. Negotiations had made possible the resolution of not only the war in Angola, but also the Iran-Iraq war, a guerrilla war in the Western Sahara and the Soviet occupation of Afghanistan. In each case long-term U.N. peacekeeping forces were needed.

The House passed the U.N. bill on Oct. 20 by voice vote, with little debate. A week earlier leaders of the Foreign Affairs Committee had sent a letter to Secretary of State George P. Shultz stating their view that the money was not to be used to support a process that did not involve the complete withdrawal of Cuban troops and reconciliation leading to free and fair elections in Angola. The administration accepted that statement, but opponents of UNITA objected to putting such language into law.

When HR 5551 reached the Senate, action on the bill was blocked by senators who demanded more explicit assurances of continued support to UNITA. Others questioned the transfer of funds from the Pentagon and foreign aid budgets and whether Congress should approve money for forces to monitor agreements not yet signed.

In the end, time ran out and the bill died.

# Iraq Sanctions

Outraged by reports that Iraq had used chemical weapons against its Kurdish minority, both chambers voted repeatedly in 1988 to impose limited sanctions against that country. But sanctions legislation never was enacted into law because of last-minute problems in the days before adjournment.

The best chance for enactment of the sanctions legislation died when House-Senate conferees stripped the Iraq provisions from a tax corrections bill (HR 4333), which cleared on Oct. 22. Iraq provisions, which had been added by the Senate as a result of compromise negotiations, would bar all exports to Iraq of weapons and high-technology items. They also would require the president to impose additional sanctions by the end of the year unless he had determined that Iraq would not use chemical weapons again.

The State Department, while denouncing Iraq, had opposed any congressionally mandated sanctions.

### Legislative Action

The Senate adopted a sanctions bill (S 2763) by voice vote on Sept. 9. Passage less than 24 hours after senior members of the Foreign Relations Committee introduced the measure represented a remarkably fast and serious response to human rights violations overseas.

The House passed a milder sanctions bill (HR 5337 — H Rept 100-981, Part I) on Sept. 27 by a vote of 388-16.

Senate Foreign Relations Committee members tried to get the House to accept a compromise as part of the conference version of the fiscal 1989 foreign aid appropriations bill (HR 4637). But the House stripped the sanctions amendment from the foreign aid bill on procedural grounds on Sept. 30, and the Senate dropped the issue in order to clear the measure. House negotiators said they were angered because the senators gave them no advance notice of what they were about to do.

Another compromise was worked out and added by the Senate to HR 4333, the tax corrections bill, by an 87-0 vote on Oct. 11. House leaders later agreed to keep it as part of that measure.

Iraq sanctions next were attached to an omnibus foreign policy bill (HR 5550), which the House passed by voice vote Oct. 20. Once the House passed HR 5550, the sanctions provisions were stripped from the tax bill, thus killing the best chance for enactment of sanctions. (Dan Rostenkowski, D-Ill., chairman of the House Ways and Means Committee, had objected to all non-tax provisions added by the Senate to HR 4333.)

Senate floor action on HR 5550 was blocked by Sen. Jesse Helms, R-N.C., and other senators who demanded action on items that the administration and House leaders refused to accept, including a provision curtailing legal immunity for foreign diplomats in the United States. Shortly before Congress adjourned early on Oct. 22, the Senate referred HR 5550 to the Foreign Relations Committee, effectively killing it for the 100th Congress.

# State Department Authorization

Congress normally put its mark on foreign policy by amending annual or biennial authorizations for foreign aid programs. But the foreign aid bill collapsed of its own political weight in 1987, so members turned to another bill to voice their sentiments on foreign affairs: the authorization bill for the State Department and related agencies (HR 1777 — PL 100-204).

The bill fulfilled its main purpose, authorizing $4.1 billion in fiscal 1988 and $4.22 billion in fiscal 1989 for the State Department; U.S. Information Agency (USIA); Board for International Broadcasting, which ran Radio Free Europe and Radio Liberty; and the Asia Foundation. Both houses of Congress had approved a smaller amount for fiscal 1988 than was ultimately agreed on in the conference version; President Reagan had requested $4.7 billion.

But beyond the dollar amounts, the legislation was filled with provisions that ranged from digs at the Soviet Union to concerns about budgeting procedures at the United Nations.

The Reagan administration opposed the bill from the outset and repeatedly attempted to block action on it. Although some of the provisions the Reagan team found most offensive were weakened or dropped in the final version, the administration still opposed several items, and State Department officials suggested all along that President Reagan might veto it.

But a law dating back to 1956 required a congressional authorization for the department before any money could be spent on its activities. This meant the State Department could not spend any of its appropriations, contained in a catchall spending measure, if Reagan vetoed the authorization bill.

Earlier, however, conferees on the catchall spending measure (H J Res 395 — PL 100-202) took steps to ease the blow: They included authority for Reagan to ignore three of the sections of the State Department bill that he opposed. One was a provision to keep the Soviet Union from occupying a new embassy atop Mount Alto in Washington, D.C., because of fears that its high-ground site would allow the Soviets to eavesdrop on sensitive U.S. communications.

# Spy Stories: Alleged Lapses at Old Embassy . . .

Two U.S.-Soviet spy scandals spawned considerable debate during the 100th Congress. The first involved security breaches at the existing U.S. Embassy in Moscow. The second involved listening devices planted in the new U.S. Embassy in Moscow and the potential for eavesdropping from the new Soviet Embassy in Washington.

President Reagan in 1988 recommended that the nearly completed U.S. Embassy office building in Moscow be demolished and a new one put in its place. Under longstanding agreements, the Soviet Union could not occupy its new embassy offices in Washington until the United States moved into its comparable facility in Moscow.

## Marine Guard Scandal

In a heavily publicized case, the Navy in 1987 arrested five U.S. Marine guards stationed at the U.S. Embassy in Moscow. It was alleged that they were lured by Soviet women into cooperating with agents of the KGB, the Soviet's spy service.

By year's end, the scope of the scandal seemed overblown. The more serious charges of conspiracy to commit espionage filed against two Marines were dropped; three were convicted of lesser charges. Amid the outcry, all 28 Marines assigned to the Moscow embassy and six in Leningrad were replaced.

## Moscow-Washington Controversies

That scandal provided the backdrop for the discovery that the new U.S. Embassy in Moscow was riddled with sophisticated listening devices.

But for some Capitol Hill hard-liners, the U.S. Embassy in Moscow was only half of the problem. Some critics feared that the location of the new Soviet Embassy on Mount Alto — one of the highest hills in Washington, D.C. — would allow the Soviets to eavesdrop on secret conservations within U.S. government agencies.

Both embassies were being constructed under a 1972 U.S.-Soviet agreement setting terms for each country to build a new embassy in the other's capital.

State Department officials said they had objected to the terms of the agreement but signed it under orders from senior Nixon administration officials.

The agreement provided for the concrete columns and beams of the U.S. building in Moscow to be precast away from the construction site — and away from supervision by U.S. officials. According to Soviet officials, this was because it was not the usual Soviet practice to fabricate such components at a building site. The concrete components subsequently were X-rayed at the construction site, but the eavesdropping devices in them were impervious to X-ray detection.

Reports in 1987 that the Moscow embassy was honeycombed with electronic listening devices brought construction to a halt and provoked a number of investigations. The most comprehensive of the inquiries was directed by James R. Schlesinger, a former CIA chief and secretary of energy under President Jimmy Carter.

In the report he forwarded to Secretary of State George P. Shultz in mid-June 1987, Schlesinger recommended that the largely completed building in Moscow be partly dismantled and rebuilt by American laborers using U.S.-made components. He also suggested that an adjacent annex be built to house the most secret activities and that the United States try to retain part of its existing complex to house embassy offices that required access by non-U.S. nationals.

Once the new Moscow complex was ready for U.S. occupancy, Schlesinger said, the Soviets should be allowed to begin using their already completed chancery building. In response to criticism that the Mount Alto location was a prime site for Soviet eavesdropping on secret communications, Schlesinger said that the new site offered no dramatic advantage as a listening post over the 10 other Soviet facilities in Washington — not to mention the dozens of properties occupied by Soviet bloc countries.

During congressional hearings in June, Schlesinger conceded that he had tried to come up with a recomendation "that would be plausibly negotiable with the Soviets." And he predicted that the Soviets

*(Embassy dispute, box, this page)*

The omnibus spending law also enabled the State Department to proceed with plans to shut down various U.S. consulates around the world, particularly in Europe, as a cost-saving step. The USIA also was allowed to close some of its foreign offices. The State Department bill had included provisions to prevent the closings. Members of Congress were reluctant to allow the department to shut down facilities that could help their constitutents when traveling abroad.

Conferees on the spending bill left untouched, how-

ever, other sections in the State Department bill that had triggered the administration's objections.

Secretary of State George P. Shultz had lobbied intensely to remove some of these items, particularly one that required some officials of his department to take lie-detector tests on counterintelligence matters. The lie-detector issue was a sensitive one for the secretary; in December 1985 he had offered to quit after vocally opposing a plan under which administration officials would be given polygraph tests in an effort to stop leaks.

Shultz also opposed a provision in the State Depart-

# ... And Soviet Bugging Devices at the New One

would regard a U.S. demand to demolish the new building as an insult.

## 1987 Congressional Action

The Senate included in its fiscal 1988 State Department authorization bill language that would require the president to void the U.S.-Soviet accords on embassy construction and begin new negotiations.

While the House joined the Senate in the tough rhetoric used to condemn the Soviet bugging of the Moscow embassy, House members were unwilling to abrogate the accord. Their proposals were more in line with Schlesinger's.

Conferees on the State Department bill (HR 1777 — PL 100-204) modified the Senate's demand to abrogate the embassy agreement but allowed the president to let the Soviets occupy their new embassy within six months if he certified that:

● Steps were being taken to guard against Soviet electronic surveillance from the diplomatic facility.

● Efforts would be made to ensure that a new U.S. Embassy site in Moscow could be "safely and securely used for its intended purpose."

● It was vital to U.S. national security not to terminate the U.S.-Soviet accords on construction of new embassies in each country.

Even with these provisos, the State Department continued to oppose any restrictions on the new U.S. and Soviet embassies. Congress yielded to the protests at the end of the year, including in a catchall spending resolution (PL 100-202) language authorizing the president to ignore the Mount Alto provision in the State Department bill. A related provision was included in an intelligence authorization bill (PL 100-178); it required the secretary of defense to report to Congress on the Soviets' ability to intercept communications at Mount Alto.

## Reagan Announcement

Reagan on Oct. 27, 1988, said the United States had "no choice" but to demolish the new U.S. Embassy in Moscow because "there's no way to rid it of the many listening devices that were built into it."

The original cost estimate for the new embassy, which was to have been completed in 1982, was $75 million. State Department officials said it could take up to five years, and cost at least $160 million and possibly $300 million, to demolish the building and replace it with a new one made from parts made in the United States and assembled in Moscow.

The Reagan administration criticized its predecessors — primarily the Nixon and Ford administrations — for letting the Soviets fabricate parts for the building. It was during that process that the listening devices apparently were implanted.

Reagan made his tear-it-down recommendation after congressional committees, his aides and outside consultants had given him numerous, and sometimes conflicting, pieces of advice. Reagan reportedly acted on a recommendation by Secretary of State Shultz for a fresh start at the embassy site.

But Congress blocked the first steps toward tearing down the building, bucking the issue to the incoming Bush administration. In December 1988 the House Appropriations Committee prevented the administration from reprogramming the first $3 million of $25 million in leftover embassy funds for a redesign of the building. Reagan did not include funds for rebuilding the embassy in his last, fiscal 1990 budget request.

And in January 1989, another variable was added to the debate over the facility's fate: a proposal by a business consortium to purchase the building.

The United States could avoid the diplomatic embarrassment of tearing down the building if it were sold, and would recoup some construction costs.

But it would mean putting private business offices in the middle of a government embassy complex, raising security and logistical concerns.

A potentially stickier problem was the 1972 U.S.-Soviet embassy agreement. Converting the embassy to private use would mean renegotiating that pact, and the United States could lose leverage in the process. Renegotiation of the pact also could reopen congressional debate over whether the Soviets should be allowed to move into their new offices at all.

ment bill that required the closing of a Palestine Liberation Organization (PLO) office in New York.

## House Action

HR 1777 was reported by the House Foreign Affairs Committee March 27 (H Rept 100-34). Three days later, as the House Rules Committee prepared to send the bill to the floor, the director of the Office of Management and Budget (OMB) sent a letter to Republican members of the Rules Committee objecting to the bill, saying the authorization levels were unacceptably low.

The stalemate continued until late June. Though no substantive changes were made in the funding levels, the House passed the measure June 23 by a vote of 303-111 after three days of debate. The bill would authorize $3.9 billion for fiscal 1988 and $4.6 billion in 1989.

In the wake of accounts of Soviet spying and in the middle of the Iran-contra hearings, members were eager to voice their views on a variety of foreign policy matters.

A shortage of other foreign policy bills on the schedule made the usually routine State Department measure a magnet for amendments to score rhetorical points. The House voted on dozens of contentious but largely symbolic amendments before passing the bill.

Several amendments were triggered by the anger of members of both parties over the reports of Soviet bugging of a new U.S. Embassy in Moscow and alleged security breaches by Marine guards at the old embassy.

The most far-reaching amendment, vigorously opposed by the administration, was adopted June 16 by 414-0. It effectively barred Soviet occupancy of their newly completed embassy building on Mount Alto in Washington, D.C. The bulk of the amendment subsequently was retained in the House-Senate conference.

The House adopted 307-103 an amendment requiring the State Department to initiate a program of drug testing for all those employees who had access to secret information.

When the debate turned to Central America, liberals and conservatives locked horns over U.S. policy toward the Sandinista government of Nicaragua. Three amendments offered by conservatives were rejected before the House on June 23 adopted, 213-201, an amendment banning travel to Central America for the purpose of assisting "the military operations" of the Nicaraguan government or any communist guerrilla group. The provision was dropped in conference.

Several hours of debate were devoted to an amendment that would delete from the bill the earmarking of $1 million for the 1990 Goodwill Games in Seattle. The House first accepted the amendment, 203-201, then later rejected it, 180-230.

## Senate Action

The Senate Foreign Relations Committee reported its version of the legislation June 18 (S 1394 — S Rept 100-75). Hours before the full Senate voted on the bill, the State Department released plans to lay off 1,300 employees and to close two dozen small embassies and consulates if the Senate version, which authorized $3.6 billion, was upheld.

Conservative Sen. Jesse Helms, R-N.C., long a critic of the State Department's policies and appointments, forced votes on numerous amendments. In the end, it took four days of floor debate and the addition of some 86 amendments, before the Senate Oct. 8 approved the $3.6 billion measure 85-8.

The Senate turned back most attempts to force major changes in U.S. policy. One of the most important actions was its tabling, by a 59-39 vote, of an amendment stating that the Senate should not have approved ratification of the Panama Canal treaties in 1978. The amendment also called on the president to void the treaties unless Panama accepted a reservation under which the United States stated its intention to defend the canal.

Most of the 86 amendments added to the bill were non-binding measures that merely stated the "sense of the Senate." A few, however, would force changes in U.S. policy or require the administration to break longstanding agreements with other countries.

As in the House debate three months earlier, much of the Senate action centered around U.S. relations with the Soviet Union. The anti-Soviet rhetoric was not dimmed by the prospect of a summit meeting between Reagan and Soviet leader Mikhail S. Gorbachev.

Indeed, conservatives used debate on the bill to voice their frustrations over the administration's determination to sign an intermediate-range missile arms control treaty in spite of what the conservatives insisted was a long history of Soviet treaty violations. *(INF treaty, p. 346)*

The Senate adopted 96-0 an amendment calling on the administration to protest Soviet missile tests — with dummy warheads — within a few hundred miles of the Hawaiian Islands.

Among other amendments directed at the Soviet Union and its allies were ones requiring the administration to begin negotiations aimed at forcing the Soviets to build a new embassy in Washington located no more than 90 feet above sea level and to apply to Soviet bloc diplomats in the United States the same travel restrictions that already were applied to Soviet diplomats.

Other amendments stated opposition to any Soviet role in a Middle East peace conference, unless the Soviets recognized Israel's right to exist; prohibited, with some exceptions, the State Department from hiring foreign nationals in communist countries to work in U.S. missions; and barred foreign nationals from being housed at diplomatic missions in the United States unless they were accredited to those missions.

Helms never attempted to disguise his belief that the State Department was peopled by weak-willed bureaucrats more interested in their careers than in national security. In the past he delayed action on ambassadorial nominations as a way of making his points. In 1987, he used his position as ranking Republican on Foreign Relations to cause fits for the State Department, especially its boss, Secretary of State Shultz.

Despite earlier defeats in committee and on the floor, Helms persisted in winning Senate support, 48-47, for an amendment barring establishment of an official residence for the secretary of state. The Senate also adopted several other Helms amendments dealing with State Department policies, as well as one limiting foreign diplomats' immunity from prosecution.

## Conference, Major Provisions

Conferees reached final agreement on the bill Dec. 8. The House approved the conference report (H Rept 100-475) Dec. 15 by 366-49. The following day, the Senate adopted it by voice vote.

As signed into law Dec. 22, 1987, HR 1777 (PL 100-204):

**Funding Levels.** Authorized $4.1 billion in fiscal 1988 and $4.22 billion in fiscal 1989 for the programs of the State Department, USIA, Board for International Broadcasting and the Asia Foundation.

**Soviet Embassy.** Prohibited the Soviets from moving into their new diplomatic facility perched atop Washington's Mount Alto, one of the highest points in the city, but allowed the president to let the Soviets occupy their new embassy within six months after the legislation became law if certain conditions were met.

**U.S.-Soviet Relations.** Instructed the secretary of state to make sure that U.S. facilities had roughly the same amount of property for residential and office purposes as did Soviet missions in the United States outside of the United Nations. The same provision prohibited the Soviets from moving into a new consulate in the United States until U.S. diplomats were able to occupy secure facilities in the Soviet city of Kiev.

● Called on the administration to protest Soviet missile

# Quandary Over PLO Mission

PL 100-204's provision ordering the closing of the Palestine Liberation Organization (PLO) observer mission to the United Nations in New York had the Reagan administration in a quandary in 1988.

As the bill made its way through Congress, the State Department had looked for strategies to keep the mission open and those efforts continued after it was signed into law. Reagan protested that the PLO provision represented Hill interference in the executive branch's powers to determine foreign policy.

The PLO controversy came as the Reagan administration was trying to bring peace to the Israeli-occupied territories, where Palestinians had been rioting and Israeli troops responding with bullets and beatings. *(Story, p. 234)*

Closing the PLO office also provoked a strong U.N. response. An emergency session of the General Assembly March 2, 1988, voted overwhelmingly for two resolutions to protest and challenge the U.S. decision to close the PLO office. The closing was denounced as a violation of the 1947 U.N. Headquarters Agreement, which, the critics said, allowed the PLO and any other U.N. observers to maintain an office in the host city.

The Justice Department announced March 10 that it had to close the office March 21 to comply with the State Department authorization law. But administration statements appeared to leave open the option of stalling, through litigation. Secretary of State George P. Shultz called the law "one of the dumber things that the Congress has done lately."

Arab groups filed suit in New York against the action and the PLO defied the March 21 order to close, forcing the federal government to take it to court.

In a second emergency session on the issue, the U.N. General Assembly March 23 voted 148-2 to denounce the closing. Israel and the United States voted against the resolution.

The International Court of Justice in the Hague ruled April 26 that the Reagan administration had to submit to international arbitration over its attempt to close the PLO mission. The State Department called the ruling premature because the United States had allowed the mission to remain open pending a U.S. court ruling. The Justice Department had asked a U.S. district court in New York to decide on the validity of the law.

Then on June 29 a New York district judge voided the congressional attempt to close the office and ruled that the December 1987 law violated the 1947 agreement allowing the U.N. headquarters in New York.

The Justice Department said Aug. 29 it would not appeal the federal court decision. That announcement drew criticism from sponsors of the anti-PLO provision.

"I hope Congress will act again as soon as possible to show the administration that we want laws we pass carried out to the letter," said Rep. Jack F. Kemp, R-N.Y.

---

tests earlier in 1987 near Hawaii.

● Permitted the State Department to restrict the travel of Soviet bloc diplomats working at missions attached to the United Nations.

● Prohibited the State Department after Sept. 30, 1989, from hiring foreign nationals in communist countries to work in U.S. diplomatic missions where classified materials were kept. The president could waive this requirement if he determined it was in the United States' national security interest.

**U.N. Support.** Placed conditions on the United States paying its full share of dues to the United Nations: 40 percent was to be paid when the bill was enacted, another 40 percent after the president reported to Congress that the United Nations was making progress on various budgetary reforms and the final 20 percent 30 days after the second installment unless Congress passed a joint resolution preventing the payment. *(Funds release, p. 244)*

**PLO Offices.** Ordered the closing of offices run by the PLO in Washington and New York. The administration already had shut down the Washington office but had resisted taking a similar step in New York because the PLO had official status there as an "observer" group at the United Nations. *(Box, this page)*

● Made it illegal for anyone in the United States to accept money from the PLO in order to spread the organization's views.

**State Department Management.** Prohibited construction of an official residence for use by future secretaries of state. Such a residence was needed, argued Secretary of State Shultz, because of security concerns.

● Prevented the State Department from declaring itself a "foreign mission" for the purpose of limiting public protests against visiting foreign officials, as it had attempted to do during a September 1987 visit by Soviet Foreign Minister Eduard A. Shevardnadze.

● Placed salary caps on senior U.S. diplomats, including ambassadors to specific countries and ambassadors-at-large.

● Required the secretary of state to name a five-person commission to study the Foreign Service personnel system.

● Ordered polygraph tests involving counterintelligence matters to be given to security officials at the State Department. The tests were modeled after a similar program applied in 1986 to the Defense Department.

● Ordered a comprehensive review of the practice of granting performance awards to employees and suspended further awards until the State Department's inspector general completed his review. The provision was prompted by unhappiness over bonuses given to officials in charge of overseeing security at the new U.S. Embassy in Moscow, where bugging devices were found.

● Placed restrictions on the State Department's ability to contract with outside groups for the purpose of boosting administration policies in support of the Nicaraguan contras. The Iran-contra inquiry had revealed irregularities in the granting of State Department contracts worth hundreds of thousands of dollars to pro-contra fund-raising and lobbying groups.

● Prevented the State Department from closing U.S. consulates around the world for money-saving reasons. But PL 100-202, the omnibus spending bill, allowed the State Department and USIA to close some overseas consulates and offices.

**Other Issues.** Required the secretary of state to submit to Congress within 90 days of the bill's enactment a report on the issue of immunity from prosecution accorded in the United States to foreign diplomatic personnel.

● Expressed the sense of Congress that the president should relax the existing U.S. trade embargo against Nicaragua to cover items that could be used to foster greater democracy in that country. The legislation suggested such items as those used by the print and broadcast media, trade unions and democratic civic opposition groups.

● Earmarked $1 million in fiscal 1988 to support democratic activities in Poland.

● Listed human rights violations in Tibet committed by the People's Republic of China, accompanied by an expression of the sense of Congress that U.S. policy toward China would be influenced by the Tibetan issue. The bill also provided U.S. college scholarships for Tibetans in exile.

● Reiterated U.S. opposition to the Soviet occupation of Afghanistan and support for anti-Soviet rebels there. (*Afghanistan, box, p. 221*)

● Called for the withdrawal of foreign military forces and Soviet military advisers from Angola. (*Angola, p. 238*)

● Stated opposition to any Soviet role in a Middle East peace conference, unless the Soviets recognized Israel's right to exist.

● Requested the secretary of state to report to Congress on actions taken by the Japanese government against the Toshiba Corp. and by the Norwegian government against the Kongsberg Corp. for their sale to the Soviet government of equipment that would make Soviet submarines much more difficult to detect. In 1983-84, Toshiba arranged to sell the Soviets a sophisticated milling machine and Kongsberg sold them a computer to control it, in violation of international agreements limiting sales of such high-technology equipment to the Soviet bloc.

# U.N. Funding

Responding in part to congressional pressure to restore full funding to the United Nations, President Reagan on Sept. 13, 1988, announced the release of $188 million in withheld dues to the organization.

Reagan also called on the State Department to develop a plan to pay $559 million in past obligations over the next three to five years. On July 15, the president had told U.N. Secretary General Javier Perez de Cuellar that a law passed by Congress in 1985 barred him from paying such arrearages until the agency revamped its budget process and other administrative practices.

But the United Nations' increasingly high-profile role in negotiating a cease-fire between Iran and Iraq and in resolving other longstanding international disputes fueled pressure on the president to release the funds before Sept. 26, when he was scheduled to make his last address to the organization.

### Background

Congress' decision in 1985 to withhold some U.N. funds was motivated by what members called excessive and careless spending. An amendment that year to the State Department authorization (HR 2068 — PL 99-93) reduced the United States' share of the U.N. total budget from 25 percent to 20 percent. Full funding was to be restored only if the agency agreed to give the United States more say in budget decisions. (*1985 action, p. 199*)

Largely as a result of this pressure, the United Nations in 1986 approved a plan under which a new Committee for Program and Coordination (CPC) would make major budgetary decisions by consensus instead of majority voting, in effect giving the United States veto power. The U.N. secretary general also ordered a 15 percent cutback in personnel to be carried out over three years, beginning in 1986.

Later, the Soviet Union agreed to resolve another major U.S. complaint by allowing a substantial portion of Soviets serving at the United Nations to take long-term assignments in New York instead of being under short-term contracts, a system known as "secondment." U.S. officials argued that secondment enabled Moscow to keep tight control of its employees at the United Nations and to more easily insert spies into its delegation. The fiscal 1988-89 defense authorization law (HR 1748 — PL 100-180) had included a provision calling on the administration to halve payments to the United Nations unless substantial progress was made on the secondment issue.

Members responded in 1987 to the changes by attaching a modification of the 1985 amendment to the fiscal 1988-89 State Department authorization bill (HR 1777 — PL 100-204). It set up a schedule for release of $144 million in U.N. funds appropriated in each of those fiscal years. (*1987 provision, p. 239*)

Of the $144 million for fiscal 1988, $44 million was withheld until the president reported Sept. 13 that the organization was following through on budget reforms and a hiring freeze. The funds were delivered the next day. The administration paid the full fiscal 1989 appropriation of $144 million after the Oct. 1 start of the fiscal year.

### Peacekeeping Money

Reagan in late September asked Congress for authority to transfer up to $150 million from Pentagon or foreign aid accounts for the U.S. share of U.N. peacekeeping efforts, such as those in Angola, Afghanistan and the Persian Gulf.

The House passed the authorizing legislation (HR 5551) by voice vote on Oct. 20, but Senate action was blocked by disputes over U.S. policy toward Angola, among other issues. (*Angola, p. 238*)

# Iran-Contra Aftermath

In the wake of the Iran-contra affair, Congress in 1988 considered several bills aimed at tightening laws governing covert operations and foreign arms sales. But only a minor change was enacted into law.

A Senate-passed bill (S 1721) requiring the president to tell Congress about all covert operations within 48 hours died a slow death in the House. The bill was intended to prevent presidents from keeping covert operations secret from all congressional leaders — as President Reagan had done in the 1985-86 arms sales to Iran.

The Senate approved the bill by a strong bipartisan margin, but in the House, Republicans objected to the measure's restraints on presidential authority. Sponsors tried for months to round up a veto-proof margin but wound up pulling the bill from the House calendar after a dispute arose over a statement made by House Speaker Jim Wright, D-Texas. Wright's comments about CIA operations in Nicaragua fueled an argument that Congress could not keep secrets, and Democrats feared that House debate on the 48-hour bill would turn into an attack on Wright. *(Wright controversy, box, p. 215)*

Another significant measure arising out of the Iran-contra affair fell victim to inaction in the Senate. It was a House-passed bill (HR 3651) imposing new restrictions on arms sales to countries that supported international terrorism. That bill would allow presidents to sell weapons to terrorist countries, such as Iran, only in narrow circumstances, and only after notifying Congress.

The only Iran-contra-related provision enacted in 1988 was language increasing Capitol Hill's involvement in sales of U.S.-made weaponry by one foreign country to another. Congress was supposed to be told about such "third-party" sales, but, as with other cases in the Iran-contra affair, it was not. Reagan in 1985 allowed Israel to sell U.S.-made anti-aircraft missiles to Iran but kept Congress in the dark. The new law, contained in the fiscal 1989 foreign aid appropriations bill (HR 4637 — PL 100-461), required the president to give Congress 30 days to pass legislation blocking such third-party transfers.

## Background

At the heart of the Iran-contra affair were covert operations, both official and semiofficial, that were kept from Congress. The official operation involved U.S. arms sales to Iran, directly and through Israel. Unofficially, CIA agents cooperated with Lt. Col. Oliver L. North's private network that supplied weapons to the Nicaraguan contras at a time when regular CIA aid was illegal. North was deputy director of political-military affairs at the National Security Council. *(Iran-contra affair, p. 253)*

Two major pieces of legislation on covert operations had been enacted: the Hughes-Ryan amendment of 1974 (PL 93-559) requiring notice about all covert operations, and a 1980 rewrite of that law (PL 96-450) saying the notice must be provided in a "timely" fashion. *(Background, Congress and the Nation Vol. V, p. 174)*

The Reagan administration interpreted those laws as giving the president the right to withhold notice to Congress indefinitely. In the case of covert arms sales to Iran, Reagan allowed 10 months to pass before formally notifying Congress, and he did so only after his secret was published in a Beirut magazine.

During the Iran-contra hearings in mid-1987, support developed in Congress for clearing up any confusion left by the timely notice requirement.

Most members of the Iran-contra investigating committees concluded that the president should be able to tell Hill leaders about even the most secret covert action within two working days after he approved it. That became the key recommendation of the committees' report, released Nov. 18, 1987.

Even before the panels issued their report, Reagan acted to make many of the changes they recommended. In August 1987 he signed National Security Decision Directive 286, ordering, among other things, that all covert-action findings be made in writing and be reviewed annually by the White House. Reagan also ordered that covert findings be reported to Congress within two working days except in "rare, extraordinary" cases.

His aides insisted that Reagan's order solved all the problems that the Iran-contra hearings had exposed.

But critics said that Reagan still reserved the right to keep Congress in the dark about covert actions. They also noted that Reagan or any future president could repeal or change the executive order — without telling Congress that the rules of the game had been altered.

## Covert-Action Measure

The Senate March 15, by a **key vote of 71-19 (R 26-17; D 45-2)**, approved legislation (S 1721) requiring the president to inform Congress ahead of time about all covert operations. The bill allowed the president to delay notice in emergencies — but in no event for more than 48 hours. *(1988 key votes, p. 981)*

The administration said that the mandatory-notice provision violated the president's right under the Constitution to carry out foreign policy as he saw fit. But supporters of the 48-hour provision argued that Congress' control over appropriations gave it an equal constitutional responsibility over such matters.

S 1721, reported by the Senate Intelligence Committee Jan. 27 (S Rept 100-276), gave the president several options as to who on Capitol Hill should receive his report. It also established several requirements for covert operations and the formal "findings" by which presidents approved them.

During floor debate, S 1721 survived several attempts to water down its 48-hour reporting requirement as well as efforts by conservative Republicans to attach unrelated amendments.

Despite the bipartisan agreement over the legislation in the Senate, on the other side of the Capitol, Republicans framed the issue in partisan terms. They called the House bill (HR 3822) an attempt by Democrats to punish Reagan for his Iran-contra sins.

Like the Senate bill, HR 3822 required advance notice of covert actions but gave the president several options for delaying it up to 48 hours under extraordinary circumstances. The bill was reported by the House Intelligence Committee on June 15 (H Rept 100-705, Part I) and Foreign Affairs Committee on July 6 (Part II), after heated, partisan debates.

Floor action on the bill was put off to allow Democratic leaders time to round up votes and also to avoid taking it up during the partisan climate of the national political conventions in July and August. But the bill got caught up in the controversy in September over Wright's remarks about Nicaragua and the furor doomed it.

## Arms Sales Limits

Another Iran-contra-related bill (HR 3651) fared no better than the 48-hour measure, suffering delays in spite of broad bipartisan support. In the end, it died in the Senate as Congress struggled to adjourn.

The legislation would require the president to notify Congress 30 days in advance of any arms sale to countries that the secretary of state had found to be supporting international terrorism. Under special circumstances, he could limit the advance notice to 15 days. Six countries were on the secretary's list at that time: Cuba, Iran, Libya, North Korea, South Yemen and Syria.

When administration officials expressed concern that the bill would reduce the president's flexibility to respond to emergencies, the bill's sponsors stipulated that under "exceptional circumstances" the president could use an existing special authority (called Section 614 of the underlying foreign aid laws) to avoid the 15-day advance notice, but that there had to be at least 24 hours notice.

The House passed HR 3651 on May 24 by voice vote. In the fall, with time running out in the session, HR 3651 was incorporated into a multipurpose foreign policy bill (HR 5550) that contained several items of unfinished business. The House passed the new measure by voice vote on Oct. 20, but Senate action was blocked by Jesse Helms, R-N.C., who insisted that provisions curtailing foreign diplomatic immunity and delaying a China satellite deal be added to the bill. The Senate referred HR 5550 back to committee, effectively killing it.

# 1988 Intelligence Authorization

For the third year in a row, Congress in 1987 substantially trimmed President Reagan's request for funding for the CIA and other intelligence agencies. As was customary, Congress kept secret the actual amounts included in the legislation (HR 2112 — PL 100-178) authorizing funds for the intelligence agencies.

But the Intelligence committees, which had readily endorsed major budget increases for those agencies during the late 1970s and early 1980s, said they cut Reagan's request, and sources said the reduction affected a wide range of intelligence programs.

The bill authorized fiscal 1988 funding for intelligence operations conducted by a host of agencies, among them the CIA, Defense Department and National Security Agency.

As in previous years, the bill barred the CIA from using its contingency fund to provide aid to the contras in Nicaragua. The CIA, however, was allowed to provide intelligence information and advice to the contras. Other provisions called for reports on ways to improve U.S. counterintelligence efforts.

## Legislative Action

HR 2112 was reported by the House Permanent Select Committee on Intelligence May 13 (H Rept 100-93, Part I) and the House Armed Services Committee June 3 (Part II).

The House passed the bill June 9 by voice vote after a brief debate and the addition of one amendment, also adopted by voice vote, requiring a report from the secretary of defense on the Soviet Union's newly constructed embassy in Washington, D.C. (*Embassy dispute, box, p. 240*)

S 1243, the Senate version, was reported May 20 by the Senate Intelligence Committee (S Rept 100-59) and the Senate Armed Services Committee July 17 (S Rept 100-117). The Senate approved an amended HR 2112 by voice vote July 23.

The conference report on HR 2112 (H Rept 100-432) was approved by the House Nov. 17 by voice vote. The Senate followed suit the next day.

## Major Provisions

As signed into law Dec. 2, 1987, major provisions of HR 2112 that were made public:

● Continued prohibitions against the use of the CIA's contingency reserve to fund the contra rebels fighting the Nicaraguan Sandinista government. The legislation was carefully worded to ensure that no funds be used to help the contras' military effort unless specifically approved by Congress. The CIA, however, was allowed to provide intelligence information and advice to the contras under the conference report.

● Called for a classified study by the National Academy of Public Administration, a federally chartered agency, to look into personnel policies of intelligence agencies and make recommendations for improving them. This and other sections of the bill were aimed at finding ways to strengthen U.S. intelligence efforts and to bolster salaries and personnel procedures in order to enhance the performance of intelligence agencies.

● Required the FBI director to study ways to recruit and keep agents in the FBI's New York field office, which tracked Soviet bloc officials at the United Nations. FBI officials had complained about their inability to keep agents in that office because of the high cost of living in and around New York City.

● Required the secretary of defense to advise Congress in a report on the Soviets' ability to intercept sensitive U.S. communications from the newly constructed but unoccupied Soviet diplomatic facilities on Mount Alto, a hilltop location in Washington, D.C., only a few miles from the White House.

● Required the attorney general to inform the Intelligence committees about any Soviet national admitted into the United States over objections from the FBI. The reporting requirement, opposed by Reagan as an interference with the constitutional prerogatives of the executive branch, represented a further attempt by Congress to establish a better balance between the number of American and Soviet employees at embassies, consulates and U.N. missions.

● Authorized $23.6 million to pay for a 237-member Intelligence Community Staff.

● Authorized $134.7 million for the CIA's retirement and disability fund.

● Extended pension and survivor benefits to certain categories of former spouses of CIA personnel.

# 1989 Intelligence Authorization

Congress in 1988 endorsed a multibillion-dollar program of new satellites and sensors to improve U.S. ability to monitor Soviet compliance with a future strategic arms reduction talks (START) treaty.

Authorization for the major new initiative was included in the fiscal 1989 authorization for U.S. intelligence agencies (HR 4387 — PL 100-453).

The bill authorized a secret amount of fiscal 1989 funds for about a dozen agencies that collected intelligence information and combatted foreign espionage in the United

States. A Senate Intelligence Committee spokesman said the bill allowed a "slight real," or after-inflation, increase in the intelligence budget for fiscal 1989.

Total U.S. spending on intelligence activities reportedly was about $25 billion a year. About half of that amount was for "national intelligence" operations, such as those of the CIA, that provided information for policy makers; the rest was for "tactical intelligence" operations by the armed services.

In the wake of the Iran-contra affair, HR 4387 broadened existing restrictions barring unauthorized aid to Nicaragua's contra guerrillas by any agency "involved in intelligence activities." The new provision barred the CIA or any other "entity" of the U.S. government from providing such aid, thus clearly applying the ban to the National Security Council (NSC) staff. The Reagan administration in 1985 secretly determined that the NSC was not an intelligence agency, thus freeing staff member Marine Lt. Col. Oliver L. North to arrange arms shipments and other forms of aid to the contras.

Also in response to the Iran-contra affair, the bill took a modest step toward boosting the status of the CIA's inspector general. The 1987 investigations into the Iran-contra affair turned up evidence that the CIA's watchdog had limited power to uncover and correct wrongdoing. Instead of making the CIA inspector general independent as in other departments, HR 4387 mandated that the CIA director keep Congress informed about the activities of the inspector general.

## Spy Satellite Dispute

The multibillion-dollar spy satellite initiative caused a budgeting dispute that threatened not only to derail the intelligence authorization bill but also to delay Senate approval of the U.S.-Soviet treaty banning intermediate-range nuclear-force (INF) missiles. *(INF treaty, p. 346)*

Because of disasters in the space program — including the 1986 explosion of the shuttle *Challenger* — the United States had only two satellites capable of taking pictures of Soviet nuclear weapons installations. One satellite, a KH-11, was months past its expected three-year life span, and the other, a KH-9 launched in 1987, was an updated version of 1970s-vintage satellites.

Senate Intelligence leaders expressed fears that those devices would not be able to monitor Soviet compliance with a future START agreement.

They pressed the administration for a commitment to a new satellite program but for a while ran into resistance from various agencies. To force the administration to boost its requests for the satellites, the Senate Intelligence Committee threatened to delay Senate action on the INF treaty and made what one source called "substantial" cuts in the intelligence budget and shifted the funds to the satellite program.

President Reagan on May 17 settled on a compromise that increased funding for the satellites but that fell short of what the Senate leaders had wanted. The agreed-on amount was classified secret but reportedly would reach several billion dollars over five years.

The House Appropriations Committee in June objected to the new program in its report on the fiscal 1989 defense spending bill (HR 4781 — H Rept 100-681). A House committee official said the administration had proposed and conferees on the intelligence authorization bill

---

# Intelligence Leaks on Hill

During Senate debate on the fiscal 1988 intelligence authorization bill (HR 2112 — PL 100-178), leaders of that chamber's Intelligence Committee publicized the panel's new, more stringent rules governing the handling of secret information by committee members.

The rules adopted in 1987 sharply restricted members' ability to remove from the committee's offices any documents containing secret information. Moreover, panel chairman David L. Boren, D-Okla., and vice chairman William S. Cohen, R-Maine, repeatedly emphasized that they would seek the resignation from the committee of any member found to have leaked classified information.

Five days later, on July 28, Patrick J. Leahy, D-Vt., announced that he had resigned from the panel on Jan. 13, 1987, after he violated committee rules by giving a reporter access to a draft report on the Iran-contra affair. The document contained no classified information, but the committee had voted not to release it.

The publicizing of the new rules and Leahy's disclosure came in the wake of claims by two former White House aides, Lt. Col. Oliver L. North and Adm. John M. Poindexter, that their earlier efforts to mislead congressional committees — including the Senate and House Intelligence panels — were justified by the risk that secret information would be leaked.

---

had accepted significant changes in the original Senate plan.

## Legislative Action

The House Intelligence Committee reported HR 4387 (H Rept 100-591, Part I) on April 29. The House Armed Services (Part II) and Foreign Affairs panels also had jurisdiction over portions of the bill and both gave informal approval, allowing the bill to go to the floor.

The House passed HR 4387 by voice vote on May 26 after adopting three minor amendments and rejecting one potentially major one. With the Nicaraguan government and the contras meeting for a third round of peace talks in Managua, the House rejected, 190-214, an amendment that would allow the CIA to resume covert aid to the guerrillas in the fall.

The Senate Intelligence Committee reported a companion measure (S 2366 — S Rept 100-334) on May 11. The Senate Armed Services Committee reported it June 28 (S Rept 100-404). The Senate passed an amended HR 4387 by voice vote on Aug. 5, without formal debate.

The House and Senate approved the conference version of HR 4387 (H Rept 100-879) by voice votes on Sept. 14 and 15, respectively.

## Major Provisions

As signed into law Sept. 29, 1988, major provisions of HR 4387 that were made public:

● Authorized funding for the first year of a long-term program — reportedly of new satellites and sensors — to improve U.S. capabilities to verify a START treaty.

● Prohibited the CIA or any other "entity" of the U.S. government from providing direct support of any kind to Nicaragua's contra guerrillas, unless Congress specifically authorized aid.

● Required, among other things, that the CIA director report to the Intelligence committees whenever he hired or fired an inspector general or placed significant restrictions on his activities. The director also was required to send the panels semiannual reports on the activities of the inspector general.

● Authorized lump-sum payments of up to $20,000, and periodic bonus payments of 20 percent to 25 percent of base pay, to attract agents to the FBI's New York City field office. *(1987 action, p. 246)*

● Stated concern about the lack of progress in improving U.S. programs to combat foreign espionage, especially by the Soviet Union and its allies. Conferees said they took several actions on counterintelligence issues in the secret parts of the bill.

● Authorized the secretary of defense to appoint an assistant secretary for intelligence.

● Extended until Dec. 31, 1989, the authority of federal intelligence agencies to obtain state and local criminal records for the purpose of conducting background security checks.

● Restricted the purchase by the Army of RC-12K Guardrail electronic surveillance planes that the House Intelligence panel said were outmoded and expensive — until the Army submitted a report to Congress.

● Required the intelligence agencies to tell next of kin about reports of live sightings of prisoners of war or servicemen missing in action from the Vietnam War.

● Authorized $23.745 million for a 244-member Intelligence Community Staff.

● Authorized $15.1 million for FBI counterintelligence activities in connection with the INF treaty. The bureau was to keep tabs on Soviet officials inspecting compliance with the treaty at some two dozen U.S. locations.

● Authorized $144.5 million for the CIA retirement and disability fund.

# Philippine Base Accord

A new base-rights agreement eased strains between Washington and Manila in 1988 but left unanswered questions about the long-term future of the U.S. presence in the Philippines.

Secretary of State George P. Shultz and Philippine Foreign Minister Raul Manglapus on Oct. 17 signed an agreement calling for a significant expansion in U.S. aid to the Philippines in fiscal 1990-91. Those were the last two years of an existing accord allowing U.S. access to Clark Air Base and Subic Bay Naval Base, two of the most important American military installations in the world.

The two countries were expected to begin negotiations in 1989 over what would happen to those bases once the new agreement had expired in 1991. Political pressure was building in the Philippines to oust the United States from the bases, and it was unclear whether the Philippine Senate would ratify a new accord keeping the bases under conditions similar to existing ones.

In signing the 1988 agreement, each side insisted it was keeping its options open — mutual code language for an implied threat to sever the military relationship should the other side fail to make enough concessions. Signaling U.S. willingness to consider drastic steps, the Pentagon had dusted off schemes to move the bases elsewhere in the Pacific — to Guam, Saipan or Palau.

The initial reaction in the Philippines demonstrated how politically contentious the base issue was. Opposition politicians and newspapers denounced the accord as a bad deal for their country, noting that Philippine negotiators settled for only about half the aid they had demanded.

On the other side of the ledger, the Oct. 17 agreement could have cleared the way for broad backing of an international aid program intended to help pull the Philippines out from under its crushing debt burden. At the instigation of congressional leaders, the administration had been negotiating with Japan, West Germany and other countries to start a "mini-Marshall plan" for the Philippines totaling at least $5 billion over the next five years.

## Philippine Aid

Under the base accord covering fiscal years 1985-89, the Philippines had been receiving about $180 million per year in U.S. aid.

During negotiations on the new two-year accord, Foreign Minister Manglapus had called for $1.2 billion a year, plus $100 million annually in Treasury bonds.

The final result, promised by President Reagan in an Oct. 17 letter to Philippine President Corazon Aquino, closely matched the U.S. aid offer: an aid package totaling $962 million over fiscal years 1990-91.

At first glance, a commitment averaging $481 million per year appeared to be a huge increase over the $180 million annual aid package that Reagan had promised in 1983 for five years. However, the new figure actually was only about $80 million more each year than the United States had been giving the Philippines. One reason was that the new agreement counted several aid programs that were not counted in the previous agreement. Also, the United States in the recent past had been giving the Philippines substantially more than the $180 million promised. The Philippines got an annual average of $370 million in fiscal years 1986-87 and $403 million in total U.S. aid in fiscal 1988. *(Philippine aid, p. 184)*

The United States also agreed to speed up the release of U.S. economic aid to the Philippines. Washington had been holding up $124 million in fiscal 1988 aid because of disagreements about how the money was to be spent. A Philippine demand for increased flexibility in using this money was one of the last major issues to be resolved. The agreement said it could be used to bolster the Philippine overall budget or to help pay off foreign debts.

## Nuclear Issue

Other than aid, the most controversial issue during the six months of negotiations involved the stationing of U.S. nuclear weapons at Clark and Subic. Echoing concerns in countries such as New Zealand and Spain, Philippine nationalists in recent years had campaigned to bar U.S. nuclear weapons. During negotiations, Philippine officials demanded greater control over the stationing of such weapons.

The final agreement, reportedly modeled after an accord with Spain, gave the Philippines the right to veto the storage or installation of nuclear and "non-conventional" weapons or components; the latter phrase was an apparent reference to chemical weapons. However, the United States would continue to be able to transit ships and aircraft with nuclear weapons. Washington also maintained its policy of neither confirming nor denying that any particular ship or aircraft was carrying such weapons.

Aquino came under heavy criticism in the Philippines for accepting this compromise, with one leftist senator calling for her impeachment because of it.

# Palau Independence Dispute

Legislation that could have cleared the way for the small Pacific island chain of Palau finally to achieve limited independence from the United States stalled at the end of the 100th Congress.

A dispute between the House and Senate over whether Palau should receive more aid than the $460 million it had been promised over 15 years in exchange for military basing rights delayed the clearing of H J Res 597. The House on Oct. 6, 1988, had passed, 406-11, the resolution, implementing a 1986 agreement on Palau's independence. The Senate passed a very different version of H J Res 597 the next day.

Only minutes before Congress adjourned Oct. 22, a compromise was reached on additional aid for Palau. But it came too late for Congress to vote on the legislation. In the end, Palau, an impoverished archipelago of 15,000 people, remained in a semi-colonial limbo without immediate prospects for economic recovery.

## Background

The United States captured Palau from the Japanese during World War II and for years loosely oversaw its affairs and those of the rest of Micronesia, including the Federated States of Micronesia (FSM) and the Marshall Islands, under a U.N. trusteeship.

FSM and the Marshall Islands received limited autonomy under a compact approved by Congress in 1985 (H J Res 187 — PL 99-239) and by the islands in 1986. *(Micronesia compact, p. 206)*

Palau was to receive the same terms under a compact tentatively approved by Congress in 1986 (H J Res 626 — PL 99-658). It would receive control over its domestic affairs and $460 million in U.S. aid over 15 years. In return, the United States would retain the right to defend the island and could claim as much as a third of Palauan land for military bases, a provision considered vital by the Pentagon in case two large U.S. military bases in the Philippines were lost. *(Philippines, p. 248)*

But Palau's residents had not ratified the deal, principally because of a clause in their constitution banning all nuclear ships or weapons from their territory, unless three-fourths of the voters agreed to overturn the ban.

The Reagan administration refused to accept the ban and wrote provisions in the compact allowing a limited U.S. presence if needed.

The result was a stalemate that put Palau at the forefront of the South Pacific anti-nuclear movement.

With the Reagan administration on one side and antinuclear activists on the other, Palau was pulled in opposite directions.

In each of six plebiscites beginning in 1983, the compact was favored by a majority of Palauan voters, but the support was short of the 75 percent required in the constitution.

A constitutional amendment changing the requirement for approval of the compact from 75 percent to a simple majority of voters was pushed through in August 1987. A new plebiscite showed 73 percent in favor of the compact, more than enough, it seemed, for approval. But later that same month the Palauan Supreme Court invalidated the vote and held that a 75 percent vote was needed after all. Palauan leaders called for an enhanced package of benefits to win approval of the compact.

# U.S.-Japan Nuclear Pact

A new nuclear-cooperation agreement between the United States and Japan rekindled non-proliferation concerns on Capitol Hill, but a Senate effort to keep it from taking effect in 1988 was defeated.

The agreement, signed by the two nations on Nov. 4, 1987, and submitted to Congress five days later, provided for the sale of U.S. uranium and uranium-enrichment supplies and services to Japan for 30 years, superseding an existing pact that was to expire in 2003.

Opponents were most alarmed by a provision that gave Japan "advance programmatic consent" for 30 years to recover and transport tons of plutonium, a radioactive substance recycled from uranium waste that could be used to make nuclear bombs. Under the existing pact, Japan needed U.S. approval each time it reprocessed and shipped spent fuel from U.S.-supplied uranium.

Under nuclear non-proliferation and export-control laws (PL 95-242, PL 99-64), the agreement automatically took effect 90 legislative days after submission to Congress. To block it, both chambers of Congress had to pass a resolution of disapproval, which would then need the president's signature.

Senate opponents mounted an effort to kill the pact, but a resolution of disapproval (S J Res 241) was rejected on March 21, by a 30-53 vote. A resolution of disapproval had been introduced in the House (H J Res 439), but the House never acted on it.

## Arguments

The administration and its supporters said the nuclear agreement would foster energy stability for Japan, an important ally, while providing a steady customer for the beleaguered U.S. nuclear industry. The Department of Energy estimated that enriched-uranium sales to Japan would be worth $250 million in 1988 alone and could amount to as much as $1 billion per year in the next decade. Given Japan's huge trade surplus with the United States, every incoming dollar from that country was welcome.

Furthermore, the administration contended the pact would increase U.S. control over Japan's use of plutonium.

But congressional critics said safety and nuclear non-proliferation objectives were abandoned in the pursuit of the commercial relationship.

Members of the Senate Foreign Relations and House Foreign Affairs committees raised concerns about the danger of Japan transporting by air large quantities of highly radioactive plutonium from recycling facilities in Europe back to Japan. They asked the president to rework the pact. Reagan refused to renegotiate but said the administration would take some of Congress' fears into account in devising a plutonium-transportation plan.

It would have been difficult for Congress to reject the pact, not only because of Japan's non-proliferation record and its strategic importance to the United States, but also because, just two and a half years earlier, it had allowed a similar agreement with the People's Republic of China, despite indications that the Chinese had aided Pakistan's nuclear weapons development program. *(China agreement, p. 207)*

## U.S. Ties to Vietnam

A surprise move by Vietnam to back off a search for Americans still missing in action (MIAs) derailed legislation aimed at improving relations between the two countries.

Although Hanoi reversed its position less than a month later and decided to let the search go forward, the move failed to get the legislation back on track in 1988.

Congress was considering non-binding resolutions (S Con Res 109, H Con Res 271) calling for the establishment of unofficial embassies, known as "interest sections," in Washington and Hanoi. The plan — supported by Vietnam but opposed by the Reagan administration — was gaining momentum on Capitol Hill.

But then Vietnam, angry over what it called the administration's "hostile policy," abruptly suspended the agreement to search for MIAs and to allow re-education camp detainees to emigrate to the United States.

Vietnam's move had the unintended effect of giving the administration what it wanted: Congress backed away from the interest-sections legislation. The administration insisted that there could be no normalization of relations until Vietnam withdrew completely from Cambodia and an acceptable settlement of the conflict had been reached. Moreover, although the United States and Vietnam in 1987 had signed a statement that humanitarian and broader political issues should not be linked, administration officials indicated diplomatic recognition could not happen without resolution of the MIA issue and other humanitarian concerns.

The break in cooperation also set back temporarily months of negotiations aimed at resolving the MIA question and other humanitarian issues that had soured U.S.-Vietnam relations for more than a decade. Approximately 1,700 Americans were still listed as missing in Vietnam.

Congress did approve a resolution (H J Res 602 — PL 100-502) urging steps to prevent the Khmer Rouge from coming back to power after Vietnam pulled out of Cambodia. Former leader Pol Pot and the Khmer Rouge, communist rulers of Cambodia from 1975 until the Vietnamese drove them from power in January 1979, were blamed for the deaths of 1 million to 2 million Cambodians.

Since 1985, the United States had provided about $3 million out of $5 million authorized each year to the non-communist resistance in Cambodia. *(Cambodia aid, pp. 193, 195, 228, 232)*

Vietnam announced in May 1987 that it would end its occupation of neighboring Cambodia by 1990. By the end of 1987, Hanoi said it had withdrawn 50,000 troops, as promised, with 50,000 still remaining. (Western diplomats estimated the number of troops remaining at about 85,000.) In January 1989, Vietnamese officials said the remaining troops would be withdrawn by September.

H J Res 602, passed by the House Aug. 8 and the Senate Sept. 16, called on the administration to continue aid to Cambodia's non-communist resistance and to urge China and Thailand immediately to stop supporting the Khmer Rouge. Although the administration opposed the provision calling for an immediate cessation of aid to the Khmer Rouge as premature, President Reagan signed H J Res 602 into law Oct. 18.

## Certifying Anti-Drug Efforts

Members of key House and Senate drug enforcement committees wrangled with the administration in 1988 over President Reagan's certification that Mexico, the Bahamas, Bolivia, Paraguay and Peru were "fully cooperating" with U.S. drug interdiction efforts. Such certificates were required by Congress for continued payments of full foreign aid to these countries. Congress could disapprove the presidential certification through passage of a joint resolution.

But in 1988, when resolutions disapproving the administration's certification of the five countries were introduced, they failed to achieve both House and Senate passage.

Hill critics and administration officials were at odds over which approach was more effective: to encourage governments to mend their ways or to threaten to punish them economically.

The 1986 Anti-Drug Abuse Act (HR 5484 — PL 99-570) required decertified countries to automatically receive a 50 percent cut in non-humanitarian U.S. foreign aid, excepting money used for drug interdiction. U.S. members of international development banks were ordered to vote against loans to decertified countries. The president also could impose harsher economic sanctions, such as suspending trade preferences. *(Drug bill, p. 723)*

In the only decertification resolution to make it to a floor vote in 1988, the Senate April 14 approved, 63-27, S J Res 268, disapproving President Reagan's assertion that Mexico was "fully cooperating" in U.S. drug-control efforts.

The resolution was put aside in the House, after Speaker of the House Jim Wright, D-Texas, requested and received a detailed letter from the Mexican government outlining its campaign against drug trafficking. The apparent shelving of the Mexico sanctions averted an embarrassing situation for Wright, a Texan with close ties to Mexico, and the Reagan administration, which had joined the Mexican government in condemning the Senate vote.

## Genocide Treaty

Nearly 40 years after a treaty to ban genocide was approved by the United Nations, Congress in 1988 cleared legislation to put the pact into effect.

The treaty was approved by the United Nations in 1948 and submitted to the Senate for ratification in 1949. It was not until 1986, however, that the pact was ratified. *(1986 action, p. 205)*

S 1851 (PL 100-606) defined genocide as acting with a "specific intent to destroy, in whole or in substantial part, a

# Joint Chiefs Chairman

Adm. William J. Crowe Jr. succeeded Army Gen. John W. Vessey Jr. as chairman of the Joint Chiefs of Staff in 1985. The Senate confirmed Crowe's nomination by voice vote July 31.

A submariner with a Princeton doctorate in political science, Crowe was highly regarded as a strategic thinker. His extensive experience in "joint" jobs — positions involving command of personnel from several armed services — suggested he might be a strong voice for "unified" military judgment, at the expense of the parochial viewpoints of the armed services.

Before his nomination to the chairmanship, Crowe capped a long string of joint positions with two years as commander in chief of all U.S. forces in the Pacific: CINCPAC.

unified commands were organized as a federation of self-contained components from each service, so that a CINC dealt with any unit only through the so-called "component commander" in charge of all the units of that service assigned to the CINC.

● Assigning command authority within his sphere of operations.

● Coordinating administrative, supply, organizational and disciplinary policy among assigned units to the degree necessary to carry out missions assigned to the CINC.

Officers could be assigned to any CINC's staff only with his concurrence, and he could suspend any officer assigned to his command.

The conference bill also required that any combat forces operating in a CINC's sphere of responsibility be assigned to his command. Also, a CINC would be allowed to monitor communications between units assigned to him and other Pentagon entities.

The conference report required the secretary of defense to submit to Congress a separate budget covering the joint training exercises and other activities of each CINC.

**'Joint' Specialists.** The compromise bill required the secretary of defense to establish an occupational category for officers in joint operations. Critics had charged that officers in joint assignments who did not support their services' points of view were punished by being denied promotion. Partly for that reason, they argued, the most talented officers eschew interservice duty.

The conference report required the secretary of defense to ensure that the officers assigned to joint duty were talented enough that they would be promoted in due course. And it required the secretary of defense to establish guidelines for each service's personnel system to prevent discrimination against officers on joint assignments.

Promotion disputes between the chairman and a service were to be resolved by the defense secretary.

**Headquarters Consolidation.** The conference report accepted in part House-passed provisions to consolidate the two parallel hierarchies at the top of the Army,

Navy and Air Force departments. Each of these agencies was headed by a civilian secretary who had a staff of civilian subordinates in charge of the service's facets. Each service also had a military headquarters, headed by a chief of staff assisted by military officers whose division of labor was similar to those of the secretary's civilian aides. The Navy Department, with one civilian secretariat, had two service headquarters: the Navy's and the Marine Corps'.

The conference report required the civilian staff to take over certain functions, including purchasing, auditing, congressional relations and public affairs.

Partly on grounds that these provisions reduced unnecessary duplication of effort, the conference report required the Pentagon to transfer 16,513 military and civilian personnel from headquarters jobs to other positions by the end of fiscal 1988. This was a reduction of 10.3 percent in the Defense Department's total headquarters staff.

# Military Retirement Cuts

Congress in 1986 approved a measure (HR 4420 — PL 99-348) that was expected to trim the cost of the military retirement system by about $3.2 billion annually. The bill reduced annuities to personnel who left active duty after less than 30 years of service. The change did not affect anyone already in the service or receiving a pension.

The House April 22 passed HR 4420 (H Rept 99-513), 399-7. The Senate May 15 passed HR 4420, 92-1, after substituting the text of its own version (S 2395 — S Rept 99-292). The Senate approved the conference version (H Rept 99-659) June 25; the House, the following day.

## Background

The existing military pension system, which allowed service members to retire after 20 years with a pension of half of their basic pay, was widely criticized as unduly generous and thus too costly. Moreover, some defense analysts objected that it provided a strong incentive for specialists to leave after 20 years, even though their experience still made them useful to the service.

Defense officials argued that some service members should retire in their early 40s, to make room for younger men able to handle the physical rigors of combat. But, they said, the military must offer these members the incentive of a considerable pension while they began a new career.

With political pressure mounting to restrain President Reagan's defense buildup, Congress in the fiscal 1986 defense authorization bill (PL 99-145) mandated a $2.9 billion reduction in funds for military retirement. Had Congress failed to act, the Pentagon would have been forced to lay off some 330,000 active-duty personnel — roughly one service member in seven. (*Authorization, p. 277*)

## Changes in Law

Under existing law, military personnel could retire after 20 years of service with an annuity equal to 50 percent of their basic pay (which excluded certain special bonuses and fringe benefits). The proportion of basic pay (or "multiplier") increased with each additional year of active duty until the 30th year, after which service members could retire with an annuity of 75 percent of their basic pay. In each case, the multiplier was applied to the person's average basic pay in his three highest-paid years of service.

Under HR 4420, the annuity for a 20-year retiree was reduced to 40 percent of a person's basic pay, averaged over his three highest-paid years. The formula for retirement after 30 years of active duty remained unchanged.

Annuities would be increased annually by a percentage equal to the annual increase in the consumer price index (CPI) minus 1 percentage point. When the retiree reached age 62, his annuity would be increased to the level it would have reached if all of his cost-of-living adjustments had equaled the increase in the CPI. But subsequent increases would be the CPI percentage minus 1 percentage point.

## Military Health Programs

Congress in a fiscal 1986 deficit reduction bill (HR 3128 — PL 99-272), cleared March 20, 1986, authorized the government to seek private health insurance payments, at the prevailing rate, for some military hospital services provided to non-active-duty military beneficiaries.

It also required hospitals that participated in Medicare to accept patients under the Pentagon's medical program for dependents and retirees, called CHAMPUS (Civilian Health and Medical Plan of the Uniformed Services), and to accept CHAMPUS payments as full payment for those patients. A small program under which CHAMPUS paid for hospital care of certain veterans also would be covered by this provision.

# 1987-88

The 100th Congress, like its predecessor, approved defense budgets resulting in real declines in the Pentagon's purchasing power. But, in contrast to the battles of earlier years, the Reagan administration in 1987 scaled down its defense budget request to an amount close to what Congress was expected to approve. In addition, a budget "summit" between the administration and Congress produced agreement on a two-year cutback for fiscal 1988 and 1989.

But, while the White House and Congress could agree on total dollar amounts, they were far apart on strategic arms issues. Over administration objections, Congress in 1987 mandated, in effect, continued compliance with the numerical ceilings on certain kinds of weapons that were set by the unratified 1979 strategic arms limitation talks (SALT II) treaty with the Soviet Union. Congress also rejected the administration's attempt to reinterpret the 1972 U.S.-Soviet treaty limiting anti-ballistic missile (ABM) weapons to permit more realistic testing of Reagan's strategic defense initiative (SDI).

Congressional attempts to go even further in its provisions on strategic weapons and arms control triggered a veto of the fiscal 1989 defense bill. A compromise was ultimately enacted.

Congress and the administration also tangled over cutbacks proposed in conventional weapons programs, with some critics charging that the reductions were being made to pay for SDI and other strategic weapons. Congress boosted production rates of some conventional weapons and blocked administration plans to phase out some others.

Efforts to delay Reagan's policy of providing U.S.

Navy escorts for Kuwaiti-owned oil tankers flying the U.S. flag in the Persian Gulf proved unsuccessful, as were subsequent moves to initiate the procedures established by the 1973 War Powers Resolution.

The Senate overwhelmingly approved the U.S.-Soviet treaty banning intermediate-range nuclear-force (INF) missiles. The treaty embodied the "zero-option," which was widely dismissed as unrealistic when Reagan first proposed it in 1981.

Congress tackled a political hot potato in 1988 when it enacted legislation providing for the first large-scale disposal of superfluous military bases in a decade.

Congress took only limited steps in response to allegations made in mid-1988 of bribery and other illegal dealings in the Pentagon procurement system.

## 1988 Defense Authorization

Hemmed in by budgetary constraints, Congress in 1987 enacted a fiscal 1988 defense authorization bill that ensured an after-inflation decline in Pentagon spending for the third consecutive year. And the bill placed new strings on President Reagan's strategic arms buildup.

When Senate-House conferees completed work on the authorization measure in early November 1987, the final word on the defense budget for fiscal 1988 still was up in the air. It was later settled as part of a White House-congressional "summit" negotiation on the budget. *(Economic summit, p. 33)*

So the conferees on the defense bill (HR 1748 — PL 100-180) provided for two authorization packages: a "high tier," yielding a total defense appropriation of $296 billion, and a "low tier," totaling $289 billion. Reagan had requested $311.9 billion.

The defense bill provided that if the defense budget for fiscal 1988 exceeded $289 billion, the higher ceilings included in the high-tier version would apply to individual programs. That was what eventually happened; the budget summit agreement, announced Nov. 20, allowed a defense budget of $292 billion. Factoring in the cost of inflation, this was 4 percent less than Congress had appropriated for defense in fiscal 1987, according to figures at the time.

The high-tier authorization for programs actually covered by HR 1748 was $218.5 billion, as compared with Reagan's request for $233.4 billion. HR 1748 did not include funds for military personnel, which were not authorized annually.

The low-tier authorization amounts — totaling $211.9 billion for HR 1748 programs — had no legal effect once the higher budget total was agreed to. But they remained a significant index of the funding priorities of the Senate and House Armed Services committees.

In addition to the cutbacks in funding levels, HR 1748 dealt dramatic reversals to the administration's nuclear arms and arms control policies. It barred for one year any tests of the strategic defense initiative (SDI) — Reagan's program to develop a nationwide anti-missile shield — that involved the use of space-based weapons. In effect, this would ensure that SDI remained consistent through fiscal 1988 with the traditional interpretation of the 1972 U.S.-Soviet anti-ballistic missile (ABM) treaty. The administration since late 1985 had claimed that certain anti-missile tests in space could be conducted without violating the ABM treaty. *(ABM treaty dispute, p. 347)*

The conferees also dealt Reagan a blow on another

# National Defense Leadership

Defense Secretary Caspar W. Weinberger announced his retirement Nov. 5, 1987, citing his wife's health as a factor. As secretary of defense since 1981, Weinberger was a seemingly indefatigable advocate of President Reagan's defense buildup and a skeptic of Soviet arms control offers. *(Weinberger background, Congress and the Nation Vol. VI, p. 1018)*

Frank C. Carlucci, a Washington insider, won Senate approval Nov. 20, 1987, to succeed Weinberger. Carlucci, who had been serving as Reagan's national security adviser, was replaced by Army Lt. Gen. Colin Powell, deputy chief of the National Security Council staff. *(Carlucci background, Cabinet profiles, p. 1044)*

Powell was the first black to be named national security adviser and was highly regarded as a field commander and a Washington operator. In 1970, as a major, Powell won a prestigious White House Fellowship and served as an intern at the Office of Management and Budget, then being run by Weinberger and Carlucci. After serving as Weinberger's military aide, he took command in 1986 of the Fifth Corps, one of the Army's most important combat commands, with headquarters in Frankfurt, West Germany.

## ACDA Director Resigns

Kenneth L. Adelman on July 30, 1987, resigned as director of the Arms Control and Disarmament Agency (ACDA), which handled arms control negotiations with the Soviet Union in Geneva, Switzerland. Adelman left the position in December.

Adelman's resignation came days after U.S. and Soviet negotiators agreed to a worldwide ban on intermediate-range nuclear forces (INF). The treaty was signed by President Reagan and Soviet leader Mikhail S. Gorbachev at a Washington summit in December 1987. *(INF treaty, p. 346)*

Adelman told reporters that he "wanted to leave at a time when . . . things were coming up roses" on arms control and when "it was clear that I was doing this without any policy implications, or for any policy disagreements." Adelman had been in the job since April 1983. *(Adelman nomination, Congress and the Nation Vol. VI, p. 233)*

Adelman's successor, Maj. Gen. William F. Burns, served as the State Department's principal deputy assistant secretary for political and military affairs and was also a representative of the Joint Chiefs of Staff to negotiations on the INF treaty. Burns was confirmed by a Senate vote of 83-0 March 4, 1988.

## Turnover at Navy Post

Carlucci's moves to cut the Pentagon's budget prompted Navy Secretary James H. Webb Jr. to resign abruptly Feb. 22, 1988. Webb, a decorated Vietnam veteran and prize-winning novelist, became secretary of the Navy in April 1987. He succeeded John F. Lehman Jr., one of the most politically combative civilians to hold a high Pentagon office in years.

Webb's break with the administration focused on Reagan's goal of a "600-ship Navy." In the late 1970s, after a decade of cutbacks, the active fleet totaled about 450 ships, including a dozen aircraft carriers. In his six years as Reagan's first Navy secretary, the hard-charging Lehman pushed for the 600-ship goal, including 15 large carriers.

Webb, too, sought to win congressional support for sustaining the expanded fleet. But with the Pentagon facing budget limits set by a November 1987 budget "summit" agreement, Carlucci elected to retire 16 frigates, among the smallest and oldest of the fleet. Webb complained that Carlucci had turned down alternative budget cuts Webb had proposed that would have spared the frigates.

But other issues also were involved. Administration officials were unhappy with Webb's public challenge of the existing commitment of military resources to the defense of Western Europe. Vital U.S. interests were increasingly to be found elsewhere, notably in the Pacific and in Latin America, Webb contended. He also said Carlucci should spend more time dealing with senior Defense Department leaders and less with the State Department and Congress.

Reagan named William L. Ball III, chief lobbyist for the White House, as Webb's successor. Ball, highly regarded on Capitol Hill as a personable and skilled legislative strategist, had been an aide to Sens. Herman E. Talmadge, D-Ga., and John Tower, R-Texas, before joining the State Department in 1985 as chief congressional lobbyist. He became assistant to the president for legislative affairs in 1986. Ball was confirmed March 23, 1988.

arms control issue — continued compliance with the unratified 1979 U.S.-Soviet strategic arms limitation talks (SALT II) treaty. The conferees required the retirement of a 25-year-old missile-launching submarine, the *Andrew Jackson*. This would largely offset planned increases during the year in the number of U.S. nuclear weapons, thus slowing dramatically the rate at which the U.S. arsenal was outstripping certain limits included in SALT II, which Reagan had vowed to ignore. *(SALT II, p. 350)*

In each case, the congressionally imposed limitation avoided explicit mention of the treaty — or treaty interpretation — that Reagan opposed.

Congress also scored a victory in the conference report's effort to reshape Reagan's budget while slicing it:

paring his proposed rapid increases for strategic arms and adding to the amounts requested for conventional forces. A dramatic instance of this was the conferees' increase in the budgeted production rates of the Army's M-1 tank and several helicopters.

## House Committee Action

The House Armed Services Committee reported on April 15 a $228.6 billion defense authorization (H Rept 100-58) that would result in a fiscal 1988 defense budget total of $305.8 billion.

But before the bill went to the House floor early in May, committee Chairman Les Aspin, D-Wis., had to draft an amendment containing some $17 billion in additional reductions to meet the ceiling on defense appropriations set by the House version of the budget resolution (H Con Res 93) adopted April 9. The amendment brought the total defense budget for fiscal 1988 down to $288.6 billion, authorizing $204.3 billion for the Pentagon and $7.8 billion for the Energy Department.

The committee bill challenged several key Reagan priorities. It sliced hefty chunks out of the Pentagon's requests for development of some controversial strategic weapons, most notably SDI. It also gave the Defense Department more than it had requested for several major Army weapons the administration wanted to slow down, such as the M-1 tank, Bradley armored troop carrier and Apache tank-hunting helicopter. Many congressional specialists charged that the administration was shortchanging the Army.

But the panel's most politically significant actions were taken on nuclear arms control issues that long had pitted the Reagan administration against liberals and political centrists.

Traditionally a source of solid pro-Pentagon majorities, the House committee backed Reagan on several issues by relatively narrow margins during the two-day markup of the bill. And on the politically supercharged question of how to interpret the 1972 U.S.-Soviet ABM treaty, the committee rejected Reagan's contention that the pact allowed testing of some space-based SDI components.

**Nuclear Offensive Forces.** The committee approved $250 million of the $591 million requested to develop a railroad launcher for the MX missile, and $1.3 billion to buy 21 additional MXs. Aspin's amendment scaled MX purchases back to 12, for $864 million.

The committee approved the funds for the mobile MX launcher over the objections of some that it might draw funds away from the smaller, single-warhead Midgetman missile that was to be carried in an armored mobile launcher. Others feared that development of a mobile MX launcher might lead to deployment of more MXs than the 50 Congress had agreed to deploy in existing launch silos. *(MX cap, p. 287)*

The committee approved the entire $2.23 billion requested to continue developing Midgetman. Aspin's plan trimmed that amount to $2.06 billion.

The committee also approved funds for a 15th Trident missile-launching submarine, Trident II missiles, a stealth bomber and a stealth cruise missile. The Aspin substitute denied funds for development of a bomber-launched missile called SRAM II with a range of a few hundred miles.

To show that the committee would come down hard on Pentagon mismanagement, Aspin and veteran Democrat Samuel S. Stratton, N.Y., one of the committee's most assertive Pentagon allies, crafted a tough stance for the panel on the most visible of the recent procurement horror stories — the Air Force's B-1 bomber.

In a critique of the program, members of the committee denounced the Air Force for not disclosing to Congress the scope of severe problems with the electronic gear intended to hide the plane from enemy radars — shortcomings that had been revealed by flight tests.

The committee bill authorized funds for additional testing and development needed to bring the B-1 up to its original specifications but denied a request for funding to upgrade the plane further to cope with unanticipated improvements in Soviet air defenses. One reason members were unwilling to keep paying for upgrades in the B-1 was their confidence that the stealth bomber would replace it within a few years for missions requiring planes to fly into Soviet territory. The B-1 then would be used for conventional missions and to lob long-range cruise missiles at Soviet targets from positions far beyond the reach of Soviet defenses.

**Strategic Defense.** The administration's budget request included $5.7 billion for SDI, of which $5.2 billion was for Pentagon programs and $481 million was for projects conducted by the Energy Department.

The committee approved $3.5 billion for the Pentagon's share and $339 million for that of the Energy Department — a total of $3.8 billion. Aspin's substitute trimmed the program further, to a total of $3.6 billion: $3.3 billion for the Pentagon and $279 million for the Energy Department.

The committee also added to the bill a provision barring tests of SDI weapons in space, in effect mandating continued compliance with the traditional interpretation of the ABM treaty. The Reagan administration argued that some tests were legally permissible under the treaty.

The Aspin substitute allowed only $50 million to continue development of the anti-satellite (ASAT) system.

**Conventional Forces.** Both the committee bill and the Aspin substitute recommended purchasing 720 M-1 tanks instead of the 600 requested. But Aspin's version reduced the number of Bradley armored troop carriers to the 616 requested by the Pentagon instead of the 656 provided for in the committee bill.

Both versions increased funding, although at different levels, for three of the Army's most important helicopter production programs — the Apache, Blackhawk and "scout" helicopters — all of which had been slashed by the Pentagon's budget request. The increases were paid for by deep cuts in the administration's request for developing a new helicopter, the LHX, that would enter production in the mid-1990s as a replacement for some 6,000 Vietnam War-era helicopters. The panel cited Pentagon reports that the LHX would not be ready for production on schedule.

Aspin's substitute approved nearly three-fourths of the request for development of a long-range tank-killer system (Joint STARS and ATACMS, or Army Tactical Missile System).

Although funds were included to build new, lethal chemical weapons, called binary munitions, Aspin's substitute eliminated funds for production of an air-dropped bomb, called Bigeye, that had failed several tests. *(Chemical weapons, box, p. 284)*

Both versions approved, with only a few minor funding adjustments, the Pentagon's request for most types of combat airplanes used by the Navy and Air Force: 42 F-15s, 180 F-16s, 12 F-14s and 84 F/A-18s. The bill also included funds — less than requested — for development of a new

# Procurement 'Czar' Resigns

Less than a year after being named the Pentagon's first procurement "czar," Richard P. Godwin on Sept. 14, 1987, quit, criticizing bureaucratic resistance to his efforts to streamline the Defense Department's weapons-buying procedures.

He was succeeded by Robert Costello as the new under secretary of defense for acquisition.

The position was created by the fiscal 1987 defense bill (S 2638 — PL 99-661) at the recommendation of the House and Senate Armed Services committees as well as a special commission established by President Reagan in 1986 to study the procurement problem. *(Background, p. 283; defense bill, p. 290)*

The commission, chaired by David Packard, a defense industry executive and former deputy secretary of defense, recommended lodging in one senior official overall authority for the entire weapons-acquisition system. That tracked closely with recommendations from the Armed Services committees.

In the wake of Godwin's failure to crack the Pentagon bureaucracy, many lawmakers wanted to understand what happened. In testimony before the two Armed Services committees Sept. 22-23, Godwin suggested that Congress clarify how much authority the procurement position should have. To bolster his view, he recounted his frustrations in trying to get Pentagon officials, particularly the secretaries of the Army, Navy and Air Force, to cooperate.

Beyond the consensus that Godwin had succumbed to fierce bureaucratic opposition, there was widespread disagreement over the extent to which other officials shared in the responsibility for Godwin's difficulties.

● While internal clashes were bound to occur in any case, given Godwin's warrant to take over power previously held by other officials, some members — and some experienced outside observers — contended that Godwin had exacerbated his own problems by maladroit tactics.

● Other members faulted Defense Secretary Caspar W. Weinberger, who at the outset opposed the creation of the Packard commission, and his deputy, William H. Taft IV. The two should have ordered other subordinates to cooperate with Godwin's proposed changes, these members said. Godwin, however, was careful not to criticize Weinberger directly.

But most members saw no effective way for Congress to give Godwin's successor a legislative guarantee of a path clear of routine bureaucratic roadblocks. Costello, a former General Motors Corp. executive with experience in defense-related research, had been an assistant secretary of defense under Godwin. The Senate confirmed his nomination by voice vote Dec. 17, 1987.

---

Air Force fighter plane scheduled to replace the F-15 in the late 1990s. Aspin's substitute would have ended production of the Marine Corps' AV-8B Harrier vertical-takeoff bomber.

The committee reined in a requested increase in the production rate of the new AMRAAM air-to-air missile on the grounds that further testing was needed.

The committee approved funds for nuclear power plants and other components for two aircraft carriers to be built in the 1990s, as well as funding to rebuild two carriers launched in the early 1960s.

The Aspin substitute called for funding four cruisers in fiscal 1988 and one in fiscal 1989, all equipped with the Aegis system of computer-controlled radars and missile launchers to defend fleets against air attack. The administration had requested two cruisers and three smaller destroyers, but the committee had approved five cruisers in fiscal 1988, in the hope that the Navy would be able to get lower bids from shipyards by putting more ships of the same design up for contract at the same time.

Also approved were three *Los Angeles*-class submarines, designed to hunt other subs, but a battle broke out over a request for funds to develop a new type of submarine to hunt Soviet subs — the *Seawolf* class. Critics argued that the *Seawolf*, the first of which was due to enter service in 1994, was outmatched by the Soviet *Akula*-class sub, which was first launched in 1984. The compromise reached gave the Navy the *Seawolf* but also provided funds to explore another attack-sub design with new technologies.

The committee approved 24 small anti-submarine helicopters requested but rejected the Navy's proposal to end production of the P-3C land-based anti-sub patrol plane before a replacement had been selected.

Also approved were funds to build a helicopter carrier intended to carry 2,000 Marines; to buy a smaller ship to carry heavy combat gear and barges; to develop the Osprey hybrid airplane/helicopter, which was intended to replace the Marines' fleet of 1960s-vintage troop-carrying helicopters; and to provide aircraft for "special operations" guerrilla units operating behind enemy lines. Funds to continue development and begin production of the C-17 cargo plane, designed to haul tanks and other heavy combat gear into primitive landing fields, were included in the bill. The bill also contained authorizations for various missiles.

### House Floor Action

After three weeks of debate, the House May 20 passed, by a vote of 239-177, a fiscal 1988 defense authorization (HR 1748) that would result in an overall defense budget authority of $289 billion, a reduction of $23 billion from Reagan's request.

Only 12 Republicans voted for the legislation. GOP members objected to the size of the budget cut but more strenuously to several arms control provisions that the

House added to the bill, as it had done in 1986 during consideration of the fiscal 1987 defense bill. *(1986 action, p. 290)*

By a vote of 249-172, the House accepted the Aspin substitute bringing the defense total down to $289 billion from the $306 billion level reported by the Armed Services Committee. A move to increase the defense total to $302 billion was rejected.

The House demanded that Reagan continue to observe limits on the numbers of certain kinds of nuclear weapons that were set by SALT II. The amendment was adopted 245-181, with only 28 Democrats voting "nay" and just 21 Republicans voting "yea." The House rejected 189-231 an amendment that would nullify the provision if the Soviet Union violated any part of SALT II. *(SALT II sublimits, p. 350)*

Members also decided, by a margin of more than 100 votes, to require continued U.S. adherence to the traditional interpretation of the U.S.-Soviet ABM treaty. A motion to strike this provision from the bill was rejected 159-262.

Immediately before passing the bill, the House rejected 172-247 a procedural motion that would, in effect, gut the provisions dealing with SALT II and the ABM treaty.

The House considered several amendments dealing with SDI funding before settling on one that reduced SDI funding by more than 45 percent. By a vote of 219-199, the House agreed to authorize $3.12 billion for SDI, about $400 million less than Congress appropriated for SDI in fiscal 1987.

The House turned down two efforts by SDI proponents to force deployment of a limited anti-missile defense. But the administration won one battle, when the House rejected an amendment that would bar tests of the "space-based kinetic kill vehicle" (SBKKV), a heat-seeking missile to be fired by a satellite at Soviet missiles in the first few minutes after they were launched. The SBKKV was the only SDI weapon that could be ready for service if the administration decided to begin deploying a partial anti-missile defense as early as 1993.

In other SDI-related actions, the House voted 418-0 for an amendment expressing the sense of Congress that the Soviet Union had violated the ABM treaty by building a large radar at Krasnoyarsk in western Siberia. *(Soviet radar, box, p. 351)*

By a **key vote of 234-187 (R 26-147; D 208-40)**, the House voted to ban practically all nuclear weapons tests, provided the Soviet Union observed the same restraint and agreed to the placement on its territory of monitoring equipment. The Reagan administration opposed this provision vehemently, but a GOP alternative, which would allow the president to waive the prohibition under certain circumstances, was rejected 201-220. *(1987 key votes, p. 965)*

For the fourth year in a row, the House also approved an amendment barring ASAT target tests, providing the Soviet Union conducted no ASAT tests. In 1987, it was approved 229-188, a 41-vote margin compared with the 25-vote margin by which the House approved the same provision in 1986. *(ASAT tests, box, p. 281)*

The House rejected four amendments that would cut back funds for the MX intercontinental ballistic missile (ICBM) and the Trident II submarine-launched missile.

Among the amendments rejected was one that would delete all funds requested to develop a rail-mobile launcher for the MX. In 1985, the liberals and centrists who favored deployment of some MXs compromised on a limit of 50 missiles to be based in existing missile silos. But Defense Secretary Caspar W. Weinberger and others did not abandon efforts to deploy 50 additional MXs.

The arms controllers tried to portray the funds to develop a new, mobile launcher for MX as a foot in the door for the second 50.

Time finally ran out in 1987 on a small but determined band of arms control advocates who for five years had blocked production of binary munitions. By a vote of 191-230, the House rejected an amendment that would bar final assembly of the new chemical weapons through fiscal 1988. *(Chemical weapons, box, p. 284)*

In other action, the House agreed to an amendment that would help Congress oversee the highly secret program to develop and produce some 130 "stealth" bombers designed to evade detection by enemy radars. The amendment grew out of the Armed Services Committee's conclusion that the Air Force had woefully mismanaged production of 100 B-1 bombers and concealed from Congress the scope of the B-1's technical shortcomings.

The tough stands taken by the committee on the B-1 and some other troubled weapons programs appeared to be a major factor in pre-empting several proposals aimed at changing the way the Pentagon bought weapons or imposing stringent conditions on specific programs that were in trouble on technical or budgetary grounds. The committee's vigilance may have persuaded some House members that the traditionally pro-Pentagon panel could be trusted to conduct firm oversight of defense purchasing.

All but one of the major "procurement-reform" amendments to HR 1748 either were rejected or were substantially watered down. The most ground the reformers won on any one issue came with a compromise amendment dealing with the Bradley vehicle: a lightly armored troop carrier equipped with a small cannon and anti-tank missiles.

Critics, having complained for years that the Army was concealing the Bradley's vulnerability to enemy weapons, insisted that the Army redesign the Bradley so that its fuel and stored ammunition would be outside the troop compartment, minimizing the risk of casualties. The Army favored a less sweeping design change, saying that moving the fuel and ammunition would cost too much and impair the Bradley's combat effectiveness. The House adopted a compromise amendment saying that the redesign should "maximize casualty reductions while considering fiscal concerns and without jeopardizing operational effectiveness."

Among the amendments rejected during debate on HR 1748 were proposals to delete some funds for two nuclear-powered aircraft carriers, to continue production of the huge C-5B cargo jet, to reduce the number of U.S. military personnel stationed overseas and to establish a panel to recommend military base closings. *(Base closings, p. 335)*

## Senate Committee Action

The Senate Armed Services Committee reported its version of the defense authorization bill (S 1174 — S Rept 100-57) on May 8. The bill authorized $224.5 billion for Department of Defense and Department of Energy defense programs, resulting in a total defense budget authority for fiscal 1988 of $302.9 billion. S 1174 also included fiscal 1989 authorizations for relatively non-controversial programs.

In reshaping Reagan's request, the Senate panel pursued the same basic priorities the House Armed Services Committee followed in drafting its version of the annual defense measure:

● Both panels made minimal reductions in the amounts requested for the combat readiness of units in the field.

● They increased the proposed production rates for some conventional weapons, particularly for the Army.

● Both panels made hefty reductions in Reagan's request for development and procurement of strategic weapons.

For years, Armed Services Committee Chairman Sam Nunn, D-Ga., had complained that the Pentagon was trying to buy too many kinds of weapons, given budget limitations. As a result, he contended, the services were paying high prices to cover the cost of inefficiently low rates of production. The Senate panel made a few of the hard choices among programs that Nunn had advocated, though he later told reporters that many more such choices would have to be made in future years.

As evidence that it was trying to focus on major policy issues instead of trivial details, the committee noted that much of its funding reduction was made in broad categories, leaving Pentagon managers a great deal of discretion in the allocation of the cuts to specific projects.

But by far the most controversial action taken by the committee was to attach a provision giving Congress veto power over any move to accelerate the timetable for testing the SDI program.

**Nuclear Offensive Forces.** The committee approved $1.16 billion for 21 MX missiles and recommended $400 million to develop an MX launcher mounted on a railroad car so it could be moved around to thwart enemy attack. The Senate panel emphasized that it was not prejudging the merits of deploying more MXs on rail launchers by funding the development program. But to keep open the option of deploying additional MXs, it recommended repealing a provision of the law that barred the manufacture of more warheads than would be needed for 50 of the 10-warhead missiles.

The panel approved only $700 million to develop the much smaller, single-warhead Midgetman ICBM.

The committee also approved funds for a 15th Trident missile-launching submarine, Trident II missiles, a stealth bomber, a bomber-launched missile (SRAM II) and a stealth cruise missile.

Like the House panel, the Senate committee approved most of the funds requested to make good the deficiencies of electronic radar-jamming equipment on the B-1 bomber but refused to fund development of any new electronic equipment.

**Strategic Defense.** When the committee took up Reagan's SDI program, it added by a 12-8 vote a requirement for congressional approval by joint resolution of tests of anti-missile devices based in space or on aircraft, ships or mobile ground vehicles. In effect, the controversial provision — proposed by Nunn and Carl Levin, D-Mich. — would require a majority of both houses of Congress to endorse a departure from the traditional interpretation of the ABM treaty, an interpretation the Reagan administration was trying to reject.

The committee approved $4.5 billion for SDI but took a broad swipe at Reagan's repeated refusal to agree to any restraints on SDI.

Strongly endorsing the ASAT missile, the committee approved $206 million for its continued development but denied the request for funds to prepare for production. The committee warned that if the moratorium on ASAT tests against a target satellite were not lifted in fiscal 1988, it might consider killing the program outright because the ASAT missile could not be kept in development indefinitely.

**Conventional Forces.** Like its House counterpart, the Senate panel authorized more than requested for procurement of major Army weapons.

The committee recommended 720 M-1 tanks instead of the 600 requested but approved only the requested 616 Bradley armored troop carriers. The panel increased funding for designing successors to the M-1 and Bradley.

The Senate panel, like the House committee, ordered the Army to continue production of existing types of helicopters and to slow down the program to develop the LHX helicopter. The committee approved 90 Apache helicopters instead of the 67 requested and 72 Blackhawks instead of the 61 requested, and added funds for improvements in the two helicopters.

The bill also included authorizations for a tank killer system (Joint STARS and ATACMS) and for binary munitions, although funds for the Bigeye bomb, which had not yet completed certain tests, were slashed.

The committee approved with only modest funding changes the requests for five of the six kinds of fighters and tactical bombers used by the Navy and Air Force: 42 F-15s, 180 F-16s, 12 F-14s, 84 F/A-18s and 32 Harriers.

But in an action as significant as its revision of the Army's helicopter plans, the committee canceled production of one of the Navy's front-line planes and ordered the service to move along with developing a replacement. The committee denied the request for the A-6 medium-sized bomber on the grounds that it was too vulnerable to anti-aircraft defenses but approved the entire secret amount to develop a new bomber, designated ATA (advanced tactical aircraft). Also approved were plans to develop a new fighter plane, the ATF (advanced tactical fighter). *(A-6 controversy, box, p. 311)*

Denouncing the Navy's desire for its own tanker fleet as "a prime example of the lack of cooperation among the services," the committee added a provision barring the Navy from acquiring any land-based tanker planes unless it was certified that the Navy and Air Force could not reach agreement on Air Force planes meeting the Navy's requirements.

Missile authorizations included funding for the first large-scale production of the new AMRAAM missile.

The panel approved funds for components of two nuclear-powered aircraft carriers and for the overhauling of a 1960s-vintage carrier. Also approved were five cruisers, all equipped with the Aegis anti-missile defense system, instead of the two cruisers and three smaller destroyers requested.

Funding for three *Los Angeles*-class attack submarines and for the new *Seawolf* attack submarine was approved, and the committee added to the bill funds for several anti-submarine programs.

The committee bill included funds for the C-17 cargo plane, aircraft for "special operations" guerrilla units, the Osprey airplane/helicopter and a large amphibious landing ship. Funds to buy a smaller ship to carry heavy combat gear and barges were denied because the Navy was considering a change in the ship's design.

## Senate Floor Action

Almost as soon as the Senate panel reported it, the defense bill became entangled in a filibuster over the SDI-ABM provision. The dispute thwarted floor debate on the bill for four months.

The debate finally began in September, after Republicans conceded they no longer had the votes to block consideration. They gave up their filibuster because, among other things, they did not want an embarrassing floor defeat during the mid-September visit of Soviet Foreign Minister Eduard A. Shevardnadze. In addition, Democrats were threatening to delay Senate action on Reagan's nomination of Robert H. Bork to the Supreme Court unless action on the defense bill and other matters was expedited first.

After three weeks of debate, the Senate passed by a 56-42 vote Oct. 2 the bill authorizing a $303.1 billion defense budget and repudiating two key positions in Reagan's arms control policy.

The items that rankled the president and congressional Republicans were those that rejected Reagan's effort to reinterpret the 1972 U.S.-Soviet treaty limiting ABM systems and mandated compliance with certain aspects of the 1979 SALT II treaty. In a statement issued Oct. 2, the president said those amendments would undercut U.S. negotiators at the U.S.-Soviet arms talks in Geneva and "undermine U.S. national security."

The Senate vote to repudiate Reagan's stand on the ABM treaty came Sept. 17, when the Senate, by a **key vote of 58-38 (R 8-37; D 50-1)**, rejected a motion to delete the Levin-Nunn provision barring tests of space-based anti-missile weapons without prior congressional approval. This would block administration efforts to accelerate the SDI program and prevent the administration from putting into effect its reinterpretation of the ABM treaty. A GOP substitute had been rejected earlier. *(1987 key votes, p. 965)*

An amendment to cut the total SDI authorization from $4.5 billion to $3.7 billion was defeated on a tabling motion Sept. 22 when Vice President George Bush broke a 50-50 tie vote on the proposal. In other SDI-related action, the Senate adopted amendments barring the awarding of SDI research contracts overseas if U.S. firms could do the work and authorizing the Pentagon to contract with a think tank for long-range studies in support of the SDI program after the contract had been reviewed by Congress. And, like the House, the Senate passed, 89-0, an amendment expressing the sense of Congress the Soviet radar near Krasnoyarsk violated the ABM treaty. *(Box, p. 351)*

Three weeks after the SDI-ABM vote, the Senate handed the Reagan administration another defeat when it adopted, by a **key vote of 57-41 (R 8-36; D 49-5)**, an amendment requiring continued compliance with three sublimits set by the unratified SALT II treaty. Administration allies argued that the provision would limit the president's flexibility to respond to Soviet treaty violations or even to threaten to do so as a bargaining tactic. They hoped their hand would be strengthened by the Soviets' testing of two ICBMs within a few hundred miles of Hawaii several days before the Oct. 2 vote, but the arms control advocates prevailed.

The administration and its allies in the Senate, however, won some battles, too. By a 51-47 vote, the Senate Sept. 22 tabled (killed) an amendment to continue an existing moratorium on tests of the ASAT missile against a target in space.

And, in the first test of Senate sentiment on a mandatory nuclear test ban, the Senate Sept. 24 tabled, by a **key vote of 61-36 (R 40-6; D 21-30)**, an amendment barring for two years nearly all but the smallest nuclear test explosions. The ban, which would have required monitoring equipment on U.S. and Soviet territory, would have lapsed automatically if the Soviet Union had violated it.

Despite one close vote, the Senate appeared to clear the way for production of binary munitions. On Sept. 24 the Senate tabled 53-44 an amendment that would defer final assembly of the new types of lethal chemical weapons through fiscal 1988. The Senate also rejected 49-48 on a tabling motion an amendment that would deny funds requested for production of one type of binary weapon, the air-dropped Bigeye bomb. The closeness of that vote reflected longstanding doubts about the weapon's technical effectiveness, rather than Senate sentiment about nerve gas.

By a vote of 62-28, the Senate tabled an amendment that would put conditions on the then-pending U.S.-Soviet treaty banning intermediate-range nuclear-force (INF) missiles. Later, three amendments were adopted calling for studies of how NATO strategy — and U.S. policy — should be modified in light of an INF treaty. Three amendments expressing the sense of Congress on the allocation of defense costs among the United States and its allies also were adopted. *(INF treaty, p. 346)*

In debating the defense bill, senators signaled their unhappiness with Reagan's policy of providing military escorts for Kuwaiti oil tankers in the Persian Gulf. But they shied away from asserting Congress' right to rein in the policy during consideration of a series of amendments. *(Persian Gulf story, p. 315)*

The White House in the summer of 1987 had ordered the Navy ships into the Gulf to protect the Kuwaiti tankers, which had been "reflagged" as U.S. vessels, from attacks by Iran in that country's ongoing war against Iraq. In a first round on the issue Sept. 18, the Senate voted 50-41 to table, and thus kill, an amendment that would force Reagan to invoke the 1973 War Powers Resolution in response to the presence of U.S. forces in the Gulf. The War Powers act set limits on the use of U.S. forces in a hostile environment without congressional approval. *(War Powers act, Congress and the Nation Vol. IV, p. 849)*

Later in the debate Senate Democrats made another attempt to end the Gulf escorting policy and triggered a filibuster threat from Republicans. On Oct. 1, the critics of reflagging claimed a symbolic victory after a motion to invoke cloture on a proposal applying a War Powers-like time limit to the reflagging operation was rejected 54-45. Although 60 votes were needed for cloture, the critics said the vote demonstrated that a majority of the Senate opposed reflagging. They then agreed to drop the issue.

Democrats' concern over the growing share of the budget absorbed by strategic weapons under the Reagan build-up was evident in a proposal to take $900 million from programs to develop the Midgetman ICBM and a rail-mobile MX missile and use the money to purchase Army helicopters and air-launched missiles. The Senate adopted a substitute that left the funding for those strategic programs intact but said its action did not constitute a commitment to proceed to production with either weapon system.

The Senate voted 56-41 to table the latest in what had become an annual effort by Senate conservatives to restrict the application to Pentagon construction projects of the

Davis-Bacon Act's wage requirements.

A number of other amendments were considered by the Senate.

## Conference, Final Provisions

House-Senate conferees reached agreement on some 5,000 differences in their two bills, but tough negotiations with the White House over arms control provisions were needed before the conference agreement was completed.

The House Nov. 18 adopted the conference report (H Rept 100-446) by a vote of 264-158. The Senate approved it the next day 86-9. President Reagan signed the bill into law (PL 100-180) Dec. 4.

**Arms Control Issues.** On two contentious arms control issues, conferees hammered out compromises giving congressional arms control advocates the substance of victory, without writing into law positions on two arms control agreements that the White House found unacceptable.

The compromise required, in effect, that:

● SDI tests conform to the traditional, restrictive interpretation of the 1972 ABM treaty. This interpretation, which the administration contested, precluded tests of space-based weapons.

The conference report allowed the Pentagon to plan future tests that would be inconsistent with the traditional interpretation, but not to acquire any equipment during the year for such tests without prior congressional approval.

● The number of multiple-warhead strategic missiles and bombers equipped with cruise missiles would increase very slowly, though remaining slightly above a ceiling on such weapons contained in the unratified SALT II treaty.

But in each case, the compromise limitation made no reference to the treaties. The White House had vowed to veto any bill enshrining the traditional reading of the ABM pact or the SALT II ceilings.

Senior White House aides negotiated the SDI provision with the two senior conferees from each chamber. The Reagan officials also were intimately acquainted with the evolution of the SALT II-related provision, though they did not explicitly agree to it, as they did with the SDI provision.

Two other arms control issues were handled the same as in the fiscal 1987 defense authorization: The ASAT test ban was continued and the House-passed nuclear test ban provision was dropped.

**Budget Options.** The compromise agreement also was uncommonly complex because the conferees were determined to produce a bill that would be relevant to whatever defense budget total emerged from bipartisan "summit" negotiations on the overall fiscal 1988 budget.

Accordingly, the conference report on HR 1748 included two parallel authorization measures. In the wake of the Nov. 20 White House-Capitol Hill budget summit agreement, the higher tier — allowing spending of $296 billion — prevailed. *(Details, p. 33)*

Technically, the conference report also authorized a certain percentage of the fiscal 1989 defense budget. But those authorizations would take effect only if the appropriations were enacted covering both fiscal years 1988 and 1989, which the Senate and House Appropriations panels seemed most unlikely to permit.

**Nuclear Offensive Forces.** The conferees authorized 12 MX intercontinental ballistic missiles (ICBMs) for $864 million, instead of the 21 missiles requested ($1.26

---

# 1988 Military Construction

Congress authorized $8.45 billion of President Reagan's $9.8 billion request for military construction and family housing in fiscal 1988.

As in the previous year, the military construction authorization was included in the defense authorization measure instead of being passed as a separate piece of legislation. The defense bill (HR 1748 — PL 100-180), which cleared Congress while budget negotiations with the White House were still under way, contained two levels of authorizations. The higher one ultimately prevailed. The lower tier would have provided $8.15 billion for military construction. *(Defense authorization, p. 302)*

The House had approved $8.1 billion for military construction in fiscal 1988, and the Senate had recommended nearly $9 billion.

The final bill also included a partial authorization for fiscal 1989. *(Fiscal 1989 authorization, box, p. 327)*

Citing severe budget constraints, conferees on HR 1748 approved $241 million of the $337 million requested to build new basing facilities at 10 locations for Navy ships. The Navy insisted that such additional "home ports" were needed to accommodate the expanding fleet. But critics charged that the plan was intended to build new pork-barrel support for the Navy. *(Homeporting issue, p. 289)*

For another of the administration's major construction initiatives — facilities for a new "lightweight" army division at Fort Wainwright, near Fairbanks, Alaska — conferees approved $65 million of the $99 million requested. This division, stripped of tanks and other heavy equipment to enable it to be flown overseas quickly, was one of two such units newly created by the Army.

The construction appropriations bill for fiscal 1987 (PL 99-591) included $221 million that was to be available in fiscal 1988 for the second new light division, which was stationed at Fort Drum in northern New York.

---

billion).

The conferees slowed the pace of development for two mobile ICBMs: a rail-carried version of the 10-warhead MX and a much smaller, single-warhead missile — informally dubbed Midgetman — that would be hauled in a mobile launcher. The conferees approved $300 million for the mobile MX and $1.5 billion for the small missile.

Many policy makers, among them Frank C. Carlucci, the new defense secretary, suggested that one of the two programs would have to be dropped under pressure of a shrinking budget. The conferees' action sought to keep both options available to a new administration in 1989.

Both houses had approved $376 million to continue

development of the B-1B bomber, instead of the $416 million requested. Previous budgets funded the purchase of 100 planes, about half of which had been delivered. Conferees agreed to a House provision authorizing a panel of outside experts to study the B-1B's capability to penetrate Soviet targets.

The secret amount requested for development of the "stealth" bomber was trimmed by one-tenth. The conferees also provided funds for an effort to prevent cost overruns or performance shortfalls in the stealth program. According to the House conferees, the kind of thing they hoped to avoid was the B-1B program's rigid timetable of putting the first planes into service by late 1986, come what may. Under the newly mandated plan, the program would move step-by-step toward stealth production only as it met intervening criteria of success.

A program to develop a stealth cruise missile with a range of more than 1,000 miles to be carried by B-1Bs and other bombers was slowed down because the new weapon had fallen short of various test goals. The secret amount requested for the project was trimmed by $511 million. Conferees decided on a $190 million authorization for development of a smaller, shorter-range bomber-launched missile (SRAM II).

For the 15th of a class of huge submarines designed to launch Trident nuclear missiles, the conferees agreed on $1.29 billion of the $1.33 billion requested.

For Trident II missiles to be carried by these subs, they authorized $1.93 billion, as requested, but they maintained that 72 missiles could be bought for that amount, instead of the 66 in the budget request.

**Strategic Defense.** To continue the SDI program (also known as "star wars"), the conference report authorized $3.9 billion of the $5.8 billion requested.

The conferees agreed to a modified version of a Senate provision setting conditions on the creation of a government-sponsored think tank to backstop the Pentagon's SDI management. The conference report attached conditions intended to ensure the institute's independence from the Pentagon viewpoint on SDI, and it delayed establishment of such an organization until Oct. 1, 1989.

The bill continued for the third consecutive year a ban on ASAT missile tests against targets in space, as long as the Soviets continued their moratorium on ASAT tests. The measure authorized $200 million of the $402 million requested to develop ASAT weapons. The conferees directed the Air Force to stop preparing for mass production of the ASAT missiles. After the completion of all testing in fiscal 1989, the remaining test missiles were to be shipped to Edwards Air Force Base in California and the system declared to be in operation, on a limited basis.

**Ground Combat.** Four major Army weapons programs symbolized Congress' boost to conventional forces, compared with Reagan's budget request. The bill authorized:

● 720 M-1 tanks ($1.61 billion). The administration had requested 600 ($1.35 billion).

● 80 Apache missile-armed anti-tank helicopters ($836 million), compared with the Pentagon's request for 67 of the aircraft ($655 million). The administration planned to buy no more Apaches after fiscal 1988, leaving half the Army's anti-tank helicopter units flying aging Cobras with far less firepower. The conferees added to the bill $36 million for components that would be used in Apaches to be funded in fiscal 1989.

● 72 Blackhawk troop-carrying helicopters ($298 mil-

lion). The administration had requested 61 ($245 million).

● Modification of 36 "scout" helicopters with lasers to spotlight tanks and other targets for laser-guided missiles and artillery shells ($138 million). The administration requested $48 million to shut down this production line.

Reagan requested $267 million for development of the new, small LHX helicopter and $135 million for an engine to be used in it. The conferees approved $170 million and $125 million, respectively, for the programs. They also added to the bill $46 million to develop new versions of the Apache and Blackhawk that could substitute for some of the planned LHXs.

The conferees approved $561 million for development of a system of long-range missiles (ATACMS) and airborne radars (Joint STARS) intended to attack enemy tank columns up to 100 miles behind their own lines.

The final bill also included $587 million for artillery rockets and shells.

The conferees approved the $59 million requested by the Pentagon for a new type of artillery shell carrying lethal nerve gas. But they denied the $25 million requested to begin production of the Bigeye aerial bomb, which had failed several field tests.

**Tactical Air Combat.** Both houses had approved, with some minor changes in cost estimates, the administration's request for the four kinds of jet fighters purchased by the Air Force and Navy for attacking other planes. The conference report authorized 42 F-15s ($1.33 billion), the long-range fighters used by the Air Force; 180 smaller F-16s ($2.17 billion) for the Air Force; 12 F-14s ($677 million), long-range planes flown by the Navy off aircraft carriers; and 84 F/A-18s ($2.32 billion), used by the Navy and Marine Corps as both fighters and small bombers.

The bill also authorized $536 million of the $537 million requested to develop a new advanced tactical fighter (ATF) that would enter service in the late 1990s as a replacement for the F-15 and — the conferees insisted — the Navy's F-14. The conference report approved the secret amount requested to develop a new attack plane (dubbed ATA for advanced tactical aircraft) to enter service late in the 1990s.

But to pay for the ATA project in an era of declining defense budgets, the report denied the request to begin production of a new "F" version of the A-6 attack plane. The final bill authorized $377 million to buy 11 more of the A-6Es bought in previous years or to modify A-6Es already in the inventory. It also authorized 24 Harriers ($428 million). *(Box, p. 311)*

The conferees slowed the production rate of the newly developed AMRAAM air-to-air missile, approving 500 ($743 million) of the 630 requested ($833 million). For other air-to-air and air-to-ground missiles, the conference report authorized about $1.13 billion.

**Naval Forces.** Both houses had approved the amounts requested to begin work on two new nuclear-powered aircraft carriers ($644 million) and to rebuild for an additional 15 years of service the 1960s-vintage carrier *Kitty Hawk.*

Both houses had revised the mix of ships equipped with the Aegis anti-aircraft system, a computer-driven network of radars and missiles designed to protect a fleet against simultaneous attacks by dozens of anti-ship cruise missiles. The conferees approved five Aegis cruisers but provided only $3.33 billion — the amount approved by the House for four cruisers — in new budget authority. The Navy could buy the fifth ship if it found the money else-

# Attack Planes Survive Budgetary Cross Fire

Senate-House conferees on the fiscal 1988 defense authorization bill (HR 1748 — PL 100-180) took the unprecedented step of singling out two major weapons programs for extinction on the grounds that the Pentagon no longer could afford them.

But the defense conferees' move proved largely symbolic. One of the programs was saved in late November 1987 by the White House-congressional "summit" agreement on an overall tax and budget package. And the other was spared by congressional appropriators, who, in a rare challenge to the authorizing committees, restored the program's funding in the final version of an omnibus continuing resolution (H J Res 395 — PL 100-202). *(Story, p. 312)*

Even so, the authorizing panels' action marked the first effort to make the Pentagon accommodate budgetary restraints by reshaping its program, instead of "stretching out" the planned rate of weapons production.

At issue were two kinds of small bombers, which the Pentagon called "attack planes": A-6Fs used by the Navy and Marine Corps, able to carry up to nine tons of bombs; and AV-8B Harriers, vertical-takeoff jets used by the Marines.

The House and Senate Armed Services committees had complained that the Marines and the Navy (of which the Marine Corps was part) were buying too many kinds of aircraft, at a high cost per copy. Counting helicopters, the fiscal 1988 budget requested funds to buy 13 kinds of aircraft for the two services in addition to hundreds of millions of dollars to develop two additional types.

The House included the A-6F funds but denied all funds for Harrier production because, according to Armed Services Committee Chairman Les Aspin, D-Wis., the Marines' own planning demonstrated they would rather cut funds for the Harrier than for other programs.

But the Senate Armed Services Committee approved the Harrier funds while dropping the A-6F money. That plane's design, dating from 1957, made it easy to detect and too vulnerable to anti-aircraft defenses, the panel argued.

The services countered that each type provided unique advantages. The A-6F — a new version of the A-6E that had been in service since the early 1970s — carried complex electronic gear used to bomb small ground targets at night and in bad weather. The Harrier, because it could take off and land in a forest clearing, was touted for giving an expeditionary force its own air power without the need for an airfield.

The conference agreement included the provision for no A-6 or Harrier funds if the defense budget fell to $289 billion or below. The Hill-White House budget agreement later cleared the way for authorization of $377 million to buy 11 more A-6Es or to modify A-6Es. It also authorized 24 Harriers ($428 million). But the Navy was ordered not to buy A-6Fs; instead, it was told to concentrate on developing a new attack plane, the advanced tactical aircraft (ATA), to replace the A-6Es and A-6Fs beginning in the mid-1990s.

When the defense conferees met in December to craft the final spending bill, however, they reversed the A-6F decision, approving $111 million to develop the plane and $610 million to begin production.

where in its budget, the conferees said.

Both houses had approved the request for three *Los Angeles*-class attack submarines, designed chiefly to hunt down other subs. The conferees reduced the amount authorized by $60 million to $1.46 billion.

They made a $3 million reduction in the $471 million requested to prepare for building the first of a new attack-sub class, dubbed *Seawolf* or SSN-21, in fiscal 1990. Also approved was the $342 million request to develop a target-finding and weapons-control system that would be used on that ship and on some existing subs.

But they also added to the bill $13 million to study potential improvements in the *Los Angeles* design and $100 million to study potential sub designs more advanced than the *Seawolf*.

Anti-submarine warfare programs approved included $424 million for sub-hunting helicopters.

**Airlift and Sealift.** Two costly new transport aircraft programs did fairly well, despite the tight budgets in prospect for the Pentagon.

For the first two C-17 long-range cargo planes, the conference report authorized the requested $618 million.

For C-17 development funds, the conference approved $1.17 billion of the $1.22 billion requested.

At the other end of the transportation spectrum, the conferees approved the $466 million requested to develop the Osprey hybrid airplane/helicopter.

The conference report authorized $753 million (including $32 million for advanced procurement) for a helicopter carrier, designed to carry nearly 2,000 Marines and the aircraft to haul them ashore, and $324 million for another ship, designated an LSD, designed to carry tanks and other large items and barges to haul them to the beach.

The conference report authorized $722 million to equip "special operations forces" (SOF) — guerrillas, Green Berets and other forces organized to operate in small units, frequently behind enemy lines.

**Pentagon Reorganization.** The conference report accepted some Senate provisions giving the Pentagon a bit more flexibility in applying provisions of the 1986 Pentagon reorganization bill (PL 99-433) dealing with officers serving in "joint" or multi-service assignments and their subsequent promotions. *(Pentagon reorganization, p. 299)*

**Defense Nuclear Programs.** The conference report contained several provisions dealing with the Energy Department's aging complex of production reactors used to manufacture the radioactive "fuel" used in nuclear weapons, including a requirement that the Energy Department give Congress by Dec. 15, 1988, a long-term plan for modernizing the nuclear-weapons production complex.

**Personnel Issues.** The conference report authorized a 3 percent pay raise for military personnel and Pentagon civilians.

The bill also required the Pentagon to begin screening military recruits for drug and alcohol use.

**Operations and Maintenance.** The final version authorized $84.8 billion for operations and maintenance. The administration had requested $87.7 billion.

# 1988 Defense Appropriations

Congress in 1987 approved a defense total for fiscal 1988 that amounted to the third consecutive year of real defense declines.

The omnibus continuing appropriations resolution (H J Res 395 — PL 100-202) brought new defense budget authority for fiscal 1988 to $291.5 billion, a reduction of $20.5 billion from President Reagan's $312 billion request. This was $1.5 billion more than the amount Congress appropriated for defense in fiscal 1987, but if the impact of inflation was taken into account, it represented a 4 percent drop in defense purchasing power, according to figures at the time. (School funds rescission, p. 889)

By late spring, the defense funding debate on Capitol Hill had stalemated, with the House trying to cap appropriations at $287 billion in its version of the budget resolution (H Con Res 93) while the Senate held out for $299 billion.

The issue was settled as part of the budget "summit" agreement between the bipartisan congressional leadership and Reagan announced Nov. 20, which set the defense total for fiscal 1988 at $292 billion. Appropriations fell slightly short of that ceiling because of the need to observe a separate limit of $285 billion on defense outlays.

The defense portion of the omnibus measure appropriated $279 billion for military personnel, operating costs and military procurement and research. Funds for military construction projects and nuclear weapons research were appropriated separately. (Military construction, p. 313)

Despite the cuts in the defense budget, House-Senate conferees managed to avoid making dramatic changes in Reagan's defense program. Even as Defense Secretary Frank C. Carlucci was pressing the services to kill off some weapons programs in their next fiscal year's budgets, the appropriations conferees were nullifying the only such move that Congress had seemed ready to make.

The Senate-passed version of the defense bill would block production of a new Navy bomber, as had the companion defense authorization bill. The conferees funded the plane — designated the A-6F — without explanation. (Box, p. 311)

The Senate version also would retire one of the Navy's oldest aircraft carriers, thus making the first major crimp in the naval expansion that had been a hallmark of Reagan's defense surge. The conference report also reversed that decision.

And conferees added $5.7 billion to the bill for two new carriers. The administration had requested only $644 million to buy components for the two ships, which it planned to request in future budgets. But the Senate, largely because of a budgetary technicality, had included the entire $6.3 billion in its version and conferees went along.

## Legislative Action

Both the House and Senate Appropriations committees reported defense appropriations bills, but neither was passed separately. Instead, they were folded into each chamber's omnibus appropriations bill for fiscal 1988.

Forced to find budget savings, the House Appropriations Committee chopped an unprecedented $27 billion from Reagan's fiscal 1988 defense request for the programs covered by the defense portion of the appropriations bill.

In its report issued Oct. 28 on the $267 billion bill (HR 3576 — H Rept 100-410), the House committee underscored the priorities Congress had observed for years in its process of paring back Reagan's defense requests.

The accounts for developing and purchasing new weapons were reduced by much larger proportions than the accounts for military personnel and operating costs, which most congressional defense specialists considered more closely linked to the day-to-day combat-readiness of forces in the field.

An extraordinarily large cut made in research funds reflected, in part, the committee's slash of more than 50 percent in funding for Reagan's anti-missile program, the strategic defense initiative (SDI), also known as "star wars." Of $5.2 billion requested in this bill (other elements were requested in the Energy Department's appropriations), the committee approved $2.5 billion.

Other large reductions were made in the amounts requested for the MX and Midgetman intercontinental ballistic missiles (ICBMs) and for the anti-satellite (ASAT) missile.

Of the three major armed services, the Army fared by far the best at the House committee's hands. This reflected the apparently widespread view among congressional defense specialists that conventional forces in general — and the Army in particular — had been shortchanged by the Reagan team's heavy emphasis on nuclear forces and SDI. The committee recommended cuts in the amounts requested for every major classification of the procurement account except one: Army aircraft, notably tank-hunting and troop-carrying helicopters.

As in the authorization bill, the appropriations measure also included several controversial arms control provisions that had provoked veto threats from the White House. These provisions banned tests of anti-satellite weapons against space targets, required U.S. compliance with certain limits in the unratified 1979 U.S.-Soviet strategic arms limitation talks (SALT II) treaty, banned all but the smallest nuclear tests and barred space-based testing of Reagan's strategic defense initiative.

The defense appropriations measure was included in the omnibus appropriations bill that passed the House Dec. 3. Although the White House and House Democrats had reached a compromise on arms control provisions included in the companion defense authorization bill, that bill still had not been signed into law. House leaders, therefore, decided to retain the Democrats' original arms control provisions in the appropriations bill as a symbolic gesture to entice liberal Democrats to support the appropriations bill. Reagan signed the authorization bill (HR 1748 — PL 100-180) Dec. 4.

# Military Construction Funding

Congress in 1987 approved $8.28 billion of the $9.85 billion President Reagan requested for military construction appropriations in fiscal 1988. Added to this was $221 million Congress had appropriated the previous year for the fiscal 1988 construction budget.

The funding, which was included in the omnibus continuing resolution for fiscal 1988 (H J Res 395 — PL 100-202) was 16 percent less than requested partly because of a long-simmering concern on Capitol Hill that U.S. allies were not paying their fair share of the defense burden.

Congress also reined in two of the administration's major construction initiatives: new Navy "home ports" to accommodate its expanding fleet, which was approaching the "600-ship Navy" that had been a 1980 Reagan campaign pledge, and facilities for one of two newly created "lightweight" Army divisions that had been stripped of heavy equipment such as tanks so they could be flown overseas quickly.

## Legislative Action

Both chambers had passed a separate military construction appropriations bill (HR 2906) but, with time running short, Congress used its past practice of including military construction appropriations in the omnibus spending bill.

The House on July 14 approved its version of HR 2906, appropriating $8.1 billion, by a vote of 371-48. The bill was passed as reported by the Appropriations Committee (H Rept 100-209). In addition to recommending cutbacks in the homeporting and light division requests, the committee, sounding a familiar congressional theme, demanded that the administration try harder to get Japan and the NATO allies to pay for more of the cost of stationing U.S. forces abroad.

Similarly, the Senate Appropriations Committee complained that U.S. allies should pay more of the cost of their own defense and slashed funds requested for projects overseas, in its version of the legislation (S Rept 100-200). The Senate Oct. 27 passed an $8.3 billion military construction appropriations bill by a vote of 93-0, after adding $9.3 million for three minor projects in the United States.

## Conference, Final Provisions

The omnibus appropriations bill cleared Congress and was signed into law on Dec. 22.

In their report (H Rept 100-498), the House-Senate conferees on the military construction bill made cuts totaling nearly 40 percent in the $921 million requested for projects in Europe, Japan and South Korea. Some of that cut reflected the sentiment that those allies should foot more of the bill for stationing U.S. forces in their territory.

But $88 million of that reduction — almost one-third of the amount cut from the request earmarked for specific projects in Western Europe — reflected a decision to block all additional spending on cruise-missile bases in Western Europe. The cruise missiles would be scrapped under the U.S.-Soviet INF treaty — banning all intermediate-range nuclear-force missiles — that was signed Dec. 8. *(INF treaty, p. 346)*

The conferees retained in the compromise version a Senate provision demanding that NATO as a whole build a new base, if necessary, for the wing of U.S. F-16 fighters based at Torrejon, Spain. The Spanish government was demanding that the unit be moved out of the country. In mid-January 1988, the Pentagon decided to bow to Spain's demands and withdraw the F-16s.

Conferees cut by about one-third the homeporting and light division requests. Conferees approved $182 million of Reagan's $277 million request for facilities at 10 new Navy home ports.

They also approved $65 million of the $99 million requested for facilities at Fort Wainwright, Alaska, to house a new "lightweight" Army division. The construction appropriations act for fiscal 1987 (PL 99-591) had contained $610 million for another light division at Fort Drum, N.Y., of which $221 million was to be available in fiscal 1988.

The Senate Appropriations Committee reported its version of the Pentagon spending bill on Dec. 4, scaling back Reagan's fiscal 1988 defense budget to the level agreed to in his Nov. 20 budget summit deal with the bipartisan congressional leadership.

The committee's defense bill (S 1923 — S Rept 100-235) appropriated $274.6 billion for Defense Department programs covered by the bill. It also allocated to the Pentagon's fiscal 1988 budget $3.5 billion left over from earlier years' budgets. That brought the bill's total funding to $278 billion, $16 billion less than the administration had requested for these programs.

In addition to making the hundreds of routine reductions that amounted to trimming around the edges of the defense budget, the Senate committee proposed some extraordinarily severe moves aimed at reorienting Pentagon spending toward a lower-than-planned level for the long haul. These included:

● Canceling plans to build a new "F" version of the Navy's A-6 bomber. Even with new engines and new radar, the panel argued, the plane's late-1950s design made it too easy for enemy radars to detect.

● Ending development of the Midgetman ICBM. The committee insisted that the Air Force could not afford both the MX and the Midgetman projects and that the MX scheme offered "sufficient survivability," given its much

# Special Report: Arms Control

President Ronald Reagan and Soviet leader Mikhail S. Gorbachev in 1988 signed a treaty banning U.S. and Soviet intermediate-range nuclear-force (INF) missiles. It was the most important arms control achievement of the Reagan presidency.

But, despite an improvement in U.S.-Soviet relations, agreement on other nuclear arms issues remained elusive. The strategic arms reduction talks (START) failed to produce an agreement before Reagan's second term ended.

And as negotiators searched for new arms agreements, battles over old U.S.-Soviet agreements raged. Congress in effect mandated — over strong White House opposition — continued compliance with the 1972 anti-ballistic missile (ABM) treaty and the unratified strategic arms limitation talks (SALT II) treaty.

The congressional actions dealing with the ABM and SALT II agreements stymied the efforts of some administration officials to dismantle those two legacies of the arms control negotiations of the 1970s — a period in which, according to Reagan and his allies, presidents of both parties negotiated arms agreements that were unduly favorable to Moscow.

The resumption in early 1985 of arms talks with the Soviet Union — broken off by Moscow in late 1983 — reflected a symbolic change in Reagan's treatment of arms control issues and of U.S.-Soviet relations in general.

In 1981-82, the president's confrontational approach toward the Soviets had fueled unprecedented domestic opposition to his nuclear arms programs. Nationwide pressure for a nuclear arms freeze had the White House on the ropes in 1982. *(Congress and the Nation Vol. VI, p. 249)*

But by the time Reagan squared off against Democratic presidential rival Walter F. Mondale in 1984, the softening of rhetoric evidently had neutralized the "war-peace" issue as a Reagan liability.

When Congress took up the defense debate in 1985, Reagan had embraced the arms control process (in general terms), "gone the extra mile" to continue the informal observance of existing treaties and scheduled a meeting with his Soviet counterpart — all things that flew in the face of his pre-1983 rhetoric.

The shift was illustrated in mid-1985, when Reagan ignored the advice of his administration hard-liners and decided to dismantle a missile-firing submarine in order to remain within a SALT II limitation.

But the ongoing arms negotiations provided the administration with a strong rhetorical weapon in its Capitol Hill battles for Reagan's military budgets. The administration argued that the resumption of arms talks vindicated a fundamental premise of Reagan policy: that Moscow would negotiate away its advantage in nuclear weaponry only if it faced a U.S. arms buildup.

## Congressional Challenges

Time and again in congressional actions on major weapons programs, members were exhorted not to cast a vote that would undercut the administration's position in Geneva, where the arms negotiations were taking place, or that would weaken the president as a summit meeting approached.

The bargaining-chip argument worked, at least initially. It contributed to Reagan victories in 1985 skirmishes over the MX intercontinental ballistic missile (ICBM) and the strategic defense initiative (SDI), Reagan's plan for an anti-missile defense system. The imminence of a summit also helped sideline congressional action on a non-binding resolution urging Reagan to resume negotiations with Moscow on a nuclear test ban.

Reagan's only defeat in 1985 in the arms control area came on the one issue that he refused to negotiate with Moscow: development of anti-satellite (ASAT) weapons. Despite vigorous White House objections, Congress barred any ASAT tests against target satellites, unless the Soviet Union ended its ASAT test moratorium.

Offsetting their victory on ASAT testing, arms control advocates lost a battle in which they had prevailed since 1982: Congress approved production of lethal chemical weapons for the first time since 1969. *(Chemical weapons, box, p. 284)*

By 1986, anti-Reagan critics in the House were able to add five amendments to the annual defense authorization (S 2638 — PL 99-661) repudiating several key facets of administration policy on nuclear arms and arms control. The most far-reaching of these would have barred all but the smallest nuclear test explosions, provided the Soviet Union observed a similar test moratorium. Another of the amendments would have required Reagan to observe numerical ceilings on certain kinds of weapons set by SALT II. Reagan had announced in May 1986 that he was ending the six-year policy of informal compliance with the SALT agreement.

The test ban and SALT II amendments were rejected by the Senate and subsequently abandoned by the House on the eve of a summit meeting between Reagan and Gorbachev. Under a barrage of demands by Reagan that Congress not undermine his bargaining position, the House leadership dropped the two issues until the following year.

In 1987, the Senate again rejected a House-passed nuclear test ban. But it concurred in a House-passed amendment requiring the administration, in effect, to stop violating the SALT II limits.

More strikingly, the Senate voted decisively in 1987 to block an administration effort to reinterpret the ABM treaty. The Reagan team's novel interpretation of the pact would have allowed much more realistic testing of SDI than would have been allowed under the traditional interpretation of the treaty.

The Senate gave its overwhelming approval to the INF treaty in 1988, but the debate was dominated by the ongoing battle over the interpretation of the ABM treaty. Senate Democrats succeeded in adding to the treaty approval resolution an amendment to prevent Reagan or any future president from asserting an interpretation of the pact that differed from the one formally presented to the Senate during consideration of the treaty.

Congress continued its pattern of imposing unprecedented arms control policy restrictions on Reagan when it considered the fiscal 1989 authorization bill. But the real significance of many of the congressional arms control initiatives was more symbolic than practical. In addition to retaining the provisions requiring continued compliance with the ABM treaty and SALT II, Congress approved provisions sharply reducing funds for one SDI project aimed at developing space-based anti-missile weapons; limiting spending on a rail-launched MX missile; and banning flight tests of missiles in a "depressed trajectory" — a lower-than-normal path that would be useful in a sneak attack. The administration did win a skirmish over ASAT tests, when an attempt to ban the tests permanently was defeated.

GOP defense specialists on Capitol Hill demanded that Reagan veto the authorization measure in protest against what they deemed excessive congressional interference in arms control negotiations. They insisted such negotiations were the prerogative of the president. The Republican activists also contended that a veto would highlight differences between the two parties' overall approaches to defense policy, to the benefit of GOP presidential nominee and then-Vice President George Bush.

Following Reagan's veto of the bill, a revised version (HR 4481 — PL 100-456) was worked out, which retained the ABM and SALT II provisions but dropped the disputed SDI restriction and the flight test ban — the Pentagon had no such tests planned, anyway — and made largely cosmetic changes in MX funding.

# Arms Control Negotiations

After discussions in early January 1985 in Geneva, Secretary of State George P. Shultz and Soviet Foreign Minister Andrei A. Gromyko announced the two countries would negotiate over three kinds of weapons: strategic nuclear missiles and bombers, intermediate-range nuclear forces located in Europe and space weaponry.

In a press conference Jan. 9, Reagan said he hoped the agreement to resume talks was "the beginning of a new dialogue between the United States and the Soviet Union." He pledged to be "flexible, patient and determined" in keeping that dialogue alive.

The March 12 opening of the Geneva talks coincided with a change at the top in the Kremlin. On March 10, Soviet leader Konstantin U. Chernenko died; Gorbachev

was named general secretary of the Soviet Communist Party the next day.

On March 13, Reagan reversed his longstanding opposition to a get-acquainted summit meeting and offered to meet with Gorbachev. The two countries on July 3 formally announced the Reagan-Gorbachev meeting. However, U.S. officials said they did not expect any important agreements to be reached at the November summit. Throughout his first term, Reagan had been reluctant to hold such a meeting unless there was a likelihood of agreement on major issues.

## Soviet Initiative

With the November summit approaching, the Soviets on Sept. 30 made a new offer at the START negotiations that, at least on its face, seemed to offer stark reductions: a 50 percent cut in strategic nuclear weapons. The Soviet offer promised particularly steep reductions in the Soviet force of land-based missiles, or ICBMs.

A major bone of contention in START — as in earlier strategic arms talks — was the Soviets' huge fleet of multiwarhead ICBMs. Unlike bombers, ICBMs could strike targets within 30 minutes. They carried warheads more powerful and more accurate than those on ballistic missiles launched from submarines. Therefore, many U.S. defense experts, especially those from the political center and right, maintained ICBMs were uniquely suited for surprise attack and thus were the most dangerous nuclear arms.

Accordingly, the Reagan administration insisted that a START deal not only reduce the number of strategic weapons but also reduce particularly those that were the most threatening — the large, multi-warhead ICBMs.

Within days of the Soviet offer, allied governments led by British Prime Minister Margaret Thatcher and West German Chancellor Helmut Kohl pressed Reagan to match Gorbachev with an equally dramatic proposal.

A month later, the Reagan team presented a counteroffer that picked up some politically catchy elements of Gorbachev's proposal — notably, the idea of a "50 percent reduction."

At the same time, the U.S. offer redefined the scope of the reduction in line with the traditional U.S. position: Only long-range ballistic missiles and intercontinental bombers would be counted against the limit.

The seeming convergence of the U.S. and Soviet positions on certain points underscored stark disagreement over SDI. The Soviets insisted on a virtual halt in the field testing of space-based and air-based anti-missile systems, which accounted for much of the SDI program, a tradeoff that Reagan rejected.

Even at half their existing size, the U.S. and Soviet strategic arsenals would number more than 5,000 weapons each, enough to destroy both countries in an all-out war.

Moreover, the proposals for dramatic cuts in strategic weapons was viewed with deep misgivings by many U.S. defense specialists from the political center and right who felt the cuts could make the nuclear balance less stable, without significantly reducing the number of fatalities in a nuclear war. Each side might be more confident of disarming the other with a surprise attack if only a few hundred missiles and bombers had to be wiped out instead of thousands. Another argument held that if each superpower's surplus of nuclear arms were greatly reduced, it would become more suspicious of prospective threats to its arsenal.

## Geneva Summit

The November 1985 summit meeting produced no surprise announcement of arms agreements. In a joint communiqué released Nov. 21, Reagan and Gorbachev called their discussions "frank and useful," while acknowledging that "serious differences remain on a number of critical issues."

On arms control issues, the communiqué called for "early progress" on weapons reduction, "particularly in areas where there is common ground." Two areas were singled out: agreement on a 50 percent reduction in nuclear weapons of the two sides and a separate agreement on medium-range nuclear missiles in Europe.

The communiqué made no reference to Moscow's demands that an agreement to ban SDI and other space weapons accompany limits on intercontinental and medium-range missiles.

But, in a post-summit news conference, Gorbachev seemed to reaffirm the Soviet position that SDI limits be part of any arms deal.

And three new bilateral initiatives were announced: a study of "nuclear risk reduction centers" to monitor nuclear weapons activity by third parties, including terrorists; discussions of ways to prevent the spread of chemical weapons; and advocacy of international cooperation to develop controlled nuclear fusion as an energy source.

The leaders also promised to continue efforts to: reduce conventional forces in Europe; ban chemical and biological weapons; and institute measures to reduce the fear of a surprise attack in Europe.

## Troubled Relations

Setting a date for the next Reagan-Gorbachev meeting proved extremely difficult because of both the general tenor of U.S.-Soviet relations and the state of progress on arms control talks.

The Soviets protested the U.S. bombing of Libya in April 1986, for example, by delaying negotiations for a time. Soviet officials consistently refused to schedule a meeting until there was evidence that the two heads of government would be able to nail down some significant arms control accord.

Prospects for improvement of U.S.-Soviet relations ran into a serious obstacle in late summer, however, after the Soviets arrested Nicholas S. Daniloff, a correspondent for *U.S. News & World Report*, on espionage charges. Daniloff had been arrested on Aug. 30, a week after the arrest in New York of Gennadi F. Zakharov, a Soviet employee of the United Nations, on espionage charges. Despite Soviet denials, U.S. observers generally agreed that the American journalist's arrest was intended to give the Soviets bargaining leverage with which to secure Zakharov's release.

The case quickly seized center stage in U.S.-Soviet relations. The Reagan administration insisted that there could be no progress toward the INF missile agreement or toward scheduling the summit until Daniloff was freed.

On Sept. 29, the two governments agreed to a settlement that included the Soviets dropping charges against Daniloff and permitting him and his wife to leave the Soviet Union. In a quick trial, Zakharov pleaded no contest to his spy charges and was sentenced to five years' probation, on the condition that he leave the United States and not return.

Reagan administration officials insisted that the arrangement did not represent a trade of Daniloff for Zakharov, but the deal was widely viewed as a straightforward swap. Some congressional hard-liners protested that Reagan had set a precedent that would lead to the arrest of a U.S. citizen in the Soviet Union every time a Soviet spy was arrested in the United States.

During the high-level negotiations over Daniloff, Gorbachev had proposed a brief presummit meeting. Reagan had agreed to the meeting, contingent on Daniloff's release.

## Reykjavik Meeting

The meeting between Reagan and Gorbachev was set for Oct. 11-12, 1986, in Reykjavik, Iceland.

The first effect of the summit occurred before the meetings even began. Anxious to show support for the president — and to avoid blame in case the talks were a failure — House Democrats announced Oct. 10 that they were putting off until 1987 their legislative efforts to mandate certain arms control policies. The Democrats agreed to drop amendments to the defense authorization bill (S 2638 — PL 99-661) barring all but the smallest nuclear weapons tests and requiring compliance with provisions of the SALT II treaty.

When the two leaders met in Reykjavik, they discussed making sweeping reductions in their countries' nuclear arsenals. In addition to making progress on an INF agreement, the two and a handful of their top national security aides apparently agreed on major elements of a START agreement, which included ceilings for each side of: 1,600 "strategic delivery vehicles" — ICBMs, submarine-launched ballistic missiles and long-range bombers; 6,000 warheads carried by those missiles and bombers; and 154 "heavy" ICBMs, carrying a total of no more than 1,540 warheads.

The two sides also agreed that the total "throw weight" of the remaining ICBMs and submarine-launched ballistic missiles would be roughly 50 percent of the current Soviet throw weight. Throw weight was a rough overall measure of the total lethality of a missile force, reflecting the number of warheads and their explosive power, or yield. Reagan administration hard-liners had demanded for years that any strategic arms agreement slash the aggregate Soviet throw weight, which was much larger than that of the U.S. missile fleet.

The talks broke down, however, over Gorbachev's demand for a 10-year moratorium on field tests of SDI components. Reagan adamantly refused to agree to limit SDI efforts, even in return for major cuts in Soviet weapons levels.

Administration officials initially described the outcome as a bitterly disappointing failure, but, after they returned to Washington, they shifted to a more positive tone, touting both the progress made on many arms issues and Reagan's fortitude in refusing to give in to Gorbachev's demands.

Sam Nunn, D-Ga., who was to become chairman of the Senate Armed Services Committee in the 100th Congress, was especially critical of Reagan's apparent willingness to consider abolition of all nuclear weapons within 10 years. Nunn warned that such a move would leave U.S. allies with little protection against the Soviet Union's stronger conventional forces. Administration officials insisted that they had only discussed doing away with nuclear missiles.

# Rules and Timetables ...

The U.S.-Soviet treaty banning intermediate-range nuclear-force (INF) missiles eliminated a total of 859 U.S. missiles and 1,836 Soviet missiles, according to data exchanged by the two governments when the treaty was signed Dec. 8, 1987.

The number of nuclear warheads to be removed from the front lines could not be directly calculated from those totals, since they included missiles that were not deployed and that carried no warheads.

According to an estimate by the staff of the Senate Foreign Relations Committee, the treaty was to remove from front-line service nearly four times as many Soviet warheads as U.S. warheads: 1,667 Soviet weapons compared with 429 U.S. ones. One-third of the Soviet missiles covered by the accord were SS-20s carrying three warheads each. The treaty:

- Required elimination within three years of all U.S. and Soviet ground-launched missiles with ranges between 1,000 and 5,500 kilometers (roughly 600-3,400 miles), including the U.S. Pershing IIs and ground-launched cruise missiles (GLCMs) and the Soviet SS-4, SS-5, SS-20 and SSCX-4 missiles.
- Required elimination within 18 months of all ground-launched missiles with ranges between 500 and 1,000 kilometers. These included the U.S. Pershing I-A (no longer deployed in Europe) and the Soviet SS-12 and SS-23 missiles.
- Required removal from Europe of U.S. nuclear warheads earmarked for use on West German Pershing I-As. The West German missiles were not explicitly mentioned.
- Specified in great detail the procedures by which the barred missiles and associated launchers had to be destroyed. For instance, it provided that GLCMs (which were small, robot jet planes) had to be cut in half, separating the wing section from the tail section.
- Permitted removal of the guidance systems and nuclear warheads from the banned weapons before they were destroyed. While the warheads might not fit other missiles, the nuclear fuel they contained could be salvaged and used to build new warheads.
- Permitted destruction of up to 100 missiles by launching them, instead of cutting them up.
- Barred all further manufacture or flight testing of missiles with ranges between 500 and 5,500 kilometers.
- Required each country to provide an inventory of all missiles covered by the treaty (and their associated launchers and support equipment) together with a list of all sites where such missiles and equipment had been manufactured, repaired, tested, deployed or stored. In the "memorandum of understanding" containing these data, the Soviet Union listed 128 sites and the United States listed 30 sites.
- Provided that either country could withdraw from the treaty on six months' notice, if it decided that events related to the subject of the treaty jeopardized its "supreme national interests." This was a standard clause in security-related treaties.
- Barred either country from "assuming interna-

## Washington Summit

The third summit meeting between Reagan and Gorbachev was held in Washington Dec. 8-10, 1987. The two leaders signed a treaty scrapping all INF missiles. There was also progress in modest but solid agreements on several START disputes. (INF treaty, p. 346)

Reagan and Gorbachev deferred a showdown on the issue that had blocked agreements at the Reykjavik summit in 1986: SDI. The joint communiqué issued on Dec. 10 was intentionally ambiguous on whether SDI tests were consistent with the 1972 ABM treaty.

The two leaders reaffirmed the previously agreed-on aspects of a START deal and directed their negotiators to work out a system for verifying the destruction of weapons and compliance with a START agreement. In part, this was to draw on the principal elements of the radically new verification arrangements embodied in the INF treaty.

But in addition to tracking over the ground newly broken in the INF treaty, Reagan and Gorbachev passed on to their negotiators instructions to draft an even more far-reaching agreement that would include:

- An overall limit on each side of 4,900 on the total number of warheads carried by ICBMs and sea-launched missiles. Within that total, U.S. negotiators were to continue pressing for an additional "subceiling" of 3,300 on the number of ICBM warheads.

However, on Dec. 3, Kenneth L. Adelman, about to depart from his position as head of the Arms Control and Disarmament Agency, suggested that the ICBM sublimit could be dispensed with if other aspects of a START deal were sufficiently attractive.

- "Counting rules" to determine the number of nuclear warheads carried by all missiles and long-range bombers.
- A limit on the number of long-range, sea-launched cruise missiles (SLCMs) above and beyond the 6,000-warhead ceiling, together with procedures for verifying the SLCM limit. Since some modern nuclear SLCMs were only the size of a torpedo, verifying an SLCM limit would be very demanding.

## Moscow Summit

Reagan and Gorbachev met again May 29-June 2, 1988, in Moscow, where they exchanged the documents of ratification of the INF treaty. The two leaders lavishly praised the newly ratified accord, although it was generally considered of secondary significance when compared with the potential for a START agreement making huge cuts in the bulk of the U.S. and Soviet nuclear arsenals.

# ... Of the INF Accord

tional obligations or undertakings" that would conflict with the treaty.

The treaty specified in considerable detail the procedures by which each country could monitor the other's compliance. Like earlier U.S.-Soviet agreements limiting longer-range "strategic" weapons, the pact forbade interference with reconnaissance satellites and other "national technical means" for each country to verify the other's compliance with the treaty.

Moreover, to prevent testing new missiles under cover of disposing of old ones, it forbade the encoding of data transmitted from the 100 missiles that could be disposed of by launching. But the most widely touted aspect of the treaty's verification regime was its extensive provision for "on-site" inspection of each country's compliance by officials of the other.

The treaty permitted:

● Teams of inspectors from each country to visit all designated sites in the other country at the start of the treaty period to verify the data concerning the number of missiles, launchers and other components at each site.

● A "close-out" inspection of each designated site after the INF missiles had been removed and the related facilities razed.

● On-site observation by each country of the other's destruction of INF missiles and equipment.

● Each country to station a team of 30 resident inspectors for 13 years at the gates of one missile assembly plant in the other country, empowered to inspect all shipments from the plant to ensure that none contained forbidden missiles. The Soviet facility was a plant in Votkinsk, near the Ural Mountains; the U.S. facility was a plant in Magna, Utah.

● Each country to conduct "short-notice" inspections of up to 20 designated sites (except for missile production facilities) during the first three years after the treaty took effect. Inspection teams would be permitted to fly into designated entry points without announcing in advance which site they intended to inspect. Once they had landed and declared their destination, the country being inspected would be obliged to transport the inspectors to that site within nine hours.

● Up to 15 such short-notice inspections in the five years beginning three years after the treaty took effect.

● Up to 10 short-notice inspections in the following five years.

The treaty also required the Soviet Union to take certain steps to facilitate U.S. verification that SS-20s were not deployed at certain sites where the similar but larger SS-25 was deployed. Six times annually during the first three years the treaty was in effect, the United States could demand that the Soviets expose to the view of reconnaissance satellites all missiles and launchers at any SS-25 base. Normally, the missiles and launchers were concealed in "garages."

Only limited progress was made toward a START agreement. The leaders ordered their Geneva negotiators to resume work on a treaty cutting arsenals of long-range nuclear weapons by 30 to 50 percent. But SDI remained the greatest obstacle. As in previous summits, Reagan and Gorbachev effectively agreed to disagree on the testing of SDI, thereby postponing the tough decisions that had to be made before a new treaty could be signed.

The two sides also appeared to make little progress on another major START issue: monitoring SLCMs. The communiqué issued June 1 merely said the two leaders "discussed the question."

However, both sides reported "substantial additional common ground" on two of the START issues that probably were the easiest to resolve: verifying limits on mobile missiles and on long-range missiles launched from airplanes.

The United States had proposed an outright ban on mobile missiles but in the face of Soviet resistance apparently had settled for strict limits on deployment of them.

A senior U.S. official also said the two sides made "considerable progress" in deciding how to distinguish between air-launched cruise missiles that carry nuclear warheads and those with conventional arms. However, there was no agreement on how to count the number of such missiles permitted on each side.

In lieu of a START pact, Secretary of State Shultz and Soviet Foreign Minister Eduard A. Shevardnadze signed two minor arms accords May 31:

● An agreement requiring each country to give the other at least 24 hours' advance notice of the test launching of any land-based or sea-based ICBM.

● An agreed-upon experiment for measuring underground nuclear tests in each country. The purpose of the experiment was to determine verification requirements for an unratified 1974 treaty establishing a limit of 150 kilotons on underground tests. The two sides also pledged to work on new agreements that would allow ratification of that treaty and a companion 1976 treaty establishing limits on peaceful nuclear explosions. (Unratified treaties, p. 352)

## Gorbachev Proposal

Six months after the Moscow summit, on Dec. 7, Gorbachev made a bold move in a wide-ranging address to the U.N. General Assembly in New York. Breaking dramatically with traditional Soviet rhetoric, he belittled the role of military force and ideological struggle in world affairs. And he backed that up with an announcement of

Soviet plans to cut 500,000 of the country's 5.1 million troops by 1991.

The Soviet leader also called for "consistent movement" toward a START agreement, "while preserving the ABM treaty."

Gorbachev's troop-cut proposal prompted cautious optimism from top officials, who noted that it seemed to meet NATO's insistence that any Soviet troop cut be tailored to hit in particular those Soviet forces in Eastern Europe that Western allies long had claimed were poised to mount a blitzkrieg against West Germany.

But that optimism was tempered by questions about how significant would be the details of Gorbachev's plans and whether he would be able to carry them out over objections of some senior military aides.

Reagan, Bush and other NATO leaders lauded the Soviet move. But Reagan warned against taking the Soviet reductions as a cue for similar U.S. cutbacks. "This still leaves them with superiority in the amount of conventional arms," Reagan said Dec. 8 at a televised press conference. "We're still way below them."

The NATO allies responded Dec. 8 with an even more sweeping cutback of their own, aimed in part at dramatizing their contention that even after Gorbachev's plan was carried out, the Soviet-led Warsaw Pact would have significantly larger military forces in Europe than did the Western allies. Their plan called for limits on tanks, infantry transports armed with missiles and cannon, and artillery pieces.

# INF Treaty

The treaty to ban all INF missiles was the first U.S.-Soviet arms agreement to be ratified since 1972.

Signed by Reagan and Gorbachev on Dec. 8, 1987, the treaty required the destruction within three years of all missiles with ranges of between 500 and 5,500 kilometers (roughly 300 to 3,400 miles), together with their associated launchers and support facilities. The ax was to fall on a total of 859 U.S. missiles and 1,836 Soviet missiles. (Treaty details, box, p. 344)

In terms of the number of nuclear warheads that would be removed from service, the ratio was lopsided in the United States' favor, since a large proportion of the scrapped Soviet weapons were triple-warhead SS-20s. All of the U.S. missiles were single-warhead Pershing II and ground-launched cruise missiles (GLCMs).

To verify compliance, the pact established an unprecedented system for each country's inspectors to visit, on very short notice, facilities in the other country where the banned missiles had been deployed, stored or serviced.

The INF treaty embodied the "zero-option," which was widely dismissed as unrealistic when Reagan first proposed it in November 1981. The pact had been viewed with profound misgivings by centrist national security experts in both parties, such as Senate Armed Services Committee Chairman Nunn and former Secretary of State Henry A. Kissinger, who feared that removal of the missiles would erode the nuclear threat on which NATO historically had relied to offset the more numerous conventional forces of the Soviet-led Warsaw Pact.

But once the treaty was signed, most of the centrists, including Nunn and Kissinger, reluctantly supported Senate approval for fear that public opinion in some Western European countries would be outraged if the agreement fell apart.

## Background

When the Soviet Union began to deploy SS-20s in 1977, some European political leaders warned that the missiles posed a unique threat against the Europeans to which NATO as a whole, including the United States, had to respond.

Hundreds of Soviet medium-range missiles had been deployed within range of Western Europe since the early 1960s. But the new SS-20 missile was a much more formidable proposition, since it could strike targets at a much greater distance and with greater accuracy.

Moreover, the missile's launcher could be hauled around the countryside in a huge truck and, since the missile was powered by solid fuel, it could be fired on a moment's notice. Those qualities made the SS-20 far less vulnerable to a pre-emptive NATO attack than the older, liquid-fueled missiles, which took hours to prepare to launch.

NATO leaders concluded that the SS-20 was dangerous because it singled out U.S. allies, subjecting them to a threat that was not directly shared by Americans. It was thought that the Soviets hoped to weaken the political ties between the United States and its allies by playing on European fears that the United States would unduly discount a menace posed to Europe by missiles that could not reach North America.

The response to the SS-20 deployment, announced in December 1979, was a "two-track" decision: NATO would match the Soviet threat by deploying in Europe Pershing IIs and GLCMs, while calling for negotiations to cut back INF missiles. In 1981, at the instigation of the Reagan administration, NATO called for abolishing all INF missiles.

Reagan and Gorbachev signed the treaty scrapping all INF missiles at their December 1987 summit meeting in Washington.

In signing the agreement, Reagan dropped his earlier insistence that arms control agreements be "linked" with other aspects of Soviet behavior. Specifically, he signed the treaty despite the fact that the Soviets still were in violation of existing arms control agreements — including the ABM treaty and SALT II — according to the administration.

As late as 1986, the administration's official position had been that no new arms treaties could be signed with the Soviets until they pulled out of Afghanistan and dismantled a huge radar built at Krasnoyarsk in western Siberia, which the United States said was in violation of the ABM treaty. (Radar, box, p. 351)

But by 1987, Reagan's commitment to the East-West struggle took on a more pragmatic aspect. In effect, he contended that useful arms agreements could safely be concluded with Moscow, so long as U.S. objections to Soviet domestic and international policy were kept in the public eye — without requiring that the objections be satisfied.

In concluding the INF treaty and making some progress toward the more far-reaching START agreement, Reagan insisted that those arms control deals proceed in the context of his continued public lambasting of the more objectionable aspects of Soviet power at home and abroad.

## Senate Approval

Senate approval of the treaty was a foregone conclusion but several disputes delayed Senate debate on the treaty into the spring of 1988. The way was cleared for Senate action only after two days of meetings in Geneva between Shultz and Shevardnadze and their top arms control advisers. On May 12, negotiators signed two addenda to the treaty settling disagreements over the scope of the pact and over detailed procedures by which officials of each country could inspect the other's facilities to verify compliance.

When the treaty reached the Senate floor, only a handful of hard-line conservatives attacked the treaty head-on. Some other conservatives tried to amend the treaty in ostensibly modest ways to exclude from its coverage certain weapons they favored, but those efforts all failed. *(Senate action, p. 332)*

Senate approval of the treaty came on May 27, 1988, by a 93-5 vote. But, before approving the landmark treaty, Senate Democrats claimed victory in another chapter of a long power struggle with the White House over the making and interpretation of treaties.

The principle at issue was whether the Senate could bind future administrations to the interpretation of the treaty presented by the Reagan administration to the Senate — the constitutional question raised by the Reagan administration's attempt to reinterpret the 1972 ABM treaty to permit more realistic testing of SDI. *(Anti-missile defense, below)*

The Senate adopted an amendment to the resolution of approval of the INF treaty stipulating that neither the current nor any future president could depart from any interpretation of the treaty that had been officially presented to the Senate.

Democratic and Republican leaders joined forces to ensure final Senate action in time for ratification at the Moscow summit. Reagan and Gorbachev exchanged the documents of ratification for the INF treaty on June 1.

Actual destruction of INF missiles began on Aug. 1, with the Soviets going first. Dramatic television footage of Soviet missiles being blown up later was used by Bush in his successful presidential campaign. As part of his peace-through-strength theme, Bush argued that Reagan administration toughness had provided the leverage needed to negotiate the treaty.

# Anti-Missile Defense

Reagan's program to develop a nationwide anti-ballistic missile defense was not only a major stumbling block in U.S.-Soviet strategic arms negotiations but also produced heated battles year after year on Capitol Hill.

Controversy had surrounded the SDI program ever since it was announced in 1983. Reagan touted it as a way to make nuclear weapons "impotent and obsolete," implying that the intent was to produce a leakproof shield over the country.

Most administration officials, however, set a more modest goal: a defense that could disrupt any Soviet attack on the U.S. nuclear force and that would dissuade Moscow from making such an attack.

Arms controllers argued that Reagan's impenetrable shield would prove physically unattainable and anything less effective would spur a Soviet offensive buildup to swamp U.S. defenses. They argued that the 1972 ABM treaty ruled out many of the exotic anti-missile weapons envisioned.

To buffer SDI against the pro-arms control backlash, Reagan and his aides said repeatedly that, for years to come, the program would be conducted in accord with the limits of the ABM treaty.

## Treaty Reinterpretation

But in October 1985, the administration announced a new interpretation of the ABM treaty: The pact did not ban development and testing — short of deployment — of space-based and air-based anti-missile weapons using lasers and other technologies not available in 1972. *(Box, p. 348)*

After a firestorm of protest from U.S. allies and members of Congress, the White House defused the issue by announcing that SDI would continue to be governed by the more restrictive "traditional" interpretation.

The issue came to a boil again late in 1986, when Defense Secretary Caspar W. Weinberger and some other officials began pressing Reagan to accelerate the timetable for SDI deployment, which would require tests that would violate the traditional interpretation.

In March 1987, Senate Armed Services Committee Chairman Nunn, a highly influential voice in defense debates, challenged the administration on the ABM treaty. After reviewing records of ABM negotiations and of the 1972 Senate debate on approval of the treaty, Nunn said the new interpretation was unfounded.

Nunn's view was backed by a majority of his colleagues on Capitol Hill. By considerable margins, the Senate and House in 1987 added amendments to the defense authorization bill in effect barring SDI tests in space that would violate the traditional interpretation of the ABM treaty. The ban was enacted again in 1988.

## 'Phase One'

But a congressional attempt in 1988 to make a deep cut in the amount within the SDI total earmarked for so-called "Phase One" space-based anti-missile weapons was a factor in Reagan's veto of the first version of the fiscal 1989 defense authorization and was abandoned in the second version (HR 4481 — PL 100-456).

In 1987, SDI had taken a large step from vision to research program, when the administration came up with a two-track plan for anti-missile deployments. The Phase One defense, using existing technologies to provide a limited defense, was to be deployed in the 1990s, with more advanced layers of defense to be added later, as they matured.

Phase One reportedly would consist of a network of satellites, each carrying dozens of "space-based interceptors," or SBIs — small and relatively inexpensive heat-seeking missiles intended to home in on Soviet missiles in the first few minutes after their launch — that would be backed up by ground-based ERIS (exo-atmospheric re-entry intercept system) missiles intended to pick off some of the attacking warheads that made it past the initial defenses and were headed toward critical targets.

The Phase One plan met strong opposition from liberals and centrists alike. Both groups denounced it as a device to build political momentum behind SDI by conducting tests and deploying equipment more for political

# The Legal Issues in the ABM Treaty ...

The domestic battle over President Reagan's effort to develop a nationwide anti-missile defense — the strategic defense initiative (SDI) — ultimately turned on the antagonists' political clout instead of on the niceties of international law.

But both sides in the SDI debate saw the issue of legality as a potent one. Both sides invested a lot of energy in the debate over whether Reagan's program was consistent with the 1972 U.S.-Soviet treaty limiting anti-ballistic missile (ABM) systems.

## The Texts

Six of the treaty's 16 articles and one appendix were at issue in the debate over SDI:

**Article I** provided that each of the two countries agreed "not to deploy ABM systems for the defense of the territory of its country and not to provide a base for such a defense and not to deploy ABM systems for defense of an individual region except as provided for in Article III."

**Article II** defined an ABM system as "a system to counter ballistic missiles or their elements in flight trajectory currently consisting of" radars, interceptor missiles and launchers for the interceptors. In the second paragraph, these three kinds of equipment were listed as "ABM system components."

**Article III** limited each country to two ABM sites, each containing no more than 100 launchers. In 1974, the two governments agreed that each would deploy ABM launchers at only one of the two permitted sites.

**Article V** provided that the two countries agreed "not to develop, test or deploy ABM systems or components which are sea-based, air-based, space-based or mobile land-based."

**Article XIV** provided that either party could propose amendments to the treaty.

**Article XV** provided that either country shall "have the right to withdraw from this treaty if it decides that extraordinary events related to the subject matter of this treaty have jeopardized its supreme interests." Six months' notice was required for withdrawal.

**Agreed Statement D** said: "In order to ensure fulfillment of the obligation not to deploy ABM systems and their components except as provided in Article III of the treaty, the parties agree that in the event ABM systems based on other physical principles and including components capable of substitut-

ing for ABM interceptor missiles, ABM launchers or ABM radars are created in the future, specific limitations on such systems and their components would be subject to discussion," according to provisions that provided for amendment by mutual agreement.

## For What Purpose?

SDI opponents read Article I as a statement that the pact's fundamental purpose was to ban precisely the kind of nationwide population shield Reagan and his aides wanted. A limited defense of one small region — including either offensive missile sites or the national capital — was permitted by the treaty.

Defense Secretary Caspar W. Weinberger was particularly insistent during the debate over SDI that he and Reagan wanted the program to defend the American public, not just missile silos. Until late in 1986, Weinberger had rejected any talk of taking the initial step of deploying a partial defense that would protect some U.S. missiles against a Soviet attack.

In 1987, Weinberger began calling for a phased deployment of anti-missile weapons, but stipulating that the initial phase would fit into an ultimate scheme that would defend people, not missiles.

## What Kind of System?

Arms control advocates insisted, practically since the treaty was signed, that the restrictions in Articles III and V were all-inclusive.

In this view, Article II defined "ABM systems" functionally: anything that could destroy a missile in flight. The reference to missiles, radars and launchers was merely illustrative of what ABM systems were "currently consisting of" at the time the treaty was signed. Accordingly, Agreed Statement D allowed only for the possible development of new kinds of ABM weapons if they were land-based and fixed.

In October 1985, the administration presented a contrary position developed by Abraham D. Sofaer, the State Department's senior lawyer. He argued that the treaty consistently used the terms "ABM system" and "component" in contexts that made it clear they referred only to the 1972-style equipment. Accordingly, he reasoned, the limits on ground-based deployment in Article III and the ban on development of space-based or mobile systems in Article V applied only to that kind of system. If those restrictions had been intended to apply to novel ABM types

show than military significance. They also objected that Phase One programs would soak up funds better spent on the more promising, exotic technologies.

An alternative to the administration plan was proposed by Nunn in early 1988. He called for studying the

value of fielding ground-based missiles, like ERIS, as permitted by the ABM treaty, to set up an "accidental launch protection system," to ward off a small number of warheads that might be launched toward the United States by accident or by the unauthorized action of a rogue Soviet

# ... Fuel Debate Over the SDI Program

as well as the 1970s version, he maintained, there would have been no need for Agreed Statement D.

A review of the negotiations that produced the pact, Sofaer said, showed that Soviet officials expressly rejected the effort of U.S. negotiators to have the treaty ban future types of ABM defenses.

The issue was central to Reagan and Weinberger's insistence that they were not developing a system that would defend only U.S. missile launchers or other military targets. To have any chance of protecting the U.S. population at large, a U.S. defense would have to include some orbiting satellites that could attack Soviet missiles almost as soon as they were launched, before they dispensed their several nuclear warheads and their dozens of decoys.

## How Exotic?

The Pentagon's efforts to press for deployment in the early 1990s of a first-phase defense system raised a new question. The exotic lasers and particle-beam weapons with which SDI first was associated — the source of its nickname, "star wars" — could not be fielded soon. Deployment in the early 1990s would have to include satellites armed with "kinetic kill vehicles" (KKVs) — small missiles designed to destroy a Soviet missile by collision. But even under Sofaer's reading of the treaty, these space-based weapons could not be developed unless they depended on "new physical principles" and thus came under the alleged exemption of Agreed Statement D.

Administration officials contended that KKVs differed from earlier ABM interceptor missiles in two respects: They would home in on the heat generated by their target instead of being guided by radar, and they would destroy their target by colliding with it, at thousands of miles per hour, instead of using the blast of a warhead.

SDI critics ridiculed this contention. Heat-seeking missiles had been used by jet fighters for decades, and the principle of destruction by physical impact was as old as the catapult, they insisted. The new missiles involved different engineering from that of older ABM weapons, but they were not based on "new physical principles," as, for instance, an anti-missile laser would have been.

Even before the administration proposed Sofaer's less-restrictive reading of the treaty, it claimed far more latitude than SDI critics and Soviet officials said was allowed for conducting research on

mobile and space-based equipment without violating Article V's ban on "development."

## What Is Development?

The treaty defined neither the term "develop," which was used in the English text, nor the corresponding word in the Russian text, which was translated as "create."

In the political maneuvering before the U.S.-Soviet summit meetings in November 1985 and October 1986, some Soviet officials insisted that any SDI-related research was banned by the ABM treaty. But from the time the treaty was signed, the most frequently expressed Soviet position on this issue was that the pact banned experiments that could be observed by the other side by virtue of their being conducted outside a laboratory. During Senate consideration of the treaty in 1972, several Nixon administration officials expressed the same view.

However, in a report to Congress in March 1985, the administration contended that the treaty "does permit research short of field testing of a prototype ABM system or component." Applying that standard, the report described several planned tests that it held to be consistent with the treaty. SDI critics charged that some of the proposed experiments would go far over the line between laboratory research and the kind of field testing that the treaty was intended to preclude.

## What Is a Component?

Paralleling the debate over the meaning of "develop" was a disagreement over the definition of an ABM system "component."

The administration had maintained that an element of a future SDI system would be a "component" under the limits of the ABM treaty only if the new item could perform all the functions that, in 1972, were performed by a radar, an interceptor missile or a missile launcher. The 1985 report listed several tests deemed permissible under the treaty since the equipment being tested either was not technically capable of fitting into an ABM system or was tested against an Earth-orbiting satellite instead of a ballistic missile.

SDI critics argued that the administration's narrow definition of "component" — like its definition of "develop" — skirted the treaty's intent.

commander.

Another alternative, labeled "Brilliant Pebbles," was developed by SDI scientists at an Energy Department laboratory in California. The plan called for orbiting thousands of small interceptor missiles, which would home in

on Soviet missiles in their boost phase. The premise was that by keeping interceptors simple and cheap, enough could be deployed that there would be no need for an elaborate control network to assign each interceptor to a separate Soviet ICBM.

## SDI Funding

Although Congress made cuts in the administration's budget requests for SDI, the program still enjoyed steady funding increases in fiscal 1985-88. But the amount appropriated in fiscal 1989 amounted to just roughly enough of an increase over the fiscal 1988 appropriation to cover inflation.

# SALT II Limits

Congress in 1987 repudiated another of Reagan's key arms control positions: It forced the administration to largely eliminate its planned increase in the number of multiple-warhead missiles and missile-armed bombers in the U.S. arsenal.

At issue were limits on the number of such weapons that were part of the U.S.-Soviet strategic arms limitation talks (SALT II) treaty, which was signed by President Jimmy Carter in 1979. *(Congress and the Nation Vol. V, p. 193)*

The agreement, among other things, set sublimits of:
● No more than 820 land-based ballistic missiles (ICBMs) with multiple warheads (MIRVs).
● No more than 1,200 MIRVed ballistic missiles altogether, including both ICBMs and submarine-launched missiles.
● No more than 1,320 MIRVed ballistic missiles, plus bombers equipped with long-range cruise missiles.

Carter dropped his effort to secure Senate approval of SALT II after the 1979 Soviet invasion of Afghanistan, and the treaty was never ratified. But the U.S. and Soviet governments announced they would informally observe the treaty's limits, on a reciprocal basis.

Reagan, who denounced SALT II for years as being advantageous to the Soviet Union, delighted liberals and confounded some of his staunchest conservative allies when he decided in June 1985 that he would "go the extra mile" to maintain SALT II. He announced on June 10 that he would dismantle a Poseidon missile-launching submarine, an action prompted by the imminence of the launch of the seventh Trident missile-launching submarine, the *USS Alaska.* The *Alaska's* missile-launch tubes would have put the total number of U.S. launchers above the SALT II limit.

For months conservatives in the Senate and in the administration, including Defense Secretary Weinberger, had urged Reagan to keep the Poseidon sub in service and to end the administration's policy of "not undercutting" SALT II. The hard-liners argued that denouncing the treaty would highlight alleged Soviet violations of this and other arms control agreements as well as signal a new firmness in dealing with Moscow.

Before Reagan announced his decision, the Senate had voted 90-5 to recommend that he continue the policy of informal adherence to the SALT limits. A more influential factor in his decision could have been intense demands by allied governments that the SALT limits be respected.

But Reagan stressed that his future policy would be dependent on Soviet compliance with existing arms treaties and progress in seeking new treaties. Administration officials and many defense experts pointed to three developments that they said represented significant Soviet violations of SALT II. They were:
● Deploying two new types of ICBMs, contrary to the SALT II provision allowing each country only one new type.
● Exceeding the treaty's limit on the total number of "strategic nuclear delivery vehicles" — long-range bombers, ICBM launchers and launchers on nuclear-missile submarines.
● Putting in code missile data radioed to Earth from test missiles. SALT II barred such encryption when it impeded verification of compliance with the treaty.

## Policy Ended

On May 27, 1986, Reagan announced that the United States would no longer observe the SALT II agreement, thus ending the six-year policy of informal compliance with the agreement. Reagan said he was taking the step because the Soviets had repeatedly violated the terms of the treaty.

Congressional critics reacted to Reagan's announcement by arguing that it was not a sensible response to Soviet treaty violations. Instead, they said, the United States should react in kind — by accelerating development of the Midgetman missile, for example, in reaction to Soviet deployment of a forbidden "second new type" of ICBM.

Critics also warned that abrogation of the treaty limits would allow Moscow to expand its nuclear force far more rapidly than the United States.

The House passed an amendment to the defense authorization bill mandating continued U.S. observation of the three key numerical sublimits on weapons in the treaty. There was no comparable provision in the Senate version of the bill, and the Reagan administration and the Republican majority in the Senate vigorously opposed the amendment in conference. After an extended deadlock, House Democrats finally agreed to drop the amendment, largely because members were loath to undercut Reagan's position on the eve of his October 1986 meeting with Gorbachev. But the final version of the defense measure (S 2638 — PL 99-661) included non-binding language urging the president to continue to observe the limits. *(Fiscal 1987 defense bill, p. 290)*

The United States formally exceeded the numerical weapons limits in the treaty on Nov. 28, 1986, when it put into service the 131st B-52 bomber equipped to carry long-range cruise missiles. That gave the United States one weapon more than the SALT II limit of 1,320 ballistic missiles with multiple-warheads and missile-armed bombers. B-52 bombers equipped to carry cruise missiles were to be deployed at a rate of two per month.

## Compliance Mandated

In 1987, both the House and Senate approved binding SALT-compliance provisions. The two houses adopted amendments to the fiscal 1988 defense authorization bill (HR 1748 — PL 100-180) imposing observance of the SALT II sublimits while not referring to the controversial treaty. Members wanted to continue observance of the sublimits as an "interim restraint" pending U.S.-Soviet agreement on a new treaty reducing strategic nuclear stockpiles.

The final version of the fiscal 1988 defense bill required the retirement of one missile-firing submarine, thus largely offsetting an increase in the number of missile-armed bombers scheduled to occur during the year. *(Fiscal 1988 defense bill, p. 302)*

# Dispute Over Soviet Radar

The 1987 visit of three liberal House Democrats to a Soviet radar site appeared to intensify the defense policy debate between the Reagan administration and congressional Democrats about the purpose of the controversial Krasnoyarsk radar facility and other arms control issues.

The three members — Thomas J. Downey, N.Y.; Bob Carr, Mich.; and Jim Moody, Wis. — returned from their visit with the view, expressed in a preliminary report to House Speaker Jim Wright, D-Texas, that the Krasnoyarsk facility could technically violate the 1972 treaty limiting anti-ballistic missile (ABM) weapons, but that it was not designed to operate effectively as a "battle management" radar — one that could control an anti-missile network.

That view differed sharply from the views of the Reagan administration, which had argued for years that the installation flagrantly violated the ABM treaty and that its battle management potential made it a particularly dangerous breach. From that perception, administration officials had derived two lessons.

First, they insisted that future arms control accords with Moscow must have very stringent, and thus very hard to negotiate, provisions for verifying Soviet compliance. Second, they argued that since the Soviets seemed to be moving toward an anti-missile system, the United States should proceed apace with the strategic defense initiative (SDI), Reagan's high-priority program to develop a nationwide ABM system.

## Downey Report

The Downey group's report, released Sept. 8, 1987, reflected a new willingness by arms control proponents to counter these arguments and oppose Reagan's arms agenda. These members, while increasingly bold on arms control, had been wary of seeming "soft" on alleged Soviet treaty violations or on potential violations of prospective agreements. For example, in January 1987, Senate Majority Leader Robert C. Byrd, D-W.Va., and Sam Nunn, D-Ga., chairman of the Senate Armed Services Committee, with the concurrence of more liberal Democrats, em-

braced Reagan's claim that new, tough verification standards were needed beyond those in two 1970s nuclear test limitation treaties. On Sept. 17, U.S. and Soviet officials announced plans to begin negotiations of new verification procedures for the testing treaties. *(Treaties, p. 352)*

The administration's critics were able to find ammunition in the Downey group's contention that while the Soviet radar might violate the treaty once it became operational, the facility was of little military significance.

But, in the wake of the Downey report, the Senate Sept. 16 passed 89-0 an amendment to the fiscal 1989 defense authorization bill expressing the sense of Congress that the radar violated the ABM treaty. The same provision had been adopted by the House in May by a 418-0 vote.

## Watching Space or Warheads?

U.S. reconnaissance satellites first observed construction of the two huge antennas at Krasnoyarsk in 1983. Within a year, the administration charged that the radar violated the ABM treaty. That view came to be widely held by U.S. arms control specialists, including some of Reagan's toughest liberal critics.

A key premise behind the treaty was that, of all the elements of an ABM system that might be deployed in violation of the pact, the easiest to detect would be the huge, "phased array" radars needed to track thousands of attacking warheads and decoys and to guide ABM missiles to their targets.

The treaty barred large phased array radars unless they were located on the periphery of the country and faced outward. From such sites, the radars could provide early warning of a missile attack, but they could not be used to coordinate an anti-missile defense of sites inside the heartland.

That prohibition did not apply to radars used to track space satellites. The Soviet Union insisted that the Krasnoyarsk facility was intended as a space-tracking radar, a contention widely rejected by U.S. experts across the political spectrum since the radar was aimed away from the equatorial orbits used by most satellites.

In effect, the compromise set an informal cap on the number of U.S. weapons at a level slightly above one of the SALT II sublimits.

In their report accompanying the compromise bill, conferees declared their intention to continue retiring the aging Poseidon subs as their turn for overhaul came due. Retiring those old ships when they required expensive overhaul could be justified as a budgetary measure, thus sparing the administration the need to accept a reduction of weapons for the sake of SALT II, which would have

enraged conservative hard-liners.

Senior conferees were particularly careful not to arouse conservative ire against Frank C. Carlucci, with whom they were dealing. Carlucci had been nominated to succeed Weinberger as secretary of defense. *(Carlucci nomination, p. 1044)*

Despite strong opposition from the White House, Congress sustained the restriction in 1988, as part of the fiscal 1989 defense authorization bill (HR 4481 — PL 100-456). *(Fiscal 1989 defense bill, p. 318)*

# MX Versus Midgetman

The MX missile had become by 1983 the central political symbol of Reagan's nuclear weapons policy. Arms control advocates warned that the missile, which was designed to carry 10 nuclear warheads, each with enough accuracy and explosive power to destroy a Soviet missile silo, would escalate the arms race with Moscow.

But Reagan and his allies contended that it was needed to counterbalance Soviet missiles powerful enough to destroy U.S. missiles in a first strike.

The president gave his opponents a major political advantage late in 1981 when he stripped the missile of one of its central technical justifications: He rejected the mobile-basing method that the Air Force and Presidents Gerald R. Ford and Jimmy Carter had proposed to protect the new missiles against Soviet attack.

Beginning in early 1983, arms controllers organized a powerful grass-roots lobbying campaign that brought them within striking distance of a House vote against the missile. Democratic leaders saw MX as a way to crystallize public frustration with Reagan's expensive military buildup. There was also widespread concern over his confrontational approach toward the Soviet Union.

The MX missile program survived the critics' assault because of a small but influential group of predominantly Democratic defense specialists who supported production of a limited number of MXs in return for changes in the administration's arms control policy.

After several years of stalemate, Congress in March 1985 approved the procurement of 21 MXs in the fiscal 1985 budget. The administration made a very forceful pitch that it needed to win the vote to preserve its bargaining leverage in the Geneva arms negotiations — which had resumed only days before the votes on MX. In the House, Reagan's narrow victory came after chief arms control negotiator Max M. Kampelman flew back to Washington from Geneva to make the case to wavering members.

Even before the dust had settled on that round of the MX fight, centrist defense experts, led by Sen. Nunn, moved to end the MX fight by "capping" the MX deployment at 50 missiles — half the number Reagan planned.

It was generally thought that the long political wrangle over the MX missile had ended. But the following year Reagan requested funds to develop a new basing method, better able to survive a nuclear attack than the existing missile silos. In 1987 the administration requested funding to develop a rail-mobile launcher for the MX.

Backers of a single-warhead missile, nicknamed Midgetman, which was to be carried in an armored mobile launcher able to roam about randomly to forestall a Soviet attack, feared the mobile MX would draw funds away from the smaller missile. Some also opposed the Pentagon request because Weinberger had linked the rail-based launch system to deployment of 50 additional MX missiles.

The chairmen of the House and Senate Armed Services committees, Rep. Les Aspin, D-Wis., and Sen. Nunn, complained that the handful of trains carrying the MX missiles would be too vulnerable in their garrisons. Instead, the powerful chairmen favored deploying hundreds of the Midgetman missile.

Many policy makers, among them Reagan's new defense secretary, Carlucci, suggested that one of the two programs would have to be dropped under pressure of a shrinking budget. Conferees on the fiscal 1988 defense authorization (HR 1748 — PL 100-180) slowed the pace of development for both of the mobile ICBMs. Their action sought to keep both options available to a new administration in 1989.

Congress did the same the following year. When Reagan objected to the limited funds allocated to the mobile MX in the first version of the fiscal 1989 defense authorization, which he vetoed, Congress increased the funding in the second version (HR 4481.— PL 100-456). But the bill still limited the amount that could be spent until a new president was in the White House.

# Nuclear Test Ban

For three years in a row, liberal arms control activists battled in vain to force Reagan to rein in the U.S. nuclear weapons testing program, so long as the Soviet Union did likewise.

A nuclear test ban long had been the priority goal of grass-roots arms control activists, who saw it as a first step toward a freeze on the testing, production and deployment of nuclear weapons.

The Reagan administration was the first in three decades not to at least pay lip service to the goal of a nuclear test ban. Administration officials argued that a test ban would be unverifiable and would be dangerous until after deep reductions in nuclear arsenals were agreed to.

The Soviet Union called for a joint test moratorium on Aug. 6, 1985 — the 40th anniversary of the atomic bomb attack on Hiroshima — and announced a temporary unilateral moratorium of its own. Moscow subsequently extended its moratorium several times during 1986 but broke it on Feb. 26, 1987. The Reagan administration continued to conduct underground tests, arguing that testing was needed to ensure that existing nuclear weapons did not lose their explosive power through aging of the nuclear materials or mechanical parts.

## Legislative Action

House action on a non-binding resolution (H J Res 3) urging Reagan to resume test ban negotiations with Moscow was sidetracked in 1985, when Reagan invoked the imminence of a U.S.-Soviet summit, then six weeks away.

But the test ban gained political momentum rapidly in the House the following year. House members in 1986 voted twice by comfortable margins in favor of bringing to an end the Reagan administration's program of underground nuclear tests. First, it passed the non-binding H J Res 3, urging Reagan to resume negotiations seeking a comprehensive test ban, and also to seek immediate ratification of two treaties negotiated in the mid-1970s that would limit underground nuclear explosions to the explosive power of 150,000 tons of TNT (150 kilotons).

And later the House — in one of the most radical arms control moves taken by Congress in recent decades — added to the fiscal 1987 defense authorization bill (HR 4428) an amendment that would have barred from January through September 1987 all but the smallest nuclear test explosions (no greater than 1 kiloton or 1,000 tons of TNT), provided the Soviet Union did likewise. The Senate added to its version of the authorization bill (S 2638) the same non-binding language as in H J Res 3.

On the eve of the Reagan-Gorbachev summit, conferees on the authorization bill dropped the House-passed provision. In return, Reagan promised to seek Senate approval in 1987 of the two unratified treaties: a 1974 "threshold" treaty limiting underground tests of nuclear weapons and a 1976 one controlling underground nuclear explosions conducted for peaceful purposes. However, unless the Soviets agreed in the meantime to tighten verification provisions, Reagan said, he would ask the Senate to approve the pacts with a reservation that would hold them in abeyance until U.S.-Soviet agreement on verification was reached.

The treaties had been approved by the Senate Foreign Relations Committee in 1977 but were never reported to the Senate, initially because President Carter and arms control advocates had higher political priorities.

After Reagan came into office, the treaties languished. The new administration insisted that Soviet compliance with the accords could not be verified without requiring on-site measurement by each country of the underground blasts conducted by the other. The Soviet Union said it would discuss additional verification methods once the treaties were ratified, a position the administration rejected.

In September 1987, U.S. and Soviet officials announced plans to begin negotiations of new verification procedures for the testing treaties. A U.S.-Soviet agreement was signed at the May 1988 Moscow summit providing for an experiment to determine verification requirements for the 1974 treaty, and the two sides pledged to work on new agreements that would allow ratification of the two treaties.

The House again in 1987 attached a nuclear test ban provision to the defense authorization bill, and it was again rejected by the Senate. Although another Reagan-Gorbachev summit was in the offing, the test ban language died in conference more as a result of Democratic leaders' eagerness to enact other tough arms control measures in the authorization bill.

In 1988, the administration won back some of the members who had supported the test ban in 1987, because it was negotiating with the Soviets over modifications in the 1974 and 1976 treaties. Nevertheless, the House test ban supporters again succeeded in adding the test ban to the defense authorization bill (HR 4264). It was dropped in conference with the Senate, but, for the first time, the House won a consolation prize: a provision ordering the Energy Department to establish a program designed to ensure the continued reliability of existing U.S. nuclear weapons if a nuclear test ban should come into force.

# 6

# Transportation and Commerce

# Transportation and Commerce

Ronald Reagan's priorities in his second term in office changed little from those advanced in his first four years. He resumed his bid to scale back the federal government's involvement in the economy, including major transportation and communications industries.

The administration sought to reduce federal subsidies for state and local governments and private-sector recipients, while it sought to free these interests from what it viewed as outdated and counterproductive regulation.

In his first term, Reagan enjoyed some success in the transportation and commerce arena. With his approval, Congress cleared legislation to deregulate the bus industry and to eliminate subsidies for new U.S. ship construction. And Reagan's appointees to the Federal Communications Commission (FCC) lifted a host of regulatory restrictions on broadcasters without interference from lawmakers.

But in his second term, resistance to the Reagan agenda stiffened in Congress. Initiatives including a proposal to eliminate remaining controls on the trucking industry died amid growing criticism linking safety hazards to transportation deregulation. Administration officials repeatedly were forced to defend the benefits of airline and rail deregulation to lawmakers alarmed about such things as deteriorating airline service and costlier rail shipments of coal and other products.

The Democrats' recapture of the Senate in the 1986 election also blunted Reagan's thrust. It brought to the chairmanship of the Commerce, Science and Transportation Committee an unbridled foe of deregulation — Ernest F. Hollings of South Carolina. At Hollings' urging, for example, Congress attached a rider to appropriations bills barring the FCC from lifting a ban on common ownership of a newspaper and television station in the same market.

Reagan did triumph over Hollings and other Democrats on one longstanding matter of contention, however: repeal of the fairness doctrine, which required broadcasters to air all sides of controversial public issues.

Lawmakers and Reagan compromised on the sale of Conrail. Although Congress rejected Reagan's proposal to sell the freight railroad to another railroad, it provided for a public stock offering of the government's Conrail shares.

Against Reagan's wishes, Congress continued to provide substantial subsidies for Amtrak as well as for mass transit grants to cities. In addition, lawmakers in 1987 overrode a veto of legislation to reauthorize highway and mass transit programs. Reagan's defeat was widely viewed as indicative of his waning influence on Capitol Hill in the wake of the 1986 election and the Iran-contra scandal.

**Conrail.** Enactment in 1986 of legislation to return Conrail to the private sector came five years after the administration first proposed such action. Reagan argued that federal subsidies were not justified and that the railroad should be privately operated. As he noted, Conrail had experienced a turnaround and had become profitable.

Many lawmakers objected to Reagan's proposal to sell the government's 85 percent share in Conrail to the Norfolk Southern Corp. on the grounds that the merger would reduce rail competition, service and employment in Conrail's base of operations in the Northeast and Midwest.

Confronted by insurmountable opposition, the administration agreed to a public stock offering to create an independent Conrail. The final legislation banned any Conrail merger with another line for one year, after which the Interstate Commerce Commission was allowed to approve a consolidation with another railroad.

**Highways, Mass Transit.** After a dramatic struggle, Congress in 1987 overrode Reagan's veto of a bill to reauthorize $88 billion for highway and mass transit programs. Reagan said the legislation was too costly and filled with wasteful "pork-barrel" projects.

Despite his trip to Capitol Hill to plead with Senate Republicans for their support, Reagan was dealt a defeat. Some who voted to override cited road projects in the bill important to their states; others pointed to a provision allowing states to raise the speed limit from 55 mph to 65 mph on rural Interstate highways.

The speed-limit change was especially popular with Western legislators. Originally enacted to save fuel at a time of oil shortages, the law gradually had attracted backing from some in Congress, particularly in the Northeast, as a safety measure. But Western legislators argued that the limit routinely was violated by motorists, that it served no safety purpose on broad stretches of rural high-

## References

Discussion of transportation and commerce policy for the years 1945-64 may be found in *Congress and the Nation Vol. I*, pp. 517-562, 1159-1185; for the years 1965-68, *Congress and the Nation Vol. II*, pp. 227-251, 779-823; for the years 1969-72, *Congress and the Nation Vol. III*, pp. 147-176, 659-700; for the years 1973-76, *Congress and the Nation Vol. IV*, pp. 433-451, 505-555; for the years 1977-80, *Congress and the Nation Vol. V*, pp. 291-362; for the years 1981-84, *Congress and the Nation Vol. VI*, pp. 261-286, 289-329.

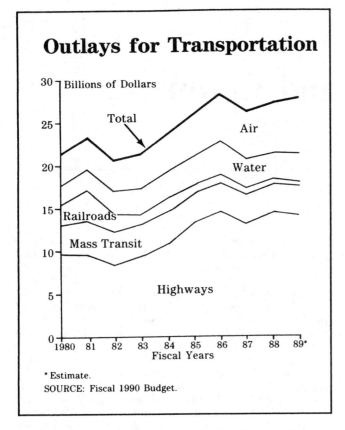

## Outlays for Transportation

30 ⌐ Billions of Dollars

Total

Air

Water

Railroads

Mass Transit

Highways

1980 81 82 83 84 85 86 87 88 89*
Fiscal Years

\* Estimate.
SOURCE: Fiscal 1990 Budget.

way and that, in any event, speed limits should be set by the states.

**Aviation.** Amid public concerns about aviation safety and shoddy airline service, Congress in 1987 enacted a $20 billion measure featuring increased funding for federal grants to airports for expansion projects and for purchases of equipment to upgrade the air-traffic control system.

Legislators left unscathed the 1978 law that lifted government controls on routes and fares.

Deregulation critics maintained that competitive pressures spawned by the law had forced airlines to cut corners on service and equipment maintenance. They pointed to increasing numbers of flight delays and near-collisions.

As complaints from passengers mounted, the House and Senate in 1987 passed bills to require public disclosure of carriers' performance records. However, pressure for the legislation eased with administration approval of agency regulations to require disclosure; no bill was cleared.

**Drug Testing.** Despite the anti-drug climate of the times, the 100th Congress could not agree on a bill to require workers in major transportation industries to submit to random drug and alcohol testing. Proponents argued that testing was needed to curtail drug-related accidents. Some lawmakers, however, were skeptical of the workability of the testing plan and were concerned about protecting workers' rights. After a yearlong battle and much parliamentary maneuvering, the legislation was abandoned.

Regulations for random drug testing of approximately 4 million transportation workers were issued by the Reagan administration after the 100th Congress adjourned.

**Communications Gridlock.** The Democratic-controlled Congress and Reagan's appointees to the FCC clashed repeatedly over major matters of policy and their appropriate institutional roles in determining policy. The result was gridlock.

On one side stood powerful congressional Democrats — notably House Energy and Commerce Committee Chairman John D. Dingell, D-Mich. — who viewed themselves as guardians of the public interest in the tradition of governmental policy since the creation of the FCC in the 1930s. The key underlying concept was that broadcasters owed a responsibility to their communities in exchange for the free licenses they received from the government.

On the other side stood Reagan-appointed deregulators committed to unshackling the communications industry from its decades-old restrictions. These individuals believed that changes in the industry, such as the explosion of television-viewing options through cable systems and videotape cassettes, had obviated the need for regulation.

The struggle come to a head over the fairness doctrine, which the FCC repealed in the summer of 1987. Dingell and other Democrats were furious, saying the FCC had acted despite a clear signal from Congress that it wished to retain the doctrine. Lawmakers charged that in this and other instances the agency had abused its discretion to set policy within guidelines set by the legislative body. However, Democrats lacked the votes to override Reagan's veto of legislation to restore the fairness doctrine.

Congress late in 1988 cleared a measure to reimpose limits abolished by the FCC four years earlier on the amount of advertising that could be shown on children's shows. Proponents said this step was needed to protect children against exploitation by commercial broadcasters and advertisers. But Reagan had the last word: Declaring that the bill ran counter to the thrust of his administration's pro-deregulation agenda, he pocket-vetoed it.

**Product Liability, Insurance.** Congress repeatedly debated but failed to clear legislation to establish the nation's first product liability law.

Since 1980 manufacturers had been pushing to supplant a patchwork of state laws with a uniform standard of liability intended to govern lawsuits filed by victims of unsafe products. Proponents said state laws tended to be conflicting and often favored the interests of accident victims — and of trial lawyers whose earnings were pegged to damage awards. Business groups also argued that escalating costs of insurance premiums were directly linked to unreasonably high damage awards for injuries.

But opponents, including consumer activists and groups representing trial lawyers, branded the manufacturers' thrust an assault on victims' rights and blamed the hike in insurance premimums not on high damage awards but on anti-competitive practices among insurers.

Persistent efforts by trial lawyers and consumers to narrow the insurance industry's exemption from federal antitrust laws also made little headway.

**Minority Business Set-Asides.** Congress in 1988 cleared a bill to overhaul a scandal-plagued Small Business Administration (SBA) procurement program designed to foster the growth of minority-owned businesses. The measure revamped a program under which the SBA contracted with other federal agencies and subcontracted the work to minority-owned firms.

Traditionally, the SBA relied on non-competitive contract awards, which critics said had led to a few, select firms securing contracts from friends in the government.

The new law required program participants to compete among themselves for top-dollar SBA contracts and to obtain an increasing portion of their sales from outside the program over the course of their participation.

# Chronology
# Of Action
# On Transportation
# And Commerce

## 1985-86

A major transportation battle waged in the 99th Congress was over the sale of Conrail, the government-owned freight railroad. It was resolved in 1986 when House and Senate negotiators agreed to a stock offering to the public for the government's share of the railroad system.

Highway authorizations also were hotly disputed: In 1985, Congress simply passed stripped-down highway authorizations that released funds held up since Oct. 1, 1983. Disputes over such matters as mass transit funding and highway projects, which had held up action in previous years, were deferred until 1986, when most major highway programs expired.

The 1986 highway authorization bill was stalled when Congress was unable to resolve key disputes over such controversial issues as relaxing the 55 mph speed limit and whether to fund special demonstration highway projects. Congress did pass legislation that withheld highway funds to states that did not pass legislation mandating a minimum drinking age of 21.

Despite intense public pressure to address the product liability insurance problem and to inhibit the wave of corporate takeovers, Congress did not enact legislation in the 99th Congress. However, Congress did pass a risk retention bill intended to make it easier for businesses, municipal groups and professionals to band together to insure themselves.

Two committees considered corporate merger legislation, but the bills never advanced.

Congress rebuffed the Reagan administration's proposal to transfer the functions of the Small Business Administration (SBA) to the Commerce Department when it reauthorized SBA's independent existence for three years, albeit with a sharply trimmed budget.

And Congress extended daylight-saving time to start on the first, instead of the last, Sunday in April.

## Conrail

Five years after the Reagan administration proposed returning Conrail to the private sector, Congress agreed to sell the government's 85 percent share of the freight railroad. However, instead of the direct sale to another railroad that the administration had sought, the legislation enacted in 1986 mandated a public stock offering.

The administration reluctantly embraced the public offering after key House members refused to consider a Senate-passed bill (S 638) that called for Conrail to be sold for $1.2 billion to the administration's selected buyer, the Norfolk Southern Corp.

A key to passage of the final stock-sale legislation was the desperate search by members to find ways to raise revenue to avoid the spending cuts that might be required under the Gramm-Rudman-Hollings anti-deficit law (PL 99-177). The sale provisions were included in reconciliation legislation (HR 5300 — PL 99-509) cleared by Congress Oct. 17, 1986, with an estimated $2.2 billion in revenues from the sale to be included in the budgetary savings of the bill. *(Gramm-Rudman, p. 44; Conrail provisions, HR 5300, p. 55)*

The administration first had proposed selling the railroad in 1981 on the grounds that federal subsidies were not justified and that Conrail should be operated by the private sector. However, the system, created by Congress in 1975 from the ashes of the Penn Central railroad and six other failing railroads, became profitable in 1982 and remained so. Administration officials then argued that Conrail needed a partner, such as Norfolk Southern, to stay off federal subsidies. *(Background, Congress and the Nation Vol. VI, p. 291)*

But the problems that the plan faced after Department of Transportation (DOT) Secretary Elizabeth Hanford Dole Feb. 8, 1985, recommended the sale to Norfolk Southern showed that even a money-making Conrail could be hard to sell.

Strong opposition to the plan came from members from the Northeast and Midwest, where Conrail operated. They said the merger, creating the nation's largest railroad with about 33,000 miles of track, would reduce competition, service and employment. Other critics raised antitrust concerns and contended that at the proposed sales price of $1.2 billion, the government was giving away valuable taxpayer property.

After key opponents agreed to drop their threatened filibuster, the Senate Feb. 4, 1986, passed the bill to implement the sale to Norfolk Southern. However, a firestorm of criticism continued in the House.

Rep. John D. Dingell, D-Mich., chairman of the Energy and Commerce Committee, refused to consider the sale of Conrail to Norfolk Southern. He called instead for a sale to the public of stock in an independent Conrail.

Confronted by that formidable opposition and the probability that pending tax-overhaul legislation could make the merger less attractive, Norfolk Southern withdrew its bid Aug. 22. The administration then endorsed the stock offering plan the same day. *(Tax-overhaul measure, p. 79)*

### Senate Action

**Committee.** Legislation (S 638) to implement the sale of Conrail to Norfolk Southern Corp. was approved by the Senate Commerce, Science and Transportation Committee by a 12-5 vote April 30, 1985.

Larry Pressler, R-S.D., offered an amendment that would protect other railroads against loss of traffic by freezing current arrangements those railroads had with Conrail and Norfolk Southern. That would prevent the merged railroad from offering lower rates for shipments on its own tracks than for shipments that moved over two railroads.

Committee Chairman John C. Danforth, R-Mo., said Pressler's amendment could hurt shippers and might cause Norfolk Southern to withdraw its offer. The plan was defeated, 3-14.

# Commerce Leadership

President Reagan Aug. 10, 1987, nominated C. William Verity Jr., a former steel industrialist, to replace Malcolm Baldrige as secretary of commerce. The Senate Oct. 13 voted 84-11 to confirm Verity. *(Verity background, Cabinet profiles, p. 1044)*

Baldrige died July 25 from injuries suffered during rodeo practice. As the head of Commerce, Baldrige was credited with pressing the administration to respond to unfair trading practices abroad, while urging Congress to avoid passing protectionist trade laws. *(Baldrige background, Congress and the Nation Vol. VI, p. 1018)*

The 1985 nomination of Terrence M. Scanlon to be chairman of the Consumer Product Safety Commission (CPSC) was opposed by consumer groups. At his confirmation hearings, Joan Claybrook, president of Public Citizen, charged that Scanlon had used his staff to further anti-abortion and real estate activities. Scanlon denied the charges, but after a CPSC employee said she had performed such work many times, Scanlon acknowledged he had requested her to perform some tasks.

Sen. John C. Danforth, R-Mo., said an investigation by the General Accounting Office showed that while CPSC staff had run errands and typed letters relating to Scanlon's personal interests, the incidents had been infrequent and minor.

The nomination was blocked Dec. 19, 1985, and Majority Leader Robert Dole, R-Kan., agreed to put off a vote on Scanlon until Congress returned in 1986. Scanlon was confirmed as CPSC chairman July 15, 1986, by a 63-33 vote. He had served as interim chairman since January 1985.

The Senate Aug. 6, 1987, voted 81-17 to confirm David S. Ruder, a Northwestern University law school professor, to succeed John Shad as chairman of the Securities and Exchange Commission (SEC). Shad later was confirmed as ambassador to the Netherlands.

The Senate Banking Committee July 28 recommended Senate confirmation of Ruder by a 17-3 vote. But dissenting committee Chairman William Proxmire, D-Wis., said the SEC needed "a tough no-nonsense enforcer," and that Ruder had "no record of concern" about securities fraud or the enforcement of securities laws.

Although Ruder had written extensively about securities fraud, he lacked practical experience in law enforcement. He had worked on securities issues for law firms in Chicago and Milwaukee and served as dean of the law school at Northwestern University from 1977 to 1985.

Ruder was nominated June 17. The SEC chairman serves a five-year term.

As reported June 27, S 638 (S Rept 99-98) allowed the transportation secretary to sell Conrail to Norfolk Southern according to the terms of a "memorandum of intent" signed by DOT and Norfolk Southern officials Feb. 8.

The legislation would forgive approximately $3.2 billion that Conrail owed in return for government aid. It also removed other statutory conditions that would prevent a private owner from operating the railroad and gave antitrust protection to Norfolk Southern for merging Conrail with the Norfolk Southern's two railroads.

The committee adopted by voice vote a series of amendments by Danforth to tighten the terms of the sale. One amendment provided that the sale would not become final until the Justice Department approved arrangements by Norfolk Southern to give smaller railroads sections of track to ensure competition.

Others required the transportation secretary to establish a complaint procedure for shippers or other railroads and to notify Congress of any waiver of covenants that DOT negotiated to protect Conrail's operations.

The committee also adopted by voice vote two amendments by Wendell H. Ford, D-Ky., to give employees of any railroad who lost their jobs as a result of the sale first rights to be hired when a vacancy occurred.

**Floor.** S 638 was listed on the Senate schedule as a priority item for several days during the first week of December, but sale opponents, led by Howard M. Metzenbaum, D-Ohio, and Arlen Specter, R-Pa., blocked floor consideration by using a variety of parliamentary tactics.

Norfolk Southern officials said they would keep their offer open after Majority Leader Robert Dole, R-Kan., announced Dec. 20, the last day of the session, that S 638 would be the Senate's first order of business in 1986.

However, when Dole tried to bring the Norfolk Southern sale measure to the floor Jan. 21, 1986, several senators objected, and Dole filed a cloture petition to limit debate.

Opponents tried to keep the bill off the floor by filibustering the motion to consider it, even though they conceded that they did not have the votes to prevail. But minutes before a Jan. 23 vote of 90-7 to impose cloture and limit debate on a motion to proceed with the bill, opponents announced they would vote to stop their own filibuster.

Specter explained the decision by saying it was difficult to mount a filibuster early in the session on a procedural motion, such as one to consider a bill, "because the sense in the Senate is not to have delay." Senators were afraid, he said, that such tactics would lead to legislative gridlock when they faced the requirements of Gramm-Rudman.

The final straw came Jan. 30 when the Senate voted 70-27 to invoke cloture, and thus limit extended debate, on the bill itself.

Metzenbaum made a last-ditch effort to stall the bill by objecting that it would raise revenue for the government and thus, under the Constitution, must originate in the House. But a motion Feb. 4 by Danforth to table (kill) Metzenbaum's point of order carried on a 70-17 vote.

The Senate rejected efforts to alter Norfolk Southern's bid or to allow new bids to be considered and on Feb. 4 approved the Norfolk Southern sale. The Senate voted 54-39 to allow the railroad to buy Conrail for $1.2 billion.

The critics of the sale took some comfort in the vote, interpreting the 39 "nay" votes as a sign of significant congressional opposition to Norfolk Southern's offer.

Floor debate centered on charges that Norfolk Southern was getting a "sweetheart deal" because its $1.2 billion offer appeared lower than some others and because of significant tax advantages a buyer would gain by acquiring Conrail.

A group of investors organized by Morgan Stanley and Co., a New York investment banking firm, had offered $1.4 billion for Conrail. A third bid — for $1.65 billion — was made Dec. 17, 1985, by Allen & Co. Inc. and First Boston Corp.

Both before and after cloture was invoked, the Senate dispensed with a number of amendments aimed at significantly altering the terms of Norfolk Southern's bid or, in some cases, allowing other bids to be considered.

On a 53-39 vote, the Senate Jan. 29 tabled an amendment by Specter to accept a $1.4 billion offer from the Morgan Stanley group.

Also, the Senate Jan. 30:

• Tabled 56-37 an amendment by Alan J. Dixon, D-Ill., to subject the proposed Conrail sale to antitrust laws. Dixon said the amendment was needed to ensure the rights of smaller railroads and other parties to challenge anti-competitive aspects of the sale.

• Tabled 51-45 an amendment by Frank R. Lautenberg, D-N.J., to allow government jurisdictions to go to court seeking traffic rights for non-Conrail lines. The amendment was designed to protect the ports of New York and New Jersey, which relied heavily on Conrail.

• Tabled 64-32 an amendment by Metzenbaum that would direct DOT to solicit new purchase bids.

• Tabled 69-27 a Metzenbaum amendment that would repeal legal immunity for fiduciaries charged with protecting the interests of Conrail's workers. Metzenbaum charged that Norfolk Southern's bid would shortchange the employees, who owned 15 percent of Conrail, and that the fiduciaries should be legally responsible for their actions.

• Tabled 63-33 an amendment by John Heinz, R-Pa., that would limit tax deductions and other benefits that would flow to Norfolk Southern after purchasing Conrail.

• Accepted by voice vote an amendment by Pressler designed to protect regional railroads in the Midwest and elsewhere that were likely to be affected by Conrail's sale.

## House Action

The administration plan immediately ran into trouble in the House. Dingell's announcement of his opposition to selling Conrail to Norfolk Southern inflicted what proved to be a fatal blow to the proposal.

Dingell's principal concerns focused on the impact of a Conrail-Norfolk Southern merger on the quality and price of rail service in the Northeast and Midwest, on competition between rail carriers in those regions and on the jobs of Conrail employees.

He also questioned the adequacy of Norfolk's $1.2 billion offer and raised the possibility of a drain on the Treasury due to tax benefits accruing to Norfolk Southern as a result of its acquisition of Conrail.

Many shippers and labor groups echoed those concerns. Shippers were worried about the monopoly that an expanded Norfolk Southern might gain over their businesses, and labor unions representing railroad workers feared that the sale would eliminate jobs on Conrail lines.

Secretary Dole in a May 6 letter to Dingell called on Norfolk Southern to raise its offer from $1.2 billion to $1.9 billion and proposed giving the Interstate Commerce Commission (ICC) a veto over the transaction.

Norfolk Southern raised its bid to $1.9 billion, but the proposed merger did not advance in Dingell's committee. On Aug. 22, Norfolk Southern withdrew its offer, saying there was "no end in sight to the legislative impasse" and indicated pending tax-overhaul legislation could make the merger less attractive.

Dingell instead called for a new plan to keep Conrail independent and to give the public "a fair opportunity" to participate in the ownership by buying stock.

However, new controversies also threatened to block the return of the railroad to the private sector. Chief among them were efforts by shippers and rail labor groups to turn a Conrail bill into an omnibus measure to address their complaints of unfair treatment under the partial deregulation of the rail industry and the ICC.

Shippers charged, among other things, that the ICC allowed monopoly railroads to overcharge them, and railroad labor groups wanted to tighten certain job protection rules.

They calculated that the determination of members and the administration to act on Conrail before adjournment would make a Conrail bill an attractive vehicle to accomplish their legislative aims.

But their efforts drew strong opposition from the administration, the Senate and rail carriers. Opponents contended that the shippers' complaints were largely unjustified and departures from current laws and ICC practices would damage the industry's economic recovery that was fostered by deregulation.

**Subcommittee.** In the Sept. 16 markup by the Energy and Commerce Subcommittee on Commerce, Transportation and Tourism, Subcommittee Chairman James J. Florio, D-N.J., offered a package embracing a public offering for Conrail, labor-protection provisions covering short-line transactions and limited changes to the 1980 railroad deregulation law known as the Staggers Act (PL 96-448). *(Staggers Act, Congress and the Nation Vol. V, p. 336)*

Florio's proposal addressed complaints made by the shippers' coalition that the ICC was allowing monopoly railroads to overcharge "captive shippers" like themselves, who had no other rail alternatives available.

Norman F. Lent, R-N.Y., raised the administration's concern that the Conrail bill should not be linked to "extraneous" issues. But his amendment to drop everything except the Conrail sale provisions failed by a 9-9 vote.

W. J. "Billy" Tauzin, D-La., offered a substitute amendment that embraced Florio's Conrail and labor provisions but gave shippers more leverage in establishing before the ICC that rates should be reduced. It also would require the ICC to order rate reductions proportionate to declines in inflation. Over the protests of Florio, who said sweeping Staggers changes could cripple the rail industry, Tauzin's substitute was adopted 10-8.

**Committee.** At full committee markup Sept. 17, Dan Coats, R-Ind., offered an amendment striking the Staggers and labor provisions.

Proponents of the Coats amendment maintained that the deregulation law was vital to the health of Conrail and the rail industry. They also argued that Conrail sale legislation that reimposed new federal regulations on the rail industry would be frowned on by Wall Street and would reduce the proceeds of a public stock offering. And they pointed out that a broad range of shippers — including some food, chemical, steel and timber companies — were against any Staggers revisions.

But opponents said that shippers not subject to monopoly pricing paid lower prices because captive shippers were being overcharged and that the Conrail bill was virtually the only legislative vehicle left in the 99th Congress to address those concerns.

The Coats amendment failed 18-23. Lent, saying that it was "very clear that a clean bill cannot win today," then offered what he called a "compromise cleanup amendment," which was adopted 22-20. While keeping the labor-protection provision, the amendment dropped most Staggers changes.

The unnumbered bill, approved by voice vote, was sent to the Budget Committee for inclusion in pending budget reconciliation legislation (HR 5300).

The bill called for a stock offering, but the sale would be barred if it would not bring in at least $1.7 billion, and Conrail must give the government another $300 million in cash.

The committee also adopted 32-9 an amendment by Dennis E. Eckart, D-Ohio, that called for at least two investment banking firms to lead the management of the public sale. The subcommittee would not have required more than one lead bank.

The amendment appeared to secure a lead role not only for Goldman Sachs & Co., which under contract advised DOT on a Conrail sale, but for the Morgan Stanley group, which had attempted to organize a public stock offering.

Other major provisions of the committee bill:
- **Public Offering.** Required the DOT secretary, in consultation with the Treasury secretary, Conrail's chairman and the investment bankers, to determine that the proceeds of a stock sale would yield at least $1.7 billion. After the first stage of the sale, the 15 percent share of Conrail vested in the employee stock ownership plan would revert to the employees, who could sell or retain their shares.
- **Board of Directors.** Provided for a transition from Conrail's current board, which included some members appointed by DOT, to a board elected by public shareholders.
- **Protective Covenants.** For five years after enactment, Conrail must make capital expenditures averaging at least $350 million per year.

Dividend payments would be allowed only if Conrail met its capital expenditure requirement and even then, common stock dividends would be subject to limitations.

For the first three years, no takeover or breakup of Conrail would be allowed, and Conrail must maintain a cash balance of at least $250 million at the end of each fiscal year.
- **Ownership Limitations.** With a few exceptions, including one for the transportation secretary, no person could own more than 7.5 percent of Conrail for five years after enactment. Total foreign ownership would be limited to 20 percent, and no major railroad would be allowed to own more than 7.5 percent.

HR 5300 was passed by the House Sept. 24 by a vote of 309-106. The Senate, before passing by an 88-7 vote its reconciliation measure (S 2706) in the session that began Sept. 19, adopted a revenue-raising amendment calling for a public offering of Conrail stock.

## Conference, Final Action

A House-Senate conference on the Conrail sale provisions of the reconciliation bill stalled soon after it began.

Conferees Sept. 29-30 discussed several issues, including whether to set a minimum price for the sale of Conrail's stock and how many investment banking firms should manage the sale, but they came to no agreement.

The most contentious item was a House labor-protection requirement, which drew sharp criticism from senators, the Reagan administration and the rail industry. The House provision closed an exemption from job protection requirements that the ICC had provided since 1980 to sales of branch lines by major railroads to new carriers.

Some industry analysts said the House provision could be devastating to growth of the short-line, or branch-line, railroad sector. But rail labor spokesmen said workers needed protection from railroads that were accelerating layoffs, reducing severance pay and denying the rights of unions to bargain collectively on the deployment of workers.

The exemption for short-line transactions generally freed the new carrier of union work rules and allowed wide latitude in making job assignments, and severance pay to laid-off workers was not required.

The ICC argued that many sales would not take place without the exemption, resulting in the abandonment of low-density branch lines and the loss of service and jobs. The administration endorsed the exemption.

However, barring the exemption did not bring workers affected by short-line transactions under an existing ICC rule that required that workers affected by mergers or abandonments receive six years' pay and benefits, which averaged about $250,000 each. The committee bill set a cap of $25,000 to be paid by the seller for each short-line worker affected.

Some senators, including Pressler, said the labor provisions were potentially devastating to the short-line industry because they might raise the cost of an acquisition. Pressler was not a Conrail conferee but threatened to filibuster the labor-protection language.

Danforth argued Sept. 29 that the labor item and other House provisions not directly related to the railroad's sale should be dropped because they would subject the bill to a point of order on the Senate floor as being "extraneous matter" not linked to the budget. He said that it would be very difficult to find the 60 votes required to overturn a parliamentary ruling that the bill was out of order.

Strenuous opposition by the Senate finally caused the House to drop the labor provision.

Danforth also objected to setting a minimum price below which Conrail could not be sold. The House set a $1.7 billion minimum for the sale of stock and required that Conrail pay another $300 million to the government. The Senate set no minimum.

Danforth said the minimum might become a ceiling, with the public deciding that Conrail was worth no more than $1.7 billion. He suggested also that the $300 million cash payment was excessive.

House members proposed dropping the minimum and lowering the cash payment to $200 million. The transportation secretary would have the discretion of requiring an additional $100 million payment. The Senate agreed to this.

There were two other non-Conrail House provisions that were not particularly controversial. One would require agricultural shippers to disclose the terms of their contracts with railroads, and the other ratified an ICC ruling requiring that large railroads adequately pay small railroads for the use of the latter's boxcars. Both provisions were retained.

The conference agreement (H Rept 99-1012) was reached and approved by both chambers Oct. 17.

# 1985 Highway Authorization

For the first time in years, Congress in 1985 released federal highway funds to the states on time. At issue were normally routine bills that Congress was supposed to approve biennially by Oct. 1. The legislation in effect would release each state's share of the Highway Trust Fund for Interstate highway construction and for highway and transit projects that states substituted for previously planned Interstate projects.

However, the scheduled Oct. 1, 1983, release of funds was blocked when the required legislation became mired in controversies over matters such as local highway projects, mass transit funding and gasoline-tax distribution formulas. Because of the impasse, the 98th Congress approved a temporary measure that gave states only six-months' worth of funds for fiscal 1984. *(Background, Congress and the Nation Vol. VI, pp. 320, 321)*

By March 1985, when 45 states were "virtually bankrupt" and could not continue work on the Interstate system, Congress agreed to drop the divisive issues and cleared two bills making available funds covering the last half of fiscal 1984 and all of 1985 and 1986.

Upon passage, the Senate March 5 completed congressional action on a cost-estimate bill (HR 1251 — PL 99-4) that was stripped of controversies. It released $7.2 billion from the Highway Trust Fund for the second half of fiscal 1984 and all of 1985. Included was $5.3 billion for Interstate construction, $979 million for substitute projects and about $960 million to ensure that states received 85 percent of the gasoline and other road-related taxes they contributed to the trust fund.

Then, Sept. 19, the House passed, and thus cleared, another streamlined bill (S 1514 — PL 99-104) that released $4.8 billion for all of fiscal 1986, including $3.6 billion for Interstate construction, $538 million for substitute highway projects and $649 million to assure that states receive at least 85 percent of their contribution to the trust fund.

The key in both cases was acknowledgment by members that the prior disagreements had created chaos in their home states, delaying highway construction and costing jobs. House and Senate leaders promised that the more divisive issues could be debated during the consideration of legislation authorizing major highway programs, which would expire when the fiscal year ended on Sept. 30, 1986. *(Story, p. 364)*

## Background

In passing the bills, Congress technically approved estimates of the cost of the construction, called an Interstate Cost Estimate (ICE) and an Interstate Substitute Cost Estimate (ISCE).

The approval was supposed to be routine, but the ICE and ISCE bills had become vehicles for members to attach special demonstration highway projects.

Members especially liked the demonstration projects because they were financed completely with federal funds, compared with the 90 percent federal share for regular Interstate work. However, the demonstration projects were criticized for being unauthorized add-ons to the construction programs proposed by state highway departments and for straining the trust fund.

In 1985 the issue of the special projects continued to cause disagreement. One especially disputed proposal was a House-backed $2.5 billion highway and tunnel project in Boston that touched the district of House Speaker Thomas P. O'Neill Jr., D-Mass.

Another issue that returned to block the 1985 bill was the insistence of House Public Works and Transportation Chairman James J. Howard, D-N.J., that the House bill include an increase in funding authorizations for mass transit capital projects. One cent of the 5-cent 1982 gasoline-tax increase was earmarked for mass transit, and Howard contended more money was available than was anticipated originally.

The Senate Banking, Housing and Urban Affairs Committee, with jurisdiction over mass transit, did not want transit authorizations included in the highway bill.

## First Highway Bill: HR 1251

**Senate Action.** Before ordering an ICE/ISCE bill reported Jan. 29, the Senate Environment and Public Works Committee voted to limit overall highway spending and to drop all special demonstration projects.

The panel voted, 15-0, to approve spending cuts by rolling back the fiscal 1986 trust fund obligation ceiling by $1.7 billion, from $14.45 billion to $12.75 billion. The special projects deleted would cost another $153.6 million. The total would be $500 million less than the fiscal 1985 level.

The committee also voted to delete 14 demonstration projects contained in the bill, which were carried over from the 1984 Senate bill.

The panel approved two measures: S J Res 8, a simple release of the funds with no other provisions, and S 178, a more complex measure that contained some programmatic changes.

Both bills released funds for the overdue period and provided for the administrative release of funds in the future to avoid entanglement in the legislative process. They would free Interstate funds for fiscal 1986-87 and funds for projects substituted for Interstate work through 1986.

S 178 also included a controversial provision proposed by Lloyd Bensten, D-Texas, that would change the way some funds were distributed.

Under existing law, states were guaranteed a return of 85 percent of their tax contributions to the trust fund, but the computations excluded several major programs. Bentsen's change would include all highway money, with the result that Texas would receive more than $64 million extra in fiscal 1985.

S 178 also preserved a provision that would keep Illinois from losing a large amount of funds for one year. That provision was added in 1984 after the two Illinois senators mounted a filibuster on the Senate floor.

In addition, the bill would make several minor changes in highway programs, such as requiring that a small proportion of landscaping funds be spent on planting wildflowers and ending federal oversight of tolls charged at certain bridges.

The more complex S 178 was reintroduced as S 391 and the report (S Rept 99-2) was filed Feb. 5.

Floor debate took place in an unusual Saturday session Feb. 23; an impasse over farm aid had tied the chamber in knots the week of Feb. 18 and delayed bringing the highway bill to the floor. When the highway bill did come up, it whisked through without amendment by a vote of 94-0.

**House, Final Action.** On Feb. 27, the Public Works and Transportation Committee decided to excise all the extraneous provisions from its bill (HR 1251 — H Rept 99-11). The House passed the bill Feb. 28 by a vote of 392-4 and demanded that the Senate accept it without change. Members complained that insisting on some provisions in the Senate bill, such as reducing the trust fund obligation ceiling, could lead to months-long delays. Although some senators bristled at the ultimatum, they agreed not to amend it and cleared the measure by voice vote.

The final legislation did include a cost estimate for Interstate work in Speaker O'Neill's state of Massachusetts that some senators suspected might be an attempt to fund the controversial highway and tunnel project. Howard said the Massachusetts estimate merely preserved the status quo in a controversy between the state and the Department of Transportation over what portion of the project was eligible for federal financing.

### Second Highway Bill: S 1514

As reported by the Senate Environment and Public Works Committee July 29, 1985, S 1514 contained none of the demonstration projects or extraneous provisions of prior years. It was passed by the Senate by voice vote July 30.

Bypassing committee, the House cleared the measure by voice vote Sept. 19.

# 1986 Highway Authorization

Because House and Senate lawmakers failed to resolve disputes over a handful of controversies, legislation (HR 3129) to reauthorize virtually all major highway and mass transit programs died in the closing hours of the 99th Congress.

Congress adjourned Oct. 18, 1986, without finishing a conference on the bill. The programs had expired when the fiscal year ended Sept. 30.

Although more than $6 billion in previously allocated funds would be available to states in fiscal 1987, anticipated new funding of $14 billion accumulating in the Highway Trust Fund could not be spent. Congress worked quickly in 1987 to pass a highway reauthorization bill, overriding a presidential veto of the legislation. *(1987-88 action, p. 378)*

The House highway bill authorized a total of about $90 billion through fiscal 1991, including about $68 billion for highway construction programs, $1.5 billion for highway safety and $21 billion for mass transit. The Senate version authorized about $52 billion for highway programs through fiscal 1990 and more than $12 billion for transit through fiscal 1990.

In addition to differences in funding, there were sharp splits over a number of issues:

● A Senate plan to allow states to raise the speed limit to 65 mph on rural Interstate highways.

● Full federal funding for 100 special demonstration highway projects included in the House bill.

● A House plan to retain compensation to billboard owners for removal of billboards.

● How Interstate construction would be funded. The

House measure extended the Interstate construction program through fiscal 1993 and retained its status as a separate funding category. In a major policy departure proposed by the administration, the Senate wrapped Interstate construction into a new program that included funding for other types of construction and for the Interstate repair program.

Despite a flurry of meetings in the final hours of the session, lawmakers could not resolve their differences on the omnibus bill. They also failed to clear an alternative one-year bill (S 2951) backed by the Reagan administration to give states more flexibility in spending the more than $6 billion in unallocated funds.

In the fiscal 1987 omnibus appropriations bill (H J Res 738 — PL 99-591), Congress provided transit systems with $2 billion in grants. *(H J Res 738, p. 57)*

### House Action

**Committee.** As reported (H Rept 99-665) July 2 by the House Public Works and Transportation Committee, HR 3129 authorized approximately $13.9 billion annually for highways through fiscal 1991. It also set an annual ceiling on spending from the Highway Trust Fund of $12.6 billion.

The bill made no major changes in existing programs and authorized funds through fiscal 1993 to complete the Interstate Highway System. The measure did alter the formula by which highway repair funds were distributed to states. The proposed formula placed more emphasis on highway usage than on the number of miles of highway in each state, as the current formula did.

The measure cut funding for Interstate highways to $3.3 billion annually — a reduction of about $750 million. In addition, the bill set aside $5 billion in fiscal 1992 and 1993 to pay for the completion of the Interstate Highway System.

The committee approved almost 100 special demonstration projects at a five-year cost of more than $1 billion.

While authorizations for programs supported by the Highway Trust Fund totaled about $14.1 billion annually, the measure limited the actual obligation of funds to $12.6 billion annually.

**Floor.** The House Aug. 15 passed HR 3129 by a vote of 345-34.

On Aug. 6, the House narrowly defeated an effort to raise the 55 mph speed limit. The amendment, by Dave McCurdy, D-Okla., would establish a five-year test program permitting states to raise the speed limit to 65 mph on rural, remote sections of the Interstate system. Federal penalties enforcing the 55 mph speed limit would be suspended.

Proponents argued that few motorists actually complied with the 55 mph limit and that states — not the federal government — should be responsible for setting speed limits. They also contended that a decline in recent years in traffic fatalities was due not merely to the 55 mph limit but to improvements in roads and safety features of automobiles.

Opponents, however, said there was "overwhelming" evidence that the 55 mph speed limit had saved thousands of lives since it was enacted in 1974 at the height of the energy crisis.

The House narrowly rejected the McCurdy amendment on a **key vote of 198-218 (R 117-57; D 81-**

161). *(1986 key votes, p. 949)*

On the issue of billboards, the House Aug. 7 by 251-159 adopted an amendment by Bud Shuster, R-Pa., as a substitute for a more restrictive proposal advanced by E. Clay Shaw Jr., R-Fla. The Shuster proposal, which was endorsed by the leadership of the Public Works panel, froze the number of billboards on federal highways while continuing the policy of reimbursing the billboard industry with federal funds for signs that were taken down. The Shaw proposal would not require cash compensation for billboards that were removed.

On Aug. 15, leaders of the Public Works Committee lost 171-214 in a bruising fight over their motion to recommit the legislation to the committee with instructions to add a provision that would exempt the Highway Trust Fund from cuts mandated by the Gramm-Rudman-Hollings anti-deficit law (H J Res 372 — PL 99-177). *(Gramm-Rudman, p. 44)*

They argued that the trust fund was self-financed by road-related user fees and had never contributed to the federal deficit. But Appropriations and Budget committee leaders successfully countered that if trust fund programs were exempt from Gramm-Rudman cuts, a deeper slash would have to be made in the rest of the budget to reach the cuts required.

Also on Aug. 15, the House reversed itself on funding for a controversial Los Angeles mass transit project. On Aug. 7 an amendment by Henry A. Waxman, D-Calif., to strike the funds was adopted 210-201. But in a second vote Aug. 15, the House rejected the Waxman proposal 153-231.

## Senate Action

**Committee.** Trying to clear the way for quick floor action, the Senate Environment and Public Works Committee July 23 deferred several controversies before approving its highway bill (S 2405). The measure was reported (S Rept 99-369) Aug. 5.

Postponed items included changes in the 55 mph speed limit and funding authorizations for mass transit programs, which were under the jurisdiction of the Senate Banking, Housing and Urban Affairs Committee.

Citing budget concerns, the committee set the obligation ceiling governing spending for most federal highway programs at $12.35 billion annually for the next four fiscal years. In addition, about $800 million was authorized for emergency aid and to ensure that each state received at least a certain amount of funds.

The committee rejected, 5-8, an amendment by the chairman of the Environment and Public Works Subcommittee on Transportation, Steven D. Symms, R-Idaho, to raise the obligation ceiling to $13.125 billion, the current level. Symms argued that cash should not be kept in the Highway Trust Fund to reduce the federal deficit.

But Budget Committee Chairman Pete V. Domenici, R-N.M., a member of Environment and Public Works, insisted that it was not realistic to expect the Senate to increase the deficit or cut other programs to raise highway spending.

By 9-4, the panel adopted an amendment to speed up removal of billboards from the nation's highways. The amendment, offered by Chairman Robert T. Stafford, R-Vt., relieved states of their obligation to compensate sign owners in cash for removal of billboards, as required in a 1978 law (PL 95-599). The amendment allowed states to use other forms of compensation, such as giving sign own-

ers a limited lease for signs that otherwise would have to be torn down.

James Abdnor, R-S.D., argued that the amendment would devastate the tourism industry, particularly in rural states. But Stafford said that there were no funds for the federal government to help states pay for removal and that some method needed to be found to speed up sign removal, which was originally required by the 1965 Highway Beautification Act (PL 89-285). *(Congress and the Nation Vol. II, p. 476)*

There was little dispute over an amendment to control special highway projects. The Senate committee by voice vote approved a Symms amendment to give state officials control over the projects and to include the projects in the state's allocation. The net effect of the change would be to give state officials greater ability to shift funds between categories of federal aid for some projects.

To avoid referral of the bill to the Banking, Housing and Urban Affairs Committee, the panel approved by voice vote an amendment by Frank R. Lautenberg, D-N.J., to strike a provision that would shift some mass transit funds from urban states to rural ones.

The panel rejected, on a 7-7 tie vote, a Symms amendment to relax a 1982 requirement (PL 97-424) that 10 percent of federal highway contracts go to minority enterprises. A Symms amendment to eliminate the program was rejected by voice vote.

Symms also proposed that the minimum value of contracts governed by the 1931 Davis-Bacon Act, requiring federal contractors to pay prevailing wages, be raised from $2,000 to $500,000. The amendment was rejected 6-7.

An amendment to exempt a Hawaii road project from environmental laws, hotly opposed by environmentalists, failed to materialize. Stafford said it would be offered on the floor.

**Floor.** The Senate passed HR 3129 Sept. 24 by a vote of 99-0, after substituting the text of its bill for the House-passed measure.

The Senate authorized $52 billion for highways and more than $12 billion for mass transit for fiscal years 1987-90. It set an annual ceiling of $12.3 billion on money from the Highway Trust Fund that could be obligated for highways.

Transit authorizations were added when the Senate adopted by voice vote an amendment by the leadership of the Banking, Finance and Urban Affairs Committee. The amendment, which was not acted on formally by the panel, froze annual funding roughly at $2 billion for formula grants and $1 billion for discretionary grants.

An amendment by leaders of the Finance Committee, also adopted by voice vote, authorized taxes for the trust fund through fiscal 1992.

On Sept. 23, the first of two days of debate on the measure, the Senate by 56-36 adopted an amendment by Symms to permit states to raise the speed limit to 65 mph on rural Interstate highways.

Opponents of the Symms amendment, most of whom represented Eastern states, argued that the 55 mph speed limit saved lives as well as fuel. A motion to table (kill) the amendment failed 40-57.

Proponents said the 55 mph speed limit might make sense in the East but was inappropriate for the lightly traveled highways of the West. They also stressed that the Symms proposal applied only to rural Interstate roads — not to rural sections of other federal highways. The Senate defeated, 36-60, an amendment by Chic Hecht, R-Nev., that would allow a speed limit of 65 mph on rural portions of all federal highways.

President Reagan had endorsed efforts, including the Symms amendment, to "restore greater authority to the states" to raise the speed limit.

Other key proposals adopted by the Senate included those by:

● Symms, by 49-46, to increase from $2,000 to $250,000 the minimum value of contracts covered by Davis-Bacon.

The House kept the threshold at $2,000. An increase in the threshold was favored by highway contractors but opposed by labor groups.

● Lawton Chiles, D-Fla., by voice vote, to relax the ban that had existed for more than seven decades on using federal funds to build toll roads, although not as much as sought by the Reagan administration. The House retained the prohibition.

Under the amendment, tolls would not be allowed on Interstate roads, and states must bear 65 percent of the cost of toll projects. The state share on non-Interstate roads was currently 25 percent.

● Symms, by voice vote, to add 50 "priority" highway projects to the 20 special projects already contained in the bill.

● Symms motion, by 56-41, to table an amendment by Thad Cochran, R-Miss., to ban the use of imported cement and cement products in federal highway construction projects. The House bill contained a ban.

● Symms, by 65-32, to drop a provision allowing state and local governments to limit highway contracts awarded to firms doing business in South Africa. The House bill had a similar provision.

The Senate rejected 16-78 a motion to table an amendment by Daniel K. Inouye, D-Hawaii, to exempt a Hawaii Interstate project from a 1984 court injunction issued on environmental grounds. The plan was adopted by voice vote. The House exempted the project.

### Conference Action

Strong, divergent views over the two measures surfaced immediately, with key House members refusing to go to conference unless the Senate agreed to drop its speed-limit provision.

Leaders of the House Public Works Committee Sept. 26 offered to allow a state to raise the limit to 65 mph on rural Interstate highways if the state demonstrated a 65 percent compliance rate for seat-belt use and banned the use by motorists of radar detectors.

Sen. Stafford said the House "precondition" to a conference threatened to kill the legislation.

House-Senate conferees did meet after House members withdrew their demands, however, and tentatively agreed Oct. 3 to drop a Senate plan to end separate funding for Interstate highway construction.

Senators also indicated they might reject the administration-backed plan ending a ban on using federal funds to construct toll roads.

House conferees accepted a Senate proposal not to shift Interstate repair money from more rural states to more densely populated states.

Despite progress on some key issues, House and Senate conferees failed to resolve the larger disputes over such items as relaxing the 55 mph speed limit and federal funding for special demonstration projects.

# Transportation Authorizations

Several fiscal 1986 funding authorizations for transportation programs were included in deficit reduction legislation (HR 3128 — PL 99-272) cleared by Congress March 20, 1986. *(HR 3128, p. 40)*

HR 3128 contained a provision, opposed by members from Vermont and Wisconsin, that stiffened penalties for states that did not set 21 as the minimum drinking age.

The measure also slowed down spending from the Highway Trust Fund, which was supported by gasoline taxes and other road-related fees. But while spending from the trust fund counted in deficit calculations, money not spent remained in the fund and could not be used for other purposes.

And members rejected President Reagan's plan to cut off funding for Amtrak.

### Major Provisions

As signed into law April 7, 1986, HR 3128 included the following transportation provisions:

● **Amtrak.** Reauthorized the federally subsidized national passenger railroad (Amtrak) at $600 million in fiscal 1986, $606.1 million in 1987 and $630.3 million in 1988.

● Required Amtrak to use capital funds to make up any shortfall instead of reducing service or maintenance.

● Prohibited Amtrak from saving expenses by reducing service on trains that operated three times a week or less.

● Allowed Amtrak to compete for government-paid travel by federal employees.

● Raised from 50 percent to 61 percent the proportion of operating costs Amtrak was expected to pay out of revenues.

● Required Amtrak and rail labor groups to report to Congress on negotiations to change labor agreements in order to reduce Amtrak expenses.

● Allowed Amtrak to transport cars on its "Autotrain" between Virginia and Florida when the cars' drivers did not ride the train. Existing law required drivers to accompany their vehicles.

● Eliminated minimum standards on the number of passengers per mile Amtrak trains must carry, while preserving standards on minimum cost efficiency per passenger mile.

● Allowed Amtrak to discontinue or adjust service on commuter trains if they exceeded cost standards, unless states agreed to subsidize the service.

● Modified the criteria under which the Interstate Commerce Commission allocated costs between Amtrak and freight railroads for use of tracks in the Northeast corridor.

● **Local Rail Service Assistance.** Reauthorized the program of federal-state matching grants for planning and rehabilitation of rail facilities at $12 million in fiscal 1986, $10 million in 1987 and $8 million in 1988.

● **Highways.** Set a ceiling on obligations from the Highway Trust Fund at $13.125 billion in fiscal 1986, $13.525 billion in 1987 and $14.1 billion in 1988. The obligation ceiling had been set in 1982 (PL 97-424) at $14.45 billion for 1986, with no ceilings set for future years.

● Reduced fiscal 1986 authorizations for repair and replacement of Interstate highways by $175 million, for bridge replacement and repairs by $150 million and for primary federal highways by $75 million.

● Increased the maximum amount of emergency highway aid for natural disasters or failures in calendar 1985 from $30 million to $55 million.

● Reprogrammed existing spending authority to allow up to $65 million to be spent for construction of three bridges over the Ohio River.

● **Minimum Drinking Age.** Provided that fiscal 1986 federal highway funds withheld from states for failure to enact a minimum drinking age of 21 could not be recovered by passage of such a law after Sept. 30, 1988. Funds would permanently be withheld for fiscal years 1989 and beyond for states that did not enact such a law. *(Background, Congress and the Nation Vol. VI, p. 322)*

● Allowed states to raise their minimum drinking age to 21 with "grandfather" clauses that would not take away the right to drink from those who currently had it.

## NTSB Authorization Veto

President Reagan Nov. 4, 1986, pocket-vetoed a bill (HR 4961) that would authorize $76.4 million in fiscal 1987-89 for the National Transportation Safety Board (NTSB).

The president called the authorizations "excessive" and objected to a requirement that the Federal Aviation Administration establish a clearinghouse to provide information on liability insurance to public airports. Saying he was not "unsympathetic" to the problems of rising premiums, Reagan argued that it would be "inequitable and unwise" for the government to address the issue on an industry-by-industry basis. Proponents argued that smaller airports did not have the staff to stay on top of the insurance market.

The bill, reported from the House Public Works and Transportation Committee Sept. 18 (H Rept 99-835, Part I), was passed Sept. 30 by the House by voice vote. The Senate, whose Commerce, Science and Transportation Committee had reported a similar bill Sept. 10 (S 2807 — S Rept 99-437), added the liability insurance provisions and passed HR 4961 by voice vote Oct. 10. The House accepted the Senate change Oct. 16, clearing the measure for the president.

Funding of $22.2 million was provided for NTSB for fiscal 1987 by the omnibus spending bill (H J Res 738 — PL 99-591). *(H J Res 738, p. 57)*

## Coast Guard Authorization

Congress Oct. 16, 1986, cleared a bill (HR 4208 — PL 99-640) authorizing $2.15 billion in fiscal 1987 funding for the U.S. Coast Guard, plus $364 million in retirement pay. The bill, signed Nov. 10 by President Reagan, increased Coast Guard spending authority by $190 million over the president's request of $1.96 billion, while rejecting the administration's perennial call for user fees to help finance certain Coast Guard activities. The administration had requested $354 million for retirement pay.

The House Merchant Marine and Fisheries Committee reported the bill (H Rept 99-547) April 18. The full House May 6 unanimously passed HR 4208 on a 374-0 vote.

The version reported Oct. 6 by the Senate Commerce, Science and Transportation Committee (S Rept 99-530)

diminished House funding levels, deleted a section the administration opposed that restricted the Coast Guard's ability to "contract out" — contract with private firms to provide services the Coast Guard had performed itself — and included an amendment revising the Coast Guard's principal maritime drug enforcement law. The last item was added to the 1986 omnibus drug bill (HR 5484 — PL 99-570). *(Story, p. 723)*

The Senate Oct. 16 passed its version of HR 4208 by voice vote; later that day, the House by voice vote agreed to the revisions and sent the bill to the president.

As signed by the president, HR 4208 authorized $1.86 billion for Coast Guard operating expenses, including law enforcement, such as stopping drug smuggling and illegal immigration and search-and-rescue missions.

The bill provided $267 million for procurement, construction and maintenance of vessels, aircraft, shore units and navigation aids; and $20 million for research and development.

## Maritime Programs Veto

President Reagan Oct. 28, 1986, pocket-vetoed legislation (HR 4175) that would authorize $400 million in fiscal 1987 for maritime programs.

However, separate legislation already signed by the president (H J Res 738 — PL 99-591), the fiscal 1987 continuing appropriations resolution, provided funding for maritime programs at virtually the same level proposed by the authorization. *(H J Res 738, p. 57)*

The president said he based his decision chiefly on the refusal of Congress to repeal the authority in existing law for federal loan guarantees to shipbuilders for the construction of commercial vessels. Concerned about defaults that required the government to pay off some of the guaranteed loans, the Reagan administration in its fiscal 1987 budget request asked to drop the program. Instead, the administration encouraged the maritime industry to rely on the private credit market as its source of capital.

Congress disputed the president's rationale for phasing out the program. Supporters said the guarantees were necessary to bolster the financially troubled industry.

Reagan also said he objected to authorization of $9 million in financial assistance for six state-run merchant marine training schools during a time of national fiscal austerity.

But supporters said that the schools played a valuable role in training personnel to be available as reserve forces in case of military emergency.

The omnibus spending bill continued the loan program and the funding for the state schools.

**Legislative History.** The House Merchant Marine and Fisheries Committee reported HR 4175 (H Rept 99-551) April 22, and the House passed it June 17 by a vote of 367-29.

The only change from the committee bill was an amendment that dropped a provision asserting the primary role of the Maritime Administration, instead of the Navy, in the management of the National Defense Reserve Fleet. The provision had met with objections from Charles E. Bennett, D-Fla., chairman of the Armed Services Subcommittee on Seapower.

The Senate Commerce, Science and Transportation Committee reported a similar version of the bill (S Rept 99-407) Aug. 14. The Senate passed the bill by voice vote

Oct. 8, and the House cleared it by accepting the Senate version Oct. 14.

The bulk of the funding in the final bill, $320 million, was for "operating differential" subsidies to U.S. shippers to make up the difference between their operating costs and the lower operating costs of foreign competitors. Labor costs typically were much higher for U.S. shippers.

The omnibus spending bill also provided $320 million for fiscal 1987 operating subsidies.

## Maritime Safety Laws Veto

Citing excessive costs and unwarranted special-interest provisions, President Reagan Feb. 14, 1986, vetoed a bill (HR 2466) that would make various revisions in laws affecting the U.S. Coast Guard and incorporate a number of private relief provisions. Congress made no attempt to override the veto.

When the bill was introduced in May 1985, it was designed primarily to correct several omissions and errors in a 1983 reorganization of maritime safety laws (PL 98-89). But by the time it cleared Congress Jan. 29, 1986, it had picked up a broad array of exemptions and amendments objectionable to the administration.

One of the changes in HR 2466 was to extend for five years an exemption from certain fire-safety requirements that had been granted to a paddle-wheel riverboat operating on the Mississippi and Ohio rivers. The boat, the *Delta Queen,* was built in 1926 and was one of two authentic paddle-wheel passenger steamboats in existence in the country, according to the House Merchant Marine and Fisheries Committee July 18, 1985, report on the bill (H Rept 99-207).

The *Delta Queen's* wooden superstructure, however, put it at odds with international boating-safety law and Coast Guard safety standards; to continue operating, it required a congressional exemption. The existing exemption was due to expire Nov. 1, 1988. The provision in HR 2466 would push the date to Nov. 1, 1993, and require the *Delta Queen* to notify potential passengers that the boat did not meet fire-safety standards.

When the House passed HR 2466 by voice vote on July 29, the administration objected to three sections of the bill: the *Delta Queen* exemption; a waiver of personnel ceilings at two Coast Guard repair facilities; and a prohibition on "contracting out" for the positioning of navigational aids in the New Jersey Intracoastal Waterway. The last provision contradicted the administration's desire to "privatize" such functions.

The Senate roughly doubled the number of provisions in the bill, passed it by voice vote on Dec. 19 and returned it to the House, where it was cleared by voice vote.

In his veto message, Reagan objected to two of the sections previously singled out, as well as others that would:

● Waive restrictions in maritime laws for several vessels. Those provisions also were contained in a bill (HR 739 — PL 99-307) that the president signed May 19, 1986.

● Require that any funds spent by the Coast Guard to alter a railroad bridge in Portland, Ore., be subject to Davis-Bacon Act prevailing-wage provisions, a change that Reagan said would add about $1.5 million to the cost of the project.

● Establish two Coast Guard advisory committees, one to address safety matters with respect to oil and gas development on the Outer Continental Shelf, the other regarding the safety of and insurance for fishing industry vessels.

## Airport Security

In response to the hijacking of a Trans World Airlines (TWA) jet with 40 Americans on board and to other terrorist acts, the House and Senate in 1985 passed legislation clarifying federal authority to assist foreign governments in improving airport security.

The measure (HR 2796), however, was not enacted, in deference to the anti-terrorist provisions contained in the foreign aid authorization bill (S 960 — PL 99-83) cleared by Congress July 31, 1985, according to an aide for the House Public Works and Transportation Subcommittee on Aviation. *(Story, p. 186)*

The House passed HR 2796 by voice vote June 19, five days after TWA flight 847 was hijacked following takeoff from the Athens, Greece, airport. The bill required the Department of Transportation to study an airport's security and notify the public within 120 days if security risks had not been improved.

The Senate July 25 by a vote of 96-0 approved a broader version (S Rept 99-113) that allowed the transportation secretary to bar U.S. carriers from using an airport identified as a security risk.

The foreign aid bill was more stringent, authorizing a boycott of foreign airports that failed to meet security standards and a cutoff of foreign aid to countries where such airports were located.

## Airport Transfer Agreement

In the final days of the 99th Congress, Congress approved legislation backed by the Reagan administration to ease federal control of two metropolitan Washington, D.C., airports.

By a 250-135 vote, the House in the early hours of Oct. 16, 1986, adopted an amendment to the continuing appropriations resolution (H J Res 738 — PL 99-591) that modified a Senate plan to lease Washington-Dulles International Airport and National Airport to a regional authority. The Senate agreed to the changes later that day. *(H J Res 738, p. 57)*

The Senate-passed version of H J Res 738 called for a regional authority to lease the airports for $150 million over 50 years. The House amendment adjusted the payments to inflation. Assuming a 4 percent annual inflation rate, the lease would cost $460 million.

The House also attached a provision that extended the legal range of non-stop flights out of National Airport from 1,000 miles to 1,250 miles. The extension would permit non-stop flights to Dallas and Houston, a change sought by House Majority Leader Jim Wright, D-Texas.

The leasing plan also called for a congressional review panel that could veto the decisions of the regional authority. The regional group could issue bonds to raise funds for improvements.

**Previous Action.** The Senate had added the airport-lease proposal to the continuing resolution, basing it on a bill (HR 5398) approved Aug. 11 by the House Public Works and Transportation Subcommittee on Aviation.

On April 11, the Senate had passed by a 62-28 vote its own measure (S 1017 — S Rept 99-193) to shift management of the two airports to a regional authority. The Senate formally took up S 1017 March 25 after voting 66-32 to cut off a five-day filibuster on a motion to consider it. Passage came after eight days of debate in which critics unsuccessfully tried to increase the $47 million price of the transaction, and Maryland senators tried with only modest success to change the membership and powers of the authority to protect the interests of Baltimore-Washington International Airport.

## Air Safety Violations

The Senate May 6, 1986, passed by voice vote a bill (S 1750) that would allow the Federal Aviation Administration (FAA) to levy stiffer civil penalties against commercial airlines for safety violations.

The full House did not act on a similar bill (HR 4403 — H Rept 99-796, Part I), reported by the Judiciary Committee Aug. 15, and the legislation died when the 99th Congress adjourned.

As passed by the Senate, the administration-backed measure would raise the maximum penalty per violation to $10,000 from the $1,000 limit established in 1938. The bill also would create a civil penalty of $1,000 for failing to notify the FAA of proposed construction that could pose a hazard to the airways.

S 1750 was reported (S Rept 99-286) April 24 by the Commerce, Science and Transportation Committee.

## Airline Worker Protection

The Senate did not act on a House-passed bill (HR 4838 — H Rept 99-822) that would require the transportation secretary to require labor protection in airline merger cases to ensure that a merger was fair to employees. The bill died at the end of the 99th Congress.

As approved by the House on a 329-72 vote Sept. 16, 1986, the bill directed the secretary to investigate merger applications to determine if the merger would reduce jobs, or adversely affect wages or working conditions, including the seniority of employees. The bill required the secretary to take whatever steps deemed appropriate "to mitigate such adverse consequences," unless the secretary found that the projected costs of protection would exceed the "anticipated financial benefits of the transaction."

It also put the burden of proof on the proponents of the merger to show that there would be no adverse employment consequences or that the projected costs of protection would be excessive.

## Air First Aid

After years of prodding by congressional and consumer critics, the federal government in 1985 began addressing complaints that the medical supplies on commercial flights were inadequate.

The Federal Aviation Administration (FAA) began drafting rules to require planes to carry more extensive supplies, including diagnostic equipment and certain drugs. The Senate July 31 approved legislation (S 63 — S Rept 99-93) that would give the agency six months after enactment to write final rules. However, House inaction caused the bill to die at the end of Congress.

Proponents of the legislation said the supplies that planes currently were required to carry were useless in dealing with conditions needing immediate treatment, such as heart attacks. Airline spokesmen said the best way to handle medical emergencies in flight was to land quickly and get the passenger appropriate medical care.

The airline industry fought the proposal, but faced with the likelihood that the requirement would be imposed, it urged Congress to provide protection against lawsuits arising from the improper use of the equipment.

The FAA did not have the authority to propose rules to relieve individuals of liability if they used the medical kit to assist others. Airline officials argued that without such protections against lawsuits, people would not take the risk of using the medical kits.

As reported June 27 by the Senate Commerce Committee, S 63 granted immunity to physicians, crew members and the airlines, unless medical supplies were used recklessly or with gross negligence. But the full Senate adopted an amendment that dropped the "good Samaritan" protections for airlines.

As approved, S 63 provided protections against lawsuits only to nurses, paramedics and crew members. Physicians were not exempted from liability because it was expected that they would be protected by malpractice insurance.

## Discrimination Loophole

Addressing complaints of groups representing handicapped individuals about a Supreme Court decision, Congress Sept. 18, 1986, cleared legislation (S 2703 — PL 99-435) that prohibited airlines from discriminating against the handicapped.

The Supreme Court June 27 ruled that section 504 of the Rehabilitation Act of 1973, which banned discrimination against the handicapped in "any program or activity" receiving federal funds, did not apply to commercial airlines because they did not receive such funds directly. The decision in *U.S. Department of Transportation v. Paralyzed Veterans of America* touched off a storm of protest from groups claiming that the ruling would sanction widespread discrimination by airlines against handicapped people solely on the basis of their ability. *(Supreme Court decision, p. 807)*

S 2703 amended the Federal Aviation Act to state that no air carrier could discriminate against individuals because they were handicapped.

The bill had been reported (S Rept 99-400) Aug. 13 by the Senate Commerce, Science and Transportation Committee and passed the full Senate by voice vote Aug. 15. The House Public Works and Transportation Committee was discharged Sept. 8, and the House cleared the Senate measure upon passage by voice vote Sept. 18. It was signed by the president Oct. 2.

## Railroad Safety Authorization

Both chambers passed legislation in 1985 aimed at strengthening U.S. rail safety programs, but members did not resolve differences over the measure and the bill died at the end of the 99th Congress.

The bill (S 1080 — S Rept 99-76), reported May 30 by the Senate Commerce, Science and Transportation Committee, passed the Senate by voice vote June 6. It authorized funding of $32.2 million in each of fiscal 1986 and 1987.

The version approved by the House Sept. 5 had been reported May 23 by the House Energy and Commerce Committee (HR 2372 — H Rept 99-147). The House amended its text to S 1080 before passing the Senate bill.

The House bill contained several provisions opposed by the Reagan administration and not passed by the Senate, including one that would allow railroad employees or their union to sue the Transportation Department to enforce safety laws.

The House bill authorized $40.9 million in fiscal 1986 and $42.9 million in 1987. The House rejected, 106-254, an amendment to cut $6.3 million over fiscal 1986-87 for reimbursements to states that conducted their own safety programs. The administration had not requested the funds.

# Other Legislation

### Sports Team Bill

The Senate Commerce, Science and Transportation Committee approved a bill to make it harder for professional sports teams to abandon one city in search of greater profits in another, but there was no further congressional action and the measure died.

The bill (S 259), which would give professional sports leagues the authority to control franchise shifts, was approved April 2, 1985, by a vote of 10-6 after two amendments to limit the power of the National Football League (NFL) to control television rights were defeated. The report (S Rept 99-69) was filed May 21.

Supporters said S 259, which was sought by the NFL, would protect communities from losing teams that were a valuable source of civic pride. Foes, including the United States Football League, argued that it would give too much power to the dominant NFL.

### Titanic Memorial

The House approved a bill Dec. 2, 1985, encouraging efforts to designate the shipwreck of the luxury liner *Titanic* as an international maritime memorial and to fend off unwarranted salvage.

The measure (HR 3272 — H Rept 99-393) would direct the secretary of state to negotiate with other nations to develop an agreement providing for the designation of the shipwreck as a memorial and for guidelines governing research, exploration and salvage. It was reported by the Merchant Marine and Fisheries Committee Nov. 21.

No action was taken by the Senate, and the bill died at the end of Congress.

# Product Liability

In the 99th Congress, the rhetoric on the liability "crisis" was not matched by action. An effort to pass a sweeping product liability bill that would set federal standards governing product liability lawsuits died on the Senate floor after a brief filibuster. Product liability legislation also stalled in the 100th Congress. *(1987-88 action, p. 398)*

Prospects for the bill faded June 26, 1986, after a sharply divided Senate Commerce, Science and Transportation Committee narrowly approved legislation (S 2760 — S Rept 99-422) that imposed limits on certain court awards to alleged victims of unsafe products. Critics said there should not be monetary restrictions on recovery for damages for "pain and suffering."

Despite the bill's poor chances for success, proponents, including Bob Kasten, R-Wis., took their fight to the floor, contending that would increase their chances of enacting legislation in 1987.

But with Ernest F. Hollings, D-S.C., prepared to filibuster the bill, the measure got only as far as approval of a motion to consider before Majority Leader Robert Dole, R-Kan., pulled it from the floor. Hollings, a former trial lawyer, blamed rising insurance costs on the industry, not on any problems with the system of federal and state tort laws. He also contended that common law tradition and state law should govern lawsuits, not a federal standard.

Kasten said that the Sept. 25 vote of 84-13 in favor of a motion to proceed with floor consideration showed "tremendous support" for new legislation and hoped legislation would be enacted in the 100th Congress.

There was no action in the House on product liability legislation, other than hearings.

The only major insurance legislation cleared by Congress was a bill (S 2129) making it easier for businesses, cities and professional groups to band together to insure themselves. *(Story, p. 372)*

### Background

The squeeze on insurance availability and affordability was concentrated in property-casualty insurance, which covered about a third of the insurance market. Within that area, it focused on commercial lines of insurance, where companies said their losses had occurred.

The industry's first response to the situation was to raise prices, which the industry contended had been cut during the late 1970s to attract funds to invest while interest rates were high. While 1985 premiums increased an average of 21 percent overall for property-casualty insurance, price hikes in certain industries were far greater. Other groups, such as day-care centers, nurse-midwives and hazardous waste disposers went through periods when no insurance was available.

Insurers were particularly wary of businesses with a "long tail of liability" — those in which an injury or illness could be discovered years after the event. Even though the policy had lapsed, the insurer was responsible for paying damages.

Insurers and industry leaders blamed the skyrocketing cost of liability insurance on the tort-law system. Insurers said that court judgments dramatically increased their costs by making it too easy for injured parties to win large damage awards. Industry leaders said that judges made insurers responsible for incidents that should not have been covered, that juries awarded outrageous sums to victims and that attorneys fueled the situation with their demands for large fees.

Insurers proposed a number of reforms. They wanted to limit awards for pain and suffering, a subjective loss going beyond medical bills and lost wages; to hold down the percentages of awards that go to attorneys; and to make each party in a multi-party lawsuit responsible only for its share of fault.

Those legal questions were the purview primarily of

states, and insurance companies pressured state courts and legislatures to make changes. Impatient with the slow pace of reform on a state-by-state basis, however, insurance companies pressed the federal government to take over in certain areas. That was notably true for product liability, where insurance represented up to 30 percent of the purchase price of some products.

Since the late 1970s, manufacturers and insurers had pushed to establish federal standards that would override state tort laws in lawsuits seeking damages caused by commercial products. They said that was necessary because products were distributed nationally, and the inconsistency of state laws made it impossible to predict losses. But legislation had been blocked by trial lawyers, consumer groups and states' rights advocates.

One idea that surfaced on the federal level was to set up alternative systems to compensate victims without the expense and delay of lawsuits. Under those systems, injured people could claim compensation for losses, but they could not receive payments for pain and suffering or punitive damages. Disputes would be settled by binding arbitration.

Many industry critics supported the idea, but one objection was that people using the alternative system would be required to give up their right to sue. Yet they might still need attorneys — paid from their own funds — to bargain effectively with large companies during settlement negotiations.

Insurance companies made little effort to obtain any sweeping federal changes in all tort laws or in federal laws that govern claims against the government.

Critics of the industry were extremely skeptical of the claim that rising court judgments were responsible for the insurance industry's problems. While insurers frequently pointed to a few instances of court judgments that seemed exceptional, critics said the companies produced no evidence to demonstrate that that was common.

Despite the insurance industry's massive ability to collect statistics, it did not publish data on the number of claims, the number going to trial, the average amount of punitive damages and the average settlement.

## Legislative History

Revision of product liability laws was fiercely contested in the 97th and 98th Congresses by manufacturers who sought a federal law, and trial lawyers, unions, consumer groups, state judges and attorneys general who opposed most changes. *(Congress and the Nation Vol. VI, pp. 269, 285)*

During the 99th Congress, members continued to hear complaints from manufacturers, doctors, municipal governments, hazardous waste disposers, truckers, tavern owners, day-care providers, pharmaceutical companies and other businesses that faced huge premium increases for liability insurance.

But while the rhetoric heated up and hearings were held, it was not clear what Congress could do to alleviate the problems of either the insurance industry or its customers.

Insurance was unfamiliar territory for Congress. The industry long had been exempted from federal regulation. And the McCarran-Ferguson Act of 1945 (PL 79-15) exempted it from antitrust laws. *(Congress and the Nation Vol. I, p. 454)*

**Senate Committee.** In May 1985 the Senate Commerce, Science and Transportation Committee considered legislation (S 100) sponsored by Kasten that pre-empted state laws to provide uniform federal standards to be applied in state courts. The key provision in S 100 required plaintiffs suing a manufacturer for injuries caused by a product to prove negligence by the manufacturer. Most state laws, to one degree or another, did not require such proof.

However, the committee failed to approve the bill when it was blocked by an 8-8 tie vote.

Citing an explosion in lawsuits that had produced a crisis affecting virtually every segment of society, the Reagan administration April 30, 1986, sent to Congress three legislative proposals to revise personal injury laws. Kasten introduced these proposals as amendments to S 100.

John C. Danforth, R-Mo., chairman of the Commerce Committee, also introduced a product liability bill (S 1999) late in 1985, which he continually revised in an effort to reach consensus and unveiled May 12, 1986.

During a June 12 committee session, Kasten, Danforth and Slade Gorton, R-Wash., worked out a compromise package of changes to product liability laws. The package (S 2760) was approved by the Commerce Committee on a 16-1 vote. The negative vote was cast by Hollings.

During committee markup on June 19, Kasten offered two amendments to the compromise legislation. The first amendment, which incorporated the administration proposals, limited contingency fees charged by lawyers representing plaintiffs who claim injuries from unsafe products. The amendment was defeated by a 5-12 vote.

A second Kasten amendment to establish a federal standard of liability that would require a plaintiff to prove the manufacturer was negligent also was defeated, 6-10. Danforth and Gorton both voted against the amendments. Arguing against fee restrictions, Danforth said the federal government had no business regulating prices in the legal marketplace.

Gorton listed three objections to the liability standard. It would, he said, fail to promote predictability in the legal system, since states would interpret the standard in varying ways; it would stir opposition from state legal officials; and it would make passage of legislation more difficult.

However, the apparent consensus of the 16-1 vote eroded in subsequent days, with several members sharply critical of a provision crafted by Danforth setting a $250,000 limit on court awards for pain and suffering. On June 26, the panel ordered the measure reported by a 10-7 vote.

The cap, contained in an expedited settlement system that Danforth labeled the heart of the Commerce package, would apply if a plaintiff rejected a pretrial settlement offer from a defendant. The Danforth plan also called for penalties against defendants who turned down offers from plaintiffs.

Although a delegation of manufacturers June 25 had urged Danforth to report legislation without the $250,000 cap and to aim for a compromise on settlement incentives that would be offered on the floor, Danforth told his colleagues that he was reluctant to eliminate the cap without substituting an equally powerful settlement incentive. No one on the committee, Danforth said, had presented an alternative that would do as much to resolve disputes in advance of a costly and time-consuming trial.

Consumer groups blasted the Commerce Committee product. They were opposed not just to the cap but to a provision sponsored by Larry Pressler, R-S.D., that restricted joint and several liability to economic losses.

The package approved by the committee:

● Required that state regulators share with the secretary of commerce data reported to them by insurance companies. Companies would be required to indicate whether compensation to claimants represented economic or noneconomic losses. Reporting also would be required from risk retention groups and self-insured manufacturers.

● Allowed punitive damages only if the plaintiff established by clear and convincing evidence the defendant's "conscious, flagrant indifference" to the safety of those who might be harmed by a product. Mere negligence, or imprudence, would not be sufficient justification for punitive damages.

● Established a "government standards" defense against punitive damages that barred award of punitive damages for injuries caused by a drug that received pre-marketing approval from the Food and Drug Administration or by an aircraft-related product certified by the Federal Aviation Administration.

● Permitted a defendant to escape liability if the plaintiff was under the influence of drugs or alcohol and was more than 50 percent responsible for the injury.

● Set a "statute of repose" that limited the length of time for which a manufacturer could be held liable.

● Established sanctions for attorneys who made frivolous claims or prolonged a trial.

● Set an expedited settlement procedure that allowed either the defendant or the plaintiff to make a settlement offer. The offer would be limited to the plaintiff's net economic loss, plus a $100,000 "dignitary" payment if the plaintiff had experienced particularly severe pain and suffering.

Net economic losses included out-of-pocket expenses, such as medical bills, less non-court benefits, such as workers' compensation. Dignitary losses represented pain and suffering arising from the death of a parent, spouse or child; serious and permanent disfigurement; loss of a limb or organ; or serious and permanent impairment of a bodily function.

If a plaintiff rejected an offer, the plaintiff's recovery would be limited to net economic loss plus $250,000 when the court found that a dignitary loss had occurred. In cases in which there was no dignitary loss, transitory pain and suffering would be capped at twice the plaintiff's recovery for economic loss or $50,000, whichever was less. Punitive damages would not be included in either cap.

If a defendant rejected a plaintiff's offer, and the court award at least equaled the rejected offer, the defendant would be liable for up to $100,000 of the plaintiff's attorneys' fees and costs from the time the offer was rejected.

The measure, which was finally numbered S 2760, was reported from the Commerce Committee Aug. 14.

**Senate Floor.** The bill, however, got only as far as the agreement of a motion to proceed with floor consideration.

After the vote Sept. 25, Majority Leader Dole yanked the measure from the floor because Hollings was prepared to filibuster. Dole had supported the measure and pushed for a floor vote.

Earlier in the day, a Hollings filibuster on the motion to take up the bill was cut off by a 97-1 vote to invoke cloture and limit debate. The filibuster began Sept. 17 when Kasten first tried to bring up the bill, and action was postponed until Sept. 23, when a cloture petition was filed.

# Risk Retention

Legislation (S 2129 — PL 99-563) that would make it easier for businesses, professionals and other groups to form cooperatives to purchase liability insurance was cleared by Congress Oct. 9, 1986.

The bill incorporated a House provision permitting states to require "risk retention groups" to show they were financially sound. Concern had been expressed by some members that groups in a hazardous financial condition might escape notice of state regulators.

Under the bill, a risk group chartered to operate in at least one state would not have to obtain a charter to operate in any other states. The bill would allow cooperatives to purchase most types of liability insurance, except for personal insurance such as homeowner's or auto.

The legislation broadened a 1981 law (PL 97-45) that allowed the formation of risk groups to provide product liability insurance only. A number of groups that had difficulty obtaining liability insurance, such as medical personnel, campaigned for the bill. Although some insurance companies did not welcome competition from risk groups, few actively opposed the legislation. *(1978 law, Congress and the Nation Vol. VI, p. 269)*

## Legislative History

The Senate July 17 voted 96-1 in favor of a new version of a bill approved March 27 by the Commerce, Science and Transportation Committee (S Rept 99-294). The new version was a compromise between state insurance regulators and potential insurance purchasers that would strengthen the powers of the regulators over risk groups.

The Senate voted 69-27 to table (kill) an amendment that would require certain qualifying states to establish guaranty funds to pay claims in the event a risk group became insolvent.

The House by voice vote passed the bill Sept. 23, amending it to include its state regulators' provision. The Energy and Commerce Committee had reported a bill (HR 5225 — H Rept 99-865) Sept. 23. The House substituted the text of HR 5225 for the Senate-passed language.

The Senate Oct. 6 accepted a compromise version of the House changes that had been worked out by House and Senate staff. Final action came when the House by voice vote Oct. 9 accepted minor amendments the Senate had approved Oct. 6. The president signed the legislation Oct. 27.

# SBA Reauthorization

A three-year reauthorization of the Small Business Administration (SBA) was included in the fiscal 1986 deficit reduction bill cleared March 20, 1986 (HR 3128 — PL 99-272).

Conferees on the bill rejected the Reagan administration's efforts to kill the SBA, but they eliminated some programs and sharply trimmed funding for others.

The legislation abolished general direct loans to small businesses, retaining only those targeted to the handicapped, disabled and Vietnam War veterans and minorities. In addition, the bill barred farmers from receiving disaster loans beginning in fiscal 1986 and dropped a non-physical disaster loan program that had been used to assist firms along the Mexican border that suffered financial loss because of the devaluation of the peso.

## Legislative History

**Administration Proposal.** The administration plan would transfer some SBA functions, such as minority set-asides and advocacy, which helped small businesses obtain government contracts, to the Commerce Department.

Office of Management and Budget Director David A. Stockman told the Senate Small Business Committee that although the SBA helped some businesses, particularly in retail and service sectors, many others in the same industries had thrived without federal aid. And, he added, the SBA had done little to aid so-called "sunrise" industries in high-technology fields.

Further, he said it was unfair for companies that made it without SBA assistance to compete with companies benefiting from federal subsidies.

Both chambers strongly opposed the administration plan to abolish the SBA.

**Senate Committee Action.** The Small Business Committee voted 16-3 March 26, 1985, to approve a bill (S 408 — S Rept 99-20) that reauthorized SBA programs for three years, while making cuts totaling $851 million in outlays and $1.1 billion in budget authority. The panel turned back an amendment that would further reduce spending.

Although the committee's action would cut the agency's budget, it was nevertheless an outright rejection of the administration's proposal to abolish the SBA, as well as the Senate Budget Committee's plan to make deep cuts in the SBA budget.

The Budget Committee had recommended that several SBA programs be eliminated and that its loan portfolio be sold to private investors at 25 cents on the dollar. In the budget resolution (S Con Res 32), the Budget panel proposed cutting the SBA's budget authority by $4.7 billion over three years.

As ordered reported, the SBA bill would authorize $690 million for fiscal 1986 but would reduce direct lending from $257 million to $86 million and reduce the amount of a loan that could be guaranteed by the SBA from 90 percent to 80 percent. S 408 would increase the fee charged to borrowers of SBA-guaranteed loans from 1 percent to 2 percent.

Disaster loans no longer would be available for non-physical misfortunes but would still be available for physical calamities such as floods and hurricanes.

The bill would freeze spending for salaries and expenses and for guaranteed business loans at their respective fiscal 1985 levels of $234 million and $3.4 billion.

But Rudy Boschwitz, R-Minn., a member of both the Small Business and Budget committees, said S 408 did not go far enough to achieve savings. He offered an amendment, which was defeated 4-15, to save an additional $1.4 billion in outlays over three years, mostly by converting direct loan programs to loan guarantees. Loan guarantees cost the federal government less in outlays than direct loans because the government only paid when a borrower defaulted, whereas each direct loan required an outlay of federal funds.

**Senate Floor Action.** The Senate July 16 overwhelmingly passed S 408 by a 94-3 vote. As approved, the bill cut more deeply into SBA programs than the version

reported March 29 by the committee.

The committee bill would trim $851 million from what would be spent over the three fiscal years if the current rate of spending were maintained. To push the savings to $2.5 billion, Small Business Committee Chairman Lowell P. Weicker Jr., R-Conn., offered an amendment making additional cuts.

One change would require Small Business Investment Corporations (SBICs) to raise funds in private capital markets, instead of the federal Treasury. SBICs raised venture capital for new small businesses by selling debentures, which were backed by an SBA guarantee. This change was expected to save $259 million.

But the major change, expected to save $817 million, would bar farmers from the SBA disaster loan program, a change critics had sought for years. In 1984 Congress passed a bill (PL 98-369) requiring farmers to seek disaster loans first from the Farmers Home Administration (FmHA) in the Department of Agriculture, before qualifying for SBA aid. *(Background, Congress and the Nation Vol. VI, p. 56)*

But Dale Bumpers, D-Ark., ranking minority member of the Small Business Committee, said that under S Con Res 32, the FmHA disaster loan program would be sharply curtailed. He offered an amendment that would allow farmers to continue to receive SBA disaster loans but capped the disaster loan program at $500 million over three years.

Weicker argued against the amendment, noting that the provision barring farmers from SBA aid represented about a third of the proposed savings called for in the budget resolution. Bumpers' change would require deep program cuts to make up the difference, he said.

The Senate rejected the Bumpers amendment, 45-52.

Senators also rejected, 24-73, an amendment that would set up a pilot project of selling loans owned by FmHA to the private sector.

**House Committee Action.** As introduced by Small Business Committee Chairman Parren J. Mitchell, D-Md., the House bill (HR 2540 — H Rept 99-222, Part I) was substantially similar to the Senate bill.

HR 2540 would cut SBA spending on direct loans to businesses to 15 percent below the fiscal 1985 level of $206 million and would freeze salaries and expenses at the fiscal 1985 level of $205 million.

The bill would reduce the authorized level of guaranteed loans by 10 percent. And the measure would eliminate a loan program for non-physical disasters.

The bill also would cap individual direct loans at $150,000 and would require businesses receiving direct loans to borrow from other sources as well. Current law capped direct loans at $350,000 each.

But the committee made deeper cuts. By a 20-19 vote, the panel adopted an amendment that would reduce the SBA's authority to guarantee repayment of privately financed loans by 10 percent, from $3.18 billion to $2.86 billion.

And, by a single 21-19 vote, the panel adopted two amendments that would eliminate the non-physical disaster loan program and require farmers to seek FmHA disaster loans, rather than through SBA. The panel agreed to recommend to the Agriculture Committee that FmHA interest rates be set to match SBA rates.

The panel also adopted, by voice vote, an amendment that would increase from 1 percent to 3 percent the fee charged to borrowers of SBA loans.

By an 18-22 vote, the panel rejected an amendment that would lower the ceiling on the amount of a privately financed loan guaranteed by SBA from 90 percent to 75 percent of the loan's principal.

The committee adopted an amendment by voice vote that would impose user fees on certain SBA services, such as publications, and would require a $100 application fee from borrowers.

**House Floor, Final Action.** To achieve its share of reconciliation savings, the Small Business Committee proposed that HR 2540 be included in a pending reconciliation bill (HR 3500). HR 3500 was passed Oct. 24, 228-199. Provisions from HR 3500 were later added to another reconciliation bill (HR 3128) for conference with the Senate.

## Major Provisions

As signed into law April 7, 1986, HR 3128 included small business provisions that:

● Reauthorized the SBA through fiscal 1988 and set spending authority at $515 million in 1986, $605 million in 1987 and $634 million in 1988. The fiscal 1985 authorization was $700.3 million.

● Authorized such sums as necessary for disaster loans for the three fiscal years, eliminating the $500 million annual ceiling.

● Abolished general direct loans that had been available to any small business and eliminated direct loans for solar and energy conservation.

● Reduced direct loans for the remaining special small business programs from $257 million authorized in fiscal 1985 to $101 million in fiscal 1986, rising to $111 million in 1987 and $116 million in 1988.

The bill earmarked $15 million each year for firms owned by the handicapped, $20 million each year for those owned by Vietnam and disabled veterans and $41 million for minority enterprises.

In addition, for firms located in areas of high unemployment or low income, direct loans were set at $25 million, $35 million and $40 million in fiscal 1986-88, respectively.

● Established total loan guarantees at $3.221 million in fiscal 1986, $3.395 million in 1987 and $3.517 million in 1988. That included guarantees for debentures issued by SBICs of $250 million in fiscal 1986, $261 million in 1987 and $272 million in 1988.

● Authorized loan guarantees of $1.05 million in fiscal 1986, $1.096 million in 1987 and $1.142 million in 1988 for the surety bonds of small business contractors and subcontractors.

● Set guarantees for pollution control bonds at $75 million each year.

● Required the SBA to utilize all available loan guarantee authority.

● Reduced the maximum guarantee on loans of $155,000 or more from 90 percent to 85 percent and left the maximum guarantee of loans for less at 90 percent.

● Increased the fee that borrowers paid for loan guarantees from 1 percent of the loan to 2 percent.

● Prohibited the Federal Financing Bank from purchasing securities issued by SBICs, in effect requiring SBICs to sell securities on the private market.

● Barred farmers from getting disaster loans, with the exception of applicants qualified during fiscal 1985.

● Eliminated non-physical disaster loans, which in the past had provided compensation for border businesses hurt by devaluation of the peso.

● Established criminal penalties of a $50,000 fine and up to five years' imprisonment for misrepresentation made in writing.

● Authorized a pilot program of selling debentures issued by capital development companies to the private market in fiscal 1986 and 1987.

# Small Business Pilot Programs

President Reagan Oct. 27, 1986, signed into law a bill (S 2914 — PL 99-567) that extended through Sept. 30, 1988, two small business pilot programs aimed at assisting minority-owned firms.

One of the pilot programs enhanced the ability of the Small Business Administration (SBA) to direct federal contracts to minority firms. The other allowed the agency to waive bonding requirements for start-up minority firms receiving contracts. The authority for both programs had expired Sept. 30, 1985. *(Background, Congress and the Nation Vol. VI, p. 276)*

Congress completed action on the bill Oct. 14 when the House passed by voice vote a measure approved by the Senate Oct. 9. There was no committee action in either chamber.

The president had vetoed an earlier extension bill (HR 2787) that also included a research project in the home state of Connecticut Republican Lowell P. Weicker Jr., chairman of the Senate Small Business Committee. The revised bill left out the Connecticut project, to which Reagan had objected. Weicker was a strident critic of Reagan's campaign to kill the SBA.

The House Small Business Committee reported HR 2787 (H Rept 99-438) Dec. 12, 1985, and the House approved it by voice vote Dec. 16. It was reported (S Rept 99-316) by the Senate Small Business panel June 5, 1986.

The Senate passed HR 2787 by voice vote June 25, after adding Weicker's amendment to authorize up to $10 million to pay 50 percent of the cost of establishing a research institute at the University of Bridgeport in Connecticut. The House accepted the Senate change Sept. 19, clearing the bill.

In his Oct. 7 veto message, the president called the project "inappropriate and unwarranted" at a time of budget constraints. Reagan also said extension of the two pilot programs was unnecessary.

# Daylight-Saving Time

Congress cleared legislation (S 2180 — PL 99-359) in 1986 to expand daylight-saving time permanently by starting it on the first Sunday in April instead of the last Sunday in April. Daylight saving would continue to end on the last Sunday in October.

The three-week extension of daylight time was attached to an unrelated measure authorizing $18.3 million in fiscal 1987 for U.S. fire prevention and control programs under the Federal Emergency Management Agency.

Extension of daylight-saving time culminated in a 10-year drive in both chambers. Congress had switched to the existing system in 1976 after experiments with yearlong and eight-month daylight-saving plans prompted by the Arab oil embargo. Extension bills stalled in 1976, 1981 and 1983. *(1976 action, Congress and the Nation Vol. IV, p. 804; 1981, 1983 action, Congress and the Nation Vol. VI, pp. 269, 277)*

The House Oct. 22, 1985, had passed a bill (HR 2095 — H Rept 99-185) that would extend daylight-saving time from the first Sunday in April to the first Sunday in November, adding an extra week in the fall to make sunset occur later on Halloween.

## Senate Action

The Senate passed S 2180 (S Rept 99-267) May 20, 1986, after rejecting a motion to kill the daylight-saving amendment on a **36-58 (R 16-33; D 20-25) key vote.** It then adopted the amendment, offered by Slade Gorton, R-Wash., and passed the bill by voice votes. *(1986 key votes, p. 949)*

Gorton attached the daylight-saving extension to the non-controversial fire prevention bill to bypass the Commerce, Science and Transportation Committee, where Wendell H. Ford, D-Ky., and other rural- and Midwestern-state senators had bottled up a daylight-saving bill (S 1433) that Gorton had introduced in July 1985. Gorton's amendment to the fire program bill, by dropping the extra week in the fall, was an effort to convert foes such as Ford and J. James Exon, D-Neb.

But when Gorton offered the amendment May 19, Ford painted the extension as "a regional issue," pitting people in the cities on the East and West coasts against rural and agricultural areas. Proponents argued that extending daylight saving would conserve energy, reduce traffic fatalities and crime and have broad economic benefits for industries dependent upon retail sales and recreation.

Much of the opposition to the daylight-saving time extension came from states that either had two time zones or were at the westernmost edge of a time zone, such as Kentucky. Because half of Kentucky was on the western fringe of the Eastern time zone, Ford said, sunrises in eastern Kentucky could occur as much as an hour and 15 minutes later than in cities on the East Coast. Ford also expressed concern that rural children would have to go to school in the dark for three extra weeks.

The National Association of Broadcasters objected to the bill's potential effect on AM stations that operated only during the day. Many of the approximately 2,450 such stations held a "pre-sunrise authorization" (PSA) from the Federal Communications Commission (FCC) allowing them to begin operating at 6 a.m. at reduced power. However, about 450 stations did not have PSAs. The amendment allowed the FCC to make adjustments to remedy any disputes raised through the extension.

## House Action

The House June 24 passed S 2180 by voice vote, clearing the bill for the president's signature.

Before approving the bill, the House by a vote of 386-28 passed its fire program authorization (HR 4252 — H Rept 99-623) with the same funding levels as in S 2180. Members agreed by unanimous consent to drop the additional week of daylight time in the fall.

# Commerce Authorizations

Congress in 1986 reauthorized an array of commerce-related programs, including a three-year reauthorization for the Corporation for Public Broadcasting (CPB), as part of its fiscal 1986 deficit reduction bill (HR 3128 — PL 99-272). Citing excessive spending, President Reagan in 1984 had vetoed two authorization bills for the corporation, which funneled federal funds to public television and radio stations and to independent producers. *(Congress and the Nation Vol. VI, p. 282; CPB, 1988 action, p. 407)*

The deficit reduction bill also reauthorized several ocean and maritime programs and instituted or raised charges for services such as nautical charts, broadcast licenses and foreign fishing permits provided by federal agencies.

## Major Provisions

As signed into law April 7, 1986, HR 3128 contained the following commerce-related provisions:

● **Public Broadcasting.** Authorized appropriations for fiscal 1987-90 for the Corporation for Public Broadcasting, which received funding authorizations several years in advance to shield it from political interference in programming decisions. The bill authorized $200 million in fiscal 1987, $214 million in 1988, $238 million in 1989 and $254 million in 1990.

● Authorized $24 million in fiscal 1986, $28 million in 1987 and $32 million in 1988 for the Public Telecommunications Facility Program, which provided aid for construction of public radio and TV outlets in unserved areas. Reagan had tried to eliminate the program.

● Eliminated a requirement under existing law that at least 75 percent of capital funds be devoted to new facilities that would reach areas not receiving public television signals. This allowed more funds to be used for replacement or repair of existing facilities.

● **FCC.** Authorized appropriations for the Federal Communications Commission (FCC) of $98.1 million in fiscal 1986 and $97.6 million in 1987.

● Required the FCC to charge fees for regulatory services, such as license approvals, certification of equipment and construction permits. Fees were not to be charged to non-commercial radio and television stations. They were to be based on the cost of providing services and were to be reviewed by the FCC every two years.

● **Boating Safety.** Transferred any unappropriated funds from the boat-safety account of the Aquatic Resources Trust Fund to the general Treasury.

● **NOAA.** Imposed higher charges for nautical and aeronautical charts produced by the National Oceanic and Atmospheric Administration (NOAA). Existing fees covered only printing costs.

● Authorized NOAA programs at $225 million in fiscal 1986 and $235 million in 1987.

● **Foreign Fishing Permit Fees.** Allowed the secretary of commerce to raise fees for fishing permits for foreign ships fishing in U.S. waters three to 200 miles from shore.

● **Coastal Zone Management.** Authorized $41.8 million in fiscal 1986, $45.2 million in 1987, $47.2 million in 1988, $49.3 million in 1989 and $51.6 million in 1990 for coastal zone management programs.

● Reduced the federal share of state management grants, currently set at 80 percent federal funds and 20 percent state funds. The new formula would phase down the federal share from 4-to-1 in 1986 to 2.3-to-1 in 1987, 1.5-to-1 in 1988 and 1-to-1 in 1989.

● **Marine Sanctuaries.** Authorized $10.6 million in fiscal 1986 and $11.1 million in 1987 for marine sanctuaries programs. *(Background, Congress and the Nation Vol. III, p. 799)*

● **Ocean Pollution Research.** Authorized $3.6 million in fiscal 1986 and $3.7 million in fiscal 1987 for ocean pollution research programs.

● **Maritime Programs.** Authorized $93.8 million in fiscal 1986 for maritime programs, including $81.9 million for the Maritime Administration and $11.9 million for the Federal Maritime Commission.

Of the Maritime Administration's budget, $19.6 million was earmarked for training at the Merchant Marine Academy at Kings Point, N.Y., and $15.2 million for state maritime academies.

A fiscal 1987 maritime programs authorization bill (HR 4175) was pocket-vetoed by President Reagan Oct. 23. *(Story, p. 367)*

# FTC Authorization

The House and Senate were unable to settle their differences in the 99th Congress on legislation (S 1078) reauthorizing the Federal Trade Commission (FTC).

The bills set similar funding levels. The House would authorize $63.9 million for fiscal 1986, $64.2 million for 1987 and $64.3 million for 1988; the Senate would authorize $65.8 million in 1986, with $1 million increases for each of the following two years.

And both versions were silent on FTC regulation of such professionals as doctors and lawyers, an issue that had helped block reauthorization since 1982. *(Congress and the Nation Vol. VI, p. 276)*

But there were substantial differences on other issues. The Senate version would extend a 1980 law barring the FTC from initiating rules on an industry-wide basis that would regulate advertising on the grounds that it was an unfair act or practice. The House-passed measure did not address the ban, and members objected to the Senate proposal.

The chambers also disagreed on how Congress should veto agency rules. The Senate bill would permit Congress to veto rules of both the FTC and Consumer Product Safety Commission (CPSC) by passing a joint resolution signed by the president. The House measure applied only to the FTC.

In addition, the Senate set up procedures to speed up a veto, while the House provided no expedited procedures. House members also disapproved of the Senate's allowing Congress to hold up appropriations to implement rules vetoed by Congress.

### Legislative History

**Senate.** S 1078 was passed by the Senate July 26, 1985, by a vote of 84-5. It had been reported (S Rept 99-81) June 11 by the Commerce, Science and Transportation Committee.

The veto provision amendment would allow FTC and CPSC regulations to be overturned if a resolution of disapproval were passed by Congress and signed by the president. If Congress did not act, rules would take effect 90 days after being submitted to Congress. The amendment was approved 67-22.

The Senate then accepted a proposal setting up procedures for amending appropriations bills to deny funds to implement FTC and CPSC rules vetoed by Congress, in the event the president vetoed the disapproval resolution. It was adopted by voice vote after a motion to table it failed, 34-56.

The Senate killed, 71-26, an amendment curbing the FTC's authority to regulate professionals. It would limit the FTC's ability to pre-empt state laws regulating the qualifications and licensing of professions, such as medicine and law. As approved, S 1078 was silent on the issue.

**House Action.** The House Sept. 17, 1985, by voice vote passed HR 2385, which had been reported June 6 (H Rept 99-162) by the Energy and Commerce Committee. It then amended its text to S 1078 and sent the measure back to the Senate.

# Consumer Product Safety

The House and Senate failed to resolve differences in legislation reauthorizing the Consumer Product Safety Commission (CPSC) after the bill became embroiled in controversy over amusement park rides. The CPSC had not been reauthorized since 1981. *(Congress and the Nation Vol. VI, pp. 267, 277)*

The Senate July 24, 1985, passed by voice vote an authorization (S 1077 — S Rept 99-60) after watering down a proposal that would restore CPSC authority to inspect amusement park rides. The Senate bill would establish a commission to study amusement park safety.

The House version (HR 3456 — H Rept 99-377) failed passage under suspension of the rules Nov. 19 but was brought up again in 1986 and passed Feb. 6 by a vote of 298-81. In passing its bill, the House refused to drop language granting the CPSC authority to regulate some fixed-site amusement park rides; it currently supervised only portable rides, such as those in traveling carnivals and fairs. An amendment to require a study of amusement park safety was defeated, 179-198.

The Senate bill reauthorized the CPSC for two years at $35 million annually, while HR 3456 set funding at $36 million for one year.

# Corporate Mergers

Throughout much of 1985 Congress struggled with complicated issues unleashed by a wave of corporate takeovers that sent buyers and their targets scrambling to Capitol Hill for legislative protection.

Although several committees held hearings on potential legislation involving tax, banking, antitrust and securities laws, only two panels advanced bills.

A House Judiciary subcommittee June 13 approved legislation (HR 2735) designed to strengthen the federal government's role in regulating corporate mergers under antitrust laws. On the same date, the Senate Commerce, Science and Transportation Committee approved a measure (S 1218 — S Rept 99-90) to inhibit the takeover of Trans World Airlines (TWA). There was no further action on either measure. *(Corporate takeovers, p. 132)*

One reason for the lack of action was that the acquisition or defense of each proposed takeover was accomplished before Congress could act. Another was caution because the area was extraordinarily complex; many proposed solutions would change the rules of the game under which the stock market operated and threatened its stability, members said.

Another major obstacle to legislation was the Reagan administration, which opposed virtually all proposals to regulate mergers as an inhibition of the free market.

## FCC Terms

President Reagan June 6, 1986, signed a bill (S 2179 — PL 99-334) that reduced the terms of Federal Communications Commission (FCC) members to five years from seven years and altered existing terms to assure that one would expire each year. Absent congressional action, no terms would expire in 1989 or 1990.

Congress in 1982 had reduced the size of the FCC to five members from seven but had not adjusted members' staggered terms of office to maintain an annual rotation system. *(Congress and the Nation Vol. VI, p. 50)*

The Senate passed S 2179 (S Rept 99-263) March 27, and the House passed the bill May 22, clearing the bill for the president.

## Pipeline Safety

Senate passage Oct. 8, 1986, by voice vote cleared a $9.2 million fiscal 1987 authorization (HR 2092 — PL 99-516) for pipeline safety programs that for the first time would require operators to report unsafe conditions that could cause an accident.

Under existing law, operators of pipelines carrying natural gas or hazardous liquids had to report only accidents. The measure, passed by voice vote by the House Sept. 16, mandated that operators report to federal and state authorities conditions that were hazardous to life or property or that could affect the safe operation of the pipelines.

The bill authorized $3.2 million to carry out the Natural Gas Pipeline Safety Act of 1968 (PL 90-481), $800,000 for the Hazardous Liquid Pipeline Safety Act of 1979 (PL 96-129) and $5.2 million in grants for states, which inspect and monitor pipeline operators. Funding would come from user fees imposed by the reconciliation bill enacted in April 1986 (HR 3128 — PL 99-272). *(1968 act, Congress and the Nation Vol. II, p. 813; 1979 act, Congress and the Nation Vol. V, p. 327; HR 3128, p. 40)*

The bill was reported May 15, 1985, by the House Public Works and Transportation Committee (H Rept 99-121, Part I), on May 21 by the Energy and Commerce Committee (Part II) and on July 8 by the Judiciary Committee (Part III). There was no Senate committee action.

## Odometer Tampering

Congress in 1986 finally cleared legislation to crack down on illegal tampering with automobile odometers. The bill (S 475 — PL 99-579), which aimed at making it easier for law enforcement officials to detect fraud, cleared Oct. 8 when the Senate approved the version of the measure that the House passed by voice vote Oct. 6. The Senate passed similar legislation in 1984 and 1985, but the House had failed to act. *(Congress and the Nation Vol. VI, p. 285)*

The bill barred state licensing of a vehicle unless the seller disclosed on the title the odometer reading at the time of the sale. The maximum penalties for tampering would be increased from one year in prison to three years,

and civil fines would be raised from $1,000 per violation to $2,000.

Sponsors said that the National Automobile Dealers Association estimated that more than 3 million cars annually were subject to rollbacks that averaged 30,000 miles at a cost to consumers in excess of $2 billion.

## Debt Collection

Congress cleared a bill in 1986 intended to protect the public from harassment by some attorneys in the debt collection business. The legislation (HR 237 — PL 99-361) would repeal an exemption for laywers that was contained in the 1977 Fair Debt Collection Practices Act (PL 95-109). *(PL 95-109, Congress and the Nation Vol. V, p. 353)*

That law did not apply to lawyers because even though they collected funds for third parties, they were not thought to be "debt collectors," explained Rep. Frank Annunzio, D-Ill., chairman of the Banking, Finance and Urban Affairs Subcommittee on Consumer Affairs.

However, some lawyers had formed collection agencies, advertised their exemption from the law and acted in an unethical manner, he charged.

Rep. John Hiler, R-Ind., opposed the bill, arguing that it was not needed and that the Federal Trade Commission already had authority to police lawyers engaged in abusive or unfair practices. He said that attorneys who collected debts on behalf of clients should continue to be exempt from the debt collection act but that the exemption should be clarified to "eliminate its abuses by misguided lawyers."

HR 237 was reported (H Rept 99-405) from the House Banking Committee Nov. 26, 1985, and passed by the full House by voice vote Dec. 2. The Senate Banking, Housing and Urban Affairs Committee reported the bill May 21, 1986, and the Senate passed the bill by voice vote June 26. President Reagan signed HR 237 July 9.

# 1987-88

One of the 100th Congress' biggest political stories in the transportation arena was a vote to override President Reagan's veto of an $88 billion highway and mass transit authorization bill. After a dramatic struggle, including a trip to Capitol Hill by the president where he pleaded with Republican senators for their support, the Senate agreed to override the veto by only one vote.

In 1987 Congress addressed a variety of concerns about air travel. Constituents swamped Capitol Hill with complaints about shoddy airline service and the news media devoted considerable attention to the increasing numbers of flight delays and near-collisions. By year's end, Congress had cleared a $20 billion package authorizing substantial funding increases for grants to airports for expansion projects and purchases of equipment to upgrade the aging air-traffic control system.

Other air travel legislation passed in 1987 included a smoking ban on domestic flights scheduled to last two hours or less. Lawmakers also directed their attention to airline industry violations of air safety reporting requirements. They passed a law to stiffen penalties for failing to file required reports or to keep mandatory records. House and Senate conferees in 1988 failed to agree on legislation to prod airlines into improving their service, which included public disclosure of carriers' perfomance records, including actual flight-arrival times.

Congress failed to clear hotly disputed legislation to require workers in the bus, truck, airline and rail industries to submit to random drug and alcohol testing. The Reagan administration issued regulations for random drug testing of some 4 million transportation workers after the 100th Congress adjourned.

Product liability was once again on the forefront of issues in Congress — and lawmakers once again failed to clear legislation to establish the nation's first product liability law. A business-backed bill, however, was approved by the House Energy and Commerce Committee in 1988. Never before in their nine-year effort to enact product liability legislation had business leaders succeeded in pushing a bill through a committee of the House.

Lawmakers in 1988 did pass a major piece of legislation to overhaul a scandal-plagued Small Business Administration (SBA) procurement program designed to foster the growth of minority-owned businesses. Traditionally, the SBA had relied on awards of non-competitive contracts.

A bill aimed at improving the quality of children's television programming was cleared in 1988. It was intended to protect children from exploitation by commercial broadcasters. However, Reagan pocket-vetoed the bill on the grounds that it would trample on broadcasters' free-speech rights.

Reagan also beat back a determined congressional bid to codify the so-called "fairness doctrine," which had required broadcasters to air controversial public issues and all sides of such issues. He vetoed 1987 legislation codifying the doctrine and no override attempt was made. Following the veto, the Federal Communications Commission voted to abolish the doctrine.

# 1987 Highway Authorization

Overriding President Reagan's veto, Congress April 2, 1987, enacted the Surface Transportation and Uniform Relocation Assistance Act (HR 2 — PL 100-17) authorizing $88 billion for highway and mass transit programs.

The 99th Congress had failed to pass a reauthorization bill, leaving states with limited transportation and road-repair funds. The 100th Congress was pressured to quickly pass the legislation because the states' funding shortage increased concerns that dozens of highway projects would be scrapped and thousands of construction industry jobs lost. *(1985-86 action, pp. 363, 364)*

The measure enacted in 1987 contained approximately $70 billion for highway construction, repair and safety programs and $18 billion for mass transit programs through fiscal 1991. The bill also set a $12.35 billion annual limit on highway spending, although funding for several key programs — including $890 million for special demonstration projects — was exempted from the cap.

Passage of the legislation was eased by funding for the 120 special demonstration road projects that were popular with their sponsors but labeled "pork-barrel" spending by the administration.

Also spurring passage was a provision in HR 2 that allowed states to raise the speed limit from 55 mph to 65

mph on rural Interstate highways located outside urban areas of 50,000 population or more. This change was especially popular with Western legislators.

In his March 27 veto message, Reagan said HR 2 "represents a failure to exercise the discipline that is required to constrain federal spending, especially pork-barrel spending." The president said the five-year reauthorization package exceeded his budget request for highway and mass transit spending by $10.1 billion.

## House Action

As introduced by leaders of the House Public Works and Transportation Committee, HR 2 was virtually identical to a measure (HR 3129 — H Rept 99-665) that died in 1986 in conference. HR 2 authorized $68 billion for highway construction and repairs and $21.2 billion for mass transit through 1991. *(HR 3129, p. 364)*

As was the case in 1986, speed limits and demonstration projects topped the list of contentious items. The House version of HR 2 retained the existing 55 mph speed limit and contained funding of $1.2 billion for nearly 100 projects over five years. No state matching funds were required for the projects in the House bill and none of the money was to be deducted from a state's regular highway apportionment. The House version also set an annual spending ceiling of $12.6 billion on highway programs.

Traditionally, annual spending ceilings were set lower than authorization levels, squeezing the amount of money that could be spent in a given year. For this reason, House members were particularly keen about leaving projects above the ceilings.

The House bill also increased from 50 percent to 85 percent the proportion of domestic products that had to be used in the manufacture of mass transit buses and rail cars. The Public Works Committee took no action on the measure, which was brought directly to the floor.

House floor action began with a debate on a rule (H Res 38) prohibiting amendments from being offered to the bill. The "closed" rule was supported by House Speaker Jim Wright, D-Texas, and James J. Howard, D-N.J., chairman of the Public Works Committee. Both men favored retaining the 55 mph speed limit and feared an open rule would lead to a vote on the speed-limit issue. They argued that consideration of controversial amendments would jeopardize quick passage of the legislation.

But James V. Hansen, R-Utah, and Dave McCurdy, D-Okla., asked colleagues to defy Wright and Howard by amending the rule to permit a vote to allow states to raise the speed limit to 65 mph on certain rural Interstates.

"There's a growing feeling across America to have some reasonable speed limits," Hansen said. "There's not a law around that's violated as much as this one. We call it 'modern-day Prohibition.' "

But H Res 38 was upheld, on a voice vote, as Democrats stood by Speaker Wright after voting 331-88 to proceed to a vote on the rule.

The House passed HR 2 on Jan. 21 by a vote of 401-20.

## Senate Action

Three Senate committees approved highway or mass transit measures that were ultimately combined into a single vehicle that went to the Senate floor.

The Environment and Public Works Committee Jan. 21 approved a measure (S 387 — S Rept 100-4) providing a

$52 billion, four-year authorization of highway programs only. Committee members blocked by an 8-8 vote an amendment by Robert T. Stafford, R-Vt., to slow the spread of new billboards along federal highways. Approved by voice vote during markup was a committee amendment by Chairman Quentin N. Burdick, D-N.D., that would permit demonstration projects as long as states contributed matching funds and the funds were deducted from a state's regular apportionment. The committee's measure also set an annual ceiling on highway construction expenditures of $12.35 billion.

The Banking, Housing and Urban Affairs panel Jan. 21 approved by voice vote a bill (S 382 — S Rept 100-3) reauthorizing $12.8 billion worth of mass transit programs over four years.

At the same time, the Finance Committee on Jan. 22 approved by voice vote a package to extend for four years the taxes in the Highway Trust Fund, the pot of road-related user fees that financed highway programs.

After three days of generally low-key debate, the Senate passed HR 2 by a 96-2 vote on Feb. 4. It included a four-year, $52 billion highway and $13 billion mass transit authorization.

The Senate bill listed 99 projects that were to be funded only at the request of the state. Matching funds were required and all of the federal money was to be deducted from a state's apportionment.

The Senate also voted to raise the speed limit on rural Interstates to 65 mph. Under a 1974 law (PL 93-643), states that did not comply with the 55 mph speed limit lost 10 percent of their highway aid. Although opponents of raising the limit contended that the current speed limit saved lives because motorists drove more slowly, the amendment carried by a vote of 65-33.

In an effort to reverse his committee defeat on controlling the proliferation of billboards, Stafford offered a compromise plan to restrict roadside ads in rural areas or near federal parks, refuges or wilderness areas. Wendell H. Ford, D-Ky., who led the opposition, charged that Stafford's amendment was anti-small business. The Senate agreed to table (kill) the amendment by a vote of 57-40.

The Senate also tabled, 65-33, an amendment by Thad Cochran, R-Miss., to prohibit the use of imported cement on federal highway projects. The House bill included the ban.

## Conference Action

There were a number of thorny issues House and Senate conferees had to iron out, but the two issues that met with strongest disagreement in the conference were the number of demonstration projects to be funded and the speed limit.

● **Demonstration Projects.** On March 4, the Senate offered to exempt 50 percent of demonstration project costs, set at $178 million annually over five years, from spending ceilings. These funds were to be split evenly between designated House and Senate projects. Thirty percent of remaining funds were to come from regular apportionments, not to be above the ceilings, and 20 percent would come from state or local sources.

House leaders objected and proposed, as in their original bill, to exempt all project costs from the ceilings. However, half of the money was to be deducted from regular apportionments.

Finally, conferees agreed to the Senate plan after

---

### Transportation Leadership

By a unanimous 74-0 vote, the Senate Nov. 30, 1987, approved the nomination of James H. Burnley IV as secretary of transportation. Burnley, who was the Department of Transportation's (DOT) deputy secretary for four years, replaced Elizabeth H. Dole, who resigned Oct. 1 to work full time on the presidential campaign of her husband, Senate Minority Leader Robert Dole, R-Kan. *(Burnley background, Cabinet profiles, p. 1047; Dole background, Congress and the Nation Vol. VI, p. 1024)*

The Senate July 17, 1987, approved by voice vote President Reagan's June 5 nomination of T. Allan McArtor of Tennessee to be the new administrator of the Federal Aviation Administration (FAA), part of DOT. McArtor had been a senior vice president of the telecommunications division of the Federal Express Corp.

McArtor succeeded Donald D. Engen, who announced March 18 that he would step down as administrator in July. Engen had served as FAA chief since April 1984 and offered no specific reason for his resignation.

---

modifications ensured that 30 percent of the money would come not from regular apportionments but from funds to be allocated at the discretion of the transportation secretary. None of the money would come from the states' regular allocation of highway funds.

The bill also exempted from the spending ceilings $890 million in federal funding for more than 120 projects over the bill's five-year life.

● **Speed Limit.** On the speed-limit issue, House conferees March 10 offered to allow the House to vote separately on a Senate plan to permit states to raise the limit to 65 mph on rural Interstates.

House Public Works Chairman Howard, a strong advocate of retaining the current 55 mph speed limit, agreed to a separate House vote on raising the limit only after Senate negotiators on HR 2 accepted much of what the House offered on demonstration project funding. Under the agreement, the House would vote on the speed-limit increase and, if approved, the Senate would vote on the measure.

● **Billboards.** After much debate, conferees also agreed not to make any changes in laws controlling the spread of billboards along federal highways.

Since a billboard control amendment was defeated on the Senate floor, the Senate bill was left without any new billboard provision. The House bill, meanwhile, carried forward a provision from 1986 that called for a cap on the total number of billboards nationwide.

House conferees — who appeared to be more sympathetic to the concerns of the outdoor-advertising industry than Senate conferees — backed away from their provision.

● **Transit Issues.** Agreement on major transit issues was reached March 13 between members of the House

Public Works Committee and the Senate Banking, Housing and Urban Affairs Committee. Negotiators compromised on a House "Buy America" provision to restrict the use of foreign products in buses and rail cars.

The House adopted the conference report (H Rept 100-27) March 18 by a vote of 407-17.

It then agreed, by a **key vote of 217-206 (R 125-50; D 92-156)**, to a concurrent resolution (H Con Res 77) that would amend HR 2 to allow for an increase in the speed limit to 65 mph, as provided by the Senate. After the vote, Howard told reporters that members opposed to "55" were swayed primarily by "anti-government feeling" among voters, especially in Western states. *(1987 key votes, p. 965)*

In a March 19 letter to congressional leaders, Reagan called HR 2 "seriously flawed" because of provisions for the demonstration projects targeted at particular districts or states and "excessive" funding for mass transit programs. Reagan threatened to veto the bill in its current form.

But immediately following receipt of this message, the Senate voted 79-17 to adopt the conference report on HR 2. The Senate also adopted H Con Res 77 by a vote of 60-21.

## Veto Override Fight

Noting the huge margins by which both the House and Senate cleared the highway measure, a number of observers said the White House's only hope of sustaining a veto was to make the vote a test of Reagan's personal leadership.

But the president's leadership had little influence on the House, where members March 31 easily voted to override the veto 350-73.

The Senate, after a lengthy battle, followed the House lead and on April 2 overrode by a **key vote of 67-33 (R 13-33; D 54-0)**.

During the politicking in the Senate, freshman Terry Sanford, D-N.C., claimed the spotlight as he first agreed to go along with the administration's wishes and then, after heavy pressure from his own party, abruptly changed his mind and voted to override.

On April 1, 13 Republicans joined with the majority in a 65-35 vote to sustain the veto. A vote of two-thirds of those present and voting, 67 in this case, was needed to override a veto.

But Majority Leader Robert C. Byrd, D-W.Va., who initially voted to override, switched his vote at the last minute to "nay." Byrd's maneuver permitted him to offer a motion that the Senate reconsider the vote, thus giving the Democratic leadership an opportunity to persuade some members to switch sides. Under intense party pressure, Sanford said he would switch his vote to support an override. His vote, with Byrd's, provided the margin to defeat Reagan's veto.

Sanford said the 65-35 vote made the point that the president was capable of demonstrating strong leadership. He said he had thought harder about problems, such as unemployment, that would result if no bill were passed, and that he believed HR 2 was the best package that could be obtained under the circumstances.

In any event, Sanford's switch on the highway bill put the heat on the 13 Republicans who had voted to override.

Minority Leader Robert Dole, R-Kan., forced a series of procedural votes to thwart Byrd's efforts to hold an immediate second vote on the override. Ultimately, Byrd agreed to postpone a vote until the following day.

On April 2, Reagan went to Capitol Hill to meet with Republicans before the second vote to override was taken. Reagan repeated his reasons for opposing the legislation, but three members of the 13 holding out told the president they could not change their votes.

The scene then shifted to Dole's office, where Reagan met with the 13 holdouts and reportedly "begged" them for their support. But when the session broke up, Dole told reporters that nothing had changed.

Among the reasons suggested for Reagan's failure was that none of the Republicans wanted to follow in the footsteps of Sanford. Changing a vote would be "an embarrassment," said Stafford.

The Senate April 2 voted 59-41 to adopt the motion to reconsider the override vote.

To no one's surprise, nothing that happened in the House came close to matching the suspense in the Senate. With Minority Leader Robert Michel of Illinois leading the way, a majority of that body's Republicans deserted the president, despite a March 25 Capitol Hill visit by Reagan when he asked House GOP members for their support.

Michel cited HR 2 funding for a demonstration project in his district, as did a number of Republicans who voted to override.

## Major Provisions

As cleared March 19, 1987, HR 2 (PL 100-17) included the following major provisions. Unless otherwise noted, the authorized funding came from the Highway Trust Fund:

● **Speed Limit.** Allowed states to raise the speed limit up to 65 mph on Interstate highway segments located outside urbanized areas of 50,000 population or more. Under existing law, states that did not comply with a 55 mph speed limit faced the loss of up to 10 percent of their federal highway aid.

● **Highway Construction, Repairs.** Set an annual ceiling of $12.35 billion for fiscal 1987-91 on obligations from the Highway Trust Fund for highway construction and repair programs. Funding for emergency relief projects and "minimum allocation payments" was not included in the ceiling. Minimum allocation payments ensured that a state received funding equal to approximately 85 percent of its estimated tax payments into the Highway Trust Fund, excluding payments into the fund's mass transit account.

Funding for special demonstration projects for particular states or districts — $890 million through fiscal 1991 — also was exempted.

● Authorized $3 billion for fiscal 1988, $3.15 billion for fiscal 1989-92 and $1.4 billion for fiscal 1993 for the Interstate highway construction program.

● Continued the apportionment of 0.5 percent of total Interstate construction funds to each state that had completed its Interstate system or whose unfinished roadways accounted for less than 0.5 percent of the national cost of completion.

● Provided for Department of Transportation (DOT) approval of apportionment of funds for Interstate construction projects and for non-Interstate projects substituted by local and state officials for previously approved Interstate work. Under previous law, congressional approval was required before states could obligate funds.

● Authorized for fiscal 1988-92 $2.81 billion annually for Interstate repair projects. Of this amount, $200 million annually was set aside for projects to be funded at the discretion of the transportation secretary.

• Authorized annually for fiscal 1987-91 $2.32 billion for primary road projects; $600 million for secondary roads; $750 million for urban roads; $80 million for Indian reservation roads; $55 million for forest highways; $40 million for public-lands highways; and $60 million for parkways and park highways.

• Authorized for fiscal 1987-91 $1.63 billion annually for bridge replacement and rehabilitation programs, $200 million of which was set aside annually for discretionary grants; $170 million annually for elimination of road hazards; and $160 million annually for rail-highway crossing projects.

Road-hazard funds were used for the installation or replacement of emergency call boxes.

• Authorized for fiscal 1987-91 $10 million annually for highway-related safety grants awarded to states by the Federal Highway Administration (FHWA) and another $10 million annually for FHWA grants for highway construction safety research and development projects.

• Authorized $58 million from the general fund for the upgrading of roads in the vicinity of the Waste Isolation Pilot Project in New Mexico. Money was made available in fiscal 1987 and would remain available in subsequent years until expended. The project provided for long-term storage of low-level nuclear wastes from around the country.

• Extended through fiscal 1991 the Disadvantaged Business Enterprise (DBE) program, which was aimed at increasing the participation of minority-owned businesses in the federal highway program.

The requirement that states award 10 percent of federal highway contracts to DBEs, unless determined otherwise by the transportation secretary, was continued. However, the secretary was required to establish uniform criteria for states to use in certifying whether a concern was a disadvantaged business enterprise.

Businesses owned by women were presumed to be disadvantaged.

• Retained the current formula for distribution of Interstate repair funds to states. The House bill would change the formula to shift funds from rural states to heavily populated states.

• Allowed states to use federal highway aid for separate projects to remove roadside obstacles, such as roadside mailboxes.

• Required states to award contracts to the most qualified bidder — not necessarily the lowest bidder — in procurement of engineering and design services. This provision did not apply in any state that adopted or already had adopted its own procedures for procurement of engineering and design services.

• Allowed for federal reimbursement for highway projects started by states in calendar year 1987 before enactment of a highway reauthorization measure, if certain conditions were met.

• Allowed states to transfer up to 20 percent of their Interstate road-repair funds each year to primary road projects without providing a justification for the transfer. Any state that desired to transfer more than 20 percent had to, as under existing law, justify the transfer.

Transferred funds had to be matched at the same rate as other primary funds — that is, the state was responsible for 25 percent of the cost.

• Added the installation of safety devices, such as traffic signs, to the list of projects and activities eligible for 100 percent federal financing of the cost of construction.

• Increased the limit on emergency relief grants for each state for each disaster from $30 million per year to $100 million per year, retroactive to disasters that occurred after Dec. 31, 1985. The federal share for a highway emergency relief project was the same as for a regular federal aid project for the road in question. However, the federal share could be 100 percent only for emergency work done in the first 90 days after the disaster occurred.

• Provided for a temporary exemption, which terminated Sept. 1, 1988, from requirements protecting Interstate bridges from undue concentrations of weight for tank trucks, ocean transport containers and dump trucks.

• Relaxed a ban on the use of federal funds for toll-road construction projects to allow federal funding for seven toll-road pilot projects. No Interstate construction projects were eligible and the federal share on any toll project was capped at 35 percent.

• Clarified federal law to permit the use of bridge project funds for the preservation of historic bridges. Current law had not always been interpreted to allow such use of funds.

• Amended the minimum allocation program to provide donor states with a return in highway funds closer to 85 percent of the amount they contributed to the Highway Trust Fund. Several major funding categories, including bridge discretionary and emergency relief, were added to the formula by which minimum allocation payments were calculated.

• Directed the transportation secretary to establish national standards for the proper safety inspection and evaluation of all highway bridges.

• Established a Strategic Highway Research Program under the direction of the transportation secretary to carry out research, development and technology transfer activities, with the goal of preserving the existing 30-year investment in the Interstate system.

• Required that 0.25 percent of federal-aid highway funds expended for landscaping on a project be for the planting of wildflowers or seedlings. Upon request of a state, the transportation secretary could waive the requirement with respect to any project.

• Authorized the transportation secretary to conduct a road demonstration program that allowed up to five states to participate in a block grant for secondary roads, urban roads and certain bridge projects.

• Made eligible for construction with Interstate funds the Central Artery and the Third Harbor Tunnel, both in Boston, Mass.

• Authorized federal funding through fiscal 1991 for more than 120 special demonstration projects for particular states or districts. Of the funding, $890 million — $178 million per year — was exempted from the annual $12.35 billion overall spending ceiling on highway projects. Another $107 million per year came from funds earmarked for accounts to be allocated at the discretion of the transportation secretary. Matching funds of $71 million per year were to be paid by state or local governments. Each state received at least 0.5 percent of the $178 million exempted from the ceiling.

The transportation secretary was required to provide Congress with an annual status report on the projects, beginning in 1988.

• Established that certain "priority" projects targeted at particular states or districts be funded from states' regular highway apportionments at the request of a state to the transportation secretary.

• Directed the transportation secretary to arrange for the Transportation Research Board of the National Research Council to conduct a study of the trucking industry, including costs and benefits of gross weight and axle-load allowances, due no later than 30 months after enactment.

● Directed the transportation secretary to conduct a study of efforts to improve safety conditions at rail-highway crossings, due no later than 24 months after enactment.

● Directed the transportation secretary to study and investigate improvement and maintenance needs for highway bridges that cross rail lines of the Amtrak national passenger railroad, due no later than 24 months after enactment.

● Directed the transportation secretary to study problems encountered by handicapped persons in parking motor vehicles, and whether each state should establish parking privileges for such persons and grant to non-residents the same privileges granted to residents, due 180 days within enactment.

● Directed the transportation secretary to arrange with the National Academy of Sciences to investigate the appropriateness of establishing minimum federal guidelines for maintenance of primary, secondary and urban roads similar to those guidelines established for Interstate highways, due 18 months after arrangements were made with the academy.

● **Highway Safety.** Authorized for fiscal 1987-91 $126 million annually for National Highway Traffic Safety Administration (NHTSA) highway traffic safety grants; and $33 million annually for NHTSA highway safety research and development programs.

● Set a ceiling of $121 million for fiscal 1987 and $126 million annually for fiscal 1988-91 on spending for NHTSA highway traffic safety grants.

● Directed the transportation secretary to commission a study by the National Academy of Sciences on school bus safety, due no later than 18 months after arrangements were made with the academy.

● Directed the transportation secretary to issue within one year of enactment regulations that required trucks to be equipped with devices that cut down on splash and spray in bad weather, unless the secretary determined that there was no available technology that could significantly reduce splash and spray from trucks and significantly improve visibility of drivers, as demonstrated in testing. The provision in the original House bill would make it easier for the secretary to determine that no standards should be issued.

● Directed the transportation secretary to commission a National Academy of Sciences study of safety problems associated with older drivers and to establish a pilot program to improve older drivers' safety and mobility.

● Approved a rescission of $148 million of unobligated contract authority that was available through federal grant programs for airport development and planning.

● **Mass Transit.** Authorized from the mass transit account of the trust fund discretionary spending of $1.1 billion for fiscal 1987, $1.2 billion for fiscal 1988, $1.25 billion for fiscal 1989, $1.3 billion for fiscal 1990 and $1.4 billion for fiscal 1991.

Of those amounts, $45 million annually was authorized for local planning activities; $35 million for programs for the elderly and handicapped and innovative research programs; and $5 million for grants to university transportation centers. Of the remaining discretionary authorization, 40 percent was allocated to start new mass transit construction; 40 percent for rail-modernization projects; 10 percent

for bus needs; and 10 percent to be allocated at the discretion of the transportation secretary.

● Authorized general fund appropriations of $2 billion in fiscal 1987 and $2.1 billion in fiscal 1988-91 for mass transit formula grants.

● Required the transportation secretary annually to submit to Congress overall funding plans for new transit construction projects and projects to modernize existing transit systems. Congressional approval of funding plans was not required, as called for in the original House bill.

● Permitted applicants for transit capital assistance from the Urban Mass Transportation Administration (UMTA) to be reimbursed for the federal share of costs incurred on a project if, among other conditions, the transportation secretary approved the project before costs were incurred and the project complied with all relevant federal requirements.

● Listed criteria that UMTA must use in deciding whether to approve requests for funding of transit rail construction projects. For example, projects approved by UMTA had to show evidence of stable and dependable funding sources for construction, maintenance and operation. Certain projects on which preliminary engineering or other work had begun were not covered by the new criteria.

● Authorized general fund appropriations for fiscal 1987-91 of $200 million annually for the Interstate transfer transit program, which permitted urban areas to use funds intended for Interstate construction projects for other highway or transit projects.

● Allowed a newly urbanized area with a population above 50,000 to use up to two-thirds of its formula grant apportionment during the first full year it received funds under the Section 9 formula program to help pay for transit operating expenses. The operating assistance cap on other urbanized areas of less than 200,000 population would be increased by a one-time inflation adjustment of 32.2 percent, effective Oct. 1, 1987.

Beginning Oct. 1, 1988, the caps for both areas would be increased by the percentage increase in the Consumer Price Index.

● Required recipients of UMTA assistance to award contracts for engineering and design services to the most qualified bidder — not necessarily the lowest bidder. The provision did not apply in states that adopted or had adopted by statute a formal procedure for procuring such services.

● Provided for a 95 percent federal share of the cost of all projects specifically targeted at improving elderly and handicapped access to public-transit systems. The federal share was 80 percent for all formula grant programs and 75 percent for discretionary grants.

● Provided that up to 0.5 percent of the annual authorizations for discretionary and formula grant programs were made available to UMTA to contract directly with independent consultants to provide construction management oversight services.

The bill also required local transit officials with major construction projects to provide detailed construction plans as a prerequisite to obtaining federal funding.

● Permitted the transportation secretary to make capital grants for improvements in transit crime prevention and security.

● Required the transportation secretary to enter into a contract to complete the first two segments of the San Fernando Valley to Downtown Los Angeles Metro Rail Project and provided Section 3 discretionary grant funds for that purpose.

● Authorized the establishment of a Rural Transit Assistance Program to coordinate various services, such as technical assistance and training, provided to rural transit operators. Funding was not to exceed $5 million per fiscal year.

● Increased domestic content requirements for buses and rail cars. Existing law required that at least 50 percent of the material in transit vehicles be domestically manufactured. The proportion would rise to 55 percent for contracts entered into after Sept. 30, 1989, and to 60 percent for contracts entered into after Sept. 30, 1991.

Any company that met the existing "Buy America" requirement was exempted from the increases for all contracts entered into before April 1, 1992.

● **Taxes.** Extended through fiscal 1993 current excise taxes that financed the Highway Trust Fund, including the 9-cents-per-gallon gasoline tax. The extension raised an estimated $75.5 billion.

● Amended the heavy-truck use tax to apply to any heavy truck driven more than 5,000 miles on U.S. roads, regardless of the country in which the truck was registered. However, the tax on trucks registered in foreign countries was 75 percent of the rate charged trucks registered in the United States.

● **Relocation Assistance.** Revised federal standards and procedures for assisting homeowners, businesses, farms or non-profit organizations displaced by federally financed activities, such as highway projects.

● Defined less restrictively the type of replacement dwellings that the government must provide displaced persons. The replacement dwelling did not have to be exactly equal to or better than the dwelling acquired by the government. However, the principal features of the acquired dwelling did have to be present in the replacement dwelling, if the displaced person so chose.

● Raised the ceiling from $15,000 to $22,500 on relocation payments to homeowners to cover expenses such as increased mortgage costs. Additional compensation for reasonable expenses — up to $10,000 — were authorized to re-establish a farm, non-profit organization or small business at its relocation site.

● DOT was designated the lead agency to issue rules implementing the relocation procedures, which every federal agency was required to follow.

## NTSB Authorization

The Senate July 6, 1988, sent to the White House a measure (S 623) to authorize $81 million for fiscal years 1989-90 for the National Transportation Safety Board (NTSB), the federal agency responsible for investigating accidents involving all modes of transportation. By voice vote, senators approved a package that was passed by the House April 12. President Reagan signed the bill (PL 100-372) July 19.

The measure included a provision, opposed by the White House, that effectively allowed the NTSB to augment its congressional appropriation with charges for training and services provided to persons from other federal agencies and state, local and foreign governments. The Reagan administration favored depositing such fees in the general Treasury.

The authorization levels in the bill slightly exceeded the administration's budget request for fiscal years 1989 and 1990.

Calling the measure excessive, Reagan in 1986 had pocket-vetoed an NTSB authorization (HR 4961) that would allow spending $76.4 million in fiscal 1987-89. *(1985-86 action, p. 367)*

**House Action.** The House passed S 623 by voice vote April 12, 1988. The bill was a compromise between the leaders of the Energy and Commerce and Public Works and Transportation panels, which had reported slightly different versions of the bill (HR 11). Public Works and Transportation reported its version (H Rept 100-158, Part I) June 17, 1987; it would authorize $106.5 million for fiscal years 1987-90 for NTSB. Energy and Commerce reported its version (Part II) March 28, 1988; it would authorize $52.4 million for fiscal years 1988-89.

Lawmakers substituted the compromise for a similar, $82.5 million package passed by the Senate. The House acted under suspension of the rules, a procedure that permitted no amendments.

**Senate Action.** The Senate Commerce, Science and Transportation Committee reported S 623 March 19, 1987 (S Rept 100-18). The full Senate passed the measure March 25 by voice vote.

As passed by the Senate, the bill would authorize $82.5 million through fiscal 1990 for NTSB.

## Truck and Bus Safety

Legislation to tighten federal truck- and bus-safety measures was enacted as part of the omnibus drug bill (HR 5210 — PL 100-690), which cleared Oct. 22, 1988. The safety provisions, similar to those passed in separate bills (HR 5321, S 861) by both houses earlier in the year, were added to the drug measure during the final negotiations on the bill. *(Drug bill, p. 748)*

The legislation eliminated decades-old exemptions from safety rules that had been provided trucks and buses operating in certain metropolitan areas known as "commercial zones." There were such zones in Washington, D.C., New York City and Chicago, among other areas.

The measure also directed the Transportation Department to examine the safety benefits of requiring on-board computerized devices that would record drivers' hours. Sponsors were concerned about widespread falsification of written logs as drivers exceeded legal hours-of-driving limits.

The transportation secretary also was required to study the effectiveness of installing speed control devices on commercial motor vehicles and to look into the possibility of requiring trucks to have anti-lock brakes, designed to prevent skidding.

The House passed HR 5321 Oct. 6 by voice vote. It had been reported (H Rept 100-1009) by the Public Works Committee Sept. 29.

The Senate had passed a similar measure, S 861, March 3 by voice vote. It had been reported (S Rept 100-267) by the Commerce Committee Dec. 19, 1987.

## Drunken Driving

The Senate's Commerce and Environment panels approved similar bills in 1988 to encourage states to crack down on drunken driving. But because of a jurisdictional wrangle — triggered by a slip-up by the Senate parliamentarian — neither measure made it to the floor. Instead, the provisions were enacted as part of the omnibus drug bill (HR 5210 — PL 100-690). *(Drug bill, p. 748)*

Frank R. Lautenberg, D-N.J., May 11 introduced a bill (S 2367) to authorize federal grants from the Highway Trust Fund to states that took certain steps to combat drunken driving, including revoking the license of a driver who failed a sobriety test.

The Senate parliamentarian referred the measure to the Environment and Public Works Committee on the grounds that the panel oversaw the Highway Trust Fund's road construction account.

But Commerce leaders cried foul. They pointed out that the Commerce Committee had jurisdiction over highway safety programs also financed by the fund, which was fed principally by federal gasoline taxes.

The parliamentarian then decided the bill should have gone to Commerce. On June 21, Lautenberg introduced an identical measure that was given a new number (S 2549) and promptly referred to the Commerce Committee.

That was not, however, the end of the matter. Senate rules allowed mistaken referrals to be corrected only by unanimous consent, and Environment and Public Works members were unwilling to allow S 2367 to slip from their grasp. On Aug. 2 they reported an amended version of the measure (S Rept 100-441).

Not to be outdone, the Commerce Committee Oct. 7 reported its own amended version of the Lautenberg bill (S Rept 100-594). Both measures authorized grants, totaling $125 million through fiscal 1991, to help states defray the costs of administering new drunken-driving programs.

Lautenberg, frustrated by the turf squabble, looked for a new vehicle and was successful in getting his legislation attached to the drug bill.

# NHTSA Authorization

The Senate April 24, 1987, passed by voice vote a bill (S 853 — S Rept 100-42) to reauthorize for two years the National Highway Traffic Safety Administration (NHTSA), the federal agency responsible for administering traffic-safety programs. However, the House did not act on the bill during the 100th Congress.

The Senate bill authorized $57 million for NHTSA in fiscal 1988 and $58.8 million in fiscal 1989. It also required lap and shoulder seat belts for back seats in all passenger cars made after Sept. 1, 1990, and allowed the transportation secretary to use $10 million in unobligated funds to encourage the use of seat belts and air bags.

The Senate basically accepted the bill as approved by the Commerce, Science and Transportation Committee but adopted one amendment by John Kerry, D-Mass., requiring states to honor other states' handicapped plates in public parking areas. Two percent of a state's highway funds would be withheld for non-compliance.

The House Appropriations Committee approved July 1 an $11.1 billion fiscal 1988 transportation appropriations package that included $96.7 million for the NHTSA, although the administration had requested only $90 million.

# Airport Authorization

Congress in December 1987 capped a year of intense public concern about air travel by clearing major legislation aimed at easing strains on congested airports and on the nation's air-traffic control network. Although President Reagan expressed concern about its cost, he signed the bill on Dec. 30 (HR 2310 — PL 100-223).

The $20 billion package featured substantial funding increases for Federal Aviation Administration (FAA) grants to airports for expansion projects and for agency purchases of equipment to upgrade the aging air-traffic control system.

The bill extended through Dec. 31, 1990, taxes on passenger tickets and other fees that flowed into the Airport and Airway Trust Fund to finance the programs.

A controversial provision requiring airlines to disclose their performance records to the public was dropped in the Senate and never considered in the House. Instead, Congress addressed that issue in separate "consumer protection" legislation (HR 3051) that eventually died in conference. *(Consumer protection bill, p. 391)*

Despite the fact that lawmakers were willing to authorize more money for the air travel system, there remained questions about whether its problems were of a sort that money could resolve.

For one thing, airport traffic congestion had increased because new construction projects were blocked by communities unwilling to tolerate aircraft noise and other problems linked to air traffic. There were few signs that such opposition was diminishing.

As for the air-traffic control network, some experts did not blame difficulties in replacing obsolete computers and other equipment on a shortage of funds but on the FAA's poor management of the modernization program and delays in contracts awarded by the FAA to equipment providers.

Earlier in 1987, the airline industry tried to galvanize support for a far-reaching plan to shift management of the air-traffic control network from the FAA to a new public corporation that would not be subject to federal procurement and civil service rules. Lawmakers and administration officials balked at the idea, concerned that such an entity would not be accountable to political officials and the public.

The Senate Commerce Committee also considered legislation (S 1600) to remove the FAA from the Department of Transportation (DOT) and establish it as an independent agency.

The aviation community in 1987 also saw the collapse of its plan to remove the Airport and Airway Trust Fund from the federal budget. Such a step, proponents said, would insulate the trust fund from pressures to cut the deficit, which was offset by trust fund surpluses. But a bid by House Public Works and Transportation Committee leaders for an "off-budget" plan fell prey to the argument of Appropriations leaders that such a change would force deeper cuts in other programs.

## House Committee Action

In the House, HR 2310 was jointly referred to Public Works and Transportation and to the Science, Space and Technology committees. The Science panel reported the bill June 3 (H Rept 100-123, Part I), and Public Works reported it June 26 (Part II).

**Public Works Bill.** Debate in the Public Works Subcommittee on Aviation occurred over an amendment by Joe Kolter, D-Pa., to add more than $200 million for 32 airport "improvement" projects — runway extensions and the like — in certain districts, particularly those of Public Works members.

Before the markup, Kolter circulated an unusual form to committee colleagues inviting them to contribute pet projects to a list he intended to offer as an amendment to the bill.

The maneuver was a challenge to Aviation Subcommittee Chairman Norman Y. Mineta, D-Calif., who had a policy against naming specific projects in airport authorizations, even though the practice had occurred in the drafting of bills appropriating funds for airport programs. Mineta maintained that Congress' proper role was to authorize funding for broad national purposes, not to decide whether any particular project had merit. That task, he believed, was best left to DOT.

Kolter's amendment was rejected by a vote of 9-18.

The subcommittee's bill as approved did not require airlines to disclose their performance records to the public, despite pressure by some members.

The full Public Works and Transportation Committee June 3 approved HR 2310 by voice vote and made no substantial changes in the bill as approved by the Aviation subcommittee. It reauthorized airport programs through fiscal 1992.

The full committee adopted by voice vote an amendment that required 10 percent of funding for airport construction projects to go to firms owned by minorities or women.

**Science, Space and Technology Bill.** The Science, Space and Technology Committee May 20 approved by voice vote a $416 million package to support federal research and development to improve the air-traffic control system.

While the bulk of the spending in the Science measure was targeted at research on the air-traffic control system, at least $25 million would be spent each year on research to expand capacity at the nation's airports.

## House Floor Action

The House Oct. 1 unanimously passed the bill after narrowly rejecting a bid to shield federal airport and airway programs from pressures to cut the federal deficit. Lawmakers voted 396-0 in favor of HR 2310.

Although members were frustrated over air travel problems, they refused to back a plan to exempt programs from cuts that could be required by a new version of the Gramm-Rudman-Hollings anti-deficit law (PL 100-119). *(Gramm-Rudman "fix," p. 67)*

The House voted 197-202 against an amendment by James J. Howard, D-N.J., chairman of the Public Works and Transportation Committee, to remove the Airport and Airway Trust Fund from the budget, a step that would protect programs from the Gramm-Rudman budget knife.

It at first appeared as if there would be no vote on the Howard off-budget plan. Under pressure from opponents, the Rules panel rejected a Public Works request that floor consideration of the amendment be allowed. However, in a surprising defeat for the leadership, whose wishes Rules generally followed, lawmakers Sept. 30 voted 178-235 to reject the rule (H Res 275).

Rules members then met hastily to approve a rule as sought by Howard, setting up the confrontation on the off-budget plan.

The ultimate verdict had less to do with policy arguments than with lawmakers having to make an unpleasant choice between antagonizing Public Works leaders or antagonizing Appropriations leaders. Both committees routinely doled out funds for home-district projects avidly sought by members.

In other action, the House:

● Adopted, 385-14, an amendment to extend for another 10 years a DOT program to guarantee airline service to small communities.

● Adopted by voice vote an amendment to require small businesses owned by minorities or women to receive at least 10 percent of revenues from airport concessions, such as food stands.

● Rejected, 198-211, an amendment to delete a provision requiring officials at the Burbank Airport in Southern California to propose a new pattern of runway use to the FAA in order to reallocate aircraft noise. Critics said it was inappropriate for Congress to legislate on such matters.

## Senate Committee Action

The Senate's airport and airway reauthorization measure (S 1184) was referred to the Commerce, Science and Transportation Committee. By voice vote, the committee May 14 approved the package to fund programs through fiscal 1990. The bill was reported July 1 (S Rept 100-99).

Wendell H. Ford, D-Ky., chairman of the Commerce Subcommittee on Aviation, favored a three-year measure to give Congress a relatively early opportunity to take another look at airport programs. House leaders had proposed a five-year bill to give airports a longer lead time for planning projects.

Like its House counterpart, the Senate package authorized substantially more spending than in previous years for airport expansion grants and for purchases of equipment to bring the air-traffic control system up to date.

On a controversial consumer issue, John C. Danforth, Mo., Commerce's ranking Republican, pushed a plan requiring ticket sellers to tell customers what the average delay had been on requested flights. When Danforth was unable to reach agreement with Ford on specific legislative language, they — Danforth and Ford — opted instead to send a letter to Transportation Secretary Elizabeth H. Dole urging the agency not to wait for a legislative directive and to issue rules in advance of the peak summer travel season. They told Dole that "there seems to be a clear consensus that consumers need the facts if they are to make meaningful comparisons between the quality of service offered by various airlines."

The panel adopted by voice vote a plan to set up a small pilot program allowing the FAA to make block grants to states for airport projects. Under the existing authorization, virtually all federal grants were made to airports.

The Senate bill, like the House measure, linked the size of grants to the volume of cargo traffic at an airport, as well as to the number of passengers served.

In addition, the bill increased from 8 percent of total grant funds to 10 percent the set-aside requirement for noise-abatement projects. The House bill contained a similar provision.

The Senate bill contained a trade-related provision — absent from the House measure — that would deny foreigners the right to bid on U.S. airport construction projects unless the bidder's country granted equivalent access to American firms. A similar provision was adopted in conference.

Also, the Senate bill provided for the hiring of 1,000 new air-traffic controllers by the end of fiscal 1988, to reach a level of 16,000 controllers. The House package did not set any target for the number of controllers. In conference, the number was set at 15,900.

## Senate Floor Action

With a few additions to the committee-approved measure, the full Senate Oct. 28 voted 96-1 to pass the airport reauthorization bill.

Before voting, the Senate inserted the text of its own bill (S 1184) in place of the House language in HR 2310.

Under the Senate measure, passenger ticket taxes and other fees that flowed into the Airport and Airway Trust Fund would be extended through calendar year 1991.

Despite repeated threats, the Senate did not add provisions to require airlines to disclose their on-time performance records.

Like the House measure, the Senate bill would extend for another 10 years, as well as expand, DOT's "essential air services" program for small communities.

Air-service provisions were tacked onto the Senate bill by an amendment, adopted by voice voice. Among other things, the amendment required subsidized airlines to upgrade service by using aircraft with 15 or more seats, two pilots and two engines.

Before adopting the amendment, the Senate voted 57-37 to kill a plan to renew the existing program for only two years.

In other action, the Senate:

● Adopted by voice vote an amendment to require the installation of collision-avoidance equipment in both private and commercial aircraft.

This provision had been adopted as a separate bill in the House Nov. 3 (HR 1517 — H Rept 100-286, Parts I and II) by a vote of 405-4.

● Adopted by voice vote an amendment that forced DOT to issue rules requiring life preservers, including ones for small children and infants, on any flight over water. Also, DOT would have to issue rules requiring interior cabins to meet tougher flammability standards.

● Adopted by voice vote an amendment to give the FAA authority to prosecute violators of air safety regulations.

The bill also extended a "penalty clause" in existing law that automatically reduced authorizations for operating expenses if appropriations for equipment and grants fell below authorized levels.

Taxes, including the 8 percent levy on airline tickets, would be extended at their existing levels through Dec. 31, 1991. However, they would be reduced by half in 1991 if the Airport and Airway Trust Fund held a surplus that was projected to exceed $3 billion. The 1987 surplus was well over $5 billion, and many aviation groups claimed some sort of "trigger" mechanism was needed to prod appropriators to spend the money faster.

## Conference Action

The Senate Dec. 17 approved the final conference package (H Rept 100-484) by voice vote; the House followed suit, by a vote of 410-1, the following day.

Although most differences between the House and Senate versions of the bill were resolved Dec. 2, the conference agreement was not filed until Dec. 15, after negotiators resolved discrepancies on the tax portion of the package.

The conferees agreed to a "trigger tax" aimed at reducing any incentive for lawmakers to use surplus trust fund revenues as a cushion against the deficit. Taxes, including an 8 percent levy, would be cut be half in calendar year 1990 if total appropriations for trust fund programs in fiscal years 1988 and 1989 were less than 85 percent of authorizations for such programs over that same period.

## Major Provisions

The airport and airway reauthorization package included approximately $20.1 billion for federal grants to airports and for upgrading the aging air-traffic control system. It also renewed taxes and other fees, set to expire Dec. 31, 1987, that were used to finance the Airport and Airway Trust Fund.

As cleared, HR 2310 included the following major provisions. Unless otherwise noted, the authorized funding came from the trust fund.

### Airport Improvement Program

● Authorized $1.7 billion annually for fiscal 1988-90 and $1.8 billion annually for fiscal 1991-92 for FAA grants to airports for expansion projects and other types of improvements.

● Required that not less than 10 percent of total grant funds be set aside for "disadvantaged" small businesses owned by racial minorities or women. Also, an airport had to ensure, to the maximum extent practicable, that at least 10 percent of concessions went to small businesses owned or leased by such individuals.

● Changed the eligibility criteria for major commercial service airports known as "primary" airports to allow about 160 additional airports to become eligible for the FAA improvement grants. In 1987 about 260 airports qualified as primary airports. The minimum amount any primary airport could receive in one year was raised from $200,000 to $300,000 and the maximum amount was raised from $12.5 million to $16 million.

● Linked the size of airport grants to the volume of cargo traffic at certain airports. Previously the size of grants was based solely on passenger volume. Some 45 airports were expected to benefit from the new cargo program, to which up to $50 million in annual grant funds could be devoted. However, no airport could receive more than 8 percent of total cargo funds.

● Retained the requirement in current law for 10 percent of grant funds to go to "reliever" airports that diverted general aviation aircraft away from commercial-service airports.

● Reduced from 5.5 percent to 2.5 percent the share of grant funds that had to be spent at small commercial-service airports. (However, the larger of such airports would be reclassified as primary airports under the bill's expanded eligibility criteria for primary airports.)

● Required that 75 percent of discretionary grant funds — those funds not based on a formula — be used for preserving and enhancing safety, capacity and security at primary and reliever airports and noise-abatement programs at such airports. Formula grants were capped at 49.5 percent of total grant funding.

● Increased from 8 percent to 10 percent the share of total grant funds that had to be set aside for noise-abatement projects, such as soundproofing of homes.

● Established a demonstration program to run from fiscal 1989-91 whereby three states would receive block grants for airport expansion projects. Previously all grants were made directly by the FAA to individual airports.

● Prohibited use of funds for airport projects using products or services of a foreign country if the U.S. trade representative determined that the country denied fair opportunities for U.S. firms to bid on construction projects that cost more than $500,000 and were funded by the foreign government. This provision was primarily intended to prod the Japanese into giving U.S. contractors a fair opportunity to bid on that country's Kansai airport project.

● Required contracts for engineering and design services related to airport projects to be awarded to the most qualified bidder — not necessarily the lowest-cost bidder.

● Directed DOT to conduct a comprehensive two-year study of long-term airport capacity needs and to come up with a plan for development of the airport system through the year 2010.

### Air-Traffic Control System

● Authorized $1.38 billion for fiscal 1988, $1.73 billion for fiscal 1989 and $2.19 billion for fiscal 1990 for FAA purchases of equipment to upgrade the air-traffic control system.

● Authorized funding to operate the air-traffic control system through fiscal 1990. Each year's authorization was to be limited to half of the funding authorization in that year for all other trust fund programs. In addition, there would be a $2 reduction in authorizations for operating expenses for every $1 that appropriations for other trust fund programs fell short of authorizations. Authorizations were capped at $1.64 billion in fiscal 1988, $1.82 billion in fiscal 1989 and $2.06 billion in fiscal 1990.

● Authorized $201 million for fiscal 1988, $215 million for fiscal 1989 and $222 million for fiscal 1990 for FAA research and development projects to improve the air-traffic control system. Of these amounts, a minimum annual authorization of $25 million was set for research and development programs to increase and preserve airport capacity.

● Set minimum levels of funding for navigational aids known as Instrument Landing Systems at primary and reliever airports of $27 million for fiscal 1988, $30 million for fiscal 1989 and $35 million for fiscal 1990.

● Required the FAA to have at least 15,900 air-traffic controllers on the job by Sept. 30, 1988. At the end of fiscal 1987, the FAA had just over 15,400 workers on the payroll.

### Safety

● Required installation, within four years, of a collision-avoidance device known as TCAS-II on planes with more than 30 seats.

● Increased from $1,000 to $10,000 the civil penalty for each violation of FAA safety rules by a commercial air carrier. Also, the FAA was given jurisdiction for two years following enactment of the bill to assess civil penalties when the total amount in a controversy was less than $50,000 and the case did not involve the seizure of aircraft. Previously the FAA had to get federal attorneys to prosecute such violations.

● Increased the penalty for interfering with accident investigations from a $5,000 fine and imprisonment of up to one year to a fine of $250,000 and imprisonment of up to 10 years.

● Directed DOT to consider requiring installation of cockpit voice recorders and flight-data recorders on commuter and general aviation aircraft.

● Directed DOT to consider requiring adequate uniform life preservers, life rafts and flotation devices on any flight that occurred over water, and adequate information on use of such devices. The bill also directed the agency to consider requiring seats on commercial aircraft to meet improved crash-worthiness standards based on the best available testing standards.

● Directed DOT to study the need for safety equipment, such as crash-resistant inner fuel tanks, to minimize the risk of fire or explosion.

● Allowed the FAA access to DOT's National Driver Register to check on the driving records, including citations for drunken driving, of pilots seeking an FAA medical certificate.

### Taxes

● Extended through Dec. 31, 1990, current taxes that financed the Airport and Airway Trust Fund, including the 8 percent tax on passenger tickets, a 5 percent tax on the amount shippers paid for domestic air-cargo transport and a $3 per-passenger tax on flights from the United States to points abroad.

● Required these taxes, except for the international departure fee, to be cut in half in calendar year 1990 if total appropriations for trust fund programs in fiscal years 1988 and 1989 were less than 85 percent of authorizations for such programs over that same period. This plan was included to reduce the incentive for lawmakers to use surplus trust fund revenues as a cushion against the federal deficit. Historically, appropriations had been held well below the level of authorizations.

● Provided a general tax exemption for emergency medical helicopters, engaged in providing emergency medical services, that did not use the federally assisted airport or airway system.

### Essential Air Services

● Extended for 10 years, through Sept. 30, 1998, the DOT's Essential Air Services program to subsidize airline service to small communities that lost service following enactment of the 1978 airline deregulation law (PL 95-504). *(Background, Congress and the Nation Vol. V, p. 311)*

With a few exceptions, aircraft providing service were required to have two engines and two pilots and seats for 15 passengers. There previously had been no minimum standards in law. Also, certain new communities were allowed to receive federal subsidies to maintain service if they agreed to pay a share of the costs. Initial estimates indicated that annual outlays of about $20 million could as much as double under the revised program.

# Smoking on Airplanes Ban

Congress cleared a $10.6 billion transportation spending package for fiscal 1988 that included a two-year ban on smoking on domestic flights scheduled to last no more than two hours. The package was folded into the continuing resolution (H J Res 395 — PL 100-202) signed by President Reagan Dec. 22, 1987.

The smoking ban was expected to affect about four-fifths of all domestic flights. Negotiators compromised between a House plan to permanently prohibit smoking on flights of two hours or less and a Senate proposal to ban for two years smoking on flights of 90 minutes or less.

Even though the House and Senate each had voted for some sort of ban, the tobacco industry and members of tobacco-industry states made a last-ditch effort to kill the proposals in conference. But House conferees Dec. 18 rejected a motion by Rep. W. G. "Bill" Hefner, D-N.C., to strike a ban from the package.

Pro-ban forces were led by flight attendants and a coalition of health groups, including the American Cancer Society. Proponents contended that the health of non-smokers was damaged by exposure to cigarette smoke in airplane cabins. Their claims were buttressed by a National Academy of Sciences study recommending a ban on smoking on all flights.

Supporters attributed their victory in part to growing public awareness of the health risks of smoking as well as a greater willingness on the part of non-smokers to assert their "right" not to have to breathe unhealthful air.

### House Action

The House Transportation Appropriations Subcommittee June 11 met in closed session and approved the fiscal 1988 transportation appropriations bill (HR 2890) by voice vote. The House Appropriations Committee reported the bill July 7 (H Rept 100-202).

Illinois Democrat Richard J. Durbin offered amendments in subcommittee and full committee that effectively would prohibit smoking on flights by withholding Federal Aviation Administration grants from airports that provided landing rights to airlines that permitted smoking on flights. The amendments were rejected.

Durbin said the segregation of passengers into smoking and non-smoking sections of airplanes failed to protect non-smokers. The opposition, led by members from tobacco-producing districts, attacked the plan on procedural grounds, saying it was against House rules to attach legislative language to an appropriations bill.

Durbin tried once again to attach a smoking ban during House floor consideration of the transportation appropriations bill July 13. After an emotional debate, lawmakers narrowly adopted an amendment by Durbin to ban smoking on planes not scheduled to be in the air for more than two hours on a **key vote of 198-193 (R 74-91; D 124-102).** *(1987 key votes, p. 965)*

Durbin's triumph on the anti-smoking bid surprised many members, including Durbin. "Based on our defeats in committee, we did not expect to win on the floor," he said. "We were pleasantly surprised."

The House then passed HR 2890 on a 282-108 vote.

### Senate Action

The Senate Appropriations Committee Oct. 1 approved its version of HR 2890 (S Rept 100-198) that included a smoking ban for commercial flights of two hours or less. The Appropriations Transportation Subcommittee had approved the ban at its markup Sept. 30.

The committee bill prohibited smoking on domestic flights of two hours or less for a trial period of three years. The bill included a civil penalty of $1,000 for each violation and also prohibited tampering with or disabling any smoke alarm on a plane with a penalty of $2,000 for each violation.

Ernest F. Hollings, D-S.C., provided the main resistance to the ban at the full Appropriations Committee meeting. Hollings insisted he objected only because the smoking ban constituted legislation attached to an appropriations bill. He noted that it was not relevant to the appropriation and that it established civil penalties.

But a moment later, Hollings was jokingly calling on other senators to support him and said of one: "I've been helping his wheat farmers for years. I need some of his help for my tobacco farmers."

Jim Sasser, D-Tenn., also complained that subcommittee Chairman Frank R. Lautenberg, D-N.J., would "wham-bam-pop this thing into the appropriations bill without having heard from the industry or those in the health field."

But Lautenberg rehearsed some of the information from recent scientific studies on passive smoking.

Before a vote was taken, Hollings suggested that committee Chairman John C. Stennis, D-Miss., strike the smoking ban from the bill as inappropriate matter on an appropriations bill. Stennis agreed to do so and spoke as if he thought that ended the matter. But after several minutes of consultation with staff and with ranking Republican member Mark O. Hatfield, Ore., Stennis called for a vote on the ban.

At that point, Lautenberg's preparation paid off. The committee had been in session for more than five hours and about half the members had left. But when the vote was taken, Lautenberg could supplement the eight votes he had in the room with nine proxies. The vote was 17-12.

Despite opposition from cigarette makers and tobacco-state lawmakers, the Senate Oct. 29 agreed by voice vote to attach a ban on smoking during commercial flights of 90 minutes or less to the $11.1 billion fiscal 1988 transportations appropriations bill. The Senate went on to vote 84-10 in favor of passage of the spending measure.

As expected, a group of tobacco-state senators, led by Jesse Helms, R-N.C., tried to kill the plan. Helms said a ban would hurt small tobacco farmers who grew a crop that was "entirely legal."

When the bill was brought up for debate Oct. 28, Helms raised a parliamentary objection to the smoking plan on the grounds that the Appropriations panel had sent a matter to the floor that was under the legislative jurisdiction of the Commerce Committee.

The parliamentarian agreed and the following day Lautenberg decided to strike the plan from the measure and offer it as a separate floor amendment.

After much wrangling, Lautenberg and Helms agreed to a compromise that not only reduced the scope of the ban from two-hour to 90-minute flights, but also shortened the trial period from three to two years.

## Airline Safety Penalties

Legislation to make it a crime to violate intentionally air safety reporting requirements was signed into law Sept. 30, 1987 (HR 1163 — PL 100-121).

The Federal Aviation Administration (FAA), acting under the 1958 Federal Aviation Act (PL 85-726), required airlines to maintain records on pilot training, maintenance, flight time and on how to handle hazardous material and the processing and certification of flight crews. Airlines filed mandatory reports of aircraft inspections with the FAA, along with reports describing the detection and correction of any aircraft defects.

The penalty under the 1958 law was a fine of not less

than $100 or more than $5,000 for failing or refusing to make or keep a report or record required by the law. Advocates of the legislation said the penalties were inadequate.

HR 1163 made intentional failure to report or keep the required records a criminal violation and set the penalty at $5,000 for an individual and $10,000 for an organization. The bill made it a felony for intentionally falsifying or concealing information in the required reports. Punishment was set at five years in prison and a fine.

The House Judiciary Committee May 18 approved the measure by voice vote. It was reported May 28 (H Rept 100-114, Part I) and referred to the Public Works and Transportation Committee, which discharged the bill June 19.

The full House approved HR 1163 under suspension of the rules June 22. In the Senate, the bill was reported by the Commerce, Science and Transportation Committee Aug. 7 (S Rept 100-146) and passed by the full Senate Sept. 16.

## Aviation Safety

Congress cleared legislation (HR 4686 — PL 100-591) in 1988 directing the Federal Aviation Administration (FAA) to undertake research on a variety of topics, including the extent to which "human factors," such as pilot error, accounted for plane accidents.

The House cleared HR 4686 on Oct. 21 when it approved the measure as amended the day before by the Senate. President Reagan signed the bill Nov. 3.

The bill also earmarked 15 percent of the FAA's fiscal 1989 and 1990 research budgets for unspecified "long-term" research and development projects that were unlikely to result in new safety regulations within five years.

The House passed the measure — reported by the Science, Space and Technology Committee (H Rept 100-894) Sept. 8 — by voice vote on Sept. 20. The Senate Commerce, Science and Transportation Committee approved a nearly identical bill (S 2746 — S Rept 100-584) the same day by voice vote.

## Aviation Whistleblowers

The House Sept. 13, 1988, approved by voice vote a measure (HR 5073) to protect from retaliation aviation workers who called company safety violations to the government's attention. But the Senate did not act on the bill.

Proponents said the measure would improve safety conditions in the airline industry. They said workers at some firms were afraid to report safety violations to the government for fear of reprisal by management.

The bill's sponsors argued that a good precedent for HR 5073 had been set by existing "whistleblower" laws that protected government workers, employees of defense contractors and nuclear power operators and others.

The Reagan administration offered no objections to the House bill. While airlines and aircraft manufacturing firms had misgivings about some provisions, they did not publicly resist the legislation.

The House-passed measure would outlaw retaliation against pilots, mechanics, aircraft assembly-line workers and others with safety tasks who reported to the Federal Aviation Administration (FAA) hazards they "reasonably"

believed constituted a safety threat or violation.

Also protected were workers who refused to permit immediate operation of an aircraft if they had "a reasonable basis for believing" that serious injury might result.

Employees who thought they had been punished for bringing safety hazards to the FAA's attention could appeal to the labor secretary for relief, including reinstatement with back pay. The secretary's ruling could be appealed to a Labor Department administrative-law judge and ultimately to the federal courts.

However, the secretary could require a worker to pay up to $5,000 of an employer's legal fees as a penalty for bringing "bad-faith" complaints against the employer. This provision helped temper airlines' opposition to the whistleblower bill.

Sponsors rejected a push by aviation firms for language that would require employees to notify their employers of safety problems before calling the FAA. Bill proponents said the public-safety imperative overrode management's right of first notification.

The House Public Works Committee approved HR 5073 (H Rept 100-883) by voice vote on Aug. 9. It made no changes to the package approved July 28 by the Aviation Subcommittee. The full House considered the measure under suspension of the rules, a procedure that permitted no amendments.

## Air-Traffic Controllers

Reacting to public concern over the safety of flying in U.S. skies, the House passed a bill March 30, 1988, that would permit the rehiring of air-traffic controllers who walked off their jobs in 1981 during a labor dispute with the Federal Aviation Administration (FAA). President Reagan fired 11,400 of the controllers in August of that year, citing a law barring strikes by federal employees.

The bill (HR 3396 — H Rept 100-375), passed by a 234-180 vote, directed the Department of Transportation and the Office of Personnel Management to rehire at least 500 former controllers in both fiscal 1988 and 1989. No other action was taken on the bill.

Reagan would have vetoed the measure, in any event, according to the Office of Management and Budget. The administration contended that the policy would threaten FAA management of the air-traffic control system and require extensive retraining of the former controllers.

But Guy V. Molinari, R-N.Y., the bill's sponsor, argued that the fired controllers' expertise was much needed. "Near midair collisions have more than doubled since 1983," he said. "Yet, there are fewer experienced controllers today than before the strike, and they are confronting higher levels of air traffic volume."

Opponents countered that rehiring the controllers would cause morale problems in the control towers for those who did not honor the strike as well as create animosity between the strikers and their replacements. Others said that rehiring the controllers would send the wrong signal to federal unions by giving them leverage in encouraging members to strike again. Still others argued that the bill was unnecessary because controller staffing levels were almost up to where they were before the strike.

In 1988 there were 15,520 air-traffic controllers, compared with 16,375 before the strike, according to the FAA. However, the number of full-performance operators — those who were fully qualified to operate all positions —

had dropped to 8,904 as opposed to 13,170 in 1981. Reagan's fiscal 1989 budget called for a controller work force of around 16,800.

According to Molinari, only the best 1,000 of the fired controllers would be hired under HR 3396. The bill also required that rehired air-traffic controllers complete a six-month probationary period before their appointments could become final. The rehired controllers also would have to complete at least six years of new service before qualifying for retirement benefits.

Molinari said he included the probationary period not only to ensure that those rehired performed their duties well, but to provide a method to remove anyone who caused morale problems. He argued that morale actually would improve with the addition of the 1,000 experienced controllers, particularly at understaffed airports.

The measure had the support of the Air Line Pilots Association and the Brotherhood of Railway and Airline Clerks.

### Air-Traffic Controller Training

The House also passed legislation (HR 3779) that directed the FAA to investigate better ways to train air-traffic controllers to use sophisticated computer equipment. Saying that the FAA was already conducting research in this area, the Reagan administration opposed the bill as unnecessary. No action was taken in the Senate.

HR 3779 was reported (H Rept 100-893) by the House Science, Space and Technology Committee Sept. 8, 1988; it passed the full House by voice vote Sept. 20.

# Independent FAA

A Senate panel June 28, 1988, approved a measure to remove the Federal Aviation Administration (FAA) from the Department of Transportation (DOT) and to establish it as an independent agency. But no further action on the bill, which was opposed by DOT, was taken during the 100th Congress.

The Commerce, Science and Transportation Committee voted 14-4 in favor of a package (S 1600 — S Rept 100-440) crafted by Aviation Subcommittee Chairman Wendell H. Ford, D-Ky. Concerned about traffic-clogged airports and unsafe planes, congressional proponents said an independent FAA was needed to shield the responsibility of ensuring safe and efficient air travel from political interference by the DOT secretary and the White House. They vowed to pursue the proposal in the 101st Congress.

But opponents feared that an independent FAA would be dominated by the aviation industry and that Ford's plan would pit the DOT secretary and FAA administrator against each other in a struggle for power over setting aviation policy. S 1600 would retain the DOT secretary's current task of promoting civil aviation.

DOT Secretary Jim Burnley threatened to recommend a presidential veto of S 1600. Burnley criticized several key provisions, including one that would provide a seven-year term for the FAA administrator. Although the president would still pick the candidate for this post, subject to Senate approval, he would not be allowed to fire a sitting administrator over policy differences. Under existing law, the FAA administrator could be fired for such reasons.

Other major provisions of S 1600:

● The FAA administrator would be permitted to grant an "incentive allowance" of up to 10 percent of base pay to induce staffers to accept transfers to high-priority locations. Proponents said existing rules hampered the ability of FAA managers to shift air-traffic controllers to areas of the country where they were most needed.

● The FAA would be permitted to issue new rules limiting requirements for competitive bids on contracts to build essential safety systems. Proponents said procurement regulators were bound by red tape that prevented timely acquisition of urgently needed equipment.

● The attorney general, in consultation with the DOT secretary and the Federal Trade Commission, would be directed to investigate anti-competitive practices by the domestic airline industry. Sponsors were concerned about a trend toward single-airline dominance of major airports that they said could eventually increase passenger fares.

In addition to opposition from DOT, Ford also faced a fight from Budget Committee leaders over his plan to protect aviation programs from budget cuts. Ford dropped several provisions from S 1600 designed to do just that after Budget leaders objected that the proposals had not been reviewed by their panel. However, he vowed to try to attach similar language to S 1600 if it reached the floor.

Key House leaders were skeptical of the need to overhaul the FAA. The chairman of the Public Works Subcommittee on Aviation, Norman Y. Mineta, D-Calif., raised a number of concerns, among them that an independent FAA administrator would lack sufficient political clout to persuade the White House to boost funding for aviation programs. His committee held hearings on revamping the FAA but took no action on a bill.

# Aircraft Liability Insurance

Legislation aimed at lowering liability insurance costs for manufacturers of small, private planes was approved by House and Senate committees but died before the end of the year. It faced strong opposition from trial lawyers representing victims of aircraft accidents and from consumer groups.

The Senate Commerce, Science and Transportation Committee June 2, 1988, reported a bill (S 473 — S Rept 100-378) that would pre-empt state liability laws with new federal standards limiting the exposure of manufacturers to victims' lawsuits.

The measure was identical to a committee bill (S 2760) that died on the Senate floor in the 99th Congress. It also was similar to a package (HR 2238 — H Rept 100-646, Part I) reported May 24 by the House Public Works and Transportation Committee. The Public Works measure was not sent to the House floor because it did not have the approval of the Judiciary and Energy and Commerce committees, which did not act before the end of the year. The Judiciary panel had long been hostile to efforts to pre-empt state liability laws.

A key provision in the Senate Commerce package would shield a manufacturer from liability for injuries that occurred more than 20 years after an aircraft's delivery. The House committee package set a more restrictive 12-year liability limit; many states had no such limits.

In nearly all circumstances, the House and Senate committee bills would restrict the liability of a defendant to his share of responsibility for damages. In many states, a defendant who was only partially responsible for an accident might have to pay more than his share if the victim could not fully recover damages from other responsible parties.

The liability standards in the Senate Commerce bill did not apply to lawsuits filed by innocent bystanders injured in an accident. The House package did not have this exemption.

Both bills applied to general aviation aircraft, defined as planes with fewer than 20 seats that did not provide commercial passenger service.

# Airline Passenger Protection

Passenger complaints about shoddy airline practices and dissatisfaction with the workings of a 1978 law (PL 95-504) that deregulated the airline industry contributed to the push in the 100th Congress for consumer legislation to protect airline travelers.

Each chamber passed its own version of legislation (HR 3051) in 1987 that contained similar provisions requiring airlines to disclose service-performance records, including data on flight delays. But conferees failed to resolve several major differences between the two versions and the measure died when the 100th Congress adjourned.

HR 3051 — the Airline Passenger Protection Act — was approved by the House Public Works and Transportation Subcommittee on Aviation July 30, 1987. The full committee approved the measure by voice vote Aug. 5 and reported it two days later (H Rept 100-293). The full House passed the measure Oct. 5 by voice vote.

The Senate Commerce Committee July 14 approved by voice vote a similar airline service bill (S 1485 — S Rept 100-138). The measure was reported Aug. 3. The full Senate inserted the language of S 1485 into HR 3051 before passing it 88-5 Oct. 30.

## Drug-Testing Plan

The standoff between conferees centered on an unrelated plan in the Senate bill to require random drug and alcohol testing in major transportation industries. House Public Works leaders refused to act on a measure that contained requirements for random testing of truck, bus and airline workers.

During consideration of its airline passenger bill Oct. 29, the Senate approved an amendment that called for random drug and alcohol testing in the airline, rail, bus and truck industries. Tests of some 3 million U.S. truckers — many of whom were self-employed — were expected to present the biggest administrative problem for regulators.

The amendment was based on a drug-testing bill (S 1041 — S Rept 100-43) that had been approved by the Commerce Committee earlier in the year.

Critics argued that the legislation was unworkable and violated personal privacy and other constitutional guarantees.

The vehement opposition by House negotiators to the drug-testing plan left HR 3051 in limbo for much of the 100th Congress. But, on Sept. 30, 1988, House Public Works Chairman Glenn M. Anderson, D-Calif., surprised Senate Commerce negotiators when he suggested reviving talks on the bill. Saying that travelers needed to be protected against workers on drugs, he declared, "We cannot afford any further delay."

But the motivation behind Anderson's sudden move was unclear. Aides said Anderson wanted to break the logjam on the three principal components of HR 3051: drug testing, provisions to require airlines to disclose their service records and language to require airlines to pay benefits to workers harmed by mergers.

But Senate Commerce aides said that at an Oct. 6 members' meeting to discuss HR 3051, Anderson seemed primarily interested in reviving the airline-labor provisions. House appropriators had been forced to drop such provisions from a transportation spending measure after encountering a veto threat from President Reagan. Airline-labor groups were pushing Public Works leaders to find a new vehicle for enacting such provisions.

In any event, the meeting resulted in no progress. Commerce negotiators balked at reviving the airline-labor matter, saying that Reagan would be sure to veto HR 3051. Members never met to discuss the bill again.

However, Commerce members did push the House to attach the drug-testing plan to the omnibus drug bill (HR 5210), a move that ultimately failed. *(Story, below)*

## Airline Mergers

The airline-labor provisions Anderson sought to revive — and that the Reagan administration opposed — were contained in both the House and Senate versions of HR 3051.

The Senate plan would shift from the transportation secretary to the labor secretary the authority to require airlines that merged to compensate workers who lost their jobs or were otherwise hurt by the transaction. No benefits were required if the labor secretary determined that the cost of payments outweighed the firms' financial gains from the transaction.

The plan also would expedite a scheduled transfer of authority to approve airline mergers from the Department of Transportation (DOT) to the Department of Justice. Existing law made the shift effective Jan. 1, 1989; the amendment would make the transfer effective upon enactment of the legislation.

The amendment was crafted by Brock Adams, D-Wash., who was transporation secretary during the Carter administration. He argued that a change was needed because DOT had been unwilling to compensate workers hurt by a rash of airline mergers. The Reagan administration was strongly opposed to such "labor protection" legislation, saying that it could make mergers prohibitively expensive.

The Senate airline merger amendment, which was adopted 64-28 Oct. 30, 1987, was identical to a bill (S 724 — S Rept 100-104) reported by the Commerce Committee July 9.

The House version of HR 3051 was similar to the Senate plan but left labor-protection authority with the DOT secretary — although the provision would make it tougher to justify not requiring payments to workers.

An identical plan was contained in an administration-opposed labor-protection bill (HR 1101 — H Rept 100-142), which passed the House June 22 by voice vote.

## Other Hurdles

Other hurdles in reaching agreement were provisions contained in the House but not the Senate bill, including:

● **Capacity Limits.** The House bill would require DOT to establish maximum numbers of takeoffs and landings at some 40 airports. Critics, including airline carriers, argued that such restrictions might result in cutbacks on flights at congested airports, leading to higher fares. There also were concerns that capacity limits might keep carriers from becoming more competitive at airports now dominated by a single airline.

● **Baggage Compensation.** The House package would require airlines to compensate consumers for lost baggage. The airline industry strongly objected to this requirement, arguing that it would increase costs as well as the potential for fraud, a problem with baggage claims.

● **Hub Requirements.** The House version would require DOT to set minimum passenger service requirements for hub airports through which many flights were routed. For example, DOT could require carriers to provide more time between flights to make it easier for passengers to make connections. Some feared that this sort of proposal could introduce "re-regulation" of the airline industry.

However, the drug-testing confrontation and differences between other issues were not the only culprits for inaction. The public furor over flight delays, lost baggage and the like abated somewhat during 1988.

The legislation took off during the 1987 summer travel season, when complaints to DOT reached record levels. But consumer complaints and media attention slackened after DOT issued its own rules requiring airlines to disclose their on-time records, and some key lawmakers became convinced that airline carriers were working harder to improve service.

The Reagan administration and the airline industry strongly objected that the disclosure of service-performance records would be costly and difficult to implement. The White House threatened to veto the legislation.

# Transportation Drug-Test Plan

The 100th Congress ended with lawmakers heartily congratulating themselves and each other on passage of sweeping legislation (HR 5210 — PL 100-690) to combat drug abuse. But little was said about a matter that failed to make it into that measure: requirements for random drug and alcohol testing of workers in major transportation industries. *(Drug bill, p. 748)*

Even though such provisions were contained in the Senate version of the drug bill — and, in the session's final weeks, key House negotiators voiced support for random testing — members were unable to work out a deal.

Senate Commerce Committee leaders said their House counterparts stayed away from the bargaining table for months and that when they finally did get there, they seemed more concerned about protecting workers' rights than the safety of the traveling public.

House negotiators said a deal could have been struck in the final days but for the adamant opposition by key senators and administration officials to language to ensure that workers who tested positive would not be fired by their employers but be allowed to enter rehabilitation programs instead.

House lawmakers also noted that Commerce leaders opposed efforts to wrap into the drug measure the provisions of a separate rail-testing bill (HR 4748) that had been passed by the House. Senate negotiators insisted that any new plan cover all major transportation modes.

The drive for a testing bill also encountered jurisdictional hurdles in the House: The Energy and Commerce panel had responsibility for rail-testing provisions, while the Public Works Committee had responsibility for airline,

bus and truck provisions. Although Energy and Commerce leaders eventually came out in favor of a rail-testing bill, there was little effort among leaders of the House panels to develop the coordinated response sought by the Senate Commerce side.

After adjournment, the Reagan administration issued regulations for random drug testing of some 4 million transportation workers. Although testing proponents in Congress welcomed this step, they said legislation remained necessary to ensure that such rules were not softened by future administrations. Labor groups vowed to fight the rules in the courts and on Capitol Hill.

Department of Transportation (DOT) leaders also preferred a bill, saying Congress' approval of random testing could help sway courts to uphold the new regulations.

## Legislative History

The clear impetus for action was the January 1987 Chase, Md., rail accident, which killed 16 people and injured 175 others. A Conrail train engineer admitted to smoking marijuana shortly before his locomotive ran stop signals and collided with an Amtrak commuter train. The accident outraged many in Congress, not least the senior Republican on the Senate Commerce panel, John C. Danforth, Mo., whose daughter had planned to be on the Amtrak train but ended up taking a car ride instead.

Soon afterwards, the panel approved an ambitious measure (S 1041) crafted by Danforth and Chairman Ernest F. Hollings, D-S.C., to direct DOT officials to require random drug and alcohol testing in the airline, bus, rail and trucking industries. It drew heavy fire from organized labor leaders and never reached the floor. However, the Senate Oct. 29, 1987, agreed to attach identical provisions to its version of an airline-consumer bill (HR 3051). *(Story, above)*

Energy and Commerce Chairman John D. Dingell, D-Mich., at first declined even to consider the rail-testing provisions. Dingell viewed random testing as legally questionable and also saw laboratories as so prone to error that they could not be relied upon to handle a massive testing program. Transportation Subcommittee Chairman Thomas A. Luken, D-Ohio, appeared to feel the same way, as both Dingell and Luken aides declined to join preliminary talks on HR 3051 between Senate and House staffers.

In those talks, Public Works aides identified the trucking provisions as a major stumbling block. In particular, they were vexed by the problem of how to administer random testing of self-employed truck drivers. The truck-driver provisions also faced opposition from the Teamsters union. Talks on the airline-consumer bill stalled.

Meanwhile, with Danforth's urging, a group representing friends and families of the victims of the Chase crash, called Safe Travel America, turned up the heat on Congress. In late April, Dr. Roger Horn, the group's leader and father of a 16-year-old girl killed in the crash, paid a personal visit to Luken's Cincinnati district to blast what he viewed as the House Democrat's intransigence on random testing. *The Cincinnati Post* and *The Cincinnati Enquirer* promptly published editorials urging Luken to push for tough testing requirements.

Shortly thereafter, Luken unveiled a proposal for random testing of rail workers, saying that he had not had a chance to focus on the matter earlier. Dingell agreed to moderate his opposition to such legislation if his concerns about lab testing and other matters were met.

Luken's bill (HR 4748) was approved by the Transportation Subcommittee on June 22, 1988 — one week after the House adopted 377-27 a non-binding motion to instruct conferees on HR 3051 to accept the Danforth-Hollings drug-testing plan. The June 15 floor vote was widely seen as a sign that House members, many of whom had embraced election-year calls for a crackdown on drug abuse, favored new testing requirements.

While Luken was hoping for full committee action on HR 4748, he also started to push for folding identical provisions into the omnibus drug package that the House leadership was beginning to put together.

However, at an early July meeting of Democratic leadership and committee aides, Public Works aides indicated that Public Works Committee Chairman Glenn M. Anderson, D-Calif., strongly opposed including the Luken rail provisions. The aides argued that wrapping in the Luken plan would create irresistible pressure to include similar provisions covering the trucking, bus and airline industries.

Norman Y. Mineta, D-Calif., chairman of Public Works' Subcommittee on Aviation, told a reporter July 14 that he viewed random testing as unreliable and an intrusion into workers' privacy, and that Anderson and others on the panel shared his concerns. Anderson declined at the time to take a public position on the issue, although aides hinted that he would seek to negotiate some sort of deal with Senate Commerce leaders.

The Luken provisions were left out of the House drug bill, but Dingell's panel approved HR 4748 (H Rept 100-940) Aug. 9; it passed the House by voice vote Sept. 20.

Under the bill, rail workers with safety-related jobs would be subject to random tests for drugs and alcohol. Tests would be required for job applicants and workers involved in accidents or suspected of drug or alcohol use.

The bill also required federal certification of laboratories to minimize testing errors, and it set civil and criminal penalties for people who altered a substance to be tested or who reported false test results.

Workers who tested positive had to be suspended without pay and referred to a drug or alcohol rehabilitation program. They had to be fired if they failed to complete the program or if they tested positive following completion. Workers who voluntarily entered a rehabilitation program before being asked to take a test could not be fired or suspended without pay. They would have to be removed from safety-related jobs.

However, Hollings opted not to act on the bill, sticking to his bid for requirements covering all major transportation modes. Commerce leaders moved to fold the Danforth-Hollings provisions into the Senate's drug bill.

On Sept. 30, Anderson issued a surprise press release calling on members to discuss the long-blocked airline-consumer bill (HR 3051). In his release, Anderson declared that Congress should no longer delay in protecting travelers against workers on drugs.

But after Senate Commerce negotiators realized that Anderson was actually more interested in reviving the bill for its airline merger labor-protection provisions, talks broke down. The labor-protection provisions were strongly opposed by President Reagan, who threatened to veto HR 3051.

### Aiming for the Drug Bill

Lawmakers' final shot at reviving transportation drug testing came on the omnibus drug bill. On Oct. 20, negotiators made their cases to a bicameral leadership group or "tribunal" established to iron out differences between the House and Senate versions.

Public Works negotiators sought to drop the Danforth-Hollings provisions on testing for aviation, truck and bus workers. Anderson now felt, according to an aide, that a testing bill would force DOT to delay issuance of its own rules and that legislative action was pointless.

However, DOT Assistant Secretary for Governmental Affairs Edward R. Hamberger later said that he had informed House and Senate negotiators on Oct. 20 that the administration preferred new legislation to bolster its case in court and that the Danforth-Hollings plan would not have unduly stalled new regulations.

Meanwhile, Luken and Dingell pressed for folding the provisions of their drug-testing bill into the final package. Hollings objected on the grounds that the proposal covered only rail workers. An aide said Hollings saw no good public policy reason for excluding other transportation workers.

In addition, both Hollings and DOT officials strongly objected to a provision in HR 4748 that was crucial to rail labor's support for the measure as well as Dingell's reluctant decision not to oppose it. Under the bill, employers could not fire workers who tested positive, as they could under the Danforth-Hollings plan. Instead, such workers would be suspended without pay and referred to a drug or alcohol rehabilitation program.

The head of the Federal Railroad Administration, John H. Riley, said this language reduced incentives for workers voluntarily to enter rehabilitation programs before being tested. Proponents disagreed, noting that the bill permitted "volunteers," unlike workers who flunked tests, to continue to receive pay.

But Riley said DOT Secretary Jim Burnley would not support any drug-testing plan that contained the mandatory-rehabilitation provision.

With no deal in sight, tribunal members and House and Senate leaders agreed to drop all transportation testing provisions from the omnibus drug bill.

# Railroad Deregulation

A shippers' campaign for protection against price gouging by monopoly railroads failed Sept. 20, 1988, when the Senate Commerce Committee rejected a measure sought by some shippers but hotly contested by railroads and other rail customers. The 9-10 vote killed the effort for the 100th Congress, but the bill's chief sponsor, John D. Rockefeller IV, D-W.Va., vowed to resume the battle in 1989.

A House Energy and Commerce subcommittee had approved a similar bill (HR 1393) in 1987. But shippers' lobbyists said they would stop pressing for a full committee markup of that measure in light of the Senate defeat.

Both the Rockefeller and Energy and Commerce packages were aimed at pushing the Interstate Commerce Commission (ICC) to lower rates for "captive" shippers dependent on monopoly railroads. They also targeted certain railroad practices that these shippers viewed as unfair.

The legislation would revise the 1980 rail deregulation law known as the Staggers Act (PL 96-448). Railroads said the law's provisions giving carriers wide scope to set rates were vital to the industry's precarious financial health. This view was shared by many conservative economists and by deregulation enthusiasts in the Reagan administration.

They cited the industry's dismal financial performance before the law was passed. *(Staggers Act, Congress and the Nation Vol. V, p. 336)*

However, captive shippers — including coal producers, electric utilities, grain producers and chemical firms — saw changes to the Staggers law as necessary to force the ICC to protect them against monopoly abuses. They pointed to recent investments by railroads in maritime and trucking firms as evidence that the industry was healthy enough to withstand any financial damage that could result from the legislation. These parties banded together in a coalition calling itself Consumers United for Rail Equity (CURE).

Also involved in the debate was a second shippers' group, the Committee Against Revising Staggers (CARS), whose members did not depend on any one railroad and generally had enjoyed favorable rates since deregulation. Members — including tissue manufacturers and washing-machine retailers — feared their own rates would go up if the ICC ordered railroads to reduce captive shippers' rates.

## House Action

A complex measure that would push the ICC to lower rates for captive shippers dependent on monopoly railroads and to address certain "unfair" railroad practices was approved by voice vote Nov. 5, 1987, by the Energy and Commerce Subcommittee on Transportation.

The vote came after the panel adopted, 9-6, an amendment by Subcommittee Chairman Thomas A. Luken, D-Ohio, to a bill (HR 1393) crafted by lawmakers backing the captive shippers. The Luken plan retained key features of the bill and was strongly opposed by railroads.

A year earlier the Energy and Commerce Committee had narrowly rejected efforts to attach similar provisions to legislation providing for a public sale of the Conrail freight railroad. *(1985-86 action, p. 359)*

Prospects for full committee action hinged in part on a separate matter that members had sidestepped at the subcommittee markup: whether to require firms to pay benefits to workers who lost their jobs or were otherwise hurt when railroads sold branch lines to new carriers. Hoping to foster growth of the short-line industry, the ICC had exempted such transactions from labor-protection requirements.

Energy and Commerce Chairman John D. Dingell, D-Mich., was a strong supporter of rail-labor proposals, opposed by railroads, to close the exemption for short-line sales. There was much speculation that Dingell, who also backed relief for the shippers, would seek to tie such proposals to a captive-shipper package.

But committee sources said Dingell was wary of losing votes of members who might be inclined to support the Luken package but were less likely to back a labor plan. Negotiations to reach some sort of deal were expected.

The Luken panel rejected, 2-11, a labor-protection amendment by James J. Florio, D-N.J. However, a number of the "nay" votes came from members who said they preferred to deal with the labor matter in full committee.

The subcommittee also rejected a series of GOP amendments to make the package more palatable to railroads.

Major elements of the legislation addressed:

● **Rate Complaints.** Under existing law, shippers could file complaints about a carrier's rates with the ICC. To determine whether it had jurisdiction to order a reduction, the agency applied several tests. It had to determine

that the challenged rate exceeded 180 percent of the railroad's operating, or "variable," costs. It also had to determine that the shipper lacked certain competitive alternatives, such as access to another carrier's system or ability to buy the product from another source. Even if the shipper met both tests, the ICC could find that the rate was reasonable because of the railroad's need to earn adequate revenues or other factors. The legal burden of proof was on the shipper to show that the rate was unreasonable.

The Luken plan retained the 180 percent threshold, but in complaints involving rates of 220 percent of variable costs or higher the burden of proof would shift to the railroad to show the rate was reasonable. Also, the ICC could reduce the rate even if a shipper were able to substitute another product or buy the same product from another supplier.

● **Competitive Access.** Some shippers charged that railroads were discouraging more efficient use of the rail system and that the ICC had cast a blind eye toward such practices. For example, shippers contended that railroads had eliminated many routes involving more than one carrier in order to keep traffic on their own lines, even if a "single line" route was not the most direct for the shipper.

The Luken plan required railroads to set competitive joint rates upon the request of a shipper or a carrier seeking access to other railroads' tracks. Also, in certain cases, the ICC would have to require one railroad to lease its tracks to another and require a carrier to move cars from its system to another carrier's system.

● **Short-Line Sales.** Although labor-protection payments would not be required in short-line sales, the ICC would be required to give the public a 60-day notice of such transactions. The agency routinely approved short-line deals with a seven-day notice.

Buried in the bill was a provision, sought by Majority Leader Thomas S. Foley, D-Wash., that would have the effect of stopping the state of Idaho from taxing the wages of Washington rail laborers who crossed the Idaho panhandle to work in Montana.

## Senate Action

The fight against the Rockefeller bill was led by J. James Exon, D-Neb., chairman of Senate Commerce's Surface Transportation Subcommittee. Exon argued that the odds were stacked against the bill's passage at such a late date in the 100th Congress and that a veto by President Reagan was a certainty even if lawmakers managed to clear the measure. He said the wisest strategy would be to postpone action pending a new administration and fresh appointments to the ICC.

Rockefeller conceded that the bill faced bleak prospects but he argued that a favorable committee vote would send an "extraordinary message of strength" to railroads and the ICC that Congress was alarmed about treatment of captive shippers under deregulation.

Major elements of the legislation addressed:

● **Simplified Rates.** The bill would revise ICC procedures for evaluating rate-gouging complaints filed by captive shippers. Critics said the process was so complicated and time-consuming that it effectively barred shippers from obtaining rate adjustments. The measure called on the ICC to develop new regulations providing for a "simplified" rate formula — left largely undefined — as a substitute for the existing one.

● **Competitive Access.** The Rockefeller bill also narrowed the ICC's discretion to reject shippers' complaints that railroads were not allowing the most efficient use of the rail system.

Existing law said the ICC "may" bar practices such as ridding of routes involving more than one carrier; the Rockefeller measure said the agency "should" stop them.

# Railroad Safety Authorization

The Senate June 9, 1988, cleared legislation (S 1539) reauthorizing rail safety programs through fiscal 1990. President Reagan signed the measure (PL 100-342) June 22.

The package enabled the Federal Railroad Administration (FRA), for the first time, to penalize an individual rail employee for a safety infraction. Previously, the FRA could only penalize the company.

The bill also increased FRA penalties from the existing cap of $2,500 per safety violation to $10,000 per violation and to as much as $20,000 for a "grossly negligent" violation or pattern of violations.

The legislation authorized $40.6 million for FRA activities in fiscal 1988, rising to $44.4 million in 1990. It also:

● Required the Department of Transportation (DOT) to establish a program for the licensing of any operator of a locomotive. The program had to include minimum training requirements and review of an individual's motor-vehicle driving record. Individuals with alcohol- or drug-related convictions on their record would be denied a license pending completion of a DOT-approved rehabilitation program.

● Required the DOT secretary to issue rules requiring trains to be equipped with so-called "event recorders," similar to those used on aircraft, which would store data on train operations and assist investigators in the event of an accident. Rules would prohibit tampering with these and other safety devices.

**House Action.** The House Dec. 18, 1987, passed by voice vote a measure (HR 3743) to reauthorize rail safety programs through fiscal 1990. Action came two days after the Energy and Commerce Committee sent to the floor a package approved Dec. 10 by the panel's Subcommittee on Transportation, Tourism and Hazardous Materials.

The committee adopted by voice vote an amendment by Doug Walgren, D-Pa., to authorize the FRA to penalize carriers for speeding violations recorded by local governments. Existing law was unclear on whether the FRA could act based on information provided by local authorities, according to Walgren.

As passed, the bill would authorize $40.6 million for rail safety programs in fiscal 1988 and slightly higher amounts the following two years.

It would allow the FRA to penalize individual rail employees for violations of safety regulations; increase the $2,500 maximum fine for rule violations by railroads to $10,000, except for grossly negligent violations, which could draw a penalty of as much as $25,000; and allow railroads to be penalized for harassing employees who reported safety violations.

The package also required installation on the main rail line between Boston and Washington, D.C., of automatic devices to stop or slow a train that had run a signal. Proponents believed such a device could have prevented a January 1987 collision in the Northeast Corridor between an Amtrak passenger train and a Conrail freight locomotive that killed 16 people. The bill instructed DOT to study the possibility of requiring automatic systems on other rail corridors on which passengers or hazardous materials were carried.

Another provision established minimum licensing requirements for train operators and engineers. Federal authorities would have access to DOT's National Driver Register to review an individual's road-driving record.

**Senate Action.** The Senate Nov. 5, 1987, voted 93-0 to reauthorize federal rail safety programs. Its bill (S 1539 — S Rept 100-153) would authorize $40.6 million in fiscal 1988 and $41.8 million the following year for such programs.

A key provision raised maximum federal penalties for violation of safety regulations by railroads from $2,500 per violation to $10,000. As in the House bill, the FRA could penalize individual rail employees for safety violations, minimum licensing requirements would be established for train operators and engineers, and railroads could be penalized for harassing employees who reported safety violations.

**Final Action.** The final version of the legislation was crafted by leaders of the House Energy and Senate Commerce committees. The House adopted the conference report (H Rept 100-637) by voice vote, under suspension of the rules, May 23. The Senate followed suit June 9.

# Local Rail Assistance

The House Sept. 26, 1988, approved by voice vote legislation to reauthorize federal funding for state projects to improve aging freight-service rail tracks. However, the Senate did not act on the legislation before adjournment. The bill (HR 4547) would authorize $15 million annually through fiscal 1991 for the rail-assistance program. Also, it would cut from 70 percent to 50 percent the federal share of such projects.

The Senate Commerce Committee Aug. 9 reported a similar package (S 2570 — S Rept 100-465) that reauthorized the program at $25 million annually and reduced the federal share to 60 percent.

The House Energy and Commerce Subcommittee on Transportation approved HR 4547 on Sept. 15. The full committee never acted.

The Federal Railroad Administration opposed the new funding on the grounds that many states had developed their own programs to preserve freight service. Created 15 years earlier, the program was intended to relieve hardships for Northeastern communities and shippers facing widespread abandonment of rail lines. The program was later expanded to all states.

# Amtrak Authorization

The Senate Commerce, Science and Transportation Committee April 26, 1988, approved by voice vote a measure (S 2320 — S Rept 100-385) to reauthorize subsidies through fiscal 1991 for the Amtrak national passenger railroad.

As he had in past years, President Reagan proposed in his fiscal 1989 budget to eliminate federal assistance to Amtrak. But federal funding of Amtrak was popular on Capitol Hill and Congress routinely rejected such requests.

The Commerce bill, adopted with almost no debate, would reauthorize $630 million in subsidies for fiscal 1989,

$656 million for fiscal 1990 and $681 million for the following year.

While no further action was taken on the authorization, Congress agreed to appropriate $584 million for Amtrak in fiscal 1989.

# Coast Guard Authorization

Congress Sept. 15, 1988, cleared a Coast Guard funding reauthorization measure after House members reluctantly bowed to a key senator's demand for a home-state project that they viewed as unnecessary.

The Senate sent to President Reagan legislation (HR 2342) that authorized $2.6 billion for the Coast Guard in fiscal 1988 and $2.9 billion the following year. Reagan Sept. 28 signed the bill (PL 100-448). Both chambers had approved the conference report by voice vote.

The bill included $10 million in fiscal 1989 to establish and operate a Coast Guard helicopter base in Charleston, S.C. The project was sought by Sen. Ernest F. Hollings, D-S.C., chairman of the Commerce Committee, which was responsible for Coast Guard authorizations.

**House Action.** The Merchant Marine and Fisheries Committee June 11, 1987, reported HR 2342 (H Rept 100-154) authorizing Coast Guard funding of $2.8 billion in fiscal 1988.

The package exceeded the administration's request by about $200 million but was $63 million less than current funding. It included a provision that future Coast Guard ships be built in U.S. shipyards.

The House July 8 passed HR 2342 by a vote of 279-126. Debate was dominated by efforts to amend the package to place limits on Reagan's plan to reflag Kuwaiti oil tankers steaming through the Persian Gulf. An amendment delaying the reflagging effort for three months was attached to the bill on the House floor, but it subsequently was dropped from the legislation.

Lawmakers rejected, 119-287, an amendment by Silvio O. Conte, R-Mass., a yachtsman, to require all recreational boaters to pay a $20 annual fee to the Coast Guard to defray costs of programs that assisted boaters, such as rescue operations for those who were lost. Opponents to the amendment said such a "user fee" would be as inappropriate as charging those who called upon the services of fire or police departments. They also noted that the Coast Guard already received some revenues from fuel taxes paid by boaters.

Citing excessive funding, the Reagan administration opposed the authorization measure. The administration also strongly objected to the provision requiring future Coast Guard ships to be built in U.S. shipyards.

**Senate Action.** The Senate Commerce Committee July 1, 1987, reported a bill (S 1459 — S Rept 100-98) authorizing $2.6 billion for the Coast Guard in fiscal 1988 and $2.8 billion the following year.

Fiscal 1988 funding fell slightly below the current appropriation but was in line with the budget request of the administration.

By a 14-4 vote, the panel adopted an amendment requiring new Coast Guard ships to be built in U.S. shipyards.

The Senate approved HR 2342 by voice vote Oct. 13, after substituting the language of S 1459 for the House-passed measure.

**Final Action.** The Senate's version was returned to the House in October with the Hollings project attached. In December the House sent the Senate a version minus the project.

Hollings wanted the base because of a heavy load of search-and-rescue operations at crowded beaches near Charleston. But Earl Hutto, D-Fla., chairman of the House Merchant Marine Committee's Coast Guard and Navigation Subcommittee, said that the agency's budget was so tight he could not support the project. After months of stalemate, Merchant Marine leaders finally accepted the project as Hollings' price for a conference agreement on the bill.

The House agreed to the conference report (H Rept 100-855) Sept. 14, 1988; the Senate approved it the following day.

HR 2342 contained $1.9 billion in fiscal 1988 and $2.1 billion the following year for salaries and other Coast Guard operating expenses. The funds supported politically popular drug interdiction programs, among others.

The bill also provided $277.9 million in fiscal 1988 and $348 million in 1989 for equipment acquisitions and improvements. And it required Coast Guard vessels to be built in U.S. shipyards, except if the president determined an exemption was in the national interest.

# Panama Canal Commission

The House Merchant Marine and Fisheries Committee June 8, 1988, approved by voice vote an authorization (HR 4449 — H Rept 100-831) of $496.5 million in fiscal 1989 for the Panama Canal Commission, which operated the canal. However, the measure was never taken up on the House floor.

The money to maintain the canal came from toll receipts, other canal revenues and borrowing by the commission. The bill included a requirement that the canal commission provide written advance notice to the House Merchant Marine and Senate Armed Services committees of any proposed change in the toll rates after fiscal 1989 and of any payments to Panama.

The commission also was required to notify the committees of any capital-improvement expenses that exceeded $10 million. The measure placed a $40 million limit on capital outlays for the canal.

# Maritime Legislation

### Fiscal 1988 Maritime Programs Authorization

Both houses passed legislation to authorize fiscal 1988 maritime programs run by the Department of Transportation (DOT) and the Federal Maritime Commission, but a final agreement was not reached before the end of the 100th Congress and the legislation died.

The House June 2, 1987, approved by voice vote a bill (HR 953 — H Rept 100-80) to authorize $391 million in fiscal 1988 for federal maritime programs. The measure exceeded the Reagan administration's fiscal 1988 budget request by $59.7 million but fell $7.8 million short of the fiscal 1987 appropriation. HR 953 was reported by the Merchant Marine and Fisheries Committee on May 5.

The bulk of the funding, $300 million, was for "operating differential" subsidies to U.S. shippers to make up the difference between their operating costs and the lower operating costs of foreign competitors. Labor expenses typically were much higher for domestic shippers.

HR 953 also continued federal loan guarantees to shipbuilders for the construction of commercial vessels. Citing its opposition to this program, the Reagan administration urged lawmakers to reject the bill. In 1986, President Reagan pocket-vetoed a similar maritime authorization bill because it extended the loan guarantees. *(Story, p. 367)*

The Senate Commerce Committee June 4 approved by voice vote and reported Oct. 6 nearly identical legislation (S 800 — S Rept 100-193), authorizing some $400 million in fiscal 1988 for maritime programs. The Senate Nov. 3 passed HR 953 by voice vote after substituting the text of S 800.

Most of the money, $300 million, was for the differential subsidies to U.S. shippers. The bill authorized nearly $75 million for operating and training expenses for the Maritime Administration within DOT.

## Fiscal 1989 Maritime Programs Authorization

The House Aug. 10, 1988, by voice vote passed a measure (HR 4200 — H Rept 100-738) authorizing fiscal 1989 appropriations of $487 million for the Maritime Administration and $15 million for the Federal Maritime Commission. However, the measure was never acted on by the Senate and died when the 100th Congress adjourned.

Like the fiscal 1988 measure, HR 4200 featured $300 million for Maritime Administration payments to U.S. owners of American ships operating in foreign trade. The subsidy primarily covered the difference between these shipowners' labor costs and the much lower costs of foreign competitors.

The Reagan administration requested $249 million for subsidy payments and opposed House passage on the grounds of costs.

The House Merchant Marine and Fisheries Committee approved the bill May 25 and reported it June 28.

## Seized Fishing Boats

The House Oct. 20, 1987, cleared for President Reagan's signature a bill (HR 2893 — H Rept 100-299) reauthorizing a program to reimburse U.S. fishermen for losses caused by improper seizure of their vessels by foreign countries. Reagan signed the bill (PL 100-151) on Nov. 3.

The one-year reauthorization was passed Sept. 29 by the House and approved with minor amendents by the Senate Oct. 14. There were no objections in the House Oct. 20 to a request by Merchant Marine and Fisheries Committee Chairman Walter B. Jones, D-N.C., to clear the bill with the Senate revisions. The legislation had been reported by the Merchant Marine Committee Sept. 14.

Most of the seized boats were distant-water tuna and shrimp vessels. Fishermen who suffered losses were paid from a fund administered by the State Department and supported by fees paid by participating boat owners.

## Fish-Processing Boats

Senate action Dec. 22, 1987, cleared a bill (HR 2598 — H Rept 100-423) to ensure that fish-processing vessels operating in U.S. waters were built in domestic shipyards.

Proponents of the measure sought to close a loophole in existing law that allowed operators of foreign-built ships

to switch registration of their vessels to the U.S. flag.

The House Dec. 21 sent the Senate an amended version of the bill, which was initially approved by the Senate on Dec. 17 and by the House on Nov. 9. The measure was reported by the House Merchant Marine and Fisheries Committee on Nov. 5. President Reagan signed the legislation into law (PL 100-239) on Jan. 11, 1988.

## Sewage Sludge

The House May 24, 1988, upon passage, cleared a bill (S 1988 — S Rept 100-327) requiring that sewage sludge brought from the United States to ocean-dumping sites be transported on domestic barges. President Reagan signed the measure (PL 100-329) June 7, although the administration had expressed earlier opposition.

The House passed a virtually identical bill (HR 82 — H Rept 100-219) in 1987, but the Senate failed to act on the measure. HR 82 was introduced by Rep. Mario Biaggi, D-N.Y., in response to New York City's 1986 decision to award a $21 million contract to a Singapore shipbuilder to build four sewage-sludge barges. The lowest U.S. bid for the city's business was $28 million.

Opponents of the contract argued that the 1920 Jones Act prevented the award. Under the Jones Act, transportation of merchandise between U.S. points had to be done by American-made, -owned and -operated vessels. But the Customs Service and a New York federal district court disagreed because the sludge was considered "valueless" cargo and because the city's dumping ground, 106 miles out to sea, was beyond U.S. territorial waters, which ended three miles from the coast.

S 1988 extended the Jones Act to such shipments. However, it did not affect the New York contract and it allowed the use of certain barges built in foreign countries by U.S. firms for transporting large platforms to offshore drilling sites.

The Senate passed S 1988 on May 18 by voice vote. The measure was approved by the Commerce Committee March 29, also by voice vote, and reported May 4. The House approved the bill under suspension of the rules by voice vote.

## Maritime Trade

The House Merchant Marine and Fisheries Committee Feb. 3, 1988, reported a bill (HR 1803 — H Rept 100-501) to bolster the ability of the Federal Maritime Commission to combat "unfair" foreign maritime trade practices, such as restrictions on containers used by U.S. shipping companies operating overseas. The commission was to have wider authority to investigate allegations of unfair practices.

However, the legislation died when the full House and the Senate did not act on the legislation before the end of the 100th Congress.

## Boat Safety

The Merchant Marine and Fisheries Committee July 26, 1988, reported a reauthorization for boat-safety programs (HR 3918 — H Rept 100-786, Part I) that would increase the amount of motorboat-gas tax revenues placed in the Boat Safety Account, a trust fund that provided money to the states and the Coast Guard for recreational boating safety programs.

Under the Merchant Marine measure, the amount of

the gas tax revenues would be increased from $45 million to $60 million until fiscal 1991, when it would jump to $70 million. HR 3918 also provided that the amounts appropriated from the account be equally divided between the Coast Guard and the state recreational boating safety program. The existing division was one-third for the Coast Guard and two-thirds for the states.

The bill also was referred to the Ways and Means Committee, which did not act before the end of the year.

### Fishing Safety

Congress Aug. 11, 1988, cleared legislation (HR 1841) that set new requirements for fishing-vessel owners to keep safety equipment on board. President Reagan signed the measure (PL 100-424) Sept. 9.

By voice vote, the Senate approved HR 1841 as passed June 28 by the House. Large vessels with more than 16 people aboard were required to carry life rafts and survival suits to protect seamen from the shock of cold water. They also would have to carry radio equipment sufficient to communicate with the Coast Guard and emergency equipment that would automatically transmit a capsized vessel's location.

The measure lacked provisions, strongly opposed by trial lawyers, to limit vessel owners' liability for temporary injuries to their employees. Such provisions had been included in the bill as reported (H Rept 100-729) June 23 by the House Merchant Marine and Fisheries Committee, but they were taken out prior to House passage to speed enactment of the measure.

The House approved the bill by voice vote, after committee leaders reluctantly dropped the liability plan.

The committee-approved bill would not set any cap on damages for permanent injuries or temporary injuries due to the owner's gross negligence. An injured seaman able to resume work in good health within 150 days of an accident would not be permitted to bring a lawsuit if the vessel operator had paid all medical bills and two-thirds of the seaman's regular pay. Participation in this compensation scheme would be mandatory for operators.

A principal goal of the legislation was to bring some financial relief to fishing operators, who faced insurance premium increases due in part to high court awards to injured workers. Sponsors hoped that workers and trial lawyers would accept liability limits if they were accompanied by improved safety requirements.

# Product Liability

The 100th Congress once again failed to clear legislation to establish the nation's first product liability law. Since 1980, manufacturers had labored in vain for a federal law to replace state statutes that businesses said often favored the interests of victims of unsafe products — and the interests of trial lawyers whose earnings were pegged to damage awards.

A business-backed bill (HR 1115 — H Rept 100-748, Part I) was approved in June 1988 by the House Energy and Commerce Committee. Never before had a product liability measure been approved by a House committee. But the legislation sparked intense opposition from trial lawyers and consumer activists who called it an assault on victims' rights.

The product liability drive stemmed from huge increases in the premiums manufacturers had to pay for insurance to protect themselves against consumer suits. Manufacturers and insurance interests blamed state laws that they said favored plaintiffs and led to higher damage awards for injuries.

But consumer leaders and trial lawyers said HR 1115 would make it more difficult for victims to collect damages. They said anti-competitive practices among insurers were the largest contributor to rising liability costs.

The measure also faced strong opposition in the Judiciary Committee and in the Senate.

On the Judiciary Committee front, product liability had become embroiled with another hot issue that, like HR 1115, involved the insurance industry. A Judiciary subcommittee June 15 approved a bill (HR 2727), backed by consumer groups and opposed by insurers, to narrow the industry's broad exemption from antitrust laws. Some in the insurance industry saw the move as an attempt by trial lawyers to thwart insurers' attempts to get a product liability bill enacted. *(Box, p. 399)*

Judiciary Chairman Peter W. Rodino Jr., D-N.J., sided with consumers in the product liability debate. Although Rodino denied it, a number of others viewed approval of HR 2727 by the Monopolies Subcommittee, also chaired by the New Jersey Democrat, as a counterthrust to Energy and Commerce Committee Chairman John Dingell's, D-Mich., drive to enact HR 1115.

There was no Senate action; business lobbyists largely avoided that body. Senate Commerce Committee Chairman Ernest F. Hollings, D-S.C., a former trial lawyer, vigorously opposed a federal product liability law. He believed such matters should be left to the states. A 1986 Senate bill died on the floor after a Hollings filibuster. However, proponents felt that Energy and Commerce's action improved chances for a bill in the 101st Congress. *(1985-86 action, p. 370)*

### Subcommittee Bill

The Energy and Commerce Subcommittee on Commerce, Consumer Protection and Competitiveness approved HR 1115 Dec. 8, 1987, on an 11-3 vote. That package set up a federal liability standard to be used by courts to determine whether victims of unsafe products should be able to recover damages from the manufacturer. Proponents, including many manufacturers, said a uniform law was needed to replace conflicting state standards.

The bill also contained provisions crafted to appeal to consumers, such as an alternative mediation plan to encourage quick settlements and avoid costly trials.

A key provision in the bill would allow a manufacturer to escape liability for damages if he could not have known of a design defect in light of reasonably available knowledge, or if there were no feasible alternative design. In many states, lack of an alternative design or a manufacturer's failure to know of a defect was treated as a partial, instead of a total, limitation on liability.

Several other provisions were aimed at appealing to consumers, including one that would make a manufacturer liable for failing to warn product buyers of a danger discovered between the time the product left the manufacturer's control and the time of the injury. The bill also did not set any limits on court awards for pain and suffering experienced by accident victims. Nor did it set any limits on the legal doctrine of joint and several liability, which allowed a plaintiff to recover the full amount of damages from a

# Insurers Derail Antitrust Exemption

Legislation to narrow the insurance industry's longstanding exemption from federal antitrust laws died in the 100th Congress amid intense opposition from insurers.

In June 1988, the House Judiciary Subcommittee on Monopolies approved a measure (HR 2727) to repeal partially the antitrust exemption contained in the 1945 McCarran-Ferguson Act (PL 79-15). This step alone was a major triumph for consumer activists, who had long argued that the McCarran exemption permitted the industry to get away with anti-competitive practices.

But the bill never came up in full committee. Although many Democrats sympathized with consumers' arguments, many also worried about political retaliation by insurance lobbyists, who said that HR 2727 would cause turmoil in the insurance industry.

## Subcommittee Action

The Monopolies Subcommittee June 15 voted 8-6 in favor of HR 2727. Members first approved a compromise substitute, offered by Jack Brooks, D-Texas, for a total-repeal measure.

Although panel leaders said the move was necessary to thwart anti-competitive practices that had raised insurance prices, industry officials saw it as retaliation for their support of legislation to overhaul the nation's product liability laws. *(Story, p. 398)*

McCarran-Ferguson protected insurers from nearly all types of federal antitrust actions. It also asserted that traditional state regulation of the insurance business was in the public interest. At the time of the law's enactment, supporters argued that federal antitrust laws need not apply to insurance because state regulators already were protecting the public from anti-competitive practices.

The Brooks package left the system of state regulation intact. It also retained federal antitrust immunity for certain activities by insurers, such as collecting historical data that assisted them in determining their risk of a loss.

Certain other activities, however, were opened to antitrust action, including efforts to fix prices and monopolize regional markets and so-called "tie-in" practices that forced a customer to buy a second type of insurance in order to receive a first. Moreover, state attorneys general and individual citizens were given broader avenues to pursue antitrust lawsuits than were currently open to them.

Proponents said there was no good reason why insurers should continue to enjoy the broad antitrust immunity that had been extended to no other American industry. They pointed, in particular, to a lawsuit filed by 19 state attorneys general charging that firms had conspired in the mid-1980s to restrict some types of liability coverage and to abandon others.

Consumer activists, as well as trial lawyers who represented plaintiffs in product liability lawsuits, applauded the panel's action. Like Peter W. Rodino Jr., D-N.J., who chaired both the subcommittee and the full committee, they blamed rising liability costs not on an explosion of lawsuits — as maintained by insurers and manufacturers — but on anti-competitive pricing practices.

Insurers, however, said Rodino and other panel leaders were responding to a bill (HR 1115), approved the day before by the Energy and Commerce Committee, aimed at making state liability laws less onerous to manufacturers.

Insurers also said the provision in the Brooks package that would continue to protect certain collective activities from antitrust scrutiny was poorly drawn. They said insurers would stop sharing many types of information for fear of exposing themselves to a lawsuit. Small firms would be the hardest hit, they added, since they were dependent on data-pooling services.

## Heavy Lobbying

The lobbying campaign mounted by insurers against the legislation was massive in scale — the most sustained, some said, that the Judiciary panel had seen in years.

At least four former members of Congress worked on the industry's behalf. They were former Rep. Tom Railsback, R-Ill. (1967-83), representing the American Insurance Association; former Rep. Robert N. Giaimo, D-Conn. (1959-81), representing Aetna Life & Casualty Co.; former Rep. Lloyd Meeds, D-Wash. (1965-79), representing the National Council on Compensation Insurance; and former Sen. Birch Bayh, D-Ind. (1963-81), representing Allstate Insurance Co., owned by Sears, Roebuck and Co.

Working alongside the former members were the industry's "shock troops" — some 220,000 independent insurance agents, based in virtually every congressional district in the country.

According to one lobbyist, "thousands of letters" from agents arrived in Capitol Hill mailboxes after the subcommittee markup. For many members, such pressure made it difficult to act on a bill with little chance of enactment.

On the other hand, consumer advocates of the bill had help from lobbyists on women's issues concerned about the availability of insurance for day-care providers and nurse-midwives.

Consumers also had powerful allies among banking industry representatives, many of whom felt that repeal of the McCarran law would advance their goal of entering into the insurance field.

defendant only partially responsible for a wrongful injury.

However, the bill specified that whatever type of conduct a state required for the award of so-called "punitive" damages, a plaintiff had to have "clear and convincing evidence" to prove such conduct by the defendant. Some states required a lesser burden of proof. States typically awarded punitive damages for flagrantly bad conduct by the plaintiff.

Morever, at the request of a manufacturer or product seller, courts would have to separate the proceeding to determine punitive damages from the trial to determine all other damages, such as for medical expenses. Consumer groups claimed this requirement would make it harder for victims to recover punitive damages.

The subcommittee package was in some respects more modest than product liability bills considered by Congress in past years, including one that died in the Senate in 1986.

## Committee Bill

The Energy and Commerce Committee June 14, 1988, handed American business a long-sought victory when it approved HR 1115 on a 30-12 vote.

All of the committee's Republicans and 13 of its 25 Democrats voted for the measure. Although by only a narrow margin, Chairman Dingell accomplished his goal of getting a majority of panel Democrats behind legislation that in the past had been championed by Republicans.

As approved by the committee, HR 1115 was expected to make it more difficult for victims of unsafe products to recover damages from the manufacturer. Like the subcommittee bill, manufacturers in most instances would enjoy total protection from liability if they did not know and could not have known of a design defect in light of knowledge reasonably available to them, or if there were no feasible alternative design.

If an injury were caused in part by misuse or alteration of a product, damages paid by a manufacturer in some cases would be limited to the extent the firm was at fault. Manufacturers would not have to pay any damages if a plaintiff's use of drugs or alcohol was at least half responsible for his injury.

In addition, manufacturers of most drugs and medical devices would be immune from punitive damages if their product had been approved by the Food and Drug Administration (FDA). Manufacturers of other products would be safe from punitive damages unless a plaintiff had "clear and convincing evidence" of flagrantly bad conduct — a greater burden of proof than required by some states.

But the bill did not contain other protections avidly sought by businesses. At consumers' insistence, for example, sponsors removed a provision that would protect manufacturers from having to pay full damages for injuries for which they were found only partially responsible. Moreover, unlike the 1986 package, the bill contained no monetary caps on court awards to victims. Efforts by Energy and Commerce Republicans to attach such caps were soundly rejected by Democrats.

## Committee Compromise

Many Democrats on the panel were clearly uncomfortable about having to make an election-year choice between business and consumer constituents.

In addition, the bill had committee Democrats squabbling with one another over whether its new federal liabil-

ity standard would hamper the ability of victims of unsafe products to recover damages. Business leaders and almost all Republicans denied this would be the case.

Dingell enlisted the help of sympathetic Democrats to try to work out some sort of compromise between business and consumer groups on the subcommittee version of the bill.

First Mike Synar, Okla., and then Rick Boucher, Va., both of whom were on Judiciary, tried to reach an accommodation. A Boucher plan would weaken manufacturers' protections against liability for design defects, but a final agreement on it could not be reached. The panel eventually adopted a Synar package that was more pro-business.

Despite consumer opposition and threats of political retaliation by trial lawyers, panel Democrats backed the measure for a number of reasons. Many panelists felt that critics of the bill had overstated their case and that consumers were abusing the legal system by refusing to take any responsibility for injuries for which they bore some fault. Some also said that important concessions had been made to consumers in the bill.

Trial lawyers, who typically took at least a third of the awards won for their clients, were portrayed by Dingell and others as leeches on a bloated system. The bill contained a plan, offered by Ralph M. Hall, D-Texas, and praised by other Democrats, to curtail frivolous lawsuits by plaintiffs and delaying tactics by defendants.

Democratic concerns also were eased by a plan, crafted by Al Swift, D-Wash., to require state insurance regulators to report data on insurance firms' pricing practices and other information to the Department of Commerce. A number of members had said they would not back a bill that did not contain a data-collection provision to allow them to assess consumers' arguments that non-competitive practices were largely responsible for the liability insurance crunch.

A proposal by Edward J. Markey, D-Mass., to change the Swift plan to allow the Commerce Department to collect data from insurance firms themselves was rejected 19-23. Insurance companies vigorously resisted the Markey plan as a federal intrusion into traditional state regulation of their industry.

The bill also contained a provision, crafted by Jim Slattery, D-Kan., and Cardiss Collins, D-Ill., aimed at making more data on unsafe products available to the public. The plan restricted secrecy agreements that manufacturers commonly required plaintiffs to enter into as a precondition of obtaining important documents. Out-of-court settlements often prevented the public and other lawyers from learning about product hazards.

Many Democrats also were supportive of a provision, crafted by Dennis E. Eckart, D-Ohio, to give parties an incentive to settle claims out of court and without having to pay exorbitant legal fees.

Energy and Commerce's final day of action on HR 1115 was not without drama. Commerce Subcommittee Chairman James J. Florio, D-N.J., announced he would oppose the package after the panel adopted an amendment that he said tipped the scales against consumers.

The committee adopted, 23-19, a plan backed by chemical manufacturers and offered by Hall, to prevent states from circumventing HR 1115 by adopting so-called environmental tort statutes. Backers feared states might follow New Jersey's example and classify as "environmental" injuries that properly fell under the scope of a product liability statute. Florio argued states should have the flexibility of crafting new laws to meet the fast pace of change in the environmental arena.

### Anti-Abortion Fight

During the bill's markup, anti-abortion activists won a major victory. On June 9 the committee voted 23-19 for an amendment by Tom Tauke, R-Iowa, to exempt abortion-inducing drugs and certain products used as contraceptives from federal liability standards contained in the bill.

Proponents of the Tauke amendment argued that the new liability standards would encourage development of abortion-inducing drugs by shielding manufacturers from having to pay damages caused by potential defects. HR 1115 would bar victims of drugs approved by the FDA from recovering punitive damages for flagrantly bad conduct by the manufacturer.

With the Tauke amendment, abortion-related products would continue to be covered by stricter state liability laws. The amendment also exempted products, commonly sold as contraceptives, that interfered with the implantation of a fertilized egg in a woman's uterus. These included many birth control pills and the intrauterine device.

Pro-choice advocates and representatives of birth control clinics said the Tauke plan would chill drug firms' development of improved contraceptives by falsely labeling such products as dangerous.

The committee rejected, 21-21, a bid by Gerry Sikorski, D-Minn., to exempt all products that could be harmful to a person's ability to generate offspring. Critics said the plan was too broadly drawn.

## SEC Authorization

The House Nov. 20, 1987, accepted by voice vote a Senate amendment to a two-year authorization (S 1452) for the Securities and Exchange Commission (SEC), clearing the bill. The president signed the authorization measure Dec. 4 (PL 100-181).

The measure authorized $158.6 million in fiscal 1988 and $172.2 million in fiscal 1989 for SEC enforcement and other activities. The authorization level, according to Senate sponsor Donald W. Riegle Jr., D-Mich., was equal to the agency's request to the administration and higher than the administration's budget request. The increased levels were to give the SEC a "long-overdue increase" and to help strengthen its enforcement of illegal stock-trading activities, he said.

The bill, reported June 30 from the Banking, Housing and Urban Affairs Committee (S Rept 100-105), passed the Senate July 10. Upon passage Sept. 10, the House pared the SEC funding back to the levels requested by the administration: $133.9 million in fiscal 1988 and $154.0 million in fiscal 1989, plus $20 million in 1988 and $15 million in 1989 for an enhanced computer-based investigations system.

The House bill also required that the fiscal 1989 funds not be spent unless the SEC met certain requirements, such as filing progress reports with the House Energy and Commerce Committee and the Senate Banking Committee.

The Senate Oct. 30 reinstated its earlier authorization levels and agreed to the other House amendment. The House accepted the Senate authorization level amendment by voice vote Nov. 20.

## SBA Minority Program Overhaul

Congress Oct. 18, 1988, cleared a measure that for the first time required minority-owned firms participating in a federal procurement program to compete for top-dollar contracts awarded by the Small Business Administration (SBA). President Reagan signed the bill (HR 1807 — PL 100-656) Nov. 15.

The Senate, by voice vote, concluded congressional action by adopting the conference report (H Rept 100-1070) on HR 1807. The House had approved the agreement Oct. 12.

The measure revamped the scandal-plagued 8(a) program, under which the SBA contracted with other federal agencies and subcontracted the work to minority-owned firms. The program's aim was to foster growth of minority enterprises.

Traditionally, the SBA relied on non-competitive contract awards. However, critics said this practice had led to a few, select firms securing contracts from friends in the government, as in the much-publicized Wedtech Corp. case, in which executives of the New York-based defense contractor admitted bribing government officials to help them win contracts.

HR 1807 required firms to bid on most contracts worth more than $3 million — a change expected to result in competitive bidding on some 40 percent of total program dollars, which were about $3 billion a year. SBA was directed to write new rules calling on firms to obtain an increasing portion of their sales from non-8(a) sales over the course of the nine years they were allowed to participate in the program.

Also, the measure stiffened criminal penalties for persons who illegally set up "front companies" posing as minority-owned firms and sharply restricted the ability of owners of minority-owned firms to sell their 8(a) contracts to non-minority enterprises.

Sponsors of the legislation hoped it would curtail fraud and abuse as well as better prepare "graduates" for life in the private sector without government assistance.

Debate lingered, however, over whether the bill fell short of these goals. Officials at the SBA and some on Capitol Hill thought the measure did too little to wean firms off 8(a) contracts. Representatives of companies that used the program feared new restrictions aimed at limiting abuse could impede legitimate minority firms that were trying to survive.

However, John J. LaFalce, D-N.Y., chairman of the House Small Business Committee and a chief architect of the bill, predicted that the 8(a) program would be much improved. "What is important is that the big contracts will have to be competed," he said.

That was the area that had minority leaders most worried. Some minority leaders predicted smaller and younger 8(a) firms would be consistently outbid by larger and older firms in the program.

But others in the 8(a) community were relieved lawmakers ultimately softened other anti-fraud provisions that contractors protested would restrict participation in the program. The final package lacked, for example, a requirement in the Senate-passed version for 8(a) owners to certify annually that their net worth fell below a certain cap.

SBA leaders had a somewhat different perspective. Officials were disappointed that conferees softened a key plan in the Senate package for participants to obtain an increasing portion of their business from non-8(a) sales as they moved through the program. The goal was to smooth the transition from the sheltered 8(a) world to the cut-throat environment of the private sector. However, fearful that many firms would be unable to meet the so-called "business-mix" bench marks, lawmakers ultimately made them "targets" and weakened mandatory penalties for firms that did not achieve those goals.

"There's a real question as to whether we've gone far enough towards cleaning this program up," said Dale Bumpers, D-Ark., chairman of the Senate Small Business Committee. Bumpers said pressure from colleagues seeking to ease the concerns of minority firms hampered efforts to write a tougher measure.

## Background

If some were skeptical that HR 1807 would put 8(a) on a sound footing, it was in part because the program had proven so resistant to past efforts by Congress to improve its workings.

The program took its name from Section 8(a) of the 1958 law (PL 85-536) that authorized the SBA to contract with other federal agencies and to subcontract the work to small firms. In the wake of the urban race riots of the late 1960s, President Lyndon B. Johnson decided to take advantage of this seldom-used provision to create jobs for minority-owned firms in run-down areas.

A decade later 8(a) encompassed several thousand companies and billions of dollars in federal contracts. But conservative critics said the program had simply spun a new web of federal dependency and that few participating companies were developing the know-how that would enable them to operate in the private sector without government help. In fact, few firms were graduating from the program at all. *(Congress and the Nation Vol. V, p. 316)*

The Wedtech scandal seemed to confirm many people's worst fears about 8(a). Despite minority leaders' protests that Wedtech was an isolated case, reporters dug up other horror stories, such as contractors' use of funds to lease expensive cars and pay themselves huge salaries.

Although the headlines prompted tough talk on Capitol Hill, things turned out differently for several reasons. For one, the Wedtech story soon receded from the front pages, dampening pressure on lawmakers to act in haste.

For another, black and Hispanic members of Congress, particularly on LaFalce's panel, rallied to 8(a)'s defense, arguing that the program remained of crucial importance to minority enterprises because of continued discrimination in the marketplace. Sympathetic blacks and Hispanics constituted nearly half of the Small Business Procurement Subcommittee that had jurisdiction over 8(a) matters.

Tensions welled up within LaFalce's committee over the shape of new legislation. The chairman and many Republicans insisted on new anti-fraud and pro-competition provisions to restore the program's tarnished credibility. Minority lawmakers fought for other provisions — such as an extension of the program from seven to nine years — to improve opportunities for 8(a) participants. All parties were concerned that, if the panel failed to act, much less desirable steps might be recommended by Bumpers' Senate panel or taken by the White House on its own.

Eventually, an accommodation was reached that gave the chairman his way on competition thresholds and included a number of concessions to the 8(a) community. In a show of unity that masked underlying tensions, LaFalce's committee voted 40-1 Nov. 9, 1987, in favor of the package (H Rept 100-460); the bill sailed through the House Dec. 1.

In the Senate, Bumpers borrowed liberally from the House bill, tacking onto the measure his plan for business-mix requirements. That set the stage for a conference in which the traditional advocates of the contracting program proved largely successful.

The Senate bill, S 1993 was reported (S Rept 100-394) June 22, 1988; the full Senate passed HR 1807 July 7 on a 92-0 vote after substituting the text of S 1993.

## Major Provisions

As cleared, HR 1807 included the following major provisions:

● **Competition Thresholds.** The bill required firms to compete for manufacturing contracts worth more than $5 million and all other contracts worth more than $3 million. Contracts worth less than these thresholds were subject to competition in limited instances at the discretion of the SBA.

● **Business Mix.** The measure directed the SBA to issue regulations to set unspecified targets for non-8(a) sales that firms would have to try to reach as they moved through the program. The SBA was authorized to take "appropriate remedial measures" to penalize firms that failed to reach the targets.

● **Contract Sales.** The bill barred firms from selling or transferring 8(a) contracts to non-minority firms unless granted waivers by the SBA. The prohibition extended to firms that had graduated from the program but were still performing work to fulfill their contracts. However, waivers could be granted if it were necessary for the minority owners to sell voting stock to raise capital, the firm had left the program, and the minority owners retained the largest block of stock and effectively controlled day-to-day operations of the business.

● **Program Length.** The bill set a nine-year term of participation. Current participants were allowed to continue in the program for the longer of nine years from the award of their first contract or their original participation term, including extensions, plus 18 months.

The 18-month extension had been avidly sought by lobbyists for firms that faced the prospect of leaving 8(a) in the near future. The extension was contained in neither the House nor the Senate bill. However, conferees said it was granted in lieu of other "transition" provisions, including a House provision to allow the bigger minority firms to participate in a separate Department of Defense procurement set-aside program from which they were otherwise excluded.

● **Eligibility.** The bill required the SBA to decide within 90 days whether an applicant was eligible for the program. Sponsors said it sometimes took as long as two years for the SBA to rule on applications.

Owners of firms seeking to enter the program had to certify that they were "economically disadvantaged." However, owners would not have to certify annually that they remained economically disadvantaged, as had been required by the Senate bill. (The SBA currently applied a threshold for personal net worth to determine whether applicants were economically disadvantaged. The bill permitted the SBA to continue this test but directed the agency not to include the value of an owner's business assets and personal residence in calculations of net worth.)

• **Political Appointees.** The measure required the associate administrator for minority small business and capital ownership development — the SBA official chiefly responsible for running the 8(a) program — to be a career civil servant, not a political appointee.

• **Reports by Firms.** Companies had to report to the SBA fees paid to consultants, lobbyists and others to help firms obtain 8(a) contracts.

• **Front Owners.** The maximum penalty for persons who illegally set up "front companies" posing as minority firms was raised from $50,000 to $500,000 and the maximum jail term from five years to 10 years.

• **Size Standards.** The measure also contained unrelated provisions to dampen complaints by large federal contractors that government agencies reserved or "set aside" too many contracts for small businesses in certain industries. Under existing law, many federal agencies had sought to channel some 20 percent of the total value of all of their contracts into the hands of small firms.

The bill directed federal agencies not to reserve construction, refuse, architectural or engineering contracts worth more than $25,000 for small firms exclusively. However, if within any of these industries small firms thereafter received less than 40 percent of the value of contracts, then agencies had to reserve future contracts for small businesses to the extent necessary to attain the 40 percent goal.

# Other SBA Legislation

## SBA Reauthorization

Congress in 1988 cleared legislation (HR 4174) reauthorizing programs of the Small Business Administration (SBA) through fiscal 1991. The Senate agreed to the conference report (H Rept 100-1029) by voice vote Oct. 20, completing congressional action. The House had agreed to the conference report by voice vote Oct. 5. President Reagan signed the bill (PL 100-590) Nov. 3.

Before final action, House and Senate lawmakers deleted a provision, opposed by Sen. Jesse Helms, R-N.C., to bar SBA assistance to firms doing business in South Africa. Helms had threatened to block this and other small business legislation — including a major bill (HR 1807) to revamp a minority-business procurement program — unless the language was struck. (Minority program bill, p. 401)

Among other things, HR 4174 permitted the SBA to guarantee $3.7 billion worth of bank loans to small businesses in fiscal 1989, rising to $3.8 billion in 1990. The fiscal 1991 authorization was left open-ended. The current authorization was $3.5 billion.

The bill also permitted an increase from $1.25 billion in fiscal 1988 to $1.5 billion in 1989 and $1.6 billion the following year in "surety-bond" guarantees of construction work performed by small business contractors. These guarantees provided payments to firms hiring such contractors who failed to perform the required work. The current authorization was $1.3 billion.

**House Bill.** The House had approved its version of the bill (H Rept 100-694) July 6 by a vote of 342-40.

Its bill would authorize $3.6 billion in fiscal 1989, rising to $3.9 billion in 1991, for SBA loan guarantees. The bill also would authorize $1.6 billion in fiscal 1989, rising to $1.7 billion in fiscal 1991, for SBA guarantees of construc-

tion work performed by small business contractors.

The House Small Business Committee voted 37-5 on April 28 to send the measure to the floor.

The committee adopted by voice vote an amendment by John Conyers Jr., D-Mich., to bar SBA assistance to small businesses that were doing business in South Africa.

The administration opposed the bill as too costly.

**Senate Bill.** The Senate July 14 approved by voice vote its version of HR 4174.

It would permit the SBA in fiscal 1989 to guarantee $3.32 billion worth of bank loans to small businesses. It also would permit an increase from $1.25 billion to $1.4 billion in surety-bond guarantees.

Senators substituted the text of a bill (S 2619 — S Rept 100-416) reported July 7 by the Small Business Committee for the House-passed version of HR 4174.

## Loan Prepayments

Congress Oct. 14, 1988, cleared legislation (S 437) to enable firms that had obtained certain loans through the Small Business Administration (SBA) to pay them back early without incurring large prepayment penalties.

However, President Reagan Oct. 31 pocket-vetoed the legislation. The administration had long opposed the bill on the grounds that, over the long run, it would reduce interest payments to the government.

But backers of the measure in Congress attacked Reagan's move as callous. They said it would force the owners of small firms saddled with high-interest loans to scale back plans to increase their payrolls and otherwise expand their businesses.

At issue was an SBA program to funnel capital-improvement loans to small firms seeking to finance plant acquisitions, construction or other business expansions. Under the program until 1986, local loan packagers, called Certified Development Companies (CDCs), issued bonds that were bought by the Treasury Department. CDCs lent the proceeds of the bond sales to small businesses and used the loan repayments to pay off the bonds. The SBA guaranteed repayment of the CDC bonds. In 1986, Congress revised the program to require sales of CDC bonds to private investors.

CDC leaders said some 1,000 small businesses wanted to refinance loans carrying interest rates that were substantially higher than existing market rates. However, they said the firms were unable to repay these early 1980s loans because of onerous prepayment penalties imposed by the Treasury.

In some instances, according to officials, penalties amounted to 40 percent of the unpaid portion of the loan. S 437 would substantially reduce this burden.

S 437 also would lower rates on other loans made by the SBA to privately owned investment firms that in turn provided financing to minority-owned small businesses.

The Senate initially passed S 437 Dec. 19, 1987, by voice vote. It cleared the bill Oct. 14, 1988, by agreeing to changes made by the House Oct. 3.

The House approved S 437 by a vote of 372-28. House members first attached a provision to lower interest rates on the loans to privately owned investment firms that provided financing to minority-owned small businesses.

The House Small Business Committee May 25 reported a similar bill (HR 3718 — H Rept 100-651) to ease the SBA loan prepayment penalties.

## Changes in SBA Programs

Congress in 1987 cleared legislation (HR 2166 — PL 100-72) making several modest changes in programs run by the Small Business Administration (SBA). The measure was approved by the House May 27 by a vote of 337-41 and by voice vote in the Senate on June 25. President Reagan signed the legislation July 11, despite initial reservations.

The bill increased by $108 million — to $1.25 billion — the fiscal 1988 authorization for federal guarantees of construction work performed by small business contractors. The program ensured that payments would be made to firms hiring such contractors even if the contractor failed to perform the work.

The bill also authorized $16 million to help small businesses that had fallen behind on payments for SBA loans used to purchase pollution control equipment.

The changes were requested by the Reagan administration. However, the White House initially opposed the bill because it failed to include more sweeping proposals, such as elimination of most direct federal loans to small businesses.

The legislation was reported (H Rept 100-94) by the House Small Business Committee on May 14 and, without change, by the Senate Small Business Committee on June 23.

## Women-Owned Businesses

Congress Oct. 12, 1988, cleared a measure (HR 5050 — PL 100-533) to speed the growth of small businesses owned by women. President Reagan signed the bill Oct. 25. Final action came when the House agreed to minor amendments — adopted in the Senate Oct. 11 by voice vote — to the version of HR 5050 that had been approved earlier by the House.

The measure:

● Established a new program through which the Small Business Administration (SBA) would guarantee commercial bank loans of up to $50,000 to small firms. Although any small business could participate, such loans were expected to be sought mainly by service-related firms, many of which were owned by women.

● Authorized an SBA demonstration project that would give $10 million to private organizations to provide management assistance and other types of help to women-owned firms.

● Created a nine-member National Women's Business Council to monitor the progress of federal, state and local governments in assisting women-owned firms. One of the Senate amendments was to disband the council five years after enactment.

The House initially approved the measure Oct. 3 by a vote of 389-7. The House Small Business Committee reported the legislation (H Rept 100-955) Sept. 22.

## New SBA Administrator

The Senate March 20, 1987, by voice vote confirmed former Sen. James Abdnor, R-S.D., to head the Small Business Administration (SBA). He was sworn into office three days later.

Members of the Small Business Committee, in approving the selection March 18 by a vote of 18-0, voiced only one concern: that Abdnor might resign the post to run for a House seat in 1988. While Abdnor did not rule that out, he indicated he was likely to remain at the SBA through President Reagan's second term.

In committee testimony March 12, Abdnor said he supported survival of the SBA as an independent agency. The administration had tried unsuccessfully to abolish the SBA and to transfer some of its functions to the Commerce Department.

The SBA had not had a permanent chief since James C. Sanders left office in April 1986.

# Children's TV Programming

Citing free-speech concerns, President Reagan Nov. 5, 1988, said he would withhold his approval from legislation aimed at improving the quality of children's television shows. Indignant sponsors of the bill vowed to resubmit it to President George Bush in 1989.

As cleared by Congress Oct. 19, the children's television measure (HR 3966) would etch a historic new requirement into the 1934 Communications Act. Federal regulators, at the time a broadcaster applied for renewal of its license, would have to consider whether the station served "the educational and informational needs of children in its overall programming."

No such directive existed on the books. The Communications Act, which had been left largely untouched over the years, required broadcasting regulation only to serve the public interest — a term left undefined.

The measure also would reimpose limits, abolished by the Federal Communications Commission (FCC) in 1984, on the amount of advertising that could be shown on children's shows.

Proponents said the bill was needed to protect children from exploitation by commercial broadcasters and advertisers. However, echoing concerns raised by Justice Department and FCC officials, Reagan said the measure would inhibit broadcasters from offering programs that might not satisfy regulators' tastes.

Ironically, broadcasters themselves had expressed no such concern. The National Association of Broadcasters (NAB), the chief trade group for commercial broadcasters, said it could live with HR 3966. NAB leaders hoped this stance would induce the next Congress to accommodate them on such matters as legislation to require cable companies to carry local television stations on their channels.

## Legislative Impetus

Legislative action in the House on children's television programming was encouraged by both Democrats and Republicans, who said they were alarmed by what they viewed as a deterioration in the quality of children's programming. Critics charged that children's minds were being warped by such things as flashy cartoons featuring characters based on a toy product. And they worried that a steady stream of ads on children's programs left little time for the show itself.

Also driving the bid for new legislation was the feeling of some lawmakers, mainly Democrats, that the FCC had tended to ignore the will of Congress, and sometimes even the courts, in its relentless effort to lift government controls from the broadcast industry. They said the FCC's pro-deregulation stance had nurtured a climate in which broadcasters felt free to lower standards for children's TV and other programming.

In a decision that many Democrats applauded, the U.S. Court of Appeals for the District of Columbia ruled in June 1988 that FCC officials had failed to justify their 1984 decision to eliminate advertising limits from children's television. "The court has slapped them down on it, and we're about to do the same thing," said Al Swift, D-Wash., a member of the House Energy and Commerce's Telecommunications and Finance Subcommittee.

Swift added that some lawmakers were still sore about the agency's repeal in 1987 of the "fairness doctrine," which had required broadcasters to air all sides of controversial issues. *(Story, below)*

### House Action

**Committee.** Members of the Telecommunications and Finance Subcommittee crafted legislation (HR 3966) that required broadcasters to limit advertising in children's programming, starting Jan. 1, 1990, to not more than 10.5 minutes per hour on weekends and not more than 12 minutes per hour on weekdays. Between 1974 and 1984, the FCC had limited advertising to 9.5 minutes per hour on weekends and 12 minutes per hour on weekdays. Under the bill, the FCC could modify the times, after Jan. 1, 1993, "in accordance with the public interest."

The bill also gave the FCC broad discretion to make educational programming a criterion for granting a license renewal.

The subcommittee approved the bill May 19; the Energy and Commerce Committee voted 39-3 on May 26 to send HR 3966 (H Rept 100-675) to the floor. The full panel made no changes to the subcommittee's package.

In both subcommittee and full committee, members rejected an amendment by Tom Tauke, R-Iowa, to suspend antitrust laws to allow stations and advertisers to work out children's television guidelines on their own.

Tauke was particularly fearful of the provision tying license renewal to an FCC judgment on whether a station's programming served children's "education and informational needs," a phrase the bill did not define. Tauke said such language not only raised a constitutional question about government restriction of broadcasters' freedom of speech but amounted to a "Trojan horse" in a broader effort to "re-regulate" the industry.

**Floor.** The House approved the bill June 8 by a vote of 328-78, despite an administration statement June 2 that it opposed the advertising and programming restrictions in the legislation.

The vote was the first to reverse FCC efforts to deregulate the broadcasting industry since Congress lost the battle over the commission's repeal of the fairness doctrine.

The legislation was passed under suspension of the rules, a procedure that required a two-thirds vote for passage and did not permit amendments.

### Senate Action

By voice vote, the Senate Oct. 19 approved HR 3966 as passed by the House, thereby sending the measure to the president.

As of Oct. 21, the White House had given no hint of Reagan's intentions. However, on Oct. 19, FCC Chairman Dennis R. Patrick said the bill was both "unnecessary and ill-advised" since the agency was weighing steps it might take on its own to improve children's TV.

For a time, it looked as if HR 3966 might not clear the Senate. Action bogged down when Timothy E. Wirth, D-Colo., protested that the measure did not do enough to improve children's TV fare. Wirth wanted to include an amendment that required stations to show programs specifically targeted at children. The House language allowed stations to serve children's needs through their "overall" programming.

Broadcasters balked at Wirth's proposed amendment, as did consumer activists and others who were generally satisfied with the House package. Ultimately, Wirth agreed to leave the bill alone in return for a pledge from Senate Commerce Committee Chairman Ernest F. Hollings, D-S.C., to hold hearings in the next Congress on a variety of children's TV issues.

## Fairness Doctrine

President Reagan in 1987 beat back a determined congressional bid to codify the so-called "fairness doctrine," which required broadcasters to air controversial public issues and to cover all sides of such issues.

The House had included the requirement in its version of the fiscal 1988 omnibus appropriations bill (H J Res 395 — PL 100-202). But negotiators backed down after Reagan insisted he would veto the bill unless the plan were dropped. *(Omnibus appropriations bill, p. 66)*

On June 19, 1987, Reagan vetoed separate legislation (S 742) codifying the doctrine, and no override was attempted. Although many lawmakers argued the fairness requirement should be retained in light of the scarcity of broadcast outlets, Reagan called it a curb on the free speech of broadcasters. Following the veto, the Federal Communications Commission (FCC) voted to abolish the 38-year-old doctrine.

Although proponents of fairness provisions vowed to resume the fight in 1988, no further action was taken.

**Senate Action.** By a vote of 14-4, the Senate Commerce Committee March 24 approved S 742 (S Rept 100-34), which would write the fairness doctrine into law.

The committee's action was prompted by a ruling in September 1986 by the U.S. Court of Appeals for the District of Columbia that the FCC could repeal the standard without congressional approval. Before the ruling, the fairness requirement was widely thought to have its basis in the 1959 amendments to the Communications Act (PL 86-274). The doctrine long had been enforced by the FCC.

But the court declared that the amendments merely ratified prior FCC enforcement of the doctrine. (The Supreme Court June 8, 1987, denied a request by a public interest group to review the decision.)

Commerce members were concerned that the FCC, under the leadership of departing Chairman Mark S. Fowler, would scrap the doctrine. Fowler often criticized it as a violation of free speech that inhibited broadcasters from airing controversial subjects for fear of having to yield time for opposing viewpoints.

Commerce Committee Chairman Ernest F. Hollings, D-S.C., author of S 742, contended that the fairness doctrine had provided the public with a greater range of views upon which to base decisions.

Committee opposition was led by Bob Packwood, R-Ore., who shared Fowler's misgivings and sponsored separate legislation (S 827) to repeal the doctrine. (Packwood's bill did not advance.)

Many in the broadcasting industry also opposed the

bill, and they contended that the proliferation of radio and cable television outlets had voided the need for governmental supervision.

Despite the opposition of the administration and broadcasters, the Senate April 21 passed S 742 by a vote of 59-31.

**House Action.** The House Energy and Commerce Subcommittee on Telecommunications and Finance May 7 agreed by voice vote to an identical measure (HR 1934 — H Rept 100-108) to codify the doctrine.

Six days later, the full Energy and Commerce panel approved the bill by a vote of 33-8. The committee defeated by voice vote an amendment that would establish a nine-member commission to review the impact of the fairness doctrine legislation.

The House June 3 sent S 742 to the White House. The action came after lawmakers voted 302-102 in favor of HR 1934, despite urging by the Reagan administration to vote against the bill. S 742 then was passed in lieu of the identical Energy and Commerce measure.

The House rejected, by a vote of 71-333, an amendment to HR 1934 by Bill Green, R-N.Y., that would exempt radio stations from the standard.

Green said the fairness requirement was not necessary, since there were already some 10,000 radio stations in the country, offering "a wide variety of points of view."

But Al Swift, D-Wash., countered that listeners in rural communities typically had limited access to the airwaves.

**Veto Confrontation.** As expected, Reagan vetoed S 742 on June 19, arguing that the fairness doctrine restricted broadcasters' freedom of speech.

Four days later, the Senate agreed to refer Reagan's veto message to the Commerce Committee, after backers of the bill acknowledged they lacked the two-thirds majority needed to override the president's veto.

Democrats said they would wait until later in the year to attach the doctrine to other legislation the White House might find more difficult to resist.

All but three Democrats supported the procedural motion by Hollings to send Reagan's message to the Commerce panel. The motion was approved 53-45.

Packwood said Democrats refused to allow a vote on the veto message because they did not want to blemish their perfect override record in the 100th Congress. Earlier, Congress had successfully overridden White House vetoes on clean water and highway and mass transit legislation. *(Clean water, p. 454; highway legislation, p. 378)*

"Very clearly, it is not in the interests of the Democrats for the president to win anything," Packwood said. "But the public can be well aware that the president would have won a victory today. The veto would have been sustained."

Eighteen Republicans initially supported the bill, but Packwood said he persuaded some of them to back the president and vote to sustain the veto.

**Further Action.** The fight over the fairness doctrine was resurrected later in the year as members of the Senate Commerce Committee tried to use a deficit reduction, or reconciliation, measure to enact the broadcasting requirement.

The committee agreed Oct. 21 to assess violators of the standard a penalty upon sale of their broadcasting outlets. On the grounds that no such fee could be collected without a doctrine on the books, the panel also included language to codify the doctrine abolished Aug. 4 by the FCC.

The provisions were part of a reconciliation package aimed at meeting a $394 million deficit reduction target set for the committee by the fiscal 1988 budget resolution (H Con Res 93). The panel rejected 6-11 a motion by the committee's ranking Republican, John C. Danforth, Mo., to strike the fairness provisions from the measure.

However, when the reconciliation bill (HR 3545 — PL 100-203) reached the Senate floor Dec. 10, Hollings agreed to drop the controversial fairness provision, in part because he hoped it would lessen opposition to another proposal he had to charge broadcasters a fee that would be used to support public broadcasting ventures. *(Fiscal 1988 reconciliation, p. 61)*

Meanwhile, the House Appropriations Committee rejected an attempt by the House leadership to include the fairness doctrine in an omnibus spending bill (H J Res 395 — PL 100-202) to keep the government running through fiscal 1988.

At the leadership's request, Neal Smith, D-Iowa, offered the fairness doctrine amendment in committee. But Chairman Jamie L. Whitten, D-Miss., opposed the move, arguing that other committees increasingly looked to Appropriations to provide cover for measures that could not be passed on their own. Smith's amendment was defeated 20-28.

When the measure came to the House floor Dec. 3, however, an amendment by Energy and Commerce Committee Chairman John D. Dingell, D-Mich., to write the fairness doctrine into law was approved 259-157.

In a conference on the legislation, Senate negotiators initially agreed to retain the House-passed provision, despite a threat by Reagan that he would veto the entire spending bill as a result.

But as the end of the year drew near, members retreated from the confrontation. At a stormy session Dec. 21, Senate conferees voted 15-12 to reconsider their earlier decision. They then voted 14-13 to leave the fairness doctrine off the bill.

House members voted 11-9 to insist on their provision and then, on a 10-10 tie, refused to reconsider. But Rep. C. W. Bill Young, R-Fla., was expected to arrive from Florida later that day and reverse the vote.

Meanwhile, House leaders became increasingly concerned that if their members continued to insist on the provision it would mean no bill would pass. When the conference resumed later that evening, the House side, directed to dump the doctrine, did so by voice vote.

# FCC Authorization

Congress Oct. 19, 1988, cleared legislation (S 1048) to reauthorize activities of the Federal Communications Commission (FCC). President Reagan signed the measure (PL 100-594) Nov. 3.

By voice vote, the House Oct. 19 adopted S 1048 as passed by the Senate Oct. 7. The measure authorized appropriations of $109 million for the FCC in fiscal 1989. A month earlier, Congress cleared a fiscal 1989 appropriations measure (HR 4782 — PL 100-459) that contained $100 million for the agency.

S 1048 also imposed a one-year deadline on investigations of the legality of rate changes by regulated telephone companies. The FCC often allowed new rates to become effective before it issued an order finding the rates lawful. Those who wanted to challenge the rates in court generally could not do so until the FCC finished its study and issued a final order.

The bill also permitted FCC officials to continue accepting travel reimbursements from private sponsors of business conferences. Lawmakers said this reimbursement policy, first approved by Congress in 1982, had not been abused by the agency.

Also, the measure contained a provision that, in effect, made permanent a new FCC policy that exempted lawmakers and congressional staffers from rules banning contacts with outside parties on matters due to be considered by the commission within seven days. The FCC adopted the new policy after lawmakers complained that they should not be treated the same as business lobbyists or others with a stake in FCC actions. Sponsors said legislative language was necessary to ensure that the FCC did not reverse the policy.

## Background

Relations between the FCC and Congress were strained through much of 1988, in part because of the commission's 1987 decision to repeal the so-called "fairness doctrine." That standard had required broadcasters to air all sides of controversial issues. Many members of Congress, especially Democrats, thought the commission had gone too far in its efforts to deregulate the industry. *(Fairness doctrine, p. 405)*

Symptomatic of the strains over who should control communications policy was a dispute over a little-noticed provision in a 1987 omnibus spending bill (PL 100-202) that barred the FCC from extending any waivers under "cross-ownership" rules prohibiting common ownership of a newspaper and TV station in the same community. The effect of the prohibition was to prevent publisher Rupert K. Murdoch from owning both a newspaper and a television station both in Boston and New York City.

Several New York legislators and conservatives argued that sponsors of the provision, Sens. Ernest F. Hollings, D-S.C., and Edward M. Kennedy, D-Mass., had sneaked the measure into the bill during the final hours of the session.

Critics claimed Kennedy was trying to punish Murdoch for unflattering coverage in the *Boston Herald*, which was owned by the publisher. Kennedy vigorously denied the charge.

Hollings, who was concerned the FCC might junk the cross-ownership rules, said he feared the commission was about to give Murdoch preferential treatment. He said he would seek legislation that would permanently codify the cross-ownership rule. However, none materialized during the year.

Those who supported the rule said it served the cause of free speech by helping to preserve a diversity of voices in the news media. Critics said the rule was no longer needed, given the growth of cable television and other broadcasting technologies.

On March 29, a federal appeals court struck down the provision in the spending bill as unconstitutional. A three-member panel of the U.S. Court of Appeals for the District of Columbia ruled 2-1 that Congress unfairly singled out Murdoch when it passed the law.

## Legislative History

**House Action.** The Energy and Commerce Committee had reported a similar FCC reauthorization measure (HR 2961 — H Rept 100-363) Oct. 9, 1987.

At the request of Energy and Commerce Republicans,

Democratic leaders deleted draft report language criticizing the FCC's abolition of the fairness doctrine. The bill was abruptly pulled from the House floor the week of Oct. 5 after Republicans protested.

Although the Energy and Commerce Committee had approved the bill July 28, Republicans were not shown a draft of the report until Oct. 2, one working day before it had to be filed with the Rules Committee. The bill initially had been scheduled for floor consideration on Oct. 7.

The full House suspended the rules and passed HR 2961 by voice vote on Oct. 13.

**Senate Action.** S 1048 was reported (S Rept 100-142) by the Commerce, Science and Transportation Committee Aug. 4, 1987. The bill passed the full Senate by voice vote on Oct. 7, 1988.

# CPB Authorization

Congress in 1988 reauthorized public broadcasting programs through fiscal 1993. The legislation (HR 4118 — PL 100-626) authorized $245 million for the Corporation for Public Broadcasting (CPB) in fiscal year 1991, rising to $285 million for fiscal 1993. It provided $200 million over this period for replacing public broadcasting satellite facilities. (CPB funding was authorized in advance to permit long-term planning of TV and radio programs.) *(1986 action, p. 375)*

The Senate cleared the bill Oct. 20; the House approved the measure the day before. President Reagan signed the bill Nov. 7.

Sponsors also directed the CPB, in consultation with public broadcasting stations, to submit to Congress by Jan. 31, 1990, a plan to divert from the CPB to the local stations federal funds for the creation of new TV programs. Some in Congress were disturbed by reports that political considerations had guided CPB funding awards for new programs.

Daniel K. Inouye, D-Hawaii, chairman of the Senate Commerce Committee's Communications Subcommittee, had inserted a plan to divert the funds to local public-television stations in a version of the bill (S 2114 — S Rept 100-444) adopted by the Commerce Committee June 28. But he agreed to drop the controversial provision before the Senate approved the bill by voice vote Oct. 7.

The House Energy and Commerce Committee reported HR 4118 (H Rept 100-825) Aug. 5. The panel made no changes in the measure as approved June 30 by its Telecommunications and Finance Subcommittee. However, a substitute plan, nearly identical to the Senate-passed version of S 2114, was brought to the House floor.

# Satellite-Dish TV

## Satellite-TV Transmissions

Legislation to permit continued transmission of television programming to owners of home satellite dishes was cleared by Congress Oct. 20, 1988. The measure was attached to a bill (S 1883 — PL 100-667) to overhaul the trademark laws, which the Senate cleared by voice vote. The plan, signed into law Nov. 16, was identical to provisions in a free-standing measure (HR 2848) passed by the House. *(Trademark legislation, p. 777)*

The legislation aimed to resolve legal uncertainties

jeopardizing satellite carriers' transmission of popular TV programs to dish owners, who were concentrated in rural areas cut off from cable TV as well as over-the-air broadcasts. Satellite firms commonly retransmitted signals to the owners from television "superstations" that distributed programs all over the country. Many retransmitters scrambled their signals to prevent reception by dish owners who did not subscribe to their systems. Copyright owners, who generally received no compensation, had challenged the legality of this practice.

The bill, championed by Robert W. Kastenmeier, D-Wis., chairman of the House Judiciary Committee Courts Subcommittee, allowed carriers to continue this activity but required them to pay copyright owners a fee.

The House Oct. 5 passed the bill by voice vote, despite an administration statement Sept. 29 that copyright royalties should be "determined in the marketplace through negotiations among carriers, broadcasters and copyright holders." However, the administration supported the trademark plan to which HR 2848 was attached.

The House Energy and Commerce Committee reported the measure (H Rept 100-887, Part II) Sept. 29. Judiciary reported a package (Part I) Aug. 18. The two panels' versions of HR 2848 were substantially the same.

The Energy and Commerce Committee's version of the bill had been approved by its Telecommunications and Finance Subcommittee Sept. 23. Kastenmeier's Courts Subcommittee acted on the measure July 7.

### Satellite-Dish Owners

The Senate Commerce Committee Dec. 21, 1987, reported a bill (S 889 — S Rept 100-272) that would require programmers who scrambled signals that were available to cable customers to make such programming available to dish owners. However, no further action was taken on the bill and it died at the end of the 100th Congress.

The legislation also mandated that if the programmer made his signal available for distribution to any third party, he also had to make it available to virtually all distributors, or middlemen, interested in selling the product to dish owners.

The bill's supporters argued that many programmers either were not making their signals available to dish owners or were refusing to sell the signal through any third-party distributor except cable operators with whom they frequently enjoyed close financial ties. Dish owners often had to pay excessive fees to receive programming as a result of a lack of competition, according to backers.

The measure also required the Federal Communications Commission to investigate whether dish owners were being denied access to programming due to high prices for, or the lack of availability of, signal-decoding, or unscrambling, equipment. Critics said programmers had not kept their promise to make decoders easily available, a charge the bill' opponents denied.

Cable operators, who vigorously opposed the bill, said the principal beneficiaries of the legislation would be sellers of satellite dishes, who traditionally had been at odds with cable operators and who were now trying to enter the signal-distribution business. The bill's opponents said programmers should have the right to distribute their product to whomever they wished.

In the House, a similar measure (HR 1885) was introduced in March. The Energy and Commerce Committee's Subcommittee on Telecommunications and Finance approved the bill for full committee action on June 30. Certain provisions of HR 1885 eventually were included in the provisions of HR 2848, the satellite-TV transmission bill, which passed Oct. 5, 1988. *(Story, above)*

# NTIA Authorization

Congress in 1988 cleared a bill (HR 2472 — PL 100-584) reauthorizing the National Telecommunications and Information Administration (NTIA). NTIA was charged with developing federal telecommunications policies.

The bill cleared when the House agreed to the Senate version of the bill. The House Energy and Commerce Committee reported HR 2472 (H Rept 100-362) Oct. 9, 1987. The full House passed the bill by voice vote Oct. 13.

The bill would authorize $14.7 million in fiscal 1988 and $15 million the following year. The agency's appropriation for 1987 was $13.2 million.

The Reagan administration opposed HR 2472, objecting to a provision that required NTIA to establish goals for recruiting minorities and women, and to report to Congress on its success in achieving such goals.

A measure (S 828 — S Rept 100-93) reported by the Senate Commerce Committee July 1, 1987, did not contain this provision. The Senate struck all after the enacting clause of HR 2472 and inserted the text of S 828 before passing HR 2472 by voice vote Aug. 4, 1988. On Oct. 19, the House agreed to the Senate amendment, completing congressional action. President Reagan signed the bill Nov. 3.

# Phone Links for the Deaf

The federal government was required to improve its telephone links with deaf and speech-impaired people under legislation cleared by Congress Oct. 14, 1988.

The Senate adopted by voice vote a measure (HR 4992) passed Oct. 12 by the House, also by voice vote. President Reagan signed the bill (PL 100-542) Oct. 28.

The legislation directed the General Services Administration (GSA) to take such steps "as may be necessary" to ensure that the government's telecommunications system was "fully accessible" to hearing- and speech-impaired individuals. Sponsors expected GSA to require federal agencies to install special equipment known as "telecommunications devices for the deaf" (TDDs). TDDs consisted of a telephone modem, a keyboard and a monitor; they ranged in price from $150 to $450.

Many deaf people owned TDDs but had to rely on a time-consuming operator-relay system to communicate with parties who did not.

As approved Sept. 27 by the House Energy and Commerce Committee, HR 4992 (H Rept 100-1058, Part I) ran into objections from Jack Brooks, D-Texas, the powerful — and highly turf-minded — chairman of the Government Operations Committee, which also had jurisdiction over the measure.

The Energy and Commerce bill directed the Federal Communications Commission (FCC), whose activities were overseen by that panel, to write the new rules requiring agencies to purchase TDDs. Proponents reasoned that the FCC was the government's expert agency on such equipment.

But Brooks thought the GSA — responsible for governmentwide procurement and overseen by the Government Operations panel — should write the new rules.

After much talk, Energy and Commerce sponsors offered on the House floor a substitute package that handed the job to GSA regulators.

A similar bill (S 2221 — S Rept 100-464) passed by the Senate Aug. 10 would put the FCC in charge of the regulations. But an aide noted that the legislation would die unless Brooks got his way. That measure had been reported from the Commerce Committee Aug. 9.

Brooks got his way on another matter as well. Unlike the Energy and Commerce and Senate packages, the House-passed bill did not specifically require purchases of TDDs. Brooks did not want the government to be locked into a single technology.

## Hearing-Aid Compatibility

Congress July 28, 1988, sent to the White House legislation that, one year after enactment, would ban U.S. sales of telephones that were not equipped to work with hearing aids.

By unanimous consent House members accepted Senate amendments to a bill (HR 2213 — H Rept 100-674) that the House had passed under suspension of the rules June 8 by a 391-15 vote. The Senate July 11 substituted by voice vote the text of a Commerce Committee package (S 314 — S Rept 100-391) for the House bill. The two versions were nearly identical.

Although the administration opposed the legislation as an unwarranted intrusion into the telephone marketplace, President Reagan signed the bill (PL 100-394) Aug. 16.

The legislation provided a three-year exemption from the sales ban for cordless telephones and permitted the Federal Communications Commission to waive compatibility requirements if they were expected to hinder the development of new phone technologies.

Some phone companies opposed the measure as unnecessary. They noted that existing law already required public telephones, as well as phones used by hearing-aid wearers at work, to be hearing-aid compatible.

But advocates of the bill said that the cost of making phones compatible with hearing aids would be minimal. Estimates ranged from 10 cents to 50 cents per phone. Proponents also said the new legislation would restore phone access to some 2 million to 3 million hearing-impaired people.

The Senate Commerce Committee approved its version of the bill May 24 by voice vote.

The House Energy and Commerce Committee May 18 sent to the floor, without amendment, a version of the bill approved April 28 by the Telecommunications and Finance Subcommittee.

## FTC Authorization

House and Senate negotiators were unable to agree on key provisions in a bill (S 677) reauthorizing the Federal Trade Commission (FTC) over a three-year period. The measure died when the 100th Congress adjourned.

Among the biggest differences between the two houses was a provision in the Senate bill to bar the FTC from using "unfairness" as a standard for determining if an industry's advertisements should be regulated. Congress had been unable to clear an FTC authorization measure

since 1980 largely because of disagreement over that issue.

Another potential stumbling block was a Senate provision to speed up passage of joint resolutions to overturn agency rules opposed by Congress and to allow lawmakers to hold up appropriations for implementing those rules. House negotiators objected to an identical Senate provision in a 1985 conference. *(99th Congress action, p. 376)*

The last FTC authorization, cleared in 1980 (PL 96-252), expired at the end of fiscal 1982, when the agency escaped a push by business and professional organizations to impose new restrictions on its powers. *(Congress and the Nation Vol. V, p. 847)*

Since 1982, the agency had operated on funds provided in annual appropriations bills, most of which continued various curbs on FTC authority contained in earlier authorizations.

Both the House and Senate versions of the new bill authorized $212.4 million for the FTC through fiscal year 1990.

### Senate Action

The Senate Commerce, Science and Transportation Committee by voice vote March 10, 1987, approved a bill (S 677 — S Rept 100-31) to reauthorize the FTC. The Senate passed S 677 by a vote of 88-9 on April 8.

The Senate bill barred the FTC from regulating advertising on an industry-wide basis on the grounds that the industry's advertising was "unfair." Instead, it required the agency to crack down on unfair advertising on a case-by-case basis. Industry-wide regulation of deceptive or factually misleading advertising was to be continued.

Unfairness as a standard for determining improper industry advertising had been suspended for three years in the 1980 law and the suspension had since been maintained in annual continuing appropriations legislation.

The ad industry strongly supported the suspension, which was enacted after advertisers lobbied heavily against an FTC proceeding on whether to restrict television ads aimed at children for such products as sugar-coated breakfast cereals.

The Senate legislation was brought to the floor April 6 and stalled the following day over an amendment by Howard M. Metzenbaum, D-Ohio, to allow the FTC to study the insurance industry without getting permission from Congress. Existing law required certain FTC inquiries to be approved by a majority of either the House or the Senate Commerce committees.

After encountering opposition, Metzenbaum scaled back the plan to require a specific FTC study of sales of health insurance to the elderly and increases in property and casualty insurance rates for small businesses, local governments, physicians, dentists and child-care centers. The amendment was adopted April 8 by an 80-18 vote.

Also on April 8, the Senate voted 71-26 to kill an amendment to lift a ban on FTC studies or investigations of agricultural marketing orders that, among other things, allowed the Department of Agriculture — with the consensus of farmers — to regulate the marketing of products by volume and quality.

As cleared by the Senate, the measure required the FTC to redirect at least $850,000 annually through fiscal 1990 to regional offices from headquarters functions in Washington, D.C. None of the redirected funds was to come from law enforcement activities.

The provision was sought by Albert Gore Jr., D-Tenn.,

chairman of the Commerce Committee's Consumer Sub-committee, who believed that although regional offices typically received a small portion of the budget, they consistently were responsible for a large slice of the agency's enforcement actions.

### House Action

**Energy and Commerce.** The Energy and Commerce Subcommittee on Transportation, Tourism and Hazardous Materials July 1, 1987, approved a bill authorizing the FTC for fiscal 1988-90. The measure authorized the same amounts called for in the Senate-passed bill, but it did not include the controversial Senate plan to bar the FTC from regulating unfair advertising on an industry-wide basis.

The House bill restricted the ability of the FTC to intervene in regulatory or other actions taken by states, local governments or federal agencies. The FTC's views had to be requested by the party taking the action, and only the commission — not the staff — could make recommendations.

The full Energy and Commerce panel approved the measure (HR 2897 — H Rept 100-271, Part I) July 14.

**Public Works.** The Public Works and Transportation Committee Sept. 23 agreed by voice vote to delete a provision in HR 2897 that would give the FTC authority to regulate airline advertising.

The provision was included in the version of the bill approved by the Energy and Commerce panel, which had primary jurisdiction over the FTC. Public Works and Transportation members argued that the power should remain with the Department of Transportation (DOT), over which their committee had jurisdiction.

Energy and Commerce members maintained that DOT had failed to protect consumers.

On Oct. 7, Public Works Committee Chairman James J. Howard, D-N.J., emerged a surprisingly easy victor in a dispute with a recognized master of territorial expansion, Energy and Commerce Chairman John D. Dingell, D-Mich.

The House voted 246-171 to strike the provision from HR 2897 that would shift authority to regulate airline advertising from DOT to the FTC. The bill was then passed on a 404-10 vote.

Howard and his troops won the battle in part by fanning widespread sentiments that, under Dingell's leadership, Energy and Commerce had often trampled on other committees' jurisdictions. Public Works leaders sent a letter to House colleagues with the headline: "Has the Energy and Commerce Committee Ever Tried to Steal Your Jurisdiction?" — a question to which many members could have, at least silently, responded, "yes."

On the floor, Howard bluntly called Energy and Commerce's advertising provision a "flimsy pretext" for "this power grab."

Dingell countered that DOT had failed to protect consumers from misleading airline ads and that the FTC would do a better job. Public Works leaders argued that it made little sense to scatter airline regulatory authority among separate agencies.

# Consumer Product Safety

Alarmed that the Consumer Product Safety Commission (CPSC) had failed to protect the public from unsafe products, Congress tried to take matters into its own hands but failed to clear legislation in 1988. House and Senate committees reported similar bills but neither were considered on the floor.

The debate focused on two broad issues: how to change CPSC's management and rulemaking procedures, and whether to require manufacturers to offer cash refunds to past purchasers of three-wheeled all-terrain vehicles (ATVs).

Although ATV manufacturers had agreed to halt sales of new three-wheelers, proponents said refunds were needed to speed removal of some 1.5 million vehicles still in circulation. They said accidents involving ATVs were killing 20 people a month, many of them children.

But manufacturers, who stood to lose hundreds of millions of dollars, argued that accidents were caused not by a design flaw but by improper use that could be corrected by consumer warnings and training that they had already agreed to provide.

A lobbying drive mounted by Japanese manufacturers against the refund plan featured some 8,000 letters to lawmakers from home-district ATV dealers. Japanese firms accounted for the vast majority of ATVs sold in the United States. Industry leaders accused ATV critics of "Japan-bashing" and of making the ATV issue a scapegoat for the general failure of the CPSC to enforce product-safety standards with sufficient vigor.

**House Action.** The House Energy and Commerce Committee reported a CPSC reauthorization measure Sept. 23 (HR 3343 — H Rept 100-962). The bill effectively would remove Terrence M. Scanlon as chairman of the commission. Congressional critics said Scanlon had not moved fast enough to reduce safety threats posed by ATVs and other products. *(Scanlon, box, p. 360)*

An amendment offered by Joe L. Barton, R-Texas, required ATV refunds. The amendment would give owners of three-wheelers the choice between a cash payment for the depreciated value of their vehicle or a manufacturer's credit against future purchases. It also would make permanent the current halt on three-wheeler sales and require improved safety standards for four-wheelers.

An Aug. 4 move to strike the cash-refund requirement from the bill was rejected by the committee, 14-28. Although Energy Committee Chairman John D. Dingell, D-Mich., raised concerns that a congressionally mandated refund might set a bad precedent that could be used against other products — including automobiles made in his Detroit-area district — he eventually found the amendment acceptable.

Among other things, the legislation also would require warning labels on toxic art materials and on toys that contained small parts that could be swallowed by children.

**Senate Action.** The Senate Commerce Committee Dec. 21, 1987, reported a CPSC reauthorization bill (S 1882 — S Rept 100-273) that left Scanlon's status intact. However, like the House measure, S 1882 pushed the CPSC to set safety standards for products if manufacturers dragged their feet on issuance of "voluntary" standards. Critics said the agency often waited too long for product makers to correct safety problems on their own.

In addition, both bills allowed the CPSC to take regulatory actions when there were only two commissioners present at a meeting, instead of the three members currently required. Proponents said the provision should speed up the work of the agency.

The Senate Commerce package required the CPSC to try to reach an agreement with ATV distributors on correcting safety risks. If an agreement was not reached, the agency was required to pursue an imminent-hazard case on its own. In any event, the CPSC had to issue a rule within one year to address safety problems. However, the rule did not have to provide for the refund option.

Senate floor action on S 1882 was blocked for an unrelated reason by Idaho's two Republican senators. James A. McClure and Steve Symms said the agency should not be reauthorized as long as it insisted on trying to halt sales of a device, made by an Idaho company, designed to assist commercial harvesters of earthworms. The senators believed the Idaho company's worm probe posed no safety threat, contrary to CPSC allegations.

McClure and Symms also objected to plans by Sens. Albert Gore Jr., D-Tenn., and Alfonse M. D'Amato, R-N.Y., to try to attach ATV refund requirements to S 1882. The two Idaho senators had a "hold" on the legislation, preventing its consideration on the floor.

### Lawn Darts

Separately, Congress Oct. 21, 1988, cleared a measure (HR 5552) to ban the sale of lawn darts — a sporting-goods product that critics said had been responsible for nearly 5,000 injuries to children since 1978. President Reagan signed the measure (PL 100-613) Nov. 5.

Similar language was contained in the stalled Senate Commerce measure (S 1882) to reauthorize the CPSC, and somewhat weaker provisions were in HR 3343.

The House Oct. 21 voted 304-51 in favor of the ban; the Senate subsequently followed suit by voice vote.

## Telemarketing Fraud

The House June 28, 1988, approved legislation (HR 4101 — H Rept 100-731) aimed at thwarting scams against consumers who bought products over the telephone. However, no action on the bill was taken by the Senate.

The measure would require the Federal Trade Commission (FTC), within six months of enactment, to issue a new rule cracking down on so-called telemarketing fraud. The agency estimated such fraud at more than $1 billion a year; others put the tab much higher.

The bill, approved by voice vote, also would authorize state attorneys general to sue violators of the new FTC rules. Lawsuits by private parties claiming losses in excess of $10,000 also would be allowed. Only FTC officials could bring legal action against scam artists under existing federal law.

The bill was approved by the Energy and Commerce Committee May 19. Committee members adopted an amendment to instruct the FTC to consider restrictions on the time of day that product-sellers could call potential consumers.

A similar measure (S 2213) was introduced in the Senate, but no action was taken before Congress adjourned.

The measure was backed by consumer activists as well as major credit card firms. The firms often got stuck with the bill if a purchaser discovered the fraud and refused to pay.

The Reagan administration did not take a position on the bill. However, the FTC raised concerns about permitting state attorneys general to sue violaters under federal regulations. The agency preferred to keep such lawsuits under tighter federal control.

## 'Gray-Market' Cars

The House Oct. 12, 1988, cleared legislation (HR 2628) to restrict imports of "gray-market" cars — foreign-manufactured vehicles that did not meet U.S. safety standards. The House by voice vote accepted the Senate's revision of the original House-passed version of the bill. President Reagan signed the measure (PL 100-562) Oct. 31.

The package required importers to prove that they were capable of modifying gray-market vehicles to meet safety standards. Sponsors said existing modification requirements were overly lax.

The House passed HR 2628 by voice vote Dec. 14, 1987. The measure was reported (H Rept 100-431) by the Energy and Commerce Committee Nov. 10.

The Senate adopted an amended version of the bill by voice vote Oct. 5, 1988. The Senate amendment, sponsored by Warren B. Rudman, R-N.H., widened the discretion the House version gave to the transportation secretary to exempt certain gray-market vehicles from the new requirements.

## Baldrige Quality Awards

Congress approved a measure (HR 812 — PL 100-107) establishing a program of presidential awards to U.S. companies that did the most to enhance the quality of their goods and services. President Reagan Aug. 20, 1987, signed the bill, the Malcolm Baldrige National Quality Improvement Act of 1987.

The Senate had amended the bill to name the awards after Commerce Secretary Baldrige, who died July 25 in a rodeo accident.

Modeled after Japan's prestigious Deming Prize, the awards were designed to recognize American businesses that offered a superior quality of goods and services.

Consisting of an inscribed medal, the award would be given by the president or the secretary of commerce to selected companies that applied for the award through the National Bureau of Standards. Companies receiving the award were allowed to use the commendation in their advertisements.

No federal funds were appropriated for the awards. The program, including administrative costs, was funded through gifts from public and private sources. If the funding was not met through contributions, then the secretary of commerce could impose fees on those organizations applying for an award.

Reported from the House Science, Space and Technology Committee May 18 (H Rept 100-96), HR 812 passed the House June 8 by voice vote under suspension of the rules.

In the Senate, the bill was reported from the Commerce, Science and Transportation Committee Aug. 4 (S Rept 100-143) and passed the full Senate Aug. 5, as amended to name the awards after Baldrige. The House agreed to the Senate amendments on Aug. 7, clearing the bill for the president's signature.

## Abandoned Shipwrecks

The House April 13, 1988, voted 340-64 in favor of legislation (S 858), passed by the Senate in 1987 and backed by the White House, to grant states the title to historic shipwrecks located within three miles of their coasts. The vote cleared the bill for President Reagan, who signed it (PL 100-298) April 28.

The bill asserted U.S. title to abandoned shipwrecks and transferred the title to the states so they could have access to historic artifacts on their underwater lands. Under existing law, absent an assertion of the federal prerogative, abandoned shipwrecks became the property of the finder.

When S 858 was brought to the House floor under suspension of the rules March 29, it failed to win the two-thirds vote required for passage. It was defeated by a vote of 263-139.

Norman D. Shumway, R-Calif., objected that the legislation did not protect the interests of sports divers because it did not require states to allow them access to sunken ships to which states would be given title. Amendments to legislation considered under suspension of the rules are not permitted.

Shumway got his chance April 13, but his amendment was rejected 134-268.

An amendment by Robert S. Walker, R-Pa., to protect the access of federal drug enforcement authorities to the shipwreck sites was defeated by a vote of 183-221.

Bruce F. Vento, D-Minn., chairman of the Interior Subcommittee on National Parks and Public Lands, argued that both amendments were unnecessary and could tie up the bill in the Senate.

The Senate had passed S 858 on Dec. 19, 1987. It had been reported (S Rept 100-241) by the Energy and Natural Resources Committee 10 days earlier.

The House Interior and Insular Affairs Committee reported the measure (H Rept 100-514, Part I) March 14; the Merchant Marine and Fisheries Committee reported it (Part II) March 28.

Shumway also had offered his amendment during Merchant Marine's markup of the legislation, but it was rejected because of concern that the Senate would not concur.

# U.S.-Soviet Fishing Pact

Senate action Oct. 21, 1988, cleared a five-year U.S.-Soviet commercial fishing agreement that allowed U.S. vessels, for the first time, to fish within 200 miles of Soviet borders. The fishing privilege long had been sought by Pacific Northwest fishermen. The measure (HR 4919 — PL 100-629) was signed by President Reagan Nov. 7.

The bill also required all foreign fishing vessels operating within 200 miles of the United States to be equipped with emergency alerting and position-indicating radio beacons.

Ratification of the agreement earlier had been blocked by an unrelated dispute between the chairmen of the House and Senate panels that oversaw such matters.

The House Sept. 26 by voice vote approved the measure (H Rept 100-968), as reported Sept. 23 by the Merchant Marine and Fisheries Committee. The Senate Oct. 1 sent it back to the House accompanied by a plan sought by Commerce Committee Chairman Ernest F. Hollings, D-S.C. The plan would transfer the *Ingham*, a decommissioned Coast Guard cutter, to the Patriots Point Naval and Maritime Museum near Charleston. At Hollings' insistence, the House Sept. 28 dropped from a transporta-

tion appropriations measure (HR 4794 — PL 100-457) language that would transfer the cutter to a New York City site.

However, House Merchant Marine Chairman Walter B. Jones, D-N.C., was unwilling to accommodate Hollings on HR 4919. The House Oct. 4 voted 412-5 to send the bill back to the Senate minus the *Ingham* amendment.

Jones had no particular objection to the language. However, an aide said the North Carolina Democrat was unwilling to accept it as long as Hollings continued to object to the Merchant Marine chairman's plan to establish a presidential commission to review federal policies related to oceans and the marine environment. A bill (HR 1171 — H Rept 100-300, Part I) to set up the commission had been passed by the House in 1987 but had seen no Senate action. A Jones aide said Hollings had objected to the commission as unnecessary.

Hollings, meanwhile, pursued other avenues for enacting the *Ingham* language with little luck. The Senate Oct. 5 by voice vote adopted his free-standing bill (S 2408 — S Rept 100-554) to base the vessel at Patriots Point. However, the House did not act on the measure during the 100th Congress.

On the final day of the first session, the Senate agreed to recede from the Hollings amendment to HR 4919, sending the bill to the president.

# Pipeline Safety

The Senate Oct. 14, 1988, completed congressional action on a bill (HR 2266 — PL 100-561) to reauthorize federal safety programs for pipelines that carried natural gas and hazardous liquids. President Reagan signed the measure Oct. 31.

The Senate, by voice vote, agreed to HR 2266 as approved by the House Oct. 12. It authorized program spending of $11 million in fiscal 1989, rising to $12.8 million in 1991. The programs, administered by the Department of Transportation, were paid for by user fees levied on the pipeline industry.

The bill also increased civil penalties for pipeline-safety violations from a maximum of $1,000 up to $10,000 for each day that the violation existed. Penalties had not been changed since 1968.

On Oct. 1, the Senate had sent back to the House a modified version of the bill based on a measure (S 2424 — S Rept 100-436) reported July 28 by the Senate Commerce Committee. It would authorize program spending of $9.6 million in fiscal 1988, the level requested by the Reagan administration, rising to $10.6 million in 1990. It also contained the penalty increases, which had not been included in the House version.

The House approved its version of HR 2266 under suspension of the rules April 19 by voice vote. The Energy and Commerce and Public Works and Transportation committees reported slightly different versions of HR 2266 to the floor. The compromise passed by the House would authorize program spending of $9.7 million for fiscal 1988, $11.5 million for fiscal 1989 and $12.1 million for the following year.

The Public Works and Transportation Committee approved the measure (H Rept 100-445, Part II) March 15 by voice vote. A similar version (Part I) had been reported by the Energy and Commerce Committee on Nov. 17, 1987.

# Other Legislation

## Tourism Authorization

The Senate July 21, 1987, approved by voice vote legislation (S 1267 — S Rept 100-116) to authorize $45 million over three years for the U.S. Travel and Tourism Administration, a Commerce Department program to promote foreign travel in the United States.

The bill was reported July 17 by the Senate Commerce, Science and Transportation Committee. Committee leaders rejected the Reagan administration's proposal to fund the agency with a passenger charge of $1 per ticket for travel to and from the United States.

The legislation would authorize $14 million for fiscal 1988, $15 million for fiscal 1989 and $16 million for fiscal 1990.

S 1267 was referred to the House Energy and Commerce Committee, but no action was taken and the bill died at the end of the 100th Congress.

## NOAA Authorization

A reauthorization for the National Oceanic and Atmospheric Administration (NOAA) was included in the fiscal 1989 National Aeronautics and Space Administration (NASA) reauthorization bill (S 2209 — PL 100-685).

The NASA bill authorized nearly $900 million in fiscal 1989 for NOAA, which included the National Weather Service. It required the service to come up with a modernization plan and called for the service to maintain a data base on the "acid content" of rain in the United States.

The House and Senate both passed two-year NOAA bills in 1987 but never reached a conference agreement. The Senate passed its NOAA bill (S 1667 — S Rept 100-151) by voice vote Sept. 10, 1987. The House passed its version (H Rept 100-406) Nov. 20 on a 341-65 vote.

● Applied provisions of Annex V of MARPOL prohibiting disposal of plastics by U.S.-flag vessels in any ocean and by vessels of foreign nations within 200 miles of the U.S. shore.

● Prohibited disposal of floating packing materials less than 25 miles offshore.

● Prohibited disposal of such non-plastic garbage as food wastes, paper, rags, glass, metals and crockery within 12 miles offshore.

● Prohibited disposal of ground-up non-plastic wastes less than three miles offshore.

● Required non-commercial government vessels (for example, Navy ships) to comply with Annex V within five years, except during time of war or national emergency.

● Required the secretary of transportation to set and enforce standards for garbage dumps at ports and terminals.

● Authorized the Transportation Department to inspect both foreign and domestic vessels in U.S. waters for compliance and to assess civil penalties of up to $25,000 for each violation or each day of a continuing violation.

● Required federal agencies operating ships to report annually to Congress on their compliance or their inability to comply with Annex V.

● Required the Environmental Protection Agency to report to Congress by Sept. 30, 1988, on land-based sources of plastic materials in the marine environment.

● Required the Commerce Department to report to Congress by Sept. 30, 1988, on the effects of plastic materials on the marine environment.

● Directed the secretary of commerce, acting through the secretary of state, to initiate negotiations immediately with foreign countries whose nationals conduct driftnet fishing in waters of the North Pacific. The negotiations would be aimed at developing agreements to obtain information on the types and amounts of U.S. marine resources taken or discarded by fishing fleets using driftnets.

● Required the secretary of commerce to develop recommendations for the use of alternative materials in driftnets that would decompose at a faster rate.

● Required the secretary of commerce to report to Congress on the impact of driftnet fishing on the marine environment.

● Required the administrator of the Small Business Administration to declare the North Carolina red-tide contamination an economic disaster, making individuals eligible for assistance from the federal government.

## Ocean Pollution

Congress in 1988 cleared a bill aimed at ending all dumping of U.S. sewage sludge in the oceans after 1991. The president signed the bill into law (S 2030 — PL 100-688) Nov. 18.

House approval Oct. 19 by voice vote of the conference report (H Rept 100-1090) merely ratified the agreement that had been reached Oct. 7 by House and Senate conferees to reconcile differences between a House bill (HR 5430) and S 2030. The Senate adopted the conference report Oct. 18.

The House passed HR 5430 Oct. 4 on a 417-0 vote, then passed S 2030 by voice vote after substituting the language of HR 5430. The Senate passed S 2030 Aug. 9 on a 97-0 vote.

Dumping of sewage sludge from New York and New Jersey had been a long-smoldering political issue, especially in the beach areas of New Jersey. Sludge dumping in the seas was supposed to stop at the end of 1981 under the 1977 Ocean Dumping Act (PL 95-153). But New York City had contended that it was unable to find any place on land to put its sludge. *(Congress and the Nation Vol. V, p. 541)*

New Jersey, whose miles of beaches bore the greatest brunt of ocean pollution, had complained loudly. The argument was no longer over whether the dumping should end, but over when, and what enforcement mechanisms could prevent further slippage in the deadline.

New York was the only major city still dumping sludge from barges, although Boston and Los Angeles continued to pipe their sludge out to sea, and some northern New Jersey communities dumped at the same site New York did, 106 miles offshore. The New Jersey legislature passed a law prohibiting ocean dumping by New Jersey municipalities after March 17, 1991.

The bill set a deadline of Dec. 31, 1991, and enforced it with an escalating schedule of fees and fines. The final deadline was one year earlier than the House had asked for in its bill.

Under the conference agreement, fees on the ocean disposal of sewage sludge started at $100 per dry ton in 1989 and escalated to $200 per ton by 1991. Most fees could be waived for a municipality that entered into an enforceable legal agreement with a schedule for phasing out the dumping.

After the Dec. 31, 1991, deadline, penalties were to be imposed for continuing ocean dumping of sludge. They started at $600 per dry ton and increased by more than 11 percent, compounded, each year.

Most of the fees and penalties from each municipality went into a special trust fund, which could be spent on developing land-based disposal facilities for that particular municipality, with concurrence of the Environmental Protection Agency (EPA).

Initially, 85 percent of the fees went into the fund. The portion of penalties going into the fund was to start at 90 percent in 1993 and to decline by 5 percent each year thereafter.

The remainder went to EPA and other federal agencies for administration and enforcement of ocean pollution laws. Unused funds also went toward pollution control.

## Degradable Plastic Holders

Another ocean pollution issue raised in Congress during 1988 was pollution by plastics, such as the plastic "six-pack" holders that had strangled birds, seals and other marine animals caught in them. Congress in 1987 enacted legislation (Treaty Doc 100-3, HR 3674 — PL 100-220) carrying out an international treaty prohibiting most plastic disposal in the oceans. *(Plastic disposal, p. 460)*

Congress cleared a bill Oct. 14 (S 1986 — PL 100-556) requiring that plastic ring carriers be degradable. The president signed the measure Oct. 28.

The Senate passed S 1986 (S Rept 100-270) May 13. The House on Oct. 4 passed by voice vote a companion bill (HR 5117 — H Rept 100-946, Parts I and II). The House then substituted the language of HR 5117 for S 1986 and passed S 1986, as amended.

New methods of manufacturing had emerged that produced plastics, at no appreciable cost increase, that decomposed after long exposure to sunlight and the elements.

The bill ordered the Environmental Protection Agency to issue rules, within two years, requiring the use of degradable materials in ring carriers.

# Medical Waste

Congress in 1988 sent the president a bill (HR 3515 — PL 100-582) to control the dumping of medical wastes such as those that washed up on East Coast beaches the summer of 1988. The president signed the measure Nov. 1.

New York and New Jersey residents had been appalled when beaches were closed after used needles and syringes, vials of blood testing positive for AIDS and hepatitis-B, used bandages and other medical waste washed up on shore. No existing federal law regulated disposal of such waste, although some state laws did.

The bill enacted set up a two-year demonstration program for tracking and handling medical wastes in New York, New Jersey, Connecticut and the Great Lakes states.

The bill cleared when the House concurred by voice vote in the Senate amendment to the bill. The House had originally passed the bill Oct. 6 by a 390-28 vote. The Senate passed the House bill, amended, Oct. 7.

As enacted, the bill forced the Environmental Protection Agency (EPA) to issue rules requiring medical waste to be separated from conventional garbage and to be properly packaged and labeled. It also beefed up EPA's enforcement powers over violations of medical waste rules.

Top civil penalties were $25,000 per day of violation, and normal criminal penalties were $50,000 per day and two years in jail. In cases where the dumper knowingly endangered the health of another person, those penalties escalated to a $250,000 fine and 15 years in jail, or a $1 million fine if the dumper was an organization.

EPA had to issue rules within six months of enactment listing the types of waste to be tracked. The bill required EPA to include cultures and stocks of infectious agents; wastes from the production of biological agents; discarded live and attenuated vaccines; pathological wastes, including tissues, organs and body parts; human blood and blood components; sharp items such as hypodermic needles, broken glass and scalpels; and various other specific wastes that had been in contact with infectious agents.

EPA also had six months to issue rules for the tracking system. The agency had to establish a standard federal form, like a freight manifest, to accompany the waste at each stage from generation to final disposal. States could adopt forms requiring more data if they chose. Hospitals and other waste generators would be able to use the system to ensure that their wastes had been received at the ultimate disposal facility.

States other than those named in the bill were allowed to petition EPA to be included in the program. Under the final amendment added by the Senate and accepted by the House, Great Lakes states could opt out of the program unconditionally. Other states could opt out if they convinced EPA that they had in place tracking programs at least as stringent as the federal one.

# Tin-Based Paints Ban

Congress cleared and sent to the president May 24, 1988, a bill (HR 2210 — PL 100-333) to limit the use of tin-based boat paints that harmed fish and shellfish. The

president signed the bill June 16.

By voice vote, the House May 24 concurred with the amendment the Senate made to the bill April 18. This was the third time the House had acted on HR 2210. The House had originally passed the bill Nov. 9, 1987, after it was reported from the Merchant Marine and Fisheries Committee Oct. 27 (H Rept 100-400). The Senate Dec. 12 passed HR 2210 after substituting the text of its own measure (S 1788 — S Rept 100-237), with an amendment. The House then concurred in the Senate amendment with a further amendment of its own Dec. 18.

The bill limited use of certain tin compounds (called organotin or tributyltin) used in anti-fouling paints to keep boat hulls free of barnacles and other organisms. The barnacles increased drag, slowing boats and raising fuel costs.

The additives, however, also harmed desirable and commercially harvested species such as mussels, oysters and salmon, especially when the paint released them at a high rate into a shallow estuary.

Under the bill, use of paints containing organotin was banned on boats less than 25 meters (82 feet) long, those most likely to be found in shallow estuaries. An exception would be made for aluminum boats and boats with outboard motors.

Boats not subject to the ban could be painted with organotin paints only if the Environmental Protection Agency (EPA) certified that the products released no more than 4 micrograms of organotin per square centimeter per day. EPA could subsequently change that requirement by regulation. The bill allowed states to set standards more stringent than federal ones.

EPA was required to monitor organotin concentrations in coastal waters for 10 years and to report its findings annually to Congress. Home ports of Navy vessels would have to be monitored quarterly and the results reported to the state. EPA was required by March 30, 1989, to publish "criteria" for organotin compounds, stating what concentrations in water were safe for various uses.

The legislation provided civil penalties as high as $5,000 per violation and criminal penalties as high as $25,000 and one year in prison. Existing stocks of tin-based paints were to be sold for up to 180 days after enactment and applied for up to one year after enactment, subject to EPA regulations.

# Clean Air

Congress in 1987-88 failed once more to get a clean air bill moving; efforts to amend and reauthorize the 1977 Clean Air Act (PL 95-95) had been stalled in Congress since 1982. *(99th Congress action, p. 435)*

When legislative efforts halted in 1987, Congress moved to extend the Dec. 31, 1987, deadline for when cities would face penalties for failing to meet existing air-quality standards. The House Dec. 3 turned up the political heat when it decided to extend the deadline to Aug. 31, 1988 — so the issue would have to be considered in the middle of the 1988 election campaign.

House action came by voice vote on a Silvio O. Conte, R-Mass, amendment to the fiscal 1988 continuing appropriations resolution (H J Res 395 — PL 100-202). Earlier, the House had rejected on a **key vote of 162-257 (R 72-99; D 90-158)** an amendment offered by John P. Murtha, D-Pa., to extend the deadline until July 31, 1989. *(1987 key votes, p. 965)*

More was at stake than simply the length of the extension. The Conte amendment would bar the Environmental Protection Agency (EPA) from imposing any sanctions at all, while the Murtha plan would leave EPA's administrator the authority to impose sanctions if he made an official finding "that the state is failing to make . . . reasonable good faith efforts."

Conferees on H J Res 395 adopted the Senate language, however, which did not exempt several locales from sanctions already imposed before the Dec. 31 deadline.

But even with an election-year deadline, various clean air measures proposed during 1988 never made it to the floor in either the House or the Senate. Finally, Sen. George J. Mitchell, D-Maine, the leader of a months-long search for a compromise bill, conceded defeat in October in a charged Senate floor speech.

Mitchell's bill was blocked from coming to the floor for almost a year by Majority Leader Robert C. Byrd, D-W.Va., who controlled the Senate schedule. Byrd had long opposed acid rain controls as a threat to coal-mining jobs in his state.

In the House, clean air legislation in the Energy Committee had been slowed by various members, including Chairman John D. Dingell, D-Mich., who was concerned that tighter tailpipe-emission standards would hurt the auto industry in his state. But Henry A. Waxman, D-Calif., a longtime advocate for tougher clean air laws, also played a role in delaying legislation when it appeared he could get a stricter bill in the next Congress.

By not acting, Congress left interpretation and enforcement of the Aug. 31 deadline to EPA by default. The agency in 1987 already had started circulating its plans for handling dirty-air cities and counties if Congress did not act.

Under the clean air law, penalties EPA could (some members said "must") impose included bans on construction of major new sources of pollution (such as factories), withholding of highway funds and withholding of air pollution control grants.

Some 14 municipal areas would have faced construction bans, but only a few faced sanctions in the near term because of Congress' failure to act: Los Angeles and the Southern California coast; Ventura County, Calif.; the Illinois and Indiana suburbs of Chicago; and perhaps Sacramento, Calif.

## House Action

The House Energy and Commerce Committee continued in 1988 to be polarized and paralyzed over a clean air bill. Waxman, from one of the smoggiest districts in the country, wanted aggressive cleanup action. He chaired the Subcommittee on Health and the Environment and tried to mark up a bill there. But full committee Chairman Dingell was opposed to strict controls.

Waxman put before his subcommittee Feb. 18 an unnumbered draft bill combining his own urban-smog bill (HR 3054) and another bill (HR 2666) by Gerry Sikorski, D-Minn., that addressed the problem of acid rain.

The draft would extend the deadlines for polluted areas from three to 10 years, depending on the severity of the pollution, while requiring cities to take additional steps toward reducing harmful emissions.

The draft measure also aimed to reduce acid rain by placing new controls on utilities, industrial boilers, automobiles and trucks.

Despite opposition from Dingell and some Republicans, the Waxman-Sikorski measure did survive a series of test votes in the subcommittee on March 1-2.

Waxman managed to fend off several attempts to amend the acid rain provisions, but just barely. Three amendments were defeated on a 10-10 tie vote. During the March markup, the subcommittee completed action only on the acid rain title of the multi-part clean air bill, which included provisions on urban smog and auto tailpipe standards.

Unable to prevail, Waxman suspended the markup. An effort to restart it in June, focusing this time on urban smog, also sputtered and was suspended.

Because of the six-year congressional hold on clean air legislation, an informal caucus of nine moderate-to-conservative House Energy Committee Democrats tried during 1988 to craft a compromise bill. They held a potential balance of power in the committee and raised hopes March 17 when they released a draft bill.

The proposal, although detailed, was not cast into legislative language, and it dealt only with urban smog and not the additional problem of acid rain. The draft relied on numerous proposals for tiny cuts in emissions of pollutants — in an effort to come up with the major air-quality improvements some cities needed.

But although the draft was at first cautiously welcomed by key players, Waxman eventually criticized it as being too weak and Dingell criticized it for being too stringent. The proposal and further negotiations in the end were not enough to bridge the gap between the two adversaries.

## Senate Action

There also was pressure in the Senate for action on a clean air bill in 1988. The Environment and Public Works Committee in 1987 had reported a clean air bill praised by environmentalists (S 1894 — S Rept 100-231), but Majority Leader Byrd did not bring the measure to the floor.

Forty-six senators from both parties signed a March 25 letter to Byrd and Republican Leader Robert Dole, Kan., urging them to schedule floor action quickly.

But it was not until September that the pace of negotiations on clean air legislation quickened, as Mitchell and the United Mine Workers of America (UMW) neared agreement on acid rain controls.

The UMW approach was to force large sulfur-dioxide ($SO_2$) reductions by a first-phase deadline in the mid-1990s. That would force utilities to use the current technology — expensive smokestack "scrubbers" — since more efficient "clean-coal technology" would not be available until later. Plants with scrubbers still could burn high-sulfur coal, and the UMW hoped that would help save Eastern mining jobs.

As outlines of the Mitchell and UMW positions began to emerge, there were clearly many common elements. Both Mitchell and the UMW would have reduced annual $SO_2$ emissions by 10 million tons — but they differed over how long this would take. Mitchell said that any deadline later than the year 2000 was unacceptable, while the UMW had asked since Aug. 31 for a deadline of 2005. Eventually they seemed to agree on the year 2003.

Both sides were proposing a new national tax of 1 mill (one-tenth of a cent) per kilowatt-hour on fossil-fueled electric power, which would be paid ultimately by the consumer. Both would use the proceeds to subsidize capital costs of the scrubbers — but only for the plants that were the biggest $SO_2$ polluters.

Western states, where many utilities already had paid for scrubbers and were burning Western low-sulfur coal, felt they would gain little under the Mitchell-UMW plan. They did not suffer nearly as much from acid rain, and they would be forced to pay a second time to clean up the Eastern companies' pollution. Key Westerners such as Sen. Alan K. Simpson, R-Wyo., raised strong doubts. But the 1 mill tax could have been small enough to get through.

Staffers for several Western senators, such as Simpson and Steve Symms, R-Idaho, said their bosses would filibuster the bill because it helped high-sulfur coal at the expense of low-sulfur coal.

But the tentative compromise worked out between Mitchell and the UMW with Byrd's support met with stiff opposition from other quarters. Among those leading the charge against the proposal to control acid rain were environmental groups, who said it did not do enough.

Those views were shared by several key senators who had backed environmental causes on the Environment Committee — Robert T. Stafford, R-Vt., John H. Chafee, R-R.I., and Max Baucus, D-Mont.

Finally, in October, Mitchell gave up trying to work out a compromise bill as the 100th Congress wound to a halt. In a highly charged Senate floor speech, Mitchell was critical of both industry and environmental groups for intransigence.

"A few who say they support the Clean Air Act joined with the many who oppose it," Mitchell said. "They remained rigid and unyielding, wholly unwilling to compromise, even when faced with the certainty that their rigidity would result in no action this year."

# Ozone Pact

The Senate gave unanimous approval March 14, 1988, to a treaty (Treaty Doc 100-10) limiting the use of chemicals that depleted the Earth's protective ozone layer.

The president signed the instrument of ratification April 5. Treaties, in the form of resolutions of ratification, are submitted to the Senate for approval by two-thirds of the senators present. The Senate Foreign Relations Committee Feb. 17 recommended approval of the treaty.

Although the House does not ratify treaties, it had passed a resolution earlier, on June 29, 1987, urging the Reagan administration to take a strong stand in international negotiations on protection of the ozone layer (H Con Res 50 — H Rept 100-176, Part I).

The treaty, known as the Montreal Protocol on Substances That Deplete the Ozone Layer, required a 50 percent cut in the production and consumption of chlorofluorocarbons (CFCs) and halons (two groups of ozone-depleting chemicals) by 1999.

Those chemical compounds, widely used in refrigeration, insulation and aerosol sprays, were long-lasting gases that scientists believed depleted the ozone layer high above the Earth. The layer filtered out about 90 percent of the sun's harmful ultraviolet rays. Scientific studies suggested that as the ozone layer became thinner, there would be a significant increase in health and environmental problems, including skin cancer.

The pact was signed by 31 countries, including the members of the European Community and Japan. The United States produced about 30 percent of the world's

CFCs, the European Community accounted for another 30 percent and Japan for about 10 percent. At least 11 countries that accounted for two-thirds of all CFC consumption and production worldwide had to ratify the treaty for it to go into effect as scheduled on Jan. 1, 1989.

Supporters said they hoped the 83-0 vote in favor of the pact would send a clear signal to other leading CFC-producing nations that they should act quickly.

Several senators, including Foreign Relations Committee Chairman Claiborne Pell, D-R.I., urged the United States to move unilaterally to impose more stringent controls.

The United States had sought a 95 percent reduction in CFCs worldwide but accepted a 50 percent cut when other nations refused to go along. The protocol imposed a graduated-reduction schedule to bring a 50 percent decline in CFC usage by 1999.

Seven months after the treaty went into effect, developed nations would have to freeze consumption and production of CFC compounds at 1986 levels. Thirty months later, levels for halon compounds would be frozen.

Industrialized nations would have until July 1, 1994, to reduce production and consumption of CFC compounds by 20 percent and until July 1, 1999, to bring them down to the 50 percent level.

Developing nations, which made and used fewer CFC compounds, would have to reduce production and consumption by a smaller percentage. And low-consuming developing nations would be allowed small increases in per capita consumption for 10 years. After that, their consumption schedules would have to match other nations'.

Nations not observing the treaty would have a tough time producing and consuming the controlled compounds. One year after the treaty took effect, imports from non-treaty countries of bulk chemicals used in CFC production would be banned. Three years after that, treaty members would be prohibited from importing any products containing CFCs from non-treaty countries.

The treaty also contained mechanisms for sharing research on the problem and on possible CFC substitutes.

# Radon Abatement

Congress in 1988 cleared a bill requiring the Environmental Protection Agency (EPA) to help states establish radon-abatement programs.

The $45 million measure (S 744 — PL 100-551) set up federal programs to study and mitigate radon contamination in homes, schools and federal buildings over the next three years. The measure included a program to certify radon measurement devices, requirements for the EPA to develop standards for building construction and a program to demonstrate radon-abatement techniques nationwide.

Radon is an invisible radioactive gas that occurs naturally from decaying uranium deposits in soil. The gas can seep into buildings and become trapped, posing a cancer threat. The EPA estimated about 8 million homes had unsafe levels of radon, and elevated radon levels had been discovered in about 200,000 homes in seven states.

The Senate passed S 744 by voice vote July 8, 1987. The House passed its own radon bill (HR 2837 — H Rept 100-1047) Oct. 5, 1988, then vacated its action and passed S 744 with the language of HR 2837.

The House bill was similar to the original Senate measure but required an EPA radon "citizen's guide" to show the health risks associated with different levels of radon exposure. Another House change added language assuring that money would be authorized to pay the National Bureau of Standards for any radon work it performed.

The Senate accepted the House changes, clearing the measure. Reagan signed the bill Oct. 28, 1988.

# Lead in Drinking Water

Congress in 1988 sent to the president a bill (HR 4939 — PL 100-572) that took aim at water coolers and school drinking fountains that added toxic lead to water. The president signed the bill Oct. 31.

The House Oct. 5 passed HR 4939 (H Rept 100-1041) by voice vote. The Senate passed the bill without amendment Oct. 14, completing congressional action.

The Environmental Protection Agency (EPA) estimated that 42 million Americans, or about one family in five, drank water with unsafe amounts of lead. Because the lead often entered the water after it left the treatment plant, normal treatment regulations did not address the problem.

The bill would control several sources from which lead entered drinking water after it had left the treatment plant. The sources included water coolers and school drinking fountains made with lead solder or lead-lined tanks.

It required the Consumer Product Safety Commission to recall drinking-water coolers with lead-lined tanks within one year of enactment. It also required the EPA to publish a list of brands and models that contained lead and prohibited their sale through interstate commerce. It also established a program for testing school water and making the results public.

To support states and school districts in finding and fixing such problems, the bill authorized grants of $30 million annually for fiscal 1989-91. Another program of grants for screening and preventing lead poisoning was authorized at $20 million for 1989, $22 million for 1990 and $24 million for 1991.

# Endangered Species

After a three-year delay, Congress finally cleared a bill revising and reauthorizing the Endangered Species Act for another five years. The bill had been bogged down by disputes over animals ranging from wolves and grizzly bears to sea turtles.

The House adopted the conference report for the bill (HR 1467 — H Rept 100-928) by voice vote under suspension of the rules on Sept. 26, 1988. The Senate had approved the conference report Sept. 15, by voice vote, after the conferees had agreed to it the day before. The president signed the bill Oct. 7 (PL 100-478).

The Endangered Species Act, which took its most recent shape in 1973 (PL 93-205), was intended to protect dwindling species from hunting, trading and habitat destruction. It also authorized existing federal and state efforts to bring about recovery of the species. *(Congress and the Nation Vol. IV, p. 289; Congress and the Nation Vol. VI, p. 477)*

The 1973 act made it a federal offense to buy, sell, possess, export or import any species listed as endangered or threatened, or any product made from such a species. Federal agencies also were required to ensure that their actions, such as building dams or allowing construction permits, did not threaten endangered species or harm their breeding and feeding grounds.

The act often was amended and reauthorized since 1973. The last reauthorization was enacted in 1982 (PL 97-304) and expired in 1985. It was funded by yearly appropriations since then.

The House passed one endangered species reauthorization in 1985, but the Senate had not followed suit. The House passed a second reauthorization, HR 1467, on Dec. 17, 1987. The Senate did not pass it until July 28, 1988.

Both Senate and House measures provided a large increase in funding for endangered species programs, raised fines for violations of the law, required the government to monitor more closely about 1,000 potentially endangered animals and plants and added new protections for endangered plants.

The Senate measure authorized about $60 million for fiscal 1988, increasing to almost $68 million in fiscal 1992. The House bill provided $57 million for fiscal 1988, increasing to $66 million in 1992. The Endangered Species Act had last been authorized at $39 million for fiscal 1985. Conferees accepted the Senate bill's authorization levels.

The final version of the bill also included provisions to establish an African elephant conservation fund to assist African nations trying to protect elephant populations. The provisions also barred ivory imports from nations whose elephant-conservation programs did not meet the bill's requirements.

One of the main obstacles that kept the Senate from passing an endangered species reauthorization before 1988 was a dispute over the reintroduction of wolves and grizzly bears in the West.

Federal agencies several years before proposed reestablishing the gray wolf in Wyoming's Yellowstone National Park, already home to one of the few surviving populations of grizzly bears in the lower 48 states.

Ranchers around Yellowstone were afraid the wolves and grizzlies would kill cattle. They wanted the law changed to make sure it allowed them to deal with predators the way they had always done — with a rifle. A 1985 Minnesota court decision said hunting of threatened species, such as wolves and grizzlies, was illegal except under certain extraordinary circumstances.

Sen. Alan K. Simpson, R-Wyo., long threatened to offer an amendment to overturn that decision. It was his "hold" on the Endangered Species Act reauthorization that kept the bill off the Senate floor. But in the end, Simpson offered no amendments and, in fact, voted for the bill.

The other controversy that dogged the bill involved sea turtles, all of which had been classified as endangered or threatened in U.S. waters.

Environmentalists complained that too many sea turtles were drowning in shrimp nets. They supported regulations drafted by the National Marine Fisheries Service requiring shrimp fishermen to use turtle excluder devices (TEDs) to keep turtles from becoming caught in their nets and drowning.

But shrimp fishermen resisted using TEDs, arguing that their size endangered the crewmen that handled them as well as reduced their catch. TEDs weighed between four and 40 pounds.

Before passing HR 1467, the House defeated an amendment proposing a two-year delay before shrimpers had to use the devices. The Senate added a controversial amendment that postponed the TEDs requirement.

As the endangered species bill hung in limbo awaiting final action, Congress enacted a separate, temporary measure designed to protect shrimpers until Congress had time to act. The disputed TEDs regulations were scheduled to go into effect Sept. 1, 1988. The stopgap measure (HR 5141 — PL 100-416), delaying their implementation until Sept. 17, was cleared Aug. 11 and signed Aug. 22.

Conferees on the bill accepted Senate-passed language delaying the TEDs until May 1989 for offshore shrimpers, and until spring 1990 for shrimp fishermen on inshore waters, such as inland bays and sounds.

The final bill also required a study by the National Academy of Sciences by April 1989 on the use of TEDs.

# Marine Mammal Protection

A measure imposing new restrictions on tuna fishermen aimed at decreasing the number of porpoises and dolphins killed accidentally by fishing nets was cleared Oct. 21, 1988.

The president signed the bill (HR 4189 — PL 100-711) Nov. 23.

The bill required the commerce secretary to review and modify each year the permits under which domestic tuna fishermen operated. The secretary could add new conditions aimed at forcing less lethal fishing methods. The legislation also required the Marine Mammal Commission to come up with guidelines for reducing the incidental kill and required the commerce secretary to prepare conservation plans for marine mammal species that were being depleted.

Of the 100,000 dolphins killed each year in the eastern Pacific Ocean, about 80 percent were killed by foreign fishing vessels. The bill prohibited foreign nations from selling tuna in American markets if they did not have dolphin protection programs similar to those in the United States.

The bill reauthorized the 1972 Marine Mammal Protection Act (PL 92-522) for fiscal years 1989-93, gradually increasing funds authorized for the Commerce Department, the Interior Department and the Marine Mammal Commission, which carried out the act. *(Congress and the Nation Vol. III, p. 812; Congress and the Nation Vol. VI, pp. 479, 481)*

The Marine Mammal Protection Act placed a moratorium on the killing of marine mammals and the importation of products made from them, although existing law allowed the incidental killing of certain marine mammals during commercial fishing.

The House originally passed HR 4189 (H Rept 100-970) on Sept. 26 by voice vote. The Senate on Oct. 14 substituted the text of its own bill (S 2810 — S Rept 100-592), passed HR 4189 and then sent it back to the House. The House responded with a further amendment on Oct. 19; the Senate concurred Oct. 21, clearing the bill.

# Water Projects

As one of its final acts, the 100th Congress cleared the Water Resources Development Act of 1988 (S 2100 — PL 100-676). President Reagan signed it Nov. 17, 1988. The measure put back on track a regular cycle of biennial water project authorizations.

The conference report on S 2100 (H Rept 100-1098) —

which authorized nearly $2 billion in flood control, navigation, erosion control and other projects — was approved by the Senate by voice vote Oct. 20.

The House adopted the conference report 355-2 Oct. 21, completing congressional action.

The promise of another water projects bill in the 101st Congress helped smooth passage of the 1988 bill, members and staff from both houses said. It took 10 years to enact the last major water projects authorization (PL 99-662) in 1986, but the offer of swift reconsideration helped to placate members whose pet projects had been dropped from S 2100. *(1986 water bill, p. 439)*

The House had approved its own version of a water projects measure (HR 5247) in September, a much larger bill that included several provisions objected to by the White House. Conferees essentially accepted the leaner Senate measure, in order to ensure the enactment of a water projects authorization bill in the 100th Congress.

## Senate Action

The Senate Environment and Public Works Committee March 29 voted 16-0 to report S 2100 (S Rept 100-313), a $1.6 billion Army Corps of Engineers water projects bill described by sponsors as "non-controversial" and squeaky clean. Quentin N. Burdick, D-N.D., the chairman of the panel, said the bill would not become "a Christmas tree."

According to committee sponsors, every project in the bill had a favorable cost-benefit ratio, providing more in economic benefits than it would cost to build. They also said all the projects had reports from the corps' chief of engineers recommending construction.

Aides said environmental impact statements had been filed, or were found to be unnecessary, on all of the projects, and that all of them were subject to funding reforms established in the 1986 omnibus water bill.

The 1986 bill had dramatically increased the share of construction costs paid by project users. Although costs varied considerably from project to project, user costs averaged about 25 percent under the 1986 bill, compared with a typical share of 5 or 10 percent under earlier legislation.

**No Hometown Favoritism.** Daniel Patrick Moynihan, D-N.Y., chairman of the Subcommittee on Water Resources, Transportation and Infrastructure, noted proudly that the bill contained no projects for his own state or the states of the other key committee and subcommittee leaders: Burdick, Robert T. Stafford, R-Vt., and Steve Symms, R-Idaho.

Although technically that was correct, the bill did contain a provision benefiting Burdick's North Dakota. The bill authorized work along the Missouri River, between Fort Peck Dam, Mont., and the Gavins Point Dam, which was between Nebraska and South Dakota. Since the work was to be done under the corps' existing operation and maintenance authority it may not have constituted a project.

The Missouri River authorization also was contained in a separate bill (S 2158) passed by the committee en bloc with the main bill.

By far, however, the biggest projects in the bill were in states not represented on the Environment Committee.

The construction of a new dam and locks on the Ohio River to replace the aging ones near Olmstead, Ill., would cost a total of $775 million, with 50 percent of that amount to come from the Inland Waterways Trust Fund. The fund consisted of revenue from a tax on fuel used by barges that plied inland waterways. Although that project was closest to Illinois and Kentucky, it benefited all states involved in bulk shipping on the Ohio-Mississippi River system.

The second biggest project, at $419 million total cost and $314 million federal cost, involved the Chicago Underflow Plan. The Chicago metropolitan area was plagued during rainstorms by sewer backups that caused street and basement flooding. As part of a larger control plan, the bill authorized floodwater storage reservoirs in quarries at McCook and Thornton, Ill.

**Reagan Plan Expanded.** The legislation had its genesis in a proposal by the Reagan administration but quickly outgrew the austere request.

The emphasis in Reagan's bill (S 2101) was on no-cost or low-cost provisions. It would authorize four new projects but would have negligible budget impact. For example, it would authorize a flood control project at Brush Creek near Kansas City, Mo., with costs borne entirely by the city. It also included authority for the Corps of Engineers to charge fees for use of recreation lands at corps facilities. That authority was left out of S 2100. Only five of the 13 provisions in Reagan's bill were included in the committee measure.

As introduced by Moynihan, S 2100 went well beyond the administration's measure, and the bill approved by the Environment Committee added still other provisions.

Spending on most of the projects could exceed the authorized amount by up to 20 percent as a result of inflation and construction-cost increases. Such increases usually were unlimited before the 1986 reforms.

Authorizations for the projects in the bill expired automatically if they did not receive appropriations to begin construction within five years — another reform instituted in 1986.

The five-year sunset helped authorizing committees keep a firmer grip on water policy. Before 1986, there had accumulated a huge backlog of projects that had been authorized but had never gotten appropriations to start construction. That resulted, according to Environment member George J. Mitchell, D-Maine, in "the decreasing significance of the authorizing committees and the increasing significance of the Appropriations and Budget committees." Mitchell and Moynihan said they wanted to reverse that trend.

Of the $1.6 billion cost of the projects in the Senate committee bill, roughly $986 million would come from the federal Treasury. The rest was to be paid by non-federal beneficiaries of the projects or through the Inland Waterway Trust Fund.

**Quiet Floor Vote.** The Senate April 26 passed S 2100 and called the bill the first of a new breed of lean, biennial water project authorizations that avoided the "pork-barrel" syndrome.

The bill was approved by voice vote with little discussion, after the Senate adopted an amendment from Environment and Public Works Committee leaders making minor changes to the version reported April 11.

The Senate adopted by voice vote an amendment offered by Majority Leader Robert C. Byrd, D-W.Va., for Environment Chairman Burdick and ranking Republican Stafford. It extended for three years, beginning in 1988, Army Corps of Engineers authority to modify existing projects for the improvement of the environment.

It also declared a part of Gravesend Bay in Brooklyn, N.Y., to be legally non-navigable, without changing dredge and fill permit requirements for the area. In addition, it directed the corps to establish a water resources planning and management service for the Hudson River Basin in New York and New Jersey and authorized annual appropriations of $400,000 for that purpose. The amendment also cut certain paperwork requirements for U.S. engineering firms receiving corps support in their work overseas.

## House Action

The House Public Works and Transportation Committee approved by voice vote a much broader, $2 billion water projects authorization measure (HR 5247 — H Rept 100-913) on Sept. 8, 1988.

Although panel members lauded their water projects authorization bill as free of parochial pork-barrel projects, they attached 29 amendments — many of them adding or modifying projects — in two days of subcommittee and committee markup.

Eighteen amendments were approved en bloc Sept. 7 by the Water Resources Subcommittee; 11 more were added as a block by the full committee at its markup the next day.

The additions included an $80,000 pilot program studying use of aluminum sulfate for algae control in California's Clear Lake and expanding by $51 million the total cost of a New Jersey beach-erosion control project.

The New Jersey project, like others authorized since 1986, was subject to requirements that provided for state and local governments to pay as much as half the cost.

Like the Senate measure, House panel members approved authorizations for the $775 million lock and dam replacement on the Ohio River near Olmsted, Ill., and the $419 million flood control project for Chicago.

The most controversial provision in the House bill was one declaring that adequate progress had been made on flood control measures for the Sacramento, Calif., area. That would have qualified new and existing development for greatly reduced flood-insurance premiums, even though flood control measures for the American River were under study. Under a 1968 law, "adequate progress" was achieved when a project's cost was fully authorized, 60 percent appropriated and 50 percent spent, and construction work was half completed.

Rep. Thomas E. Petri, R-Wis., who was known for crusading against fellow members' sacred cows, said the Sacramento provision would set a wrong precedent. "It's a bad policy to set rates below the risk," he said.

Petri was ready to offer an amendment to strike the provision, but committee leaders told him that as an insurance matter, it was under the Banking Committee's jurisdiction.

**More Floor Amendments.** The full House passed HR 5247 by voice vote Sept. 30, then passed in lieu S 2100 amended with the language of HR 5247.

During House debate, 45 amendments were added in a block, which included four new projects and canceled the deauthorization of three.

The provision reducing flood-insurance rates for the Sacramento, Calif., area was changed in a separate amendment to limit the special rates to four years and to prevent additional development in flood-prone areas. The amendment by Vic Fazio, D-Calif., headed off the effort by Petri to strike the provision entirely.

The Congressional Budget Office estimated that the projects in the original bill, before amendments, if fully funded, would cost the federal government $222 million between fiscal 1989 and 1993, and about $1.7 billion from fiscal 1994 to 2004.

## Final Action

House conferees on the water projects bill agreed with the Senate to eliminate several provisions of the larger House-passed measure, including a series of authorizations that were made conditional upon favorable review in reports forthcoming from the U.S. Army Corps of Engineers.

The White House threatened to veto the bill because of the conditional authorizations.

Also dropped was the provision that would lower flood-insurance premiums for the Sacramento, Calif., area. But the Sacramento provision survived on another vehicle; it was tacked on to reauthorization of the Stewart B. McKinney Homeless Assistance Act (HR 558 — PL 100-77), which was sent to the president Oct. 20. (*McKinney Homeless Act, p. 677*)

Compromise also was reached on a demonstration project allowing the Corps to dump a "thin layer" of dredged material from the Gulfport Harbor, Miss., navigation project into Mississippi Sound.

The 1986 authorization required dredged material to be dumped in open waters of the Gulf of Mexico, instead of in the shallower coastal waters of the sound. Environmentalists feared the experiment could cause ecological damage; the conference bill limited the shallow-water dumping to 3 million cubic yards of dredged material, 6 to 12 inches deep.

## Major Provisions

As cleared, S 2100:

### New Authorizations

- **Lower Mission Creek, Calif.** Improved channel and replaced bridges near Santa Barbara, Calif., at a total cost of $10.4 million, with the federal share at $5.9 million.
- **Fort Pierce Harbor, Fla.** Deepened and widened existing channels and provided an additional channel at a total cost of $6.7 million, with the federal share at $4.3 million.
- **Nassau County, Fla.** Filled approximately 3.6 miles of beach and kept 4.3 miles of shore filled along Amelia Island, Fla., at a total cost of $5.8 million, with the federal share at $4.6 million.
- **Port Sutton Channel, Fla.** Deepened to 43 feet at a total cost of $2.7 million, with an estimated federal share of $1.2 million; construction began only after the Army secretary determined that the project served more than one beneficiary.
- **Chicagoland Underflow Plan, Ill.** Built two reservoirs near Chicago, Ill., at a total cost of $419 million, with a federal share of $314.3 million. The reservoirs were to be built in existing quarries at McCook and Thornton, Ill. They were intended to relieve storm-sewer backups by storing storm water temporarily.
- **Lower Ohio River, Ill. and Ky.** Built a new dam and locks near Olmsted, Ill., to replace existing Locks and Dams 52 and 53 at a total cost of $775 million, with half of the cost coming from appropriations and half from the Inland Waterways Trust Fund.
- **Hazard, Ky.** Cleared and widened approximately six miles of the North Fork Kentucky River at a total cost of $7.5 million, with a federal share of $5.6 million.
- **Mississippi and Louisiana Estuarine Areas, Miss. and La.** Diverted water from the Mississippi River into Lake Pontchartrain and the Mississippi Sound at a total cost of $59.3 million, to be paid entirely by federal funds.
- **Wolf and Jordan Rivers, Miss.** Deepened, widened and extended channel of Bayou Portage near Pass Christian, Miss., at a total cost of $2.2 million, with a federal share of $1.6 million.
- **Truckee Meadows, Nev.** Constructed levees, flood walls and overflow storage on the Truckee River and tributaries near Reno, Nev., at a total cost of $78.4 million, with a federal share of $39.2 million, plus $4.1 million for fish and wildlife enhancement.
- **West Columbus, Ohio.** Pumping-station and levee/flood-wall work on approximately 3.3 miles of the Scioto River at a total cost of $31.6 million, with a federal share of $23.7 million.
- **Delaware River, Pa. and Del.** Deepened channel and built turning basin on the Schuylkill River near Philadelphia, Pa., and the Delaware River near Camden, N.J., at a total cost of $17.2 million, with a federal share of $9.1 million.
- **Cypress Creek, Texas.** Enlarged channel and built recreation facilities on approximately 29 miles of Cypress Creek near Houston, at a total cost of $114.2 million, with a federal share of $85 million.
- **Falfurrias, Texas.** Built 5.6 miles of levee, plus pilot channel and other work, along Palo Blanco and Cibolo Creeks at a total cost of $31.8 million, with a federal share of $15.9 million.
- **Guadalupe River, Texas.** Enlarged channel from the Gulf Intracoastal Waterway near Victoria, Texas, at a total cost of $23.9 million, with a federal share of $15.1 million.
- **McGrath Creek, Wichita Falls, Texas.** Constructed new spillway for Sikes Lake and new channel in McGrath Creek at a total cost of $9.1 million, with a federal share of $6.8 million.

### Project Modifications

- **Redondo Beach, Calif.** Changed cost-sharing requirements for the King Harbor project to allow hurricane and storm-damage control to be considered as project purposes. As a result, the local share of project costs was reduced.
- **San Pedro Bay, Calif.** Allowed non-federal interests to receive credit against their share of costs for work they themselves performed on the projects to improve Los Angeles and Long Beach harbors.
- **Los Angeles, Calif.** Directed the Army Corps of Engineers to perform dredging of the existing federal project at the mouth of the Los Angeles River to the authorized depth of 20 feet.
- **Sunset Harbor, Calif.** Added wetland restoration as a purpose of the demonstration project authorized in 1986. All additional costs were to be paid by non-federal interests.
- **Stumpy Lake, La.** Authorized the corps to acquire 300 acres as part of the project to mitigate losses of fish and wildlife habitat along the Red River Waterway.
- **Annapolis, Md.** Directed the corps to realign the harbor channel for more efficient mooring operations by using non-structural dredging measures.

● **Deale Island, Md.** Authorized the corps to pay the remaining cost for the navigation project for Deale Island (Lower Thorofare). The amount authorized was estimated at $277,000 plus any interest due to the construction contractor.

● **Marshall, Minn.** Increased the authorized cost ceiling for the Redwood River flood control project to a total cost of $6.9 million, with a federal cost of $5 million.

● **Root River Basin, Minn.** Added clarifying language to permit the project to be constructed under standing legal authority for construction of small flood control projects.

● **Roseau River, Minn.** Permitted part of the project to be constructed under standing legal authority for construction of small flood control projects.

● **Gulfport Harbor, Miss.** Authorized a demonstration program to study effects of disposing of dredged materials in a "thin layer" in Mississippi Sound, rather than more expensive disposal in open waters of the Gulf of Mexico. The program was limited to 3 million cubic yards of material, 6-12 inches deep.

● **Brush Creek, Mo. and Kan.** Authorized construction of extensions to the flood control project for Brush Creek and tributaries at the expense of non-federal parties.

● **Libby Dam, Mont.** Authorized additional recreational and low-water access facilities on Lake Koocanusa. The bill also directed the corps to protect Indian archaeological sites at an estimated total additional cost of $750,000.

● **Sea Bright to Monmouth Beach, N.J.** Authorized additional work on the beach-erosion control, Sandy Hook to Barnegat Inlet, N.J. Total initial cost for first increment of federal work was authorized at $91 million (previously $40 million), and an additional $1.2 million was authorized annually for beach replenishment. Standard cost-sharing requirements applied to costs above $40 million.

● **Blair and Sitcum Waterways, Wash.** Raised the cost ceiling from $38.2 million to $51 million on the project for navigation at Tacoma Harbor.

● **Wynoochee Lake, Wash.** Authorized non-federal interests to operate and maintain the multipurpose project for Wynoochee Lake.

● **Beaver Lake, Ark.** Included the Agriculture Department's Soil Conservation Service in development of plans to clean up the lake.

## Other Provisions

● **West Virginia, Maryland and Pennyslvania.** Directed the corps to enhance recreation opportunities through its operation of the projects at Beechfort Lake, W.Va.; Bluestone Lake, W.Va.; East Lynn Lake, W.Va.; Francis E. Walter Dam, Pa.; Jennings Randolph Lake (Bloomington Dam), Md. and W.Va.; R. D. Bailey Lake, W.Va.; Savage River Dam, Md.; Youghiogheny River Lake, Pa. and Md.; Summersville Lake, W.Va.; Sutton Lake, W.Va.; and Stonewall Jackson Lake, W.Va.

● **Juniata River, Pa.** Authorized a flood warning and response system at a federal cost of $2 million.

● **Buffalo, N.Y.** Authorized the corps to undertake emergency repairs in the dike at the small boat harbor, Buffalo Harbor, with ceilings of $2 million on the total cost and $1 million on the federal share.

● **Lakeport Lake, Calif.** Reauthorized the flood control project at Lakeport Lake, which was deauthorized in 1986.

● **Sacramento, Calif.** Required the president to in-clude in his 1990 budget a schedule for completing the feasibility study on the Northern California Streams project, American River Watershed.

● **Duluth, Minn.** Authorized the corps to dredge the Hearding Island Inlet, Duluth Harbor, to increase circulation in an area of stagnant water, at a total cost of $500,000.

● **Bayou Lafourche, La.** Directed the corps to review periodically any water shortages related to drought at the Bayou Lafourche Reservoir in Louisiana and to take appropriate action under existing emergency authorities.

● **Great Lakes Dredged Spoil.** Authorized continued use of facilities for the disposal of dredged spoil in the Great Lakes and conducted a study of whether the spoil materials contained toxic substances and whether they were leaking.

● **Charlevoix, Mich.** Directed the corps to restore any recreational uses at the South Pier of Charlevoix Harbor lost because of reconstruction.

● **Los Angeles County, Calif.** Authorized the corps to convey to the city of South El Monte land within the flood control basin of the Whittier Narrows Dam project, subject to an easement to the United States for flood control purposes.

● **Ottawa, Illinois.** Authorized the corps to convey 5.3 acres of federal land at the junction of the Fox and Illinois rivers to the City of Ottawa.

● **Whitman County, Wash.** Directed the corps to exchange 171 acres of federal land for a tract owned by the Port of Whitman County suitable for wildlife habitat.

● **Cabell and Mason Counties, W.Va.** Prohibited the conveyance of the Lesage/Greenbottom swamp to the state of West Virginia.

● **Puerto Rico.** Authorized the corps to pay tuition for children of federal employees working on construction of the Portuguese and Bucana Rivers Project.

● **Sandy Hook, N.J.** Required the Environmental Protection Agency to send Congress within 120 days a plan for a dredged-spoil disposal site to replace the offshore "Mud Dump" area.

● **Montana, South Dakota and Nebraska.** Directed the corps to alleviate bank erosion and other problems caused along the Missouri River by reservoir releases between Fort Peck Dam and a point 58 miles downstream from Gavins Point Dam, at a cost of no more than $3 million annually.

● **New York, N.Y.** Changed the cost ceiling for the New York Harbor Drift Removal Project from an overall total of $30.5 million to $6 million annually.

● **Ventura, Calif.** Authorized emergency repairs to a beach-erosion control groin between Ventura and Pierpont Beach.

● **Philadephia, Pa.** Declared portions of the Delaware River in Philadelphia to be non-navigable (thus exempting wetlands dredge-and-fill projects there from corps permit requirements) unless the corps determined that projects proposed for that area were not in the public interest. The projects involved were Liberty Landing, Marina Towers and World Trade Center, Marine Trade Center, the National Sugar Co. "Sugar House," and Rivercenter.

● **Brooklyn, N.Y.** Declared portions of Coney Island Creek and Gravesend Bay, N.Y., to be non-navigable (thus exempting wetlands dredge-and-fill projects there from corps permit requirements) unless the corps determined that projects proposed for that area were not in the public interest.

● **Everglades National Park, Fla.** Extended through

1991 the corps' authority to modify schedules for the delivery of water from the Central and Southern Florida Flood Control Project to provide a more natural flow of water.

● **Wadsworth, Ill.** Authorized a project to restore wetlands adjacent to the Des Plaines River.

● **Kissimmee River, Fla.** Directed the corps to proceed with work on the Kissimmee River Demonstration Project.

● **Bartlett, Ill.** Directed the corps to consider the impact on the Newark Valley Aquifer of a proposed municipal landfill near Bartlett, Ill., and to report to Congress before issuing a dredge-and-fill permit.

● **Great Lakes-St. Lawrence Seaway.** Directed the corps, with other agencies, to conduct a study of ways to finance navigational improvements on the Great Lakes-St. Lawrence Seaway and to report to Congress within 18 months.

● **Hudson River Basin, N.Y. and N.J.** Directed the corps to establish a water-resource management and planning service for the Hudson River Basin in New York and New Jersey, with annual appropriations authorized at $400,000, to help develop local initiatives.

● **Red River Basin, Minn. and N.D.** Directed the corps to establish a Technical Resource Service for the Red River Basin in Minnesota and North Dakota, with annual appropriations authorized at $500,000, to help develop local projects.

● **Ridgefield, N.J.** Declared three bodies of water in Ridgefield, N.J., to be non-navigable (thus exempting wetlands dredge-and-fill projects there from corps permit requirements).

● Raised the limit on reimbursement to certain non-federal sponsors for work they did on projects under the 1968 Flood Control Act, from $3 million or 1 percent of project cost (whichever was greater) to $5 million annually.

● Extended the existing requirement that beneficiaries of a federal flood control project complied with flood-plain management and flood-insurance programs to cover projects for reduction of hurricane or storm damage as well.

● Required the corps to provide opportunity for public comment before making any change in reservoir operation that would require reallocation of storage capacity or significantly affect any project purpose.

● Authorized the corps to use its laboratories and research centers for collaborative research and development projects with non-federal entities on a cost-shared basis.

● Authorized the corps to undertake a two-year demonstration program of technical assistance to U.S. engineering firms seeking or performing work outside the country if the firms covered all federal costs in advance.

● Required the corps to provide non-federal project sponsors with periodic statements of project expenditures if they requested it. The bill also authorized the corps to grant private companies a license to use any invention conceived by a federal employee while providing such assistance.

● Extended, from two years to five years, a 1986 authority for environmental improvements in existing projects.

# Western Water Measures

## Indian Water Rights

Congress Oct. 20, 1988, cleared a bill (S 795 — PL 100-675) designed to supply enough water for 400,000 Southern Californians — without building any dams and at no cost to the federal government. The president signed the legislation Nov. 17.

The measure eliminated seepage from the All-American Canal, which carried water from the Colorado River to irrigate vegetable farms in California's Imperial and Coachella valleys. The earthen parts of the canal that were not lined with waterproof materials lost as much as 100,000 acre-feet (enough water to cover an acre to a one-foot depth) per year.

Authority to line the All-American Canal was included in S 795, which was introduced to settle decades-long water-rights claims by various bands of San Luis Rey River Indians in San Diego County, Calif. The bands of Mission Indians long had claimed that they were entitled, as a result of the 1891 law that settled them on reservations, to water from the San Luis Rey River. Settlement of those claims was made difficult by the fact that all the water in the San Luis Rey River already was taken by other parties.

S 795 was originally passed by the Senate (S Rept 100-254) on Dec. 19, 1987. In that form, it was a simple water-rights settlement, in which the Indians would relinquish their claims in return for water from the federally sponsored Central Valley Project (CVP) 200 miles to the north.

Subsequently, objections arose from the users of CVP water. After further negotiations, the House Interior Committee in June 1988 ordered reported its version of the bill (H Rept 100-780), which took another tack. It included authorization for the Metropolitan Water District of Southern California and other parties to fund the lining of the canal. This would save enough water to satisfy the Indians' claims with 16,000 acre-feet yearly, with much more than that to spare for other users in the region. The bill also established a Tribal Development Trust Fund and authorized federal appropriations of $30 million to go into it.

The House passed that bill, 405-12, on Oct. 4.

## Central Utah Project

A one-year, $45.3 million bill to allow continuing construction on the sprawling Central Utah water project went to the president Oct. 12, 1988. The president signed it Oct. 31.

The bill (HR 3408 — PL 100-563) funded continued construction on some non-controversial parts of the project, primarily the Bonneville Unit, leaving for 1989 further congressional work on broader legislation to overhaul the whole Central Utah Project.

The Central Utah Project was meant to bring water from the Colorado River system to towns along the state's Wasatch Front and to irrigators in other parts of the state. As originally introduced, the bill would raise the authorization ceiling by $754 million. Of the scaled-down total in the final bill, about $26.6 million was to go to fish, wildlife and recreation purposes. Most of the remainder would go toward municipal and industrial water supply in the Salt Lake City area.

Several add-ons drew fire from the Reagan administration. One authorized a $15 million payment to ranches around the Strawberry Reservoir, east of Salt Lake City. In return, the ranchers gave up surface rights to 56,775 acres of government-owned pasture, which was to become part of the Uinta National Forest.

The bill originally passed the House on Sept. 13 (H Rept 100-915), and the Senate passed its own version Sept. 30. The House subsequently amended the Senate version

Oct. 6, and the Senate sent the House a further amendment Oct. 11. House agreement Oct. 12 to the amendment completed congressional action.

## South Dakota Drinking Water

The president signed on Oct. 24, 1988, a bill that sponsors said would provide drinking water for some 20,000 residents of South Dakota.

The Mni Winconi project, as it was named in the bill (HR 2772 — PL 100-516), was really a network of three interconnected rural water supply systems serving the Oglala Sioux of the Pine Ridge Indian Reservation and residents of seven rural counties in the southwest part of the state.

The pump-and-pipeline project served an area of about 11,000 square miles, or about 15 percent of the state, where groundwater was scarce and often unhealthful, by bringing in water drawn from the Missouri River system near Fort Pierre.

The bill authorized a total of $87.5 million in federal funds for construction of all three components: the Oglala Sioux Rural Water Supply System, the West River Rural Water System and the Lyman-Jones Rural Water System. That limit could be increased for normal rises in construction costs. The bill limited the federal share of the costs of the West River and Lyman-Jones systems to 65 percent, requiring the water users, through state and local governments, to pay the remaining 35 percent.

The bill cleared Oct. 7 when the Senate agreed by voice vote to amendments added Oct. 4 by the House.

The House had first passed the bill (H Rept 100-733) on June 28, and the Senate passed it with its own amendments (S Rept 100-490) on Sept. 8.

The Reagan administration had opposed the earlier House version.

## Animas-La Plata Project

Congress in October 1988 sent to the president a bill (HR 2642 — PL 100-585) clearing the last obstacles to construction of the $577 million Animas-La Plata water project in Colorado. President Reagan signed the bill Nov. 3.

While sponsors said the project was necessary to settle water-rights claims of the Colorado Ute Indians, environmentalists and the Reagan administration had opposed the bill.

The House passed HR 2642 (H Rept 100-932) on Oct. 3 by a 249-146 vote, and the Senate passed it by voice vote Oct. 14. That same day, the Senate also passed S Con Res 162, to correct enrollment of the bill, making last-minute adjustments as part of a compromise worked out with House managers. The House passed S Con Res 162 Oct. 19 by voice vote.

The Animas-La Plata project was actually authorized in 1968 in the Colorado River Storage Projects Act, but construction was not funded.

In 1976, the Colorado Ute Indian tribes went to court claiming a right, as part of the federal reservation established for them in 1868, to the water in southwestern Colorado rivers. That water already was being used by hundreds of farmers and ranchers and by several towns.

The Indian tribes and other parties eventually started negotiating a settlement whose keystone was the Animas-La Plata project, which would increase the total supply instead of forcing the parties to take smaller shares.

In 1985, Congress mandated under PL 99-88 that no federal funds could go to the project until non-federal parties agreed to pay a share of its costs as part of an overall water-rights settlement. And in 1986 all parties signed such an agreement.

HR 2642 ratified that settlement. Under it, non-federal parties agreed to pay $212 million, or about 37 percent, of the project's $577 million overall cost. Water from the project also would go to the Navajo reservation and towns and ranches in northwest New Mexico.

Environmentalists had opposed the project, saying it would hurt streams used for whitewater rafting and trout fishing. Reps. George Miller, D-Calif., and Thomas E. Petri, R-Wis., who opposed the project on the House floor, criticized it as wasteful and more beneficial to farmers than Indians. Petri said the project would pay $5,800 per acre to irrigate land that would be used to grow crops that were already in surplus, and for which the government then would have to pay surplus subsidies. The Office of Management and Budget had opposed the bill because the terms under which the federal government financed the local share of costs were more generous than those that were standard for other water projects.

# Rivers and Land Conservation

**Michigan Wilderness.** Congress cleared legislation in 1987 (HR 148 — PL 100-184) designating 91,500 acres in Michigan as a federal wilderness area. The House April 7 suspended the rules and passed the bill by voice vote designating 92,056 acres as federal wilderness. The measure passed the Senate also by voice vote Nov. 19, reducing the number of acres to 91,500. The House agreed to that number Nov. 20, clearing the bill. The president signed it Dec. 8.

The measure shielded from development 11 areas in the Manistee, Ottawa and Hiawatha national forests. Most motor vehicles, mineral extraction and logging would be banned permanently, although hiking, hunting and fishing would be allowed. The bill released for development about 21,000 other acres that were under consideration as possible wilderness areas.

**Kings River.** Also signed by the president in 1987 was a bill (HR 799 — PL 100-150) designating the Kings River in California as part of the National Wild and Scenic Rivers System. The measure protected 92 miles of the river and more than 50,000 acres of riverside land.

The House passed the measure by voice vote April 21, and the Senate passed the bill amended Oct. 1. The House accepted the Senate amendments Oct. 13, thus clearing the measure. The president signed the bill Nov. 3.

**Kern River.** Congress in 1987 cleared a bill (S 247 — PL 100-174) that prevented development on portions of the Kern River in California. The president signed the bill Nov. 24.

The bill designated about 78.5 miles of the north fork and 72.5 miles of the south fork of the Kern River for protection under the federal Wild and Scenic Rivers Act. Most of those two river reaches was still free-flowing and any further dam building would be prohibited under the law.

Both river segments flowed out of the Sierra Nevada. The north fork dropped some 10,000 feet from its headwaters on Mount Whitney, passing through the Sequoia National Park and the Golden Trout Wilderness Area.

The Senate passed S 247 (S Rept 100-184) Oct. 1. The House agreed Nov. 9 to suspend the rules and pass S 247 (H Rept 100-424) on a 363-26 vote, clearing the measure.

**Washington Wilderness.** Congress in 1988 cleared a bill (S 2165 — PL 100-668) to designate wilderness areas within national parks in the state of Washington. The bill designated as wilderness approximately 877,000 acres in the Olympic National Park, 217,000 acres in the Mount Rainier National Park and 635,000 acres in the North Cascades National Park area. The bill also limited the number of hydroelectric projects allowed in the Lake Chelan and Ross Lake national recreation areas.

The House cleared the bill upon passage by voice vote on Oct. 19, a day after the Senate acted. The president signed the measure into law Nov. 16.

**Zuni-Cibola National Park.** A National Historic Park on the Zuni Indian Reservation in New Mexico was created under a bill (HR 4182 — PL 100-567) cleared Oct. 12, 1988. The president signed the legislation Oct. 31.

This was the first such park on Indian lands. The Reagan administration initially opposed the measure. A White House statement said the bill would create expectations by the Zuni tribe that federal lands would go to the park. No federal land acquisition was required for the unit, however, which was named the Zuni-Cibola National Historic Park. Sponsors estimated the park would cost about $250,000 annually to run. The bill authorized "such sums as may be necessary."

The House passed HR 4182 (H Rept 100-942) on Sept. 20, and the Senate passed its own version of the bill (S 2162 — S Rept 100-354) the same day. The Senate amended the House bill Oct. 11 to include compromise language, and the House Oct. 12 concurred.

**Oregon Rivers.** Congress in 1988 cleared a landmark river-protection bill for Oregon, one of the states with the most wild rivers to protect. President Reagan signed the measure (S 2148 — PL 100-557) Oct. 28.

The House passed the bill by voice vote Oct. 12; the Senate (S Rept 100-570) had acted Oct. 7.

The bill added to the National Wild and Scenic Rivers System segments of 40 rivers totaling some 1,400 miles. That status protected them from federal activities, such as dam building, and many kinds of private development that could spoil their pristine state. The majority of the land adjoining the rivers was federally owned.

Another title in the bill authorized construction of the Umatilla Basin water project in Oregon — a key to easing the objections of Rep. Robert F. Smith, R-Ore., the only member of the state's delegation to oppose the bill.

The Umatilla title, which had moved separately as S 1613, authorized a $42.2 million pumping project aimed at settling conflicting water demands. Indians on the Umatilla Reservation wanted water to support fishing in the Umatilla River, while farmers were drawing down the river for irrigation. The project was to pump more water out of the Columbia River to increase the supply. The Senate had passed S 1613 (S Rept 100-488) Sept. 8.

The Oregon river-protection bill was one of the largest of its kind since the original Wild and Scenic Rivers Act (PL 90-542) became law two decades earlier. The 1,400 river-miles in the bill were a major addition to the 7,700 total river-miles in the system at the start of 1988. *(Congress and the Nation Vol. II, p. 472)*

Oregon previously had only four river segments totaling 317 miles in wild and scenic status.

As introduced, the bill named some 1,700 river-miles for protection, but the amount was cut to eliminate objections, especially those of private landowners. The final bill left out all rivers where more than 50 percent of the adjacent lands were privately owned. But the bill did authorize studies of six other segments for possible later inclusion.

**Rio Chama River.** The 100th Congress also sent the president a bill putting part of the Rio Chama in northern New Mexico off-limits to development by naming it a wild and scenic river. The bill (S 850 — PL 100-633) cleared Oct. 20, 1988, when the Senate agreed by voice vote to House amendments to the bill. The measure had been passed by the Senate on Oct. 7 and the House on Oct. 19. The president signed it Nov. 7.

Wild and scenic status prohibited dam building and certain other development activities. The segment of the Rio Chama named extended for 24.6 miles downstream from the dam at El Vado Lake. Another segment four miles long immediately below that received a slightly less protective status. The bill specified that the Rio Chama designation would not interfere with operation of the Abiquiu Dam, which supplied water for Albuquerque, N.M.

**West Virginia Rivers.** Congress in 1988 cleared a scaled-back bill for conservation of three scenic-river segments in West Virginia. The president signed the bill (HR 900 — PL 100-534) Oct. 26.

The measure cleared Oct. 7 when the Senate agreed by voice vote to the House amendments to the bill, which protected segments of the New, Gauley and Lower Bluestone rivers. Protections for the Greenbrier River were dropped from the bill.

The New River, believed by geologists to be one of the oldest rivers on the continent, had already been protected from development as a "national river" under the National Park System. The bill modified the boundaries of the protected area, authorized cooperative agreements with the state and local governments, authorized a study of a manmade flow regime set by reservoir releases and authorized new public access and visitor facilities.

The bill also authorized designation of a Gauley River National Recreation Area and a Bluestone National Scenic River — classifications that would protect them from development. Included in the Gauley recreation area was 5.5 miles of its tributary, the Meadow River. HR 900 was passed by the House (H Rept 100-106) on May 27, 1987, and by the Senate (S Rept 100-481) Sept. 8, 1988.

**Sipsey River and Wilderness.** Congress in 1988 sent the president a bill (HR 5395 — PL 100-547) to protect wilderness and a wild river in Alabama.

The bill named about 52 miles of the Sipsey River, in the Bankhead National Forest, as a federal wild and scenic river, a status that protected it from dam building and many forms of development. The protection covered 5,085 acres of forested river canyon.

The bill also added 13,260 acres to the existing Sipsey Wilderness and 710 acres to the Cheaha Wilderness. It authorized a study of a proposed dam-and-lake construction project within the Bankhead forest. It also gave the Forest Service authority to control fire and insects (including the southern pine beetle) within the Sipsey Wilderness — measures usually avoided in wilderness lands.

The House passed HR 5395 (H Rept 100-1057, Parts I and II) Oct. 6, and the Senate followed suit Oct. 11. The president signed the bill on Oct. 28.

The Senate had passed a similar bill (S 2838 — S Rept 100-578) Oct. 5.

# Carter Historic Site

Congress in 1987 cleared legislation (HR 2416 — PL 100-206) to establish the Jimmy Carter National Historic Site in Plains, Ga., in honor of the 39th president. President Reagan signed the bill Dec. 23.

The bill, passed by the House (H Rept 100-342) on Oct. 5, mandated preservation of Carter's home in Plains and 2.9 acres across from it; his boyhood home in nearby Archery, Ga.; the Plains High School, which he attended; and the railroad depot that served as his presidential campaign headquarters.

In addition to the Carter historic site, the bill established a preservation district in and around Plains to preserve and interpret life in that rural Southern town. The bill authorized $3.5 million for acquisition of property, preservation easements and development, plus $300,000 annually for operating and related expenses.

The Senate (S Rept 100-250) passed the measure Dec. 12, completing congressional action.

# Montana Wilderness

President Reagan announced on Nov. 3, 1988, a pocket veto of a bill that would create additional Montana wilderness preserves.

Reagan said the bill (S 2751) to put about 1.4 million acres of National Forest System land in Montana off-limits to logging, road building and other development "could cost jobs and eliminate vast mineral development opportunities."

A pocket veto occurred when the president declined to sign a bill and was unable to return it to Congress because Congress had adjourned.

The Senate had approved a final version of the Montana wilderness bill by voice vote Oct. 18, and the House followed suit Oct. 20, after a last-minute compromise broke a long impasse over the measure. The House had passed a different Montana wilderness bill (HR 2090 — H Rept 100-369, Part I) a year before, on Oct. 13, 1987.

Congress had previously designated 3.4 million acres as wilderness in Montana.

Besides setting aside land as wilderness, the vetoed bill also would identify some 680,000 acres for special management or further study. At the same time, the bill would release from development restrictions another 4 million acres that had been managed as wilderness while Congress was considering whether they should be permanently set aside.

# Manassas Battlefield Land

Land preservationists and Civil War historians claimed a last-minute victory in their effort to save land from development by adding it to the Manassas National Battlefield Park in a Northern Virginia suburb of Washington, D.C.

A provision in the tax technical-corrections bill (HR 4333 — PL 100-647), cleared during the last day of the 100th Congress, Oct. 22, 1988, expanded the battlefield by about 600 acres. *(Corrections bill, p. 100)*

The provision required that the federal government take immediate possession of the land, which had been slated to become a shopping mall. The area included the site of Gen. Robert E. Lee's headquarters during the second battle of Manassas in 1862.

The price of the property, estimated to be between $50 million and $300 million, was to be decided in federal court.

Sen. Dale Bumpers, D-Ark., had attached the Manassas provision to the technical-corrections measure as a floor amendment Oct. 7 to shield it from possible veto by President Reagan. Bumpers' amendment was virtually the same as a measure (HR 4526 — H Rept 100-809, Parts I and II) to save the land that the House passed Aug. 10, 1988. The House bill had been introduced by Robert J. Mrazek, D-N.Y., and Michael A. Andrews, D-Texas, and had 203 cosponsors.

Under the legislation, the developer was to receive "just compensation" — a price to be worked out either through negotiation or through the courts.

The Board of Supervisors of Prince William County, Va., where the battlefield was located, supported plans by the Hazel/Peterson Co. to build a 1.2 million square foot shopping mall adjacent to the battlefield park because it would bolster the tax base. But preservationists said it would ruin the national park site.

The bill authorized a study to plan how to shut down U.S. Routes 29 and 234, which ran through the battlefield. It also authorized construction of a bypass, with 75 percent of costs to be paid by the federal government and 25 percent by state and local governments. It authorized $30 million for the study and federal share of the bypass.

An Aug. 9 letter from the Office of Management and Budget (OMB) reinforced Interior Department opposition to the bill and said OMB would recommend a veto because it was too costly. Opponents on the House floor tried to challenge the bill at every step, beginning with the rule providing for its consideration. But the House approved HR 4526 over Reagan administration objections by a 307-98 vote.

# Cave Protection

In the final days of the 100th Congress, lawmakers cleared a bill to beef up protections for caves on federal lands against vandalism, looting and misuse.

The bill (HR 1975 — PL 100-691) was cleared by Congress Oct. 21, 1988, and signed by the president Nov. 18.

About 40,000 caves had been discovered in the United States, and 4,200 of those were on the lands of the Bureau of Land Management and National Forest Service. Those caves often were rich in fossils, archaeological relics and biological and geological specimens. Spelunkers (recreational cave explorers) enjoyed such caves, but vandalism and commercial exploitation had sometimes destroyed irreplaceable resources.

The bill required the Interior Department to issue new rules for managing federal caves. It authorized the department to keep secret the location of certain caves to protect them, and to require permits for the collection and removal of cave resources. It made it a federal offense to destroy, deface, alter, remove or harm cave resources without authorization, to enter a cave with the intent of doing so or to possess or sell such resources. Civil penalties went as high as $10,000 per violation, and criminal penalties included up to three years in prison for second-offenders.

The House passed the bill (H Rept 100-534) by voice

vote on March 28. The Senate passed an amended version (S Rept 100-559) by unanimous consent on Oct. 21, and the House agreed to the Senate amendments by unanimous consent the same day, clearing HR 1975.

# Rails-to-Trails

Congress in 1988 cleared a bill (S 1544 — PL 100-470) to encourage the preservation of abandoned railroad rights of way as recreational trails.

The House passed its version of the bill (HR 2641 — H Rept 100-572) earlier in the year on April 19. The Senate passed S 1544 (S Rept 100-408) July 6 by voice vote. The House Aug. 2 took up S 1544, amended it and passed it by voice vote. The Senate then agreed to the House amendments, clearing the bill Sept. 19 for the president, who signed it Oct. 4.

In previous decades, thousands of miles of track had been abandoned as unprofitable by railroad companies, and when that happened, title to the land often reverted to the United States. The bill authorized the Interior Department to convert such rights of way to use as public recreational trails wherever possible.

If the rights of way ran through a national park, national forest or other federal conservation unit, the bill required that they be added to the park or forest. The interior secretary also could give land to a state or local government or a private group for public recreational use. When such a conversion was not feasible, the rights of way could be sold and the proceeds were to be placed in the Land and Water Conservation Fund, which was used to acquire federal park land.

Many of the rights of way held by railroads were given to them from federal lands in the 19th century, to encourage railroad expansion. Legal title for many of these lands reverted to the United States once they were no longer used as railroads, unless they were part of a public highway.

But a 1922 law (43 USC 912) changed that. It made an abandoned right of way the property of the adjacent landowner or the municipality through which it passed. The key purpose of the rails-to-trails measure was to cancel the 1922 law. Under the bill, the United States kept title to the land.

Some 30,000 miles of the 150,000-mile total U.S. rail system came from federal grants. Most of it was in the West, although small amounts were found in Florida, Michigan, Illinois, Mississippi, Alabama, Minnesota and Iowa.

# National Park Fees

Congress in 1987 enacted legislation authorizing increases in entrance fees to the national parks for the first time in a decade and a half. But under a separate piece of legislation, visitors could not be charged a fee at the Statue of Liberty.

The fee hike in its final form was cleared Dec. 22, 1987, as part of the fiscal 1988 deficit reduction bill (HR 3545 — PL 100-203) and signed by President Reagan later the same day. (Deficit reduction bill, p. 61)

The final provisions were similar to ones passed by the House April 1, 1987, in a separate bill (HR 1320 — H Rept 100-33).

Reagan had repeatedly asked for park fee increases as a way of paying for park operations and reducing the deficit. But many in Congress balked at charging the public to see national monuments or raising the price of admission to parks.

In 1986, Congress met the president part way, when it included in the continuing appropriations resolution for fiscal 1987 (PL 99-591) temporary authority for entrance fee increases at most parks. That authority expired Sept. 30, 1987. HR 1320 extended it permanently but limited further increases.

In February 1987, the Interior Department had imposed a $1-per-visitor fee at the Statue of Liberty under the temporary authority. It was the first time an entrance fee had been charged at the statue, although visitors already had to pay $3.25 for the ferry to Liberty Island and another 25 cents for the elevator to the top of the statue.

Some congressional members thought charging a fee was inappropriate, since citizen donations had raised $250 million for a restoration of the statue in 1986.

The bill barring an entrance fee at the Statue of Liberty (S 626 — PL 100-55) cleared when the House (H Rept 100-136) suspended the rules and passed it June 8 by voice vote; the Senate (S Rept 100-32) had passed it April 7. The president signed the bill June 19.

The House vote of 416-5 on passage of HR 1320 reflected broad agreement that it was time to raise the fees, which had remained essentially unchanged from 1972 until 1986.

As enacted, the final legislation set a maximum fee of $10 at Yellowstone and Grand Teton national parks, $5 at Glacier National Park and, beginning Oct. 1, 1991, $10 at Grand Canyon National Park. Fees were prohibited at urban parks with many access points. Fee revenues were subject to appropriation until 1991. Ten percent of the revenue went to a discretionary fund to be allocated by the director of the National Park Service among various park units on the basis of need.

# Arizona-Idaho Land

Congress in 1988 cleared a bill (S 2840 — PL 100-696) that wrapped up various legislation of interest to Arizona and Idaho and included the final text of a controversial Arizona-Florida land exchange that had started as separate legislation. The president signed the bill Nov. 18.

The House passed S 2840 Oct. 20 by a 316-32 vote. The Senate, which had passed its own version Oct. 13, agreed by voice vote to the House amendments the same day, clearing the measure.

The separate bill (HR 4519) was passed by the House July 27, on a 281-125 vote, and allowed the Interior Department to exchange some prime real estate in downtown Phoenix, Ariz., for a much larger piece of land to fill out some federal wildlife refuges in Florida.

Also included in S 2840 was authorization of a complex swap of some 240,000 acres of land between the federal government and Arizona, primarily in the Santa Rita Range, which had been introduced as HR 4565. The legislation also included a bill (HR 568) to establish a 56,431-acre San Pedro Riparian National Conservation Area in Arizona.

Other language authorized the Mississippi National River and Recreation Area in the Minneapolis-St. Paul area and provided funds for the National Capital Commission to assist in the preservation of the U.S. Capitol.

The Arizona-Florida land exchange bill that was wrapped into S 2840 received strong House approval, even though critics assailed it as being too generous to a private real estate company.

The bill allowed the U.S. government to trade 68 acres of prime real estate in downtown Phoenix to the Barron Collier Co. for 108,000 acres of southern Florida wetlands and $34.9 million in cash. The Florida land was used to extend existing wildlife refuges. The money from the exchange went to finance a trust fund for the education and welfare of Arizona Indian children because the land in Phoenix was the site of a former government-owned boarding school for Indian children.

In addition to the 68 acres that the government traded to Collier, another 20 acres went to the city of Phoenix for a public park, 11.5 acres to the Veterans Administration (VA) to expand an existing VA hospital and 4.5 acres to the state of Arizona for construction of a state nursing home for veterans.

Interior Committee Chairman Morris K. Udall, D-Ariz., said painstaking negotiations had produced a proposal "that I believe to be fair to all the parties and in the best interests of the United States."

Although the measure required the Interior Department to solicit other competitive bids for the Phoenix property, Collier then was given 30 days to match the highest bid. George Miller, D-Calif., called it a "sweetheart deal," because the other parties could not come back and bid again. "We are giving away valuable government assets at bargain-basement prices," Miller said.

But Florida Republican Tom Lewis said if the measure had been voted down, southern Florida would lose land desperately needed to preserve its water supply, as well as to help endangered species.

## Land Exchanges

The 100th Congress created uniform procedures for various federal land exchanges under a bill (HR 1860 — PL 100-409) cleared Aug. 3, 1988, and signed by the president Aug. 20.

Federal agencies often identified cases where the public could have benefited from swapping parcels of federal land for state, local or private land, allowing both parties to consolidate holdings and get lands they would rather have. While certain exchanges had to be approved by Congress, many smaller ones were conducted by the agencies on their own authority under a complicated web of laws.

HR 1860 created uniform procedures for such exchanges. The measure required prompt appraisal of the lands involved and provided for resolution of appraisal disputes through arbitration or negotiation. The measure made exchanges of small parcels (less than $150,000 in value) easier, and it granted more flexibility in compensation of costs needed to prepare the land for exchange.

The House passed HR 1860 (H Rept 100-165, Parts I and II) Dec. 14, 1987. The Senate passed an amended version (S Rept 100-375) June 13, 1988.

## Fish and Wildlife

A bill cleared in 1987 raising the annual authorization for the National Fish and Wildlife Foundation. President

Reagan signed the measure (S 1389 — PL 100-240) Jan. 11, 1988.

Congress created the foundation in 1984 (PL 98-244) as an independent conservation organization to develop private support for programs and activities of the U.S. Fish and Wildlife Service. The 1984 law authorized $1 million per year to match private donations to the foundation on a one-to-one basis. S 1389 increased the authorization to $5 million annually for fiscal years 1988 to 1993, maintaining the requirement for a one-to-one match.

S 1389 was passed by the Senate (S Rept 100-255) Dec. 18, 1987, and by the House Dec. 21.

## Fighting Wildfires

The 100th Congress cleared legislation designed to help firefighters deal with wildfires that raged during the summer of 1988 at Yellowstone National Park and in other parts of the West.

The bill (S 2641 — PL 100-428) allowed the secretaries of interior and agriculture to enter into an agreement with Canada, under which the United States would reimburse Canada for firefighting equipment and services needed on an emergency basis. The bill was rushed through the Senate and the House in a matter of hours on voice votes Sept. 8. President Reagan signed the bill Sept. 9.

## Polluted Lands

Congress in 1988 cleared a bill (HR 4362 — PL 100-648) to keep Western towns from accepting gifts of federal land, filling them with hazardous wastes and then giving them back to the federal government. The president signed the measure Nov. 10.

Such situations had occurred under the Recreation and Public Purposes Act of 1926 (43 USC 869), which authorized the Bureau of Land Management (BLM) to give tracts to municipalities that could put them to use. Often, they became the city dump.

The law specified that if the municipality misused or abandoned the land, title would revert to the federal government — which often could bring with it liability for the costs of cleaning up a hazardous waste dump. To avoid such situations, the BLM had in February 1987 imposed a moratorium on such transfers until the law was amended.

HR 4362 amended the 1926 act to exempt land conveyed for purposes of solid-waste disposal from the usual reversion clause. Before BLM conveyed the land to a local or state government, it would have to be inspected to ensure there were no hazardous wastes already on it. To get the land, a municipality had to warrant that its use met all applicable state and federal laws, especially those on waste disposal. The bill also authorized BLM to renounce its reversionary interest in contaminated land.

The House passed the bill (H Rept 100-934) on Sept. 20. The Senate amended and passed it Oct. 21, and the House agreed to the Senate amendments the same day, clearing the measure.

## Grand Canyon Flights

Congress in 1987 moved to restrict sightseeing flights in the Grand Canyon and two other national parks after a sightseeing helicopter and a small plane collided in June 1986 over the Grand Canyon, killing 25 people.

The legislation (HR 921) not only restricted air tours over the canyon but also directed the Interior Department to conduct a three-year study to determine the minimum altitude for flights over national parks and monuments. The bill authorized $3 million.

Although the Reagan administration said the bill was unnecessary because the Interior Department already had the authority to conduct a study, President Reagan Aug. 18 signed the bill into law (PL 100-91).

During the three-year study period and for two years thereafter, aircraft were required to fly at least 2,000 feet above the surface of Yosemite National Park in California and 9,500 feet above sea level over Haleakala National Park in Hawaii.

At the Grand Canyon, the National Park Service was required to develop a flight control plan that provided for a "substantial restoration of the natural quiet" of the canyon, including a ban on flights below the rim.

HR 921 was reported from the House Interior and Insular Affairs Committee April 28 (H Rept 100-69, Part I) and passed the House May 4 under suspension of the rules.

Referred to the Senate Energy and Natural Resources Committee May 5 and reported out July 1 (S Rept 100-97), the bill then went to the Commerce, Science and Transportation Committee where it was reported out July 24 (S Rept 100-125). It passed the Senate with amendments on July 28. The House agreed by voice vote to the Senate amendments Aug. 3, clearing the bill.

# Strip-Mining Restrictions

Congress cleared legislation in 1987 to curb abuses of the 1977 Surface Mining Control and Reclamation Act (PL 95-87). The bill (HR 1963 — PL 100-34) became law when the president signed it May 7.

HR 1963 repealed a two-acre mine exemption written into the 1977 law so that small "pick and shovel" operations would not have to comply with environmental standards imposed on larger mines. *(Congress and the Nation Vol. V, p. 544)*

Over the years, however, several large coal companies were accused of using the exemption to circumvent the law. Abuses included using dummy corporations to mine adjoining two-acre sites or leaving a few feet of unmined land between a series of two-acre mines, said House Interior Committee Chairman Morris K. Udall, D-Ariz., chief sponsor of the bill.

HR 1963 also allowed states to set aside up to 10 percent of their abandoned-mine/land-reclamation grants for use after the taxes that supported the grants expired in 1992. Previously grants had to be used within three years or were forfeited. Sponsors said the provision would give states more flexibility to repair damage from mining.

The bill was reported from the House Interior and Insular Affairs Committee April 21 (H Rept 100-59). It passed the House the same day, under suspension of the rules. The Senate Energy and Natural Resources Committee reported its bill (S 643 — S Rept 100-37) April 10. But by unanimous consent, the Senate voted to accept the House version and passed HR 1963 April 23. All votes were by voice.

# Alaskan Refuge Drilling

The Alaska delegation fought hard during the 100th Congress for a bill that would lift a ban on oil drilling in the Arctic National Wildlife Refuge (ANWR), but, in the end, no measure made it to either the House or Senate floor.

Oil companies and the Reagan administration also wanted to open the refuge to drilling, which they hoped contained the nation's richest remaining oil reservoir. They said it would keep oil flowing down the trans-Alaska pipeline and ease the nation's dependence on imported oil. Existing law prohibited leasing for oil operations in the refuge.

Environmentalists, however, said oil drilling would ruin the nation's last remaining example of a natural arctic ecosystem and threaten the survival of the biggest migratory U.S. caribou herd.

They also questioned whether the ANWR oil was needed and said there were cheaper and less destructive ways to find oil. They compiled volumes of alleged environmental violations and damages from other oil company operations on Alaska's North Slope, although the oil companies denied most of the charges.

Drilling advocates saw the 100th Congress as a possibly unique opportunity to gain their goal — while they had a sympathetic president and powerful allies in congressional leadership posts. But any impression of momentum vanished as opposition grew and Congress ended in prolonged stalemate on the legislation.

## Background

ANWR was a 19.3 million-acre expanse of mountains and tundra bigger than any wildlife refuge in the lower 48 states and second in size only to one other in Alaska. It was located in Alaska's extreme Northeast corner, mostly above the Arctic Circle. The refuge included the mountains of the Brooks Range, a major formation running east-west for most of the width of the state.

Some 8 million of the refuge's acres already had been designated by Congress as wilderness, a federal category that meant development, including oil drilling, was banned.

The refuge was so large that it encompassed a range of linked arctic ecosystems. It provided habitat for grizzly and polar bear, caribou, musk ox, Dall sheep, wolf, wolverine, peregrine falcon and gyrfalcon.

Congress created ANWR in 1960. Then in 1980 with the Alaska National Interest Lands Conservation Act (ANILCA, PL 96-487), Congress divided up Alaska's lands among the state government, native groups and various federal management categories. ANILCA also doubled the size of the arctic refuge, and it put the 1.5 million-acre ANWR coastal plain off-limits while requiring the Interior Department to study oil potential and environmental threats there. After that, an affirmative action of Congress still would be required before any drilling could occur. *(Congress and the Nation Vol. V, p. 577)*

The Interior Department finally came back to Congress with its official report in April 1987, and Secretary Donald P. Hodel recommended that the entire area be opened to drilling. The report also included an environmental impact statement that described what would happen if Congress left the area undrilled, opened it up part way or opened it up completely.

Despite the seasonally intense profusion of life, the coastal plain could be classified as a desert. Average annual rainfall there was less than ten inches. In the winter, the average temperature was below zero Fahrenheit. During much of the winter, nearly continuous winds blew a thin snow cover over most of the landscape.

For almost three months of the year, the sun did not really shine on this land at all, only the perpetual twilight of the Arctic winter.

Environmentalists argued that the Arctic Refuge's unique ecosystems would be disturbed by oil drilling, and perhaps permanently damaged. Of particular concern was the affect of development on the caribou.

The Porcupine caribou herd migrated to the ANWR coastal plain every summer for females to give birth to calves. The area offered them a number of advantages, including protection from natural predators, escape from hungry insects and a preferred climate. Environmentalists said oil exploration would ruin the coastal plain as a calving ground. The oil companies disagreed.

An oil-drilling program also could affect 25 percent to 50 percent of the area's musk oxen, according to the Interior Department's impact statement, either by displacing them or reducing their numbers. Musk oxen, native to the arctic range, were exterminated in the 19th century by hunters. After musk oxen from Greenland were transplanted to ANWR, the population grew rapidly from about 40 to about 500 by 1987.

Environmentalists argued that the issues raised by petroleum operations in the ANWR went beyond simple displacement or loss of wildlife populations. The land itself would be significantly changed, they said. The best available guess on the amount of oil underneath the refuge was the Interior Department study, which estimated there was a 19 percent chance of there being enough oil to be worth the trouble of finding it, bringing it to the surface and transporting it to market.

Environmentalists said this was too low an estimate to be worth the ecological disruption of the Arctic Refuge.

## Jumping the Gun?

A skirmish broke out in July 1987 when the Interior Department, even before Congress had ruled on the issue, went ahead and tentatively divided up some of the prime-prospect lands among Alaskan native corporations that wanted to lease them to oil companies.

George Miller, D-Calif., chairman of the Interior Subcommittee on Water and Power Resources, and other House Interior Committee leaders, protested that the department was prejudicing a decision that was Congress' to make and doing it behind closed doors.

A bill (HR 2629 — H Rept 100-262, Part I) introduced in the Interior and Insular Affairs Committee, which dealt with the broader issue of Alaskan lands distribution, added provisions in July that blocked any land exchanges in the refuge without congressional approval. Hodel later assured members he would not go ahead without their approval.

HR 2629 originally was introduced to settle a long dispute over how to count lands beneath lakes and rivers in dividing up Alaska's lands under the Alaska Native Claims Settlement Act of 1971 (PL 92-203). Under the bill, rivers wider than 198 feet and lakes bigger than 50 acres would not be counted against the amount of federal land the state and natives could claim. (Congress and the Nation Vol. III, p. 783)

The House passed HR 2629 by voice vote Aug. 3, 1987, and the Senate passed it July 14, 1988. The president signed it Aug. 16 (PL 100-395).

## Senate Action

On Feb. 25, 1988, the Senate Energy and Natural Resources Committee approved, 11-8, a measure (S 2214 — S Rept 100-308) that would lift the drilling ban. But the Environment and Public Works Committee also claimed jurisdiction over the bill, a fact that helped prevent it from reaching the floor.

The Energy Committee's ANWR measure would capture half of the royalties and fees from oil companies and devote them to federal land acquisition and conservation programs.

That would have been a departure from the usual formula, under which the state of Alaska received 90 percent of the revenues from most mineral leasing there. State officials said that was one of the terms under which Alaska joined the Union, and they threatened to challenge the constitutionality of the bill in court if it became law.

The committee adopted two amendments offered by Timothy E. Wirth, D-Colo., who led the opposition to the bill, to address such a lawsuit.

One amendment would require any action challenging the revenue split to be brought within 90 days of the bill's enactment. The second specified that if the courts held the 50-50 state-federal revenue split to be invalid, then all the rest of the bill would be void. The amendment also stipulated that the Interior Department could not sell any leases in ANWR until judicial review was final.

After extensive debate, the committee rejected an amendment by Wyche Fowler Jr., D-Ga., that would set a stricter standard for wildlife protection in order for drilling to go forward. But committee Chairman J. Bennett Johnston, D-La., argued against the amendment, saying the bill would adequately protect Alaska wildlife, and that Fowler's amendment would effectively prevent drilling from going forward.

All nine Republicans on the Energy Committee voted to report the bill. Johnston and John Melcher, D-Mont., were the only Democrats to vote for it.

## House Action

The House Merchant Marine and Fisheries Committee on May 3, 1988, approved, 28-13, legislation (HR 3601 — H Rept 100-670, Part I) that would open up the refuge to oil drilling. The bill required the Interior Department to sell leases to oil companies but would place off-limits most of the caribou herd's central calving area, some 260,000 acres.

The Merchant Marine Subcommittee on Fisheries and Wildlife Conservation had approved the measure April 27.

HR 3601 would create a 23.5 million-acre wildlife refuge out of the existing National Petroleum Reserve-Alaska, where exploratory drilling had produced nothing but dry holes. And it would split revenues from ANWR leasing with the state of Alaska. Most of the federal half, however, would be earmarked for fish and wildlife purposes with only 5 percent of total receipts going to offset the deficit.

In the May 3 markup, committee members again rejected several amendments that also had been offered unsuccessfully at the subcommittee level.

One was an amendment by Mike Lowry, D-Wash., and Claudine Schneider, R-R.I., that would require the interior secretary to come up with a national energy plan in two to three years and would prohibit any leasing in ANWR until authorized by Congress. The amendment was defeated 14-26.

The committee did approve two other amendments. One, adopted 29-8, was offered by Thomas J. Manton, D-N.Y., and would require any company obtaining a lease in ANWR to pay the prevailing wage for construction and maintenance work at associated facilities.

Members also adopted by voice vote an amendment by Curt Weldon, R-Pa., that would delay drilling on certain Eskimo corporation lands near the refuge, so that oil companies leasing those lands would not have the advantage of extra geologic information when bidding began for leases on federal lands nearby.

The measure also was referred to the Interior Committee, whose chairman, Morris K. Udall, D-Ariz., opposed any drilling in the arctic refuge. It died in his committee, despite strong pressure from Speaker Jim Wright, D-Texas, to get the committee to act quickly.

Udall had introduced his own legislation (HR 39) that would declare ANWR a federal wilderness, making it permanently off-limits to either leasing or drilling. Eleven of the 41 members (counting the four non-voting delegates) on the Interior Committee cosponsored Udall's bill, and 16 cosponsored a bill (HR 1082) by Don Young, R-Alaska, that — like the Merchant Marine Committee bill — would open up the refuge to drilling. But neither one of those measures went anywhere during the 100th Congress.

## Oil, Gas Leasing Overhaul

Congress in 1987 overhauled the system of leasing federal lands for oil and gas drilling and production, as part of its fiscal 1988 deficit reduction, or reconciliation, bill. *(Reconciliation bill, p. 61)*

Reconciliation conferees blended House and Senate provisions to set a national minimum bid of $2 per acre (up from 50 cents per acre) with authority for the energy secretary to increase the minimum at a later date. They also prohibited the federal government from deducting its administrative costs before it shared drilling revenues with the states.

The legislation did not apply to offshore tracts leased by the federal government, which were covered under different laws. It revised the onshore leasing program under the Mineral Leasing Act of 1920. *(Congress and the Nation Vol. I, p. 1000; Congress and the Nation Vol. VI, p. 339)*

Western Republicans fought hard but lost Sept. 23, 1987, when the House Interior Committee approved a bill overhauling the leasing system.

Led by Dick Cheney, R-Wyo., opponents of the bill (HR 2851 — H Rept 100-378, Part I) sought to strip out various provisions that they said would unfairly penalize Western drillers. But all they succeeded in removing was an unrelated restriction on coal imports that the bill's chief sponsor, Nick J. Rahall II, D-W.Va., had included.

With the committee's liberal and Eastern Democrats rallying behind their own plan engineered by Rahall, the bill was approved by a 24-16 party-line vote. It was largely unchanged from the version adopted Sept. 15 by Rahall's Subcommittee on Mining and Natural Resources.

Rahall called the bill a "moderate" attempt to overhaul a system that critics said shortchanged the Treasury. But Cheney rejected claims that the bill represented a compromise.

Over Republican objections, the committee voted to report the bill as part of the panel's proposals for inclusion in a fiscal 1988 budget reconciliation package.

The Senate Energy Committee had approved different oil and gas leasing reforms in its proposed reconciliation package.

The oil leasing program was suspended in 1983-84 as a result of congressional criticism and was later resumed at a scaled-back pace.

The legislation attempted to prevent undervaluation of public land leased to oil companies by establishing a comprehensive competitive bidding process.

Under a two-tier system, any tracts that failed to draw competitive bids when first offered would become available for a one-year period to the first applicant. If no one claimed them, they would have to go through competitive bidding again to be leased.

The plan drew the ire of Westerners, who feared that competition from large oil companies would cut smaller drillers out of the bidding. Cheney offered an amendment to retain the two-tier system but set a comparatively high minimum bid of $20 per acre. The idea, he said, was to dissuade speculation and thus "preserve a segment of those leases for the independent operator."

But George Miller, D-Calif., said, "We want a competitive system, not one that precludes people from bidding."

The amendment was rejected 18-21. Later, by voice vote, the committee adopted a $2 per acre minimum bid.

The Senate bill required all tracts to be offered competitively first but would move to a non-competitive system any tract not receiving a $10 per acre minimum bid.

The Rahall bill also strengthened environmental controls on drilling. It required the mapping of oil and gas reserves and assessments of the environmental consequences of drilling before leases could be issued for lands with high petroleum potential.

The Senate bill had no new environmental planning requirements.

Cheney offered an amendment to remove the environmental requirements from the bill. But even with the support of several Democrats, including Bill Richardson of New Mexico and George "Buddy" Darden of Georgia, the amendment drew only enough votes for a 20-20 tie and thus failed.

The House committee did alter the environmental language in the bill slightly. Before a tract of land was leased, the "most likely" consequences of oil and gas exploration and development would have to be determined. Originally, the bill required a determination of "reasonably foreseeable" consequences, but members agreed that the language was too vague.

## Oil Shale Land Claims

The House on June 2, 1987, passed a bill (HR 1039 — H Rept 100-43) that Interior Committee Chairman Morris K. Udall, D-Ariz., said was meant to stop an administration "giveaway" of federal oil shale lands.

In the 295-93 vote, only one Democrat voted against it. White House officials said the administration opposed the bill, preferring that the matter be left to the Interior Department to handle.

The Senate did not act on the bill, and it died at the end of the 100th Congress.

At issue were some 1,700 claims to federal oil shale lands under the 1872 Mining Act, which allowed individuals and companies to claim title to such lands. The 1920 Mineral Lands Leasing Act put an end to that practice, reserving title for the government and allowing mining companies only to lease the land. It did, however, "grandfather" valid claims made before 1920 if holders were actively developing the claims. *(Congress and the Nation Vol. I, p. 1000)*

A furor was set off in 1986 when the Interior Department settled with oil companies, giving them title to some 82,000 acres of the land for $2.50 per acre. HR 1039 would block similar action on about 260,000 acres still being claimed.

The bill required claim holders either to convert their claims to leases or to develop them. Holders could not gain title unless they had completed a patent application by Feb. 5, 1987.

# Nuclear Insurance

Congress in 1988 amended and reauthorized the 1957 Price-Anderson Act, which limited the liability of the nuclear power industry in case of an accident and provided a system for paying some of the damage claims that would result from such an accident.

The new law (HR 1414 — PL 100-408) raised the previous coverage of about $700 million for a single accident to about $7 billion. President Reagan signed the measure Aug. 20.

The Price-Anderson Act of 1957 (PL 85-256) set up a system to handle damage claims from an accident at either a government-run reactor or a private nuclear-generating plant. It had last been renewed in 1975. *(Congress and the Nation Vol. IV, p. 247)*

To encourage the then-fledgling nuclear power industry, Congress limited the financial risks from damage claims — to about $700 million to be paid by all the 100 or so nuclear plants in the country. To protect victims, it also set up a "no-fault" procedure to avoid courtroom delays in payment of claims. Victims, however, could not be paid more than the $700 million unless Congress found the money somewhere and appropriated it.

The total amount of coverage depended on the number of commercial reactors in service, and because that number grew during the years Congress worked on the legislation, the figures cited often varied.

The law also authorized the Department of Energy (DOE) to "indemnify" its nuclear contractors. This meant that contractors were guaranteed they would not have to pay any damage claims against them; instead, the federal Treasury would have to pick up the tab.

## House Action

The House passed its Price-Anderson reauthorization on July 30, 1987, a bill backed by the nuclear power industry and the Reagan administration.

The 396-17 vote on final passage (HR 1414 — H Rept 100-104, Parts I, II and III) did not reflect the degree of underlying controversy.

A group of insurgent Democrats made three efforts to amend the bill to beef up its victim-compensation and safety-incentive provisions. But the insurgents were unable to overcome the threat of a veto and strong opposition from the nuclear industry, and all three amendments were defeated.

Floor manager Philip R. Sharp, D-Ind., called the bill "a bargain" that provided potential accident victims with a simpler, no-fault legal process and greater certainty of financial compensation for damage or injury. Sharp said the bill, by increasing possible compensation more than tenfold, was a major improvement over existing law.

But Dennis E. Eckart, D-Ohio, a leader of the insurgency, retorted that while the bill might be a bargain for some people, it was a "K-Mart blue-light special for the nuclear-power industry" and a "raw deal for the taxpayers of this country."

HR 1414 would raise the total funds available for victim compensation in case of an accident at a nuclear plant, from about $650 million under existing law to more than $7.4 billion. That amount would come from a combination of private commercial insurance and a unique form of industry self-insurance whereby each of the nation's nuclear utilities could pay up to $63 million in "deferred premiums" after an accident at any one reactor.

Both the law and the bill left unsettled what would happen if the $7.4 billion ran out. The bill would require the president to submit a plan to Congress for paying damages but would not authorize spending for such payments. Sharp called that a "promise" by Congress to pay. But Eckart said the promise was "not worth the paper it's written on."

**Committee.** The full Interior Committee approved HR 1414 on May 6, after a showdown over how to pay lawyers fighting nuclear-damage claims.

The bill raised tenfold, from about $650 million to about $6.5 billion, the limit on how much compensation electric utilities would have to pay victims of a nuclear accident. Its main sponsor was Interior Committee Chairman Morris K. Udall, D-Ariz.

The measure approved by the committee allowed a portion of the compensation fund set up under the bill to be used to pay the fees of lawyers who were hired to defend the utilities against claims from the victims of a nuclear accident.

The use of compensation funds for legal fees long had been the subject of controversy. In a 1975 reauthorization (PL 94-197) of Price-Anderson, Congress enacted language intended to prevent the funds from being used for such fees. But Justice Department lawyers concluded informally that, because of a drafting error, the provision was invalid and fees could be taken out of the funds.

As introduced, HR 1414 would reverse the Justice Department position. But at the May 6 markup, the committee chose instead to compromise. The bill finally approved allowed the use of the compensation fund to cover up to 70 percent of eligible lawyers' fees.

The question of legal fees was also paramount when the House Energy Committee took up HR 1414. Under the bill approved by the Energy Subcommittee on Energy and Power June 3, lawyers would be fully protected from financial risk — although accident victims would not be.

The subcommittee, chaired by Sharp, was overruled when the full Energy Committee voted June 30 to pay nuclear accident victims before paying utility lawyers if damage from a nuclear disaster exceeded a $7 billion compensation fund.

The Energy Committee adopted, by a 24-18 vote, an amendment offered by Gerry Sikorski, D-Minn., that in effect moved victims to the head of the line at the pay window. The subcommittee version of the bill put lawyers in front.

The Sikorski victory, however, proved to be short-lived. Under heavy lobbying pressure, the Energy Committee met again July 8 and reversed itself, voting to allow electric utility lawyers to get paid before victims, at a judge's discretion. The reversal on legal costs came on an amendment by Ralph M. Hall, D-Texas, which the committee adopted 22-20.

The other close contest in the July 8 markup was over an amendment by Ron Wyden, D-Ore., to make DOE nuclear contractors pay for negligence or safety violations. The committee rejected it on a 21-21 tie vote.

The Energy Committee then approved HR 1414 by voice vote.

**Floor.** Committee leaders finished negotiations the week of July 20 on a substitute amendment resolving their different versions of HR 1414 and took the bill to the floor under an open rule on July 30.

When they did, Eckart and his allies, backed by environmental, consumer and taxpayer groups, sought unsuccessfully to add a series of amendments that would increase the nuclear industry's financial responsibility for a major accident.

Democrats split for and against them, but all were resisted by a comparatively solid phalanx of Republicans. The White House and DOE also opposed all amendments and actively lobbied against them. Equally solid in opposition were the various segments of the nuclear industry — groups representing investor-owned utilities, nuclear-insurance companies and the suppliers, contractors and design firms that built nuclear plants.

Democratic committee leaders tended usually to support the compromise vehicle and resist amendments. Even when some committee leaders joined the insurgents, however, they did not bring enough Democrats with them to overcome the nearly monolithic Republican-industry coalition.

The House first rejected, 119-300, an amendment offered by Eckart that would remove any limit on how much damage utilities could be forced to pay collectively through the deferred-premium system. Eckart's amendment, however, would limit the amount a utility would have to pay in any one year to $10 million per reactor.

Ranking Energy Committee Republican Norman F. Lent, N.Y., said Eckart's amendment "guts the entire premise of Price-Anderson," which was to encourage the fledgling civilian nuclear power industry by limiting the risks that could drive investors away.

Eckart, however, argued that it was time to "take the training wheels off" the 30-year-old industry.

The House also rejected an amendment by Wyden and Sharp aimed at making DOE nuclear contractors financially accountable for unsafe practices. Wyden's amendment was defeated 193-226, with Democrats split 164-87.

Voting for the amendment were Udall, Energy Chairman John D. Dingell, D-Mich., and Majority Leader Thomas S. Foley, D-Wash.

But Science, Space and Technology Chairman Robert A. Roe, D-N.J., and Marilyn Lloyd, D-Tenn., whose Science subcommittee had jurisdiction over the bill, voted against the Wyden amendment. They typified a significant number of Democrats whose districts had strong ties to the multibillion-dollar industry doing nuclear research, fuels processing, weapons production and waste handling for DOE.

Wyden's amendment set civil penalties for DOE contractors who violated the agency's safety rules. Fines were up to $100,000 per violation. The amendment also allowed the government, in the event of an accident caused by a DOE contractor, to sue the contractor to recover some of the damages — but only if the accident was caused by the gross negligence or willful misconduct of top officials of the contracting firm.

The House also rejected, on a **183-230 (R 24-145; D 159-85) key vote**, an amendment offered by Sikorski, on how legal costs would be paid in the event that damages from an accident exceeded the $7.4 billion pool of coverage. *(1987 key votes, p. 965)*

## Senate Action

**Energy Committee.** The battle over Price-Anderson in the Senate also was long and difficult and included the same kind of back-and-forth swings that characterized the House debate.

When the Senate Energy Committee turned to the Price-Anderson Act on April 8, 1987, it focused on the portion of the law that was set to expire Aug. 1. The Energy Committee took up a bill (S 748 — S Rept 100-70) reauthorizing only the part of the Price-Anderson Act that dealt with nuclear facilities that performed work for DOE.

Committee Chairman J. Bennett Johnston, D-La., the sponsor of S 748, told the committee that if Congress did not renew the law by the Aug. 1 date, DOE would not be able to continue shielding contractors from having to pay for damages in a nuclear accident. Most of DOE's nuclear contracts were for development and production of atomic weapons, building submarine reactors, advanced reactor research, enrichment of uranium and other fuels and disposal of reactor wastes.

Under the expiring authority in the Price-Anderson Act, DOE regularly signed agreements to "indemnify" its contractors (or pay for any damages for which the contractor was found liable). Those federal damage payments were capped at $500 million. Beyond that, accident victims had no assurance of compensation.

Existing DOE contracts and the accompanying indemnification agreements were not all due to expire at once on Aug. 1. But executive branch officials testified that if Congress missed the Aug. 1 date there would be increasing disruption of federal nuclear programs as old contracts came up for renewal or new ones needed to be written.

S 748 would raise the limit on DOE indemnification of its contractors from $500 million to $6 billion and extend the authorization for DOE to make such agreements until Aug. 1, 2007.

Howard M. Metzenbaum, D-Ohio, a strong critic of the nuclear industry, had been poised as the markup began to offer three amendments he felt would strengthen the protection of victims and the accountability of contractors.

But Metzenbaum did not offer the amendments April 8. Johnston, instead, offered his own amendment. It required DOE, upon finding gross negligence or willful misconduct on the part of a contractor in an accident, to assess administratively a civil penalty of up to $10 million. The fine could be appealed or enforced in court.

Metzenbaum found that amendment unacceptable, saying that a maximum penalty closer to $100 million would be appropriate. After negotiations, Johnston and Metzenbaum seemed to agree on a civil penalty of up to $30 million, subject to appeal, in place of the three amendments Metzenbaum had originally planned to offer. Johnston offered that formula as a modification of his original amendment. When the markup continued on April 22, the committee voted 15-2 for Johnston's plan to impose civil penalties of up to $30 million.

But the committee failed at its April 22 session to complete action on the bill, and when it reconvened May 20, it reversed itself.

Under a storm of protest from the nuclear industry, the committee approved much softer penalties for safety violations by Energy Department contractors.

The revision set maximum civil fines for safety violations at $100,000 per day and top criminal penalties for persons committing knowing and willful violations at $25,000 and two years in jail. It also established a new DOE inspector general for nuclear safety and an independent safety review panel.

Johnston opened the May 20 session by disavowing the action of April 22. "It is clear in my judgment that we acted improvidently," he said. Johnston also said that there was "no hearing record to support a pattern of violations," and that nuclear contractors "do not make the kind of profit to support that kind of penalties."

After the April 22 markup, nuclear contractors promptly complained that they would not be able to keep doing business with the government under the stiff penalties that would be imposed.

Metzenbaum told the committee that Energy Secretary John S. Herrington "summoned" more than a dozen nuclear contractors to a meeting May 4 in "an effort to mobilize the troops" for lobbying against the penalty provisions. Herrington maintained the session was purely informational.

Herrington wrote Johnston May 5 urging that the penalty language be changed. After the committee did just that, Metzenbaum denounced the action as a "capitulation" to DOE and industry demands. "All of a sudden the Senate of the United States stands up and says, 'Yes, sir, whatever you say.'" He called it "a reflection on the integrity of Congress."

Johnston called Metzenbaum's remarks "insulting."

"If you think there's some kind of grand conspiracy to let nuclear contractors off with greedy profits ... so they can endanger the public," Johnston told Metzenbaum, "you're just dead wrong."

The Johnston amendment to revise the penalties section was adopted 12-7.

Voting against adoption of the amendment were Bradley; Bumpers; Daniel J. Evans, R-Wash.; Mark O. Hatfield, R-Ore.; John Melcher, D-Mont.; Metzenbaum; and Timothy E. Wirth, D-Colo.

The vote on reporting the bill was 17-2. The "nay" votes were cast by Metzenbaum and Bill Bradley, D-N.J.

**Environment Committee.** The Senate Environment Committee came up with a different, broader Price-Anderson bill, which covered civilian reactors as well as DOE facilities. The bill (S 1865 — S Rept 100-218) was sponsored by Nuclear Regulation Subcommittee Chairman John B. Breaux, D-La., and Alan K. Simpson, R-Wyo.

The Breaux-Simpson bill would pay damages above a $7 billion limit from the U.S. Treasury if Congress and the president did not come up with another way to do it. The backstop mechanism was to be a permanent, indefinite appropriation to pay whatever judgment was awarded in an incident by the courts. This unusual mechanism, called the "judgment appropriation," had been set up in 1956 to meet other claims. The bill also would set up expedited congressional procedures for acting on an alternative-payment mechanism.

The full Environment Committee Aug. 4 voted 16-0 to approve the bill, but it drew an immediate veto threat from Reagan administration officials such as Energy Secretary Herrington.

The Environment bill also set forth two alternative procedures by which Congress and the president could decide on a backstop funding mechanism. Each involved specific timetables. If Congress did not come up with other funds by a certain time, the judgment appropriation would be used.

**Floor.** The bills reported in the summer of 1987 by the two Senate committees, Energy and Environment, went significantly beyond the House-passed bill in encouraging nuclear safety and guaranteeing compensation of victims. The Energy bill authorized civil fines as high as $100,000 per day against contractors who violated DOE safety rules. The Environment bill guaranteed payment to victims of an accident at a commercial plant if damages exceeded $6.6 billion. Neither of those provisions was in the House bill.

After months of negotiations that failed to reconcile differences, leaders of the two Senate committees finally agreed among themselves to bring the House bill to the floor instead of either of the two Senate bills.

It was not until March 18, 1988, that the Senate passed the House Price-Anderson bill (HR 1414) by voice vote, after rejecting a move to make Energy Department contractors liable for accidents caused by their own gross negligence. The Senate also rejected a plan to beef up safety supervision at the Energy Department's nuclear plants.

The Senate decision on contractor liability came March 16, when members on a **key vote of 53-41 (R 35-10; D 18-31)** tabled (killed) an amendment by Metzenbaum, which would allow DOE to sue contractors for limited damages in case of an accident at a weapons-production plant or research reactor. *(1988 key votes, p. 981)*

Metzenbaum won an important victory, however, before the bill reached the Senate floor. By threatening to block the measure, he got Energy Committee Chairman Johnston to agree to language setting potentially stiff civil and criminal penalties for contractors who violated DOE safety rules.

**Senate Amendments.** Although the Senate bill was similar to the House-passed version, some changes were made.

One amendment approved by the Senate struck the House bill's unlimited federal liability for accidents involving nuclear waste. Another required the Nuclear Regulatory Commission (NRC) to indemnify nuclear pharmacies. The Senate also adopted amendments providing expedited consideration by Congress of a compensation plan if damages exceeded the limit and making DOE indemnification of contractors mandatory instead of optional. Another provided equivalent coverage in cases where DOE did nuclear-waste work itself, instead of contractors.

The Senate set the length of its Price-Anderson reauthorization at 20 years. The original act and two later reauthorizations had set 10-year intervals. The House bill set a 10-year period.

A voice vote March 16 to approve a 20-year period was vitiated March 17, after Gordon J. Humphrey, R-N.H., and several others complained it had been done so quickly they had not had a chance to debate it. Utilities and the nuclear industry favored a 30-year period, to avoid uncertainties such as the 1987-88 legislative delay. Breaux said that as reactors aged and went out of service, coverage for victims (which was pegged to the number of reactors) would drop over 30 years from $7.4 billion to only $3.75 billion.

James A. McClure, R-Idaho, then offered an amendment to extend the law for 30 years. Breaux offered a substitute to make the period 20 years, which the Senate approved by a 50-34 vote.

The Senate approved the underlying McClure amendment by 45-36. Some saw that as a choice between the 20-year period and the 10-year cycle in current law.

The Senate rejected, 21-72, an amendment by Breaux to double the $7.4 billion cap on how much victims could be sure of getting in an accident at a commercial nuclear power plant.

"This legislation is not to protect the companies, it is to protect the victims," Breaux said.

**DOE Safety.** The Senate tabled, and thus killed, an amendment by John Glenn, D-Ohio, to improve outside oversight of safety practices at DOE nuclear facilities.

The final 49-42 vote to table the Glenn amendment reversed an earlier vote of 44-47 on a Johnston motion to table. Johnston switched from "yea" to "nay" so he could offer a motion to reconsider, and there followed a long series of intervening procedural votes before he reversed his earlier defeat.

Glenn chaired the Governmental Affairs Committee, which had reported a bill (S 1085 — S Rept 100-173) that was the prototype of his amendment. It established an independent nuclear-safety board to oversee DOE, investigate accidents and recommend prevention measures. It also required DOE work sites to be regulated by the Occupational Safety and Health Administration (OSHA) and set up a new study board on health effects of radiation.

Glenn said he became interested in DOE nuclear-safety issues when he discovered a DOE plant in Fernald, Ohio, had rained some 300,000 pounds of uranium dust on the surrounding community, causing serious contamination problems. In the seven or eight years since, he said, he broadened the scope of his inquiries to include all DOE operations, amassing 21 GAO reports.

"We let some horrible things happen around those plants," he said. The Reagan administration opposed such proposals as Glenn's and said that an oversight group recently set up by the DOE itself should be given a chance to work.

Johnston opposed the amendment partly on the grounds that it was duplicative and would complicate the problem of enacting the Price-Anderson bill by moving it into the jurisdiction of many more committees.

**Pre-Floor Maneuvers.** Metzenbaum had in early February 1988 announced that he would block Johnston's plans to bring the House bill to the Senate floor, because it lacked contractor penalties in the bill reported by Johnston's Energy Committee (S 748).

Johnston and Breaux had agreed in January to use the House-passed HR 1414 as a vehicle. That agreement resolved months of stalemate over how to meld the Price-Anderson bill reported by the Energy Committee and the one reported by Environment.

Metzenbaum's threat was effective. After the bill had been held up for more than a month, Johnston agreed to an amendment putting his committee's language back into it.

Johnston offered, and Metzenbaum cosponsored, the amendment, which was adopted by a 94-0 vote after it had been agreed to behind the scenes.

The amendment authorized the energy secretary to impose civil penalties of up to $100,000 for each violation of a DOE safety rule, or $100,000 per day if the violation was a continuing one. For knowing and willful violations, the amendment provided criminal penalties of up to $25,000 and two years in jail for the first offense and a $50,000 fine and five years in jail for subsequent ones.

But, as Metzenbaum was quick to point out, the civil penalties were left entirely up to the secretary's discretion. The amendment required the secretary, in setting any civil fine, to consider the nature, circumstances, extent and gravity of the violation, as well as the violator's history of past violations, the violator's ability to pay and the effect of the fine on the violator's ability to continue to do business. The penalties could be appealed in court.

"Frankly," argued Metzenbaum, "the penalties are minimal."

Johnston called the language "a good balance."

**Contractor Liability.** There remained a Johnston-Metzenbaum disagreement on the issue of contractor liability.

Under existing law the Treasury would have to pick up the tab for a nuclear accident at a contractor-run DOE facility — up to a limit of $500 million. HR 1414 raised the limit to about $7.4 billion — the same as in other nuclear accidents — and lifted the limit altogether if the accident involved nuclear waste.

After victims had been paid, Metzenbaum wanted to give the federal government the chance to go to court and recover its own costs from the contractor if the accident resulted from the contractor's gross negligence or willful misconduct.

"As long as DOE contractors are completely shielded from financial penalty for irresponsible behavior," Metzenbaum argued, "there is no reason to expect them to improve the terrible safety record at DOE facilities."

Johnston said that the responsibility for any safety problems lay not with the contractors, but with the government. "These ... plants are in fact owned by the federal government," he said. "The regulations are put out by DOE. The regulations are enforced by DOE. And these contractors are simply acting under DOE."

One of the key arguments the nuclear industry and its supporters had used when they defeated a similar amendment in the House in July 1987 was that exposure to liability would drive contractors out of business. Since the Price-Anderson authority for DOE to indemnify its contractors expired on Aug. 1, 1987, five contractors had signed new contracts, even though exposed to some liability.

Metzenbaum said contractors came to the Hill claiming they would never be able to operate these contracts if exposed to financial liability.

Because contractors objected to earlier versions of Metzenbaum's amendment, saying they would not renew DOE contracts if all their corporate assets were at risk, Metzenbaum scaled it back. His original floor amendment stipulated that the government could not collect more than the value of the contract and could collect no funds from any university.

Industry and many in the Senate still objected. Metzenbaum further diluted his amendment by accepting a perfecting amendment from Dale Bumpers, D-Ark. Bumpers further limited what the government could collect to the value of the contract's "award fee," if any. That fee was usually less than 5 percent of the total value of government business a company received in a DOE contract.

"That means," Metzenbaum said, "that a contractor ... would only stand to lose his potential profit from the contract. No corporate assets would be put at risk."

The Metzenbaum amendment failed even as amended by Bumpers, who said his amendment would broaden its chance of winning votes.

### Final Action

Instead of appointing a House-Senate conference, the bill's managers chose to negotiate informally and work out their differences in amendments to the bill.

On Aug. 2, the House adopted 346-54 a motion by Interior Committee Chairman Udall that the House accept the compromises agreed to in talks by House and Senate managers.

Udall called the compromise substitute "a good bill" that would preserve the basic benefits of the Price-Anderson Act.

"The act ensures that adequate funds will be available to compensate the public in the event of a nuclear accident," he said. "It streamlines the claims process to ensure speedy compensation for victims."

But Rep. Dennis E. Eckart, who had led the 1987 floor insurgency, urged a vote against the substitute, saying it protected the economic interests of the utility companies, nuclear-engineering firms and uranium-mining companies — "not necessarily the economic interests of the average American taxpayer, or the health and environmental interests of American citizens."

The Senate agreed to the compromise Aug. 5, clearing the bill for the president.

### Major Provisions

As cleared, HR 1414:

● **Length of Reauthorization.** Extended for 15 years the authority of the Department of Energy to indemnify its contractors (shield them from liability) and the authority of the Nuclear Regulatory Commission to indemnify commercial power plants.

● **Safety Penalties.** Authorized civil penalties of up to $100,000 per day for violations of DOE safety rules and criminal penalties of up to $50,000 and five years in jail for repeat offenders.

● **Expedited Procedures.** Required the president to send Congress, if damages from a nuclear accident exceeded the $7 billion limit on coverage, a plan for compensating victims for some or all of the additional damages. Under the compromise agreement, expedited procedures were established for the Senate but not for the House for considering the president's plan.

● **Sovereign Immunity.** Required DOE to continue to pay damages in accidents caused by its contractors at one of its facilities. If the accident was the fault of an employee of DOE itself, however, private parties could sue for damages only under the Federal Tort Claims Act, the standard law governing damage suits against the government.

● **Radiopharmaceuticals.** Required the NRC to undertake rulemaking proceedings to determine whether it should indemnify hospitals and laboratories dealing with nuclear medicines (such as radioactive tracer dyes) or com-

pel them to buy private insurance.

● **Recent Contracts.** Retroactively applied the indemnification authority to DOE contracts signed since the previous authority expired.

# Nevada: Nuclear Waste Site

House and Senate negotiators agreed Dec. 17, 1987, on a plan to put all of the nation's nuclear waste in Nevada. The plan was added to the fiscal 1988 deficit reduction, or reconciliation, bill (HR 3545 — PL 100-203), which President Reagan signed Dec. 22. *(Reconciliation, p. 61)*

The plan reversed a decision Congress made in the 1982 Nuclear Waste Policy Act (PL 97-425), which declared that selection of a site would be based purely on science and safety, not politics. *(Congress and the Nation Vol. VI, p. 361)*

"We've done it in a purely political process," said Al Swift, D-Wash., commenting on the agreement announced Dec. 17. "We are going to give somebody some nasty stuff."

Working under the 1982 law, the Department of Energy (DOE) had narrowed down the search for the first nuclear waste repository to three Western states: Nevada, Washington and Texas. The House-Senate compromise took Washington and Texas "off the hook," as the chief sponsor of the plan, Energy Committee Chairman J. Bennett Johnston, D-La., put it. By doing so, Johnston was able to convert Texas and Washington from resistance to support of the plan.

It also let the eastern half of the country off the hook by canceling language in the 1982 law calling for a second repository in the East.

That left only Nevada still in the running.

This "will turn our state into a federal colony," said Rep. Barbara F. Vucanovich, R-Nev. "Congress is behaving like a pack of wolves going in for the kill."

But Johnston predicted Nevada would get over its outrage when it realized the waste site would bring jobs and federal money — up to $20 million annually. "If I were a Nevadan living in the real world, I would be happy with this bill," Johnston said. "I would bet that in a very few years, Nevada will deem this one of their most treasured industries."

But Nevadans would have none of that.

"When you rub all the fog off this window," said Sen. Harry Reid, D-Nev., "you look in and you see base power politics at its worst."

"No one from our state has been permitted to participate or argue for our interests," said Vucanovich, referring to the House-Senate conference committee on reconciliation.

Reid echoed that charge, saying the state had been "shut out completely."

"They weren't shut out," Johnston responded. "They just weren't appointed to the conference."

### Major Provisions

The agreement explicitly named Yucca Mountain, Nev., as the site where DOE was to drill the first exploratory shaft for a permanent repository for the nation's civilian highly radioactive waste.

Although years of study and procedural steps would remain after that, the investment of an estimated $1 billion to $2 billion to test the geological suitability of the site was viewed by most members as a virtual commitment to put the waste there.

Under the agreement, if DOE found the Yucca Mountain site unsuitable, it had to cease work on finding a repository, report to Congress and await further direction.

The agreement also authorized a temporary waste site, called a monitored retrievable storage (MRS) facility, but not until the permanent repository got licensed. Members from Tennessee and South Carolina, whose states were likely sites for the MRS, feared they could be stuck with the waste if a permanent repository was stymied. The postponement in setting up the MRS, added during the conference, assured support from MRS-candidate states.

Theoretically, Nevada could still delay or block the nuclear waste dump. The 1982 law gave the chosen state a veto, and that was kept in the plan. But that veto could be overridden by a vote of both houses of Congress. Given what both chambers had done, Johnston said, "that veto would be, I am sure, overridden."

Nevada also could take the issue to court. The conferees' bill left appeals under the jurisdiction of the federal appeals courts, instead of under a speeded-up Temporary Emergency Court of Appeals, which Johnston sought.

Nevada would get compensated for taking the dump. The final plan included authorization of federal payments to the host state of $10 million per year after agreeing to the repository, going up to $20 million per year once the repository actually started accepting waste.

The catch, of course, was that to get the benefits, Nevada would have to surrender its right to exercise the veto over its selection.

## Senate Energy Committee

Johnston seized the initiative in the nuclear waste debate by coming up with a plan for picking a site and moving on three fronts to get it written into law. He secured Energy Committee approval for the plan as free-standing legislation (S 1668); he succeeded in attaching it to fiscal 1988 deficit reduction legislation; and he managed to add it to the fiscal 1988 appropriations bill (HR 2700) for energy and water development.

The first Johnston victory came July 29, 1987, when the Energy Committee approved the plan 7-2 and attached it to the reconciliation bill.

Johnston's plan was to save money by characterizing only one site in the West instead of three as the 1982 nuclear waste law required, on the premise that the scientific problem of finding a geologically suitable site would be much easier than the political problem of finding a state that was willing to take the waste.

Johnston estimated the plan would save $634 million over three years ($139 million in fiscal 1988, $248 million in 1989 and $247 million in 1990). That provided the bulk of the $730 million in savings the Energy Committee needed to meet its three-year reconciliation target.

Johnston's plan gave states incentives designed to make acceptance of a site a little more palatable. Johnston originally proposed that a state would get $50 million per year after signing up for a repository and, once it actually began receiving waste, $100 million per year for the life of the facility. For an MRS, the state would get $20 million per year for signing up and $50 million once it began taking waste. States would sign a "benefits agreement" under which DOE would give them the benefits and they would not oppose the site.

The Energy Committee's plan evolved from legislation (S 839, S 1481) introduced by Johnston and the panel's ranking Republican, James A. McClure of Idaho.

As approved by the panel, it required DOE to select by Jan. 1, 1989, one site for characterization as a possible first repository. DOE would have to choose one of the three candidate sites in the West: Yucca Mountain, Nev.; Deaf Smith County, Texas; or Hanford, Wash. If drilling and testing proved the chosen site suitable, it would be licensed and constructed. If not, DOE would have to select one of the other two for characterization.

The plan suspended further study or selection of specific sites for a second repository and required DOE to report to Congress by the year 2110 on the need for a second site.

The Johnston-McClure plan authorized an MRS facility for the first time. It annulled DOE's selection of Oak Ridge, Tenn., as its first-choice location, as well as two other backup sites in Tennessee, and directed the agency to start the selection process over. If a state volunteered to host an MRS, DOE could go ahead with a benefits agreement and build the facility. If not, DOE must select a site between Jan. 1 and Oct. 1, 1989.

One of the "nay" votes on the Johnston plan was cast by Republican Chic Hecht of Nevada. During the panel markup, Hecht succeeded in beefing up the federal incentives for the repository state but still voted against the plan.

"I am adamantly, unalterably, absolutely opposed," he told reporters. "The people in my state are scared. . . . The bureaucrats at DOE have done nothing to allay their fears."

The other "nay" vote came from Pete V. Domenici, R-N.M., who expressed reservations about putting the nuclear waste plan on a reconciliation bill. Domenici also was the ranking minority member on the Budget Committee.

## Johnston's Step Two

Johnston moved next to win approval of his plan as separate legislation. At his prodding, the Energy Committee reported S 1668 (S Rept 100-152) Sept. 1.

Part three of the Johnston plan called for adding it to the appropriations process, and on Sept. 15, Johnston persuaded the Appropriations Committee to add the waste plan to HR 2700, the $15.96 billion fiscal 1988 energy and water appropriations bill. Johnston also was chairman of the Appropriations Subcommittee for Energy and Water Development.

Committee members Reid and Jim Sasser, D-Tenn., twice tried to eliminate the plan but were voted down by wide margins.

Reid moved to strike the Johnston plan from the bill, but the full committee rejected the motion by a 6-19 vote. Reid then moved to substitute the text of HR 2888 — a House bill that would delay selection of a site for 18 months — for that of S 1668 in the appropriations bill, but that was rejected 8-17.

When all his efforts in committee failed, Reid then let it be known that he planned to filibuster the bill — a threat that kept the measure off the Senate floor for several weeks.

Several House members also objected to trying to settle the waste question with a rider on the appropriations bill.

In a Sept. 29 letter to Appropriations Committee

Chairman Jamie L. Whitten, D-Miss., three influential House chairmen voiced blunt objections to a move that bypassed their authorizing panels. They were Interior Committee Chairman Morris K. Udall, D-Ariz.; Energy Committee Chairman John D. Dingell, D-Mich.; and Energy and Power Subcommittee Chairman Philip R. Sharp, D-Ind.

"A complex and controversial issue such as high-level nuclear waste should be considered through the normal legislative process," they wrote.

## Senate Environment Committee

Further opposition to the Johnston plan surfaced in the Senate Environment Committee, which approved its own reconciliation language on nuclear waste on Oct. 20.

Unlike Johnston's plan, which was aimed at speeding up the selection of a site, the Environment Committee called for new layers of environmental and scientific review of DOE's choice of a site, effectively delaying the process.

Johnston reacted strongly to the move. In a letter to the Environment Committee, he warned that "more indecision and more delay sends the public the message that there are technical reasons not to proceed with site characterization, which is not the case."

The Environment Committee language required DOE to develop a plan in consultation with the states for surface-based testing of the three sites already chosen as finalists. DOE would have to give special consideration to how surface-based testing could disqualify sites for full-fledged below-ground characterization.

The Environment panel did not reject the Energy panel's concept of characterizing the three sites one at a time (if the first one were found to be qualified, it would be chosen). But Environment did specify that DOE would have to finish surface testing for all three before it chose one for characterization. No shaft could be drilled before then.

In addition to the surface-testing plan, the Environment plan said DOE must propose within 180 days of enactment a plan stating just how it would choose a site. That plan would have to be made final, after public comment, within 18 months of enactment.

Before choosing a single site for characterization, DOE would have to make available to all parties the technical information it would consider in choosing a site.

DOE would have to choose a preferred site for characterization after it finished surface testing, or no later than Jan. 1, 1991. (The Energy Committee plan gave DOE until Jan. 1, 1989.) Once it chose, DOE would have to issue a "comprehensive statement of the basis" for the decision, suitable for use in court appeals. DOE would be forbidden to discard any documents relating to its decision. Charges by members of Congress that it had done so weakened the credibility of its last round of decisions.

The Environment Committee kept the Energy panel's provisions for expediting court appeal of DOE's decision. Both gave jurisdiction to a Temporary Emergency Court of Appeals, which would not be burdened with other cases. The Energy Committee imposed a time limit on the appeal of 150 days from DOE's decision; Environment lengthened that to 300 days.

Unlike the Energy Committee, the Environment Committee explicitly preserved pending lawsuits on DOE's nuclear waste decisions — more than 40 of which had been filed to date. Candidate states wanted that language be-cause they were arguing in court that they should not be on the list of three finalists in the first place.

The Environment Committee bill also would establish an Oversight Board of experts under the National Academy of Sciences to review the scientific and technical adequacy of DOE's site evaluation and selection. The board's comments on DOE's work would be put into the public record and thus be useful for legal appeals.

Another potential delay the committee added was environmental review. The 1982 nuclear waste law tried to speed up a siting decision by limiting the delays that would be imposed by the National Environmental Policy Act (NEPA) of 1969 (PL 91-190). That law required assessment of the environmental impacts of most major federal action. The 1982 law limited NEPA review to DOE's final choice of a site (exempting all the decisions leading up to it) and excluded from the scope of NEPA review questions about the need for a repository or the alternatives to it. *(Congress and the Nation Vol. III, p. 842)*

The Environment Committee would amend the 1982 law to make NEPA broadly applicable to the site-selection process, specifically requiring environmental assessment for site characterization as well as for site approval and construction of a repository.

## Senate Floor Action

The energy and water appropriations bill finally reached the floor Nov. 4 and, as threatened, Reid began his filibuster.

While Johnston pressed his plan to make Nevada the site for storage of the nation's nuclear waste, Reid resisted with sheer physical strength, staying on his feet hour after hour, his voice sometimes getting raspy as he explained why he thought the choice of his state scientifically unfounded and procedurally unfair.

"What is happening is wrong and it's unfair," Reid said in an interview. "It's just not right to run over people."

Reid called it the "Screw Nevada Bill" and said his state was being picked on "because we're the small kid on the block."

Joining him in the filibuster was Brock Adams, D-Wash., whose state also had been targeted by DOE as a possible permanent waste site. Both men won their Senate seats in 1986 by emphasizing the nuclear waste issue, with Adams charging that his opponent was not staunch enough in resisting the nuclear repository.

Reid and Adams showed surprising strength on a test vote Nov. 4. The Senate voted 55-30 to table, or kill, an Adams amendment that would strike Johnston's nuclear waste language from the bill.

Johnston sought to conquer his opponents by dividing them. He negotiated a separate deal with Sasser to keep a temporary waste site out of Tennessee for two years.

An aide confirmed that the results of Sasser's negotiations were embodied in an amendment Johnston offered Nov. 4, setting up a commission to study whether an MRS was necessary.

Sasser had stood with Reid against Johnston during the Appropriations Committee markup Sept. 15, but when they were unsuccessful, Sasser went his own way.

Under the amendment, the three-member blue-ribbon commission, appointed by the Speaker of the House and president pro tempore of the Senate, would have until January 1989 to report.

Once the commission reported, DOE could go ahead

and build an MRS facility even if the commission recommended against it, although Congress would have 90 days to stop the MRS with a resolution of disapproval.

The January 1989 date was important in several ways. Tennesseans had tried to keep an MRS from being authorized before a permanent repository was selected as a way to avoid being stuck indefinitely with the waste; January 1989 was the year when DOE had to make its final choice of a permanent site. The date also would put the MRS decision off until after 1988 — when Sasser came up for re-election. The date also put the decision in the hands of whatever administration succeeded President Reagan's.

## Parliamentary Chess

Adams said the nuclear waste legislation was an authorization that did not belong on an appropriations bill. "The real issue here is whether or not we want to sanction attempts to bypass the authorizing committees," he said. "On institutional grounds, that ought to be unacceptable."

Reid said Johnston wanted the matter on the appropriations bill because, when it came to conference with the House, Johnston would be sitting opposite Appropriations Chairman Jamie L. Whitten, D-Miss., and Energy and Water Subcommittee Chairman Tom Bevill, D-Ala., both friends of nuclear power.

Adams said that while the best approach was a separate bill, he would agree to limit debate if the nuclear waste plan were considered as part of reconciliation. That would give the authorizing committees, two of which had different proposals, seats at the conference table.

As the battle over the appropriations bill stretched into a second — and then a third — week, the tide continued to run against Reid and Adams, but they yielded ground slowly.

The two sides reached an agreement Nov. 10 allowing a clear vote on a number of nuclear issues in exchange for a delay in final passage of the bill until Nov. 18.

A key element was a separate vote on whether the nuclear waste plan should be included in the bill. When it came, Johnston won 63-30.

Another important vote came on an amendment offered by Reid. It stipulated that DOE was to make public health and safety the foremost consideration in its choice of a site for an exploratory shaft. The Senate rejected it on **a key vote of 37-56 (R 8-35; D 29-21).** *(1987 key votes, p. 965)*

The final hurdle to passage of the appropriations bill came Nov. 18, on a motion by Breaux to resubmit the bill to the Appropriations Committee with instructions to add the nuclear waste provisions favored by the Environment Committee. The vote was 34-61. The Senate then passed the bill by a vote of 86-9.

Because of the continued opposition of Reid and House members, conferees were unable to reach agreement on HR 2700 and the bill was eventually added to the omnibus spending bill (H J Res 395 — PL 100-202) that the Senate passed in December.

## House Committee Action

The House entered the 1987 debate over nuclear waste June 30, when Udall, the main architect of the 1982 nuclear waste law, declared "the program is in ruins" and called on Congress to try again to solve the disposal problem.

Udall and a bipartisan group of 52 cosponsors introduced HR 2888, which would suspend specific site-selection activities by DOE for at least 18 months. It called for appointment of a special commission to come up with ideas for a viable program.

Udall said DOE had politicized the program set up under the 1982 law and that "the public and many of us in Congress have lost all faith in the integrity of the process."

Udall's bill would set up a bipartisan three-member commission within the legislative branch, to be appointed by the Speaker of the House and the president pro tempore of the Senate. This panel would have 18 months to study the problem and DOE's handling of it to date. It then would recommend to Congress any additional legislation needed to ensure safe disposal of nuclear waste.

## Plan Approved

The Interior Subcommittee on Energy and the Environment, which Udall chaired, approved an amended version of the Udall bill — with a new number (HR 2967) — by voice vote Oct. 20.

The subcommittee first adopted two amendments by Nevada Rep. Vucanovich.

The first Vucanovich amendment lengthened the commission's study period from six months to 12 months. It also barred DOE from sinking an exploratory shaft at any site for six months after that, bringing the total moratorium to 18 months.

The second Vucanovich amendment gave federal aid to state and local governments affected by the underground studies called "site characterization." States, Indian tribes and local governments could ask for financial or technical aid to offset any adverse effects of site-study activities, such as the major construction work on an exploratory shaft.

Local governmental units such as school districts and water districts would qualify, as well as cities, counties and other general-purpose governments. Local governments also could ask for funds to replace what they could have gotten by taxing the site-study activities, which were exempt from local taxes because they were carried out by the federal government. No dollar limit was set on such aid.

The committee also expanded the new commission's purview to include DOE's past decisions. That amendment was offered by Wayne Owens, D-Utah, and supported by Nevada and other finalist states.

The bill directed the commission to "review the adequacy" and "identify any deficiencies" of various decisions by DOE leading up to the current list of sites. These included DOE's siting guidelines, environmental assessments, ranking methods and consultation with states.

The commission even would be required to study whether DOE should continue to run the waste program and must rethink basic principles underlying the 1982 Nuclear Waste Policy Act (PL 97-425), such as the schedule for building a repository and the presumption that deep burial was the right disposal method. It also would have to review whether a temporary storage facility should be built.

The full Interior Committee approved HR 2967 on a voice vote Oct. 28, and it was reported (H Rept 100-425, Part I) Nov. 5.

## Conference Committee

With Johnston's nuclear waste plan a part of both the reconciliation bill and the omnibus spending bill — both of which went to conference in the closing days of the session — the first step was to decide which set of conferees would make the decision.

The opposing parties agreed that the reconciliation conferees would get first crack at negotiating a compromise, but if they failed, the decision would fall to the spending bill conferees.

The House and Senate started the reconciliation conference with positions so different that some of the conferees said they looked irreconcilable.

The core of the House position was still HR 2967, the bill reported by the Interior Committee that called for an 18-month moratorium on the study of specific nuclear waste sites.

Johnston's plan called for speeding up the process instead of slowing it down. His plan changed the site-study process from three at once, with language that strongly pushed the decision toward Nevada. Johnston's bill sought to sweeten the bitter pill by authorizing federal payments of $100 million yearly to the state taking the waste. But it left to DOE the choice of a state, even if the state were unwilling. Johnston also wanted to authorize an MRS temporary waste site, while the House plan made no provision for one.

The first signs of movement came at a Dec. 14 meeting of the nuclear waste subconference, when Texans from the House Energy Committee, led by Republican Jack Fields, pushed the House closer to the Johnston plan. They had earlier insisted on provisions taking their state out of the final-three contest. Their demands had to be heeded. Five of the 21 members of the Energy and Power Subcommittee were from Texas.

One of the items they wanted was a stipulation that DOE could not choose a repository site that lay below an aquifer, which could presumably leak into the repository or be contaminated by it.

Both the Texas and Washington sites lay below aquifers. Yucca Mountain did not.

Swift, the Washington state Democrat who was a key actor on the Energy Committee, told House conferees that forces beyond his control were turning the process from a scientific one to a political one, and that if other states were getting off for political reasons, then he wanted his state to get off, too.

Neither of Nevada's two House members was on the Energy Committee.

"My disappointment," said Reid, "is that the House just capitulated."

Swift, afterward called the plan "a goddamned outrage," but said he had to protect his constituents. "If we are going to have to do it over a barrel, then this configuration gives me the parochial things that I need."

The House conferees Dec. 14 made the Senate an offer. The key feature was that it explicitly chose Nevada for the first and only exploratory shaft, "calling a spade a spade," as some put it. But it contained no authorization for the MRS Johnston wanted. After a Senate counteroffer Dec. 15 that included an MRS, the two sides again appeared to be at an impasse.

What tipped the balance, according to several reports, was a 2 p.m., Dec. 16 meeting attended by House Speaker Jim Wright, D-Texas, Udall, Dingell, Rules Committee member Butler Derrick, D-S.C., and some of the other House conferees. They reportedly won Wright's assurance that if necessary they would be allowed a floor vote to substitute their own language for any Johnston provision

they disagreed with. The results of that meeting were made known to Johnston.

Johnston at that point was faced with the prospect of a House floor vote in which he would be going up against not only the two committee titans, Dingell and Udall, but also Speaker Wright and Majority Leader Thomas S. Foley, D-Wash., whose states would be let off the hook by the House plan.

That was the point, sources say, at which Johnston started to compromise on the MRS, making its authorization conditional, and thus paving the way for an agreement.

# NRC Changes, Uranium Industry

The 100th Congress wrestled with a collection of bills that promised to help revive the ailing domestic nuclear power industry, but most were not enacted.

Electric utilities had stopped ordering new nuclear generating plants in the late 1970s. Public safety concerns since the 1979 near-meltdown at Pennsylvania's Three Mile Island generating plant had been one reason for the halt, but cost overruns, regulatory delays and uncertainty and the failure of demand for electricity to live up to high growth estimates also contributed.

The nuclear power industry asked Congress in the ensuing years for a number of legislative changes in economic and political conditions its lobbyists said were needed if new nuclear plants were to become viable again.

One such change, reauthorization of the 1957 Price-Anderson Act to limit the financial risks faced by utilities and reactor manufacturers in case of a catastrophic accident, did win enactment. *(Story, p. 421)*

Others on the list included streamlining the reactor licensing procedures at the Nuclear Regulatory Commission (NRC), standardized reactor designs and restructuring of the commission itself. The industry wanted the five-member commission replaced by a single commissioner, while industry critics wanted more watchdogs watching the industry and the agency itself.

Still another agenda was put forward by the U.S. uranium industry that fueled the nuclear plants, including both the companies that mined uranium and the many contractors and individuals employed by the government in enriching it. Those industries were suffering devastating economic woes, not only because electric power plants were demanding less uranium than expected, but because of other problems as well.

## Senate Package Fails

The Senate easily passed a bill to reorganize the NRC and to shore up the failing domestic uranium industry on Aug. 8, 1988, but the bill failed to clear in the waning hours of Congress. It was an effort to package and pass the most viable items on the industry's legislative shopping list.

Sen. Alan K. Simpson, R-Wyo., said it would "help to restore public confidence in nuclear power" and "lay the groundwork for a new generation" of reactors.

The House already had passed the bill (HR 1315), as a simple two-year reauthorization of the NRC without reorganization, on Aug. 5, 1987, by a 389-20 vote. The Senate Aug. 8, 1988, called up its own NRC reform bill (S 2443 — S Rept 100-364), amended it, substituted the text of that bill for HR 1315 and then passed HR 1315.

The main body of the bill, to reorganize the five-member NRC into a new Nuclear Safety Agency (NSA) under a single administrator, was a compromise worked out in long negotiations between critics and advocates of nuclear power. The 89-6 vote on passage indicated a wide consensus had been reached.

The new NSA would be run by a single administrator, appointed by the president and confirmed by the Senate. The bill also would establish an Office of Investigations to probe possible criminal wrongdoing by licensees and a three-member Nuclear Reactor Safety Investigations Board to look into nuclear incidents. It also would establish an Office of Inspector General to look into internal agency abuses, operating under the standard rules for such offices at most other agencies.

The Senate adopted, by voice vote, an amendment by James A. McClure, R-Idaho, directing the new NSA, within one year of enactment, to issue a proposed rule providing for standardized nuclear power plant designs. The industry had asked Congress to mandate standardization as a way to cut licensing delays and cost overruns.

The principal notes of dissent came from the Reagan administration, which threatened to veto the bill on the grounds that the new agency's structure and ground rules undermined the president's constitutional powers. But the bill's sponsors argued that they were actually making the agency more responsive to the president.

On Oct. 5, 1988, the House approved a less ambitious NRC reorganization plan. That bill (HR 4140 — H Rept 100-878, Parts I and II) would place the NRC Office of Investigations directly under the authority of the NRC's five commissioners. Investigators currently reported to the executive director, a position below the commissioner level.

In report language accompanying the fiscal 1988 continuing resolution (PL 100-202), Congress had in 1987 directed the NRC to merge its investigations office with other inspection offices that reported to the executive director, in order to streamline the commission's hierarchy.

The office's director, Ben B. Hayes, said the change seriously hampered investigations. Hayes said because the office's work was highly sensitive, its investigators should report directly to the NRC's five head commissioners.

## Senate Environment Committee

The Senate Environment Committee had approved S 2443 by voice vote March 29, 1988.

The bill's key sponsor, John B. Breaux, D-La., had held more than a dozen hearings to probe the structure of the NRC and its relation to the nuclear industry it regulated. Breaux chaired the Subcommittee on Nuclear Regulation.

The full committee adopted three Breaux amendments before approving the bill. One specified that the NSA, like the old NRC, would be independent of the Office of Management and Budget (OMB) in its regulatory decisions, although it would still have been subject to OMB budget discipline.

Another amendment required the agency to set up a program of drug testing of nuclear power plant personnel whose performance affected safety, similar to that which the Federal Aviation Administration set up for airline pilots. Testing was to be for both drugs and alcohol. The program would include testing before employment, at periodic and random intervals, after an accident and upon reasonable suspicion.

The amendment took authority for licensing the nation's nuclear waste repository away from the NSA and vested it in a special licensing board created just for that function. The board would have three members, all appointed by the NSA administrator.

Harry Reid, D-Nev., whose state was the prime candidate for the repository, said the amendment would solve a potential conflict of interest that the NSA administrator would have if he were the one considering the waste site license application. The waste site would be proposed by the president, at whose pleasure the administrator would serve.

## Seabrook/Shoreham Controversy

Before the House passed HR 1315, the NRC reauthorization, it rejected an effort to prevent the startup of two controversial Northeastern nuclear power plants.

After an acrimonious debate and a large-scale lobbying effort, the House Aug. 5 rejected in a 160-261 vote an amendment by Edward J. Markey, D-Mass.

The Markey amendment was aimed at the Shoreham nuclear plant in Long Island, N.Y., and another nuclear plant in Seabrook, N.H., 10 miles from Massachusetts. Construction of both was complete, but neither had yet gotten an NRC license for full operation. They had been unable to meet an NRC rule requiring state and local government agreement with evacuation plans for all people within a 10-mile radius.

The governors of Massachusetts and New York had argued that a mass evacuation in such heavily populated areas was impossible.

The Markey amendment would bar the NRC from relaxing its rules to let Shoreham and Seabrook generate power. Supporters of the amendment, many of whom represented the plants' neighbors, called the reactors unsafe and said the rule change would violate states' rights.

The amendment's supporters — most of whom were liberal Democrats — took on an unaccustomed role as defenders of states' rights. "Should this decision rest with millions of citizens through their highest elected state officials or with a handful of bureaucrats here in Washington?" asked Joseph E. Brennan, D-Maine, a former governor of that state.

Opponents, backed by the nation's utilities and the Reagan administration, argued that the Markey amendment would set a precedent that could destroy the nuclear power industry. They said the national interest was at stake because nuclear power was needed to reduce American dependence on foreign oil.

The amendment drew scores of lobbyists, and Markey blamed them for the defeat. "The most powerful lobbying group in the country was able to flex its muscles tonight," he said, but he warned that "it would be foolish to say that this is the end of the battle."

Proponents of the Markey amendment tried throughout the debate to prove that the bill was not anti-nuclear and would not affect the 107 nuclear plants now in operation. They said Seabrook and Shoreham were unique in that no emergency plan had been found to give local citizens as much protection as the neighbors of other nuclear plants received.

HR 1315 was a two-year reauthorization of the Nuclear Regulatory Commission. It authorized $427.8 million for fiscal 1988 and $422.6 million for fiscal 1989.

By voice vote, the House adopted an amendment, by

Jim Slattery, D-Kan., requiring nuclear plants to underwrite the entire NRC budget, instead of 75 percent of it, as proposed in the bill. That would mean paying an average of $3.3 million per nuclear plant.

Under the budget reconciliation bill (HR 3545 — PL 100-203), NRC fees were eventually increased to cover 45 percent of the agency's costs — up from the current level of 33 percent. *(Reconciliation, p. 61)*

The House also approved by voice vote an amendment by Dennis E. Eckart, D-Ohio, to bar the NRC from closing meetings to the public.

HR 1315 was approved by the Interior and the Energy and Commerce committees (H Rept 100-90, Parts I, II and III). Differences between the committees' reports were resolved in HR 3037, a clean compromise measure that was then offered as a substitute for the text of HR 1315.

## Uranium Bailout

Before passing HR 1315, the full Senate voted 78-17 to adopt an amendment by Wendell H. Ford, D-Ky., adding the uranium-industry rescue plan.

The Senate had previously passed another uranium-industry rescue bill, S 2097, on March 30, which was similar to a measure (S 1846 — S Rept 100-214) approved by the panel in 1987.

S 2097 contained a plan to charge fees on imported uranium, but critics said it threatened the U.S.-Canada Free Trade Agreement. (Canada was a major supplier of U.S. uranium imports.) The fee idea was dropped after uranium-state legislators won Reagan administration support for a plan to bolster the domestic industry by establishing a $750 million federal fund to buy up domestic uranium.

The administration at first agreed to attach the buy-up plan to the free-trade agreement, but it drew objections from the Senate Finance Committee and the House Ways and Means, Energy and Commerce, and Interior and Insular Affairs committees. As a result, the administration dropped it from the U.S.-Canada pact it ultimately submitted to Congress July 25. *(U.S.-Canada trade agreement, p. 159)*

Ford put the substance of the plan into his amendment, which was cosponsored by Pete V. Domenici, R-N.M. It combined the $750 million domestic uranium buy-up with a $1 billion program to clean up uranium mill wastes and to reorganize uranium-enrichment operations carried out by the Energy Department under a government-owned corporation.

**Background.** Uranium, as it came from nature, was a mixture of a small amount (0.7 percent) of a fissionable isotope, U-235, and a large amount of the heavier U-238. To be used as reactor fuel, it had to be "enriched" — an elaborate and expensive process — to a concentration of about 3 percent U-235.

Congress, in the Atomic Energy Act of 1954, set up the uranium-enrichment industry as a government monopoly. At the time, the United States was concerned about keeping other nations from developing atomic weapons, as well as public health and safety.

Under the 1954 act, all enrichment plants had to be owned by the government. To promote a "viable domestic uranium industry," Congress at first allowed no foreign uranium to be enriched and used by U.S. utilities. Until 1978, the United States had a near-monopoly on the sale of enriched uranium to other Western nations, and the do-

mestic uranium-mining industry had been expanding rapidly.

Between 1974 and 1984, the ban on uranium imports was gradually lifted, because the domestic uranium industry had flourished. In the early 1980s, a world market in enriched uranium developed. The new competition for customers, and a supply exceeding demand, pushed the world price downward.

During that same time span, the U.S. commercial nuclear power industry hit hard times. The expectation that more and more raw uranium would be needed to fuel an ever-growing nuclear power industry was deflated. New uranium deposits from foreign countries such as Canada began displacing U.S. uranium because the deposits were cheaper to mine. Utilities with long-term contracts to buy uranium ended up with surpluses on their hands. When they attempted to sell their surpluses, at discount prices, they undercut U.S. uranium mining even further.

The number of operating U.S. uranium mines dropped from 362 in 1979 to only three in 1986. Employment dropped similarly, from about 22,000 in 1981 to scarcely 2,000 in 1986. Historically, almost half the nation's uranium was mined in New Mexico. By 1988, the biggest amounts came from phosphate operations in Florida and Louisiana, as well as mines in Arizona. Other states with uranium were Utah, Colorado, Texas and Wyoming.

But the problem extended beyond the uranium-mining industry, which was in private hands. The enrichment industry, which was run by the Department of Energy (DOE), had suffered as well during the 1980s for other reasons.

After President Reagan took office in 1981, OMB budget-cutters began looking at DOE's enrichment program, one of the few federal programs actually capable of making money instead of losing it, as ammunition against the deficit.

DOE raised the price of enrichment to as much as $135 per work-unit, but foreign enterprises were offering enrichment for as little as $100 per unit. Not surprisingly, DOE lost customers. U.S. utilities for the first time in 1982 began buying enrichment services abroad, although 90 percent of their needs were still met by DOE. The U.S. share of the foreign enrichment market, however, dropped from almost 100 percent in 1978 to 40 percent by 1986.

**Senate Energy Committee Bill.** The Senate Energy Committee approved its bipartisan bill to bolster the U.S. uranium industry by a 13-2 vote on Oct. 1, 1987.

The bill was pushed by senators from New Mexico and Kentucky, where hundreds of jobs were at stake. But some senators from other parts of the country, saying the bill helped the uranium industry at the expense of taxpayers and electric utility customers, vowed to challenge it on the floor. Voting against the bill in committee were Daniel J. Evans, R-Wash., and Bill Bradley, D-N.J.

The bill (S 1846 — S Rept 100-214) was a blend of proposals from Domenici and Ford. It was modeled after a bill approved by the Energy Committee in 1986 (S 1004 — S Rept 99-464).

The bill attempted to boost demand for domestically mined uranium by imposing charges on electric utilities using foreign uranium as fuel. It also would set up a new government-owned corporation to make the federal uranium-enrichment program more independent of DOE.

It would settle a longstanding accounting dispute over how much money the enrichment program owed the government for past capital costs. It also would settle another dispute between DOE and the Tennessee Valley Authority (TVA) over compensation for electric power DOE contracted to buy but never used.

And it would set up a new $1 billion fund, paid for by the mining companies, utilities and federal government, to pay for cleanup of potentially dangerous uranium mill wastes, or tailings.

Before approving the bill, the committee amended it to make sure OMB could not capture revenue from the uranium-enrichment program for the Treasury.

The bill was designed as a compromise between the U.S. uranium industry, which wanted a bigger market and protection from foreign competition, and the U.S. nuclear utilities, which wanted a cheap and stable supply of fuel. But the uranium producers were happier with the result.

The bill effectively would restrict the use of uranium mined in foreign countries. If a utility used more than 37.5 percent foreign uranium, it would have to pay charges on a sliding scale that ranged as high as $500 per kilogram. (A typical plant used 37,000 kilograms per year.)

The Reagan administration opposed the import charges, although it generally accepted the other major features of the bill, according to DOE. The administration had proposed selling the uranium-enrichment enterprise to private industry.

**New Corporation.** The Energy Committee's bill would establish the "United States Enrichment Corporation," which would be wholly owned by the federal government and subject to the Government Corporation Control Act of 1958 (PL 85-477), to run the enrichment enterprise.

The corporation would be operated "as a continuing, commercial enterprise, on a profitable and efficient basis." Energy Committee Chairman J. Bennett Johnston, D-La., said that would prohibit the Reagan administration's policy of "harvesting" the corporation's assets for short-term deficit reduction at the risk of weakening its long-term viability.

The corporation would be run by an administrator, appointed by the president and confirmed by the Senate, and overseen by a five-member advisory board.

The bill would authorize DOE to transfer its uranium stocks and enrichment plant to the corporation and declare a nominal capital value for those assets of $3.2 billion. It authorized the corporation to borrow up to $2.5 billion in the private bond market.

If the corporation was highly profitable, it would be authorized to pay dividends to the Treasury out of its earnings, but that would be entirely at the administrator's option.

Domenici, Ford and Johnston said they thought the enterprise could be quite profitable, and they were optimistic that it could yield revenues to the Treasury over and above the basic $364 million debt. Committee staffers cited estimates that the new corporation could sell enrichment services at rates undercutting the world price — putting the United States back into competition and winning back a bigger share of the world market. DOE was forced to sell above the world market price under the circumstances that existed in 1987, they said, because it was servicing the $8.8 billion debt they viewed as artificial.

Domenici and others voiced concern during the Energy Committee markup that the secretary of energy could simply order the corporation administrator to declare dividends or be fired. They drew up amendments, approved by voice vote, stiffening his independence. One specified that, although the administrator was under the general supervision of the secretary on matters like national security, he was solely responsible for fiscal decisions, especially the setting of dividends.

Another specified that the administrator could be removed only by the president, and only for inefficiency, neglect or malfeasance, after 30 days' notice to Congress.

**Payback Issue.** The bill approved by the Energy Committee was meant to settle an issue that had dogged the enrichment program in recent years: how much the DOE enrichment program owed the general Treasury for "unrecovered costs."

Most of the argument was over capital costs, including the cost of the shut-down enrichment plant at Oak Ridge, Tenn., and two plants still running at Paducah, Ky., and Portsmouth, Ohio.

The General Accounting Office (GAO) told a House Committee on April 8, 1987, that DOE owed $8.8 billion to the Treasury. OMB agreed with GAO. The Edison Electric Institute, representing utilities whose customers would ultimately pay such charges through enrichment fees, said the program owed the Treasury nothing. The committee's bill would set the payback at $364 million.

The dispute was one that involved not only platoons of accountants and lawyers, but also leaders of the House and Senate Budget committees.

Apart from being an architect of the bill and a member of the Energy Committee, Domenici was ranking Republican on the Budget Committee. "The government thinks we owe more money to them than . . . every outside auditor thinks we owe," he said. "We have taken this huge, fictitious [$8.8 billion] bookkeeping entry, and we have reduced it to what most people think is real [$364 million]."

But House Budget Committee Chairman William H. Gray III, D-Pa., saw it very differently. While it did not specify exactly how much the total payback should be, the original House-passed fiscal 1988 budget resolution (H Con Res 93) assumed the utility industry could afford to pay, through some mechanism, up to $200 million per year toward the debt over a three-year period. The Senate knocked out that item in conference.

The National Taxpayers Union, a non-partisan citizen group, shared GAO's view that DOE owed $8.8 billion. It said the law required full repayment and that anything else was a subsidy to the nuclear utilities.

# Other Nuclear Legislation

## Nuclear Plant Security

By voice vote, the House Dec. 14, 1987, passed a bill to strengthen security at nuclear facilities.

The bill (HR 2683) would amend the Atomic Energy Act of 1954 and expand the authority of the Nuclear Regulatory Commission (NRC) to withhold information about security at nuclear plants.

It also would make it a federal crime to take a weapon onto the site of a nuclear plant or any other facility regulated by the NRC without authorization. The measure made it a federal crime to sabotage a nuclear power plant or any other nuclear facility under construction if the resulting damage could pose a threat to public health and safety. And it would clarify requirements that nuclear licensees notify NRC of any rules violations or safety hazards.

HR 2683 was reported July 15 by the Interior Committee and Oct. 19 by the Energy and Commerce Committee (H Rept 100-223, Parts I and II).

The Senate did not act on the bill, which died at the end of the 100th Congress.

## Nuclear Emergencies

The House May 10, 1988, passed a bill (HR 1570 — H Rept 100-243, Part I) that would allow officials at the headquarters of the Nuclear Regulatory Commission (NRC) in Washington, D.C., to read instruments at a remote nuclear power plant in an emergency, like the one that occurred in 1979 at the Three Mile Island plant in Pennsylvania.

The House passed the bill on a 341-77 vote. The bill died at the end of the 100th Congress, because the Senate did not act on it.

The bill would require the NRC to establish a 24-hour electronic system for transmission of data about the operating condition of a commercial nuclear power reactor during an emergency. That would have included information such as the temperature, pressure and water level in the reactor core as well as whether radiation was being released from the containment building. It also would allow NRC engineers to transmit back to reactor operators advice to help avert a catastrophic meltdown.

The measure also would require power plant operators to maintain a "black box" similar to cockpit flight recorders that would record operating data for each 24-hour period. The NRC had to have the system operating within five years of enactment. Most of the costs of these requirements would be paid by the utility companies.

# 'Windfall Profits' Tax Repeal

At the urging of the oil industry and the Reagan administration, Congress in 1988 finally repealed the so-called "windfall profits" tax on oil.

The tax — passed in 1980 with much fanfare — was meant to capture for the Treasury some of the added revenues the oil companies were expected to earn after decontrol of domestic oil prices. It was a keystone of Congress' response to the "energy crisis" of the 1970s. President Jimmy Carter staked his personal prestige on it, while oil-state senators fought unsuccessfully to stop it.

Little fanfare, however, attended efforts to repeal it. Oil-state members convinced many colleagues that since low oil prices had stopped collection of the tax nothing would be lost by repealing it. The repeal had backing from powerful committee chairmen and was attached by the Senate in 1987 to two bills on Congress' list of critical legislation: the omnibus trade bill (HR 3) and the deficit reduction, or reconciliation, bill (HR 3545 — PL 100-203). But it was not included in the House version of either of those bills. Conferees on reconciliation dropped the repeal in the closing days of 1987. A decision on the trade bill was postponed until 1988. *(Trade bill, p. 148; reconciliation, p. 61)*

The tax repeal was finally enacted as part of a refurbished trade bill (HR 4848 — PL 100-418) cleared by Congress Aug. 3, 1988, and signed by President Reagan Aug. 23.

After two years of work, Congress cleared the trade bill a first time in April 1988, but President Reagan vetoed it May 24 because of plant-closing provisions unrelated to the oil tax. Only after Congress split off the plant-closing provisions and sent the president a new, veto-proof trade bill (HR 4848) did oil tax repeal become law.

## Background

As gas station lines lengthened and world oil prices climbed in the 1970s, the price of oil drilled or pumped in the United States still was controlled by the federal government and kept at less than world market prices. Oil companies said they had no incentive to produce and called for decontrol of the domestic price.

During 1979 world oil prices doubled from about $16 to more than $30 per barrel. Oil-company profits headed the same way, with record profits reported for the first three quarters in 1979.

Skeptics in the 1970s suspected oil companies were contriving shortages to jack up the price, and it was high prices that were being blamed for inflation and recession.

The tax that Congress finally passed in 1980 (PL 96-223) was part of a much more comprehensive package meant to address energy problems — a package that included decontrol of oil prices. *(Congress and the Nation Vol. V, p. 503)*

A good many of the items in the package — for example, a $20 billion synthetic fuels program — were later judged grandiose and wasteful. Over the next half-decade, many of them were repealed and discarded. The windfall profits tax was to be one of the last.

The windfall profits tax was key to the 1980 package. It made decontrol of oil prices politically possible by defusing suspicions that oil companies were getting away with something.

## How It Worked

During the trade bill debate, senator after senator remarked that windfall profits tax was a misnomer.

"Let me dispel a myth surrounding the windfall profits tax. The windfall profits tax, despite its name, has nothing to do with windfalls or profits and never has had," said Malcolm Wallop, R-Wyo. Nonetheless, the name was commonly used to refer to the tax. Congress officially named it the windfall profits tax when it was enacted.

The tax was collected only on the amount by which the market price of crude oil exceeded the old price ceiling. If the current market price went below the base price, no tax was collected.

"Windfall profit. It sounds so evil," said Wallop, "but whatever it costs anybody to lift a barrel of oil from the ground was never considered. Only the price that was received for it was considered."

Nor were profits considered. The tax was due whether or not the producer was making a profit.

Built into the 1980 law, however, was the assumption that if oil companies were making record profits at the controlled price, they would be making higher profits at a higher price.

Oil companies argued that if their revenues were taxed away, they would have no incentive to look for new oil. Consumer advocates said such arguments could not apply to wells already drilled and producing. In response to these arguments, Congress structured the "windfall" tax to distinguish between oil discovered before 1979 and oil discovered in years after 1979.

Pre-1979 oil was taxed at a rate of 70 percent of the difference between the base price and the market price. Oil tapped after 1978 was taxed at 30 percent of the difference. The base price used to calculate the tax was much lower for old oil as well — further exaggerating the differential. In short, the government took most of the benefit oil companies could have reaped from decontrol of old oil, but left them a greater share of the benefits from discovering new reserves.

Those base prices were indexed for inflation, as a way of keeping increases in the cost of exploration and production from nibbling away at the producers' margin. In 1987, the base price for old oil was about $19 per barrel, and the base price for new oil was about $29 per barrel. Because oil prices were lower than $19, revenue from the tax in 1986 and 1987 was negligible.

When the price of oil plunged from $26 to $11 in 1986, a devastating shakeout took place in the U.S. oil industry. The damage was worse on the "upstream" end of the industry, the end of the pipeline closest to the wellhead. Producers could no longer be sure they could sell oil for a price high enough to pay for finding and pumping it. Banks stopped lending oilmen money and started calling their loans. Exploratory drilling came almost to a stop, devastating the economies of states such as Texas, Louisiana and Oklahoma.

"Downstream" petroleum enterprises — the refiners, transporters and marketers — did better. Lower crude prices meant they earned a higher margin on the finished, delivered product. Big, integrated companies that included both upstream and downstream operations simply cut back their drilling and weathered the storm.

By mid-1987, crude prices had regained more than half the ground they had lost and hovered around $19 per barrel. The upstream end of the industry had begun making some recovery, but drilling still was far below earlier levels.

Oil companies and oil-state members were still asking Congress for relief that summer, but by late October, most of the big oil companies were reporting that their earnings in the third quarter had increased substantially. Net earnings more than tripled for the Shell Oil Co. They were up 75 percent for the Mobil Oil Corp.

## Would It Help?

One of the oil industry's main arguments in favor of repeal was that, as domestic production fell, the nation's increasing dependency on imported oil presented a national security threat. The industry said the answer was to give the oil companies an incentive to find and produce more domestic oil.

Critics like Howard M. Metzenbaum, D-Ohio, were dubious: "Now oil companies like to talk about what they would do if they had these dollars. . . . They would use the profits to expand oil exploration and development. History shows, however, that they will in fact be exploring and developing oil company mergers."

Bill Bradley, D-N.J., reiterated that the tax was not collected on new oil until it reached the $29-per-barrel base price. Repeal "would not be an incentive for new exploration because the price of oil has to go up nearly $10 before we get to the time where the windfall profits tax would even kick in on newly discovered oil," he said.

One of the most potent arguments in favor of repeal was based on the trade deficit — an issue that had broader

political appeal and more legislative momentum than energy security.

The nation's oil imports accounted for one of the biggest shares of the deficit. In July 1987 the United States spent $4.1 billion on foreign crude — twice what was spent on Japanese cars.

## What It Cost

One of the main arguments in favor of the tax repeal was put succinctly by Phil Gramm, R-Texas: "We are basically talking about an action that does not cost any money because the windfall profits tax is not collecting any revenue."

Another key argument oil companies made was that the tax was, as Gramm said, "a dead-weight-burden cost of over $100 million on the American economy for record keeping, paperwork, accountants, lawyers — all spent in the name of a tax that is not being collected."

That estimate of paperwork costs was provided by the American Petroleum Institute, the industry's main lobbying arm.

Whether or not the market price of oil had triggered the tax, companies had to file a form with the Internal Revenue Service, which estimated it received about 4 million of them a year.

Much of the industry's argument for the repeal was psychological: The idea was that while it might not really relieve them of any major financial burden, the symbolic relief of repeal would provide a morale boost to a depressed industry.

# Fuel Use Act Repeal

The 100th Congress repealed a Carter-era law that forced utilities to burn coal instead of oil or natural gas.

After utilities, gas companies and the coal industry compromised on key points, Congress cleared and sent to the president May 7, 1987, a bill (HR 1941 — PL 100-42) repealing and amending sections of the 1978 Powerplant and Industrial Fuel Use Act (PL 95-620). The president signed the bill May 21.

## Background

The Fuel Use Act was enacted when oil and gas resources were expected to become scarce. The law flatly barred new power plants from burning gas or oil as their primary energy source. (Congress and the Nation Vol. V, p. 482)

But the main goal of the 1978 law, shifting the nation's electric power generation from petroleum to coal, had been achieved by 1987, whether the Fuel Use Act was effective or not. The nation's utilities were burning more coal as the amount of electricity generated from gas and oil dropped from 30.3 percent in 1978 to 15.9 percent in 1985, according to utility groups.

Since the 1970s, however, the nation was producing far more natural gas than experts had predicted, resulting in a glut of gas and a drop in gas prices. The low price made gas competitive with coal for "baseload" generating plants (those plants that ran all the time to meet continuous demand).

A requirement in the 1978 law that existing oil- or gas-fired plants convert to coal was already repealed in 1981.

*(Congress and the Nation Vol. VI, p. 383)*

But it was questionable whether the repeal of the Fuel Use Act would have much impact on the already economically depressed U.S. petroleum industry.

Many "peakload" utility power plants — auxiliary power plants used for handling temporary peaks in electricity demand — already burned oil, through Energy Department exemptions.

The coal industry in 1986 blocked a bill to repeal the Fuel Use Act because it did not provide language requiring new power plants to be "coal capable," that is able to burn coal when they were built.

## Senate Action

It was the Senate Energy and Natural Resources Committee that paved the way for repeal of the fuel use bill. The committee March 31 by an 18-0 vote reported a bill (S 85 — S Rept 100-30) to repeal.

The compromise reached in the Senate committee required that new baseload power plants be convertible to coal someday, if necessary, rather than be capable of burning coal when they were built.

The compromise was worked out between Senate Energy Chairman J. Bennett Johnston, D-La., who represented a major oil producing state, and Wendell H. Ford, D-Ky., whose state produced large amounts of coal.

Ford was expected to launch a fight for an amendment to require that new baseload power plants be "convertible" to coal. Johnston and the gas industry were expected to oppose such an amendment.

Gas and utility companies had argued that the convertibility requirement would raise the price of a $500 million plant to $650 million because extra land had to be purchased to provide for coal handling and pollution control facilities.

The compromise adopted by the Energy Committee eased the convertibility requirement significantly from what Ford had originally proposed. It prohibited a new plant from being "physically, structurally or technologically precluded from using coal as its primary energy source." But the compromise removed language requiring new plants to have adequate land space for coal-handling facilities; however, land must be available for pollution-control equipment.

The full Senate April 8 passed the bill by voice vote without amendment.

## House Action

The House Energy Subcommittee on Energy and Power April 7 also approved 22-0 a bill (HR 1941) to repeal the Fuel Use Act, and the full Energy and Commerce Committee May 4 reported the bill (H Rept 100-78). Most of the provisions of HR 1941 were identical to those in S 85.

The House May 4 passed HR 1941 by voice vote under suspension of the rules. The bill's manager, Philip R. Sharp, D-Ind., chairman of the Energy and Power Subcommittee, added an amendment to the committee-approved version before presenting it to the House.

The amendment repealed "incremental pricing" provisions of the 1978 law, which required that industries using gas to fire their boilers pay a surcharge for it.

The Senate May 7 agreed to the bill as passed by the House and sent the bill to the White House.

# Appliance Efficiency Standards

The National Appliance Energy Conservation Act of 1987 (S 83 — PL 100-12) was signed into law March 17 by President Reagan. The bill, pocket-vetoed by Reagan in 1986, required manufacturers to meet minimum nationwide energy-efficiency standards for such appliances as refrigerators, freezers, furnaces, room and central air conditioners, water heaters, dishwashers, washers and dryers, televisions and kitchen ranges and ovens.

The standards, which provided a 15 percent to 25 percent improvement in efficiency, were different for each appliance and took effect in 1988, 1990, 1992 or 1993, depending on the product. Manufacturers had at least five years after the effective date to redesign their appliances for compliance.

In subsequent years, the Department of Energy (DOE) could revise the standards to cover new appliances or to make them stricter — but not to make them less strict. The bill also outlined criteria and procedures for DOE to follow in setting such standards.

The federal standards pre-empted state standards. States, however, could petition DOE for waivers from the standards to meet "unusual and compelling state and local interests" substantially different from national interests. DOE could not grant waivers if interested parties showed that the state standard would burden or disrupt commerce nationally or make a product type unavailable in the state.

Manufacturers and environmentalists began negotiating for an appliance standards bill in early 1986 and came up with legislation (HR 5465) that both sides could support. Both the House and Senate passed the 1986 bill by voice vote. *(1986 bill, p. 453)*

The 1987 bill (S 83) was approved unanimously by the Senate Energy and Natural Resources Committee Jan. 28 and reported Jan. 30 (S Rept 100-6). The bill was virtually identical to the one passed in 1986.

The bill went to the Senate floor Feb. 5 and triggered a parliamentary dispute when Phil Gramm, R-Texas, tried to prevent Majority Leader Robert C. Byrd, D-W.Va., from calling up the bill. Gramm had asked leaders of both parties for a delay to give the administration time to come up with a compromise offer.

Byrd, however, decided to proceed. "As majority leader of the Senate, I have a responsibility to try to keep the Senate moving and to act on the calendar," he said.

But through a series of delaying tactics, Gramm succeeded in keeping the bill from the floor Feb. 5. By unanimous consent the Senate agreed to take up the measure Feb. 17, when it was passed by a vote of 89-6.

Before final action, the Senate agreed by voice vote to adopt an amendment to the bill put forth by Gramm that lifted a requirement that DOE review appliance efficiency standards every five years. Gramm said the amendment satisfied one of the administration's main objections to the bill.

The House Subcommittee on Energy and Power marked up a companion appliance standards bill (HR 87) Feb. 24, and the full Energy and Commerce Committee approved it two days later (H Rept 100-11). The subcommittee adopted by voice vote the same amendment, easing DOE review requirements, that passed in the Senate. Carlos J. Moorhead, R-Calif., offered the amendment.

After passing HR 87 March 3 by voice vote, the House set it aside and passed the Senate's measure, S 83. Floor

# ... For Most Federal Farm Programs

which gave it considerable influence over international trade.

## A Peculiar Entitlement

Although the CCC was an entitlement program, it was unique in that its funds were provided by the regular congressional appropriations process. Once Congress established the eligibility criteria under an entitlement program, it had no further discretion on how much money the program would cost in any year. All farmers who met the eligibility requirements were guaranteed full benefits.

Unlike other entitlements, the CCC could not spend money independently the way Social Security or unemployment compensation was distributed. Its only funding source was Congress. The CCC borrowed money from the Treasury and other lenders to finance its farm programs. As farmers repaid their loans and as CCC commodity stocks were sold, the CCC recovered funds and paid off its debts. But the CCC typically did not recover as much money as it spent. Sometimes there were big losses, such as when commodities were sold at prices significantly lower than the CCC paid for them, or when it made direct payments to support farmers' incomes. And when such losses were incurred, the CCC had to turn to Congress and request an appropriation.

Another factor that gave the CCC less flexibility than other entitlements was that Congress placed a ceiling on how much the agency could borrow — currently $25 billion. Until recent years the cap was not a problem. When CCC operations bumped up against the cap, Congress routinely raised the ceiling. But the mounting cost of farm subsidies caused the CCC to reach the ceiling more frequently. Even the Agriculture Department consistently fell short in its predictions of the CCC's annual budget.

## Proposed Funding Solutions

The Reagan administration tried repeatedly to take the CCC out of the financial merry-go-round with a proposal for a "permanent, indefinite" appropriation to reimburse the corporation's losses. But until 1987 Congress refused to consider the proposal. Whitten maintained that the existing procedure of limited funding was the only way Congress could keep an eye on farm program spending. He also complained that non-price-support programs were being funded through the CCC, such as crop insurance, conservation projects, the whole-herd dairy buyout program, meat purchases for schools and the military, and subsidies for ethanol plants.

Some lawmakers suggested a compromise. Called a "current, indefinite" appropriation, it would give the CCC unlimited reimbursements on a year-to-year basis and free it from the annual ritual of a supplemental appropriation. The proposal was approved in 1987 by the Senate Agriculture and Budget committees when they considered the budget deficit reduction bill (HR 3545 — PL 100-203). Congress approved the Senate's indefinite funding provision, but later that same year it also approved the regular, limited appropriation for the CCC in a catchall spending bill (H J Res 395 — PL 100-202). The Agriculture Department subsequently ruled the conventional funding procedure took precedence, killing the Senate initiative.

Whitten won out again in 1988 when the Senate, in the fiscal 1989 Agriculture appropriations bill (HR 4784 — PL 100-460), once more tried to enact an indefinite appropriation for the CCC. He succeeded in reducing the Senate's much higher appropriation for the CCC in the House-Senate conference negotiations on HR 4784. And in doing so, conferees also eliminated the Senate's indefinite funding language.

Thus the CCC's budget remained subject to the vagaries of the farm economy and the weather. Sudden changes in prices or production could drive the costs of farm stocks well beyond expectations, forcing the administration to return to Congress for supplemental funding. The question remained whether Congress would ever choose to abandon CCC supplemental funding, a "must-pass" measure used by urban as well as rural legislators to enact controversial proposals and pet projects that could not win a majority of votes on their own.

the weaker banks in many of the Midwestern states.

Compromises eventually were reached that imposed new loan restructuring and borrowers' rights requirements on the Farmers Home Administration (FmHA), and created a new secondary market that commercial banks and insurance companies could use to pool agricultural loans for sale as tradable securities. The committee rejected all proposals for bond issues or direct appropriations to give the system a financial infusion. Instead of approving a federal bailout, the panel voted to send the politically sensitive decision about money to the Appropriations Committee. The fiscal 1988 budget resolution (H Con Res 93) did not provide for additional funds for farm credit, and constraints imposed by the Gramm-Rudman-Hollings deficit reduction law (PL 99-177) made it difficult to pass legislation increasing the federal deficit. *(1988 budget resolution, p. 58; Gramm-Rudman, p. 44)*

The committee also voted to eliminate the 12 regional boundaries in the banking system and trim the 37-bank network down to no more than seven institutions. In place of the array of credit banks and land banks that distribute funds to local lending associations, the committee favored creation of up to six full-service banks. The 12 regional cooperative banks also would be merged with the Central Bank for Cooperatives. A new federally appointed board would supervise farm bailout money and impose conditions on banks that received it.

**Floor.** The House overwhelmingly passed HR 3030 on Oct. 6. But before the bill was approved a major turf battle developed over the provision to create a secondary market for agricultural loans, which was deemed necessary to win the pivotal support of the banking and insurance industries. Proponents said a secondary market would allow small agricultural banks and insurance companies to greatly expand their ability to make farm real estate loans. The banking industry wanted the secondary market to be given federal sponsorship or agency status to avoid expensive start-up costs.

While the Agriculture panel backed the provision, leading members of committees that would supervise the banking and securities markets were concerned about the implications of the new market. And administration officials contended a secondary market within the Farm Credit System would force the federal government eventually to guarantee commercial lenders' securities. They also worried about the impact a secondary market might have on the credit system's ability to compete with private lenders for good borrowers.

The administration, top House Republicans and some influential Democrats from non-farm districts, including Energy and Commerce Committee Chairman John D. Dingell, D-Mich., and Banking Committee Chairman Fernand J. St Germain, D-R.I., attempted to strip the provision from the bill. Floor action was temporarily suspended while the two committees held hearings on the issue. Eventually a compromise was reached. The provision's language giving brokers an exemption from state and federal securities regulations and anti-fraud laws was dropped. Dingell said Farmer Mac securities should not be exempted because such loans were more volatile than Ginnie Maes and Fannie Maes. Other restrictions also were added.

The Agriculture Committee succeeded in adding an amendment providing a funding scheme to pay for the Farm Credit System bailout. It avoided having to come to Congress for a new appropriation by requiring the FmHA to sell $2.5 billion worth of water and sewer bonds. And the House handily adopted a compromise on credit system reorganization.

## Senate Action

**Committee.** The Senate Agriculture Committee reported its version of the farm credit rescue plan (S 1665 — S Rept 100-230) on Nov. 20.

As in the House, the Senate committee had difficulty reaching a consensus. The administration and farm and banking lobbies all offered different solutions, which prevented the committee from acting quickly. Attempts in April and May to mark up a bill were thwarted. Even farm-state senators themselves were divided. In the interim, the Senate on April 8 tried to stem an exodus of worried borrowers from the system by passing a non-binding resolution (S Res 185) urging the FCA to seek financial assistance if borrower credit conditions worsened.

Most of the work on the bill occurred in the Agricultural Credit Subcommittee, chaired by David L. Boren, D-Okla. It took the subcommittee until Oct. 30 to finish its work. Various senators sponsored bills representing par-

ticular agricultural interests such as the American Farm Bureau Federation and corn, wheat, cotton, cattle and pork producers. In addition to disagreements over how much money was needed for the bailout and how to structure the aid, senators were divided on how to overhaul the highly decentralized credit system. Some Democrats wanted to concentrate on helping farmer-borrowers, while financial interests pressed for a secondary market. The panel's version included provisions to protect and aid farmer-borrowers and facilitate some restructuring of the credit system.

The committee bill included a two-year, $30 million program of matching grants to states that set up mediation procedures for farmers and their creditors. Funding for the bailout would be provided by the issuance of up to $4 billion in 15-year bonds, with Washington paying all the interest for the first five years and half the interest for the next five. The cost to the federal government over the 10-year period was estimated at $1.5 billion. The bill delayed the first interest payment until 1989. The committee agreed to a secondary market for farm mortgage loans but imposed a cap on the amount of federally backed loans that could be sold in the secondary market during the first three years. But members could not agree on what limit to impose.

S 1665 also contained provisions to help borrowers having difficulty repaying FmHA loans. This represented a compromise with the White House by giving the agriculture secretary leeway in treating delinquent borrowers. A final compromise was needed, however, to allow farmers in foreclosure proceedings to use up to $18,000 of their farm income for household and operating expenses.

**Floor.** The Senate passed the farm credit bill (HR 3030) Dec. 4. Before passage, senators exacted a promise from Agriculture Committee leaders that the bailout scheme would not cost the U.S. Treasury a cent in fiscal 1988 and no more than $190 million in fiscal 1989.

Few additional changes were made on the floor. A key budgetary hurdle was cleared when the Office of Management and Budget (OMB), after lengthy negotiations with key Agriculture Committee senators, agreed that the corporation created to administer the funding would not be designated a government entity. But it would be treated as a federally sponsored enterprise having the same legal standing as the Farm Credit System. Thus the new bonds would not be considered federal borrowing, and the distribution of $4 billion in 15-year notes would not be considered budget outlays even though payment would be guaranteed by the Treasury. The only cost to the government came from the requirement that the Treasury pay the interest on the bonds. If the corporation had been designated a government entity, the outlays would have been much higher.

## Conference Action

House-Senate conferees reached agreement (H Rept 100-490) on HR 3030 Dec. 16. After the financing arrangements were approved by OMB, working out a final compromise was much easier. Also spurring final action was an announcement in early December that the Jackson, Miss., Federal Land Bank was close to bankruptcy.

Conferees quickly agreed to the Senate funding mechanism and to a compromise on the rescue and the "borrowers' rights" requirements for the credit system and the FmHA. The House reorganization plan was agreed to with revisions. While the House had required the 37-bank credit system to pare itself down to no more that seven regional lending centers, the final bill opted generally for a reorganization plan suggested by the credit system directors. Once the banks had merged within the 12 districts, system directors would have to allow farmer-borrowers who had controlling shares in the system to vote on whether to merge the districts. Shareholders in the 13 Banks for Cooperatives also would vote on whether to merge into a single national Bank for Cooperatives. The system could end up with as few as six districts and seven banks.

The last hurdle in conference was the secondary market provision. With time running out in the session, the Senate side gave in completely to the House demand to bring the new Farmer Mac loans under strict federal securities regulation.

The House approved the conference report Dec. 18 and the Senate gave its approval Dec. 19, clearing the bill.

## Major Provisions

As signed into law Jan. 6, 1988, HR 3030 (PL 100-233):

### Financial Assistance

● Required the Farm Credit System to establish a new Farm Credit System Assistance Board, replacing the Capital Corporation that was created by Congress in 1985 (PL 99-205), to take over bad loans and supervise financial assistance to system banks. The new assistance board would be overseen by a three-member board of directors: the secretaries of agriculture and Treasury and an agricultural producer with experience in financial matters appointed by the president. The board's authority was set to expire Dec. 31, 1992.

● Empowered the board to authorize financial assistance for troubled system institutions. If certified, an institution would issue preferred stock, which would be purchased by another new entity, the Farm Credit System Assistance Corporation. Troubled institutions were allowed to apply for aid when borrower stock, which made up the bulk of the system's remaining capital reserves, was "impaired," or used to cover the institutions' losses. The assistance board was required to approve assistance when the value of stock dropped to 75 percent or less of par value, unless the institution was to be liquidated.

● Allowed the assistance board to impose conditions on institutions receiving assistance, giving it power over debt issuances, interest rates on loans and business and investment plans. The board was empowered to request the FCA to order the liquidation of an institution.

● Established the financial assistance corporation as a sibling of the Federal Farm Credit Banks Funding Corporation, which raised money for the system on Wall Street, using the same board of directors and employees. The new corporation would create a revolving fund by issuing up to $4 billion in 15-year, uncollateralized bond obligations, with the principal and interest guaranteed by the U.S. Treasury. Up to $2.8 billion in bonds could be issued between the date of enactment and Jan. 1, 1989. Another $1.2 billion could be issued after that date until Sept. 30, 1992, if necessary.

In addition, the corporation would set up a special trust fund to help banks repay the bonds, using the proceeds of a one-time assessment on system institutions. The assessments were to be set at the amount by which each institution's surplus (unallocated retained earnings) exceeded either 5 percent of assets (for district banks) or 13 percent of assets (for local associations).

● Required the U.S. Treasury to pay interest on the guaranteed bonds during the first five years. The payments were to be made in annual installments to the assistance corporation, beginning in fiscal 1989.

During the second five years, interest was to be shared by system institutions and the Treasury. Each institution would have to pay a proportionate share based on performing, or good, loan volume. System institutions were required to pay all the interest in the last five years. The maximum amount of interest to be paid by Treasury without repayment by the system was set at $2 billion.

When the bonds matured, the trust fund would be used to pay part of the principal due. The entire system would be responsible for repaying the rest of the principal. However, the system as a whole would not be responsible for repayment of the principal on the assistance received by a district that voted not to merge with another of the system's 12 districts. Such districts would be solely liable for repayment of assistance they received. System banks would be jointly responsible for repaying the Treasury's interest expenses when they were able to do so without impairing borrower stock or jeopardizing their financial viability.

● Required the assistance corporation to pay out of the trust fund any interest due from a system institution in default. After 15 years, if the assistance corporation determined that a system institution would not be able to pay the 15-year obligations, the Treasury was required to purchase the preferred stock and the defaulting institution would be liable to the Treasury.

● Returned to system institutions the assessments that were ordered previously by the capital corporation. The measure also canceled "third-quarter" loss-sharing agreements among banks, and the assistance corporation was required to make up the difference.

### Borrower Stock Guarantee

● Required Farm Credit System institutions to guarantee their borrowers' stock for five years, so that farmer-borrowers could retire the stock at face value. The guarantee covered borrower stock outstanding on the date of enactment; stock that was frozen or retired for less than par by an association after Jan. 1, 1983; and stock that was purchased either within nine months of enactment or before approval of an institution's new capitalization plan, whichever was earlier.

### Loan Restructuring, Borrowers' Rights

● Required all federal land banks and production credit associations to restructure "distressed" loans if restructuring would cost less than foreclosing on the loan and liquidating the collateral. A loan was distressed when a borrower missed payments or showed evidence that he was undercollateralized or did not have the financial capacity to meet the terms of the loan. Restructuring included action to modify the terms of, or forbear on, a loan that would make it probable that the farm operations of the borrower would become financially viable.

Each system institution certified to receive assistance was required to review each non-accrual loan that had not been restructured, and to determine whether it would be. And each district receiving assistance was required to es-

# Farm Credit System Boomed, Went Bust ...

For most of seven decades, the Farm Credit System enjoyed the reputation of being a government enterprise that worked. This quasi-federal network of banks and lending associations provided cheap loans to family farmers, who were the owners and directors of their own lending cooperatives. Together they paid the government back and even turned a hefty profit.

But the romance began to sour in 1985, when the system reported its first losses since the Depression. A total of $4.8 billion in losses in two years and the prospect of going another $3 billion in debt by 1989 prompted system officials to come to Capitol Hill for help for the third time in three years — this time to the tune of $6 billion.

In addition to sending congressional leaders hunting for ways to shore up the system without increasing the deficit, the issue set off a debate on how to protect the original mission of the system — to help farmers in every region of the country get credit to buy land. These efforts were complicated by the fact that since the system was one of the country's largest banking institutions, its fate touched the financial underpinnings of the entire nation.

In the end, Congress agreed to let the system have up to $4 billion through a complicated bond scheme designed to minimize federal budget outlays. The legislation (HR 3030 — PL 100-233) also restructured the system, created a new secondary market for agricultural loans and included provisions to protect farmers from foreclosure.

## Roots of the System

The Farm Credit System had its genesis at the turn of the century, when farmers experienced difficulty buying good farm land and government officials noted an alarming increase in farm tenancy. Farmers could not get long-term financing to buy land. Most of the money centers were concentrated on the East Coast, and small country banks only offered loans that came due in two to five years.

As farmers' political influence began to build, President Theodore Roosevelt in 1908 created a "Country Life Commission" to study how the government could help farmers obtain credit. The study resulted in a land-bank system, based on a Scandinavian model, that was organized as a borrower-owned cooperative. In 1916, the government provided the start-up money through a special bond issue, and farmer-borrowers were required to buy stock in their local associations to help the system pay off its government loan.

Recapitalized in the 1930s, the system paid off the last of its loans in 1968 and went on to rack up big profits during the following decade. It then fell on hard times, a victim of its own success.

## Boom Followed by Bust

The full weight of a sodden farm economy in the 1980s fell hard on the 37 money centers and 387 local associations that made up the lending network.

The system's gains in the 1970s were based largely on soaring farm-land values — jacked up by export-driven farm prices — and were helped by legislation that liberalized the system's lending powers. A 1971 law (PL 92-181) allowed system banks to make larger loans and to base them on speculative land values, not just agricultural uses. Many banks aggressively marketed bigger loans to farmers. *(Congress and the Nation Vol. III, p. 346)*

The system also found a way to offer relatively low interest rates during a period of high inflation. Unlike commercial banks, Farm Credit System institutions did not take deposits. They raised capital by selling bonds and discount notes on corporate securities markets. During the 1970s, as interest rates on new bond issues were rising, system banks were able to charge farmers far lower rates than commercial lenders. They could base their interest rates not on their most recent issues, but on the average cost of all their outstanding debts — dominated by the lower interest rates of the previous decade.

But when inflation and interest rates dropped in the 1980s, the system was caught by its own gambit. Commercial banks could significantly undercut system banks, whose outstanding bond obligations were gradually being dominated by higher-priced issues.

At the same time, export prices for farm products tumbled and farm-land values followed suit. Farmers holding mortgages with system banks increasingly were unable to meet their payments, and if the banks foreclosed the value of the land would not cover the mortgages.

As a result, the system found itself holding a bundle of bad debts. Nearly one-fourth of the system's $55 billion loan portfolio in 1987 consisted of questionable-to-failing loans. Borrowers were required to purchase stock when they took out loans; many of the most credit-worthy borrowers, fearful that their stock would be used to cover the system's losses, began paying off their loans and turning to commercial lenders.

A number of system lenders were left with such negligible assets that 11 major system institutions were threatened with bankruptcy. The 26 still-profitable banks were responsible for the debts of the others, fomenting divisions within the system.

In 1985 and 1986, Congress moved to shore up the system without spending any hard cash. A 1985 measure (PL 99-205) significantly restructured the system, set up a program for loss-sharing among the districts and strengthened the Farm Credit Adminis-

# ... Leaving Congress With a Complex Issue

tration, the federal regulatory agency in charge of overseeing the system's operations. The bill also authorized direct financial assistance but required the system to apply for it through a separate appropriation. *(Story, p. 514)*

In 1986, when it appeared assistance might be necessary for some banks, Congress used an omnibus deficit reduction bill (PL 99-509) to loosen accounting requirements to let system banks stretch out some losses over 20 years. *(Story, p. 514)*

## Loose Confederation

The Farm Credit "system" was actually a confederation of regional money centers and local lending associations, without a central decision-making authority. It was divided into 12 regions of the country. Each district contained a self-supporting federal land bank for real estate loans and a self-supporting federal intermediate credit bank for shorter-term production loans, plus a bank for cooperatives. There was also a Central Bank for Cooperatives.

Real estate and operating loans were made to farmers through local land bank associations and production credit associations run by farmers.

This decentralized structure was a fiercely protected feature, since each lending association and each bank could control its own destiny. But it also bred suspicion and turmoil among different institutions, largely along regional lines.

## Wall Street, Farmers Lobby Hard

Two major political forces combined to put pressure on Congress to save the system: the farmer-borrowers and the financial investors.

The cooperative nature of the system was its most meaningful characteristic. The system affected nearly every agricultural producer in the country and financed every type of agricultural product through loans for land, equipment, seed and feed. Each of the local lending associations was organized as a cooperative of farmer-borrowers, which elected its own board of directors and formed a ready-made political network of farmers and ranchers who could get in touch with representatives in Congress.

Wall Street, where the system raised its cash, provided a political force with equal power. Urban members of Congress became concerned about the system's financial health because its collapse could be felt in other financial markets. System bonds were technically backed only by the system's assets — that is, the land farmers used as collateral. But investors bought them on the assumption that they were guaranteed by the U.S. Treasury. This implied federal guarantee gave the system a status on Wall Street that came close to matching that of a government agency. This so-called "agency status" allowed the system to sell its bonds at much lower interest rates than bonds issued by private corporations.

If a system bank were to declare bankruptcy and the federal government did not step in to guarantee the outstanding debt, it could impair investor confidence in other agency status bonds, such as the Federal National Mortgage Association (Fannie Mae) — and perhaps even U.S. Treasury bonds, since some foreign investors did not differentiate between implied and explicit federal guarantees.

## Banks Pressed for 'Farmer Mac'

Another political force was the banks and insurance companies that were the system's competitors. In return for supporting a bailout, they demanded a "secondary market" for agricultural loans that would be patterned after the three cousins that dominated the home loan business: Fannie Mae, Freddie Mac (Federal Home Loan Mortgage Corporation) and Ginnie Mae (Government National Mortgage Association). The proposed new secondary market was quickly dubbed "Farmer Mac."

In its simplest form, a secondary-market transaction occurred when a group of loans were packaged and sold by the original lender to someone else who collected future payments on them. The financial community perceived that securities sold through Fannie Mae and Freddie Mac were almost as good as if they were directly backed by the government. Thus they were said to have agency status, although such implicit guarantees had never been tested.

A secondary market for farm loans would enable private lenders to diversify their risk by pooling loans of varying geographic location and commodity type. They also could get their money back quickly by selling loans instead of waiting for payments to trickle in over years and years.

## Pressure to Help Farmers Directly

Some farm-state Democrats wanted to broaden the "institutional" aspects of the bailout to include aid that would benefit farmers directly. For example, they demanded specific forbearance requirements to stall foreclosures by the system and by the Farmers Home Administration, the government agency designed to lend money to farmers who could not get credit from private lenders. But that ran counter to the position of the Reagan administration.

Instead of a direct or indirect cash infusion, the Reagan administration favored steps that would let the stronger banks move into the areas of the weaker ones, eventually taking over their territory.

tablish a special asset group to review each determination of an institution against restructuring and, if necessary, to overrule that decision. The assistance board was required to create a national special asset council to monitor and regulate compliance with restructuring standards.

● Required system banks to send statements of their restructuring policies to borrowers. At least 75 days prior to giving notice of foreclosure, the lender was required to again give the borrower notice of his right to have restructuring considered as an alternative. Whenever a loan became delinquent, the lender was required to notify the borrower of the restructuring option and to facilitate the drafting of restructuring proposals by the borrower. The lender was required to meet with the borrower personally and to consider, in reviewing the loan, the borrower's proposals for restructure.

● Retained the right of a system lender and the assistance corporation to foreclose if they had reasonable grounds to believe that, due to future actions of the borrower, the collateral would be dissipated or diverted.

● Required borrowers whose loans were restructured to forfeit the same dollar amount of stock that was written off by the lender. The borrower could retain one share of stock to maintain voting interest in the institution.

● Required each system lender and the assistance corporation to develop a "right of first refusal" policy for the disposition and leasing of acquired agricultural real estate to the previous owner. Also, upon foreclosure, borrower bankruptcy or liquidation, the lender was encouraged to make arrangements that would still allow the borrower to retain possession of the residence and a reasonable amount of adjoining land.

● Established federal matching grants for states that created mediation programs for farmers and their lenders. The programs could receive up to 50 percent federal funding, not exceeding $500,000 a year per state. The bill authorized appropriations of $7.5 million a year through 1991.

### Farmers Home Administration

● Required the agriculture secretary to establish a program to modify delinquent FmHA loans to the maximum extent possible to avoid losses to the government, placing emphasis on writing down principal and interest and on debt set-aside, whenever this would help keep a borrower on the property.

● Required the secretary of agriculture to provide notice of all available loan-service programs to each FmHA borrower who was 180 days delinquent on an FmHA loan, before taking any adverse foreclosure action against the borrower.

● Gave priority for purchasing or leasing farm land acquired by the FmHA through foreclosure to the previous owner or his spouse or child, to a buyer actively engaged in farming, to operators of family-sized farms and to Indian tribes (if the farm was on reservation lands or Indian allotments).

● Required the agriculture secretary to release income for household and operating expenses (not to exceed $18,000 per borrower) to an active farmer who applied for loan restructuring, if the borrower was required to accelerate payments between Nov. 1, 1985, and May 7, 1987.

● Established a demonstration program using loan authority from an interest-subsidy program to allow FmHA-eligible borrowers to buy up to $250 million worth of system-owned land. Farmers were given a 4 percent interest discount.

### System Reorganization

● Required the federal land bank and the federal intermediate credit bank in each of the system's 12 districts to merge within six months after the enactment of the bill.

● Required farmer-stockholders of each production credit association and federal land bank association in a district to vote, within six months after the merger of district banks, whether to merge those local associations.

● Required the voting stockholders in the existing 12 districts to vote on reorganizing the system's district structure to allow for no fewer than six districts. The plan was to be developed within one year of enactment by a special committee composed of one representative from each district. The FCA and the assistance board would have to approve the committee's plan before the vote.

● Required stockholders of the 12 district banks for cooperatives and the Central Bank for Cooperatives to vote within six months of enactment on a plan of merger into a National Bank for Cooperatives. Approval would take a majority of cooperatives, weighted by loan volume, and a majority of individual banks. If eight or more, but not all, Banks for Cooperatives voted to merge into a national bank, each bank would be given an exception to current territorial service limitations on doing business outside its district.

● Allowed an institution to terminate its status as a system institution if it received an appropriate federal or state charter as a bank, savings and loan or other financial institution; if it got the approval of shareholders and the FCA board; and if it paid to the system's new reserve account the amount by which total capital exceeded 6 percent of assets.

● Authorized the breakup of previously merged institutions, subject to stockholder approval.

● Authorized banks for cooperatives to lend to subsidiaries of cooperative borrowers, and removed the existing statutory sunset date of 1990 for the authority for banks for cooperatives to finance agricultural exports and for federal intermediate credit banks to provide access to funds to other financing institutions.

● Maintained existing permission for land banks to make loans up to 85 percent of the appraised market value of the land used as collateral.

But the FCA was authorized to require, by regulation, that loans not exceed 75 percent of the appraised value.

● Required each board within the system districts to appoint two new voting members who were not borrowers or employees of the system, and who had not been associated with the system for two years, but who possessed knowledge and experience in agricultural finance.

● Gave the FCA power to assess civil penalties of up to $500 a day for violations by system officers and directors, similar to powers given to other regulators of financial institutions.

### Capitalization

● Required the FCA to establish minimum permanent-capital adequacy standards, to be phased in over five years, for all system institutions. The standards were to include fixed percentages representing the ratio of permanent capital to an institution's assets, similar to standards imposed on commercial banks.

● Required each system institution's board of directors to develop new bylaws for the capitalization of the system that would allow banks to build up capital while discouraging credit-worthy borrowers from abandoning the system. Under these plans, permanent capital was defined as allocated and unallocated earnings, all surpluses (less allowances for losses) and stock other than stock that could be retired by the holder on repayment of a loan or that was protected under the borrower stock-guarantee provisions of the bill.

System institutions were prohibited from issuing stock that could be retired by the holder when he repaid a loan. System banks and local associations would have to set up a capital structure providing for classes of stock and loan-origination fees. Voting stock would have to cost at least $1,000 or 2 percent of the amount of the loan, whichever was less. Prior to HR 3030, borrowers were required to purchase stock equal to 5-10 percent of the loan but paid no origination fees.

Banks were required to issue voting stock to borrowers who were farmers, ranchers or farm cooperative associations. Institutions also could issue non-voting stock to non-borrowers. The stock could be sold or transferred. Voting stock would be converted to non-voting stock two years after a loan was repaid.

● Prohibited system institutions from reducing permanent capital through the payment of dividends or from retiring stock or allocated equities, as long as the permanent capital of the institution failed to meet the minimum standards. Some exceptions were allowed for an institution that was exempt from federal income tax, and for an institution subject to income tax that paid dividends in cash to qualify for tax deductions.

## Bond Insurance

● Established a Farm Credit System Insurance Corporation to insure bonds, notes, debentures and other obligations issued by system banks through the Federal Farm Credit Banks Funding Corporation. The insurance corporation was to be chartered by the FCA and would operate much the way the Federal Deposit Insurance Corporation (FDIC) did.

● Established a three-member board of directors for the new insurance corporation, consisting of the board members of the FCA, with a different chairman.

● Required each system bank to have insurance as a condition for retaining its charter. The reserve fund for the insurance corporation would equal 2 percent of outstanding system bonds. The fund's start-up capital would come from the FCA's revolving fund (about $260 million), and each system bank, beginning in January 1990, was to be assessed an annual premium of 0.15 percent of accruing loans and 0.25 percent of non-accruing loans, which would be the maximum premium rates once the fund was fully capitalized. The reserve would be used as needed in the future to provide assistance to system institutions to enable them to honor their bond obligations and to ensure retirement of borrower stock at par value.

Insurance coverage became available after five years. As a backstop to the new insurance program, system banks would retain "joint and several liability" for system obligations, which could be invoked by the FCA as needed if the insurance fund were exhausted by a future crisis.

● Gave the FCA powers to liquidate or effect a merger of failing system institutions, or provide financial assistance to the institution if that were the least-cost alternative. These powers were similar to those given to the FDIC.

## Secondary Market

● Created a secondary market for agricultural real estate and certain rural housing loans, establishing a Federal Agricultural Mortgage Corporation (Farmer Mac) within the Farm Credit System. System land banks and other commercial farm lenders could package their agricultural real estate loans for resale to investors as tradable, interest-bearing securities. The mortgage corporation would have a 15-member board, consisting of five members from the system, five from commercial banks and insurance companies and five appointed by the president with the consent of the Senate. The corporation itself could purchase or sell securities for investment purposes but could not originate or pool loans. It would set underwriting standards, determine the eligibility of pooling firms and provide repayment guarantees for approved pools.

● Allowed system institutions to qualify as pooling firms, with authority to originate, underwrite and service loans in the secondary market.

● Limited any one agricultural real estate loan in a guaranteed pool to no more than $2.5 million, or 1,000 acres, whichever was greater. In no case could any loan be included if it exceeded 3.5 percent of the total amount in the pool, or if it was in excess of 80 percent of the agricultural value of the land. Each guaranteed pool would have to have at least 50 loans, spread among various commodities and over a wide geographical area.

● Limited rural housing loans that could be sold in the secondary market to those on single-family residences of less than $100,000 in communities with less than 2,500 population.

● Required each pooling firm to maintain a reserve, equal to 10 percent of the unpaid balance of each loan in a pool, to qualify for repayment guarantees. The lenders and pooling firm shared responsibility for the reserve.

● Required the mortgage corporation to guarantee to investors that they would receive timely payments of principal and interest on the securities. The mortgage corporation would create a special reserve for this purpose, assessing each pooling firm a fee of up to 0.5 percent of the face value of each loan in the first year, and not more than 0.25 percent annually thereafter.

● Required the Treasury to underwrite (lend) the mortgage corporation up to $1.5 billion, subject to appropriations, to cover loan losses that exceeded the poolers' reserves and the corporation's reserve.

● Limited the amount of commercial loan pools that could receive repayment guarantees in the first year of operation to no more than 2 percent of all outstanding commercial and Farm Credit System agricultural real estate debt; no more than 4 percent in the second year; and no more than 8 percent in the third year. Farm Credit System loans were excluded from these percentage limitations.

● Specified that guaranteed securities in the secondary market would not be treated as government securities, which were exempt from regulation by the Securities and Exchange Commission (SEC). Thus, Farmer Mac securities would come under SEC regulations. The secretary of the Treasury was directed to report to Congress within six months if this caused the sale price of Farmer Mac securities to exceed comparable government-guaranteed securities by 0.25 percent. Furthermore, banks would be allowed no new authority for underwriting Farmer Mac securities. Individual states were given eight years to impose registration or qualification standards, at which time state regulations would be pre-empted.

● Authorized lenders who participated in the FmHA 90 percent guaranteed loan program for farm real estate loans to pool the guaranteed portion of the loans for sale on a separate secondary market. The agriculture secretary would administer and regulate the market and the U.S. Treasury would provide the underlying guarantee on repayment of pool certificates.

### Farm Credit Correction

Congress in 1988 was forced to revisit the Agriculture Credit Act to restore a provision that had inadvertently been omitted from the final version of PL 100-233. The House Feb. 23 and the Senate Aug. 3 passed a bill (HR 3980 — PL 100-399) restoring language that exempted mergers of Farm Credit System institutions from state transfer taxes. The provision was especially important to California institutions, which would have been subject to stiff taxes as a result of mergers.

## Farm Program Funding Changes

During the 1987 session, Congress made relatively minor changes in federal funding of farm programs, resisting attempts at wholesale revision of the basic agriculture law enacted in 1985.

As part of the fiscal 1988 reconciliation bill (HR 3545 — PL 100-203), Congress agreed to a package of cost-saving farm program adjustments, drafted by House and Senate Agriculture committee leaders, designed to cut agriculture spending by $969 million in fiscal 1988 and $1.497 billion in fiscal 1989. This was slightly more than the $2.5 billion in two-year savings that had been agreed to by congressional leaders and the Reagan administration at meetings held to reduce the federal budget deficit. *(Reconciliation, p. 61)*

The farm adjustments included moderate cuts in target prices for major commodities, although Congress did not adhere to the administration's interpretation that target prices were to be cut by an additional 2 percent a year beyond previously agreed upon reductions for fiscal 1988-89. Instead, these prices, which determined farmers' income subsidies, were reduced by only an additional 1.4 percent, which translated into cuts estimated at $207 million in fiscal 1988 and $489 million in 1989.

The farm provisions in HR 3545 also limited the reductions that could be made in rates for crop loans, which determined the price at which the federal government bought up surplus commodities. The existing farm law allowed the Agriculture Department to reduce loan rates by 5 percent a year. Under HR 3545, reductions in loan rates for 1988 crops were limited to 3 percent. But the agriculture secretary was given discretion to make up the difference by further lowering loan rates.

Additional budget savings in farm programs focused on various schemes to pay farmers for not growing their crops. Some $425 million in savings for fiscal 1989 were expected through an optional diversion program under which wheat and feed grain farmers who did not plant any

of their crops would still receive 92 percent of their usual income subsidies. *(Farm disaster assistance, below)*

## 1987 Disaster Relief

Congress in 1987 passed a limited farm disaster relief bill (HR 1157 — PL 100-45) that expanded farmer eligibility for the government's existing disaster assistance program, enacted in 1986. The 1986 law (H J Res 738 — PL 99-591) had provided $400 million in disaster assistance. *(1986 bill, p. 518)*

Disaster assistance was extended to Midwestern winter wheat growers and some other farmers who had not been eligible for aid under the earlier law. The Agriculture Department estimated that approximately 3 million acres of winter wheat had not been planted in 1986 because of flooded farm land. That wheat crop would have been harvested in 1987.

PL 100-45 authorized an additional $135 million for the expanded aid coverage. The new measure also extended the deadline for applying for farm disaster relief.

The disaster relief funding authorized by PL 100-45 subsequently was provided by Congress in a supplemental appropriations bill (PL 100-71).

### Legislative History

The Senate Agriculture Committee reported a disaster relief bill (S 341) on Jan. 29, and the Senate quickly passed the bill the same day without opposition. The Senate version merely expanded disaster relief eligibility as it had been defined in H J Res 738. The bill's sponsors decided not to press for an increase in farm disaster funding beyond the level set in the 1986 law.

The Senate-passed bill ran into opposition in the House Agriculture Committee, which insisted the $400 million in disaster relief already authorized by law was inadequate to cover all eligible farmers. On March 16 it reported an entirely new bill (HR 1157 — H Rept 100-25) that expanded relief coverage to include the wheat growers in the Senate bill as well as certain feed grain producers who also were prevented by 1986 floods from planting their crops.

The bill incorporated a new policy giving growers of winter wheat and feed grain producers the option of taking 92 percent of their normal price-support subsidies if they agreed not to plant a different crop in 1987. This "0-92" policy was a variation of a plan proposed by the Reagan administration and farm-state lawmakers to "decouple" the farm income-support subsidy program from farmers' planting decisions for major farm crops. The 0-92 scheme had been included in the administration's fiscal 1988 budget, which proposed to give all wheat and corn farmers the option of getting their income subsidies without planting any acres in these crops. The 1985 farm law (PL 99-198) had provided a "50-92" scheme for farmers of price-support crops who planted 50 percent of their normal acreage. *(1985 farm bill, p. 501)*

It was the White House's position that overproduction, which led to the huge farm surpluses, was encouraged by existing rules that based a farmer's subsidies on the quantity of grain he produced. By decoupling federal payments from planting decisions, administration officials believed that farmers would be free to limit their production to what they thought they could sell on the open market.

The House passed HR 1157 on March 17.

The Senate passed HR 1157 on April 23 with relatively minor amendments. The Senate insisted that the House's 0-92 program be limited to disaster relief, and it resisted all attempts to broaden the scope of the bill. An amendment that would waive Senate budget restrictions and incorporate a new, and expensive, price-support mechanism for soybean farmers was rejected decisively on a **key vote of 33-63 (R 18-25; D 15-38)**. *(1987 key votes, p. 965)*

A House-Senate conference committee quickly approved a compromise on May 12 (H Rept 100-91). Most of the Senate-passed amendments were approved, including provisions expanding the bill's eligibility to farmers of crops other than winter wheat and a discretionary price-support program for sunflower growers.

The Senate gave final approval to the conference report on May 12 and the House on May 13, clearing the Farm Disaster Assistance Act of 1987 for the president.

# 1988 Disaster Relief

Congress in 1988 approved a comprehensive emergency relief assistance bill for American farmers who suffered major financial losses from a disastrous summer drought. Much of the U.S. Corn Belt had withered under a drought considered worse than the Dust Bowl of the 1930s.

The legislation (HR 5015 — PL 100-387) granted drought relief aid to farmers who had lost at least 35 percent of any crop. Also eligible for federal assistance under certain conditions were ranchers and other livestock producers. Many livestock producers had sent their herds to slaughter prematurely because it became too expensive to feed them.

The bill proved to be a boon to members seeking reelection in November 1988. HR 5015 reached many farmers. As of mid-July 1988, 2,110 counties in 41 states had been declared eligible for some form of disaster relief. Speaker Jim Wright, D-Texas, said the bill had been drafted in a bipartisan manner, that drought was "non-respective of political affiliations."

The cost of the bill initially was set by the Agriculture Department (USDA) at $3.9 billion. But after the bill was cleared congressional estimates based on updated drought damage reports raised the price tag to $5.1 billion. The cost to the government was not as high as that figure implied, however. Because of the widespread drought, some of the money Congress had appropriated for farm deficiency payments — payments that made up the difference between congressionally mandated target prices and the prices farmers actually received for their crops — was not needed. This was because falling supplies of farm crops translated into higher demand and thus higher prices. Thus there was less of a gap, or deficiency, for the government to make up. The Agriculture Department was able to use much of the appropriation set aside for these deficiency payments, amounting to about $10 billion in 1988, for drought relief.

PL 100-387 was the third drought relief measure approved by Congress in as many years. Major, though less severe, droughts and other natural disasters had cut farm production in 1983 and 1986, and in both cases Congress had passed limited relief legislation. *(1983 drought, Congress and the Nation Vol. VI, p. 507; 1986 legislation, p. 518; 1987 legislation, above)*

Before HR 5015 was cleared, Congress eliminated a costly Senate-passed provision that would aid drought-affected livestock owners who did not grow their own feed grain. Elimination of that provision reduced the bill's cost by $2 billion.

The 1988 farm relief bill also contained a feature not in earlier disaster relief legislation: language assuring that all farm producers were treated equitably. Congress in the past had fashioned drought relief aimed at assisting only growers of crops that were covered by the government's price- and income-support programs. These crops consisted chiefly of wheat, feed grains, cotton, rice, soybeans, peanuts, sugar, tobacco and dairy products. PL 100-387, on the other hand, covered producers of fruits and vegetables as well as the major farm crops.

## Legislative History

**Committee Action.** The Senate and House Agriculture committees considered farm disaster relief measures in July 1988, just before the Democratic National Convention. Both panels tried, but with only limited success, to keep drought relief free from costly special-interest amendments. When farm bills were considered there always was the risk that major changes would be proposed in the basic federal farm law. The committees' leaders warned that drought relief would lose the support of urban legislators if it was loaded down with non-drought aid and additional farm benefits. The Senate Agriculture Committee reported its version of the bill (S 2631 — S Rept 100-426) July 25. House Agriculture reported HR 5015 (H Rept 100-800, Part I) July 27.

The Senate Agriculture Committee succeeded in fending off dozens of special-interest amendments. Nevertheless the bill as reported contained new provisions for soybean, dairy and ethanol producers.

Despite calls for equitable treatment for all farmers, members of the Senate panel complained that various drought relief formulas favored producers of one major crop over another. And a regional fight developed over a non-drought issue: a proposal to establish a new federal program allowing additional plantings of soybean and sunflowers. Over objections of members from the Midwest, Southerners on the committee succeeded in winning adoption of the plan on an experimental basis, along with a new marketing-loan program. Under a marketing loan, farmers were allowed to take out crop loans from the government at one rate and then repay the government only as much as the crop brought at the market.

The panel's ethanol provision, sponsored by two Corn Belt members, granted the ethanol industry additional federal aid in the form of cheap surplus corn.

The House Agriculture Committee approved a controversial provision pushed by the dairy industry and by Vermont and Upper Midwest lawmakers to increase the federal price-support payments to dairy farmers by 50 cents per hundredweight. This provision was in addition to language contained in both House and Senate versions canceling a 50-cent price-support cut mandated by the 1985 omnibus farm bill that was scheduled to take effect in January 1989. *(Farm bill, p. 501)*

The House panel added language to require farmers who received drought aid to purchase federal crop insurance. The committee also approved a soybean marketing-loan program and a provision providing for the shipment of cheap water to Western farmlands.

**Floor Action.** Both the House and Senate gave overwhelming approval to drought relief legislation. The House passed HR 5015 July 28 on a 368-29 vote. The Senate, acting the same day, approved S 2631 unanimously, 94-0. HR 5015 as amended passed the Senate July 29 by voice vote. The House-passed version had an estimated price tag of $5.8 billion, the Senate's $6.6 billion. The key disaster relief provisions of both versions were similar. They provided payments to farmers who suffered at least a 35 percent loss in production. The payment rate was 65 percent of the pre-drought expected production. Additional payments were allowed to farmers who suffered near total crop losses. Both versions prohibited any payments to farmers whose gross income in 1988 was more than $2 million, and the bills placed a $100,000 cap on the amount paid to any one farmer.

Before passing its version, the House debated and amended the controversial dairy price-support provision approved in committee. Many members complained that the proposed price-support increase violated the spirit of the 1985 farm bill, which called for the gradual lowering of federal price supports for most subsidized commodities. It also offended members who felt such a change would give an edge to one segment of the agriculture community over another. This was the argument of cattlemen, in particular, who competed for the same feed supplies as dairy farmers. And higher dairy prices would result in larger herds, they said, which eventually would depress meat prices as the dairy herds were sent to slaughter. Consumer groups argued against the change on the ground it would lead to higher retail milk prices.

The combined opposition to the amendment, with the threat that it might be dropped altogether, prompted proponents to accept a compromise that allowed the 50-cent increase but only for the period from April through June 1989, when dairy farmers would be hardest hit by drought-related high feed costs.

The House also adopted a drought-related amendment providing assistance to migrant farm workers whose jobs were threatened by the drought.

Amendments were adopted in both chambers to provide additional compensation for the hardest hit farmers in the Midwest — those who lost all or nearly all of their crops. Few of these farmers had crop insurance.

**Conference Action.** A compromise resolving the difference between House and Senate versions of HR 5015 was quickly reached by a conference committee. A conference report (H Rept 100-830) was filed Aug. 8.

Conferees tried to provide drought relief to as many farmers and agriculture-related interests as possible while keeping the cost of the aid package low enough to make it acceptable to President Reagan. As agreed to, the bill provided assistance estimated at $3.9 billion, almost $2 billion less than the House bill and $2.7 billion less than the Senate version.

The most controversial section of the legislation that had to be negotiated was livestock feed compensation. While both versions provided for compensation to livestock owners who grew their own animal feed, the Senate bill went further by allowing compensation to livestock owners who bought their feed instead of growing their own. Agriculture Secretary Richard E. Lyng termed this the most objectionable provision in the bill, and the administration opposed various attempts at compromise. Eventually the Senate side gave in and dropped the provision.

The key compromises worked out by House and Senate conferees were:

● **Dairy Price Supports.** The House won this fight when the Senate went along with the House-passed amendment to increase price supports for milk by 50 cents per hundredweight for a three-month period beginning April 1, 1989. Both chambers were in agreement on a provision to eliminate a 50-cent price-support cut that was scheduled for January 1989.

● **Crop Insurance.** The House wanted to require farmers to purchase crop insurance for 1989 and 1990 if they received disaster payments or other benefits from HR 5015. The Senate-passed bill had no such requirement. The compromise required insurance for only one year, and it could be waived by local Agriculture Department offices. In addition, the insurance requirement would apply only to producers who lost more than 65 percent of their normal yield due to the drought.

● **Ethanol Producers.** The Senate-passed bill would have provided aid to ethanol producers by allowing them to purchase cheaper government-owned corn. The House had no such provision. The agreement reduced the amount of corn to be made available, from 16 million bushels to 12 million, and it excluded producers that used more than 30 million bushels a year. Most importantly, the program would be instituted at the administration's discretion.

● **Breadth of Relief.** The Senate bill limited relief to those suffering losses from drought or related conditions. The House wanted to provide coverage to drought, hail, flood or natural disasters. The compromise covered "drought, hail, excessive moisture or related conditions," but not if they occurred in 1987, as some House members wanted.

## Major Provisions

As signed into the law, HR 5015 (PL 100-387):

● **Disaster Payments.** Provided payments to producers of commercial crops who lost at least 35 percent of their 1988 crop due to drought, hail, excessive moisture or related conditions.

● Provided payments for wheat, feed grains, cotton and rice program participants at a rate of 65 percent of the 1988 price-support level.

● Provided payments for peanuts, sugar beets, sugar cane and tobacco producers at a rate of 65 percent of the 1988 price-support level.

● Provided payments for soybeans and other non-program crop producers at a rate of 65 percent of the average producer market price over the last five years.

● Provided additional direct payments to those who suffered crop losses in excess of 75 percent. The payments would equal 25 percent of the applicable target price, price-support level or five-year average market price. Target prices (so-called "ideal" prices for individual commodities) were set by Congress.

● **Insurance Coverage.** Required those who elected to receive disaster payments and who suffered more than 65 percent crop losses to purchase the minimum amount of federal crop insurance for the 1989 crop year. The requirement did not apply if insurance premiums exceeded 25 percent of the benefits received under the disaster program, or if the premiums increased more than 25 percent between 1988 and 1989. Farmers could appeal to local Agriculture Department offices to waive the requirement if they could demonstrate that the requirement would create undue hardship.

● Limited combined crop-insurance benefits and disaster payments to an amount that did not exceed income that would result from normal crop yields.

● **Minimum Yields.** Permitted USDA to establish a minimum yield for each crop eligible for disaster payments in order to reduce farmer incentives to abandon crops to receive larger disaster payments.

● **Advance Deficiency Payments.** Excused producers from repaying advance deficiency payments on portions of crops that failed or could not be planted due to adverse weather, unless that portion of the crop received a disaster payment. For portions of crops for which a disaster payment was received, producers would not have to make a repayment before July 31, 1989.

● **Feed Assistance.** Established a new program, effective 15 days after enactment, for livestock producers who lost feed crops they grew on their farms. The new program included government donations of feed, hay and forage, emergency water assistance and livestock-transportation assistance.

● Specified that eligible livestock included cattle, sheep, goats, swine, poultry, fish for food, and horses and mules used for food or food production.

● **Emergency Forage.** Directed USDA to conduct a limited emergency forage program for pastures damaged by drought, with USDA paying for half the cost of seeding and fertilizing certain forage crops to facilitate grazing and haying in late fall of 1988 and early spring of 1989.

● **Livestock Producers.** Capped benefits at $50,000 in federal feed assistance and prohibited payments to those producers with gross revenues of more than $2.5 million a year.

● **Combined Payments.** Capped payments to any one agricultural producer at $100,000, including livestock assistance.

● **Food Stamp Benefits.** Provided that food stamp benefits to migrant and seasonal farm-worker families not be reduced because of the receipt of emergency assistance.

● Allowed such workers a 30-day grace period to submit documentation for food stamp recertification without loss of benefits. *(Food stamps, p. 607)*

● **Job Training.** Transferred $5 million from the disaster relief program of the Federal Emergency Management Agency to fund farm-worker programs under the Job Training Partnership Act.

● **Loan Guarantees.** Extended Farmers Home Administration (FmHA) loan guarantees to help producers who had borrowed from the Farm Credit System or other commercial lenders and could not repay all or part of their 1988 operating loans or scheduled installments on farm ownership, farm equipment or farm structures loans.

● **Forbearance and Loan Restructuring.** Encouraged USDA to aid producers affected by disaster by exercising forbearance on the collection of loan proceeds, restructuring credit and encouraging commercial lenders to exercise forbearance before declaring loans in default.

● **Emergency Loans.** Authorized USDA to provide emergency loans for producers whose crops were affected by disasters in 1988, whether or not the producer had previously purchased federal crop insurance.

● **Operating Loans.** Directed USDA to take steps to assist businesses affected by the drought by making operating loans available for 1989.

● **Soybeans and Sunflowers.** Permitted producers to plant soybeans and sunflowers on not less than 10 percent, or more than 25 percent, of their acreage for wheat, feed grain, upland cotton or rice in 1989 without affecting their base acres eligible for federal assistance under those pro-

grams. USDA had discretion to extend this program through 1990.

● **Oats.** Allowed producers, under certain conditions, to plant any portion of their farm acreage base with oats in 1989 and 1990.

● **Water Supplies.** Authorized the Interior Department to sell farmers and other water-users in 17 states west of the Mississippi River available supplies of water to help alleviate drought damage.

● **Emergency Loans.** Established an emergency loan program within the Interior Department to provide funds for management, conservation, acquisition and transportation of water and to help pay increased pumping costs resulting from the drought.

● **Spending Cap.** Authorized a maximum of $25 million for both the loan program and emergency actions by the Interior Department.

● **Loan Guarantees.** Directed USDA to establish a new program to guarantee loans to rural businesses and organizations to assist them in dealing with drought-caused losses. Guarantees could not exceed a total of $200 million, and no individual could receive a loan greater than $500,000.

● **Drought Survey.** Directed USDA to conduct a survey of agribusinesses affected by the drought.

● **Dairy Price Supports.** Directed USDA to increase temporarily the price support for milk by 50 cents per hundredweight, effective April 1, 1989, through June 30, 1989. Deleted the 50-cents-per-hundredweight price-support cut scheduled to begin Jan. 1, 1989.

● **Assistance to Ethanol Producers.** Permitted USDA to sell corn held in government reserves at reduced prices to ethanol producers. The maximum amount of corn to be made available for sale was limited to 12 million bushels per month. Furthermore, the sale was limited to ethanol producers who used no more than 30 million bushels of corn per year.

● **Forestry Assistance.** Directed USDA to pay for 65 percent of the costs of replanting tree seedlings that produced an annual crop or were grown for commercial harvest. Benefits were limited to tree farmers and commercial growers who owned 1,000 acres or fewer and who planted within the last two years. Assistance was capped at $25,000 per person.

● **Tobacco Quotas.** Allowed USDA to adjust burley tobacco producers' quotas for 1989. The adjustment could not exceed 125 percent of the producers' basic quotas.

# Trade Bill Provisions

In the omnibus trade bill cleared in 1988, Congress incorporated provisions broadening several government programs to boost U.S. farm exports.

The core of the Trade and International Economic Policy Reform Act (HR 4848 — PL 100-418) focused on unfair foreign trade practices and U.S. government relief for domestic industries significantly hurt by imports. But the massive bill was not concerned only with the traditional foreign trade issues of import relief, tariffs and quotas but also with foreign policy and defense considerations as well as Third World debt, foreign business practices and U.S. agriculture policy. *(Trade bill, p. 148)*

The trade legislation, which was debated by Congress for three years and vetoed by President Reagan in its first version (HR 3), dealt with agricultural issues on two broad fronts: export incentive programs and new marketing loans for major U.S. crops if international trade negotiations failed to make progress toward reducing or eliminating foreign government agriculture subsidies.

## Legislative History

**House Action.** The House Agriculture, Merchant Marine and Fisheries, and Small Business committees contributed to the agriculture provisions of the omnibus trade bill. All three approved measures to enhance exports of U.S. farm products and crack down on unfair foreign trading practices.

The major initiatives were added by the Agriculture Committee. It approved a provision to extend a program that used government-owned grain as subsidies for farm exports. But the panel backed away from language forcing the Reagan administration to greatly expand the program. Under the export enhancement program (EEP), created in 1985 as part of the omnibus farm bill (PL 99-198), the Agriculture Department was mandated, over a three-year period, to distribute at no charge to farm exporters $1 billion worth of government-owned surplus commodities, plus an additional $500 million worth at the agriculture secretary's discretion. This was to be used as an incentive for farm exporters to lower the price of their commodities. *(1985 farm bill, p. 501)*

In the first two years following enactment of PL 99-198, the Agriculture Department had used the surplus commodities to fashion U.S. sales to about 40 countries where the United States had lost market share to the 12-nation European Economic Community (EEC).

The Agriculture Committee amended the EEP sales provision of the 1985 farm bill by increasing to $2.5 billion the amount of surplus commodities to be used in the export promotion program and extending it through fiscal 1990. Another change set the price of the surplus commodities at prevailing market levels, instead of at the rate in effect at the time the government first took possession. Current market prices were well below the book value of most government-owned commodities, so more could be disbursed if released at market rates.

The committee also approved a series of new import quotas on lamb, milk protein products (casein) and any other items that contained at least 25 percent of products already under import restrictions. HR 3 was passed by the House April 30, 1987.

**Senate Action.** The Senate Agriculture Committee agreed to the House provision extending through 1990 the EEP program and increasing the total value of the program to $2.5 billion.

The Senate committee also approved with modifications a proposal to require the president to implement over two years a marketing-loan program for wheat, corn and soybeans if no progress was made in talks with the EEC and other nations to reduce agricultural subsidies. The Senate version of the trade bill, which generally paralleled the House bill, was passed July 21.

**Conference, Final Action.** The House-Senate conference committee began its negotiations in September 1987. Agricultural issues settled before the end of the 1987 session included agreement on additional funding for the Agriculture Department's targeted export assistance (TEA) program, which was used to counter unfair trading practices of another country, and an increase in certain food donations authorized by a 1949 agriculture law, in-

cluding grains, oilseeds and dairy products.

Major issues not resolved until the committee reconvened in March 1988 included basic U.S. farm policy guidelines to be presented at the next round of the General Agreement on Tariffs and Trade (GATT) talks, including the Senate provision requiring the president to put into effect a marketing loan for major crops if the GATT negotiations failed to produce results by 1990. Marketing loans allowed farmers who received price supports in the form of government loans to repay the loans at whatever price their crops brought at the market, instead of at the original price-support rate. Also resolved was the final form of a "Buy America" Senate provision requiring that labels on imported meat and poultry products specify the country of origin.

The conference committee finally wrapped up its negotiations on HR 3 at the end of March 1988. The conference report (H Rept 100-576) was filed April 20.

The agriculture marketing-loan provision was one of several in the conference bill expressly opposed by the administration. Reagan threatened to veto the legislation if it was not removed.

The House debated and approved the conference version of the trade bill April 21, and the Senate adopted it April 27. The Senate vote was three votes shy of the two-thirds majority needed to override a presidential veto. Republican support for the bill was eroded by concerted White House lobbying. Individual GOP members also disagreed with particular provisions, including one agriculture entry. One Midwestern GOP senator from a corn-producing state maintained that a loophole could let foreign ethanol into the United States duty-free. (Existing U.S. ethanol production was protected by a 60-cents-per-gallon duty.) But the chief issues that jeopardized the trade bill's enactment were non-agricultural.

A last-minute attempt by House Democrats to avoid a presidential veto by reconsidering HR 3 and dropping a controversial Alaskan oil exports provision was blocked in the Senate, and Reagan vetoed the bill May 24.

The House May 24 voted to override the veto by a substantial margin, but in the Senate the override attempt failed by five votes on June 8.

Following the defeat of HR 3, a new trade bill (HR 4848) was drafted that was identical to the vetoed bill except for the controversial provision on Alaskan oil exports and another on plant-closing notice requirements. This time the bill easily passed both chambers, the House on July 13 and the Senate on Aug. 3, and it was signed by the president Aug. 23.

Before the final vote on the bill in each house, GOP attempts to eliminate the ethanol provision were unsuccessful.

## Major Provisions

As signed into law, the major agriculture-related provisions in the omnibus trade bill (HR 4848 — PL 100-418):

● **Triggered Marketing Loan.** Required the president to implement a new federal price-support loan for wheat, feed grains and soybeans in 1990 if he could not certify that GATT negotiations had produced significant progress toward reducing or eliminating agricultural subsidies. The so-called marketing loans could permit farmers to avoid full repayment, because they were repaid at the prevailing market prices for the crop serving as collateral, and not at the official loan rate, which was often higher.

This structure was meant to keep high loan rates from artificially inflating world commodity prices.

The president could refuse to go ahead with the loan program if he determined that it would impede GATT negotiations; he would be required instead to expand existing Agriculture Department export-subsidy programs. He also could refuse to carry out the expansion of existing programs if that would harm further negotiations. The president could cancel either program if it had the intended effect of spurring negotiations.

The bill required that if the marketing-loan program went into effect the Agriculture Department also would offer a price-support program for the 1990 crop of sunflower seeds and cottonseeds.

● **Export Incentives.** Reauthorized through 1990 the export enhancement program, which gave bonuses of surplus, government-owned commodities to foreign buyers of U.S. crops. The bill increased to $2.5 billion, from $1.5 billion, the value of surplus commodities that might be used in the incentive program. It required the Agriculture Department to use prevailing market prices in determining its compliance with the annual $1 billion statutory minimum for program activity.

The bill also increased to $215 million, from $110 million, the 1988 authorization for a second export-subsidy program that assisted private U.S. producer/processor organizations in developing foreign markets. The program provided money or surplus agricultural commodities to these groups. The bill authorized the secretary of agriculture to use the money or equivalent surplus commodities to pay legal fees of the Corn Growers Association that were incurred defending a complaint brought in Canada against U.S. corn subsidies.

● **Foreign Agricultural Service (FAS).** Increased FAS funding by $20 million in fiscal years 1988 through 1990, set a statutory minimum of FAS personnel and upgraded senior agency officers.

● **Wood Products.** Included wood and wood products among agricultural products eligible for federal export subsidies.

● **Studies.** Required studies of the Canadian system of licensing wheat imports to that country, of the so-called "intermediate" export credit and of U.S. imports of eggs, roses, dairy products, sugar and honey.

● **Ethanol.** Extended to Dec. 31, 1989, a provision under the Caribbean Basin Initiative program that permitted certain Caribbean-owned ethanol-production facilities to ship ethanol with minimal Caribbean processing to the United States duty-free. The extension was an exception to the program's general rule that to get duty-free status at least 35 percent of a products' value had to consist of Caribbean parts and labor. The bill added two plants to those eligible for the exception under existing law.

## Nutrition Programs

Food stamp benefits to approximately 19 million Americans were increased and emergency feeding programs were extended for two years, through fiscal 1990, under legislation (S 2560 — PL 100-435) cleared by Congress Aug. 11, 1988. The measure provided additional food for the homeless through food banks and soup kitchens.

PL 100-435 represented the largest expansion of the food stamp program since 1977. The estimated cost of the bill was about $288 million in fiscal 1989, growing to an estimated $590 million by fiscal 1991.

Related legislation (HR 1340 — PL 100-237) to revise the way government-owned commodities were distributed to schools and by other federal food assistance programs cleared Dec. 19, 1987, just before Congress adjourned. Food commodities, including cheese and milk, had been distributed through programs assisting the elderly, children and American Indians.

The key point of contention in the debate over the bill was who best could determine which surplus commodities should be distributed — recipients or the agriculture secretary. A compromise was reached that required the Agriculture Department (USDA) to gather data from recipient agencies to determine the most acceptable and preferred commodities. The secretary, assisted by a new advisory council, would give serious weight to the recipient recommendations when deciding USDA purchases.

The bill also included a provision that loosened some restrictions in the women, infants and children (WIC) supplemental food program to allow states to use some of their savings on food purchases to increase the number of recipients in the program.

The House passed HR 1340 Aug. 3 (H Rept 100-216, Parts I and II), and the Senate followed suit Aug. 5, after consideration of its own version of the bill (S 305 — S Rept 100-127).

## Cap on Honey Loans

Congress in 1988 imposed new limits on honey subsidy programs administered by the Agriculture Department. The limitation, incorporated in the fiscal 1989 agriculture appropriations bill (HR 4784 — PL 100-460) that cleared Sept. 30, was a variation of a short-lived restriction imposed on beekeepers from October 1986 to December 1987.

Like other agriculture producers, beekeepers already had a cap on the total amount of federal subsidies they could receive under a provision of the 1985 omnibus farm bill (PL 99-198). *(1985 farm bill, p. 501)*

Rep. Silvio O. Conte, R-Mass., ranking Republican on the House Appropriations Committee, temporarily succeeded in winning enactment of a $250,000 cap on the amount of loans individual beekeepers could receive from the government. But the 15-month cap quietly was removed in 1987 by a House-Senate conference committee that wrote the fiscal 1988 budget reconciliation bill (HR 3545 — PL 100-203). Conte contended that a relatively small group of beekeepers was given disproportionate financial benefits by the Agriculture Department through both price supports and subsidized loans.

The House in 1988 approved an amendment by Conte to HR 4784 that would resurrect the $250,000 cap on federal loans to honey producers. But in the House-Senate conference on the appropriations legislation, Conte's amendment was revised. Instead of a cap on the amount of loans a honey producer could receive from the government, lawmakers approved a $250,000 cap on the amount of honey that beekeepers could forfeit to the government if they chose not to repay their honey marketing loans. The cap applied to federal payments to honey producers in both price-support and income-support programs.

Under the honey marketing-loan program, producers could get federal loans to finance their operations. Once a beekeeper harvested his honey, he could take it to an Agriculture Department field office, put the honey up as

saccharin, the controversial artificial sweetner linked to bladder cancer in laboratory animals.

Passage of the bill marked the fourth extension of the prohibition since Congress in 1977 first blocked the Food and Drug Administration (FDA) from banning saccharin. The most recent ban approved in 1983 expired April 22, 1985. *(1983 action, Congress and the Nation Vol. VI, p. 541)*

Under S 484, the moratorium was extended through May 1, 1987. It did not entirely prevent FDA from taking action against saccharin but only barred the agency from actions based on research findings from before 1978. If new evidence of health risks was discovered, FDA had authority to ban use of the sweetner.

The Senate Labor and Human Resources Committee April 22 by voice vote reported S 484 (S Rept 99-36). Before approving the bill, the committee rejected an amendment to require special labeling of aspartame, another popular artificial sweetner.

The full Senate May 7 passed the bill 94-1, after rejecting an amendment that would require special labeling of soft drinks that contained aspartame. The House by voice vote May 14 approved S 484, clearing the measure for the president.

Congress extended the moratorium another five years, until May 1, 1992, in the fiscal 1987 supplemental appropriations bill (HR 1827 — PL 100-71). *(Fiscal 1987 supplemental appropriations, p. 57)*

## Help for AIDS Victims

Less than two weeks after a government report predicted geometric increases in the number of people who would be diagnosed with acquired immune deficiency syndrome (AIDS) over the next five years, the Senate Labor and Human Resources Committee on June 25, 1986, approved legislation to improve services to AIDS victims. But the measure went no further.

The bill (S 2345 — S Rept 99-337) described AIDS, a fatal disease with no known cure, as the nation's "No. 1 public health priority." It authorized the Public Health Service (PHS) to make $40 million in grants to public and private organizations for the development, establishment or expansion of support systems for AIDS patients.

Under the bill, approved by voice vote, grants could be made to groups that coordinate outpatient or home health-care services, counseling and mental health services, case management and education for health workers about AIDS and how it is spread.

The committee action came as the PHS predicted that AIDS cases in the United States would total more than 270,000 by 1991, compared with 21,726 as of June 1986.

# 1987-88

Action on health legislation in the 100th Congress was overshadowed by debate over adoption of catastrophic health insurance. Approval of the measure after a long struggle marked the largest expansion of the Medicare program since its inception in 1965. Although the concept of helping older people cope with the often crushing financial burdens of serious illness enjoyed broad support, the measure's provision requiring Medicare recipients to pay for the new program was extremely controversial, with critics predicting it would lead to a tidal wave of political anger among older people hit with substantially higher Medicare premiums.

Other key health legislation approved included a significant expansion of federal AIDS (acquired immune deficiency syndrome) research and control efforts, cuts in some Medicare spending and toughening of federal standards for nursing homes and clinical laboratories. Rejected, however, were major initiatives in the areas of long-term health-care costs and mandatory health insurance benefits by employers.

## Catastrophic Health Insurance

President Reagan July 1, 1988, signed legislation (HR 2470 — PL 100-360) amending the Social Security Act to provide protection against catastrophic medical expenses under Medicare. The measure constituted the largest expansion of the federal Medicare program since its inception in 1965.

Under assault by senior citizens angry at having to pay the entire cost of their new benefits, Congress in November 1989 virtually repealed the Medicare Catastrophic Coverage Act. Members, however, did leave intact several expansions of the joint federal-state Medicaid program for the poor.

After some 18 months of legislative work, the Senate cleared HR 2470 for the president on June 8. The House adopted the conference report (H Rept 100-661) on the bill June 2.

The measure aimed to shield Medicare's 32 million beneficiaries from catastrophic hospital and doctors' bills related to acute illnesses, and it provided Medicare's first broad coverage of outpatient prescription-drug costs. But it did not cover most costs associated with long-term care, which analysts described as the principal source of catastrophic health-care costs for the elderly. *(Long-term care, p. 591)*

HR 2470 capped at approximately $2,000 in 1990 the amount Medicare beneficiaries could be required to pay for services covered under Medicare's Part A (including hospital, home health and some nursing home care) and Part B (which covered physician and other outpatient costs). It also helped pay the costs for prescription drugs after beneficiaries met a deductible, set at $600 in 1991, the first year such drug coverage was to be available.

The new law also made some significant changes in the Medicaid program, and it sought to ensure that private insurance companies adjusted their "Medigap" policies to avoid duplication with the new benefits provided to those eligible for Medicare.

As cleared, HR 2470 went well beyond the relatively modest new benefits envisioned by Reagan when he first urged development of a catastrophic insurance measure in his 1986 State of the Union address. In that speech, Reagan had asked his secretary of health and human services (HHS), Otis R. Bowen, to report on the issue by year's end. *(1986 State of the Union address, p. 1067)*

To the dismay of some conservatives, Bowen's report — issued Nov. 20, 1986 — suggested expansion of the Medicare system to provide catastrophic coverage for the elderly and disabled. He proposed capping at $2,000 per year the amount any Medicare beneficiary would have to pay for covered services, with the new benefit to be paid for through an increase in the monthly premium paid by Part B subscribers.

Critics said that approach would intrude on the market for private Medigap policies. But Bowen's plan received a generally warm reception on Capitol Hill, and the 100th Congress used it as a starting point when it went to work on catastrophic insurance early in 1987.

## The Financing Mechanism

With the budget deficit precluding substantial new federal spending, sponsors decided to make Medicare beneficiaries themselves pay for the new catastrophic costs program. The measure gradually increased the monthly premium beneficiaries already paid for the optional Part B program. The premium, which went up every year with inflation anyway, was raised by an extra $4 per month beginning in 1989, rising to $10.20 per month in 1993, for the catastrophic benefits.

But sponsors feared that any further premium increases would be too steep for beneficiaries with modest incomes, so they decided to collect just over 60 percent of the costs of the new program via an income-related "supplemental premium" that increased according to a beneficiary's federal income tax liability. The 60 percent of beneficiaries who owed less than $150 in income tax per year were to pay only the flat Part B premium increase, but the remaining 40 percent could be required to pay up to $800 extra per year per person in 1989, and up to $1,050 per year in 1993.

The supplemental premium operated like a surtax, since beneficiaries were to calculate and pay what they owed right along with their federal income taxes each year.

For 1989, the supplemental premium was $22.50 per $150 of federal tax liability, up to a cap of $800 for those with a tax bill of $2,858 or more. As the new benefits were phased in, the premium rate rose, to $42 per $150 of tax liability, with a cap of $1,050 (at $3,750 of tax liability) in 1993.

According to estimates prepared by the accounting firm of Price Waterhouse, in 1989 single individuals with "average" amounts of non-taxed income (including most Social Security payments) would pay no supplemental premium if their total income was $10,000 or less; their supplemental premium would be $68 per year if their total income was about $15,000, and it would not reach the $800 cap until total income reached $45,000. For married beneficiaries, the per-person supplemental premium would be zero up to $10,000 total joint income, $23 per year at about $20,000 and would hit the $800 cap at roughly $90,000.

Those hit hardest by the new premiums, in percentage terms, were single beneficiaries with roughly $40,000 in total income, who would pay a total annual (supplemental and flat) catastrophic premium of $768, or 1.92 percent of total income, and married beneficiaries whose roughly $80,000 in total income, whose total catastrophic premium of $1,671 would represent 2.09 percent of total income.

While beneficiaries could avoid paying the basic premium increases by dropping their Part B coverage, the supplemental premium was mandatory for the estimated 40 percent of beneficiaries with federal income tax liabilities greater than $150 per year.

## House Action

**Ways and Means.** In the House, a catastrophic health-care measure was referred jointly to two committees — Energy and Commerce and Ways and Means.

The Ways and Means Health Subcommittee approved catastrophic-care legislation April 9, 1987, by a 9-2 vote. The benefits, which were more generous than the administration proposed in Bowen's plan but less than senior citizens' groups wanted, would be financed by charging Medicare beneficiaries higher premiums. The measure also required that Medicare patients who were not poor pay income taxes on a portion of their benefits.

By a 3-8 vote, members rejected the more modest administration proposal (HR 1245) proposed by Bowen.

As it emerged from Ways and Means, the bill would expand Medicare coverage by about $5 billion per year and would relieve the program's beneficiaries of financial responsibility for long hospital stays by providing unlimited coverage after payment of a deductible; in 1987 the deductible was $520. Under the bill, the deductible would rise annually at the same rate as Social Security's cost-of-living adjustment (COLA). The bill also extended current Medicare coverage for short-term nursing home and home care and capped the out-of-pocket costs for beneficiaries for Medicare-covered doctor and outpatient services.

These benefits were largely the same as those that emerged from the Health Subcommittee. What was different in the full committee markup was financing.

Under the plan that came from the subcommittee, the new benefits would be financed by making beneficiaries pay income tax on the subsidized portion of Medicare coverage. The subcommittee plan was abandoned in favor of a two-tier Medicare premium.

Under the full committee plan, the Part B monthly premium, which was $17.90 in 1987, would rise by $1 in 1990, and by $1.50 in 1991. In addition, the roughly 40 percent of beneficiaries who had incomes high enough to incur a tax liability would be assessed an annual "supplemental premium" to help cover the costs of the new benefits. This premium would be assessed regardless of whether a beneficiary chose Part B coverage, although those that did not choose Part B would not be eligible for the catastrophic coverage offered under that portion of the program.

The two measures considered by the subcommittee (HR 1280, HR 1281) were merged into a single, clean bill, HR 2470, which was reported by Ways and Means May 22 (Rept 100-105, Part I).

On June 24, the committee voted 24-12 to ask the Rules Committee to add an amendment on coverage of outpatient prescription drugs.

**Energy and Commerce.** The Energy and Commerce Committee June 17 approved its version of HR 2470 by a 30-12 vote, including a slightly different prescription-drug benefit. The committee reported the bill July 1 (Part II).

As approved by the committee, Medicare would pay the full cost of outpatient prescription drugs after a $500 annual deductible was met.

The Energy Committee's Subcommittee on Health and the Environment first approved its version of a catastrophic-care bill June 9 that expanded Medicare to insure beneficiaries against expenses of more than $1,768 annually resulting from acute medical problems, including extended hospital stay.

# Catastrophic Health Insurance: Definitions

Below is a brief explanation of Medicare and the proposed catastrophic health insurance plan considered by the 100th Congress, along with definitions of some of the terms used in the debate:

**Catastrophic Health Insurance**—While some link "catastrophic" to the severity of an illness, policy makers used the term to refer to the financial cost. Some diseases or maladies — Alzheimer's disease, for example, or a severe car accident requiring a lengthy hospital stay — were catastrophic for anyone, but something as seemingly innocuous as a broken leg could be catastrophic for someone with a low income and no health insurance. The legislation was aimed at protecting Medicare beneficiaries from these catastrophic costs.

**Medicare**—The federally funded program helped 28 million elderly and 3 million disabled Americans pay acute-care health costs. Medicare was funded from three sources: general revenues; beneficiaries who paid premiums, deductibles and copayments; and the 1.45 percent payroll tax collected with Social Security withholding.

**Medicare-Covered Services**—Medicare had traditionally paid only for illness-related health expenses, not for preventive services. Medicare also did not cover the costs of routine dental care, eyeglasses and hearing aids, and outpatient prescription drugs. Medicare did pay (although restrictions were numerous and many patients failed to qualify) the costs for care in a so-called skilled nursing facility, but it did not pay for care that was more custodial (such as feeding and bathing) than medical. Medicaid, the joint federal-state health program for the poor, did pay for custodial nursing home care (costing an average of $22,000 per year), but only after a beneficiary had used up virtually all of his savings and income.

**Medicare Part A**—Officially known as the Hospital Insurance (HI) program, Part A helped pay the costs of inpatient hospital and skilled nursing care under Medicare. Anyone aged 65 or older who was eligible for Social Security or railroad retirement benefits was automatically eligible for Part A coverage. People under 65 who received Social Security disability payments (or railroad retirement disability) also were covered by Part A after a two-year waiting period. Just over 100,000 individuals with end-stage kidney disease also received Part A coverage. Persons aged 65 or older who did not otherwise qualify for Part A could purchase coverage. The 1987 premium was $226 per month. Part A was financed primarily by an earmarked portion of the Social Security payroll tax. For 1987, the HI share was 1.45 percent of income up to $43,800 for both employers and employees.

**Medicare Part B**—Officially the Supplemental Medical Insurance (SMI) program, this was the optional portion of Medicare available to those covered by Part A. About 98 percent elected Part B coverage, which paid 80 percent of covered physician and outpatient charges after a $75 annual deductible. The 1987 Part B monthly premium was $17.90. Premiums financed 25 percent of the cost of the Part B program. The remainder came from general revenues.

**Supplemental Premium**—Under current law, all Medicare beneficiaries paid the same premium, regardless of income. The legislation, however, would impose an additional annual premium based on income. This supplemental premium for 1988 would range from $10 for an individual with an adjusted gross income of between $6,000 and $6,143, up to $580 for an individual who had an adjusted gross income of more than $14,166.

**Long-Term vs. Acute Care**—Acute care referred to services provided by a hospital or doctor. Long-term care referred to care provided in a nursing home, the patient's home or anywhere other than a hospital, generally for a chronic condition from which the patient was not expected to recover quickly. Acute care was covered by Medicare, but there were strict limits on long-term care.

**'Medigap' Insurance**—More than 72 percent of the elderly purchased additional health insurance to pay costs not covered by Medicare. Those policies meeting certain standards could be marked as federally certified "Medigap" policies. At an average cost of $300-$400 annually, most Medigap policies paid Medicare-required premiums, copayments and deductibles, but few covered services, such as long-term care, not covered by Medicare.

**Spousal Impoverishment**—When a married person was institutionalized, Medicaid covered those costs after the couple "spent down" their income and assets to well below the poverty line. Medicaid rules, however, continued to require that most of the couple's joint income be used to pay for the cost of the institutional care. The spouse remaining at home (often referred to as the community spouse) was allowed to keep only a "personal needs allowance," which averaged about $340 per month, usually too little to meet basic living costs.

**Skilled Nursing Facility**—This could be a nursing home or a portion of a hospital specifically dedicated to providing nursing care or rehabilitation services that could be performed only by or under the supervision of licensed nursing personnel. Most nursing homes, however, provided "intermediate" instead of skilled nursing care, and many that did provide skilled care were not certified by Medicare. To qualify for Medicare nursing coverage, the beneficiary also had to have been recently hospitalized for at least three days, and a doctor had to certify that skilled care was required on a daily basis.

Subcommittee Chairman Henry A. Waxman, D-Calif., added an amendment to include payment of outpatient drugs. Under his plan, Medicare would pay all the costs of outpatient prescription drugs after a beneficiary met a $400 annual deductible. His plan was to be financed by raising the premium for Part B coverage.

Before Energy and Commerce agreed on the Waxman drug benefit, members rejected, 16-26, a Republican amendment that would replace Waxman's plan with one that would require states to cover the full cost of prescription drugs for elderly Medicare beneficiaries whose incomes were 200 percent or less of the federal poverty level.

But committee members adopted a Waxman amendment raising the annual deductible from $400 to $500 and limiting the increase in the premium that covered the benefit to 20 percent in any given year.

Groups representing senior citizens had been pushing hard for a prescription-drug benefit since plans for catastrophic-care legislation were first announced.

Among those behind the push for the prescription-drug coverage was House Speaker Jim Wright, D-Texas, who argued that adding a drug benefit would help put a Democratic stamp on a catastrophic-care plan that first began as a Reagan administration initiative.

The Reagan administration reacted negatively to the bill approved by the two committees. In a June 15 letter, Bowen argued that the bill would "contort the concept the president endorsed: to provide an acute care, catastrophic benefit under Medicare. Instead, it appears that the legislation has become a vehicle for modifications and add-ons to the basic Medicare program."

Other criticisms came from committee Republicans, who warned that the cost of the new benefits, particularly the new drug benefit, could quickly outpace the ability — or desire — of beneficiaries to pay for them. Estimates of the costs of the bill varied widely. The Congressional Budget Office (CBO) put the cost of the original Ways and Means proposal for 1989 at about $750 million, while HHS said it would be $6.4 billion. Similarly, HHS said the Energy and Commerce plan approved by the subcommittee would cost $8.9 billion for 1989, while CBO set the figure at $1.2 billion.

**Floor.** The House approved HR 2470 by a 302-127 vote July 22.

The way for House consideration of HR 2470 was cleared after Democratic leaders assured Rules Committee Chairman Claude Pepper, D-Fla., of later floor consideration of two of his bills. His measures would authorize "long-term home care" coverage for persons needing assistance in daily activities (HR 2762) and providing coverage of all outpatient prescription-drug costs after an annual $250 deductible (HR 2761).

Although 61 Republicans voted for HR 2470, many of their colleagues were harshly critical of the legislation. "This bill shows how Congress cannot control its insatiable appetite to spend and spend," said Minority Whip Trent Lott, R-Miss.

Democrats said they feared that if cost estimates turned out to be too low and steep premium increases were required, senior citizens would balk, and the federal government would ultimately have to foot the bill. But most Democrats voted "yea" on the theory that something was better than nothing.

As approved by the House, HR 2470 contained the text of HR 2941, a compromise bill combining versions of the legislation reported May 22 by the Ways and Means Com-

mittee and July 1 by the Energy and Commerce Committee. The rule to accept the text of HR 2941 was passed by the House July 22 by a vote of 248-174. Many members expressed frustration that the bill did not go further toward solving the problem of catastrophic medical expenses. They were disturbed that the bill lacked provisions to address the problem of long-term care, by far the leading cause of catastrophic health expenses for the elderly. But sponsors of the bill said long-term care had to be left out because it would be far too costly.

Although they were limited by the rule providing for floor consideration of the bill from offering many amendments, Republicans were able to propose an overall substitute measure. The plan, introduced as HR 2970, was based on the proposal set out by HHS Secretary Bowen, with the addition of the home-health and spousal-impoverishment provisions from the Democratic version, and a limited prescription-drug benefit for the elderly poor.

The GOP substitute was defeated on a **key vote of 190-242 (R 175-1; D 15-241).** *(1987 key votes, p. 965)*

Republicans also attacked the prescription-drug benefit in HR 2470, on the grounds that it would saddle the nation's senior citizens with underwriting the costs of expensive drug therapy for those under age 65 suffering from AIDS (acquired immune deficiency syndrome). That was because AIDS patients who had paid into the Social Security system were eligible for Medicare after a substantial waiting period.

Democratic sponsors argued, however, that most AIDS patients died before becoming eligible for Medicare.

Philip M. Crane, R-Ill., offered a motion to recommit the bill to committee with instructions to determine the cost to senior citizens of coverage of drug payments for AIDS patients. The motion was rejected 187-244.

The House also defeated an amendment, offered by Andrew Jacobs Jr., D-Ind., to strike language encouraging the use of less-costly generic substitutes for brand-name prescription drugs. The amendment was rejected 161-265.

### Senate Action

**Committee.** The Senate catastrophic-care bill (S 1127) was sponsored by Finance Committee Chairman Lloyd Bentsen, D-Texas, and cosponsored by all of the Democrats on Finance and five of the committee's nine Republicans, including Minority Leader Robert Dole, Kan. With that broad, bipartisan support, S 1127 sailed through the Finance Committee on a unanimous vote May 29.

Although it was similar in many respects to the House bill, S 1127 contained some significant differences. Unlike the House measure, for example, the program created under Bentsen's bill would be completely optional. Under the Bentsen bill, both the supplemental and basic premiums would be deductible as medical expenses for federal income tax purposes, while under the House bill only the basic Part B premium would remain deductible. Although the House version was more progressive in its treatment of the low-income elderly, S 1127 was more progressive in its determination of the supplemental premium.

As in the House, a number of members of the Finance Committee were concerned about what was left out of the bill.

"The bill does not cover the cost of long-term care services, prescription drugs or balance-billing by physicians," complained John H. Chafee, R-R.I. Although they agreed that the long-term care and prescription-drug issues needed to be addressed, sponsors worked successfully in most cases to fend off amendments that would add to the cost of the bill. However, the committee approved two amendments that were expected to raise the supplemental premium from $12 to about $13.50 per $150 of tax liability.

The first, offered by Donald W. Riegle Jr., D-Mich., eliminated the three-day prior hospitalization requirement for Medicare coverage of stays in skilled nursing homes. The second, offered by Dave Durenberger, R-Minn., for the first time brought preventive services into the purview of the Medicare program.

**Floor.** Because of cost objections raised by Senate Republicans and White House officials, S 1127 did not reach the Senate floor until October. But sponsors eventually negotiated with White House officials and got them to agree to the Senate version, with an amendment adding prescription-drug benefits for Medicare beneficiaries with high annual drug expenses.

In exchange, Senate negotiators agreed to raise the so-called "catastrophic threshold" from $1,700 per year to $1,850. Negotiators also agreed to an administration request to index annual Medicare premiums paid by beneficiaries to the yearly increase in the catastrophic's program costs, not to the slower-rising Consumer Price Index, which measured inflation in the economy as a whole.

The Senate passed 86-11 an amended HR 2470 Oct. 27.

After the prescription-drug amendment was approved 88-9, members practically breezed through another two dozen proposed add-ons, adopting 18 of them, before completing work on the bill.

The drug amendment provoked by far the most prolonged debate, with supporters citing the need for such coverage under Medicare while opponents expressed concern about future costs. In an effort to control costs of the program in future years, and to win administration support, a number of provisions were added to the amendment, including the imposition of a statutory cap on monthly premiums that could be charged to beneficiaries. Members also adopted a series of amendments designed to rectify what sponsors described as an unintended inequity that the bill created for Medicare beneficiaries whose pensions were primarily from sources other than Social Security.

Because Social Security was largely not taxable, and because the new supplemental premium would be calculated on the basis of tax liability, many beneficiaries with non-Social Security pensions would be required to pay more for the benefits than others with identical incomes.

To try to address the problem, members adopted an amendment offered by David Pryor, D-Ark., and Pete V. Domenici, R-N.M., that provided those with non-Social Security pensions an adjustment, for purposes of calculating their supplemental premium, equal to 15 percent of the average Social Security benefit. The Senate rejected, by a 18-77 vote, a Malcolm Wallop, R-Wyo., amendment to permit beneficiaries to forgo the new catastrophic coverage without giving up Part B coverage.

## Conference Action

House-Senate conferees officially began work on the catastrophic insurance bill in mid-March 1988, amid stepped-up efforts by various lobbying groups to torpedo the measure or at least alter its provisions significantly.

The American Association of Retired Persons (AARP) and most other major groups representing the nation's senior citizens strongly supported the thrust of the bill. But support for the measure, while broad-based, was not universal.

Most notably, the National Committee to Preserve Social Security and Medicare asked its members to urge their representatives and senators to defeat the conference report on the bill. The group, founded in 1983, was headed by James Roosevelt, President Franklin D. Roosevelt's eldest son.

The Roosevelt group objected to the fact that, under HR 2470, Medicare beneficiaries would be required to pay for their new benefits through premium increases, and that the bill did not address the issue of long-term care — by far the leading cause of health-related financial catastrophe for the elderly. The group's newsletters and mailings asked senior citizens to urge enactment of a separate measure (HR 3436, S 1616) that sought to provide long-term home care. That legislation was sponsored by Rep. Pepper, in the House, and in the Senate by presidential candidate Paul Simon, D-Ill.

At the same time all members of Congress were being flooded with mail prompted by the Roosevelt group, the Pharmaceutical Manufacturers Association (PMA) was underwriting a narrower campaign targeted at the conferees.

The object of that exercise was to kill the House version of a provision that provided broad Medicare coverage of prescription-drug costs. Instead, the organization was lobbying for adoption of the less-expensive Senate version of the drug program. A PMA spokesman said the drug makers were concerned about estimates showing that within a few years, the increased premiums envisioned in the House bill would fail to cover the program's costs. At that point, the PMA feared, Congress would find itself in a bind. Reluctant to impose new increases in premiums that beneficiaries had to pay, and unable to cover the shortfall from general revenues while budget deficits remained a problem, members might turn instead to price controls on prescription drugs.

**Clearing the Underbrush.** Despite the lobbying currents swirling around them, conferees on the catastrophic costs bill made steady progress as spring rolled around. House and Senate staffers had worked on the bill since February, producing two offers designed to reconcile what were officially called minor and technical issues.

At a meeting April 14, conferees officially approved most of the contents of the first offer, dubbed "Underbrush 1." Under that agreement, among other things, beneficiaries with Medicare-covered stays in skilled nursing homes would pay coinsurance equal to 20 percent of the cost of an average day for each of the first eight days. (The House bill proposed 20 percent for seven days, while the Senate bill envisioned 15 percent for the first 10 days.) Also under that agreement, House conferees acceded to a Senate provision designed to prevent federal retirees from having to pay more for the new coverage than retirees whose pensions came primarily from Social Security. The unintended glitch in the bill the provision sought to address affected an estimated 760,000 federal retirees who were eligible for Medicare.

"Underbrush 2," an offer relating to financing and the prescription-drug-coverage provisions, actually contained a compromise of some significance. It based the new "supplemental" premium on a beneficiary's federal income tax liability. The House bill would base the premium on the beneficiary's adjusted gross income (AGI).

**Indexing.** Conferees turned toward their central challenge the week of April 18: devising a package with benefits generous enough to win the support of the beneficiaries who had to pay for them, but not so extravagant as to price some people out of the Medicare program entirely.

In general, the House version of the bill offered more benefits than the Senate's package, but at a greater cost.

House conferees April 21 made their first substantive offer to Senate negotiators.

The House offer envisioned a bill with a price tag of about $11.6 billion by 1993, the first year all the new benefits were expected to be fully in effect. The original House bill was estimated to cost $12.2 billion in 1993, compared with $8.1 billion for the Senate measure.

Although the April 21 House offer covered a number of issues, its authors focused most intently on the issue of how to structure premium increases to keep up with anticipated rises in the cost of the new program.

The House offer of April 21 took a small step in the direction of benefiting fewer people at less cost. As originally passed, the House bill would increase the out-of-pocket cap by the amount of each year's Social Security COLA. That COLA, however, grew more slowly than medical costs, so the effect would be to provide benefits to an increasing percentage of Medicare recipients each year.

By contrast, the cap provided in the Senate bill was indexed in a manner that would hold constant the percentage of program participants qualifying for catastrophic cost benefits.

The House offer acceded to the Senate scheme that assumed that a constant percentage of beneficiaries would trip the cap, although the offer anticipated that the percentage would be closer to 10 percent than the 5.7 percent envisioned by the Senate bill.

**Separate Caps.** Senate conferees April 29 presented a formal offer to their House counterparts that closed a significant portion of the gap remaining between the two versions of HR 2470.

Senators, for example, agreed to accept a House provision setting separate out-of-pocket limits for Medicare Part A hospital expenses and Part B physician and other outpatient costs. Under the plan, after a beneficiary spent up to either cap, Medicare would pay 100 percent of the cost of covered services for the remainder of the year.

The Senate originally proposed a single cap, set at $2,030 for 1989. Senate conferees also proposed essentially to split the difference with the House over what percentage of beneficiaries should qualify for the new benefits. The House earlier had agreed to the Senate's plan to increase the out-of-pocket cap each year by enough to keep the percentage of qualifying beneficiaries constant. The House, however, sought to ensure that about 10 percent of Medicare beneficiaries would receive the catastrophic costs benefits each year, compared with the Senate's 5.7 percent. Under the new Senate offer, about 7.9 percent of beneficiaries would qualify.

The Senate also showed movement on how to allocate costs for the new program, the vast majority of which were to be borne by beneficiaries themselves via higher premiums. The House wanted nearly 80 percent of the costs to be paid by a new "supplemental" premium that would be assessed according to ability to pay. The remaining 20 percent would be raised by increasing the flat monthly premium (currently $24.80) most beneficiaries paid for the optional Part B program. The Senate originally wanted to split the costs almost evenly between the flat and supplemental premiums but offered to move to a 60-40 split.

**Drug Benefit Disputes.** During the week of May 9, conferees struggled with the issue of outpatient prescription-drug costs.

The House bill originally envisioned no delay in implementing the drug benefit, which would pay 80 percent of the cost of drugs after an annual deductible had been met. The Senate bill called for phasing in the benefit over four years, with only certain classes of drugs to be covered each year.

Led by Ways and Means Health Subcommittee Chairman Fortney H. "Pete" Stark, D-Calif., House conferees offered a variation of the phase-in plan, which would cover all drugs from the outset but require a relatively high copayment by beneficiaries that would later drop to 20 percent.

Senior citizen groups supported the Senate plan because they feared that phasing in by level of copayments would tempt lawmakers to re-examine the drug benefit if costs were running too high. Makers of brand-name drugs, represented by the PMA, opposed the House's version of the drug benefit because, they said, it would open the door to price controls if costs escalated too high or too fast.

Also weighing in were Reagan administration officials, who earlier threatened to recommend a veto of any bill containing a prescription-drug benefit but after painstaking negotiations endorsed the Senate plan.

In a May 10 letter, HHS Secretary Bowen urged conferees to limit the number of beneficiaries who could qualify for drug coverage, allow program administrators to take steps to ensure that program costs did not exceed projected financing and provide HHS enough lead time to implement the program.

**Final Agreement.** Exhausted but jubilant House and Senate negotiators completed work May 25.

Conferees had been optimistic about finishing work on the measure since May 20, when a subconference reached agreement on the complex and controversial portion of the bill providing broad Medicare coverage for outpatient prescription drugs.

The agreement provided that, beginning in 1991, Medicare was to pay 50 percent of the cost of most outpatient drugs after payment of a $600 deductible. Medicare's share would increase to 60 percent in 1992 and 80 percent in 1993 and thereafter; the deductible would rise at the rate required to keep constant, at about 16.8 percent, the percentage of beneficiaries who qualify.

But even after an agreement was reached on drug coverage, several key issues remained unresolved, including overall financing of the program, whether all beneficiaries should be required to pay for the new benefits or if participation should be voluntary, and what to do about the House's proposal for a respite-care benefit, not included in the Senate bill and strongly opposed by the Reagan administration. In meetings May 24-25, conference leaders agreed to make coverage mandatory, as envisioned by the House, but to move closer to the Senate's financing scheme, which would keep constant each year the percentage of beneficiaries eligible for the new benefits.

Respite-care coverage, however, was left to the full conference to decide. Bowen made clear early in the deliberations that the administration opposed inclusion of the benefit.

And while most Senate conferees seemed to agree with Bowen, a small cadre, led by Bill Bradley, D-N.J., and Durenberger pushed hard for its inclusion. Bradley offered a Senate proposal that would limit the benefit by tightening eligibility standards. Stark, however, was unhappy with the proposal, because it would be financed by raising the out-of-pocket cap, thus reducing the number of people who would qualify for the bill's major new benefit.

But just as Stark made a counteroffer, Bowen made a startling turnabout. If the conference would accept the Bradley amendment, said Bowen, he was prepared to drop his opposition to a respite-care benefit.

With no further debate, Bradley's proposal was adopted.

### Final Approval

The House acted first on the conference report (HR 100-661) on HR 2470, adopting it June 2 by a **key vote of 328-72 (R 98-63; D 230-9)**. *(1988 key votes, p. 981)*

Three of the 10 Republican conferees on the measure — Sen. Dole and Reps. Norman F. Lent, N.Y., and John J. Duncan, Tenn. — did not sign the conference report. But House Minority Leader Robert H. Michel, R-Ill., added his name to a June 1 "Dear Colleague" letter urging approval of the measure. Backers of the bill considered Michel's support significant, since he spearheaded opposition to the version of the bill passed by the House July 22, 1987.

Despite the strong vote for the bill, debate on the conference report was marked by strong criticism of its failure to provide coverage for long-term care for those with chronic conditions.

The Senate put the final congressional stamp of approval on HR 2470 on June 8, clearing the measure for the president.

The **key vote was 86-11 (R 34-11; D 52-0)**. Reagan signed the legislation into law July 1. While the president took credit for originating the idea, he warned Congress not to let costs of the features it had added get out of hand.

### Major Provisions

As cleared, HR 2470:

### Medicare Part A

● **Inpatient Hospital Services.** Beginning Jan. 1, 1989, covered all hospitalization costs of Medicare beneficiaries after the patient paid a single annual deductible, estimated at $564 in 1989. Someone who entered a hospital in December of one year and remained there into the next year need not pay a second deductible. However, a second deductible must be paid if the beneficiary left and re-entered the hospital during the second year.

● **Skilled Nursing Facilities.** Beginning Jan. 1, 1989, extended to 150 days, from 100 days, Medicare coverage for qualified stays in a certified skilled nursing facility (SNF).

● Required beneficiaries to pay coinsurance equal to 20 percent of the nationwide average per-day cost of SNF care for the first eight days (estimated at $20.50 per day for 1989).

● Eliminated the current requirement that a beneficiary be hospitalized for at least three days prior to entry into an SNF to qualify for Medicare coverage.

● **Hospice Care.** Eliminated, beginning Jan. 1, 1989, the current 210-day limit on hospice care if the beneficiary was recertified as terminally ill by the attending physician or hospice medical director.

● **Blood Deductible.** Altered existing requirements so that beginning Jan. 1, 1989, beneficiaries would be responsible for payment of a single annual deductible equal to the cost of the first three pints of whole blood (or equivalent quantities of packed red blood cells) furnished to the beneficiary. The cost would be waived to the extent the blood was replaced by the beneficiary or on his behalf. The Part A deductible also could be waived to the extent a beneficiary already had met the deductible under Part B.

● **Premium Formula.** Beginning in 1989, required the HHS secretary to use a new formula to set the Part A monthly premium, which was paid by those who did not qualify for free Part A coverage by virtue of Social Security-covered employment. The new formula made the premium equal to the actuarial value of the Part A benefit, estimated at $158 per month in 1989.

● **Supplemental Premium.** Imposed a supplemental premium on all individuals with a federal income tax liability of $150 or more who were eligible for Medicare Part A for more than six months in any year. Those eligible for six months or less in any year were exempt from payment, although those eligible for more than six months but less than a full year were liable for the full-year premium.

The supplemental premium for a married couple in which only one member was Medicare-eligible was based on half the couple's total tax liability. (Thus, if a couple owed a total of $302 in taxes, the lone enrollee would pay a supplemental premium based on a tax liability of $151; an enrollee in a couple with a total tax liability of $200 would be exempt, because only $100 would be attributed to the enrollee.)

The premium was to finance approximately 63 percent of the catastrophic and prescription-drug benefits, with the remaining 37 percent financed through increases in the flat Part B premium. The supplemental premium could not be counted as a medical expense for income tax purposes.

● For 1989, set the supplemental premium at $22.50 per $150 of federal income tax liability, up to a cap of $800 per enrollee. For 1990-93, the premium rate and caps were set as follows: for 1990, $37.50 per $150 of tax liability, with a cap of $850 per enrollee; for 1991, $39 per $150 of tax liability, capped at $900 per enrollee; for 1992, $40.50 per $150 of tax liability, up to a cap of $950 per enrollee; and for 1993, $42 per $150 of tax liability, capped at $1,050 per enrollee.

● Provided that government retirees, whose pensions were not tax-exempt like most Social Security payments, receive a special adjustment to their tax liability before calculating their supplemental premium.

● After 1993, indexed the premium to costs of the catastrophic benefits and prescription-drug programs, plus specified contingency reserves. The supplemental premium, however, could not rise by more than $1.50 per $150 of tax liability from the previous year. If the increase needed to maintain the program would be more than $1.50, the rest of the funds would be raised via increases in the flat Part B premium.

● Indexed the premium cap to increases in program costs, rounded to the nearest $50 increment.

● Beginning in 1993, required HHS and the Treasury Department to publish, by July 1, a preliminary notice of premium rates for the subsequent year. The final premium rates were to be published by Oct. 5.

## Medicare Part B

● **Part B Premium.** Notwithstanding other increases, raised the monthly Part B premium ($24.80 in 1988) by $4.00 in 1989 to pay for the new catastrophic and prescription-drug coverage. In 1990, the increase was to be $4.90; in 1991, $7.40; in 1992, $9.20; and in 1993, $10.20.

● After 1993, increased the flat premium in relation to program costs, with the proviso that no person's monthly Social Security check could decrease from the year before as a result of the combined effect of the premium increase and the annual COLA in the person's Social Security benefit, from which the premiums were deducted. Special rules for calculating the additional Part B premium would apply to residents of U.S. commonwealths and territories and to individuals enrolled in Part B who were not eligible for Part A benefits.

● **Cap on Out-of-Pocket Costs.** Beginning Jan. 1, 1990, limited out-of-pocket expenses for covered Part B services to $1,370. After the limit was reached, Medicare would pay 100 percent of its approved charge for covered services, instead of the 80 percent it otherwise paid. The limit was to be increased annually by the amount needed to hold constant, at 7 percent, the proportion of beneficiaries who reached the cap each year. CBO estimated that to keep the percentage of beneficiaries constant, the cap was likely to rise to $1,530 in 1991, to $1,700 in 1992 and to $1,900 in 1993.

Beneficiaries could count as expenses toward the out-of-pocket cap the Part B annual deductible (currently $75), the Part B blood deductible and all Part B coinsurance.

● Required Medicare carriers (insurance companies that processed Medicare claims on behalf of the government) to notify beneficiaries when they have incurred expenses high enough to exceed the cap and thus qualify for the catastrophic costs benefits.

● Required the HHS secretary to provide for "an appropriate adjustment" in rates paid by Medicare to health maintenance organizations or other prepaid providers to reflect the new catastrophic coverage.

● Prohibited providers (including hospitals, nursing homes and home health agencies) that had agreements to receive payment directly from Medicare from billing beneficiaries for costs in excess of the Medicare payments.

● **Mammogram Screening.** Beginning Jan. 1, 1990, provided for Medicare coverage of biennial screening mammograms to detect breast cancer in beneficiaries over age 65. (Mammograms for diagnostic purposes already were covered.)

For Medicare-eligible disabled women under age 65, a baseline screening would be covered between ages 35 and 40, along with annual mammograms for women aged 40-49 who were considered at high risk for breast cancer, and biennial exams for other women that age. Medicare would cover annual exams for all disabled beneficiaries between ages 50 and 64. Beginning in 1992, the HHS secretary, after consultation with the director of the National Cancer Institute, could revise the frequency of mammograms that could be covered.

As with other Part B benefits, Medicare would pay 80 percent of the cost of mammograms, up to a limit of $50 in 1990. That limit was to be indexed to the measure of non-hospital medical inflation. Beginning in 1992, the HHS secretary also could adjust Medicare payment rates.

● Required the HHS secretary to prescribe standards to ensure safety and accuracy, effective when the benefit began in 1990. The Physician Payment Review Commission was required to report, by July 1, 1990, results of a study of the costs of providing mammography in various settings, including doctors' offices, hospital outpatient departments and outpatient radiology facilities. Due on that same date was a study by the General Accounting Office of the quality of mammograms conducted in doctors' offices as compared with other facilities.

● **In-Home Health Services.** Beginning Jan. 1, 1990, allowed Medicare-covered home health services to be provided to beneficiaries seven days per week for up to 38 days if a physician certified the need for such care on a daily basis. Current interpretations of the law generally allowed care five days per week for no more than 21 days.

● Extended, through October 1990, the "waiver of liability" for skilled nursing facilities, hospices and home health agencies that permitted them to receive Medicare payment for beneficiaries later declared ineligible for coverage if the provider had no reason to believe that the beneficiary was ineligible when the services were provided.

● Required the creation of an 11-member Advisory Committee on Home Health Claims, to study the reasons for an increase in the denial rate for home health claims during 1986 and 1987, the ramifications of such an increase and the need to reform the process involved in such denials. The committee was required to report its findings to the Health Care Financing Administration (Medicare's administrative office) and to Congress within one year of enactment.

● **Respite Care.** Beginning Jan. 1, 1990, provided coverage of up to 80 hours per year of paid care to give a respite to an unpaid family member or friend who lived with and cared for a "chronically dependent" Medicare beneficiary. Care could include homemaking duties, personal care or nursing care.

To be eligible, a beneficiary would have to meet the following requirements: be unable, for at least three months, to perform two or more "activities of daily living," including eating, dressing, bathing, toileting or moving into or out of a bed or chair; and have incurred medical expenses high enough to have exceeded either the Medicare prescription-drug deductible or the Part B out-of-pocket cap. Once these requirements were met, the patient would be eligible for respite services for the following 12 months, although in no case could more than 80 hours of care be paid for in any calendar year.

Persons receiving care could be required to pay coinsurance of 20 percent, even if they had exceeded the Part B cap, which relieved them of copayment requirements for other Part B services. The coinsurance, however, could be counted toward the cap if it had not already been reached.

● Required the HHS secretary to study out-of-home services, such as adult day care, and to report to Congress within 18 months of enactment. The secretary was to look at the advisability of providing out-of-home services to beneficiaries eligible for in-home services.

● **Notice of Medicare Benefits.** By Jan. 31, 1989, and annually thereafter, required the HHS secretary to mail to all Medicare beneficiaries a notice detailing the benefits available and categories of care not covered by Medicare. The notice was to describe the limitations of Medicare payments, particularly for long-term care services, and outline all required premiums, deductibles and coinsurance.

● Amended the current requirement that beneficiaries be notified annually of the existence of the "participating physician" program, which consisted of physicians who agreed, for all Medicare patients, not to charge more than the Medicare-approved amount for services. Required a brochure to be sent annually to all beneficiaries describing the program and explaining the financial advantages to the beneficiary of using a "participating physician." The brochure also was to explain how to locate such physicians and was to give the local Medicare carrier's toll-free number for inquiries concerning the program and requests for free copies of directories of such physicians in the beneficiary's geographical area.

● **At-Home Drug Therapy.** Beginning Jan. 1, 1990, provided coverage for at-home intravenous drug therapy and associated services, including supplies and equipment, nursing and pharmacy services. No deductible or coinsurance was required, although the drugs themselves were subject to the same deductible and coinsurance requirements as other outpatient prescription drugs. The deductible and coinsurance requirements could be waived if the home therapy was part of a continuous course of therapy initiated in a hospital.

Initially, only intravenous antibiotics were covered, although other drugs could be added if the HHS secretary found they could be administered safely and effectively in the home.

Certification was required for providers of in-home intravenous drug therapy, and the HHS secretary had to establish sanctions short of decertification (including civil fines and suspension of payments) for providers who violated established standards. In addition, except in certain narrowly defined cases, physicians could not refer patients to a provider in which the physician had an ownership interest or from whom the physician received compensation.

## Prescription-Drug Coverage

● **Coverage Phase-in.** Beginning in 1991, phased in coverage of the cost of outpatient prescription drugs after payment of an annual deductible, to be set that year at $600. Medicare was to pay 50 percent of the costs after the deductible had been met in 1991, 60 percent of the costs in 1992 and 80 percent of the costs in 1993 and thereafter.

All prescription drugs certified as safe and effective by the federal Food and Drug Administration (FDA) were to be covered, as well as those marketed before 1938 (which were exempt from FDA review), and the HHS secretary was expressly prohibited from implementing a formulary to exclude from coverage any drug otherwise covered.

In 1990, Medicare was to cover two classes of outpatient prescription drugs: those used for home intravenous therapy and immunosuppressive drugs for organ transplant recipients. The deductible for those drugs that year was set at $550. Medicare currently covered 100 percent of the costs of immunosuppressives for one year after a transplant that was financed by Medicare. This coverage was retained, as was coverage after the first year, regardless of whether Medicare paid for the original transplant. Immunosuppressives were subject to the 50 percent coinsurance requirement in 1990 and 1991, with the coverage increasing in the same manner as for other drugs in future years.

● **Deductible.** Required beneficiaries to meet the drug deductible separately from the basic catastrophic out-of-pocket limit, but they could begin receiving drug benefits before reaching the separate threshold and vice versa.

● **Indexing.** Indexed the deductible to keep constant, at approximately 16.8 percent, the proportion of beneficiaries who qualified for the drug benefit each year.

● **Financing.** Financed the drug benefit through an additional premium (included within the supplemental premium and increases in the flat premium) that was to be set to cover anticipated costs of the program, plus contingency reserves. Required contingency reserves were set at 100 percent in 1991 (so premiums would have to collect twice the amount the benefit was estimated to cost), 75 percent in 1992 and 50 percent in 1993. After 1993, premiums would be set to achieve a reserve of 25 percent in 1994 and 1995, and 20 percent after 1995.

● **Trust Fund.** Created within the U.S. Treasury the Federal Catastrophic Drug Insurance Trust Fund, to which the drug portion of the supplemental and flat premiums was to be paid, and which, in turn, was to be drawn down to pay for the new prescription-drug benefits, including payments for home intravenous drug therapy. The trust fund had no authority to borrow from other Medicare accounts.

● **Report to Congress.** Required that the trustees of the drug trust fund report to Congress by April 1 of each year on the operation and status of the trust fund for the preceding fiscal year and on projected status for the current fiscal year and the next two fiscal years.

● **'Participating Pharmacies.'** Created a "participating pharmacy" program. Pharmacies seeking such designation could not refuse to dispense covered drugs in stock to Medicare beneficiaries. They also had to keep patient records; assist Medicare beneficiaries in determining when and if they had exceeded the annual drug deductible; and notify Medicare carriers when the deductible was met. The HHS secretary was required to make available to each participating pharmacy a distinctive emblem suitable for display, indicating that the pharmacy was a member of the program.

● **Electronic Tracking.** By 1991, required the HHS secretary to create a system for computer tracking of all drug purchases by Medicare beneficiaries at the point of sale. Participating pharmacies were required to join this system.

● **Payment in Full.** Prohibited pharmacies from charging beneficiaries more than Medicare would pay for a particular drug, once the required copayment was met.

● **Limits on Charges.** Prohibited pharmacies from charging Medicare beneficiaries more than they charged the general public, with violators subject to civil penalties of $2,000 per offense.

For drugs made by a single company, or for generic drugs for which a doctor had specified a certain brand (either in handwriting on the prescription or by written confirmation within 30 days in the case of telephoned prescriptions), Medicare was to pay the lowest of the pharmacy's actual charge, the amount equal to the 90th percentile of pharmacy charges, or the average wholesale price for the drug dispensed plus an administrative allowance for the pharmacy. The HHS secretary was required to establish the average wholesale price by conducting a semiannual survey of direct sellers, wholesalers or pharmacists to determine the applicable wholesale price. The secretary could, however, rely on published sources instead of a survey for low-volume drugs, as well as for intravenous drugs and immunosuppressive drugs that would be covered in 1990.

For all other drugs, payment was to be the lower of the pharmacy's actual charge or the median of the average wholesale price, plus an administrative allowance.

● **Administrative Costs.** Allowed administrative charges of $4.50 per prescription for participating pharmacies and $2.50 for other pharmacies for 1990 and 1991. The allowances then were to be adjusted for inflation on an annual basis. The administrative allowance could be reduced for mail-service pharmacies.

● **Prescribing Limits.** In general, covered no more than a 30-day supply of a drug, although the secretary could authorize payment for supplies for up to 90 days (or beyond, in certain exceptional circumstances).

● **Report to Congress.** Beginning June 30, 1989, required the HHS secretary to submit a report every six months to the House Ways and Means and Energy and Commerce committees and the Senate Finance Committee that included drug-price changes and use of outpatient drugs by Medicare beneficiaries. To control price increases that could be prompted by the creation of the program, the secretary had to use as a starting point drug prices from Jan. 1, 1987. Between October 1991 and April 1993, the secretary was required to report monthly to Congress the total outlays and receipts of the drug trust fund.

Based on information in those reports the HHS secretary, beginning in 1992, was required to submit an annual report to Congress on the budgetary status of the trust fund, including recommended changes necessary to achieve the contingency reserve required for the subsequent year.

● **Trouble-Shooting.** To assure appropriate use of drugs, required the HHS secretary to establish a program to identify instances and patterns of unnecessary or inappropriate prescribing or dispensing practices, instances of substandard care and potential adverse drug reactions. The secretary also was required to establish prescribing standards based on accepted medical practice.

● **Review Panel.** Created an 11-member Prescription Drug Payment Review Commission to provide Congress with recommendations concerning administration of the drug program.

● **Studies.** Called for a series of studies, to be performed by various entities (including the HHS secretary, CBO and Office of Technology Assessment) on such issues as beneficiary drug costs, the possibility that including coverage under Medicare could increase demand for covered drugs and the potential of mail-service pharmacies to reduce the costs of drugs for both beneficiaries and the Medicare program.

### 'Medigap' Supplemental Insurance

● **Certification Procedures.** Amended procedures for federal certification of "Medigap" policies — private insurance policies that sought to supplement Medicare benefits and that have been certified by the HHS secretary as meeting or exceeding standards developed by the National Association of Insurance Commissioners (NAIC). Among other things, the current standards set forth minimum benefits; required that a buyer be provided a "free-look" period during which the individual could decide to forgo the policy and receive a refund of any premiums paid; and required that expected benefits equal at least 60 cents of every premium dollar for individual policies and at least 75 cents of every dollar for group policies.

● Required that if the NAIC revised its standards for Medigap policies within 90 days after enactment, those standards would apply for federal certification. If the NAIC did not act within 90 days, the HHS secretary would

be required to issue federal model standards within 60 days, to take effect one year later. In either case, Medigap policies could not duplicate existing Medicare benefits and had to provide for a refund or premium adjustment in cases in which such duplication occurred.

● Provided that policies sold before enactment but still in effect as of Jan. 1, 1989, would not be deemed duplicative if they complied with the NAIC model transition rule, which provided for refunds or premium adjustments, when appropriate, for duplicative portions. Policies sold after enactment had to meet the requirements of the NAIC transition rule before they could be sold.

● Required Medigap companies to send to policyholders, by Jan. 31, 1989, a letter explaining the improved benefits enacted by Congress and how they affected the policy's benefits and premiums. Insurers whose existing policies contained duplicative coverage as a result of the new catastrophic benefits had to notify beneficiaries by Jan. 1, 1989, of proposed changes in coverage; of resulting premium adjustments or refunds; and of when such adjustments or refunds were to be made.

● Required insurance companies to provide consumers a 30-day free-look period for all Medigap policies, regardless of whether sold by agents or through the mail. Under the current standards, customers were allowed to change their minds within 10 days for policies sold by agents, and 30 days for those sold by mail.

● Required certified Medigap insurers to submit to state insurance commissioners copies of all advertisements for review, in accordance with state law.

● Required that states with their own Medigap certification programs use forms developed by the NAIC to collect information on actual (as opposed to expected) loss ratios (the portion of each premium dollar returned in benefits).

● Required the HHS secretary to inform Medicare beneficiaries about current laws that prohibited certain marketing and sales abuses and how they could report any marketing or sales abuse, and to publish the HHS toll-free telephone number beneficiaries could use to report prohibited practices.

● Required the HHS secretary to report to Congress in March 1989 and in July 1990 on actions states had taken in adopting standards equal to or more stringent than the NAIC model transition regulation or any forthcoming NAIC revised standard or federal model standard.

### Third-Party Coverage

● **Duplicative Policies.** Required employers, including state and local governments, who provided health insurance to workers or retirees that duplicated the new Medicare catastrophic benefits to provide either additional benefits or cash refunds equal to the actuarial value of the duplicated benefits. The transitional benefits were to last for one year for coverage that duplicated the new Part A benefits, two years for coverage that duplicated the new Part B benefits or until the expiration of any collective-bargaining agreement governing health benefits.

● **Prepaid Health Plans.** Required prepaid health plans that contracted with Medicare to adjust their benefit packages to take the new benefits into account.

● **Federal Employees.** Beginning Jan. 1, 1989, required the Office of Personnel Management (OPM), in consultation with companies offering health insurance under the Federal Employee Health Benefits Program (FEHBP), to reduce the rates charged Medicare-eligible participants. The reduction was to be equal to the cost of services that were to be provided by Medicare that would have been provided by the plan, but for enactment of the new benefits, prorated for the number of Medicare-eligible participants.

● **Study of Federal Medigap Plans.** Required the director of OPM to report by April 1, 1989, to the Senate Committee on Governmental Affairs and the House Committee on Post Office and Civil Service regarding changes in the FEHBP that would make it more efficient and effective in serving the needs of participants who also were Medicare beneficiaries. The OPM director was required to submit a study on the feasibility of creating Medigap plans within the FEHBP.

## Medicaid-Medicare Changes

● **Payment of Premiums.** Required states to pay Medicare-required premiums, deductibles and coinsurance charges for elderly and disabled Medicare beneficiaries with incomes below the federal poverty line ($5,770 per year for an individual in 1988) and resources at or below twice the standard allowed under the Supplemental Security Income (SSI) program ($3,800 in 1988), but who were not poor enough to otherwise qualify for Medicaid coverage. Coverage was to be phased in, requiring states to cover all beneficiaries with incomes below 85 percent of poverty by Jan. 1, 1989, with income thresholds rising by 5 percent per year until the 100 percent threshold was reached in 1992. The five states whose Medicaid income standards were more restrictive than those for SSI (Hawaii, Illinois, North Carolina, Ohio and Utah) were to be given an additional year to phase in the coverage, being required in 1989 to cover only those with incomes up to 80 percent of poverty.

For outpatient prescription drugs, states had the option of paying the Medicare drug deductible for a low-income beneficiary or extending the same drug coverage the state provided to other Medicaid recipients.

● **Medicaid for Pregnant Women, Infants.** By July 1, 1989, required states to provide Medicaid coverage of prenatal care and other pregnancy-related services to women, and full Medicaid coverage for infants up to age 1, for families with incomes too high to otherwise qualify for Medicaid but still below 75 percent of the federal poverty threshold ($9,690 for a family of three in 1988). That threshold was to rise to 100 percent of poverty on July 1, 1990.

To prevent states from pulling resources from other needy individuals to pay for the new coverage, states were prohibited from reducing already approved optional Medicaid coverage of pregnant women or children with incomes under 185 percent of poverty. States also were prohibited from reducing cash-assistance payments under the Aid to Families with Dependent Children (AFDC) program below levels in effect on May 1, 1988.

● **Spousal Impoverishment/Nursing Home Care.** Limited the assets and income of a married couple that must be "spent down" before Medicaid would pay for nursing home care for one of the pair.

Current law required a person to exhaust his or her income and most assets before Medicaid would begin paying the cost of nursing home care. After a person had been institutionalized for more than one month, spouses were no longer considered to be living together, and only the income of the institutionalized spouse was considered for determining Medicaid eligibility. If the wife was in an institution and the husband remained at home, the husband could keep income in his name. More often, however, it was the husband in the nursing home and the wife at home. If the wife had no income in her own name, as was frequently the case, she had to subsist on a welfare-level maintenance allowance from the husband's income, while the rest went toward the cost of his nursing home care. This situation was commonly referred to as "spousal impoverishment."

Under the bill, in any month in which a married person was in a nursing home, no income of the at-home spouse was to be considered available to the institutionalized spouse, and income paid solely to one spouse was to belong to that spouse alone. Income paid in both names was to be considered available in equal portions to both spouses.

At the beginning of a continuous period of institutionalization, a couple's total assets would be counted and split in two, with half considered available to each spouse. (The couple's house, household goods and personal effects, however, were exempt.) If, after division of the assets, the at-home spouse was left with less than $12,000 (indexed to general inflation beginning in 1989), the institutionalized spouse could transfer an amount sufficient to allow the at-home spouse to hold $12,000 worth of assets in his or her own name. However, amounts greater than $60,000 (also indexed to inflation) would be attributed to the institutionalized spouse, and thus become available to pay the nursing home bill. States could, at their option, raise the $12,000 minimum to any level below the $60,000 maximum.

Beginning Sept. 30, 1989, states had to permit the at-home spouse to keep a "maintenance needs allowance" from the other spouse's income sufficient to bring total income to at least 122 percent of the monthly federal poverty threshold for a two-person household ($786 in 1988). On July 1, 1991, the minimum allowance would rise to 133 percent of that threshold, and to 150 percent on July 1, 1992. The maintenance needs allowance could not exceed $1,500 per month, except where a higher level was determined by administrative decree or court order.

Court orders for support for the at-home spouse from the institutionalized spouse would supersede either the asset or income limitations set forth.

● **Fraud Prevention.** Required states to delay Medicaid eligibility for institutionalized individuals determined to have disposed of assets at less than fair-market prices within 30 months of applying for Medicaid in order to avoid having to "spend down." The transfer prohibition did not apply in several instances, including if the transfer was of the applicant's home to his or her spouse, child under 21 or blind or disabled adult child; if the resources were transferred to the at-home spouse; if the applicant demonstrated that the individual intended to dispose of the assets at fair-market value; or if the state determined that postponing eligibility would cause undue hardship.

● **Exempt Expenditures.** Required states to allow nursing home residents to deduct from their incomes uncovered medical costs (such as those for eyeglasses or hearing aids) before contributing to the cost of their nursing home care. States retained the ability to place "reasonable limits" on a resident's expenditures for medical or remedial care.

● **Medicare-Medicaid Counseling.** Required the HHS secretary to establish a three-year demonstration project with a public or private non-profit agency for the purpose of training volunteers to provide counseling regarding Medicare and Medicaid to elderly individuals aged 60 or over. Counselors also could assist in the preparation of forms required to apply for benefits. Authorized "such sums as necessary" to be paid from the Part A and Part B trust funds to help provide the training and to reimburse volunteers for transportation, meals and other expenses incurred during training or counseling.

### Miscellaneous

● **Actuarial Soundness of Premiums.** Required that the trustees of the Medicare trust funds identify in their annual reports receipts and outlays attributable to the new catastrophic coverage.

● **Commission on Comprehensive Care.** Authorized $1.5 million for the establishment of a bipartisan commission on comprehensive health care to examine shortcomings in the current health-care delivery and financing mechanisms that limited or prevented access to comprehensive care. The commission was to make specific recommendations to Congress on measures to assure the availability of comprehensive long-term care for Medicare beneficiaries, along with comprehensive health care for all citizens. Defined comprehensive services to include inpatient hospital care, skilled and intermediate nursing home care, home health services, physician and other outpatient care, preventive health care, prescription drugs, eyeglasses, hearing aids, orthopedic equipment and dentures.

● Called for a commission of 15 members: three appointed by the president; six (no more than four of whom may be from the same party) appointed by the Senate leadership; and six (with the same stipulation) appointed by the House leadership.

● Required the commission to submit to Congress within six months a report of findings and recommendations regarding ways to provide long-term care services to Medicare beneficiaries, including detailed recommendations for appropriate legislative initiatives. Within one year, the commission was to submit to Congress a report of findings and recommendations regarding ways to provide comprehensive health services for both Medicare beneficiaries and the general public.

● **Long-Term Care.** Authorized $5 million annually for fiscal 1989-93 for research on the delivery and financing of long-term care services, defined to include nursing home care, home care, custodial care and community-based services. Studies were to examine the financial characteristics of Medicare beneficiaries who received or required long-term care services, how financial or other characteristics of Medicare beneficiaries affected their use of institutional or non-institutional care, the quality of available long-term care and the effectiveness of, and need for, consumer protections for those who received long-term care outside nursing homes.

● Required the HHS secretary to submit interim reports to the House committees on Ways and Means and Energy and Commerce and the Senate Finance Committee by Dec. 1, 1990, and Dec. 1, 1992, and a final report by June 1, 1994.

● Required the Treasury Department to study and make recommendations before Nov. 30, 1988, regarding tax policies to encourage the private financing of long-term care. The Treasury secretary was required to seek the views of the insurance industry and of providers of long-term care.

● Required the HHS secretary to survey adult day-care services in the United States. Such services included medical or social services provided in an organized, non-residential setting to chronically impaired individuals. Within one year of enactment, the secretary was to report to Congress his findings, including recommendations concerning appropriate standards for coverage of adult day-care services under Medicare and establishment of a reimbursement mechanism.

● **Case Management.** Required the establishment of at least four two-year projects to demonstrate the feasibility of applying case management to Medicare beneficiaries with selected catastrophic illnesses, defined as those that threaten to become high-cost or long hospital-stay illnesses. Case management involved designating a person or organization to oversee and coordinate all health services for particular individuals. The projects were to evaluate the appropriateness and determine the most effective approaches for providing case-management services to Medicare beneficiaries with high-cost illnesses.

● **Ventilator-Dependent Patients.** Required the HHS secretary to conduct up to five demonstration projects for up to three years each to review the appropriateness of Medicare paying for services of hospital units for patients who were chronically dependent on ventilators in the same manner that it paid for hospital rehabilitation services.

● **Misuse of Name, Symbols.** Prohibited the use of the name, emblem or symbols of Social Security or Medicare in a manner that would convey a false impression that any item was approved, endorsed or authorized by the federal government, and provided for civil fines for offenders of up to $25,000 for a single violation and $100,000 in any one year for multiple violations.

● **Reconciliation Law Technical Corrections.** Made technical and conforming changes to provisions of PL 100-203, the fiscal 1988 budget reconciliation law, affecting Medicare, nursing home quality requirements and rural health.

# AIDS

Congress Oct. 13, 1988, cleared for the president an omnibus health package that contained the first significant federal policy outlines for dealing with the deadly AIDS (acquired immune deficiency syndrome) epidemic.

Despite reservations about some of the items in the catchall bill, President Reagan signed the measure into law on Nov. 4 (S 2889 — PL 100-607).

The final version of the legislation combined more than a dozen separate measures into a single nine-title bill.

S 2889 included two measures — reauthorizing federal aid for the training of nurses and other health professionals — that the president had earlier threatened to veto. It contained three others — reauthorizing programs encouraging the donation and transplanting of human organs, providing funds to states for preventive health services and reauthorizing health programs for the homeless — that included what the administration considered objectionable language or excessive authorization totals.

The AIDS portion of the measure authorized a minimum of $270 million over three years for AIDS education and a total of $400 million over two years for anonymous blood testing and counseling and for home and community-based health services for AIDS patients. It also authorized $2 million for operating costs for a new national AIDS commission.

The title expedited federal AIDS research activities, ordered the hiring of 780 new workers for the Public Health Service and formally authorized several elements of the federal government's war on AIDS that had already been launched.

At the insistence of Sen. Jesse Helms, R-N.C., who threatened to block the entire package otherwise, sponsors dropped some controversial elements of an AIDS bill (HR 5142) passed overwhelmingly by the House in September. Excluded were provisions authorizing $1.2 billion for voluntary blood testing and counseling, with guaranteed confidentiality of test results.

## Background

Although the AIDS epidemic had been the leading public health concern of the nation's medical community for several years, Congress was relatively slow to address the problem. Lawmakers pumped increasing funds into AIDS research, but until the 100th Congress, they shied away from policy decisions on combating the deadly disease.

The delay was due to several factors, including a deep schism among members over the best way to slow the march of the disease, which was transmitted primarily through sexual contact (especially among male homosexuals) and intravenous drug use.

Public health experts and their congressional allies, led by Rep. Henry A. Waxman, D-Calif., chairman of the Energy and Commerce Subcommittee on Health and the Environment, argued for intensive public education coupled with confidential blood testing and counseling of high-risk individuals.

Congressional conservatives, led by Helms and Rep. William E. Dannemeyer, R-Calif., urged mandatory, routine testing of large groups within the population, with the names of those testing positive being reported to public health authorities. They also wanted to require that sexual contacts of all those testing positive be contacted and warned of their risk.

In 1987, for example, Helms and Dannemeyer attempted on several occasions to add amendments reflecting their concerns to a number of different bills. On June 2, the Senate adopted a Helms amendment to a midyear spending bill (HR 1827), requiring that AIDS be added to the list of diseases for which immigrants could be refused entry into the United States.

On May 21, the Senate rejected a Helms amendment to require states to test those applying for marriage licenses.

Helms succeeded in attaching an amendment to the fiscal 1988 Health and Human Services appropriations bill (HR 3058) to prohibit AIDS-education funds from being used for activities that promoted homosexuality.

In the House, Dannemeyer was able to persuade colleagues to agree to instruct conferees on HR 3058 to accept Helms' language about barring funds for "promotion" of homosexual activities.

## The President's Commission

The split on Capitol Hill was mirrored within the Reagan administration. Throughout 1987, Surgeon General C. Everett Koop had squared off against Education Secretary William J. Bennett.

Koop argued that moral judgments about homosexuality and drug abuse had no place in a public health debate, and that those at greatest risk of AIDS would be driven underground by mandatory testing requirements. Bennett and other conservatives contended that the general public had a right to be protected to the maximum extent possible and that AIDS education should stress sexual abstinence and other moral values.

In June 1987, Reagan appointed a special commission to study the AIDS epidemic and recommend policy directions for the federal government. The panel almost foundered before it began on exactly the kinds of bitter arguments that split the politicians. But after months of bickering and turmoil, followed by the appointment of a new chairman, the commission finally settled down to work in late 1987.

To the surprise of many, the commission, led by retired Adm. James D. Watkins, developed detailed suggestions regarding health care for AIDS victims, basic research and development and the need to stem intravenous drug abuse. In an interim report issued Feb. 25, 1988, Watkins said the federal and state governments should ensure that drug abusers who wanted to quit had access to "treatment on demand," an undertaking that could cost some $1.5 billion in new spending in the next year alone.

The panel drew more cheers from public health experts (and criticism from conservatives) when it issued its final report in June, urging anti-discrimination protections for those who tested positive for exposure to the Human Immunodeficiency Virus (HIV), the virus that caused AIDS. Existing law already shielded AIDS victims from discrimination, but it did not protect HIV carriers.

Watkins called discrimination against those who tested positive for HIV "the foremost obstacle to progress" in stemming the epidemic. Watkins' call for a federal anti-bias law was one of 579 recommendations in the commission's final report. The panel also urged about $3 billion in added federal and state AIDS spending by 1990.

The AIDS commission delivered its final report to the White House June 24, but Reagan declined to comment on it at that time. Instead, he directed his drug abuse adviser, Dr. Donald Ian Macdonald, to review the report and make recommendations for its implementation.

The "AIDS action plan" outlined by Macdonald Aug. 2 was more notable for what it lacked — anti-bias recommendations — than for what it contained.

At a breakfast meeting with reporters and again later at a White House briefing, Macdonald stressed that more than 40 percent of the AIDS commission's 340 recommendations pertaining to the federal government were already being implemented, with another 30 percent to be included in the administration's fiscal 1990 budget request.

The Reagan plan directed the Food and Drug Administration to take steps to protect the nation's blood supply and instructed the secretary of health and human services to conduct a study of the current system of health-care financing and to seek ways to promote out-of-hospital care for AIDS patients.

The plan also ordered all federal agencies to adopt AIDS policies based on guidelines issued in March by the Office of Personnel Management (OPM). Those guidelines directed federal managers to treat employees with AIDS the same as workers with any other serious illness and permitted managers to discipline workers who refused to work with those with AIDS.

The president had been expected to issue an executive

# Efforts to Ban or Limit Abortion ...

Abortion continued to be a divisive issue in 1985-88.

Legislative debates on abortion in the 99th and 100th Congresses generally centered on public funding. The pro-choice side, outnumbered on abortion funding issues, had been less active in Congress, relying instead on the courts to uphold abortion rights. It was forced to become more organized, however, in the face of strong anti-abortion sentiment from the Reagan administration.

Abortion foes suffered a major defeat in 1986 when the Supreme Court, ruling in *Thornburgh v. American College of Obstetricians and Gynecologists*, upheld a woman's right to have an abortion. The court, declaring that there is "a certain private sphere of individual liberty" that should "be kept largely beyond the reach of government," reaffirmed its 1973 decision in *Roe v. Wade*, legalizing abortions and strictly limiting state power to regulate them. *(Decision, p. 802)*

Anti-abortion activists also were disheartened by the 1987 defeat of Supreme Court nominee Robert H. Bork, an abortion rights opponent and critic of *Roe*. *(Bork nomination, p. 714)*

Following are summaries of action on legislation considered by the 99th and 100th Congresses that involved abortion-related issues:

**Prisoners.** Sen. Jesse Helms, R-N.C., in 1985 offered an amendment to the fiscal 1986 Commerce, State and Justice appropriations bill (HR 2965 — PL 99-180) that would bar federal women's prisons from providing abortions to inmates, except to save the life of the pregnant woman. The Senate judged the amendment unconstitutional and dropped it.

A similar amendment, offered by Rep. Bob Dornan, R-Calif., was offered in 1986 as part of the omnibus fiscal 1987 spending bill (H J Res 738 — PL 99-591), which included funding for the Commerce, Justice and State departments, the federal judiciary and several related agencies. The House adopted the amendment, which would bar the Justice Department from using funds to pay for abortions for female inmates in federal prisons or for providing facilities for abortion, unless the life of the woman would be endangered by carrying the fetus to term.

**Tax-Exempt Status.** In 1985 three senators — Helms, Gordon J. Humphrey, R-N.H., and William L. Armstrong, R-Colo. — considered offering an amendment to the 1986 tax-overhaul bill (HR 3838 — PL 99-514) that would terminate the tax-exempt status of any organization that performed or financed abortions or permitted its facilities to be used for them.

They dropped their plans after consultation with President Reagan, however, because he wanted no amendments added to the bill. Reagan promised to support their amendment if they offered it later to another piece of legislation.

During 1986 Senate consideration of the fiscal 1987 continuing appropriations measure (H J Res 738 — PL 99-591), Humphrey offered an amendment to revoke the tax-exempt status of institutions providing abortions. The Senate judged the amendment non-germane, effectively killing it.

Senators in 1988 rejected a Humphrey attempt to repeal the tax-exempt status of non-profit abortion clinics. His amendment, offered during consideration of a tax bill that corrected technical errors in past tax laws (HR 4333 — PL 100-647), would terminate the tax-exempt privilege for any business that earned more than 1 percent of its income from performing abortions.

**CSBG Funds.** The House Education and Labor Committee in April 1986, while considering an omnibus human services authorization bill (HR 4421 — PL 99-425), rejected an amendment to deny Community Services Block Grant (CSBG) funds to organizations that provided abortion counseling or referrals.

**'Morning-After Pill.'** A time limit on 1987 House floor debate on the fiscal 1988 continuing appropriations measure (H J Res 395 — PL 100-202), which included funding for Labor, Health and Human Services (HHS) and Education, effectively prevented amendments from being offered on sensitive social issues that in years past mired the funding bill in controversy. Among the proposals never offered was one by Dornan that would ban federal funds from being spent on research on RU 486, a so-called "morning-after pill" that induced abortion.

**Labor-HHS-Education Appropriations.** A backroom deal in 1986 helped avoid a messy floor fight over abortion during consideration of the fiscal 1987 omnibus continuing appropriations measure (H J Res 738 — PL 99-591), which included funding for the departments of Labor, HHS, Education and related agencies. Opponents of language added by the Senate Appropriations Committee that would allow federal funds to be used to pay for abortions in cases of rape or incest agreed not to seek to delete or otherwise restrict the appropriation provided in the bill for federal family planning programs in exchange for dropping the rape/incest language.

The Senate in 1988 cleared the way for final congressional action on the fiscal 1989 Labor-HHS-Education appropriations bill (HR 4783 — PL 100-436) when it abandoned its efforts to loosen constraints on the use of federal funds for abortion. Members had wanted to allow use of Medicaid funds to pay for abortions in "promptly reported" cases of rape or incest, in addition to cases where continuing a pregnancy would endanger the life of the woman.

Since 1976, Congress had forbidden the use of

allowed to sponsor HMOs without having to set up separate legal entities. HMOs likewise were permitted to offer a wider variety of health insurance products, including mental health, substance abuse, visual or dental plans.

The legislation prohibited the Department of Health and Human Services from changing current regulations, policy statements, interpretations or practices regarding abortion services offered by federally qualified HMOs. Finally, at the insistence of Sen. Dan Quayle, R-Ind., a member of the Labor and Human Resources Committee, the bill ended, as of Oct. 1, 1993, the federal requirement that employers who offered health coverage of any type offer coverage by a federally qualified HMO as well.

## Legislative History

HR 3235 was passed by the House on Nov. 3, 1987. The bill had been reported by the Energy and Commerce Committee Oct. 30 (H Rept 100-417).

The Senate Labor and Human Resources Committee reported the bill on March 22, 1988 (S Rept 100-304). The Senate passed the measure Aug. 11.

The Reagan administration opposed the bill on the grounds that HMOs "no longer need special support from the federal government, either to develop as an industry or to expand their portion of the health care marketplace."

The measure amended a 1973 law (PL 93-222) that set federal standards for HMO services and offered a variety of incentives to encourage the creation of these and other prepaid alternatives to traditional fee-for-service arrangements. (Congress and the Nation Vol. IV, p. 327)

# Mandated Benefits

The Senate Labor and Human Resources Committee on Feb. 17, 1988, approved a controversial bill (S 1265) that would require all employers to provide health insurance for their workers. The measure went no further in the 100th Congress, however. The measure sought to aid the estimated 37 million Americans who lacked any health insurance coverage, public or private.

The chief sponsor of the bill was Edward M. Kennedy, D-Mass., chairman of the Labor panel. Kennedy said his bill would provide health coverage to about 23 million of those people who worked or were dependents of those in the work force.

"For more than half a century, we have required employers to pay a minimum wage, to participate in Social Security, to contribute to unemployment compensation and to purchase workman's compensation insurance," said Kennedy. "In 1988, it is time to require basic health-insurance coverage as well."

Opponents, led by the committee's ranking Republican, Orrin G. Hatch of Utah, warned the measure would do more harm than good. It could cost the economy jobs and billions of dollars, and drive health costs up, Hatch said.

"This bill is too big, too costly and too ineffective for what it does," complained Hatch, who called the proposal "socialism, pure and simple." Nonetheless, Hatch and other critics agreed that something needed to be done about the problem of the uninsured. "This is a well-intentioned bill," said Hatch. "The motives are good."

The Reagan administration vigorously opposed the Kennedy bill. "We believe S 1265 would impose an unduly intrusive and centralist solution, one wholly disproportion-ate to the dimensions of the problem being addressed," said Otis R. Bowen, secretary of the Department of Health and Human Services, in a Feb. 16 letter to Kennedy. "The proposal would open the door to broad new federal regulation of the private health care sector, exacerbate health care inflation, and upset settled wage and benefit arrangements. . . ."

**Provisions.** As approved by the committee, S 1265 (S Rept 100-360) would require all employers to offer a package of minimum health benefits to all adult employees working more than 17.5 hours per week and their dependents. Employees would be required to accept their employer's coverage. The package was to include:

● Coverage of at least 80 percent of costs of medically necessary hospital and physician care and lab tests.

● A "catastrophic" provision limiting out-of-pocket costs to $3,000 per year per family.

● A ban on exclusions based on health status or pre-existing conditions.

● A mental health benefit covering at least 45 days of inpatient care and up to 20 outpatient visits annually for psychotherapy or counseling. Workers could be required to pay half the costs of the outpatient care.

● Coverage of 100 percent of costs for prenatal and routine "well-baby" care, which could not be made subject to an annual deductible.

● A waiting period of no more than 30 days for employers offering health benefits for the first time. Businesses that previously had a longer waiting period could require waits up to six months but had to provide catastrophic coverage for the period between 30 days and the date when full coverage began.

● An employer contribution of at least 80 percent of the premium (100 percent for workers with incomes under 125 percent of minimum wage, which was then $3.35 per hour), and annual deductibles not to exceed $250 per individual and $500 per family.

Employers who offered more generous plans could require larger deductibles and coinsurance payments, or require employees to contribute a larger percentage of the premium, so long as the total value of the employer's contribution to the plan was "actuarially equivalent" to the contribution required under the minimum plan.

The bill also contained special provisions designed to ease the burden the requirements would place on small businesses.

For example, employers with fewer than 10 workers who had been in business less than two years would have to offer employees only a low-cost catastrophic plan to cap out-of-pocket medical costs.

Employees of small family farms would be excluded from coverage until such time as prices for the major commodity produced by the farm had been at 70 percent of parity for two years.

The bill also would create a series of regional "pools" for businesses with fewer than 25 employees. Sponsors said such pools would allow firms to purchase group insurance at lower rates and would reduce administrative overhead.

Finally, in a move much sought by the business community, the bill would pre-empt state regulation of the content of health insurance. State mandates, which typically required coverage of costs of mental health care, treatment for alcoholism or drug abuse or reimbursement for certain non-physician health professionals, resulted in increased administrative costs and drove up the cost of insurance for everyone, according to the U.S. Chamber of Commerce.

# Medical Abuses

President Reagan Aug. 18, 1987, signed legislation making it easier for the Department of Health and Human Services (HHS) to bar unfit, abusive or incompetent health-care practitioners from participation in a raft of health programs.

The House cleared the measure (HR 1444) July 30 when, by voice vote, it accepted the version of the bill passed by the Senate July 23.

In signing the bill (PL 100-93), Reagan overlooked administration objections to a provision clarifying that the HHS secretary could not impose sanctions on states that offered Medicaid coverage on the basis of income and resource thresholds that were less restrictive than the thresholds for cash assistance programs such as Aid to Families with Dependent Children (AFDC).

HR 1444 widely expanded the HHS secretary's authority to bar unfit or incompetent health-care providers (or facilities that employed them) from participating in and receiving payment from the federal Medicare program for the elderly and disabled. It also expanded the secretary's authority to order states to bar providers from participation in Medicaid, the Maternal and Child Health Block Grant program and the Social Services Block Grant program.

Prior to enactment of HR 1444, HHS could exclude practitioners from specific programs if they committed fraudulent acts against those programs and their beneficiaries. It also could exclude them from the programs in any state that had revoked or suspensed their licenses. But HHS was powerless to act against doctors who moved to another state to evade one state's jurisdiction.

An earlier version of the bill nearly became law during the 99th Congress but was derailed when it was caught up in electoral politics. *(99th Congress action, p. 554)*

HR 1444 was approved March 31 by voice vote by the Energy and Commerce Subcommittee on Health and the Environment. The full committee reported it (H Rept 100-85, Part I) May 7.

The Ways and Means Subcommittee on Health, which also had jurisdiction, approved the measure April 1; the full committee reported it (Part II) May 21.

The House passed the bill under suspension of the rules June 2 by a vote of 402-0. On July 14, the Senate Finance Committee reported an almost identical bill (S 661 — S Rept 100-109) on a unanimous vote.

The Senate passed HR 1444 July 23 after substituting the text of S 661.

On July 30, the House accepted the Senate's version of HR 1444, clearing the measure for the president.

## Major Provisions

As cleared, HR 1444:

### Mandatory Exclusions

● Required the HHS secretary to exclude from participation in Medicare and to direct states to exclude from participation in Medicaid, the Maternal and Child Health Block Grant program and the Social Services Block Grant program: An individual or entity convicted of a criminal offense relating to the delivery of services under any of the programs. Exclusions would be for a minimum of five years

unless a state requested otherwise because the individual or entity was the sole community physician or the sole source of essential specialized services in the community.

An individual or entity convicted under federal or state law of a criminal offense related to neglect or abuse of patients. The conviction would not have to be related to the programs in question. The same minimum five-year exclusion would apply, with the same state option for sole community providers.

### Optional Exclusions

● Permitted the HHS secretary to exclude from participation in Medicare and to direct states to exclude from participation in Medicaid, the Maternal and Child Health Block Grant program and the Social Services Block Grant program: An individual or entity convicted under federal or state law of a criminal offense relating to fraud, theft, embezzlement, breach of fiduciary responsibility or financial abuse if the offense was committed either in connection with the delivery of health care or with respect to a health-care program financed in any part by the federal government or any state or local government.

An individual or entity convicted of interfering with the investigation of health-care fraud or of unlawfully manufacturing, distributing, prescribing or dispensing a controlled substance.

An individual or entity whose license to provide health care was suspended or revoked by a state licensing authority or whose license was otherwise lost for reasons bearing on the individual's professional competence, professional conduct or financial integrity.

An individual who surrendered his license while a formal disciplinary proceeding was pending before a state licensing authority.

An individual or entity suspended or excluded from participation in any other federal or state health-care program for reasons related to professional competence, professional performance or financial integrity.

An individual or entity determined by the HHS secretary to have claimed excessive charges or to have furnished items or services substantially in excess of patients' needs or of a quality that failed to meet professionally recognized standards.

A health maintenance organization or competitive medical plan, approved under Medicare or Medicaid, that failed substantially to provide medically necessary services if the failure adversely affected, or had the likelihood of adversely affecting, Medicare or Medicaid beneficiaries.

An entity owned or controlled (defined as a 5 percent interest or greater) by an individual, or that had an officer, director, agent or managing employee who was convicted of program-related offenses, or who had had a civil penalty assessed, or who had been excluded from participation in any of the programs.

An individual or entity who failed to grant access to the HHS secretary, state agency, HHS inspector general or state Medicaid fraud-control unit seeking access for the purpose of performing their statutory functions.

A hospital that failed to act within a stipulated time period to correct inappropriate admission or practice patterns identified by a peer review organization.

An individual in default of repayment of scholarship obligations or loans in connection with health profession education.

● Made all exclusions effective after a period (to be

determined by regulation) long enough to provide "reasonable" notice to the public, as well as to the individual or entity being excluded.

• Permitted the HHS secretary to impose civil fines at current statutory limits ($2,000 per item plus twice the amount claimed for services not actually provided) on: An individual who filed false or fraudulent claims.

An individual who filed claims for services provided by someone whose physician's license was wrongfully obtained or for services provided by someone who falsely represented to the patient that he was board-certified in a medical speciality.

An individual who submitted, or caused to be submitted, claims for payment during a period when the person furnishing the services was excluded from participation. An individual who knowingly gave false or misleading information that could influence a decision on when to discharge a Medicare patient from a hospital.

• Established criminal penalties of $25,000 or five years in prison or both for persons who presented or caused to be presented claims for physician services when the person knew that the individual delivering service was not a licensed physician.

• Required states to have systems for reporting information about formal proceedings concluded against a health-care practitioner or entity by a state licensing authority.

• Required states to make available to the HHS secretary information concerning adverse actions taken by a state licensing authority.

• Required the HHS secretary to provide information to other state licensing authorities, as well as other state and federal officials, for the purpose of determining fitness of such individuals to provide health-care services and to protect the health and safety of beneficiaries.

• Required the HHS secretary to provide suitable safeguards to ensure the confidentiality of the information.

• **Clarification of Medicaid Moratorium.** Clarified the provision of the Deficit Reduction Act of 1984 (PL 98-369) that prohibited the HHS secretary from imposing sanctions on states that offered Medicaid coverage to those deemed "medically needy" using income and resource thresholds less restrictive than for cash assistance programs (such as Aid to Families with Dependent Children and Supplemental Security Income).

## Programs for Handicapped

Congress Oct. 13, 1987, cleared legislation reauthorizing for three years programs that provided assistance for individuals with severe mental or physical handicaps.

The Senate July 21 passed S 1417 (S Rept 100-113), which was a complete rewrite of the programs. The House Aug. 4 passed HR 1871 (H Rept 100-265), a straight reauthorization. The House then passed S 1417 with the language of HR 1871. The Senate agreed to the House changes with further amendments Sept. 30. The House accepted the compromise version Oct. 13. The Developmental Disabilities Assistance and Bill of Rights Act was signed into law (PL 100-146) Oct. 29.

As cleared, S 1417 authorized $209.5 million over fiscal 1988-90 for basic state grants, which helped fund planning, advocacy and service activities for the developmentally disabled. It authorized a total of $66.2 million for special grants to support state systems to protect the legal and human rights of the developmentally disabled.

The bill also authorized a total of $45.6 million over the three years for university-affiliated research grants and $3.7 million in each of the three years for special projects "of national significance."

## Devices for the Disabled

Congress in 1988 cleared legislation (S 2561 — PL 100-407) creating a new grant program to help the nation's 36 million disabled people obtain devices and services that could aid them at home and on the job.

The president signed the bill Aug. 19.

The measure, passed by the Senate Aug. 2 and by the House Aug. 8, authorized $9 million in fiscal 1989 and "such sums as necessary" for four years thereafter for grants to the states to promote the distribution of "assistive technology" to the disabled. It also authorized $6.5 million for 1989 and an open-ended amount in the following years for training personnel to provide technical aid to the handicapped and for various studies and demonstration projects.

Grant funds also could be used to train disabled individuals and their families in the use of assistive devices.

The grants were to be awarded on a competitive basis, with up to 10 states funded the first year and 20 the second. Funding would be fixed at $500,000 to $1 million in each of the first two years and up to $1.5 million in the third year.

The measure mandated a study on the financing of assistive technology devices, to be undertaken by the National Council on the Handicapped. It also required the secretary of education to conduct a feasibility study of setting up a nationwide information and referral network.

The House Education and Labor Committee approved its version of the bill (HR 4904 — H Rept 100-819) on July 12; the Senate Labor and Human Resources Committee reported S 2561 (S Rept 100-438) on July 28.

## 'Gray Market' for Drugs

Congress in 1988 cleared legislation (HR 1207 — PL 100-293) seeking to close the "gray market" by which prescription drugs that were counterfeit, adulterated, too old to be used safely or had been improperly stored could end up in the hands of unwitting consumers.

By voice vote, the Senate March 31 passed HR 1207, which had been approved by the Finance Committee Dec. 11, 1987, and formally reported March 18, 1988 (S Rept 100-303). The final measure was virtually identical to a version passed by the House May 4, 1987, after being reported by the Energy and Commerce Committee April 30 (H Rept 100-76).

The president signed the measure April 22.

The bill sought to choke off the gray market by outlawing the sale or purchase of drug manufacturers' samples, prohibiting in most cases the return to the United States of prescription drugs exported for sale in other countries and barring resale of drugs purchased in bulk by hospitals and other health facilities for their own use.

The bill also imposed storage, handling and accounting standards for drug samples, barred the sale or trade of coupons that could be redeemed for drug samples and set civil and criminal penalties for violators.

The legislation, originally introduced by House Energy

and Commerce Committee Chairman John D. Dingell, D-Mich., grew out of a series of hearings conducted by the Oversight Subcommittee he chaired. At those hearings, witnesses told of drug samples sitting in uninsulated garages or cars, unprotected from high temperatures, and of samples used as payments for doctor bills or goods obtained from pharmacies. The panel also was told of cases in which samples were sold to consumers after being removed from their original packaging.

During legislative action on the bill, the Reagan administration expressed opposition, arguing that "there is insufficient evidence of significant health problems" due to consumers receiving improperly diverted drugs.

## Major Provisions

As cleared, HR 1207:

● Prohibited the import of drugs made in the United States and later exported, except by the manufacturer or if the secretary of health and human services (HHS) authorizes importation in times of medical emergency.

● Made it a federal crime to sell, purchase or trade, or offer to do so, prescription-drug samples or coupons redeemable for them.

● Created penalties for violators of up to 10 years in prison or fines of up to $250,000 or both.

● Required manufacturers or distributors to notify the HHS secretary whenever their representatives were convicted of such a crime, and imposed civil penalties of up to $100,000 for failure to make such a report.

● Required drug makers to control more strictly distribution of samples.

● Required that samples be stored under conditions that maintained their sterility and potency.

● Made it a crime for private hospitals or other facilities to sell, purchase or trade, or offer to do so, drugs purchased at discounts for their own use.

● Required that wholesale distributors of prescription drugs be licensed in the state in which they did business, and that state licensing requirements meet certain minimum standards.

# Vaccine Compensation

One year after it established a program to compensate families whose children were injured or killed by required childhood vaccines, Congress in 1987 created a mechanism to finance the program.

As part of the fiscal 1988 budget reconciliation bill (HR 3545 — PL 100-203) that cleared Dec. 22, lawmakers approved an excise tax on vaccines to finance a trust fund that was to be used to compensate those injured after Oct. 1, 1988. *(Budget reconciliation, p. 61)*

But the compensation program was scaled back significantly to keep the tax low enough to ensure that vaccines remained affordable.

To compensate those injured prior to Oct. 1, 1988, members authorized $80 million in appropriations annually for fiscal 1989-92 to provide compensation for all medical costs and up to $30,000 in attorneys' fees, lost earnings and miscellaneous costs.

HR 3545 also strictly limited the number of compensation awards that could be made from the trust fund.

Finally, the bill moved jurisdiction for administering the compensation system from the U.S. district court to the

U.S. claims court in an effort to address concerns about possible constitutional problems.

## Legislative Action

Capping several years of work, the 99th Congress created a no-fault system through which families of children injured or killed as a result of adverse vaccine reactions could receive compensation without having to prove negligence on the part of those who made or administered the vaccines. *(99th Congress action, p. 547)*

The law (PL 99-660) aimed at ameliorating a liability insurance crisis that was threatening the nation's supply of vaccines to prevent common childhood diseases.

Members of the House Ways and Means Committee complained that they did not have enough time in 1986 to consider an excise tax that had been proposed to fund the compensation system, so a decision on the financing mechanism was postponed until 1987.

A funding plan proposed but set aside in 1986 called for an excise tax on each dose of DPT (diphtheria-pertussis-tetanus) vaccine, polio vaccine and the MMR vaccine, which prevented measles, mumps and rubella. The tax meant higher costs for parents who paid to have their children vaccinated and for state public health programs that offered the shots to those who could not afford them.

The House Ways and Means Select Revenue Subcommittee took up the issue on July 13, 1987. The panel agreed to recommend that the full Ways and Means Committee use general revenues to create a trust fund to compensate 3,500 children injured or killed by vaccines prior to enactment of PL 99-660.

The subcommittee deferred a recommendation on financing compensation for future cases, however, because cost estimates were still uncertain. Rep. Henry A. Waxman, D-Calif., chairman of the Energy and Commerce Subcommittee on Health and author of the original plan, then went back to the drawing board.

On Oct. 14, the full Energy and Commerce Committee approved a Waxman plan that substantially altered the original program. It:

● Required that all compensation be paid in a lump sum, instead of as bills arose.

● Provided separate funding for future vs. past cases.

● Limited the number of cases paid from the trust fund to an average of 150 each 12 months. Taking into account the changes proposed by Energy and Commerce, the Ways and Means Committee approved creation of the trust fund and excise taxes Oct. 15. But it authorized the taxes for only four years.

Even with the new changes, the administration opposed the compensation plan. Secretary Otis R. Bowen of the Department of Health and Human Services (HHS) said in an Oct. 8 letter to Energy and Commerce Chairman John D. Dingell, D-Mich., "We continue to believe that the [compensation program] is so flawed that action should not be taken to activate the program."

Members ignored such objections, however, and added the financing provisions to the budget reconciliation bill.

## Major Provisions

As cleared, the budget reconciliation bill (HR 3545 — PL 100-203) contained the following vaccine compensation provisions:

● **Financing Mechanism Established.** Implemented

a financing mechanism for the vaccine-compensation program established in 1986, thus allowing it to take effect.

● **Jurisdiction.** Placed jurisdiction for vaccine-injury claims under the no-fault system within the U.S. Claims Court.

● **Two-Part Compensation.** Provided that deaths or injuries occurring before Oct. 1, 1988, be compensated from appropriations, authorized at $80 million per year for fiscal 1988-91. Deaths or injuries incurred after that date would be paid from a new Vaccine Injury Compensation Trust Fund, financed from excise taxes on vaccines.

Those with injuries occurring after Oct. 1, 1988, and before Oct. 1, 1992, had to go through the new compensation process and reject any offered award, before suing a vaccine manufacturer in federal court. Those with injuries incurred prior to Oct. 1, 1988, could either seek no-fault compensation or file a damage suit that would not be subject to the liability revisions applicable to cases arising after that date.

● **Excise Tax.** Set excise taxes at $4.56 per dose for the vaccine against diphtheria, tetanus and pertussis (whooping cough); $4.44 per dose for the measles-mumps-rubella vaccine; 29 cents per dose for the polio vaccine; and 6 cents per dose for the tetanus-diphtheria vaccine.

Directed that the tax became effective on vaccines sold after Dec. 31, 1987, and terminated Jan. 1, 1993.

● **Cost Minimum Eliminated.** Eliminated the requirement that persons incurred at least $1,000 in medical, rehabilitative or certain other expenses before becoming eligible to file compensation claims.

● **Lump-Sum Payment.** Provided that all compensation awarded from the Vaccine Compensation Trust Fund under the no-fault system be paid in a lump sum, instead of periodically, as originally envisioned in PL 99-660.

● **Installment Payments.** Provided that payments from appropriated funds be made in four equal, annual installments.

● **Payment Ceiling.** Capped at $30,000 the amount that those eligible for compensation to be paid from appropriations would recover for attorneys' fees, costs, lost earnings, and pain and suffering. The cap would not apply to medical expenses.

● **Limit on Awards.** Provided that the compensation system be terminated if an unexpectedly large number of awards were made and accepted in any year. The HHS secretary was required to notify Congress if more than 150 awards had been made in the first 12 months that the system was in effect. Six months following that notification, unless Congress took affirmative action, no new petitions would be accepted and the tort revisions would lapse. The secretary would be required to examine the number of awards quarterly after the first year, and if at any time they exceeded the 150-per-year average, notify Congress and take steps to shut down the system to new petitions.

● **Tort-Revision Applicability.** Stipulated that only those eligible to file petitions under the no-fault system were subject to the tort law revisions.

● **Speedy Consideration.** Permitted anyone who filed a petition seeking no-fault compensation to withdraw it if the petition had not been adjudicated within one year, and to file a civil suit without regard to the tort revisions.

● **Vaccine Administrators.** Required those seeking damages from the person or clinic administering the vaccine to first pursue compensation through the no-fault system. If an award was made and accepted, no further action would be allowed. If no award was made, or an award was rejected, the family could file a civil action without restriction.

# 'Orphan' Drugs

Congress in 1988 cleared legislation that reauthorized for three years federal grants for the development of treatments for rare diseases. The president signed the bill (HR 3459 — PL 100-290) on April 18. *(Previous authorization, p. 558)*

HR 3459, reauthorizing the 1983 Orphan Drug Act (PL 97-414), had been passed by the House March 22 and the Senate March 31. *(1983 Act, Congress and the Nation Vol. VI, p. 536)*

The bill authorized $10 million for fiscal 1988, $12 million for 1989 and $14 million for 1990 for grants to independent scientists to develop treatments for so-called "orphan diseases," which were loosely defined as those afflicting fewer than 200,000 people. It also:

● Permitted grants to be awarded for the development of special foods and devices needed to treat orphan diseases.

● Required manufacturers of designated orphan drugs who intended to halt production to notify the federal Food and Drug Administration (FDA) one year in advance so the agency could try to find a new production source.

The House Energy and Commerce Committee had approved HR 3459 on Oct. 14, 1987, and formally reported it on Dec. 10 (H Rept 100-473). As approved by the committee, the bill contained a controversial proposal designed to prevent drug companies from reaping big profits from orphan drugs.

The Orphan Drug Act authorized tax credits and grants to pharmaceutical companies to encourage the development of drugs. It also granted the companies seven-year exclusive marketing rights to products given "orphan" status by the FDA.

Rep. Henry A. Waxman, D-Calif., chairman of the Health and the Environment Subcommittee, expressed concern that some drug companies might be taking advantage of the short-term monopoly to charge exorbitant prices for orphan drugs. As a result, the committee bill would modify the exclusivity provision so that competing drug companies could gain approval of their own versions of an orphan drug after going through the FDA drug-approval process separately. The Pharmaceutical Manufacturers Association vigorously protested the proposed change.

Before the bill reached the House floor, Waxman agreed to drop the provision, clearing the way for quick action in both chambers.

# Abandoned Babies

Congress Oct. 4, 1988, cleared legislation aimed at helping find foster homes or other residential settings for babies abandoned in hospitals because their parents were unable or unwilling to care for them.

Final action on the bill (S 945 — PL 100-505) came when the Senate concurred in amendments adopted by the House before it passed the measure Sept. 13. The president signed the bill Oct. 18.

The measure was directed particularly toward infants with AIDS (acquired immune deficiency syndrome), many of whom had no immediate medical need to be in a hospital but had nowhere else to go. Babies born to drug-abusing mothers also often were stranded in hospitals.

The bill authorized $37 million over three years for demonstration projects helping parents to care for their afflicted babies or finding foster homes for the children.

The measure required the secretary of health and human services to report to Congress within a year on the number of abandoned infants in hospitals and on how many of them had AIDS.

A separate title of the bill required a study to determine the most cost-effective ways of caring for all AIDS patients, and an estimate on how much the federal government was spending on AIDS patients through the Medicaid program.

The Senate originally passed S 945 on Aug. 5, 1987.

The House Energy and Commerce Committee reported a companion bill (HR 4843 — H Rept 100-821, Part I) on Aug. 4, 1988.

## Crisis Nurseries

Congress in 1988 cleared legislation (HR 4676 — PL 100-403) to reauthorize demonstration programs to provide crisis care for children at risk of abuse. The president signed the measure into law Aug. 19.

The bill, which was passed by the House July 26, authorized programs to offer temporary child care for disabled children, who often were at high risk of abuse. Such care could provide parents a much-needed respite from the constant pressures of coping with a disabled child, House sponsors said. The measure also reauthorized demonstration programs to provide crisis nurseries for other children at risk of abuse or neglect.

The bill reauthorized grants to states first created in 1986 (PL 99-401). *(1986 bill, p. 744)*

The Senate passed, and cleared, the bill without debate Aug. 9.

## Infant Health

The House and Senate both passed legislation in 1987 to step up federal efforts to combat infant mortality. Neither measure became law, however.

The Senate passed its bill (S 1441) Aug. 6. The House passed its bill (HR 1326) Nov. 9. The House measure would boost by a total of $30 million the fiscal 1988 authorization levels for community and migrant health centers, stipulating that appropriations from the added authorization levels be used for services designed to reduce the incidence of infant mortality.

HR 1326 was reported (H Rept 100-416) by the Energy and Commerce Committee Oct. 30.

The $42-million Senate bill would authorize increased funding for federal community and migrant health centers to be directed toward improving maternal and child health-care services. The bill had been reported by the Labor and Human Resources Committee Aug. 3 (S Rept 100-137).

## Family Planning Program

Legislation to reauthorize the federal family planning program stalled during the 100th Congress, as it had in the 99th, in a swirl of controversy over abortion. *(99th Congress action, p. 557)*

The Senate Labor and Human Resources Committee Nov. 12, approved a four-year reauthorization (S 1366) of the so-called Title X program, but the measure failed to reach the Senate floor by the end of the year. Instead, Congress continued the family planning program through appropriations legislation, as it had every year since fiscal 1985.

And bowing to a White House veto threat, House-Senate conferees dropped from the year's omnibus funding bill (H J Res 395 — PL 100-202) a Senate provision aimed at blocking the Reagan administration from implementing stiff new anti-abortion regulations for the family planning program.

The Reagan regulations, first published Sept. 1 and due to take effect in early 1988, barred Title X grantees from making abortion referrals, mentioning abortion as an option or using non-federal money for abortions or abortion-related services unless the facilities were physically and financially separate from those getting Title X funds.

The proposed regulations drew cheers from anti-abortion groups and threats of lawsuits from a number of Title X grantees, including the National Family Planning and Reproductive Health Association Inc.

In March 1988, however, the Department of Health and Human Services postponed implementation of the regulations. The decision came after a March 3 ruling by a federal judge in Boston that the regulations, scheduled to be phased in beginning that day, were unconstitutional and contrary to congressional intent for the Title X program.

The new rules had been published in final form Feb. 2.

## 'Chastity' Program

The Senate Labor and Human Resources Committee Aug. 10, 1988, approved legislation to reauthorize a controversial program aimed at reducing teenage pregnancies, but the measure went no further.

By voice vote, the panel approved S 1950, which would authorize $60 million annually in fiscal 1989-91 for the Adolescent Family Life program. The bill was formally reported Oct. 7 (S Rept 100-591).

The program, created in 1981, funded demonstration projects to discourage teenagers from engaging in sex, as well as projects to promote adoption and provide services for teen parents.

The so-called "chastity" program, which contained controversial bans on abortion counseling and on providing services without parental consent, had been unauthorized since 1985 and had been the subject of a heated court battle because it funded religious groups to teach about sex.

In June 1988, a divided Supreme Court narrowly upheld the program's constitutionality in *Bowen v. Kendrick*, with a five-judge majority declaring that the program "has a valid secular purpose, does not have the primary effect of advancing religion and does not create an excessive entanglement of church and state." *(Supreme Court decision, p. 814)*

But Justice Sandra Day O'Connor — who provided the necessary fifth vote — said in a concurring opinion that the act, while valid on its face, "appears to have been administered in a way that led to violations of the Establishment Clause."

S 1950 would eliminate current requirements for parental consent or notification before services could be provided; it also would lift the ban on abortion counseling or referrals, although a ban on the use of funds for abortions would remain.

## Alcohol Warning Labels

Congress' election-year push to get tough on illegal drugs provided an unexpected opening for legislators who wanted to discourage the use of alcohol as well.

A measure (S 2047) to require health warning labels on all containers of alcoholic beverage containers was attached to the omnibus anti-drug bill (HR 5210 — PL 100-690) cleared Oct. 22, 1988. Also made part of the drug bill was a reauthorization of programs under the auspices of the Alcohol, Drug Abuse and Mental Health Administration. *(Drug bill, p. 748)*

Efforts to require warning labels failed in the 99th Congress. *(1986 action, p. 559)*

The Senate Commerce Committee Sept. 20 unanimously approved a compromise version of S 2047 (S Rept 100-596) in a move that represented a surprise turnaround from years past. The bill was sponsored by Strom Thurmond, R-S.C., who had been pushing warning label legislation without success every year since 1971. The measure required that within 12 months of enactment, all containers of alcoholic beverages carry "in a conspicuous and prominent place" the following message: "GOVERNMENT WARNING: (1) According to the Surgeon General, women should not drink alcoholic beverages during pregnancy because of the risk of birth defects. (2) Consumption of alcoholic beverages impairs your ability to drive a car or operate machinery, and may cause health problems."

The bill prohibited states from requiring any different warnings.

Officially, the alcoholic beverage industry remained opposed to the bill. But observers said the industry did not actively work against the measure and actually favored health warning labels.

Supporters of the bill attributed the industry's apparent switch to the desire to avoid having to deal with similar legislation in each of the states and to obtain possible protection against future product liability lawsuits.

They noted that the cigarette industry, which had been the target of numerous product liability suits, had defended itself successfully against almost all of them, in part by arguing that federally required warning labels on tobacco products gave consumers ample notice of the health dangers associated with smoking.

## Nutrition Monitoring

Legislation (S 1081) in 1988 aimed at better coordination of the government's nutrition-monitoring efforts drew a pocket veto from President Reagan, who criticized it as unnecessary and cumbersome. Advocates of the bill vowed to pass it again in the 101st Congress.

In the works for nearly a decade, the bill would force the Departments of Agriculture (USDA) and Health and Human Services (HHS) to develop a 10-year plan for coordinating federal nutrition-monitoring efforts, which involved determining what Americans ate and how good that food was for them. At least six different agencies gather such information, resulting in the publication of 19 different government reports and surveys on dietary habits and

## New Smoking Report

A new surgeon general's report on the addictive nature of nicotine set off a chorus of antismoking rhetoric on Capitol Hill in 1988, but no new federal smoking curbs were enacted.

U.S. Surgeon General C. Everett Koop May 16 officially released the 19th volume of surgeon generals' reports on the health consequences of smoking. In what was in fact a long-delayed 1987 report, Koop — an ardent smoking foe — likened nicotine's addictive qualities to those of illegal substances such as heroin and cocaine.

The 618-page report revealed no new research documenting the addictive nature of nicotine but, like many past reports, compiled existing information and drew conclusions from the whole.

Koop acknowledged that the report's ultimate significance lay not in its findings, but in the way it was used to further initiatives aimed at discouraging tobacco use — termed by some as its "legislative bounce."

Smoking and health reports issued by the surgeon general long had had a significant bounce. The first report detailing the link between cigarette smoking and lung cancer, issued in 1964 by Surgeon General Luther L. Terry, was credited with providing the impetus for the first congressionally required warning labels on cigarette packs. *(Congress and the Nation Vol. I, p. 1184)*

And many said it was Koop's 1986 report, which found that so-called secondhand smoke represented a health hazard to non-smokers, that prompted Congress in 1987 to ban smoking on airplane flights of less than two hours. *(Smoking ban, p. 387)*

Koop proposed that labels on tobacco products carry a notice that they contain an addictive substance. He also suggested that Congress increase the excise tax on cigarettes, but similar tax increases had been repeatedly rebuffed in the past. And a major objective of the surgeon general was finding ways to discourage children and teenagers from starting to smoke in the first place.

Industry spokesmen were quick to attack Koop's report. "Claims that smokers are 'addicts' defy common sense," said the Tobacco Institute, which represented tobacco manufacturers. "Smoking is truly a personal choice which can be stopped if and when a person decides to do so."

Tobacco-state lawmakers took offense as well. Said Sen. Terry Sanford, D-N.C., "In the middle of a supposed war on drugs, the surgeon general has mistaken the enemy. In comparing tobacco — a legitimate and legal substance — to insidious narcotics such as heroin and cocaine, he has directed 'friendly fire' at American farmers and businessmen."

nutrition. Similar legislation passed the House in 1986 but died in the Senate. *(1986 action, p. 560)*

Under the 1988 bill, the two departments were required to issue jointly, at least every five years, a report called "Dietary Guidelines for Americans." The bill also would set up a system under which the two departments would review any such guidance issued by other federal agencies, to prevent the release of conflicting advice.

The White House issued a statement Nov. 8, 1988, in which Reagan said his administration "supports the principal goals of this legislation." But, he added, "the bill would create a substantial amount of unnecessary and complex federal bureaucracy that would hamper the achievement of the bill's goals."

Advocates of the bill had been stymied in their decade-long effort not only by the administration but by some commodity groups, which feared that the bill would result in the government declaring certain foods unhealthful. A key compromise resulted in endorsements from a wide variety of health groups and food producers, aligning the American Heart Association and the American Public Health Association with the National Cattlemen's Association, the National Pork Producers Council and United Egg Producers.

The compromise sought to ensure that the government would speak with one voice when issuing dietary advice to the public. The secretaries of HHS and USDA were required to review all dietary guidance proposed by any federal agency to assure that it was either consistent with the government's latest dietary guidelines or based on new scientific evidence that they considered valid. If the two officials disagreed on whether to approve the proposed new guidance, the public had to be given a chance to comment on the proposal. Thus, the producers of the food involved had a chance to fight negative advice. If the officials still disagreed after reviewing public comments, either could approve release of the advice.

The House Science Committee approved a reworked version of the bill (H Rept 100-1067, Part I) Oct. 3. The Senate Governmental Affairs Committee reported the measure (S Rept 100-409) June 29. It was passed by the Senate Aug. 9 and and House Oct. 12. Final congressional acton came Oct. 18 when the Senate accepted the House-passed version.

# Animal-Drug Patents

Legislation (S 2843 — PL 100-670) to give animal drugs the same patent treatment as drugs for humans was cleared by Congress Oct. 13, 1988, after both chambers approved a compromise version by voice vote.

The bill, signed by the president Nov. 16, made it easier for manufacturers of generic copies of animal drugs to win marketing approval for their products while granting brand-name manufacturers extended patents to make up for time lost in the federal government's drug-approval process.

The measure was designed to bring animal drugs under a 1984 law (PL 98-417) making similar changes for human drugs. *(Congress and the Nation Vol. VI, p. 547)*

Under the legislation, makers of generic animal drugs seeking marketing approval from the Food and Drug Administration (FDA) would have to show only that their products were equivalent to brand-name drugs already approved. In exchange, makers of brand-name drugs could extend their 17-year patents by up to five years (during which time no generic copies could be marketed) to make up for time lost in the approval process.

S 2843 did differ somewhat from the 1984 law. For example, the legislation required that additional safety studies be conducted for drugs given to food-producing animals.

The House version of the bill was approved Aug. 9 by the Energy and Commerce Committee and Sept. 27 by the Judiciary Committee (HR 4982 — H Rept 100-972, Parts I and II).

The full House passed HR 4982 on Oct. 6 by voice vote. House-Senate negotiators then worked out the final version.

# Stolen Animals

The Senate by voice vote passed legislation Aug. 10, 1988, that was designed to help curb the sale of stolen pets to research facilities. But the measure was never acted on by the House.

The bill, S 2353, effectively would ban federally licensed animal dealers who sold to research facilities from purchasing dogs and cats at auctions. The Department of Agriculture, which enforced the Animal Welfare Act of 1966, had uncovered numerous instances in which stolen pets had been sold at auction to licensed dealers.

S 2353 would require that dealers obtain animals not specifically bred for research only from state or local animal shelters and only after the animals had been held at least seven days, to give owners the opportunity to reclaim lost pets.

# Chronology
# Of Action
# On Human Services

# 1985-86

The 99th Congress cleared major human services legislation extending food stamp benefits and eligibility and making substantive changes in federal welfare laws.

Reauthorized were programs that offered child care, education, nutritional services, energy aid and other community assistance to the poor; five child nutrition programs; training programs for the handicapped; and a program that helped provide millions of meals to senior citizens.

Congress created, as part of reauthorization legislation of major domestic volunteer programs, a new "literacy corps" to help resolve problems of illiteracy.

Made permanent was a program that encouraged the disabled who received Supplemental Security Income benefits to work if they were able. And Congress established new legal protection and advocacy services for the mentally ill.

## Food Stamps

Responding to reports of increased hunger in the United States, Congress in 1985 voted to expand benefits and eligibility for the largest federal food aid program — food stamps.

The final version of the omnibus farm bill (HR 2100 — PL 99-198) cleared by Congress Dec. 18 authorized food stamp spending of up to $13.03 billion in fiscal 1986, rising to $15.97 billion in 1990. Over the five-year life of the law, $523 million more would be spent on food stamps than would have been spent by extending the existing level of funding, which was $13.93 billion in fiscal 1985. *(Omnibus farm bill, p. 501)*

Most of the additional spending was caused by increases in the allowances recipients could deduct from gross income, which raised benefit levels. Also, the bill relaxed limits on a family's assets — such as cash resources and certain automobiles — that were used to determine eligibility for the program. In addition, the measure prohibited states from charging sales tax on purchases made with food stamps, which increased the buying power of food stamp recipients.

For the first time, all states were required to set up employment and training programs for eligible food stamp recipients. About 40 states had some type of work requirement, but they varied in effectiveness.

The final bill permitted states to design their own programs, subject to approval by the secretary of agriculture. States could provide job search, job training, "workfare" or other means to help recipients gain skills, training or experience to increase their ability to gain employment.

According to official poverty figures released in August 1985 by the Census Bureau, in 1984 14.4 percent of the nation — 33.7 million Americans — were living below the poverty line of $10,609 for an urban family of four. A study, conducted by the Physicians Task Force on Hunger in America at the Harvard University School of Public Health, found that up to 20 million Americans were hungry at least sometime each month. The task force concluded that the problem was getting worse, and that it was the result of federal cutbacks in food and nutrition programs. The food stamp program had been cut by about $2 billion a year since 1981.

As signed into law Dec. 23, 1985, HR 2100 (PL 99-198) included food assistance provisions that:

● Required state agencies to provide a method for distributing food stamps to the homeless.

● Revised the definition of "disabled" to allow for special treatment in determining eligibility and benefits for: certain disabled persons who received state-financed Supplemental Security Income (SSI) payments, but who did not receive the basic federal SSI benefits; recipients of public disability retirement pensions who had permanent disabilities; veterans receiving pensions for non-service connected disabilities; and certain railroad retirement disability annuitants.

● Prohibited states from charging sales taxes on food stamp purchases. This provision was to take effect at the beginning of the fiscal year following the first session of the state legislature.

● Made households automatically eligible for the food stamp program if members already received benefits under the program for Aid to Families with Dependent Children (AFDC) or under SSI. In addition, the bill prohibited the automatic denial of eligibility or termination of food stamp benefits if a recipient was denied AFDC or SSI benefits.

● Emphasized that any federal Pell Grant not used for tuition and mandatory school fees was to be counted as income for food stamp eligibility purposes, and any organization fees or insurance premiums that reduced the amount of a student loan would not be counted as income for food stamp purposes.

● Permitted farmers and other self-employed persons to deduct business losses when determining net income for food stamp eligibility.

● Required that payments to third parties by state and local governments would count as income, including student grants, loans and scholarships, but excepting medical assistance, energy assistance, child care and other basic assistance programs comparable to general assistance.

● Required that all allowances, earnings and payments received under the Job Training Partnership Act be counted as income.

● Allowed states to exclude from income the first $50 a month of child support received by an AFDC recipient family, if the state were to reimburse the federal government for the estimated food stamp benefit cost of doing so.

● Increased the "earned income deduction" from 18 percent to 20 percent to increase food stamp benefits available to low-income working families, effective May 1, 1986. The bill also increased the deduction for shelter expenses from $139 a month to $147 a month and created a separate deduction of up to $160 a month for child-care costs. The deductions were to be subtracted from gross income to arrive at the net income on which stamp benefits were based.

● Prohibited households receiving low-income energy assistance from taking deductions for utility costs, if the amount of the energy assistance were to exceed the utility allowance. States were given the option of establishing a separate utility allowance for families receiving energy assistance.

● Required states to have households with earnings or recent work history, except for migrant farm workers and families with elderly and handicapped members, report monthly on factors affecting their eligibility, but allowed the requirement to be waived if the state were to show that it would result in unwarranted administrative expenses.

● Raised liquid asset limits on most eligible households from $1,500 to $2,000 in fiscal 1987. For households with one or more members, at least one of whom was elderly, the limit was set at $3,000. The existing level was $3,000 for households of two or more with one elderly member and $1,500 for others. Excluded from assets were property with liens or related to maintenance; use of a vehicle used to produce income or transport a disabled person; and burial plots.

● Disqualified a household if the head of the household failed to comply with food stamp work requirements; made subject to work requirements heads of households 16 or older not attending school half-time or more.

● Required states to set up job training and employment programs for employable food stamp recipients, designed by the state. A state could exempt recipients from participation if the state determined that it would be impractical or not cost-effective to require them to participate in job programs. States could exempt entire geographic areas and persons receiving food stamps for less than 30 days, but participation could not exceed 50 percent through fiscal 1989. The bill also authorized $40 million in fiscal 1986, $50 million in fiscal 1987, $60 million in fiscal 1988 and $75 million in fiscal 1989 and 1990 in grants to states to carry out their employment and training programs. If states were to incur greater costs, the federal government would share in 50 percent of the additional cost.

● Permitted insurance of food stamp benefits at various times during a month, providing that no more than 40 days elapsed between issuances.

● Permitted federally insured credit unions with wholesale or retail grocers within their field of membership to redeem food stamps.

● Prohibited financial institutions from imposing or collecting from retail food stores a fee or other charge for redemption of coupons.

● Required one adult member of a household to attest, under penalty of perjury, that the household's statements on the food stamp application were true, and required states to verify income and other eligibility factors.

● Required that in areas serving more than 5,000 food stamp households, states would have to set up fraud detection units to investigate and assist in the prosecution of fraud.

● Required that if a disqualified store were sold, the previous owner would be subject to a civil money penalty to reflect the remaining disqualification period.

● Required a study of the quality control and error-rate sanction system, and prohibited the collection of sanctions from states for six months, pending the results of the study.

● Required the secretary to develop, in consultation with states, a plan by Feb. 1, 1987, for the use of an automated data processing and information retrieval system to administer the food stamp program. States were required to develop a plan based on the secretary's model by Oct. 1,

1987, to improve computer operations and to implement the plan by Oct. 1, 1988.

● Authorized for the food stamp program up to $13.037 billion in fiscal 1986, $13.936 billion in 1987, $14.741 billion in 1988, $15.435 billion in 1989 and $15.970 billion in 1990.

● Authorized for the Puerto Rico nutrition assistance block grant $825 million in fiscal 1986, $853 million in fiscal 1987, $880 million in 1988, $908 million in 1989 and $937 million in 1990.

● Extended the Temporary Emergency Food Assistance Program for two years, and authorized $50 million a year for state and local administrative costs. The bill also required states to match 80 percent of the federal contribution and allowed the match to include in-kind contributions. It also reauthorized the Commodity Supplemental Food Program and allowed local officials operating the program to serve elderly persons within available funding if the local agencies determined that the funds were in excess of what was necessary to serve eligible women, infants and children.

● Required the cooperative extension services of states to carry out an expanded program of nutrition and consumer education for low-income individuals, and authorized $5 million in fiscal 1986, $6 million in fiscal 1987 and $8 million in fiscal 1988, 1989 and 1990 for the program.

# Welfare Program Changes

Significant changes in federal welfare laws were included in the fiscal 1986 omnibus deficit reduction bill (HR 3128 — PL 99-272) cleared by Congress March 20, 1986. *(Fiscal 1986 reconciliation bill, p. 40)*

Although both the House and Senate versions of HR 3128 included changes to the nation's welfare laws that would result in increased federal spending, most so-called "add-on" programs were dropped either in the December 1985 conference report (H Rept 99-453) or during the negotiations that followed.

Among the last add-ons dropped was a provision mandating that Aid to Families with Dependent Children (AFDC) benefits be paid to two-parent households in which the primary wage earner was unemployed. Under existing law, states had the option of offering such benefits under AFDC, the principal federal-state welfare program. The Reagan administration strongly opposed the proposal, which later was dropped from the fiscal 1987 reconciliation bill (HR 5300 — PL 99-509) as well. *(Fiscal 1987 reconciliation bill, p. 48)*

Post-conference negotiations also resulted in the demise of a proposal to give states a reprieve from sanctions for failure to comply with federally set administrative error rates in Medicaid, the federal-state health insurance program for the poor. But similar sanctions were delayed for AFDC, which, like Medicaid, was jointly funded by the federal and state governments and administered by the states.

On March 28, 1986, 26 states, the District of Columbia and three California counties filed suit to void both the AFDC and Medicaid penalties. A federal trial court dismissed the case in November, saying it was brought prematurely.

One add-on program that emerged intact authorized $45 million for both fiscal 1987 and 1988 to help children aged 16 and over in the AFDC foster-care program prepare for independent living.

The proposal was championed by Sen. Daniel Patrick Moynihan, D-N.Y., who cited studies showing that former AFDC foster children in New York City were twice as likely to end up on public assistance as other young people aged 18-21, and that half of all youths in the city's shelters for the homeless were formerly in foster care.

Under the program, states could use the funds to provide services to help former foster children finish high school or obtain vocational training, as well as to provide training in daily living skills such as budgeting.

**Major Provisions.** As signed into law April 7, 1986, HR 3128 (PL 99-272) included welfare provisions that:

● Altered the way in which a state could satisfy the federal requirement that it "pass through" increases in Supplemental Security Income (SSI) payments, which provided assistance to needy aged, blind or disabled individuals. The change was sought by members from Oklahoma, because that state stood to lose its federal funding due to non-compliance.

● Provided that the federal government, through the Social Security Administration, administer state supplementary payments to institutionalized persons eligible for the $25 per month federal SSI personal needs allowance, if the state requested it. A number of states currently supplemented the personal-needs allowance, which allowed institutionalized Medicaid patients to purchase toiletries and other personal goods not covered by Medicaid.

● Provided that disabled widows and widowers between the ages of 50 and 59 who became ineligible for SSI and Medicaid because of a 1984 increase in their Social Security benefits have their eligibility reinstated. These individuals were given an additional 15 months to file for Medicaid benefits.

● Imposed a two-year moratorium on the collection of sanction payments from states not in compliance with federally set error rates for AFDC.

Under existing law, states that did not keep error rates below federal targets could be required to pay back to the federal government the federal share of the cost of improperly issued benefits.

During the moratorium, HHS and the National Academy of Sciences were to conduct quality control studies. Based on the results of the studies, the existing quality control system was to be restructured and criteria established for recalculating the amount owed by states liable for sanctions. The AFDC sanctions assessed but not yet collected amounted to more than $155 million for 1981 and 1982.

● Directed the secretary of health and human services to take action to recover 40 percent of the amounts spent on automated AFDC claims-processing and information-retrieval systems from any state that failed to implement those systems in a timely manner.

The federal government currently paid 90 percent of the cost of development and installation of automated systems if the plans were approved in advance. States would be liable if their systems were not operational on the date specified in the approved planning document; however, the bill also expanded the secretary's authority to extend the deadline if delays resulted from circumstances beyond the state's control.

● Directed the General Accounting Office to conduct a one-year study of per capita payments to American Indians from various funds based on their status as members of an Indian tribe or organization. The study also would document how those payments were treated for purposes of eligibility for means-tested federal programs, and justifications for exemptions.

Under existing law, many per capita payments to Indians were exempt from being counted as income for the purpose of determining eligibility for federally funded benefit programs.

● Required, as a condition of eligibility for AFDC, that recipients cooperate in identifying third parties who might be liable for their health coverage. Such a requirement already was in place for Medicaid eligibility.

● Added a number of provisions to make it easier for adopted and foster children to receive Medicaid benefits. The provisions removed the need for actual adoption assistance payments to be made before an adopted child could be deemed eligible for Medicaid; provided that, should the child move to another state, the new state would provide the child's Medicaid benefits; and established Medicaid eligibility at the time a child was placed for adoption, as long as an adoption assistance agreement was in effect.

Previously, Medicaid eligibility did not begin until the issuance of an interlocutory or judicial decree of adoption.

● Extended through 1987 the ceiling on AFDC foster-care funds below which states could transfer unused funds to other child welfare services.

● Extended through 1987 AFDC foster-care payments for children removed from their home under a voluntary placement agreement.

● Authorized a new program funded at $45 million in each of fiscal 1987 and 1988 to help AFDC foster-care children prepare for independent living, by providing career counseling and other services. Money would be distributed to states by their percentage of AFDC foster children. States would not have to match the federal assistance.

# Human Services Funds

President Reagan Sept. 30, 1986, signed an omnibus human services bill (HR 4421 — PL 99-425) authorizing $15.79 billion through fiscal 1990 for programs that offered child care, education, nutritional services, energy aid and other community assistance to the poor.

The legislation reauthorized for four years Head Start, Dependent Care, Community Services Block Grant (CSBG), Community Food and Nutrition, and the Low Income Home Energy Assistance Program (LIHEAP).

In its fiscal 1987 budget, the administration had called for outright termination of the Dependent Care and Follow Through programs and zero funding for CSBG. The programs were last reauthorized in 1984. *(1984 action, Congress and the Nation Vol. VI, p. 603)*

### Legislative Action

The House Education and Labor Committee April 10 unanimously approved HR 4421 (H Rept 99-545). The panel rejected an amendment that would deny CSBG funds to organizations that provided abortion counseling or referrals.

The LIHEAP reauthorization was reported in a separate bill (HR 4422 — H Rept 99-556, Part I).

The House, making no major alterations in the programs, approved HR 4421 April 29 by a vote of 377-33.

Before passage, the House rejected, 161-245, an amendment by Tom Tauke, R-Iowa, to kill the Follow Through program. Members also rejected, 140-267, an amendment by Robert S. Walker, R-Pa., to freeze fiscal 1987 funding for CSBG at its fiscal 1986 outlay level.

The Senate Labor and Human Resources Committee May 20 unanimously approved S 2444 (S Rept 99-327). After substituting the text of S 2444 for the House bill, the Senate passed HR 4421 by voice vote July 14.

The Senate bill called for the establishment of a $6 million scholarship program for low-income candidates pursuing a Child Development Associate (CDA) credential. The CDA credential was a prerequisite for licensing day-care providers in 31 states and the District of Columbia.

By voice vote, the chamber agreed to a number of amendments to HR 4421, one of which consisted of a modified version of a bill (S 140) that sought to improve the treatment of victims of child abuse. The Senate passed S 140 in 1985, but the House version (HR 2999) was tied up in three different committees. *(Child abuse bill, p. 744)*

Another amendment, offered by Dan Quayle, R-Ind., would amend the Fair Labor Standards Act to allow 14- and 15-year-olds to serve as bat/ball boys or girls for professional baseball teams. The Labor Department ruled that the use of children under age 16 by the minor-league Indianapolis Indians violated child labor standards under the act.

Most of the debate in the House-Senate conference committee was devoted to the provision by Quayle. House conferees, led by Education and Labor Chairman Augustus F. Hawkins, D-Calif., and Austin J. Murphy, D-Pa., chairman of the Labor Standards Subcommittee, criticized the measure, objecting that it removed the bat boys/girls from minimum wage requirements. In the conference's final order of business, the Senate conferees agreed to remove the exemption from the bill and instead to request the secretary of labor to study the issue for a year.

The conferees also killed two plans — contained in the Senate bill — to hold a national conference on poverty and to make a New York primate research laboratory eligible for federal grants.

The conference committee Aug. 13 by voice vote approved HR 4421. The House Sept. 16 approved the conference report (H Rept 99-815) by voice vote. The Senate followed suit Sept. 18, clearing the bill.

## Major Provisions

As signed into law Sept. 30, 1986, HR 4421 (PL 99-425):

● Authorized a total of $5.2 billion for the Head Start program — $1.2 billion for fiscal 1987, $1.3 billion for fiscal 1988, $1.3 billion for fiscal 1989 and $1.4 billion for fiscal 1990.

● Required that Head Start programs for Indians and migrant workers be funded for 1987-90 at no less than fiscal 1985 levels.

● Authorized $31.85 million for the Follow Through program, with $7.5 million for fiscal 1987, $7.8 million for fiscal 1988, $8.1 million for fiscal 1989 and $8.4 million for fiscal 1990.

● Renamed Dependent Care the State Dependent Care Development Grants, and authorized a total of $80 million for the program — $20 million annually for fiscal 1987-90.

● Eliminated a provision in existing law that permitted before- and after-school child-care programs to be provided at community centers only when school facilities were not available.

● Changed the definition of school-age children to include those under age 5 in states that provided younger children free public education.

● Authorized a total of $1.68 billion for the CSBG program — $390 million for fiscal 1987, $409.5 million for fiscal 1988, $430 million for fiscal 1989 and $451.5 million for fiscal 1990.

● Permitted CSBG training funds to be used for national conferences, newsletters and the collection and dissemination of data about CSBG programs and projects.

● Extended eligibility for CSBG funds to organizations created in fiscal 1982 as direct successors to a Community Action Agency.

● Required the secretary of health and human services (HHS) to report annually to the chairmen of the House Education and Labor and the Senate Labor and Human Resources committees on programs and projects funded under the secretary's discretionary authority and to make publicly available a catalog of such programs.

● Authorized a total of $12 million for the Community Food and Nutrition program, with $3 million for each of fiscal 1987-90.

● Authorized $15 million, or $5 million for each of fiscal 1987-89, for grants for a new CSBG demonstration program. These grants were to help fund new approaches to meeting critical needs of the poor. Grants were to be made only for activities not previously funded by the federal government and could not finance more than 50 percent of the costs of any program. In addition, no single grant could exceed $250,000.

● Authorized a total of $8.71 billion for LIHEAP — $2.05 billion for fiscal 1987, $2.13 billion for fiscal 1988, $2.22 billion for fiscal 1989 and $2.31 billion for fiscal 1990.

● Permitted certain community-based organizations to be designated to provide LIHEAP payments for energy crisis intervention, including providing space heaters, blankets, payments and alternative shelter arrangements.

● Stipulated that LIHEAP payments could not be considered as income for the purpose of determining a recipient's eligibility to receive food stamps.

● Authorized the HHS secretary to make grants to states receiving funds under Title XX of the Social Security Act (PL 93-647) to fund scholarships for those working toward a CDA credential, required by many states as a condition for licensing.

● Authorized a total of $6 million for the grants — $1.5 million for each of fiscal 1987-90.

● Defined as eligible to receive scholarship assistance a candidate for a CDA credential whose income did not exceed the federal poverty line by more than 50 percent.

● Required each state receiving grants under the program to provide annually information on the number of eligible individuals assisted under the program, their positions and their salaries before and after receiving their CDA credentials.

● Directed the secretary of labor to study and inform the president and Congress whether changing the permissible hours of employment for bat boys and bat girls would be detrimental to their well-being.

● Required the secretary of education to compile a complete list, by name, of beginning reading instruction programs and methods, including phonics. The listing must be publicized and disseminated nationally on an annual basis.

# Volunteer Programs

Congress Oct. 8, 1986, cleared for the president a bill (HR 4116 — PL 99-551) reauthorizing major domestic volunteer programs for three years, through fiscal 1989.

HR 4116 authorized a total of $555.36 million for the Volunteers in Service to America (VISTA) program, the Older American Volunteer Programs and administrative costs for ACTION, the agency that administered them.

The legislation also created a new "literacy corps" within VISTA to help existing public and private efforts aimed at resolving problems of illiteracy. (Previous reauthorization, Congress and the Nation Vol. VI, p. 610)

## Legislative History

The House Education and Labor Committee (H Rept 99-588) by voice vote April 23 approved the reauthorization of VISTA and five other programs first established under the Domestic Volunteer Service Act of 1973 (PL 93-113). The committee added to the bill the language of HR 4607, reauthorizing for three years the Older American Volunteer Programs. (Domestic Volunteer Service Act, Congress and the Nation Vol. IV, p. 412)

After heated debate, the House June 17 passed HR 4116 by a vote of 360-52. Debate on the bill grew partisan over an amendment offered by Tom Tauke, R-Iowa, to lower the bill's authorization levels. Tauke's amendment, which failed on a 189-221 vote, would reduce the 1987 authorization to the amount approved in the 1986 appropriation.

The chamber also defeated, by a vote of 204-208, an amendment offered by Lynn Martin, R-Ill., to freeze the funding floor levels for VISTA at fiscal 1986 levels. The floor levels mandated the number of VISTA volunteer hours funded before money could be spent on the Service Learning and Special Volunteer Programs.

By voice vote, the Senate Labor and Human Resources Committee June 25 approved S 2324 (S Rept 99-332), legislation reauthorizing domestic anti-poverty volunteer programs for three years.

S 2324 included a controversial provision requested by the Reagan administration that allowed volunteers to participate in the Senior Companions and Foster Grandparents program without receiving stipends. Those programs were open to low-income senior citizens.

After substituting the text of S 2324, the Senate by voice vote July 14 passed HR 4116.

The conference report on the bill (H Rept 99-954) was filed Oct. 2. Conferees agreed to authorization levels that were slightly higher than those approved by the Senate and slightly lower than those approved by the House. Overall authorization levels represented a small increase over previous years.

House and Senate conferees agreed on "funding floors" for VISTA of 2,400 full-time volunteers for 1987, 2,500 for 1988 and 2,600 for 1989.

The main sticking point in conference involved the Senate provision permitting non-needy senior citizens to participate in two senior volunteer programs. The final version permitted non-needy individuals to serve in the programs without receiving stipends, provided that the costs associated with their efforts came from outside gifts or the volunteers themselves, not from appropriated funds. Senate conferees, however, insisted on striking the House provision allowing Foster Grandparents to serve mentally retarded adults, as well as children.

Final action came Oct. 8 when the Senate adopted the conference report on the bill by voice vote. The House had approved the report by a 366-33 vote Oct. 2.

## Major Provisions

As cleared by Congress, HR 4116:

● Authorized a total of $78.04 million in stipends for VISTA volunteers: $25 million for fiscal 1987, $26 million for fiscal 1988 and $27.04 million for fiscal 1989.

● Authorized an additional $10 million for a new VISTA Literacy Corps: $2 million for fiscal 1987, $3 million for fiscal 1988 and $5 million for fiscal 1989.

● Authorized a total of $5.4 million for the Service Learning Programs: $1.8 million for each of fiscal 1987, 1988 and 1989.

● Authorized a total of $5.952 million for Special Volunteer Programs: $1.984 million for each of fiscal 1987, 1988 and 1989.

● Authorized a total of $75.94 million for administrative costs for ACTION: $25.31 million for each of fiscal 1987, 1988 and 1989.

● Authorized a total of $99.89 million for the Retired Senior Volunteer Program: $32 million for fiscal 1987, $33.28 million for fiscal 1988 and $34.61 million for fiscal 1989.

● Authorized a total of $187.3 million for the Foster Grandparents program: $60 million for fiscal 1987, $62.4 million for fiscal 1988 and $64.9 million for fiscal 1989.

● Authorized a total of $92.84 million for the Senior Companions Program: $29.74 million for fiscal 1987, $30.93 million for fiscal 1988 and $32.17 million for fiscal 1989.

● Authorized non-needy persons to serve without pay as senior companions and foster grandparents, provided no appropriated funds were used for their expenses.

● Directed ACTION to spend up to $250,000 to recruit individuals to serve as VISTA volunteers.

● Established a VISTA Literacy Corps to develop, strengthen, supplement and expand efforts of local, state and federal public and private, non-profit organizations working to address the problem of illiteracy.

● Stipulated that funds made available for the literacy corps be used to supplement and not supplant other VISTA services, and directed that volunteers be assigned with priority going to programs or projects assisting illiterate individuals in unserved or underserved areas with the highest concentrations of illiteracy and of low-income individuals and families.

● Directed ACTION to conduct an evaluation of the impact of senior volunteer programs that assist families caring for frail and disabled adults.

# Child Nutrition Programs

One of the 99th Congress' last acts was to approve a three-year reauthorization of five child nutrition programs that had been stalled in a House-Senate conference since early 1986. But the pursuit of a viable vehicle to carry the bill produced a legal headache of some magnitude.

Just before adjournment, Congress attached nearly identical versions of the nutrition legislation to two bills — the fiscal 1987 defense authorization bill (S 2638 — PL 99-661) and the $576 billion continuing appropriations resolution (H J Res 738 — PL 99-591). (Defense authorization, *p. 290; continuing appropriations, p. 57)*

The two bills included slightly different language for three provisions, raising questions about which should prevail. The sole discrepancy for two provisions lay in the date that they were to take effect. There was a substantive difference between the two versions of the other provision.

The matter pitted congressional intent against the normal legal precedent of enforcing the last version to be signed by the president. Lawyers at the Department of Agriculture finally decided that the defense bill, the last version to become law, must prevail.

## Overdue Reauthorization

Both bills extended authorization through fiscal 1989 for five child nutrition programs: the supplemental feeding program for needy pregnant women, infants and children (WIC); the summer food service program for children; a surplus commodity distribution program; payments to states for administrative expenses; and the nutrition and education training program. In addition, the bills made some changes to the school lunch and breakfast programs and to WIC.

Authorization for the programs expired at the end of fiscal 1984. They were extended under appropriations measures in fiscal 1985 and 1986.

The House passed a new authorization (HR 7 — H Rept 99-96) Sept. 18, 1985, providing a $121 million increase overall in child nutrition programs over three years. The Senate Nov. 22, 1985, bypassed the Agriculture, Nutrition and Forestry Committee and passed a bare-bones, four-year reauthorization containing no increase in funding. President Reagan had requested an $800 million cut.

On Feb. 5, 1986, House-Senate conferees reached a tentative compromise on funding levels, paring the bill's total increase to $46 million. House conferees signed a conference agreement, but Senate Agriculture Chairman Jesse Helms, R-N.C., objected to any increase and did not circulate the agreement to Senate conferees.

The bill languished until Sen. Paula Hawkins, R-Fla., a chief proponent of the child nutrition programs reauthorization, offered the conference agreement as an amendment to the defense authorization bill. The Senate adopted Hawkins' amendment Aug. 9 by voice vote, then passed the bill later that day.

On Oct. 2, Hawkins again offered the nutrition conference agreement as a floor amendment — this time, to the measure providing continuing appropriations for the government.

Hawkins said it was unclear whether Congress would complete action on the defense authorization bill and added, "I feel it is important to include this amendment in the continuing resolution to ensure that the president will have the opportunity to sign" it into law. Her amendment was adopted by voice vote after the Senate voted 78-17 that the amendment was germane.

An earlier attempt to attach the child nutrition provisions to the continuing resolution failed as part of a farm-aid amendment by David L. Boren, D-Okla. By a vote of 45-53, the Senate rejected a motion to waive a budget act limitation with respect to that amendment.

## Provisions in Dispute

The version of HR 7 that had been appended to the defense authorization bill was the same as the conference agreement reached earlier in the year. In that proposal, three provisions were scheduled to take effect Oct. 1, 1986.

One of the provisions allowed partial-day (or "split-session") kindergartens to participate in a program that offered free or subsidized milk, at an estimated cost in fiscal 1987 of $10 million. Another provision provided an additional 6 cents per breakfast to supplement the school breakfast program — 3 cents in cash and 3 cents in commodities. That change was estimated to cost $24 million in 1987. The third provision raised from $1,500 to $2,000 the maximum tuition a private school could charge and remain in the school lunch and breakfast programs — at an approximate cost in 1987 of $2 million.

Oct. 1 had already passed, however, by the time the continuing resolution was being debated. To stave off bookkeeping nightmares by changing the law in the midst of the school year, and to keep the bill as close to revenue neutrality as possible, conferees on H J Res 738 decided to advance the effective dates of the three provisions to July 1, 1987.

In addition, House Appropriations Committee member Richard J. Durbin, D-Ill., persuaded conferees to drop the tuition cap altogether, reasoning that the overriding factor in determining eligibility for federal assistance should be the parents' income, not the school's tuition. The fiscal 1987 cost of eliminating the tuition cap — since it would not be removed until July — was estimated at $2 million; it was expected to have an annual cost of $6 million.

## Timing Problem

The conference report on S 2638 (H Rept 99-1001) was filed Oct. 14; the report on H J Res 738 (H Rept 99-1005) was filed the next day.

The defense authorization bill was cleared for Reagan Oct. 15; the continuing resolution was cleared Oct. 17. Because the spending bill had to be enacted to keep the government running, Reagan signed it Oct. 18. On Oct. 30 he signed a second version (PL 99-591) that contained two pages inadvertently omitted from the earlier bill.

Reagan did not sign the defense authorization bill until Nov. 14.

As a general rule, when conflicting versions of legislation are passed, the last version enacted prevails. In this case, that was the defense bill.

Congressional intent, however, also plays a key role in disputes of this type. House staffers on the Appropriations and the Education and Labor committees argued that since the last nutrition bill to have been worked on — and, indeed, the last version to be cleared by Congress — was the one on the continuing resolution, that version, with its effective date of July 1, 1987, and removal of the tuition cap, should prevail.

The decision to enforce the defense bill provisions meant that school districts around the country had to implement the disputed provisions immediately, in the middle of a school year. The Senate tuition cap increase also was adopted.

## Major Provisions

As enacted, the legislation:
● Set funding levels for WIC at $1.58 billion in 1986; "such sums as may be necessary" for 1987 and 1988; and

$1.78 billion in 1989. The other programs were extended at their existing levels.

The Congressional Research Service had estimated fiscal 1986 spending for those programs at $511.8 million for the commodity distribution program; $121.9 million for the summer food service; $48.9 million for state administrative expenses; and $5 million for the nutrition education and training program.

● Made a state ineligible to participate in the WIC program if it collected state or local taxes on food purchased with WIC funds.

● Allowed a state to carry up to 1 percent of a year's grant for supplemental foods into the next fiscal year without affecting the amount of funds allocated to that state in that year. In addition, a state was allowed to use up to 1 percent of a fiscal year's grant in the preceding fiscal year. This provision was designed to improve program management by reducing states' fears of having to forfeit unused funds at the end of a year.

● Required that nine-tenths of 1 percent of WIC appropriations be available first for providing WIC services to migrants.

● Required that if a state determined that benefits had been overissued to participants, the state must recover the cash value of the benefits overissued, unless it determined that it would not be cost-effective to pursue the matter.

● Required the agriculture secretary to report to Congress on March 1, 1987, and every two years thereafter, on the income, nutritional risk and other characteristics of WIC participants.

● Provided automatic eligibility for free meals for children who were members of households receiving food stamps or Aid to Families with Dependent Children (AFDC), in states where the standard for AFDC eligibility did not exceed 130 percent of poverty-level income.

● Required schools to offer whole milk as part of the lunch program.

● Permitted schools to allow students to refuse up to one item in each school breakfast, without having that refusal affect the charge to students or the amount of federal reimbursement for the breakfast. A similar provision was contained in the school lunch program.

● Clarified that it was legal to offer federally assisted school cafeterias and food service equipment or personnel to nutrition programs for the elderly.

● Changed the dates by which the secretary must make an estimate of the value of agricultural commodities to be delivered to schools, and by which the secretary must provide cash payments for any difference between the estimates of available commodities and the amount of commodity support mandated by law. The date for the estimate was changed from May 15 to June 1 of each year; the date to make cash compensation was changed from June 15 to July 1.

● Raised from $1,500 to $2,000 the maximum tuition a private school could charge and remain in the school lunch and breakfast programs.

● Reduced from $75,000 to $50,000 a year the minimum amount of funds a state could receive in any fiscal year for conducting nutrition education and training.

● Allowed local school districts that had been participating in a pilot project studying alternatives to the traditional commodity distribution program to continue their participation, and authorized $50,000 for any expenses related to carrying out the project.

# Vocational Rehabilitation

A five-year reauthorization of popular vocational training programs for the handicapped was cleared by Congress Oct. 3, 1986. The legislation (HR 4021 — PL 99-506) extended through fiscal 1991 programs created under the Rehabilitation Act of 1973 (PL 93-112). The programs, which assisted more than 900,000 people a year, were designed to help the handicapped become self-sufficient through employment. *(Background, Congress and the Nation Vol. VI, p. 567)*

The House Education and Labor Committee March 11 approved HR 4021 (H Rept 99-571). As reported, the bill called on the states to pay 25 percent of the cost of their vocational rehabilitation programs after fiscal 1988. Existing law required states to supply 20 percent of the cost. Bill sponsor Pat Williams, D-Mont., said the increased matching requirement was designed to prod states into spending more on a program that served only a small fraction of those eligible. But the proposal met with opposition from William D. Ford, D-Mich., and several other Democratic panel members who were worried that states would not be able to afford more money for rehabilitation training when they were facing federal budget cuts in other social services.

The House May 7 by a 401-0 vote passed HR 4021. To avoid a floor fight over the increased matching requirement, Williams offered a compromise backed by Ford that would phase in the 25 percent match over five years, beginning in 1989. But even when effective, the match would apply only to sums that states received in excess of their 1988 allotment.

The Senate Labor and Human Resources Committee Aug. 6 approved S 2515 (S Rept 99-388) by voice vote. On Sept. 8 the Senate approved HR 4021 by voice vote after substituting the text of S 2515.

Senate-House differences were reconciled in staff negotiations without convening a formal conference. The Senate accepted the House provision calling for a 5 percent increase in states' share of the cost of rehabilitation programs.

The House accepted a Senate proposal to set up a separate grant program to foster "supported employment" programs and a provision countering a 1985 Supreme Court decision limiting the application of federal anti-bias laws to state governments.

The House also accepted Senate provisions awarding grants to various agencies and institutions in the home states of key members of the Senate Labor and Human Resources Committee. Augustus F. Hawkins, D-Calif., chairman of the House Education and Labor Committee, said he asked Senate negotiators to meet in conference to discuss the issue, but they had refused. The House had to accept the projects to ensure enactment of the bill before adjournment, he said.

The House adopted the conference report (H Rept 99-955) on the bill Oct. 2 by a 408-0 vote. The Senate approved it by voice vote Oct. 3.

As cleared by Congress, HR 4021:

● Authorized $1.28 billion in fiscal 1987 in basic grants to the states for rehabilitation programs. In the succeeding four years, the grants would total at least that much — plus an increase pegged to inflation. Grants would be capped at $1.41 billion in fiscal 1988, $1.55 billion in 1989, $1.71 billion in 1990 and $1.875 billion in 1991.

● Authorized $200 million in fiscal 1987 for an array of smaller related programs, such as joint training projects with industry, allowing 5 percent increases annually in 1988-91. Of the total, $25 million was earmarked in fiscal 1987 for new supported-employment grants.

● Gradually increased, beginning in fiscal 1989, the existing requirement that states put up at least 20 percent of rehabilitation program costs to qualify for federal funds. By fiscal 1993, the bill would increase the matching rquirement to 25 percent, but only on sums states received in excess of their fiscal 1988 allotments.

● Required states to spend no less on rehabilitation programs than the average of the amounts they spent in the previous three years.

● Authorized states to use funds from their basic rehabilitation grants for supported employment programs.

● Authorized demonstration projects and a new program of grants to help states provide training and on-the-job services of limited duration for severely handicapped individuals capable of supported employment.

● Required states to include in their rehabilitation plans, which were required in order to receive federal rehabilitation grants, assurances that they had acceptable proposals for using funds made available under the new supported-employment program.

● Required the involvement of an impartial hearing officer in the process of resolving disputes over the provision of rehabilitation services, although that officer's decisions would be subject to final review by a state rehabilitation director.

● Authorized demonstration projects to provide incentives for the development and manufacture of devices to assist individuals with handicaps so rare that firms were not otherwise likely to market such devices.

● Authorized grants to help severely handicapped youths make the transition from school to work.

● Specified that states were not immune from lawsuits if they violated anti-bias laws, including Section 504 of the Rehabilitation Act, which barred discrimination against the disabled by recipients of federal funds.

The provision overturned a 1985 Supreme Court decision in *Atascadero State Hospital v. Scanlon*, which held that the 11th Amendment gave states immunity from such suits unless the state or Congress explicitly waived or overrode the immunity. *(Court decision, p. 830)*

## SSI Work Program Renewal

President Reagan Nov. 10, 1986, signed into law a bill (HR 5595 — PL 99-643) making permanent a program that encouraged disabled individuals receiving Supplemental Security Income (SSI) benefits to work if they were able.

SSI was the federal-state welfare program for the needy blind, elderly and disabled. The work program allowed disabled individuals who worked to retain a portion of their SSI benefits as well as eligibility for Medicaid. The program, created in 1980 and extended in 1984, was scheduled to expire June 30, 1987. *(Background, Congress and the Nation Vol. V, p. 705; Congress and the Nation Vol. VI, p. 667)*

The House originally passed the bill, which included a number of other minor changes to SSI, on Sept. 30 (H Rept 99-893). On Oct. 8, the Senate approved a version of the bill extending the work program but eliminating the House's other changes.

The House Oct. 15 added back one of the changes, allowing payment of retroactive SSI benefits to the spouse or parents of a deceased individual who was eligible for SSI. The Senate accepted the change Oct. 18, clearing the bill. All votes were by voice.

## Senior Citizens' Meals

Congress March 18, 1986, cleared for the president legislation (HR 2453 — PL 99-269) to continue a popular federal program that helped provide 225 million meals for senior citizens in 1985.

The bill raised authorization levels through fiscal 1987 for commodity and cash distributions under the Older Americans Act of 1965.

HR 2453 was introduced in May 1985, after the Agriculture Department announced that the 1985 authorization level would not only preclude its granting a 4 percent cost-of-living increase but also would force a reduction of 2 cents to 4 cents in the 56.5-cents-per-meal reimbursement rate. The House Select Aging Subcommittee on Human Services estimated that a 3-cent drop in reimbursements would mean a daily reduction of 2 million meals.

In late 1985, Congress appropriated an additional $11 million for the program for fiscal 1986, but some $4 million of that was eliminated in the first round of cuts under the Gramm-Rudman-Hollings anti-deficit law. Much of the remaining $7 million would be used to pay outstanding reimbursements from 1985.

The House Education and Labor Committee reported HR 2453 Sept. 23, 1985 (H Rept 99-286), and the House passed it the next day by voice vote. The bill would raise the authorized levels by "such sums as necessary" to provide reimbursement rates of 56.76 cents per meal for fiscal 1985 and 1986, and an inflation-adjusted rate for fiscal 1987.

The Senate passed HR 2453 by voice vote Feb. 5, 1986, after substituting the language of a bill reported by the Labor and Human Resources Committee Jan. 31 (S 1858 — S Rept 99-232). It called for the same 56.76-cent reimbursement rate and authorized $127.8 million for 1985 and $144 million each for 1986 and 1987 to achieve that rate.

Conferees accepted the Senate bill's authorization levels. Those levels were expected to be sufficient to reimburse states at the 56.76-cents-per-meal rate through 1987.

The Senate adopted the conference report on the bill (H Rept 99-487) by voice vote March 13, and the House approved the report, 344-0, on March 18. The president signed HR 2453 April 1.

## Protections for Mentally Ill

Congress May 14, 1986, completed action on legislation (S 974 — PL 99-319) to create new legal protection and advocacy services for the institutionalized and recently discharged mentally ill.

S 974 extended to the mentally ill protection and advocacy services already available to the "developmentally disabled" under a 1975 law that was last reauthorized in 1984 (PL 98-527). Developmentally disabled persons included most of the institutionalized mentally retarded and individuals with physical handicaps, such as cerebral palsy, that affect mental function. *(PL 98-527, Congress and the Nation Vol. VI, p. 609)*

The new legislation was developed in response to continuing reports of abuse and neglect of patients in state mental institutions.

The bill authorized the Department of Health and Human Services (HHS) to provide funds to independent statewide agencies with access to facilities and records and authority to investigate alleged instances of abuse and neglect. Eligible agencies must be able to pursue administrative, legal and other remedies on behalf of mental patients. Agencies also must have an advisory board to recommend policies and priorities in protecting and advocating for the mentally ill. The protection services program was reauthorized in the 100th Congress. *(100th Congress action, p. 632)*

## Legislative History

S 974 originally was passed by the Senate, by voice vote, on July 31, 1985. The Senate bill (S Rept 99-109) stemmed from a six-month staff investigation into the treatment of residents of state mental institutions.

The House passed its version (HR 4055) on Jan. 30, 1986. The bill had been reported as HR 3492 (H Rept 99-401) by the Energy and Commerce Committee in 1985. It passed on a 290-84 vote, despite conservatives' complaints that the action contradicted lawmakers' avowed determination to eliminate the federal budget deficit.

Conferees filed their report May 5 (H Rept 99-576). The conference agreement authorized a total of $31.53 million for the program over three years: $10 million for fiscal 1986, $10.5 million for fiscal 1987 and $11.025 million for fiscal 1988. These were the figures contained in the Senate version of the bill; House-approved authorization levels were $1.5 million higher.

The $10 million for fiscal 1986 already had been appropriated, on a conditional basis, in the funding bill for HHS (PL 99-178) that was cleared in December 1985. Those funds became available when President Reagan signed S 974 into law May 23.

Conferees agreed to delete a controversial Senate provision that would limit fees for publicly funded attorneys who prevailed in legal actions on behalf of a mentally ill individual. The provision would limit the amount that could be collected to attorneys' actual costs, instead of the prevailing market rates generally available under current practice.

Sen. Edward M. Kennedy, D-Mass., said this cap would "set up an unfair two-tiered system of protection for mentally ill people" that would hinder poor patients' access to legal representation.

House conferees agreed to accept Senate language requiring agencies to exhaust all administrative remedies before going to court.

They also agreed to drop a provision that would preclude states from receiving funds under the federal alcohol, drug abuse and mental health block grant unless the states agreed to establish the advocacy agencies.

Conferees retained a House provision to promote the creation of a national network of support groups for victims of Alzheimer's disease and related memory disorders and their families. No new funds were authorized for the program.

The House approved the conference report May 13, by a 383-21 vote, and the Senate followed suit by voice vote May 14.

## Major Provisions

As signed into law May 23, 1986, S 974 (PL 99-319):

● Defined abuse as "any act or failure to act by an employee of a facility rendering care or treatment ... performed knowingly, recklessly or intentionally, and which caused or may have caused injury to a mentally ill individual." Abuse could include rape or sexual assault, striking an individual, use of excessive force or use of bodily or chemical restraints not in compliance with federal or state laws or regulations.

● Defined neglect as a "negligent act or omission" by anyone responsible for providing care to the mentally ill that caused or might have caused injury, or that placed a mentally ill individual at risk of injury. Neglect could include failure to establish or carry out a treatment plan; failure to provide adequate food, clothing or health care; or failure to provide a safe environment for a mentally ill individual.

● Specified that to be eligible for grants, advocacy agencies — whether public or private — must be independent of any agency providing treatment or services. Agencies also must have access to facilities providing treatment and their records, and authority to investigate allegations of abuse and neglect. They must have authority to pursue administrative, legal and other appropriate remedies on behalf of institutionalized individuals and patients discharged within the preceding 90 days.

● Required that advocacy agencies set up boards to advise them on policies and priorities. Board members must include attorneys, mental health professionals, members of the public knowledgeable about mental illness and a provider of mental health services. At least half the board members must be individuals who had received or were receiving mental health services, or family members of such individuals.

● Required agencies to exhaust all administrative remedies before instituting legal action on behalf of a patient or former patient.

● Authorized $10 million for fiscal 1986, $10.5 million for fiscal 1987 and $11.025 million for fiscal 1988.

● Restated the "bill of rights for mental health patients" included in Title V of the Mental Health Systems Act of 1980 (PL 96-398) and encouraged states to review and, if necessary, revise laws to conform to that bill of rights. *(PL 96-398, Congress and the Nation Vol. V, p. 646)*

● Stipulated that such restatement should not be construed as establishing any new rights for mentally ill individuals.

● Directed the secretary of HHS, using available appropriations, to promote the establishment of family support groups for victims of Alzheimer's disease or related memory disorders, and for their families. Such groups would provide educational, emotional and practical support. The secretary also was to promote a national network to coordinate the activities of the family support groups.

# 1987-88

Action on human services issues in the 100th Congress centered on a massive overhaul of the federal system of aid to the poor. The successful completion of the bill capped decades of efforts to improve the much-criticized system by both expanding benefits and creating greater incentives and requirements for welfare recipients to work in order to become self-supporting.

Although Congress cleared several less-controversial welfare-related bills, including an extension of nutrition and support programs for the elderly, it was unable to reach agreement on the increasingly prominent issue of federal subsidies for day-care programs.

# Welfare Reform

President Reagan Oct. 13, 1988, signed into law landmark welfare-overhaul legislation (HR 1720 — PL 100-485).

The bill, said Reagan, "responds to the call in my 1986 State of the Union message for real welfare reform — reform that will lead to lasting emancipation from welfare dependency." *(1986 State of the Union address, p. 1067)*

The final product, a compromise in which both liberals and conservatives gained what they wanted most and swallowed provisions each earlier had vowed to fight to the death, strengthened child support enforcement procedures; required states to implement work, education and training programs for welfare mothers; required states to pay welfare benefits to poor two-parent families; and offered extended child-care and medical benefits to families in which parents left the welfare rolls for a job.

Conservatives, spurred on by Reagan, insisted on Senate provisions requiring that states enroll set percentages of recipients in the job and skills program created under the bill and that one parent in two-parent welfare families spend at least 16 hours a week performing community service or other unpaid work.

Liberals opposed both provisions, saying the participation rates would spread state resources too thinly and the work requirement would be costly to administer and punitive. But the liberals relented when both provisions were watered down slightly. In exchange, conservatives agreed to mandate welfare coverage for poor two-parent families (only 27 states currently offered such benefits) and to provide a year of child-care and Medicaid benefits to those leaving welfare for jobs.

In the end, the 100th Congress produced the most significant overhaul of the welfare system in half a century because sponsors could not bear to see the measure die.

"When people looked up and realized we almost killed it, that was the turning point," said Sen. Daniel Patrick Moynihan, D-N.Y., chairman of the Senate Finance Subcommittee with jurisdiction over welfare, lead sponsor of the Senate version of the bill and a veteran of nearly every welfare reform battle of the preceding three decades.

HR 1720 cleared Sept. 30, when the House approved the conference report (H Rept 100-998) by a vote of 347-53. The Senate overwhelmingly gave its assent the previous day, by a 96-1 vote.

## Background

The bill cleared in 1988 represented Congress' third attempt in 20 years to revamp the welfare system. The two previous efforts — in 1969 and in 1977 — foundered over many of the same philosophical differences about how best to reduce welfare dependency that threatened to doom HR 1720.

President Richard Nixon tried unsuccessfully in 1969 to sell Congress his Family Assistance Plan (FAP). FAP would set a minimum benefit nationwide under the Aid to Families with Dependent Children (AFDC) program, the principal federal-state welfare program. It also would provide assistance to the "working poor," who did not earn enough to escape poverty.

Attacked by liberals as too stingy and conservatives as too generous, FAP was never enacted. But out of the battle came the federalization of welfare plans for the aged, blind and disabled, which were consolidated into what became the Supplemental Security Income (SSI) program. *(Congress and the Nation Vol. III, p. 622)*

Welfare reform next topped the national agenda in 1977, when President Jimmy Carter proposed his Program for Better Jobs and Income. The Carter plan would eliminate AFDC, SSI and food stamps and replace them with cash payments for about 32 million persons, including the working poor. At the same time, it would create up to 1.4 million public service jobs. Once again, competing interests and philosophies doomed the proposal. *(Congress and the Nation Vol. V, p. 685)*

Both liberals and conservatives began the 100th Congress with high hopes that they could succeed where past efforts had failed. They were banking on a newfound if tenuous consensus among experts that the welfare system should be transformed from one emphasizing income maintenance to one stressing education and training so that welfare parents could gain and keep jobs that paid enough to support their families.

Advocates of the legislation were buoyed by Reagan's vow in his 1986 State of the Union message to make welfare reform a priority. They also were encouraged by the commitment of the nation's governors to push for a welfare overhaul. The governors in 1987 had made welfare reform their top priority.

The plan proposed by the governors had two major parts. The first called for changing the emphasis of the welfare system from income maintenance to work and training. The plan envisioned that every "employable" welfare recipient, including mothers of children aged 3 or older, would be required to seek self-sufficiency, either by completing education or training programs or by beginning a job search, in return for training and job search assistance, child care and medical insurance.

The second part of the plan called for a reformation of AFDC, the government's major cash-assistance program. An income-support program would replace AFDC and would aim to ensure that all families, including poor two-parent families in which someone worked full time, had incomes at least as great as a regionally adjusted standard of living approximating the current official poverty line.

Another key proposal was put forward in HR 1720, sponsored by Rep. Harold E. Ford, D-Tenn., chairman of the Ways and Means Subcommittee on Public Assistance. Backed by House Democratic leaders, the bill sought to create a work training and education program for AFDC recipients and to remove disincentives in the current welfare system that, for many recipients, made welfare more economically advantageous than work. The centerpiece of Ford's bill was the NETWork program. It was designed to replace the Work Incentive (WIN) program, which also was aimed at training welfare recipients so they could move into the work force.

One of the key differences between NETWork and WIN was that NETWork would be open-ended. States

# Key Issues in Welfare Debate

In the sea of discord over welfare reform, there was one island of bipartisan consensus: provisions that significantly increased government involvement in forcing absent fathers to support their children.

Congress for some time had recognized the need for the federal government to help states see to it that absent fathers supported their children. And that concern extended not only to children on welfare (in whom both the state and federal governments had a direct financial interest), but also to those in families above the poverty line. Indeed, when Congress last beefed up federal requirements regarding child support in 1984, the measure (PL 98-378) passed unanimously in both houses. *(PL 98-378, Congress and the Nation Vol. VI, p. 605)*

For all welfare families, and for others seeking state help, that law required automatic withholding of court-ordered child support payments when the absent parent fell behind by an amount equal to 30 days' worth of payments. It also required states to intercept income tax refunds to collect past-due payments. And, to bring some uniformity to the system, the law required states to establish guidelines that judges or other officials could use in determining the amount of child support to order.

Even with the new requirements, however, statistics from the Department of Health and Human Services (HHS) showed that more than half (52 percent) of all women with children under 21 still did not receive part or all of the child support legally due them. And nearly 40 percent of households with children in need of support did not have court orders or legal support agreements.

The key provisions in both the House- and Senate-passed welfare reform bills required that in most cases, court-ordered child support be withheld from the paycheck of the parent who owed it, instead of when the parent fell a month or more behind on payments.

Both versions of the bill also sought to introduce some consistency to the calculation of child support amounts. They required judges or other officials to use the guidelines that the 1984 law ordered states to create to set award payments, unless extraordinary circumstances existed.

Although popular in Congress, the automatic-withholding provisions were criticized by groups representing divorced fathers, who complained that automatic wage withholding could result in fathers losing their jobs, because businesses would rather not deal with withholding requirements, and that handing over the monthly support check was often the only leverage fathers had in forcing mothers to obey visitation orders.

A far more controversial issue, however, involved the AFDC-UP program, which extended welfare benefits to two-parent families in which the principal wage earner was unemployed. (UP stood for "unemployed parent.")

Both the House and Senate welfare bills required states to adopt the program, which was currently optional, although the Senate bill (S 1511) permitted states to limit benefits to six months out of every 12.

The Reagan administration was adamantly opposed to making the program mandatory in any form.

Before AFDC-UP was created in 1961, an able-bodied father had to leave his family for it to qualify for welfare benefits, no matter how low the family's income.

That was still the case in nearly half the states. In fiscal 1987, 28 of the nation's 54 AFDC jurisdictions (50 states plus the District of Columbia and the territories) operated AFDC-UP programs.

But while 71 percent of the nation's 3.8 million welfare families lived in jurisdictions with AFDC-UP, the program paid benefits to an average of only 236,156 families each month — about 6.2 percent of the overall caseload. That was because AFDC-UP included other restrictions. One was the so-called "100-hour rule," which precluded eligibility for families in which the principal wage earner (defined as the parent who earned more over the previous two years) worked more than 99 hours per month.

The other major obstacle to eligibility was the program's work-history requirement. A family could not receive AFDC-UP benefits unless the principal wage earner worked, collected unemployment or participated in training in at least six of the 13 calendar quarters within a year of applying for benefits. Going to school currently did not qualify as work experience, which generally shut out most young families.

The fight to mandate AFDC-UP was hardly new. Both Democrats and Republicans in Congress repeatedly had sought to make the program mandatory, charging that failure to offer benefits to two-parent families encouraged fathers to leave home.

More recently, the House, in fiscal 1986 and 1987 budget reconciliation bills, voted to require states to offer the program. The Senate indirectly voted for it once, in approving a tentative conference agreement on the fiscal 1986 measure that later unraveled. But each time, the provision was dropped at the insistence of White House officials, who threatened that Reagan would veto the entire reconciliation package unless the AFDC-UP provision was removed.

The White House claimed that mandating the program would add people to the welfare rolls, that states should be able to decide how to administer welfare programs without federal mandates and, not least, that the program was not worth its cost, which estimates put at about $1.3 billion over five years.

would be able to receive as much in federal funds as they were willing to match (at a rate of 75 percent federal and 25 percent state). WIN paid 90 percent to a state's 10 percent but was capped each year.

Another difference was that NETWork made states give priority to those who were — or were most likely to become — long-term welfare dependents: families with teenage parents, families in which the parents were teenagers when the first child was born and families receiving AFDC for two or more years continuously.

NETWork made participation in an education or job-training program mandatory for recipients with children over age 6. It offered states the option of reducing the mandatory age to as low as 6 months, provided child care was available.

James C. Miller III, director of the Office of Management and Budget (OMB), lambasted the program. Miller argued for a Reagan administration alternative called Greater Opportunities Through Work, or GROW. Like NETWork, GROW was open-ended, although it offered states only a 50 percent match. It also required that states enroll an increasing percentage of AFDC recipients in the program. Up to 60 percent of recipients would be required to participate by 1992, an estimated 1.4 million people.

## House Committee Action

**Ways and Means.** Three House committees had jurisdiction over welfare reform — Ways and Means, Education and Labor, and Energy and Commerce. The Agriculture Committee also added food stamp provisions to HR 1720.

The Ways and Means Subcommittee on Public Assistance approved HR 1720 on April 9, 1987, but not before scaling back the measure enough to cut its $11.8 billion five-year cost roughly in half.

By cutting the measure back, Ford was able to meet the budget limits set by the House leadership. Republicans on the subcommittee opposed the measure, but it still passed by voice vote.

Republicans instead backed a bill (HR 1985), sponsored by Hank Brown, Colo., that would grant state governments broad authority to experiment with new approaches toward welfare.

Before the full Ways and Means Committee undertook consideration of Ford's measure, however, he was forced to give up his subcommittee chairmanship after being indicted on charges of tax, mail and bank fraud. He was replaced as head of the panel and chief manager of the bill by Thomas J. Downey, D-N.Y.

The full committee then approved HR 1720 June 10 on a straight party-line vote. The bill was reported June 17 (H Rept 100-159, Part I). Sponsors had to scramble to win over some committee Democrats. All of the panel's 23 Democrats signed on in the end, but only after sponsors agreed during a closed-door, two-day markup to trim an additional $880 million from the bill's estimated five-year cost of just over $6.1 billion. Republicans charged that portions of the bill that sought to increase benefits, to extend benefits to two-parent families in which the principal wage-earner was unemployed and to protect recipients from being forced to accept jobs that paid less than the welfare benefits they received would create impediments for welfare families trying to move into the working world.

Republican efforts to eliminate or scale back those provisions, however, were rejected, generally along party lines.

Downey offered the amendment to cut $880 million from the bill's estimated five-year cost through a variety of changes affecting Medicaid and other programs. In addition, the amendment also eliminated one of the bill's most controversial provisions — one that would require states, beginning in 1993, to offer welfare benefits equal to at least 15 percent of a state's median income. Eighteen states offered benefits lower than that.

**Education and Labor.** The Education and Labor Committee reported HR 1720 (Part II) on Aug. 7. The panel had approved a plan in July that was far more lenient in its work, education and training requirements for welfare recipients than the plan that emerged from the Ways and Means Committee.

The Education and Labor plan, offered by committee Chairman Augustus F. Hawkins, D-Calif., would exempt from mandatory participation welfare mothers with children under age 15 unless day or after-school care for their children was guaranteed. The Ways and Means plan exempted mothers of children under the age of 3. The Hawkins bill also differed from the Ways and Means measure in that it permitted AFDC recipients to satisfy the education and training requirement by attending college.

The Hawkins plan also explicitly prohibited traditional "workfare," in which recipients were required to perform work in exchange for receiving welfare payments. It would authorize, however, up to a year of government-subsidized "transitional" employment for recipients who completed training and job-search activities yet still found themselves jobless.

**Energy and Commerce.** The Energy and Commerce Committee reported HR 1720 (Part III) on Sept. 15. The committee approved by voice vote July 1 amendments to HR 1720 that would allow families who left federal welfare rolls when they moved into paying jobs to retain their public health insurance coverage for up to 42 months.

The Ways and Means version of the welfare bill increased the period within which former recipients could get coverage to six months, from the four in existing law. Henry A. Waxman, D-Calif., argued, however that six months still was not enough time to make the transition to regular health coverage. So he offered an amendment, included in the Commerce Committee bill, to require states to extend at least some coverage to a family, after expiration of its six-month full coverage, if its income remained relatively low.

**Agriculture.** The Agriculture Subcommittee on Domestic Marketing, Consumer Relations and Nutrition, which oversaw the food stamp program, approved a plan in September for coordinating requirements of the food stamp program with the rest of the welfare reform package. The legislation was drafted by subcommittee Chairman Leon E. Panetta, D-Calif., who inserted language into the proposal that the coordination provisions would not become effective unless Congress met specified budget targets.

The legislation increased incentives for child care and child support payments with increased deductions and exclusions from income.

## House Floor Action

It took four attempts by the Democratic leadership before welfare reform legislation passed the full House in December, largely because of controversy over the rule providing only a limited opportunity to amend the bill on the floor.

deadlock that had doomed all previous judicial review bills.

In addition to negotiating the details of the judicial review provisions, key House and Senate members agreed to attach a section authorizing a 4.1 percent COLA for veterans' compensation recipients.

The measure (HR 4741) had previously been passed by the Senate with a section providing temporary benefits for veterans suffering from cancers that were associated with "Agent Orange," a defoliant used widely during the Vietnam War. *(Agent Orange, p. 644)*

But that Agent Orange provision was dropped when the House combined the COLA bill with the judicial review legislation and passed S 11, as amended. Other minor Agent Orange provisions were retained. The Senate Oct. 20 accepted the House version of S 11, clearing the bill for the president.

### Major Provisions

As cleared, S 11:
● Retained the Board of Veterans Appeals as the first avenue of appeal for veterans.
● Made the BVA somewhat more independent of the VA by requiring the chairman of the board to be appointed by the president and confirmed by the Senate. Furthermore, BVA board members were given nine-year appointments.
● Created an independent specialty court based in Washington, D.C., effective Sept. 1, 1989. This tribunal — the U.S. Court of Veterans' Appeals — was given authority to review veterans' appeals of decisions made by the BVA.
● Allowed the new court to consider appeals if the BVA decisions were deemed "clearly erroneous."
● Permitted veterans to appeal cases challenging laws and regulations — but not individual questions of fact — to the U.S. Court of Appeals.
● Lifted a Civil War-era statutory $10 limit on the amount a lawyer could be paid for representing a veteran in a claims case. S 11 permitted payment of "reasonable fees" in cases that went beyond the BVA hearing stage.
● Authorized a 4.1 percent cost-of-living adjustment for recipients of veterans' disability compensation.

## Veterans and Radiation

Congress on May 2, 1988, cleared legislation (HR 1811 — PL 100-321) mandating disability benefits for veterans who developed certain cancers after exposure to radiation during and after World War II.

The president signed the bill May 20.

An estimated 250,000 veterans were thought to have been exposed to radiation. Under existing law, however, veterans could receive compensation for cancers only if they could prove the illness was service-related. Rep. J. Roy Rowland, D-Ga., chief sponsor of the bill, noted that only 44 of the 6,000 veterans who had applied for such benefits had received them by 1988.

The legislation was expected to cost an estimated $36 million a year.

The House had passed HR 1811 (H Rept 100-235) on July 28, 1987. But further action on the measure was delayed because the provisions of the bill were included in the omnibus veterans' health legislation (HR 2616).

After President Reagan voiced objections to the cancer-related provisions, however, conferees on HR 2616 decided to split those provisions off from the larger bill, in hopes of avoiding a veto. *(Omnibus health bill, p. 638)*

The Senate then passed HR 1811 by a 48-30 vote April 25, 1988. The House accepted the Senate's amendment to the bill — dropping colon cancer from the list of covered diseases — by a 326-2 vote May 2, clearing the measure.

As cleared, HR 1811:
● Established, for the first time, a "presumptive link" between a veteran's exposure to atomic fallout and the subsequent development of any of 13 forms of cancer.
● Provided benefits to servicemen, and their survivors, who were part of U.S. occupation forces in Japan after nuclear bombs were dropped on Hiroshima and Nagasaki, or who were among those exposed to radiation during atomic tests during the 1950s and 1960s.
● Covered the following cancers: leukemia; multiple myeloma; lymphomas; and cancers of the thyroid, breast, pharynx, esophagus, stomach, small intestine, pancreas, bile ducts, liver and gall bladder.

## Veterans' Job Bill

Congress April 28, 1988, cleared legislation (S 999 — PL 100-323) authorizing veterans' employment, training and counseling programs aimed primarily at long-term unemployed veterans who served in the Korean and Vietnam wars.

The measure extended a veterans' job-training program for two years and provided additional funding for 1,600 local veterans' employment representatives nationwide.

The Senate passed the bill Dec. 19, 1987 (S Rept 100-128).

The House passed its version of the bill on April 27, 1988, by a 417-0 vote, and the Senate accepted the House changes the following day.

President Reagan signed the bill May 20.

As cleared, S 999:
● Required the Department of Labor to operate a National Veterans' Employment and Training Services Institute to train outreach program specialists and local employment counselors.
● Required the Department of Labor to conduct a biennial study of unemployment among Vietnam-era and disabled veterans.
● Broadened membership on the secretary of labor's Committee on Veterans' Employment.
● Authorized $60 million in each of fiscal years 1988 and 1989 for the Veterans' Job Training Act (VJTA, PL 98-77).
● Required the Veterans Administration administrator to disapprove employers' participation in VJTA if it was determined too few veterans were successfully completing the employers' programs because of deficiencies in the programs.
● Extended until March 31, 1990, the deadline by which a veteran participating in VJTA must be enrolled in a job-training program.
● Required that funds be available for support of disabled veterans' outreach program specialists (DVOPs) and local veterans' employment representatives (LVERs).
● Required that funding be made available in the states to support 1,600 full-time local employment representatives.
● Required the secretary of labor to develop a prototype set of performance standards to be used in setting such standards for DVOPs and LVERs.

# Vets COLA, Agent Orange

An effort to provide new disability benefits to veterans who were exposed to the herbicide "Agent Orange" during the Vietnam War failed during the last days of the 100th Congress when lawmakers stripped the provision from other veterans' legislation.

The Agent Orange provision was originally included in a Senate measure (S 2011) that also authorized a cost-of-living adjustment (COLA) for veterans' disability compensation.

The House version of the COLA bill (HR 4741 — H Rept 100-760) did not include the Agent Orange provisions. When members decided to merge the COLA bill with a measure authorizing judicial review for veterans' claims cases, the Agent Orange provisions were dropped. The COLA provisions and some minor Agent Orange sections became law as part of the judicial review measure (S 11 — PL 100-687). *(Judicial review, p. 642)*

The Senate's key Agent Orange provision temporarily would grant disability and death benefits to Vietnam War veterans suffering from non-Hodgkins lymphoma or any soft-tissue sarcoma.

The benefits would extend until at least six months beyond the completion of a comprehensive Veterans Administration (VA) study of the health effects of Agent Orange.

The legislation would create the official presumption that contact with Agent Orange caused the cancer. Under those circumstances, the veteran would not have had to prove the origins of the cancer.

S 2011, the Agent Orange/COLA measure, was reported by the Senate Veterans' Affairs Committee Aug. 1 (S Rept 100-439). The House passed its separate COLA bill, HR 4741, by a vote of 395-0 July 26.

The Senate passed HR 4741 — with its Agent Orange language — on Oct. 18.

The next day, the House attached HR 4741 to S 11, the judicial review measure, minus the Agent Orange provisions.

The Senate, anxious to win passage of the judicial review measure, accepted the House amendment Oct. 20.

# VA Housing Supplemental

Congress in 1988 cleared a $709 million supplemental appropriations measure for fiscal 1988 to keep a veterans' housing program running.

The measure (H J Res 552) also provided money for education, training assistance and rehabilitation programs.

H J Res 552 passed the House on April 27, and the Senate the following day. The action in both chambers was by voice vote. President Reagan signed the measure April 29 (PL 100-304).

H J Res 552 provided $526.6 million for the Veterans Administration (VA) home loan fund, which helps veterans, active duty servicemen and certain surviving spouses buy, build, repair or refinance homes.

Without the supplemental appropriations, funds were expected to run out by the first week of May. That was because expenditures for the program had far outpaced projections, as loan defaults skyrocketed.

Also included in the supplemental funding was $182.5 million for veterans' education programs and readjustment benefits.

# 10

# Education Policy

# Education Policy

Education issues in the mid-to-late 1980s were dominated by the continuing efforts to reform the nation's public schools.

By 1988 — five years after the release of the landmark report *A Nation at Risk*, which had launched the movement — reformers could point to evidence of major changes aimed at correcting what many saw as the woeful inadequacies of the educational system.

The first wave of reform, which was largely carried out at the state level, focused on two major themes: raising the standard for both teachers and students — for example, by toughening high school graduation requirements; and improving the status of teaching, most importantly by raising teachers' pay.

By 1988, some of the initial impetus for reform appeared to have waned. And polls showed that many people were skeptical that the substantial increases in state and local spending for the schools that had accompanied reform had resulted in major improvements.

Nevertheless, education remained a major topic on the public agenda, as was shown by the 1988 presidential campaign. In the fall of 1987, for example, nine candidates for the White House had staged the first presidential debate devoted solely to education. And Vice President George Bush promised as a candidate to be the "education president" if elected.

Interest and involvement in education was particularly evident in the nation's business community, which faced increasing difficulties in hiring workers with adequate basic skills. Many business leaders warned that the United States would be unable to compete in the increasingly technological world economy unless its workers received better preparation in English, science and mathematics. Business involvement in education included both political support for reform efforts and direct "partnerships" with individual schools.

## Reform and Restructuring

With the completion of the early burst of reform activity at the state level, efforts to improve the schools began to shift to a variety of other strategies.

A major concern continued to be the need to improve the condition of teaching as a profession. Although teachers in many areas had won substantial pay increases, advocates of change argued that more was needed to be done to raise the status of teaching.

One key area of activity concerned standards for teachers. In 1987, the Carnegie Corporation's Forum on Education and the Economy, which had released a major report on teaching in 1986, created a National Board for Professional Teaching Standards. The board was aimed at developing a set of standards on which teachers could be certified nationally.

In addition, the National Education Association pressed to make state teacher-licensing boards more accountable to the profession by having a majority of their members be teachers, as had not been the case in the past.

A related reform concept was implemented in Rochester, N.Y., Dade County, Fla., and other areas. In Rochester, teachers were to earn up to $70,000 a year in return for taking on greater responsibilities and helping other teachers.

More broadly, some reformers called for a thorough restructuring of school decision making. Instead of simply mandating changes from above, they said, officials should give greater authority and responsibility to educators at the level of individual schools, and then judge them on their success in educating children.

Other restructuring ideas called for giving greater authority to parents. The most dramatic example of this occurred in Chicago, where community protests forced officials to consider fundamental changes in what many considered to be one of the worst school systems in the nation. The effort led to legislation, adopted by the Illinois legislature in 1988, to establish parent-dominated governing boards for each school.

The most popular and controversial reform proposal was parental "choice," under which parents would have greater authority to decide which schools their child would attend. Minnesota was a state leader in the area, approving legislation to allow students to enroll in any school district in the state, accompanied by a share of state funding. Other states adopted similar proposals.

## References

Discussion of education policy for the years 1945-64 may be found in *Congress and the Nation Vol. I*, pp. 1195-1215; for the years 1965-68, *Congress and the Nation Vol. II*, pp. 709-733; for the years 1969-72, *Congress and the Nation Vol. III*, pp. 581-604; for the years 1973-76, *Congress and the Nation Vol. IV*, pp. 377-402; for the years 1977-80, *Congress and the Nation Vol. V*, pp. 655-677; for the years 1981-84, *Congress and the Nation Vol. VI*, pp. 555-580.

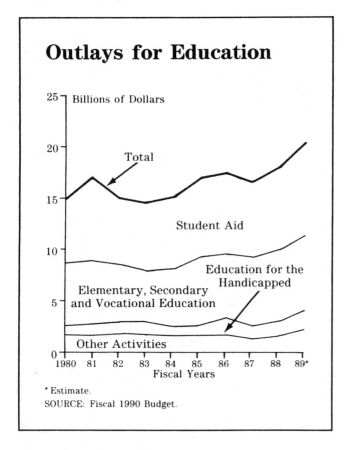

## Outlays for Education

Billions of Dollars

25 —

20 —

Total

15 —

Student Aid

10 —

Education for the
Handicapped

Elementary, Secondary
and Vocational Education

5 —

Other Activities

0 —
1980  81  82  83  84  85  86  87  88  89*
Fiscal Years

* Estimate.
SOURCE: Fiscal 1990 Budget.

the past. The Justice Department under President Reagan opposed mandatory desegregation plans and undertook efforts to drop longstanding desegregation cases against many school districts and state higher education systems.

Two new social problems drew increasing attention from the schools. One was illegal drugs, which polls showed the public viewed as the schools' biggest problem — even though other surveys found evidence of declining drug use by students. Efforts to require teachers to submit to drug testing were blocked by the courts, although some school systems began testing students involved in extracurricular activities. Educators also devoted increasing resources to drug-education programs.

Education programs on AIDS (acquired immune deficiency syndrome) were more controversial. U.S. Surgeon General C. Everett Koop called in 1986 for beginning AIDS-education efforts in the early grades. But many conservatives argued that such programs should be decided at the local level and should stress abstinence as the best way to prevent infection. By 1988, a majority of states had mandated some sort of AIDS instruction. Enrollment of students infected with the AIDS virus also generated heated debate, with some communities refusing to admit such students. Subsequently, however, AIDS-infected students generally were admitted without major obstacles, as experts concluded that spread of the disease through casual contact was highly unlikely.

### Higher Education

The forces of change affecting higher education during Reagan's tenure were considerably less dramatic than those buffeting elementary and secondary education.

Perhaps the most significant development was by no means a new one: the growth of college costs. Despite the overall slackening of inflation, tuition costs at both public and private schools rose at a steady pace. Tuition and fees at public institutions during the 1987-88 school year were 6 percent above the previous year's level, while those at private institutions were 8 percent above. At some prestigious colleges and universities, tuition and room and board exceeded $20,000 a year.

While federal grant and loan programs picked up some of the costs, hard-pressed parents turned to state governments for help. In 1986, Michigan passed legislation allowing parents to pay specified annual amounts, while their children were still very young, in exchange for a guarantee that their children's full tuition costs at public institutions in the state would be covered when they reached college age. Other states followed, or they established tax incentives for college saving.

Higher education managed to maintain its enrollment levels despite a fall in the number of college-age youths. The difference was made up by an increase in the percentage of youths going to postsecondary schools and a swelling in the ranks of older students.

While the public appeared less dissatisfied with higher education than with that at the pre-collegiate level, one sharp critique of college curricula achieved widespread popularity. In *The Closing of the American Mind*, University of Chicago scholar Alan Bloom blasted the shift that had occurred since the 1960s away from a core curriculum, arguing that the spread of "relativism" on campus had been an "unmitigated disaster."

Supporters of choice argued that it would make schools compete for students and thus force them to improve in order to survive in a "free-market" economy. But critics warned that it would benefit only schools that were already satisfactory, while leaving poor and disadvantaged students even worse off.

### Social Issues

The schools also struggled to cope with a variety of social ills. Perhaps the most important long-range issue was the growth in the ranks of "at-risk" students — minorities, disadvantaged, handicapped and other children who began their school careers with a significantly greater chance than other children of not finishing high school or not receiving an adequate education. Because of demographic trends, such students constituted an increasing percentage of all enrollment, and the vast majority of many urban systems. Warning of the problems that the existence of the "educational underclass" could pose for the economy, a 1987 report by the Committee for Economic Development called for a variety of early-intervention and other programs to aid at-risk students.

Meanwhile, schools systems continued the desegregation efforts that had begun with the Supreme Court's 1954 decision in *Brown v. Board of Education of Topeka, Kan.* Studies released in 1986 and 1987 showed that these efforts had been at least partially successful, with a substantial fall in the percentages of students attending racially unbalanced schools. Mandatory busing plans continued in effect in many areas, but they were far less controversial than in

# Chronology Of Action On Education

## 1985-86

A five-year extension of college aid programs headed the list of education bills produced by the 99th Congress during its two-year lifespan. Other legislation included a three-year extension of education programs for handicapped children and a measure to spur the cleanup of hazardous asbestos in the nation's schools.

## Higher Education Aid

Congress in 1986 approved legislation that renewed for five years, through fiscal 1991, popular aid programs for colleges and their students under the Higher Education Act.

The measure (S 1965 — PL 99-498) set stricter eligibility rules for student loans and made other changes designed to target aid to the neediest students. The bill also raised loan limits and, for the first time, made aid available to students enrolled less than half time.

Most of the bill's funding was to pay for the two largest student aid programs, Pell Grants and Guaranteed Student Loans (GSLs), which were expected to cost $3.9 billion and $3.1 billion, respectively, in fiscal 1987. That left a total of $3.2 billion for all other programs — a ceiling that was to be increased to compensate for inflation in 1988-91.

The bill cut student loan subsidies paid to banks and made other changes in GSLs designed to reduce projected outlays by $445 million over three years. The cuts were required as part of Congress' deficit reduction efforts.

S 1965 represented a bipartisan rejection of President Reagan's proposals for deep cuts in higher education. But the bill did draw on some proposals backed by the administration, such as tightened financial needs requirements for students seeking guaranteed loans.

Faced with rising college costs, Congress was under pressure to permit students to borrow more per year. Since 1976, the per-student limit had been $2,500 a year for undergraduates and $5,000 for graduate students. Senate-House conferees on the bill allowed only a small increase, to $2,625 per year, for freshmen and sophomores, but juniors and seniors were allowed to borrow $4,000 annually and graduate students $7,500. The total students could borrow through college and graduate school was more than doubled, from $25,000 to $54,750.

The measure included a revised program of support for continuing education, new grants for campus child-care programs and provisions allowing students to postpone repayment of past college loans if they returned to school part time.

The bill included several important provisions designed to prevent abuses of financial aid programs. It made it harder for undergraduates under age 24 to declare financial independence from their parents simply to improve their chances of getting financial aid. Students were required to maintain a C average, or grades consistent with graduation requirements, to keep getting aid after their sophomore year. Other provisions were designed to crack down on schools that had taken advantage of the availability of federal aid to recruit students for shoddy programs or courses for which they were unprepared.

Although most of the money under S 1965 was to go directly to needy students, the bill also reauthorized a wide array of smaller programs aiding colleges. The Senate tried to resist pressure to create new college aid programs or to maintain existing ones that had not received appropriations in recent years. However, Senate negotiators did accept numerous House proposals to provide new aid in such areas as graduate education and teacher training. And both chambers supported proposals to expand aid to historically black colleges and other institutions serving minority students.

### Background

The Higher Education Act of 1965 authorized guaranteed loans to college students, grants for library books and materials and for university extension programs and funds to help small colleges. *(Congress and the Nation Vol. II, pp. 716, 722; 1980 extension, Congress and the Nation Vol. V, p. 672)*

In amending the act over the years, Congress began to channel most higher education aid to needy students rather than to colleges. By 1985, roughly half of all college students were receiving some form of federal financial aid for their college costs. Student aid totaled about $9 billion in the fiscal year ending Sept. 30, 1985. The largest programs were Pell Grants for low-income students and low-interest Guaranteed Student Loans, which helped low- and middle-income students pay college bills.

The growing student aid programs became targets of Reagan administration efforts to reduce federal spending. At first Congress went along with the administration: Federal aid to college students was cut sharply by 1981 deficit reduction legislation. In subsequent years, however, Congress resisted administration efforts to cut aid. *(Congress and the Nation Vol. VI, pp. 562, 566, 575)*

### Deficit Reduction, Fiscal 1986

In 1985, Reagan proposed $4 billion in student aid cuts over fiscal 1986-88. The cuts were to be accomplished by setting an annual cap on the amount of federal aid a student could receive and by tightening income eligibility for subsidized loans.

Congress early in 1986 approved a variety of cost-cutting changes in the GSL program as part of a fiscal 1986 deficit reduction bill (HR 3128 — PL 99-272). That bill aimed to cut costs primarily through administrative changes, including a variety of measures to improve collections of defaulted student loans and a new requirement that banks disburse loans in at least two installments a year instead of in one lump sum.

Conferees on HR 3128 dropped two of the most controversial proposals in the original House and Senate versions of the bill. They dropped a Senate provision to trim the subsidies paid to banks that made the low-interest GSLs. And the House agreed to back down from a proposal to require all students to undergo a financial needs test to qualify for loans. That issue was left for the full-scale higher education reauthorization bill. *(HR 3128, p. 40)*

## House Action, 1985

The House Education and Labor Committee reported a five-year reauthorization of the Higher Education Act (HR 3700 — H Rept 99-383) Nov. 20, 1985. The full House passed the measure Dec. 4 on a 350-67 vote. Before passing the bill, the House defeated, 127-289, an amendment to freeze spending for several programs at fiscal 1985 levels.

Rejecting charges that the bill was a "budget-buster," proponents noted that it had a lower price tag than current authorizations. The House bill authorized roughly $10.5 billion for fiscal 1987, $1 billion less than authorized for fiscal 1986 under existing law but $1.3 billion more than the amount appropriated for fiscal 1985.

HR 3700 reflected widespread concern that low-income students were going too deeply into debt to finance their college education. The bill generally attempted to shift student aid funding from loans to grants. It allowed a gradual increase in the ceiling on Pell Grants from $2,100 to $3,100 in fiscal 1991. Student grants would continue to be limited to no more than 60 percent of college costs, however. The bill also liberalized grants to the lowest-income students and increased aid to the growing number of mid-career adults enrolling in college.

The measure included an administration-backed proposal requiring all student loan recipients to demonstrate their financial need for the loans. Under existing law, only students from families with annual incomes exceeding $30,000 had to pass a financial needs test. The bill also made it harder for student aid applicants to claim they were financially independent of their parents simply to improve their chances of getting aid.

## Senate Action, 1986

The Senate Labor and Human Resources Committee unanimously reported S 1965 on May 13, 1986 (S Rept 99-296).

S 1965 increased the existing $2,100 annual limit on Pell Grants to $2,400 in fiscal 1987. In fiscal 1991, a $3,200 maximum grant would be authorized. In a significant change not included in the House bill, S 1965 for the first time barred students from getting Pell Grants if they had more than $30,000 annual family income. The bill barred undergraduates from receiving Pell Grants for more than five years.

In another departure from the House bill, S 1965 required aid recipients, by the end of their second year in college, to achieve a C average. Students with lower grades would remain eligible if their academic standing was deemed "consistent with the requirements for graduation."

For the guaranteed loans, S 1965 raised the $2,500 annual limit on the amount undergraduates could borrow to $3,000 in the first two years of college and $4,000 a year thereafter. S 1965, like the House measure, required all GSL applicants to undergo a financial needs test to establish eligibility.

In other areas, the committee adopted a compromise for restructuring aid to financially struggling colleges — a politically sensitive program that had been a major but dwindling source of aid to historically black colleges. The program, authorized by Title III of the Higher Education Act, was one of the few that provided aid directly to col-

leges with few strings attached. The bill set up a separate program within Title III for historically black colleges, authorized at $55 million in 1987. Other financially struggling colleges would compete for aid under another section of Title III, for which $85 million was authorized for fiscal 1987.

The Senate June 3 passed S 1965 by a 93-1 vote. Only Jesse Helms, R-N.C., voted against the bill.

Before approving S 1965, the Senate adopted, 60-34, an amendment to scale back proposed increases in Pell Grants and make other cost-saving changes in an effort to accommodate Reagan administration complaints. But even with those cuts, the bill's fiscal 1987 authorization of $9.5 billion far exceeded the $6.2 billion higher education budget proposed by Reagan.

## Conference, Final Action

House and Senate conferees approved a compromise version of S 1965 on Sept. 12, 1986. The final bill authorized about $10.2 billion in fiscal 1987, compared with existing authorizations of roughly $12 billion and fiscal 1986 appropriations of about $8.5 billion.

To comply with the 1987 budget resolution, which called for changes that would reduce projected GSL outlays by $395 million over three years, conferees cut the subsidies paid to banks to make up the difference between the low interest paid by borrowers and market rates. In addition, a new fee would be levied on state agencies that helped administer the GSL program, with higher fees charged to agencies whose borrowers had high default rates.

The compromise allowed borrowers to defer repayment of GSLs for up to two years if they were unemployed — a deferment limited to one year under existing law.

Reaching a compromise on one of the most controversial issues before the conference, negotiators agreed to allow only the poorest students to qualify for grants to attend less than half time — and they would not qualify until fiscal 1988. A somewhat larger pool of part-time students would qualify after fiscal 1991.

The House adopted the conference report on the bill (H Rept 99-861) on a 385-25 vote Sept. 24. The Senate approved it by voice vote the next day, completing congressional action.

## Major Provisions

As signed into law Oct. 17, 1986, S 1965 (PL 99-498) contained the following major provisions:

● **Authorization Levels.** Authorized $10.2 billion for higher education programs in fiscal 1987. That figure included enough to accommodate projected costs for Pell Grants and GSLs and the specific ceilings set for other programs. The limits on programs other than Pell Grants and GSLs were to be adjusted for inflation in fiscal 1988-91; no fixed ceilings were set for individual programs after fiscal 1987.

● **Guaranteed Student Loans.** Required all students to pass a financial needs test to qualify for loans and forbade them to borrow more than they needed; under existing law those requirements applied only to students from families with more than $30,000 annual income. Family assets had to be considered in the needs assessment, not just income as was the case under existing law.

● Increased the $2,500 annual limit on the amount undergraduates could borrow to $2,625 for freshmen and sophomores, and $4,000 for upperclassmen. Graduate students were allowed to borrow $7,500 a year. The aggregate limits on borrowing were raised from $12,500 to $17,250 for undergraduates, and from $25,000 to $54,750 for those who went on to graduate school.

• Increased the interest rate from 8 percent to 10 percent beginning in the fifth year of repayment.

• Reduced the special allowance paid to banks that made GSLs by 0.25 percent. Under existing law the allowance was pegged quarterly to a rate equal to 3.5 percent above the rate paid on Treasury bills.

• Required state loan guarantee agencies that helped administer the GSL program to pay a new reinsurance fee to the federal government, with higher fees charged to agencies whose borrowers had high default rates.

• Allowed borrowers to defer repaying GSLs for up to two years if they were unemployed — an extension of the one-year deferment previously allowed.

• Allowed borrowers to defer repaying GSLs if they became teachers in regions or of academic subjects suffering teacher shortages.

• Allowed borrowers to defer repaying past student loans if they returned to school part time and had to borrow again. Existing law allowed such deferments only if borrowers returned to school full time.

• Required banks to inform borrowers of their projected levels of indebtedness on graduation and their estimated monthly repayments.

• Imposed new restrictions on loans to students attending foreign medical schools, allowing GSLs to be used at such schools only if at least 60 percent of the students there were citizens of the country in which the school was located, or if at least 45 percent of its students passed a standardized test of medical knowledge that was administered to foreign students before they could practice in the United States. That minimum pass rate was to rise to 50 percent in fiscal 1989.

• Barred state guarantee agencies from offering inducements to employees and schools to recruit loan applicants.

• Allowed students with more than $5,000 in federal loans to consolidate their debts and take longer to repay them. The repayment period could be extended from 10 years to as much as 25 years, depending on how much students had borrowed.

• Raised the limit on borrowing under a separate program of higher interest "auxiliary loans" currently available to parents of college students as well as to self-supporting and graduate students. The cap was raised from $3,000 to $4,000 a year.

• Lowered the interest on auxiliary loans from the existing level of 12 percent to a rate tied to Treasury bill rates, but no more than 12 percent. Borrowers currently holding 12 percent auxiliary loans could refinance them at the lower rate.

• **Pell Grants.** Increased the existing $2,100 per-student annual limit on Pell Grants to $2,300 in fiscal 1987. The maximum was increased in $200 annual increments thereafter. Grants continued to be limited to no more than 60 percent of a student's college costs.

• Allowed some students enrolled in college less than half time to receive Pell Grants beginning in fiscal 1989. Initially, eligibility was extended only to the poorest students, whose families could not afford to contribute at all toward college costs. In fiscal 1991, eligibility was to be expanded to include students whose expected family contribution to college costs was up to $200, as determined by a federal formula for assessing financial need.

• Barred students from receiving Pell Grants for more than five years. The limit could be waived for students in five-year degree programs and for other special cases.

• **Campused-Based Financial Aid.** For students who attended less than half time, expanded access to aid under the three "campus-based" aid programs administered by college officials: Supplemental Educational Opportunity Grants (SEOG), College Work-Study (CWS) and National Direct Student Loans (NDSL). Colleges were required to award such students a "reasonable proportion" of their campus-based funds.

• Revised the formula for distributing campus-based aid, specifying that each school receive no less than it did in fiscal 1985. For appropriations beyond that level, 75 percent of the money was to be distributed by a new formula that based allocations on the financial need of each college's students.

• Raised the annual limit on supplemental grants from $2,000 to $4,000.

• Required colleges, in distributing supplemental grants and direct loans, to give priority to students with exceptional financial need.

• Increased the existing limits on direct loans by 50 percent, allowing students to borrow up to $4,500 over their first two years and $9,000 over all their undergraduate years. Those who went on to graduate school could accumulate up to $18,000 in debt.

• Barred schools from receiving additional direct loan funds if their alumni default rate exceeded 20 percent. The existing cutoff was 25 percent.

• Extended from six months to nine months the period allowed borrowers after leaving school before they had to begin repaying their direct loans.

• Allowed students at proprietary schools to participate in the College Work-Study program.

• Raised from $2,000 to $2,500 the annual limit on awards under the State Student Incentive Grants, a program that provided federal matching funds to states to encourage them to set up and expand their own scholarship programs.

• **Other Student Aid Provisions.** Required aid recipients, to remain eligible, to achieve by the end of their second year a C average or academic standing consistent with their college's graduation requirements.

• Required colleges, to participate in student aid programs, to certify that they had a drug abuse prevention program.

• Authorized $5 million a year for a pilot project making student loans that were to be repaid in installments geared to the borrowers' income after they left school.

• Allowed students who had not earned a high school diploma or its equivalent to qualify for financial aid only if they received counseling and remedial instruction or passed a nationally recognized test assessing their ability to benefit from the postsecondary program they wanted to enter.

• Specified key elements of two formulas for assessing applicants' financial need, with separate needs analysis systems for Pell Grants and for other financial aid programs. The new systems would take effect in fiscal 1988.

• Took account of child-care costs in assessing a student's need for aid.

• Specified that home equity not be considered in assessing the financial need of workers seeking mid-career retraining or homemakers preparing to enter the work force.

● Authorized the secretary of education annually to propose changes in the needs analysis formulas, subject to congressional approval by a joint resolution. If the proposal was not approved, the formulas would be automatically updated and adjusted to reflect inflation.

● Barred aid applicants under the age of 24 from qualifying as financially independent of their parents unless they met specified standards. Graduate and professional students and married students under 24 could qualify as independent if their independence was affirmatively demonstrated to campus officials. Older students would automatically qualify as financially independent.

● **Institutional Aid.** Overhauled aid to "developing institutions" into a three-part program under Title III of the Higher Education Act:

1) Under Part A, authorized $120 million for aid to financially struggling colleges to improve their management and academic quality, with $51.4 million earmarked for community colleges. In addition, 25 percent of appropriations for Title III above the fiscal 1986 levels was earmarked for institutions serving the highest percentages of minority students.

2) Under Part B, authorized $100 million for 1987 for a new program for historically black colleges to improve their academic programs and facilities, and $5 million for historically black graduate and professional schools.

3) Under Part C, renewed existing challenge grants to help build the endowments of struggling colleges, which were required to put up matching funds.

● **Other College Aid Programs.** Overhauled federal aid for continuing education to improve programs for such "non-traditional" students as adults seeking mid-career retraining and homemakers preparing to enter the work force.

● Reauthorized grants to college libraries, with a new stipulation that institutions must demonstrate their need for such aid to qualify.

● Renewed the "TRIO" program, which encouraged students from disadvantaged backgrounds to enroll in college.

● Authorized $60 million for new and revised programs to train and recruit schoolteachers, including grants for teacher training centers and joint school-college projects.

● Reauthorized grants for international education and foreign language studies, and set up a new program to help colleges buy foreign periodicals.

● Reauthorized loans to colleges for student housing construction, and expanded their use to include renovation of academic facilities.

● Required the education secretary to sell $579 million worth of loan assets in fiscal 1987 and $314 million in fiscal 1988 under programs that provided loans for construction of college housing and other academic facilities.

● Set up a government-sponsored private corporation to increase the availability of private capital for campus construction and renovation projects by insuring and reinsuring bonds and loans.

● Reauthorized grants for cooperative education, which supported programs that allowed students to link off-campus work experience with their classroom studies.

● Established a new graduate education program to recruit more minority students and another to provide fellowships for graduate students in areas of national need, such as engineering and computer science.

● Reauthorized existing graduate and professional fel-

lowships for women and minority groups, raising the stipend from $4,500 to $10,000.

● Reauthorized without major change the Fund for the Improvement of Postsecondary Education and a program to help colleges serving large numbers of minority students to improve their science programs.

● Renewed grants to urban universities and authorized new ones to other colleges to work with local governments, unions and business groups to promote economic development.

● Renewed aid to colleges for programs to encourage the children of migrant farm workers to finish high school and enroll in college.

● Authorized a new program of grants to institutions for child-care services for disadvantaged students.

● **Other Provisions.** Renewed programs supporting educational research and statistics gathering through fiscal 1991.

● Required universities to report to the Education Department certain information about donations from foreign sources that exceeded $250,000.

● Set up a National Commission on Responsibility for Financing the Cost of Postsecondary Education.

● Reauthorized through fiscal 1988 the U.S. Institute of Peace. The institute was dedicated to the study of peace and conflict resolution. *(Congress and the Nation Vol. VI, p. 579)*

# Handicapped Education

In 1986 Congress approved legislation (S 2294 — PL 99-457) reauthorizing handicapped education programs for three years, with increased emphasis on helping preschool children.

The measure bolstered incentive grants to states that began special education for handicapped children at age 3, and it authorized new grants for serving even younger children.

The final version of the measure was a compromise drafted by the House Education and Labor Committee as a substitute for a far more sweeping Senate-passed bill. In a key change, the compromise dropped provisions of the earlier Senate bill that would expand existing handicapped education mandates by requiring states to provide services for all handicapped children beginning at age 3.

Even the incentive-based final version was opposed by the Reagan administration, which objected to its cost and its "hasty enactment."

The legislation amended the Education for All Handicapped Children Act (PL 94-142), which provided grants to states and required them to provide a "free, appropriate public education" for all handicapped children beginning no later than age 5. *(Congress and the Nation Vol. IV, p. 389)*

Those state grants were permanently authorized, but an array of smaller handicapped education programs was due to expire Sept. 30, 1986. S 2294 reauthorized those programs, involving such activities as research and teacher training, through fiscal 1989. *(Previous reauthorization, Congress and the Nation Vol. VI, p. 567)*

Under PL 94-142, many states already began special education at age 3, but an estimated 70,000 handicapped children between the ages of 3 and 5 were not being served. S 2294 did not require states to cover those preschool students, but it authorized significant increases in grants to states that did.

Sponsors of the original Senate bill predicted the compromise's financial incentives would have the same practical effect as mandating services for preschool children, but they vowed to monitor the bill's implementation to make sure that was the case.

### Legislative History

The Senate Labor and Human Resources Committee May 20, 1986, approved S 2294 (S Rept 99-315), and the Senate passed the bill without change June 6.

The Senate version of the bill, approved by voice vote, would require states to provide special education services for handicapped children beginning at age 3. The bill also would set up a new $100 million-a-year program of grants to states that began services for handicapped infants at birth.

The bill also reauthorized through fiscal 1989 a variety of special-purpose handicapped education programs in such areas as teacher training and research.

S 2294 was passed over the objection of Education Secretary William J. Bennett, who described the bill as "unduly prescriptive, burdensome and costly." He singled out the new $100 million program for serving infants as "clearly excessive."

The House Education and Labor Committee Sept. 17 approved its less extensive version of the legislation (HR 5520 — H Rept 99-860). As approved, 33-0, the bill boosted incentive grants to states that served disabled children aged 3 to 5, and it authorized a new $50 million program to help states develop services for infants up to age 2. The measure also reauthorized a number of small education programs for the handicapped.

HR 5520 was a compromise put together in staff negotiations that included Senate aides, to ensure that the end result would be supported by Lowell P. Weicker Jr., R-Conn., principal sponsor of the Senate bill and a leading congressional advocate for the handicapped.

The House passed its version Sept. 22, and the Senate agreed to the House changes two days later, completing congressional action on the bill.

### Major Provisions

As signed into law Oct. 8, 1986, S 2294 (PL 99-457) contained the following major provisions:

• Revised and increased incentive grants to states for serving handicapped children aged 3 to 5. In the fourth year of the program, states would have to serve all handicapped children from age 3 to 5 or lose federal funds for that age group.

That mandate would be postponed until the fifth year of the program if funding for the grants had not totaled $656 million in fiscal 1987-89 and $306 million in 1990.

• Authorized $50 million in fiscal 1987, $75 million in 1988 and "such sums" as Congress considered necessary in 1989-91 for new grants to help states provide services to handicapped children from birth to age 2.

After the fourth year of the program, any state that chose to participate must serve all eligible children in the age group.

• Authorized $585 million over fiscal 1987-89 for several existing handicapped programs, including teacher training, research, postsecondary programs and centers for the deaf and blind.

---

## Education Leadership

Controversial and outspoken, William J. Bennett was unanimously confirmed as education secretary Feb. 6, 1985, succeeding T. H. Bell. Bennett repeatedly asserted throughout the course of his tenure that he believed the Cabinet-level status of the Department of Education was unnecessary. *(Bell background, Congress and the Nation Vol. VI, p. 1018)*

Lauro F. Cavazos became the first Hispanic to hold a Cabinet position when he succeeded Bennett Sept. 20, 1988. Cavazos was serving as president of Texas Tech University at the time of his nomination. President Bush retained Cavazos in the education post. *(Cabinet profiles, p. 1046)*

---

• Authorized $31.75 million over fiscal 1987-89 for a new program of grants to promote the use of new technologies in handicapped education.

## Legal Fees for Handicapped

Congress in 1986 enacted legislation (S 415 — PL 99-372) to allow parents to recover the legal cost of defending the education rights of handicapped children.

The conference report (H Rept 99-687), which authorized courts to award attorneys' fees to parents who prevailed in special-education legal disputes, was adopted by the Senate by voice vote July 17 and cleared by the House July 24, also by voice vote. The Senate originally passed S 415 (S Rept 99-112) July 30, 1985. The House passed its version (HR 1523 — H Rept 99-296) Nov. 12, 1985.

The compromise was reported by a conference committee after Senate negotiators agreed to drop a controversial proposal to impose new limits on fee awards to publicly funded legal aid lawyers in handicapped education cases. That provision was one of the principal stumbling blocks to an agreement on the bill, which had been in conference since late 1985.

The legislation was drafted in response to a 1984 Supreme Court ruling. In the case of *Smith v. Robinson*, the court held that nothing in existing law allowed parents to recover their attorneys' fees when they prevailed in court cases brought under the Education for All Handicapped Children Act (PL 94-142). *(PL 94-142, Congress and the Nation Vol. IV, p. 389; 1984 ruling, Congress and the Nation Vol. VI, p. 730)*

That law guaranteed handicapped children a free, appropriate public education. It set up special administrative procedures for resolving disagreements between schools and parents about what special services and education programs were appropriate for a disabled child. When differences could not be resolved in those proceedings, parents could take school officials to court.

Congress did not authorize the award of attorneys' fees in the handicapped education law, but before *Smith v.*

*Robinson*, some courts had allowed parents to recover legal costs under related anti-bias statutes.

The Supreme Court foreclosed that possibility by ruling that Congress intended the handicapped education law to be the exclusive legal avenue for enforcing the rights of disabled school children. Sponsors of S 415 said the ruling misread congressional intent and denied court access to families that could not afford hefty legal expenses.

S 415 authorized the award of reasonable attorneys' fees under the handicapped education law.

### Resolving Differences

While similar in their basic thrust, House and Senate versions of S 415 differed on several controversial points. The provision imposing stricter limits on fee awards to lawyers who worked for publicly funded legal aid groups had been pushed by Sen. Orrin G. Hatch, R-Utah, chairman of the Labor and Human Resources Committee, which handled S 415.

The Senate bill would allow such lawyers to receive only their actual litigation costs. By contrast, most awards of attorneys' fees were based on prevailing market rates, which generally were higher than litigation costs.

Conferees agreed to include other provisions that Hatch said would "protect against excessive reimbursement" of lawyers, such as fee reductions if attorneys unreasonably prolonged disputes.

The bill that emerged from conference allowed awards to cover attorneys' fees incurred in administrative proceedings as well as in court disputes. Conferees dropped a House provision to cut off after four years the authority for courts to award attorneys' fees incurred at the administrative level.

### Major Provisions

As signed into law Aug. 5, 1986, S 415 (PL 99-372) contained the following major provisions:

● Authorized courts to award reasonable attorneys' fees to parents who prevailed in legal disputes brought under the Education for All Handicapped Children Act.

● Specified that awards should not be calculated by using "bonuses and multipliers," applied in rare instances by courts to increase fee awards to lawyers in exceedingly complicated cases.

● Stipulated that no fees could be awarded for legal services provided after a school district made a written offer of a settlement if the offer was rejected but proved to be at least as favorable as the relief parents eventually won. An exception was provided to allow reimbursement if the parent was "substantially justified" in rejecting the settlement offer.

● Provided for the reduction of fee awards if a parent unreasonably delayed resolution of a dispute or if the time spent and fees charged by an attorney were excessive. Reductions would not be made in such cases if school officials delayed resolution of the controversy unreasonably or otherwise violated the handicapped education law.

● Required parents to exhaust administrative remedies under the handicapped education law before filing suits under other anti-bias statutes.

● Specified that the bill applied to all cases initiated after July 3, 1984, and to cases pending on July 4, 1984 — the day before the *Smith* decision.

# School Asbestos Cleanup

President Reagan Oct. 22, 1986, signed legislation (HR 5073 — PL 99-519) mandating that the nation's schools clean up hazardous asbestos and requiring the Environmental Protection Agency (EPA) to issue standards for school inspection, cleanup and disposal of the insulating material.

The legislation arose from congressional dissatisfaction with existing EPA efforts to regulate asbestos, a once-common building material that can cause cancer and other diseases. Under regulations issued in 1982, schools were required to inspect for asbestos and to notify parents and employees of the results. However, the agency rules did not require schools to take remedial action if asbestos hazards were found, nor did they set standards for determining when the presence of asbestos posed a health hazard. *(Background, Congress and the Nation Vol. VI, p. 572; Congress and the Nation Vol. V, p. 676)*

EPA officials argued that such assessments and decisions were best made at the local level. They said on-site observers were best able to decide whether, as was often the case, it was more dangerous to remove asbestos and risk releasing fibers into the air than to seal it off or take other, less drastic actions.

But critics complained that school officials needed more guidance because, lacking clear federal standards, many schools had undertaken unnecessary removal work or hired incompetent contractors who made the problem worse. Rep. James J. Florio, D-N.J., a leading sponsor of HR 5073, cited EPA estimates that 75 percent of all school cleanup work had been done improperly.

The House originally passed HR 5073 (H Rept 99-763) by voice vote Aug. 12, 1986. The Senate passed HR 5073 Sept. 10 after substituting its own measure (S 2083 — S Rept 99-427). Staff negotiators worked out a compromise bill, which was approved by the House Oct. 1 and the Senate Oct. 3.

As signed into law, HR 5073:

● Required EPA, within one year of enactment, to issue regulations prescribing procedures for mandatory school inspections and reinspections, and to set standards for the safe disposal of asbestos. The agency also would be required to set standards spelling out what steps should be taken to protect "human health and the environment" in different circumstances when asbestos was found.

● Required EPA to develop a model program for states to certify contractors hired to remove asbestos, conduct inspections and help schools develop plans for handling asbestos. States would be required to adopt a program at least as stringent as the EPA model, and schools would have to use accredited contractors.

● Required the National Bureau of Standards to develop a program for accrediting laboratories that did asbestos-related work.

● Spelled out backup standards that would take effect if EPA failed to issue the required regulations by the deadlines set by the bill. The backup provisions would require schools, following a specified timetable, to inspect and clean up asbestos in keeping with an existing EPA guidance document.

● Required school districts, after conducting building inspections, to submit to their state governors for approval plans for cleaning up asbestos in their schools.

● Provided for civil penalties of up to $5,000 a day per

violation to be levied against school districts that violated the law, although courts could return funds to schools with an order that they be used to pay the costs of complying with the law.

● Authorized citizens to bring suit against EPA if the agency did not comply with the statutory deadlines.

● Required EPA to study asbestos problems in commercial and public buildings other than schools, and recommend whether they should also be subject to removal requirements.

● Increased by $25 million a year the authorization for aid to schools for abating asbestos hazards by recapturing repayment money from loans made under the 1984 Asbestos School Hazard Abatement Act (PL 98-377).

# 1987-88

Much of the 100th Congress' work on education issues focused on a single piece of legislation — the massive reauthorization of federal programs aiding elementary, secondary and adult education. Although action on that bill stirred up several controversies — some related to education, such as that concerning methods of bilingual instruction for students of limited English proficiency, and some unrelated, such as efforts to ban telephone pornography — the broad popularity of the measure as a whole reflected the growing public interest in efforts to improve the nation's public schools.

Debate over higher education programs, which had been reauthorized for five years during the 99th Congress, centered largely around concern about the growth of federal student loan programs because of a high default rate. The issue remained unresolved at the end of 1988, however, although Congress did clear a bill aimed at cracking down on abuses in the much smaller Supplemental Loan for Students program.

## Education Reauthorization

Congress cleared an education reauthorization bill (HR 5 — PL 100-297) on April 20, 1988. The bill, which authorized a total of $8.3 billion in spending in fiscal 1989, extended the full panoply of federal elementary, secondary and adult education programs for five years, through fiscal 1993.

Action on HR 5, during most of its journey through Congress, had been marked by a clear bipartisan desire to avoid presidential politicking, while capitalizing on voter support for education. The versions of the measure passed by the House and Senate in late 1987 were strikingly similar in both philosophy and scope.

Before the bill could be cleared for the president, however, sponsors had to steer it through a last-minute election-year battle over a non-germane provision to ban telephone services that allowed a caller to dial a toll number to listen to sexually oriented messages. Originally tacked onto the Senate version of HR 5 by Jesse Helms, R-N.C., the "dial-a-porn" provision quickly became the major obstacle to final action. Ultimately, opponents of the provision were defeated and it became law.

HR 5 was officially named for its two chief sponsors: Augustus F. Hawkins, D-Calif., chairman of the House Education and Labor Committee; and Robert T. Stafford, R-Vt., ranking Republican on the Senate Labor and Human Resources Subcommittee on Education.

The bill as cleared made few major changes in the program of compensatory education for low-income children that was created by the 1965 Elementary and Secondary Education Act (PL 89-10) and last reauthorized in 1981 by the wide-ranging budget reconciliation law (PL 97-35). The Chapter 1 program, which provided aid to school districts in which at least 10 percent of children came from families with incomes below the poverty level, was the centerpiece of federal education assistance, with nearly 90 percent of the nation's school districts receiving funds. *(PL 89-10, Congress and the Nation Vol. II, p. 720; PL 97-35, Congress and the Nation Vol. VI, p. 559)*

But the legislation made a major significant change in the concentration-grant program, which targeted districts with a high number or percentage of poor children. HR 5 altered the formula for distribution of grants, to the benefit of rural and Southern schools. The existing formula, which favored urban districts, had been established in 1981.

The bill also authorized block grants (Chapter 2) to state and local educational agencies. And it created a number of new prorgrams: "Even Start," to provide educational and social services to very young children and their parents; "star schools," to support education by satellite technology; and a dropout-prevention program for secondary-school students. In addition, HR 5 provided more funding for alternative bilingual-education programs, such as "English as a second language" and immersion in English. The Reagan administration had sought the change to give local school districts more flexibility in designing programs for lesser-English-proficiency students.

### House Subcommittee Action

By far the most difficult issue facing the House Education and Labor Committee in its work on HR 5 was the bilingual-education issue. Panel Republicans, backed by the Reagan administration, were determined to insert into the bill provisions allowing greater use of federal funds for "alternative" programs, which were not based on giving lesser-English-proficiency students instruction in some academic subjects in their native languages. *(Bilingual education, box, p. 657)*

Committee Democrats had more than enough votes to defeat such GOP efforts. But chief sponsor Hawkins wanted to ensure that the bill had strong bipartisan support so that it could move through the House quickly. Since he was in accord on most other issues with the chief Republicans on the committee, led by James M. Jeffords, Vt., and Bill Goodling, Pa., he did not want to create political problems by forcing a confrontation on bilingual education.

Moreover, Democratic sponsors could not be sure of support on the issue in the full House. Although Hispanic organizations were strongly against alternative programs, their members were concentrated in relatively few congressional districts. In many other parts of the country, educators were struggling to find alternatives for teaching the influx of Asian and Middle Eastern immigrants, in whose languages it was frequently difficult to find qualified instructors.

The bilingual issue was not to be resolved within the

Subcommittee on Elementary, Secondary and Vocational Education, however. The panel voted April 9, 1987, to approve the bill while leaving it to the full committee to settle the question.

During subcommittee consideration of the bill, Steve Bartlett, R-Texas, offered a compromise amendment to raise the maximum amount of federal money that could go to alternative programs from 4 percent to 25 percent. The proposal was opposed by leading Democrats, who warned that it could destroy bilingual programs. The administration, on the other hand, wanted to open up the program entirely and allow local educators to use any method they wanted.

Finally, moderate Republicans and some Democrats wanted a compromise that would increase school districts' flexibility in using federal bilingual aid, while still requiring that most of the money go for native-language instruction.

After agreeing not to settle the fate of the amendment until the full committee met, the subcommittee quickly approved the rest of the bill, backing a version of HR 5 that authorized some $600 million in new spending for education programs.

## House Committee Action

In the full Education and Labor Committee, Democratic sponsors of HR 5 gave panel Republicans and the Reagan administration much of what they wanted on bilingual-education issues, in return for a promise of unobstructed floor passage for the bill.

The committee then approved the bill by voice vote April 22 (H Rept 100-95).

To get bipartisan backing for the bill, leading Democrats grudgingly agreed to let the administration increase spending on alternative bilingual-education programs. The compromise proposal was worked out by Dale E. Kildee, D-Mich., and Bartlett.

The proposal was criticized by Hispanic members, who complained that the bill set a new federal policy for bilingual education and handed the administration a major victory in its efforts to loosen congressional controls on bilingual programs.

As approved by the committee, the bill would give English-only programs 75 percent of any increases in future appropriations for bilingual-education programs. Native-language programs were guaranteed at least as much as they were given in 1987, plus adjustments for inflation, before any new money could be allocated to English-only programs.

## House Floor Action

Because of the compromise worked out in the Education and Labor Committee, HR 5 was able to speed through full House action without any major fights. The bill passed by a 401-1 vote May 21. Philip M. Crane, R-Ill., cast the lone negative vote.

The only notable floor amendment was offered by Bill Grant, D-Fla., who called for a ban on the use of block grants for suicide-prevention programs until a study determined whether such programs could aggravate the problem. The amendment was rejected by voice vote.

Recognizing that their efforts were certain to be defeated, Bill Richardson, D-N.M., and other Hispanic members decided not to offer a floor amendment to change the bill's provisions on bilingual education.

As approved by the House, HR 5 expanded remedial-education services for the poor and added several new programs that, taken together, would add a total of $780 million in new budget authority for elementary and secondary education.

The bill also called for expansion of Chapter 1 programs by authorizing a new $50 million effort for preschool children, another $100 million in new programs for high schools and $30 million to help school districts provide compensatory services to children in private schools.

The measure also included new requirements for targeting existing grants to low-income pupils and forcing school districts to show progress in teaching the disadvantaged.

Otherwise, the bill contained no major changes in existing law, including the block grant program established in 1981 at the urging of the Reagan administration. The bill renewed the block grant program, which sought to give school districts more leeway in spending federal dollars, with only a token attempt to limit how funds were spent.

## Senate Committee Action

Senate education leaders at first had considered delaying action on the reauthorization bill until 1988 to gauge the mood of the Senate for new spending. But approval of the budget resolution (H Con Res 93), which contained a healthy boost for education, and passage of an omnibus trade bill (HR 3), which provided more than $500 million in new budget authority for education, convinced sponsors that the time was right to move on the overall education bill.

The Labor and Human Resources Subcommittee on Education approved its version of the reauthorization (S 373) by an 11-0 vote Oct. 1, at a five-minute markup session. The 253-page bill had been drafted in private conferences between panel members and their staffs.

The bill as approved by the subcommittee added $400 million for the Chapter 1 program of compensatory education and also added a new "concentration" grant formula to increase aid to school districts with high levels of poverty.

The bill contained bilingual-education provisions that were based on a bill (S 857) approved by the committee in May. As attached to S 373, the provisions allowed the education secretary to reserve up to 25 percent of bilingual-education grants for special alternative methods. The bill also contained protections for existing native-language programs, however, and provided that new money for alternative programs would go first to school districts where many languages were spoken or where there were not enough qualified bilingual teachers.

The full committee then approved S 373 (S Rept 100-222) by a 16-0 vote Oct. 14. The bill contained several provisions previously included in the Senate's version of the trade bill. It provided for a $330 million program of grants for math and science education, and a $100 million "star schools" program for telecommunications projects. The star schools proposal had already passed the Senate as a free-standing bill (S 778) April 23.

In addition, the Senate education and trade bills each would expand Chapter 1 with a separate $400 million authorization for secondary-school programs and would create a $50 million dropout-prevention program. The House education bill would provide only $100 million for secondary schools and dropout prevention combined.

# Bilingual Education

Although they represented a small fraction of all federal spending for elementary and secondary education — $143 million in 1987, out of a total of $9.4 billion — bilingual-education programs were perhaps the single greatest subject of controversy during debate on the fiscal 1989 omnibus education reauthorization bill (HR 5).

Arguments over bilingual education in part reflected disagreements about the best pedagogical methods for teaching students with limited ability in English. More fundamentally, however, they also resulted from differences over the role of English in American life. President Reagan and others argued that to succeed in the United States students must be taught English as quickly as possible. But others saw in that demand an attempt to curb the growing power and presence in society of non-white Americans.

There were an estimated 4 million students in America with limited English ability. Roughly three-quarters of that total were Hispanics, who represented an even larger share of students who spent an extended period in bilingual education.

The first Bilingual Education Act (PL 90-247) was enacted in 1968. The roots of the law lay, however, in the Civil Rights Act of 1964, which prohibited discrimination in education on the basis of a student's limited English ability and called for steps to rectify language deficiencies. The 1968 law established a federal policy of helping school districts develop new programs for such students.

A key turning point in the bilingual debate came in 1974, when the Supreme Court ruled in the case of *Lau v. Nichols* that schools had a responsibility under the Constitution to ensure that limited-English-proficient children received special help. As a result, Congress in the same year passed legislation making native-language instruction a prerequisite for school districts applying for federal bilingual-education grants.

Advocates of such an approach argued that students needed to receive instruction in basic subjects in a language they understood, so that they could progress academically even as they were learning English. But critics said that the native-language programs did not do enough to teach children English as fast as possible and had become strongholds for those who wanted to remain culturally separate from other Americans.

Reagan was among those critics, and his administration began pressing for bilingual-education changes soon after taking office in 1981. Administration officials, who argued that local schools should have the right to determine the best methods for helping limited-English students, pushed for legislation making "alternative" programs that did not use native-language instruction eligible for federal aid.

In 1984, Congress approved a bill (PL 98-511) that allowed up to 4 percent of federal bilingual funds to be used for alternative programs. Such alternatives usually involved "English as a second language," which gave pupils intensive English instruction but did not include separate instruction in other tongues, and an updated version of the traditional "immersion" technique, in which students were taught in English but received some supplemental help in their own language. *(PL 98-511, Congress and the Nation Vol. VI, p. 573)*

## Senate Floor Action

Senate passage of S 373 was routine and uneventful; it was approved by a 97-1 vote Dec. 1. But senators unanimously agreed to the addition of an amendment that was to cause major problems in conference negotiations with the House.

The Senate added several relatively non-controversial amendments related to education. One was an Indian education bill (S 1645 — S Rept 100-233), which had been reported by the Select Indian Affairs Committee. The amendment authorized $149 million for Indian education programs in fiscal 1989. The amendment also contained a provision, strongly criticized by the Interior Department, establishing a new financing mechanism for the Bureau of Indian Affairs schools.

The Senate also added a bill (S 1542 — S Rept 100-141), sponsored by Labor Committee Chairman Edward M. Kennedy, D-Mass., authorizing a $25 million early-childhood intervention program based on the "Beethoven" project in the Robert Taylor Homes, a low-income housing project in Chicago.

A compromise reached in the conference on the trade bill also was included in the Senate bill during floor action. The $100 million star schools program had been accepted by House conferees on the condition that appropriations not exceed $20 million a year.

The star schools provisions were added to the bill on an amendment by Claiborne Pell, D-R.I., chairman of the Education Subcommittee. It was approved by voice vote. The amendment also resolved another key difference between the House and Senate bills — on the new concentration grant formula to supplement the existing distribution method for the Chapter 1 program of compensatory education grants for disadvantaged schoolchildren. The amendment reduced the minimum amounts guaranteed for small states.

The only controversy on the bill came when Helms offered his amendment to repeal a section of the Communications Act of 1934 that he said allowed "dial-a-porn" businesses to operate legally. The amendment had been approved by the Senate in 1986, as an amendment to the anti-drug bill, but it was dropped in conference.

Although Pell voiced questions about the constitutionality of Helms' amendment, he eventually voted for it, allowing for a unanimous 98-0 vote of approval. Bill sponsors expressed confidence that the amendment would be dropped in conference. That did not happen.

## Conference Action

The Senate's anti-pornography rider proved to be by far the most difficult and controversial issue during conference action on the education bill. Nevertheless, there were a number of significant differences between the House and Senate versions of the legislation on education issues that needed to be resolved. They included:

**Concentration Grants.** The House bill directed the new concentration grants under the Chapter 1 program to school districts in which at least 6,500 children, or 15 percent of enrollment, were classified as disadvantaged. The Senate version used a two-part formula, under which half the money was to go to districts with more than 5,000 poor children, or 20 percent of enrollment, and the other half was to be distributed through a new grant formula.

**Bilingual Education.** The House measure guaranteed that traditional bilingual programs would receive at least the 1987 level of grants. Above that level, 75 percent of the funding would go to alternative programs and 25 percent to traditional efforts.

The Senate bill, however, gave the Education Department the authority to spend 25 percent of all bilingual funds on alternative programs, regardless of funding levels. Unlike the House measure, the Senate version limited to five years the amount of time a student could remain in a bilingual program.

**Impact Aid.** HR 5 as approved by the House extended the program of assistance to school districts with military bases, Indian reservations or other federal activities without major changes. The Senate bill created a new payment formula, modified entitlement levels and made a number of other technical changes.

**Magnet Schools.** The Senate bill called for a new program of support for districts with high percentages of minority students but whose magnet-school programs were not aimed at desegregation.

## Education Agreement

House and Senate conferees reached agreement on the education provisions of HR 5 on March 31, 1988. That left only the anti-pornography amendment to be resolved.

The hottest educational issue debated involved the magnet-school program. The Senate bill called for an expansion of the existing program of grants, which by law could go only to districts implementing a desegregation plan. Backers of the Senate provision said the grants also should go to heavily minority districts that were not undergoing desegregation but that were attempting to create exemplary schools.

But House opponents warned that allowing federal grants to go to magnet schools not directed toward desegregation would encourage the resegregation of the schools, as well as dilute the resources of an already underfunded program.

Conferees finally agreed to set up a parallel program that could be funded only after the existing magnet-school program received all of its authorized funding. So-called "alternative-curriculum" schools could get up to $35 million after the existing program had received $165 million.

While some House members were not satisfied with the compromise, it helped pave the way for Senate acceptance of House provisions on concentration grants. Conferees adopted the House formula for distributing the grants, which favored Southern and rural districts. The Senate's formula would favor urban districts.

Conferees also agreed to:

● Guarantee states at least 0.25 percent of Chapter 1 basic grants if appropriations totaled more than $700 million and the concentration grants were not funded.

● Provide funding — 0.25 percent of state and local educational agency funding for fiscal years 1989-91 and 0.5 percent for 1992-93 — for state-local cooperation in improving local educational programs.

● Abolish the National Advisory Council on Women's Educational Programs and stress the need for a national council to deal with the general concerns of women.

● Delete a Senate provision to provide for open enrollment within school districts.

● Authorize a $4 million demonstration project to develop a statewide network to provide educational and other special services to the handicapped and those with limited English proficiency.

## Dial-a-Porn Amendment

While conferees were working out an agreement on the education provisions of HR 5, a separate group of conferees was struggling with the Senate dial-a-porn amendment.

The Helms amendment, which simply struck one paragraph and 14 words from the Communications Act of 1934, prohibited the use of a telephone for "any obscene or indecent communication for commerical purposes," whether directly or by recording. Violations were to be punishable by a $50,000 fine or six months in jail.

Before the conference, House advocates sought to put the House on record in favor of the Senate provision. Initially, however, the House voted to instruct conferees to "agree to language that offers a solution to the dial-a-porn problem." That language, offered by Edward R. Madigan, Ill., a senior Republican on the Energy and Commerce Committee, was effectively approved on a parliamentary motion by a vote of 200-179 Feb. 17.

But two weeks later, William E. Dannemeyer, R-Calif., a vocal advocate of the dial-a-porn ban, was able to win House approval of a motion calling for acceptance of the Senate amendment. Dannemeyer's amendment was adopted 274-17 March 1.

Even with that instruction, conferees sought to resolve the issue by approving a compromise amendment denying access to dial-a-porn services unless a person subscribed to them. But the effort did little to satisfy backers of a complete ban, who argued that both the House and the Senate had voted to outlaw the services.

The issue came to a head in the House Rules Committee, which met to consider a rule providing for floor consideration of the conference report. Republican backers of the Helms amendment sought a rule allowing an up-or-down vote on the compromise proposal, after which the House would then get a chance to vote on a new package that included the Helms ban.

Although the committee initially approved such a rule, Democratic leaders eventually forced through a resolution allowing only an up-or-down vote on the conference report, following by a separate vote on a new bill (HR 4401) embodying the Helms amendment.

Democratic leaders then brought HR 4401 to the House floor, hoping that passage of the bill would defuse demands that the anti-pornography provision be included in the education bill. The House passed HR 4401 by a 380-22 vote under suspension of the rules April 19.

However, advocates of the ban still wanted to include it in HR 5. When House leaders sought to proceed to consideration of the rule providing for floor consideration of the conference report on the education bill, House members voted 131-272 against the motion.

Action on the education bill proceeded rapidly following that vote, as members agreed by voice vote to defeat the compromise dial-a-porn language and create a new bill that included the education portions of the conference report and the Helms ban. The conference report was then approved 397-1 April 19. The following day, the Senate approved the bill by voice vote, clearing the measure.

## Technical Fix

Shortly after, however, backers of the education bill realized that they had created an inadvertent problem with the effective date of the bill.

At issue was when the new grant formula for such programs as Chapter 1 would take effect. Federal education grants normally were determined at the beginning of the fiscal year on Oct. 1.

However, the Education Department determined that since the effective date of the reauthorization law was July 1, 1988, all remaining grants in fiscal 1988 were to be determined by the new formulas. That interpretation delayed needed payments to some districts and changed the amounts they were to receive in that year.

The House Education and Labor Committee May 24 approved a bill (HR 4638 — PL 100-351) changing the effective date of the new law from July 1 to Oct. 1. The House passed the measure June 7, and the Senate followed suit June 14, clearing the bill.

# Trade Bill Provisions

The omnibus trade bill cleared by the 100th Congress (HR 4848 — PL 100-418) contained significant provisions related to education and training. *(Trade bill, p. 148)*

The provisions were aimed at facilitating the United States' changing role in the world economy by aiding the basic, foreign language and technological skills of American students. In addition, the bill authorized a major new retraining program for workers who lost their jobs as a result of economic trends, including foreign competition.

The education and training sections of HR 4848, which authorized more than $1 billion in new spending, enjoyed broad bipartisan support, as did most of the bill's trade-related provisions. However, final action on the bill was held up for several months during 1988 as a result of a dispute between President Reagan and congressional Democrats over the issue of notification of plant closings and layoffs. *(Plant-closing bill, p. 704)*

## House Action

The House Education and Labor Committee on April 1, 1987, approved a comprehensive amendment to HR 3,

the original version of the trade bill. The legislation was in the form of a bill (HR 90) authorizing $1.48 billion in new spending for education and job training.

The bill as approved authorized $980 million for a new retraining program for dislocated industrial and rural workers. Reagan had requested an identical amount for retraining but had sought to replace existing dislocated-worker assistance with the new program.

Under the bill, half of the money would go for federal and state emergency services for such workers, while the rest would go for states that set up longer-term worker-readjustment programs of job-search assistance, counseling and on-the-job training.

The bill also authorized $325 million for literacy, science and math, and foreign language programs in elementary, secondary and vocational schools.

Another $175 million in matching grants was authorized for higher education programs for scientific research, high-technology centers and summer workshops in science and math.

The House passed HR 3 April 30.

## Senate Action

The Senate Labor and Human Resources Committee June 12, 1987, approved a bill (S 406 — S Rept 100-73), authorizing more than $1 billion in new spending for education, to attach to the trade measure. Dan Quayle, R-Ind., was the only committee member opposed to the bill.

The bill included a five-year reauthorization of a math and science grant program. It recommended funding the program at $350 million, although annual appropriations for it had not exceeded $80 million since it was created in 1985.

S 406 also authorized an additional $400 million in Chapter 1 spending for compensatory education, to be targeted on secondary-school students. Other provisions authorized $35 million for foreign language aid to schools, authorized $20 million for demonstration grants for education-business partnerships and increased to $80 million funding for programs for retraining dislocated workers.

The committee added to S 406 a new five-year, $100 million program to set up telecommunications networks, or "star schools," for teaching math, science and foreign languages. The Senate passed an identical bill (S 778) on April 23.

The Senate passed HR 3 July 21.

## Final Action, Provisions

Congress cleared the conference report on HR 3 (H Rept 100-576) on April 27, 1988.

Citing opposition to the plant-closing provisions, Reagan vetoed the bill. The Senate sustained the veto.

Democratic leaders then reintroduced the trade and education provisions as a new bill (HR 4848) and the plant-closing section as a separate measure. Both measures cleared both House and Senate by comfortable margins.

Under election-year pressures, Reagan then announced that he would sign the plant-closing bill.

Soon after, on Aug. 3, Congress cleared HR 4848, which including the following education provisions:

● **Elementary and Secondary Education.** Reauthorized for fiscal 1988 a variety of elementary, secondary and vocational education programs, including those for literacy, math, science and foreign language training, and dropout retention. These programs also were reauthorized for fiscal 1989-93 in a more comprehensive elementary and secondary education bill (HR 5 — PL 100-297), signed into law April 28. Both bills created a program of star schools for special math, science and foreign language instruction.

● **Literacy.** Authorized a new $30 million demonstration program providing matching grants for basic skills programs, including literacy, in the work place. The bill also authorized $25 million for grants to aid adults who were not proficient in English, and $10 million in grants to higher education institutions for literacy corps programs in which students would get academic credit for tutoring.

● **Foreign Language.** Authorized $20 million in matching grants for model elementary- and secondary-school programs in foreign language instruction, and $1 million for presidential awards to teachers for excellence in foreign language teaching.

● **Partnerships for Excellence.** Authorized $10 million for demonstration grants to create partnerships among local school districts, state education departments, institutions of higher education, businesses and chambers of commerce to enhance education.

● **Technology.** Authorized $19 million for a variety of programs aimed at increasing training in uses of technology.

● **Rural Education.** Authorized $5 million in discretionary grants to regional laboratories or certain other institutions to create rural education assistance centers.

● **Vocational Education.** Enhanced worker training, retraining and job-placement services in high-technology occupations by authorizing a new $25 million adult retraining program and increasing to $30 million, from $20 million, funding for cooperative industry-education training programs in high technology.

● **Secondary Education.** Authorized a new $200 million demonstration program providing basic skills to secondary-school students, and a new $50 million demonstration program to prevent students from dropping out of high school and to encourage the return of those who had dropped out.

● **Higher Education.** Authorized $115 million for a variety of higher education programs: $85 million for upgrading university research facilities; $21.5 million for science, engineering and mathematics; $5 million for joint graduate degrees in business and international affairs; and $3.5 million for general library assistance and acquisition of foreign journals.

● **Dislocated Workers.** Authorized $980 million in fiscal 1989 and an unlimited amount in future years for a new training program for workers who lost their jobs because of economic factors, including plant closings and mass layoffs. The program replaced the dislocated-worker training program of the Job Training Partnership Act (JTPA) and retained some of that program's eligibility requirements and its formula for distributing money.

In addition to those workers eligible under JTPA, the bill made some laid-off workers eligible. Displaced homemakers — mostly women — with no salable job skills and who were divorced or widowed and needed to support their families would also be eligible, provided no other eligible workers were adversely affected.

Money was to be distributed for national and state training programs: 20 percent to the secretary of labor; 80 percent to the states. States were to be allocated money under JTPA criteria (one-third based on unemployment; one-third on unemployment in excess of 4.5 percent; one-

third on unemployment in excess of 15 weeks), but at a certain point data on plant closings, mass layoffs and farmer and rancher dislocation also were considered.

The bill specified that half of a state's money go to designated "substate areas" of 200,000 or more people, on the basis of formulas determined by individual governors. Another 40 percent was to be retained by governors for statewide training programs and the remaining 10 percent was to be allocated to substate areas based on need.

# Education Tax Breaks

Reacting to the continuing rise in the cost of higher education, Congress in 1988 approved two income tax breaks for college expenses.

The first, a new provision, made interest on U.S. savings bonds tax-exempt if the funds were used to defray tuition costs. The second restored for one year a previous tax provision, which had expired at the end of 1987, to exclude from an employee's taxable income tuition or other educational assistance provided by an employer.

Both measures were part of a year-end miscellaneous tax bill (HR 4333 — PL 100-647) cleared in the session that began Oct. 21. *(Tax bill, p. 100)*

The Senate added the savings-bond plan to the tax bill as a floor amendment on a 94-0 vote Oct. 6.

The plan provided a full tax exemption on savings-bond interest for families with an adjusted gross income of up to $60,000 (joint returns) or $40,000 (single taxpayers and heads of households). As income increased, the exclusion diminished and was unavailable for taxpayers with adjusted gross incomes exceeding $90,000 (joint returns) or $55,000 (single taxpayers and heads of households). It also was unavailable to married persons filing separately.

Parents could purchase the bonds through weekly payroll deductions, and the money could be used at any postsecondary school.

The estimated three-year, $60 million cost was offset by limiting the dependent's exemption for an adult, full-time student that parents could claim on their income tax returns to students under age 24. Existing law set no age limit.

The extension of the tax exclusion for employer-provided educational assistance was contained in both the House version of HR 4333 and in the Senate Finance Committee's amended version. Because of concern over the provision's cost, however, Congress agreed to make it apply only to undergraduate courses and to limit it to 1988.

## Savings Bonds

The Reagan administration supported the savings-bond proposal, which had been first introduced as separate legislation (S 1817) by Sen. Edward M. Kennedy, D-Mass.

The proposal enjoyed strong political support because of the growing public concern over rising college costs. Between 1980 and 1988, costs for private colleges grew by 90 percent, while those of public institutions increased by 70 percent. As a result, Pell grants for low-income students covered only 29 percent of the average college-tuition bill in 1988, forcing many students to rely increasingly on loans to cover their expenses.

At a March 15, Finance Committee hearing, O. Donaldson Chapoton, assistant secretary of the Treasury for tax policy, said that the Reagan administration favored a plan that differed only slightly from the Kennedy proposal.

The key difference between the two proposals concerned the upper limits on family incomes eligible for the savings-bond exemptions. Kennedy called for phasing out the exemption for families with incomes between $75,000 and $150,000, while the administration wanted to phase it out between $60,000 and $80,000.

The Joint Committee on Taxation estimated that the exemption would cost the government $300 million a year in tax revenues. But, Kennedy noted, the loss would be offset by increased sales of savings bonds, which carried lower interest rates than other financial instruments sold by the Treasury to finance the federal debt.

### Employer-Paid Tuition

Before 1988, workers were allowed to receive up to $5,250 in employer-paid tuition without paying income taxes on that sum. The exclusion proved to be a major incentive for workers and companies to develop tuition-assistance plans.

In the preceding 10 years, nearly 7 million workers had taken advantage of the fringe benefit. A survey by the American Society for Training and Development showed that 97 percent of companies with more than 43 employees provided some form of education assistance. Many unions negotiated the benefit in collective-bargaining agreements.

The tax benefit also was indirectly important to many postsecondary institutions, which collected millions of dollars a year from businesses that paid to send their employees to college.

However, the exemption expired at the end of 1987. In 1988, only "job-related" education — expressly designed to enhance worker's performance in his current job — remained tax-free.

As a result, some colleges reported that they were losing students who could not afford to pay taxes on the value of the tuition assistance they received.

In response to complaints from education, labor and business groups, the House version extended the benefit through 1991 but limited the amount of tax-free tuition to $1,500 a year. The Senate version, ultimately passed by Congress, retained the $5,250 cap but ended it after 1988 and limited it to undergraduates.

The administration opposed any renewal of the benefit. Chapoton told the Finance Committee that the provision was discriminatory, since it was available only to workers whose employers offered the tuition benefits.

## Supplemental Student Loans

Although the 100th Congress failed to complete action on legislation aimed at curbing abuses in the Guaranteed Student Loan (GSL) program, it did clear a bill (HR 4639 — PL 100-369) directed against problems in the smaller Supplemental Loans for Students (SLS) program.

The SLS program permitted students to borrow up to $4,000 a year with a minimum of paperwork and without meeting a needs test.

The SLS program had grown rapidly in recent years, with the total of student loans rising from $200 million in 1986 to $1.8 billion in 1988. One reason for the rapid growth was the ease of obtaining an SLS loan — students did not have to show that they needed the money for school, or even that the entire loan would be used to cover college costs.

However, the costs of SLS loans were higher, with up to 12 percent interest rates, and repayment of loans was required to begin 60 days after they were made.

The easy accessibility of SLS loans had made them particularly attractive to students attending trade schools, which frequently had high rates of default.

As cleared, HR 4639 required students to seek a guaranteed loan or Pell Grant before applying for a supplemental loan. If a student received aid from either of the programs, the SLS loan would be reduced by the amount received. The measured also required banks to send SLS money directly to the borrower's school and to do so in installments so that if the student dropped out of the school the total sum would not be owed.

The bill also renamed the guaranteed-loan program the Stafford Loan Program, in honor of retiring Sen. Robert T. Stafford, R-Vt.

The Reagan administration supported the measure, while arguing that it did not go far enough to curb abuses by "unscrupulous schools."

The House Education and Labor Committee approved HR 4639 by voice vote May 24, 1988, and formally reported it June 3 (H Rept 100-669).

The House passed the measure June 8 by a vote of 408-0. The Senate approved the measure by voice vote June 15, with minor amendments. The House approved the Senate changes June 28, thus clearing the bill for the president.

## Student Loan Defaults

Despite growing concern over the escalating cost of defaults on federally guaranteed student loans, both Congress and the Reagan administration postponed action during the 100th Congress on measures addressing the problem.

The Senate Sept. 15, 1988, approved legislation (S 2647) aimed at curbing abuses. The House Education and Labor Committee earlier, on July 12, had approved a related measure (HR 4986 — H Rept 100-820).

Meanwhile, the Education Department proposed regulations implementing an even more stringent crackdown on schools with students who had consistently high rates of defaults. Many of the targeted institutions were proprietary trade schools that enrolled large numbers of low-income students.

House leaders and Education Department officials agreed in September 1988 to hold off further work on the issue until the next year. The House pulled HR 4986 from the floor schedule, while the department put off proposing a final version of its regulations until the spring of 1989.

The Education Department estimated that students would fail to repay nearly $1.6 billion in federally backed education loans in 1988. Default payments were the third most expensive program in the department, with the 1990 cost projected at $2 billion. In 1978, by contrast, students defaulted on $224 million in loans.

The department's proposed regulations, published Sept. 16, would crack down on any postsecondary school with a default rate in excess of 20 percent. The department would be able to limit such schools' participation in federal student-aid programs or drop them from the programs entirely.

The House and Senate bills would give high-default schools three years to bring their problems under control.

Other parts of the regulations, which were similar to provisions of the congressional legislation, would:

● Require schools to explain to prospective student borrowers how their loans would work and the consequences of defaulting.

● Require schools to refund a student's financial aid on a pro-rata basis if the student withdrew before the end of the term.

● Institute a "truth in advertising" program requiring schools to publish information on the percentage of students graduating and finding work in their field.

Unlike the administration's proposals, both the House and Senate bills also would expand significantly eligibility for aid programs by making changes in the formula for determining how much students could receive. The changes were aimed at eliminating consideration of the value of certain "non-liquid" assets — the family home, farm or small business — when calculating aid amounts. The House bill would allow an estimated 200,000 more students to receive guaranteed loans, while another 700,000 current borrowers could receive larger amounts.

## House Action

The Education and Labor Committee approved HR 4986 by voice vote July 12. The Postsecondary Education Subcommittee had approved an earlier version of the bill (HR 4798) by voice vote June 30.

The bill sought to attack loan-default problems in two ways. First, it expanded the Pell Grant program to provide grants, instead of loans, to more low-income students. The bill as approved increased the maximum Pell Grant awards from the existing $2,200 limit to $2,400 in 1990 and $2,500 in 1991.

Moreover, the bill made the Pell Grant program an entitlement, thus ensuring that Congress would have to provide funding to enable students to receive the full amount to which they were eligible.

Committee Republicans had strongly objected to the entitlement provision, arguing that it was too costly and did not address the loan-default issue. E. Thomas Coleman, R-Mo., sought unsuccessfully in both subcommittee and full committee to delete the Pell provisions, failing in the larger panel by a 12-21 vote.

Second, the bill sought to force schools to take a more active role in preventing defaults. Those with the highest default rates would be required to enter into a "default-reduction agreement" with the Department of Education. If, after three years, a school failed to reduce defaults but had fully complied with the agreement, no further action would be taken. If a school refused to cooperate, however, the department could move to deny that school access to federal aid programs.

The bill also offered a one-time "amnesty" to those currently in default. It gave those borrowers a six-month window in which to repay or begin to repay their debt, in return for having their bad-credit records expunged and becoming eligible for future student loans.

Before approving the bill, the committee accepted a number of amendments but rejected a Coleman proposal to deny aid to students who had been convicted on drug-related charges.

As approved by the committee, HR 4986 contained the following major provisions:

● Required schools with the worst loan-default problems to undertake efforts to reduce their rates. Schools that did not comply could be cut off from aid eligibility.

● Required the Department of Education to spend between $20 million and $25 million a year to improve control of loan programs.

● Required lenders to notify students if their loans had been sold to another lender, and limited disbursement of the full loan amounts to the schools until the student had shown evidence of academic progress.

● Required schools to provide testing and counseling for "ability to benefit" students, who were allowed to enroll in postsecondary schools even though they had not completed high school.

● Allowed students who had defaulted or fell behind on their loans to consolidate them for repayment purposes, and authorized a six-month amnesty period for defaulters to repay their loans.

● Made the Pell Grant program into an entitlement.

● Authorized maximum Pell Grants of $2,400 in the 1990-91 school year, and $2,500 in 1991-92.

● Eliminated consideration of certain non-liquid assets — the principal home, family-owned farm or business — when determining a student's eligibility for loans.

## Senate Action

The Senate Labor and Human Resources Committee approved S 2647 (S Rept 100-487) Aug. 10, and the Senate passed it by voice vote Sept. 15.

The provisions of the Senate measure generally were similar to those of the House bill as they applied to loan defaults. However, the Senate bill did not convert Pell Grants into an entitlement, as the House bill did, or raise the cap on grant amounts.

The Senate's provisions on non-liquid assets also differed from the House's, in that they applied only to students with family incomes below $30,000 and covered grants as well as loans.

# Geography Centers

Congress on Oct. 13, 1988, cleared legislation (HR 4416 — PL 100-569) to underwrite the creation of a network of regional geography centers.

The bill also reauthorized the U.S. Institute of Peace for five years.

As originally reported by the House Education and Labor Committee (H Rept 100-666) June 3 and passed by the House June 7, HR 4416 consisted of a one-year extension of the authorizations for federal programs aiding state and local public libraries to acquire foreign language materials and support literacy programs.

During action on the bill Oct. 4, the Senate added amendments extending the peace institute and creating the geography centers.

The peace institute, created in 1984, received a $10 million annual authorization in 1989-91 and $15 million a year in 1992-93.

The geography centers were to be sponsored by the Education Foundation of the National Geographic Society. They were to provide teacher training, model curricula and other assistance to school districts to help improve the teaching of geography. The bill authorized $5 million for the centers.

# Labor and Pension Policy

In many ways the years of the second Reagan administration represented a marked improvement for American workers over the preceding four years. Yet workers, their unions and retirees continued to face strong economic pressures during the period, some of which originated in basic changes in the nation's role in the world economy. Those fundamental shifts provided much of the backdrop for much of the labor-related legislation considered by the 99th and 100th Congresses.

Perhaps most importantly, the years 1985-88 saw a major decline in the unemployment rate. After reaching a post-World War II high of 10.7 percent in 1982, the ranks of the jobless steadily shrank throughout the mid-1980s, falling to 5 percent by the end of 1988 — a level that many economists believed represented as close to "full employment" as the economy could safely attain. Indeed, by the late 1980s some areas and industries were experiencing labor shortages, which experts predicted could lead to inflationary pressures.

As the 100th Congress came to a close, however, there was little evidence of a strong upward movement of either prices or wages. Despite tight labor markets, the wages of many workers rose at only a modest rate. In 1986, for example, average hourly wages for production and non-supervisory employees were 12 cents below their 1970 level, once inflation had been taken into account.

The static wage levels were even more apparent among the economy's lowest-paid workers. The minimum wage of $3.35 an hour, which had not been raised since 1981, had lost a quarter of its purchasing power.

While the paucity of real wage gains was due to a number of different factors, one major cause was the increasing competition faced by U.S. companies in the world economy. Unable to compete with low-wage competitors in other countries, many employers were forced to shut their plants or move production "off-shore." Although many workers who lost their jobs as a result of plant closings eventually found other employment, they frequently were forced to settle for low-paying jobs in service businesses.

And for workers who were unemployed, there was less government help than in earlier eras. In part because of tightened eligibility requirements imposed by the Reagan administration, only 33 percent of all jobless workers in 1988 collected federal unemployment benefits.

## Organized Labor

The strong foreign competition faced by many American companies during the period added to the problems faced by organized labor. Unions continued their long decline in membership, both because of changes in the economy and shifts in some workers' attitudes toward belonging to a union. Total membership in AFL-CIO unions, which had stood at 14 million in 1975, fell to 12.7 million in 1987.

Declines were greatest among aging "rust belt" industries that were having growing problems surviving in the increasingly international economy. Membership in the steel workers' union — once among the largest and most powerful unions — fell from 1.1 million in 1975 to 494,000 in 1987. But unions had major successes among public-sector workers; membership in the union of state- and local-government workers rose from 647,000 in 1975 to more than 1 million in 1987.

The AFL-CIO experienced a 13 percent jump in membership in 1987, when union leaders agreed to readmission of the Teamsters' union, which had been expelled during the 1950s. But the massive union, which often split from the rest of organized labor by supporting Republican presidential candidates, came under heavy pressure from the Reagan administration, which sought to remove the Teamster leadership on the grounds that it was under the influence of organized crime.

Unionized workers also scored what were at best modest gains in collective-bargaining agreements. In many cases, unions agreed to concessions on wages and other issues to prevent a threatened loss of jobs.

The common danger posed by foreign competition also inspired some employers and unions to begin moving toward a more cooperative relationship. This was most apparent in the automobile industry, which once had been largely characterized by confrontation and mistrust between the two sides. The auto-workers' union and General Motors, for example, established a wide range of programs providing for worker participation in problem-solving

## References

Discussion of labor and pension policy for the years 1945-64 may be found in *Congress and the Nation Vol. I,* pp. 565-657, 1220-1224; for the years 1965-68, *Congress and the Nation Vol. II,* pp. 601-622, 734-743; for the years 1969-72, *Congress and the Nation Vol. III,* pp. 703-742; for the years 1973-76, *Congress and the Nation Vol. IV,* pp. 681-713; for the years 1977-80, *Congress and the Nation Vol. V,* pp. 399-425; for the years 1981-84, *Congress and the Nation Vol. VI,* pp. 643-672.

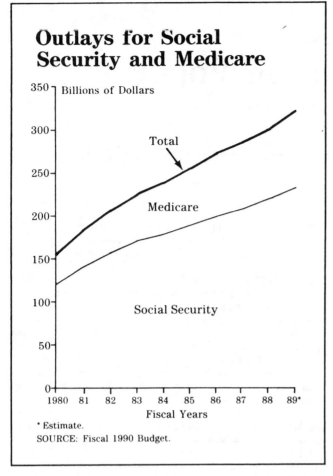

## Outlays for Social Security and Medicare

Billions of Dollars

Total

Medicare

Social Security

1980  81  82  83  84  85  86  87  88  89*

Fiscal Years

* Estimate.

SOURCE: Fiscal 1990 Budget.

teams, training programs and union involvement in some aspects of management.

The mid-1980s also saw a marked change in the AFL-CIO's approach to presidential politics, after being criticized for its early backing of Walter F. Mondale for the 1984 Democratic presidential nomination. Federation leaders decided to remain neutral during the 1988 nomination campaign, while openly backing Democrat Michael S. Dukakis in the general election.

## Pensions

The drastic decline in the fortunes of the domestic steel industry had a major impact on retired workers as well as on unions. Although Congress in the first Reagan administration appeared to have solved, at least for the time being, the financial problems facing the Social Security system, many private pension funds — and the government agency that insured them — were coming under growing pressure.

By 1987, the Pension Benefit Guaranty Corporation (PBGC), the federal agency that insured private pension plans, was staggering under a $3.8 billion deficit brought about in large part by a virtual collapse of the steel industry.

The PBGC received no money from the U.S. Treasury. Instead, the agency financed its single- and multi-employer pension insurance operations through two programs, each consisting of a revolving fund and a trust fund. The revolving funds were derived from premiums charged to employers and the income from investment of those premiums. The trust funds consisted of assets received from terminated pension plans and money received in settlements with employers whose pension obligations had been taken over by the PBGC.

Since the insurance program took effect in 1975, the PBGC's assets had consistently trailed its liabilities. But the deficit skyrocketed as the PBGC stepped in to take control of the two largest underfunded pension plans it had to rescue in its history: $500 million in unfunded benefit obligations in connection with the bankruptcy of Wheeling-Pittsburgh Steel Corp. in 1985 and the $2.2 billion in liabilities stemming from the 1986 collapse of LTV Steel. Altogether, the beleaguered steel industry accounted for 80 percent of the PBGC's deficit.

Other economic currents also were buffeting pension systems during this time. A key change was the growing interest in leveraged buyouts, junk bonds and other financial tactics for gaining control of corporations. This shifting business background forced many companies to become more aware of ways to utilize their financial assets. Previously, many companies had allowed their pension plans to build up healthy surpluses over the amounts needed to provide future benefits. But they rarely thought of terminating the plans in order to siphon off the excess cash.

In 1980, however, a West German company bought control of the A&P supermarket chain, terminated its pension plan and captured $273 million from it. Retirees sued and settled for $50 million in 1984.

As a result of the A&P experience, between 1980 and 1987 nearly $16 billion in excess funds had been taken from more than 1,300 overfunded pension plans, according to the PBGC. While many companies subsequently established new pension plans, some did not. Although federal law regulated companies that had pension plans, it did not require them to have a plan at all.

In 1987, the PBGC insured the pension benefits of about 30 million workers enrolled in 110,000 single-employer private pension plans. Another 8 million workers participated in 2,300 multi-employer plans guaranteed by the government corporation.

# Chronology Of Action On Labor And Pension Policy

## 1985-86

Action on labor legislation in the 99th Congress largely reflected a standoff between labor union allies and their conservative, business-oriented opponents. Unlike during President Reagan's first administration, pro-labor forces were generally able to prevent major cuts in jobs and other programs, although Reagan did force congressional leaders to accept the death of a program that provided special assistance to the long-term unemployed. At the same time, labor groups were unable to win congressional approval of a number of bills, including ones banning polygraphs in most employment-related uses and cracking down on anti-union tactics by construction industry employers.

The 99th Congress also continued the work of recent years in shoring up the nation's retirement system. Following the 98th Congress, which approved legislation strengthening the Social Security system, the 99th Congress acted to help the financially troubled system that guarantees private-employer pensions. *(Congress and the Nation Vol. VI, p. 659)*

## Pension Safeguards

Faced with the mounting financial problems of the Pension Benefit Guaranty Corporation (PBGC), Congress in 1986 cleared legislation aimed at safeguarding workers' pensions. The measure was included in the fiscal 1986 budget reconciliation bill (HR 3128 — PL 99-272). *(Fiscal 1986 reconciliation, p. 40)*

The main thrust of the pension legislation was to shore up the PBGC's single-employer insurance fund, which provided financial coverage for pension plans owned by individual firms. The bill sought to do that by raising the premium paid by employers for each employee from $2.60 to $8.50. The bill also sought to prevent companies from terminating their pension plans arbitrarily, thus leaving the PBGC with considerable liability for retirees.

Despite the action taken by the 99th Congress, the PBGC faced continued difficulties, which the 100th Congress was forced to address. *(100th Congress action, p. 696)*

### Background

The PBGC had been established by the Employee Retirement Income Security Act (ERISA) of 1974 (PL 93-406), which set federal standards for private pension plans that promised a guaranteed benefit at retirement. If a company went out of business or terminated its pension plan, the PBGC, a federal corporation, guaranteed the benefits of workers and retirees, up to certain statutory limits. *(Congress and the Nation Vol. IV, p. 690)*

The 1974 law established two kinds of pension plans — single-employer and multi-employer. The latter were collectively bargained plans of employers in the same industry, who contributed to a single industry-wide pension plan.

By the early 1980s, problems with the single-employer pension program were causing serious financial difficulties for the PBGC. In 1984, the agency for the first time had to pay out more in benefits than it collected in premiums, dipping into its reserves to make up the difference. Officials predicted that by 1990 the fund would no longer be able to pay benefits when they were due.

In response to the PBGC's financial problems, officials sought an increase in the existing $2.60-per-participant premium paid by employers, to $7.50. Opponents said a higher premium could discourage small- and medium-sized companies from adopting pension plans.

Critics of the program also said that part of PBGC's financial problems could be traced to loopholes in the pension law that allowed companies to dump pension debts on the PBGC even if they were solvent. PBGC officials said that one-fifth of the agency's losses could be attributed to companies that took advantage of weaknesses in the law.

### Legislative History

Congress deadlocked for several years over how to restructure the program. Beginning in 1982, key members of Congress and the PBGC pushed for tightening the program and raising premiums. But they were unable to gain business and labor support for a reform package.

The 98th Congress considered legislation to crack down on abuses and raise premiums. House and Senate panels approved bills, but neither measure went any further.

Frustrated by the stalemate and concerned about the PBGC's mounting deficits, legislative sponsors in 1985 dropped many of the more controversial proposals in the earlier measure, although they retained a requirement that employers prove economic hardship before being allowed to turn pension debts over to the PBGC.

The House Ways and Means Committee approved an $8-per-participant premium rate in a deficit reduction bill (HR 3128 — H Rept 99-241, Part I) reported on July 31, 1985. Then the Education and Labor Committee reported its version (Part II) on Sept. 11. It called for an $8.50 premium and contained provisions aimed at barring employers from unloading pension debts.

The Education and Labor provisions also were included in another reconciliation bill (HR 3500 — H Rept 99-300) reported by the House Budget Committee on Oct. 3 and passed by the House Oct. 24. The committee estimated that the measure would reduce federal spending by $300 million a year.

The House passed HR 3128 Oct. 31, and both it and HR 3500 went to conference with the Senate-passed version of HR 3128, which called for an $8.10 premium.

Conferees agreed to raise the premium to $8.50. HR 3128 was cleared by Congress on March 20.

### Provisions

As signed into law April 7, 1986, HR 3128 (PL 99-272):
* Raised from $2.60 to $8.50 the premium that employers paid for each employee to the PBGC single-employer

insurance fund. The premium increase was retroactive to Jan. 1, 1986.

Congress also agreed to require the PBGC to study the insurance premium structure and make recommendations for change.

• Clarified an employer's authority to freeze future benefits by requiring at least 15 days' notice to each participant in the plan and to each beneficiary. Existing law included no advance-notice requirement.

• Clarified the circumstances under which an employer could terminate a pension plan, distinguishing between "standard terminations" in which there were sufficient assets to pay all benefits and "distress terminations." Distress terminations involved employers who had petitioned bankruptcy court seeking liquidation of assets or reorganization, or cases where pension costs had become unreasonably burdensome because of a declining work force.

• Established a formula for an employer's liability to the PBGC under a distress termination. Under existing law, an employer was liable to the PBGC for 30 percent of his net worth payable at the date of termination of the plan. Under HR 3128, an employer was still liable for 30 percent of his net worth upon termination of a pension plan. In addition, an employer was liable for 75 percent of unfunded guaranteed benefits, less the 30 percent already paid.

• Established a general framework for repayment to the PBGC when liability for unfunded guaranteed benefits exceeded 30 percent of net worth. The bill specified that payment of the excess was to be made at "commercially reasonable" terms under a repayment schedule worked out between the PBGC and an employer. The agreement provided further for a one-year deferral of 50 percent of the amount owed in any year in which the PBGC determined an employer had no pre-tax profits.

• Set up new procedures within the PBGC for distributing benefits under a distress termination to active employees and retirees who had suffered benefit losses. An employer would be liable to a "termination trust" for the lesser of two amounts: 75 percent of the difference between all non-forfeitable, or vested, benefits under the terminated plan and benefits guaranteed by the PBGC, or 15 percent of total non-forfeitable benefits.

The bill specified that a payment schedule would be negotiated between the employer and the termination trust administrator at "commercially reasonable terms."

If the amount owed was less than $100,000, payment could be made in equal annual installments along with interest, and the PBGC was given the authority to increase the $100,000 ceiling by regulation.

The bill also provided for deferral of 75 percent of the amount owed to the trust in any year in which the employer had no pre-tax profits.

• Required 60 days' notice of intent to terminate a plan to participants, beneficiaries and unions.

• Required the PBGC to conduct annual audits of selected terminated plans to determine if participants and beneficiaries had received the benefits to which they were entitled.

• Barred the PBGC from proceeding with the voluntary termination of a plan if the termination would violate a collective-bargaining agreement.

• Required the PBGC to begin proceedings to terminate a pension plan if the PBGC determined that the plan did not have assets available to pay benefits currently due under the terms of the plan.

• Authorized the Internal Revenue Service to require

security before waiving the requirement of minimum funding for a pension plan.

• Gave virtually all parties involved in a pension plan, including the employer, the employee and those individuals handling benefit trusts, the right to sue in federal district court to stop acts or practices of any other party that violated the employer liability provisions. The PBGC's right to sue under existing law was retained.

• Established detailed procedures governing pension plan terminations pending prior to or at the time of enactment. These requirements were designed to make sure that the PBGC could determine if sufficient assets existed to pay employees and to give employees time to file complaints concerning plan terminations.

Exceptions could be made allowing a speedy plan termination if an employer could demonstrate to the PBGC that he was "experiencing substantial business hardship." This was defined to mean operating at an economic loss.

• Established Jan. 1, 1986, as the effective date for all provisions except those covering specified studies to be delivered to Congress.

• **Railroad Unemployment.** Made permanent the authority of the railroad unemployment insurance program to borrow from the railroad retirement program. The borrowing authority previously had been permanent, but in 1983 Congress set an expiration date of Sept. 30, 1985.

• Established an automatic surcharge of 3.5 percent for any loan from the retirement program to the unemployment insurance program. This surcharge applied only to new loans made after Sept. 30, 1985.

• Increased the tax levied on the unemployment system for repayment of loans from the retirement account.

• **Unemployment Compensation.** Allowed states to enter into agreements with one another and the federal government to recoup unemployment benefits that were overpaid to an individual. For example, if a state made an overpayment to someone who later moved to another state, that state could withhold the person's unemployment benefits and reimburse the first state for its overpayment.

# Mandatory Retirement Ban

Congress cleared legislation Oct. 17, 1986, barring most employers from setting mandatory retirement ages. A seven-year exemption was included for firefighters and law enforcement officers and for colleges and universities.

The bill (HR 4154 — PL 99-592) amended the 1967 Age Discrimination Act, which had been amended in 1978 to raise the mandatory retirement age from 65 to 70. The law protected employees after they had reached the age of 40 and covered those businesses with 20 or more workers. Mandatory retirement for most federal employees was abolished in 1978. *(Congress and the Nation Vol. V, p. 414)*

While the legislation was hailed by groups representing senior citizens, it was opposed by business groups such as the U.S. Chamber of Commerce and the National Association of Manufacturers, who said it would mean a disruption in turnover cycles, slower advancement for qualified workers and fewer jobs for young people.

According to John Heinz, R-Pa., the chief Senate sponsor of the bill, there were 1.1 million Americans aged 70 and over in the work force in 1986. A Department of Labor study projected that some 200,000 workers who would otherwise have retired would remain in the work force because of the legislation.

The Congressional Budget Office estimated that lifting the ban would save the federal government $25 million annually by 1991 in reduced Social Security and Medicare payments.

The biggest fight on HR 4154 was over the exemptions for law enforcement groups. The push for the exemption was motivated by a 1985 Supreme Court decision in which the justices ruled that the city of Baltimore could not require that all firefighters retire at the age of 55.

The age discrimination law included a general exemption allowing employers to set maximum ages when "age is a bona fide occupational qualification reasonably necessary to the normal operation of the particular business."

But the court said Baltimore could not justify its policy under this language.

The House-passed bill exempted law enforcement personnel and firefighters. But the Senate modified that by limiting the exemption to seven years and adding a similar exception for colleges and universities. The Senate also required the Labor Department and the Equal Employment Opportunity Commission (EEOC) to make studies during this period. The House accepted that change.

### Legislative History

The House Education and Labor Committee July 24, 1986, approved HR 4154 (H Rept 99-756) by voice vote, after the committee turned back efforts to exempt firefighters, law enforcement officers and tenured university professors. The bill's chief sponsor, Rep. Claude Pepper, D-Fla., had warned the committee that any exemptions would start a stampede of similar requests and have the practical effect of killing the legislation.

The crucial fight came on an amendment by Austin J. Murphy, D-Pa., allowing state and local governments to set mandatory retirement ages for firefighters and law enforcement officers. Murphy's amendment was replaced by a substitute calling for a study of the issue by the EEOC.

The committee also rejected an amendment, offered by E. Thomas Coleman, R-Mo., that provided an exemption for tenured university professors. Coleman argued that without mandatory retirement, tenured faculty jobs would, in effect, be guaranteed jobs for life, depriving universities of regular turnover. When HR 4154 reached the floor Sept. 23, Murphy offered his amendment again and this time he won. The House voted 291-103 to allow an exemption for state and local public safety officers.

HR 4154 was then passed by the House, 394-0.

The Senate passed the bill by voice vote Oct. 16. Final action came the next day when the House, by voice vote, accepted the Senate version of the bill.

## Public Workers' Overtime

Congress Nov. 7, 1985, cleared a bill to ease the impact of a Supreme Court decision requiring overtime pay for state and local government workers.

The measure, signed into law by President Reagan Nov. 13 (S 1570 — PL 99-150), instead allowed public employers to provide time-and-a-half compensatory time off for employees who worked more than 40 hours in a week.

---

## Labor Leadership

Ann Dore McLaughlin was confirmed as labor secretary by a 94-0 Senate vote Dec. 11, 1987. She was the 19th labor secretary and the first woman to serve in that capacity since Frances Perkins in the Franklin D. Roosevelt administration.

McLaughlin replaced William E. Brock III, who resigned Nov. 1 to head the presidential campaign of Sen. Robert Dole, R-Kan. (Cabinet profiles, p. 1047)

Brock had succeeded Raymond J. Donovan, who resigned March 15, 1985, to stand trial on charges of larceny and fraud. Donovan later was acquitted of all charges. (Donovan background, Congress and the Nation Vol. VI, pp. 656, 1023)

---

The Supreme Court had ruled Feb. 19, in *Garcia v. San Antonio Metropolitan Transit Authority*, that the overtime pay requirements of the Fair Labor Standards Act (FLSA) applied to state and local government workers. The *Garcia* ruling, decided by a 5-4 vote, reversed a 1976 high court decision that exempted state and local government workers from FLSA coverage. (Garcia *ruling, p. 829*)

In its 1976 decision, *National League of Cities v. Usery*, the court ruled that the minimum wage and overtime provisions of the FLSA could not be constitutionally applied to "integral governmental functions" at the state and local level. The court specifically found that such functions included fire prevention, police protection, sanitation, public health and parks and recreation. (1976 decision, Congress and the Nation Vol. IV, p. 651)

Public employer groups — in particular, the National League of Cities, the U.S. Conference of Mayors and the National Association of Counties — sought relief from the *Garcia* ruling, claiming it would cost them more than $1 billion in overtime pay in the next year.

Organized labor, which represented about 3 million of the 9 million state and local government workers, hailed the decision for giving government workers parity with the private sector.

But sensing that city and county officials might be able to press Congress into drastically revising the FLSA, a 1938 labor law that set minimum pay and overtime requirements, union lobbyists offered in September to bargain with the public employers. Within days of their first meeting, union and employer negotiators struck a deal.

As a result of that agreement, Congress was able to complete action on the legislation in short order. The Senate Labor and Human Resources Committee reported the measure Oct. 17 (S Rept 99-159), and the Senate passed it by voice vote Oct. 24.

The companion bill (HR 3530), reported by the Education and Labor Committee Oct. 24 (H Rept 99-331), passed the House by voice vote under suspension of the rules Oct. 28. Both chambers adopted the conference report (H Rept 99-357) Nov. 7.

## Provisions

As signed into law Nov. 13, 1985, S 1570 (PL 99-150):

● Allowed public employers to give employees time-and-a-half compensatory time off, instead of cash, for each hour of overtime worked over 40 hours. Existing collective-bargaining agreements that called for cash payment for overtime or provided employees the option of either cash or time off would not be affected. However, compensatory time after the effective date would have to be at the time-and-a-half rate.

● Established a cap of 480 hours of compensatory time earned for public safety and seasonal employees. Overtime hours worked after this cap would have to be compensated in cash. Other employees, such as clerical workers, would get cash after working 240 hours of overtime.

● Provided that an employee who left a job with unused compensatory time should be paid for the unused time either at the average regular rate received over the last three years of work or at the final regular rate the employee received, whichever was greater.

● Made the bill effective April 15, 1986.

● Exempted volunteers, such as firefighters, from coverage even if the volunteers were paid expense money.

● Exempted state and local legislative staff, except library employees, from FLSA coverage.

● Provided that firefighters and law enforcement employees, including security and prison personnel, who voluntarily did part-time work different from their regular jobs be considered as working two separate jobs.

● Barred state and local governments from discriminating against employees by changing wages or other working conditions because the employee asserted that he was covered by the FLSA after the *Garcia* decision.

# Unemployment Benefits

President Reagan April 4, 1985, signed legislation (HR 1866 — PL 99-15) phasing out special assistance for the long-term unemployed, after his repeated veto threats squelched congressional efforts to extend the program.

Reagan had wanted benefits cut off immediately when the federal supplemental unemployment compensation program, enacted in 1982, expired on March 31. But in signing HR 1866, he allowed a more gradual elimination of benefits for those on the rolls.

The Democratic-controlled House removed a potential obstacle to quick action when it abandoned a proposed three-month extension of the program. That move embittered some House Democrats who wanted to challenge Senate Republicans and Reagan by pushing an extension.

However, many Democrats, even traditional supporters of aid to the out-of-work, agreed that such benefits were ill-suited to targeting aid to pockets of high unemployment and suggested the whole system should be revamped.

HR 1866 provided that no new beneficiaries could qualify for the supplemental compensation program, which provided up to 14 weeks of additional aid for jobless people who had exhausted regular unemployment benefits.

But to cushion the effects of terminating the program, the bill allowed people already on the rolls to draw their remaining benefits. More than 300,000 persons were receiving benefits under the program.

The cost of the phase-out was estimated at $160 million to $180 million.

## Legislative History

The House Ways and Means Committee reported HR 1866 April 2 (H Rept 99-36), after rejecting a three-month extension recommended by the Subcommittee on Public Assistance and Unemployment Compensation.

That proposal was dropped in the face of a threat by committee Republicans to delay floor consideration of the bill. Instead, an amendment offered by Carroll A. Campbell Jr., R-S.C., replacing the extension with the phase-out was approved 20-16.

The bill was rushed to the floor later April 2 and approved by voice vote.

The Senate Finance Committee approved the House bill without change also on that same day.

When the bill reached the Senate floor, Arlen Specter, R-Pa., sought to add an amendment providing for a six-month extension of the program. His amendment was rejected 34-58.

The Senate also rejected, by a 32-62 vote, an amendment by Carl Levin, D-Mich., to liberalize another program that provided up to 13 weeks of additional aid to workers in states with very high unemployment rates.

The Senate then passed the bill 94-0 on April 3.

# Social Security Funds

Whenever the 99th Congress pondered questions of spending and deficits, the talk seemed inevitably to turn to a discussion of the Social Security system. Schemes to reduce the federal deficit by slowing payment of Social Security inflation adjustments and the Treasury Department's manipulation of the system's trust fund to ward off federal default weakened partisan loyalties and spurred congressional-administration ill will.

Social Security's status as the most politically untouchable domestic program was confirmed by broad congressional agreement to exempt the system from the across-the-board cuts mandated by the Gramm-Rudman-Hollings budget-balancing measure. Gramm-Rudman also contained provisions placing the system beyond the reach of budget-cutters. *(Gramm-Rudman, p. 44)*

The fights over Social Security took place against the background of the 1982 elections, when House Republicans lost 26 seats after a campaign in which Democrats tarred the GOP as intent on destroying Social Security. In 1985, all members sought to portray themselves as staunch supporters of Social Security to fend off potential opponents' charges in the 1986 elections.

In May 1985, the Senate approved a budget resolution that would eliminate the 1986 cost-of-living adjustment (COLA) for the 36 million Social Security recipients, while providing an inflation increase for the Pentagon. The House passed a package freezing military spending and protecting COLAs for Social Security and other retirement programs. *(Budget resolution, p. 39)*

The Reagan administration initially backed the Senate budget, but House Republicans rapidly ran from it. Eventually, President Reagan reversed himself and supported the House position on Social Security.

## Debt Limit Debate

Congress again debated Social Security as part of the government's debt crisis at the end of 1985. When the government was about to run out of money Nov. 1, Treasury Department officials sold some long-term investments controlled by the Social Security trust fund to tide the government over.

Some members of Congress were outraged, not so much because the Treasury officials redeemed some of the system's investments, but because a similar reshuffling of money had occurred before — during debt crises in September and October 1985 and in October 1984 — and no one on Capitol Hill had been told.

The shuffling of funds involved the cashing-in of long-term government securities that had been purchased with Social Security surplus funds. Redeeming the securities reduced the government's indebtedness and allowed the Treasury Department to sell new securities to raise cash.

Treasury Secretary James A. Baker III had warned Congress in an Oct. 22 letter that he would take the "extraordinary" step of "disinvestment" if a debt extension had not been enacted. Provisions to make up the losses incurred by the early redemption of the securities were included in a temporary debt limit measure (PL 99-155) passed Nov. 14 and in the final version of Gramm-Rudman (PL 99-177). All the funds had been restored by early January 1986, according to Treasury officials.

Gramm-Rudman also removed Social Security from the unified federal budget in fiscal 1986 and thereafter exempted the program from legislated limitations on spending. Congress in 1983 had voted to remove the system from the budget in 1993, but sentiment to do it sooner grew during 1985. *(Congress and the Nation Vol. VI, p. 658)*

Proponents argued that because the system's trust funds ran a surplus, Social Security did not contribute to the deficit and, therefore, benefits should not be cut to help pay for shortfalls in other federal programs.

However, "removal" of Social Security from the budget had more political than practical implications. The Treasury Department borrowed from the Social Security surplus to help finance the federal debt, and it could continue to do so even if the program were "off budget." As a result, overall government borrowing from the public would remain the same.

Those opposed to putting Social Security off budget argued that the deficit was so serious that all spending programs should be reviewed for possible cuts. They noted that Social Security made up a large portion — approximately one-fifth — of government outlays and removing it from the budget would have presented a distorted view of government activities.

### 1986 Legislation

Congressional anger over the 1985 use of Social Security investments to keep the government running led to efforts in 1986 to prevent a recurrence. Although both House and Senate passed measures aimed at restricting such use, none became law.

On July 22, 1986, the House unanimously approved legislation (HR 5050) prohibiting any future disinvestment of Social Security trust funds. The legislation would allow the managers of the funds to redeem long-term assets only if needed to handle an internal Social Security funding crisis.

The measure also would take the Social Security Administration out of the Department of Health and Human Services (HHS) and establish it as an independent agency, as it had been from its creation in 1935 until 1939.

The measure had been approved by the House Ways and Means Committee on June 25.

The Senate, as part of a bill (H J Res 668 — S Rept 99-335) to increase the debt limit, approved provisions that would allow the Treasury secretary to disinvest the Social Security trust funds under certain limited conditions. The House refused to accept the proposal, however, and the measure died.

As approved by the Senate Aug. 9, the legislation would permit disinvestment during debt limit crises only to provide enough money to pay Social Security benefits and administrative expenses, not to pay other government costs.

### Social Security Adjustments

Also in 1986, Congress made minor adjustments in the Social Security program as part of the omnibus deficit reduction bill cleared March 20 (HR 3128 — PL 99-272). *(Story, p. 40)*

As signed into law April 7, the bill:

● Exempted from Social Security payroll taxes the wages of federal judges who reached retirement age but continued working. Their pay also could not be used in calculating earnings to see if benefits should be reduced under the Social Security retirement earnings test.

● Extended for five years the HHS secretary's authority to waive legal requirements that otherwise would prevent recipients of Social Security disability payments from participating in demonstration projects to ease their return to work.

A 1980 law authorized HHS to develop the projects, but the department had not done so.

● Eliminated U.S. tax withholding on Social Security payments to American Samoans, consistent with tax treatment of citizens of other U.S. possessions.

● Allowed great-grandchildren who were dependent on a Social Security recipient and under age 18 to receive benefits. Children and grandchildren could get benefits under existing law.

● Clarified that an individual's Social Security disability payments were to be reduced by the amount of all disability benefits paid under a federal or state worker-compensation program.

# Polygraph Ban

The 99th Congress considered but did not pass legislation barring most private employers from requiring employees to take lie detector tests to get or keep a job.

The bill passed the House and was approved by a Senate committee, but it never reached the Senate floor.

A similar bill, however, was cleared by the 100th Congress and became law in 1988. *(1987-88 action, p. 700)*

Sponsors of the legislation said it was needed to halt "the epidemic growth" in the use of the tests, which attempt to detect deception by measuring physiological responses to questions.

According to estimates, as many as 2 million of the tests, known as polygraphs, were being given annually, about 98 percent of them in private industry. Nearly 75 percent of the tests were given prior to employment, the rest during investigations.

Supporters of the polygraph ban, led by organized labor, argued that the tests were not reliable. Their widespread use in making employment decisions, they said, was unfair. While 31 states and the District of Columbia had laws regulating the use of lie detectors in the work place, the report said they had not been effective and that a national law was needed to give workers uniform protections.

Opponents of the bill, including some business groups, argued that the tests had been shown to be relatively accurate and were a useful tool in combating employee theft and other crimes.

### Legislative History

The House Education and Labor Committee Dec. 5, 1985, reported the polygraph bill (HR 1524 — H Rept 99-416).

The committee had approved HR 1524 by voice vote Oct. 23. The bill, sponsored by Pat Williams, D-Mont., and Matthew G. Martinez, D-Calif., chairman of the Employment Opportunities Subcommittee, exempted state, local and federal government employers from coverage. It also made clear that lie detector tests might be used in counter-intelligence work and that persons under contract with the CIA or the National Security Agency would be subject to the tests. Individuals under contract with the FBI also could be subject to polygraph tests when doing counter-intelligence work for the bureau.

By a 20-9 vote, the panel adopted an amendment by Dennis E. Eckart, D-Ohio, allowing companies that manufactured drugs to use lie detector tests under very specific circumstances involving missing or stolen narcotics.

Under HR 1524, an employer could be fined up to $10,000 for violating the law. The Labor Department, which would implement and enforce the law, could seek a court order to restrain an employer from violating it, and individuals would have the right to sue an employer for violations.

The House passed HR 1524 by a 236-173 vote March 12, 1986. Before approving the bill, the House accepted amendments adding several exemptions from the polygraph ban. The amendments allowed use of polygraph tests on employees of nursing homes and day-care centers, if they had "direct contact" with children or the elderly; on security guards at nuclear power facilities, financial institutions and toxic waste sites; and on public utility workers.

The House rejected efforts to allow continued polygraph testing of all employees of financial institutions, and of gambling casino employees. Also rejected was an amendment allowing private-sector testing as long as the employer followed certain standards.

The Senate Labor and Human Resources Committee approved its polygraph ban (S 1815 — S Rept 99-447) by an 11-5 vote June 25.

# Plant-Closing Notice

Legislation aimed at softening the impact of mass layoffs and plant closings by requiring employers to give advance notice of their intentions made little progress during the 99th Congress. Despite ardent support by organized labor, the measure was defeated by the House in 1985.

However, a similar bill cleared Congress in 1988 and was signed by President Reagan, amidst intense election-year political pressures. *(1987-88 action, p. 704)*

The 1985 rejection of the plant-closing bill (HR 1616)

was a major setback for organized labor, particularly since the version rejected was already significantly weaker than the original proposal. Moreover, many of labor's traditional allies opposed the bill. On the final **203-208 (R 20-154; D 183-54) key vote**, 54 Democrats voted in the negative. *(1985 key votes, p. 933)*

Supporters of advance notification of closings said it would give workers time to seek retraining or a new job and would allow state and local governments to anticipate loss of tax revenues and increased demand for social services.

The bill faced bitter opposition from the U.S. Chamber of Commerce and other employer groups, which argued that the advance-notice requirement would prevent financially troubled companies from getting credit or working out deals that might keep them afloat.

### Legislative History

The Education and Labor Committee July 23 approved HR 1616 by a 20-12 vote.

As reported Oct. 29 (H Rept 99-336), HR 1616 required employers to provide three months' notice before permanently laying off 50 or more employees. Employers would have to consult with employees in the interim about alternatives to plant closings.

In addition to the notice and consultation requirements, HR 1616 included provisions to:

• Exempt from coverage temporary layoffs, where employees would be recalled in 90 days.

• Allow the three-month notice requirement to be reduced if the business in question demonstrated that "unavoidable business circumstances prevent the employer from withholding the closing or layoff."

• Authorize the labor secretary to get a court order within 10 days of determining that there was "reasonable cause to believe" an employer had ordered a plant closing or layoff in violation of the act.

• Allow an employee to file a civil suit in federal court for any layoff in violation of the act.

By the time the bill reached the House floor Nov. 14, it was in serious trouble. Recognizing the danger that it might be defeated, chief sponsor William D. Ford, D-Mich., developed a substitute eliminating a number of remedies for laid-off workers.

After the House voted 215-193 to delete a key provision requiring employers to consult with workers about a plant closing, Ford was forced to pull the bill off the floor.

When the measure returned to the floor a week later, James M. Jeffords of Vermont, the ranking Republican on the Education and Labor panel, proposed a substitute version that further restricted employees' remedies. The amendment was adopted 211-201.

Nevertheless, the House then voted down the bill by a five-vote margin, 203-208, ending its chances in the 99th Congress.

# Double-Breasting Restrictions

Union-backed legislation aimed at preventing companies from circumventing labor laws to hire non-union workers for construction projects passed the House in the 99th Congress. The measure received no Senate action, however.

The issue again was brought up in the 100th Congress, but no legislation was cleared. *(1987-88 action, p. 707)*

The bill (HR 281) sought to prevent the practice of

"double breasting," under which a unionized company set up a non-union subsidiary to do the same work as the original firm.

HR 281 was intended to prohibit the practice by specifying that separate firms performing similar construction work would be considered a single employer if their management or ownership was directly or indirectly in common. The terms of a union contract in one entity of the combined business would be applied to other entities as well.

Critics of the bill said construction companies usually resorted to double breasting not to take work away from union employees but to make it possible for them to bid for contracts where union wages would not be competitive.

HR 281 also would strengthen "pre-hire" agreements, under which construction firms and unions signed a contract for a construction job before workers were hired. Democrats claimed recent court decisions had made it too easy for employers to repudiate their pre-hire pacts. HR 281 would give the pacts the same binding status as collective-bargaining agreements.

The bill was reported by the Education and Labor Committee in 1985 (H Rept 99-311, Parts I and II).

Before passing the bill by a 229-173 vote on April 17, 1986, the House rejected several amendments by Republican critics, who sought to narrow the scope of the measure.

## Job Training Expansion

Legislation to expand coverage of a job training program was signed by President Reagan Oct. 16, 1986.

The measure (S 2069 — PL 99-496) was cleared by the House Oct. 1. The Senate had given final approval Sept. 29.

S 2069 amended the 1982 Job Training Partnership Act (PL 97-300), which sought to help youths and unskilled adults find work and to aid displaced workers. Under the law, money was sent to states to set up job training programs, with an emphasis on involving the private sector. *(Congress and the Nation Vol. VI, p. 655)*

The 1986 amendment allowed unemployed farmers to participate in the job training partnership programs. It also added new training programs for older individuals and authorized summer youth employment programs to make educational projects part of the job training.

A summary of the legislation prepared by the Senate Labor and Human Resources and House Education and Labor committees said the educational project provision was included because the "deficit of basic education skills among the targeted population of youth is so acute."

The legislation also established presidential awards to acknowledge outstanding private sector involvement in operating job training programs.

## Conservation Corps

For the third year in a row, the House in 1985 approved legislation to create an American Conservation Corps (ACC) to put unemployed teenagers to work on conservation projects, primarily rehabilitating public and Indian lands.

However, the measure (HR 99) passed by only a two-vote margin, far short of the support needed to override a veto. The July 11 vote on passage of the bill was 193-191.

The Senate did not act on the proposal, and it died at the end of the 99th Congress. President Reagan pocket-vetoed a similar bill in 1984. Some changes were made in the 1985 version to ease White House opposition, but the administration continued to oppose the legislation. *(Congress and the Nation Vol. VI, p. 671)*

In past years, the House had voted by wide margins to create the ACC. The hair's-breadth margin of victory for HR 99 was attributed to pressures to cut federal spending. Opponents said Congress should not be creating new programs at a time when lawmakers were struggling to rein in spending for existing programs.

The bill approved by the House had been reported by the Education and Labor Committee on May 2. Earlier, the Interior Committee had reported its version of the measure (H Rept 99-18, Parts I and II).

The program, modeled on the Civilian Conservation Corps of the 1930s, was designed to provide about 85,000 jobs in the beginning, including year-round jobs for 16-to-25-year-olds and summer jobs for 15-to-21-year-olds. While open to all eligible youths, special efforts would be made to enroll and recruit economically disadvantaged youth.

## Risk Notification

Legislation to establish a national system for identifying and notifying employees exposed to dangerous substances in the work place was approved by a House committee in 1986 but went no further.

The bill (HR 1309 — H Rept 99-691) was approved by a 20-8 vote in the Education and Labor Committee June 25.

The legislation would create a Risk Assessment Board of public health professionals who would evaluate medical and scientific data to identify groups of workers who were "at risk" of contracting diseases as a result of work place exposure. Once the board identified such a group, the Department of Health and Human Services would notify individual workers of the potential dangers and of the type of testing recommended. No treatment would be provided, however.

The Reagan administration opposed the bill, arguing that it would create a new, unnecessary bureaucracy.

The issue again was considered in the 100th Congress. *(1987-88 action, p. 708)*

## Parental Leave

The House Education and Labor Committee June 24, 1986, approved legislation to require most public and private employers to grant their workers unpaid family and disability leave under certain conditions.

The Family and Medical Leave Act of 1986 (HR 4300 — H Rept 99-699, Part II) was approved by the panel on a voice vote, but it never reached the House floor.

Although the bill was supported by labor, women's rights and health groups, spokespersons for the business community vehemently opposed it, saying it would impose unreasonable burdens on many businesses.

As approved, the bill required public and private employers with 15 or more workers to grant up to 18 weeks of unpaid family leave to employees to care for newborn, newly adopted or seriously ill children or parents. The legislation also required employers to grant up to 26 weeks of unpaid disability leave to employees with serious medical conditions.

In both cases, employers would be required to continue health insurance benefits while the employee was on leave, and the employee upon return to work would have a right to reclaim his old job, or a comparable one, with full benefits and seniority.

The version approved by the committee was a compromise worked out between William L. Clay, D-Mo., chairman of the Subcommittee on Labor-Management Relations, and a number of Republican members, including James M. Jeffords of Vermont, the full committee's ranking Republican.

After the parental leave legislation was approved by the subcommittee June 12, Jeffords and others had expressed concerns that some of the bill's provisions could place an intolerable burden on small businesses. The substitute adopted by the full committee increased the small business exemption from five to 15 workers, instituted a vesting period of three months before workers could become eligible for leave, limited the combined leave an employee could take to 36 weeks per year and required certification of medical conditions before leave could be taken. The substitute also contained a new provision requiring employees to give prior notice and to schedule leave to accommodate the employer, when possible.

Republican members, including some who voted for the Clay substitute on grounds that it was an improvement over the original version, expressed deep reservations about the legislation. "This bill clearly establishes a new precedent for federal involvement in employer-employee relations," said Tom Tauke of Iowa. "This is a very serious issue that has not been handled today in a very serious manner." *(100th Congress action, p. 706)*

# 1987-88

The return of the Democrats in the 100th Congress to a majority in both chambers guaranteed that there would be intensive action on labor issues, as union allies pushed a wide range of bills that had had little chance when the Republicans were in control of the Senate. Particularly during the election year of 1988, Democrats fought hard for such bills as parental-leave legislation and an increase in the minimum wage, in hopes of forcing the bills' Republican opponents into accepting the measures or taking politically unpopular stands against them.

On most issues, Democrats and their labor allies were unsuccessful. Among major bills backed by labor and opposed by many business groups, only a ban on employer use of polygraphs became law. However, Congress did complete action on two other major bills — restructuring federal pension protections and reforming the railroad unemployment system.

## Pension Safeguards

Congress in 1987 made the most sweeping changes in the nation's pension protection law, the Employee Retirement Income Security Act (ERISA), since its enactment in 1974.

As part of the fiscal 1988 budget reconciliation bill (HR 3545 — PL 100-203), lawmakers increased minimum funding requirements for private pension plans, sharply boosted the premium employers had to pay the federal Pension Benefit Guaranty Corporation (PBGC) for insurance of those plans and made it less enticing for companies to terminate overfunded pension plans to get at the surplus for non-pension purposes. *(Fiscal 1988 reconciliation, p. 61)*

Calls for an ERISA overhaul were spurred by the desperation of workers from the troubled U.S. steel industry and by soaring deficits of the PBGC, which had seen its coffers drained by steel company bankruptcies.

The Reagan administration put forward a comprehensive proposal for overhauling ERISA that provided a starting point for congressional action.

Lawmakers eventually adopted one key element of the administration proposal, requiring companies with underfunded pension plans to pay a higher PBGC premium than those with fully funded plans. But Congress rejected the administration's request, backed by business, that companies be allowed to withdraw surplus funds from pension plans without terminating those plans.

### Background

Although Congress had acted in 1986 to bail out the PBGC, by raising the annual premium from $2.60 per worker to $8.50, the government corporation continued to face serious financial difficulties. *(1986 action, p. 689)*

The gap between liabilities and assets widened to a chasm in the mid-1980s, as the result of three major corporate bankruptcies: Wheeling-Pittsburgh Steel Corp. and Allis-Chalmers Corp. in 1985 and LTV Steel in 1986. The LTV bankruptcy, the largest reorganization in U.S. history, forced PBGC to take over pension plans covering 108,600 workers, 60,000 of them retirees, at a cost of $2.2 billion.

The monthly $32 million in payments to LTV retirees alone exceeded the agency's annual premium income.

Agency officials warned that the situation could lead to the collapse of government pension protections. Although the PBGC might be able to continue to write checks until 1996, its executive director, Kathleen P. Utgoff, warned that it could go broke sooner if other large firms with many retirees were added to the books.

In response to the looming PBGC problem, the Reagan administration in 1987 proposed a new financial plan for the agency. The package had three overriding objectives:

● To force companies to put sufficient funds into their pension plans, so that those plans did not end up as wards of the PBGC.

● To discourage terminations of healthy plans by allowing companies to withdraw surplus cash from them without halting the plans entirely.

● To combat the PBGC deficit by assessing companies with underfunded pension plans an additional premium on top of the standard fee charged all businesses.

Virtually every aspect of the proposal proved to be controversial. But two issues dominated congressional debate: whether the proposals to bail out the PBGC would drive struggling industries further into debt and thus threaten more jobs, and whether excess funds in healthy pension plans belonged to a company or to its workers.

To prevent more companies with pension plans from turning over their responsibilities to the PBGC, the administration also called for legislation to:

● Require companies to amortize anticipated pension liabilities more rapidly, which would have the effect of requiring a larger contribution per worker per year.

● Require employers to make quarterly, instead of annual, contributions to their pension plans.

● Reduce from five to three the number of waivers from minimum funding requirements that a company could obtain within a 15-year period.

● Prohibit a company from investing more than 10 percent of its workers' pension funds in its own stock.

● Increase the level of assets a company must leave in a plan when a withdrawal is made.

● Require an employer seeking to terminate an underfunded plan to transfer assets from other, adequately funded plans to cover the liability of the terminating plan.

## Reversion Issue

Nothing in the administration's proposal stirred more controversy than the proposal to allow employers to withdraw excess cash from "overfunded" pension plans without terminating them.

Under current law, all money in a pension fund had to be used for the benefit of the workers unless the plan was terminated. Company managers could then "capture" the excess funds if they met certain requirements, a process known as reversion.

Reversions were not a problem in the early years of ERISA. Companies with healthy pension plans never thought of terminating them to siphon off cash. But in 1980, a West German firm bought control of the A&P supermarket chain, terminated its pension plan and captured $273 million from it.

The example inspired imitators. Since 1980, nearly $16 billion in excess funds had been taken from more than 1,300 overfunded pension plans, according to the PBGC.

Often, companies that terminated a plan to tap its surplus funds turned around and established a new pension plan, but with only enough assets to cover current liabilities. In other cases, however, plans were not replaced or employers switched to defined-contribution plans, in which no set benefits were promised and employees bore the risk of how the plans performed.

By 1987, some $218 billion surplus funds remained in unterminated accounts, according to the Labor Department.

The administration's plan would permit an employer to withdraw assets from a defined-benefit plan — without terminating it — if the company left behind an asset "cushion," generally 125 percent of the plan's liability if it were to terminate at that moment.

The employer could either remove the excess funds entirely or transfer them to another pension plan that was underfunded. Alternatively, some or all of the money could be transferred to a separate fund to pay retirees' health benefits, without losing tax-favored status.

Business groups favored reversions. An employer should have access to surplus pension funds, they said, because the company took a financial risk when it promised to provide pension benefits at certain defined levels. That position had been upheld by the courts, under an interpretation that excess funds were the result of actuarial errors.

But union leaders adamantly opposed the administration's proposal to give employers easier access to the funds, since the surplus funds did not go to help pension plan participants. And retiree groups warned that removal of assets often meant there was not enough left in a pension fund to pay cost-of-living increases, which were not required by law.

## Variable Funding

To bail out the PBGC and discourage companies from deliberately underfunding their pension plans, the administration proposed a variable-rate structure for insurance premiums, instead of the current flat $8.50 per worker annual rate.

"The PBGC's backing makes underfunded pensions almost as valuable as those that are fully funded," said Utgoff. "In effect, the present rules permit a few companies to pay their workers using somebody else's money."

If flat-rate premiums continued to rise, she warned, many would decide to do away with defined-benefit pension plans, replacing them with defined-contribution plans.

Utgoff said the vast majority of companies with defined-benefit plans would continue to pay a flat premium. The minority that were significantly underfunded — with less than 125 percent of the money needed to meet their current obligations — would be required to pay a variable rate, with premiums adjusted along a sliding scale. The more underfunded a plan, the higher the premium a company would pay, up to a maximum of $100 per worker per year.

The funding formula would mean no rate hike for about 92 percent of the companies insured by PBGC, Utgoff said.

Union officials warned, however, that the proposal could cost jobs, since it would hit struggling companies with premium increases just when they could least afford them.

## Legislative History

From the begining, it was clear that the ERISA overhaul would be handled as part of the budget reconciliation bill.

The measure had to make its way through two committees in the House and two more in the Senate before it was rolled into HR 3545. Each of the four panels produced its own version of the bill, and there were some significant differences among them.

Neither the House nor the Senate attempted to settle on a single set of pension provisions; all four versions eventually wound up before House-Senate conferees on the reconciliation legislation.

The House Ways and Means Committee marked up its package of proposals on July 22. The Education and Labor Committee approved its version July 28.

Both House panels had three goals: to strengthen financially shaky pension plans by tightening funding standards; to give PBGC greater financial stability; and to encourage companies with excess funds in their pension plans to keep the plans going instead of terminating them to get at surplus cash.

The two committees differed on a number of points, including:

● **Premiums.** The Labor panel called for boosting the $8.50 premium to $19 per person, plus a charge of $200 per employee for any defined-benefit plan terminated after July 1, 1987.

The Ways and Means bill, however, called for an increase to $14, with an additional variable charge for pension plans that currently did not contain sufficient funds to meet their obligations.

● **Asset Withdrawals.** The Labor Committee bill allowed withdrawal of excess funds, but only if a plan had a cushion equal to 125 percent of the amount owed to vested employees and to those who were accruing pension benefits but were not fully vested.

The Ways and Means bill did not permit asset withdrawals from ongoing plans; it allowed a company to use surplus pension funds only if it terminated the plan first. To discourage such terminations, the committee proposal assessed a 20 percent excise tax against all surplus funds not used for other pension purposes.

● **Minimum Funding.** Both bills required faster funding of pension plans. But the Labor panel put an annual limit on the percentage of increase in funding required for plans that had at least 50 percent of their future obligations funded.

Ways and Means did not place any cap on the annual percentage increase, except for plans in the financially distressed steel industry.

In the Senate, two committees also drafted pension provisions for the reconciliation bill.

The Labor and Human Resources Committee approved its bill Oct. 9, while the Finance Committee acted on Oct. 16.

The Senate Labor Committee called for increasing the annual premium to $20 per employee. The Finance bill increased the premium to $14 but demanded more from companies that had let their pension funds fall short of benefits owed to retirees. The latter were required to make "risk exposure" payments of $6 for every $1,000 that a plan fell short of obligations.

The two panels also differed over plan terminations by employers seeking to withdraw money from pension plan surpluses. The Labor Committee allowed employers to withdraw surpluses as long as they left a cushion that would cover 125 percent of current liabilities. But the Finance measure retained current law, which prohibited employers from withdrawing any money from pension plans, unless the employer terminated the plan.

## Major Provisions

As cleared by Congress, HR 3545 included the following major provisions affecting pension law:

### Minimum Funding Requirements

● **Full-Funding Limitation.** Limited the amount of tax-deductible contributions employers could make to pension plans. Under the provision, once a pension plan was funded to 150 percent of its current obligations, no additional employer contributions would be tax-deductible.

● **'Current Liability.'** Defined "current liability" of a pension plan as all liabilities to employees and their beneficiaries under the plan.

● **Unfunded Old and New Liabilities.** Defined the unfunded "old liability" as the unfunded current liability at the beginning of the first plan year starting after Dec. 31, 1987. "New liability" was the current liability of the plan for the year without regard to the unamortized portion of the unfunded old liability or the liability for an "unpredictable contingent event," such as a plant shutdown.

● **Amortization Periods.** Required that for single-employer plans, the growth in liabilities beyond expectations because of changing economic conditions or other experience-related changes be amortized over five years, instead of the current 15 years. Increases in predicted liabilities resulting from changes in actuarial assumptions had to be amortized over 10 years, instead of the current 30 years (40 years for plans started before 1974).

● **Benefit Increases Under Existing Collective-Bargaining Agreements.** Required that if a plan's benefits increased because of terms of a collective-bargaining agreement ratified before Oct. 17, 1987, any unfunded old liability for a plan year be increased by the amount needed to amortize the raise in benefits in equal annual installments over 18 years. The 18 years were to start either the plan year in which the benefit increase occurred or, if the taxpayer chose, the first plan year starting after Dec. 31, 1988.

● **'Unpredictable Contingent Event.'** Required additional contributions for pension plans that fell below obligations because of an "unpredictable contingent event" for which special benefit was one, such as a plant shutdown, that resulted from something other than age, service, compensation, death or disability, or any other event that could reasonably be predicted.

● **Special Rules for Small Plans.** Exempted from the minimum funding rules plans that had fewer than 100 participants every day of the preceding plan year. For plans with more than 100 but less than 150 participants during the preceding plan year, the amount of required additional funding was equal to the product of: the increase in funding liability, without regard to this paragraph, multiplied by 2 percent for the highest number of participants in excess of 100 on any such day.

● **Aggregation of Plans.** Treated all plans held or controlled by one employer as one plan.

● **Interest Rates Used.** Required that the interest rates used in calculating a plan's assets and necessary employer contributions to the plan fall within 10 points of the weighted average of 30-year Treasury certificates for the four preceding years.

● **Certain Service Disregarded.** Determined the percentage of service counted toward current liabilities for employees who worked before becoming participants in the plan. The percentage was: 20 percent for one year of participation; 40 percent for two years; 60 percent for three years; 80 percent for four years; 100 percent for five or more years. This applied to employees who had not accrued any other benefits under any other plan maintained by the employer and who first became participants after Dec. 31, 1987.

● **Valuation of Bonds.** Allowed the secretary of the Treasury to draft, with respect to the 1986 Internal Revenue Code, regulations for determining the value of any dedicated bond portfolio.

● **Special Rules for Steel Companies.** Limited the required contribution to steel company pension plans by a formula intended to prevent excessive funding burdens on those companies.

● **Time When Contributions Were Deemed Made.** Determined that, for single-employer plans, any contributions made during the period beginning the day after the last day of the plan year and ending the 15th day of the eighth month after the close of the plan year would be considered made on the last day of the plan year. For multi-employer plans, contributions made after the last day of the plan year but not more than two and one-half months thereafter would be considered made on the last day. The period for multi-employer plans could be extended up to six months by the secretary.

● **Quarterly Estimated Payments.** Required four installments, on April 15, July 15, Oct. 15 and Jan. 15, for plan years starting Jan. 1. For plans with fiscal years starting on other days, the required installment dates would be adjusted accordingly.

● **Amount of Required Installment.** Determined the amount as the "applicable percentage" of the required annual payment. The required annual payment was the lesser of: 90 percent of the amount required contribution to the plan or 100 percent of the amount required for the preceding year. The applicable percentage was 6.25 percent for plans years beginning in 1989, 12.5 percent for 1990, 18.75 percent for 1991 and 25 percent for 1992 and thereafter. If a non-multi-employer plan failed to pay the full amount of a required installment for any plan year, then the rate of interest was to be the greater of: 175 percent of the federal midterm rate or a rate within 10 points of the weighted average of 30-year Treasury certificates.

● **Underpayment Amount.** Determined the amount of underpayment as the excess of: the required installment divided by the amount of the installment contributed to or under the plan on or before the due date before the installment.

● **Period of Underpayment.** Required that interest be paid for the period starting from the due date for the installment to the date the contribution was made.

● **Special Rules for Unpredictable Contingent Event Benefits.** Provided that, for a plan with benefit liabilities for an unpredictable contingent event, the liabilities not be taken into account in computing the required payment.

● **Increase in Excise Tax.** Raised the initial tax on failure to meet minimum funding standards from 5 percent to 10 percent of the amount of funding deficiency; applied these rules for plan years beginning after 1988.

● **Failure to Meet Minimum Funding Standards.** Required an employer with a single-employer plan who failed to make a required installment before the 60th day after the due date to notify each plan participant by means approved by the secretary.

● **Imposition of Lien.** Required that, if any member of the pension plan control group failed to make a required installment or any other required payment before the due date, and the unpaid balance, including interest and previously unpaid balances, exceeded $1 million, a lien be placed, in favor of the plan, upon all property and property rights belonging to that person and any other person of the pension-control group. This applied to any single-employer defined-benefit plan with a funded liability percentage of less than 100 percent.

● **Lien Amount.** Set the lien amount as the lesser of: the amount of the unpaid balance over $1 million or the aggregate unpaid balance of required installments for plan years starting after 1987 for which payment was not made before the due date. The person failing to make the payments had to inform the Pension Benefit Guaranty Corporation within 10 days of the due date. The lien started on the 60th day after the due date and continued through the end of the plan year. Any amount with respect to which the lien was imposed was to be treated as taxes due the United States. The lien was to be enforced by the PBGC.

● **Tax Liability of Controlled Group.** Imposed the 10 percent excise tax for failure to meet minimum funding requirements on the employer responsible for contributing to the plan.

● **Joint and Several Liability.** Made all members of the controlling group of a single-employer plan jointly and severally liable for the tax imposed.

● **Funding Waivers.** Prohibited waivers of funding requirements for single-employer plans, unless an application was submitted by the 15th day of the third month after the end of the plan year (or the 15th day of the sixth month if the plan year started during calendar 1988). Waivers were allowed only for a temporary business hardship; the hardship also had to affect the entire controlled group if the employer belonged to one.

● Reduced from five to three the number of waivers allowed in a 15-year period and required employers to notify all plan participants of any waiver obtained. Waivers for funding deficiencies were to be allowed only if the deficiency was less than $1 million, compared with the current $2 million. The provision was effective after Dec. 31, 1987.

## Terminations

● **Plan Termination/Distribution of Assets.** Required that, upon termination of a plan, after paying all other obligations, assets attributable to employee contributions be distributed "equitably" to the participants.

● Defined a participant with respect to a termination as someone currently participating in the plan or a person who received, during the three-year period ending with the termination date, a single-sum distribution of his earned benefit from the plan.

● **Liability to PBGC.** Set an employer's liability to the PBGC at the total amount of unfunded benefit liabilities at the time of termination, plus interest. A lien of up to 30 percent of the net value of all members of the plan's controlling group could be imposed for failure to meet liabilities.

● **Additional Payment to Participants.** Required that, in addition to other obligations to participants, the corporation pay each participant a portion of the amount of assets remaining in the plan, if so provided under the plan itself.

● **Standards for Termination.** Restricted standard terminations — meaning voluntary terminations — to fully funded pension plans, in which assets were adequate to meet benefit liabilities.

● **PBGC Premium Increase.** Raised from $8.50 per employee to $16 per worker the annual premium an employer with a defined-benefit pension plan had to pay the PBGC.

● **Added Premium for Underfunded Plans.** Required employers with underfunded pension plans to pay an added premium for underfunded vested benefits of $6 per $1,000 of underfunding, capped at $34 per employee. This meant the maximum premium per employee required under the law would be $50 annually.

● **Joint and Several Liability.** Made all members of a controlled group jointly and severally liable for the premiums.

● **Deposits in Revolving Funds.** Established a seventh PBGC fund, to be filled through premiums, penalties, interest charges for premiums in excess of $8.50 and earnings on investments by the fund or assets credited to it after enactment. Amounts in the fund could be transferred to other funds but could not be used to pay administrative costs of the PBGC or benefits for any plan terminated before Oct. 1, 1988, unless no other funds were available.

● **Penalties for Failure to Supply Information.** Authorized the PBGC to assess a penalty against any person or company failing to provide required information or notice of up to $1,000 a day for each day the failure continued.

● **Security for Plan Amendment That Resulted in Underfunding.** Required that, beginning Jan. 1, 1989, if a defined-benefit plan adopted an amendment that increased liabilities and the result was that assets covered less than 60 percent of liabilities, the controlled group had to furnish security for a percentage of the unfunded liabilities.

● Required companies to file an annual report showing the percentage of pension liabilities covered by assets. Failure to do so could result in a civil penalty of $1,000 per day.

● **Treatment of 'Floor-Offset' Arrangements.** Specified that after Dec. 17, 1987, a plan consisting of a defined-benefit plan and an individual account plan was to be considered a single plan.

● **Stock.** Allowed company stock to qualify as employer security only if no more than 25 percent of the same class was held by the plan and at least 50 percent was held outside the company. This did not apply until Jan. 1, 1993, for stock held before Dec. 17, 1987.

### 1988 Pension Legislation

Two issues that had been left unresolved by the 1987 pension law (PL 100-203) — termination of overfunded pension plans and pension portability — were the occasion for further congressional debate during 1988. Neither issue resulted in major changes in pension law, however.

Conferees on the 1987 bill had sought to work out a permanent solution to the "reversion" problem, under which companies scrapped their overfunded pension plans and used the surplus to fund such corporate quests as mergers and takeovers. But last-minute disagreements stymied those efforts, leaving what some called a major loophole in ERISA.

In the wake of the deadlock on the reversion issue during consideration of the ERISA overhaul, labor unions, retiree groups and their allies in Congress continued in 1988 to push for legislative steps to ensure that workers received at least part of the surplus from overfunded pension plans.

The leader in this effort was Sen. Howard M. Metzenbaum, D-Ohio, chairman of the Senate Labor and Human Resources Subcommittee on Labor. "Companies have turned their pension plans into corporate piggy banks," Metzenbaum argued. But business groups said that Congress should not try to dictate how companies used pension assets. Any proposal to share surplus funds with workers was "basically the confiscation of an employer's property," said Sen. Don Nickles, R-Okla.

In April, Metzenbaum introduced legislation (S 2284) to put a moratorium on reversions, by requiring employers who terminated overfunded plans within the next year either to distribute the surplus to workers and retirees or put the funds into escrow.

Metzenbaum added his moratorium proposal to the Senate Appropriations Committee version of the fiscal 1989 spending bill (HR 4783) for the Departments of Labor, Health and Human Services and Education.

When the Senate took up HR 4783 on July 26, however, members voted to replace the moratorium language with a non-binding resolution urging Congress to enact legislation to force companies to pay a 60 percent excise tax on the excess assets of a terminated plan. The penalty was to expire on May 1, 1989, giving Congress time to consider a permanent solution to the problem.

The Senate Finance Committee on Sept. 8 incorporated Metzenbaum's proposal for a 60 percent excise tax into its version of the tax technical corrections bill (HR 4333). During conference action on the bill, however, conferees decided to replace the provision with one raising the existing 10 percent excise tax to 15 percent — a change that was expected to increase federal revenues by $59 million over three years.

**Pension Portability.** Also in 1988, Congress considered legislation aimed at permitting workers to have their accumulated pension benefits transferred into an Individual Retirement Account (IRA) when they changed jobs. The measure went no further than approval by a House committee, however.

Under existing law, pension savings for an employee who left his job before retirement age frequently were "cashed out" — paid in a lump sum to the worker, who often spent them on immediate needs.

A bill (HR 1961 — H Rept 100-676, Part I) reported by the House Education and Labor Committee June 7 would give workers another option: transferring pension savings to an IRA or other tax-deferred retirement fund.

To encourage the creation of pension plans by employers who did not offer them because of the red tape involved, the bill also allowed a private-sector investment manager — a bank, for example — to set up a "portable pension plan" in the form of an IRA or simplified employee pension (SEP). A portable pension plan could receive a worker's pension benefits when the employee changed jobs or his company terminated its pension plan.

The Ways and Means Committee did not act on the measure, however, and it died at year's end.

# Polygraph Ban

Despite initial administration opposition, President Reagan June 27, 1988, signed into law a measure (HR 1212 — PL 100-347) limiting the use of lie detectors by private-sector employers.

Congress had cleared the bill June 9.

The product of a lengthy legislative struggle led by labor unions and their allies, the bill prohibited private-sector employers from testing employees or job applicants with polygraphs, deceptographs, voice-stress analyzers, psychological-stress evaluators or any similar devices. Only companies providing security services for specified purposes, and those manufacturing and distributing controlled drugs, were exempted from the ban.

Polygraph tests were also allowed in connection with an ongoing criminal investigation if the employer had a "reasonable suspicion" that one of his workers was involved in a crime causing economic harm to the company. In all cases, the test results could not be the sole basis for adverse employment actions against a person.

Federal, state and local governments were exempted from the ban, as were consultants to national security agencies, such as the CIA.

Proponents of the ban said that polygraphs were unreliable and were too often used to intimidate innocent people. The Office of Technology Assessment reported that about 98 percent of the 2 million polygraph tests conducted each year were administered for private-sector employers, and 75 percent of those were given to job applicants.

Opponents of the legislation contended that the issue should be dealt with by the states, 20 of which already had laws regulating polygraph use. They also said that the tests could be useful tools in uncovering potentially dishonest workers and in solving on-the-job crimes.

## House Action

During the 99th Congress, the House approved polygraph legislation, and the Senate Labor and Human Resources Committee reported a companion bill. The measure died when the full Senate declined to act on the bill, however. *(1985-86 action, p. 693)*

In 1987, a new polygraph bill (HR 1212) began moving through the House. On June 10, the Education and Labor Committee approved the bill by a 25-9 vote.

Before approving the bill, the panel had rejected several amendments to allow polygraph use in selected businesses. Marge Roukema, R-N.J., offered an amendment to exempt a number of "security services," such as armored-car firms and those providing security at nuclear power plants. It was rejected 10-23. Another Roukema amendment, exempting federally regulated financial institutions, was rejected by voice vote.

Other defeated amendments would allow the pharmaceutical industry, day-care centers, nursing homes and pest control firms to use polygraphs. Also rejected was a Steve Gunderson, R-Wis., substitute amendment allowing polygraph testing in certain cases where a theft or crime had occurred.

House floor debate on Nov. 4 followed a similar pattern, with critics offering a series of amendments to exempt different types of businesses from the ban.

However, the House did adopt two amendments. Roukema again offered her amendment exempting certain security firms, and it was adopted on a 210-209 vote. In addition, the House by a wide margin accepted a Bill Richardson, D-N.M., amendment allowing polygraph use in connection with a criminal investigation involving a manufacturer of controlled drugs.

The House then passed HR 1212 by a 254-158 vote.

## Senate Action

The Senate Labor and Human Resources Committee, which had approved a polygraph-ban bill in 1986, approved S 1904 (S Rept 100-284), its version of the polygraph bill, by a 12-3 vote Feb. 3, 1988.

The bill was cosponsored by both the panel's chairman, Edward M. Kennedy, D-Mass., and its ranking member, Orrin G. Hatch, R-Utah. The measure prohibited private employers from using polygraphs during interviews with job applicants and in nearly all other situations, but it permitted polygraph use when an employer was investigating a specific criminal incident. In those cases, the test could only be used as supporting evidence, not as the sole grounds for action against an employee.

The measure faced strenuous opposition from a group of conservative Republicans on the Senate floor. Opponents did succeed in adding an amendment by Strom Thurmond, R-S.C., to exempt companies that operated armored cars or installed security systems at facilities in-

volving public health and safety. But other Republican-sponsored amendments were rejected.

The Senate March 3 passed, without major changes, HR 1212 after substituting the text of S 1904. The vote was 69-27.

## Conference Action

Conferees approved the final version of HR 1212 May 17.

The main issue facing conferees had been House and Senate differences over exemptions for various types of businesses. The House version of the bill was more restrictive than the Senate's, banning testing of job applicants and workers across the board.

In addition, the Senate bill — and the final compromise version — allowed all employers to use polygraphs in connection with an ongoing criminal investigation, as long as an employer had good reason to suspect the worker in question was involved.

The only other notable difference between the two bills was the issue of employer liability. The House bill would allow an employee who had suffered a loss due to an employer's violation of the polygraph ban to sue for damages, while the Senate bill allowed only recovery of lost employment, wages and benefits. Conferees adopted the Senate approach.

Final action came June 9, when the Senate adopted the conference report (H Rept 100-659) by a 68-24 vote. The House had approved the conference report June 1, by a 251-120 vote.

## Major Provisions

As enacted, HR 1212 (PL 100-347):

### Definitions

● Defined "lie detector" as a polygraph, deceptograph, voice-stress analyzer, psychological-stress evaluator or any similar mechanical or electrical device used to reach an opinion about an individual's honesty or dishonesty.

● Defined "polygraph" as an instrument that recorded "continuously, visually, permanently and simultaneously changes in cardiovascular, respiratory and electrodermal patterns" or the individual tested for the purpose of reaching an opinion about that person's honesty. In cases where lie-detector tests were not banned, the employer had to use a polygraph, instead of another type of lie detector.

### Prohibitions

● Forbade a private employer from directly or indirectly requiring or suggesting that an employee or job applicant take a lie-detector test and from inquiring about or using the results of any such test previously taken by the person.

● Prohibited an employer from discharging, disciplining, discriminating against or denying employment or promotion to any employee or job applicant who refused to take a lie-detector test or who had filed a complaint or started a lawsuit against the employer for violating the law prohibiting such tests. Even in the instances when a polygraph test was allowed, an employer was forbidden to take an adverse job action based solely on the results of the test.

## Exemptions

- Exempted federal, state and local governments, and their subdivisions, from the lie-detector ban.
- Exempted consultants or experts under contract to the Defense Department, the FBI or the Department of Energy (in connection with atomic-energy defense activities). The exemption also applied to a contractor's employees.
- Exempted anyone employed by, assigned to or detailed to the following government intelligence agencies: the National Security Agency, the CIA and the Defense Intelligence Agency. Job applicants, consultants and employees of contractors for the above agencies could be required to take a lie-detector test, as could any federal government employee with access to top-secret materials.
- Allowed polygraph tests in connection with an ongoing criminal investigation. Any employer who had "a reasonable suspicion" that one of his workers was involved in a crime such as theft, embezzlement, misappropriation or unlawful industrial espionage or sabotage could request that that employee undergo a polygraph test, provided that: the employee had access to the property under investigation; the employer made a statement available to the worker prior to the test that outlined the specific incident under investigation and the basis of the employer's suspicions; and the statement was signed by a person authorized to legally bind the employer to his statement and was kept on file for at least three years.
- Exempted job applicants for security-related businesses, such as companies that provided armored-car personnel, installation and maintenance of security alarm systems, and security personnel to protect facilities that affected national security or public health and safety. The latter included electric power generating and transmission facilities; public water supply facilities; public transportation; and shipment or storage of radioactive and other toxic materials. The exemption also applied to applicants for jobs protecting valuables such as currency and precious commodities. Security-service employers could not request a job applicant to take a polygraph test if the individual would not have access to the above valuables or facilities.
- Exempted companies involved in the manufacture, distribution and sale of controlled drugs. An employer could test any job applicant who would have access to such drugs and any current employee suspected of criminal wrongdoing.

## Limits

- Mandated that the exemptions specified by federal law should not diminish an employer's responsibility to comply with state and local law or with any negotiated collective-bargaining agreement that prohibited the use of lie-detector tests on employees and job applicants.
- Provided that the exemptions not apply if the results or analysis of a polygraph test were used as the sole basis of adverse employment action taken against an employee or job applicant, even in the case of a criminal investigation. A refusal to submit to a polygraph also could not be the sole basis for an adverse job action.

## Testing Procedures

- Required that no test be shorter than 90 minutes and that no examiner conduct and complete more than five polygraph tests on a given day.

- Provided that prior to taking a lie-detector test, the examinee must: receive a reasonable written notice of the date, time and place of the examination and of his right to obtain legal counsel; be informed in writing of the nature of the test and the instruments involved; be informed in writing whether the test was to be observed through a two-way mirror or any other such device and whether it was to be recorded; read and sign a notice informing the examinee of his legal rights under the act, including provisions that the examinee could not be required to take a lie-detector test as a condition of employment and that the results of such a test could be used as supported evidence to fire, discipline or refuse to hire an individual; receive a copy of the questions to be asked during the test; be informed that he could terminate the test at any time.
- Provided that during the test, the examinee: could end the test at any time; could not be asked questions that were not presented to the examinee in writing prior to the test; could not be asked questions in a manner designed to degrade the examinee nor questions that dealt with race, religion, politics, sex and union affiliation; could be excused from the test if there was sufficient evidence from his doctor that he was suffering from a medical or psychological condition, or was undergoing treatment, that might adversely affect the test results.
- Provided that after the test, and before any adverse action was taken against the examinee, an employer had to: further interview the employee on the test results, provide the employee with a written copy of the test results, a copy of the questions and the examinee's responses.
- Prohibited the results of a polygraph test from being used as the sole basis for disciplining, firing or refusing to hire an individual.

## Examiner Qualifications

- Required that a polygraph examiner: be licensed by the state in which the test was to be conducted; maintain at least a $50,000 bond or the equivalent in professional liability insurance; submit in writing any conclusion or opinion based on the test results. The conclusion was to be based solely on the results of the polygraph charts and could not include any recommendations concerning the employment status of the examinee. Also required the examiner to retain all records relating to a polygraph test for at least three years after administering the test.

## Disclosure

- Prohibited disclosure of information obtained during a polygraph test except to the examinee, or someone designated by the examinee; the employer, or governmental agency, who requested the test; or any person, court or government agency with a warrant for the information.

## Secretary of Labor

- Required the labor secretary to prepare and distribute a notice summarizing the provisions of the act. An employer was to post the notice in a conspicuous place.
- Required the secretary to issue rules and regulations needed to carry out the provisions of the polygraph ban.
- Authorized the labor secretary to cooperate with regional, state and local agencies and provide technical assistance to employers, labor unions and employment agencies.

### Enforcement

● Authorized the labor secretary to investigate and inspect companies suspected of violating the act's provisions and to keep records relating to the administration of the act.

● Provided the labor secretary with the authority to issue subpoenas for the purpose of any hearing or investigation in connection with the act's provisions.

● Set a fine of up to $10,000 in civil penalties for any employer who violated the act.

● Allowed the labor secretary to bring court cases against any employer who violated the act. The solicitor of labor was authorized to appear for and represent the secretary in any litigation brought under the act.

● Allowed an employee or job applicant to sue an employer who had violated the provisions of the act. The suit had to be brought within three years of the alleged violation and an employer could be held liable for legal and equitable relief, including employment, reinstatement, promotion and the payment of lost wages and benefits.

# Railroad Unemployment Funds

Congress in 1988 approved legislation providing for a long-delayed overhaul of the railroad unemployment system. The measure was included in a miscellaneous tax bill (HR 4333 — PL 100-647) cleared by Congress in the session that began Oct. 21.

The bill included the first increase in benefits for unemployed rail workers since 1976 and revised the system's funding mechanism to shield it from financial catastrophe. For the first time, rail employers were required to pay unemployment taxes geared to the cost of providing for the workers they laid off.

Backers of the legislation, who included both rail management and labor, said that the measure would make the system much sounder financially than it had been for several decades.

## Background

Since the late 1930s, the rail industry had been a world unto itself in terms of unemployed and retired workers. Instead of paying into Social Security to provide for their workers' retirement, railroad employers contributed to a special Railroad Retirement Account. And instead of relying on state unemployment benefits, laid-off rail workers were aided by a special employer-financed unemployment fund.

The two funds were independent. Beginning in 1959, however, the unemployment fund had been allowed to borrow from the pension account when it ran short of cash. Having borrowed funds in 20 of 28 years, the unemployment fund by 1988 owed the pension account some $600 million. Most of the debt was racked up during the recession of the early 1980s. The heavy borrowing by the unemployment fund threatened the solvency of the retirement account.

In response, Congress in 1983 cleared legislation (PL 98-76) that imposed a new employer-paid tax. The repayment tax was increased in the fiscal 1986 reconciliation act (PL 99-272) but was due to expire in 1990 — when the unemployment fund would still have owed some $580 million. *(1983 law, Congress and the Nation Vol. VI, p. 666;*

*fiscal 1986 reconciliation, p. 40)*

The unemployment fund faced other problems as well. Basic benefits for jobless rail workers fell far behind those provided by most states. The most a laid-off rail worker could hope to receive was $25 a day.

## Legislative History

The House Energy and Commerce Committee reported its version of rail unemployment legislation (HR 2167 — H Rept 100-102, Part I) on May 21, 1987. The bill then went to the Ways and Means Committee, which reported it Oct. 19 (Part II).

When the bill reached the House floor, the Reagan White House issued a statement opposing it. The administration called for merging the railroad unemployment system with the larger federal and state unemployment insurance system.

Nevertheless, HR 2167 enjoyed broad bipartisan support among House members. The only note of criticism came from Bill Frenzel, R-Minn., who argued that the bill would in fact require additional federal spending during its first two years.

The bill passed by a 366-24 vote Nov. 9.

The Senate did not move quickly on the measure, however. After negotiations were held between members of the Finance and Labor and Human Resources committees, the provisions of the rail unemployment bill were rolled into a technical tax bill (S 2238 — S Rept 100-445) reported by the Finance Committee on Aug. 3, 1988. Thereafter, the fate of the legislation was tied up with Senate and conference action on the tax bill.

## Major Provisions

HR 4333 increased the daily maximum unemployment benefit to $30 from $25. More importantly, it made future increases automatic, based on the annual rise in average national wages.

To pay for higher benefits, the measure similarly indexed the current wage base — the first $600 of each worker's monthly paycheck — used to calculate how much in taxes an employer should pay into the unemployment fund. The measure also specified that all unemployment taxes were to be based on the new, indexed wage base.

In a cost-saving move, the bill required workers to wait 14 days after being laid off before receiving benefits — instead of immediately, as under previous law.

For the first time, the basic tax paid by employers was to be pegged to their actual unemployment experience. Previously, all railroad employers had paid the same flat rate of between 0.5 percent and 8 percent of each worker's base wage, depending on the financial strength of the unemployment fund.

HR 4333 required all railroads except public commuter lines to pay an 8 percent tax through 1990. Starting in 1991, the new "experience-rated" tax was to be phased in for all railroad employers. Employers who maintained a steady work force would no longer subsidize those who repeatedly laid off workers.

The bill also increased the administrative tax used to run the fund and imposed a surcharge designed to make sure there was always enough money in the unemployment fund. But it limited the total tax a railroad would have to pay in any given year to no more than 12.5 percent.

HR 4333 also indefinitely extended the existing employer repayment tax until the entire debt to the retirement account was paid off — sometime in the late 1990s, experts predicted.

In addition, the bill made some relatively minor changes in the retirement fund, affecting such issues as severance payments, spousal benefits, earned income by disabled workers and the treatment of prior military service by retired workers.

Although the retirement fund was on a firm financial footing in 1988, experts warned that it might run into trouble later, when the number of retired workers exceeded those active. Congress in 1987 had created a seven-member commission to study reform of financing methods for the fund. HR 4333 extended the deadline for that panel's report until Oct. 1, 1990.

# Plant-Closing Notice

Congress in 1988 cleared legislation (S 2527 — PL 100-379) to require companies to give 60 days' notice of plant closings and large-scale layoffs to workers and affected local governments.

President Reagan opposed the issue so strongly that he had vetoed an omnibus trade bill (HR 3) primarily because of his opposition to its plant-closing provisions. The idea of giving workers advance warning that they would lose their jobs enjoyed strong support in Congress, however, and the new version of the notification legislation became law Aug. 4, without Reagan's signature. Washington observers speculated that Reagan decided not to veto the popular bill a second time so as not to jeopardize the presidential campaign of Vice President George Bush. Before S 2527 became law, the plant-closing issue had become a major point of partisan contention. *(Trade bill, p. 148)*

## House Action

Plant-closing legislation had for several years been a pet project of Rep. William D. Ford, D-Mich., whose home state and region had been hit hard by economic dislocations and plant closings. He sought to bring a plant-closing bill to the House floor in 1985, but it was defeated even after sponsors agreed to water down its provisions substantially. *(1985 action, p. 694)*

In 1987, however, the progress of the bill was considerably smoother. The Education and Labor Committee, on which Ford was a senior member, approved a plant-closing bill (HR 1122 — H Rept 100-285) by a 23-11 vote on June 9.

Backers of the measure said that helping workers readjust to changing economic conditions was in the national interest. They also contended that business groups' fears about the adverse effects of giving advance notice of closings were not well-founded.

But committee Republicans, led by Marge Roukema of New Jersey and James M. Jeffords of Vermont, the ranking member on the panel, opposed the legislation, particularly its provisions requiring companies to consult with labor and local government officials about proposed shut-downs.

Before approving the bill, the committee by a 10-22 vote rejected a Roukema amendment to eliminate the consultation requirement and substantially reduce the notice requirement.

The bill as approved by the committee required 90 days' notice of closings or layoffs involving 50 to 100 workers, 120 days' notice for those involving between 100 and 500 employees and a six-month notice period if more than 500 employees were affected.

The provisions of the bill were later included in HR 3.

## Senate Action

The Senate Labor and Human Resources Committee reported a plant-closing bill (S 538) on May 19 (S Rept 100-62). Similar provisions were inserted July 9 into the Senate's omnibus trade bill (S 1420).

The provisions of the trade bill required companies with more than 100 employees to give at least 60 days' notice before a plant closing or layoff involving at least one-third of the work force.

The Senate provisions were not only weaker than the House bill, but they also were a watered-down version of S 538. The principal sponsors, Howard M. Metzenbaum, D-Ohio, and Edward M. Kennedy, D-Mass., agreed to modify the bill to strengthen their position on the Senate floor, where they faced strong opposition from business allies led by Dan Quayle, R-Ind. Critics claimed the bill's mandatory notice provisions would have an anti-competitive effect and would discourage the creation of new companies.

The mandatory notice was added by voice vote July 8. Quayle moved the next day to strike the provisions but was defeated 40-60.

## Second Measure

The plant-closing measure eventually cleared Congress as part of the omnibus trade bill.

An important moment in the legislative history of the bill came when the conference version of HR 3 came to the House floor. Republican leader Robert H. Michel of Illinois moved to delete the plant-closing provisions from the bill, but his motion was rejected on a **167-253 (R 144-29; D 23-224) key vote** April 21, 1988. *(1988 key votes, p. 981)*

Reagan continued to oppose the notice provisions strongly, however, and vetoed the bill as a result. A veto override attempt in the Senate then failed.

In response, the Democratic leadership decided to introduce the notice requirement as a separate bill.

S 2527 passed the Senate July 6 by a vote of 72-23 — more than the two-thirds majority needed to override a veto. The bill passed with the support of 10 Republicans and 2 Democrats who had voted against the override of the trade bill in June.

The House then passed S 2527 by a 286-136 vote July 13. Again, the margin was more than enough to override a veto. The bill passed without change, despite strong Republican criticism of a rule that allowed only one amendment to be offered on the floor.

## Major Provisions

As cleared, S 2527:

● Required employers, in certain circumstances, to give 60 days' advance notice of a plant closing that would cause 50 or more workers at one site to lose their jobs. The bill required 60 days' notice for layoffs of longer than six months, if the layoff would cause 50 or more workers at one site to lose their jobs and if affected workers constituted 33 percent or more of the work force at a site.

In the case of a layoff causing 500 or more workers to

lose their jobs, notice would be required whether one-third of the work force was affected or not.

● Barred plant closure or a mass layoff, for which notice had been given, before the end of the notice period.

● Exempted from the notice requirement employers with fewer than 100 full-time workers. In determining whether an employer would be covered, employees working fewer than 20 hours per week or for less than six months were not to be counted. Employees who had been offered transfers within commuting distance, or who would be employed by the purchaser of a business, also were not to be included.

● Exempted from the notice requirement "faltering" businesses whose owners were actively seeking capital or business to keep a firm going at the time notice should have been given. The bill also exempted businesses affected by circumstances, such as price changes or drought, that could not have been "reasonably" foreseen.

● Exempted from the notice requirement closures or layoffs from projects that employees know would be temporary when they were hired.

Strikes or lockouts were exempted, so that an employer would not be required to give notice to "economic" strikers (as defined by the National Labor Relations Act) if he replaced them with other workers. The bill specified that the legislation neither violated nor invalidated rulings on the hiring of replacements for economic strikers under the labor act.

● Authorized penalties for violations of the notice requirement. A company would have to pay its workers the equivalent of a day's pay and fringe benefits for each day the required notice was not given. It would have to pay local communities up to $500 per day, to a maximum of $30,000. But a firm would not have to make the community payments if it had made penalty payments to workers expeditiously.

# Minimum Wage Increase

Despite a major effort by organized labor, the 100th Congress refused to approve the first increase in the federal minimum wage since 1981.

The immediate cause of the death of legislation (S 837) raising the minimum wage was a Senate Republican filibuster in the final weeks of the 1988 session. But the measure also had created deep schisms between Democrats in both chambers.

In fact, House Democrats never brought their version of the measure (HR 1834) to the floor, even though it was approved in March 1988 by the Education and Labor Committee. Democratic leaders were unsure whether they had enough votes to pass the bill.

S 837 would raise the minimum wage from its existing $3.35 an hour to $4.55 over a three-year period. HR 1834 would boost the minimum to $5.05 over four years.

The minimum wage issue touched off an all-out lobbying war between organized labor and the business community.

Labor supporters of the measure, joined by civil rights, church and other lobby groups, argued that the nation's lowest-paid workers deserved a raise. Since 1981, they pointed out, the minimum had lost 25 percent of its purchasing power to inflation. Past minimum wage hikes, they said, had resulted in little or no overall loss of jobs in the economy.

But opponents, who were led by the National Federation of Independent Business, the U.S. Chamber of Commerce and other employer groups, waged a major effort to convince members of Congress that the legislation would cost jobs and hurt the economies of their states and districts. Critics mounted a sophisticated campaign that was able in most cases to bring far more public pressure on members than the coalition of groups supporting the bill were able to mobilize.

## House Action

The troubles facing a minimum wage bill were clearly shown in the House Education and Labor Committee, which on most issues is strongly sympathetic to labor unions. But the Labor Standards Subcommittee did not even take up HR 1834 until almost a year after it was introduced and approved the measure only after making major changes. The subcommittee supported the bill by a 6-3 party-line vote March 3, 1988.

Subcommittee Democrats agreed to make changes in the bill in hopes of expanding support for the controversial measure. One key alteration removed from the bill a provision automatically increasing the minimum wage each year after it had reached $4.65 to ensure that the wage level would be at 50 percent of the average wage nationally. The provision evoked strong doubts among moderate and conservative Democrats, as well as Republicans, who warned that it could fuel unending inflation. The subcommittee also agreed to exempt businesses with annual incomes of less than $500,000 from the wage requirements.

But the panel rejected several Republican amendments, the most significant of which was offered by Thomas E. Petri of Wisconsin. His amendment would raise the minimum wage to $4 over three years, provide for a "training wage" for new workers and increase the earned income tax credit (EITC) for the working poor. The proposal would increase the amount of income eligible for the 14 percent credit to $7,143, from $5,714, and allow even larger credit for families with more than one child.

Supporters of increasing the EITC, including both liberals and conservatives, argued that it would be a more effective means of helping the working poor than raising the minimum wage. A number of subcommittee Democrats expressed interest in the idea but argued that it was too complex to be included in the minimum wage bill. The amendment was rejected 3-6.

In the full Education and Labor Committee, sponsors moved to strengthen the bill's provisions, both to satisfy labor lobbyists unhappy with the elimination of the indexing provision and to give House negotiators more to bargain with if the bill ever reached a conference committee with the Senate.

The change approved by the committee added a fourth-year raise in the minimum wage to $5.05. The amendment, offered by Carl C. Perkins, D-Ky., was adopted by the panel on an 18-14 vote.

The committee rejected a number of Republican amendments, including ones temporarily to block a minimum wage increase for workers in federally funded programs, such as Head Start, and another to set a $3.35 subminimum training wage for new workers.

The committee then approved HR 1834 by voice vote March 16. The panel reported the bill March 31 (H Rept 100-560).

Prospects for the bill on the House floor quickly dimmed, however, after the Congressional Budget Office released a report estimating that the increase in the minimum wage would lead to higher prices and the loss of nearly 500,000 jobs in the economy.

## Senate Action

Sponsors turned to the Senate in hopes of speeding action. The Labor and Human Resources Committee soon accommodated backers, approving S 837 June 29.

Before approving the bill, the Labor panel adopted a substitute amendment, offered by Edward M. Kennedy, D-Mass., raising the minimum to $4.55 per hour over three years and exempting businesses with annual sales volumes of less than $500,000.

Only two Republicans, Lowell P. Weicker Jr., Conn., and Robert T. Stafford, Vt., voted for the measure, which was formally reported by the Labor Committee July 26 (S Rept 100-430). The fact that bill sponsors did not allow Republicans to offer a number of other proposed amendments in committee ensured that the bill would face a long string of suggested changes when it reached the Senate floor.

There was no action on the measure for several months, however, as House and Senate leaders called on each other to move on the bill. But Republican presidential candidate George Bush added new impetus to the bill in September, when he called for a slight increase in the minimum wage. Bush called for a raise in the rate combined with a lower, "training" wage for new workers.

The Senate then plunged into a heated partisan debate on the bill, beginning Sept. 16. The first amendment offered was by Orrin G. Hatch, R-Utah, to allow employers to pay new hires a wage equal to 80 percent of the minimum for 90 days.

The Senate postponed a vote on the amendment, however, and by the week of Sept. 19 had become thoroughly bogged down, as Republicans blocked all attempts by Democrats to move forward on the bill.

Democratic leaders decided to pull the bill from the floor, thus killing it, after two cloture votes fell short of the 60 votes needed. The second attempt in as many days failed Sept. 23 on a **key vote of 56-35 (R 8-32; D 48-3)**. *(1988 key votes, p. 981)*

# Parental Leave

After a major partisan battle, the 100th Congress failed to complete action on legislation requiring many employers to grant their employees up to 10 weeks of unpaid leave to care for parents or newborn or seriously ill children.

The legislation was killed by a Republican filibuster in the final weeks of the 1988 session, after weeks of intense maneuvering for political advantage in the November election.

The final version of the measure that was blocked in the Senate was part of a "pro-family" bill that combined parental leave, child care and a crackdown on child pornography.

It was the third year that Congress had worked on parental leave legislation, which had taken on growing political importance in the wake of increasing attention to family issues and the greater presence of women in the

work force. *(1985-86 action, p. 695)*

Proponents of the legislation pointed out that the United States was all but alone among industrialized nations in failing to guarantee parents job-protected leave to care for newborns. Since the bill applied only to businesses with 50 or more workers, it would not be an unreasonable sacrifice by businesses to aid their employees in raising the next generation.

But critics insisted that mandated leave would disrupt companies and undermine their international competitiveness. Opponents ranged from small business groups to the National Association of School Boards, which feared possible interference with school schedules because of teacher leave.

## House Action

The House Education and Labor Committee approved its parental leave bill (HR 925 — H Rept 100-511, Part II) by a 21-11 vote Nov. 17, 1987. Action on the measure was marked by heated partisan debate, with only two Republicans — committee ranking member James M. Jeffords, Vt., and Marge Roukema, N.J. — joining Democrats in support.

The bill represented a compromise between Democratic sponsors and Roukema, who agreed on a bill that was significantly more modest in scope than the bill considered in the 99th Congress. The new version raised the floor on business size to 50 employees from 15 and reduced the total amount of time that an employee could take for parental leave in two years to 10 weeks from 18. In addition, employees would have to work for an employer for at least a year before being eligible to take leave without losing their job position.

The General Accounting Office estimated that the 50-employee floor for coverage would exempt 95 percent of all businesses, although only about 60 percent of all workers.

Nevertheless, the bill continued to face strong opposition from committee Republicans, who offered a series of amendments, including one to exempt elementary and secondary schools. All were rejected.

The bill also went to the Post Office and Civil Service Committee, which had jurisdiction over the provisions affecting federal workers. The bill (H Rept 100-511, Part I) as reported by the committee March 8, 1988, guaranteed federal employees 18 weeks of leave during any two-year period.

## Senate Action

Although Christopher J. Dodd, D-Conn., had introduced parental leave legislation early in the 100th Congress, the idea did not receive much attention in the Senate until June 1988, when he brought forth a new, scaled-down version (S 2488). The bill allowed up to 10 weeks of parental leave and applied only to businesses with 20 or more employees.

The Labor and Human Resources Committee approved S 2488 by an 11-5 vote July 14 and reported it Aug. 3 (S Rept 100-447). A key part of the bill would require employers to maintain employees' health insurance coverage while they were on leave — a potentially major cost for employers.

During committee action on the measure, Dan Quayle, R-Ind., offered an amendment to limit the scope of the bill to requiring employers to provide only up to four months unpaid leave for pregnancy or caring for a newborn baby.

The amendment, which would require continuation of health insurance coverage, was rejected by a 4-10 vote.

S 2488 came to the Senate floor in the midst of an openly partisan struggle over key domestic issues in the months before the general election. Majority Leader Robert C. Byrd, D-W.Va., called up the bill shortly after Republicans had successfully blocked action on the minimum wage bill.

Chief sponsor Dodd acted quickly to strengthen support for the bill, which had less than a majority of firm backers. He offered an amendment to reduce unpaid medical leave for a worker's own illness from 13 weeks to 10 weeks and limited coverage of the bill only to companies with 50 or more workers.

But the bill, which President Reagan threatened to veto, continued to become entangled in other controversial issues geared to gaining electoral advantage. First, Strom Thurmond, R-S.C., offered an amendment to crack down on child pornography. It was approved Sept. 28 on a 97-0 vote.

After a week of debate, Byrd moved to tack onto the bill the provisions of the "ABC" child-care bill (S 1885). Democrats hoped that Republican opponents of the bill would be wary of voting against a bill that had both parental leave and child care. When the bill reached a decisive vote Oct. 7 — on a cloture motion against the ongoing Republican filibuster — Democratic sponsors were 10 votes short (50-46) of the level needed to cut off debate. Byrd then pulled the bill from the floor. *(Child-care bill, p. 628)*

# Davis-Bacon Amendments

House Democrats were unsuccessful during the 100th Congress in efforts to make modest reforms in the Davis-Bacon Act, the 50-year-old federal law that required most federal contractors to pay workers the prevailing local wage rate, as determined by the Labor Department.

The legislation, which was passed by the House as an amendment to a defense authorization bill, was dropped in conference at the insistence of the Senate.

Pushed by organized labor and its Democratic allies, the legislation represented an effort to stave off growing pressure to make major changes in the law. The Reagan administration and business groups argued that the minimum size of contracts covered by the law should at least be raised from its existing $2,000 level, so that small- and medium-sized businesses would be exempted from its coverage.

Critics of the law said its wage standard, which was usually interpreted as meaning the union scale wage paid in the area, made it difficult for small and minority-owned businesses, who could not afford union wages, to compete for federal contracts.

Enacted in 1931, the Davis-Bacon Act was intended to prevent fly-by-night construction companies from underbidding local companies for federal contracts by paying substandard wages, thereby depressing the local wage rate. In 1935, it was expanded to include public works, and the threshold for coverage was set at $2,000. The law remained virtually unchanged thereafter.

Critics of the law argued that it inflated the cost of federal projects, since companies were required to pay union wages. A Congressional Budget Office study estimated it increased federal costs by nearly $1 billion a year.

Business groups argued that the threshold should be as high as $1 million, as the administration proposed. In 1986, there were three separate attempts to increase the threshold to $250,000, but all were unsuccessful.

## House Action

The House Education and Labor Committee approved its Davis-Bacon bill (HR 2216 — H Rept 100-504) on Aug. 4, 1987.

The bill as approved raised the threshold for coverage to $50,000 for new construction projects and $15,000 for remodeling or repair work. The bill also barred splitting of contracts on a project to avoid coming within the Davis-Bacon provisions. Other provisions of the bill cut reporting requirements for employers and beefed up enforcement of the law.

Republicans said the new threshold in the bill was far too low. Harris W. Fawell, Ill., sought to raise the minimum to $1 million, but his amendment was defeated by voice vote.

Opponents also attacked other provisions of the bill, including a provision allowing court challenges of decisions concerning coverage of the act. Their efforts to change it were unsuccessful, however.

No further action was taken on HR 2216 as a separate bill. Instead, sponsors moved to add the bill as a floor amendment to the fiscal 1989 defense authorization bill (HR 4264). The amendment adding the bill, offered by Austin J. Murphy, D-Pa., was approved by a 213-195 vote May 3, 1988. *(Defense authorization, p. 318)*

The effort to attach the Davis-Bacon measure to the defense bill was a surprise to many House members, who had expected to consider it as separate legislation.

However, in mid-April House Education and Labor Committee Chairman Augustus F. Hawkins, D-Calif., asked the Rules Committee for a rule allowing consideration of the Davis-Bacon changes as an amendment to the defense authorization bill. On April 27, the Rules panel approved a rule allowing for consideration of both the Murphy amendment and one offered by Charles W. Stenholm, D-Texas, to raise the threshold to $250,000.

The Rules Committee's action prompted some last-minute lobbying by small business groups, who strongly backed the Stenholm plan and opposed that offered by Murphy. Organized labor did little lobbying in response, however, and the disparity of effort was reflected in the narrow margin by which the Stenholm amendment was rejected: 204-210.

When the defense authorization bill went to conference, Senate conferees were adamantly opposed to retaining the Murphy amendment, arguing that it did not belong on a bill relating to national security. Eventually, House conferees relented, and the provision died.

# Double-Breasting Restrictions

The House in 1987 passed legislation (HR 281) that virtually barred construction companies from setting up subsidiaries to do the same work as the parent firm to evade union contracts.

The Senate Labor and Human Resources Committee also approved a companion bill. But the measure went no further and died at the end of the 100th Congress.

The practice of setting up dual shops was known as "double breasting," and it was not, in itself, illegal. But construction unions contended that companies abused the practice to avoid paying union-level wages.

As approved by the House, HR 281 would curb the practice of double breasting by redefining a "single employer." Under the bill, two or more business entities in the construction industry would be treated as a single employer if they worked within the geographical area covered by a union contract, performed the type of work described in the contract and were under common ownership.

Other provisions of the bill related to "pre-hire" agreements, under which a union could negotiate a contract with a company before any workers were employed. The measure made clear that pre-hire agreements could be repudiated only after the National Labor Relations Board certified that a majority of employees had selected another bargaining unit or decided not to have union representation.

### House Action

The House Education and Labor Committee approved HR 281 May 19 (H Rept 100-137).

When the bill reached the House floor, supporters said it was needed to keep order in the construction industry. Double breasting, they argued, denied workers a voice in union representation.

But Republican critics of the bill said it helped building-trades unions impose themselves on workers. Republicans offered a long series of amendments to the bill, all of which were defeated. The strongest amendment, offered by James M. Jeffords, R-Vt., would make the provisions of the bill apply only to contracts entered into after the date of enactment. It was rejected 203-221. Another proposal, offered by Steve Bartlett, R-Texas, would define companies as being a single employer only if they had common management, central control of labor relations, interrelated operations and common ownership. It was defeated 179-247.

The House passed the bill by a 227-197 vote June 17.

### Senate Action

The subject of double breasting also stirred up heated debate in the Senate Labor and Human Resources Committee, which approved its version of the bill (S 492 — S Rept 100-314) Dec. 9.

Backers of the bill, led by Chairman Edward M. Kennedy, D-Mass., said it was needed to ensure that construction employers abided by their contracts with unions. But critics, notably ranking member Orrin G. Hatch, R-Utah, said it would hurt businesses, particularly minority-owned firms.

Before approving the bill, the committee rejected a series of amendments proposed by Hatch. The amendments were defeated by a solid core of Democratic members, joined by Republicans Lowell P. Weicker Jr. of Connecticut and Robert T. Stafford of Vermont. Among the rejected amendments was one that would allow single employers to withdraw from union contracts for two years after enactment of the bill. Another would strip from the 1959 Landrum-Griffin Act the so-called "hot cargo" exemption for the construction industry.

Existing law prohibited agreements in which a union or employer refused to handle material sold or produced by a company that had been struck, but exempted the construction industry.

# Risk Notification

The 100th Congress considered legislation requiring workers who might be exposed to disease-causing chemicals and other hazardous substances in the work place to be informed of the possible threat to their health. The measure (HR 162) passed the House in 1987. But a companion Senate bill (S 79) died the following year as a result of a successful filibuster.

The bill would create a Risk Assessment Board to review medical research and identify groups of workers at risk of developing occupational diseases. It required notification of those workers and entitled them to employer-paid medical monitoring and testing. It also set procedures for transfer of workers to other jobs, without loss of earnings or benefits, if that was medically indicated.

The legislation was backed by organized labor and opposed by most business groups. The Reagan administration also was against the bill.

Supporters argued that the legislation was needed to combat the growing danger placed by work-place chemicals. Since 1968, according to the Centers for Disease Control, more than 19 million people had been exposed to toxic substances on the job, increasing their risk of contracting cancer, respiratory disease or other serious health problems.

Critics warned that the bill would impose a heavy burden of legal fees on companies to deal with legal challenges under the law. Such groups as the National Federation of Independent Business (NFIB) predicted that the bill would drive many small businesses into bankruptcy and would duplicate the work of existing federal agencies.

The bill sought to close a gap in the protection of workers left by the 1970 Occupational Safety and Health Act (PL 91-596). That law established the National Institute on Occupational Safety and Health to study occupational diseases, but it did not establish any way of notifying workers at risk as a result of exposure. *(Congress and the Nation Vol. III, p. 713)*

The House Education and Labor Committee had approved similar legislation in the 99th Congress. *(1985-86 action, p. 695)*

### House Action

The House Education and Labor Committee approved HR 162 May 19, 1987, and reported it June 26 (H Rept 100-194).

Although the bill was easily approved by the panel, action on it in both the Health and Safety Subcommittee and the full committee revealed the intensity of business and Republican opposition. While everyone agreed that workers should be notified of job-related health risks, opponents of the bill said current law was sufficient. Proponents countered that existing law had proved inadequate.

Republican members, including ranking committee member James M. Jeffords, Vt., and Paul B. Henry, Mich., offered several amendments aimed at restricting coverage of the law, particularly as it applied to small business. Their amendments — including a Henry substitute giving primary responsibility for work-place chemical dangers to the Occupational Safety and Health Administration — were rejected.

The House passed HR 162 by a 225-186 vote Oct. 15.

Democratic sponsors were able to beat back a major Republican alternative to the bill, offered by Jeffords and Henry. The amendment, defeated 191-234, would mandate more stringent enforcement of existing occupational safety laws and require a two-year study of the need for a risk-notification program.

However, sponsors did agree to modify the bill somewhat on the House floor. The amendments exempted small businesses, and those with good safety records, from some provisions of the bill. Moreover, floor managers were unable to defeat an amendment, offered by William E. Dannemeyer, R-Calif., to require all medical professionals and emergency-care workers to be warned that they were at risk of contracting AIDS (acquired immune deficiency syndrome).

### Senate Action

Action on S 79 in the Senate Labor and Human Resources Committee was dominated by the efforts of its chief sponsor, Howard M. Metzenbaum, D-Ohio, to reach a compromise on the bill with its chief Republican opponent, Dan Quayle of Indiana.

In both the Labor Subcommittee and full committee, Metzenbaum and Quayle reached agreements on a number of points, which led to amendments to modify the bill. For example, one amendment would exempt companies with fewer than 10 employees from the requirements of the law. But the changes were not enough to satisfy Quayle, who unsuccessfully offered several other amendments. One such amendment would give the secretary of health and human services more authority over the risk-assessment board.

The committee approved the bill by an 11-5 vote July 17 and filed its report on the measure Sept. 23 (S Rept 100-166).

Democratic leaders brought S 79 to the floor in March 1988. Floor action proved to be long, difficult and ultimately fatal for the bill. Aided by a strong lobbying effort by the NFIB and the U.S. Chamber of Commerce, Republicans were able to wage a filibuster that bill sponsors could not even come close to overcoming.

The first move on S 79 came when Majority Leader Robert C. Byrd, D-W.Va., filed a cloture motion limiting debate before there had been any discussion of the bill, irking many Republicans. That motion was defeated March 23 on a vote of 33-59, far short of the 60 votes needed to invoke cloture.

For the next week, the Senate debated amendments to the bill. Several were rejected, including one by Jesse Helms, R-N.C., to designate health and emergency workers as being at risk as a result of possible exposure to AIDS.

Democratic sponsors also moved to try to expand their support by exempting farmers and small businesses from the bill. Ultimately, however, floor managers pulled the bill, but not before three more motions to invoke cloture were defeated, 2-93, 41-44 and 42-52. The bill died upon adjournment.

# International Labor Pact

The Senate Feb. 1, 1988, approved ratification of two conventions of the International Labor Organization (ILO) — the first time in 35 years that the United States had done so.

Still, the United States, one of 10 nations in the ILO's governing executive council, had accepted only nine of the organization's 162 conventions.

Senators voted 81-2 in favor of Convention No. 144 (Treaty Doc 99-20) calling for governments to work with organized labor and business in implementing international labor standards.

The second pact, No. 147 (Treaty Doc 99-21), was approved 84-0. It set minimum living and working standards for merchant seamen.

The United States quit the ILO in 1977, charging it had grown increasingly politicized and complacent about labor violations in communist countries. After several reforms by the international agency, the United States rejoined in 1980.

personal appeal to the senators. Referring to the preceding arguments, he said, "I kind of feel like a piece of meat that is thrown out to a couple of dogs, jerked back and forth for possession ... between the House managers and my lawyers." He again claimed he was innocent of wrongdoing and repeated that he was the victim of a vendetta by federal officials who wanted to force him off the bench.

There was some concern expressed by senators about Claiborne's charge, and David Pryor, D-Ark., a member of the special committee, voted to acquit Claiborne "because of the long and abusive arm of the federal government." He said of the FBI and the Internal Revenue Service that "without their involvement, without their targeting, without their harassment, I have great doubt that he would have been convicted in the first place."

**Senate Votes.** On Article I the Senate Oct. 9 found Claiborne guilty by a vote of 87-10 — 21 more than the two-thirds majority required to convict.

On Article II, the vote was 90-7 for conviction.

On Article III, the vote was 46-17, with 35 senators voting present. Since a two-thirds vote of the members present and voting (66) was required for conviction, Claiborne was adjudged not guilty on this article.

On Article IV, the vote was 89-8 for conviction.

# Federal Anti-Fraud Law

Congress in 1986 amended the 123-year-old False Claims Act, the primary statute for fighting fraud against the federal government — particularly by defense contractors.

The legislation (S 1562 — PL 99-562), cleared Oct. 7, made four key changes in the existing federal statute: (1) penalties were increased against those who defrauded the government; (2) the standards and procedures in existing law for bringing suits were clarified and the Justice Department was given new pretrial investigative tools; (3) incentives were provided for private citizens to report suspected fraud; and (4) new protections were established for whistleblowers who reported fraud against the government and as a result suffered job discrimination.

Proposed provisions dealing with new, streamlined administrative procedures for handling small-dollar fraud were dropped from the final version because of complaints they would deny due process. However, these provisions, which applied to cases of fraud where the amounts involved were less than $150,000, were incorporated in HR 5300 (PL 99-509), the fiscal 1987 reconciliation bill. That legislation was cleared by Congress Oct. 17, 1986.

## Background

The False Claims Act was enacted in 1863 to curb defense contractor fraud during the Civil War. It had never been brought up to date to deal with modern fraud against a much larger federal government. And because of ambiguous language in the statute, government lawyers were experiencing difficulties using the law to bring suits for alleged fraud.

House and Senate sponsors of the bill charged that the $2,000 fraud penalty in the 1863 law was woefully out of date. Rep. Peter W. Rodino Jr., D-N.J., chairman of the Judiciary Committee, which considered the House version, pointed out that while fraud had become "more sophisticated, the law through which the government prosecutes fraud and recoups its losses has not followed the same

pattern." Other members who helped draft the bill stressed the importance of strengthening the anti-fraud laws during a period of growing budget deficits to retain the confidence of the American public that all federal means were being employed to address the problem.

The defense industry lobbied aggressively against the bill, contending the existing statute was sufficient to discourage fraud. But sponsors, including those who consistently supported a large defense establishment, said more tools were needed to investigate waste, abuse and, especially, fraud in the huge Pentagon budget.

## Legislative History

The House Judiciary Committee acted first to amend the False Claims Act. On June 26 it reported HR 4827 (H Rept 99-660) after rejecting efforts that would weaken any powers proposed for the Justice Department to fight fraud. The committee's bill included a separate section designed to handle small-dollar fraud cases.

The committee rejected an amendment to bar the Justice Department from sending written questionnaires to individuals or companies suspected of defrauding the government. Its sponsors said giving such authority to the department was tantamount to letting officials engage in "fishing expeditions" for fraud. Opponents charged the amendment would "take the guts out" of the bill, and it was rejected by a 15-19 vote. The panel, however, adopted an amendment requiring the Justice Department to get court approval before it could share with other agencies any information it gathered during a pretrial investigation.

Also adopted were amendments that clarified the government's administrative remedies when the alleged fraud involved beneficiaries of federal programs, such as food stamps and Medicare, and restored a provision in current law allowing the government to recover double the damages it could prove.

Before passing the bill Sept. 9, the House dropped the section establishing new streamlined administrative procedures for dealing with small-dollar fraud. The provisions were similar to a Senate bill (S 1134 — S Rept 99-212) that ran into strong opposition from defense contractors as well as groups representing beneficiaries of federal welfare programs. They said that such administrative procedures would deny them the constitutional right of a trial. But supporters pointed out that such cases were not being investigated because of the time and cost of going to court.

The House, after considering HR 4827, passed in lieu S 1562, amended with the language of HR 4827.

The Senate Judiciary Committee reported its version (S Rept 99-345) on July 28, and the full Senate passed S 1562 Aug. 11. Like the House bill, S 1562 clarified ambiguous language in the existing law and increased penalties for fraud, allowing a judge to impose double or triple the amount involved in the fraud plus a penalty of between $5,000 and $10,000.

One floor amendment was adopted. The committee bill established a new standard on the degree of knowledge about fraudulent activity a person had to have before the government could pursue a case against the person. He would be liable if he knew a statement was false or if he acted in "gross negligence of the duty" to inquire about fraud. Defense and other industry groups contended this was too broad, and the Senate amended this to conform to the narrower language in the House bill.

After the House acted Sept. 9, the Senate made additional changes Oct. 3, and the House accepted these Oct. 7, clearing S 1562.

## Major Provisions

As cleared, S 1562 made the following changes in the False Claims Act:

• Raised the fine for violations from $2,000 to between $5,000 and $10,000.

• Allowed a judge to require defendants to pay triple the amount of damages sustained by the government.

• Allowed a judge to reduce the award to double the government's damages if the defendant could prove that he cooperated fully with the government once the fraud was detected.

• Raised the term of imprisonment for a criminal violation from five years to 10 years and increased the criminal fine from $10,000 for individuals and corporations to $250,000 for individuals and $500,000 for corporations.

A criminal prosecution would occur when the Justice Department determined that the fraud was too serious for civil penalties only. An example would be a conspiracy to commit fraud against the government.

• Clarified the standard of knowledge a person must have before the government could pursue a case against that person. The bill specified that a person must have actual knowledge of information involving fraud or act in deliberate ignorance or reckless disregard for the truth or falsity of the information.

• Allowed an individual who uncovered fraud to bring a lawsuit seeking to recover damages for the fraud.

• Authorized a judge to limit the participation of the individual in the lawsuit if the government decided to join the litigation.

• Provided the individual who initiated the suit with a damage award of between 15 percent and 25 percent if the government entered the case. The individual could receive at least 25 percent of the damage award but not more than 30 percent if the government did not enter the case.

Under the old law, there was a cap of 10 percent on the individual's award if the government entered the case and 25 percent if the government did not.

• Required the offender to pay attorneys' fees to a citizen who prevailed in a suit.

• Provided whistleblowers with protection from harassment, firing, demotion or suspension by allowing them "all relief necessary to make the employee whole." Such relief could include reinstatement with seniority, twice the back pay owed and compensation for any special damages sustained, such as the cost of litigation to get his job back.

• Authorized the attorney general to issue "civil investigative demands," which are requests for documentary material or information, in advance of filing a lawsuit under the act.

• Barred the attorney general from delegating the authority to issue such demands.

• Required any civil investigative demand to state the conduct allegedly in violation of the false claims law and to describe with specificity the material sought.

# Attorneys' Fees

Congress approved legislation in 1985 allowing individuals, small businesses and certain local governments to collect attorneys' fees when they prevailed in legal disputes with federal agencies. Under the new law (HR 2378 — PL 99-80), the U.S. government would not have to pay any fees if it proved its position in a particular case was "substantially justified."

The final version of the bill represented a compromise that had the support of the administration, various business groups and the House and Senate Judiciary committees. A similar bill had been pocket-vetoed in 1984 by President Reagan because of provisions that he said would require the government, in order to avoid paying a fee award, to justify every step of the process in bringing a lawsuit or administrative proceeding. The 1985 version was changed so that the government would have to justify an agency's position only at the administrative level or in court. *(Congress and the Nation Vol. VI, p. 709)*

## Background

Historically in U.S. jurisprudence each party in litigation bore its own legal expenses. But as early as 1875, when the first fee-award provision was approved as part of a civil rights law, Congress recognized that citizens should not have to pay legal fees to enforce rights guaranteed to them by law. While fee provisions helped citizens fight the government on an equal footing, they also were a boon to lawyers. Some fee awards totaled millions of dollars and regularly ran into thousands of dollars, Justice Department figures showed.

A 1975 Supreme Court decision had prompted a spate of new fee provisions. In *Aleyska Pipeline Service Co. v. Wilderness Society,* the court ruled that without specific authorization from Congress, courts could not award attorneys' fees. Before that ruling, lawyers believed courts could award fees when they determined that prevailing litigants were enforcing important rights. But the high court rejected that idea, stating that it was difficult for the courts, without legislative guidance, to consider some statutes important and others unimportant for the purpose of awarding attorneys' fees.

Within a year of the 1975 ruling Congress cleared the Civil Rights Attorneys' Fees Awards Act (PL 94-559), which allowed fees to prevailing parties in suits to enforce all civil rights laws passed since 1866. And in 1980 Congress cleared the Equal Access to Justice Act (PL 96-481), which allowed individuals and small businesses to collect attorneys' fees when they prevailed in legal disputes with the federal government. Many other laws also permitted attorneys' fees awards, covering areas from black lung compensation to antitrust challenges and consumer product safety to environmental protection. *(Congress and the Nation Vol. IV, p. 607; Congress and the Nation Vol. V, p. 346)*

Virtually all of these laws gave judges great discretion in making awards, specifying only that lawyers' fees be "reasonable." But that was open to wide interpretation, and in 1982 the administration sought to impose a $75 per hour cap on legal fees under civil rights and other laws. In 1984 it sought to write such a cap into law, but Congress did not approve the legislation. A 1985 survey revealed that private attorneys hired by more than 20 federal government agencies were paid at least $50 million in 1983-84, at rates as high as $285 per hour.

## Legislative History

The House Judiciary Committee reported HR 2378 on May 15 (H Rept 99-120). An amendment to expand coverage of fee awards to Social Security recipients was rejected on a 12-19 vote. The amendment would allow fee recoveries for recipients who prevailed after their cases were remanded to the agency in an administrative proceeding. (The measure did allow recovery of fees in such cases if they were settled in court.) The House easily passed the bill June 24 as approved in committee.

To speed enactment, HR 2378 was placed directly on the Senate calendar without first going to the Judiciary Committee. The Senate passed the bill without amendment July 24, clearing the legislation.

### Major Provisions

As signed into law, Aug. 5, 1985, HR 2378 (PL 99-80):
● Made permanent the authorization for awarding attorneys' fees to individuals, small businesses and certain local governments that prevailed in legal disputes with the government.
● Required fees to be paid by the agency that lost the case, from any funds available to it.
● Exempted the government from paying attorneys' fees when its position was "substantially justified."
● Defined "position of the government" to mean the government's action or non-action in an administrative or court proceeding. The determination of the government's position would be based on the record made at the adversary proceeding or at the proceeding to award attorneys' fees.
● Made eligible for fee awards individuals with a net worth of $2 million or less at the time the adversary adjudication was initiated, and small businesses or local governments with a net worth of $7 million or less and no more than 500 employees.

Under the 1980 law, the limits had been $1 million for individuals and $5 million for small businesses and local governments.
● Allowed private litigants to appeal a decision on attorneys' fees to a federal court within 30 days of the fee determination.
● Required an attorney who collected a fee under this law in a Social Security case to use that amount to offset any fee he was awarded under the Social Security Act for handling the same case.

This provision was designed to prevent "double dipping" by lawyers.

## Sentencing Commission

Congress cleared legislation (HR 3837 — PL 99-217) Dec. 18, 1985, extending for one year the deadline by which a government sentencing commission had to set guidelines for establishing penalties and punishments in federal crimes.

The House passed HR 3837 on Dec. 16, and the Senate cleared the bill Dec. 18.

The commission was charged with writing guidelines that judges were required to follow in sentencing. The intent of the guidelines was to lessen the disparity in punishments for similar crimes.

The commission was created under a 1984 measure (PL 98-473) that made sweeping changes in federal criminal laws. Sentencing reform was a primary objective of PL 98-473, which also included tougher bail and drug laws and restrictions on the insanity defense. (Congress and the Nation Vol. VI, p. 698)

The 1984 law required the guidelines to be written within 18 months of enactment. But the task took longer than expected, and the commission asked Congress for an extension. Under PL 99-217, the commission was given until mid-April 1987 to finish drafting the guidelines.

Congress earlier in 1985 had cleared legislation (HR 1847 — PL 99-22) making minor changes in the commission in order to lessen the burden on sitting federal judges. Under the 1984 law three of the seven commission members had to be active judges. HR 1847 modified this requirement to allow judges in "senior" status to serve on the board. Such judges handled a variety of cases but were not in regular active service. The U.S. Judicial Conference, the policy-making arm of the federal judiciary, had expressed concern about the effect on the courts' dockets if even three active judges were taken out of service to work on the commission.

HR 1847 was passed by the House April 2 and by the Senate April 3.

## Affirmative Action/Procurement

Disputes in Congress over the adequacy of the Justice Department's enforcement under a 1984 law intended to promote competition in federal procurement and the department's alleged failure to fully enforce affirmative action plans stymied action on legislation authorizing programs for the Justice Department for fiscal 1986.

The House Judiciary Committee May 15, 1985, reported a fiscal 1986 authorization bill (HR 2348 — H Rept 99-113) that included new restrictions on department activities. Committee Democrats were angry at the department's refusal to enforce a "competition in contracting" law and its attempts to scale back affirmative action remedies for past discrimination against women and minorities. HR 2348 was never brought to the floor for House consideration.

The Senate Judiciary Committee did not complete action on a related Justice Department authorization bill (S 1065) that also got tangled up in a dispute over the department's performance in enforcing affirmative action plans.

### House Committee Amendments

By a 21-12 vote largely along party lines, the committee adopted an amendment barring any expenditures by the attorney general's office in fiscal 1986 unless the attorney general directed federal agencies to enforce the 1984 Competition in Contracting Act. That law allowed an unsuccessful bidder for a federal contract to file a protest with the General Accounting Office (GAO), and the GAO was authorized to suspend the awarding of the contract until the challenge was resolved. (Congress and the Nation Vol. VI, p. 790)

Administration officials contended the law unconstitutionally breached the separation of powers between the branches of government. They said GAO was a legislative office that had no constitutional authority to compel an executive branch agency to act in a particular way. Congressional legal experts insisted the GAO was not a legislative agency, even though it performed studies for Congress, because its head was appointed by the president and confirmed by the Senate, like any executive agency chief.

Attorney General Edwin Meese III told Judiciary

## Reynolds Rejection

The Senate Judiciary Committee June 27, 1985, decisively rejected the nomination of William Bradford Reynolds to be associate attorney general, the third-ranking post in the Justice Department.

Reynolds was head of the department's civil rights division and remained in that job. It was the decisions he made there, and the way he defended them at his confirmation hearings, that led to his rejection for the higher position. As associate attorney general, Reynolds would have been in charge of all civil law matters.

The Judiciary Committee first refused, 8-10, to report the nomination favorably. It then tied 9-9 on motions to report it without recommendation or with an unfavorable recommendation. The tie vote prevented the nomination from coming before the full Senate. What ultimately swung key committee members against Reynolds were conflicts between his testimony and information provided by other witnesses and by documents from his own department regarding certain decisions he had made.

In his confirmation hearings, Reynolds defended his record and claimed that in several controversial voting rights cases he had talked with civil rights lawyers before making the decisions they disliked — decisions that in some cases overrode the recommendations of his own staff. However, civil rights lawyers challenged his assertions.

Critics claimed Reynolds had failed to enforce civil rights laws — particularly the Voting Rights Act — and had misapplied federal court decisions to suit his own policy ends. President Reagan contended that some members of the Judiciary Committee "chose to use the confirmation process to conduct an ideological assault" on Reynolds.

In a move that angered Democrats on the Senate Judiciary Committee, Attorney General Edwin Meese III in 1987 gave Reynolds additional duties and the title "counselor to the attorney general," a post not requiring Senate confirmation.

has the 'obligation' to revise or rescind any law which is inconsistent with his interpretation of the Constitution."

The other restriction in HR 2348 barred the department from reopening any litigation that had resulted in a court order establishing numerical goals and quotas "to remedy illegal discrimination." The section also established new procedures the department had to follow to open up any "consent decree" reached among parties in a civil rights suit.

William Bradford Reynolds, head of the department's Civil Rights Division, was an outspoken opponent of numerical goals and quotas and had moved aggressively to curtail the use of such remedies. *(Reynolds, box, this page)*

The Supreme Court had ruled 6-3 in June 1984 that federal judges could not override a valid seniority system in making layoffs, even to preserve the jobs of black workers hired under a court-approved affirmative action plan.

That decision, in *Firefighters Local Union No. 1784 v. Stotts,* left considerable confusion in legal circles about the permissible boundaries of affirmative action plans, but Reynolds interpreted the ruling broadly. He asserted that the decision meant federal courts "may not require or permit race- or gender-conscious hiring, promotion or layoff quotas" as a remedy for discrimination. *(Court ruling, Congress and the Nation Vol. VI, p. 726)*

After the *Stotts* decision, the department sent letters to 50 jurisdictions asking them to modify substantially consent decrees that included numerical goals and quotas as a remedy for past discrimination.

The Justice Department also took three cities to court in an effort to remove hiring goals from consent decrees requiring the jurisdiction to bring more women, blacks and Hispanics into municipal jobs.

In response, Don Edwards, D-Calif., drafted provisions in HR 2348 to restrict any future attempts to modify affirmative action agreements.

One of the provisions inserted by Edwards barred the Justice Department from reopening any affirmative action decree unless the appeals court governing the district court had previously endorsed the department's claim that goals or quotas to remedy employment discrimination were improper. A second section barred the attorney general from seeking to modify a consent decree in civil rights cases unless certain specific conditions were met.

## Civil Rights

A dispute over abortion stalled action during the 99th Congress on legislation to overturn a 1984 Supreme Court decision that restricted enforcement of four federal civil rights laws.

The bill (HR 700) would reverse the court's decision in *Grove City College v. Bell,* which narrowed the coverage of Title IX of the 1972 Education Act Amendments and three other civil rights laws. Title IX banned sex discrimination in educational institutions that received federal funding. But the court said that provision of the law applied only to a particular education "program or activity" receiving the federal aid, not the entire institution. *(Court decision, Congress and the Nation Vol. VI, p. 735)*

Civil rights proponents and their allies in Congress charged that the court had misread Title IX, that Congress had intended an entire educational institution to be barred from discriminating if any of its components received federal aid.

members during an oversight hearing in April that the department would not enforce the law even though its constitutionality was upheld March 27 by a federal district court in New Jersey. Meese said the court was "not competent" to rule on the law's validity.

Jack Brooks, D-Texas, sponsored the provision intended to force adherence to the contracting act. Brooks was chairman of the Government Operations Committee, which wrote the 1984 law. He said the administration's actions "strike at the very heart of our constitutional form of government. In effect, the president has decreed that he

The ruling also restricted enforcement of three other laws: Title VI of the 1964 Civil Rights Act, Section 504 of the Rehabilitation Act of 1973 and the Age Discrimination Act of 1975. All three contained language similar to Title IX pertaining to discrimination by institutions receiving federal assistance.

The Education Department's Office of Civil Rights had ended or restricted the force of dozens of anti-discrimination lawsuits in the wake of the court's 1984 ruling.

In 1985 two House committees — Education and Labor and Judiciary — by wide margins approved legislation to restore the full reach, or broad interpretation, of the four laws. But HR 700 (H Rept 99-963, Parts I and II) was never considered by the full House because of the abortion controversy. Related Senate bills remained stuck in the Labor Committee.

The abortion dispute in HR 700 centered on assertions by the Catholic Conference that provisions of the legislation could broaden abortion rights, forcing Catholic hospitals that received federal money, for example, to perform abortions. Sponsors of HR 700 disputed this interpretation, asserting that the measure merely restored to their previous scope the four civil rights laws in question. *(Abortion, p. 574)*

In 1984 the House had passed similar legislation to reverse the court's ruling, but that measure died in the Senate. *(Congress and the Nation Vol. VI, p. 708)*

The issue was considered again in the 100th Congress, and new legislation reversing the Supreme Court's decision ultimately was enacted into law in March 1988 over President Reagan's veto. *(100th Congress action, p. 763)*

# School Prayer

The controversial issue of prayer in the public schools confronted Congress in two guises in 1985, but as in previous years advocates failed to win enactment of any legislation permitting school prayer. There was no action on the prayer issue in 1986.

The Senate on Sept. 10 decisively rejected legislation (S 47) designed to allow organized, recited prayer in the public schools. S 47, sponsored by Sen. Jesse Helms, R-N.C., would facilitate school prayer by prohibiting the federal courts — including the Supreme Court — from hearing cases involving prayer in public schools. If a state or local government chose to adopt a policy allowing prayer, opponents would not have any means of challenging it in the federal courts.

Related efforts to enact legislation proposing a constitutional amendment allowing individual or group silent prayer in public schools also failed to win congressional approval in 1985. A measure was approved by the Senate Judiciary Committee, but it was never considered by the full Senate. No action was taken in the House on several constitutional amendments submitted to the Judiciary Committee.

The Supreme Court since 1962 had barred virtually all forms of public school prayer on the ground that they violated the Constitution's First Amendment, which says government "shall make no law respecting an establishment of religion."

Helms had first introduced his school prayer legislation in 1979 in the form of a non-germane amendment to a bill establishing the Department of Education. It caught school prayer opponents by surprise, and the proposal was adopted by the Senate. It subsequently died in the House, however. A similar Helms proposal was considered in 1982 when the Senate debated an unrelated debt ceiling bill, but this time the amendment was tabled by a 51-48 vote. In all, the Senate had considered school prayer measures on 10 occasions since 1979.

## Organized School Prayer Bill

Helms in 1985 bypassed the Senate Judiciary Committee and had S 47 placed directly on the Senate calendar. The bill was considered on Sept. 10 and decisively tabled (killed) by a **key vote of 62-36 (R 24-28; D 38-8)**. The vote marked the lowest level of Senate support for a school prayer proposal since the Helms bill was first debated in 1979. The Helms bill had the backing of President Reagan. *(1985 key votes, p. 933)*

Opponents called S 47 a "court-stripping" measure and contended it represented an unconstitutional exercise of congressional authority. In contrast to previous years, the debate was short and desultory. Both Helms and Sen. Lowell P. Weicker Jr., R-Conn., who led the opposition to the bill, agreed the subject had been discussed so much in recent years there was no need for lengthy debate. Sen. Barry Goldwater, R-Ariz., who had moved twice in 1982 to kill an earlier Helms prayer bill, chided Helms for bringing up the issue again. Goldwater said he was "surprised that [Helms] . . . decided to outlaw the Supreme Court from our life."

Leaders of both parties in the Senate said the vote tally reflected changed political circumstances. Weicker contended the public was "becoming more sensitive" to the issues involved in the prayer fight. "The more times the television preachers go ahead and talk about what Congress ought to do, the more people realize it is these people who are bringing government into religion, and they don't want it," he said.

## Proposed Constitutional Amendment

The Senate Judiciary Committee Oct. 3, 1985, approved a proposed constitutional amendment (S J Res 2 — S Rept 99-165) to allow silent prayer in the public schools. Committee approval was by a 12-6 vote. S J Res 2 was never brought to the Senate floor, however, and the proposal died at the end of the 99th Congress. Proposed constitutional amendments require the approval of a two-thirds majority in each chamber of Congress and then must be ratified by three-fourths (38) of the states to take effect. In 1984 several proposed school prayer amendments were rejected by the Senate. *(Congress and the Nation Vol. VI, p. 572)*

The 1985 version stated: "Nothing in this Constitution shall be construed to prohibit individual or group silent prayer or reflection in public schools. Neither the United States nor any state shall require any person to participate in such prayer or reflection nor shall they encourage any particular form of prayer in schools."

S J Res 2 was drafted in response to a June 1985 decision by the Supreme Court that struck down an Alabama law allowing a minute of silence in the schools for "meditation or voluntary prayer." Although the constitutional amendment had considerable support in the committee, it did not go far enough for fundamentalist groups such as the Moral Majority, which favored the Helms bill allowing organized, recited prayer in the schools. *(Supreme*

*Court decision, Congress and the Nation Vol. VI, p. 703)*

In the House, several proposed constitutional amendments allowing some form of school prayer were pending in the Judiciary Committee, but no action was taken on any of them in the 99th Congress. The panel had consistently opposed such measures in the past.

# Child Abuse, Pornography

Bills directed at the growing problems of child abuse and child pornography were enacted in 1986.

● S 140 (PL 99-401), cleared Aug. 12, was intended to help states deal with child abuse, especially sexual abuse. It authorized federal assistance to states that enacted reforms making it easier to prosecute and convict persons who sexually abused children.

Under S 140, the secretary of health and human services could make grants to states that took steps to improve their investigation and prosecution of child abuse cases. To remain eligible for the grants, states would have to implement suggested reforms. Some $2.7 million from the Crime Victims Funds would be made available immediately, increasing in subsequent years to $10 million.

The Senate originally passed S 140 (S Rept 99-123) on Aug. 1, 1985. It was sponsored by Sen. Paula Hawkins, R-Fla., who disclosed in 1984 that she had been a victim of child abuse. *(Background, Child Abuse Prevention Act Amendments of 1984, Congress and the Nation Vol. VI, p. 606)*

The House passed an amended version Aug. 4, 1986. Subsequently, the Senate agreed to the House changes Aug. 12, clearing the measure.

● H J Res 738 (PL 99-591), the fiscal 1987 continuing appropriations resolution, cleared Oct. 17, included provisions that strengthened federal laws against child pornography by increasing penalties for repeat offenders and providing victims an opportunity to get compensation from those who exploited them.

The penalty for a second child pornography conviction was increased to five years from two years. In addition, the child pornography provisions of H J Res 738 gave victims who were minors the right to sue for damages anyone who enticed or forced them into helping to produce pornographic materials. A minor was entitled to a minimum of $50,000 and attorneys' fees. *(Appropriations bill, p. 57)*

# Communications Privacy

In legislation cleared Oct. 2, 1986, Congress extended privacy protection to communications transmitted by new forms of transmission. Existing federal privacy guarantees applying to conventional telephones were expanded to cover cellular telephones that operated by high-frequency radio waves, and transmissions by private satellite, paging devices and "electronic mail" — messages transmitted by and stored in computers.

HR 4952 (PL 99-508) made violators of communications privacy regulations subject to fines and prison terms. Government officials would have to get approval through the courts before they could intercept any "high-tech" communications.

The bill was the result of two years of negotiations among the American Civil Liberties Union (ACLU), the electronics industry, the Justice Department and members of Congress. Many groups had an interest in ensuring communications privacy. The ACLU said protections were needed to prevent eavesdropping and abuse. Industry groups argued that without such protections consumers would lose interest in these new forms of communication. The Justice Department at first opposed the privacy legislation out of concern it would tie the hands of law enforcement officials. But a compromise eventually was reached that met the Reagan administration's objections.

The legislation expanded and updated a 1968 law (PL 90-351) that specified when and how the government could wiretap conventional telephones. *(Background, Congress and the Nation Vol. II, p. 323; Congress and the Nation Vol. III, p. 266)*

The House passed HR 4952 (H Rept 99-647) June 23. The Senate passed it Oct. 1, amending it to conform with an almost identical bill (S 2575 — S Rept 99-541). The House then accepted the Senate version, completing congressional action.

## Major Provisions

As cleared, HR 4952:

● **Definitions and Exemptions.** Rewrote the 1968 wiretap law to protect "electronic communications" and "electric communications systems."

● Defined electronic communications to include "any transfer of signs, signals, writing, images, sounds, data or intelligence of any nature" that was transmitted "in whole or in part by wire, radio, electromagnetic, photoelectronic or photo-optical system that affects interstate or foreign commerce."

● Defined electronic communications system to mean any wire, radio, electromagnetic, photo-optical or photo-electronic facilities for the transmission of electronic communications, and any computer facilities or related electronic equipment for the electronic storage of such communications.

● Exempted from coverage — and thus left unprotected from intrusion — any radio communication that was "readily accessible to the general public."

Also exempted were the radio portion of a cordless telephone communication, which was transmitted between the cordless telephone handset and the base unit; any communication made through a tone-only paging device; communications between amateur radio operators; general mobile radio services; marine and aeronautical communications systems; police, fire, civil defense and other public safety radio communications systems; and specified satellite transmissions.

● Protected radio signals in several instances: if the signal were scrambled or put into code that was "encrypted"; if the signal's frequency were changed to one withheld from general use by the Federal Communications Commission; if the signal were transmitted through a common carrier, such as a cellular telephone company, that served the public; or if the signal were transmitted via specific radio frequencies set out in the bill.

● **Private Interception.** Made it illegal for individuals intentionally to intercept electronic communications as defined in the bill.

● Made the offense a felony with a penalty of a fine, a prison term of up to five years or both when the interception was for any illegal purpose, such as gathering stock information for insider trading; was for direct or indirect commercial gain; or was an interception of a scrambled or encrypted signal. Fines could range up to $10,000 if the interception was for commercial advantage.

● **Government Interception.** Allowed the government to intercept electronic communications after obtaining a court order. A judge could grant the order after he had determined that the interception "may provide or has provided" evidence of any federal felony.

● Made it a felony for any person to divulge information about a possible communication interception by the government in order to obstruct, impede or prevent such interception.

● **Stored Communications.** Protected the privacy of stored communications, either before or after delivery if a copy was kept.

● Made it a misdemeanor to break into any electronic system holding copies of messages either before or after delivery or to exceed authorized access in the system to alter or obtain the stored messages.

● Provided a fine for a first offense of up to $250,000, a maximum one-year prison term or both, if the offense were committed for commercial advantage or "malicious destruction or damage." There would be a two-year prison term for a second offense.

● Provided a maximum fine of $5,000 or imprisonment of up to six months for an offense that was not for commercial gain or for malicious destruction or damage.

● Allowed the government to require disclosure of copies of electronic mail under certain conditions.

● **Pen Registers, Trap and Trace.** Generally barred government use of "pen registers" and "trap and trace devices" except pursuant to a court order.

● Defined a pen register as a device that recorded or decoded numbers dialed or otherwise transmitted by telephone. Devices used to monitor calls involving billing were not covered.

● Defined a trap and trace device as one that captured an incoming electronic or other impulse and could identify the number from which a call was made.

● Provided a penalty for knowingly violating this section of a fine and imprisonment of up to one year or both.

● Required a government agency seeking a court order to use a pen register or trap and trace device to certify that the information "likely to be obtained is relevant to an ongoing criminal investigation being conducted by the applying government agency."

## Constitutional Convention

The Senate Judiciary Committee approved legislation (S 40) in July 1985 outlining specific procedures for holding constitutional conventions to debate proposed amendments to the Constitution. The committee had approved a similar bill in 1984, but as was the case that year the full Senate in 1985 never acted on the bill. *(Background, Congress and the Nation Vol. VI, pp. 679, 709)*

All 26 amendments to the Constitution had been proposed by Congress and then ratified by at least three-fourths of the states. The other amendment procedure outlined in Article V of the Constitution — through the calling of a constitutional convention upon the approval of two-thirds of the states — had never been used. Article V did not specify procedures for conducting constitutional conventions and was silent on what a convention could debate, how long a state's call for a convention remained in effect, who could be delegates, how many there would be

and who would preside. For example, could a convention debate and propose any constitutional amendment or only proposals specifically approved by two-thirds of the states that called a constitutional convention? Unless procedures were established, some member of Congress feared, a convention could become a "runaway" session that would expose the entire Constitution to amendment.

S 40 (S Rept 99-135), reported Sept. 10, specified the number of delegates from each state, how long a state's call for a convention would be valid (seven years) and how long a convention could last (six months), unless extended by Congress. In requesting Congress to convene a convention, the states would be required to specify the subject matter of the proposed amendments to be considered. No amendment could be considered that differed from the subject matter stated in the resolution adopted by the states calling for a convention. The Speaker of the House and president pro tempore of the Senate would convene the convention and preside until convention delegates elected their own presiding officer.

There was considerable opposition to some of the committee's recommendations. Some groups objected that the delegate selection rules violated the Supreme Court's one-person, one-vote rule. And there was uncertainty about whether Congress had the authority to limit the scope of a convention.

There was no further action on the issue in the 99th Congress.

# Other Legislation

## Marriage Fraud

HR 3737 (PL 99-639), cleared Oct. 18, 1986, increased the penalties for sham marriages used to gain entry into the United States. The legislation established a fine of up to $250,000 and up to five years in prison for those who committed marriage fraud. It made a fraud conviction grounds for deportation. A two-year conditional-permanent resident status was created for alien spouses and their immediate relatives. By the end of the two-year period, spouses would have to file a petition, under penalty of perjury, that their marriage had been legal, was still intact and was not aimed at evading the U.S. immigration laws.

## Judges' Survivor Benefits

HR 3570 (PL 99-336), cleared May 22, 1986, increased benefits for surviving spouses and children of deceased federal judges. HR 3570 allowed a survivor of a judge who had served a minimum of 18 months on the federal bench to receive at least 25 percent of the judge's annual salary. Previously, there had been no minimum survivor benefit. The maximum survivor benefit was increased to 50 percent, from 40 percent. In 1986 district court judges' annual salary was $78,700; appeals court judges' salary was $83,200 and Supreme Court justices' was $104,100 (the chief justice made $108,400).

To help pay for the increased benefits, the bill increased to 5 percent from 4.5 percent of salary judges' contributions to a survivor fund. The government's contribution to the fund could not exceed 9 percent of a judge's salary.

## Computer Tampering

HR 4718 (PL 99-474), cleared Oct. 6, 1986, expanded and clarified federal laws prohibiting computer fraud. The bill was aimed at stopping persons who illegally gained access to computer files for the purpose of defrauding the government. HR 4718 made it a felony, punishable by five years in prison, to "access," or enter, a "federal interest" computer without authorization in order to alter or damage information stored there or to obtain anything of value. Federal interest computers were defined as those owned or used by the federal government or a federally insured financial institution, or used in interstate communication. The law covered computers used by stockbrokers registered with the Securities and Exchange Commission.

The bill also made it a felony to illegally enter and maliciously damage such computers or to tamper with computerized medical records. And the legislation established a misdemeanor for "pirate bulletin board" activities, in which computer "pirates" displayed passwords to computers for others to use. The government could prosecute only when the passwords were to federal computers or computers that affected interstate or foreign commerce.

## Bankruptcy Court Expansion

HR 5316 (PL 99-554), cleared Oct. 3, 1986, authorized 52 new federal bankruptcy judges to help eliminate a backlog in bankruptcy cases. The increase brought the total of such judges to 284. HR 5316 also expanded a 1978 pilot bankruptcy trustee program, operated by the Justice Department, to speed up the handling of cases. The Judicial Conference, the policy-making arm of the federal judiciary, opposed the expansion of the trustee program, contending that the bankruptcy courts, not the Justice Department, should supervise bankruptcy cases. (1978 action, Congress and the Nation Vol. V, p. 723)

The bill also amended the bankruptcy laws to permit small farmers to reorganize without the consent of their creditors, as was required under existing law. The intent of the change was to grant family farmers the same rights enjoyed by small business men. It was hoped that this would save many financially stricken farmers from having to liquidate. (Background, p. 516)

## Nuclear Plant Security

S 274 (S Rept 99-143), passed by the Senate Oct. 3, 1985, would allow companies that owned nuclear power plants to use FBI criminal history files to conduct background checks on persons with access to critical areas of the plants. The bill would give plant operators more complete criminal histories of persons before deciding whether employees should have access to such areas of a plant.

According to the Nuclear Regulatory Commission (NRC), there were 85 operating nuclear plants in the United States as of 1985 and construction permits for 37 others. The NRC said it had investigated more than a dozen incidents of suspected sabotage by plant employees. A commission report noted that between 1974 and 1982 there were 32 possibly deliberate acts of sabotage at 24 reactors and reactor construction sites.

There was no House action on the legislation in the 99th Congress.

## Military Malpractice Suits

HR 3174 (H Rept 99-288), passed by the House Oct. 7, 1985, would allow active-duty military personnel to sue the federal government for medical or dental malpractice in government facilities. The legislation was prompted by increasing concern in Congress about incidents of medical malpractice at military hospitals.

In a 1950 Supreme Court decision, Feres v. United States, members of the armed forces were barred from suing for injuries suffered while on active duty. Yet civilians with access to government medical facilities, including dependents of active-duty service members and retired military personnel, were allowed to do so. HR 3174 would not change substantive personal injury law but would give service members the right to seek damages for certain types of injuries not related to combat.

The Reagan administration opposed the bill, contending that the Feres decision was correct in barring active-duty personnel from filing malpractice suits and that to overturn it would disrupt military operations.

There was no Senate action on HR 3174 or on a companion bill (S 489) in the 99th Congress.

## Legal Services Corporation

HR 2468 (H Rept 99-448), reported by the House Judiciary Committee Dec. 18, 1985, would reauthorize Legal Services Corporation (LSC) programs for fiscal years 1986-88. The counterpart Senate committee refused to report an authorization bill, and there was no further action on the measure. Senate Judiciary Committee Chairman Orrin G. Hatch, R-Utah, and many other Republicans were ardent critics of the corporation.

The LSC had not had an authorization, or approval of its programs by Congress, since 1979. The corporation, which provided legal help to the nation's poor, had remained in operation despite the Reagan administration's continuing effort to abolish it. For the first time since Reagan took office, the LSC in 1985 had a board of directors confirmed by the Senate.

The LSC stayed in business because Congress continued to appropriate money for the corporation, albeit at a reduced rate, even though its programs had not been formally reauthorized. Funding had dropped from $321 million in fiscal 1981 to $241 million in fiscal 1982-83, $275 million in 1984 and $305 million in 1985. (Background, Congress and the Nation Vol. VI, pp. 677, 683, 695, 705; 1988 action, p. 765)

## Bankruptcy Law

HR 5490 (H Rept 99-917), passed by the House Sept. 29, 1986, and by the Senate with amendments Oct. 3, would clarify the bankruptcy law to specify that companies filing for bankruptcy could not unilaterally terminate a retiree's benefits. The two chambers were unable to reconcile their differences, and the bill died at the end of the 99th Congress.

HR 5490 was the outgrowth of a 1984 law (PL 98-353) that restructured the bankruptcy courts and included provisions establishing special criteria for determining when bankrupt companies could terminate labor contracts. (Background, Congress and the Nation Vol. VI, p. 702)

## Patent Process Protection

HR 2434 (PL 99-607), cleared Oct. 18, 1986, barred any increase in patent fees beyond those needed to compensate for inflation. In 1980 and 1982 Congress revised the patent commissioner's authority to set fees to cover the costs of processing patent and trademark applications so as to recoup 100 percent of patent application and maintenance costs incurred by large firms, while individual inventors, small firms and non-profit organizations paid at a rate designed to recoup 50 percent of such costs. The Reagan administration in 1985 sought to cut the annual appropriation for the U.S. Patent and Trademark Office and rely more heavily on fees to operate the office.

The House (H Rept 99-104) passed HR 2434 June 24, 1985. The Senate (S Rept 99-305) passed an amended version June 6, 1986.

Two other patent-related measures failed to clear in the 99th Congress:

● HR 4899 (H Rept 99-807) would extend U.S. patent protections to some products manufactured abroad. The bill would create patent infringement liability for goods made abroad by a process patented in the United States. Process patents protect the technique, art or method of creating a product. They were especially important in the pharmaceutical and biotechnology industries and to the development of solid-state electronics.

HR 4899 was passed by the House Sept. 16, 1986, and by the Senate with amendments Oct. 3. The Reagan administration opposed the Senate version, and the House Oct. 16 approved a compromise version that had the administration's backing. But the Senate failed to take up the compromise, and HR 4899 was not enacted.

The chief opposition to the bill came from importers of generic drugs, who claimed the bill would lead to a flood of frivolous, time-consuming lawsuits filed by brand-name drug manufacturers. The Senate version made it more difficult than the House-passed bill to file an infringement suit against someone who unknowingly imported or sold products manufactured abroad under a process patent.

● HR 4316 (H Rept 99-788, Parts I and II), passed by the House Sept. 16, 1986, would amend the U.S. patent code to make it apply to activities on all space vehicles under the jurisdiction of the United States. The bill would require anything invested, used or sold in outer space to be covered by U.S. patent law.

## Drug Use by Vehicle Operators

S 850, passed by the Senate Nov. 21, 1985, would make it a federal crime for anyone to operate a train, plane or ship while under the influence of drugs or alcohol. The bill levied a penalty for violating the law of a fine up to $10,000, imprisonment up to five years or both. The Judiciary Committee cited Transportation Department figures in arguing for federal penalties. Since 1975, the committee said, there had been 48 alcohol-related or drug-related train accidents, resulting in at least 41 deaths and more than $34 million in property damage.

There was no further action in either house during the 99th Congress; however the 1988 anti-drug bill (HR 5210 — PL 100-690) provided stiff penalties for such offenses. *(Drug bill, p. 748)*

## Bank Bribery

HR 3511 (PL 99-370), cleared June 26, 1986, narrowed coverage of a 1984 law aimed at curbing bribery in the banking industry.

Banking officials had complained that the 1984 omnibus anti-crime law (PL 98-473) made certain conduct that was appropriate in the banking industry a crime. PL 98-473 barred employees, officers, directors, agents and attorneys in a variety of financial institutions from accepting, in most circumstances, anything of value connected with transactions or the business of the financial institution. Since the law did not require showing of intent to commit a crime, a person could violate it if he paid for a bank official's lunch while the two discussed bank business. *(1984 law, Congress and the Nation Vol. VI, p. 698)*

HR 3511 clarified the law by making it clear that violations occurred only if a person "corruptly" gave, offered or promised anything of value to a bank official or if an official "corruptly" solicited or demanded a benefit in exchange for doing work for the person. The bill specified fines and imprisonment for violations.

The Justice Department strongly opposed the legislation, claiming existing law was adequate, including guidelines to federal prosecutors to curb any abuses that could occur under the 1984 law.

The House passed HR 3511 (H Rept 99-335) Oct. 29, 1985. The Senate passed an amended version Feb. 4, 1986. President Reagan signed the bill Aug. 4.

## Intercircuit Tribunal

S 704 (S Rept 99-431), reported by the Senate Judiciary Committee Sept. 3, 1986, would create a temporary new U.S. court of appeals to help ease the Supreme Court's workload. The bill was backed by Chief Justice Warren E. Burger and five other justices. But it was criticized by some federal appeals judges, who worried that their authority would be diluted and their own workload problems exacerbated by creation of the court, whose members would be taken from the ranks of the appellate judges.

Burger had campaigned for years for ways to lighten the court's workload, which reached a high of 5,311 cases in the 1981-82 term. However, three justices, John Paul Stevens, William J. Brennan Jr. and Thurgood Marshall, said the proposed court — known as the intercircuit tribunal — was not necessary.

There was no further action on S 704 in the 99th Congress. House and Senate subcommittees had approved similar legislation in the 98th Congress, and the House, but not the Senate, had passed a court jurisdiction bill in 1982 as another way for the Supreme Court to better control its growing workload. *(Congress and the Nation Vol. VI, p. 693)*

## Beer Industry Antitrust

S 412 (S Rept 99-259), reported by the Senate Judiciary Committee March 13, 1986, would make it easier for beer distributors to have exclusive markets for their products. S 412 would protect from antitrust challenge a distributor's arrangement with a brewery for an exclusive market as long as competition in the area was not weakened. And it would modify the "rule of reason," which required a judge to determine on a case-by-case basis whether such arrangements were anti-competitive.

The bill was similar to a 1980 law protecting exclusive marketing arrangements in the soft drink industry. The beer industry had sought similar protection since then. *(Congress and the Nation Vol. V, p. 742)*

The legislation was opposed by key committee members, including Chairman Strom Thurmond, R-S.C. It prompted intense opposition from consumer groups, which said it would mean higher beer prices, and also from the Federal Trade Commission. S 412 was never considered by the full Senate, and a companion House bill languished in the House Judiciary Committee.

# 1987-88

A plethora of controversial law and law enforcement issues were debated by the 100th Congress. The first session was preoccupied with the confirmation hearings and eventual Senate rejection of Robert H. Bork, President Reagan's first of three choices to fill a vacancy on the Supreme Court. *(Bork nomination, p. 785)*

Probably the most emotional debates occurred during consideration of a comprehensive anti-drug bill that, as enacted, included the death penalty for major drug traffickers who killed police officers or private citizens during drug transactions, created a Cabinet-level "drug czar," established stiffer penalties for both drug dealers and users and provided more funds for drug treatment and rehabilitation. The most hotly contested battle, however, was over a provision in the original House bill to require a seven-day waiting period before a person could purchase a handgun. The National Rifle Association once again showed its political muscle by successfully lobbying the House to kill the provision.

After a four-year legislative fight, Congress voted to restore four broad civil rights laws — barring certain types of discrimination in education — that had been crippled by a 1984 Supreme Court decision, *Grove City College v. Bell.* First debated in 1985, the legislation was not enacted until Congress overrode a 1988 veto of the measure. Reagan argued that the bill represented an unwarranted expansion of federal power.

Among other key actions were: approval of a bill providing a formal apology by Congress and $1.25 billion in reparations for Japanese-Americans who were forced into internment camps during World War II; a ban on the manufacture, importation, sale or delivery of non-detectable firearms — those mostly made of plastic; an extension and revision of the independent counsel (special prosecutor) law; and a revision of the immigration laws to allow more Irish and citizens from some other countries to enter the United States. Congress set aside a more ambitious revision of U.S. immigration laws.

Finally, Congress once again had to consider formal charges against a U.S. district judge, Alcee L. Hastings of Miami. In August 1988 he was impeached for "high crimes and misdemeanors" stemming from an alleged 1981 bribery scheme and the leak of wiretap information during a 1985 undercover investigation. He was the first judge to be impeached who previously had been acquitted by a jury. It marked the second impeachment of a federal district judge in less than three years.

And Congress postponed until 1989 an impeachment investigation of still another district judge, Walter L. Nixon Jr., of Mississippi.

# Anti-Drug Bill

One of the last major acts of the 100th Congress in election-year 1988 was passage of a comprehensive anti-drug bill. Cleared Oct. 22 after months of debate, HR 5210 (PL 100-690) contained a federal death penalty for major drug traffickers, a controversial provision sought by President Reagan. The bill attempted to dramatize Washington's concern about the nation's drug problem by establishing a Cabinet-level "drug czar" to coordinate federal efforts to stem the flow of drugs into the United States and reduce drug abuse.

The bill incorporated many provisions sought by the Republican and Democratic parties. These generally were intended to demonstrate to the voters that both parties were tough on drugs. The final version eliminated or reduced some of the harsher measures sought by Republicans to crack down on drug use that many Democrats felt could violate citizens' constitutional rights. And HR 5210 was modified enough to provide some protections for those who ran afoul of the law. Nevertheless, the bill included much stiffer penalties for convicted drug dealers, increased the amount of money that could be made available for drug treatment programs, established new penalties for child pornographers, expanded federal drug interdiction programs and required tighter record-keeping in certain banking transactions to combat money laundering.

The bill placed a new emphasis on the need to reduce illegal drug use by incorporating a controversial provision denying certain federal assistance and other welfare benefits to repeat drug-use offenders. In all, the legislation authorized $2.8 billion for the government's war on drugs.

The final version did not include several key provisions backed by the Reagan administration, including language to relax the exclusionary rule — which prohibited evidence seized without a search warrant from being admitted in criminal trials.

## Background

HR 5210 was the second major drug bill to be approved by Congress within two years. In October 1986 lawmakers, responding to growing voter concern over illegal drug use, cleared legislation (HR 5484 — PL 99-570) to beef up federal drug interdiction, eradication, enforcement, education, treatment and rehabilitation efforts. That measure increased the penalties for most federal drug crimes. *(99th Congress action, p. 723)*

Two years before that law was enacted, Congress had passed the omnibus crime bill of 1984 (PL 98-473), which contained numerous provisions to combat drug trafficking. *(Congress and the Nation Vol. VI, p. 698)*

The 1988 legislation was drafted in the midst of the presidential election campaign, with each party accusing the other of not doing enough to combat drugs. Reagan maintained that his administration had brought to bear the full weight of the federal government against drug traffickers and had addressed the demand side of the drug problem through first lady Nancy Reagan's "Just Say No" campaign. But other administration officials conceded that the fight was being lost.

The drug issue initially put Republican presidential candidate George Bush on the defensive because of the Reagan administration's previous ties with Panamanian strongman Gen. Manuel Antonio Noriega, who in 1988 was indicted by a U.S. district court in Miami of drug smuggling and related charges.

Bush subsequently went on the offensive, portraying himself as the tougher candidate on the drug issue and challenging the Democratic Party to commit itself to strong penalties against both drug users and dealers, including the death penalty for drug dealers convicted of murder.

A White House Conference for a Drug-Free America in May 1988 had recommended creation of a drug czar as well as a proposal to commit the armed forces to land and sea surveillance of drug smuggling at U.S. borders. The administration originally opposed both ideas. But the Defense Department agreed to a limited commitment to the war against drug smugglers so long as arrest powers remained the exclusive province of civilian authorities.

## Legislative History

**House Action.** Major anti-drug proposals were introduced early in 1988. House Republicans called for suspending federal benefits for persons convicted of drug dealing or on two drug-possession offenses. Republicans labeled these "user accountability" provisions. They also proposed that, as a precondition for getting federal highway funds, states would have to enact laws suspending a person's driver's license upon conviction of a drug offense.

House Democrats' proposal addressed the AIDS (acquired immune deficiency syndrome) link to drug abuse by proposing creation of treatment programs and promotion of programs to get AIDS warnings to addicts. They called for a federal commitment to expand community-based drug treatment programs and give the armed forces a greater role in protecting U.S. borders from drug smugglers.

Nine House committees contributed major sections to what became the 1988 anti-drug bill (HR 5210). Many sections were approved and reported as separate legislation and then combined into the omnibus bill. In some cases these sections had been proposed as amendments to other bills. For example, the House approved an amendment to a 1988 defense authorization bill that required use of the military to halt the penetration of U.S. borders by aircraft and ships transporting illegal drugs.

The House Banking, Finance and Urban Affairs Committee June 9 approved provisions on money laundering that made it tougher for drug dealers to cover up their financial interests through use of legal financial institutions and markets. The committee imposed a heavy fine on banks that willfully violated Treasury Department regulations requiring that certain in-house customer banking records be kept for five years. Such records were important to the Treasury in establishing a paper trail on money laundering.

The Ways and Means Committee June 9 approved a significant increase in the authorization for the U.S. Customs Service to provide 500 new positions for enforcement and operations. The penalty for failure to report a controlled substance was increased from 200 percent of the value of the product to 1,000 percent.

The House Foreign Affairs Committee June 15 added provisions for international narcotics control efforts, provisions originally added to foreign aid legislation. The panel

## Death Penalty Provision

Enactment of HR 5210 (PL 100-690) in 1988 marked the end of a decadelong effort by proponents of capital punishment to win approval of the death penalty for drug traffickers who murdered people or conspired in the murder of someone. The death penalty also covered persons involved in drugs who killed police officers.

The enacted provision was narrower than a separate death penalty provision passed by the Senate before the drug bill was debated. That version was never considered by the House, whose Judiciary Committee had a history of opposition to capital punishment. A death penalty provision had been rejected when that committee considered HR 5210. It became law only because proponents in September succeeded, on a **299-111 (R 161-9; D 138-102) key vote**, in winning approval of a death penalty amendment to HR 5210 on the House floor. *(1988 key votes, p. 981)*

The Senate had approved the death penalty as early as 1984. The 1988 version was championed by Sen. Alfonse M. D'Amato, R-N.Y., who waged a successful campaign to force the Senate to vote on a separate death penalty bill (S 2455) in June. That debate showed clearly that a majority of the Senate favored the provision. A proposal to substitute life imprisonment without the possibility of parole for drug kingpins was rejected by better than a 2-1 margin. Other attempts to narrow the reach of the death penalty, including one to make it apply only when drug dealers killed police officers, were easily rejected before the bill itself was approved by a **65-29 (R 37-6; D 28-23) key vote**.

also recommended that the State Department revoke passports of convicted drug violators and that economic and military aid be withheld from countries known to be involved in drug trafficking.

The Education and Labor Committee June 23 added to HR 5210 provisions of a bill (HR 4872 — H Rept 100-779) dealing with drug abuse education, prevention and rehabilitation targeted at juvenile drug offenders. A major dispute developed over whether to bar federal school loans to convicted drug users. An amendment to make persons ineligible for such assistance for five years upon conviction of two or more drug-possession offenses or one offense to distribute drugs was rejected, 13-19.

The Merchant Marine and Fisheries Committee's contribution (HR 4658 — H Rept 100-814, Part I), June 21, was aimed at improving the Coast Guard's drug enforcement activities. Additional authorizations for fiscal 1989 amounting to $346 million were approved. The committee proposed giving the Coast Guard additional powers to prosecute U.S. citizens aboard vessels seized with drugs outside U.S. territorial waters, particularly if another na-

# Juvenile Justice Act

Both the House and Senate in 1988 passed legislation extending the Juvenile Justice and Delinquency Prevention and Runaway and Homeless Youth Acts (PL 93-415). However, the bill (HR 1801) never cleared. Instead, its provisions were incorporated in the omnibus anti-drug bill (HR 5210 — PL 100-690). The acts were reauthorized through fiscal 1992.

The Reagan administration opposed HR 1801 as unnecessary, arguing that its goals had been achieved to the extent practicable and that the money could be put to better use within the Justice Department. *(Previous reauthorization, Congress and the Nation Vol. VI, p. 700)*

The House had passed HR 1801 following a contentious debate over an amendment to require any person or organization receiving money under the bill to provide a drug-free work place. The debate proved to be the forerunner of a raucous floor battle on the issue when the House took up the drug bill in August. The originator of the idea, Rep. Robert S. Walker, R-Pa., aggressively promoted the provision in debates on several bills. His success was related directly to its use as a hot election-year issue. He got his way by repeatedly threatening to embarrass his colleagues with soft-on-drug charges. In addition to the detailed provision in HR 5210, shorter versions became law in five other bills.

tion did not intend to prosecute. The Coast Guard was authorized to prosecute the owners of a ship based on their citizenship rather than on where the boat was registered, in order to prevent drug smugglers from sinking a boat to hide its ownership.

The panel also adopted a provision to limit use of the Reagan administration's "zero tolerance" policy by restricting the power of the Coast Guard and Customs Service to seize boats if there was no evidence of wrongdoing by the owners and operators. The provision's backers said the policy often penalized innocent boat owners for the actions of passengers and crew members.

The Public Works and Transportation Committee's provisions (HR 4844 — H Rept 100-891), approved June 21, were aimed at enhancing the role of the Federal Aviation Administration (FAA) in assisting law enforcement agencies' attempts to stop the flow of drugs coming in through the nation's airspace. The new regulations would aid in the prosecution of pilots and aircraft owners using small planes for drug smuggling. Penalties for violations of aircraft registration requirements were increased.

The Energy and Commerce Committee on June 28 approved HR 4907 (H Rept 100-927), which increased funding authorizations for programs to combat drug and alcohol abuse through the Alcohol, Drug Abuse and Mental Health Administration. It also replaced two existing drug abuse prevention programs with block grants, some of which would help states treat intravenous drug abusers as a way of preventing the spread of AIDS. States would be required to institute mandatory AIDS testing and counseling of persons convicted of prostitution, sexual assault or intravenous drug use. The committee also approved language subjecting the nation's railroad workers to random drug and alcohol testing.

The Government Operations Committee approved its drug-related provisions (HR 4719 — H Rept 100-829) on June 29. A controversial section required recipients of federal grants and contracts to maintain drug-free work places by following certain guidelines. It required a contractor to prepare a policy statement prohibiting drug use in the work place and specified appropriate punishment for violators. Employees would have to certify that they understood the policy, and employers would have to establish drug-free awareness programs. Contracts awarded by the federal government could be suspended or terminated if the new guidelines were not followed or if too many employees were convicted of violations on the job.

Much of the controversy over the content of the bill developed in the Judiciary Committee, which after contentious markup sessions ordered its bill (HR 4916) reported June 30. The committee was divided in particular over provisions requiring a seven-day waiting period for handgun purchases and prohibiting persons convicted of repeated drug-use offenses from receiving certain federal benefits. The panel also recommended greater government control over chemicals used to process and create drugs, a Cabinet-level drug czar and additional funding for state and local law enforcement and for the federal Drug Enforcement Administration (DEA).

The gun control provision required a seven-day waiting period so that a background check could be run on anyone wanting to purchase a handgun. Though it eventually was approved in committee by voice vote, it generated heated debate by members backing the position of the National Rifle Association (NRA). An NRA substitute, offered by Bill McCollum, R-Fla., requiring the U.S. attorney general to develop a system for identifying any felon attempting to purchase a firearm, was rejected 12-22.

Republican attempts to add the death penalty for major drug traffickers failed on several close votes. Generally, these amendemtns called for the death penalty for persons involved in multiple criminal drug enterprises or whenever a law enforcement official was killed during a drug-related investigation. The initial proposal was rejected on a 17-17 tie vote. Under another rejected version the death penalty could be applied where a drug trafficker had dealt in at least 300 kilos of cocaine, even if no killing occurred. Some members objected that it was unconstitutional because the Supreme Court had ruled that in cases where no death occurred the death penalty could not be used.

An attempt was made to eliminate the section denying certain federal benefits, such as housing, education and job-training loans, to persons convicted of distributing drugs or using drugs twice within a 10-year period. Instead, a substitute was accepted that allowed a drug-use offender who completed a supervised drug rehabilitation program to again receive federal benefits.

The House passed HR 5210 overwhelmingly on Sept. 22 after three weeks of debate. Under a Rules Committee resolution (H Res 521) adopted before floor action began Aug. 11, only 36 of some 150 proposed amendments could

firearms — those made primarily of plastic. The final version of the bill (HR 4445 — PL 100-649) was a compromise between two groups that had been at loggerheads with each other for two years on gun issues: the National Rifle Association (NRA) and the Law Enforcement Steering Committee, a coalition of 11 police groups.

At the time the bill was passed no guns were being made that were made completely of plastic. But the bill's sponsors said the technology for producing such weapons soon would outstrip detection systems, allowing terrorists to smuggle firearms onto airplanes or into government buildings.

The NRA initially opposed the legislation, arguing that it was unnecessary and the first step toward banning handguns. At first this position was backed by Attorney General Edwin Meese III, but the police groups pressured Meese into changing his mind. Meese subsequently directed Justice Department staff to work with the police and the NRA to work out a compromise both could support.

### Legislative History

HR 4445 was reported by the House Judiciary Committee on May 10 (H Rept 100-612) and passed by the full House the same day by a near unanimous vote. The House version originally had been included as a section of the 1988 omnibus drug bill (HR 5210 — PL 100-690). Sponsors later decided they wanted a separate bill and deleted the gun section from HR 5210. *(Drug bill, p. 748)*

The Senate Judiciary Committee on May 12 reported a different version (S 2180). The bill had the unexpected support of the NRA, which determined that the measure would not ban any existing firearms. The Senate passed an amended HR 4445 on May 25. The House agreed to the Senate version with an amendment Oct. 20. The Senate proposed a further amendment Oct. 21, and the House, upon acceptance of the Senate change, cleared the bill the same day.

As signed Nov. 10, 1988, HR 4445 (PL 100-649):

● Banned all guns that failed to trigger detection devices in the same manner as firearms made with 3.7 ounces of stainless steel. Required that all guns be detectable by the cabinet X-ray systems used in airports in the United States. It did not ban any guns already on the market.

● Required federal officials to conduct research and development over one year for improvements in the effectiveness of airport metal detectors and X-ray machinery. After the first year, the secretary of the Treasury was required to amend the test-gun standard to comport with the new technology. The secretary could rewrite the regulations to decrease the weight requirement of the test gun and would have to continually review the state of detection technology to see if further reductions in the test-gun standard were warranted. Once the test-gun standard was lowered, a future Treasury secretary could not raise it.

● Permitted the conditional import of firearms that might otherwise be banned if they were for testing purposes.

● Exempted firearms that might fall below the standard specified in HR 4445 but were used by the military or for intelligence purposes.

● Provided a fine, imprisonment for up to five years, or both, for violations of the law.

# Special Prosecutor Law

Legislation cleared Dec. 2, 1987, extending and revising the Watergate-era law that authorized the appointment of independent counsels (special prosecutors) to investigate alleged wrongdoing by top federal officials. The measure (HR 2939 — PL 100-191) was strongly opposed by the Reagan administration. Nevertheless, the bill received overwhelming support in both chambers, inducing President Reagan to sign the measure despite his misgivings that the bill encroached on executive powers.

The original law established a procedure whereby the attorney general could request a special three-judge court to appoint a special prosecutor to investigate suspected misconduct by high-level executive branch officials. HR 2939 amended the original law by limiting the attorney general's discretion in deciding when to implement the law. And it extended the law for five more years.

The special prosecutor law (PL 95-521) originally was enacted in 1978 in the wake of the Watergate scandal. It was reauthorized (PL 97-409) in 1982 for five years. The special prosecutor was renamed independent counsel in PL 97-409. *(Congress and the Nation Vol. V, p. 829; Congress and the Nation Vol. VI, p. 681)*

The Justice Department opposed both the original law and the revised legislation, contending they violated the separation of powers and thus were unconstitutional. The judicial branch was given power to appoint prosecutors — officers of the executive branch. Reagan said he was disappointed "Congress had not heeded these concerns, apparently convinced that it is empowered to divest the president of his fundamental authority to enforce our nation's laws." But he signed the bill, he said, "in order to ensure that public confidence in government not be eroded while the courts are in the process" of resolving the constitutional issues.

PL 100-191 was almost immediately thrown into question when the U.S. Court of Appeals for the District of Columbia on Jan. 22, 1988, struck down the law as unconstitutional. However, it was upheld by the Supreme Court the following June 29. The high court ruled 7-1, in *Morrison v. Olson*, that the law did not violate the Constitution's separation-of-powers doctrine by encroaching on executive branch prerogatives. *(Supreme Court decision, p. 834)*

As Congress debated HR 2939, several administration officials were under investigation by independent counsels, including Attorney General Edwin Meese III and those involved with the Iran-contra affair. *(Box, p. 756)*

### Legislative History

**House.** HR 2939 was drafted by the House Judiciary Subcommittee on Administrative Law and Governmental Relations. It was approved, with amendments, by the full committee on Sept. 15, 1987, by a 21-14 vote that closely broke along party lines. The bill was reported by the Judiciary Committee Sept. 23 (H Rept 100-316).

The committee approved several amendments, including a new section establishing an ethics code for independent counsels and a series of provisions limiting the discretion of the attorney general in deciding when and whether to initiate an investigation by an independent counsel. The latter were sponsored by committee Democrats and generally opposed by Republican members. The Democrats charged that Meese had subverted the law's intent by declining to proceed with investigations against some Reagan administration officials and by limiting the scope of other probes. Republicans argued that the amendments took too much power away from the attorney general.

A Republican proposal to extend the existing law without change while the constitutional issues were decided by the courts was rejected, as were two other controversial GOP initiatives. One would allow the attorney general to remove an independent counsel from a case for any reason, without appeal; the other would make members of Congress subject to the special prosecutor law. HR 2939 permitted the attorney general to remove the independent counsel "only for good cause, physical disability [or] mental incapacity" and allowed his decision to be overturned by a court if it was "based on error of law or fact." The current special prosecutor law had no authority to target lawmakers for independent counsel investigations.

The House passed the bill Oct. 21 by a wide margin, but only after a lengthy debate touched off by another Republican attempt to add a provision to include members of Congress within the scope of the special prosecutor law. In addition to the Reagan administration's ethics problems, several congressional Democrats also were under fire for ethics violations. The amendment eventually was rejected, 169-243, with only 11 Democrats voting for it.

A critical moment on the House floor occurred when Republican opponents to the legislation called upon Congress to wait for the courts to decide whether the special prosecutor law was constitutional before extending it for five years. A substitute was offered that would extend the law, unchanged, for only one year. The amendment was defeated by a **key vote of 171-245 (R 165-10; D 6-235)**. *(1987 key votes, p. 965)*

Other Republican floor attacks on the bill also were largely unsuccessful. These included attempts to narrow the independent counsel's jurisdiction to investigate certain crimes and delete provisions limiting the attorney general's flexibility in deciding whether to invoke the law. The House did adopt GOP-sponsored amendments renewing the law for five years (instead of making the law permanent, as originally recommended) and specifying a full-time salary of $77,500 annually for the independent counsel.

**Senate.** A Senate Governmental Affairs subcommittee drafted its own version — S 1293 — on June 19, 1987, and the full committee approved it July 1 by a 13-1 vote. It made the special prosecutor law permanent while limiting the attorney general's discretion to determine whether to seek appointment of an independent counsel. The Governmental Affairs Committee reported S 1293 (S Rept 100-123) on July 24.

The Senate Nov. 3 overwhelmingly passed HR 2939 after incorporating the committee's version of the legislation. As in the House, the Senate killed an amendment that would make members of Congress suspected of wrongdoing subject to an independent counsel investigation. A vote on a motion to table (kill) the amendment was agreed to 49-46.

**House-Senate Compromise.** House and Senate conferees reached agreement on a compromise bill Nov. 18. The two versions were identical on most provisions. A five-year extension of the original law was agreed to, and conferees quickly resolved the remaining key differences involving how long government officials would be subject to the law after leaving office, additional investigative authority sought by the independent counsel and the circumstances under which the attorney general could unilaterally close a case and not request an independent counsel.

The final version of HR 2939 (H Rept 100-452) was approved by the Senate Nov. 20 and by the House Dec. 2, completing congressional action.

## Major Provisions

As cleared, HR 2939:

● **Length of Coverage.** Extended from two to three years the period of time individuals subject to independent counsel investigations were covered by the statute after they left their office or position.

● **Information.** Specified that the attorney general could consider only the "specificity of the information received" and the source's credibility in a "threshold inquiry" to determine whether a preliminary investigation (to decide whether to appoint an independent counsel) was warranted.

● **State of Mind.** Prohibited the attorney general from closing a case during the threshold inquiry on the basis of the subject's alleged "state of mind," such as by making a determination that the individual in question lacked criminal intent.

● Prohibited the attorney general from deciding against seeking a special prosecutor because the subject lacked the state of mind to commit the crime unless the attorney general had "clear and convincing evidence" to that effect.

● **Time Limit.** Required the attorney general to determine whether to begin a preliminary investigation within 15 days after first receiving information on the subject's alleged misconduct.

● Allowed the attorney general to close the case if he found that the information was not specific or from a credible source. However, if the attorney general failed to determine the credibility of the information within the 15-day period or determined that further investigation was warranted, he had to begin a preliminary investigation based on the information by the end of such period.

● **Recusal.** Required the attorney general to recuse (or remove) himself from the case if he had a current or recent personal or financial relationship with the subject. The attorney general was required to specify in a written request for recusal why he felt it was necessary to remove himself from the case, and to submit that request to the special three-judge court responsible for appointing independent counsels.

● Designated, in the event of the attorney general's recusal, the next most senior official within the Justice Department who did not have a similar conflict of interest to perform the duties of the attorney general with respect to the case.

● **Notification.** Required the attorney general to inform the special court of the date when the preliminary investigation began. The attorney general then had 90 days in which to decide whether to seek appointment of an independent counsel and a one-time option to extend the preliminary investigation for up to 60 days.

● **Disclosure of Information.** Specified that requirements prohibiting members of the Justice Department or the independent counsel's office from disclosing any materials specific to an ongoing case without the express permission of the special court should not be construed as an authorization to withhold such information from Congress.

● **Congressional Requests.** Required, within 30 days after receiving a request for an independent counsel investigation from the House or Senate Judiciary Committee, or from a majority of either party's members on one of those committees, that the attorney general submit a written report on the status of the investigation to the committee or to the members making the request. The report had to specify whether a preliminary investigation had begun, or when it would begin, and the reasons behind the attorney general's decision to pursue or drop the case.

● Required that the committee or members making a request for an independent counsel investigation receive copies of all documents, materials or memorandums concerning the case supplied to the special court over the course of the preliminary investigation.

● Required the attorney general, upon the request of any congressional committee that had jurisdiction over the independent counsel law, to provide within 15 days the dates on which he received information about alleged criminal misconduct by an executive branch official, as well as information on whether a preliminary investigation was being conducted and when it began, and on whether an independent counsel had been requested and when he was appointed. The requirement applied only to investigations that were a matter of public knowledge.

● **Qualifications of the Independent Counsel.** Required the three-judge court to appoint, upon the request of the attorney general, an independent counsel who would conduct the investigation and any subsequent prosecution in a "prompt, responsible and cost-effective manner" and who would complete the case "without undue delay." The candidate for independent counsel must have had "appropriate experience," such as investigative or prosecutorial experience, or an extensive background in the area of law allegedly violated by the subject.

● **Jurisdiction.** Expanded the independent counsel's jurisdiction, as defined by the court, to include the authority to investigate and prosecute all federal crimes, other than petty offenses, related to the subject already under investigation that were discovered in the process of investigating the original case. Those crimes included "perjury, obstruction of justice, destruction of evidence and intimidation of witnesses."

● Required, if the independent counsel discovered possible criminal violations that did not fall within his prosecutorial jurisdiction, that he inform the attorney general. The attorney general then was required to begin a preliminary investigation into the alleged criminal violation. The preliminary investigation into new allegations of criminal misconduct by a subject already involved in an independent counsel case could not exceed 30 days.

● Allowed the attorney general to request the special court to expand the jurisdiction of the current prosecutor or to appoint a new prosecutor if he decided that another independent counsel investigation was necessary based on new allegations. If the attorney general decided the new information did not warrant another investigation or the extension of the current investigation, the special court did not have the power to override that decision.

● Allowed the special court to ask the attorney general, if he decided during any stage of an investigation to close the case, to provide the court with a complete explanation of the reasons for the attorney general's finding that there were no reasonable grounds to believe that further investigation was warranted.

● **Restitution for Attorneys' Fees.** Required the court to notify the attorney general when the subject of an independent counsel investigation asked to be reimbursed for the cost of hiring a defense attorney. The subject could

---

## Officials Under Inquiry

As President Reagan Dec. 15, 1987, signed HR 2939, the special prosecutor law, officials in his administration were under investigation by independent counsels or standing trial. The day after Reagan signed the bill, former presidential aide Michael K. Deaver became the first person convicted under the special prosecutor law. He was found guilty in federal district court of committing perjury during an investigation of his lobbying activities after he left the White House. On Feb. 11, 1988, another former White House aide, Lyn Nofziger, was convicted of illegal lobbying. (His conviction subsequently was overturned by a federal appeals court panel June 27, 1989.)

An independent counsel also was looking into the role of Marine Corps Lt. Col. Oliver L. North and several other White House officials in the secret sale of arms to Iran to finance the insurgency in Nicaragua. North was found guilty in May 1989 on three felony counts of obstructing Congress, altering documents and taking an illegal gratuity. *(Iran-contra affair, p. 253)*

In addition, Attorney General Edwin Meese III was accused of improper involvement in helping Wedtech Corp., a bankrupt Bronx, N.Y., defense contractor. Independent counsel James C. McKay concluded his inquiry into that case July 5, 1988, by saying that Meese "probably violated the criminal law" in certain instances but that "no prosecution is warranted." *(Details, p. 756)*

---

request reimbursement only when the investigation did not result in his indictment or when the fees would not have been incurred except for the independent counsel investigation.

● Limited reimbursement to cover only "reasonable" attorney fees and required the Justice Department to file a written evaluation of the request for reimbursement.

● Allowed the special court to disclose any information related to the subject's request for reimbursement and the Justice Department's evaluation of the request.

● **Friend-of-the-Court Briefs.** Allowed the court to disclose information on cases involving significant legal issues with ramifications beyond the specific case, in order to allow interested parties to file amicus curiae briefs.

● **Independence.** Specified that the independent counsel and his staff were "separate from and independent of" the Justice Department and therefore not subject to federal conflict-of-interest provisions that defined ethical standards for government employees. HR 2939 set up a separate ethical code for an independent counsel, members of his staff and members of his private-sector law practice.

● **Standards of Conduct.** Prohibited an independent counsel, any member of his staff and any member of his private-sector law firm from representing anyone under investigation by a special prosecutor during the period in which the independent counsel was involved in such an investigation.

• Prohibited, for three years following the conclusion of a case, an independent counsel or any member of his staff from representing the individual who was the subject of the independent counsel's investigation.

• Prohibited, for one year following the conclusion of a case, an independent counsel, any member of his staff or any member of his law firm from representing any individual who was the subject of another independent counsel's investigation or prosecution.

• **Costs.** Required the Justice Department to pay all of the independent counsel's expenses in setting up his office and conducting his investigation or prosecution.

• Required the comptroller general to audit the expenditures of the independent counsel and his office at the conclusion of the counsel's investigation, and to submit a report to the appropriate congressional committees.

• **Reporting Requirements.** Required the attorney general to submit to Congress no later than 30 days after the end of a fiscal year a report on an independent counsel's expenses. The report had to include a statement of all payments made by the Justice Department for the special prosecutor's activities, but it could not reveal the identity or prosecutorial jurisdiction of any counsel unless such information was public knowledge.

• Required an independent counsel to file an expenditure report every six months with the special court.

• Required the independent counsel to file a final report with the special court that included a complete description of the counsel's work, the disposition of the case and reasons for not prosecuting any matter within the counsel's jurisdiction.

• **Removal.** Allowed an independent counsel who was removed from office to appeal to the U.S. District Court for the District of Columbia and, if ordered by the court, gain reinstatement or other "appropriate relief." A special prosecutor could be removed by impeachment and conviction or by the personal action of the attorney general for "good cause, physical disability, mental incapacity or any other condition that substantially impairs the [counsel's] performance."

• **'Sunset' Provision.** Reauthorized for five years, effective upon the date of enactment, the independent counsel law. Cases pending when the law expired would be continued if, in the special prosecutor's opinion, further investigation was warranted.

• **Record-Keeping.** Required that all records connected with an independent counsel investigation be transferred from the counsel's office to the Archives of the United States upon conclusion of the case. The counsel had to identify which records were potential material for a grand jury and which were classified as national security information.

• Allowed the Justice Department access to records for use in ongoing law enforcement investigations or court proceedings if the department submitted a request for such records in writing.

# Patent Law Clarification

A bill (HR 4972 — PL 100-703) cleared in 1988 reauthorizing the activities of the Patent and Trademark Office for fiscal years 1989-91 contained a section directed at the doctrine of "patent misuse" — actions by a patent owner that went beyond those allowed by law in protecting the owner's exclusive marketing rights.

The doctrine was activated when a patent owner accused someone of infringing his patent. The defendant then could claim that the patent owner misused his patent, for example, by seeking a marketing monopoly beyond the 17 years that customarily belonged to patent owners, by fixing prices for a patented item or by forcing third parties to sign agreements not to sell products that competed with the patented item.

Once a judge found that the patent owner had misused his patent, the owner lost his right to enforce his patent protections until the conduct that constituted the misuse stopped and the effects of the misuse were eradicated.

A Senate Judiciary Committee report on a similar bill concluded that judges had been inconsistent in their application of the doctrine and that judges were finding patent misuse even when an owner's conduct had no anti-competitive effect nor caused injury to the patent infringer who had raised the issue.

HR 4972 stated that it was not misuse of a patent to refuse to license use of the patented item. And it was not misuse of a patent to require the purchase of a second product as a condition of using the patented product, unless a judge found that the patent owner controlled enough of the market for the relevant products to keep prices above competitive levels.

As cleared, the bill also provided $117 million for Patent Office operations for fiscal 1989, $125 million for 1990 and $111.9 million for 1991. It also contained provisions to ensure that the public was provided free access to Patent Office files and documents. *(Related legislation, p. 777)*

HR 4972 was passed by the House on Oct. 5 under suspension of the rules and by the Senate with revisions on Oct. 14. The House then approved a compromise version Oct. 20, and the Senate gave final approval Oct. 21.

# Price-Fixing Regulations

Legislation making changes in federal antitrust laws that would benefit consumers ran into administration opposition in 1987 and was not enacted. The measure (HR 585) would promote tougher scrutiny of pricing disputes between manufacturers and retailers.

The House Nov. 9 passed HR 585, to amend the Sherman Antitrust Act regarding so-called vertical price fixing, which occurs when a manufacturer or distributor sets a minimum retail price for a product. But the Senate never considered the measure during the 100th Congress.

Vertical price fixing, also known as resale-price maintenance, was prohibited by the Sherman Act, but decisions by the Supreme Court had created some ambiguity about what constituted sufficient evidence to warrant a jury trial when accusations of price fixing were made. Such complaints usually arose when a distributor decided he wanted to discount a manufacturer's product. And another distributor, usually a much larger one who was unwilling to lower his prices to meet the competition, persuaded the manufacturer to terminate the contract with the distributor selling the product at a discount.

A 1984 Supreme Court decision, *Monsanto Co. v. Spray-Rite Service Corp.*, made it difficult to prove vertical price fixing. The court upheld a $10.5 million judgment against Monsanto, finding that the company improperly terminated its contract with Spray-Rite, which had consistently undercut the prices of other distributors. *(Supreme Court decision, Congress and the Nation Vol. VI, p. 743)*

But the court said that to prove such a violation, the complaining party had to provide either direct or circumstantial evidence showing that the manufacturer and others consciously intended to maintain resale-price levels.

Some antitrust lawyers and their allies in Congress believed that *Monsanto* was incorrectly decided by the court and that it led to confusing results in cases before the federal appeals courts. The chief sponsor of HR 585, Judiciary Committee Chairman Peter W. Rodino Jr., D-N.J., said that the court "seemed to set up an almost impossible evidentiary standard for plaintiffs."

HR 585, in effect, would overturn the *Monsanto* decision and establish specific guidelines for the kind of evidence needed to prove a price-fixing violation.

The Justice Department lobbied against HR 585, contending it would eliminate the "flexible language" of the Sherman Act and replace it with inflexible statutory language on resale-price maintenance. Sponsors of the bill accused the department of undermining the antitrust laws. A provision in HR 585 stated unequivocally that resale-price maintenance in all its forms was illegal per se under the antitrust law.

### Legislative History

The House Judiciary Committee reported HR 585 (H Rept 100-421) Nov. 4, 1987. The committee approved language to protect the right of a defendant to get a dismissal of a discounter's lawsuit in the early states of litigation. The purpose of the amendment was to make sure the defendant manufacturers and retailers could seek summary judgment — dismissal without a full trial — if the evidence presented showed "no inference of concerted action."

The Senate Judiciary Committee reported similar legislation (S 430 — S Rept 100-280) on Feb. 1, 1988. Like the House version, S 430 would make it easier for a plaintiff to prove a price-fixing charge. The committee's bill represented a compromise between Democrats and Republicans that provided a tougher standard of proof than the version introduced by the committee's Democrats.

S 430 would specify what kind of evidence was sufficient for a judge or jury to conclude that there was a concerted effort to fix resale prices. The bill said the plaintiff was allowed to present evidence showing that a manufacturer received "an express or implied suggestion, request or demand" that the manufacturer take steps to curtail or eliminate price competition by the plaintiff. The plaintiff also could attempt to show that because of that suggestion the manufacturer refused to supply the plaintiff some or all of the goods or services he requested. It then was up to the judge or jury to determine whether the manufacturer's action violated antitrust laws.

Senate sponsors of S 430 charged the Reagan administration's Justice Department had not brought a single vertical price-fixing case in six years and actually had intervened on behalf of defendants who were seeking to overturn existing anti-price-fixing rules.

## Lottery Advertising

In legislation cleared Oct. 19, 1988, Congress provided another exemption in a decades-old law banning advertising for most gambling activities.

The bill (HR 3146 — PL 100-625) allowed certain privately run, non-profit gambling enterprises, such as church-sponsored bingo games, to advertise on radio and television as well as through the mails. The new law required such lotteries or games of chance to be legal in the state in which they were being conducted. PL 100-625 took effect 18 months after enactment.

The legislation also allowed advertising of certain activities related to commercial gambling. A travel agency, for example, was allowed to advertise a raffle for a free trip to a resort that had a casino as long as the advertising was for promotional reasons and incidental to the primary business of the commercial organization that ran the ad.

In addition, the legislation expanded advertising rights for state-run lotteries. It allowed states to advertise lists of prizes, although the bill retained an existing prohibition on using the mails for sending lottery tickets, money or other lottery paraphernalia.

### Background

Federal restrictions on lotteries existed since 1895. In 1935 Congress enacted restrictions on broadcasting or mailing of advertisements or information regarding lotteries. After several states established state-run lotteries in the 1960s and 1970s, however, Congress exempted such games from the advertising ban. Sponsors of HR 3146 said a change in the advertising law was necessary to put privately run lotteries on an equal footing with state-run gambling games. *(Congress and the Nation Vol. II, p. 271; Congress and the Nation Vol. IV, p. 591)*

The federal law barring advertising was at the center of two cases pending before the Supreme Court in 1988. Various Minnesota newspapers had challenged the law on constitutional grounds, contending that it in effect barred them from accepting advertising for legal, non-profit games because most newspapers had some mail subscriptions.

### Legislative History

The House passed HR 3146 (H Rept 100-557, Part I) on May 25, 1988. The bill initially had been defeated May 10 under suspension of the rules, a shortcut parliamentary procedure requiring a two-thirds majority vote for passage.

Before passing the bill, some members charged that HR 3146 was a "relief" measure designed to aid Las Vegas and Atlantic City casinos. The House approved an amendment barring advertising of "any casino gambling game conducted or operated by a gambling establishment."

The Senate approved HR 3146 with amendments Oct. 14, and the House agreed to the compromise version Oct. 19, clearing the bill.

## Trademark Protection

Congress in 1988 cleared legislation to make it easier for U.S. companies to protect their trademarks. The bill (S 1883 — PL 100-667) was the product of more than two years of work by the U.S. Trademark Association (USTA), a private group that conducted a study of trademark law.

After a survey of trademark owners, lawyers practicing in the field and government officials, the association recommended changes in trademark law. In September 1987 the association issued its report, which formed the basis of S 1883. The bill revived and modernized the Lanham Act, a

1946 trademark statute. The statute was last amended in 1982. *(Congress and the Nation Vol. VI, p. 686)*

## Legislative Action

The Senate Judiciary Committee reported S 1883 (S Rept 100-515) on May 12, and the Senate passed the bill the next day without opposition.

The House Judiciary Committee reported a different bill (HR 5372 — H Rept 100-1028) on Oct. 3. HR 5372 contained consumer provisions that were absent from the Senate version. These allowed consumers to file lawsuits against trademark owners for false advertising. These and several other House provisions led the USTA to oppose HR 5372. In addition, the House bill omitted a section in the Senate's bill that allowed owners of famous trademarks to file lawsuits to prevent others from diluting or disparaging their trademark or from advertising the product with a "material omission" of information about the product. Various media groups opposed this provision on the ground that it could subject them to lawsuits for running stories comparing two different products or for doing satires or spoofs that included references to trademarked products.

Various attempts in the Judiciary Committee to drop the consumer-lawsuit provision were rejected.

Before the bill went to the House floor, members and aides on the House and Senate Judiciary committees held private negotiations to resolve the differences between S 1883 and HR 5372. The House side agreed to give up its controversial consumer provisions, and the Senate members agreed to drop the provision that would allow trademark owners to file lawsuits to prevent others from diluting or disparaging the trademark or advertising the product with a material omission of information. The House then took up and passed the Senate bill Oct. 19 after amending it to contain the earlier compromises. Before passing S 1883, the House also incorporated the provisions of HR 2848, a bill the House passed earlier in the year that permitted continued transmission of television programming to owners of home satellite dishes. *(Satellite-TV transmissions, p. 407)*

The Senate approved the compromise version of S 1883 on Oct. 20, sending the bill to the president, who signed it Nov. 16.

## Major Provisions

A key provision in the legislation allowed a company to apply for registration of a trademark with the U.S. Patent and Trademark Office based on a bona fide intent to use the trademark in commerce. Trademark owners were to present supporting information to demonstrate that they intended to put the trademark into circulation.

Under existing law, the company actually had to have used the trademark before it could file for registration and protection against unauthorized use by others. Foreign companies did not have to meet this requirement, and American companies complained that this placed them at a disadvantage.

The bill gave trademark owners six months to get their trademarked product into commerce after they applied for registration with the Trademark Office. The owner could get another automatic six-month extension if he made a written request for the extra time. Further extensions of up to two years could be granted if the applicant showed good cause why the trademarked product was not actually in commerce.

S 1883 also expanded the right of trademark owners to sue other parties for false advertising claims about the trademarked product. However, this provision would cover only false and misleading comments used for advertising or promotion for business purposes. It would not cover the dissemination of false information by the media unless such dissemination was malicious. It also would not cover false information that was part of a political campaign.

# Government Contract Fraud

Legislation (HR 3911 — PL 100-700) cleared Oct. 20, 1988, created a new federal crime to deal specifically with fraud in government contracts. The new law applied to contracts worth at least $1 million and covered anyone who knowingly executed or attempted to execute a scheme to defraud the federal government by making false or fraudulent representations or promises.

HR 3911 expanded upon a law enacted in 1986 (S 1562 — PL 99-562) that increased the penalties against those who defrauded the government and protected whistleblowers in the federal bureaucracy who reported fraud. *(PL 99-562, p. 739)*

Although there were several existing federal laws that dealt with fraud, none specifically addressed fraud by contractors. Federal prosecutors had to use novel interpretations of laws that covered fraud by mail, wire or conspiracy to get at contractors' schemes.

Sponsors of the legislation succeeded in overcoming the concerted opposition of the defense industry. Industry spokesmen argued strenuously that there already were enough laws in force to handle government fraud. However, disclosures in the summer of 1988 of fraud in the defense industry gave the legislation the push it needed to get through Congress. *(Defense scandals, p. 340)*

Under HR 3911, violators could be fined up to $1 million or imprisoned for up to 10 years, or both. The fine could be increased to $5 million if the gross loss to the government or the gain to the defendant was at least $500,000 or if the offense involved "a conscious or reckless risk of serious personal injury." In cases where multiple instances of fraud occurred a defendant could be fined up to $10 million. However, a judge was given the discretion of fining a defendant up to twice the amount of the government's gross loss or the defendant's gross gain.

The bill provided protections for individuals who came forward with information about government fraud. These persons were given the right to file a civil action for, among other things, reinstatement if they were fired and twice the amount of back pay, plus interest, they would have earned during the period following their termination.

Another provision limited to 80 percent the legal costs contractors could recover from the government when they had to defend against a charge of violating a federal or state statute or regulation. Under previous law, contractors were allowed to recover the full cost of expenses incurred in a variety of legal proceedings.

## Legislative History

The House Judiciary Committee reported HR 3911 (H Rept 100-610) on May 9, 1988, and the full House passed the measure under suspension of the rules May 10. The Senate Judiciary Committee reported the bill (S Rept 100-503) with amendments on Sept. 12, and the Senate passed it Oct. 18.

Both versions of HR 3911 initially contained a provision that provided rewards for individuals who came forward with fraud information that led to a conviction. Although sponsors felt they had carefully drafted the provision, some members strongly opposed it on the ground it could lead to serious abuses. Reluctantly, the Senate sponsors agreed to drop the provision from the bill.

The House then approved the Senate version without change, completing congressional action.

# Copyright Convention

The United States in 1988 became the 77th nation to join the Berne Convention for the Protection of Literary and Artistic Works. After nearly 100 years of on-and-off debate, Congress Oct. 12 cleared legislation (HR 4262 — PL 100-568) authorizing the United States to participate in the convention, which was established in 1886 to provide international copyright protection for works from countries that were members of the convention.

HR 4262 made minor changes in U.S. copyright laws so that they would conform with the Berne Convention requirements. In considering the bill, lawmakers had to balance the interests of the creator to protect and profit from his work, the ability of distributors to transmit those works and ultimately the ability of the public to use and enjoy such works.

The legislation was the product of extensive negotiations among Republicans and Democrats in Congress, publishing houses, magazines, the motion picture industry and broadcasters.

## Background

The Berne Convention set minimum copyright standards defining what was protected and how long the protection lasted. The convention prohibited members from discriminating against copyrighted works of other signers. And the convention provided copyright protection without government-imposed formalities such as providing official notice of a copyright. (Berne Convention, Congress and the Nation Vol. I, p. 658)

Proponents of joining the Berne Convention said such action was necessary to give U.S. copyright owners adequate worldwide protection for their works. They noted that because the United States was not a party to the convention, companies had to develop often very expensive separate arrangements with foreign countries to secure such protection.

At hearings before a subcommittee of the Senate Judiciary Committee, IBM official Kenneth W. Dam said his company spent about $10 million annually to protect its computer software by releasing the products in a foreign country at the same time they were released in the United States. Dam, a former State Department official, said that process was not only expensive but also provided uncertain copyright protection. He said that domestic software sellers lost about $800 million annually in overseas sales due to piracy.

Lawmakers faced a dilemma over a so-called "moral rights" issue, which was not provided for in the final legislation. Moral rights were the rights of an artist or writer to protect the integrity of his creative endeavor against what he believed to be misuse or damaging alterations. If film directors, for example, objected to the addition of color to black-and-white films, they could argue that this was a violation of moral rights. U.S. copyright law did not explicitly cover moral rights, but they surfaced in the Berne Convention debate because the convention required signers to protect in law — though not necessarily in copyright law — the right of artists to ensure the integrity of their work and to see that it was properly attributed.

Artists had argued for strong moral rights coverage in U.S. law and believed it was necessary for compliance with the Berne agreement. Groups in publishing, broadcasting and film making argued that new laws would be unworkable.

A majority of committee members also felt that artists' rights were adequately protected in the United States through means other than moral rights protection, such as through case law that had been developed regarding defamation, the right to privacy and unfair competition. The final version of HR 4262 did not contain any moral rights provisions.

Lawmakers also had to face the thorny issues of coverage for architectural works and what copyright specialists call "the formalities issue" — what kind of notice, filing or registration of a copyrighted work would be required, to protect against unauthorized use.

HR 4262 addressed the architectural issues by recognizing architectural plans as a type of pictorial, graphic or sculptural work entitled to protection.

The final agreement worked out between the House and Senate on the formalities issues provided a two-tiered registration system. Works created in a foreign country that was a Berne signatory were exempted from the registration requirement. Infringement lawsuits thus could be filed without prior registration with the copyright office. Works that originated in the United States still had to be registered with the office.

## Legislative History

The Senate Judiciary Committee reported a version of the legislation implementing the convention on May 20, 1988 (S 1301 — S Rept 100-352), and the House Judiciary Committee reported another version (HR 4262 — H Rept 100-609) on May 6.

The House passed its bill unanimously on May 10, and the Senate 90-0 passed S 1301 Oct. 5. The Senate then substituted its text for HR 4262 and passed it amended. The House accepted the Senate changes Oct. 12, clearing the bill. President Reagan signed the bill Oct. 31, thus putting the convention into effect.

# Protection for Retirees

On its third try, Congress approved legislation to protect retirees who worked for companies that were seeking to reorganize under Chapter 11 of the bankruptcy laws. HR 2969 (PL 100-334), signed June 16, 1988, guaranteed retired workers health and life insurance benefits in cases where their former employers declared bankruptcy.

The legislation originally was drafted in 1986 in response to problems that arose when the LTV Steel Co. filed for Chapter 11 protection and contended that under existing federal law it was required to stop paying retiree benefits. Congress disagreed and passed several stopgap measures to protect the company's retired employees while it worked on a permanent clarification of the bankruptcy laws.

## Legislative History

Congress thought it had taken care of the retiree issue in 1984 when it enacted a law (PL 98-353) that contained provisions barring changes in benefits owed to workers under collective-bargaining agreements, except after negotiations and approval by a bankruptcy court. Members believed the law applied to all benefits covered by a union contract and included former as well as current employees. *(Congress and the Nation Vol. VI, p. 702)*

However, in 1986 the LTV Steel Co. declared bankruptcy and tried to end paying for life and health insurance benefits owed to retirees under a collective-bargaining agreement. The House and Senate reacted by passing HR 5490, explicitly protecting retirees' benefits in bankruptcy cases, but differences were not reconciled before adjournment and the bill died. *(1986 action, p. 746)*

Congress then enacted a temporary measure as part of the fiscal 1987 continuing appropriations resolution (H J Res 738 — PL 99-591) to require that companies in bankruptcy continue paying benefits. It was the first of several such measures enacted while Congress tried to write a permanent bill. The Senate on July 24, 1987, passed a permanent bankruptcy law revision bill (S 548 — S Rept 100-119). The House followed by passing a similar bill (HR 2969) on Oct. 13. The Senate passed an amended version of HR 2969 on Oct. 30, which contained several unrelated bankruptcy provisions on farm bankruptcies and student loans. It also would add one bankruptcy judge in Arizona and another in Colorado.

The House further amended the bill May 23, 1988, and the Senate relented and approved the House version May 26, completing congressional action.

## Provisions

As cleared, HR 2969 gave bankruptcy courts the discretion to order a modification of the amount paid in benefits to retirees while the bankruptcy case was pending, if modification was required for successful reorganization. But the company's reorganization plan would have to include provisions for paying retirees' benefits.

Before seeking a court reduction in benefits, a company would have to propose the reduction to retirees, and the company would be required to negotiate in good faith with a retiree representative.

The administrator of a health plan or a health-care provider was empowered to collect from the employer for services rendered to employees before the company went bankrupt. The bill ensured that retirees would not be left footing the bill for health care received before the bankruptcy.

# Crimes Against Religions

A bill (S 794 — PL 100-346) cleared June 14, 1988, made it a federal crime to damage or deface religious property or to interfere with an individual's free exercise of religion.

Penalties established under the bill included a fine and life imprisonment when a death resulted, a prison term of up to 10 years and a fine when serious bodily injury resulted, and imprisonment of up to one year and a fine in other cases.

Congressional action was spurred in part by a report by the Anti-Defamation League of B'nai B'rith citing a rise in anti-Semitic crimes. The league reported 638 incidents of vandalism against Jewish homes and institutions in 1985 and 306 reports of threats or assaults against Jews. Rep. Dan Glickman, D-Kan., the chief sponsor of the legislation, said it would target white-supremacist groups such as The Aryan Nations and The Order.

The House approved one version of the bill (HR 3258 — H Rept 100-337) on Oct. 5, 1987. The Senate passed S 794 (S Rept 100-324) on May 18, 1988. Unlike the House bill, the Senate version required proof of an intention to damage property or to interfere with another's exercise of religion; required written notification from an attorney general that a prosecution under the act was under way; and included a mosque in the definition of religious property. The House on June 14 then approved the Senate bill, clearing the measure.

**Related Action.** The House passed legislation (HR 3193 — H Rept 100-575) in 1988 to require the Justice Department to collect and publish data on certain crimes committed against individuals on the basis of race, religion, ethnicity or homosexuality. The bill covered crimes committed between 1988 and 1992 such as homicide, assault, robbery, burglary, theft, arson, vandalism and threats.

The Senate Judiciary Committee reported a similar bill (S 702 — S Rept 100-514) Sept. 15, but the full Senate did not act before adjournment.

The Reagan administration opposed the legislation, arguing it would impose burdensome and costly requirements on law enforcement personnel.

# Bankruptcy Law Changes

Congress in 1988 cleared two bills clarifying federal bankruptcy law to ensure that these statutes did not interfere with investor rights or certain commercial licensing transactions.

## Safeguards for Municipal Bondholders

A measure (S 1863 — PL 100-597) cleared Oct. 20 strengthened the ability of municipalities to sell revenue bonds for public works projects. S 1863 was the outgrowth of revisions Congress made in the bankruptcy code in 1978. *(Congress and the Nation Vol. V, p. 723)*

At a House subcommittee hearing held earlier in 1988, city officials and bankruptcy experts testified that existing law could cause problems for municipalities, particularly small- and medium-sized cities, when they needed to sell special revenue bonds. These bonds frequently were used to raise money for public works, such as water or electric plants and sewer systems. The bonds were repaid with the revenues generated by the public works systems built with the proceeds from the sales of the bonds.

Bond buyers expected to get a return on their investment, but under current bankruptcy law the bondholder's lien on the revenue bond could be terminated if the municipality filed for bankruptcy. As a result, the bond buyer would lose his investment. Thus, without a change in the law, the bill's sponsors said, potential buyers of such bonds would be reluctant to take the risk.

The initial version of the legislation (HR 5347 — H Rept 100-1011) was reported by the House Judiciary Committee on Sept. 30. The Senate Judiciary Committee reported S 1863 (S Rept 100-506) Sept. 14, and the Senate passed the bill Sept. 20. The House Oct. 19 then passed the Senate bill with amendments, which were accepted by the Senate Oct. 20, completing congressional action.

As cleared, S 1863 revised existing bankruptcy law so that bondholders would not lose all or part of their investments if a municipality filed for bankruptcy.

## Licensing Protection

A bill (S 1626 — PL 100-506) cleared Oct. 4 allowed businesses that had been licensed to use a particular technological process to continue doing so even though the originator of the process — who had legal ownership rights to it — filed for bankruptcy and tried to terminate the contract.

S 1626 was drafted in response to a 1985 federal appeals court decision in which a bankrupt company that owned a metal-coating process was permitted to terminate a licensing contract it had given to another company for use of the process. The owner of the process hoped to improve his financial situation by marketing the process to others at a higher price.

The House Judiciary Committee reported a version of the legislation (HR 5348 — H Rept 100-1012) Sept. 30. The Senate Judiciary Committee reported S 1626 (S Rept 100-505) on Sept. 14, and the Senate passed it Sept. 20. The House then approved the Senate version without change Oct. 4, clearing the bill.

# Immigration Policy

Following up on its ambitious reform (S 1200 — PL 99-603) in 1986 of the nation's immigration laws, the House and Senate considered numerous refinements and additions in the 100th Congress. *(PL 99-603, p. 717)*

## McCarran-Walter Act Revision

Congress debated but did not clear a major change in immigration policy that would prohibit the federal government from denying foreigners entry to the United States because of their past or current political associations and beliefs.

The bill (HR 4427) revised a controversial provision of the 1952 McCarran-Walter Act (PL 82-414) that allowed the government to bar foreigners because of their political beliefs. The provision was targeted primarily at communists. *(McCarran-Walter Act, Congress and the Nation Vol. I, p. 222)*

The House Judiciary Committee approved HR 4427 by a 21-14 vote June 22, 1988, after a contentious markup session. It was reported (H Rept 100-882) on Aug. 12. The bill's sponsor, Barney Frank, D-Mass., said the purpose of revising the McCarran-Walter Act was to make a person's behavior, instead of his political beliefs, the only grounds for exclusion and deportation. The committee's bill restricted the government's right to exclude people because of past, present or expected beliefs, statements or associations. It allowed the government to bar individuals from entering the United States only for health-related, criminal or national security grounds, including past terrorist activity. It also barred persons who had posed a danger abroad or were considered an espionage or terrorist risk.

An amendment was accepted that allowed the exclusion, under the terrorist clause, of any officer, official, representative or spokesman of the Palestine Liberation Organization (PLO). Several other amendments were adopted that extended the grounds for exclusion. HR 4427 never was considered by the full House, and no comparable legislation was considered by the Senate.

A similar measure, however, was incorporated in the fiscal 1988-89 State Department authorization bill (HR 1777 — PL 100-204), cleared Dec. 16, 1987. But this version remained in effect for only one year. It was intended to spur Congress into finishing action on HR 4427 to make the change permanent.

HR 1777 was reported (H Rept 100-34) by the House Foreign Affairs Committee March 27 and passed by the House June 23. The Senate Foreign Relations Committee reported its version (S 1394 — S Rept 100-75) June 18. The full Senate passed an amended HR 1777 Oct. 8. Backers of the change in the 35-year-old law were given a lift by the Supreme Court in October 1987 when the high court let stand an appeals court ruling requiring the State Department to certify, before denying entry to a foreigner, that the person represented a danger to national security because of his communist affiliation.

A House-Senate conference committee filed its report on HR 1777 (H Rept 100-475) on Dec. 14. Addressing the issue, the conference negotiators noted that "a large number of well-known" foreigners as well as thousands of ordinary persons had been kept out of the United States. As a result, Americans "have been denied the opportunity to have access to the full spectrum of international opinion, and the reputation of the United States as an open society, tolerant of divergent ideas, has suffered."

The House adopted the conference report Dec. 15 and the Senate followed suit the next day. President Reagan signed HR 1777 Dec. 22.

## European Immigration Expansion

Legislation (HR 5115 — PL 100-658) cleared Oct. 21, 1988, allowed more Irish citizens and those from some other countries to enter the United States. Other provisions of HR 5115 were designed to ease a shortage of nurses in the United States.

The bill expanded a provision of the 1986 immigration law (S 1200 — PL 99-603) that provided 5,000 visas annually to citizens of countries that had had little immigration to the United States over the previous 20 years. Under HR 5115, an additional 10,000 visas were made available to these countries in both 1989 and 1990.

Another provision of HR 5115 helped, in particular, residents from Ireland, other Western European nations and some African countries. Residents from these countries had not been able to immigrate in large numbers because they had few immediate relatives in the United States and could not meet other requirements that allowed visas to foreigners with special skills. These visas were known as the "Donnelly" visas, named after Rep. Brian J. Donnelly, D-Mass., who had inserted the provision in the 1986 law. The bill made 10,000 additional visas available in 1990 and 1991 for persons from countries that had not been able to take advantage of the existing visa preference system.

The nurses provision allowed foreign nurses already in the United States whose visas expired at the end of 1988 to remain in the country legally for another year, to Dec. 31, 1989.

A comprehensive immigration bill (S 2104 — S Rept 100-290) was passed by the Senate 88-4 March 15. The Senate Judiciary Committee had considered another bill (S 1611) but reported the compromise measure (S 2104) instead Feb. 26. S 2104 would completely rewrite the family-based preference system for awarding visas to foreigners and would give the government more flexibility to admit foreigners based on the financial contributions they made to the United States. It would reduce the percentage of legal immigration based on family ties from about 90 percent to about 80 percent. It also would set an overall annual cap of 590,000 on the number of foreigners who could enter the country.

The House Judiciary Committee was reluctant to move another major immigration bill so soon after enactment of the 1986 bill. Instead, on Oct. 3 it reported HR 5115 (H Rept 100-1038). The full House passed HR 5115 on Oct. 5, after intense lobbying from America's Irish population. Given the House's reluctance to consider the Senate's more sweeping bill, the Senate accepted the House version without amendment on Oct. 21, sending the measure to the president.

## Status of Salvadorans, Nicaraguans

The Senate never considered legislation passed by the House in 1987 to temporarily suspend the deportation of Salvadorans and Nicaraguans who had come to the United States illegally. The bill (HR 618) would grant these illegal aliens "extended voluntary departure" — a form of temporary legal residence, for approximately two years. A similar program had been approved by the House in 1986 as part of the omnibus immigration bill (S 1200 — PL 99-603), but it was knocked out of the House-Senate compromise version that ultimately was enacted into law. Approximately 500,000 Salvadorans and 200,000 Nicaraguans would be covered by HR 618.

The Reagan administration lobbied against the legislation in both chambers. The White House argued that HR 618 would undercut current U.S. immigration policy, specifically a provision in the 1986 law aimed at curbing the flow of illegal aliens. Republicans also charged the bill would create loopholes in a 1980 law (PL 96-212) that revised U.S. refugee policy. U.S. policy was to admit refugees if they could demonstrate that they were fleeing their homeland because of persecution. Opponents said most of the illegal immigrants from the two Central American countries were seeking a better life economically, not fleeing persecution. *(PL 96-212, Congress and the Nation Vol. V, p. 740)*

Congressional action became entangled with the larger political debate over President Reagan's Central America policies. While supporters called the legislation a response to very difficult problems in both El Salvador and Nicaragua, opponents contended the sponsors' real intention was to embarrass the administration and Salvadoran President José Napoleón Duarte, whom Reagan helped put in office. While some supporters of HR 618 implicitly criticized Duarte's inability to protect his countrymen, the bill's mainly Republican opponents in both chambers defended the Salvadoran president, arguing that civil rights conditions in El Salvador had greatly improved under his leadership.

Ironically, Duarte supported the bill and even wrote Reagan requesting that he change his position. Duarte's main concern was the economic conditions in his country. He told Reagan the Salvadorans were sending home between $350 million and $600 million. And Duarte said there was high unemployment in his country, which could not easily absorb the additional Salvadorans who would be forced to return home.

Daniel Ortega, president of the Sandinista government in Nicaragua, did not support the legislation.

Congressional action was further politicized when Attorney General Edwin Meese III announced in July that any Nicaraguan exile who could show a well-founded fear of persecution at home could stay in the United States. The bill's backers charged Meese's action was done for political reasons because the administration backed Durate but opposed Ortega. They said U.S. immigration officials were willing to find a fear of persecution for Nicaraguans but would not make a similar finding for illegal aliens from El Salvador.

Although a subcommittee of the House Judiciary Committee was evenly divided on the bill and failed to recommend its approval, the full committee approved HR 618 by a 20-15 vote June 30. The committee reported the bill July 13, 1987 (H Rept 100-212, Part I). It also was reported by the House Rules Committee (Part II), which had jurisdiction over a section of the bill.

The House passed HR 618 on July 28 by a 237-181 vote without amendment. Pressure from the government of El Salvador and from religious groups in the United States helped to provide the necessary votes for passage.

The Senate Judiciary Committee reported its own bill (S 332 — S Rept 100-213) on Nov. 4. But Senate opponents were able to block floor action on S 332, and the bill's sponsors tried without success to attach the bill to other legislation.

## Amnesty Program Extension

The Senate in 1988 blocked a House initiative to extend for seven months a one-time amnesty program for illegal aliens. The House-passed measure (HR 4222) was killed when an attempt by the bill's backers to cut off a filibuster fell 20 votes short of the three-fifths majority required by Senate rules.

An extension of the federal government's amnesty program was needed, proponents said, because the Immigration and Naturalization Service (INS) had been slow in implementing the program. The amnesty, or legalization, program was established by the 1986 immigration law (S 1200 — PL 99-603). The yearlong amnesty was set to expire on May 4, 1988, and it was from that date that the bill would extend the deadline for seven more months.

Aliens who had come to the United States before Jan. 1, 1982, lived in the country continuously since then, spoke English and met certain other requirements were eligible for temporary residence and a chance to become citizens six and one-half years later. The purpose of the amnesty program in PL 99-603 was to get rid of a "shadow class" of people who had been contributing to the U.S. economy through their work but were highly exploitable because of their illegal status.

A coalition of Hispanic, civil rights, religious and labor groups lobbied for extension of the deadline. But the INS commissioner opposed the bill, maintaining the agency had caught up with its backlog and the program had served its purpose. According to INS records, approximately 1.8 million persons had come forward by the May 1988 deadline. Another 1.2 million had applied for a special amnesty program for foreign farm workers that expired Nov. 30, 1988.

The House Judiciary Committee reported HR 4222 (H Rept 100-569) on April 14, 1988. Opponents in the committee pointed out that the legalization provision had escaped defeat in the House in 1986 by only seven votes and an extension amounted to making a bad idea worse. The House narrowly passed HR 4222 April 20 by a 213-201 vote. A close House vote on amnesty in 1986 coupled with the narrow margin on the extension bill demonstrated that legalization was one of the most sensitive elements of U.S. immigration policy.

When the bill was sent to the Senate, opponents threatened to block any move to take up the bill, forcing supporters to file a cloture petition to end a threatened filibuster. Senate debate showed there was no consensus on the need for an extension.

**Related Legislation.** A related bill (HR 4379) to provide a "safe-haven" plan also failed to win congressional approval. The bill would set up new procedures for allowing foreigners to remain in the United States temporarily because of special circumstances in their homeland. These circumstances included armed conflict, an environmental disaster that significantly disrupted living conditions or other extreme conditions that presented humanitarian concerns. HR 4379 was reported by the House Judiciary Committee May 17 (H Rept 100-627) and was passed by the House Oct. 5. The Senate did not take up the bill.

# Other Legislation

## Video Rentals Privacy

In an unusual aftermath to the 1987 Senate fight over Robert H. Bork's unsuccessful nomination to the Supreme Court, Congress approved legislation (S 2361 — PL 100-618) to protect the privacy of videocassette consumers. During the Bork confirmation hearings, a reporter had obtained and published a list of the movies the Bork family had rented, prompting an angry response from members of both political parties who charged Bork's privacy had been invaded. *(Bork nomination, p. 785)*

As cleared, S 2361 barred video stores from disclosing their customers' names and addresses or the specific videotapes rented or both by customers except in specifically defined circumstances. These included instances when the customer consented to release of the information, when law enforcement officials had obtained a warrant or when there was a court order specifying a "compelling need" for release of the information.

An individual who believed his privacy under the law had been violated could file a civil lawsuit in federal court. A judge could award attorneys' fees, damages of at least $2,500 and punitive damages in egregious cases.

The Senate passed S 2361 (S Rept 100-599) on Oct. 14, 1988, and the House passed it without amendment Oct. 19, clearing the bill.

## Record Rentals Ban

Legislation (S 2201 — PL 100-617) cleared Oct. 21, 1988, extending for eight years a ban on the commercial rental of most phonograph records without the copyright owner's permission. The bill extended a 1984 law (PL 98-450), due to expire in 1989, that was aimed at curbing a practice in which record stores were renting records for a small fee and then selling blank tapes to customers. The customers taped the records at home and returned the albums to the store, thus depriving the copyright holder of any royalty on the sale of the record. Exempted were nonprofit libraries and other organizations that were renting for educational uses. *(Congress and the Nation Vol. VI, p. 707)*

As passed by the Senate June 7, 1988, S 2201 (S Rept 100-361) made the record ban permanent. The version (HR 4310 — Rept 100-776) passed by the House Aug. 1 provided a five-year extension of the record ban. The House passed S 2201 amended Sept. 26. The Senate agreed to the House changes Oct. 21, clearing the measure.

## Appeals Procedure Changes

Legislation (HR 1162 — PL 100-236) cleared Dec. 19, 1987, sought to end a situation that lawyers called "the race to the courthouse" when they were appealing orders from federal agencies.

Under previous law, appeals from an agency order could be filed in more than one courthouse. Attorneys sometimes went to elaborate lengths to get papers filed before judges they believed would be most favorable to their case. Under the old law, the case was heard in the court that first received the appropriate papers. HR 1162 changed the procedure to allow each party in a case 10 days to appeal an agency order. If multiple appeals were filed, a special judicial panel on multi-district litigation would pick the proper appellate court by lottery. The panel could transfer the case to a more convenient forum if a party could show good cause for the transfer.

The House passed HR 1162 (H Rept 100-72) on May 27, 1987, and the Senate passed the bill without amendment Dec. 19, clearing the measure.

## Semiconductor-Chip Protection

Congress in 1987 cleared legislation (S 442 — PL 100-159) extending a 1984 law (PL 98-620) providing copyright-style protection for 10 years for semiconductor-chip designs of U.S. companies in order to keep them from being copied and reproduced by other companies, both foreign and domestic. Silicon semiconductor chips formed the heart of the microcomputer revolution. The 1984 law was set to expire Nov. 8, 1987. S 442 extended the copyright protections until July 1, 1991. *(1984 law, Congress and the Nation Vol. VI, p. 706)*

S 442 (S Rept 100-66) was passed by the Senate June 26. The House passed an amended version on Oct. 27. The Senate Nov. 4 agreed to the House-passed amendments, clearing the bill.

## Government Personnel Claims

Legislation enacted in 1988 (HR 3685 — PL 100-565) increased, to $40,000 from $25,000, the maximum amount the federal government could pay to settle claims filed by U.S. military or civilian government personnel. Such claims covered the loss of property during government service. HR 3685 amended a 1964 law that established the process for paying claims by the government. That law had been amended several times. In 1980, in response to the Iran hostage crisis, Congress amended the law to allow government officials who were targets of hostile actions abroad to collect up to $40,000. The most recent previous revision of the law was made in 1983. HR 3685 was passed by the House Oct. 5, 1988 (H Rept 100-1037), and by the Senate without amendment Oct. 14, completing congressional action.

## Federal Employee Legal Protection

Congress in 1988 approved legislation (HR 4612 — PL 100-694) to protect federal employees from the threat of lawsuits brought about by their performance at work. The bill was drafted in response to a 1988 Supreme Court decision, *Westfall v. Erwin*, in which the court said a federal employee could be sued in his individual capacity for alleged negligence even if acting within the scope of his employment. *(Supreme Court decision, p. 837)*

HR 4612 specified that the government would be the sole defendant in cases where employees were sued for conduct within the scope of their employment.

The House passed HR 4612 (H Rept 100-700) on June 28. The Senate passed it Oct. 12 after adding an amendment to include employees of the Tennessee Valley Authority in the bill's coverage. The House then accepted the Senate change Oct. 20, clearing the measure.

## Antitrust Enforcement

The 100th Congress did not complete action on a legislative package (S 1068) designed to improve antitrust enforcement. The Senate July 31, 1987, passed a compendium of three bills that was reported by the Judiciary Committee, but the House did not act on the legislation.

● S 431 (S Rept 100-88), reported June 25, would let the Justice Department and the Federal Trade Commission (FTC) review proposed mergers of large partnerships. Under existing law partnerships that launched takeover bids were not covered by reporting provisions of the antitrust laws that applied to mergers. S 431 required review of mergers involving partnerships if at least $10 million in assets was involved and one partner was a general partner or one partner had the right to at least 50 percent of the profits of the partnership.

● S 432 (S Rept 100-115), reported July 17, would give the Justice Department and FTC more time to review proposed mergers to determine their effect on competition in the marketplace.

Both S 431 and S 432 amended a 1976 antitrust law (PL 94-435) that created new procedures for reviewing mergers. *(Congress and the Nation Vol. IV, p. 610)*

● S 1068, reported June 25 (S Rept 100-89), contained provisions that revised the antitrust law barring a person from serving as a director of two competing corporations — so-called interlocking directorates. Under existing law directors had to comply with the ban if they served on two competing companies worth at least $1 million. S 1068 raised the floor to $10 million.

## Military Malpractice

The House passed legislation (HR 1054) in 1988 to allow active-duty members of the armed forces to sue the government for medical and dental malpractice in military hospitals within the United States. Sponsors of the bill argued that members of the armed forces were entitled to the same right of compensation for malpractice as civilians. But the Reagan administration was adamantly opposed to the idea. Congressional opponents said the legislation would lead to higher costs and that a better remedy was to revise the Military Claims Act by increasing compensation for victims of improper medical care.

HR 1054 would cover all active-duty members of the armed forces, including Coast Guard and National Guard units on full-time duty.

Peter W. Rodino Jr., D-N.J., chairman of the Judiciary Committee that reported HR 1054 (H Rept 100-279) on Aug. 6, said legislation was needed because a 1950 Supreme Court ruling, *Feres v. United States,* said armed forces personnel could not use the Federal Tort Claims Act to sue the government for malpractice. Rodino said there was no justification for the ruling. Before passing the bill Feb. 17, the House adopted an amendment limiting suits by armed forces personnel to $300,000.

There was no Senate action on the legislation. The Senate also did not act on a similar bill (HR 3174) passed by the House in the 99th Congress. *(99th Congress action, p. 746)*

## Limits on Anti-Racketeering Law

The full Senate never considered legislation (S 1523 — S Rept 100-459) reported by the Senate Judiciary Committee Aug. 8, 1988, to limit the use of a federal anti-racketeering law to settle private business disputes.

The measure would revise the 1970 Racketeer Influenced and Corrupt Organizations Act (RICO) to make it harder for private parties — particularly businesses — to sue one another in order to collect the triple damages that were available under the law if the party won the case. *(RICO, Congress and the Nation Vol. III, p. 272)*

The 1970 law was designed to combat organized crime by allowing both criminal prosecutions for specified activities and civil suits aimed at corrupt business practices. The triple damages were intended to provide a deterrent against illegal activity and an incentive to plaintiffs. But there was a growing perception that civil suits under the 1970 law were being used by businesses to harass competitors.

In 1985 the Supreme Court refused to limit use of the law, saying it was up to Congress to make changes. Since that time, the business community had pressured Congress to revise the act. *(Background, Sedima S.P.R.L. v. Imrex Co. Inc. and American National Bank and Trust Co. of Chicago v. Haroco Inc., p. 802)*

The bill as approved by the Judiciary Committee would allow triple-damage awards only when the defendant had been convicted of a criminal racketeering offense; when a suit alleged insider-trading violations; or when a suit was filed by a consumer or by the federal, state or local government.

# The Supreme Court

Ronald Reagan spent eight years, six nominations and dozens of arguments trying to change the brand of law and justice dispensed by the U.S. Supreme Court. Success, in some measure, finally came, but only after he had left the White House.

Reagan's 1980 landslide election victory convinced him that he had a mandate to change the way the federal government served the American people. A large part of that change focused on the federal courts, by then thoroughly imbued with the activist philosophy exemplified by the Supreme Court of the 1960s, the court led by Chief Justice Earl Warren.

In 1981, his first year in office, Reagan named one member of the court — Sandra Day O'Connor, the first woman justice. Although O'Connor was a strong new conservative voice and an equally strong conservative vote, a single appointment was not enough to bring about the philosophical shift that Reagan desired.

Over the next five years, Reagan had mixed success with his arguments for judicial restraint. In the October 1983 term the court seemed to move into a more conservative posture. But in the next two terms, the court reasserted its liberal character, reaffirming landmarks such as *Roe v. Wade* (1973), which legalized abortion; *Baker v. Carr* (1963), which made legislative malapportionment a subject for judges to review; and *Engel v. Vitale* (1962), which banned officially sanctioned prayer in public schools.

More important even than the stand which the court took and maintained on the issues that were the subjects of these rulings was the effect these decisions had of underscoring certain liberal tenets with which Reagan sharply disagreed. In decisions on issues such as jury selection, voting rights and affirmative action, the court declared again and again that the nation must continue to work actively toward the goal of equality for all citizens.

Reagan, while espousing a colorblind society, nonetheless argued that enough progress had been made toward that goal. He contended it was time to discard some of the more aggressive civil rights tools, such as affirmative action.

The court also showed no signs of shrinking from its major role in preserving and protecting individual rights. With equal forcefulness, the court refused to curb a woman's right to an abortion — or to curtail access to the courts. This, again, ran counter to Reagan's argument that judges should do less and elected officials more.

Reagan supporters were gloomy as the 1985-86 term ended. "This term witnessed the most significant defeats for the policy objectives of a chief executive in half a century," said Bruce Fein, an adjunct scholar at the American Enterprise Institute for Public Policy Research and former Reagan Justice Department official. "Not since the Supreme Court scuttled President Franklin D. Roosevelt's efforts to fashion a domestic New Deal program in a flurry of 1935 rulings has a president's policy agenda fared so poorly before the high court," Fein added.

## Chief Justice Rehnquist

During the early 1980s, only two members of the court consistently supported the administration: Chief Justice Warren E. Burger and Associate Justice William H. Rehnquist. Moves they made in the summer of 1986 had a dramatic effect on the subsequent success of Reagan's efforts to refocus the federal judiciary.

In June, Chief Justice Burger, 79, announced his retirement, giving Reagan the chance every president covets — the chance to name the nation's chief justice.

Reagan moved quickly, promoting Rehnquist, 61, the most conservative member of the court and a veteran of 15 years' service there, to the court's center seat. To take the seat vacated by Rehnquist, Reagan named the brilliant young conservative, Antonin Scalia, 50.

Scalia was confirmed easily; Rehnquist had a rougher time. Senators opposed his confirmation because of his views on minority and individual rights; civil rights groups mounted an all-out effort to defeat the nomination. They failed, and two weeks before the October 1986 term convened, the Senate confirmed Rehnquist on a **65-33 (R 49-2; D 16-31) key vote**. The 33 "nay" votes were the largest number ever cast by the Senate against a court nominee who won confirmation. *(1986 key votes, p. 949)*

## References

Discussion of the Supreme Court for the years 1945-64 may be found in *Congress and the Nation Vol. I*, pp. 1441-1454; for the years 1965-68, *Congress and the Nation Vol. II*, pp. 335-340; for the years 1969-72, *Congress and the Nation Vol. III*, pp. 289-327; for the years 1973-76, *Congress and the Nation Vol. IV*, pp. 619-659; for the years 1977-80, *Congress and the Nation Vol. V*, pp. 755-791; for the years 1981-84, *Congress and the Nation Vol. VI*, pp. 711-768.

## Judicial Salaries

Judicial salaries increased in the 1980s. For the chief justice, they moved from $75,000 in 1980 to $115,000 in 1989; the comparable boost for associate justices was from $72,000 to $110,000. District court salaries moved up to $89,500 from $67,100, and appeals court judges got a raise from $70,900 to $95,000.

Steeply rising salaries for attorneys in private practice almost erased the impact of those increases, particularly for lower court judges. And in 1989, Chief Justice William H. Rehnquist engaged in some serious lobbying for a raise for all federal judges. After Congress failed to approve a recommended raise early in the year, Rehnquist broke precedent to appear before a congressional committee, meet privately with congressional leaders and hold a press conference to urge Congress to increase judicial salaries.

Rehnquist was successful. Late in 1989, Congress approved a pay raise for federal judges that was to take effect in 1990.

Rehnquist's first term as chief justice, the 1986-87 term, was unique: For only 10 months did the nine justices on this court sit together. As the term ended, its pivotal member, Justice Lewis F. Powell Jr., 79, announced his retirement.

The departure of this courtly Southerner came at a particularly unstable point in the court's history. The major decisions of the 1986-87 term emerged from an institution that was more deeply divided on more important issues than it had been in years.

A first look at that year's rulings would lead one to think that the court had resolved some perennial disputes. It had ruled in support of affirmative action, for continued use of the death penalty and against efforts to inject religion into public school classrooms. But even before Powell's decision to retire was known, the longevity of some of those rulings was in question.

More than half the decisions of the term emerged from a court divided 5-4 or 6-3. Two years earlier, in the 1984-85 term, only one-third of the rulings divided the court that closely. The future was foreshadowed when one looked at the prevailing majority in these close cases. Conservatives won well over half of them, most on matters of criminal law and economic and property rights. The court's more liberal rulings came on questions of individual and civil rights. The deep divisions within the court underscored the impact that Powell's successor would have. Powell's vote had determined on what issues the court was conservative and on what issues it was liberal.

### The Battle for the Seat

Reagan's effort to fill Powell's seat turned into one of his more embarrassing episodes as president. Civil rights and women's groups, well aware of the extent to which their recent victories at the court had depended upon Powell's vote, went all out to ensure that the public at large, and the Senate in particular, was cognizant of the importance of the next Supreme Court nominee. When Reagan named Robert H. Bork, a 60-year-old judge on the Court of Appeals for the District of Columbia, as his choice to succeed Powell, he set off one of the most vociferous confirmation battles in history. Even before the nomination, the opposition had been rallying. Less than an hour after the July 1 nomination, Edward M. Kennedy, D-Mass., was on the Senate floor declaring, "Robert Bork's America is a land in which women would be forced into back-alley abortions, blacks would sit at segregated lunch counters, rogue police could break down citizens' doors in midnight raids ... and the doors of the Federal courts would be shut on the fingers of million of citizens for whom the judiciary is often the only protector of the individual rights that are the heart of our democracy."

Bork's supporters portrayed him as a scholar who favored judicial restraint — an attitude of deference to Congress and state legislatures in the belief that the right of elected bodies to make political choices took precedence over the views of courts. They said Bork's long legal career, including his tenure as a Yale University law professor, solicitor general and a judge on the U.S. Court of Appeals for the District of Columbia, demonstrated his commitment to a strict interpretation of the Constitution.

Bork's opponents, meanwhile, insisted his reputation for judicial restraint was undeserved. They read his writings as a teacher and scholar and his decisions as an appeals court judge as demonstrating an appetite for conservative activism as extreme as any liberal's passion for judicially imposed change.

The opposition to Bork was led by civil rights groups that pointed to Bork's criticism of major civil rights legislation as proof that he would turn the clock back two decades. That argument was cited by Southern senators whose decision to vote against Bork doomed the nomination. They explained that they could not support him without risking the reopening of old wounds, old issues now resolved.

Bork was questioned extensively during Judiciary Committee hearings that were unprecedented in their scope and detail. Unlike many other nominees, Bork agreed to explain his judicial philosophy and to discuss specific cases.

The Bork episode also reopened an informal debate over the Senate role in the confirmation process. Republicans argued that the president was entitled to his choice unless the nominee was unqualified. But Democrats said the Senate should be an equal partner and insisted that it was proper to examine a nominee's judicial philosophy, as well as his qualifications.

The ensuing battle over Bork lasted 3½ months, polarizing the Senate and inflaming political passions across the country. On Oct. 23, 1987, Bork became the first Supreme Court nominee to be rejected since G. Harrold Carswell in 1970. Bork's nomination was rejected on a **42-58 (R 40-6; D 2-52) key vote.** (1987 key votes, p. 965)

Following Bork's defeat, Reagan nominated Douglas H. Ginsburg, a 41-year-old colleague of Bork's on the Court of Appeals for the District of Columbia. Ginsburg's nomination was announced Oct. 29, and within days questions were raised about his background. He was accused of a conflict of interest during his tenure as a Justice Department official, and there were charges that he had not been candid in filling out a 1986 questionnaire about his court experience. But what sealed Ginsburg's fate was the admission Nov. 5 that he had used marijuana during the 1960s and 1970s. The disclosure proved extremely embarrassing for the Reagan administration, which had cultivated a strong anti-drug image, and on Nov. 7 Ginsburg asked that his name be withdrawn from consideration.

On Nov. 11, Reagan named as his third choice for the vacant seat — appeals court Judge Anthony M. Kennedy of California. Although a conservative and an advocate of judicial restraint, Kennedy was viewed as a moderate who was chosen more because he stood a good chance of being confirmed than because he would guarantee a conservative swing in the court.

In introducing his nominee, Reagan appealed for bipartisan cooperation toward confirmation. The court was back in session, operating with only eight members, never an easy situation. The very day that Senate confirmation hearings began for Kennedy, the court divided 4-4 on an abortion case, signaling again both the need for — and the significance of — its ninth member.

In his dozen years as a judge on the U.S. Court of Appeals for the 9th Circuit, Kennedy had written on a variety of social and constitutional issues, but in such careful and narrow terms that there was far less for critics to seize upon than had been the case with Bork. Kennedy's confirmation, on a 97-0 vote, came Feb. 3, 1988. Later in February, eight months after Powell had retired, Kennedy took his seat.

Despite the fact that O'Connor, Scalia and Kennedy were in their 50s, the court that ended the decade of the 1980s was still one of the oldest courts in history. The average age was almost 69; five years earlier — when Burger and Powell, both nearing 80, still sat on the court — the average age had been 70.

## The Conservative Court

The 1987-88 term of the court was a holding action. Kennedy, who joined the term at midpoint, participated in about half of the decisions.

The next term — the term which began just before the election of George Bush as Reagan's successor and ended five months after Reagan had left the White House — was the term Reagan had been waiting and working for for almost a decade. His campaign for change came to fruition. Kennedy proved a powerful conservative force, allied with Scalia, O'Connor, Rehnquist and Byron R. White. By the end of the term, it was clear that this had been a watershed year.

The court struck down an affirmative action plan that set aside a fixed percentage of city contracts awarded by Richmond, Va., for minority-owned firms. In other job bias cases, it moved away from its usual concern for the victims and back to a more neutral stance, balancing the needs of minority and majority, employer and employee.

On questions of criminal law, it took an even harder line than in recent years, permitting states to execute young murderers — and mentally retarded ones.

Advocates of personal liberty were particularly unhappy when the court upheld two federal drug testing programs, even while acknowledging that the obligatory urine tests were searches within the meaning of the Constitution's ban on unreasonable searches and seizures. In both cases, the court found that the public interest in-

---

## The Court of 1989

The members of the U.S. Supreme Court in 1989 were:

- Justice William H. Rehnquist, born in 1924, appointed to the court by President Nixon in 1971, promoted to chief justice by President Reagan in 1986.
- Justice William J. Brennan Jr., born in 1906, appointed by President Eisenhower in 1956.
- Justice Byron R. White, born in 1917, appointed by President Kennedy in 1962.
- Justice Thurgood Marshall, born in 1908, appointed by President Johnson in 1967.
- Justice Harry A. Blackmun, born in 1908, appointed by President Nixon in 1970.
- Justice John Paul Stevens, born in 1920, appointed by President Ford in 1975.
- Justice Sandra Day O'Connor, born in 1930, appointed by President Reagan in 1981.
- Justice Antonin Scalia, born in 1936, appointed by President Reagan in 1986.
- Justice Anthony M. Kennedy, born in 1936, appointed by President Reagan in 1987.

---

volved outweighed the individual's right. Justice Kennedy wrote both opinions.

The most closely watched case of the term was *Webster v. Reproductive Health Services*, Missouri's defense of its law regulating abortion. It had been 16 years since the court legalized abortion with its ruling in *Roe v. Wade*. Of the seven-man majority in that case, only Brennan, Marshall and Blackmun remained. Both dissenters, Rehnquist and White, were still on the court. When the court reaffirmed *Roe v. Wade* in 1983, the majority had slipped to six. One retiring member, Potter Stewart, had been replaced by O'Connor — she dissented with Rehnquist and White. The court's next abortion ruling, three years later, in 1986, came by the bare margin of 5-4. Chief Justice Burger moved into dissent. Powell was the deciding vote. His resignation left the court evenly divided.

With the *Webster* ruling late in the 1988-89 term, the balance finally tipped. Kennedy, as anticipated, joined Rehnquist, White, O'Connor and Scalia to uphold Missouri's law. Rehnquist wrote the opinion, never mentioning the right of privacy that underlay the entire line of abortion rulings.

## Keeping the Powers Separate

The separation of powers is a tenet of the American system of government, implicit in the structure created by the Constitution, allocating powers among the judicial, executive and legislative branches.

The Supreme Court had had only infrequent opportunity to consider this aspect of the national system, but it had three such opportunities during the 1980s. One came during Reagan's first term — when the court struck down

## U.S. Supreme Court Caseload

| | 1984-1985 | 1985-1986 | 1986-1987 | 1987-1988 |
|---|---|---|---|---|
| Number of Cases on Docket | 5,006 | 5,158 | 5,123 | 5,268 |
| Cases Decided Summarily | 73 | 102 | 109 | 87 |
| Cases Argued and Decided | 185 | 175 | 179 | 175 |
| Number of Signed Opinions | 159 | 161 | 164 | 151 |

SOURCE: U.S. Supreme Court.

the legislative veto as infringing too far on executive powers.

In Reagan's second term, two more occasions presented themselves for judicial consideration of this issue. The president won one; Congress won the other.

In an almost-desperate effort to rein in the ungovernable federal deficit, Congress devised a new mechanism in legislation referred to as Gramm-Rudman, named after its two primary sponsors, Sens. Phil Gramm, R-Texas, and Warren Rudman, R-N.H. The law called for the comptroller general, the head of the General Accounting Office, to tell the president how much had to be cut out of the budget if Congress failed to meet the deficit target established by Gramm-Rudman. Not surprisingly, the president did not like to be dictated to and challenged this device as unconstitutional, a violation of the separation of powers. The court agreed with the challenge. The comptroller general was responsible to Congress, therefore to allow him to control executive branch affairs was improper.

In the aftermath of Watergate, Congress had passed legislation authorizing the appointment of an independent counsel (special prosecutor) to investigate alleged wrongdoing by high-level government officials. The counsel was to be appointed by a panel of three judges. By giving judges appointment power, the president contended, Congress usurped some of his power in breach of the separation of powers.

The Supreme Court did not agree, upholding the independent counsel statute as appropriate and constitutional. Chief Justice Rehnquist wrote the opinion. There was even more sting in this ruling for President Reagan. The rejection of this constitutional challenge left intact the convictions of two of his former close White House aides; both convictions were obtained by independent counsel appointed under the challenged law.

The evenly divided court affirmed a ruling by the 2nd U.S. Circuit Court of Appeals that a city cannot rely on the First Amendment's ban on state action establishing religion as its reason for denying a request from a citizens' group that a creche be displayed in a public park during the Christmas season.

**Tony and Susan Alamo Foundation v. Secretary of Labor** (471 U.S. 290), decided by a 9-0 vote, April 23, 1985. White wrote the opinion.

Commercial enterprises of churches or religious foundations are subject to minimum wage, overtime and record-keeping requirements of the Fair Labor Standards Act. They cannot claim exemption from such laws by citing the First Amendment freedom of religion guarantees.

Even if employees consider themselves associates, rather than employees, and are paid in benefits, not cash wages, the federal law applies. This law must be applied broadly to accomplish its goal of outlawing goods produced under conditions that do not meet minimum standards of decency.

**Wallace v. Jaffree** (472 U.S. 38), decided by a 6-3 vote, June 4, 1985. Stevens wrote the opinion; Burger, Rehnquist and White dissented.

Moment-of-silence laws intended to restore prayer to the nation's public schools are unconstitutional. The court struck down an Alabama law that permitted a moment of silence for prayer or meditation at the beginning of each school day.

The legislative history of the law made clear that it had no secular purpose but was specifically designed to endorse religion and to encourage students to pray. Such state endorsement of religion is unconstitutional, a violation of the First Amendment ban on state action establishing religion.

**Jensen v. Quaring** (472 U.S. 478), affirmed by a 4-4 vote, June 17, 1985. *Per curiam* (unsigned) opinion. Powell did not participate.

The evenly divided court affirmed a decision by the 8th U.S. Circuit Court of appeals that Nebraska violated the First Amendment rights of a qualified motorist by denying her a driver's license after she refused, based on her religious beliefs, to have her photograph taken for the license.

**Estate of Thornton v. Caldor Inc.** (472 U.S. 703), decided by an 8-1 vote, June 26, 1985. Burger wrote the opinion; Rehnquist dissented.

It is not constitutional for states to require employers to give workers a day off on their Sabbath. The court invalidated a Connecticut law that gave all employees the right to refuse with impunity to work on their Sabbath.

By giving workers this unqualified right, the state elevated religious concerns over all other interests that might be involved in setting work schedules. Thus a primary effect of the law was to advance a religious practice, in violation of the First Amendment ban on establishment of religion.

**Grand Rapids School District v. Ball** (473 U.S. 373), decided by votes of 7-2 and 5-4, July 1, 1985. Brennan wrote the opinion; White and Rehnquist dissented; Burger and O'Connor dissented in part.

Grand Rapids, Mich., school officials violated the First Amendment ban on establishment of religion by providing remedial and enrichment classes to students at 41 non-public schools, all but one religiously affiliated.

These classes were either conducted during the regular school day by public school teachers in a "shared time" program, or after school by parochial school teachers who were paid for this extra work from public funds.

By 7-2, the justices held that the school-day classes were impermissible, primarily because the "symbolic union of church and state inherent in the provision of secular, state-provided instruction in the religious school buildings threatens to convey a message of state support for religion." Burger and O'Connor agreed that this program was unconstitutional. By 5-4, the justices held the after-school classes similarly impermissible.

**Aguilar v. Felton** (473 U.S. 402), decided by a 5-4 vote, July 1, 1985. Brennan wrote the opinion; Burger, White, Rehnquist and O'Connor dissented.

New York's system for providing Title I remedial and counseling services to disadvantaged students who attend non-public schools violates the First Amendment, because the city uses federal funds to send teachers and other educational personnel into private and parochial schools to provide these services to these students during the regular school day.

The New York system, like the Grand Rapids system, effectively advanced religion symbolically and practically, by providing services the private or parochial school would otherwise have had to provide. In addition, New York actively monitored its program to ensure that participating personnel were not involved in religious activities, but that monitoring itself inevitably entangled church and state too far, the court held.

**Witters v. Washington Department of Services for the Blind** (474 U.S. 481), decided by a 9-0 vote, Jan. 27, 1986. Marshall wrote the opinion.

It does not violate the First Amendment's ban on government establishment of religion for a state to grant vocational rehabilitation aid to a blind man studying to become a minister.

"The Establishment Clause is not violated every time money previously in the possession of a state is conveyed to a religious institution," the court held, particularly since this aid would be paid directly to the student and would then flow to a religious college "only as a result of the genuinely independent and private choice of [the] aid recipient."

**Bender v. Williamsport Area School District** (475 U.S. 534), decided by a 5-4 vote, March 25, 1986. Stevens wrote the opinion; Burger, Rehnquist, White and Powell dissented.

An individual school board member and parent lacks standing to pursue an appeal that the full board has declined to pursue. In this case, the appeal was from a court decision permitting a high school student religious group to meet during the school day on school grounds. The school officials denied the group permission to meet because they were concerned that such a meeting would violate the Establishment Clause; the district court reversed the officials' decision.

**Goldman v. Weinberger** (475 U.S. 503), decided by a 5-4 vote, March 25, 1986. Rehnquist wrote the opinion;

Brennan, Marshall, Blackmun and O'Connor dissented.

The First Amendment guarantee of freedom of religion does not require the Air Force to permit an officer who is also an Orthodox Jewish rabbi to wear his yarmulke, or skullcap, indoors while in uniform and on duty.

**Bowen v. Roy** (476 U.S. 693), decided by an 8-1 vote, June 11, 1986. Burger wrote the opinion; White dissented.

Freedom of religion is not violated by a requirement that citizens applying for food stamps report Social Security numbers for all members of their family, even if obtaining and using a Social Security number for a child is against the religious beliefs of the parents.

**Hobbie v. Unemployment Appeals Commission of Florida** (480 U.S. 136), decided by an 8-1 vote, Feb. 25, 1987. Brennan wrote the opinion; Rehnquist dissented.

A state violates the First Amendment's guarantee of freedom of religion when it denies unemployment benefits to a woman who was fired from her job because she would not work on her Sabbath.

"The state may not force an employee to choose between following the precepts of her religion and forfeiting benefits ... and abandoning one of the precepts of her religion in order to accept work," wrote Brennan for the court.

**Edwards v. Aguillard** (482 U.S. 578), decided by a 7-2 vote, June 19, 1987. Brennan wrote the opinion; Rehnquist and Scalia dissented.

A Louisiana law requiring public schools that teach the theory of evolution also to teach "creation science" violated the Establishment Clause because it was clearly intended to advance religious beliefs that depend upon the creation of the world by a divine intelligence.

**Corporation of the Presiding Bishop of the Church of Jesus Christ of Latter-Day Saints v. Amos, United States v. Amos** (483 U.S. 327), decided by a 9-0 vote, June 24, 1987. White wrote the opinion.

Congress did not violate the Establishment Clause when, as part of Title VII of the 1964 Civil Rights Act, it exempted religious organizations from the general prohibition against job discrimination based on religion. The exemption is valid, even when extended to the secular nonprofit activities of a church.

**Karcher v. May** (484 U.S. 72), decided by an 8-0 vote, Dec. 1, 1987. O'Connor wrote the opinion.

Two former New Jersey legislators who participated, as leaders of the legislature, in a suit to defend the constitutionality of the state's moment-of-silence law cannot pursue the suit after they lost their positions of legislative leadership.

**Lyng v. Northwest Indian Cemetery Protective Association** (485 U.S. 439), decided by a 5-3 vote, April 19, 1988. O'Connor wrote the opinion; Brennan, Marshall and Blackmun dissented. Kennedy did not participate.

Incidental effects of government programs, which may interfere with the practice of certain religions but have no tendency to coerce individuals into acting contrary to their religious beliefs, do not require the government to assert a compelling justification for its otherwise lawful actions. The Free Exercise clause of the First Amendment is written in terms of what the government cannot do to the individual, not in terms of what the individual can exact from the government. In this case, the government was not barred from building a road near sacred Indian grounds in California.

**Employment Division v. Smith, Employment Division v. Black** (485 U.S. 660), decided by a 5-3 vote, April 27, 1988. Stevens wrote the opinion; Brennan, Marshall and Blackmun dissented. Kennedy did not participate.

The First Amendment protects legitimate claims to the free exercise of religion, not activity a state has validly proscribed. The state court must determine whether religious use of peyote is legal, before the high court can determine whether the state violates the First Amendment by withholding unemployment benefits from American Indians who used peyote for religious purposes.

**Bowen v. Kendrick**, decided by a 5-4 vote, June 29, 1988. Rehnquist wrote the opinion; Blackmun, Brennan, Marshall and Stevens dissented.

The Adolescent Family Life Act (PL 97-35), which channels federal funds to religious groups to promote sexual abstinence, does not on its face abridge the constitutional separation of church and state. The court found that the law had a secular purpose, the prevention of pregnancy, and did not have the primary effect of advancing religion or entangling church and state.

## Freedom of the Press

**Harper & Row Publishers Inc. v. Nation Enterprises** (471 U.S. 539), decided by a 6-3 vote, May 20, 1985. O'Connor wrote the opinion; Brennan, White and Marshall dissented.

The First Amendment does not shield the press from suits for copyright infringement in cases involving extensive use of quotations from unpublished copyrighted material without the permission of the copyright holder.

The court held that *The Nation* magazine violated federal copyright law when it used significant quotations from President Gerald R. Ford's then-unpublished memoirs in an April 1979 article about Ford's decision to pardon his predecessor, Richard Nixon.

This use of Ford's material did not come within the "fair use" exception to the copyright law for "criticism, comment, news reporting, teaching, scholarship or research," the court held. The magazine could have reported on the information in the Ford book without risk, but it had no right to quote large segments from the memoirs without authorization.

**Philadelphia Newspapers Inc. v. Hepps** (475 U.S. 767), decided by a 5-4 vote, April 21, 1986. O'Connor wrote the opinion; Stevens, Burger, Rehnquist and White dissented.

Private persons who sue for libel must prove the falsity of the challenged report as well as fault on the part of the media before they can recover damages. The court applied this standard to cases in which the alleged libel involves some issue of public concern.

The court held invalid a Pennsylvania law that required the media defendant in such a case to prove the truth of the contested report in order to avoid a damage award. At least eight other states had such laws.

**Anderson v. Liberty Lobby Inc.** (477 U.S. 242), decided by a 6-3 vote, June 25, 1986. White wrote the opinion; Brennan, Rehnquist and Burger dissented.

Judges should summarily dismiss libel charges brought by a public figure unless they find "clear and convincing evidence" of actual malice in the challenged report, the same standard of proof that a plaintiff must meet to prevail at trial.

**Press-Enterprise Co. v. Superior Court** (478 U.S. 1), decided by a 7-2 vote, June 30, 1986. Burger wrote the opinion; Rehnquist and Stevens dissented.

The First Amendment guarantees that pretrial criminal proceedings be open to the public unless they must be closed to preserve some higher value, and unless closure is narrowly tailored to serve that interest.

**Hazelwood School District v. Kuhlmeier** (484 U.S. 260), decided by a 5-3 vote, Jan. 13, 1988. White wrote the opinion; Brennan, Marshall and Blackmun dissented.

Public school officials have wide latitude to censor student publications and other "expressive activities" so long as an official's action is "reasonably related to legitimate pedagogical concerns."

**Hustler Magazine Inc. v. Falwell** (485 U.S. 46), decided by an 8-0 vote, Feb. 24, 1988. Rehnquist wrote the opinion. Kennedy did not participate.

Public figures and public officials cannot collect damages in libel suits for intentional infliction of emotional distress even if they are caricatured and parodied in "outrageous" and offensive manner. To prevail, the public figure or official must meet the actual malice standard, proving that the offensive statements were false or made with reckless disregard of whether the information was false.

**U.S. v. Providence Journal Co.** (485 U.S. 693), decided by a 6-2 vote, May 2, 1988. Blackmun wrote the opinion; Stevens and Rehnquist dissented. Kennedy did not participate.

The court dismissed this case of criminal contempt against the Providence paper after it found that the special prosecutor appointed by a federal district court to prosecute the contempt had no authority to represent the United States before the high court and had not requested such authority from the U.S. solicitor general.

**City of Lakewood v. Plain Dealer Publishing Co.** (486 U.S. 750), decided by a 4-3 vote, June 17, 1988. Brennan wrote the opinion; White, Stevens and O'Connor dissented. Rehnquist and Kennedy did not participate.

A licensing statute that gives unbridled discretion to a government official to grant or deny permits for placing newspaper racks on public property (sidewalks) constitutes a prior restraint in violation of the First Amendment.

## Right of Petition

**McDonald v. Smith** (472 U.S. 479), decided by an 8-0 vote, June 19, 1985. Burger wrote the opinion. Powell did not participate.

The First Amendment right to petition the government does not shield those who exercise it from being sued for libel by persons who allege that they are defamed by the petition or letter.

**Walters v. National Association of Radiation Survivors** (473 U.S. 305), decided by a 6-3 vote, June 28, 1985. Rehnquist wrote the opinion; Brennan, Marshall and Stevens dissented.

Congress did not deny veterans due process, nor did it limit their right effectively to petition the government for redress of grievances, when it limited to $10 the amount that a veteran can pay an attorney for representing him in pursuing death or disability claims before the Veterans Administration.

The court upheld the 1862 law, emphasizing that Congress did not intend for such benefit disagreements to become adversary proceedings.

## Obscenity

**Brockett v. Spokane Arcades, Eikenberry v. J-R Distributors** (472 U.S. 491), decided by a 6-2 vote, June 19, 1985. White wrote the opinion; Brennan and Marshall dissented. Powell did not participate.

The First Amendment does not permit a state to ban material merely because it incites "lust."

The portion of Washington state's anti-obscenity law permitting regulation or banning of such material is unconstitutional because it covers material that "does no more than arouse 'good, old-fashioned, healthy' interest in sex." But the appeals court went too far in striking down the entire law as unconstitutional; only the "lust" provision is invalid.

**Pope v. Illinois** (481 U.S. 497), decided by a 6-3 vote, May 4, 1987. White wrote the opinion; Brennan, Marshall and Stevens dissented.

Community standards should not be applied in deciding whether allegedly obscene materials have scientific, literary or artistic value. A less parochial standard must be used for this determination, although community standards may be used in deciding whether material appeals to a prurient interest in sex and is patently offensive.

**Virginia v. American Booksellers Association** (484 U.S. 383), decided by an 8-0 vote, Jan. 25, 1988. Brennan wrote the opinion.

The court declined to address the constitutional issues raised in a challenge to a Virginia law barring stores from "knowingly" displaying sexual or sadomasochistic material where individuals under 18 might "examine and peruse" the material. The court said it needed more information about how the statute would operate before it could rule and sent the case to the Virginia Supreme Court with specific questions to be answered.

## Trademarks

**San Francisco Arts & Athletics Inc. v. United States Olympic Committee (USOC)** (483 U.S. 522), decided by votes of 7-2 and 5-4, June 25, 1987. Powell wrote the opinion; O'Connor, Blackmun, Brennan and Marshall dissented.

Congress did not violate the First Amendment when it granted the USOC the power to deny other groups the right to use the word "Olympic" for commercial and promotional purposes. The decision of Congress to give the USOC a limited property right in the word falls within the traditional scope of trademark law protection.

# Election Laws

## Voting Rights

**NAACP v. Hampton County Election Commission** (470 U.S. 166), decided by a 9-0 vote, Feb. 27, 1985. White wrote the opinion.

Counties subject to the "pre-clearance" requirements of the Voting Rights Act must seek federal approval of a decision to hold a special election for school board officials and to limit candidates in that election to those who had qualified to run prior to the last general election.

**Hunter v. Underwood** (471 U.S. 222), decided by an 8-0 vote, April 16, 1985. Rehnquist wrote the opinion. Powell did not participate.

A provision of Alabama's Constitution denying the right to vote to people convicted of certain non-prison offenses involving moral turpitude was adopted in 1901 with racially discriminatory intent and operates in a racially discriminatory manner. It therefore violates the Equal Protection Clause of the U.S. Constitution.

**Davis v. Bandemer** (478 U.S. 109), decided by votes of 6-3 and 7-2, June 30, 1986. White wrote the opinion; O'Connor, Burger and Rehnquist dissented in part; Powell and Stevens dissented in part.

Political gerrymanders are subject to constitutional challenge and review by federal courts, even if the disputed districts meet the "one person, one vote" test, the court held 6-3.

By 7-2, however, the justices upheld a 1981 Indiana reapportionment plan that heavily favored the Republican Party — saying that more than one election's results are necessary to prove a gerrymander unconstitutional.

**Thornburg v. Gingles** (478 U.S. 30), decided by votes of 9-0 and 6-3, June 30, 1986. Brennan wrote the opinion; Stevens, Blackmun and Marshall dissented in part.

The court agreed with a lower court that six of North Carolina's multi-member legislative districts impermissibly diluted the strength of black votes in violation of the Voting Rights Act.

This was the first time that the court applied 1982 amendments to the Voting Rights Act (PL 97-205) that required courts to look at the results of a challenged practice, not just its intent, in deciding whether it was discriminatory.

Those amendments were adopted to reverse a 1980 Supreme Court decision, *Mobile v. Bolden* (446 U.S. 55), that required proof of discriminatory intent before a violation of the Voting Rights Act could be found.

The court rejected the argument that once one or more black candidates have been elected from a challenged district, the district is immune from challenge under the Voting Rights Act.

**City of Pleasant Grove v. United States** (479 U.S. 462), decided by a 6-3 vote, Jan. 21, 1987. White wrote the opinion; Powell, Rehnquist and O'Connor dissented.

The annexation of uninhabited land by a city with a history of discrimination is a change in voting law or practice that must be pre-cleared by the attorney general or a federal court under the Voting Rights Act of 1965. The court backed the attorney general's refusal to approve such an annexation by the Alabama city of Pleasant Grove.

## Campaign Finance

**Federal Election Commission v. National Conservative Political Action Committee (NCPAC), Democratic Party of the United States v. NCPAC** (470 U.S. 480), decided by votes of 5-4 and 7-2, March 18, 1985. Rehnquist wrote the opinion; Marshall and White dissented; Brennan and Stevens dissented in part.

Congress cannot limit independent spending by political action committees (PACs) in presidential campaigns, the court ruled 7-2. The court held unconstitutional, as a violation of the First Amendment guarantee of free speech, a provision of the Federal Election Campaign Act Amendments (PL 93-443) that limited to $1,000 the amount a PAC could spend independently to promote or prevent the election of publicly funded presidential candidates.

In the context of a national presidential campaign, the majority found this limit curtailed freedom of speech in the same way as "allowing a speaker in a public hall to express his views while denying him the use of an amplifying system."

By 5-4, the court held that Congress did not intend to permit one private group, the Democratic Party, to sue another, the National Conservative Political Action Committee, for violating the $1,000 limit. Only the Federal Election Commission can move to enforce the law against NCPAC or another party in such circumstances without first going through administrative proceedings.

**Federal Election Commission v. Massachusetts Citizens for Life** (479 U.S. 238), decided by a 5-4 vote, Dec. 15, 1986. Brennan wrote the opinion; Rehnquist, White, Blackmun and Stevens dissented.

The First Amendment's guarantee of free speech protects ideological advocacy groups from strict federal limitations on their political expenditures. Non-profit ideological corporations do not have to comply with federal election laws that require all corporations to form separate political action committees (PACs) to engage in political activities and that ban the use of funds from the general corporate treasury to fund such activities.

The court exempted corporations formed to promote political ideas, provided they have no shareholders or other persons who benefit financially from their operations, were not set up by a business corporation or labor union and do not receive funds from either.

# Business Law

## Antitrust

**Marrese v. American Academy of Orthopaedic Surgeons** (470 U.S. 373), decided by a 7-0 vote, March 4, 1985. O'Connor wrote the opinion. Blackmun and Stevens did not participate.

Although federal antitrust claims are within the exclusive jurisdiction of the federal courts, a federal court hearing such a claim cannot ignore state law and automatically hold that federal courts are barred from hearing that claim by a prior state judgment arising out of the same facts but resolving a differently based claim.

**Town of Hallie v. City of Eau Claire** (471 U.S. 34), decided by a 9-0 vote, March 27, 1985. Powell wrote the opinion.

Allegedly anti-competitive conduct by a city, if authorized by state law, is immune from challenge under antitrust laws as "state action" — even if the state does not actively supervise the city's implementation of policy. Such active supervision is necessary only when a private party is carrying out a state policy and hopes to claim the protection of the "state action" exemption from antitrust laws.

**Southern Motor Carriers Rate Conference Inc. v. United States** (471 U.S. 48), decided by a 7-2 vote, March 27, 1985. Powell wrote the opinion; Stevens and White dissented.

Collective rate making by common carrier rate bureaus for submission to state public service commissions is protected from federal antitrust challenge under the "state action" exemption so long as the activities are authorized by states in which the rate bureaus operate.

**Northwest Wholesale Stationers Inc. v. Pacific Stationery and Printing Co.** (472 U.S. 284), decided by a 7-0 vote, June 11, 1985. Brennan wrote the opinion. Powell and Marshall did not participate.

A wholesale purchasing cooperative does not commit a per se violation of Section 1 of the Sherman Antitrust Act — which declares every restraint of trade illegal — when it expels a member without notice, hearing or the opportunity to challenge the expulsion decision.

Such action is not clearly a group boycott or concerted refusal to deal in violation of Section 1 but should be reviewed under the "rule of reason" standard to determine whether it constitutes an unreasonable restraint of trade.

**Aspen Skiing Co. v. Aspen Highlands Skiing Corp.** (472 U.S. 585), decided by an 8-0 vote, June 19, 1985. Stevens wrote the opinion. White did not participate.

Evidence in an antitrust case that a firm with monopoly power exercised that power in violation of the Sherman Act by refusing to deal with a competitor is sufficient to justify a jury's conclusion that an antitrust violation did occur.

**Mitsubishi Motors Corp. v. Soler Chrysler-Plymouth Inc.** (473 U.S. 614), decided by a 5-3 vote, July 2, 1985. Blackmun wrote the opinion; Brennan, Marshall and Stevens dissented. Powell did not participate.

American courts have power to order international arbitration of antitrust disputes between foreign manufacturers and their distributors in the United States. Antitrust claims by a Puerto Rican car dealer against a Japanese manufacturer and another foreign distributor are arbitrable under the arbitration clause of their sales agreement.

**Fisher v. City of Berkeley, Calif.** (475 U.S. 260), decided by an 8-1 vote, Feb. 26, 1986. Marshall wrote the opinion; Brennan dissented.

Federal antitrust law forbidding price-fixing conspiracies does not prevent cities from adopting and enforcing rent control ordinances. Such laws are unilaterally imposed by the city and thus do not represent the sort of concerted action that the antitrust laws were written to prevent.

**Matsushita Electric Industrial Co. Ltd. v. Zenith Radio Corp.** (475 U.S. 574), decided by a 5-4 vote, March 26, 1986. Powell wrote the opinion; White, Brennan, Blackmun and Stevens dissented.

Zenith Radio failed to present sufficient evidence to justify a trial on its claim that Japanese television manufacturers conspired to sell television sets at particularly low prices in order to push U.S. manufacturers out of the market. Therefore, the federal district court was correct in dismissing the suit, a decision the appeals court was wrong to overturn.

This decision moved this long-running antitrust case, first filed in 1970, closer to a conclusion. The court sent the case back to the appeals court, pointing out that it was free to consider whether Zenith had any additional evidence to present.

**Square D Co. v. Niagara Frontier Tariff Bureau Inc.** (476 U.S. 409), decided by an 8-1 vote, May 27, 1986. Stevens wrote the opinion; Marshall dissented.

Under *Keogh v. Chicago & Northwestern Railway Co.* (1922), private parties may not sue regulated truckers for treble damages, arguing that the truckers' rates, filed with the Interstate Commerce Commission (ICC), are in fact illegal price fixing in violation of antitrust laws. By virtue of ICC approval, these rates are legal and cannot be used as the basis for such a suit.

**Federal Trade Commission v. Indiana Federation of Dentists** (476 U.S. 477), decided by a 9-0 vote, June 2, 1986. White wrote the opinion.

Dentists may not escape the reach of federal antitrust laws by arguing that their coordinated decision to refuse to supply insurance companies with patients' X-rays was necessary to preserve the moral and ethical standards of their profession.

**Cargill Inc. v. Monfort of Colorado Inc.** (479 U.S. 104), decided by a 6-2 vote, Dec. 9, 1986. Brennan wrote the opinion; Stevens and White dissented. Blackmun did not participate.

A company may win a court order to block the acquisition of one competitor by another only if it can show that the acquisition will have negative effects on competition.

**Business Electronics Corp. v. Sharp Electronics Corp.** (485 U.S. 717), decided by a 6-2 vote, May 2, 1988. Scalia wrote the opinion; Stevens and White dissented. Kennedy did not participate.

A vertical restraint of trade — in this case a manufacturer's termination of a discounting retailer after complaint by another retailer — is not a per se violation of the antitrust law unless there is some agreement on price or price levels charged by the remaining dealer. Such restraints of trade must be judged on a case-by-case basis by the rule of reason.

**Patrick v. Burget** (486 U.S. 94), decided by an 8-0 vote, May 16, 1988. Marshall wrote the opinion. Blackmun did not participate.

Oregon doctors are not protected from federal antitrust liability for their activities on hospital peer review committees.

The activities in question — determining whether a doctor can have hospital privileges — are not supervised by state officials, which is a requirement in order to be covered by the "state action" exemption from challenge under antitrust laws.

**Allied Tube & Conduit Corp. v. Indian Head** (486 U.S. 492), decided by a 7-2 vote, June 13, 1988. Brennan wrote the opinion; White and O'Connor dissented.

When competition is restrained by valid governmental action, those urging that governmental action are immune from antitrust liability for the restraint of competition. Such immunity is not available to a corporation that tried to influence a private association without official authority that sets standards for its members. Such an organization cannot be treated as "quasi-legislative" simply because legislatures routinely adopt its code.

## Aviation

**Air France v. Saks** (470 U.S. 392), decided by an 8-0 vote, March 4, 1985. O'Connor wrote the opinion. Powell did not participate.

A passenger who suffers a permanent hearing loss as a result of normal and usual operation of the aircraft's pressurization system is not injured by an accident within the meaning of the Warsaw Convention, which governs the liability of air carriers to their passengers, and thus may not sue the airlines for damages under it.

**Eastern Air Lines Inc. v. Mahfoud** (474 U.S. 213), affirmed by a 4-4 vote, Dec. 10, 1985. Brennan did not participate.

After two rounds of argument, the court left intact a lower court ruling permitting awards of both pre- and post-judgment interest in wrongful-death lawsuits brought under the Warsaw Treaty, which governs suits growing out of international airplane crashes.

## Banking

**Northeast Bancorp Inc. v. Board of Governors of Federal Reserve System** (472 U.S. 159), decided by an 8-0 vote, June 10, 1985. Rehnquist wrote the opinion. Powell did not participate.

Existing regional banking agreements — under which states permit acquisition of in-state banks by banks located in some, but not all, other states — are neither illegal nor unconstitutional.

The Douglas amendment to the Bank Holding Company Act generally prohibits interstate banking but permits state legislatures to lift that barrier by specifically authorizing interstate bank acquisitions. The language of the amendment allows states to permit some or all interstate bank acquisitions.

Because Congress specifically gave states this power, laws permitting regional banking are immune from challenge as unconstitutional impediments to the flow of interstate commerce.

**Board of Governors of the Federal Reserve System v. Dimension Financial Corp.** (474 U.S. 261), decided by a 9-0 vote, Jan. 22, 1986. Burger wrote the opinion.

The Board of Governors exceeded its authority to administer the Bank Holding Company Act of 1956 when it redefined key terms in that law — "demand deposits" and "commercial loans" — in an effort to bring limited-service banks within the scope of federal regulation. These "non-bank banks" either make commercial loans or accept demand deposits, but not both.

**Federal Deposit Insurance Corp. v. Philadelphia Gear Corp.** (476 U.S. 426), decided by a 6-3 vote, May 27, 1986. O'Connor wrote the opinion; Blackmun, Marshall and Rehnquist dissented.

Standby letters of credit are not federally insured bank deposits. Such letters of credit are simply not the sort of assets that Congress intended to protect by setting up a federal deposit insurance plan.

**Clarke v. Securities Industry Association, Security Pacific National Bank v. Securities Industry Association** (479 U.S. 388), decided by an 8-0 vote, Jan. 14, 1987. White wrote the opinion. Scalia did not participate.

National banks can set up discount brokerage arms outside the states where they have branches. The court upheld a 1982 decision by the comptroller of the currency permitting a California bank to set up an affiliate offering discount brokerage services both at branch offices and at other locations, including some outside California. The court held that discount brokerage services are not "the general business" of a national bank that must be limited to its headquarters and branches.

**Langley v. Federal Deposit Insurance Corp.** (484 U.S. 86), decided by an 8-0 vote, Dec. 1, 1987. Scalia wrote the opinion.

Federal regulators have the right to collect debts owed to failed banks they take over even when the debtor claims that the debt was invalid.

**Federal Deposit Insurance Corp. v. Mallen** (486 U.S. 230), decided by a 9-0 vote, May 31, 1988. Stevens wrote the opinion.

The constitutional guarantee of due process is not violated by the law that authorizes the Federal Deposit Insurance Corp. to suspend an indicted bank official from his job for up to 90 days without the benefit of a post-suspension ruling or the right of the official to testify at any hearing. Such action is justified by the government's interest in protecting depositers and ensuring public confidence in banks.

## Bankruptcy

**Commodity Futures Trading Commission v. Weintraub** (471 U.S. 343), decided by an 8-0 vote, April 29, 1985. Marshall wrote the opinion. Powell did not participate.

The trustee of a bankrupt corporation has the authority to waive the corporation's attorney-client privilege with regard to conversations that occurred before the bankruptcy filing.

**Kelly v. Robinson** (479 U.S. 36), decided by a 7-2 vote, Nov. 17, 1986. Powell wrote the opinion; Marshall and Stevens dissented.

Convicted criminals who have been ordered by courts to make restitution to their victims may not invoke the federal bankruptcy law to avoid paying up.

**United Savings Association of Texas v. Timbers of Inwood Forest Associates Ltd.** (484 U.S. 365), decided by an 8-0 vote, Jan. 20, 1988. Scalia wrote the opinion.

Undersecured creditors in a bankruptcy proceeding

are not entitled to reimbursement under the bankruptcy code for delays caused by an automatic stay provision relating to the foreclosure on the collateral in question.

**Norwest Bank Worthington v. Ahlers** (485 U.S. 197), decided by an 8-0 vote, March 7, 1988. White wrote the opinion. Kennedy did not participate.

Financially troubled farmers may not avoid foreclosure under federal bankruptcy law by promising to use their labor and expertise to continue operating their farm. The court said a creditor's right to protection under the bankruptcy law cannot be met by such a promise.

## Communications

**Louisiana Public Service Commission v. Federal Communications Commission (FCC)** (476 U.S. 355), decided by a 5-2 vote, May 27, 1986. Brennan wrote the opinion; Burger and Blackmun dissented. Powell and O'Connor did not participate.

Congress, in passing the Communications Act of 1934, specifically forbade the FCC to interfere in setting intrastate telephone rates. The FCC's 1983 order requiring local telephone companies to accelerate their depreciation of plant equipment is therefore invalid, pre-empting a decision that Congress intended to be left to the states.

**Public Service Commission of Maryland v. Chesapeake and Potomac Telephone Company of Maryland** (476 U.S. 445), vacated by a 7-0 vote, May 27, 1986. *Per curiam* (unsigned) opinion. Powell and O'Connor did not participate.

The court sent back to the U.S. Court of Appeals for the 4th Circuit a case in which that court had required Maryland utility regulators to use the Federal Communications Commission's (FCC) new depreciation method. The court directed that a second look at this case be taken in light of the ruling in *Louisiana Public Service Commission v. FCC.*

**Federal Communications Commission (FCC) v. Florida Power Corp.** (480 U.S. 245), decided by a 9-0 vote, Feb. 25, 1987. Marshall wrote the opinion.

The FCC does not "take" private property for public use when it implements the Pole Attachments Act, which authorizes it to determine the rates that public utilities may charge to cable television systems for using space on the telephone poles to string their cable.

**City of New York v. Federal Communications Commission (FCC)** (486 U.S. 57), decided by a 9-0 vote, May 16, 1988. White wrote the opinion.

The FCC did not exceed its statutory authority by forbidding local authorities to impose more stringent technical cable signal quality standards than those established in commission regulations.

## Copyright/Trademark

**Mills Music Inc. v. Snyder** (469 U.S. 153), decided by a 5-4 vote, Jan. 8, 1985. Stevens wrote the opinion; White, Brennan, Marshall and Blackmun dissented.

A music publisher may continue to receive some royalties from its recordings of a copyrighted song that qualify as derivative works within the meaning of the 1976 Copyright Act even after the heirs to one of the song's writers have reacquired the copyright from the publisher. The song involved in this case was "Who's Sorry Now?"

**Park 'n Fly Inc. v. Dollar Park and Fly Inc.** (469 U.S. 189), decided by an 8-1 vote, Jan. 8, 1985. O'Connor wrote the opinion; Stevens dissented.

A person charged with infringing upon the use of a trademark may not defend himself against that charge by arguing that the allegedly infringing practice simply describes his business.

**K Mart Corp. v. Cartier Inc.** (485 U.S. 176, 486 U.S. 28), decided by a 5-3 vote, March 7, 1988. Brennan wrote the opinion; Scalia, Rehnquist and O'Connor dissented. Kennedy did not participate. The case was reargued and decided by a 5-4 vote, May 31, 1988. Blackmun joined the dissenters in the second ruling; Kennedy wrote the court's opinion.

Federal district courts have jurisdiction over a trademark dispute over "parallel" imports, or "gray-market" goods. The court called for a second round of arguments on the issue of whether a conflict between the 1930 Tariff Act and Customs Services regulation involved an embargo and should come under the exclusive jurisdiction of the Court of International Trade.

In the second ruling the court held that the disputed Customs Service regulation was valid. It allowed retailers to buy trademarked, foreign goods — watches, cameras, perfumes and other products — from independent distributors and sell them in the United States at reduced prices without the consent of the U.S. trademark holders. The court said the regulation was valid when the U.S. trademark was owned by a U.S. company that is either the parent or subsidiary of the foreign manufacturer. Most gray-market sales, the court held, are exempt from the Tariff Act, which bars importation of products bearing a trademark that is owned in the United States.

Kennedy was joined by Scalia, Rehnquist, O'Connor and Blackmun in holding that gray-market sales are illegal when the owner of the U.S. trademark authorizes its use abroad by an independent foreign manufacturer. On that point, Brennan, Marshall, White and Stevens dissented.

## Postal Service

**Regents of the University of California v. Public Employment Relations Board** (485 U.S. 589), decided by a 6-2 vote, April 20, 1988. O'Connor wrote the opinion; Stevens and Marshall dissented. Kennedy did not participate.

The University of California properly refused to carry letters in its internal mail system from the American Federation of State, County and Municipal Employees to university employees. To do so would violate the Private Express Statutes, which establish the postal monopoly and generally prohibit the private carriage of letters over postal routes without paying the U.S. Postal Service. The union's letter did not fall within the exceptions to the statute.

**Loeffler v. Frank, Postmaster General of the United States** (486 U.S. 549), decided by a 5-3 vote, June 13, 1988. Blackmun wrote the opinion; White, Rehnquist and O'Connor dissented. Kennedy did not participate.

Prejudgment interest may be awarded in a suit against the Postal Service brought under Title VII of the 1964 Civil Rights Act. When Congress put the Service into the commercial world, and included a sue-and-be-sued clause in the Postal Reorganization Act, Congress gave it the status of a private commercial enterprise, and the Service's liability is the same as that of any other business.

## Product Liability

**East River Steamship Corp. v. Transamerica Delaval Inc.** (476 U.S. 858), decided by a 9-0 vote, June 16, 1986. Blackmun wrote the opinion.

Product liability claims based on negligence and theories of strict liability may be decided under general maritime law. But in a case that causes injury only to the product, not to any other property or individual, the manufacturer is not liable; economic losses by a commercial product user can only be recovered under contract law.

**Boyle v. United Technologies Corp.**, decided by a 5-4 vote, June 27, 1988. Scalia wrote the opinion; Brennan, Marshall, Blackmun and Stevens dissented.

Government contractors may not be held liable under state law for defects in their products sold to the government, if the government approved precise specifications for those products, the products met those specifications and the contractors warned the government about the dangers involved in using the products.

## Railroads

**National Railroad Passenger Corp. v. Atchison, Topeka and Santa Fe Railway Co.** (470 U.S. 451), decided by an 8-0 vote, March 18, 1985. Marshall wrote the opinion. Powell did not participate.

Congress acted within constitutional limits when it amended the Rail Passenger Service Act to require privately owned railroads to reimburse Amtrak for the free or reduced-fare travel that Amtrak provides for the employees of the private railroads and their families.

**Interstate Commerce Commission (ICC) v. Texas** (476 U.S. 450), decided by a 9-0 vote, Jan. 20, 1987. Stevens wrote the opinion.

The ICC is authorized by the Staggers Rail Act of 1980 to exempt from state regulation some intrastate rail and truck transportation provided by an interstate rail carrier.

**Interstate Commerce Commission (ICC) v. Brotherhood of Locomotive Engineers** (482 U.S. 270), decided by a 9-0 vote, June 8, 1987. Scalia wrote the opinion.

Federal judges are not authorized to review a decision by the ICC to reject a petition to reconsider its decision approving a railroad merger, unless the parties seeking to appeal have new evidence.

## Regulation

**Thomas v. Union Carbide Agricultural Products Co.** (473 U.S. 568), decided by a 9-0 vote, July 1, 1985. O'Connor wrote the opinion.

The Federal Insecticide, Fungicide and Rodenticide Act does not violate the Constitution in permitting the Environmental Protection Agency to use data submitted by one company in support of a second company's application for registration of a pesticide, so long as the second company agrees to compensate the first for use of the data

— and insofar as the law provides for binding arbitration with limited judicial review, of any dispute over the amount of compensation.

**Transcontinental Gas Pipe Line Corp. v. State Oil and Gas Board of Mississippi** (474 U.S. 409), decided by a 5-4 vote, Jan. 22, 1986. Blackmun wrote the opinion; Rehnquist, Powell, Stevens and O'Connor dissented.

In deregulating the price of natural gas through the Natural Gas Policy Act of 1978, Congress did not intend to allow states to require interstate gas pipeline companies to buy gas from all owners of a common gas pool. Such "ratable taking" laws are still pre-empted by federal law.

**United States v. City of Fulton** (475 U.S. 657), decided by a 9-0 vote, April 7, 1986. Marshall wrote the opinion.

The secretary of energy has the power to impose interim rate increases for electricity generated by federal hydroelectric projects, subject to eventual approval by the Federal Energy Regulatory Commission.

**Young v. Community Nutrition Institute** (476 U.S. 974), decided by an 8-1 vote, June 17, 1986. O'Connor wrote the opinion; Stevens dissented.

The Food and Drug Administration is within its authority in using informal, rather than formal, methods to regulate the level in foods of aflatoxin, a cancer-causing mold that grows naturally on crops such as corn.

**Nantahala Power & Light Co. v. Thornburg** (476 U.S. 953), decided by a 7-0 vote, June 17, 1986. O'Connor wrote the opinion. Powell and Stevens did not participate.

North Carolina lacks authority to order a utility to sell power to in-state customers at rates lower than recommended by the Federal Energy Regulatory Commission.

**Brock v. Roadway Express** (481 U.S. 252), decided by a 6-3 vote, April 21, 1987. Marshall announced the judgment of the court in an opinion joined by Blackmun, Powell and O'Connor; Brennan and Stevens concurred in part; White, Rehnquist, Scalia and Stevens dissented in part.

A trucking employer was denied due process when the secretary of labor failed to provide him with the evidence upon which the secretary ordered the temporary reinstatement of a worker discharged for refusing to operate a vehicle that he believed to be unsafe. The secretary was not, however, required to give the employer a full evidentiary hearing complete with cross examination when ordering reinstatement of an employee discharged in violation of the Surface Transportation Assistance Act.

**Agency Holding Corp. v. Malley-Duff & Associates Inc.** (483 U.S. 143), decided by a 9-0 vote, June 22, 1987. O'Connor wrote the opinion.

The four-year statute of limitations contained in the Clayton Act is the most appropriate standard to apply to civil suits brought under the Racketeer Influenced and Corrupt Organizations Act, because of the similarity in both structure and purpose between those two laws.

**Federal Energy Regulatory Commission v. Martin Exploration Management Co.** (486 U.S. 20), decided by an 8-0 vote, May 31, 1988. Brennan wrote the opinion. White did not participate.

The court upheld a Federal Energy Regulatory Commission regulation determining that any gas that qualified for both deregulated and regulated treatment would be treated as deregulated.

**Huffman v. Western Nuclear Inc.** (486 U.S. 663), decided by a 9-0 vote, June 15, 1988. Blackmun wrote the opinion.

The Department of Energy is required to restrict the enrichment of imported uranium only if that step would help the viability of the domestic uranium production industry. If such restriction would not help the domestic industry, then no restrictions are necessary.

## Securities

**Dean Witter Reynolds Inc. v. Byrd** (470 U.S. 213), decided by a 9-0 vote, March 4, 1985. Marshall wrote the opinion.

A federal district court faced with a case in which there are claims of federal securities law violations and claims that under state law may be settled by arbitration must grant a motion to compel arbitration of the state claims while the federal court hears the securities complaint.

**Landreth Timber Co. v. Landreth, Gould v. Ruefenacht** (471 U.S. 681), decided by an 8-1 vote, May 28, 1985. Powell wrote the opinion; Stevens dissented.

Federal securities law applies to the sale of stock in a closely held company even when the purpose of the sale is the purchase of the entire business.

The court rejected the argument that the "sale of business" doctrine left resolution of disputes arising out of such transactions to state courts.

**Schreiber v. Burlington Northern Inc.** (472 U.S. 1), decided by a 7-0 vote, June 4, 1985. Burger wrote the opinion. Powell and O'Connor did not participate.

Federal securities law may not be used to challenge tender offers that are simply "unfair." Securities lawsuits charging fraud in a tender offer must show that a company's management misrepresented or failed to disclose certain crucial information.

**Bateman Eichler, Hill Richards Inc. v. Berner** (472 U.S. 299), decided by an 8-0 vote, June 11, 1985. Brennan wrote the opinion. Marshall did not participate.

Investors may pursue a private damages suit under federal securities law charging corporate officials and securities brokers with inducing them to buy stocks by giving them false "inside information" — even though the investors themselves, by trading on such information, also violated the law.

**Randall v. Loftsgaarden** (478 U.S. 647), decided by an 8-1 vote, July 2, 1986. O'Connor wrote the opinion; Brennan dissented.

An investor who sues for damages after he has been defrauded by a tax shelter promotion does not face having his damages reduced by the amount of tax shelter benefits he enjoyed.

**Commodity Futures Trading Commission v. Schor** (478 U.S. 833), decided by a 7-2 vote, July 7, 1986.

O'Connor wrote the opinion; Brennan and Marshall dissented.

The Commodity Futures Trading Commission has the authority to decide counterclaims based on state law when those counterclaims arise in the course of resolving complaints based on charges that federal commodities trading laws have been violated.

**Shearson/American Express Inc. v. McMahon** (482 U.S. 220), decided by votes of 9-0 and 5-4, June 8, 1987. O'Connor wrote the opinion; Blackmun, Brennan, Marshall and Stevens dissented.

Securities-fraud claims brought under the 1934 Securities Exchange Act can be forced to arbitration, rather than litigation, under the arbitration clause that is standard in most contracts between brokerages and their clients, the court held, 5-4. The court ruled 9-0 that many charges brought under the Racketeer Influenced and Corrupt Organizations Act also should be arbitrated instead of litigated.

**Carpenter v. U.S.** (484 U.S. 19), decided by votes of 8-0 and 4-4, Nov. 16, 1987. White wrote the opinion.

Federal mail and wire fraud statutes reach the use by a *Wall Street Journal* reporter of the paper's confidential business information for his financial benefit. The newspaper had a tangible interest in the confidentiality of the contents and timing of release of the information.

The court was evenly divided on whether the defendant had knowingly breached a duty of confidentiality by misappropriating prepublication information, and so it affirmed the lower court's ruling that his deliberate breach of confidentiality and concealment of the scheme was securities fraud.

**Basic Inc. v. Levinson** (485 U.S. 224), decided by votes of 6-0 and 4-2, March 7, 1988. Blackmun wrote the opinion; White and O'Connor dissented in part. Rehnquist, Scalia and Kennedy did not participate.

Preliminary merger negotiations can be "material" to disclosures required by federal securities laws, and companies and their officials can be held liable for falsely denying the existence of negotiations whenever a reasonable investor would consider negotiations significant, the court held unanimously. There does not have to be an "agreement-in-principle" about the price and structure of a deal for negotiations to be material. What is "material" will depend on the facts available in a case-by-case analysis, the court held. It is appropriate for a court, in handling a stockholder dispute, to rely on a "fraud-on-the-market" theory so that each aggrieved stockholder does not have to show that he personally relied on faulty information, the court held, 4-2. The presumption of reliance is rebuttable, however.

**Pinter v. Dahl** (486 U.S. 622), decided by a 7-1 vote, June 15, 1988. Blackmun wrote the opinion; Stevens dissented. Kennedy did not participate.

When sellers of unregistered securities are sued by investors over a loss, they can defend themselves by claiming that the investors were equally at fault because they knew the securities were not registered.

## Taxation

**Paulsen v. Commissioner of Internal Revenue** (469 U.S. 131), decided by a 6-2 vote, Jan. 8, 1985. Rehnquist wrote the opinion; O'Connor and Burger dissented.

Powell did not participate.

The merger of a stock savings and loan association with a mutual savings and loan association, in which the stockholders in the first exchanged their stock for accounts and certificates of deposit in the second, is not a tax-free reorganization under federal tax laws. The shareholders involved must pay income tax on the gain they realize through the exchange of stock for accounts and certificates.

**United States v. Boyle** (469 U.S. 241), decided by a 9-0 vote, Jan. 9, 1985. Burger wrote the opinion.

A taxpayer who files a late estate tax return is not excused from the penalty for late filing because he relied on his attorney to meet the deadlines.

**Tiffany Fine Arts Inc. v. United States** (469 U.S. 310), decided by a 9-0 vote, Jan. 9, 1985. Marshall wrote the opinion.

When the Internal Revenue Service (IRS) serves a summons on a holding company and its subsidiaries with the dual purpose of obtaining information about their tax liabilities and the tax liabilities of unnamed persons they have licensed to sell a certain device, the IRS is not required to obtain prior judicial approval for the summons.

Prior judicial approval is required only when the IRS seeks information on the tax liability of unnamed taxpayers, not when the person to whom the summons is issued also is the target of such an investigation.

**United States v. National Bank of Commerce** (472 U.S. 713), decided by a 5-4 vote, June 25, 1985. Blackmun wrote the opinion; Powell, Brennan, Marshall and Stevens dissented.

The Internal Revenue Service may seize the assets of a delinquent taxpayer contained in a joint bank account, even if only one of the account holders is delinquent in paying his taxes.

**United States v. American College of Physicians** (475 U.S. 834), decided by a 9-0 vote, April 22, 1986. Marshall wrote the opinion.

A tax-exempt organization that realizes a profit on the advertising it sells in its journal must pay federal income tax on that profit unless it can show that its solicitation and coordination of the advertising is substantially related to the organization's primary reason for being.

**Sorenson v. Secretary of the Treasury** (475 U.S. 851), decided by an 8-1 vote, April 22, 1986. Blackmun wrote the opinion; Stevens dissented.

Congress intended, under a provision included in the Omnibus Budget Reconciliation Act of 1981 (PL 97-35), to permit the Treasury to intercept tax refunds owed to persons who have failed to meet their child support obligations, including refunds resulting from excess earned-income credits.

**United States v. Hughes Properties** (476 U.S. 593), decided by 7-2 vote, June 3, 1986. Blackmun wrote the opinion; Stevens and Burger dissented.

A gambling casino using the accrual method of tax accounting may deduct the amount shown on its progressive slot machines' jackpot indicators at the close of a taxable year as an ordinary business expense incurred during that taxable year.

**United States v. Hemme** (476 U.S. 558), decided by a 9-0 vote, June 3, 1986. Marshall wrote the opinion.

Changes in federal estate taxes enacted in October 1978 apply retroactively to transactions during the previous month.

**United States v. American Bar Endowment** (477 U.S. 105), decided by a 6-1 vote, June 23, 1986. Marshall wrote the opinion; Stevens dissented. Powell and O'Connor did not participate.

Tax-exempt organizations must pay federal taxes on the profits earned from selling group insurance to their members; no portion of the premium paid for such insurance may be claimed as a charitable contribution.

**Jersey Shore State Bank v. United States** (479 U.S. 442), decided by a 9-0 vote, Jan. 20, 1987. Rehnquist wrote the opinion.

No notice or demand for payment is required by the law before the Internal Revenue Service brings a civil suit to collect unpaid withholding taxes from the creditors of delinquent employers.

**Commissioner of Internal Revenue v. Groetzinger** (480 U.S. 23), decided by a 6-3 vote, Feb. 24, 1987. Blackmun wrote the opinion; Rehnquist, White and Scalia dissented.

A full-time gambler is engaged in a "trade or business" within the meaning of the tax code and thus may deduct his gambling losses for federal tax purposes.

**United States v. General Dynamics Corp.** (481 U.S. 239), decided by a 6-3 vote, April 22, 1987. Marshall wrote the opinion; O'Connor, Blackmun and Stevens dissented.

Taxpayers using an accrual method of accounting may not deduct as a liability health benefits that are due employees but for which claims have not yet been filed or paid.

**Commissioner of Internal Revenue v. Fink** (483 U.S. 89), decided by an 8-1 vote, June 22, 1987. Powell wrote the opinion; Stevens dissented.

When a shareholder who holds the majority of a company's shares voluntarily hands over some of those shares to the company while retaining control, he does not immediately suffer a loss that he can deduct from his taxable income. Instead he must deduct the loss, if any, when he disposes of the remaining shares.

**Arkansas Best Corp. v. Commissioner of Internal Revenue** (485 U.S. 212), decided by an 8-0 vote, March 7, 1988. Marshall wrote the opinion. Kennedy did not participate.

A taxpayer's motivation in purchasing an asset is irrelevant in determining whether the asset is a "capital asset," income from the sale of which is taxed as capital, not ordinary, income. A business that sells stock and loses money may not claim that as ordinary, non-capital loss for federal income tax purposes.

**Commissioner of Internal Revenue v. Bollinger** (485 U.S. 340), decided by an 8-0 vote, March 22, 1988. Scalia wrote the opinion. Kennedy did not participate.

Individuals or business partnerships that form corporations to obtain financing for business enterprises are the owners of those ventures from the point of view of federal income tax. While the IRS has a right to make sure that the corporation and enterprise are for genuine purposes, the court said that when it is clear that a corporation functions as an agent for its shareholders, the losses incurred by those ventures are attributable to the partnerships who own them.

**U.S. v. Wells Fargo Bank** (485 U.S. 351), decided by an 8-0 vote, March 23, 1988. Brennan wrote the opinion. Kennedy did not participate.

A provision of the 1937 Housing Act, which exempts obligations of state and local public housing agencies from taxation does not exempt these notes from federal estate taxes.

# Labor Law

**National Labor Relations Board (NLRB) v. Action Automotive Inc.** (469 U.S. 490), decided by a 6-3 vote, Feb. 19, 1985. Burger wrote the opinion; Stevens, Rehnquist and O'Connor dissented.

Unions do not have to represent employees who are close relatives of management. The NLRB acted within its powers when it excluded from a union representation election employees who were related to the owner of the employer corporation.

**Herb's Welding Inc. v. Gray** (470 U.S. 414), decided by a 5-4 vote, March 19, 1985. White wrote the opinion; Marshall, Brennan, Blackmun and O'Connor dissented.

Workers on offshore drilling platforms in state waters are not engaged in maritime employment within the meaning of the Longshoremen's and Harbor Workers' Compensation Act and so are not covered by that law's death and disability benefits.

**Allis-Chalmers Corp. v. Lueck** (471 U.S. 202), decided by an 8-0 vote, April 16, 1985. Blackmun wrote the opinion. Powell did not participate.

An employee who feels that his employer violated state law by exhibiting bad faith in handling his claim for disability insurance cannot sue his employer in state courts. Such a suit must either be dismissed as pre-empted by the Labor Management Relations Act, which governs claims alleging violations of labor contracts, or be treated as a claim arising under that law and subject to arbitration.

**Cornelius v. Nutt** (472 U.S. 648), decided by a 6-2 vote, June 14, 1985. Blackmun wrote the opinion; Marshall and Brennan dissented. Powell did not participate.

The same standard — "harmful error" — applies to review of a federal agency's decision to discipline an employee whether or not that employee belongs to a union.

If the employee belongs to a union, that review usually is conducted by an arbitrator; if he does not, the review is by the Merit Systems Protection Board. Either way, the standard to be used is the same — the action should be overturned only if there is a showing of "substantial prejudice" to the individual employee's rights.

**National Labor Relations Board (NLRB) v. International Longshoremen's Association (ILA)** (473 U.S. 61), decided by a 6-3 vote, June 27, 1985. Brennan wrote the opinion; Rehnquist, Burger and O'Connor dissented.

ILA rules requiring that most containers to be loaded on ships must be loaded and unloaded by longshoremen if the process takes place within 50 miles of port are a valid work-preservation agreement.

The court overturned an NLRB ruling that the rules, adopted to preserve work for ILA members in the face of increasing containerization of freight, were invalid because they acquired for longshoremen work traditionally done by others.

**Pattern Makers' League of North America, AFL-CIO v. National Labor Relations Board (NLRB)** (473 U.S. 95), decided by a 5-4 vote, June 27, 1985. Powell wrote the opinion; Blackmun, Brennan, Stevens and Marshall dissented.

Unions violate the 1947 Taft-Hartley Act and the national policy of "voluntary unionism" when they discipline members who resign during a strike and return to work in violation of union rules.

The court upheld the NLRB's finding that it was illegal for unions to enforce rules forbidding members to resign during a strike.

**National Labor Relations Board (NLRB) v. Financial Institution Employees of America, Local 1182** (475 U.S. 192), decided by a 9-0 vote, Feb. 26, 1986. Brennan wrote the opinion.

An NLRB rule requiring non-union employees to be permitted to take part in elections to decide whether a local union would affiliate with an international union is irrational. Unless the board has reason to believe that the affiliation would change the union into a different entity, the NLRB should not interfere in this matter but should consider it an internal union affair.

**Chicago Teachers Union Local #1 v. Hudson** (475 U.S. 292), decided by a 9-0 vote, March 4, 1986. Stevens wrote the opinion.

Public employee unions must take special care and set up clear procedures to ensure that non-members who pay representation fees are not being forced to contribute to support "ideological" activities of the union with which they disagree.

The First Amendment protects non-union members from being forced to fund such activities.

Unions that collect representation fees from non-members must provide an adequate explanation of the size of the fee and a "reasonably prompt opportunity" to challenge the amount before a neutral decision maker, and must see that the disputed amount is placed in escrow pending a decision.

**AT&T Technologies v. Communication Workers of America** (475 U.S. 643), decided by a 9-0 vote, April 7, 1986. White wrote the opinion.

Whether a contractual arbitration agreement obligates parties to arbitrate a particular dispute is an issue for courts to decide, not to pass on to the arbitrator.

**Equal Employment Opportunity Commission v. Federal Labor Relations Authority** (476 U.S. 19), dismissed by a vote of 7-2, April 29, 1986. *Per curiam* (unsigned) opinion; White and Stevens dissented.

The court dismissed, after argument, a case concerning the negotiability of a union proposal requiring a federal agency to comply with federal guidelines for contracting-out work.

**Brock v. Pierce County** (476 U.S. 253), decided by a 9-0 vote, May 19, 1986. Marshall wrote the opinion.

Under the Comprehensive Employment and Training Act, the secretary of labor could move to recover misspent funds from grant recipients — even if he did not meet the law's 120-day deadline for resolving charges that funds had been misused.

**International Longshoremen's Association, AFL-CIO v. Davis** (476 U.S. 380), decided by votes of 8-1 and 5-4, May 27, 1986. White wrote the opinion; Rehnquist, Powell, Stevens and O'Connor dissented in part; Blackmun dissented in part.

The court with only one dissenting vote upheld a jury award against the International Longshoremen's Association to a man who lost his job because he tried to organize an affiliate of the union. He sued the union for failing to make good on its pledge to get his job back. The National Labor Relations Board's regional office rejected his unfair labor practice claim, holding that he was a supervisor, not an employee; at that point he successfully sued the union in state court for misrepresentation. The court upheld the award because the union had failed to show that this case was subject to federal labor law.

The court also held, 5-4, that the union was entitled to resolution of its belated claim that state court jurisdiction over this case was pre-empted by federal labor law.

**Offshore Logistics Inc. v. Tallentire** (477 U.S. 207), decided by votes of 9-0 and 5-4, June 23, 1986. O'Connor wrote the opinion; Powell, Brennan, Marshall and Stevens dissented in part.

A state tort law may not be applied to an accident that occurs on the high seas. The federal Death on the High Seas Act pre-empts application of state tort law beyond the state's territorial waters.

**International Union, United Automobile, Aerospace and Agricultural Implement Workers of America v. Brock** (477 U.S. 274), decided by a 5-4 vote, June 25, 1986. Marshall wrote the opinion; White, Burger, Powell and Rehnquist dissented.

A labor union has standing to sue the government in a dispute over trade readjustment benefits allegedly due some of its members. Associations are permitted to bring such cases on behalf of aggrieved members, as an alternative to class action suits.

**Atchison, Topeka & Santa Fe Railroad Co. v. Buell** (480 U.S. 557), decided by a 9-0 vote, March 24, 1987. Stevens wrote the opinion.

A railroad worker can sue his employer under the Federal Employers' Liability Act to recover damages for injuries suffered on the job as a result of working conditions that may also be subject to arbitration under the Railway Labor Act.

**Alaska Airlines v. Brock** (480 U.S. 678), decided by a 9-0 vote, March 25, 1987. Blackmun wrote the opinion.

Unconstitutional legislative veto provisions do not always invalidate the statutes of which they are a part, unless they were critical to the decision of Congress to pass the law in the first place.

The court reaffirmed its traditional standard for deciding when an unconstitutional provision can be severed from the rest of a law. "The unconstitutional provision must be severed unless the statute created in its absence is legislation that Congress would not have enacted," said the court. The result of the ruling in this case was to uphold an employee protection plan that was part of the Airline Deregulation Act of 1978 (PL 95-504).

**West v. Conrail** (481 U.S. 35), decided by a 9-0 vote, April 6, 1987. Stevens wrote the opinion.

The six-month statute of limitations imposed by federal law on unfair labor practice lawsuits does not apply to a worker's two-part suit against his employer for breaching a collective-bargaining agreement and against his union for failing to provide him fair representation.

**Burlington Northern Railroad Co. v. Brotherhood of Maintenance of Way Employees** (481 U.S. 429), decided by a 9-0 vote, April 28, 1987. Brennan wrote the opinion.

The Norris-LaGuardia Act denies federal judges the jurisdiction to order railroad union workers to stop secondary picketing; that is, picketing against railroads that are not clearly aligned with the railroad with which the union has its primary disagreement.

**National Labor Relations Board v. International Brotherhood of Electrical Workers, Local 340** (481 U.S. 573), decided by a 6-3 vote, May 18, 1987. Brennan wrote the opinion; O'Connor, Rehnquist and White dissented.

The National Labor Relations Act was not violated by a union that punished a supervisor who was a union member but did not participate in collective bargaining or deal with contract grievances.

**International Brotherhood of Electrical Workers v. Hechler** (481 U.S. 851), decided by votes of 9-0 and 8-1, May 26, 1987. Blackmun wrote the opinion; Stevens dissented.

A union member may not use state courts to sue union officials for breach of duty by failing to provide her with a safe place to work; that duty is too close to those imposed on the union by its collective-bargaining agreement (as well as by state law) to avoid being pre-empted by federal labor law and thus is a matter for resolution in federal courts.

**Fall River Dyeing & Finishing Corp. v. National Labor Relations Board** (482 U.S. 27), decided by a 6-3 vote, June 1, 1987. Blackmun wrote the opinion; Rehnquist, Powell and O'Connor dissented.

A business that takes over many of the assets of a previous business that has closed down, and does basically the same work, is a "successor employer" obligated by federal labor law to deal with the union that represented the employees of the previous business.

**Caterpillar Inc. v. Williams** (482 U.S. 386), decided by a 9-0 vote, June 9, 1987. Brennan wrote the opinion.

An employer sued by a worker for breach of an individual employment contract cannot remove the case from state to federal court by arguing that because the claim requires an interpretation of the collective-bargaining agreement, the claim thus arises under federal law.

**Perry v. Thomas** (482 U.S. 483), decided by a 7-2 vote, June 15, 1987. Marshall wrote the opinion; Stevens and O'Connor dissented.

The Federal Arbitration Act, which mandates enforcement of arbitration agreements, pre-empts a state law permitting a worker's suit for non-payment of his wages to be heard in state courts regardless of any prior agreement to arbitrate.

**Citicorp Industrial Credit Inc. v. Brock** (483 U.S. 27), decided by a 7-2 vote, June 22, 1987. Marshall wrote the opinion; Stevens and White dissented.

A creditor who acquires from a debtor goods produced in violation of the minimum wage and maximum-hour provisions of federal labor law may not introduce those goods into interstate commerce without violating the Fair Labor Standards Act.

**United Paperworkers International Union, AFL-CIO v. MISCO Inc.** (484 U.S. 29), decided by an 8-0 vote, Dec. 1, 1987. White wrote the opinion.

A federal court may not refuse to enforce an arbitration award pursuant to a collective-bargaining agreement because the court feels that the award conflicts with public policy.

**National Labor Relations Board v. United Food and Commercial Workers Union, Local 23** (484 U.S. 12), decided by an 8-0 vote, Dec. 14, 1987. Brennan wrote the opinion.

A court may not review an informal settlement by National Labor Relations Board officials of an unfair labor practice dispute.

**Mullins Coal Co. v. Director, Office of Workers' Compensation Programs** (484 U.S. 135), decided by a 6-2 vote, Dec. 14, 1987. Stevens wrote the opinion. Marshall and Brennan dissented.

A single piece of medical evidence that a miner has black lung disease is not sufficient to allow the miner to receive interim disability benefits unless there is a preponderance of evidence that the miner has the disease.

**Trans World Airlines (TWA) Inc. v. Independent Federation of Flight Attendants** (485 U.S. 175), decided by a 4-4 vote, March 2, 1988. *Per curiam* (unsigned) opinion. Kennedy did not participate.

The court deadlocked on an appeal by TWA from an appellate court ruling that it was obligated to continue collecting union dues from flight attendants after expiration of their union's contract in 1984.

**Lyng v. International Union, United Automobile, Aerospace and Agricultural Implement Workers** (485 U.S. 360), decided by a 5-3 vote, March 23, 1988. White wrote the opinion; Marshall, Brennan and Blackmun dissented. Kennedy did not participate.

Federal law that allows the government to bar food stamps to strikers does not infringe on First Amendment rights of freedom of association or freedom of speech.

**Edward J. DeBartolo Corp. v. Florida Gulf Coast Building & Construction Trades Council** (485

U.S. 568), decided by an 8-0 vote, April 20, 1988. White wrote the opinion. Kennedy did not participate.

It is not an unfair labor practice for unions to distribute handbills at a mall urging consumers to boycott "neutral employers" in the mall, even though the unions have no grievance against them but only one with the mall builder.

**Landers v. National Railroad Passenger Corp.** (485 U.S. 652), decided by a 9-0 vote, April 27, 1988. White wrote the opinion.

The Railway Labor Act does not entitle a railroad employee to be represented at company-level grievance or disciplinary proceedings by a union other than his collective-bargaining representative.

**U.S. Postal Service v. Letter Carriers** (485 U.S. 680), decided by a 9-0 vote, April 27, 1988. *Per curiam* (unsigned) opinion.

The court dismissed the writ of certiorari as improvidently granted in a case posing the question of whether an arbitrator's decision ordering reinstatement of an employee convicted of willfully failing to deliver the mail can be set aside as contrary to public policy.

**McLaughlin v. Richland Shoe Co.** (486 U.S. 128), decided by a 6-3 vote, May 16, 1988. Stevens wrote the opinion; Marshall, Brennan and Blackmun dissented.

To qualify for three years of back-pay for violations of the Fair Labor Standards Act, an individual must prove that his employer acted willfully to violate the law; that is, he either knew or showed reckless disregard for whether his conduct violated the law.

**Lingle v. Norge Division of Magic Chef Inc.** (486 U.S. 399), decided by a 9-0 vote, June 6, 1988. Stevens wrote the opinion.

State law giving an aggrieved worker the right to sue his employer for mistreatment is generally not pre-empted by federal labor law. Such pre-emption occurs only when application of the state law requires interpretation of a collective-bargaining agreement.

**Monessen Southwestern Railway Co. v. Morgan** (486 U.S. 330), decided by votes of 9-0 and 7-2, June 6, 1988. White wrote the opinion; Blackmun and Marshall dissented in part.

Federal law, not state law, governs the question of whether prejudgment interest on a damage award can be allowed under the Federal Employers' Liability Act. Divided 7-2, the court held that prejudgment interest is authorized by federal law.

**Communications Workers v. Beck**, decided by votes of 8-0 and 5-3, June 29, 1988. Brennan wrote the opinion; Blackmun, O'Connor and Scalia dissented in part. Kennedy did not participate.

A union cannot spend funds collected from dues-paying non-member employees on activities that are not related to collective bargaining. The National Labor Relations Act does not permit such use of those monies.

## Pensions

**Central States, Southeast and Southwest Areas Pension Fund v. Central Transport Inc.** (472

U.S. 559), decided by votes of 9-0 and 6-3, June 19, 1985. Marshall wrote the opinion; Burger, Rehnquist and Stevens dissented.

Officials of a multi-employer benefit plan regulated by the Employee Retirement Income Security Act (ERISA) have the right to audit the records of participating companies to ensure that contributions are being made for all eligible workers.

**Massachusetts Mutual Life Insurance Co. v. Russell** (473 U.S. 134), decided by a 9-0 vote, June 27, 1985. Stevens wrote the opinion.

The provision of the Employee Retirement Income Security Act that makes the fiduciaries of an employee benefit plan personally liable "to such plan" for any losses to it resulting from a breach of fiduciary duties does not give workers with complaints about the payment of benefits under the plan the right to sue the plan administrators for damages.

**Connolly v. Pension Benefit Guaranty Corp.** (475 U.S. 211), decided by a 9-0 vote, May 26, 1986. White wrote the opinion.

Provisions of the Multi-Employer Pension Plan Amendments of 1980 (PL 96-364) that require employers who withdraw from such plans to pay a share of the cost of future benefits to be paid under the plan do not violate the Constitution's ban on the taking of private property for public use without just compensation.

"In the course of regulating commercial and other human affairs, Congress routinely creates burdens for some that directly benefit others," the court observed. "Given the propriety of the governmental power to regulate, it cannot be said that the Taking Clause is violated whenever legislation requires one person to use his or her assets for the benefit of another."

**Metropolitan Life Insurance Co. v. Taylor** (481 U.S. 58), decided by a 9-0 vote, April 6, 1987. O'Connor wrote the opinion.

The civil enforcement provisions of the Employee Retirement Income Security Act (ERISA) were intended to be the only remedy for ERISA plan participants who were challenging a denial of benefits. Therefore, such a challenge — even if it only makes claims under state law — may be removed to federal court.

**Pilot Life Insurance Co. v. Dedeaux** (481 U.S. 41), decided by a 9-0 vote, April 6, 1987. O'Connor wrote the opinion.

The Employee Retirement Income Security Act (ERISA) pre-empts all state law claims about pensions regulated under that law.

The only remedies available to people covered under such plans are the remedies provided by ERISA.

**Pension Benefit Guaranty Corp. v. Yahn & McDonnell Inc.** (481 U.S. 735), decided by a 4-4 vote, May 18, 1987. *Per curiam* (unsigned) opinion. White did not participate.

An equally divided court simply left standing a lower court decision that upheld the Multi-Employer Pension Plan Amendment Act's provision that presumes that pension plan trustees are correct in determining the amount of an employer's liability when he withdraws from the plan.

**Fort Halifax Packing Co. Inc. v. Coyne** (482 U.S. 1), decided by a 5-4 vote, June 1, 1987. Brennan wrote the opinion; Rehnquist, White, O'Connor and Scalia dissented.

State law requiring employers whose plants close to provide severance pay to the plant employees is not pre-empted by the Employee Retirement Income Security Act nor by the National Labor Relations Act.

**Laborers Health and Welfare Trust Fund for Northern California v. Advanced Lightweight Concrete Co. Inc.** (484 U.S. 539), decided by an 8-0 vote, Feb. 23, 1988. Stevens wrote the opinion. Kennedy did not participate.

Companies cannot be sued in federal court to force them to contribute to multi-employer union benefit funds once a collective-bargaining agreement expires. Although Congress amended the 1980 Employee Retirement Income Security Act in 1980 to provide the courts with authority to order collection of delinquent contributions to benefit funds, that authority does not encompass requiring contributions after a union agreement has expired.

## Federal Employees

**United States v. Fausto** (484 U.S. 439), decided by a 5-4 vote, Jan. 25, 1988. Scalia wrote the opinion; Stevens, Brennan and Marshall dissented.

The 1978 Civil Service Reform Act, which does not provide for administrative or judicial review of suspensions or removals of non-veteran government workers, precludes judicial review for these employees under another federal law allowing claims for back pay.

**Department of the Navy v. Egan** (484 U.S. 518), decided by a 5-3 vote, Feb. 23, 1988. Blackmun wrote the opinion; White, Brennan and Marshall dissented. Kennedy did not participate.

The Merit Systems Protection Board does not have the authority to review whether a federal employee's denial of a security clearance was justified.

**Federal Labor Relations Authority v. Aberdeen Proving Ground** (485 U.S. 409), decided by a 9-0 vote, April 4, 1988. *Per curiam* (unsigned) opinion.

Federal employers are not required to negotiate with employees' unions over rules or regulations until the Federal Labor Relations Authority determines whether those rules and regulations have been imposed without any "compelling need." The Federal Labor Relations Authority may not rule in an unfair labor practice proceeding that the employer has to negotiate such an issue; that determination must be made before the proceeding begins.

**Webster v. Doe** (486 U.S. 592), decided by a 6-2 vote, June 15, 1988. Rehnquist wrote the opinion; O'Connor and Scalia dissented. Kennedy did not participate.

Employees in the CIA and other national security organizations can sue their employers when they believe their constitutional rights have been violated. In a case involving the CIA, the majority said nothing in the existing national security law demonstrated that Congress meant to preclude consideration of constitutional claims stemming from the CIA director's actions relating to employment termination decisions.

# Environment

**Ohio v. Kovacs** (469 U.S. 274), decided by a 9-0 vote, Jan. 9, 1985. White wrote the opinion.

A businessman's obligation, under a state court order, to clean up a hazardous waste disposal site is a debt that can be discharged if the businessman declares bankruptcy. Congress did not include such obligations as one of the specific categories of obligations that are exempt from discharge under the bankruptcy law.

**Chemical Manufacturers Association v. Natural Resources Defense Council (NRDC), Environmental Protection Agency (EPA) v. NRDC** (470 U.S. 116), decided by a 5-4 vote, Feb. 27, 1985. White wrote the opinion; Marshall, Blackmun, O'Connor and Stevens dissented.

The EPA may grant individual plants exceptions from the industry-wide Clean Water Act standards requiring pre-treatment of toxic wastes before they are dumped into a sewage system. Such variances are granted to plants that are in some way fundamentally different from others in the industry, and for whom compliance with the industry-wide standard is particularly difficult.

**United States v. Locke** (471 U.S. 84), decided by a 6-3 vote, April 1, 1985. Marshall wrote the opinion; Powell, Stevens and Brennan dissented.

The Federal Land Policy and Management Act, which deems unpatented mining claims abandoned if the owner does not file a timely claim with state and federal officials each year of his intention to hold the claim or evidence of work on claim, is not unconstitutional. The law's requirement that this claim must be filed "prior to December 31" makes clear that claims must be filed on or before December 30 — and thus owners filing December 31 have not met the filing deadline.

**United States v. Riverside Bayview Homes Inc.** (474 U.S. 121), decided by a 9-0 vote, Dec. 4, 1985. White wrote the opinion.

The court approved the government's broad definition of "wetlands" protected by the Clean Water Act against development without the approval of the Army Corps of Engineers. Under the approved definition, "wetlands" need not be frequently flooded but need only be sufficiently saturated by surface or groundwater to support vegetation typical of swamps, marshes and bogs.

**Midlantic National Bank v. New Jersey Department of Environmental Protection, O'Neill v. City of New York** (474 U.S. 494), decided by a 5-4 vote, Jan. 27, 1986. Powell wrote the opinion; Rehnquist, Burger, White and O'Connor dissented.

The trustee of a bankrupt company whose property includes sites contaminated with toxic waste may not simply abandon those sites, forcing the state to clean them up.

The fact that federal bankruptcy law permits a trustee to abandon burdensome property does not permit abandonment of sites that create a major threat to public health. This provision of federal law does not pre-empt state environmental laws.

**Exxon Corp. v. Hunt** (475 U.S. 355), decided by a 7-1 vote, March 10, 1986. Marshall wrote the opinion; Stevens dissented. Powell did not participate.

The federal "superfund" law, the Comprehensive Environmental Response, Compensation and Liability Act (PL 96-510), pre-empts states' power to levy their own taxes against oil and chemical companies to fund cleanups of abandoned hazardous waste dumps. States are free under the law to impose such taxes for other purposes, such as victim compensation and other costs not covered by the federal law.

**Japan Whaling Association v. American Cetacean Society, Baldrige v. American Cetacean Society** (478 U.S. 221), decided by a 5-4 vote, June 30, 1986. White wrote the opinion; Marshall, Brennan, Blackmun and Rehnquist dissented.

Neither the Pelly amendment to the 1967 Fisherman's Protective Act nor the Packwood amendment to the Magnuson Fishery Conservation and Management Act requires the secretary of commerce to certify Japan for refusing to abide by whale harvest quotas established by international commission — and thereby to impose economic sanctions on Japan — so long as Japan complies with an executive agreement providing for an end of all commercial whaling by 1988.

**Pennsylvania v. Delaware Valley Citizens' Council** (478 U.S. 746), decided by votes of 6-3 and 9-0, July 2, 1986. White wrote the opinion; Brennan, Marshall and Blackmun dissented in part.

The Clean Air Act authorizes awards of attorneys' fees for work before administrative agencies as well as before courts. It is not appropriate for courts to award higher-than-usual fees based on the court's view of the quality of the legal work involved.

The court agreed to hear reargument in the October 1986 term on a related question — whether a higher-than-usual fee can be awarded because of the risk of losing in the particular case.

**International Paper Co. v. Ouellette** (479 U.S. 481), decided by votes of 9-0 and 5-4, Jan. 21, 1987. Powell wrote the opinion; Blackmun, Marshall, Brennan and Stevens dissented in part and concurred in part.

Citizens of one state affected by pollution originating in another may sue the polluter for creating a public nuisance in their state. The Clean Water Act does not pre-empt state law to the point of blocking such suits, the court held unanimously. However, the court ruled 5-4 that such a suit is governed by the law of the state in which the polluter is located, not the law of the state where the suit is brought.

**Keystone Bituminous Coal Association v. DeBenedictis** (480 U.S. 470), decided by a 5-4 vote, March 9, 1987. Stevens wrote the opinion; Rehnquist, Powell, O'Connor and Scalia dissented.

Pennsylvania did not "take" property from coal mine operators, requiring it to compensate them for that taking, when it passed a law requiring them to leave up to half of the coal in an area in the ground to prevent damage to buildings on the surface from cave-ins or sinking.

**California Coastal Commission v. Granite Rock Co.** (480 U.S. 572), decided by votes of 9-0 and 5-4, March 24, 1987. O'Connor wrote the opinion; Powell, Stevens, Scalia and White dissented.

State environmental regulations affecting activities on federal lands are not pre-empted by federal law unless they conflict with federal law.

The court required a company that wished to mine for limestone in Los Padres National Forest to comply with California's environmental law requiring a permit for such mining.

**Amoco Production Co. v. Village of Gambell, Hodel v. Village of Gambell** (480 U.S. 531), decided by votes of 9-0 and 7-2, March 24, 1987. White wrote the opinion; Stevens and Scalia dissented in part.

The Alaska National Interest Lands Conservation Act of 1980, intended to protect Eskimo hunting and fishing rights, does not apply to federal waters on the Outer Continental Shelf adjacent to Alaskan waters. The court was unanimous on this point.

Federal courts should not issue injunctions more readily in cases in which environmental damage is alleged than in other types of cases, unless Congress chooses to direct them to do so — which, so far, it has not. The court by 7-2 threw out an injunction halting further exploration for oil and gas on certain offshore leases.

**Tull v. United States** (481 U.S. 412), decided by votes of 9-0 and 7-2, April 28, 1987. Brennan wrote the opinion; Scalia and Stevens dissented.

A company or individual charged by the government with violating the federal Clean Water Act is entitled, under the Seventh Amendment, to a jury trial to determine liability.

**Gwaltney of Smithfield v. Chesapeake Bay Foundation Inc.** (484 U.S. 49), decided by an 8-0 vote, Dec. 1, 1987. Marshall wrote the opinion.

Citizens filing suit under the 1972 Clean Water Act must allege continuing or intermittent violations of law. Suits for wholly past violations of the law's anti-pollution standards are not permissible.

**ETSI Pipeline Project v. Missouri** (484 U.S. 495), decided by an 8-0 vote, Feb. 23, 1988. White wrote the opinion. Kennedy did not participate.

Reservoirs built by the U.S. Army Corps of Engineers are not reclamation projects under the control of the Interior Department. As a result, the interior secretary cannot contract to provide water from the reservoir for industrial uses — in this case a coal slurry line — without first getting the approval of the secretary of the army.

**Phillips Petroleum Co. v. Mississippi** (484 U.S. 469), decided by a 5-3 vote, Feb. 23, 1988. Justice White wrote the opinion; O'Connor, Stevens and Scalia dissented. Kennedy did not participate.

States have control over all underwater lands affected by the ebb and flow of the tides even if that land is miles from the ocean and those waters non-navigable.

# State Powers

## Antitrust

**324 Liquor Corp. v. Duffy** (479 U.S. 335), decided by a 7-2 vote, Jan. 13, 1987. Powell wrote the opinion;

O'Connor and Rehnquist dissented.

New York violates federal antitrust laws by setting the minimum price that liquor retailers must charge for liquor sold in the state; this is resale price maintenance, which clearly conflicts with federal law.

**CTS Corp. v. Dynamics Corp. of America** (481 U.S. 69), decided by a 6-3 vote, April 21, 1987. Powell wrote the opinion; White, Blackmun and Stevens dissented.

Indiana did not burden interstate commerce when it passed a 1986 law that gave shareholders of Indiana corporations power to approve any change in corporate control. The law provided that when someone sought to acquire stock that would give him at least 20 percent of the voting power in an Indiana corporation, that stock would carry voting rights only if a majority of the existing, disinterested (non-management) shareholders approved.

The Indiana law was one of several passed by states since *Edgar v. MITE Corp.* (457 U.S. 624, 1982) struck down earlier versions of state laws regulating hostile takeovers. Unlike those laws, which had affected securities transactions, this law amended state laws regulating corporations, a traditional area of state responsibility. The court found Indiana's law "justified by the state's interest in defining the attributes of shares in its corporations and in protecting shareholders," adding that "Congress has never questioned the need for state regulation of these matters." The Indiana law, the court said, was not pre-empted by the 1968 Williams Act, the federal law governing corporate stock-tender offers.

## Boundaries

**United States v. Maine** (469 U.S. 504), exceptions overruled and the report of the special master confirmed by a vote of 9-0, Feb. 19, 1985. Blackmun announced the court's decision.

Long Island, N.Y., is legally part of mainland New York. Block Island Sound is a bay, an internal state waterway. New York and Rhode Island may continue to require ships using the sound to have state-licensed pilots.

The federal government had argued that Long Island, which is surrounded by water, should be considered an island, and Block Island Sound therefore part of the high seas not subject to state regulation.

The court rejected that argument, however, holding that Long Island functions as a peninsula, an extension of the mainland, forming the southern headland of Block Island Sound.

**United States v. Louisiana** (470 U.S. 93), exceptions to the report of the special master overruled and report confirmed by a vote of 8-0, Feb. 26, 1985. Blackmun announced the court's decision. Marshall did not participate.

Mississippi Sound is a historic bay that belongs entirely to the states of Alabama and Mississippi and contains no high seas to be claimed by the federal government.

**United States v. Maine** (475 U.S. 89), exception to the report of the special master overruled by an 8-0 vote, Feb. 25, 1986. Stevens wrote the opinion. Marshall did not participate.

Nantucket Sound does not constitute "internal waters" of Massachusetts; its seabeds belong to the United States. A state must establish its claim to coastline jurisdiction by evidence "clear beyond doubt."

the legislation during the 100th Congress. The House passed the bill (HR 3875) Feb. 2, 1988, on a 365-21 vote.

HR 3875 would give appeal rights to most of the estimated 500,000 "excepted-service" workers employed by the federal government. These were persons not hired through competitive civil service tests. They included attorneys, chaplains, scientists, interpreters, handicapped workers and other specially trained employees.

On Jan. 25, 1988, the Supreme Court ruled that excepted-service employees were not granted protections afforded to most federal civil service workers under the Civil Service Reform Act of 1978. (United States v. Fausto, *p. 826*)

The provisions of the bill originally were part of HR 25 (H Rept 100-274) to protect federal employees who reported waste or fraud in government agencies, a whistleblower protection bill. The measures were separated just before House passage of HR 3875. S 508, the Senate version of HR 25, cleared Congress but was pocket-vetoed by President Reagan. *(Whistleblower bill, p. 858)*

## Prompt Payment

Federal agencies faced new penalties for late payment of bills to private businesses under the provisions of legislation (S 328 — PL 100-496) cleared in 1988.

S 328 amended the Prompt Payment Act of 1982 (PL 97-177). Many government agencies found loopholes in the 1982 law that permitted them to delay payments. A 1986 General Accounting Office study found that nearly 25 percent of government payments were late and that the required interest penalties were seldom made. *(Prompt Payment Act, Congress and the Nation Vol. VI, p. 783)*

The bill eliminated the 15-day grace period previously enjoyed by federal agencies for payment of bills and specified that federal agencies that were late in paying their bills must pay the interest penalty prescribed by law, even if the contractor did not request a penalty payment.

The Senate passed S 328 (S Rept 100-78) on Oct. 9, 1987. The House Government Operations Committee reported a similar version of the measure (H Rept 100-784) July 22. The House passed the bill July 26 on a 394-0 vote. On Sept. 23, the Senate accepted the House-passed version. The president signed the bill Oct. 17.

## Procurement Policies

Congress Oct. 20, 1988, cleared legislation (S 2215 — PL 100-679) to strengthen the authority of the Office of Federal Procurement Policy, the federal agency assigned to oversee the awarding of contracts between the federal government and private contractors.

Action came in the wake of a long-running investigation into procurement policies by the Department of Defense. That probe also spawned legislation (HR 3911 — PL 100-700) making procurement fraud against the federal government a crime in its own right. *(Procurement fraud, p. 340)*

The Senate intially passed S 2215 (S Rept 100-424) Aug. 11. The House approved the bill Sept. 13, after substituting the language of HR 3345 (H Rept 100-911). Final congressional action came after key House and Senate members met informally to resolve differences. The Senate approved S 2215 Oct. 19, and the House approved the bill

under suspension of the rules the next day. President Reagan signed the measure Nov. 17.

## Census Questionnaire

President Reagan in 1988 pocket-vetoed a bill (HR 4432) that would require the Census Bureau to design its questionnaire so that respondents who were members of none of 11 Asian or Pacific Islander ethnic groups could check an appropriate box instead of having to write-in their ethnic background.

The measure also would require the Census Bureau to include questions about plumbing and heating facilities in respondents' homes.

Reagan, in a Nov. 8 "memorandum of disapproval," said the legislation would increase administrative costs and add to the paperwork burden imposed on the public by the census. He also argued that the information on plumbing and heating facilities and heating and cooling equipment would not produce data sufficiently useful to justify their inclusion on the census form.

HR 4432 (H Rept 100-951) passed the House by voice vote Sept. 26. The Senate approved a slightly different version of the measure Oct. 18, also by voice vote. The next day, the House accepted the Senate-passed version, clearing it for the president.

Two other census-related bills were considered in 1988 but stalled short of enactment.

HR 4720 would include federal employees and dependents stationed overseas, who number more than 1 million, in their home states' census total. The overseas personnel would be counted as residents of the last state in which they lived for more than six months. HR 4720 was defeated on the House floor Sept. 28 by a 93-317 vote.

The House Administration Committee Sept. 28 killed, 10-11, a bill (HR 3511) that would order the Census Bureau to perform a statistical adjustment after the 1990 headcount was completed. The adjustment would increase the census figures to make up for the expected omission of millions of people, mostly blacks and Hispanics in large cities.

## Agency Relocation

The House Sept. 20, 1988, passed a bill (HR 2524 — H Rept 100-853) that would permit certain federal agencies to move their operations out of the District of Columbia to surrounding areas in suburban Virginia and Maryland. The legislation, however, died when it failed to receive Senate action.

Proponents cited cost-savings as the main reason for the bill. Rep. Glenn M. Anderson, D-Calif., said lease rates in the District averaged $27 to $37 a square foot. In certain Maryland and Virginia suburbs those rates would be about $18 to $31 a square foot, he said.

## Post Office 'Off Budget'

Despite signing up about three-fourths of the members of both the Senate and House as cosponsors, backers of legislation that would remove the U.S. Postal Service (USPS) from the unified federal budget failed to win final approval before the 100th Congress adjourned.

The full Senate did not act on its measure (S 2449 — S Rept 100-427). Sponsors had hoped that an 85-8 vote April 13, 1988, on a non-binding amendment to the fiscal 1989 budget resolution (S Con Res 113) urging off-budget status for the USPS was an indication of the bill's support.

The House passed its version (HR 4150 — H Rept 100-656, Parts I and II) by a 390-16 vote June 21.

Off-budget status would mean that most of the Postal Service's revenues and expenditures would not be counted in calculating the national debt, which would make it virtually immune to any cuts designed to lower the deficit. Under a November 1987 deficit reduction agreement between the White House and congressional leaders, the USPS was required to reduce spending by $1.2 billion over fiscal years 1988-89. Those cuts forced the Postal Service to curtail services and defer or cancel construction projects. Members heard complaints from constituents about reduced service hours.

## Mailings Restrictions

Congress in 1988 cleared legislation (HR 5199 — PL 100-574) imposing new prohibitions on the mailing of plants, fruits, vegetables and other agricultural commodities through the U.S. Postal Service.

The bill was aimed at discouraging individuals from mailing products that possibly carried insects and diseases that could spread to crop lands. A major target of the bill was the mailing of "food gifts," such as guava or pineapple.

Under the bill, such products could be mailed only if they were certified by the Agriculture Department to be free of disease and pests. Postal officials were given authority to open suspicious packages after obtaining warrants. The legislation established criminal penalties for mailing certain plants and other agricultural items that had not been inspected first by the government.

HR 5199 was reported Sept. 22 from the House Post Office and Civil Service Committee (H Rept 100-954, Part I). The House passed the bill Oct. 4 by a vote of 415-2. The Senate approved the measure by voice vote Oct. 12. It was signed into law Oct. 31.

## Curbs on Deceptive Mail

Legislation to curb mail solicitations that falsely implied a connection with the U.S. government died at the end of the 100th Congress for want of Senate action. The bill (HR 4478), which passed the House by a voice vote Aug. 8, 1988, would require "conspicuous" disclaimers on mailings that mimicked government documents or that offered to sell a service the government provided for less or for free. The all-capital-letters disclaimer would warn readers: "THIS IS NOT A GOVERNMENT DOCUMENT."

The Postal Service would be authorized to throw away such solicitations that displayed no disclaimers and to fine the violators. Backers of the measure said that questionable mailings typically came from organizations with Washington, D.C., return addresses and bore official-sounding names. The chief offenders were said to be groups that sought to capitalize on the fears of senior citizens about the safety of their Social Security or Medicare benefits.

The House Post Office and Civil Service Committee approved HR 4478 (H Rept 100-772, Part I) June 8.

# Fiscal 1989-93 NSF Funding

Congress in 1988 put the government back in the business of granting money to university research facilities from a common pool of funds. It thereby tried to reduce the growing congressional practice of "earmarking" funds for favored home-state institutions.

In authorizing National Science Foundation (NSF) spending to double the 1988 level of $1.7 billion by fiscal 1993, Congress provided for the Academic Research Facilities Modernization Program. By 1992, the program was expected to spend $250 million a year.

Since the 1970s few research facilities received funding from that kind of program. Instead, Congress increasingly designated money in appropriations bills for specific institutions, averting merit-based awards on the basis of selection among competing colleges and universities. It was generally conceded in Congress that earmarking had created an "academic pork barrel" and that many university research buildings were badly in need of repair.

The same bill (HR 4418 — PL 100-570) also authorized the establishment of several interdisciplinary research centers, constituting one of the biggest science initiatives in President Reagan's fiscal 1989 budget. The bill authorized $85 million in 1989-91; the spending level for 1992-93 was not specified.

HR 4418 was reported (H Rept 100-649) May 24 by the House Science, Space and Technology Committee. The full House passed the bill June 9 by a vote of 405-5. The Senate Commerce, Science and Transportation Committee approved its version of the measure (S 1632 — S Rept 100-331) April 26. The Senate passed HR 4418 June 17 by a vote of 88-1, after substituting the language of S 1632.

The legislation cleared Congress with unanimous Senate passage Oct. 14 and was signed into law Oct. 31. The measure was the result of a compromise worked out without an official House-Senate conference; the House passed the agreement by a vote of 402-2 Sept. 27.

Reagan had been pushing Congress to approve such a five-year authorization plan since early 1987, as had researchers whose work was funded by the foundation. But to increase the funding to the authorized levels of $3.5 billion by 1993 would be difficult; in 1989, for instance, the agency's appropriations' bill (PL 100-404) fell $100 million short of the year's $2.05 billion authorization.

Congress had passed just two science foundation authorization bills since 1980, for fiscal years 1986 and 1987. In other years, the appropriations bills fell victim to a jurisdictional fight between the Senate Commerce and Labor committees. In 1988, however, the panels worked out their differences and persuaded the House Science, Space and Technology Committee to go along with a five-year authorization they had crafted. (*Fiscal 1986 and 1987 bills, p. 848*)

Lobbying groups for the nation's colleges and universities had been pressing for the research-facilities program for several years. Big-name universities, long used to faring quite well in competition for individual research grants, complained bitterly when they saw money for facilities being earmarked mostly for smaller schools.

Defending the earmarks, individual lawmakers argued that smaller schools could not compete for research grants because they did not have the needed facilities and because peer-review panels evaluating research-grant applications were stacked with researchers from the bigger schools.

The bill included several provisions aimed at spreading the money around: No institution could get more than $7 million in five years; priority was given to those that did not get much federal money; different types of institutions had to vie for money separately so big-name schools were not pitted against smaller schools; and schools attended primarily by minority students were to receive 12 percent of the money.

## Computer Security

Legislation (HR 145 — PL 100-235) cleared in 1987 that empowered the National Bureau of Standards to create a computer security program for all federal agencies and to train government employees on it.

The bill emerged from a committee investigation of a secret order intended to protect unclassified government computer files. Members and civil liberties groups feared that the National Security Agency (NSA) would use the order, National Security Decision Directive (NSDD) 145, to justify a censorship campaign that would extend its power to domestic as well as international affairs.

HR 145 replaced a presidential order issued in 1984, as well as NSDD 145, which was issued in October 1986 by Adm. John M. Poindexter, shortly before he resigned as national security adviser to the president. Poindexter's successor, Frank C. Carlucci, rescinded the orders in March. They empowered the NSA to guard a new category of information called "sensitive but unclassified."

The measure was designed to protect information such as records of air-traffic control, taxes, Social Security and census data. However, it defined "sensitive information" far more narrowly than did Poindexter, and it specifically excluded from regulation all information covered under the Freedom of Information Act, as well as privately owned data and information in the public domain.

HR 145 was reported by the House Science, Space and Technology and the Government Operations committees (H Rept 100-153, Parts I and II) on June 11. The full House passed the bill by voice vote June 22. The Senate cleared the legislation Dec. 21, and the president signed it Jan. 8, 1988.

## Computer Safeguards

Congress in 1988 imposed new safeguards on the federal government's use of computer records pertaining to individuals' income, employment and other personal matters. There was concern about invasion of privacy in the federal agencies' use of computer records to detect fraud, abuse or overpayments of government benefits.

As cleared Oct. 3, 1988, and signed into law Oct. 18, the legislation (S 496 — PL 100-503) required federal agencies to establish safeguards to govern the release of records, including the establishment of a "data integrity board" at every agency involved in computer-matching programs. Agencies were prohibited from reducing, suspending or terminating financial assistance to an individual without first verifying the accuracy of the computerized data and giving the individual 30 days to contest the action.

The Senate first passed S 496 (S Rept 100-516) on May 21, 1987. The House then passed the text of its bill (HR 4699 — H Rept 100-802) as an amendment to S 496 on Aug. 1, 1988.

The Senate passed an amended version of S 496 by voice vote Sept. 20. The House Oct. 3 accepted the latest Senate version of the bill, clearing the measure for the president.

## Fiscal 1988 NASA Authorization

President Reagan on Oct. 30, 1987, signed a $9.57 billion fiscal 1988 National Aeronautics and Space Administration (NASA) authorization bill (HR 2782 — PL 100-147).

NASA's plan to develop an advanced solid rocket motor (ASRM) for the space shuttle, which had been grounded since the Jan. 28, 1986, explosion of the *Challenger*, was at the heart of the differences between the House and Senate. The final bill balanced Senate desires that NASA proceed with ASRM with House concerns that the program could fail. The Senate eventually agreed to a provision requiring the agency to make production of the motor more competitive. As cleared, HR 2782 required NASA to select a second supplier or reopen the competition among private firms seeking to produce the ASRM, if the program stalled in 1988. *(Space program review, p. 850)*

The bill also authorized $1.17 billion for the revitalization of the space shuttle program, up from $1 billion in fiscal 1987. The measure included only $60 million for NASA to resume buying "expendable launch vehicles" (ELVs) to put satellites into orbit. The agency stopped buying the unmanned rockets years earlier when it decided to rely on the shuttle. The Senate wanted $100 million for ELVs but eventually accepted the lower House figure.

After a heated fight over military uses of the proposed space station, the House accepted a Senate provision requiring that use of a future space station be covered by the Outer Space Treaty. Under the terms of that treaty, the station could not be used to place nuclear weapons or other weapons of mass destruction into orbit. But the provision left open the possibility of military-related research being conducted in the space station. By 1987 estimates, the space station would cost between $15 billion and $20 billion and could be launched in the late 1990s. The bill required NASA to submit an analysis in 1988 of the cost, schedule and design of the space station. At the insistence of the House, the analysis also had to consider "low-cost alternatives" to the space station.

The House Science, Space and Technology Committee reported HR 2782 (H Rept 100-204) June 26. The full House July 9 voted 372-34 to pass the bill.

The Senate Commerce, Science and Transportation Committee approved its version of the authorization bill (S 1164 — S Rept 100-87) May 14. The Senate passed HR 2782 by voice vote July 10, after substituting the text of S 1164.

## Fiscal 1989 NASA Authorization

In a last-minute compromise, an ambitious National Aeronautics and Space Administration (NASA) reauthorization bill (S 2209 — PL 100-685) won final congressional approval Oct. 21, 1988, and was signed into law Nov. 17.

The bill called for spending nearly $6 billion in fiscal years 1989-91 for a proposed manned space station and created an advisory National Space Council — an idea that prompted a pocket veto of the fiscal 1987 NASA authorization bill. S 2209 also endorsed manned exploration of the solar system outside of Earth's orbit and unmanned probes far beyond. *(Fiscal 1987 authorization, p. 852)*

The bill also included reauthorization for the National Oceanic and Atmospheric Administration. *(Story, p. 413)*

The House approved the bill by voice vote Oct. 19, but Senate acceptance of the House-amended version was left in doubt almost until the time, two days later, that it too gave approval by voice vote. As the 1988 session was drawing to a close, House and Senate negotiators appeared unwilling to compromise their differences. House Science Committee Chairman Robert A. Roe, D-N.J., was holding out for a full-blown three-year authorization for the space agency, while his counterpart in the Senate, Commerce Committee Chairman Ernest F. Hollings, D-S.C., was not yet ready to commit to a three-year plan.

A version passed by the House June 2 (HR 4561 — H Rept 100-650) included fiscal 1989-91 authorizations. The version passed by the Senate Aug. 9 (S 2209 — S Rept 100-429) included no multi-year authorizations.

The compromise included fiscal 1989 authorizations of $11.2 billion, dropping all multi-year authorizations except for the space station, which the administration had requested. The House approved the president's budget request of $11.5 billion, whereas the Senate approved only $11.1 billion. Actually, an even smaller amount, $10.7 billion, was appropriated (HR 4800 — PL 100-404) for fiscal 1989. In giving in on most of the multi-year authorizations, Roe managed to get a key concession: The bill required NASA to submit two-year funding requests starting with its fiscal 1990 budget. Roe and his committee colleagues on the Science, Space and Technology Committee favored the multi-year approach as a way of bringing a measure of stability to the space program.

The compromise deleted House provisions requiring seven detailed "five-year capital development plans" that would force NASA to commit itself to a slew of far-reaching goals endorsed by the Science Committee, including a U.S.-Soviet manned mission to Mars. In keeping with Roe's insistence on long-range goals and planning, however, the final bill required one overall five-year capital-improvement plan and five 10-year "strategic" plans. The bill also contained several reach-for-the-stars provisions in which Congress implicitly or explicitly endorsed manned "space settlements," moon outposts, manned missions to Mars and elsewhere in the solar system and the "robotic" exploration of other solar systems.

NASA ended up getting $900 million of the nearly $1 billion it had requested for a manned space station, but it was a tough fight. The authorization bill called for more than $2 billion in 1990 and close to $3 billion in 1991. But the bill left in doubt until 1989 the linchpin of Reagan's space policy — a commercially developed space facility.

Proposed by a politically well-connected Houston firm, Space Industries Inc., the idea of a relatively tiny private space station was endorsed by Reagan. Under the proposal, the government would be the prime tenant for five years at a cost of up to $700 million. Under the fast track that was key to the administration's plans, the private station was to be in orbit in the early 1990s. If it was delayed much beyond that, its main attraction — early access to space for microgravity researchers — could be subverted because the manned space station was expected to be in orbit by the mid-to-late 1990s. But the Senate refused its approval, saying the idea needed further study.

**Appropriations Action.** In the budget-conscious times of the late 1980s, Congress was faced with having to make difficult choices between favored programs. During consideration of the fiscal 1989 appropriations bill for the Department of Housing and Urban Development (HUD) and independent agencies (HR 4800 — PL 100-404), both the House and Senate voted to retain funds for NASA provided by the measure.

Rep. Charles E. Schumer, D-N.Y., offered an amendment to shift $400 million from NASA to programs to benefit the homeless, veterans, the elderly, Environmental Protection Agency grants and Urban Development Action Grants (UDAGs). The amendment was defeated June 22 on a **key vote of 166-256 (R 40-133; D 126-123)**. *(1988 key votes, p. 981)*

The Senate July 12 on a **key vote of 34-63 (R 9-36; D 25-27)** rejected a John Heinz, R-Pa., amendment to shift $30 million from NASA to HUD for UDAGs.

Congress' actions demonstrated its commitment to the space program.

# Rocket-Launch Insurance

Congress Oct. 21, 1988, cleared a bill (HR 4399) aimed at reducing the cost of insurance for the fledgling U.S. launch industry by having the government share liability risks with private firms. President Reagan signed the measure (PL 100-657) on Nov. 15.

The administration had long opposed the idea but gave in after protracted negotiations. Reagan's advisers threatened to recommend a veto for a House version of the bill because it was open-ended, requiring the government to pay for all launch-accident damage not covered by a private firm's insurance. The final version, drafted by the Senate Commerce Committee and accepted by the administration, limited the government's liability to $1.5 billion per accident and made any large payments subject to the appropriations process.

It also had called for the government's liability to end after 10 years, but objections raised by Sen. Howard M. Metzenbaum, D-Ohio, forced advocates of the bill to shorten the "sunset" provision to five years just before the Senate approved the measure by voice vote Oct. 14. House advocates grudgingly accepted the compromise; the bill was cleared by the House by a vote of 355-1.

The House initially passed HR 4399 May 24 by voice vote. The measure was unanimously approved by the Senate Commerce, Science and Transportation Committee (S Rept 100-593) on Sept. 20.

### China-Launch Deal

The insurance victory for the rocket industry was tempered by the Reagan administration's Sept. 9 decision to allow China to launch U.S.-made satellites. Industry lobbyists and some of their congressional advocates fought hard to derail the deal, saying it would hurt American rocket firms. Sen. Jesse Helms, R-N.C., on Sept. 30 tried to kill the deal with an amendment to the foreign aid spending bill (HR 4637 — PL 100-461), but the House rejected the amendment overwhelmingly.

Under terms of the deal, export licenses were to be issued allowing three American-made satellites to be shipped to China, which offered cut-rate launch services. Some U.S. companies objected that they would be hurt by unfair competition. Proponents of the deal stressed the need to open doors with China as part of America's effort to reduce its trade deficit. Reagan promised to delay the satellite shipments until China agreed to several conditions, one of which would be designed to protect the U.S. industry from subsidized prices.

Foreign Relations Chairman Claiborne Pell, D-R.I., joined Helms in asking the administration to withdraw its decision to give Congress a chance to review the conditions in 1989. The administration refused but promised to work closely with interested members of Congress in drafting the conditions. Subsequently, the two senators drafted a multipurpose foreign policy bill that included an amendment blocking the license until at least 1989. But that measure died in the final hours of the session.

# Supercollider Funding

The 100th Congress intensely debated but provided no construction money for the superconducting supercollider (SSC), a gigantic and costly science research facility that had been sought by 25 states. After Congress adjourned in 1988, Department of Energy (DOE) Secretary John S. Herrington announced the government's decision to build the SSC at Waxahachie, Texas, 25 miles south of Dallas.

His announcement set the stage for a heated funding battle in the 101st Congress. Since the government began studying the supercollider concept in 1984, $205 million had been appropriated for the project. An additional $3.6 billion would be required over the next six years to build it, according to DOE estimates. Including operating costs, the department calculated the spending would reach $11 billion in 25 years.

The SSC would be a pair of underground tunnels laid out like race tracks, some 53 miles long. Extremely powerful magnets would be used to whirl protons around, smashing them into one another. Scientists would study the resulting subatomic debris in an attempt to uncover secrets about the basic nature of matter and energy. Physicists consider the facility to be the necessary next step to advance their science after years of work at other big atom smashers, such as the Fermi National Accelerator Laboratory near Chicago.

After President Reagan endorsed the SSC on Jan. 30, 1987, there was great enthusiasm on Capitol Hill — fueled by the hopes of the 25 states competing for the project and the hordes of jobs it would create. Building the supercollider would require up to 4,500 workers, and 2,500 people would be needed to staff it permanently.

But support dropped off sharply after Jan. 16, 1988, when DOE whittled the field of contending states to seven — Arizona, Colorado, Illinois, Michigan, North Carolina, Tennessee and Texas. The decision to make Texas home to the SSC enhanced the project's political clout by giving it several powerful allies, including House Speaker Jim Wright, D-Texas, and Senate Finance Committee Chairman Lloyd Bentsen, D-Texas. But the project also could suffer from opponents' charges of political favoritism.

Sen. Dennis DeConcini, D-Ariz., collected signatures of members from losing states for a letter to Reagan calling for the creation of a commission to review the decision. DeConcini also wanted the General Accounting Office to undertake a similar study.

Although the lawmakers balked at construction funds for the project, they approved $100 million in the fiscal 1989 energy and water appropriations bill (HR 4567 — PL 100-371) specifically to continue SSC research.

The House May 17 passed HR 4567 (H Rept 100-618), which contained $100 million for the SSC. Lawmakers continued, however, to debate the SSC component of the fiscal 1989 reauthorization of the DOE's civilian research and development programs. That measure (HR 4505 — H Rept 100-636), approved 290-27 June 3, authorized $100 million for research.

The Senate Appropriations Committee June 9 reported HR 4567 (S Rept 100-381), which also provided $100 million for the SSC. The Senate passed the bill June 15.

The House agreed to the conference report on HR 4567 (H Rept 100-724) June 30. The Senate followed suit July 7, clearing the measure for the president.

HR 4505, the authorization measure, was referred to Senate Energy and Natural Resources, where it was completely rewritten and stripped of its SSC provision. The bill passed by Senate by voice vote Oct. 21.

# Technology Administration

Congress in 1988 created a Technology Administration within the Commerce Department with the intent of overseeing programs aimed at keeping American industry technologically competitive with the rest of the world. A bill (HR 4417 — PL 100-519) creating the new agency received final congressional approval Oct. 5 upon its unanimous passage in the Senate. President Reagan signed the legislation Oct. 24.

HR 4417 was the fiscal 1989 reauthorization for the old National Bureau of Standards — renamed the National Institute of Standards and Technology (NIST) in a trade bill (PL 100-418) enacted Aug. 23. The Technology Administration embraced NIST; the Office of Technology Policy, a renamed version of the existing Office of Productivity, Technology and Innovation (OPTI); and the National Technical Information Service (NTIS), an existing self-supporting agency that collected and sold technical reports written by federal agencies.

The House unanimously approved HR 4417 Sept. 26 after replacing the text of the legislation with a compromise measure drafted after the Science and Energy and Commerce committees marked up conflicting versions of the bill (H Rept 100-673, Parts I and II).

The Senate Commerce Committee June 28 approved its own version of the bill (S 2701 — S Rept 100-466) similar to the House-passed measure.

# Energy Research

The end result of legislative ping-pong between the House and Senate in 1988 over several energy-research bills was a relatively simple measure aimed at coordinating federal efforts in the research and development of superconductivity.

Superconductivity is the absence of resistance to electricity in certain materials at extremely low temperatures. Research is aimed at significantly increasing the temperatures at which superconductivity can be reached — an achievement that is expected to greatly improve the efficiency of electricity.

The House tooks its final action on the superconductivity bill (HR 3048 — H Rept 100-900) Oct. 21 when it voted 353-0 to lop off two bills that the Senate had attached earlier in the month. Later that day, the Senate gave in, sending the shortened measure to President Reagan by a voice vote. He signed the measure Nov. 19, although the administration had protested that the bill duplicated existing superconductivity planning mechanisms.

Provisions stripped from the bill in the House would permit private industries to share in the technological advances made at the Department of Energy's national laboratories and would provide a $1 billion authorization for research aimed at developing new sources of energy. The provisions — based on S 1480 (S Rept 100-544) and S 1554 (S Rept 100-523), respectively — were added to the bill when it was approved unanimously by the Senate Oct. 5.

Members of the House Armed Services Committee objected to the technology-transfer measure because they feared it might compromise secret technology based on military research — the staple of the labs' work — by imprudently transferring it to the private sector. Some Republicans on the House Science Committee objected to the alternative-energy proposal as too costly.

## Continental Drilling

The House Sept. 9, 1988, cleared legislation (S 52 — PL 100-441) calling for all federal agencies involved in research drilling of the Earth's crust to coordinate their efforts. Such drilling was used to help scientists in the detection of earthquakes and volcanoes, aid in the search for mineral resources and increase the nation's development of geothermal energy resources.

The Senate Energy and Natural Resources Committee reported S 52 (S Rept 100-67) June 11, 1987. The full Senate passed the measure June 17.

The House version of the bill (HR 2737) was reported by the Interior and Insular Affairs Committee (H Rept 100-580, Part I) April 26, 1988, and by the Space, Science and Technology Committee (Part II) May 2. The House passed S 52 May 23, after substituting the language of HR 2737.

## Metals Research

Congress in 1988 cleared a bill (S 2470) that authorized $56 million in fiscal 1989-91 for a program based on the government's so-called Steel Initiative. President Reagan signed the measure (PL 100-680) Nov. 17, although his advisers had opposed the bill as unnecessary.

The bill called for public-private research partnerships, with funding coming from both sectors. It was aimed at teaming up the expertise of the industry with the research know-how of the Department of Energy's national laboratories and the National Bureau of Standards (renamed the National Institute of Standards and Technology).

Advocates of the bill said tough times in the early 1980s prompted substantial research cutbacks by the industry. At the same time, foreign governments were spending a great deal of money on research to improve the energy efficiency of their metals industry.

The Senate passed S 2470 (S Rept 100-443) Aug. 9. The House passed an amended version of the bill (H Rept 100-1061) Oct. 12. The Senate accepted the House changes Oct. 21, clearing the measure.

## Animal Patents

Farmers won a significant but short-lived victory over the biotechnology industry when the House Sept. 13, 1988, unanimously decided they should be exempted from patent-infringement laws in the breeding, use or sale of offspring from genetically engineered animals. Although the bill (HR 4970 — H Rept 100-888) was never acted on by the Senate, it was considered a test of legislative sentiment.

While the bill did not prevent inventors from placing use and sale restrictions in contracts with farmers who bought their patented animals, it denied the inventors the extra protection of patent-infringement law in enforcing such contracts. The bill was seen as a response to a decision by the U.S. Patent and Trademark Office to issue a patent to Harvard University for a mouse genetically engineered to be more susceptible to cancer. HR 4970, introduced by Robert W. Kastenmeier, D-Wis., was supported by Charlie Rose, D-N.C., who had earlier sponsored a bill (HR 3119) calling for a two-year ban on such patents.

Biotechnology industry advocates said the exemption would remove potential economic rewards and thus render farm-animal patents useless, thereby stifling research aimed at finding more productive animals. Farmers argued that the patenting of animals threatened their livelihood because they could be forced to pay hefty royalties.

## Indian Gambling

Almost six years after Congress first started grappling with the issue, the House on Sept. 27, 1988, cleared legislation (S 555 — PL 100-497) to regulate high-stakes bingo games and other forms of gambling on Indian reservations. The president signed the measure Oct. 17.

The Senate passed the bill (S Rept 100-446) Sept. 15 by voice vote. Final action came 12 days later when the House passed the bill, 323-84, under suspension of the rules.

Facing cutbacks in federal funding, Indian tribes in the 1980s began taking advantage of their unique status to set up gaming operations as a source of revenue. In 1988, various tribes sponsored more than 100 gambling operations, most often high-stakes bingo. Collectively, those games generated more than $100 million annually in revenue for the tribes.

Indian-sponsored bingo games proliferated after 1982, when the U.S. Supreme Court left standing a ruling by a lower court that Florida — and by implication other states — could not regulate bingo on Indian reservations if the game was legal elsewhere in the state. In 1987, the high court explicitly stated the same thing in *California v. Cabazon Band of Mission Indians. (1987 ruling, p. 840)*

The proliferation of gambling activities on tribal lands stirred considerable anxiety among state and federal law-enforcement authorities, who feared that organized crime figures would corrupt the games and fleece both Indian tribes and their customers. Bills were introduced and hearings commenced during the 98th Congress. In 1986, the House passed a bill to assert some federal control over Indian gambling operations, but the measure died in the Senate during the closing days of the 99th Congress. *(1986 action, p. 854)*

## Major Provisions

As cleared, S 555:
● Established three classes of gambling, applying differing degrees of regulation to each:

Class I, defined as traditional ceremonial gaming or social games for prizes of limited value, would be under sole control of the tribes.

Class II games — bingo, lotto and certain card games (but not blackjack, chemin de fer or baccarat) — were subject to oversight by a five-member National Indian Gaming Commission appointed by the president and confirmed by the Senate. Three of the commissioners would have to be members of federally recognized Indian tribes.

Class III activities, defined as casino gambling, slot machines, horse and dog racing, and jai alai, would be prohibited unless they were legal in the state and a tribe entered into a compact with the state for their operation.
● Permitted the continuation, under a "grandfather clause," of Indian-sponsored blackjack or other prohibited card games in operation as of May 1, 1988, in four states: Michigan, North Dakota, South Dakota and Washington. The clause did not allow expansion of the existing operations to new sites.
● Authorized $2 million for the first year of operations of the gaming commission, with at least half of the funding to be raised by the tribes from gambling revenues.

The commission had the power to approve and enforce tribal gaming ordinances, close down games that violated the law, conduct background investigations of the contractors who operated games, collect civil fines and audit all books and records of gaming operations.

# Indian Relocation and Business

Two bills concerned with Indian issues, one continuing a relocation program and the other providing loans for Indian business development, cleared Congress in 1988, but President Reagan pocket-vetoed the business-development measure.

The bill that became law (S 1236 — PL 100-666) renewed a program to entice Navajo Indians to leave land they had settled in Arizona that belonged to Hopi Indians. The Navajo-Hopi dispute went back to the 1880s, when nomadic Navajo herders remained on land the federal government granted the Hopis as a reservation.

Congress tried to settle the dispute with a 1974 law (PL 93-531) dividing the disputed land equally between the two tribes. As the July 1986 deadline for relocation neared, a small number of Navajos remained on Hopi land. Congress mandated, in the fiscal 1987 continuing appropriations bill (H J Res 738—PL 99-591), that relocation was to be voluntary and appropriated more than $22 million to pay for new homes for relocated Navajo families. By October 1988, only about 250 families had not been resettled. S 1236 doubled the authorized annual spending for housing and moving expenses to $30 million during 1989-91 and provided some additional incentive payments to Navajos. *(1974 law, Congress and the Nation Vol. IV, p. 809)*

Despite the administration's opposition, the Senate passed the bill (S Rept 100-425) Aug. 8 by voice vote. The House passed S 1236 (H Rept 100-1032) by a 298-120 vote on Oct. 4. And the Senate cleared the measure Oct. 13 when it accepted the House amendments.

The pocket-vetoed measure (HR 3621) would establish an Indian Development Finance Corporation to make loans to Indian-operated businesses from a $100 million pool of funds to be appropriated by Congress. The purpose of the bill was to develop Indian enterprises that would contribute to Indian tribal economies. The corporation could provide loans, loan guarantees and other financial services to new and existing Indian businesses, as well as technical and managerial assistance and training.

Reagan, in his veto message of Nov. 2, 1988, said, "The bill would have created an expensive and unnecessary new bureaucracy and duplicated currently existing programs."

The House passed HR 3621 (H Rept 100-811) under suspension of the rules Aug. 8. The Senate passed the bill (S Rept 100-581) Oct. 1. The House agreed to the conference report (H Rept 100-1084) Oct. 12. The Senate followed suit Oct. 14, clearing the measure for the president.

# Indian Health

Congress Oct. 14, 1988, cleared legislation (HR 5261 — PL 100-713) reauthorizing health programs for American Indians and native Alaskans.

The House Oct. 12 approved the conference report (H Rept 100-1075) on the bill to reauthorize Indian Health Service programs through fiscal 1992 at a total funding level of more than $400 million over the four years. The Senate followed suit Oct. 14. The president signed the bill Nov. 23.

HR 5261 reauthorized programs initiated in 1976 after a series of studies indicated that the health status of Native Americans ranked far below that of the rest of the population. The bill also created several new programs aimed at beefing up health personnel, facilities and services.

Authorizations for the existing programs officially expired at the end of fiscal 1984, although the programs continued to be funded.

President Reagan pocket-vetoed a 1984 reauthorization measure, and both houses approved similar bills at the end of the 99th Congress that died on the last day with only minor details left unresolved. *(99th Congress action, p. 853)*

As cleared, HR 5261 was similar to the House version of the bill, which an official Reagan administration position statement termed "highly objectionable" because, among other things, of its "numerous micromanagement provisions." Also in the final measure was a provision pertaining to health services for Indians in Montana that led to the Reagan veto in 1984. Nonetheless, the president signed HR 5261.

The House Interior and Insular Affairs Committee reported HR 2290 (H Rept 100-222, Part I) July 15, 1987. The House Energy and Commerce Committe reported the bill (Part II) Dec. 8.

Leaders of the Interior and Commerce committees then worked out a new version of the bill, which was introduced as HR 5261. The House passed HR 5261 by voice vote Sept. 13, 1988.

The Senate approved HR 5261 on Sept. 28 by voice vote, after substituting the text of S 129 (S Rept 100-508).

The Senate adopted a number of amendments, including ones by John Melcher, D-Mont., to extend ongoing demonstration programs in Montana and Arizona for the prevention and treatment of child sexual abuse. Melcher also appended to the bill an amended version of S 1475 (S Rept 100-212), to help the Indian Health Service recruit and retain staff. The Senate passed S 1475 on Nov. 18, 1987.

The Senate Oct. 14, 1988, also cleared a related measure (S 136 — PL 100-579) to authorize a total of $19.6 million over three years for health programs for native Hawaiians. The House approved the final version of the bill Oct. 12, and the president signed it Oct. 31.

# Earthquake Hazards

President Reagan signed a bill (HR 1612 — PL 100-252) Feb. 29, 1988, reauthorizing for three years the Earthquake Hazards Reduction Act of 1977, even though his administration believed it cost too much and had urged members to vote against it.

The bill authorized $73 million in fiscal 1988, $80 million in 1989 and $85 million in 1990 for planning and research to reduce earthquake-related deaths. Reagan's fiscal 1988 budget requested $67 million.

The House initially passed HR 1612 (H Rept 100-89, Parts I and II) June 8, 1987. The Senate passed the measure, amended, Dec. 22. The House agreed to the Senate version under suspension of the rules Feb. 16, 1988, clearing the measure.

# Fire Safety

Legislation (HR 4419 — PL 100-476) was enacted in 1988 that authorized $53.2 million in fiscal 1989-91 for the U.S. Fire Administration and the National Fire Academy in Emmitsburg, Md. The authorization was more than had been sought by the Reagan administration, which wanted to cut by two-thirds travel stipends given to firefighters who attended the academy.

HR 4419 was approved by the House Science, Space and Technology Committee April 21 (H Rept 100-589). The House passed the bill by voice vote May 24. In the Senate, the Commerce, Science and Transportation Committee reported the bill (S Rept 100-435) July 27. The full Senate passed the bill, amended, Aug. 10. The House accepted the Senate change Sept. 26, clearing the measure.

# Presidential Transitions

With the approach of a national election and forthcoming change of presidents, Congress in 1988 authorized far more funds than it previously had for both the outgoing and incoming presidents in the transition between administrations.

The bill (HR 3932 — PL 100-398), cleared by Congress Aug. 2, 1988, and signed by President Reagan Aug. 17, reauthorized the 1964 Presidential Transition Act (PL 88-277) to ease the transfer of power from one administration to another. The law was amended in 1976 (PL 94-499), boosting the funding for incoming presidents to $2 million and departing presidents to $1 million. Previously, they received the same amount, $450,000 each. *(Congress and the Nation Vol. I, p. 1438; Congress and the Nation Vol. IV, p. 979)*

The 1988 bill authorized a combined $3.5 million to incoming presidents and vice presidents and $1.5 million to outgoing presidents and vice presidents to cover transition costs. However, the $1.5 million figure would be reduced by

$250,000 if the outgoing vice president was the incoming president — as was the case in 1988.

During the transition period, from Election Day in November until Inauguration Day in January, the president-elect must begin filling about 3,000 key government positions, developing a budget and laying the foundation for his domestic and foreign policies.

John Glenn, D-Ohio, chairman of the Senate Governmental Affairs Committee and chief sponsor of the bill in the Senate, argued that the president elected in 1988 would need about $4 million to match the purchasing power that $2 million offered in 1976. More money was needed, Glenn said, so that a new president did not "have to hire a fundraiser as his first act after the election." Presidents Nixon, Carter and Reagan all raised money from private sources to help pay for their transitions. But the sources, amounts or expenditures of the funds were not disclosed.

Congress continued to permit contributions from private sources, providing they were publicly reported and limited to $5,000 per person or organization. The federal funding level would be indexed for inflation. The incoming president and vice president were required to file reports disclosing the names of all transition personnel, full time or part time, and listing their most recent employment and the source of funds used to pay them.

The House Government Operations Committee March 22 approved HR 3932 (H Rept 100-532). The full House passed the bill March 31 by a 374-15 vote.

The Senate Governmental Affairs Committee April 14 voted 9-0 to approve S 2037 (S Rept 100-317). By voice vote April 26 the Senate passed S 2037. On April 29 the Senate substituted the text of S 2037 for that of the House-passed measure and then passed HR 3932.

The Senate passed a compromise version of the bill Aug. 2 by voice vote after informal negotiations with the House. The compromise had been approved by the House, also by voice vote, on July 26.

# 'Stars and Stripes'

By act of Congress, John Philip Sousa's "Stars and Stripes Forever" became the national march of the United States. This was proclaimed in a bill (S 860 — PL 100-186) President Reagan signed Dec. 11, 1987.

The Senate passed S 860 Nov. 6. The House, after substituting the language of its own version of the bill (HR 613), passed S 860 on Dec. 1. The Senate agreed to the House version the following day.

Rep. James H. Quillen, R-Tenn., said Congress made official "what all Americans have known for years — that no musical composition arouses patriotism and pride more than 'The Stars and Stripes Forever.' " Sousa composed the march Christmas Day 1896.

# Uniform Poll-Closing Time

For the second straight year, the House in 1987 passed a bill (HR 435) to require every state in the continental United States to close its polls simultaneously in presidential elections. Passed by a vote of 208-189 on Nov. 10, the bill would set a 9 p.m. EST closing time for all states except Alaska and Hawaii in presidential general elections.

It was identical to a bill passed by the House in January 1986. That bill, approved by a 204-171 vote, died in the

Senate at the close of the 99th Congress. *(99th Congress action, p. 856)*

Sponsors said the poll-closing measures addressed the problem of presidential-election results being announced before all people in the country vote. Westerners complained that broadcast reports of election returns from Eastern states tended to diminish the voter turnout in the West — that Western voters might think the election's outcome had already been determined and not go to the polls.

"Thousands of voters are told that the election has been held without them, and that their votes do not count," said Al Swift, D-Wash., chairman of the House Administration Subcommittee on Elections. HR 435 was reported June 2 by the House Administration Committee (H Rept 100-117, Part I) and Oct. 29 by the Energy and Commerce Committee (Part II). An ardent opponent of poll-closing legislation, Bill Frenzel, R-Minn., said HR 435 would create unimaginable confusion and drive voters from the polls by requiring 37 states to alter voting hours. "There will be massive disenfranchisement under this Rube Goldberg device," he said.

# Chronology
# Of Action
# On Congress:
# Election Issues

# 1985-86

It took the House four months to resolve a contested election in Indiana's 8th District. The nearly party-line vote in favor of the incumbent Democrat triggered a walkout by Republicans.

The Senate voted twice in 1986 to place new limits on campaign fund raising but in the end failed to pass legislation to that effect.

## Contested Elections

Three 1984 House races were so close that the losers contested the results. One race, in Indiana's 8th, led to four months of acrimony between Democrats and Republicans over what appeared to be the closest House contest in the 20th century. Debate on the race took up far more time than almost any other issue the House considered in 1985.

### McCloskey-McIntyre Contest

After the Nov. 6, 1984, election, incumbent Democrat Frank McCloskey appeared to have won re-election to his Indiana 8th District seat by 72 votes. But correction of an arithmetical error (ballots in two precincts were counted twice) gave Republican challenger Richard D. McIntyre an apparent 34-vote victory. On that basis, the Indiana secretary of state Dec. 14 certified McIntyre the winner.

But when Congress convened Jan. 3, 1985, the Democratic-controlled House refused to seat McIntyre, voting instead to declare the seat vacant pending an investigation of alleged irregularities in the election. Three times after that — in February, March and April — Republicans pushed the seating of McIntrye to a vote, losing each time while picking up no more than a handful of votes from the Democrats.

A recount completed Jan. 22 showed McIntyre's lead had increased to 418 votes, after more than 4,800 ballots were thrown out for technical reasons. But a House Administration Committee task force, with auditors from the General Accounting Office, conducted its own recount and, on a 2-1 partisan split, found McCloskey the winner by four votes.

Republicans then tried to get a new election by declaring the seat vacant. Their attempt (H Res 148) lost by a **key vote of 200-229 (R 181-0; D 19-229)** on April 30. *(1985 key votes, p. 933)*

The next day, before the House Administration Committee's recommendation to seat McCloskey (H Res 146 — H Rept 99-58) came to a vote, Republicans moved to send the issue back to the panel with orders to count 32

controversial absentee ballots that the task force had decided, on a 2-1 vote, not to count. That motion was rejected, 183-246.

The House then approved the resolution 236-190, with 10 Democrats joining the Republicans in voting against it. GOP members walked out of the House chamber in protest, accusing Democrats of stealing the election. *(Box, p. 892)*

The Supreme Court May 28 refused to get involved in the dispute. Without a dissenting vote, it denied Indiana permission to sue the House in the Supreme Court.

A U.S. District Court judge in Washington, D.C., dismissing a suit brought by McIntyre against House Democrats and House officers, ruled March 1 that the House had the constitutional right to judge its own membership.

On Feb. 7, a federal district court in Indiana had dismissed a separate suit filed by McIntyre challenging recount procedures in two of the district's counties and ruled that the House alone was responsible for determining the validity of contested ballots.

### Other Contested Elections

Results in two other close House races also were contested, but those challenges, in Guam and Idaho, were unsuccessful.

On July 24, the House agreed by voice vote to H Res 229 (H Rept 99-220) dismissing a challenge by Democrat Antonio Borja Won Pat, the former non-voting delegate from Guam, against Republican Ben Blaz. Won Pat, who had represented Guam in Congress since 1973, had lost the November 1984 election by about 350 votes. Won Pat had protested, among other things, that Blaz had not won an absolute majority of the votes cast, as required by law.

On Oct. 2, the House threw out a challenge by former Rep. George Hansen, R-Idaho (1965-69, 1975-85), against Democrat Richard H. Stallings. Hansen, who was convicted in 1984 of filing false financial disclosure forms, charged, among other things, vote fraud in his 170-vote loss to Stallings. The House approved H Res 272 (H Rept 99-290) dismissing the challenge by a 247-4 vote, with 169 members, mostly Republicans, voting "present." *(Hansen appeal rejected, p. 879)*

---

## Contribution Credit Repeal

A massive tax-overhaul bill enacted in 1986 (HR 3838 — PL 99-514) repealed the existing $50 credit ($100 for joint returns) for contributions to political campaigns and certain political campaign organizations.

The House version of the bill would replace the $50 tax credit, which applied to any kind of political contribution, with a $100 tax credit ($200 for joint returns) for contributions to congressional candidates in a taxpayer's state. This provision, adopted by the House Dec. 17, 1985, by a 230-196 vote, was not included in the final bill.

---

## GOP 'Guerrilla Warfare'

The May 1, 1988, walkout of House Republicans to protest the seating of Indiana Democrat Frank McCloskey climaxed several months of "guerrilla warfare" by the GOP. *(Contested election, p. 891)*

The Republicans, outnumbered 182-253, had been angry for years at what they viewed as the arrogance of the Democratic majority. They complained that partisan committee ratios stacked the deck for Democrats and that other rules unfairly favored the majority. But more than any other issue, the Indiana election contest galvanized them.

GOP bitterness over the failure to seat Indiana Republican Richard D. McIntyre grew, reaching a peak in late April, when angry members kept the House in session all night April 22 and blocked later floor action with parliamentary guerrilla tactics.

In what they called "sample Thursday" on April 25, Republicans brought the House to a halt with a display of parliamentary procedures and votes. They forced roll-call votes on minor procedural questions and then delayed those by switching their votes, finally forcing the House to adjourn without completing its business.

They showed more of the same the week of April 29 with motions to adjourn and votes on procedures or bills that normally would not receive time-consuming roll-call votes.

Although Minority Leader Robert H. Michel, R-Ill., said the May 1 walkout was "just the beginning" of GOP efforts to create public awareness of "the autocratic, tyrannical rule of the Democratic majority," the "war" appeared to wind down after the seating of McCloskey.

The walkout had not been without precedent. On Sept. 23, 1890, Democrats, then in the minority, left the chamber during debate on another contested election. In that case, Republicans decided to seat Republican Thomas E. Miller to represent the 7th District of South Carolina.

## Campaign Finance

The Senate went on record twice in 1986 in favor of strict new controls on campaign fund raising. However, the bill (S 655) ended up mired in partisan maneuvering over who should get credit (or blame) for reforming campaign finance guidelines, and which party would suffer the most under the proposed restrictions.

An amendment sponsored by David L. Boren, D-Okla., would put caps on what a candidate could take from political action committees (PACs) overall and singly. It also would close loopholes on PAC giving that generally favored Republicans. Rudy Boschwitz, R-Minn., offered a countermeasure to stifle PAC contributions to party organizations, which Democrats relied on more heavily than the GOP.

Both amendments were approved Aug. 12, Boren's by a lopsided margin of 69-30, and Boschwitz' on a more partisan tally of 58-42. But the bill itself went no further. Republican leaders were willing to press for passage of S 655, and Boren and other Democrats were ready to go along. But Boschwitz blocked a final vote on the grounds that the issues had become lost in partisan gamesmanship.

The last time either chamber of Congress had voted on PAC-related legislation was in 1979, when the House passed a bill to limit PAC spending but Senate opponents filibustered it to death. Legislation in the 100th Congress would suffer a similar fate. *(1979 bill, Congress and the Nation Vol. V, p. 947; 1987-88 action, p. 894)*

"Special-interest" campaign contributions were a touchy political issue on Capitol Hill. Boren and other supporters of PAC limits repeatedly invoked statistics that showed PAC spending on congressional campaigns had risen nearly tenfold in the past decade. In 1974, PACs gave candidates for Congress a total of $12.5 million. In the 1983-84 election cycle, House and Senate candidates received $105.3 million from PACs. The total number of registered PACs — not all of which gave to congressional candidates — had grown from 608 in 1974 to 4,009 in 1984.

The rise in the number of PACs and their influence in political campaigns had put lawmakers on the defensive against a public perception that special-interest groups had undue influence on politicians.

### Boren Proposal

Boren had offered his proposal in 1985 as an amendment to S 655, an unrelated bill dealing with low-level radioactive waste, but the Senate sidestepped a definitive vote on the bill, effectively agreeing instead to postpone the issue until 1986. The outcome of a vote had been far from certain, with neither side on the campaign finance issue claiming a majority.

A much-anticipated showdown on the proposal dissipated when supporters and critics joined together in calling for hearings by the Senate Rules and Administration Committee on Boren's plan and other campaign finance measures. That paved the way for an overwhelming 7-84 vote on Dec. 3, 1985, against tabling (killing) the PAC proposal. Under a previous agreement, the bill then was pulled from further consideration, but Boren was promised a floor vote in 1986.

The Boren proposal would:

● Limit overall PAC contributions to $100,000 for House candidates and between $175,000 and $750,000 for Senate candidates, depending on the populations in their states. Increases would be permitted to allow for contested primaries and runoff elections.

● Reduce from $5,000 to $3,000 the ceiling on individual PAC contributions, while increasing the limit on maximum individual gifts to $1,500 from $1,000.

● Close a loophole in existing campaign finance law that allowed a PAC to exceed existing limits by "bundling" further donations from individuals and passing those on to candidates.

● Require television and radio broadcasters to provide free response time to candidates opposed by groups operating "independent expenditure" campaigns.

# Campaign Spending's Upward Spiral

The 100th Congress considered legislation (S 2) to limit campaign spending against a backdrop of statistics showing record-breaking spending by House and Senate candidates and unprecedented contributions from political action committees (PACs) in the 1985-86 congressional election cycle.

Figures released May 10, 1987, by the Federal Election Commission (FEC) showed that candidates for Congress spent $450 million during the two years between Jan. 1, 1985, and Dec. 31, 1986. This represented a 20 percent increase over the previous record, the $374.1 million spent during the 1983-84 cycle.

Spending by Senate candidates topped $211 million, a 24 percent increase. House candidates spent $239 million, 17 percent more than in 1983-84.

Groups and individuals not formally linked to any campaign or candidate made independent expenditures of another $8.5 million to influence congressional elections.

The FEC said that PACs and other non-party committees gave a record $132.2 million to congressional candidates in 1985-86, up from $105.3 million in 1983-84. PAC funds represented 28 percent of total receipts, up from 26 percent in 1983-84.

Senate candidates received $45 million from PACs, 21 percent of their total receipts, compared with 17 percent in 1983-84. House candidates got $87.2 million from PACs, 34 percent of their funds, the same percentage as in 1983-84.

PACs continued to favor incumbents over challengers by a wide margin. Incumbents in both houses got $89.5 million from PACs; challengers got $19.2 million. The rest went to open-seat candidates.

## Steady Upward Trend

The increase in campaign spending continued a pattern. Spending rose in each of the five election cycles monitored by the FEC since 1977-78, when the agency began releasing complete figures. In that cycle, candidates for both houses spent a total of $194.8 million. Two years later, in 1979-80, the figure rose to $239 million. In 1981-82, it reached $342.4 million.

Furthermore, in the four previous election cycles, the number of announced candidates decreased from 2,288 to 1,868, meaning that spending per candidate actually rose at a higher rate than was apparent from the overall spending figures.

## Boschwitz Countermeasure

Opponents of the proposed limits insisted that Boren's bill would do little to contain the flow of PAC money into campaigns, because PACs would merely funnel their funds into more negative advertising and other forms of independent expenditures.

"The Boren plan will only worsen the problems that he seeks to resolve," Boschwitz said, adding that PACs were formed in the post-Watergate era of the mid-1970s as a result of campaign reforms that sought to control the influence of wealthy individuals.

Boschwitz offered a countermeasure to prohibit PAC contributions to national political parties, which included the partisan campaign committees run by leaders of the House and Senate.

His amendment also would require political parties to disclose the so-called "soft money" they accepted from corporations, unions and other donors that currently went unreported.

Soft money was used for general "party-building" purposes, such as paying for campaign headquarters or bolstering the coffers of state party organizations, instead of for a particular candidate's campaign. The practice allowed wealthy donors to exceed limits on individual contributions and allowed party organizations to provide indirect support for candidates with money that would be illegal if given directly to a candidate.

Boschwitz' amendment was assailed as a blatantly partisan attempt to embarrass Democrats, who traditionally relied more heavily on PAC contributions to party organizations than did Republicans, who got most of their donations from individuals.

In the 1984 congressional elections, national Democratic Party organizations, such as the Democratic Senatorial Campaign Committee and the Democratic Congressional Campaign Committee, received $6.5 million in contributions from PACs, compared with $58.3 million from individuals, according to the Federal Election Commission.

Republican organizations, including the National Republican Senatorial Committee and the National Republican Congressional Committee, received only $1.7 million from PACs, compared with $262 million from individual contributors.

Boschwitz acknowledged that his amendment was crafted with a political strategy in mind. The amendment and the rules governing the two votes were designed to give Republicans a way to vote successively for the Boren amendment and the Boschwitz alternative, working on the assumption that the Democratic-controlled House would probably not want to act on a bill that contained both measures.

# 1987-88

The Senate took up more comprehensive campaign finance legislation in the 100th Congress but failed to overcome partisan divisions. Parliamentary fireworks early in the session overshadowed some progress toward compromise, leaders said.

# Campaign Finance

Legislation to overhaul campaign finance law was killed by a Republican filibuster in the Senate, despite a determined drive by Majority Leader Robert C. Byrd of West Virginia. It was the most far-reaching campaign finance bill to come before Congress since 1974, when sweeping reforms were enacted in the wake of the Watergate scandal.

The bill (S 2), which would provide financial incentives for senatorial candidates to abide by campaign spending limits, was shelved in 1988 after a record-setting eight cloture votes in 1987-88 failed to cut off debate.

Most Republicans bitterly opposed the bill, which they said would put the GOP at a disadvantage in efforts to win a majority of seats in Congress.

Proponents of S 2 promised to revisit the issue, saying they gained momentum from the protracted debate in the 100th Congress — debate marked by extraordinary partisanship, elaborate parliamentary maneuvering, two all-night sessions and the arrest of a senator.

While the two parties remained deeply divided over the central issues of whether there should be public financing of campaigns or a limit on campaign spending, gaps were narrowed on other issues. These included limits on the role of political action committees (PACs), disclosure of in-kind contributions (non-cash support), limits on so-called independent expenditures (spending for or against a federal candidate without consulting the campaign) and reductions in the cost of television campaign advertising.

Congressional campaigns had been left largely untouched since the passage of comprehensive campaign finance reform legislation in 1974. Twice, however, one chamber had passed legislation to limit PACs. In 1979, the House passed legislation to limit PAC contributions to House candidates, but the bill died from a filibuster threat in the Senate. *(Congress and the Nation Vol. IV, p. 991; Congress and the Nation Vol. V, p. 947)*

The Senate in 1986 approved a proposal by David L. Boren, D-Okla. — who also was the chief sponsor of S 2 — to limit PAC contributions to all candidates. A political war ensued, in which the GOP won passage of an amendment to restrict fund raising by national party committees. The measure died without a final Senate vote. *(Story, p. 892)*

## Original Bill Revised

In the 100th Congress, the cornerstone of the Democratic bill was a proposal for overall campaign spending limits, specified on a state-by-state basis, which S 2 backers saw as the key to curbing skyrocketing election costs. But such limits were anathema to Republicans, who thought a spending cap would institutionalize the Democrats' majorities in Congress.

Another key element that many Republicans hated was to provide public financing for Senate candidates who agreed to abide by the spending limits. Most Republicans said it represented a government intrusion into what generally had been a private realm.

For Boren and the Democrats, however, public funding was essential because it was needed to impose spending

limits legally. Under the Supreme Court's 1976 ruling in *Buckley v. Valeo*, spending limits could not constitutionally be imposed in political campaigns unless they were adopted voluntarily as, for example, a condition for receiving public financing. *(Congress and the Nation Vol. IV, p. 995)*

In the course of 1987, Byrd and Boren made modifications in S 2 designed to pick up additional support — principally by scaling back the proposed system of public financing for Senate campaigns.

In the version brought to the floor in 1988, the Byrd-Boren bill would provide financial incentives — such as reduced broadcasting and postal rates — for senatorial candidates to abide by specified campaign spending limits. It would provide public funds only to candidates whose opponents did not abide by limits in the bill. As reported, S 2 would provide public finds to all qualified candidates who abided by the limits.

S 2 also would impose limits on contributions from PACs. Under it, no Senate candidate would be allowed to accept more than 30 percent of the primary spending limit set for the candidate's state, up to a maximum in 1988 of $825,000.

Republicans criticized such an aggregate limit. They said it would favor well-organized, well-funded PACs that could donate early in an election cycle, freezing out other PACs that wanted to donate later.

Republicans countered with a proposal to lower the existing $5,000 per-candidate limit on donations a PAC was allowed to make each election. Democrats argued that the vast majority of PAC contributions were already below the $5,000 ceiling. Because of Democrats' dominance in fund raising from PACs, some Republicans began to talk about banning PAC contributions altogether.

## 1987 Action

S 2 had been reported with deceptive ease by the Senate Rules and Administration Committee on May 14, 1987 (S Rept 100-58). But the bill was shelved in 1987 after more than three months of on-and-off debate.

S 2 ran into parliamentary roadblocks almost as soon as floor debate began on June 3. After Republicans launched their filibuster, a frustrated Byrd resorted to a maneuver called "double-tracking" that permitted the Senate to consider other legislation while S 2 remained pending. The majority leader's frustration was compounded by a simultaneous, ongoing filibuster on the fiscal 1988 defense authorization bill.

Republicans staved off Byrd's first attempt to invoke cloture during a largely party-line vote of 52-47 on June 9. Sixty votes were needed to cut off debate.

Although modifications were made in the bill, Byrd lost six more cloture votes by similar margins on June 16, 17, 18, 19, Sept. 10 and 15. The Sept. 15 cloture attempt, which was rejected by a **key vote of 51-44 (R 3-42; D 48-2)**, marked a minor turning point in Senate history: The Senate had never taken more than six cloture votes on a single issue. *(1987 key votes, p. 965)*

Several Republican alternatives were offered, none of which gained much Democratic support, in part because they did not contain overall spending limitations. They sought mainly to reduce the amount individual PACs could contribute to candidates and to require more disclosure of campaign finance data.

# A Senator's Arrest: Rare and Dramatic Event

An arcane tool of Senate discipline was wielded in the wee hours of Feb. 24, 1988, during acrimonious debate over campaign finance legislation (S 2).

When the episode was over, Oregon Republican Bob Packwood had been arrested and physically carried onto the Senate floor at 1:19 in the morning.

Touching off the skirmish was Majority Leader Robert C. Byrd's decision to resurrect the Senate's little-known power, last used in 1942, to call for the arrest of absent members to bring them to the floor.

## Stalking the Hallways

The escapade began Feb. 23, the first night of the Senate's three-day non-stop session on S 2. Byrd attempted to wear down the opposition by forcing them to talk all night.

Republicans responded with a maneuver that allowed them, in effect, to sustain a midnight filibuster without showing up. Only one Republican remained stationed on the floor to keep watch over the proceedings. The GOP tactic was to force a series of quorum calls and then boycott the votes, forcing the Democrats to come up with the 51 bodies needed to establish a quorum and keep the Senate in session.

When Democrats around midnight found themselves one vote short of a quorum, they approved, 45-3, Byrd's motion to request the sergeant-at-arms, Henry K. Giugni, to arrest absent senators and bring them to the floor.

Giugni gathered a posse of Capitol police, armed them with arrest warrants and began combing Capitol Hill for delinquent senators who had scattered.

Giugni and company finally tracked down Packwood in his office, where the senator had bolted one door and blocked the other with a heavy chair.

Giugni unbolted the door with a pass key and, when Packwood tried to hold it shut with his shoulder, forced it open. In the process, Packwood re-injured a finger he had broken a few weeks earlier.

Packwood agreed to walk over to the Senate chamber but refused to go inside under his own steam. Two of Giugni's officers lifted Packwood carefully and carried him feet-first to the Senate floor.

"Here," Packwood said, at last establishing the quorum of 51. He was jocular after the incident, but other Republicans were bitter over Byrd's tactics.

## A Rarely Used Power

The Packwood arrest sent Capitol Hill history buffs scrambling for precedents, but it remained unclear whether Packwood was the first, second, third or fourth senator to be arrested to compel attendance. One thing was certain: Packwood was the first senator to be carried into the chamber under arrest.

Article 1, Section 5 of the Constitution says: "Each house . . . may be authorized to compel the attendance of absent members, in such manner, and under such penalties as each house may provide."

The Senate's history included several attempts to address the attendance problem. In 1798, the Senate changed its rules to allow use of the sergeant-at-arms to enforce attendance. Attempts also were made to require absent senators to cover the cost of fetching them. The Senate also tried to force attendance by paying its members on a per-day basis, but in 1856, it switched to an annual salary. The result: Sessions got shorter, from an average 265 days to 203.

In 1864, the Senate tried to shame members into showing up by recording members as "absent" for missed votes. Thirty years later, that method was abandoned, and the phrase "not voting" was used.

Frustrated by failed attempts to adjourn for lack of a quorum, the Senate in 1877 loosened its rules to allow adjournment motions without a quorum.

One of the first times the Senate approved a motion to order the arrest of absent members was on Feb. 23, 1927, during a debate over the construction of what became the Hoover Dam. The sergeant-at-arms, dispatched with warrants, returned without any senators at 6:30 a.m., reporting a variety of excuses, including one by a senator who said he was just too tired.

The next test came on Nov. 14, 1942, during a debate over a bill to abolish poll taxes. The Senate issued warrants for eight members, seven of them Southerners opposed to the bill. It was unclear, however, how many were actually arrested, if any.

Press accounts of the time said three senators — Burnet Maybank, D-S.C.; Berkeley Bunker, D-Nev.; and Kenneth D. McKellar, D-Tenn. — were arrested.

Bunker, however, insisted in a 1988 interview that he was not arrested and walked into the chamber unescorted. Maybank, who died in 1954, said on the floor in 1950 that he and Joseph Lister Hill, D-Ala., had been arrested that day. But the sergeant-at-arms said in a report in the *Congressional Record* of the day that he could not find Hill. (The report did not say who was arrested.) And press accounts said that Maybank only accepted a ride to the Capitol from a deputy sergeant-at-arms and walked into the chamber on his own. McKellar was taken by car from a nearby hotel by another deputy although he was not told he was under arrest, nor was the warrant actually produced. He, too, walked into the chamber on his own. "He was hotter than a pistol," Bunker recalled.

Until 1988, there were only two other successful motions to arrest absent senators, in 1950 and 1976, but no one was arrested either time because the threat itself prompted a quorum.

## 1988 Action

In February 1988 Byrd appointed a bipartisan task force to search for a breakthrough on S 2 before the bill was brought back to the floor. But after some discussions, the group reported that both sides regarded their positions on overall spending limits as non-negotiable.

With negotiations stalled, Byrd said he would fight it out on the floor and made it known he would not let Republicans conduct the kind of "gentleman's filibuster" against S 2 they did in 1987, when they were not forced to make good on their threats to talk around the clock.

Byrd said he would force Republicans to hold the floor around the clock beginning the night of Feb. 23, or else push the bill to a vote if the GOP was not there to stop him.

On that evening, Republicans responded in kind. They moved repeatedly for quorum calls, then boycotted the floor. That forced Democrats to keep enough members present to maintain the quorum needed for the Senate to remain in session.

When the Democrats came up short around midnight of Feb. 23-24, Byrd resorted to seeking the arrest of absent senators and had Sen. Bob Packwood, R-Ore., carried onto the floor. That night's events were followed by a day of vitriolic debate about the propriety and legality of the arrest. *(Box, p. 895)*

Party leaders reached a truce late Feb. 24. They agreed to restrict the second all-night debate to the substance of the bill and to call off the talkathon the next day at the dinner hour, with a final cloture vote Feb. 26.

S 2 was pulled from the floor after a record-setting eighth cloture attempt was defeated by a **key vote of 53-41 (R 3-39; D 50-2)**. *(1988 key votes, p. 981)*

## Constitutional Amendment Fails

The issue resurfaced in a different and less confrontational form in April 1988, when the Senate conducted two test votes on a measure (S J Res 282) to amend the Constitution to allow Congress and state governments to impose limits on campaign spending. It was designed to overcome the *Buckley v. Valeo* decision forbidding mandatory campaign spending limits.

The resolution, sponsored by Ernest F. Hollings, D-S.C., was an alternative to S 2; it was pulled after Democratic supporters twice failed to impose cloture.

# Chronology
# Of Action
# On Congress:
# Pay and Benefits

# 1985-86

The Senate in 1985 raised that chamber's limit on members' honoraria — fees paid to members by outside groups for speeches and the like. The House followed suit in 1986 but, fearful of political reverberations, quickly reversed itself.

Budget constraints forced both houses of Congress to take steps to limit their use of the cherished franking privilege, which allowed them to send mail to constituents at taxpayers' expense.

## Outside Income Limits

The 99th Congress grappled with the politically sensitive issue of limits on members' outside income.

In late 1985 the Senate raised the limit on senators' ability to earn honoraria — outside earnings from speeches, articles and appearances — from 30 percent to 40 percent of their official salary. This amounted to a jump from a cap of about $22,500 in 1986 to about $30,000. The change, included in the fiscal 1986 continuing appropriations resolution (H J Res 465 — PL 99-190), applied to the House as well, but it could not take effect in that chamber until and unless the House voted to alter a House rule limiting members' honoraria to 30 percent.

The House attempted to do just that in 1986, when it unexpectedly approved April 22 a resolution (H Res 427) raising its cap on outside income to 40 percent of a member's salary. However, fearing political fallout — especially in an election year — members quickly reversed themselves, voting the next day to restore the 30 percent cap (H Res 432 — H Rept 99-553).

Senators did the opposite in 1986. An amendment to the fiscal 1986 supplemental appropriations bill (HR 4515 — PL 99-349) that would return the Senate cap to 30 percent was blocked June 5 by a 68-30 vote on a procedural motion.

The House had last raised the ceiling on all outside earned income — honoraria as well as professional fees — in 1981, when it adopted a rule increasing the cap from 15 percent of official salary to 30 percent. (Congress and the Nation Vol. VI, p. 823)

The Senate in 1983 had agreed to accept a 30 percent cap on honoraria in return for a pay hike in 1984. (Congress and the Nation Vol. VI, p. 830)

A study by Common Cause, the self-styled citizens' lobby, showed that outside earnings had jumped in 1985. House members had collected almost one-third more in speaking fees and other honoraria in 1985 then they had the year before, according to the study.

Based on an analysis of House members' financial disclosure forms, Common Cause calculated that the 420 House members who filed the documents had received a total of $4.6 million in honoraria. In 1984, members reported receiving $3.5 million.

In the Senate, Common Cause said, honoraria earnings hit a total of $2.4 million — up 20 percent from the year before. Of that total, some $723,038 was donated to charity, leaving about $1.7 million in senators' pockets.

### 1985 Action

The original Senate version of H J Res 465 would restrict members' ability to earn outside income from law practices and business enterprises. The House had more lenient rules in this area than the Senate, and House conferees said the provision would seriously disrupt many members' legitimate activities outside of Congress.

Conferees compromised on deleting the provision and raising the honoraria cap to 40 percent of members' annual salary.

### 1986 Action

H Res 427 was offered by John P. Murtha, D-Pa., on April 22, 1986, when only a few members were on the floor. It was brought to the floor under expedited procedures that circumvented committee consideration. The resolution was approved by unanimous consent. The maneuver was a replay of action in 1981, when Murtha had pushed through an outside income hike in seconds.

But in 1986 when members discovered what they had done, many were distressed. Even though some in Congress felt they were not adequately compensated, at an annual salary of $75,100 in 1986, few were willing to vote for increased pay or benefits.

Backers said Murtha's plan would simply put the House on an equal footing with the Senate. However, opponents said it would do more.

H Res 427 deleted the House rule setting the 30 percent limit and specified that the only limit on outside income would be that fixed by law — in other words, the 40 percent limit imposed by PL 99-190. Critics charged this would eliminate limits on outside income from sources other than honoraria. They noted that under the House rule, the 30 percent limit applied to all outside income, including professional fees; the 40 percent limit established by law applied only to honoraria.

Faced with angry complaints about the Murtha resolution and its fast-track consideration, House Speaker Thomas P. O'Neill Jr., D-Mass., agreed to give members the opportunity to vote on overturning it.

The House Rules Committee sent H Res 432, a resolution reversing the Murtha resolution, to the floor the next day. In a key procedural move, members voted 333-68 to consider the new measure and thus reimpose the old limit. The resolution itself, like the one lifting the cap, was then approved by voice vote.

## Franking Privilege

After years of escalating costs, budget limits forced the 99th Congress to reduce subsidies covering members' free-mail privilege, one of their most prized perquisites.

# Congressional Mailing Costs

The Senate in 1985 revealed for the first time how much individual members spent on mass mailings, after last-minute efforts to postpone the disclosure failed.

According to a report released Dec. 9 by the secretary of the Senate, 79 senators spent a total of $10.95 million on mass mailings during the three-month period covered by the report (July-September 1985). The cost was paid by the taxpayers.

Twenty-one senators sent out no mass mailings.

Alan Cranston, D-Calif., ran up the single biggest postage bill — $1.63 million — during the three-month reporting period. Next on the list were Arlen Specter, R-Pa.; John Heinz, R-Pa.; Christopher J. Dodd, D-Conn.; Charles E. Grassley, R-Iowa; and Donald W. Riegle Jr., D-Mich.

With the exception of Heinz and Riegle, who were up in 1988, all of the top mailers faced re-election in 1986. The top two spenders, Cranston and Specter, both were considered vulnerable.

The spending disclosures were required under a rule pushed through the Rules and Administration Committee in May by Chairman Charles McC. Mathias Jr., R-Md.

Mathias had criticized the growing cost of congressional mail as "an embarrassing example of the waste of the taxpayers' money" and "the congressional equivalent of the Pentagon's $500 hammer." He said disclosure would remind senators that "mailings are not cost-free and that the real control of this rests with the voters."

The House declined to disclose mailing information on its members.

The franking privilege, which allowed members to mail out virtually unlimited amounts of correspondence to voters back home, had become an increasingly sensitive political issue as mail costs soared.

Incumbents said it was an essential means of letting constituents know about special town meetings and important congressional action — for some, the only way around hostile or indifferent local news media. But critics, such as the self-styled citizens' lobby Common Cause, called it a weapon of protection for incumbents. They pointed to the tendency of incumbents to boost their mailings during campaign years and slack off during non-election years.

---

The fiscal 1987 omnibus spending bill (H J Res 738 — PL 99-591) included $91.4 million for mail, down from $95.7 million in fiscal 1986 (HR 2942 — PL 99-151). Fiscal 1986 was the first in many years that members' costs for sending mail to constituents dropped in an election year.

The franking privilege allowed members of Congress to send their constituents newsletters, press releases, meeting notices, calendars and other mail simply by stamping their signatures on the envelope. In theory, the practice was limited by the size of Congress' annual appropriation for reimbursing the Postal Service, but members typically increased the account as it was depleted.

## Fiscal 1986 Funds

Congress in 1985 purposely underestimated its mailing expenses when it approved fiscal 1986 appropriations for the legislative branch. Although staff projected that franked mail would cost $144 million ($56 million in the Senate, $88 million in the House), Congress voted only $100 million to help keep its overall budget ostensibly frozen at 1985 levels. Several members denounced the move at the time and predicted that Congress would end up passing a supplemental appropriation.

The total fiscal 1986 appropriation was reduced to $95.7 million in February 1986 as part of the across-the-board reductions required by the new Gramm-Rudman-Hollings anti-deficit law (PL 99-177).

That same month the Postal Service notified members that, unless they cut back, Congress would spend $146.2 million in fiscal 1986, $50.5 million more than appropriated.

That would have handily broken the $111 million record set in election-year 1984, which in turn broke the 1982 record of $100 million. Since the 1982 elections, there had been only one postal rate increase, which took effect in February 1985.

Without an increase, it was estimated the postal account could run out in May. Since 1986 was an election year, members did not want their mailing fund to dry up.

Members spent most of the year stewing and squabbling over the likelihood that they would exceed the fiscal 1986 appropriation and what should be done about it.

The House Appropriations Committee in March 1986 included $42.2 million for Congress' mail in an omnibus supplemental spending bill (HR 4515 — H Rept 99-510). Also approved were several rules changes designed to save money.

The rules changes, negotiated by a bipartisan House group, included proposals for 1986 that reduced the number of mass-mailing newsletters from six to four, limited town-meeting notices to one per household, required certain materials without time value (such as calendars) to be mailed at the lowest postal rate and required members to submit mailings to Congress' franking commission for possible advice on cost-saving measures.

After reports of the attempt to boost the free-mail subsidy — when many other government programs were being cut — received widespread publicity, the funds were dropped from the supplemental, and the House shifted its focus to conserving the remaining funds.

The franking debate was given a new twist by a May 2 ruling by the U.S. comptroller general, who interpreted the franking law as effectively giving Congress a blank check.

The comptroller general said that whatever Congress appropriated for its mail had to be accepted as payment in full by the U.S. Postal Service.

Although the ruling appeared to undermine any incentive for Congress to bring its postal spending under control, it fanned the fury of those seeking new restrictions on the franking privilege. On May 14, the Senate approved a measure (S Res 374 — S Rept 99-285) to limit each senator's mailing allowance for the rest of the fiscal year. Funds were divided among senators based on their states' populations.

Although the Senate passed a second resolution (S Con Res 139) that would impose a similar system for rationing mail funds on both chambers, that plan went nowhere.

By the end of July, congressional officials said the funding shortfall would be far smaller than expected. And in the end the formal restraints imposed in the Senate and the informal methods in the House kept the postal budget within bounds.

### Fiscal 1987 Funds

The Senate in August 1986 approved an amendment to the fiscal 1987 legislative appropriations bill (HR 5203) to set up separate appropriations accounts for House and Senate mail.

The amendment split the postal funds for fiscal 1987 equally between the 435-member House and the 100-member Senate. Historically, the House had spent considerably more than half of the mailing allowance.

As expected, the proposed 50-50 funding split did not sit well with the House. The amendment was dropped from the conference version of HR 5203 (H Rept 99-805).

By voice vote, the Senate Oct. 8, 1986, approved a resolution (S Res 500) allocating funds to pay for senators' official mail in fiscal 1987, which began Oct. 1. The resolution continued the cost-saving steps first implemented in fiscal 1986 under S Res 374.

Under S Res 500, senators from states with small populations were allotted $100,000 apiece for mailing costs, while California's two senators received the top allocation — $2,100,478 each.

S Res 500, like the earlier resolution, covered only senators' mail costs. The House continued to resist Senate pleas that it adopt a similar measure.

## Congressional Pay

Members of Congress and other white-collar federal employees received a 3 percent cost-of-living increase effective Jan. 1, 1987, under the fiscal 1987 continuing appropriations resolution (H J Res 738 — PL 99-591) cleared in 1986. The raise boosted most congressional salaries from $75,100 to $77,400 a year. Certain members of the leadership earned more.

The last pay hike on Capitol Hill was at the beginning of 1985, when congressional salaries rose from $72,600 to $75,100. *(Congress and the Nation Vol. VI, p. 832)*

The Senate in 1985 narrowly defeated an attempt to lower congressional salaries. On a 49-49 tie vote, the Senate May 3 rejected a move to recommit the first congressional budget resolution (S Con Res 32) to the Budget Committee with instructions to lower the salaries of members of Congress by 10 percent and use the resulting savings to lower the federal budget deficit.

# 1987-88

Congressional pay rose from $75,100 to $89,500 during the 100th Congress and an even larger pay raise — up to $135,000 — was proposed. But that pay hike — which was linked to a ban on honoraria — was rejected by the next Congress.

## Congressional Pay

Proposals for congressional pay raises sparked heated debate in the 100th Congress.

Despite members' fears of being accused of lining their own pockets while cutting programs that helped constituents, Congress in 1987 accepted two pay raises before blocking a third.

Members received a 3 percent cost-of-living increase Jan. 1, 1987, raising their annual salaries from $75,100 to $77,400. Then, after elaborate parliamentary maneuvering, members in February accepted another raise, to $89,500, that had been proposed by President Reagan based on the study of a special commission. *(1986 action, this page)*

But the political sensitivity of accepting a third raise within a year led members to exempt themselves and other top federal officials from the 2 percent cost-of-living increase for most federal employees that was included in the fiscal 1988 continuing appropriations resolution (H J Res 395 — PL 100-202). House Republicans gave politically embarrassing publicity to an early version of the legislation that would allow the raise, and Democratic leaders then moved to kill it.

Anticipating another pay increase proposal in 1988, congressional leaders began laying the groundwork in June 1988, when both the House and Senate voted to exempt themselves from a 4 percent cost-of-living raise approved for other federal employees in the fiscal 1989 budget resolution (H Con Res 268).

In December 1988, the presidential commission recommended that the pay of most members be raised by 51 percent, from $89,500 to $135,000 annually. Reagan in 1989 adopted the recommendation as part of his fiscal 1990 budget. Both the commission and the president said that if members got a higher salary, they should ban the practice of accepting honoraria, the fees members collected from outside groups for appearances and speaking engagements. *(Honoraria limits, p. 897)*

But after months of behind-the-scenes maneuvering, the 51 percent pay hike went down to defeat in February 1989 under a heavy barrage of public criticism.

### Background

Members of Congress had two mechanisms for increasing their salaries.

One was the annual cost-of-living pay increase that, under legislation (PL 97-51) adopted in 1981 and effective in fiscal 1983, was automatic unless Congress voted to block it. *(1981 legislation, Congress and the Nation Vol. VI, p. 821)*

The second mechanism was the Commission on Executive, Legislative and Judicial Salaries, known as the Quadrennial Commission, which was supposed to meet every four years to make recommendations to the president about pay levels for approximately 2,500 top federal officials, including members of Congress, Cabinet officers and federal judges.

Under a procedure approved in 1985 as part of the fiscal 1986 continuing appropriations legislation (PL 99-190), whatever pay raise the president recommended in his annual budget was to take effect within 30 days unless both chambers of Congress passed a joint resolution rejecting it and the president signed that resolution.

## 1987 Pay Raise

The Quadrennial Commission recommended in 1986 — two years later than it was supposed to — a $135,000 salary for most members. (Leaders receive higher pay.) Reagan pared the proposal to $89,500 when he submitted his budget. The salary at that time was $77,400.

Despite the political unpopularity of a big pay raise, the Quadrennial Commission argued that compensation for top federal officials had been badly eroded by inflation over the years, estimating that the purchasing power of a congressional salary had dropped 40 percent since 1969 — when members were paid $42,500 per year.

The panel also cited a surge in resignations by federal judges, many of whom left for economic reasons. More judges had resigned since 1969 than in the previous 180 years; 15 judges resigned in 1980-84 alone. Most federal judges made $81,100 or $85,700 a year — roughly half of what they could earn in private law practice, according to the commission.

Cabinet secretaries earned $88,800 in 1986. If their salaries had kept pace with inflation since 1969, the commission said, they would be paid more than $180,000 — still far less than what their executive counterparts in the corporate world earned.

In Congress, there was widespread support for a pay raise and harsh rhetoric opposing it. Members acknowledged that their constituents had little sympathy with claims that they could not make ends meet on $77,400 a year. And many also acknowledged that given record budget deficits, there could hardly have been a worse political and fiscal climate in which to enact a pay increase.

The Senate took several steps on Jan. 29, 1987, to block the proposed pay hike. It passed 88-6 a bill (S J Res 34) to prevent the pay raises. Then, by voice vote, it added an amendment with similar language to a House-passed bill (H J Res 102) providing emergency aid to the homeless. Democrats in the House had made homeless aid a priority and were infuriated when the Senate added the pay-hike rejection to their pet legislation.

With careful maneuvering, the House cleared H J Res 102 (PL 100-6) with the Senate-sponsored rider opposing the raise on Feb. 4 — one day after the 30-day deadline for rejecting the pay raise. "Vote 'no' and take the dough" was how critics described the strategy.

Reagan declared the pay boost in effect, and on June 30 a U.S. District Court judge dismissed a lawsuit by six members of Congress alleging that the raise was enacted unconstitutionally.

## 1988 Recommendation

The Quadrennial Commission on Dec. 13, 1988, recommended a 51 percent pay hike — but only if members stopped supplementing their salaries with honoraria.

The higher pay would be more than enough to make up for the loss of honoraria — even for those who had collected the maximum allowed.

Under rules allowing members to supplement their income with honoraria, House members could keep up to 30 percent more, or $26,850 at 1988 pay levels, and senators could keep up to 40 percent more, or $35,800.

Thus, House members had been able to earn a total of $116,350 a year, and senators $125,300, if they earned the maximum honoraria allowed. Congressional leaders could make more.

But most members, particularly in the House, did not collect the full amount allowed. According to Common Cause, the self-styled citizens' lobby that was a leading opponent of honoraria, nearly half of all senators bumped up against the ceiling on honoraria in 1987; only about 20 percent of House members did.

But the prospect of this quid pro quo did not quiet critics who saw the proposed honoraria ban as a moral fig leaf for an unjustified pay grab. Railing against pay raises was a potent populist issue, since congressional pay looked plenty generous by the standards of most members' constituents.

Despite populist opposition, advocates of the raise said that continued erosion of congressional salaries would turn lawmaking into a profession only the wealthy could afford. They emphasized that members faced unusually high living costs, including the maintenance of two residences, one back home and another in Washington.

Pay-raise advocates hoped their cause would be fueled by concern that the judiciary and executive branch were suffering because of Congress' failure to enact regular pay hikes — or to sever the link between the three branches' pay scales.

They also hoped that burgeoning public criticism of the honoraria system would change the political dynamics of the issue. Total honoraria receipts had grown vastly over the years and totaled nearly $9.4 million in 1987.

The Democratic leadership's strategy to accomplish both the pay increase and the honoraria ban, at least in the House, hinged on avoiding a vote on salaries, on the assumption that any roll call would kill the increase

But that strategy failed. The House Feb. 7, 1989 — the day before the salary increase was to take effect automatically — approved, 380-48, a resolution (H J Res 129) to kill the pay raise, and the Senate followed suit by a 94-6 margin.

**President of the Senate**—Under the Constitution, the vice president of the United States presides over the Senate. In his absence, the president pro tempore, or a senator designated by the president pro tempore, presides over the chamber.

**President Pro Tempore**—The chief officer of the Senate in the absence of the vice president; literally, but loosely, the president for a time. The president pro tempore is elected by his fellow senators, and the recent practice has been to elect the senator of the majority party with the longest period of continuous service.

**Previous Question**—A motion for the previous question, when carried, has the effect of cutting off all debate, preventing the offering of further amendments and forcing a vote on the pending matter. In the House, the previous question is not permitted in the Committee of the Whole. The motion for the previous question is a debate-limiting device and is not in order in the Senate.

**Printed Amendment**—A House rule guarantees five minutes of floor debate in support and five minutes in opposition, and no other debate time, on amendments printed in the *Congressional Record* at least one day prior to the amendment's consideration in the Committee of the Whole. In the Senate, while amendments may be submitted for printing, they have no parliamentary standing or status. An amendment submitted for printing in the Senate, however, may be called up by any senator.

**Private Calendar**—In the House, private bills dealing with individual matters such as claims against the government, immigration or land titles are put on this calendar. The private calendar must be called on the first Tuesday of each month, and the Speaker may call it on the third Tuesday of each month as well.

When a private bill is before the chamber, two members may block its consideration, which recommits the bill to committee. Backers of a recommitted private bill have recourse. The measure can be put into an "omnibus claims bill" — several private bills rolled into one. As with any bill, no part of an omnibus claims bill may be deleted without a vote. When the private bill goes back to the House floor in this form, it can be deleted from the omnibus bill only by majority vote.

**Privilege**—Relates to the rights of members of Congress and to the relative priority of the motions and actions they may make in their respective chambers. The two are distinct. "Privileged questions" deal with legislative business. "Questions of privilege" concern legislators themselves.

**Privileged Questions**—The order in which bills, motions and other legislative measures are considered by Congress is governed by strict priorities. A motion to table, for instance, is more privileged than a motion to recommit. Thus, a motion to recommit can be superseded by a motion to table, and a vote would be forced on the latter motion only. A motion to adjourn, however, takes precedence over a tabling motion and thus is considered of the "highest privilege." *(See also Questions of Privilege.)*

**Pro Forma Amendment**—*(See Strike Out the Last Word.)*

**Public Laws**—*(See Law.)*

**Questions of Privilege**—These are matters affecting members of Congress individually or collectively. Matters affecting the rights, safety, dignity and integrity of proceedings of the House or Senate as a whole are questions of privilege in both chambers.

Questions involving individual members are called questions of "personal privilege." A member rising to ask a question of personal privilege is given precedence over almost all other proceedings. An annotation in the House rules points out that the privilege rests primarily on the Constitution, which gives him a conditional immunity from arrest and an unconditional freedom to speak in the House. *(See also Privileged Questions.)*

**Quorum**—The number of members whose presence is necessary for the transaction of business. In the Senate and House, it is a majority of the membership. A quorum is 100 in the Committee of the Whole House. If a point of order is made that a quorum is not present, the only business that is in order is either a motion to adjourn or a motion to direct the sergeant-at-arms to request the attendance of absentees.

**Readings of Bills**—Traditional parliamentary procedure required bills to be read three times before they were passed. This custom is of little modern significance. Normally a bill is considered to have its first reading when it is introduced and printed, by title, in the *Congressional Record*. In the House, its second reading comes when floor consideration begins. (This is the most likely point at which there is an actual reading of the bill, if there is any.) The second reading in the Senate is supposed to occur on the legislative day after the measure is introduced, but before it is referred to committee. The third reading (again, usually by title) takes place when floor action has been completed on amendments.

**Recess**—Distinguished from adjournment in that a recess does not end a legislative day and therefore does not interrupt unfinished business. The rules in each house set forth certain matters to be taken up and disposed of at the beginning of each legislative day. The House usually adjourns from day to day. The Senate often recesses, thus meeting on the same legislative day for several calendar days or even weeks at a time.

**Recognition**—The power of recognition of a member is lodged in the Speaker of the House and the presiding officer of the Senate. The presiding officer names the member who will speak first when two or more members simultaneously request recognition.

**Recommit to Committee**—A motion, made on the floor after a bill has been debated, to return it to the committee that reported it. If approved, recommittal usually is considered a death blow to the bill. In the House, a motion to recommit can be made only by a member opposed to the bill, and, in recognizing a member to make the motion, the Speaker gives preference to members of the minority party over majority party members.

A motion to recommit may include instructions to the committee to report the bill again with specific amendments or by a certain date. Or, the instructions may direct that a particular study be made, with no definite deadline for further action. If the recommittal motion includes instructions to "report the bill back forthwith" and the motion is adopted, floor action on the bill continues; the committee does not actually reconsider the legislation.

**Reconciliation**—The 1974 budget act provides for a "reconciliation" procedure for bringing existing tax and spending laws into conformity with ceilings enacted in the congressional budget resolution. Under the procedure, Congress instructs designated legislative committees to approve measures adjusting revenues and expenditures by a certain amount. The committees have a deadline by which they must report the legislation, but they have the discretion of deciding what changes are to be made. The recommendations of the various committees are consolidated without change by the Budget committees into an omnibus reconciliation bill, which then must be considered and approved by both houses of Congress. The orders to congressional committees to report recommendations for reconciliation bills are called reconciliation instructions, and they are contained in the budget resolution. Reconciliation instructions are not binding, but Congress must meet annual Gramm-Rudman deficit targets to avoid the automatic spending cuts of sequestration, which means it must also meet the goal of reconciliation. *(See also Budget Resolution, Sequestration.)*

**Reconsider a Vote**—A motion to reconsider the vote by which an action was taken has, until it is disposed of, the effect of putting the action in abeyance. In the Senate, the motion can be made only by a member who voted on the prevailing side of the original question or by a member who did not vote at all. In the House, it can be made only by a member on the prevailing side.

A common practice in the Senate after close votes on an issue is a motion to reconsider, followed by a motion to table the motion to reconsider. On this motion to table, senators vote as they voted on the original question, which allows the motion to table to prevail, assuming there are no switches. The matter then is finally closed and further motions to reconsider are not entertained. In the House, as a routine precaution, a motion to reconsider usually is made every time a measure is passed. Such a motion almost always is tabled immediately, thus shutting off the possibility of future reconsideration, except by unanimous consent.

Motions to reconsider must be entered in the Senate within the next two days of actual session after the original vote has been taken. In the House they must be entered either on the same day or on the next succeeding day the House is in session.

**Recorded Vote**—A vote upon which each member's stand is individually made known. In the Senate, this is accomplished through a roll call of the entire membership, to which each senator on the floor must answer "yea," "nay" or, if he does not wish to vote, "present." Since January 1973, the House has used an electronic voting system for recorded votes, including yea-and-nay votes formerly taken by roll calls.

When not required by the Constitution, a recorded vote can be obtained on questions in the House on the demand of one-fifth (44 members) of a quorum or one-fourth (25) of a quorum in the Committee of the Whole. *(See Yeas and Nays.)*

**Report**—Both a verb and a noun as a congressional term. A committee that has been examining a bill referred to it by the parent chamber "reports" its findings and recommendations to the chamber when it completes consideration and returns the measure. The process is called "reporting" a bill.

A "report" is the document setting forth the committee's explanation of its action. Senate and House reports are numbered separately and are designated S Rept or H Rept. When a committee report is not unanimous, the dissenting committee members may file a statement of their views, called minority or dissenting views and referred to as a minority report. Members in disagreement with some provisions of a bill may file additional or supplementary views. Sometimes a bill is reported without a committee recommendation.

Adverse reports occasionally are submitted by legislative committees. However, when a committee is opposed to a bill, it usually fails to report the bill at all. Some laws require that committee reports — favorable or adverse — be made.

**Rescission**—An item in an appropriations bill rescinding or canceling budget authority previously appropriated but not spent. Also, the repeal of a previous appropriation by Congress at the request of the president to cut spending or because the budget authority no longer is needed. Under the 1974 budget act, however, unless Congress approves a rescission within 45 days of continuous session after receipt of the proposal, the funds must be made available for obligation. *(See also Deferral.)*

**Resolution**—A "simple" resolution, designated H Res or S Res, deals with matters entirely within the prerogatives of one house or the other. It requires neither passage by the other chamber nor approval by the president, and it does not have the force of law. Most resolutions deal with the rules or procedures of one house. They also are used to express the sentiments of a single house such as condolences to the family of a deceased member or to comment on foreign policy or executive business. A simple resolution is the vehicle for a "rule" from the House Rules Committee. *(See also Concurrent and Joint Resolutions, Rules.)*

**Rider**—An amendment, usually not germane, that its sponsor hopes to get through more easily by including it in other legislation. Riders become law if the bills embodying them are enacted. Amendments providing legislative directives in appropriations bills are outstanding examples of riders, though technically legislation is banned from appropriations bills. The House, unlike the Senate, has a strict germaneness rule; thus, riders usually are Senate devices to get legislation enacted quickly or to bypass lengthy House consideration and, possibly, opposition.

**Rules**—The term has two specific congressional meanings. A rule may be a standing order governing the conduct of House or Senate business and listed among the permanent rules of either chamber. The rules deal with issues such as duties of officers, the order of business, admission to the floor, parliamentary procedures on handling amendments and voting and jurisdictions of committees.

In the House, a rule also may be a resolution reported by its Rules Committee to govern the handling of a particular bill on the floor. The committee may report a "rule," also called a "special order," in the form of a simple resolution. If the resolution is adopted by the House, the temporary rule becomes as valid as any standing rule and lapses only after action has been completed on the measure to which it pertains. A rule sets the time limit on general debate. It also may waive points of order against provisions of the bill in question such as non-germane language or against certain amendments intended to be proposed to the bill from the floor. It may even forbid all amendments or all amendments except those proposed by the legislative committee that handled the bill. In this instance, it is known as a "closed" or "gag" rule as opposed to an "open" rule, which puts no limitation on floor amendments, thus leaving the bill completely open to alteration by the adoption of germane amendments.

**Secretary of the Senate**—Chief administrative officer of the Senate, responsible for overseeing the duties of Senate employees, educating Senate pages, administering oaths, handling the registration of lobbyists and handling other tasks necessary for the continuing operation of the Senate. *(See also Clerk of the House.)*

**Select or Special Committee**—A committee set up for a special purpose and, usually, for a limited time by resolution of either the House or Senate. Most special committees are investigative and lack legislative authority — legislation is not referred to them and they cannot report bills to their parent chamber. *(See also Standing Committees.)*

**Senatorial Courtesy**—Sometimes referred to as "the courtesy of the Senate," it is a general practice — with no written rule — applied to consideration of executive nominations. Generally, it means that nominations from a state are not to be confirmed unless they have been approved by the senators of the president's party of that state, with other senators following their colleagues' lead in the attitude they take toward consideration of such nominations. *(See Nominations.)*

**Sequestration**—A procedure established by the 1985 Gramm-Rudman-Hollings deficit reduction law, as amended in 1987, to cancel (or withhold) budgetary resources. Gramm-Rudman set up a declining deficit target timetable so the deficit would be zero by fiscal year 1993. If the federal budget exceeded the deficit target in any year, the president would be required to issue a sequester order — based on a deficit estimate report issued by the Office of Management and Budget — to make across-the-board cuts in budget programs. The sequester order would be issued twice; the first order (issued Aug. 25) withholding funds to give Congress time to meet the deficit target by regular budget actions (such as reconciliation), and the second order (issued Oct. 15) actually canceling funds. *(See also Budget Process.)*

**Sine Die**—*(See Adjournment Sine Die.)*

**Slip Laws**—The first official publication of a bill that has been enacted and signed into law. Each is published separately in unbound single-sheet or pamphlet form. *(See also Law, Statutes at Large, U.S. Code.)*

**Speaker**—The presiding officer of the House of Representatives, selected by the caucus of the party to which he belongs and formally elected by the whole House.

**Special Session**—A session of Congress after it has adjourned sine die, completing its regular session. Special sessions are convened by the president.

**Spending Authority**—The 1974 budget act defines spending authority as borrowing authority, contract authority and entitlement authority for which budget authority is not provided in advance by appropriation acts.

**Sponsor**—*(See Bills Introduced.)*

**Standing Committees**—Committees permanently established by House and Senate rules. The standing committees of the House were last reorganized by the committee reorganization of 1974. The last major realignment of Senate committees was in the committee system reorganization of 1977. The standing committees are legislative committees — legislation may be referred to them and they may report bills and resolutions to their parent chambers. *(See also Select or Special Committee.)*

**Standing Vote**—A non-recorded vote used in both the House and Senate. (A standing vote also is called a division vote.) Members in favor of a proposal stand and are counted by the presiding officer. Then members opposed stand and are counted. There is no record of how individual members voted.

***Statutes at Large***—A chronological arrangement of the laws enacted in each session of Congress. Though indexed, the laws are not arranged by subject matter, and there is not an indication of how they changed previously enacted laws. *(See also Law, Slip Laws, U.S. Code.)*

**Strike From the Record**—Remarks made on the House floor may offend some member, who moves that the offending words be "taken down" for the Speaker's cognizance, and then expunged from the debate as published in the *Congressional Record*.

**Strike Out the Last Word**—A motion whereby a House member is entitled to speak for five minutes on an amendment then being debated by the chamber. A member gains recognition from the chair by moving to "strike out the last word" of the amendment or section of the bill under consideration. The motion is pro forma, requires no vote and does not change the amendment being debated.

**Substitute**—A motion, amendment or entire bill introduced in place of the pending legislative business. Passage of a substitute measure kills the original measure by supplanting it. The substitute also may be amended. *(See also Amendment in the Nature of a Substitute.)*

**Supplemental Appropriations Bill**—Legislation appropriating funds after the regular annual appropriations bill for a federal department or agency has been enacted. A supplemental appropriation provides additional budget authority beyond original estimates for programs or activities, including new programs authorized after the enactment of the regular appropriation act, for which the need for funds is too urgent to be postponed until enactment of the next year's regular appropriation bill.

**Suspend the Rules**—Often a time-saving procedure for passing bills in the House. The wording of the motion, which may be made by any member recognized by the Speaker, is: "I move to suspend the rules and pass the bill . . ." A favorable vote by two-thirds of those present is required for passage. Debate is limited to 40 minutes and no amendments from the floor are permitted. If a two-thirds favorable vote is not attained, the bill may be considered later under regular procedures. The suspension procedure is in order every Monday and Tuesday and is intended to be reserved for non-controversial bills.

**Table a Bill**—Motions to table, or to "lay on the table," are used to block or kill amendments or other parliamentary questions. When approved, a tabling motion is considered the final disposition of that issue. One of the most widely used parliamentary procedures, the motion to table is not debatable, and adoption requires a simple majority vote.

In the Senate, however, different language sometimes is used. The motion may be worded to let a bill "lie on the table," perhaps for subsequent "picking up." This motion is more flexible, keeping the bill pending for later action, if desired. Tabling motions on amendments are effective debate-ending devices in the Senate.

**Teller Vote**—This is a largely moribund House procedure in the Committee of the Whole. Members file past tellers and are counted as for or against a measure, but they are not recorded individually. In the House, tellers are ordered upon demand of one-fifth of a quorum. This is 44 in the House, 20 in the Committee of the Whole.

The House also has a recorded teller vote, now largely supplanted by the electronic voting procedure, under which the votes of each member are made public just as they would be on a recorded vote.

**Treaties**—Executive proposals — in the form of resolutions of ratification — which must be submitted to the Senate for approval by two-thirds of the senators present. Treaties are normally sent to the Foreign Relations Committee for scrutiny before the Senate takes action. Foreign Relations has jurisdiction over all treaties, regardless of the subject matter. Treaties are read three times and debated on the floor in much the same manner as legislative proposals. After approval by the Senate, treaties are formally ratified by the president.

**Trust Funds**—Funds collected and used by the federal government for carrying out specific purposes and programs according to terms of a trust agreement or statute such as the Social Security and unemployment compensation trust funds. Such funds are administered by the government in a fiduciary capacity and are not available for the general purposes of the government.

**Unanimous Consent**—Proceedings of the House or Senate and action on legislation often take place upon the unanimous consent of the chamber, whether or not a rule of the chamber is being violated. Unanimous consent is used to expedite floor action and frequently is used in a routine fashion such as by a senator requesting the unanimous consent of the Senate to have specified members of his staff present on the floor during debate on a specific amendment.

**Unanimous Consent Agreement**—A device used in the Senate to expedite legislation. Much of the Senate's legislative business, dealing with both minor and controversial issues, is conducted through unanimous consent or unanimous consent agreements. On major legislation, such agreements usually are printed and transmitted to all senators in advance of floor debate. Once agreed to, they are binding on all members unless the Senate, by unanimous consent, agrees to modify them. An agreement may list the order in which various bills are to be considered, specify the length of time bills and contested amendments are to be debated and when they are to be voted upon and, frequently, require that all amendments introduced be germane to the bill under consideration. In this regard, unanimous consent agreements are similar to the "rules" issued by the House Rules Committee for bills pending in the House.

**Union Calendar**—Bills that directly or indirectly appropriate money or raise revenue are placed on this House calendar according to the date they are reported from committee.

***U.S. Code***—A consolidation and codification of the general and permanent laws of the United States arranged by subject under 50 titles, the first six dealing with general or political subjects, and the other 44 alphabetically arranged from agriculture to war. The *U.S. Code* is updated annually, and a new set of bound volumes is published every six years. (See also *Law, Slip Laws*, Statutes at Large.)

**Veto**—Disapproval by the president of a bill or joint resolution (other than one proposing an amendment to the Constitution). When Congress is in session, the president must veto a bill within 10 days, excluding Sundays, after he has received it; otherwise, it becomes law without his signature. When the president vetoes a bill, he returns it to the house of origin along with a message stating his objections. (See also *Pocket Veto, Override a Veto*.)

**Voice Vote**—In either the House or Senate, members answer "aye" or "no" in chorus, and the presiding officer decides the result. The term also is used loosely to indicate action by unanimous consent or without objection.

**Whip**—(See *Majority and Minority Whip*.)

**Without Objection**—Used in lieu of a vote on non-controversial motions, amendments or bills that may be passed in either the House or Senate if no member voices an objection.

**Yeas and Nays**—The Constitution requires that yea-and-nay votes be taken and recorded when requested by one-fifth of the members present. In the House, the Speaker determines whether one-fifth of the members present requested a vote. In the Senate, practice requires only 11 members. The Constitution requires the yeas and nays on a veto override attempt. (See *Recorded Vote*.)

**Yielding**—When a member has been recognized to speak, no other member may speak unless he obtains permission from the member recognized. This permission is called yielding and usually is requested in the form, "Will the gentleman yield to me?" While this activity occasionally is seen in the Senate, the Senate has no rule or practice to parcel out time.

# The Legislative Process in Brief

*Note: Parliamentary terms used below are defined in the glossary.*

## Introduction of Bills

A House member (including the resident commissioner of Puerto Rico and non-voting delegates of the District of Columbia, Guam, the Virgin Islands and American Samoa) may introduce any one of several types of bills and resolutions by handing it to the clerk of the House or placing it in a box called the hopper. A senator first gains recognition of the presiding officer to announce the introduction of a bill. If objection is offered by any senator, the introduction of the bill is postponed until the following day.

As the next step in either the House or Senate, the bill is numbered, referred to committee, labeled with the sponsor's name and sent to the Government Printing Office so that copies can be made for subsequent study and action. Senate bills may be jointly sponsored and carry several senators' names. Until 1978, the House limited the number of members who could cosponsor any one bill; the ceiling was eliminated at the beginning of the 96th Congress. A bill written in the executive branch and proposed as an administration measure usually is introduced by the chairman of the congressional committee that has jurisdiction.

**Bills**—Prefixed with HR in the House, S in the Senate, followed by a number. Used as the form for most legislation, whether general or special, public or private.

**Joint Resolutions**—Designated H J Res or S J Res. Subject to the same procedure as bills, with the exception of a joint resolution proposing an amendment to the Constitution. The latter must be approved by two-thirds of both houses and is thereupon sent directly to the administrator of general services for submission to the states for ratification instead of being presented to the president for his approval.

**Concurrent Resolutions**—Designated H Con Res or S Con Res. Used for matters affecting the operations of both houses. These resolutions do not become law.

**Resolutions**—Designated H Res or S Res. Used for a matter concerning the operation of either house alone and adopted only by the chamber in which it originates.

## Committee Action

With few exceptions, bills are referred to the appropriate standing committees. The job of referral formally is the responsibility of the Speaker of the House and the presiding officer of the Senate, but this task usually is carried out on their behalf by the parliamentarians of the House and Senate. Precedent, statute and the jurisdictional mandates of the committees as set forth in the rules of the House and Senate determine which committees receive what kinds of bills. An exception is the referral of private bills, which are sent to whatever committee is designated by their sponsors. Bills are technically considered "read for the first time" when referred to House committees.

When a bill reaches a committee it is placed on the committee's calendar. At that time the bill comes under the sharpest congressional focus. Its chances for passage are quickly determined — and the great majority of bills falls by the legislative roadside. Failure of a committee to act on a bill is equivalent to killing it; the measure can be withdrawn from the committee's purview only by a discharge petition signed by a majority of the House membership on House bills, or by adoption of a special resolution in the Senate. Discharge attempts rarely succeed.

The first committee action taken on a bill usually is a request for comment on it by interested agencies of the government. The committee chairman may assign the bill to a subcommittee for study and hearings, or it may be considered by the full committee. Hearings may be public, closed (executive session) or both. A subcommittee, after considering a bill, reports to the full committee its recommendations for action and any proposed amendments.

The full committee then votes on its recommendation to the House or Senate. This procedure is called "ordering a bill reported." Occasionally a committee may order a bill reported unfavorably; most of the time a report, submitted by the committee chairman to the House or Senate, calls for favorable action on the measure since the committee can effectively "kill" a bill by simply not taking any action.

After the bill is reported, the committee chairman instructs the staff to prepare a written report. The report describes the purposes and scope of the bill, explains the committee revisions, notes proposed changes in existing law and, usually, includes the views of the executive branch agencies consulted. Often committee members opposing a bill include dissenting minority statements in the report.

Usually, the committee "marks up" or proposes amendments to the bill. If they are substantial and the measure is complicated, the committee may order a "clean bill" introduced, which will embody the proposed amendments. The original bill then is put aside and the clean bill, with a new number, is reported to the floor.

The chamber must approve, alter or reject the committee amendments before the bill itself can be put to a vote.

## Floor Action

After a bill is reported back to the house where it originated, it is placed on the calendar.

There are five legislative calendars in the House, issued in one cumulative calendar titled *Calendars of the United States House of Representatives and History of Legislation*. The House calendars are:

# Progress of Legislation

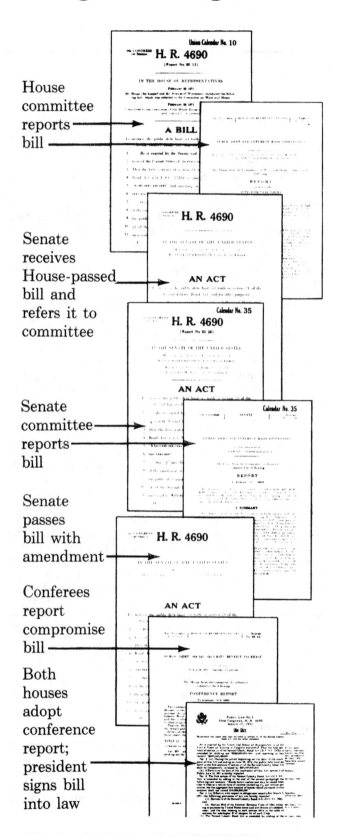

House committee reports bill

Senate receives House-passed bill and refers it to committee

Senate committee reports bill

Senate passes bill with amendment

Conferees report compromise bill

Both houses adopt conference report; president signs bill into law

*The Union Calendar* to which are referred bills raising revenues, general appropriations bills and any measures directly or indirectly appropriating money or property. It is the Calendar of the Committee of the Whole House on the State of the Union.

*The House Calendar* to which are referred bills of public character not raising revenue or appropriating money or property.

*The Consent Calendar* to which are referred bills of a non-controversial nature that are passed without debate when the Consent Calendar is called on the first and third Mondays of each month.

*The Private Calendar* to which are referred bills for relief in the nature of claims against the United States or private immigration bills that are passed without debate when the Private Calendar is called the first and third Tuesdays of each month.

*The Discharge Calendar* to which are referred motions to discharge committees when the necessary signatures are signed to a discharge petition.

There is only one legislative calendar in the Senate and one "executive calendar" for treaties and nominations submitted to the Senate. When the Senate Calendar is called, each senator is limited to five minutes' debate on each bill.

**Debate.** A bill is brought to debate by varying procedures. If a routine measure, it may await the call of the calendar. If it is urgent or important, it can be taken up in the Senate either by unanimous consent or by a majority vote. The majority leader, in consultation with the minority leader and others, schedules the bills that will be taken up for debate.

In the House, precedence is granted if a special rule is obtained from the Rules Committee. A request for a special rule usually is made by the chairman of the committee that favorably reported the bill, supported by the bill's sponsor and other committee members. The request, considered by the Rules Committee in the same way that other committees consider legislative measures, is in the form of a resolution providing for immediate consideration of the bill. The Rules Committee reports the resolution to the House where it is debated and voted upon in the same fashion as regular bills. If the Rules Committee should fail to report a rule requested by a committee, there are several ways to bring the bill to the House floor — under suspension of the rules, on Calendar Wednesday or by a discharge motion.

The resolutions providing special rules are important because they specify how long the bill may be debated and whether it may be amended from the floor. If floor amendments are banned, the bill is considered under a "closed rule," which permits only members of the committee that first reported the measure to the House to alter its language, subject to chamber acceptance.

When a bill is debated under an "open rule," amendments may be offered from the floor. Committee amendments always are taken up first but may be changed, like all amendments up to the second degree; that is, an amendment to an amendment to an amendment is not in order.

Duration of debate in the House depends on whether the bill is under discussion by the House proper or before the House when it is sitting as the Committee of the Whole House on the State of the Union. In the former, the amount of time for debate either is determined by special rule or is allocated with an hour for each member if the measure is under consideration without a rule. In the Committee of the Whole the amount of time agreed on for general debate is equally divided between proponents and opponents. At the end of general discussion, the bill is read section by section for amendment. Debate on an amendment is limited to five minutes for each side; this is called the "five-minute rule." In practice, amendments regularly are debated more than ten minutes, with members gaining the floor by offering pro forma amendments or obtaining unanimous consent to speak longer than five minutes.

Senate debate usually is unlimited. It can be halted only by unanimous consent by "cloture," which requires a three-fifths majority of the entire Senate except for proposed changes in the Senate rules. The latter requires a two-thirds vote.

The House considers almost all important bills within a parliamentary framework known as the Committee of the Whole. It is not a committee as the word usually is understood; it is the full House meeting under another name for the purpose of speeding action on legislation. Technically, the House sits as the Committee of the Whole when it considers any tax measure or bill dealing with public appropriations. It also can resolve itself into the Committee of the Whole if a member moves to do so and the motion is carried. The Speaker appoints a member to serve as the chairman. The rules of the House permit the Committee of the Whole to meet when a quorum of 100 members is present on the floor and to amend and act on bills, within certain time limitations. When the Committee of the Whole has acted, it "rises," the Speaker returns as the presiding officer of the House and the member appointed chairman of the Committee of the Whole reports the action of the committee and its recommendations. The Committee of the Whole cannot pass a bill; instead it reports the measure to the full House with whatever changes it has approved. The full House then may pass or reject the bill — or, on occasion, recommit the bill to committee. Amendments adopted in the Committee of the Whole may be put to a second vote in the full House.

**Votes.** Voting on bills may occur repeatedly before they are finally approved or rejected. The House votes on the rule for the bill and on various amendments to the bill. Voting on amendments often is a more illuminating test of a bill's support than is the final tally. Sometimes members approve final passage of bills after vigorously supporting amendments that, if adopted, would scuttle the legislation.

The Senate has three different methods of voting: an untabulated voice vote, a standing vote (called a division) and a recorded roll call to which members answer "yea" or "nay" when their names are called. The House also employs voice and standing votes, but since January 1973 yeas and nays have been recorded by an electronic voting device, eliminating the need for time-consuming roll calls.

Another method of voting, used in the House only, is the teller vote. Traditionally, members filed up the center aisle past counters; only vote totals were announced. Since 1971, one-fifth of a quorum can demand that the votes of individual members be recorded, thereby forcing them to take a public position on amendments to key bills. Electronic voting now is commonly used for this purpose.

After amendments to a bill have been voted upon, a vote may be taken on a motion to recommit the bill to committee. If carried, this vote removes the bill from the chamber's calendar and is usually a death blow to the bill. If the motion is unsuccessful, the bill then is "read for the third time." An actual reading usually is dispensed with. Until 1965, an opponent of a bill could delay this move by objecting and asking for a full reading of an engrossed

# Bills and Resolutions

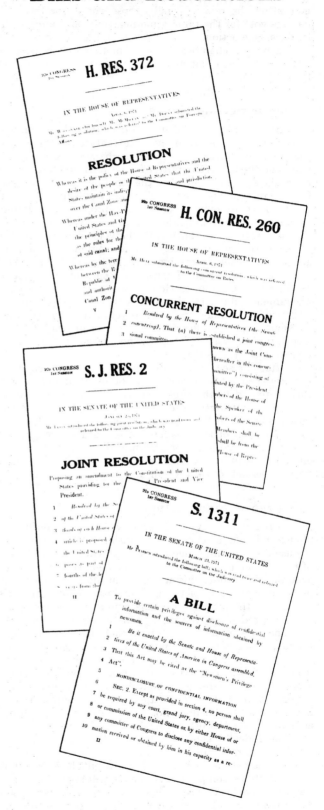

(certified in final form) copy of the bill. After the "third reading," the vote on final passage is taken.

The final vote may be followed by a motion to reconsider, and this motion may be followed by a move to lay the motion on the table. Usually, those voting for the bill's passage vote for the tabling motion, thus safeguarding the final passage action. With that, the bill has been formally passed by the chamber. While a motion to reconsider a Senate vote is pending on a bill, the measure cannot be sent to the House.

## Action in Second House

After a bill is passed it is sent to the other chamber. This body may then take one of several steps. It may pass the bill as is — accepting the other chamber's language. It may send the bill to committee for scrutiny or alteration, or reject the entire bill, advising the other house of its actions. Or it simply may ignore the bill submitted while it continues work on its own version of the proposed legislation. Frequently, one chamber may approve a version of a bill that is greatly at variance with the version passed by the other house, and then substitute its contents for the language of the other, retaining only the latter's bill number.

A provision of the Legislative Reorganization Act of 1970 permits a separate House vote on any non-germane amendment added by the Senate to a House-passed bill and requires a majority vote to retain the amendment. Previously the House was forced to act on the bill as a whole; the only way to defeat the non-germane amendment was to reject the entire bill.

Often the second chamber makes only minor changes. If these are readily agreed to by the other house, the bill then is routed to the president. However, if the opposite chamber significantly alters the bill submitted to it, the measure usually is "sent to conference." The chamber that has possession of the "papers" (engrossed bill, engrossed amendments, messages of transmittal) requests a conference and the other chamber must agree to it. If the second house does not agree, the bill dies.

## Conference, Final Action

**Conference.** A conference works out conflicting House and Senate versions of a legislative bill. The conferees usually are senior members appointed by the presiding officers of the two houses, from the committees that managed the bills. Under this arrangement the conferees of one house have the duty of trying to maintain their chamber's position in the face of amending actions by the conferees (also referred to as "managers") of the other house.

The number of conferees from each chamber may vary, the range usually being from three to nine members in each group, depending upon the length or complexity of the bill involved. There may be five representatives and three senators on the conference committee, or the reverse. But a majority vote controls the action of each group so that a large representation does not give one chamber a voting advantage over the other chamber's conferees.

Theoretically, conferees are not allowed to write new legislation in reconciling the two versions before them, but this curb sometimes is bypassed. Many bills have been put into acceptable compromise form only after new language was provided by the conferees. The 1970 Reorganization Act attempted to tighten restrictions on conferees by forbidding them to introduce any language on a topic that neither chamber sent to conference or to modify any topic beyond the scope of the differing versions of the bill.

Frequently the ironing out of difficulties takes days or even weeks. Conferences on involved appropriations bills sometimes are particularly drawn out.

As a conference proceeds, conferees reconcile differences between the versions, but generally they grant concessions only insofar as they remain sure that the chamber they represent will accept the compromises. Occasionally, uncertainty over how either house will react, or the positive refusal of a chamber to back down on a disputed amendment, results in an impasse, and the bills die in conference even though each was approved by its sponsoring chamber.

Conferees sometimes go back to their respective chambers for further instructions, when they report certain portions in disagreement. Then the chamber concerned can either "recede and concur" in the amendment of the other house or "insist on its amendment."

When the conferees have reached agreement, they prepare a conference report embodying their recommendations (compromises). The report, in document form, must be submitted to each house.

The conference report must be approved by each house. Consequently, approval of the report is approval of the compromise bill. In the order of voting on conference reports, the chamber which asked for a conference yields to the other chamber the opportunity to vote first.

**Final Steps.** After a bill has been passed by both the House and Senate in identical form, all of the original papers are sent to the enrolling clerk of the chamber in which the bill originated. He then prepares an enrolled bill, which is printed on parchment paper. When this bill has been certified as correct by the secretary of the Senate or the clerk of the House, depending on which chamber originated the bill, it is signed first (no matter whether it originated in the Senate or House) by the Speaker of the House and then by the president of the Senate. It is next sent to the White House to await action.

If the president approves the bill, he signs it, dates it and usually writes the word "approved" on the document. If he does not sign it within 10 days (Sundays excepted) and Congress is in session, the bill becomes law without his signature. Should Congress adjourn before the 10 days expire, and the president fails to sign the measure, it does not become law. This procedure is called the pocket veto.

A president vetoes a bill by refusing to sign it and, before the 10-day period expires, returning it to Congress with a message stating his reasons. The message is sent to the chamber that originated the bill. If no action is taken on the message, the bill dies. Congress, however, can attempt to override the veto and enact the bill, "the objections of the president to the contrary notwithstanding." Overriding a veto requires a two-thirds vote of those present, who must number a quorum and vote by roll call.

Debate can precede this vote, with motions permitted to lay the message on the table, postpone action on it or refer it to committee. If the president's veto is overridden in both houses, the bill becomes law. Otherwise it is dead.

When bills are passed finally and signed, or passed over a veto, they are given law numbers in numerical order as they become law. There are two series of numbers, one for public and one for private laws, starting at the number "1" for each two-year term of Congress. They are then identified by law number and by Congress — for example, Private Law 21, 97th Congress; Public Law 250, 97th Congress (or PL 97-250).

# How a Bill Becomes Law

This graphic shows the most typical way in which proposed legislation is enacted into law. There are more complicated, as well as simpler, routes, and most bills never become law. The process is illustrated with two hypothetical bills, House bill No. 1 (HR 1) and Senate bill No. 2 (S 2). Bills must be passed by both houses in identical form before they can be sent to the president. The path of HR 1 is traced by a solid line, that of S 2 by a broken line. In practice most bills begins as similar proposals in both houses.

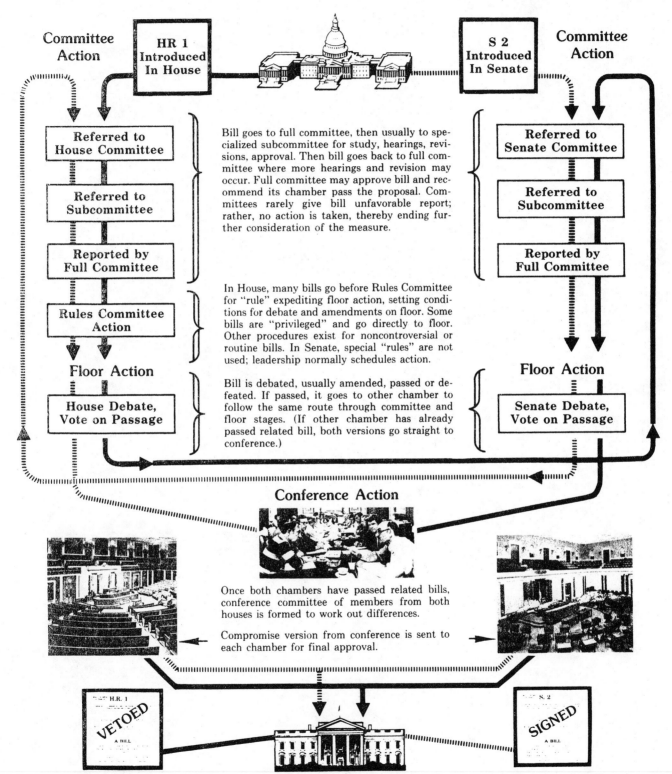

**Committee Action**

**HR 1 Introduced In House**

**S 2 Introduced In Senate**

**Committee Action**

**Referred to House Committee**

**Referred to Subcommittee**

**Reported by Full Committee**

Bill goes to full committee, then usually to specialized subcommittee for study, hearings, revisions, approval. Then bill goes back to full committee where more hearings and revision may occur. Full committee may approve bill and recommend its chamber pass the proposal. Committees rarely give bill unfavorable report; rather, no action is taken, thereby ending further consideration of the measure.

**Referred to Senate Committee**

**Referred to Subcommittee**

**Reported by Full Committee**

**Rules Committee Action**

In House, many bills go before Rules Committee for "rule" expediting floor action, setting conditions for debate and amendments on floor. Some bills are "privileged" and go directly to floor. Other procedures exist for noncontroversial or routine bills. In Senate, special "rules" are not used; leadership normally schedules action.

**Floor Action**

**House Debate, Vote on Passage**

Bill is debated, usually amended, passed or defeated. If passed, it goes to other chamber to follow the same route through committee and floor stages. (If other chamber has already passed related bill, both versions go straight to conference.)

**Floor Action**

**Senate Debate, Vote on Passage**

## Conference Action

Once both chambers have passed related bills, conference committee of members from both houses is formed to work out differences.

Compromise version from conference is sent to each chamber for final approval.

**H.R. 1 VETOED A BILL**

**S. 2 SIGNED A BILL**

Compromise bill approved by both houses is sent to the president, who can sign it into law or veto it and return it to Congress. Congress may override veto by a two-thirds majority vote in both houses; bill then becomes law without president's signature.

# Key Votes, 1985-88

Congressional Quarterly each year selects a series of key votes on major issues.

**Selection of Issues.** An issue is judged by the extent it represents one or more of the following:

- A matter of major controversy.
- A test of presidential or political power.
- A decision of potentially great impact on the nation and lives of Americans.

**Selection of Votes.** For each series of related votes on an issue, only one key vote usually is chosen. This vote is the roll call in the House or Senate that in the opinion of Congressional Quarterly was the most important in determining the outcome.

In the description of the key votes, the designation ND denotes Northern Democrats, and the designation SD denotes Southern Democrats.

# 1985 Key Votes

## Senate

### 1. Emergency Farm Credit

In an early show of bipartisan opposition to Reagan administration farm policy, the Senate Feb. 27 voted in favor of advancing crop-loan payments to financially strapped farmers. The vote came on a measure providing emergency, non-food assistance to drought- and famine-stricken areas in Africa (HR 1096).

Years of low farm profits and collapsing land values, particularly in the Midwest, had created a credit crisis for many farm communities.

The administration had been pressing for scaled back federal aid to farmers, and argued that it had done enough to help out farmers with serious debts. Notwithstanding the administration's veto threat, and attempts by Majority Leader Robert Dole, R-Kan., to hold the Senate to a goal of serious deficit reduction, eight Republicans voted with all but one Democrat to add the farm credit provisions to the Africa aid bill.

The Senate then passed HR 1096, with the farm-credit provisions, 62-35: R 16-34; D 46-1 (ND 32-1, SD 14-0).

The House accepted the Senate version March 5, and, true to his promise, President Reagan vetoed the bill March 6, calling it a "massive new bailout that would add billions to the deficit." Only a small minority of farmers were in need, Reagan said, despite unpublished Agriculture Department studies that showed 17 to 18 percent of U.S. farms with severe financial problems.

Neither chamber attempted to override the veto, but the Senate coalition of Democrats and farm-state Republicans continued to dominate as Congress worked to rewrite basic farm policy until the end of the 1985 session. And ultimately, Dole had to offer a contradictory amalgam of "sweeteners" to win away enough votes to get a farm bill passed in the Senate. *(Senate key vote 14)*

### 2. MX Missile Production

The Senate struck a major blow against a coalition of opponents of the MX intercontinental missile March 19 when it approved continued production of the controversial weapon by an unexpectedly large margin.

In 1984, the Senate had cast a tie vote on an amendment that would have blocked MX production, and the missile survived only because of Vice President George Bush's tie-breaking vote in favor. But in the key vote less than a year later — on a joint resolution (S J Res 71) approving procurement of 21 missiles in the fiscal 1985 budget — production was approved March 19, 55-45: R 45-8; D 10-37 (ND 3-30, SD 7-7).

Since MX became the central symbolic battle over Reagan administration nuclear arms policy in early 1983, liberal arms controllers had concentrated their anti-MX lobbying effort in the Democratically controlled House. So when they nearly won in the Senate in 1984 — partly because the particular amendment offered by moderate Democrat Lawton Chiles, Fla., was unexpected — it came as a great morale booster to opponents.

By the same token, their decisive Senate defeat in 1985 hit opponents hard and set the stage for Reagan's companion MX win in the House a week later. *(House key vote 1)*

After the House also approved the fiscal 1985 MX production, an influential group of moderate Democrats led by Sam Nunn, Ga. — all of whom had voted for production on March 19 — called for a legislative cap of 40 on the total number of MXs deployed in existing missile silos, compared with the 100 Reagan had proposed. This formula — with the cap raised to 50 — helped resolve the MX issue in 1985.

### 3. Fiscal 1986 Budget Resolution

The Senate's new majority leader, Robert Dole, R-Kan., made deficit reduction a top priority during his first months in office. In the early morning hours of May 10, Dole engineered a cliffhanger vote to pass a sweeping fiscal 1986 budget plan (S Con Res 32) that called for the largest reductions in the spending growth in the nation's history. The vote was 50-49: R 48-4; D 1-45 (ND 1-31, SD 0-14).

The 15-minute deadline for a vote, often bent in the Senate, was stretched well beyond custom as the Senate waited for Pete Wilson, R-Calif., en route by ambulance from a suburban hospital where he had undergone an appendectomy the day before.

An ashen Wilson, garbed in pajamas and robe and still receiving intravenous fluids, finally appeared in a wheelchair and cast his "aye" while senators of both parties cheered. His vote made for a 49-49 tie, which was then broken by Vice President George Bush. (Illness prevented two other senators, Republican John P. East, N.C., and Democrat J. James Exon, Neb., from voting.)

The vote was an important victory for Dole. He had had to persuade GOP senators, particularly 22 skittish colleagues up for re-election in 1986, that constituents were so concerned about the deficit that an "aye" would be a political asset, even though the legislation made substantial reductions in a number of popular programs and froze politically sensitive Social Security spending for a year.

Dole also had to convince the White House not to torpedo the legislation, even though it cut into the president's top-priority buildup in defense spending.

The narrow 53-47 Republican majority in the Senate had forced Dole and Senate Budget Committee Chairman

Pete V. Domenici, R-N.M., to struggle hard for every vote. The two spent months in exhaustive, private negotiations with Senate Republicans and the White House. Dole did not turn to Democrats for help, except at the last minute when concessions on farm spending won an "aye" from Edward Zorinsky, D-Neb.

## 4. Strategic Defense Initiative

The Senate approved a reduction in President Reagan's request for anti-missile research that was recommended by its Armed Services Committee for budgetary reasons. It did so after rejecting several amendments that would have sliced more money from the project.

The deeper reductions in the so-called strategic defense initiative (SDI) or "star wars" anti-missile defense program were proposed by arms control advocates who warned that the project would end any hope of an agreement to sharply reduce the number of U.S. and Soviet long-range nuclear missiles.

The critics' best effort came on an amendment to the fiscal 1986 defense authorization bill (S 1160) that would have trimmed the SDI ceiling from the $2.96 billion recommended by the Armed Services Committee to $1.9 billion. The amendment was rejected June 4, 38-57: R 6-45; D 32-12 (ND 25-7, SD 7-5).

Reagan had requested $3.96 billion.

Other amendments proposing larger and smaller reductions from the committee-recommended level were rejected by larger margins.

## 5. Contra Aid

President Reagan's policy of aiding Nicaragua's anti-government guerrillas, called contras, long had enjoyed wide bipartisan support in the Senate. But that support weakened in 1984 following revelations of the CIA's bungled attempt to mine harbors in Nicaragua, and Congress suspended arms shipments and all other aid to the contras.

Members of both parties in 1985 complained that the administration appeared to have no long-term policy for ending the civil war in Nicaragua. Reagan's request for renewed aid to the contras was rejected by the House in April — but a few days later Nicaraguan President Daniel Ortega angered many in Congress by flying to Moscow for meetings with top Soviet leaders.

Reagan once again sought congressional approval for renewed aid to the contras. The Senate complied on June 6, approving an amendment to a State Department authorizations bill (S 1003) authorizing $24 million for new "humanitarian" aid to the guerrillas and releasing conditions on another $14 million. The vote was 55-42: R 41-10; D 14-32 (ND 4-28, SD 10-4).

Although the aid was supported by members of both parties, the vote demonstrated for the first time that the overwhelming majority of Senate Democrats had joined their House counterparts in opposing U.S. involvement in Nicaragua's wars. *(House key vote 5)*

Nearly two months later, Congress gave final approval to $27 million in non-military aid to the contras in fiscal 1985.

## 6. United Nations Budget

With its frequently anti-American slant and seemingly out-of-control budget, the United Nations had been the target of growing congressional criticism over the years. That criticism came to a head in 1985, with Congress approving a provision threatening a major pullback in U.S. support for the world forum.

"The United Nations can no longer be a sacred cow," said Kansas Republican Nancy Landon Kassebaum, who followed up on her views with a key Senate amendment to restrict U.S. support for the U.N. budget. Kassebaum's proposal was added to the 1985 State Department authorizations bill (S 1003) June 7 by a vote of 71-13: R 41-4; D 30-9 (ND 18-8, SD 12-1). A modified version of the amendment cleared Congress in the final version of the bill.

Kassebaum and many of her allies said that they were not opposed to a strong U.S. role in the world body. But, they argued, the United States could no longer continue to provide a substantial share of the funding for a U.N. budget that had tripled in the preceding decade without gaining a greater voice in how the money was spent. So Kassebaum's amendment called for a reduction in U.S. contributions to the U.N. operating budget unless the institution moved to a system of proportional voting, which would give the United States voting clout on budget matters equal to its financial contribution.

## 7. Gun Control

Almost since the day the 1968 Gun Control Act was enacted, Westerners in Congress, urged on by the National Rifle Association (NRA), had been trying to undo major elements of the law. On July 9 in the Senate, they took a large step toward that goal.

The Senate handily approved a bill (S 49) relaxing many of the provisions in the 1968 law, including allowing interstate sales of rifles, shotguns and handguns. The vote was 79-15: R 49-2; D 30-13 (ND 18-13, SD 12-0).

The wide margin demonstrated the political clout of the NRA, which was able to overcome strong opposition from major police organizations that claimed the bill would undercut law enforcement efforts. James A. McClure, R-Idaho, chief sponsor of S 49, said the overwhelming vote for his bill was in part a reaction to "abusive enforcement" of the law since 1968 by the federal government.

Edward M. Kennedy, D-Mass., the Senate's leading gun-control advocate, tried to strengthen the bill by banning interstate sales of small handguns and by requiring a 14-day waiting period for gun purchases. But his efforts were rejected by substantial margins.

## 8. Line-Item Veto

President Reagan suffered a defeat in the Senate when the Republican leadership was prevented from bringing to the floor a measure (S 43) granting Reagan authority to veto individual items in appropriations bills. The attempt was blocked by a bipartisan filibuster, led by Appropriations Committee Chairman Mark O. Hatfield, R-Ore.

Hatfield and others argued that the so-called "line-item veto" would result in an unnecessary and dangerous transfer of power from the legislative branch to the executive branch of government. Under existing law, the president could only veto an entire appropriations bill if he did not like one or two individual items within it.

Sponsor Mack Mattingly, R-Ga., argued that ongoing attempts to trim the federal deficit had been unsuccessful, and that Congress should give the new veto authority a chance. Reagan, who had asked repeatedly for the line-item veto to control government spending, lobbied hard to get the measure to the floor. From his hospital bed at the Bethesda Naval Medical Center in Maryland where he was recuperating from cancer surgery, Reagan made a number of personal calls and wrote a letter to all senators asking for their support.

But three attempts by Republican leaders to cut off debate on the motion to proceed to S 43 failed to get the required 60 votes. After the final cloture motion was rejected July 24, 58-40: R 46-7; D 12-33 (ND 8-24, SD 4-9), Senate Majority Leader Robert Dole, R-Kan., withdrew the pending motion to proceed to the bill.

## 9. School Prayer

Advocates of organized, recited public school prayer suffered their worst defeat in seven years when the Senate Sept. 10 decisively rejected a bill designed to allow prayer in the schools. The vote on the motion to table, and thus kill, the measure (S 47) was 62-36: R 24-28; D 38-8 (ND 31-1, SD 7-7).

The legislation, sponsored by Jesse Helms, R-N.C., would have barred the federal courts, including the Supreme Court, from hearing any case involving school prayer. Thus, if a state or local government chose to adopt a policy allowing public school prayer, opponents would have no means of challenging it in federal court.

The Senate had voted on similar legislation 10 times in the past seven years. But the Sept. 10 vote marked the lowest level of support for the measure since 1979, when the Senate passed it.

Helms said the vote demonstrated that, although Republicans controlled the chamber, "this is really a liberal Senate." But Lowell P. Weicker Jr., R-Conn., the leading opponent of the bill, contended that there had been "a change in sentiment" about the prayer issue. He said the vote demonstrated that the public was "becoming more sensitive" to the issues involved and that citizens were encouraging their representatives to vote against measures that were "bringing government into religion."

## 10. Seasonal Workers

Heavy lobbying by Western agricultural growers convinced the Senate Sept. 17 to add a new foreign "guest-worker" program to an overhaul of the nation's immigration laws (S 1200).

The vote to adopt the program, sponsored by Pete Wilson, R-Calif., was 51-44: R 36-15; D 15-29 (ND 6-25, SD 9-4). It reversed the Senate's action Sept. 12 when a similar Wilson amendment was killed, 50-48.

Immigration reform, which the Senate has passed three times since 1982, would create a new system of penalties against employers who knowingly hired illegal aliens. Western growers, who relied heavily on an illegal work force, said they would support the sanctions provisions, but they had insisted on new guarantees of sufficient labor to harvest crops.

The Sept. 17 vote was a blow to Alan K. Simpson, R-Wyo., the chief sponsor of S 1200. He had been unalterably opposed to any guest-worker program, and accused the growers of being greedy in their quest for foreign labor.

The guest-worker program also had repercussions in the House Judiciary Committee, where members were deeply divided about the issue. Although the House Subcommittee on Immigration, Refugees and International

Law approved an immigration bill (HR 3080), it bypassed the farm worker issue to give a group of Democrats, led by committee member Charles E. Schumer, D-N.Y., more time to develop a compromise that could be presented to the full committee early in 1986.

## 11. Toxic Waste Victims' Aid

A decision to limit the federal role in aiding victims of toxic waste dumps was settled in a close vote Sept. 24 during debate on Senate passage of the "superfund" hazardous waste cleanup bill (S 51).

The vote came on a motion by William V. Roth Jr., R-Del., to strike from the bill a provision establishing a demonstration program for medical aid to victims of toxic spills and leaks. The vote in favor of the Roth amendment was 49-45: R 40-11; D 9-34 (ND 3-28, SD 6-6).

Although titled the Comprehensive Environmental Response, Compensation and Liability Act, the superfund program never included liability or compensation provisions for victims. Sponsors dropped those provisions in the closing days of the 96th Congress to get superfund enacted, but vowed to try again in 1985 when the law came up for renewal.

The "Victim Assistance Demonstration Program," proposed by George J. Mitchell, D-Maine, was added to the bill during markup by the Senate Environment and Public Works Committee. Mitchell had drastically pared down earlier victim aid schemes in hopes of picking up enough support.

The program would have been funded at $30 million annually for 1986-90 and have been conducted in five to 10 geographic areas around the country, which could qualify only if scientific studies showed that toxic exposure caused health threats. The U.S. government would have paid only medical expenses not covered by other insurance.

But Roth and other opponents charged that individual victims would not have had to prove that their ailments were specifically caused by a certain toxic release. They said it would be politically difficult to keep the program from expanding.

## 12. Gramm-Rudman-Hollings

Anger at the prospect of continued high federal deficits, exacerbated by the upcoming 1986 congressional elections, drove Congress to approve a radical overhaul of budgetary procedures with remarkable speed.

First introduced in September, the legislation received emphatic approval on Oct. 9 when the Senate voted to add it to a measure raising the ceiling on the federal debt (H J Res 372). The vote was 75-24: R 48-4; D 27-20 (ND 15-18, SD 12-2).

The following day, Oct. 10, the debt bill bearing the budget amendment passed the Senate by a 51-37 vote, with Republicans voting 38-8 in favor of the measure, and Democrats registering a negative 13-29 vote.

Advocates said that the plan, by requiring forced deficit reductions for a period of five years, would eliminate the federal budget deficit by the beginning of fiscal 1991. Opponents warned that it would have perverse and damaging effects on the nation's economy, on key priorities including defense, and that it entailed an unconstitutional shift of power away from Congress.

Those voting for the plan ranged from conservatives, such as sponsors Phil Gramm, R-Texas, Ernest F. Hollings,

D-S.C., and Warren B. Rudman, R-N.H., to liberals such as Edward M. Kennedy, D-Mass.

Each bloc of supporters believed that the plan would foster its own preferred solution to the deficit. Gramm's agenda was to shrink the federal government; others argued that the plan would force defense spending reductions and protect social programs. A strong theme was that the measure would confront President Reagan with a choice of defense spending cuts or higher taxes, and that would make Reagan finally agree to a tax hike. *(House key vote 12)*

## 13. Textile Imports

Legislation (HR 1562) limiting textile imports was the most prominent of the many trade bills that drew increasing congressional interest in 1985. Despite strong lobbying support from domestic textile manufacturers and unions, however, sponsors of the measure had to fight tooth-and-nail for nearly two months to get their proposal through the Senate.

The complex interplay of regional and economic factors influencing congressional action on trade legislation was clearly illustrated by the intense maneuvering over the textile bill. Not content with winning just a majority of the Senate, bill backers worked to expand their base of support by bringing in other trade interests in order to secure the two-thirds majority needed to override President Reagan's expected veto of the bill.

The first move of bill sponsors was to add import protections for shoes to the House-passed textile bill. That helped shore up support from members from shoe-producing states. Another change scaled back the House bill's import limits, in an effort to allay concerns that the application of deep cutbacks on Chinese products would damage trade relations with that country. Those shifts brought the proposal to a comfortable majority, but still well short of two-thirds; sponsors won key procedural votes by margins of 53-42 and 54-42. *(House key vote 10)*

Two other moves lifted the bill somewhat closer to its goal. Sponsors finally secured a promise from the GOP leadership for an up-or-down vote on the House-passed bill, thus avoiding a threatened filibuster as well as quieting objections from the backers of the unrelated bills to which textile forces earlier had sought to attach their proposal as amendments. Finally, an amendment aiding hard-pressed copper producers added strength among Western senators, bringing the bill to its high-water mark. The vote on final passage Nov. 13 was 60-39: R 25-28; D 35-11 (ND 23-10, SD 12-1).

## 14. Farm Bill

Stymied by an alliance of Democrats and farm-state Republicans, Majority Leader Robert Dole, R-Kan., took personal reins of a farm programs reauthorization measure (S 1714) on the Senate floor and fashioned a catchall compromise that managed to placate the various interests whose disagreement had blocked the bill, and kept the door open for an administration proposal to reduce price- and income-supports for farmers.

Dole put together a package that he acknowledged to be contradictory and over budget, but with its passage managed to avoid both an embarrassing defeat for the administration and a prolonged filibuster by Democrats.

The Agriculture Committee, dominated by an alliance of Democrats and farm-state Republicans, had reported out a bill with a four-year freeze on the "target" prices that determine government income subsidies for farmers. The administration had insisted on no more than a one-year freeze on target prices, although neither a one-year freeze nor a four-year freeze could garner a majority of votes in the full Senate.

To break the logjam, Dole substituted a dual system of income supports, putting both a one-year provision and a four-year provision in the bill, adding other "sweeteners" for nearly every special farm interest in the Senate, and prohibiting the Democrats from attempts to amend it to their advantage.

Dole won over 11 Democrats, mainly from sugar- and rice-producing states, and lost only six farm-state Republicans. The Nov. 20 vote on Dole's package was 56-41: R 45-6; D 11-35 (ND 4-28, SD 7-7).

Dole's maneuver, coupled with some tactical missteps by the Democrats, effectively blunted the organized opposition to his bill and put the GOP firmly back in control of the Senate. He later had to strike a last-minute compromise with three maverick Democrats who continued to hold out the threat of a filibuster. But the product of that deal, a one-year freeze with in-kind payments making up the slack in the second year, gave Dole all the leverage he needed to negotiate a compromise with the House, which had passed a bill containing a five-year freeze on target prices.

The final version of the bill contained a two-year freeze on target prices, with only a 2 percent cut in the third year and a total reduction of 10 percent over the five-year life of the bill.

# House Key Votes

## 1. MX Missile Production

In what may have been the last significant vote of a battle that dominated the congressional defense debate for nearly three years, the House March 26 cleared the way for production of the MX missile.

The vote came on a joint resolution (S J Res 71) that approved spending $1.5 billion in fiscal 1985 to build 21 MXs. This roundabout way of settling the question of MX production had been agreed to in October 1984 by the White House and the House Democratic leadership — which opposed the missile — after conferees on the fiscal 1985 defense authorization bill deadlocked on the issue.

The House approved the resolution by the same kind of narrow margin by which it had resolved MX battles since late 1983. Production was approved 219-213: R 158-24; D 61-189 (ND 15-154, SD 46-35).

Designed to carry 10 nuclear warheads, each with enough accuracy and explosive power to destroy a Soviet missile silo, MX had become by 1983 the central political symbol of President Reagan's nuclear weapons policy. Arms control advocates warned that it would escalate the arms race with Moscow, while Reagan and his allies contended that it was needed to counterbalance Soviet missiles powerful enough to destroy U.S. missiles in a first strike.

Reagan gave his opponents a major political advantage late in 1981 when he stripped the missile of one of its central technical justifications: He rejected the mobile basing method that the Air Force and Presidents Gerald R. Ford and Jimmy Carter had proposed to protect the new missiles against Soviet attack.

Beginning in early 1983, arms controllers organized a powerful grass-roots lobbying campaign that brought them within striking distance of a House vote against the missile. What finally swung the balance was the increasing involvement of the Democratic leaders, who saw MX as a way to crystallize public frustration with Reagan's expensive defense buildup, and widespread concern over his confrontational approach toward the Soviet Union.

Reagan was supported by a small but influential group of Democratic defense specialists who backed limited MX production in return for changes in the administration's arms control policy.

After more than a year of legislative battles, MX opponents eked out a narrow House victory in late May 1984, thus setting the stage for the final compromise that led to the March 26, 1985, House vote. Reagan won that final test by insisting that a vote against MX would undermine U.S. bargaining leverage in arms control talks with the Russians — a message carried to House members by Max M. Kampelman, Reagan's chief arms control negotiator.

In the fiscal 1986 defense bills, Congress seemed to end the MX fight — at least for the next several years — by capping the total MX deployment at 50 missiles, though more would be purchased to allow for testing. *(Senate key vote 2)*

## 2. McIntyre-McCloskey Contested Election

The winner of the 1984 election in Indiana's 8th Congressional District was not settled until May 1, when the House voted to seat Democrat Frank McCloskey instead of Republican Richard D. McIntyre, who had been certified the winner by Indiana.

The decision to declare McCloskey the winner followed four months of acrimony between Democrats and Republicans over what appeared to be the closest House contest in this century. Republicans, outnumbered 182-252 in the House, charged that Democrats stole the election. Democrats claimed there were inconsistencies in the Indiana ballot-counting and said a recount was necessary.

After the Nov. 6, 1984, election, incumbent McCloskey appeared to win by 72 votes. But in two precincts in one of the district's 15 counties, ballots had been counted twice. Correction of that arithmetical error gave McIntyre an apparent 34-vote victory. On that basis, the Indiana secretary of state certified McIntyre as the winner on Dec. 14.

When the House convened Jan. 3, members voted along party lines to hold vacant the Indiana 8th seat, pending a House Administration Committee investigation of alleged election irregularities. Three times after that, Republicans pushed the seating of McIntyre to a vote, but they lost to the Democratic majority.

After conducting its own recount, a House Administration Committee task force concluded April 18, on a 2-to-1 partisan split, that McCloskey had won by four votes.

On April 30, Republicans tried to get a new election by declaring the seat vacant. This was the key vote in the controversy — the best chance Republicans had and the one in which the most Democrats sided with the GOP. The vote on the Republican attempt (H Res 148) was 200-229: R 181-0; D 19-229 (ND 6-161, SD 13-68).

The recommendation of House Administration to seat McCloskey (H Res 146 — H Rept 99-58) came to a vote May 1. The House passed the resolution 236-190, with 10 Democrats voting against it. As Democrats prepared to

swear in McCloskey immediately after the vote, Republicans stormed out of the House chamber in protest.

## 3. South Africa Sanctions

During his first term, one of President Reagan's most controversial foreign policies was his "constructive engagement" approach to South Africa — friendly persuasion of the white minority government to ease its repressive racial system and to participate in regional peace-making efforts.

Constructive engagement came under increased scrutiny in 1985 as civil rights groups staged well-publicized protests at Pretoria's embassy in Washington and as racial violence mounted in South Africa.

To force a change in U.S. policy, congressional activists drew up legislation imposing economic sanctions against South Africa. The idea of sanctions drew broad bipartisan support in both chambers of Congress, with the main debate centering over how tough they should be.

On June 5, the Foreign Affairs Committee took to the House floor HR 1460, which would have imposed immediate sanctions on South Africa, including a ban on bank loans to the government and prohibitions against the sale of computers and nuclear power supplies. Subject to review by the president and Congress, the bill also would have barred new U.S. investment in South Africa and prohibited imports of South African coins called Krugerrands. Over the administration's opposition, the House passed the bill 295-127: R 56-121; D 239-6 (ND 166-0, SD 73-6).

The Senate later passed its own, somewhat weaker sanctions legislation, and on July 31 a House-Senate conference committee produced a surprisingly strong sanctions bill. Rather than face outright congressional repudiation of his policy, Reagan on Sept. 9 imposed his own limited set of sanctions, including a ban on Krugerrand imports, derailing the legislation.

## 4. Water Projects

On a cliffhanger vote June 6, the House signaled its unwillingness to fund politically popular water projects without program reform that would cut federal costs.

The key vote came on an amendment to the fiscal 1985 supplemental appropriations bill (HR 2577 — PL 99-88) having to do with funds to start construction on new water projects. The amendment, offered by Bob Edgar, D-Pa., cut from $150 million to $51 million the amount in the bill for new Army Corps of Engineers projects. It passed by one vote, 203-202: R 108-69; D 95-133 (ND 80-75, SD 15-58).

Authorization, funding and construction of new water projects had been stalled for almost a decade over how to divide costs between the federal government and local beneficiaries. The federal government had traditionally paid most of the cost, but reformers said fewer wasteful projects would be built if users had to put up a bigger share.

Although authorizing legislation had not been enacted, the House Appropriations Committee put funds for new construction starts into HR 2577. It contained 62 new projects, 31 of which had not yet been authorized. The unauthorized projects had been removed from the bill on the House floor by a point of order, and Edgar's amendment, in effect, blocked the funding that went with them.

The vote was an expression of fiscal austerity. But it also upheld the jurisdiction of the authorizing committee, Public Works and Transportation, whose leaders had jealously opposed what they saw as an effort to short-circuit the authorizing process. Because the omnibus water projects authorizing bill contained many projects not in the supplemental, committee leaders could call on the loyalty of a considerable number of members.

The demonstration of strength by reformers made its mark on the legislation as cleared. The final bill contained $48.8 million for 41 new Army Corps of Engineers projects (21 of them unauthorized), but under the condition that funds could not be spent on the unauthorized projects until Congress passed authorizing legislation (which did not happen in 1985) or the administration reached a cost-sharing agreement with local sponsors of individual projects.

## 5. Contra Aid

Since President Reagan took office, no foreign policy question had caused such deep divisions within Congress, and between Congress and the administration, as U.S. involvement in the war in Nicaragua. Reagan in 1981 ordered the CIA to organize a paramilitary force that would harass the leftist Sandinista government in Managua. By 1983, that force had grown to several thousand guerrillas who were receiving about $40 million a year worth of weapons and other supplies from the CIA.

Responding to a bungled CIA attempt to mine Nicaraguan harbors, Congress in 1984 ordered a halt to all U.S. backing for the guerrillas, widely known as contras. Reagan early in 1985 asked Congress to renew U.S. aid to the guerrillas. The House, long the center of opposition to intervention in Nicaragua, rebuffed that request April 23-24. A few days later, Nicaraguan President Daniel Ortega flew to Moscow for a meeting with top Soviet officials. That trip angered many House Democrats who had voted against aiding the contras; they said Ortega had forfeited a chance for political reconciliation between his government and the anti-communist guerrillas.

In a new political atmosphere caused by the Ortega trip, Reagan once again sought aid for the contras, promising that it would be used only for "humanitarian" or non-military purposes. The House approved that request in a stunning turnaround on June 12, during consideration of a fiscal 1985 supplemental appropriations bill (HR 2577).

The key House vote came on an amendment by Edward P. Boland, D-Mass., who sought to continue indefinitely his 1984 Boland amendment barring aid to the contras by any U.S. intelligence agencies. Democratic opponents of the contra aid saw that amendment as their best shot at defeating Reagan's request. The House rejected Boland's new amendment 196-232: R 7-174; D 189-58 (ND 156-11, SD 33-47). The House then approved $27 million in non-military assistance to the contras. That aid, with some strings attached, was included in the final version of the supplemental spending bill (PL 99-88). *(Senate key vote 5)*

## 6. Chemical Weapons

After blocking the move for three years, the House June 19 finally gave conditional approval to President Reagan's request to resume production of lethal chemical weapons for the first time since 1969.

The key vote came on an amendment to the fiscal 1986 defense authorization bill (HR 1872) that authorized $124 million for production of the so-called binary chemical weapons, provided they were formally requested by the NATO alliance. The amendment — which, in effect, substituted for a proposed amendment that would have con-

tinued the ban on binary production — was agreed to 229-196: R 143-34; D 86-162 (ND 30-138, SD 56-24).

According to the administration, new weapons were needed to replace the existing chemical weapons which, it warned, were militarily ineffective and were in danger of leaking because of age. Moreover, it argued, a U.S. chemical weapons modernization plan would induce the Russians to agree to a mutual ban on chemical weapons.

Opponents warned the weapons were unnecessary since existing chemical weapons were safe and militarily adequate. Moreover, they argued, chemical weapons are particularly repugnant and production would erode U.S. influence with its allies. The amendment skirted that diplomatic argument by making production contingent on NATO approval.

## 7. Strategic Defense Initiative

The effort of liberal arms control advocates to rein in development of anti-missile defenses reached its high-water mark on June 20. The House rejected an effort to trim the project — called the strategic defense initiative (SDI) or "star wars" — to $2.1 billion for fiscal 1986.

President Reagan had requested $3.96 billion for SDI in the fiscal 1986 defense budget and the House Armed Services Committee recommended a funding ceiling of $2.5 billion in its version of the fiscal 1986 defense authorization bill (HR 1872). The key vote came on an amendment to cut the figure to $2.1 billion, which was rejected 195-221: R 12-167; D 183-54 (ND 147-11, SD 36-43).

Reagan touted SDI as a way to make nuclear weapons "impotent and obsolete," implying that the program was intended to produce a leakproof shield over the country. But most administration officials set a more modest goal: a defense that could disrupt any Soviet attack on the U.S. nuclear force, and that would thus dissuade Moscow from making such an attack.

Arms controllers argued that Reagan's impenetrable shield would prove physically unattainable and anything less effective would spur a Soviet offensive buildup to swamp U.S. defenses.

## 8. Repeal of the Clark Amendment

In late 1975 and early 1976, reacting to the war in Vietnam and revelations of CIA misdeeds in the guise of "covert operations," Congress halted a Ford administration program of aiding one of the three guerrilla groups then battling for the control of Angola. Sponsored by Sen. Dick Clark, D-Iowa (1973-79), the Clark amendment stopped what was supposed to be secret CIA aid to rebels, called the Union for the Total Independence of Angola (UNITA).

In subsequent years, the Clark amendment became a symbol of congressional intervention in foreign policy; except for a short-lived 1984-85 ban on CIA action in Nicaragua, the Clark amendment was the only law specifically excluding U.S. intervention in a foreign country. To liberals it was a statement that the United States would step into foreign civil wars only when its vital interests were at stake and when the goals were clearly defined to the American public. Conservatives, including President Reagan, said the amendment showed that the United States no longer had the stomach to confront communist expansionism.

Congress weakened the Clark amendment in 1980,

while retaining its essential thrust. Reagan persistently demanded its outright repeal, but Democrats in the House fought to retain it.

The time for change came in July 1985, shortly after the House had reversed itself and approved renewed aid for the contras in Nicaragua. When the House was considering the fiscal 1986-87 foreign aid authorizations bill (HR 1555), a coalition of Democrats and Republicans banded together to offer a floor amendment to repeal the entire Clark measure. Their leading spokesman was Claude Pepper, D-Fla., chairman of the House Rules Committee.

The House July 10 adopted the Clark amendment repealer by a surprisingly wide margin of 236-185: R 176-6; D 60-179 (ND 14-150, SD 46-29). The vote was one of several actions the House took on the foreign aid bill demonstrating a new willingness to aid anti-communist insurgents. The Senate a month before had voted a similar measure, and the repealer was included with little controversy in the final version of the foreign aid authorization bill (PL 99-83) cleared in August.

## 9. Farm Bill

The administration, generally rebuffed in its efforts in the House to reform federal farm price-support programs, successfully lobbied against a measure to let farmers vote on what direction federal farm programs should take.

The House stripped a provision from the farm programs reauthorization bill (HR 2100 — PL 99-198) calling for a referendum among wheat and feed grain farmers on the question of instituting strict marketing controls in place of the government's regular price supports.

The proposal to give farmers direct control over the structure of federal agriculture policy developed slowly over the summer. The referendum was put into the Agriculture Committee bill at the last minute to keep mutinous Democrats from voting against a bill that would lower price-support protection for major crops, while freezing the "target" prices that determine income subsidies.

The referendum was a compromise version of a plan that would let farmers impose mandatory acreage cutbacks themselves as a way to reduce supply and drive up prices. The compromise, "voluntary" plan would place controls on production for domestic consumption and allow farmers to grow as much as they wanted for export.

On the floor, Democratic leaders hoped to keep the referendum in the bill as a "populist" proposal to embarrass President Reagan's administration in key farm states where House members planned to challenge Republican senators in the 1986 elections. The president vowed to veto the bill if it contained a referendum, and several Democratic members saw political advantage in that prospect.

But on Oct. 3, after intense lobbying against the referendum by agriculture organizations and the administration, the House voted in favor of a motion by Edward R. Madigan, Ill., ranking Republican on Agriculture, to strike the referendum. The vote was 251-174: R 169-10; D 82-164 (ND 53-112, SD 29-52).

The Senate-passed bill also contained a referendum measure after Republican leaders included it to buy Democratic votes for their package of price- and income-support cuts. It was quickly dropped in conference, however. And the five-year farm bill shaped up as a compromise between the administration's hard-line stance against price supports and Democrats' equally fervent desire to maintain an income "safety net."

## 10. Textile Imports

Worried about the prospect of a record international trade deficit of nearly $150 billion in 1985, members of Congress shifted sharply in favor of a tougher stance in dealing with America's trading partners. The cutting edge of that surge of "protectionist" sentiment was legislation (HR 1562) to force substantial reductions in the quantities of clothing and other textiles imported from Taiwan, South Korea, Hong Kong and other Third World nations.

The textile bill had strong support from textile manufacturers and unions, who warned that their industry faced a bleak future if something was not done to stem the tide of low-cost imports. But an equally important factor in rounding up overwhelming initial support for the legislation — some 290 House members signed on as cosponsors — was the widespread irritation over President Reagan's "free-trade" policies. Reagan enraged many members by refusing to provide import relief for the shoe industry and other hard-pressed domestic producers.

Unfortunately for backers of the bill, however, Reagan shifted to a more activist trade stance before they could get their bill through Congress. Reagan's new policy, announced in late September, had two key elements — attacks on unfair trading practices of other countries and joint efforts with other leading industrialized countries to bring down the high value of the U.S. dollar.

Reagan's moves were enough to take some of the wind out of the textile bill's sails. The measure passed the House Oct. 10 by a comfortable margin, 262-159: R 75-97; D 187-62 (ND 118-49, SD 69-13). But it lacked the two-thirds majority needed to override an anticipated veto.

Congress later cleared a version of the bill that was considerably less restrictive than the original measure, but support remained inadequate to surmount Reagan's Dec. 17 veto. House sponsors decided to put off an override vote until August 1986, in hopes of pressuring the administration to pursue a tough line in international textile negotiations.

## 11. Latta Amendment on Reconciliation

When the House considered an omnibus deficit reduction package (HR 3500) Oct. 24, the rule for debate permitted only three amendments, one of which was a controversial proposal to strike all provisions authorizing new or increased spending. The amendment failed by a close vote, 209-219: R 166-15; D 43-204 (ND 15-151, SD 28-53).

Republicans made the amendment a referendum on who was serious about cutting $200 billion deficits. All but 15 Republicans voted for the amendment, agreeing with sponsor Delbert L. Latta of Ohio, senior Republican on the House Budget Committee, that a deficit reduction bill was no place to attach spending items, no matter how desirable.

Latta's main target was a package of housing program authorizations that had been added to the bill with bipartisan support in the House Banking, Finance and Urban Affairs Committee.

Another provision called for many states to receive $150 million in 1988 from a new block-grant program for coastal resources. Another authorized 5 percent pay raises in fiscal 1987 and 1988 for federal civilian employees — including members of Congress; some members said they supported the Latta amendment out of fear that otherwise they would be accused of sneaking in a pay raise, even though it required later approval through appropriations.

Latta estimated his amendment would save an additional $3.5 billion over three years beyond the $60.9 billion that the bill would cut. Technically, however, the authorizations would not have added to the deficit since the programs would have required appropriations.

The budget-cutting package, known as a reconciliation bill, combined proposals for spending cuts from most committees to achieve the deficit goals set in the annual budget resolution. The Banking Committee had included the text of a pending housing bill (HR 1) with its proposed spending cuts, after whittling costs elsewhere so it could meet its required savings target.

Committee members argued that without allowing the housing bill to piggyback on the important reconciliation bill, the Senate Banking, Housing and Urban Affairs Committee would never consider housing programs.

After defeating Latta's amendment, the House went on to approve HR 3500 by a 228-199 vote. A second, revenue-raising reconciliation bill (HR 3128) passed a week later, on Oct. 31. The two bills ultimately were combined and the Senate passed its version of HR 3128 Nov. 14, by a 93-6 vote.

In the last days of the 1985 session, a conference agreement on HR 3128 became snared in a House-Senate dispute over a Senate tax provision and Congress adjourned without clearing what would have been the second-largest deficit reduction package ever.

## 12. Gramm-Rudman-Hollings

House Democrats cheered themselves when, in a rare moment of unity, all but two voted Nov. 1 for an amended version of the Senate-passed Gramm-Rudman-Hollings plan to balance the federal budget by fiscal 1991 (H J Res 372 — PL 99-177). The vote to substitute the Democratic alternative was 249-180: R 1-178; D 248-2 (ND 167-2, SD 81-0).

The party-line vote and the cheering did not denote any great fondness among House Democrats for the budget plan itself. Nor did the Republican vote signify that members of that party opposed the concept of the legislation. House leaders of both parties had made the vote a matter of partisan loyalty. The procedural vote clearing the way for floor consideration of the Senate measure — which passed 288-134 with 131 Democrats voting against — was a better gauge of outright support or opposition.

But House Democratic leaders had faced a stampede by their own members toward the Senate's budget measure. Conservative Democrats were philosophically in tune with the legislation, and there was very strong pressure from members representing marginal House districts. This group believed that, given the concern in the nation about federal deficits, they could not vote against the very conspicuous budget plan and survive the 1986 elections. *(Senate key vote 12)*

The Democratic leadership rallied its troops at the last moment, arguing among other things that the Senate version was deeply flawed and should not become law without some improvements reflecting Democratic priorities. The House alternative called for forced deficit reductions immediately, in fiscal 1986, so as to expose sponsors to any political fallout from spending cuts. It also exempted several anti-poverty programs from automatic spending cuts mandated by the legislation.

## 13. Plant Closings

By a five-vote margin Nov. 21, the House rejected a compromise version of a bill (HR 1616) designed to cushion the effect of plant closings and mass layoffs. Organized labor, which had tried for 11 years to get plant-closing legislation to the House floor, suffered a disappointing defeat in the close vote of 203-208: R 20-154; D 183-54 (ND 153-5, SD 30-49).

The bill would have required employers to give employees advance notice of intent to close plants or lay off large numbers of workers. A strong business lobby led by the U.S. Chamber of Commerce and deep philosophical differences among members about this labor-management issue led to the bill's defeat.

The final version of HR 1616 was substantially weaker than the original version. Gone from the bill was a requirement that employers consult with employees before closing plants and the right of employees to get court orders halting shutdowns. But some members said even the notice provision could be burdensome for financially troubled companies trying to find lenders to stay in business.

## 14. 'Superfund' Petrochemical Tax

A vote that set business against business and House against Senate came Dec. 10 when the House chose a method of paying for the "superfund" hazardous waste cleanup program. The House voted to increase the existing tax on petroleum and chemical raw materials instead of imposing a new excise tax on a broader base of general manufacturers and producers of raw goods.

A bitterly divided Ways and Means Committee had sent to the floor a tax package that relied largely on the broad-based tax to finance superfund (HR 2817, later renumbered as HR 2005), similar to a Senate-passed tax. Opponents called it a "value-added tax" — a tax on the increase in value of a product at each stage of production.

The vote came on a proposal by Thomas J. Downey, D-N.Y., to increase the tax on oil and chemicals. The vote was structured so that if Downey's amendment were defeated, the broad-based tax automatically would have been adopted. The vote for the Downey amendment was 220-206: R 73-105; D 147-101 (ND 127-42, SD 20-59).

Oil and chemical companies lobbied hard for the broader tax and against Downey's amendment, claiming that it would harm their ability to compete with overseas producers and cost American jobs. On the other side were Republican fiscal conservatives who feared that once a value-added tax got started, Congress would turn to it again and again as a way of raising revenue. Administration officials warned of a veto of any new tax.

Senate backers of the broad-based tax attached their superfund taxing package to the fiscal 1986 budget reconciliation bill (HR 3128). Conferees on HR 3128 agreed to accept the proposal, but the House refused to pass HR 3128 with the tax and the bill failed to clear.

## 15, 16. Tax Overhaul

In what could have been a devastating blow to President Reagan and his tax-overhaul initiative, almost every House Republican joined a minority of Democrats Dec. 11 to defeat a rule allowing a Ways and Means Committee tax bill (HR 3838) to come to the floor. The rule was rejected 202-223: R 14-164; D 188-59 (ND 135-33, SD 53-26).

The size of the Republican defection on the president's top domestic priority came as a shock to just about everyone, including Republicans. Reagan had said he was not completely happy with the Ways and Means rewrite of the tax code, but had urged members to support it to keep the "process" moving so that improvements could be made in the Senate.

But White House lobbyists had failed to detect widespread unhappiness about the tax bill among the GOP ranks. Republicans complained that they had been virtually ignored by the administration during markup of the bill in the Democrat-controlled Ways and Means Committee. They also felt slighted because Reagan appeared to ignore their earlier warnings that few GOP members were excited about overhauling the tax code.

In addition, many Republicans were unhappy with what they saw as HR 3838's anti-business cast. And they had little confidence that their Republican colleagues in the Senate would be able to reshape the bill to their liking.

The startling vote finally got House Republicans the attention they sought. With Democrats refusing to bring the bill back to the floor without at least 50 Republican votes confirmed, the administration got to work. Reagan finally won his way after he made an unusual visit to Capitol Hill to assure wavering Republicans he would veto any bill that did not include several significant changes to HR 3838.

By a vote of 258-168: R 70-110; D 188-58 (ND 138-28, SD 50-30), the House Dec. 17 approved a slightly modified rule. Later that day, it passed HR 3838 by voice vote and sent the bill to the Senate.

# Appendix

| | 1 | 2 | 3 | 4 | 5 | 6 | 7 |
|---|---|---|---|---|---|---|---|
| **ALABAMA** | | | | | | | |
| *Denton* | Y | Y | Y | N | Y | Y | Y |
| Heflin | Y | Y | N | N | Y | Y | Y |
| **ALASKA** | | | | | | | |
| *Murkowski* | Y | Y | Y | N | Y | Y | Y |
| *Stevens* | Y | Y | Y | N | Y | Y | Y |
| **ARIZONA** | | | | | | | |
| *Goldwater* | ? | Y | Y | N | ? | Y | Y |
| DeConcini | Y | Y | N | Y | Y | Y | Y |
| **ARKANSAS** | | | | | | | |
| Bumpers | Y | N | N | Y | N | ? | Y |
| Pryor | Y | N | N | Y | N | Y | Y |
| **CALIFORNIA** | | | | | | | |
| *Wilson* | N | Y | Y | N | Y | Y | Y |
| Cranston | Y | N | N | Y | N | ? | N |
| **COLORADO** | | | | | | | |
| *Armstrong* | N | Y | Y | N | Y | ? | ? |
| Hart | Y | N | N | Y | N | N | N |
| **CONNECTICUT** | | | | | | | |
| *Weicker* | Y | N | Y | Y | N | N | Y |
| Dodd | Y | N | N | Y | N | Y | N |
| **DELAWARE** | | | | | | | |
| *Roth* | N | Y | Y | N | Y | Y | Y |
| Biden | Y | N | N | # | N | N | Y |
| **FLORIDA** | | | | | | | |
| *Hawkins* | Y | Y | N | N | Y | Y | Y |
| Chiles | Y | N | N | Y | Y | Y | Y |
| **GEORGIA** | | | | | | | |
| *Mattingly* | N | Y | Y | N | Y | Y | Y |
| Nunn | Y | Y | N | N | Y | Y | Y |
| **HAWAII** | | | | | | | |
| Inouye | Y | N | N | Y | N | N | N |
| Matsunaga | Y | N | N | Y | N | N | N |
| **IDAHO** | | | | | | | |
| *McClure* | N | Y | Y | N | Y | Y | Y |
| *Symms* | N | Y | Y | N | Y | Y | Y |
| **ILLINOIS** | | | | | | | |
| Dixon | Y | N | N | N | Y | Y | Y |
| Simon | Y | N | N | Y | N | ? | ? |
| **INDIANA** | | | | | | | |
| *Lugar* | N | Y | Y | N | Y | Y | Y |
| *Quayle* | N | Y | Y | N | Y | Y | Y |
| **IOWA** | | | | | | | |
| *Grassley* | Y | N | Y | Y | Y | Y | Y |
| Harkin | Y | N | N | Y | N | Y | Y |
| **KANSAS** | | | | | | | |
| *Dole* | N | Y | Y | N | Y | Y | Y |
| *Kassebaum* | N | N | Y | Y | Y | Y | Y |
| **KENTUCKY** | | | | | | | |
| *McConnell* | N | Y | Y | N | Y | ? | Y |
| Ford | Y | N | N | Y | Y | Y | Y |
| **LOUISIANA** | | | | | | | |
| Johnston | Y | N | N | Y | Y | Y | Y |
| Long | Y | Y | N | N | Y | N | ? |
| **MAINE** | | | | | | | |
| *Cohen* | N | Y | Y | N | N | ? | Y |
| Mitchell | Y | N | N | Y | N | Y | Y |
| **MARYLAND** | | | | | | | |
| *Mathias* | Y | Y | N | Y | N | N | N |
| Sarbanes | Y | N | N | Y | N | N | N |
| **MASSACHUSETTS** | | | | | | | |
| Kennedy | Y | N | N | Y | N | ? | N |
| Kerry | Y | N | N | Y | N | N | N |
| **MICHIGAN** | | | | | | | |
| Levin | Y | N | N | Y | N | Y | N |
| Riegle | Y | N | N | Y | N | Y | Y |
| **MINNESOTA** | | | | | | | |
| *Boschwitz* | N | Y | Y | N | Y | Y | Y |
| *Durenberger* | Y | N | N | Y | Y | Y | Y |
| **MISSISSIPPI** | | | | | | | |
| *Cochran* | N | Y | Y | N | Y | Y | Y |
| Stennis | Y | Y | N | ? | Y | Y | ? |
| **MISSOURI** | | | | | | | |
| *Danforth* | Y | Y | Y | N | Y | Y | Y |
| Eagleton | Y | N | N | Y | N | Y | Y |
| **MONTANA** | | | | | | | |
| Baucus | Y | N | N | Y | N | Y | Y |
| Melcher | Y | N | N | Y | N | ? | Y |
| **NEBRASKA** | | | | | | | |
| Exon | Y | N | + | N | Y | Y | Y |
| Zorinsky | Y | Y | Y | N | N | Y | Y |
| **NEVADA** | | | | | | | |
| *Hecht* | N | Y | Y | N | Y | Y | Y |
| *Laxalt* | N | Y | Y | N | Y | ? | Y |
| **NEW HAMPSHIRE** | | | | | | | |
| *Humphrey* | N | Y | Y | N | Y | Y | Y |
| *Rudman* | N | Y | Y | N | ? | Y | Y |
| **NEW JERSEY** | | | | | | | |
| Bradley | Y | N | N | N | N | ? | ? |
| Lautenberg | Y | N | N | Y | N | Y | N |
| **NEW MEXICO** | | | | | | | |
| *Domenici* | N | Y | Y | N | Y | Y | Y |
| Bingaman | Y | N | N | N | N | Y | Y |
| **NEW YORK** | | | | | | | |
| *D'Amato* | Y | Y | N | N | Y | Y | Y |
| Moynihan | Y | N | N | Y | N | N | N |
| **NORTH CAROLINA** | | | | | | | |
| *East* | N | Y | + | ? | Y | Y | Y |
| *Helms* | N | Y | Y | N | Y | Y | Y |
| **NORTH DAKOTA** | | | | | | | |
| *Andrews* | Y | N | N | Y | N | Y | Y |
| Burdick | Y | N | N | Y | N | Y | Y |
| **OHIO** | | | | | | | |
| Glenn | Y | N | N | N | N | Y | Y |
| Metzenbaum | Y | N | N | Y | N | Y | N |
| **OKLAHOMA** | | | | | | | |
| *Nickles* | N | Y | Y | N | Y | Y | Y |
| Boren | Y | Y | N | X | Y | Y | Y |
| **OREGON** | | | | | | | |
| *Hatfield* | Y | N | Y | Y | N | N | + |
| *Packwood* | N | Y | Y | N | Y | Y | Y |
| **PENNSYLVANIA** | | | | | | | |
| *Heinz* | N | Y | Y | N | Y | Y | Y |
| *Specter* | Y | Y | N | ? | N | Y | Y |
| **RHODE ISLAND** | | | | | | | |
| *Chafee* | N | Y | Y | Y | N | N | N |
| Pell | Y | N | N | Y | N | N | N |
| **SOUTH CAROLINA** | | | | | | | |
| *Thurmond* | N | Y | Y | N | Y | Y | Y |
| Hollings | Y | N | N | Y | N | Y | Y |
| **SOUTH DAKOTA** | | | | | | | |
| *Abdnor* | Y | Y | Y | N | Y | Y | Y |
| *Pressler* | Y | N | Y | N | Y | Y | Y |
| **TENNESSEE** | | | | | | | |
| Gore | Y | Y | N | Y | N | Y | Y |
| Sasser | Y | N | N | Y | N | Y | Y |
| **TEXAS** | | | | | | | |
| *Gramm* | N | Y | Y | N | Y | Y | Y |
| Bentsen | Y | Y | N | N | Y | Y | Y |
| **UTAH** | | | | | | | |
| *Garn* | - | Y | Y | N | Y | Y | Y |
| *Hatch* | N | Y | Y | N | Y | Y | Y |
| **VERMONT** | | | | | | | |
| *Stafford* | N | N | Y | N | N | Y | Y |
| Leahy | Y | N | N | Y | N | ? | Y |
| **VIRGINIA** | | | | | | | |
| *Trible* | N | Y | Y | N | Y | Y | Y |
| *Warner* | N | Y | Y | N | Y | Y | Y |
| **WASHINGTON** | | | | | | | |
| *Evans* | N | Y | Y | N | N | Y | Y |
| *Gorton* | N | Y | Y | N | N | + | Y |
| **WEST VIRGINIA** | | | | | | | |
| Byrd | Y | Y | N | N | Y | Y | Y |
| Rockefeller | Y | N | N | Y | + | ? | Y |
| **WISCONSIN** | | | | | | | |
| *Kasten* | Y | Y | Y | N | Y | ? | Y |
| Proxmire | N | N | N | Y | N | Y | Y |
| **WYOMING** | | | | | | | |
| *Simpson* | N | Y | Y | N | Y | Y | Y |
| *Wallop* | ? | Y | Y | N | + | + | Y |

ND - Northern Democrats     SD - Southern Democrats (Southern states - Ala., Ark., Fla., Ga., Ky., La., Miss., N.C., Okla., S.C., Tenn., Texas, Va.)

**1. HR 1096. African Relief/Farm Credit.** Passage of the bill to authorize $175 million in non-food aid for emergency relief to Africa, to authorize $100 million to offset interest on restructured private farm loans guaranteed by the Farmers Home Administration (FmHA), to increase the FmHA loan guarantee program by $1.85 billion and revise certain eligibility rules and to authorize advances to eligible farmers of Commodity Credit Corporation commodity price-support loans. Passed 62-35: R 16-34; D 46-1 (ND 32-1, SD 14-0), Feb. 27, 1985. A "nay" was a vote supporting the president's position.

**2. S J Res 71. MX Missile Authorization.** Passage of the joint resolution to reaffirm the authorization of $1.5 billion in the fiscal 1985 defense budget to purchase 21 MX missiles. Passed 55-45: R 45-8; D 10-37 (ND 3-30, SD 7-7), March 19, 1985. A "yea" was a vote supporting the president's position.

**3. S Con Res 32. First Budget Resolution, Fiscal 1986.** Dole, R-Kan., perfecting amendment to the Dole-Domenici, R-N.M., amendment to the instructions of the Dole motion to recommit the concurrent resolution to the Budget Committee, to set budget targets for the fiscal year ending Sept. 30, 1986, as follows: budget authority, $1,069.5 billion; outlays, $965 billion; revenues, $793.6 billion; deficit, $171.4 billion. The amendment also established dual, annual caps on defense appropriations and on non-defense, discretionary (non-entitlement) appropriations as follows: fiscal 1986, defense, $303.2 billion, non-defense $140.8 billion; 1987, defense, $324.1 billion, non-defense $143.8 billion; 1988, defense, $347.6 billion, non-defense, $149.3 billion. It revised budget levels for fiscal 1985, and included reconciliation instructions requiring the Budget committees to recommend legislative savings to meet the budget targets by June 30, 1985. Adopted 50-49: R 48-4; D 1-45 (ND 1-31, SD 0-14), with Vice President George Bush casting a "yea" vote to break the 49-49 tie, in the session that began May 9, 1985. (The effect of this Dole amendment was to substitute, for the Senate GOP-White House budget package approved April 30, a revised version of that package providing, among other things, for $17.7 billion less in defense spending in fiscal 1986-88, and $15.7 billion more in domestic program spending for those three fiscal years.) (S Con Res 32, as amended by the Dole plan, subsequently was adopted by voice vote.)

**4. S 1160. Department of Defense Authorization, Fiscal 1986.** Proxmire, D-Wis., amendment to reduce from $2.96 billion to $1.9 billion the authorization for research on anti-missile defenses. Rejected 38-57: R 6-45; D 32-12 (ND 25-7, SD 7-5), June 4, 1985.

**5. S 1003. State Department Authorizations, Fiscal 1986-87.** Nunn, D-Ga., amendment to authorize $24 million for fiscal year 1986 for humanitarian assistance to the Nicaraguan rebels and to direct the National Security Council to monitor the use of the funds. The amendment also releases the $14 million approved for fiscal 1985 for the rebels but restricts the use of those funds to humanitarian assistance, and it urges the president to lift the economic sanctions on Nicaragua if that country agrees to a cease-fire and talks with the rebels, to call upon the rebels to remove from their ranks any individuals who have engaged in human rights abuses, and to resume bilateral negotiations with the government of Nicaragua. Adopted 55-42: R 41-10; D 14-32 (ND 4-28, SD 10-4), June 6, 1985. A "yea" was a vote supporting the president's position.

**6. S 1003. State Department Authorizations, Fiscal 1986-87.** Kassebaum, R-Kan., amendment to limit U.S. contributions to the United Nations and related organizations to 20 percent of those organizations' annual budgets, unless the secretary of state certified to Congress that such organizations had adopted procedures for proportionate voting on budgetary matters and had adopted plans to reduce employee salaries and pensions to levels comparable to those of the U.S. Civil Service. Adopted 71-13: R 41-4; D 30-9 (ND 18-8, SD 12-1), June 7, 1985.

**7. S 49. Firearm Owners' Protection.** Passage of the bill to revise the Gun Control Act of 1968 to exempt many gun collectors from licensing requirements, remove the ban on interstate sales of rifles, shotguns and handguns, require advance notice for routine compliance inspections, and impose a mandatory five-year sentence on anyone convicted of using a firearm in a violent federal crime. Passed 79-15: R 49-2; D 30-13 (ND 18-13, SD 12-0), July 9, 1985. A "yea" was a vote supporting the president's position.

## KEY

- **Y** Voted for (yea).
- **#** Paired for.
- **+** Announced for.
- **N** Voted against (nay).
- **X** Paired against.
- **-** Announced against.
- **P** Voted "present."
- **C** Voted "present" to avoid possible conflict of interest.
- **?** Did not vote or otherwise make a position known.

*Democrats*  *Republicans*

| | 8 | 9 | 10 | 11 | 12 | 13 | 14 |
|---|---|---|---|---|---|---|---|
| **ALABAMA** | | | | | | | |
| *Denton* | Y | N | Y | Y | Y | Y | Y |
| Heflin | Y | N | Y | Y | Y | Y | N |
| **ALASKA** | | | | | | | |
| *Murkowski* | Y | N | Y | Y | Y | N | Y |
| *Stevens* | Y | Y | Y | Y | Y | N | Y |
| **ARIZONA** | | | | | | | |
| *Goldwater* | Y | Y | Y | Y | Y | N | Y |
| DeConcini | # | Y | Y | N | Y | Y | Y |
| **ARKANSAS** | | | | | | | |
| Bumpers | N | Y | Y | N | Y | Y | Y |
| Pryor | N | Y | Y | N | Y | Y | Y |
| **CALIFORNIA** | | | | | | | |
| *Wilson* | Y | Y | Y | Y | Y | N | Y |
| Cranston | N | Y | N | N | N | N | Y |
| **COLORADO** | | | | | | | |
| *Armstrong* | Y | N | Y | Y | Y | N | Y |
| Hart | N | Y | N | N | N | N | N |
| **CONNECTICUT** | | | | | | | |
| *Weicker* | N | Y | N | Y | N | Y | Y |
| Dodd | N | Y | N | N | Y | Y | N |
| **DELAWARE** | | | | | | | |
| *Roth* | Y | N | N | Y | Y | Y | Y |
| Biden | Y | Y | N | N | Y | Y | N |
| **FLORIDA** | | | | | | | |
| *Hawkins* | Y | N | Y | Y | Y | Y | Y |
| Chiles | N | Y | N | N | N | ? | Y |
| **GEORGIA** | | | | | | | |
| *Mattingly* | Y | N | Y | Y | Y | Y | Y |
| Nunn | Y | Y | Y | Y | Y | Y | Y |
| **HAWAII** | | | | | | | |
| Inouye | N | Y | ? | N | N | N | ? |
| Matsunaga | N | Y | N | N | N | N | Y |
| **IDAHO** | | | | | | | |
| *McClure* | Y | N | Y | Y | Y | Y | Y |
| *Symms* | Y | N | Y | Y | Y | N | Y |
| **ILLINOIS** | | | | | | | |
| Dixon | Y | Y | N | N | Y | Y | N |
| Simon | N | Y | N | N | Y | Y | N |
| **INDIANA** | | | | | | | |
| *Lugar* | Y | Y | Y | Y | Y | N | Y |
| *Quayle* | Y | N | Y | Y | Y | N | Y |
| **IOWA** | | | | | | | |
| *Grassley* | Y | N | N | Y | Y | N | N |
| Harkin | N | Y | N | N | N | N | N |
| **KANSAS** | | | | | | | |
| *Dole* | Y | N | Y | Y | Y | Y | Y |
| *Kassebaum* | Y | Y | Y | Y | N | N | Y |
| **KENTUCKY** | | | | | | | |
| *McConnell* | Y | N | Y | Y | Y | Y | Y |
| Ford | N | N | N | N | Y | Y | N |
| **LOUISIANA** | | | | | | | |
| Johnston | N | N | N | Y | N | Y | Y |
| Long | X | N | N | Y | Y | Y | Y |
| **MAINE** | | | | | | | |
| *Cohen* | Y | Y | N | N | Y | Y | Y |
| Mitchell | N | Y | Y | N | N | Y | N |
| **MARYLAND** | | | | | | | |
| *Mathias* | N | Y | N | N | ? | Y | Y |
| Sarbanes | N | Y | N | N | N | N | Y |
| **MASSACHUSETTS** | | | | | | | |
| Kennedy | Y | Y | N | Y | N | Y | N |
| Kerry | N | Y | N | N | Y | Y | N |
| **MICHIGAN** | | | | | | | |
| Levin | N | Y | N | N | Y | Y | N |
| Riegle | N | Y | Y | N | N | Y | N |
| **MINNESOTA** | | | | | | | |
| *Boschwitz* | Y | Y | Y | Y | Y | N | Y |
| *Durenberger* | N | Y | N | N | N | N | N |
| **MISSISSIPPI** | | | | | | | |
| *Cochran* | Y | N | Y | Y | Y | Y | Y |
| Stennis | N | N | ? | ? | Y | Y | N |
| **MISSOURI** | | | | | | | |
| *Danforth* | Y | Y | N | Y | Y | N | Y |
| Eagleton | N | Y | N | N | N | Y | N |
| **MONTANA** | | | | | | | |
| Baucus | N | Y | Y | - | Y | N | N |
| Melcher | N | Y | N | N | Y | Y | N |
| **NEBRASKA** | | | | | | | |
| Exon | Y | N | Y | N | N | N | N |
| Zorinsky | Y | Y | X | Y | Y | N | N |
| **NEVADA** | | | | | | | |
| *Hecht* | Y | N | Y | Y | Y | N | Y |
| *Laxalt* | Y | N | Y | Y | Y | Y | Y |
| **NEW HAMPSHIRE** | | | | | | | |
| *Humphrey* | Y | N | Y | N | Y | N | Y |
| *Rudman* | Y | Y | Y | Y | Y | Y | Y |
| **NEW JERSEY** | | | | | | | |
| Bradley | N | Y | N | N | N | N | N |
| Lautenberg | N | Y | N | N | N | N | N |
| **NEW MEXICO** | | | | | | | |
| *Domenici* | Y | Y | Y | Y | Y | Y | Y |
| Bingaman | N | Y | N | Y | N | Y | N |
| **NEW YORK** | | | | | | | |
| *D'Amato* | Y | Y | Y | N | Y | Y | Y |
| Moynihan | N | Y | N | ? | N | Y | N |
| **NORTH CAROLINA** | | | | | | | |
| *East* | Y | ? | # | ? | Y | Y | ? |
| *Helms* | Y | N | Y | Y | Y | Y | Y |
| **NORTH DAKOTA** | | | | | | | |
| *Andrews* | N | Y | N | ? | Y | N | Y |
| Burdick | N | + | N | N | Y | N | N |
| **OHIO** | | | | | | | |
| Glenn | N | Y | N | N | Y | N | Y |
| Metzenbaum | N | Y | N | N | N | N | N |
| **OKLAHOMA** | | | | | | | |
| *Nickles* | Y | N | Y | Y | Y | N | N |
| Boren | Y | Y | Y | ? | Y | N | N |
| **OREGON** | | | | | | | |
| *Hatfield* | N | Y | + | Y | N | N | N |
| *Packwood* | N | Y | N | N | Y | N | Y |
| **PENNSYLVANIA** | | | | | | | |
| *Heinz* | Y | Y | N | N | Y | Y | Y |
| *Specter* | Y | Y | Y | Y | Y | Y | Y |
| **RHODE ISLAND** | | | | | | | |
| *Chafee* | Y | Y | N | N | Y | Y | Y |
| Pell | Y | Y | N | N | N | Y | N |
| **SOUTH CAROLINA** | | | | | | | |
| *Thurmond* | Y | N | Y | Y | Y | Y | Y |
| Hollings | Y | Y | Y | Y | Y | Y | N |
| **SOUTH DAKOTA** | | | | | | | |
| *Abdnor* | Y | N | Y | Y | Y | N | N |
| *Pressler* | Y | N | N | Y | Y | N | N |
| **TENNESSEE** | | | | | | | |
| Gore | N | Y | Y | N | Y | Y | N |
| Sasser | N | N | Y | N | Y | Y | N |
| **TEXAS** | | | | | | | |
| *Gramm* | Y | N | Y | Y | Y | N | Y |
| Bentsen | N | N | Y | Y | Y | Y | Y |
| **UTAH** | | | | | | | |
| *Garn* | Y | N | Y | Y | Y | Y | Y |
| *Hatch* | Y | Y | Y | N | Y | Y | Y |
| **VERMONT** | | | | | | | |
| *Stafford* | N | Y | N | N | N | N | ? |
| Leahy | Y | Y | Y | N | Y | Y | N |
| **VIRGINIA** | | | | | | | |
| *Trible* | Y | N | Y | Y | Y | Y | Y |
| *Warner* | Y | N | Y | Y | Y | Y | Y |
| **WASHINGTON** | | | | | | | |
| *Evans* | Y | Y | Y | N | Y | Y | Y |
| *Gorton* | Y | Y | Y | Y | Y | N | Y |
| **WEST VIRGINIA** | | | | | | | |
| Byrd | N | Y | N | N | N | Y | N |
| Rockefeller | N | Y | N | N | Y | Y | N |
| **WISCONSIN** | | | | | | | |
| *Kasten* | Y | N | N | Y | Y | N | Y |
| Proxmire | Y | Y | N | Y | N | Y | Y |
| **WYOMING** | | | | | | | |
| *Simpson* | Y | N | N | Y | Y | N | Y |
| *Wallop* | Y | N | Y | Y | Y | N | Y |

ND - Northern Democrats     SD - Southern Democrats (Southern states - Ala., Ark., Fla., Ga., Ky., La., Miss., N.C., Okla., S.C., Tenn., Texas, Va.)

**8. S 43. Line-Item Veto.** Dole, R-Kan., motion to invoke cloture (thus limiting debate) on the Dole motion to proceed to consideration of the bill to give the president power to veto individual spending items by requiring that appropriations bills be split by paragraph or section into separate bills before being sent to the White House. Motion rejected 58-40: R 46-7; D 12-33 (ND 8-24, SD 4-9), July 24, 1985. A three-fifths majority vote (60) of the total Senate is required to invoke cloture. A "yea" was a vote supporting the president's position.

**9. S 47. School Prayer.** Weicker, R-Conn., motion to table (kill) the bill to bar the federal courts, including the Supreme Court, from considering cases involving prayer in public schools. Motion agreed to 62-36: R 24-28; D 38-8 (ND 31-1, 7-7), Sept. 10, 1985. (The effect of the bill would have been to restore the right of states or local communities to permit prayer in public schools without being subject to challenges in the federal courts.)

**10. S 1200. Immigration Reform and Control Act.** Wilson, R-Calif., amendment to create a "seasonal worker" program to allow foreign workers into the country for up to nine months each year for agricultural work, with a cap allowing no more than 350,000 of these workers in the United States at any one time. Adopted 51-44: R 36-15; D 15-29 (ND 6-25, SD 9-4), Sept. 17, 1985.

**11. S 51. Superfund Reauthorization, Fiscal 1986-90.** Roth, R-Del., amendment to strike from the bill a section establishing a new demonstration program to pay for medical expenses of victims of hazardous-substance releases, and to authorize appropriations of $30 million annually during fiscal 1986-90 for that purpose. Adopted 49-45: R 40-11; D 9-34 (ND 3-28, SD 6-6), Sept. 24, 1985. A "yea" was a vote supporting the president's position.

**12. H J Res 372. Public Debt Limit.** Dole, R-Kan. (for Gramm, R-Texas, Rudman, R-N.H., Hollings, D-S.C.), amendment to set maximum allowable federal deficits for fiscal years 1986-91, declining annually to zero in 1991, and to require the president, if projected deficits exceed those allowed, to issue an emergency order reducing all federal spending except for Social Security, interest on the federal debt and existing contractual obligations, by enough to reduce deficits to the maximum established by the bill. The amendment also revises congressional budgeting procedures and removes Social Security from the unified federal budget in fiscal 1986 and thereafter. Adopted 75-24: R 48-4; D 27-20 (ND 15-18, SD 12-2), Oct. 9, 1985. A "yea" was a vote supporting the president's position.

**13. HR 1562. Textile Import Quotas.** Passage of the bill to establish a worldwide system of quotas for imports of textiles and apparel, limit shoe imports to 60 percent of the domestic shoe market and require negotiations leading to an international agreement limiting copper production. Passed 60-39: R 25-28; D 35-11 (ND 23-10, SD 12-1), Nov. 13, 1985. A "nay" was a vote supporting the president's position.

**14. S 1714. Farm Programs Reauthorization, Fiscal 1986-89.** Dole, R-Kan., perfecting amendment to the Dole amendment to the Dole motion to recommit the bill to the Agriculture, Nutrition and Forestry Committee with instructions, to freeze current target prices for wheat, feed grains, cotton and rice titles for the life of the bill; to freeze target prices for corn, cotton and rice in fiscal 1986 and allow maximum 5 percent annual reductions thereafter; to provide a sliding scale of target prices for wheat based on levels of production; to authorize the agriculture secretary to increase the maximum acreage limitation for wheat, feed grains, cotton and rice by 5 percent; to reduce the conservation reserve in 1986 and require some of the reserve to be devoted to trees; to change provisions dealing with loans for rice; to provide for payments to soybean and sunflower farmers; to expand disaster payments to farmers of soybeans, sugar cane and sugar beets; and to require the president to operate the sugar program at no cost to the government. Adopted 56-41: R 45-6; D 11-35 (ND 4-28, SD 7-7), Nov. 20, 1985.

**1. S J Res 71. MX Missile Authorization.** Passage of the joint resolution to approve authorization of $1.5 billion to procure 21 MX missiles in fiscal 1985. Passed 219-213: R 158-24; D 61-189 (ND 15-154, SD 46-35), March 26, 1985. A "yea" was a vote supporting the president's position.

**2. H Res 148. Indiana 8th District Seat.** Adoption of the resolution to declare a vacancy in the 99th Congress from the 8th District of Indiana. Rejected 200-229: R 181-0; D 19-229 (ND 6-161, SD 13-68), April 30, 1985.

**3. HR 1460. Anti-Apartheid Act.** Passage of the bill to impose sanctions immediately against South Africa, including a ban on bank loans to the South African government, and prohibitions against the sale of computer goods and nuclear power equipment and supplies to that country. Subject to review by the president and Congress, the bill also would bar new U.S. business investment in South Africa and prohibit the importation into the United States of South African gold coins, called Krugerrands. Passed 295-127: R 56-121; D 239-6 (ND 166-0, SD 73-6), June 5, 1985. A "nay" was a vote supporting the president's position.

**4. HR 2577. Supplemental Appropriations, Fiscal 1985.** Edgar, D-Pa., amendment to the Whitten, D-Miss., amendment, to reduce from $150 million to $51 million the funds added for water projects of the U.S. Army Corps of Engineers. Adopted 203-202: R 108-69; D 95-133 (ND 80-75, SD 15-58), June 6, 1985. (The Whitten amendment was subsequently adopted.

**5. HR 2577. Supplemental Appropriations, Fiscal 1985.** Boland, D-Mass., amendment to the McDade, R-Pa., amendment to continue indefinitely the prohibition of any funding by U.S. intelligence agencies that would support, directly or indirectly, military or paramilitary operations in Nicaragua. Rejected 196-232: R 7-174; D 189-58 (ND 156-11, SD 33-47), June 12, 1985. A "nay" was a vote supporting the president's position.

**6. HR 1872. Department of Defense Authorization, Fiscal 1986.** Skelton, D-Mo., amendment to the Porter, R-Ill., amendment, to authorize the appropriation of $124 million to produce binary chemical weapons subject to certain conditions. Adopted 229-196: R 143-34; D 86-162 (ND 30-138, SD 56-24), June 19, 1985. A "yea" was a vote supporting the president's position.

**7. HR 1872. Department of Defense Authorization, Fiscal 1986.** Dicks, D-Wash., amendment to the Price, D-Ill., amendment, to reduce from $2.5 billion to $2.1 billion the authorization for the strategic defense initiative. Rejected 195-221: R 12-167; D 183-54 (ND 147-11, SD 36-43), June 20, 1985. A "nay" was a vote supporting the president's position.

**8. HR 1555. Foreign Assistance Authorization, Fiscal 1986.** Stratton, D-N.Y., amendment to repeal the so-called Clark amendment to the International Security and Development Cooperation Act of 1980, prohibiting assistance for military or paramilitary operations in Angola. Adopted 236-185: R 176-6; D 60-179 (ND 14-150, SD 46-29), July 10, 1985. A "yea" was a vote supporting the president's position.

---

[1] *Because of a seating challenge, Rep. Frank McCloskey, D-Ind., was not sworn in until May 1, 1985.*

[2] *Rep. Cathy (Mrs. Gillis) Long, D-La., was sworn in on April 4, 1985, to succeed Gillis W. Long, D, who died Jan. 20, 1985.*

[3] *Rep. Sam B. Hall Jr., D-Texas, resigned May 27, 1985.*

## KEY

Y Voted for (yea).
# Paired for.
+ Announced for.
N Voted against (nay).
X Paired against.
- Announced against.
P Voted "present."
C Voted "present" to avoid possible conflict of interest.
? Did not vote or otherwise make a position known.

Democrats    *Republicans*

| | 1 | 2 | 3 | 4 | 5 | 6 | 7 | 8 |
|---|---|---|---|---|---|---|---|---|
| **ALABAMA** | | | | | | | | |
| 1 *Callahan* | Y | Y | N | N | N | Y | N | Y |
| 2 *Dickinson* | Y | Y | N | N | N | Y | N | Y |
| 3 Nichols | Y | N | Y | N | N | Y | N | Y |
| 4 Bevill | Y | N | Y | N | N | Y | N | Y |
| 5 Flippo | Y | N | Y | N | N | Y | N | ? |
| 6 Erdreich | Y | N | Y | N | N | N | N | Y |
| 7 Shelby | Y | N | Y | N | N | Y | N | Y |
| **ALASKA** | | | | | | | | |
| AL *Young* | Y | Y | Y | N | N | Y | N | Y |
| **ARIZONA** | | | | | | | | |
| 1 *McCain* | Y | Y | N | N | N | Y | N | Y |
| 2 Udall | N | ? | Y | N | Y | ? | Y | N |
| 3 *Stump* | Y | Y | N | N | N | Y | N | Y |
| 4 *Rudd* | Y | Y | N | N | N | Y | N | Y |
| 5 *Kolbe* | Y | Y | N | N | N | Y | N | Y |
| **ARKANSAS** | | | | | | | | |
| 1 Alexander | N | N | Y | N | Y | Y | N | N |
| 2 Robinson | Y | N | Y | N | N | Y | N | Y |
| 3 *Hammerschmidt* | Y | Y | N | N | N | Y | N | Y |
| 4 Anthony | N | N | Y | N | Y | Y | Y | N |
| **CALIFORNIA** | | | | | | | | |
| 1 Bosco | N | N | Y | Y | ? | Y | Y | N |
| 2 *Chappie* | Y | Y | N | N | N | Y | N | Y |
| 3 Matsui | N | N | Y | ? | Y | N | Y | N |
| 4 Fazio | Y | N | Y | N | Y | Y | Y | N |
| 5 Burton | N | N | Y | N | Y | N | Y | N |
| 6 Boxer | N | N | Y | ? | Y | N | Y | N |
| 7 Miller | N | N | ? | ? | Y | N | Y | N |
| 8 Dellums | N | N | Y | N | Y | N | Y | N |
| 9 Stark | N | N | Y | ? | Y | N | ? | ? |
| 10 Edwards | N | N | Y | Y | Y | N | Y | N |
| 11 Lantos | N | N | Y | Y | Y | N | Y | N |
| 12 *Zschau* | N | Y | N | Y | N | Y | N | Y |
| 13 Mineta | N | N | Y | N | Y | N | Y | N |
| 14 *Shumway* | Y | Y | N | N | N | Y | N | Y |
| 15 Coelho | N | N | Y | N | Y | N | Y | N |
| 16 Panetta | N | N | Y | N | Y | N | Y | N |
| 17 *Pashayan* | Y | Y | N | N | N | Y | N | Y |
| 18 Lehman | N | N | Y | ? | Y | N | Y | N |
| 19 *Lagomarsino* | Y | Y | N | N | N | Y | N | Y |
| 20 *Thomas* | Y | Y | - | Y | N | Y | N | Y |
| 21 *Fiedler* | Y | Y | N | ? | N | Y | N | Y |
| 22 *Moorhead* | Y | Y | N | N | N | Y | N | Y |
| 23 Beilenson | N | N | Y | Y | Y | N | Y | N |
| 24 Waxman | N | N | Y | Y | Y | N | Y | ? |
| 25 Roybal | N | N | Y | N | Y | N | Y | N |
| 26 Berman | N | N | Y | Y | Y | N | Y | N |
| 27 Levine | N | N | Y | Y | Y | N | Y | N |
| 28 Dixon | N | N | Y | N | Y | X | ? | N |
| 29 Hawkins | N | N | Y | N | ? | N | Y | N |
| 30 Martinez | N | N | Y | Y | Y | N | Y | N |
| 31 Dymally | N | N | Y | Y | Y | N | Y | N |
| 32 Anderson | Y | N | Y | Y | Y | N | Y | N |
| 33 *Dreier* | Y | Y | N | Y | N | Y | N | Y |
| 34 Torres | N | N | Y | Y | Y | N | Y | N |
| 35 *Lewis* | Y | Y | N | Y | N | Y | N | Y |
| 36 Brown | N | N | Y | N | Y | N | Y | N |
| 37 *McCandless* | Y | Y | N | Y | N | Y | N | Y |
| 38 *Dornan* | Y | Y | N | N | N | Y | N | Y |
| 39 *Dannemeyer* | Y | Y | N | N | N | Y | N | Y |
| 40 *Badham* | Y | Y | N | N | N | Y | N | Y |
| 41 *Lowery* | Y | Y | N | N | N | Y | N | Y |
| 42 *Lungren* | Y | Y | N | Y | N | Y | N | Y |

| | 1 | 2 | 3 | 4 | 5 | 6 | 7 | 8 |
|---|---|---|---|---|---|---|---|---|
| 43 *Packard* | Y | Y | N | Y | N | Y | N | Y |
| 44 Bates | N | N | Y | Y | Y | N | Y | N |
| 45 *Hunter* | Y | Y | N | N | N | Y | N | Y |
| **COLORADO** | | | | | | | | |
| 1 Schroeder | N | N | Y | + | Y | N | Y | N |
| 2 Wirth | N | N | Y | ? | Y | N | Y | N |
| 3 *Strang* | Y | Y | N | N | N | + | X | Y |
| 4 *Brown* | Y | Y | Y | N | N | Y | N | Y |
| 5 *Kramer* | Y | N | N | N | Y | N | N | Y |
| 6 *Schaefer* | Y | N | Y | N | ? | N | N | Y |
| **CONNECTICUT** | | | | | | | | |
| 1 Kennelly | N | N | Y | Y | Y | N | Y | N |
| 2 Gejdenson | N | N | Y | Y | Y | N | Y | N |
| 3 Morrison | N | N | Y | ? | Y | N | Y | N |
| 4 *McKinney* | N | Y | Y | N | Y | N | Y | N |
| 5 *Rowland* | Y | Y | N | Y | N | Y | N | Y |
| 6 *Johnson* | Y | Y | Y | N | Y | N | Y | N |
| **DELAWARE** | | | | | | | | |
| AL Carper | N | N | Y | Y | Y | N | Y | Y |
| **FLORIDA** | | | | | | | | |
| 1 Hutto | Y | Y | N | ? | N | Y | N | Y |
| 2 Fuqua | Y | N | Y | N | N | Y | N | Y |
| 3 Bennett | N | N | Y | N | Y | N | N | N |
| 4 Chappell | Y | N | N | N | Y | N | Y | N |
| 5 *McCollum* | Y | Y | N | Y | N | Y | N | Y |
| 6 MacKay | N | N | Y | Y | Y | N | Y | N |
| 7 Gibbons | N | N | Y | N | Y | Y | Y | N |
| 8 *Young* | Y | Y | N | N | N | Y | N | Y |
| 9 *Bilirakis* | Y | Y | N | ? | N | Y | N | Y |
| 10 *Ireland* | Y | Y | N | Y | N | Y | N | Y |
| 11 Nelson | Y | N | Y | N | Y | N | N | # |
| 12 *Lewis* | Y | Y | N | N | N | N | N | Y |
| 13 *Mack* | Y | Y | N | Y | N | Y | N | Y |
| 14 Mica | N | N | Y | N | Y | Y | Y | N |
| 15 *Shaw* | Y | Y | N | N | N | Y | N | Y |
| 16 Smith | N | N | Y | N | Y | N | # | N |
| 17 Lehman | N | N | Y | N | Y | N | Y | N |
| 18 Pepper | Y | N | Y | N | Y | # | # | Y |
| 19 Fascell | N | N | Y | N | N | N | N | Y |
| **GEORGIA** | | | | | | | | |
| 1 Thomas | Y | N | Y | N | N | Y | N | Y |
| 2 Hatcher | Y | N | Y | ? | N | Y | N | Y |
| 3 Ray | Y | Y | Y | Y | N | Y | N | Y |
| 4 *Swindall* | Y | Y | N | Y | N | Y | N | Y |
| 5 Fowler | N | N | Y | Y | N | Y | N | Y |
| 6 *Gingrich* | Y | Y | N | Y | N | Y | N | Y |
| 7 Darden | Y | N | N | N | N | Y | N | Y |
| 8 Rowland | Y | N | Y | N | N | Y | N | Y |
| 9 Jenkins | N | N | Y | N | N | Y | N | Y |
| 10 Barnard | Y | Y | N | N | N | Y | N | Y |
| **HAWAII** | | | | | | | | |
| 1 Heftel | N | N | Y | Y | N | Y | Y | ? |
| 2 Akaka | N | N | Y | N | Y | Y | Y | N |
| **IDAHO** | | | | | | | | |
| 1 *Craig* | Y | Y | N | N | N | Y | N | Y |
| 2 Stallings | N | Y | ? | ? | Y | N | Y | N |
| **ILLINOIS** | | | | | | | | |
| 1 Hayes | N | N | Y | N | Y | N | Y | N |
| 2 Savage | N | N | Y | Y | Y | N | ? | N |
| 3 Russo | N | N | Y | N | Y | N | Y | N |
| 4 *O'Brien* | Y | Y | N | N | N | ? | X | Y |
| 5 Lipinski | N | Y | N | N | Y | N | ? | N |
| 6 *Hyde* | Y | N | Y | N | Y | N | Y | Y |
| 7 Collins | N | N | Y | Y | Y | N | Y | N |
| 8 Rostenkowski | N | N | Y | N | Y | N | ? | N |
| 9 Yates | N | N | Y | Y | Y | N | Y | N |
| 10 *Porter* | Y | Y | Y | Y | Y | N | Y | N |
| 11 Annunzio | N | N | Y | N | Y | N | Y | N |
| 12 *Crane* | Y | Y | N | N | N | Y | N | Y |
| 13 *Fawell* | Y | Y | N | Y | N | Y | N | Y |
| 14 *Grotberg* | Y | N | Y | N | Y | N | Y | N |
| 15 *Madigan* | Y | Y | N | N | N | Y | N | Y |
| 16 *Martin* | Y | Y | Y | N | N | Y | N | Y |
| 17 Evans | N | N | Y | Y | Y | N | Y | N |
| 18 *Michel* | Y | Y | N | Y | N | Y | N | Y |
| 19 Bruce | N | N | Y | N | Y | N | Y | N |
| 20 Durbin | N | N | Y | N | Y | N | Y | N |
| 21 Price | Y | N | Y | Y | Y | N | Y | N |
| 22 Gray | N | N | Y | Y | Y | Y | N | X |
| **INDIANA** | | | | | | | | |
| 1 Visclosky | N | N | Y | N | Y | N | Y | N |
| 2 Sharp | N | N | Y | Y | Y | N | Y | N |
| 3 *Hiler* | Y | Y | Y | Y | N | Y | N | Y |
| 4 *Coats* | Y | Y | N | N | N | Y | N | Y |
| 5 *Hillis* | Y | Y | N | ? | N | Y | N | Y |

ND - Northern Democrats        SD - Southern Democrats

| | 9 | 10 | 11 | 12 | 13 | 14 |
|---|---|---|---|---|---|---|
| **ALABAMA** | | | | | | |
| Heflin | Y | N | Y | N | N | Y |
| Shelby | Y | N | Y | N | N | Y |
| **ALASKA** | | | | | | |
| *Murkowski* | Y | N | Y | Y | N | Y |
| *Stevens* | Y | N | Y | Y | Y | Y |
| **ARIZONA** | | | | | | |
| DeConcini | N | N | N | N | + | Y |
| *McCain* | Y | N | N | Y | N | Y |
| **ARKANSAS** | | | | | | |
| Bumpers | N | Y | N | N | Y | Y |
| Pryor | Y | Y | Y | N | Y | Y |
| **CALIFORNIA** | | | | | | |
| Cranston | N | Y | N | N | N | Y |
| *Wilson* | Y | ? | N | Y | + | Y |
| **COLORADO** | | | | | | |
| Wirth | N | Y | Y | N | N | Y |
| *Armstrong* | Y | N | N | Y | N | Y |
| **CONNECTICUT** | | | | | | |
| Dodd | N | Y | Y | N | N | Y |
| *Weicker* | N | Y | Y | N | N | Y |
| **DELAWARE** | | | | | | |
| Biden | ? | Y | N | N | Y | Y |
| *Roth* | Y | N | Y | Y | N | Y |
| **FLORIDA** | | | | | | |
| Chiles | Y | N | Y | N | N | Y |
| Graham | Y | Y | Y | N | Y | Y |
| **GEORGIA** | | | | | | |
| Fowler | N | Y | Y | N | Y | Y |
| Nunn | Y | Y | Y | N | N | Y |
| **HAWAII** | | | | | | |
| Inouye | N | Y | Y | N | Y | Y |
| Matsunaga | N | Y | Y | N | Y | Y |
| **IDAHO** | | | | | | |
| *McClure* | Y | N | N | Y | N | Y |
| *Symms* | Y | N | N | Y | N | Y |
| **ILLINOIS** | | | | | | |
| Dixon | Y | Y | Y | N | Y | Y |
| Simon | - | Y | ? | N | ? | Y |
| **INDIANA** | | | | | | |
| *Lugar* | Y | N | N | Y | ? | Y |
| *Quayle* | Y | N | N | Y | N | Y |

| | 9 | 10 | 11 | 12 | 13 | 14 |
|---|---|---|---|---|---|---|
| **IOWA** | | | | | | |
| Harkin | N | Y | Y | N | Y | Y |
| *Grassley* | Y | N | Y | Y | N | Y |
| **KANSAS** | | | | | | |
| *Dole* | Y | N | N | Y | Y | Y |
| *Kassebaum* | Y | N | N | Y | N | Y |
| **KENTUCKY** | | | | | | |
| Ford | Y | Y | Y | N | N | Y |
| *McConnell* | Y | N | N | Y | ? | Y |
| **LOUISIANA** | | | | | | |
| Breaux | Y | Y | Y | N | Y | Y |
| Johnston | Y | Y | Y | N | N | Y |
| **MAINE** | | | | | | |
| Mitchell | N | Y | Y | N | Y | Y |
| *Cohen* | Y | Y | Y | Y | Y | Y |
| **MARYLAND** | | | | | | |
| Mikulski | N | Y | Y | N | Y | Y |
| Sarbanes | N | Y | Y | N | Y | Y |
| **MASSACHUSETTS** | | | | | | |
| Kennedy | N | Y | N | N | Y | Y |
| Kerry | N | Y | N | N | + | Y |
| **MICHIGAN** | | | | | | |
| Levin | N | Y | Y | N | N | Y |
| Riegle | N | Y | Y | N | Y | Y |
| **MINNESOTA** | | | | | | |
| *Boschwitz* | Y | N | N | Y | N | Y |
| *Durenberger* | Y | Y | Y | N | Y | Y |
| **MISSISSIPPI** | | | | | | |
| Stennis | Y | Y | ? | N | N | Y |
| *Cochran* | Y | N | N | Y | N | Y |
| **MISSOURI** | | | | | | |
| *Bond* | Y | N | N | Y | N | Y |
| *Danforth* | N | N | N | Y | N | Y |
| **MONTANA** | | | | | | |
| Baucus | N | Y | Y | N | Y | Y |
| Melcher | N | Y | Y | N | N | Y |
| **NEBRASKA** | | | | | | |
| Exon | Y | Y | Y | N | N | Y |
| *Karnes* | Y | N | N | Y | N | Y |
| **NEVADA** | | | | | | |
| Reid | Y | Y | Y | N | Y | Y |
| *Hecht* | Y | N | N | Y | Y | Y |

| | 9 | 10 | 11 | 12 | 13 | 14 |
|---|---|---|---|---|---|---|
| **NEW HAMPSHIRE** | | | | | | |
| *Humphrey* | Y | N | N | Y | N | N |
| *Rudman* | Y | N | N | Y | N | Y |
| **NEW JERSEY** | | | | | | |
| Bradley | Y | Y | Y | N | Y | Y |
| Lautenberg | N | Y | Y | N | Y | Y |
| **NEW MEXICO** | | | | | | |
| Bingaman | Y | Y | Y | N | N | Y |
| *Domenici* | Y | N | N | Y | N | Y |
| **NEW YORK** | | | | | | |
| Moynihan | N | Y | Y | N | Y | Y |
| *D'Amato* | Y | N | N | Y | N | Y |
| **NORTH CAROLINA** | | | | | | |
| Sanford | N | Y | Y | N | Y | Y |
| *Helms* | Y | N | N | Y | N | Y |
| **NORTH DAKOTA** | | | | | | |
| Burdick | N | Y | Y | N | Y | Y |
| Conrad | N | Y | Y | N | N | Y |
| **OHIO** | | | | | | |
| Glenn | Y | Y | Y | N | Y | Y |
| Metzenbaum | N | Y | Y | N | Y | Y |
| **OKLAHOMA** | | | | | | |
| Boren | Y | Y | N | Y | N | Y |
| *Nickles* | Y | N | N | Y | Y | Y |
| **OREGON** | | | | | | |
| *Hatfield* | N | Y | Y | N | Y | Y |
| *Packwood* | Y | N | Y | N | Y | Y |
| **PENNSYLVANIA** | | | | | | |
| *Heinz* | Y | Y | Y | N | Y | Y |
| *Specter* | N | Y | Y | N | Y | Y |
| **RHODE ISLAND** | | | | | | |
| Pell | N | Y | Y | N | N | Y |
| *Chafee* | N | Y | N | N | N | Y |
| **SOUTH CAROLINA** | | | | | | |
| Hollings | Y | N | Y | Y | N | Y |
| *Thurmond* | Y | N | N | Y | N | Y |
| **SOUTH DAKOTA** | | | | | | |
| Daschle | N | Y | N | N | N | Y |
| *Pressler* | Y | N | N | Y | N | Y |
| **TENNESSEE** | | | | | | |
| Gore | - | Y | Y | N | ? | Y |
| Sasser | Y | Y | Y | N | Y | Y |

| | 9 | 10 | 11 | 12 | 13 | 14 |
|---|---|---|---|---|---|---|
| **TEXAS** | | | | | | |
| Bentsen | Y | Y | Y | N | Y | Y |
| *Gramm* | Y | N | N | Y | Y | Y |
| **UTAH** | | | | | | |
| *Garn* | Y | ? | N | Y | N | Y |
| *Hatch* | Y | N | N | Y | N | Y |
| **VERMONT** | | | | | | |
| Leahy | N | Y | N | N | Y | Y |
| *Stafford* | N | Y | Y | N | N | Y |
| **VIRGINIA** | | | | | | |
| *Trible* | Y | N | N | Y | N | Y |
| *Warner* | Y | N | Y | N | N | Y |
| **WASHINGTON** | | | | | | |
| Adams | N | Y | N | N | Y | Y |
| *Evans* | Y | N | N | Y | N | Y |
| **WEST VIRGINIA** | | | | | | |
| Byrd | Y | Y | Y | N | N | Y |
| Rockefeller | N | Y | Y | N | Y | Y |
| **WISCONSIN** | | | | | | |
| Proxmire | N | Y | N | N | N | Y |
| *Kasten* | Y | N | N | Y | N | Y |
| **WYOMING** | | | | | | |
| *Simpson* | Y | N | Y | Y | N | Y |
| *Wallop* | Y | N | N | Y | N | Y |

**KEY**

| | |
|---|---|
| Y | Voted for (yea). |
| # | Paired for. |
| + | Announced for. |
| N | Voted against (nay). |
| X | Paired against. |
| - | Announced against. |
| P | Voted "present." |
| C | Voted "present" to avoid possible conflict of interest. |
| ? | Did not vote or otherwise make a position known. |

Democrats    *Republicans*

ND - Northern Democrats    SD - Southern Democrats (Southern states - Ala., Ark., Fla., Ga., Ky., La., Miss., N.C., Okla., S.C., Tenn., Texas, Va.)

**9. S 1174. Fiscal 1988-89 Defense Authorization/Nuclear Testing.** Reid, D-Nev., motion to table (kill) the Hatfield, R-Ore., amendment to prohibit in fiscal 1988-89 nuclear test explosions with an explosive power of more than 1 kiloton, subject to certain conditions. Motion agreed to 61-36: R 40-6; D 21-30 (ND 7-27, SD 14-3), Sept. 24, 1987. A "yea" was a vote supporting the president's position.

**10. S 1174. Fiscal 1988-89 Defense Authorization/SALT II Limits.** Bumpers, D-Ark., amendment to bar the deployment of more than 820 multiple-warhead intercontinental ballistic missiles, more than 1,200 multiple-warhead strategic missiles of any sort, or more than 1,320 multiple-warhead strategic missiles and missile-armed bombers. Adopted 57-41: R 8-36; D 49-5 (ND 35-1, SD 14-4), Oct. 2, 1987. A "nay" was a vote supporting the president's position.

**11. S J Res 194. War Powers Compliance.** Byrd, D-W.Va., and Warner, R-Va., substitute to require the president to send Congress a report on U.S. military operations in the Persian Gulf that would not trigger the time limits set by the War Powers Resolution, but which would set in motion another time limit for action on an unspecified joint resolution dealing with the subject of the report. Adopted 54-44: R 13-33; D 41-11 (ND 26-9, SD 15-2), Oct. 21, 1987. A "nay" was a vote supporting the president's position.

**12. Bork Nomination.** Confirmation of President Reagan's nomination of Robert H. Bork of the District of Columbia to be an associate justice of the Supreme Court. Rejected 42-58: R 40-6; D 2-52 (ND 0-36, SD 2-16), Oct. 23, 1987. A "yea" was a vote supporting the president's position.

**13. HR 2700. Energy and Water Appropriations/Nuclear-Waste Repository.** Reid, D-Nev., amendment to direct the secretary of energy to give primary consideration to public health and safety in selecting a site for study as a possible permanent repository for nuclear wastes. Rejected 37-56: R 8-35; D 29-21 (ND 21-12, SD 8-9), Nov. 12, 1987.

**14. S 825. Housing and Community Development/Budget Waiver.** Cranston, D-Calif., motion to waive the spending-limitation requirement contained in the 1974 Budget and Impoundment Control Act (PL 93-334) with respect to the conference report on the bill to authorize $15 billion in fiscal 1988 and the same amount plus inflation in fiscal 1989 for housing, rural housing and community development assistance, and to make permanent the loan-insuring authority of the Federal Housing Administration. Motion rejected 57-43: R 8-38; D 49-5 (ND 31-5, SD 18-0), Nov. 17, 1987. A three-fifths majority (60) of the total Senate is required to waive certain Gramm-Rudman requirements.

**1. HR 1. Clean Water Act Reauthorization.** Passage, over President Reagan's Jan. 30 veto, of the bill to amend and reauthorize the Clean Water Act of 1972 authorizing $18 billion through fiscal 1994 in federal aid to state and local governments for construction of sewage treatment plants and more than $2.14 billion for other water pollution control programs. Passed 401-26: R 147-26; D 254-0 (ND 170-0, SD 84-0), Feb. 3, 1987. A two-thirds majority of those present and voting (285 in this case) of both houses is required to override a veto. A "nay" was a vote supporting the president's position.

**2. H Con Res 77/HR 2. Speed Limit/Omnibus Highway Reauthorization.** Adoption of the concurrent resolution to make a correction in the enrollment of the bill, HR 2, to allow states to raise the speed limit to 65 mph on Interstate highways located outside urbanized areas of 50,000 population or more. Adopted 217-206: R 125-50; D 92-156 (ND 45-121, SD 47-35), March 18, 1987.

**3. H Con Res 93. Fiscal 1988 Budget Resolution.** Gray, D-Pa., substitute to set fiscal 1988 budget totals as follows: new budget authority, $1.142 trillion; outlays, $1.039 trillion; revenues, $930.9 billion; deficit, $107.6 billion. Adopted 230-192: R 0-173; D 230-19 (ND 159-10, SD 71-9), April 9, 1987. A "nay" was a vote supporting the president's position.

**4. HR 1827. Fiscal 1987 Supplemental Appropriations/ Across-the-Board Cut.** MacKay, D-Fla., amendment to reduce discretionary budget authority by an across-the-board cut of 21 percent in order to keep total appropriations within the ceiling set by the 1987 budget resolution. Adopted 263-123: R 121-39; D 142-84 (ND 82-69, SD 60-15), April 23, 1987.

**5. HR 3. Omnibus Trade Bill/Gephardt Amendment.** Gephardt, D-Mo., amendment to require identification of countries with excess trade surpluses with the United States and quantify the extent to which unfair trade practices contribute to that surplus, to mandate negotiations to eliminate those unfair trade practices, and, if negotiations fail or an agreement is not fully implemented, to mandate imposition of tariffs or quotas to yield annual 10 percent reductions in that country's trade surplus. Adopted 218-214: R 17-159; D 201-55 (ND 137-34, SD 64-21), April 29, 1987. A "nay" was a vote supporting the president's position.

**6. HR 27. FSLIC Rescue.** St Germain, D-R.I., amendment to increase the bill's $5 billion, two-year recapitalization borrowing authority to $15 billion over five years. Rejected 153-258: R 72-98; D 81-160 (ND 62-99, SD 19-61), May 5, 1987. A "yea" was a vote supporting the president's position.

**7. HR 1748. Fiscal 1988-89 Defense Authorization/ Nuclear Testing.** Schroeder, D-Colo., amendment to bar nuclear test explosions larger than one kiloton provided the Soviet Union observes the same limitation. Adopted 234-187: R 26-147; D 208-40 (ND 160-9, SD 48-31), May 19, 1987. A "nay" was a vote supporting the president's position.

**8. HR 2342. Coast Guard Authorization/Reflagging Kuwaiti Ships.** Lowry, D-Wash., amendment to delay until 90 days after enactment the registration under U.S. ownership of any ships owned by Kuwait. Adopted 222-184: R 22-146; D 200-38 (ND 149-12, SD 51-26), July 8, 1987. A "nay" was a vote supporting the president's position.

[1] Rep. Nancy Pelosi, D-Calif., was sworn in June 9, 1987, to succeed Sala Burton, D, who died Feb. 1, 1987.
[2] Rep. Stewart B. McKinney, R-Conn., died May 7, 1987.

## KEY

- **Y** Voted for (yea).
- **#** Paired for.
- **+** Announced for.
- **N** Voted against (nay).
- **X** Paired against.
- **-** Announced against.
- **P** Voted "present."
- **C** Voted "present" to avoid possible conflict of interest.
- **?** Did not vote or otherwise make a position known.

Democrats   *Republicans*

| | 1 | 2 | 3 | 4 | 5 | 6 | 7 | 8 |
|---|---|---|---|---|---|---|---|---|
| **ALABAMA** | | | | | | | | |
| 1 *Callahan* | Y | Y | N | N | N | N | N | N |
| 2 *Dickinson* | ? | Y | N | N | N | N | N | N |
| 3 Nichols | Y | Y | N | Y | N | N | N | N |
| 4 Bevill | Y | Y | Y | Y | Y | N | ? | |
| 5 Flippo | Y | N | Y | Y | Y | N | Y | N |
| 6 Erdreich | Y | Y | Y | Y | N | Y | N | |
| 7 Harris | Y | Y | N | Y | Y | N | N | N |
| **ALASKA** | | | | | | | | |
| AL *Young* | Y | Y | N | Y | N | Y | N | ? |
| **ARIZONA** | | | | | | | | |
| 1 *Rhodes* | Y | Y | N | N | N | Y | N | N |
| 2 Udall | Y | Y | Y | N | Y | ? | Y | Y |
| 3 *Stump* | N | Y | N | Y | N | N | N | N |
| 4 *Kyl* | Y | Y | N | N | N | N | N | N |
| 5 *Kolbe* | Y | Y | N | Y | N | N | N | N |
| **ARKANSAS** | | | | | | | | |
| 1 Alexander | Y | Y | Y | N | Y | N | Y | Y |
| 2 Robinson | Y | N | Y | Y | N | N | N | N |
| 3 *Hammerschmidt* | Y | N | N | Y | N | N | N | N |
| 4 Anthony | Y | N | Y | Y | Y | N | Y | Y |
| **CALIFORNIA** | | | | | | | | |
| 1 Bosco | Y | N | Y | Y | N | N | Y | Y |
| 2 *Herger* | N | Y | N | N | N | Y | N | N |
| 3 Matsui | Y | N | Y | N | N | Y | Y | Y |
| 4 Fazio | Y | Y | Y | N | Y | N | Y | Y |
| 5 Pelosi [1] | | | | | | | | Y |
| 6 Boxer | Y | N | Y | Y | Y | N | Y | Y |
| 7 Miller | Y | N | Y | Y | N | Y | Y | Y |
| 8 Dellums | Y | N | Y | Y | Y | Y | Y | Y |
| 9 Stark | Y | # | Y | Y | Y | N | Y | Y |
| 10 Edwards | Y | N | Y | N | Y | N | Y | Y |
| 11 Lantos | Y | N | Y | Y | Y | N | Y | Y |
| 12 *Konnyu* | Y | Y | N | Y | N | Y | N | Y |
| 13 Mineta | Y | N | Y | N | Y | N | Y | Y |
| 14 *Shumway* | Y | Y | N | Y | N | N | N | N |
| 15 Coelho | Y | N | Y | Y | Y | N | Y | Y |
| 16 Panetta | Y | Y | Y | Y | N | Y | N | Y |
| 17 *Pashayan* | Y | Y | N | Y | N | N | N | N |
| 18 Lehman | Y | Y | Y | N | Y | N | Y | Y |
| 19 *Lagomarsino* | Y | Y | N | Y | N | Y | N | N |
| 20 *Thomas* | Y | Y | N | Y | N | Y | N | N |
| 21 *Gallegly* | Y | Y | N | Y | N | N | N | N |
| 22 *Moorhead* | Y | Y | N | Y | N | N | N | N |
| 23 Beilenson | Y | X | Y | N | N | Y | ? | |
| 24 Waxman | Y | N | Y | ? | N | Y | Y | Y |
| 25 Roybal | Y | Y | Y | N | N | N | Y | Y |
| 26 Berman | Y | N | Y | Y | Y | N | Y | Y |
| 27 Levine | Y | N | Y | Y | N | ? | Y | Y |
| 28 Dixon | Y | N | Y | N | Y | N | Y | Y |
| 29 Hawkins | Y | N | Y | N | Y | N | Y | Y |
| 30 Martinez | Y | N | Y | ? | Y | N | Y | Y |
| 31 Dymally | Y | N | Y | ? | Y | N | Y | ? |
| 32 Anderson | Y | N | N | Y | N | N | Y | Y |
| 33 *Dreier* | Y | Y | N | Y | N | N | N | N |
| 34 Torres | Y | N | Y | N | Y | N | Y | Y |
| 35 Lewis | N | Y | N | Y | N | N | N | N |
| 36 Brown | Y | Y | Y | N | N | N | Y | Y |
| 37 *McCandless* | Y | N | N | Y | N | N | N | ? |
| 38 *Dornan* | N | Y | N | Y | N | N | N | N |
| 39 *Dannemeyer* | N | Y | N | Y | N | N | N | N |
| 40 *Badham* | N | Y | N | N | N | N | N | N |
| 41 *Lowery* | Y | # | N | Y | N | N | N | N |
| 42 *Lungren* | N | Y | N | Y | N | Y | N | N |

| | 1 | 2 | 3 | 4 | 5 | 6 | 7 | 8 |
|---|---|---|---|---|---|---|---|---|
| 43 *Packard* | Y | N | N | Y | N | N | N | N |
| 44 Bates | Y | N | Y | Y | N | N | Y | Y |
| 45 *Hunter* | Y | Y | N | N | N | Y | N | N |
| **COLORADO** | | | | | | | | |
| 1 Schroeder | Y | Y | Y | Y | N | N | Y | Y |
| 2 Skaggs | Y | Y | Y | Y | N | Y | Y | Y |
| 3 Campbell | Y | Y | N | N | Y | N | Y | Y |
| 4 *Brown* | Y | Y | N | ? | Y | N | Y | Y |
| 5 *Hefley* | Y | Y | N | N | N | N | N | N |
| 6 *Schaefer* | Y | Y | N | ? | N | N | N | N |
| **CONNECTICUT** | | | | | | | | |
| 1 Kennelly | Y | N | Y | Y | Y | N | Y | Y |
| 2 Gejdenson | Y | N | Y | Y | N | Y | Y | Y |
| 3 Morrison | Y | N | Y | Y | Y | Y | Y | Y |
| 4 *McKinney* [2] | Y | Y | N | ? | ? | ? | ? | |
| 5 *Rowland* | Y | N | N | Y | N | N | N | N |
| 6 *Johnson* | Y | Y | N | N | N | N | N | N |
| **DELAWARE** | | | | | | | | |
| AL Carper | Y | N | Y | Y | Y | Y | Y | N |
| **FLORIDA** | | | | | | | | |
| 1 Hutto | Y | Y | N | ? | N | N | N | N |
| 2 Grant | Y | Y | Y | N | N | N | Y | Y |
| 3 Bennett | Y | N | N | Y | N | N | Y | Y |
| 4 Chappell | Y | Y | N | Y | N | N | Y | Y |
| 5 *McCollum* | Y | N | Y | N | N | N | N | N |
| 6 MacKay | Y | Y | Y | Y | Y | N | Y | Y |
| 7 Gibbons | Y | N | Y | Y | N | N | Y | Y |
| 8 *Young* | Y | N | N | Y | N | N | N | Y |
| 9 *Bilirakis* | Y | Y | N | Y | N | N | N | N |
| 10 *Ireland* | Y | Y | N | N | N | N | N | N |
| 11 Nelson | Y | N | Y | Y | N | N | N | N |
| 12 *Lewis* | Y | Y | N | Y | N | N | N | N |
| 13 *Mack* | Y | N | N | N | N | N | N | N |
| 14 Mica | Y | Y | Y | Y | N | Y | Y | Y |
| 15 *Shaw* | Y | N | Y | N | N | N | N | N |
| 16 Smith | Y | N | Y | Y | N | Y | Y | Y |
| 17 Lehman | Y | N | Y | N | N | N | Y | Y |
| 18 Pepper | Y | N | Y | ? | Y | Y | Y | Y |
| 19 Fascell | Y | N | Y | Y | Y | N | Y | Y |
| **GEORGIA** | | | | | | | | |
| 1 Thomas | Y | N | Y | N | Y | N | Y | Y |
| 2 Hatcher | Y | Y | Y | ? | Y | N | Y | Y |
| 3 Ray | Y | N | Y | # | N | N | ? | Y |
| 4 *Swindall* | Y | N | Y | N | Y | N | N | N |
| 5 Lewis | Y | N | Y | Y | Y | N | Y | Y |
| 6 *Gingrich* | Y | Y | N | N | N | N | N | N |
| 7 Darden | Y | Y | Y | Y | N | N | N | Y |
| 8 Rowland | Y | N | Y | Y | Y | N | Y | Y |
| 9 Jenkins | Y | N | Y | Y | Y | N | Y | Y |
| 10 Barnard | Y | Y | Y | Y | N | Y | N | N |
| **HAWAII** | | | | | | | | |
| 1 *Saiki* | Y | Y | N | N | N | Y | N | N |
| 2 Akaka | Y | N | Y | N | Y | N | Y | ? |
| **IDAHO** | | | | | | | | |
| 1 *Craig* | Y | Y | N | Y | N | N | N | Y |
| 2 Stallings | Y | Y | N | Y | N | N | Y | Y |
| **ILLINOIS** | | | | | | | | |
| 1 Hayes | Y | N | Y | N | Y | N | Y | Y |
| 2 Savage | Y | N | Y | N | Y | N | Y | Y |
| 3 Russo | Y | Y | Y | Y | Y | N | Y | Y |
| 4 *Davis* | Y | N | Y | Y | N | N | N | N |
| 5 Lipinski | Y | N | Y | Y | Y | N | N | N |
| 6 *Hyde* | N | Y | N | N | N | N | N | N |
| 7 Collins | Y | ? | Y | ? | Y | N | Y | Y |
| 8 Rostenkowski | Y | Y | Y | ? | N | N | Y | ? |
| 9 Yates | Y | N | Y | ? | N | Y | Y | Y |
| 10 *Porter* | Y | Y | N | Y | N | N | N | N |
| 11 Annunzio | ? | N | ? | ? | ? | ? | ? | Y |
| 12 *Crane* | N | Y | N | ? | N | N | N | N |
| 13 *Fawell* | Y | N | N | Y | N | N | N | N |
| 14 *Hastert* | Y | N | N | Y | N | N | N | N |
| 15 *Madigan* | N | Y | N | ? | N | N | N | N |
| 16 *Martin* | Y | N | N | Y | N | N | N | N |
| 17 Evans | Y | N | Y | N | Y | N | Y | Y |
| 18 *Michel* | N | Y | N | N | N | N | N | N |
| 19 Bruce | Y | N | Y | Y | Y | N | + | Y |
| 20 Durbin | Y | Y | Y | Y | Y | Y | Y | Y |
| 21 Price | Y | Y | Y | N | Y | Y | Y | Y |
| 22 Gray | Y | Y | N | Y | Y | Y | Y | ? |
| **INDIANA** | | | | | | | | |
| 1 Visclosky | Y | N | Y | Y | Y | N | Y | Y |
| 2 Sharp | Y | Y | Y | Y | Y | N | Y | Y |
| 3 *Hiler* | Y | N | Y | N | Y | N | N | N |
| 4 *Coats* | Y | N | N | Y | N | N | N | N |
| 5 Jontz | Y | Y | Y | Y | N | Y | Y | Y |

ND - Northern Democrats   SD - Southern Democrats

| | 1 | 2 | 3 | 4 | 5 | 6 | 7 | 8 |
|---|---|---|---|---|---|---|---|---|
| 6 ***Burton*** | N | Y | X | N | N | ? | N | N |
| 7 ***Myers*** | Y | Y | N | N | N | N | N | ? |
| 8 McCloskey | Y | Y | N | Y | Y | N | Y | Y |
| 9 Hamilton | Y | Y | Y | Y | Y | N | Y | N |
| 10 Jacobs | Y | N | N | Y | Y | N | Y | Y |
| **IOWA** | | | | | | | | |
| 1 ***Leach*** | Y | N | N | ? | N | Y | Y | Y |
| 2 ***Tauke*** | Y | Y | N | Y | N | Y | Y | N |
| 3 Nagle | Y | Y | Y | N | Y | Y | Y | N |
| 4 Smith | Y | Y | Y | N | N | Y | Y | ? |
| 5 ***Lightfoot*** | Y | Y | N | N | N | Y | N | N |
| 6 ***Grandy*** | Y | Y | N | N | N | Y | Y | N |
| **KANSAS** | | | | | | | | |
| 1 ***Roberts*** | Y | Y | N | Y | N | N | N | ? |
| 2 Slattery | Y | Y | Y | Y | Y | N | Y | N |
| 3 ***Meyers*** | Y | Y | N | Y | N | Y | Y | N |
| 4 Glickman | Y | Y | Y | Y | N | N | Y | Y |
| 5 ***Whittaker*** | Y | Y | N | Y | N | N | X | N |
| **KENTUCKY** | | | | | | | | |
| 1 Hubbard | Y | Y | Y | Y | Y | Y | N | N |
| 2 Natcher | Y | N | Y | N | Y | N | N | Y |
| 3 Mazzoli | Y | N | Y | N | Y | Y | Y | Y |
| 4 ***Bunning*** | Y | Y | N | Y | N | Y | N | N |
| 5 ***Rogers*** | Y | N | N | Y | N | N | N | ? |
| 6 ***Hopkins*** | Y | Y | N | Y | N | N | N | N |
| 7 Perkins | Y | N | Y | N | Y | Y | Y | Y |
| **LOUISIANA** | | | | | | | | |
| 1 ***Livingston*** | Y | Y | X | ? | N | N | N | Y |
| 2 Boggs | Y | N | Y | N | Y | Y | ? | Y |
| 3 Tauzin | Y | ? | # | Y | Y | ? | N | Y |
| 4 Roemer | Y | Y | N | Y | Y | Y | # | ? |
| 5 Huckaby | Y | Y | Y | Y | Y | Y | Y | Y |
| 6 ***Baker*** | Y | Y | N | Y | N | Y | N | N |
| 7 Hayes | Y | Y | N | Y | Y | N | Y | Y |
| 8 ***Holloway*** | Y | Y | N | Y | N | N | N | N |
| **MAINE** | | | | | | | | |
| 1 Brennan | Y | N | Y | Y | Y | N | Y | N |
| 2 ***Snowe*** | Y | N | N | Y | Y | Y | Y | N |
| **MARYLAND** | | | | | | | | |
| 1 Dyson | Y | N | Y | Y | Y | Y | N | Y |
| 2 ***Bentley*** | Y | N | N | Y | Y | Y | N | N |
| 3 Cardin | Y | N | Y | N | Y | Y | Y | Y |
| 4 McMillen | Y | N | Y | Y | Y | N | Y | N |
| 5 Hoyer | Y | N | Y | N | Y | Y | Y | Y |
| 6 Byron | Y | N | Y | Y | Y | N | N | N |
| 7 Mfume | Y | N | Y | N | Y | N | Y | Y |
| 8 ***Morella*** | Y | N | N | N | N | Y | Y | Y |
| **MASSACHUSETTS** | | | | | | | | |
| 1 ***Conte*** | Y | N | N | N | Y | Y | Y | Y |
| 2 Boland | Y | N | Y | N | Y | Y | Y | Y |
| 3 Early | Y | N | Y | ? | Y | Y | Y | ? |
| 4 Frank | Y | Y | Y | Y | Y | Y | Y | Y |
| 5 Atkins | Y | Y | Y | N | Y | Y | Y | Y |
| 6 Mavroules | Y | N | Y | N | Y | Y | Y | Y |
| 7 Markey | Y | N | Y | N | Y | Y | Y | Y |
| 8 Kennedy | Y | Y | Y | N | N | Y | Y | Y |
| 9 Moakley | Y | N | Y | N | Y | Y | Y | Y |
| 10 Studds | Y | N | Y | N | Y | ? | Y | Y |
| 11 Donnelly | Y | N | Y | Y | Y | Y | Y | Y |
| **MICHIGAN** | | | | | | | | |
| 1 Conyers | Y | N | Y | ? | Y | N | Y | Y |
| 2 ***Pursell*** | Y | N | N | N | N | N | N | N |
| 3 Wolpe | Y | N | Y | Y | Y | N | Y | Y |
| 4 ***Upton*** | Y | Y | N | Y | N | N | N | N |
| 5 ***Henry*** | Y | Y | N | Y | Y | N | Y | N |
| 6 Carr | Y | Y | N | N | Y | N | Y | Y |
| 7 Kildee | Y | N | Y | N | Y | Y | Y | Y |
| 8 Traxler | Y | ? | Y | N | Y | Y | Y | Y |
| 9 ***Vander Jagt*** | N | Y | N | ? | N | N | N | N |
| 10 ***Schuette*** | Y | N | N | N | N | N | N | N |
| 11 ***Davis*** | Y | Y | N | Y | Y | N | N | N |
| 12 Bonior | Y | N | Y | Y | Y | Y | Y | Y |
| 13 Crockett | Y | Y | Y | ? | Y | N | Y | Y |
| 14 Hertel | Y | N | Y | Y | Y | Y | Y | Y |
| 15 Ford | Y | N | Y | N | Y | N | Y | Y |
| 16 Dingell | Y | N | Y | Y | Y | ? | Y | Y |
| 17 Levin | Y | N | Y | Y | Y | Y | Y | Y |
| 18 ***Broomfield*** | N | Y | N | N | N | N | N | N |
| **MINNESOTA** | | | | | | | | |
| 1 Penny | Y | N | Y | Y | N | N | Y | Y |
| 2 ***Weber*** | Y | Y | N | N | N | N | N | N |
| 3 ***Frenzel*** | Y | Y | N | Y | N | Y | Y | Y |
| 4 Vento | Y | ? | Y | Y | Y | N | Y | Y |
| 5 Sabo | Y | N | Y | N | Y | N | Y | Y |
| 6 Sikorski | Y | Y | Y | Y | Y | N | Y | Y |

| | 1 | 2 | 3 | 4 | 5 | 6 | 7 | 8 |
|---|---|---|---|---|---|---|---|---|
| 7 ***Stangeland*** | Y | N | N | Y | N | N | N | N |
| 8 Oberstar | Y | N | Y | N | Y | N | Y | Y |
| **MISSISSIPPI** | | | | | | | | |
| 1 Whitten | Y | N | Y | N | Y | N | N | Y |
| 2 Espy | Y | Y | Y | N | Y | N | Y | Y |
| 3 Montgomery | Y | Y | Y | Y | N | N | N | N |
| 4 Dowdy | Y | Y | Y | ? | Y | N | Y | Y |
| 5 ***Lott*** | N | Y | N | N | N | N | N | N |
| **MISSOURI** | | | | | | | | |
| 1 Clay | Y | N | Y | N | Y | Y | Y | Y |
| 2 ***Buechner*** | N | Y | N | Y | N | N | Y | N |
| 3 Gephardt | ? | N | Y | N | Y | ? | Y | ? |
| 4 Skelton | Y | Y | Y | Y | Y | N | N | N |
| 5 Wheat | Y | N | Y | N | Y | N | Y | Y |
| 6 ***Coleman*** | Y | Y | N | N | N | N | N | N |
| 7 ***Taylor*** | Y | N | N | ? | N | N | N | N |
| 8 ***Emerson*** | Y | Y | N | Y | N | N | N | N |
| 9 Volkmer | Y | N | Y | Y | Y | N | Y | Y |
| **MONTANA** | | | | | | | | |
| 1 Williams | Y | Y | Y | N | Y | N | Y | Y |
| 2 ***Marlenee*** | N | Y | N | Y | N | N | N | N |
| **NEBRASKA** | | | | | | | | |
| 1 ***Bereuter*** | Y | Y | N | Y | N | Y | N | N |
| 2 ***Daub*** | Y | Y | N | Y | N | N | N | N |
| 3 ***Smith*** | Y | Y | N | Y | N | Y | N | Y |
| **NEVADA** | | | | | | | | |
| 1 Bilbray | Y | Y | Y | Y | Y | N | N | Y |
| 2 ***Vucanovich*** | Y | Y | - | Y | N | Y | N | N |
| **NEW HAMPSHIRE** | | | | | | | | |
| 1 ***Smith*** | Y | Y | N | Y | N | Y | N | N |
| 2 ***Gregg*** | Y | Y | N | Y | N | Y | Y | N |
| **NEW JERSEY** | | | | | | | | |
| 1 Florio | Y | N | Y | N | Y | N | Y | Y |
| 2 Hughes | Y | N | Y | Y | N | Y | Y | Y |
| 3 Howard | Y | N | Y | N | Y | Y | Y | Y |
| 4 ***Smith*** | Y | N | N | Y | Y | N | Y | N |
| 5 ***Roukema*** | Y | N | N | Y | N | Y | N | N |
| 6 Dwyer | Y | N | Y | N | Y | N | Y | ? |
| 7 ***Rinaldo*** | Y | N | N | Y | Y | N | N | N |
| 8 Roe | Y | N | Y | Y | Y | ? | Y | Y |
| 9 Torricelli | Y | N | Y | ? | Y | N | Y | Y |
| 10 Rodino | Y | N | Y | N | Y | Y | Y | Y |
| 11 ***Gallo*** | Y | N | N | Y | N | Y | N | N |
| 12 ***Courter*** | Y | N | N | ? | N | Y | N | N |
| 13 ***Saxton*** | Y | N | N | Y | N | Y | N | N |
| 14 Guarini | Y | N | Y | Y | Y | Y | Y | Y |
| **NEW MEXICO** | | | | | | | | |
| 1 ***Lujan*** | Y | Y | N | Y | N | N | N | N |
| 2 ***Skeen*** | Y | Y | N | Y | N | N | N | N |
| 3 Richardson | Y | Y | Y | Y | Y | N | Y | N |
| **NEW YORK** | | | | | | | | |
| 1 Hochbrueckner | Y | N | Y | Y | Y | Y | Y | Y |
| 2 Downey | Y | N | Y | Y | N | Y | Y | Y |
| 3 Mrazek | Y | N | Y | N | N | Y | Y | Y |
| 4 ***Lent*** | Y | N | N | Y | N | Y | N | N |
| 5 ***McGrath*** | Y | N | N | Y | N | Y | N | N |
| 6 Flake | Y | N | Y | N | Y | N | Y | Y |
| 7 Ackerman | Y | N | Y | Y | Y | Y | Y | Y |
| 8 Scheuer | Y | N | Y | ? | Y | Y | Y | Y |
| 9 Manton | Y | N | Y | N | Y | N | Y | Y |
| 10 Schumer | Y | N | Y | Y | N | Y | Y | Y |
| 11 Towns | Y | N | Y | ? | Y | Y | Y | Y |
| 12 Owens | Y | N | Y | N | Y | N | Y | Y |
| 13 Solarz | Y | N | Y | N | Y | Y | Y | Y |
| 14 ***Molinari*** | Y | N | N | Y | N | N | N | N |
| 15 ***Green*** | Y | N | N | N | N | Y | Y | N |
| 16 Rangel | Y | N | Y | N | Y | Y | Y | Y |
| 17 Weiss | Y | X | Y | Y | Y | Y | Y | Y |
| 18 Garcia | Y | N | # | ? | Y | Y | Y | + |
| 19 Biaggi | Y | N | Y | N | Y | Y | Y | Y |
| 20 ***DioGuardi*** | Y | Y | N | Y | N | Y | Y | N |
| 21 ***Fish*** | Y | N | N | N | N | Y | Y | N |
| 22 ***Gilman*** | Y | N | N | N | Y | N | N | N |
| 23 Stratton | Y | N | Y | N | N | Y | N | N |
| 24 ***Solomon*** | Y | Y | N | ? | N | N | N | N |
| 25 ***Boehlert*** | Y | N | N | N | Y | ? | Y | Y |
| 26 ***Martin*** | Y | Y | N | N | N | N | N | N |
| 27 ***Wortley*** | Y | N | N | Y | N | Y | N | N |
| 28 McHugh | Y | N | Y | N | N | Y | Y | Y |
| 29 ***Horton*** | Y | Y | N | N | Y | ? | Y | Y |
| 30 Slaughter | Y | N | Y | Y | Y | N | Y | Y |
| 31 ***Kemp*** | N | ? | X | ? | N | Y | N | ? |
| 32 LaFalce | Y | N | Y | ? | Y | Y | Y | Y |
| 33 Nowak | Y | N | Y | N | Y | Y | Y | Y |
| 34 ***Houghton*** | Y | Y | N | Y | N | Y | N | N |

| | 1 | 2 | 3 | 4 | 5 | 6 | 7 | 8 |
|---|---|---|---|---|---|---|---|---|
| **NORTH CAROLINA** | | | | | | | | |
| 1 Jones | Y | N | Y | N | Y | N | ? | Y |
| 2 Valentine | Y | N | Y | Y | Y | N | N | N |
| 3 Lancaster | Y | N | Y | Y | Y | N | N | Y |
| 4 Price | Y | N | Y | Y | Y | N | Y | Y |
| 5 Neal | Y | Y | Y | Y | Y | N | Y | Y |
| 6 ***Coble*** | Y | Y | N | Y | N | N | N | N |
| 7 Rose | Y | Y | Y | Y | Y | N | Y | Y |
| 8 Hefner | Y | N | Y | Y | Y | N | Y | Y |
| 9 ***McMillan*** | Y | Y | N | Y | N | Y | N | N |
| 10 ***Ballenger*** | Y | Y | N | Y | Y | Y | N | N |
| 11 Clarke | Y | Y | Y | Y | Y | N | Y | Y |
| **NORTH DAKOTA** | | | | | | | | |
| AL Dorgan | Y | Y | Y | ? | Y | N | Y | Y |
| **OHIO** | | | | | | | | |
| 1 Luken | Y | N | Y | Y | Y | N | Y | ? |
| 2 ***Gradison*** | Y | Y | N | Y | N | Y | N | N |
| 3 Hall | Y | Y | Y | Y | Y | N | Y | Y |
| 4 ***Oxley*** | Y | Y | N | Y | N | N | N | N |
| 5 ***Latta*** | N | N | N | ? | N | N | N | N |
| 6 ***McEwen*** | Y | N | N | Y | N | N | N | N |
| 7 ***DeWine*** | Y | N | N | Y | N | N | N | N |
| 8 ***Lukens*** | N | Y | N | ? | N | N | N | N |
| 9 Kaptur | Y | N | Y | Y | Y | N | Y | Y |
| 10 ***Miller*** | ? | Y | N | N | N | N | N | N |
| 11 Eckart | Y | N | Y | Y | Y | N | Y | Y |
| 12 ***Kasich*** | Y | Y | N | N | N | N | N | N |
| 13 Pease | Y | N | Y | Y | Y | Y | Y | Y |
| 14 Sawyer | Y | N | Y | Y | Y | N | Y | Y |
| 15 ***Wylie*** | Y | N | N | Y | N | Y | N | N |
| 16 ***Regula*** | Y | N | N | Y | Y | Y | N | Y |
| 17 Traficant | Y | N | Y | N | Y | N | Y | Y |
| 18 Applegate | Y | N | N | Y | Y | N | Y | Y |
| 19 Feighan | Y | N | Y | Y | Y | N | Y | Y |
| 20 Oakar | Y | N | Y | ? | Y | N | Y | Y |
| 21 Stokes | Y | N | Y | N | Y | Y | Y | Y |
| **OKLAHOMA** | | | | | | | | |
| 1 ***Inhofe*** | N | Y | N | Y | N | N | N | N |
| 2 Synar | Y | N | Y | N | N | Y | Y | Y |
| 3 Watkins | Y | Y | Y | Y | N | N | Y | Y |
| 4 McCurdy | Y | Y | Y | Y | N | N | N | ? |
| 5 ***Edwards*** | Y | Y | N | Y | N | N | N | N |
| 6 English | Y | Y | N | Y | N | N | N | Y |
| **OREGON** | | | | | | | | |
| 1 AuCoin | Y | N | N | N | N | N | Y | Y |
| 2 ***Smith, R.*** | Y | Y | N | Y | N | N | N | N |
| 3 Wyden | Y | Y | Y | Y | N | N | Y | Y |
| 4 DeFazio | Y | Y | Y | Y | Y | N | Y | Y |
| 5 ***Smith, D.*** | Y | Y | N | Y | N | N | N | N |
| **PENNSYLVANIA** | | | | | | | | |
| 1 Foglietta | Y | Y | Y | ? | Y | N | ? | Y |
| 2 Gray | Y | N | Y | ? | Y | Y | Y | Y |
| 3 Borski | Y | N | Y | Y | Y | N | Y | Y |
| 4 Kolter | Y | N | N | Y | Y | ? | Y | Y |
| 5 ***Schulze*** | Y | N | N | N | N | N | N | Y |
| 6 Yatron | Y | N | Y | Y | Y | ? | Y | Y |
| 7 ***Weldon*** | Y | Y | N | Y | N | N | N | N |
| 8 Kostmayer | Y | N | Y | Y | Y | N | Y | Y |
| 9 ***Shuster*** | Y | N | N | Y | N | Y | N | N |
| 10 ***McDade*** | ? | N | N | ? | Y | Y | N | ? |
| 11 Kanjorski | Y | N | Y | Y | Y | N | Y | Y |
| 12 Murtha | Y | N | Y | N | Y | N | N | N |
| 13 ***Coughlin*** | Y | N | N | Y | N | Y | Y | N |
| 14 Coyne | Y | N | Y | N | Y | Y | Y | Y |
| 15 ***Ritter*** | Y | Y | N | Y | Y | Y | ? | N |
| 16 ***Walker*** | Y | Y | N | N | N | Y | N | N |
| 17 ***Gekas*** | Y | Y | N | Y | N | N | N | N |
| 18 Walgren | Y | N | Y | Y | Y | ? | Y | Y |
| 19 ***Goodling*** | Y | N | N | Y | N | N | Y | N |
| 20 Gaydos | Y | Y | Y | Y | Y | N | N | Y |
| 21 ***Ridge*** | Y | N | N | Y | Y | Y | Y | Y |
| 22 Murphy | Y | Y | Y | ? | Y | N | Y | Y |
| 23 ***Clinger*** | + | N | N | Y | N | N | N | N |
| **RHODE ISLAND** | | | | | | | | |
| 1 St Germain | Y | N | ? | Y | Y | Y | Y | ? |
| 2 ***Schneider*** | Y | N | N | N | N | N | Y | Y |
| **SOUTH CAROLINA** | | | | | | | | |
| 1 ***Ravenel*** | Y | Y | N | Y | N | Y | N | N |
| 2 ***Spence*** | Y | Y | N | Y | N | N | N | N |
| 3 Derrick | Y | N | Y | Y | Y | N | Y | N |
| 4 Patterson | Y | N | N | Y | Y | N | N | N |
| 5 Spratt | Y | N | Y | Y | Y | N | Y | Y |
| 6 Tallon | Y | Y | Y | Y | Y | N | N | Y |
| **SOUTH DAKOTA** | | | | | | | | |
| SD Johnson | Y | Y | Y | N | Y | N | Y | Y |

| | 1 | 2 | 3 | 4 | 5 | 6 | 7 | 8 |
|---|---|---|---|---|---|---|---|---|
| **TENNESSEE** | | | | | | | | |
| 1 ***Quillen*** | Y | N | N | N | N | N | N | N |
| 2 ***Duncan*** | Y | N | N | Y | N | N | ? | N |
| 3 Lloyd | Y | Y | ? | Y | Y | N | N | Y |
| 4 Cooper | Y | N | Y | Y | Y | ? | Y | N |
| 5 Boner | Y | Y | Y | Y | Y | ? | Y | ? |
| 6 Gordon | Y | Y | Y | Y | Y | N | Y | Y |
| 7 ***Sundquist*** | Y | Y | N | Y | N | N | N | Y |
| 8 Jones | Y | Y | Y | ? | Y | Y | N | Y |
| 9 Ford | Y | N | Y | ? | Y | N | ? | ? |
| **TEXAS** | | | | | | | | |
| 1 Chapman | Y | Y | Y | Y | Y | Y | Y | N |
| 2 Wilson | Y | Y | Y | ? | Y | Y | N | N |
| 3 ***Bartlett*** | N | Y | N | ? | N | Y | N | N |
| 4 Hall | Y | Y | Y | Y | Y | N | N | N |
| 5 Bryant | Y | Y | Y | Y | Y | Y | Y | Y |
| 6 ***Barton*** | N | Y | N | Y | N | Y | N | N |
| 7 ***Archer*** | Y | Y | N | Y | N | Y | N | N |
| 8 ***Fields*** | Y | Y | N | Y | N | Y | N | N |
| 9 Brooks | Y | Y | Y | N | Y | N | Y | Y |
| 10 Pickle | Y | Y | # | Y | N | N | Y | N |
| 11 Leath | Y | Y | Y | Y | Y | N | Y | ? |
| 12 Wright | | | | | Y | | | |
| 13 ***Boulter*** | Y | Y | N | X | N | N | N | N |
| 14 ***Sweeney*** | Y | Y | N | Y | N | Y | N | N |
| 15 de la Garza | Y | Y | Y | Y | Y | N | Y | N |
| 16 Coleman | Y | Y | Y | N | Y | Y | Y | Y |
| 17 Stenholm | Y | Y | Y | Y | N | Y | N | N |
| 18 Leland | Y | N | Y | N | Y | Y | Y | Y |
| 19 ***Combest*** | N | Y | N | Y | N | + | N | N |
| 20 Gonzalez | Y | Y | Y | N | N | Y | Y | Y |
| 21 ***Smith*** | Y | Y | N | Y | N | Y | N | N |
| 22 ***DeLay*** | N | Y | N | Y | N | Y | N | N |
| 23 Bustamante | Y | Y | Y | Y | Y | N | Y | Y |
| 24 Frost | Y | N | Y | Y | Y | N | Y | Y |
| 25 Andrews | Y | N | Y | Y | Y | Y | Y | N |
| 26 ***Armey*** | Y | Y | N | Y | N | Y | N | N |
| 27 Ortiz | Y | Y | Y | Y | Y | Y | Y | Y |
| **UTAH** | | | | | | | | |
| 1 ***Hansen*** | Y | Y | N | Y | N | N | N | N |
| 2 Owens | Y | Y | N | Y | Y | N | Y | Y |
| 3 ***Nielson*** | Y | Y | N | Y | N | Y | N | N |
| **VERMONT** | | | | | | | | |
| AL ***Jeffords*** | Y | Y | N | N | N | Y | Y | Y |
| **VIRGINIA** | | | | | | | | |
| 1 ***Bateman*** | Y | Y | N | N | N | C | N | N |
| 2 Pickett | Y | Y | Y | Y | N | N | N | N |
| 3 ***Bliley*** | Y | Y | N | Y | N | N | N | N |
| 4 Sisisky | Y | Y | Y | Y | N | N | N | N |
| 5 Daniel | Y | ? | ? | ? | Y | N | N | N |
| 6 Olin | Y | N | Y | Y | N | N | Y | Y |
| 7 ***Slaughter*** | Y | N | N | Y | N | ? | N | N |
| 8 ***Parris*** | Y | Y | N | N | N | N | N | N |
| 9 Boucher | Y | Y | Y | Y | Y | ? | Y | ? |
| 10 ***Wolf*** | Y | N | N | N | N | Y | N | N |
| **WASHINGTON** | | | | | | | | |
| 1 ***Miller*** | Y | N | N | Y | N | N | N | N |
| 2 Swift | Y | Y | Y | Y | N | N | Y | Y |
| 3 Bonker | Y | Y | Y | Y | N | N | Y | Y |
| 4 ***Morrison*** | Y | Y | N | Y | N | N | N | N |
| 5 Foley | Y | N | Y | Y | N | Y | Y | Y |
| 6 Dicks | Y | N | Y | N | N | N | Y | Y |
| 7 Lowry | Y | N | Y | Y | N | ? | Y | Y |
| 8 ***Chandler*** | Y | Y | N | Y | N | N | N | N |
| **WEST VIRGINIA** | | | | | | | | |
| 1 Mollohan | Y | N | Y | N | Y | N | N | Y |
| 2 Staggers | Y | N | Y | Y | Y | N | Y | Y |
| 3 Wise | Y | N | Y | Y | Y | N | Y | Y |
| 4 Rahall | Y | N | Y | N | Y | N | Y | Y |
| **WISCONSIN** | | | | | | | | |
| 1 Aspin | Y | Y | Y | ? | Y | Y | Y | Y |
| 2 Kastenmeier | Y | N | Y | N | Y | N | Y | Y |
| 3 ***Gunderson*** | Y | Y | N | N | N | Y | N | N |
| 4 Kleczka | Y | N | Y | Y | Y | Y | Y | Y |
| 5 Moody | Y | N | Y | Y | Y | N | Y | Y |
| 6 ***Petri*** | Y | Y | N | Y | N | N | N | Y |
| 7 Obey | Y | N | Y | N | Y | N | Y | Y |
| 8 ***Roth*** | Y | Y | N | Y | N | Y | N | Y |
| 9 ***Sensenbrenner*** | Y | Y | N | Y | N | N | N | Y |
| **WYOMING** | | | | | | | | |
| AL ***Cheney*** | N | Y | N | Y | N | Y | N | - |

Southern states - Ala., Ark., Fla., Ga., Ky., La., Miss., N.C., Okla., S.C., Tenn., Texas, Va.

**9. HR 2890. Fiscal 1988 Transportation Appropriations/In-Flight Smoking.** Durbin, D-Ill., amendment to deny federal grants to any airport that permits any airline to provide service between its facilities and any other airport with an aircraft scheduled to be in the air for two hours or less on which smoking is permitted. Adopted 198-193: R 74-91; D 124-102 (ND 102-48, SD 22-54), July 13, 1987.

**10. HR 2470. Catastrophic Health Insurance Bill.** Michel, R-Ill., amendment to substitute the text of HR 2970, which would expand the Medicare program to protect beneficiaries from catastrophic medical expenses in a more limited way than would HR 2470. The Congressional Budget Office estimated that over five years the Michel bill would cost about $18.2 billion, while HR 2470 would cost $33,9 billion. Rejected 190-242: R 175-1; D 15-241 (ND 5-167, SD 10-74), July 22, 1987.

**11. HR 1414. Price-Anderson Amendments.** Sikorski, D-Minn., amendment to prohibit courts from awarding legal costs for any party from the Price-Anderson funds if it would jeopardize compensation of victims of a nuclear accident. Rejected 183-230: R 24-145; D 159-85 (ND 138-28, SD 21-57), July 30, 1987. A "nay" was a vote supporting the president's position.

**12. HR 2939. Independent Counsel Law.** Shaw, R-Fla., substitute to reauthorize through the end of 1988 the current independent counsel law providing for court-appointed special prosecutors to investigate allegations of misconduct by high-level executive-branch officials. Rejected 171-245: R 165-10; D 6-235 (ND 3-163, SD 3-72), Oct. 21, 1987.

**13. HR 3545. Fiscal 1988 Budget Reconciliation.** Passage of the bill to raise $11.9 billion in revenues and make spending cuts in accordance with the fiscal 1988 budget resolution (H Con Res 93). Passed 206-205: R 1-164; D 205-41 (ND 143-21, SD 62-20), Oct. 29, 1987. A "nay" was a vote supporting the president's position.

**14. H J Res 395. Fiscal 1988 Continuing Appropriations/Clean Air.** Murtha, D-Pa., substitute to the Conte, R-Mass., amendment, to postpone economic sanctions against areas that fail to meet pollution standards of the Clean Air Act from Dec. 31, 1987, until July 31, 1989. Rejected 162-257: R 72-99; D 90-158 (ND 45-124, SD 45-34), Dec. 3, 1987.

**15. HR 1720. Welfare Reform.** Adoption of the rule (H Res 331) to provide for House floor consideration of the bill to convert Aid to Families with Dependent Children into a national program of education, training and work to help welfare recipients gain permanent private-sector jobs. Adopted 213-206: R 0-170; D 213-36 (ND 155-12, SD 58-24), Dec. 15, 1987.

---

[1] Rep. Christopher Shays, R-Conn., was sworn in Sept. 9, 1987, to succeed Stewart B. McKinney, who died May 7, 1987.
[2] Rep. Bill Boner, D-Tenn., resigned Oct. 5, 1987, to become mayor of Nashville.

**KEY**

| | |
|---|---|
| Y | Voted for (yea). |
| # | Paired for. |
| + | Announced for. |
| N | Voted against (nay). |
| X | Paired against. |
| - | Announced against. |
| P | Voted "present." |
| C | Voted "present" to avoid possible conflict of interest. |
| ? | Did not vote or otherwise make a position known. |

*Democrats*  ***Republicans***

| | 9 | 10 | 11 | 12 | 13 | 14 | 15 |
|---|---|---|---|---|---|---|---|
| **ALABAMA** | | | | | | | |
| 1 Callahan | N | Y | N | Y | N | Y | N |
| 2 Dickinson | N | Y | N | Y | N | Y | X |
| 3 Nichols | N | Y | N | N | N | Y | N |
| 4 Bevill | N | N | N | N | N | Y | Y |
| 5 Flippo | N | N | N | N | Y | Y | Y |
| 6 Erdreich | Y | N | N | N | N | Y | N |
| 7 Harris | N | N | N | N | N | Y | N |
| **ALASKA** | | | | | | | |
| AL Young | N | Y | N | Y | X | Y | N |
| **ARIZONA** | | | | | | | |
| 1 Rhodes | N | Y | N | Y | N | N | N |
| 2 Udall | Y | Y | N | N | Y | N | Y |
| 3 Stump | N | Y | N | Y | N | Y | N |
| 4 Kyl | N | Y | N | Y | N | N | N |
| 5 Kolbe | Y | Y | N | Y | N | N | N |
| **ARKANSAS** | | | | | | | |
| 1 Alexander | Y | N | Y | ? | Y | N | Y |
| 2 Robinson | N | N | N | N | Y | N | Y |
| 3 Hammerschmidt | N | Y | ? | Y | Y | N | Y |
| 4 Anthony | N | N | ? | N | Y | Y | Y |
| **CALIFORNIA** | | | | | | | |
| 1 Bosco | ? | N | Y | N | Y | Y | ? |
| 2 Herger | N | Y | N | Y | N | Y | N |
| 3 Matsui | Y | N | Y | N | Y | N | Y |
| 4 Fazio | Y | N | Y | N | # | N | Y |
| 5 Pelosi | Y | N | Y | N | Y | N | Y |
| 6 Boxer | Y | N | Y | N | Y | N | Y |
| 7 Miller | Y | N | Y | N | N | N | Y |
| 8 Dellums | Y | N | Y | N | Y | N | Y |
| 9 Stark | Y | N | Y | N | N | N | Y |
| 10 Edwards | Y | N | Y | N | Y | N | Y |
| 11 Lantos | Y | N | Y | N | Y | N | Y |
| 12 Konnyu | N | Y | N | Y | N | N | N |
| 13 Mineta | N | N | Y | N | Y | N | Y |
| 14 Shumway | Y | Y | N | Y | N | Y | N |
| 15 Coelho | N | N | Y | N | Y | N | Y |
| 16 Panetta | Y | N | Y | N | Y | N | Y |
| 17 Pashayan | N | Y | N | Y | N | N | N |
| 18 Lehman | Y | N | Y | N | Y | N | Y |
| 19 Lagomarsino | Y | Y | N | Y | N | N | N |
| 20 Thomas | Y | Y | N | Y | N | X | N |
| 21 Gallegly | Y | Y | N | N | N | Y | N |
| 22 Moorhead | Y | Y | N | Y | N | N | N |
| 23 Beilenson | Y | N | Y | N | Y | N | Y |
| 24 Waxman | Y | N | Y | N | # | N | Y |
| 25 Roybal | Y | N | Y | N | Y | N | Y |
| 26 Berman | Y | N | Y | N | Y | N | Y |
| 27 Levine | Y | N | Y | N | Y | N | Y |
| 28 Dixon | N | N | Y | N | Y | N | Y |
| 29 Hawkins | ? | N | ? | N | Y | X | Y |
| 30 Martinez | Y | N | Y | N | Y | N | Y |
| 31 Dymally | N | N | ? | N | Y | N | Y |
| 32 Anderson | Y | N | Y | N | Y | N | Y |
| 33 Dreier | Y | Y | N | Y | N | N | N |
| 34 Torres | Y | N | + | N | Y | N | Y |
| 35 Lewis | N | Y | N | Y | N | N | N |
| 36 Brown | ? | N | ? | ? | Y | N | Y |
| 37 McCandless | ? | Y | N | Y | N | N | N |
| 38 Dornan | Y | Y | N | Y | N | Y | N |
| 39 Dannemeyer | Y | Y | N | Y | N | Y | N |
| 40 Badham | N | Y | N | Y | ? | N | N |
| 41 Lowery | Y | Y | N | Y | N | N | N |
| 42 Lungren | Y | Y | N | Y | N | N | N |

| | 9 | 10 | 11 | 12 | 13 | 14 | 15 |
|---|---|---|---|---|---|---|---|
| 43 Packard | Y | Y | N | Y | N | N | N |
| 44 Bates | Y | N | Y | N | Y | N | Y |
| 45 Hunter | N | Y | N | Y | N | N | N |
| **COLORADO** | | | | | | | |
| 1 Schroeder | Y | N | Y | N | Y | N | N |
| 2 Skaggs | N | N | Y | N | Y | N | Y |
| 3 Campbell | Y | N | Y | N | Y | N | N |
| 4 Brown | N | Y | N | N | N | N | N |
| 5 Hefley | Y | Y | Y | Y | N | N | N |
| 6 Schaefer | Y | Y | N | Y | N | N | N |
| **CONNECTICUT** | | | | | | | |
| 1 Kennelly | Y | N | ? | N | Y | N | Y |
| 2 Gejdenson | Y | N | N | N | Y | N | Y |
| 3 Morrison | Y | N | ? | N | Y | N | Y |
| 4 Shays [1] | | | | N | N | N | N |
| 5 Rowland | Y | Y | ? | Y | N | N | |
| 6 Johnson | Y | Y | ? | Y | N | N | N |
| **DELAWARE** | | | | | | | |
| AL Carper | N | Y | N | N | N | N | N |
| **FLORIDA** | | | | | | | |
| 1 Hutto | Y | N | Y | N | Y | N | N |
| 2 Grant | N | N | N | N | Y | Y | Y |
| 3 Bennett | Y | N | Y | N | Y | N | N |
| 4 Chappell | N | N | N | N | Y | Y | Y |
| 5 McCollum | Y | Y | N | Y | N | N | N |
| 6 MacKay | Y | N | Y | N | Y | - | Y |
| 7 Gibbons | Y | N | N | N | Y | N | N |
| 8 Young | Y | Y | Y | N | N | N | N |
| 9 Bilirakis | N | Y | N | Y | N | N | N |
| 10 Ireland | Y | Y | N | Y | N | N | N |
| 11 Nelson | N | Y | N | Y | N | Y | N |
| 12 Lewis | Y | Y | N | Y | N | N | N |
| 13 Mack | N | Y | N | Y | N | Y | N |
| 14 Mica | Y | N | N | N | Y | N | Y |
| 15 Shaw | N | Y | N | Y | N | Y | N |
| 16 Smith | Y | N | Y | N | Y | N | Y |
| 17 Lehman | N | N | Y | N | Y | N | Y |
| 18 Pepper | Y | N | N | N | Y | Y | Y |
| 19 Fascell | Y | N | Y | N | Y | N | Y |
| **GEORGIA** | | | | | | | |
| 1 Thomas | N | N | N | N | Y | Y | N |
| 2 Hatcher | N | Y | N | N | Y | Y | Y |
| 3 Ray | ? | Y | N | N | N | Y | N |
| 4 Swindall | Y | Y | N | Y | N | Y | N |
| 5 Lewis | N | N | N | N | Y | Y | N |
| 6 Gingrich | N | Y | N | Y | N | N | N |
| 7 Darden | N | N | N | N | Y | Y | Y |
| 8 Rowland | N | N | N | N | Y | Y | N |
| 9 Jenkins | N | N | N | N | Y | Y | Y |
| 10 Barnard | Y | Y | N | N | N | Y | N |
| **HAWAII** | | | | | | | |
| 1 Saiki | N | Y | Y | Y | N | Y | N |
| 2 Akaka | N | N | Y | N | Y | Y | # |
| **IDAHO** | | | | | | | |
| 1 Craig | N | Y | N | Y | N | N | N |
| 2 Stallings | Y | Y | N | N | N | Y | N |
| **ILLINOIS** | | | | | | | |
| 1 Hayes | Y | N | Y | N | Y | Y | Y |
| 2 Savage | Y | N | Y | N | Y | N | Y |
| 3 Russo | Y | N | Y | N | N | N | Y |
| 4 Davis | Y | Y | Y | Y | N | Y | Y |
| 5 Lipinski | Y | N | Y | N | ? | N | Y |
| 6 Hyde | Y | Y | ? | Y | N | N | N |
| 7 Collins | Y | N | N | N | Y | N | Y |
| 8 Rostenkowski | ? | N | N | N | Y | N | Y |
| 9 Yates | Y | N | Y | N | Y | N | Y |
| 10 Porter | Y | Y | Y | Y | N | Y | N |
| 11 Annunzio | ? | N | N | N | Y | N | Y |
| 12 Crane | N | Y | N | Y | N | ? | N |
| 13 Fawell | Y | Y | N | Y | N | N | X |
| 14 Hastert | N | Y | Y | Y | N | Y | N |
| 15 Madigan | ? | Y | N | Y | ? | N | N |
| 16 Martin | N | Y | N | Y | N | Y | N |
| 17 Evans | Y | N | Y | N | Y | N | Y |
| 18 Michel | N | Y | N | Y | N | N | N |
| 19 Bruce | N | N | N | N | Y | Y | Y |
| 20 Durbin | Y | N | Y | N | Y | Y | Y |
| 21 Price | N | N | N | N | Y | Y | Y |
| 22 Gray | Y | N | Y | N | # | Y | Y |
| **INDIANA** | | | | | | | |
| 1 Visclosky | Y | N | Y | N | Y | N | Y |
| 2 Sharp | N | N | N | ? | Y | Y | Y |
| 3 Hiler | N | Y | N | Y | N | Y | N |
| 4 Coats | N | Y | N | Y | N | Y | N |
| 5 Jontz | Y | N | Y | N | Y | N | Y |

ND - Northern Democrats    SD - Southern Democrats

| | 9 | 10 | 11 | 12 | 13 | 14 | 15 |
|---|---|---|---|---|---|---|---|
| 6 ***Burton*** | Y | Y | N | Y | N | Y | N |
| 7 ***Myers*** | N | Y | N | Y | N | Y | N |
| 8 McCloskey | Y | N | Y | N | Y | Y | Y |
| 9 Hamilton | N | N | Y | N | N | Y | N |
| 10 Jacobs | Y | N | Y | N | Y | N | Y |
| **IOWA** | | | | | | | |
| 1 ***Leach*** | Y | Y | Y | N | N | N | N |
| 2 ***Tauke*** | Y | Y | Y | Y | N | N | N |
| 3 Nagle | N | N | N | N | Y | N | Y |
| 4 Smith | Y | N | N | N | Y | N | Y |
| 5 ***Lightfoot*** | N | Y | N | Y | N | N | N |
| 6 ***Grandy*** | N | Y | N | Y | N | N | N |
| **KANSAS** | | | | | | | |
| 1 ***Roberts*** | N | Y | N | Y | N | N | N |
| 2 Slattery | Y | N | Y | N | Y | N | N |
| 3 ***Meyers*** | Y | Y | Y | Y | N | N | N |
| 4 Glickman | Y | N | Y | N | Y | N | Y |
| 5 ***Whittaker*** | Y | Y | N | Y | N | N | N |
| **KENTUCKY** | | | | | | | |
| 1 Hubbard | N | N | ? | N | N | Y | Y |
| 2 Natcher | N | N | N | N | Y | Y | Y |
| 3 Mazzoli | Y | N | N | N | N | N | N |
| 4 ***Bunning*** | N | Y | N | Y | N | Y | N |
| 5 ***Rogers*** | N | Y | N | Y | N | Y | N |
| 6 ***Hopkins*** | N | Y | N | Y | N | Y | N |
| 7 Perkins | N | N | N | N | Y | Y | Y |
| **LOUISIANA** | | | | | | | |
| 1 ***Livingston*** | ? | Y | N | ? | N | N | N |
| 2 Boggs | N | N | Y | ? | Y | Y | Y |
| 3 Tauzin | ? | N | ? | ? | N | N | Y |
| 4 Roemer | ? | N | ? | ? | N | ? | Y |
| 5 Huckaby | N | N | N | N | N | N | Y |
| 6 ***Baker*** | Y | Y | N | Y | ? | Y | N |
| 7 Hayes | N | N | N | ? | N | Y | Y |
| 8 ***Holloway*** | N | Y | N | Y | N | Y | N |
| **MAINE** | | | | | | | |
| 1 Brennan | Y | N | Y | N | Y | N | Y |
| 2 ***Snowe*** | N | Y | Y | N | N | N | N |
| **MARYLAND** | | | | | | | |
| 1 Dyson | N | N | N | N | Y | Y | N |
| 2 ***Bentley*** | N | Y | N | Y | N | Y | N |
| 3 Cardin | Y | N | Y | N | Y | N | Y |
| 4 McMillen | N | N | Y | N | N | Y | Y |
| 5 Hoyer | Y | N | Y | N | Y | N | Y |
| 6 Byron | Y | N | N | N | N | N | N |
| 7 Mfume | Y | N | Y | N | Y | N | Y |
| 8 ***Morella*** | Y | Y | N | N | N | N | N |
| **MASSACHUSETTS** | | | | | | | |
| 1 ***Conte*** | N | N | N | N | N | N | N |
| 2 Boland | Y | N | Y | N | Y | N | Y |
| 3 Early | N | N | Y | N | Y | N | Y |
| 4 Frank | Y | N | Y | N | Y | N | Y |
| 5 Atkins | Y | N | Y | N | Y | N | Y |
| 6 Mavroules | Y | N | Y | N | Y | N | Y |
| 7 Markey | Y | N | Y | N | Y | N | Y |
| 8 Kennedy | Y | N | Y | N | Y | N | Y |
| 9 Moakley | Y | N | Y | N | Y | N | Y |
| 10 Studds | Y | N | Y | N | Y | N | Y |
| 11 Donnelly | Y | N | Y | N | Y | N | Y |
| **MICHIGAN** | | | | | | | |
| 1 Conyers | ? | N | N | N | Y | N | Y |
| 2 ***Pursell*** | Y | Y | N | Y | N | ? | N |
| 3 Wolpe | Y | N | Y | N | Y | Y | Y |
| 4 ***Upton*** | N | Y | Y | Y | N | N | N |
| 5 ***Henry*** | Y | Y | N | Y | N | N | N |
| 6 Carr | N | N | N | N | N | Y | Y |
| 7 Kildee | Y | N | Y | N | Y | Y | Y |
| 8 Traxler | N | N | N | N | Y | Y | Y |
| 9 ***Vander Jagt*** | N | Y | N | Y | N | N | N |
| 10 ***Schuette*** | N | Y | N | Y | N | N | N |
| 11 ***Davis*** | Y | Y | N | Y | N | Y | N |
| 12 Bonior | N | N | Y | N | Y | Y | Y |
| 13 Crockett | ? | N | Y | N | Y | Y | Y |
| 14 Hertel | Y | N | Y | N | Y | Y | Y |
| 15 Ford | N | N | Y | N | Y | Y | Y |
| 16 Dingell | N | N | Y | N | Y | Y | Y |
| 17 Levin | Y | N | Y | N | Y | Y | Y |
| 18 ***Broomfield*** | Y | Y | N | Y | N | N | N |
| **MINNESOTA** | | | | | | | |
| 1 Penny | Y | Y | Y | N | N | N | N |
| 2 ***Weber*** | Y | Y | Y | Y | N | N | N |
| 3 ***Frenzel*** | Y | Y | N | Y | N | N | N |
| 4 Vento | # | N | Y | N | Y | N | Y |
| 5 Sabo | N | N | Y | N | Y | N | Y |
| 6 Sikorski | Y | N | Y | N | Y | N | Y |
| 7 ***Stangeland*** | N | Y | N | Y | N | N | N |
| 8 Oberstar | Y | N | Y | N | Y | N | Y |
| **MISSISSIPPI** | | | | | | | |
| 1 Whitten | N | N | N | N | Y | Y | Y |
| 2 Espy | N | N | N | N | Y | N | Y |
| 3 Montgomery | Y | Y | N | N | Y | ? | N |
| 4 Dowdy | N | N | N | ? | Y | ? | ? |
| 5 ***Lott*** | N | Y | ? | Y | N | ? | N |
| **MISSOURI** | | | | | | | |
| 1 Clay | ? | N | Y | N | Y | N | Y |
| 2 ***Buechner*** | N | Y | N | Y | N | N | N |
| 3 Gephardt | ? | ? | ? | ? | # | ? | # |
| 4 Skelton | N | N | N | N | N | Y | Y |
| 5 Wheat | Y | N | Y | N | Y | N | Y |
| 6 ***Coleman*** | Y | Y | N | Y | N | N | N |
| 7 ***Taylor*** | N | Y | N | Y | N | Y | N |
| 8 ***Emerson*** | N | Y | N | Y | N | Y | N |
| 9 Volkmer | N | N | Y | N | Y | N | N |
| **MONTANA** | | | | | | | |
| 1 Williams | N | N | Y | N | Y | N | Y |
| 2 ***Marlenee*** | Y | Y | N | Y | N | Y | N |
| **NEBRASKA** | | | | | | | |
| 1 ***Bereuter*** | Y | Y | N | Y | N | N | N |
| 2 ***Daub*** | Y | Y | N | Y | N | N | N |
| 3 ***Smith*** | Y | Y | N | Y | N | N | N |
| **NEVADA** | | | | | | | |
| 1 Bilbray | N | N | Y | N | N | N | Y |
| 2 ***Vucanovich*** | N | Y | N | Y | N | N | N |
| **NEW HAMPSHIRE** | | | | | | | |
| 1 ***Smith*** | Y | Y | Y | Y | N | N | N |
| 2 ***Gregg*** | N | Y | N | Y | N | N | N |
| **NEW JERSEY** | | | | | | | |
| 1 Florio | Y | N | Y | N | Y | N | Y |
| 2 Hughes | N | N | Y | N | Y | N | N |
| 3 Howard | X | N | N | N | Y | N | # |
| 4 ***Smith*** | Y | Y | N | Y | N | N | N |
| 5 ***Roukema*** | Y | Y | N | Y | N | N | N |
| 6 Dwyer | N | N | Y | N | Y | N | Y |
| 7 ***Rinaldo*** | Y | Y | N | Y | N | N | N |
| 8 Roe | ? | N | N | N | Y | N | Y |
| 9 Torricelli | Y | N | Y | N | Y | N | Y |
| 10 Rodino | Y | N | Y | N | Y | N | Y |
| 11 ***Gallo*** | N | Y | N | Y | N | N | N |
| 12 ***Courter*** | Y | Y | N | Y | X | N | N |
| 13 ***Saxton*** | N | Y | N | Y | N | N | N |
| 14 Guarini | Y | N | Y | N | Y | N | Y |
| **NEW MEXICO** | | | | | | | |
| 1 ***Lujan*** | N | Y | N | Y | N | N | N |
| 2 ***Skeen*** | N | Y | N | Y | N | N | N |
| 3 Richardson | Y | N | Y | N | N | N | Y |
| **NEW YORK** | | | | | | | |
| 1 Hochbrueckner | Y | N | Y | N | Y | N | Y |
| 2 Downey | Y | N | Y | N | Y | N | Y |
| 3 Mrazek | Y | N | Y | N | Y | N | Y |
| 4 ***Lent*** | Y | Y | N | Y | N | Y | N |
| 5 ***McGrath*** | N | Y | N | Y | N | N | N |
| 6 Flake | ? | N | Y | N | Y | N | Y |
| 7 Ackerman | ? | N | Y | N | Y | N | Y |
| 8 Scheuer | # | N | Y | N | Y | N | Y |
| 9 Manton | N | N | Y | N | Y | Y | Y |
| 10 Schumer | ? | N | Y | N | Y | N | Y |
| 11 Towns | ? | N | Y | N | Y | Y | Y |
| 12 Owens | ? | N | Y | N | Y | N | Y |
| 13 Solarz | Y | N | Y | N | Y | ? | Y |
| 14 ***Molinari*** | N | Y | N | Y | N | N | N |
| 15 ***Green*** | N | Y | N | N | N | N | N |
| 16 Rangel | Y | N | Y | N | Y | N | Y |
| 17 Weiss | Y | N | Y | N | Y | N | Y |
| 18 Garcia | + | N | Y | N | Y | N | Y |
| 19 Biaggi | N | N | Y | ? | ? | ? | ? |
| 20 ***DioGuardi*** | ? | Y | N | Y | N | N | N |
| 21 ***Fish*** | Y | Y | N | Y | N | N | N |
| 22 ***Gilman*** | Y | Y | N | N | N | N | N |
| 23 Stratton | Y | N | N | Y | Y | Y | Y |
| 24 ***Solomon*** | N | Y | N | Y | N | N | N |
| 25 ***Boehlert*** | N | Y | Y | N | N | N | N |
| 26 ***Martin*** | N | Y | N | Y | N | N | N |
| 27 ***Wortley*** | N | Y | N | Y | N | N | N |
| 28 McHugh | Y | N | Y | N | Y | N | Y |
| 29 ***Horton*** | N | Y | N | Y | N | N | N |
| 30 Slaughter | Y | N | Y | N | N | N | Y |
| 31 ***Kemp*** | ? | Y | ? | ? | X | ? | ? |
| 32 LaFalce | Y | N | Y | N | N | N | Y |
| 33 Nowak | Y | N | Y | N | Y | N | Y |
| 34 ***Houghton*** | N | Y | N | Y | N | Y | N |
| **NORTH CAROLINA** | | | | | | | |
| 1 Jones | N | N | Y | N | Y | Y | N |
| 2 Valentine | N | N | N | N | Y | N | N |
| 3 Lancaster | N | N | Y | N | Y | N | Y |
| 4 Price | N | N | Y | N | N | N | Y |
| 5 Neal | N | N | N | N | Y | N | N |
| 6 ***Coble*** | N | Y | N | Y | N | Y | N |
| 7 Rose | N | N | N | N | ? | N | Y |
| 8 Hefner | N | N | N | N | Y | N | Y |
| 9 ***McMillan*** | N | Y | N | Y | N | Y | N |
| 10 ***Ballenger*** | N | Y | N | Y | N | Y | N |
| 11 Clarke | N | N | N | ? | Y | N | Y |
| **NORTH DAKOTA** | | | | | | | |
| AL Dorgan | Y | N | Y | N | Y | N | Y |
| **OHIO** | | | | | | | |
| 1 Luken | Y | Y | Y | N | N | Y | Y |
| 2 ***Gradison*** | Y | Y | N | Y | N | Y | N |
| 3 Hall | Y | N | N | N | Y | Y | ? |
| 4 ***Oxley*** | N | Y | N | Y | N | Y | N |
| 5 ***Latta*** | Y | Y | ? | Y | N | ? | N |
| 6 ***McEwen*** | ? | Y | Y | Y | N | Y | ? |
| 7 ***DeWine*** | Y | Y | N | Y | N | Y | N |
| 8 ***Lukens*** | Y | Y | Y | Y | N | Y | ? |
| 9 Kaptur | Y | N | Y | N | Y | N | Y |
| 10 ***Miller*** | ? | Y | N | Y | N | Y | N |
| 11 Eckart | Y | N | Y | N | N | N | Y |
| 12 ***Kasich*** | Y | Y | N | Y | N | Y | N |
| 13 Pease | Y | N | Y | N | Y | N | Y |
| 14 Sawyer | Y | N | Y | N | Y | N | Y |
| 15 ***Wylie*** | ? | Y | N | Y | ? | Y | N |
| 16 ***Regula*** | Y | Y | N | Y | N | Y | N |
| 17 Traficant | N | N | Y | N | # | Y | Y |
| 18 Applegate | N | N | N | N | N | Y | N |
| 19 Feighan | Y | N | Y | N | Y | N | Y |
| 20 Oakar | N | N | Y | N | Y | N | Y |
| 21 Stokes | N | N | Y | ? | Y | N | Y |
| **OKLAHOMA** | | | | | | | |
| 1 ***Inhofe*** | N | Y | N | Y | N | Y | N |
| 2 Synar | Y | N | Y | N | Y | N | Y |
| 3 Watkins | N | N | Y | N | Y | Y | Y |
| 4 McCurdy | Y | Y | N | N | Y | N | N |
| 5 ***Edwards*** | ? | Y | N | Y | N | Y | N |
| 6 English | Y | N | N | N | N | N | N |
| **OREGON** | | | | | | | |
| 1 AuCoin | Y | N | Y | N | Y | N | Y |
| 2 ***Smith, R.*** | N | Y | N | Y | ? | Y | N |
| 3 Wyden | Y | N | Y | N | Y | N | Y |
| 4 DeFazio | N | N | Y | N | N | N | Y |
| 5 ***Smith, D.*** | N | Y | N | Y | N | Y | N |
| **PENNSYLVANIA** | | | | | | | |
| 1 Foglietta | ? | N | Y | N | Y | Y | Y |
| 2 Gray | ? | N | Y | N | Y | Y | Y |
| 3 Borski | N | N | Y | N | Y | Y | Y |
| 4 Kolter | N | N | N | N | ? | Y | Y |
| 5 ***Schulze*** | N | Y | N | Y | ? | N | N |
| 6 Yatron | Y | N | Y | N | N | Y | Y |
| 7 ***Weldon*** | N | Y | N | Y | N | N | N |
| 8 Kostmayer | Y | N | Y | N | Y | N | Y |
| 9 ***Shuster*** | N | Y | N | Y | N | Y | ? |
| 10 ***McDade*** | N | Y | N | Y | N | N | N |
| 11 Kanjorski | N | N | Y | N | Y | Y | Y |
| 12 Murtha | N | N | N | N | Y | Y | Y |
| 13 ***Coughlin*** | N | Y | Y | Y | N | N | N |
| 14 Coyne | N | N | Y | N | Y | N | Y |
| 15 ***Ritter*** | Y | Y | N | Y | N | Y | N |
| 16 ***Walker*** | N | Y | Y | Y | N | N | N |
| 17 ***Gekas*** | Y | Y | Y | Y | N | N | N |
| 18 Walgren | Y | N | N | N | Y | N | Y |
| 19 ***Goodling*** | Y | Y | N | Y | N | N | N |
| 20 Gaydos | N | N | N | N | Y | Y | Y |
| 21 ***Ridge*** | Y | Y | N | Y | N | N | N |
| 22 Murphy | Y | Y | N | Y | ? | Y | N |
| 23 ***Clinger*** | N | Y | Y | Y | N | Y | N |
| **RHODE ISLAND** | | | | | | | |
| 1 St Germain | N | N | Y | ? | Y | N | Y |
| 2 ***Schneider*** | Y | Y | Y | N | N | N | N |
| **SOUTH CAROLINA** | | | | | | | |
| 1 ***Ravenel*** | Y | Y | Y | Y | N | N | N |
| 2 ***Spence*** | N | Y | N | Y | X | Y | N |
| 3 Derrick | N | N | Y | N | Y | N | Y |
| 4 Patterson | N | Y | Y | N | N | N | Y |
| 5 Spratt | N | N | N | N | Y | N | N |
| 6 Tallon | N | Y | N | N | N | Y | Y |
| **SOUTH DAKOTA** | | | | | | | |
| SD Johnson | Y | N | Y | N | N | N | Y |
| **TENNESSEE** | | | | | | | |
| 1 ***Quillen*** | N | Y | N | Y | N | Y | N |
| 2 ***Duncan*** | N | Y | N | Y | N | N | N |
| 3 Lloyd | N | Y | N | N | Y | Y | N |
| 4 Cooper | ? | N | N | N | Y | Y | Y |
| 5 Boner [2] | X | N | ? | | | | |
| 6 Gordon | N | N | N | N | Y | Y | Y |
| 7 ***Sundquist*** | N | Y | N | Y | N | Y | N |
| 8 Jones | N | N | N | N | Y | Y | Y |
| 9 Ford | Y | N | Y | N | Y | N | Y |
| **TEXAS** | | | | | | | |
| 1 Chapman | N | N | N | N | Y | Y | N |
| 2 Wilson | ? | N | N | N | Y | Y | Y |
| 3 ***Bartlett*** | N | Y | N | Y | N | Y | N |
| 4 Hall | N | N | N | Y | N | N | N |
| 5 Bryant | ? | N | Y | N | Y | N | Y |
| 6 ***Barton*** | N | Y | N | Y | N | Y | N |
| 7 ***Archer*** | Y | Y | N | Y | N | Y | N |
| 8 ***Fields*** | N | Y | N | Y | N | Y | N |
| 9 Brooks | N | N | N | N | Y | Y | Y |
| 10 Pickle | N | N | N | Y | Y | N | Y |
| 11 Leath | N | N | N | N | Y | Y | N |
| 12 Wright | | | | | | | |
| 13 ***Boulter*** | Y | Y | N | Y | N | Y | N |
| 14 ***Sweeney*** | N | Y | N | Y | N | Y | N |
| 15 de la Garza | N | N | N | N | Y | Y | Y |
| 16 Coleman | N | N | N | N | Y | N | Y |
| 17 Stenholm | Y | N | N | N | N | Y | N |
| 18 Leland | Y | N | Y | N | Y | Y | Y |
| 19 ***Combest*** | N | Y | N | Y | N | Y | N |
| 20 Gonzalez | N | N | N | N | Y | N | Y |
| 21 ***Smith*** | Y | Y | N | Y | N | Y | N |
| 22 ***DeLay*** | N | Y | N | Y | N | Y | N |
| 23 Bustamante | N | N | N | ? | Y | Y | Y |
| 24 Frost | ? | N | N | N | Y | N | Y |
| 25 Andrews | Y | N | N | N | Y | Y | Y |
| 26 ***Armey*** | N | Y | N | Y | N | Y | N |
| 27 Ortiz | N | N | N | N | Y | Y | Y |
| **UTAH** | | | | | | | |
| 1 ***Hansen*** | Y | Y | N | Y | N | Y | N |
| 2 Owens | Y | N | Y | N | Y | N | Y |
| 3 ***Nielson*** | Y | Y | N | Y | N | Y | N |
| **VERMONT** | | | | | | | |
| AL ***Jeffords*** | N | Y | N | Y | Y | N | N |
| **VIRGINIA** | | | | | | | |
| 1 ***Bateman*** | N | Y | N | Y | N | Y | N |
| 2 Pickett | Y | N | N | N | Y | Y | Y |
| 3 ***Bliley*** | N | Y | N | Y | N | Y | N |
| 4 Sisisky | N | N | N | N | Y | Y | Y |
| 5 Daniel | N | Y | ? | Y | N | Y | N |
| 6 Olin | N | N | N | N | Y | Y | N |
| 7 ***Slaughter*** | N | Y | N | Y | N | Y | N |
| 8 ***Parris*** | N | Y | N | Y | N | N | N |
| 9 Boucher | N | N | Y | N | Y | Y | Y |
| 10 ***Wolf*** | Y | Y | N | Y | N | N | N |
| **WASHINGTON** | | | | | | | |
| 1 ***Miller*** | Y | Y | Y | Y | N | N | N |
| 2 Swift | N | N | Y | N | Y | N | Y |
| 3 Bonker | ? | N | Y | N | Y | N | Y |
| 4 ***Morrison*** | Y | Y | N | Y | N | N | N |
| 5 Foley | N | N | Y | N | Y | Y | Y |
| 6 Dicks | Y | N | Y | N | Y | N | Y |
| 7 Lowry | Y | N | Y | N | Y | N | Y |
| 8 ***Chandler*** | Y | Y | N | Y | N | N | N |
| **WEST VIRGINIA** | | | | | | | |
| 1 Mollohan | N | N | N | Y | Y | Y | Y |
| 2 Staggers | N | N | Y | N | Y | Y | Y |
| 3 Wise | N | N | Y | N | Y | Y | Y |
| 4 Rahall | N | N | Y | N | Y | Y | Y |
| **WISCONSIN** | | | | | | | |
| 1 Aspin | ? | N | Y | ? | Y | N | Y |
| 2 Kastenmeier | N | N | Y | N | Y | N | Y |
| 3 ***Gunderson*** | X | Y | Y | Y | N | N | N |
| 4 Kleczka | Y | N | N | N | Y | N | Y |
| 5 Moody | Y | N | Y | N | Y | N | Y |
| 6 ***Petri*** | Y | Y | Y | Y | N | N | N |
| 7 Obey | N | N | Y | N | Y | N | Y |
| 8 ***Roth*** | N | Y | N | Y | N | # | N |
| 9 ***Sensenbrenner*** | Y | Y | N | Y | ? | N | N |
| **WYOMING** | | | | | | | |
| AL ***Cheney*** | # | Y | N | Y | N | Y | N |

Southern states - Ala., Ark., Fla., Ga., Ky., La., Miss., N.C., Okla., S.C., Tenn., Texas, Va.

# 1988 Key Votes

## Senate

### 1. Campaign Finance

Senate Democrats failed to break a Republican-led filibuster against legislation (S 2) overhauling campaign finance laws, despite a record-setting eight attempts to invoke cloture. But the measure, which had become practically an idée fixe for Majority Leader Robert C. Byrd of West Virginia, was pushed harder and farther than any other campaign finance bill in years.

It was pulled from the floor only after Byrd resorted to a game of parliamentary hardball that provoked one of the most bitter displays of partisanship in the 100th Congress. The battle set a tone of confrontation between the parties that persisted through much of 1988.

Having failed seven times to cut off the GOP filibuster in 1987, Byrd resurrected the campaign finance measure, which would have limited campaign spending and the role of political action committees, as one of the first major bills to be debated in 1988. Determined to wear down the opposition and heighten public awareness of the problems of the current system, Byrd kept the Senate in session round-the-clock for three days in February. When Republicans boycotted a midnight quorum call, Byrd dusted off a rarely used disciplinary tool and had the Senate vote to order the arrest of absent senators. Bob Packwood, R-Ore., was arrested by the sergeant-at-arms and carried onto the Senate floor feet-first.

The uproar surrounding such tactics largely overshadowed substantive debate on the bill. In the end, S 2 proponents fell seven votes shy of the 60 needed to cut off a filibuster. The Feb. 26 vote on the final motion to invoke cloture was 53-41: R 3-39; D 50-2 (ND 35-0, SD 15-2).

The debate dramatized the growing frustration members of both parties felt with the unending fund-raising demands they faced under the existing system. But the vote laid bare a schism between Republicans and Democrats over what was needed to be done. Democrats insisted that the key lay in limits on campaign spending. S 2 would have provided financial incentives to senatorial candidates who agreed to abide by such limits, which would be set on a state-by-state basis. But such limits were anathema to Republicans, who maintained that a spending cap would hurt challengers and cement Democrats' current grip on both chambers. The GOP proposed an alternative that included new limits on the sort of in-kind contributions (e.g., union telephone banks) that Democrats relied on more than Republicans.

Despite the partisan divisions, there was some movement toward consensus on other issues, including limits on the role of political action committees and reductions in the cost of television campaign advertising.

### 2. Covert Operations

A law in effect since 1980 said the president must notify Congress about covert actions overseas. But in 1985-86, when President Reagan authorized secret arms sales to Iran, he used legal loopholes to keep Congress in the dark.

One of the major recommendations of the special Iran-contra committees in 1987 was that Congress eliminate any possibility that the president could conduct covert operations without telling at least a few congressional leaders. Consequently, key members of the House and Senate Intelligence committees drafted legislation (HR 3822, S 1721) requiring the president to tell Congress in advance about all covert operations. The bills would have allowed the president to delay notice in emergencies — but in no event for more than 48 hours.

The Senate Intelligence Committee approved S 1721 on Jan. 27, after making modifications to satisfy most Republicans, and the full Senate passed the measure on March 15 by an overwhelming 71-19 vote: R 26-17; D 45-2 (ND 31-2, SD 14-0).

However, the bill later died in the House, despite winning approval from the Foreign Affairs and Intelligence committees. House Republicans refused to join their Senate colleagues in supporting the bill, and the Democratic leadership dropped it in September following a partisan controversy over allegations that House Speaker Jim Wright, D-Texas, had disclosed classified information about CIA operations in Nicaragua.

### 3. Nuclear Accidents

The nuclear industry won a major test of its influence on Capitol Hill when the Senate March 18 rejected an effort to make Energy Department contractors liable for accidents caused by their own gross negligence.

The Senate at the time was considering a bill (HR 1414) to renew the 1957 Price-Anderson Act, which limited the liability of commercial nuclear power companies for damages caused in a nuclear accident and provided for partial compensation of victims.

The act also authorized the Department of Energy (DOE) to indemnify (shield from liability) the contractors in its far-flung, multibillion-dollar enterprise devoted primarily to production of nuclear materials and weapons. If the contractor's actions caused a release of radioactivity that injured someone, the federal government assumed responsibility for compensating the victims. Damages above a certain limit, which the bill raised from $500 million to $7.4 billion, would not be compensated.

Howard M. Metzenbaum, D-Ohio, voiced concerns that the arrangement took away any incentive contractors could have to operate safely. He offered a Senate floor amendment aimed at increasing contractor accountability. After the government had paid victims of a DOE-contractor accident, Metzenbaum wanted to require the government to sue the contractor to recover its costs, if the accident resulted from the contractor's gross negligence or willful misconduct. Environmental and consumer groups supported his amendment.

But Metzenbaum's amendment was opposed by the nuclear industry and by Energy Committee Chairman J. Bennett Johnston, D-La. Johnston argued that because the government owned, regulated and managed the weapons-production plants, the government should be held accountable rather than the contractors.

When Johnston on March 16 moved to table (kill) Metzenbaum's amendment, the Senate agreed 53-41: R 35-10; D 18-31 (ND 7-26, SD 11-5). President Reagan ultimately signed the measure into law Aug. 20 as PL 100-408.

## 4. Civil Rights Restoration

After the Senate forced an abortion compromise into a major civil rights bill, Congress in March first cleared the measure and then overrode President Reagan's veto of it. The new law (S 557 — PL 100-259) overturned a controversial 1984 Supreme Court decision and restored broad coverage of four civil rights laws.

The final outcome was not unexpected. The bill had passed both chambers by overwhelming margins, and relatively few members switched sides in the veto showdown. The Senate went first, voting on March 22 to override the veto by 73-24: R 21-24; D 52-0 (ND 35-0, SD 17-0). The margin was eight more than the two-thirds vote needed.

Eight Republicans who had voted for the bill when the Senate passed it Jan. 28 voted to sustain Reagan's March 16 veto. But supporters of the bill overcame that loss by picking up the votes of seven senators who had been absent when the Senate first passed S 557.

The law that resulted from the veto override overturned the high court's ruling in *Grove City College v. Bell.* In that case, the court ruled that Title IX of the 1972 Education Act Amendments applied only to the specific "program or activity" of an institution receiving federal aid and not to the entire institution.

Title IX barred discrimination on the basis of sex. But the court's ruling also limited enforcement of three other civil rights laws that barred discrimination on the basis of race, handicap or age in any federally funded "program or activity": Title VI of the 1964 Civil Rights Act, Section 504 of the Rehabilitation Act of 1973 and the 1975 Age Discrimination Act.

S 557 made clear that if any part of an entity received federal aid, the entire entity must not discriminate. The law also picked up a provision from Title IX exempting from coverage any "operation of an entity controlled by a religious organization."

Civil rights advocates portrayed S 557 as a simple restoration of the four laws as they had been interpreted prior to the *Grove City* decision. But in his veto message, Reagan contended that the measure was an extraordinary and unwarranted expansion of federal power.

The most hotly contested section of the bill — and the one that eventually cleared the way for its passage — was a provision specifying that nothing in the measure either prohibited or required any person or entity to provide or pay for services related to abortion. That superseded administrative regulations requiring health benefits for abortions when health benefits were provided for pregnancies. *(House key vote 2)*

## 5. AIDS Policy

Six years after the disease was first identified in 1981, Congress began to develop policies to deal with the AIDS (acquired immune deficiency syndrome) epidemic. Appropriators for several years had provided increasing amounts for research into the disease, whose death toll in the United States was nearly 42,000 as of September 1988. Total funding for fiscal 1989 reached some $1.3 billion.

But those attempting to set policy on sensitive issues such as testing for the virus that caused AIDS and providing education to those at risk of acquiring the disease — primarily homosexual males and intravenous drug users — found themselves mired in morality debates.

Public health officials, led by Surgeon General C. Everett Koop, argued that AIDS was a disease that made no moral distinctions. To stem its spread, they were prepared to take such steps as providing explicit "safe sex" information to homosexuals and concealing the identity of those carrying the HIV virus that causes AIDS. But a small cadre of conservatives, led by Jesse Helms, R-N.C., argued that AIDS was as much a moral as a public health problem, and that the rights of the uninfected should take precedence over those of persons who were sick or carrying the virus.

Helms won several votes during 1988 by crafting the wording of his amendments in such a way that those voting against him would appear to be condoning homosexuality. During the April 28 debate of an AIDS research and education authorization (S 1220) that had been approved unanimously by the Senate Labor and Human Resources Committee, Helms offered an amendment virtually identical to one he successfully appended to a fiscal 1988 appropriations bill. It barred use of federal funds for educational materials that "promote or encourage, directly, homosexual sexual activity."

Labor Committee Chairman Edward M. Kennedy, D-Mass., and Lowell P. Weicker Jr., R-Conn., were concerned that the language, already in force via the appropriations bill, was preventing federal funding of needed health information. They had hoped to dilute Helms' amendment to S 1220, but the North Carolinian outmaneuvered them. Helms offered his language as a second-degree amendment to an unrelated amendment offered by Don Nickles, R-Okla., thus preventing further changes. When Kennedy moved to table (kill) the Helms amendment, his motion failed and Helms prevailed 22-73: R 7-36; D 15-37 (ND 13-22, SD 2-15).

In October, as Congress was pushing to clear an omnibus health bill (S 2889 — PL 100-607) that contained major AIDS policy provisions, the mere threat of a Helms filibuster was enough to force House-Senate negotiators to drop provisions that would have ensured confidentiality of blood-test results. Public health advocates considered such protections vital to encourage at-risk individuals to submit to testing. But Helms contended that those who live or work with people infected with the HIV virus have a right to know if someone close to them tests positive. Once more, he prevailed.

## 6. Strategic Defense Initiative

The key Senate battle in 1988 over the strategic defense initiative (SDI), Reagan's program to develop a nationwide anti-missile shield, occurred over whether to cut the president's $4.9 billion budget request to $4.5 billion or $3.8 billion.

During debate in May over the fiscal 1989 defense authorization bill (HR 4264, S 2355), the Armed Services Committee, chaired by Sam Nunn, D-Ga., had recommended the higher amount to counterbalance a $3.5 billion SDI authorization approved by the House. In the Senate-House conference, Nunn argued that the time-honored practice of "splitting the difference" on disputed programs would result in an SDI authorization of about $4.1 billion, a slight increase above the fiscal 1988 SDI budget after an allowance for inflation was counted.

Nunn and his allies favored such a slight "real" increase in SDI funding, partly on grounds that it would provide bargaining leverage in arms control negotiations with the Soviet Union.

But J. Bennett Johnston, D-La., who had emerged as the Senate's most influential SDI skeptic, proposed an amendment that would have had the effect of slicing $700 million from the $4.5 billion Nunn and his panel recommended. Johnston's amendment would have transferred $700 million from SDI to the National Aeronautics and Space Administration (NASA), to reimburse the space agency for a share of the cost of building a new space shuttle orbiter to replace the *Challenger*, destroyed by an explosion Jan. 28, 1986.

On May 11, a motion to table (kill) Johnston's amendment was adopted 50-46. But immediately, Johnston blocked a normally routine procedural motion that would have killed his amendment once and for all, defeating the maneuver 47-50.

On a key third vote, which Johnston had to win to resuscitate his amendment, the Senate confirmed its initial vote against his amendment, defeating Johnston by the closest margin of the day. The vote was 48-50: R 6-39; D 42-11 (ND 30-5, SD 12-6).

## 7. SALT II Limits

The Senate in May rejected an amendment aimed at keeping the U.S. strategic arsenal roughly in compliance with provisions of the unratified 1979 U.S.-Soviet strategic arms limitation treaty (SALT II).

At issue were provisions of the treaty allowing each country to have no more than:

● 820 intercontinental ballistic missiles (ICBMs) equipped with multiple warheads known as MIRVs.

● 1,200 MIRVed ballistic missiles, including ICBMs and submarine-launched missiles.

● 1,320 MIRVed ballistic missiles, plus strategic bombers equipped with long-range cruise missiles.

The United States had informally observed those limits until late 1986, when Reagan dropped that policy, saying that the Soviets were violating SALT II and other arms control accords.

In 1987, Congress had added to the annual defense authorization bill a provision that made no explicit reference to SALT II, but mandated the retirement of an aging missile submarine. This had the effect of offsetting most planned deployments of new weapons, thus minimizing the extent to which the U.S. arsenal outran the SALT II limits.

In 1988, Dale Bumpers, D-Ark., who had pushed the successful 1987 amendment, offered an amendment to the annual defense bill (HR 4264, S 2355) that would have barred the United States from deploying more weapons in any of the three SALT II categories than it had deployed on Jan. 25, 1988. That was the date Reagan transmitted to the Senate the U.S.-Soviet treaty banning intermediate-range nuclear-force (INF) missiles.

Senate Armed Services Committee Chairman Sam Nunn, D-Ga., who had supported Bumpers' 1987 amendment, opposed the 1988 version, arguing that it would freeze in place the Soviet Union's current advantage in the number of MIRVed ICBMs. Bumpers pointed out that the Pentagon planned no additional ICBM deployments for at least three years, but Nunn objected to the symbolic impact of establishing a lower ICBM ceiling for the United States than for the Soviet Union.

Bumpers' amendment was tabled (killed) by a vote of 51-45: R 39-5; D 12-40 (ND 3-32, SD 9-8), May 11, 1988.

## 8. INF Treaty Limits

Senate approval of the U.S.-Soviet treaty banning intermediate-range nuclear-force (INF) missiles was a foregone conclusion even before the pact was signed by President Reagan and Soviet leader Mikhail S. Gorbachev in December 1987.

The treaty (Treaty Doc 100-11) was extremely popular with the U.S. public, a broad, bipartisan spectrum of Congress and major U.S. allies. It was energetically supported by the most hawkish president of modern times. And it incorporated dramatic new departures in U.S.-Soviet arms control dealings, such as elaborate provisions for each country's officials to inspect the other's missile facilities.

In that political context, most defense specialists from the political right and center, though dubious about the treaty's merits, concluded that derailing it would cause more damage to the NATO alliance than it would be worth.

But some of those conservatives, led by Sens. Dan Quayle, R-Ind., and Ernest F. Hollings, D-S.C., tried to narrow the scope of the INF ban to allow for future kinds of weapons they insisted would be needed to offset the numerical advantages of the conventional forces fielded against NATO by the Soviet-led Warsaw Pact.

The closest test of Senate sentiment on this issue came on a Hollings amendment that would have exempted from the treaty ban INF-range ground-launched cruise missiles armed with non-nuclear warheads. The Reagan negotiating team had banned all ground-launched missiles of INF range for fear that senators would believe it too difficult to verify a ban that exempted non-nuclear armed versions.

Hollings' amendment was rejected on May 25 by a vote of 28-69: R 18-28; D 10-41 (ND 3-32, SD 7-9).

## 9. INF Treaty Interpretation

The most heated fight in the Senate debate on the intermediate-range nuclear-force (INF) missile treaty (Treaty Doc 100-11) actually related to a battle between Senate Democrats and the Reagan administration over another treaty altogether.

The principle at issue was whether the Senate could bind future administrations to the interpretation of the treaty presented by the Reagan administration to the Senate. That constitutional question had surfaced with a vengeance in the course of a lengthy battle over the Reagan administration's contention in 1985 that the 1972 U.S.-Soviet treaty limiting anti-ballistic missile (ABM) weapons was substantially less restrictive than had been thought for the preceding 13 years.

The more permissive interpretation proposed by the administration would have permitted tests in space of ABM weapons developed under the strategic defense initiative (SDI) — tests that would have been illegal under the traditional interpretation of the 1972 pact.

Senate Armed Services Committee Chairman Sam Nunn, D-Ga., and other Democrats insisted that executive branch officials had expressed the traditional interpretation during Senate hearings on the treaty in 1972, a point disputed by President Reagan and his allies.

On May 26, the Senate adopted 72-27 an amendment to the resolution approving the INF treaty stipulating that neither the current president nor any future president could depart from any interpretation of the treaty that had been officially presented to the Senate.

The key vote in this fight came the following day on an amendment by Arlen Specter, R-Pa., that was intended to nullify the earlier amendment. Specter's proposal was tabled (killed) 64-33: R 13-33; D 51-0 (ND 33-0, SD 18-0), May 27, 1988.

## 10. Omnibus Trade Bill

By highlighting little-noticed provisions of omnibus trade legislation (HR 3) designed to stiffen the U.S. response to unfair trading practices of other nations, administration lobbying corralled enough GOP votes in the Senate June 8 to sustain the president's veto of the bill.

The tactic somewhat diffused attention to a controversial plant-closing notice requirement, which was seen as the primary reason that President Reagan vetoed the bill. Democrats had discovered that the provision, which required employers to give workers 60 days' notice of plant closings or mass layoffs, was playing very well with voters. They seized upon the issue to amplify their argument that GOP economic policies benefited the well-to-do at the expense of working Americans. For the record, GOP leaders said they were not worried about opposing the notice requirement, or seeming to sacrifice the huge trade bill to it. But a number of Republicans were clearly anxious to go on record for the notice requirement, and to save the trade measure.

When the vetoed bill returned to the Senate floor after a successful House override vote, some Republicans began saying they planned to oppose it because of a reaffirmation of existing restraints on exports of Alaskan oil, and because of another section permitting a temporary exemption for duty-free imports of Caribbean ethanol that hadn't been fully processed in the islands. Both provisions had been mentioned in Reagan's veto message, but neither had excited much visible opposition before the bill was vetoed.

The June 8 override vote of 61-37 fell five short of the two-thirds majority needed: R 10-35; D 51-2 (ND 33-2, SD 18-0).

Two Democrats voted to sustain the veto. One, William Proxmire, Wis., objected to the bill's revisions of rules against business-related bribery abroad by U.S. firms. The second, Majority Leader Robert C. Byrd, D-W.Va., voted "no" as a parliamentary maneuver, which reserved to him the right to move for another Senate vote on the vetoed bill later in the year.

The threat of reviving the vetoed trade bill was meant to spur action on a second version, which was ultimately enacted (HR 4848 — PL 100-418) without the controversial plant-closing notice requirement that also became law separately (S 2527 — PL 100-379). *(House key vote 7)*

## 11. Catastrophic Health Insurance

The Senate June 8 cleared for the president historic legislation to expand Medicare to shield its 33 million beneficiaries from catastrophic costs due to acute illness or injury. The final vote of 86-11 was overshadowed, however, by a House vote the same day to spurn an opportunity to address a far more pervasive source of medical-cost catastrophe: long-term care for chronic conditions.

Ironically, many of the 11 senators — all Republicans — who voted against approval of the conference report on the catastrophic insurance bill (HR 2470 — PL 100-360) said they did so because the measure was too expensive and failed to address the long-term care problem. Sponsors agreed that the long-term care problem was a serious one, but they said budget constraints and a lack of consensus on how to address the issue made the catastrophic insurance bill more practical in the short term.

HR 2470 did plug some major gaps opened in the Medicare program since its creation in 1965. Health-care inflation by 1987 had left most Medicare beneficiaries spending a larger percentage of their income on medical costs than they did before Medicare was enacted. The catastrophic costs bill put a cap on the amount any beneficiary would have to pay for hospital care, doctor bills, lab fees and other expenses covered by Medicare.

The bill also instituted the program's first broad coverage for outpatient prescription drugs and sought to ameliorate the situation in which one member of a couple would become impoverished in order for the federal-state Medicaid program to pay the costs of nursing home care for the other spouse.

Final action came by an 86-11 vote on June 8: R 34-11; D 52-0 (ND 35-0, SD 17-0). *(House key vote 8)*

## 12. Death Penalty

To show that Congress was eager to get tough on crime, the Senate by more than a 2-1 margin June 10 passed legislation authorizing the death penalty for drug traffickers who killed during the course of a drug transaction.

The vote on the bill (S 2455), sponsored by Alfonse M. D'Amato, R-N.Y., was 65-29: R 37-6; D 28-23 (ND 15-19, SD 13-4).

The Senate had passed a more sweeping death penalty bill in 1984, but the measure went nowhere in the House. In 1988, however, a provision similar to the D'Amato bill was enacted into law in October as part of an omnibus anti-drug bill (HR 5210 — PL 100-690). Passage of the separate death penalty bill in June was an important step. When a Senate task force drafted its version of HR 5210, its members decided to include the death penalty provision, citing the overwhelming June vote. No one wanted to force proponents of the provision to offer it as a floor amendment, using up precious late-session time, when it was certain to be put into the drug bill in the end.

In 1986, Senate opponents of capital punishment were able to keep a death penalty out of that year's big anti-drug bill. But Vice President George Bush's continued attacks on Democratic presidential nominee Michael S. Dukakis, a death penalty opponent, for being soft on crime left few in Congress eager to invite the same criticism. *(House key vote 15)*

## 13. Welfare Overhaul

Senate approval of an amendment by Minority Leader Robert Dole, R-Kan., to create the first-ever federal work requirement for some welfare recipients was arguably *the* turning point in the 100th Congress' two-year effort to overhaul the welfare system. The amendment turned out to be the single provision that President Reagan demanded before he would sign the bill (HR 1720) into law (PL 100-485).

It was Reagan who put welfare reform on the congressional agenda in the first place in 1986, calling for such legislation in his State of the Union address that year. But the $7 billion bill approved by the House in December 1987 was vehemently opposed by the administration as too expensive and too generous to welfare recipients. Administration officials were somewhat more sympathetic to the $2.8 billion bipartisan measure that emerged from the Senate Finance Committee in April 1988, but even that bill had a veto threat hanging over it as it came to the Senate floor.

Democratic sponsors, including Finance Chairman Lloyd Bentsen, Texas, and Daniel Patrick Moynihan, N.Y., negotiated furiously with administration officials the week of June 12, but to no avail. They then set about negotiating with Republican holdouts on the Finance Committee, with the result being Dole's amendment to require one parent in two-parent welfare families to "work off" their welfare grant for at least 16 hours each week the family received benefits.

The amendment was opposed by liberals, who said it was punitive, as well as by many of the nation's governors, who argued that two-parent families were the wrong group on which to target the scarce resources the new bill would make available. Because two-parent families must have extensive prior work experience in order to qualify for aid, the governors said, they would benefit little from unpaid community work programs that are designed to give experience to those who have worked little or not at all.

But Dole and others argued that there was virtually no chance that Reagan would sign a welfare bill without the amendment, and even less prospect of overriding a veto on such a politically distasteful issue as welfare.

Moynihan's motion to table (kill) Dole's amendment was rejected June 16 by 41-54: R 3-40; D 38-14 (ND 27-7, SD 11-7). *(House key vote 12)*

## 14. UDAG vs. NASA

For seven years, President Reagan railed against urban development action grants (UDAGs) as the epitome of wasteful government largess.

But the program thrived, steadfastly protected by a Congress loath to kill anything that produced bacon for the folks back home. Under orders from Capitol Hill, Reagan's administration had handed out roughly $3.5 billion in UDAGs since he took office.

On July 12, the death knell finally sounded. "We stand looking over the grave," lamented John Heinz, R-Pa. Backed against a wall, the Senate overwhelmingly rejected a Heinz amendment to shift $30 million, a relative pittance, from the National Aeronautics and Space Administration (NASA) to the Department of Housing and Urban Devel-

opment (HUD) to give UDAGs at least the appearance of life. The decision had little to do with Reagan's persuasiveness and much to do with budget realities and politics.

The budget summit agreement of 1987 had capped domestic spending and prohibited raids on defense funds. That made it difficult for appropriators to pay for everything they wanted in the HUD-independent agencies spending bill (HR 4800 — PL 100-404), which also included NASA, the Environmental Protection Agency and the Veterans Administration. The chief problem: The space program's ambitious goals required a hefty funding increase.

Something had to go, so UDAG was offered as the sacrificial lamb to the lame-duck president.

By 1988, the oft-criticized program was a weakened target. Created in 1978 under President Carter, it was designed to encourage private investment in distressed urban areas. Federal money would spur projects that otherwise would not be built. To date, the government's $4.6 billion investment has been matched by some $30 billion in private money to build nearly 3,000 developments, which in turn provided nearly 600,000 jobs.

But the program was vulnerable on several fronts. It was meant to help the poor, but it produced many upscale projects that were easy targets for critics: fancy hotels, marinas, ritzy malls, ski resorts and corporate headquarters. Further, fewer than 60 percent of the jobs went to moderate- and low-income people. And there was significant debate over whether those jobs were "new" or just shifted from somewhere else.

UDAG's biggest political weakness was the formula under which the grants were awarded. The program, intended to aid blighted areas, favored areas with older housing. The result: The industrialized Northeast got most of the money.

Ironically, changes intended to spread the money out and widen the program's support base eventually quickened its demise. Under prodding from UDAG-poor states, Congress in 1987 decided to set aside 35 percent of the money for projects judged without regard to economic considerations, giving Southern and Western states a better shot.

That done, however, traditional UDAG supporters on the House Appropriations Committee — including subcommittee Chairman Edward P. Boland, D-Mass., and ranking Republican Bill Green, N.Y. — had a good excuse to abandon it. Although most hard-core supporters in the Senate refused to jump ship, the populous Northeast had no numerical advantage in that chamber, so Heinz' amendment didn't have a chance — despite scattered support from the South and West. The vote was 34-63: R 9-36; D 25-27 (ND 21-14, SD 4-13).

Supporters argued that UDAG would be impossible to revive with no new money, even though there might have been leftover HUD funds, from previous appropriations, to hand out — estimated at $50 million worth. "Table scraps," Heinz sniffed. *(House key vote 9)*

## 15. Contra Aid

Ever since 1983, contra aid had been one of the most divisive issues on Capitol Hill. But it had rarely been a strictly party-line issue. In both chambers, significant minorities of Democrats had supported President Reagan's requests for aid to the Nicaraguan guerrillas, and smaller minorities of Republicans had opposed the president.

After the collapse in July of peace talks between the contras and the leftist Nicaraguan government, Senate leaders sought to craft a broadly supported, bipartisan measure on the contra-aid issue. They almost succeeded during two weeks of closed-door negotiations.

With the active participation of White House officials, leading Democrats and Republicans developed a compromise plan approving a renewed dose of non-military aid for the contras and establishing a procedure for the president to ask Congress for permission to give the contras some $16.5 million in military supplies that had been warehoused in Honduras.

But at the last minute, as the Senate was about to debate the issue on Aug. 10, the White House and staunch contra-aid backers in the Senate refused to support the aid plan. They complained that it did nothing to give the contras immediate military aid, and they insisted that Democrats were merely trying to sweep aside contra aid as an embarrassing political issue.

In a burst of partisan acrimony, the Senate approved the aid plan as an amendment to the fiscal 1989 defense appropriations bill (HR 4781). The vote was 49-47: R 0-43; D 49-4 (ND 31-4, SD 18-0). The four Democrats who opposed the plan said they could never support contra aid in any form.

The House later accepted the Senate provision, and it was included in the fiscal 1989 defense appropriations bill (PL 100-463) sent to Reagan on Sept. 30. *(House key vote 1)*

## 16. Minimum Wage

After a year of bitter partisan wrangling over labor-backed issues, Senate Democrats Sept. 23 failed to overcome Republican delaying tactics on a bill (S 837) raising the minimum wage from its current $3.35 an hour to $4.55 over three years.

When the party-line vote fell four votes short of the 60 needed to limit debate, Majority Leader Robert C. Byrd, D-W.Va., abruptly pulled the measure from the floor and castigated Republicans for "delaying economic justice for millions of Americans." For the second time in as many days, the Senate had failed to invoke cloture — this time, by a vote of 56-35: R 8-32; D 48-3 (ND 34-1, SD 14-2).

Only eight moderate Republicans, including four up for re-election in 1988, voted to cut off the GOP filibuster: John H. Chafee, R.I.; Mark O. Hatfield, Ore.; John Heinz, Pa.; Bob Packwood, Ore.; William V. Roth Jr., Del.; Arlen Specter, Pa.; Robert T. Stafford, Vt.; and Lowell P. Weicker Jr., Conn.

Three conservative Democrats defected from their party's ranks, voting against cloture: David L. Boren, Okla.; J. James Exon, Neb.; and Richard C. Shelby, Ala.

The wage measure, earlier stalled in both chambers for a lack of votes, was brought to the floor in the last weeks of the congressional session to capitalize on GOP presidential candidate George Bush's indication that he would support a modest increase in the minimum wage. But Bush's "election-year conversion" did little to soften Republican opposition to the wage bill.

In fact, some GOP votes against cloture were more a protest against Democratic political strategy than a reflection of opposition to the measure itself. The Democrats had waited until the end of the session to bring up a parade of last-minute social legislation, including the minimum-wage bill, child-care and parental leave measures, which they wanted to highlight before the Nov. 8 elections.

And the time pressure to complete action on the bill, combined with Byrd's habit of immediately filing cloture on controversial measures to prevent or limit members from offering their alternatives, only exacerbated the gulf between Democrats and Republicans on the wage issue.

The cloture vote also could have been a litmus test for many of the "labor agenda" issues debated in 1988.

In March, a bill (S 79) requiring employers to notify their workers of on-the-job health hazards was derailed by a GOP filibuster after four attempts to cut off debate fell short. At the time, Dan Quayle, R-Ind., confidently predicted that S 79's fate would "make it more difficult to get the so-called labor agenda through Congress."

And right after the minimum-wage fiasco, Senate Democrats pressed a bill (S 2488) combining child-care provisions with a requirement that all but the smallest businesses provide unpaid, job-protected leave for parents of newborn or ill children. But that, too, was foiled by GOP delaying tactics. Unable to cut off debate, Byrd pulled the parental leave bill from the Senate floor.

On all three bills, the party-line cloture votes underscored the ideological chasm on key labor issues. While Democrats sought to require employers to provide better benefits for their workers, Republicans fought to preserve an employer's right to run his business without government interference.

# House

## 1. Contra Aid

Contra aid was a major political issue all through 1988, and President Reagan repeatedly attacked Congress for its unwillingness to provide military backing for the Nicaraguan guerrillas. But Reagan himself sent Congress only one request for aid to the contras during all of 1987: In January, he sought $36.25 million, for military aid.

The House on Feb. 3 rejected that request on a narrow vote of 211-219: R 164-12; D 47-207 (ND 6-166, SD 41-41). The margin was typical for contra aid votes in the House, demonstrating the deep divisions on the issue both on Capitol Hill and in the country at large.

Reagan submitted no more requests during the remainder of 1988 and instead allowed Congress to take the lead on the issue. Congress approved a stopgap dose of non-military aid to the contras in late March, following the signing of a cease-fire agreement by the contras and the Nicaraguan government.

And in July and August, the Senate agreed to allow additional non-military aid through March 1989. That amendment, providing $27.1 million in food and other supplies, was enacted into law as part of the fiscal 1989 defense appropriations bill (HR 4781 — PL 100-463). *(Senate key vote 15)*

## 2. Civil Rights Restoration

Congress handed President Reagan a sharp, but not unexpected, blow when the Senate and House overrode his veto of legislation that restored broad coverage of four civil rights laws (S 557).

The measure had passed both chambers by veto-proof margins, the result of four years of negotiations to overturn a 1984 Supreme Court decision that had restricted the reach of the anti-bias laws.

The final chapter in the long saga came March 22, when the House voted 292-133 to override the veto: R 52-123; D 240-10 (ND 167-1, SD 73-9). The tally was eight more than the required two-thirds majority of those present and voting. A few hours earlier, the Senate had voted 73-24 to override the president — eight votes more than required. *(Senate key vote 4)*

The law enacted over Reagan's veto (PL 100-259) overturned the high court's ruling in *Grove City College v. Bell*. In that case, the justices held that Title IX of the 1972 Education Act Amendments applied only to the specific "program or activity" of an institution receiving federal aid and not to the entire institution.

Title IX barred discrimination on the basis of sex in education programs. Because three other laws prohibiting discrimination on the basis of race, age or handicap carried the same "program or activity" language, their enforcement was also restricted.

The new law made clear that if one part of an entity received federal aid, the entire entity must not discriminate. The law also picked up a provision from Title IX exempting from coverage any "operation of an entity controlled by a religious organization."

The most hotly contested section of the law — and the one that eventually cleared the way for its passage — was a provision specifying that nothing in the measure either prohibited or required any person or entity to provide or pay for services related to abortion. That superseded administrative regulations requiring health benefits for abortions when health benefits were provided for pregnancies.

Civil rights advocates portrayed the new law as a simple restoration of legal interpretations in force prior to the *Grove City* decision. But in his veto message, Reagan contended that the measure was an extraordinary and unwarranted expansion of federal power.

## 3. Fiscal 1989 Budget Resolution

An unprecedented show of support from both Democrats and Republicans swept a $1.1 trillion budget through the House March 23, offering the first clear signal that congressional fiscal policy would not be contentious in the election year.

Presented with a delicately crafted document designed to appeal to many interests, the House responded with an overwhelming vote of 319-102: R 92-78; D 227-24 (ND 152-17, SD 75-7).

The unusually quiet floor action followed two weeks of even more unusual working harmony within the House Budget Committee, which in previous years had been known for its partisan divisions and rancor.

The fiscal 1989 budget resolution (H Con Res 268) called for no new taxes and, other than a prearranged deal with President Reagan on defense slowdowns, asked no important constituencies to take big cuts in spending. At the same time, the budget appeared to conform with the $136 billion deficit target set by the Gramm-Rudman-Hollings law.

The budget was largely a reconfirmation of a two-year bargain sealed during a November 1987 "summit" between the Reagan White House and bipartisan leaders of Congress. The summit accord set hard numbers for three categories of federal spending — defense, international affairs and domestic programs. That left the Budget Committee

with the relatively inconsequential task of setting priorities among the various discretionary domestic spending programs.

Nevertheless, the process of crafting a budget resolution had important political consequences for the House Democratic leadership, which wanted to show it could produce a bipartisan agreement early in 1988. Early adoption of the budget cleared the way for the Appropriations Committee to begin marking up the 13 regular spending bills for fiscal 1989. And even though House and Senate Budget panels later bogged down over their differing versions of the budget, the appropriators were able to move their bills quickly through both chambers.

As a result, Congress managed to clear all 13 bills before the Oct. 1 start of the new fiscal year, a feat not achieved since 1976. It thus avoided the need for a catchall spending bill, or "continuing resolution," which had been used to keep the government operating for fiscal years 1986, 1987 and 1988.

## 4. Plant Closings

The notion that businesses should be required to warn their employees in advance of plant closings or mass layoffs became politically hot in 1988, after languishing in Congress for more than a decade. A first signal that the requirement could become law over the strong objections of President Reagan came April 21, when House Republicans forced a procedural vote on whether to strip the controversial requirement from omnibus trade legislation (HR 3).

With Reagan threatening to veto the big trade bill unless the plant-closing language was removed, GOP leaders hoped to show that they had enough allies among conservative Democrats to sustain the veto. But the plan backfired when Southern Democrats, generally cool to such labor-backed initiatives, split on the issue. The showdown vote came on a motion by Republican leader Robert H. Michel of Illinois to send the final version of the trade bill back to conference, with instructions to drop the notice requirement. The motion was rejected 167-253: R 144-29; D 23-224 (ND 0-168, SD 23-56).

House Democratic leaders had seized on the easily understood notice requirement, and the president's objections, to symbolize all they thought wrong with GOP economic policies. And the Democrats worked effectively with textile and oil interests to corral votes. The petroleum industry wanted the trade bill passed because another section would repeal the "windfall" tax on certain oil revenues. Their hunger for the tax repeal blunted anti-labor sentiment among Southwestern Democrats, as did textile lobbying among Southeastern Democrats.

Democratic strategists said later that by creating an extra vote, the GOP had given wavering members a chance to straddle the fence by voting against plant closing on the procedural motion, but for the trade bill — including the notice requirement — on final passage.

Another version of the trade bill (HR 4848 — PL 100-418) was later enacted without the plant-closing notice requirement, which also became law separately (S 2527 — PL 100-379). *(Senate key vote 10)*

## 5. Nuclear Test Ban

For the third year in a row, the House added to the annual defense authorization bill (HR 4264, S 2355) an amendment banning all nuclear test explosions with an explosive power greater than 1,000 tons of TNT.

A test ban long had been a priority goal of grass-roots arms control activists, who saw it as a first step toward a freeze on the testing, production and deployment of all nuclear weapons.

The test ban had gained powerful momentum in the House in 1986 because the Reagan administration appeared hostile to the very idea of trying to negotiate a comprehensive ban — a goal to which previous administrations had at least paid lip service.

But after passing the House in 1986 and 1987, despite strong White House opposition, the ban was rejected by the Senate and in the Senate-House conference on the annual defense bill — as happened again in 1988.

In 1988, the administration won back some of the members who had supported the test ban in 1987, because it was negotiating with the Soviets over modifications in two treaties signed in the mid-1970s but never ratified that would have limited underground nuclear explosions to the explosive power of 150,000 tons of TNT.

Nevertheless, the House again added the test ban to the defense authorization bill by a vote of 214-186: R 18-148; D 196-38 (ND 151-9, SD 45-29), April 28, 1988.

## 6. Strategic Defense Initiative

The hottest House battle in 1988 over the strategic defense initiative (SDI) — President Reagan's program to develop a nationwide anti-missile shield — focused on administration proposals for an interim anti-missile system designed to intercept only a fraction of the Soviet warheads that could be fired at the United States in an all-out attack.

Promoted by the administration as the first step toward a comprehensive anti-missile defense, this "phase one" deployment was derided by congressional critics as a militarily insignificant ploy to generate political momentum for SDI.

The proposed phase-one system would consist of a network of satellites, each carrying dozens of "space-based interceptors" or SBIs — small and relatively inexpensive heat-seeking missiles intended to home in on Soviet missiles in the first few minutes after their launch.

John M. Spratt Jr., D-S.C., led a small but influential group of centrist Democrats who were intrigued by the possibility of a "thin" anti-missile defense to guard against unauthorized missile launches by a rogue Soviet commander. But Spratt and his allies regarded SBIs as too expensive for their limited effectiveness and too easily nullified by Soviet countermeasures. Moreover, SBIs would violate the 1972 U.S.-Soviet treaty limiting anti-ballistic missile (ABM) weapons, whereas up to 100 ground-based anti-missile rockets could be deployed under the treaty.

Spratt offered an amendment slicing by nearly three-fourths the $350 million Reagan requested for SBIs. House adoption of Spratt's amendment was one factor cited by Reagan to justify his veto of the first fiscal 1989 defense authorization bill (HR 4264, S 2355), and the amendment was dropped from the second version (HR 4481 — PL 100-456). But initially, the House agreed to the SBI limitation by a vote of 244-174: R 27-146; D 217-28 (ND 163-2, SD 54-26), May 4, 1988.

## 7. Omnibus Trade Bill

The House demonstrated the broad political appeal of requiring employers to warn workers of plant closings and layoffs when it voted May 24 to override President Reagan's veto of a trade bill (HR 3) that included the notice requirement. Other strong factors in the vote were members' determination to salvage the massive trade bill, and the hunger of oil-state members for repeal of the so-called "windfall profits" tax on oil. Repeal was included in the omnibus trade measure.

The vote to override was 308-113: R 60-112; D 248-1 (ND 167-1, SD 81-0), substantially exceeding the two-thirds majority of members present and voting (281 in this case) required. The lone Democratic "nay" was not from a conservative Southerner, as might have been expected. It was instead cast by Robert J. Mrazek, N.Y., who represented a trade-sensitive district.

The override attempt ended unsuccessfully when the Senate subsequently failed to muster the necessary two-thirds majority of members present and voting. But congressional leaders subsequently separated the notice requirement from the trade measure and passed both bills a second time. With members of his own party pleading with him not to veto the plant-closing bill (S 2527), lest they suffer the political consequences, Reagan permitted it to become law (PL 100-379) on Aug. 4 without his signature. Reagan signed the modified trade bill (HR 4848 — PL 100-418) on Aug. 23. *(Senate key vote 10)*

## 8. Catastrophic Health Insurance

Congress successfully completed its top legislative priority in the health realm in June, approving the largest expansion of the federal Medicare program since its inception in 1965. But in the House, the vote on the catastrophic-insurance bill (HR 2470 — PL 100-360) was overshadowed by an impending decision the following week over what was likely to be the 101st Congress' biggest health headache — figuring out how to help the elderly pay the staggering costs of long-term care at home or in nursing homes.

President Reagan's endorsement of catastrophic health insurance in his 1986 State of the Union message put the issue firmly on the 100th Congress' agenda. But if the measure endorsed by Reagan in February 1987 was a light bulb, then the package approved by Congress was a full-fledged chandelier. The Reagan plan, the brainchild of Otis R. Bowen, secretary of health and human services, was a relatively modest proposal to cap the hospital and doctor's bills that the nation's 33 million Medicare beneficiaries would have to pay annually. HR 2470 did that — and a whole lot more. Among other things, it offered the first broad Medicare coverage for outpatient prescription drugs and for mammography examinations to detect breast cancer in women.

Tempering the enthusiasm for the bill somewhat was its financing mechanism, a combination of increased premiums for all beneficiaries and a "supplemental premium" — a surtax by another name — that would be charged the estimated 40 percent of beneficiaries with incomes high enough to owe federal income tax. But with Bowen's blessing, and with senior citizens' groups — led by the influential American Association of Retired Persons — firmly behind the bill, the conference report breezed through June 2 on a vote of 328-72: R 98-63; D 230-9 (ND 159-5, SD 71-4).

Among those who voted "nay," the most oft-expressed complaint was that the measure did little to help Medicare beneficiaries pay for long-term care. Just six days later, though, the House refused a chance to take up a long-term care measure (HR 3436) championed by Claude Pepper, D-Fla., chairman of the Rules Committee and superhero of the senior citizens' lobby. Members rejected by 169-243 a rule on the bill, which would have raised the Medicare tax to pay for long-term care at home. Although many supported the concept, members were skittish about the measure's estimated cost of some $28 billion over five years. Pepper also faced opposition from the powerful chairmen of the Ways and Means and Energy and Commerce committees, whose panels he had circumvented in seeking to bring HR 3436 to the floor. *(Senate key vote 11)*

## 9. NASA and Housing Aid

Congress in 1988 resembled a child chafing at the constraints of a strict allowance. Barred from defense-spending cuts by the two-year budget "summit" agreement reached in November 1987, Congress was forced to make tough choices among treasured domestic programs.

Never was its quandary better defined, nor its discomfort more apparent, than when the House June 22 had to choose between the space program and aid for the homeless and other domestic programs. After a heated debate in which both sides decried the process that led to such a fight, the space agency won by a wide margin. Its victory was due in part to a healthy dose of parochial interests.

The appropriations bill in question (HR 4800 — PL 100-404) seemed almost designed to prompt emotional disputes over priorities. Lumped in the same money pot with the government's most futuristic endeavors were some of its most noble social goals. The National Science Foundation and the National Aeronautics and Space Administration (NASA) vied against the Department of Housing and Urban Development (HUD), the Environmental Protection Agency (EPA) and the Veterans Administration (VA).

After agreeing in the budget summit to limit domestic spending increases to roughly 2 percent, President Reagan proposed putting nearly all $3.3 billion of the available money into science programs. Many appropriators at first balked, but it quickly became apparent that NASA's ambitious goals — a manned space station and a revitalized shuttle program — required a hefty increase.

Faced with intense pressure from the administration and Capitol Hill space advocates, the House Appropriations Committee gave NASA a large increase by limiting funding for the 1987 Stewart B. McKinney Homeless Assistance Act, the EPA and HUD.

Members of the Banking Committee's Housing Subcommittee led the charge to shift the bill's priorities. Charles E. Schumer, D-N.Y., offered an amendment to shift $400 million from NASA to a variety of programs and causes with wide support: the homeless, veterans, the elderly, EPA grants for construction of sewage-treatment plants and long-treasured Urban Development Action Grants. Although Schumer structured his amendment to protect the bill's nearly $1 billion for the space station, few believed the cut would leave it unscathed.

The debate featured emotional speeches on the plight of the poor and the promise of space. But in the end, Schumer's amendment was defeated 166-256: R 40-133; D 126-123 (ND 111-58, SD 15-65).

Its opponents built on a solid block of well over 100 members with state-based or committee-based interests. The Science Committee was nearly unanimously opposed, as were states that got substantial sums from NASA:

Texas, Florida, Alabama and Louisiana.

The vote provided momentum to keep the space station alive through a subsequent conference with the Senate, where the project had been shortchanged. It also gave Democratic space advocates badly needed fodder for a meeting two months later with a top presidential campaign aide to nominee Michael S. Dukakis, who had questioned the need for a manned space station. On Aug. 15 — long after presidential candidate George Bush announced that he was for it — Dukakis followed suit.

With White House support for a space station thus assured for at least four more years, and actual construction to begin in 1989, it appeared certain that the House's June 22 decision would be hard to reverse. *(Senate key vote 14)*

## 10. Fair Housing and Families

Congress cleared legislation in August that for the first time protected families with young children and individuals with handicaps from discrimination in housing.

A critical vote on the issue occurred June 23, when the House refused to delete a provision from the measure (HR 1158 — PL 100-430) that prohibited those who sell or rent homes from discriminating against families.

The vote was 116-289: R 95-73; D 21-216 (ND 11-150, SD 10-66). A "yea" was a vote supporting the president's position.

The provision exempted housing for older individuals, defining with some specificity what types of housing complexes could refuse to admit families with minor children. The provision was drafted with the help of senior citizens' organizations, but opponents, led by Rep. E. Clay Shaw Jr., R-Fla., said the section was unworkable and would put an end to senior citizens' housing.

In addition to its expanded anti-bias protections, HR 1158 created a new mechanism for enforcement of the 1968 Fair Housing Act, as amended. The bill in effect gave both complainants and housing owners a choice of resolving disputes through a new administrative-law-judge procedure within the Department of Housing and Urban Development or going to trial in federal court.

## 11. D.C. Funding and Abortions

On June 28, House members declared that the District of Columbia should not be allowed to use its own money to pay for abortions. That language, part of an amendment restricting the use of federal funds for abortion as well, was added to a fiscal 1989 D.C. appropriations bill (HR 4776 — PL 100-462) by a vote of 222-186: R 138-31; D 84-155 (ND 51-112, SD 33-43).

The vote opened the floodgates to what became the greatest intrusion on home rule since Congress first granted autonomy to the District in 1973. By the time the funding bill cleared Congress it was laden with congressional directives. For example, the District was given until Sept. 30, 1989, to scrap its requirement that D.C. employees must live in the city. Another provision exempted religious institutions, such as Jesuit-run Georgetown University, from a D.C. law prohibiting discrimination based on sexual preference.

The vote also sparked a showdown over abortion between Congress and the administration.

Since 1980, Congress had prohibited the District from using federal funds for abortions except in cases where the mother's life was in danger or the pregnancy resulted from rape or incest. But lawmakers had managed to rebuff the administration's attempts to extend that ban to city funds, defusing veto threats by rolling the D.C. appropriations into massive spending bills, known as continuing resolutions, which included funding for programs desired by the administration.

In 1988, however, with lawmakers vowing to pass each appropriations bill separately and on time, the D.C. bill had to stand alone. After days of conference negotiations during which lawmakers deadlocked several times over the abortion issue (the House had agreed to restrict city funds; the Senate had not), the House position prevailed.

President Reagan, aided by an election-year frenzy to be on the "right" side of issues, had defied his lame-duck status and prodded lawmakers to make already strict abortion funding rules even more stringent.

## 12. Welfare Overhaul

An initial display of bipartisanship in the 100th Congress' attempt to overhaul the nation's welfare system broke down by late 1987, when the House passed a $7 billion bill (HR 1720) by a relatively narrow 230-194 margin. Republicans and conservative Democrats considered the measure far too costly and disliked provisions in it that they felt made welfare too attractive.

The Senate on June 16 passed a far more modest, $2.8 billion measure (S 1511) by a 93-3 margin. That version included work and participation requirements stringent enough ultimately to gain a presidential endorsement.

The Senate's action gave House Republicans their opening, and on July 7, Hank Brown, R-Colo., ranking Republican on the Ways and Means subcommittee that wrote HR 1720, successfully pushed through a non-binding motion that ordered House conferees to move closer to the Senate bill.

By 227-168: R 162-4; D 65-164 (ND 24-130, SD 41-34), members instructed conferees to keep the final bill's five-year cost to no more than the Senate's $2.8 billion, and "to permit no impediments to work beyond those in the Senate" bill.

Despite that vote, and an even larger 249-130 margin Brown won on a Sept. 16 rerun of the same motion, the final bill (PL 100-485) carried a five-year price tag of $3.34 billion and a slightly watered-down work requirement. *(Senate key vote 13)*

## 13. Military Base Closings

The key to a bill intended to clear the way for the first large-scale disposal of obsolete or superfluous military bases in more than a decade was insulating the base-closing decisions from congressional interference.

Proponents of a change in the law argued that members whose constituents would be displaced by the closure of a base would always feel compelled to try to stop it. Moreover, they said, such members would be well positioned to call in their chits with other members to block the move, since no single closure would promise dramatic immediate savings.

To break that cycle of political protection, base-closing proponents, led by Dick Armey, R-Texas, proposed the establishment of an independent commission that would choose the bases to be closed — with no congressional interference permitted.

When the House took up the base-closing measure (HR 4481) in July, it added to the bill provisions that diluted the impact of Armey's proposal. These provisions also would have advanced the interests of certain congressional committees, or of members who wanted to protect specific bases.

But the magnitude of political support for the Armey concept was dramatically demonstrated by the unexpectedly large majority that approved an amendment intended to tilt the bill's procedures back toward the original concept. The amendment, by John R. Kasich, R-Ohio, provided that the bases nominated by the independent panel would be closed unless Congress adopted (and the president signed) a joint resolution to block all of the closures en bloc. Since the burden of initiating action would be on those opposed to the closures, Kasich argued, the odds would be against Congress blocking the list.

The amendment was adopted by a 250-138 vote: R 139-23; D 111-115 (ND 77-75, SD 34-40) on July 7, 1988.

Congress subsequently passed a new base-closing measure (S 2749), which was signed into law (PL 100-526) Oct. 24.

## 14. Reparations for Japanese-Americans

Forty-six years after the United States government removed Japanese-Americans from their homes and forced them into internment camps, Congress formally apologized to the 60,000 surviving internees and set up a $1.25 billion trust fund to provide them with tax-free payments of $20,000 apiece. Under the measure, the oldest former internees were to be paid first.

The House cleared the bill (HR 442) for the president on Aug. 4, adopting the conference report by a vote of 257-156: R 72-100; D 185-56 (ND 151-14, SD 34-42).

The Senate had approved the conference report by voice vote July 27.

The new law was an emotional milestone for Japanese-Americans, who had worked hard with their allies in Congress to get the legislation passed. Many Japanese-Americans lost homes and businesses that were left behind when they were ordered to internment camps and lived for decades with what a spokesman called the "stigma" of their internment.

The Japanese-Americans, many of them U.S. citizens, were ordered to camps in February 1942, after Japan had bombed Pearl Harbor Dec. 7, 1941. Opponents of the legislation said it was inappropriate to second-guess government decisions made during wartime. But proponents said the bill represented a long overdue acknowledgment of one of the most shameful episodes of U.S. history. A special government commission in 1982 concluded that the internment of Japanese-Americans was "not justified by military necessity," but was "shaped by race prejudice, war hysteria and a failure of political leadership." It was the commission's report that led to the legislation enacted in 1988.

Although President Reagan initially opposed HR 442, he signed the final version into law (PL 100-383) on Aug. 10.

## 15. Death Penalty

Reflecting election-year concerns about the spread of crime and drug abuse, the House Sept. 8 handily approved a death penalty for drug traffickers as part of an omnibus drug bill (HR 5210 — PL 100-690). The vote was 299-111:

R 161-9; D 138-102 (ND 70-93, SD 68-9).

Approval of the death penalty, which could be imposed on someone convicted of a killing in the course of a major drug transaction, set the stage for Senate approval of a similar measure in that chamber's version of the drug bill.

The House had included a death penalty in its drug bill in 1986, but the Senate refused to go along then. It was a different story in 1988, however, largely because Vice President George Bush had hammered on criminal justice issues in his race against Democratic presidential nominee Michael S. Dukakis. The death penalty, which Bush favored and Dukakis opposed, became something of a litmus test for toughness on crime.

While agreeing to the death penalty, the House also accepted a number of procedural amendments, later included in the final drug bill, to make sure that defendants in capital cases had adequate legal counsel and that juries were given proper instructions for considering whether to impose capital punishment. *(Senate key vote 12)*

## 16. Handgun Purchases

The National Rifle Association (NRA) proved that it still was a power on Capitol Hill when it launched a relentless and successful lobbying campaign against a national seven-day waiting period for the purchase of handguns.

The waiting period had been strongly supported by a coalition of the nation's law enforcement groups, the Law Enforcement Steering Committee. But the police groups were outspent and outmanned by the NRA.

On the critical vote Sept. 15 to strip the waiting-period provision from an omnibus anti-drug bill (HR 5210 — PL 100-690), the NRA forces prevailed 228-182: R 127-45; D 101-137 (ND 45-117, SD 56-20).

The vote came on an amendment to replace the waiting period with language proposed by Rep. Bill McCollum, R-Fla., to require the Justice Department to come up with a system enabling gun dealers to tell whether would-be gun buyers were convicted felons and thus ineligible, under existing law, to purchase handguns. Critics said technology was insufficient for such a system.

A revised version of the McCollum amendment was eventually included in the final drug bill. It gave the attorney general a year to prepare a system for identifying convicted felons and then gave Congress 30 days to approve it or block it.

The attorney general had 18 months to come up with another system for identifying other individuals, such as fugitives from justice and mental patients, who were barred from handgun ownership.

| ALABAMA | 1 | 2 | 3 | 4 | 5 | 6 | 7 | 8 |
|---|---|---|---|---|---|---|---|---|
| Heflin | N | ? | Y | Y | N | Y | Y | Y |
| Shelby | N | Y | Y | Y | N | N | Y | Y |
| **ALASKA** | | | | | | | | |
| *Murkowski* | N | Y | Y | Y | N | N | Y | Y |
| *Stevens* | ? | Y | Y | Y | N | N | Y | N |
| **ARIZONA** | | | | | | | | |
| DeConcini | Y | Y | Y | Y | N | Y | Y | Y |
| *McCain* | N | N | Y | Y | N | N | Y | Y |
| **ARKANSAS** | | | | | | | | |
| Bumpers | Y | Y | N | Y | N | Y | N | N |
| Pryor | Y | Y | N | Y | N | Y | N | N |
| **CALIFORNIA** | | | | | | | | |
| Cranston | Y | Y | N | Y | Y | Y | Y | N |
| *Wilson* | N | Y | N | Y | N | N | Y | Y |
| **COLORADO** | | | | | | | | |
| Wirth | Y | Y | N | Y | Y | Y | N | N |
| *Armstrong* | N | N | Y | N | N | N | Y | N |
| **CONNECTICUT** | | | | | | | | |
| Dodd | Y | Y | N | Y | Y | Y | Y | N |
| *Weicker* | N | Y | N | Y | Y | Y | Y | N |
| **DELAWARE** | | | | | | | | |
| Biden | ? | ? | ? | ? | ? | ? | ? | ? |
| *Roth* | N | Y | Y | Y | N | N | Y | N |
| **FLORIDA** | | | | | | | | |
| Chiles | Y | Y | N | Y | N | Y | Y | ? |
| Graham | Y | Y | N | Y | N | Y | Y | N |
| **GEORGIA** | | | | | | | | |
| Fowler | Y | Y | Y | Y | N | N | N | N |
| Nunn | Y | ? | Y | Y | N | Y | N | N |
| **HAWAII** | | | | | | | | |
| Inouye | Y | Y | N | Y | Y | Y | Y | N |
| Matsunaga | Y | ? | ? | Y | N | Y | N | N |
| **IDAHO** | | | | | | | | |
| *McClure* | N | N | Y | N | N | N | Y | Y |
| *Symms* | N | N | Y | N | ? | N | Y | Y |
| **ILLINOIS** | | | | | | | | |
| Dixon | Y | N | Y | Y | N | N | Y | Y |
| Simon | Y | ? | ? | Y | Y | Y | N | N |
| **INDIANA** | | | | | | | | |
| *Lugar* | N | Y | Y | N | N | N | Y | N |
| *Quayle* | N | N | Y | N | N | N | Y | Y |

| IOWA | 1 | 2 | 3 | 4 | 5 | 6 | 7 | 8 |
|---|---|---|---|---|---|---|---|---|
| Harkin | Y | Y | N | Y | N | Y | N | N |
| *Grassley* | N | Y | Y | Y | N | N | N | Y |
| **KANSAS** | | | | | | | | |
| *Dole* | ? | ? | Y | ? | N | N | Y | N |
| *Kassebaum* | Y | Y | Y | Y | N | N | Y | N |
| **KENTUCKY** | | | | | | | | |
| Ford | Y | Y | Y | Y | N | Y | N | Y |
| *McConnell* | N | Y | Y | N | N | N | Y | N |
| **LOUISIANA** | | | | | | | | |
| Breaux | Y | Y | Y | Y | N | Y | Y | Y |
| Johnston | Y | Y | Y | Y | N | Y | N | Y |
| **MAINE** | | | | | | | | |
| Mitchell | Y | Y | N | Y | N | Y | N | N |
| *Cohen* | N | Y | N | Y | N | N | N | N |
| **MARYLAND** | | | | | | | | |
| Mikulski | Y | Y | N | Y | N | Y | N | N |
| Sarbanes | Y | Y | N | Y | N | Y | N | N |
| **MASSACHUSETTS** | | | | | | | | |
| Kennedy | Y | Y | N | Y | Y | Y | N | N |
| Kerry | Y | Y | N | Y | Y | Y | N | N |
| **MICHIGAN** | | | | | | | | |
| Levin | Y | Y | N | Y | N | Y | N | N |
| Riegle | Y | Y | N | Y | N | Y | N | N |
| **MINNESOTA** | | | | | | | | |
| *Boschwitz* | N | Y | N | Y | N | N | Y | N |
| *Durenberger* | N | Y | N | Y | N | Y | Y | N |
| **MISSISSIPPI** | | | | | | | | |
| Stennis | Y | ? | ? | ? | ? | Y | ? | N |
| *Cochran* | ? | N | Y | N | N | N | Y | N |
| **MISSOURI** | | | | | | | | |
| *Bond* | N | ? | Y | Y | N | N | Y | N |
| *Danforth* | N | N | N | N | N | N | Y | N |
| **MONTANA** | | | | | | | | |
| Baucus | Y | Y | N | Y | N | Y | N | N |
| Melcher | Y | Y | N | Y | N | Y | N | N |
| **NEBRASKA** | | | | | | | | |
| Exon | Y | Y | Y | Y | N | N | Y | N |
| *Karnes* | N | Y | Y | N | ? | ? | ? | N |
| **NEVADA** | | | | | | | | |
| Reid | Y | Y | N | Y | N | N | N | N |
| *Hecht* | N | N | Y | N | N | N | ? | Y |

| NEW HAMPSHIRE | 1 | 2 | 3 | 4 | 5 | 6 | 7 | 8 |
|---|---|---|---|---|---|---|---|---|
| *Humphrey* | N | ? | N | N | N | N | Y | Y |
| *Rudman* | N | Y | Y | Y | N | N | Y | Y |
| **NEW JERSEY** | | | | | | | | |
| Bradley | Y | Y | N | Y | Y | Y | N | N |
| Lautenberg | Y | Y | N | Y | N | Y | N | N |
| **NEW MEXICO** | | | | | | | | |
| Bingaman | Y | Y | Y | Y | N | N | N | N |
| *Domenici* | N | Y | Y | Y | N | N | Y | N |
| **NEW YORK** | | | | | | | | |
| Moynihan | Y | Y | Y | Y | Y | Y | N | N |
| *D'Amato* | N | Y | Y | Y | N | N | Y | N |
| **NORTH CAROLINA** | | | | | | | | |
| Sanford | Y | Y | N | Y | Y | Y | N | ? |
| *Helms* | N | N | Y | N | N | N | Y | Y |
| **NORTH DAKOTA** | | | | | | | | |
| Burdick | Y | Y | Y | Y | N | Y | N | N |
| Conrad | Y | Y | N | Y | N | N | N | N |
| **OHIO** | | | | | | | | |
| Glenn | Y | Y | N | Y | N | Y | N | N |
| Metzenbaum | Y | Y | N | Y | N | N | N | N |
| **OKLAHOMA** | | | | | | | | |
| Boren | Y | Y | Y | Y | N | N | Y | N |
| *Nickles* | N | N | Y | N | N | N | Y | Y |
| **OREGON** | | | | | | | | |
| *Hatfield* | N | Y | N | Y | Y | Y | N | N |
| *Packwood* | N | Y | N | Y | N | Y | N | N |
| **PENNSYLVANIA** | | | | | | | | |
| *Heinz* | N | Y | Y | Y | Y | N | N | N |
| *Specter* | N | Y | Y | Y | Y | N | N | N |
| **RHODE ISLAND** | | | | | | | | |
| Pell | Y | Y | Y | Y | Y | Y | N | N |
| *Chafee* | Y | Y | N | Y | Y | Y | N | N |
| **SOUTH CAROLINA** | | | | | | | | |
| Hollings | Y | Y | Y | Y | N | N | Y | Y |
| *Thurmond* | N | Y | N | N | N | N | Y | N |
| **SOUTH DAKOTA** | | | | | | | | |
| Daschle | Y | Y | N | Y | N | Y | N | N |
| *Pressler* | N | N | Y | N | N | N | Y | Y |
| **TENNESSEE** | | | | | | | | |
| Gore | ? | + | ? | Y | Y | N | N | N |
| Sasser | Y | Y | Y | Y | N | Y | N | Y |

| TEXAS | 1 | 2 | 3 | 4 | 5 | 6 | 7 | 8 |
|---|---|---|---|---|---|---|---|---|
| Bentsen | Y | Y | Y | Y | N | Y | Y | N |
| *Gramm* | ? | N | Y | N | N | N | Y | Y |
| **UTAH** | | | | | | | | |
| *Garn* | N | N | Y | N | N | N | Y | Y |
| *Hatch* | N | N | Y | N | N | N | Y | Y |
| **VERMONT** | | | | | | | | |
| Leahy | Y | Y | N | Y | Y | Y | N | N |
| *Stafford* | Y | Y | ? | Y | Y | N | N | N |
| **VIRGINIA** | | | | | | | | |
| *Trible* | N | Y | Y | N | N | N | Y | N |
| *Warner* | N | Y | Y | N | N | N | Y | N |
| **WASHINGTON** | | | | | | | | |
| Adams | Y | Y | N | Y | Y | Y | N | N |
| *Evans* | N | Y | Y | Y | ? | Y | Y | N |
| **WEST VIRGINIA** | | | | | | | | |
| Byrd | Y | Y | N | Y | N | Y | N | Y |
| Rockefeller | Y | Y | N | Y | N | Y | N | N |
| **WISCONSIN** | | | | | | | | |
| Proxmire | Y | N | N | Y | Y | Y | N | N |
| *Kasten* | N | N | Y | Y | N | N | Y | Y |
| **WYOMING** | | | | | | | | |
| *Simpson* | N | N | Y | N | N | N | Y | N |
| *Wallop* | N | N | Y | N | N | N | Y | Y |

**KEY**

Y Voted for (yea).
\# Paired for.
+ Announced for.
N Voted against (nay).
X Paired against.
- Announced against.
P Voted "present."
C Voted "present" to avoid possible conflict of interest.
? Did not vote or otherwise make a position known.

Democrats    *Republicans*

ND - Northern Democrats    SD - Southern Democrats (Southern states - Ala., Ark., Fla., Ga., Ky., La., Miss., N.C., Okla., S.C., Tenn., Texas, Va.)

**1. S 2. Campaign Finance/Cloture.** Byrd, D-W.Va., motion to invoke cloture (thus limiting debate) on the bill to overhaul federal campaign finance law. S 2 would limit campaign spending and the role of political action committees in Senate elections. Motion rejected 53-41: R 3-39; D 50-2 (ND 35-0, SD 15-2), Feb. 26, 1988. A three-fifths majority vote (60) of the total Senate is required to invoke cloture.

**2. S 1721. Intelligence Oversight/Passage.** Passage of the bill to require the president to notify Congress of all covert activities. Under "ordinary circumstances," the president would be required to tell Intelligence committees in advance of a covert operation. But in "rare occasions when time is of the essence," the president could wait up to 48 hours after a covert activity begins. Passed 71-19: R 26-17; D 45-2 (ND 31-2, SD 14-0), March 15, 1988.

**3. HR 1414. Price-Anderson Amendments.** Johnston, D-La., motion to table (kill) the Metzenbaum, D-Ohio, amendment to require recovery of funds paid by the United States to a federal contractor for compensation of claims by accident victims, if the contractor is guilty of gross negligence or willful misconduct. Motion agreed to 53-41: R 35-10; D 18-31 (ND 7-26, SD 11-5), March 16, 1988. A "yea" was a vote supporting the president's position.

**4. S 557. Civil Rights Restoration Act/Veto Override.** Passage, over President Reagan's March 16 veto, of the bill to provide broad coverage of four civil rights laws by making clear that, if one entity of an institution receives federal funds, the entire institution must abide by the anti-discrimination laws. Passed 73-24: R 21-24; D 52-0 (ND 35-0, SD 17-0), March 22, 1988. A two-thirds majority of those present and voting (65 in this case) of both houses is required to override a veto. A "nay" was a vote supporting the president's position.

**5. S 1220. AIDS Research and Education/Restrictions on Information Activities.** Kennedy, D-Mass., motion to table (kill) the Helms, R-N.C., amendment to the Nickles, R-Okla., amendment. The Helms amendment would prohibit the use of funds authorized under the bill on activities that "promote or encourage, directly, homosexual sexual activity." Motion rejected 22-73: R 7-36; D 15-37 (ND 13-22, SD 2-15), April 28, 1988. (The underlying Nickles amendment, subsequently adopted by voice vote, would require that federally funded AIDS information and education programs warn that "homosexual and bisexual activities, multiple sex partners and intravenous drug use" place individuals at high risk of acquiring AIDS.)

**6. S 2355. Fiscal 1989 Defense Authorization/SDI Funding and NASA.** Exon, D-Neb., motion to reconsider the vote by which the Senate tabled (killed) the Johnston, D-La., amendment to provide that $700 million of the amount authorized for the strategic defense initiative (SDI) be used to reimburse NASA for some of the cost of restoring operation of the space shuttle. Motion rejected 48-50: R 6-39; D 42-11 (ND 30-5, SD 12-6), May 11, 1988. A nay was a vote supporting the president's position.

**7. S 2355. Fiscal 1989 Defense Authorization/SALT II Limits.** Nunn, D-Ga., motion to table (kill) the Bumpers, D-Ark., amendment to bar the deployment of multiple-warhead (MIRVed) intercontinental ballistic missiles, MIRVed ballistic missiles of any type, and MIRVed ballistic missiles plus bombers armed with long-range cruise missiles in excess of the number of each of those weapons categories that were deployed on Jan. 25, 1988. Motion agreed to 51-45: R 39-5; D 12-40 (ND 3-32, SD 9-8), May 11, 1988. A "yea" was a vote supporting the president's position.

**8. Treaty Doc 100-11. INF Treaty/Ground-Launched Cruise Missile Definition.** Hollings, D-S.C., amendment to provide that references in the intermediate-range nuclear-force (INF) treaty to ground-launched cruise missiles apply only to those with nuclear warheads. The treaty would ban missiles that carry either conventional or nuclear warheads. Rejected 28-69: R 18-28; D 10-41 (ND 3-32, SD 7-9), May 25, 1988.

| | 9 | 10 | 11 | 12 | 13 | 14 | 15 | 16 |
|---|---|---|---|---|---|---|---|---|
| **ALABAMA** | | | | | | | | |
| Heflin | Y | Y | Y | Y | N | N | Y | Y |
| Shelby | Y | Y | Y | Y | N | N | Y | N |
| **ALASKA** | | | | | | | | |
| *Murkowski* | N | N | Y | Y | N | N | N | N |
| *Stevens* | Y | N | Y | Y | N | N | N | N |
| **ARIZONA** | | | | | | | | |
| DeConcini | Y | Y | Y | Y | N | N | Y | Y |
| *McCain* | N | N | N | Y | N | N | N | N |
| **ARKANSAS** | | | | | | | | |
| Bumpers | Y | Y | Y | Y | N | N | Y | Y |
| Pryor | Y | Y | Y | Y | Y | N | Y | Y |
| **CALIFORNIA** | | | | | | | | |
| Cranston | Y | Y | Y | N | Y | N | Y | Y |
| *Wilson* | N | N | Y | Y | N | N | N | ? |
| **COLORADO** | | | | | | | | |
| Wirth | Y | Y | Y | N | Y | N | Y | Y |
| *Armstrong* | N | N | N | Y | N | N | N | N |
| **CONNECTICUT** | | | | | | | | |
| Dodd | Y | Y | Y | Y | Y | Y | Y | Y |
| *Weicker* | Y | Y | Y | N | Y | Y | - | Y |
| **DELAWARE** | | | | | | | | |
| Biden | ? | ? | ? | ? | ? | ? | ? | Y |
| *Roth* | Y | Y | N | Y | N | N | N | Y |
| **FLORIDA** | | | | | | | | |
| Chiles | Y | Y | + | ? | Y | N | Y | ? |
| Graham | Y | Y | Y | Y | Y | N | Y | Y |
| **GEORGIA** | | | | | | | | |
| Fowler | Y | Y | Y | N | Y | Y | Y | Y |
| Nunn | Y | Y | Y | N | N | N | Y | Y |
| **HAWAII** | | | | | | | | |
| Inouye | Y | Y | Y | N | Y | Y | Y | Y |
| Matsunaga | Y | Y | Y | N | Y | N | Y | Y |
| **IDAHO** | | | | | | | | |
| *McClure* | N | N | N | Y | ? | N | N | ? |
| *Symms* | N | N | N | Y | N | N | N | N |
| **ILLINOIS** | | | | | | | | |
| Dixon | Y | Y | Y | N | Y | N | Y | Y |
| Simon | Y | Y | Y | N | Y | Y | Y | Y |
| **INDIANA** | | | | | | | | |
| *Lugar* | Y | N | Y | Y | N | N | N | N |
| *Quayle* | N | N | Y | Y | N | N | N | ? |

| | 9 | 10 | 11 | 12 | 13 | 14 | 15 | 16 |
|---|---|---|---|---|---|---|---|---|
| **IOWA** | | | | | | | | |
| Harkin | Y | Y | Y | N | Y | Y | Y | Y |
| *Grassley* | N | N | Y | Y | N | Y | N | N |
| **KANSAS** | | | | | | | | |
| *Dole* | Y | N | Y | Y | N | N | N | N |
| *Kassebaum* | Y | N | N | Y | N | N | N | N |
| **KENTUCKY** | | | | | | | | |
| Ford | Y | Y | Y | Y | Y | N | Y | Y |
| *McConnell* | N | N | Y | Y | N | N | N | N |
| **LOUISIANA** | | | | | | | | |
| Breaux | Y | Y | Y | Y | Y | N | Y | Y |
| Johnston | Y | Y | Y | Y | Y | N | Y | Y |
| **MAINE** | | | | | | | | |
| Mitchell | Y | Y | Y | N | Y | Y | Y | Y |
| *Cohen* | Y | Y | Y | ? | N | Y | N | N |
| **MARYLAND** | | | | | | | | |
| Mikulski | Y | Y | Y | N | Y | Y | Y | Y |
| Sarbanes | Y | Y | Y | Y | Y | Y | Y | Y |
| **MASSACHUSETTS** | | | | | | | | |
| Kennedy | Y | Y | Y | N | Y | Y | Y | Y |
| Kerry | Y | Y | Y | N | Y | Y | Y | Y |
| **MICHIGAN** | | | | | | | | |
| Levin | Y | Y | Y | N | ? | Y | Y | Y |
| Riegle | Y | Y | Y | Y | Y | N | Y | Y |
| **MINNESOTA** | | | | | | | | |
| *Boschwitz* | N | N | Y | Y | N | N | N | N |
| *Durenberger* | Y | Y | Y | N | ? | Y | N | N |
| **MISSISSIPPI** | | | | | | | | |
| Stennis | Y | Y | Y | N | Y | N | Y | Y |
| *Cochran* | Y | N | Y | Y | N | ? | N | N |
| **MISSOURI** | | | | | | | | |
| *Bond* | N | Y | Y | Y | N | N | N | N |
| *Danforth* | N | Y | Y | N | N | N | N | N |
| **MONTANA** | | | | | | | | |
| Baucus | Y | Y | Y | Y | Y | N | Y | Y |
| Melcher | Y | Y | Y | N | Y | N | Y | Y |
| **NEBRASKA** | | | | | | | | |
| Exon | Y | Y | Y | N | Y | N | Y | N |
| *Karnes* | N | N | Y | N | N | N | N | N |
| **NEVADA** | | | | | | | | |
| Reid | Y | Y | Y | N | N | N | Y | Y |
| *Hecht* | N | N | Y | Y | ? | N | N | ? |

| | 9 | 10 | 11 | 12 | 13 | 14 | 15 | 16 |
|---|---|---|---|---|---|---|---|---|
| **NEW HAMPSHIRE** | | | | | | | | |
| *Humphrey* | N | N | N | ? | N | N | N | N |
| *Rudman* | N | N | Y | N | N | N | N | N |
| **NEW JERSEY** | | | | | | | | |
| Bradley | Y | Y | Y | Y | Y | Y | Y | ? |
| Lautenberg | Y | Y | Y | N | Y | Y | Y | Y |
| **NEW MEXICO** | | | | | | | | |
| Bingaman | Y | Y | Y | Y | Y | N | Y | Y |
| *Domenici* | N | N | Y | N | N | N | N | N |
| **NEW YORK** | | | | | | | | |
| Moynihan | Y | Y | Y | Y | Y | Y | Y | Y |
| *D'Amato* | N | N | Y | N | Y | N | N | N |
| **NORTH CAROLINA** | | | | | | | | |
| Sanford | Y | Y | Y | N | Y | Y | Y | Y |
| *Helms* | Y | N | N | Y | N | ? | N | N |
| **NORTH DAKOTA** | | | | | | | | |
| Burdick | Y | Y | Y | N | Y | N | Y | Y |
| Conrad | Y | Y | Y | N | Y | N | Y | Y |
| **OHIO** | | | | | | | | |
| Glenn | ? | Y | Y | N | Y | N | Y | Y |
| Metzenbaum | ? | Y | Y | Y | Y | Y | Y | Y |
| **OKLAHOMA** | | | | | | | | |
| Boren | Y | Y | Y | N | Y | N | Y | N |
| *Nickles* | N | Y | N | Y | N | N | N | N |
| **OREGON** | | | | | | | | |
| *Hatfield* | Y | N | Y | N | N | N | N | Y |
| *Packwood* | N | Y | Y | N | N | N | N | Y |
| **PENNSYLVANIA** | | | | | | | | |
| *Heinz* | N | Y | Y | N | Y | N | Y | Y |
| *Specter* | N | ? | ? | Y | N | Y | N | Y |
| **RHODE ISLAND** | | | | | | | | |
| Pell | Y | Y | Y | N | Y | Y | Y | Y |
| *Chafee* | Y | Y | Y | N | Y | N | Y | Y |
| **SOUTH CAROLINA** | | | | | | | | |
| Hollings | Y | Y | Y | Y | Y | N | Y | Y |
| *Thurmond* | N | N | Y | Y | N | N | N | N |
| **SOUTH DAKOTA** | | | | | | | | |
| Daschle | Y | Y | Y | Y | Y | Y | Y | Y |
| *Pressler* | N | N | Y | Y | N | N | N | N |
| **TENNESSEE** | | | | | | | | |
| Gore | Y | Y | Y | N | N | N | Y | Y |
| Sasser | Y | Y | Y | Y | Y | Y | Y | Y |

| | 9 | 10 | 11 | 12 | 13 | 14 | 15 | 16 |
|---|---|---|---|---|---|---|---|---|
| **TEXAS** | | | | | | | | |
| Bentsen | Y | Y | Y | Y | N | ? | Y | ? |
| *Gramm* | N | N | N | ? | N | N | N | ? |
| **UTAH** | | | | | | | | |
| *Garn* | N | N | N | Y | N | N | N | N |
| *Hatch* | N | N | Y | Y | N | N | N | N |
| **VERMONT** | | | | | | | | |
| Leahy | Y | Y | Y | N | Y | Y | Y | N |
| *Stafford* | Y | N | Y | N | N | N | N | Y |
| **VIRGINIA** | | | | | | | | |
| *Trible* | N | N | Y | N | N | N | N | N |
| *Warner* | N | N | Y | N | N | N | N | N |
| **WASHINGTON** | | | | | | | | |
| Adams | Y | Y | Y | ? | Y | Y | N | Y |
| Evans | N | N | Y | N | Y | N | N | N |
| **WEST VIRGINIA** | | | | | | | | |
| Byrd | Y | N | Y | N | Y | Y | Y | Y |
| Rockefeller | Y | Y | Y | N | Y | Y | Y | Y |
| **WISCONSIN** | | | | | | | | |
| Proxmire | Y | N | Y | N | N | N | N | Y |
| *Kasten* | N | N | Y | Y | N | Y | - | N |
| **WYOMING** | | | | | | | | |
| *Simpson* | N | N | Y | Y | N | N | N | N |
| *Wallop* | N | N | Y | N | N | N | N | ? |

ND - Northern Democrats    SD - Southern Democrats (Southern states - Ala., Ark., Fla., Ga., Ky., La., Miss., N.C., Okla., S.C., Tenn., Texas, Va.)

**9. Treaty Doc 100-11. INF Treaty/Treaty Interpretation.** Byrd, D-W.Va., motion to table (kill) the Specter, R-Pa., amendment to reverse the thrust of a previously passed amendment, which barred reinterpretation of a treaty without Senate approval, by stating that the Senate did not intend to alter existing international or constitutional law. Motion agreed to 64-33: R 13-33; D 51-0 (ND 33-0, SD 18-0), May 27, 1988.

**10. HR 3. Omnibus Trade Bill/Veto Override.** Passage, over President Reagan's May 24 veto, of the bill to revise statutory procedures for dealing with unfair foreign trade practices and import damage to U.S. industries, to clarify the law against business-related bribes abroad by U.S. businesses, to streamline controls on militarily sensitive exports, to revise agriculture and education programs, to repeal the windfall-profits tax on oil and to require certain employers to provide workers with 60 days' notice of plant closings or layoffs. Rejected 61-37: R 10-35; D 51-2 (ND 33-2, SD 18-0), June 8, 1988. A two-thirds majority of those present and voting (66 in this case) of both houses is required to override a veto. (The House overrode the veto May 24.) A "nay" was a vote supporting the president's position.

**11. HR 2470. Catastrophic Health Insurance/Conference Report.** Adoption of the conference report on the bill (thus clearing the measure for the president) to cap the amounts for which Medicare beneficiaries will be financially liable for Medicare-covered services and to make other changes in the program. Adopted 86-11: R 34-11; D 52-0 (ND 35-0, SD 17-0), June 8, 1988.

**12. S 2455. Death Penalty for Drug-Related Killings/Passage.** Passage of the bill to allow the death penalty for "drug kingpins" who intentionally kill or who order a killing. The bill would provide a separate hearing before a judge or jury on the issue of punishment, where the judge or jury would have to weigh aggravating and mitigating circumstances before determining whether the death penalty was appropriate. The jury would have to be unanimous in imposing the death penalty. Passed 65-29: R 37-6; D 28-23 (ND 15-19, SD 13-4), June 10, 1988. A "yea" was a vote supporting the president's position.

**13. S 1511. Welfare Reform/'Workfare' Amendment.** Moynihan, D-N.Y., motion to table (kill) the Dole, R-Kan., amendment to require that by 1994, states require at least one parent in two-parent families receiving welfare to work a minimum of 16 hours per week in either unpaid community work experience or subsidized jobs. Motion rejected 41-54: R 3-40; D 38-14 (ND 27-7, SD 11-7), June 16, 1988. A "nay" was a vote supporting the president's position.

**14. HR 4800. Fiscal 1989 HUD Appropriations/NASA and UDAG Program.** Heinz, R-Pa., amendment to shift $30 million from NASA to the Urban Development Action Grant (UDAG) program. Rejected 34-63: R 9-36; D 25-27 (ND 21-14, SD 4-13), July 12, 1988.

**15. HR 4781. Fiscal 1989 Defense Appropriations/Contra Aid.** Byrd, D-W.Va., perfecting amendment to make technical changes to his own amendment to authorize $27.14 million in humanitarian aid to the Nicaraguan contras and to establish procedures for congressional consideration of a request by the president for authority to release up to $16.5 million worth of stockpiled military aid to the contras as well. Adopted 49-47: R 0-43; D 49-4 (ND 31-4, SD 18-0), Aug. 10, 1988.

**16. S 837. Minimum-Wage Restoration/Cloture.** Kennedy, D-Mass., motion to invoke cloture (thus limiting debate) on the bill to raise the minimum wage to $4.55 an hour over three years, from $3.35. Motion rejected 56-35: R 8-32; D 48-3 (ND 34-1, SD 14-2), Sept. 23, 1988. A three-fifths majority vote (60) of the total Senate is required to invoke cloture.

# Appendix

**1. H J Res 444. Contra Aid/Passage.** Passage of the joint resolution to approve President Reagan's request of $36.25 million for continued military and non-military aid to the Nicaraguan contras. Rejected 211-219: R 164-12; D 47-207 (ND 6-166, SD 41-41), Feb. 3, 1988. A "yea" was a vote supporting the president's position.

**2. S 557. Civil Rights Restoration Act/Veto Override.** Passage, over President Reagan's March 16 veto, of the bill to provide broad coverage of four civil rights laws by making clear that, if one entity of an institution receives federal funds, the entire institution must abide by the anti-discrimination laws. Passed (thus enacted into law) 292-133: R 52-123; D 240-10 (ND 167-1, SD 73-9), March 22, 1988. A two-thirds majority of those present and voting (284 in this case) of both houses is required to override a veto. A "nay" was a vote supporting the president's position.

**3. H Con Res 268. Fiscal 1989 Budget Resolution/Adoption.** Adoption of the concurrent resolution to set forth the congressional budget for the U.S. government for fiscal 1989, 1990 and 1991. The resolution sets fiscal 1989 ceilings of $1.2321 trillion in total new budget authority and $1.0982 trillion in total outlays; establishes a revenue floor of $964.1 billion, with an expected deficit of $134.1 billion; assumes savings of $6.8 billion, a 3 percent pay increase for military and civilian federal employees; and recommends general spending levels for the various functions of government. Adopted 319-102: R 92-78; D 227-24 (ND 152-17, SD 75-7), March 23, 1988.

**4. HR 3. Omnibus Trade Bill/Plant Closings.** Michel, R-Ill., motion to recommit to the conference committee the conference report on the bill, with instructions to eliminate the requirement to provide workers with 60 days' notice of plant closings or layoffs. (Recommittal of a conference report would permit conferees to reconsider any provision in the legislation.) Motion rejected 167-253: R 144-29; D 23-224 (ND 0-168, SD 23-56), April 21, 1988.

**5. HR 4264. Fiscal 1989 Defense Authorization/Nuclear Testing Ban.** Gephardt, D-Mo., amendment to ban nuclear tests with an explosive power greater than one kiloton and tests conducted outside of designated test areas, if the Soviet Union observes the same ban. Adopted 214-186: R 18-148; D 196-38 (ND 151-9, SD 45-29), April 28, 1988. A "nay" was a vote supporting the president's position.

**6. HR 4264. Fiscal 1989 Defense Authorization/SDI Funding.** Spratt, D-S.C., amendment to provide that no more than 40 percent of the funds authorized for the strategic defense initiative (SDI) can be used for the "phase one" version using current technology. Adopted 244-174: R 27-146; D 217-28 (ND 163-2, SD 54-26), May 4, 1988. A "nay" was a vote supporting the president's position.

**7. HR 3. Omnibus Trade Bill/Veto Override.** Passage, over President Reagan's May 24 veto, of the bill to revise statutory procedures for dealing with unfair foreign trade practices and import damage to U.S. industries, to clarify the law against business-related bribes abroad by U.S. businesses, to streamline controls on militarily sensitive exports, to revise agriculture and education programs, to repeal the windfall-profits tax on oil and to require certain employers to provide workers with 60 days' notice of plant closings or layoffs. Passed 308-113: R 60-112; D 248-1 (ND 167-1, SD 81-0), May 24, 1988. A two-thirds majority of those present and voting (281 in this case) of both houses is required to override a veto. A "nay" was a vote supporting the president's position.

**8. HR 2470. Catastrophic Health Insurance/Conference Report.** Adoption of the conference report on the bill to cap the amounts for which Medicare beneficiaries will be financially liable for Medicare-covered services and to make other changes in the program. Adopted 328-72: R 98-63; D 230-9 (ND 159-5, SD 71-4), June 2, 1988.

---

[1] *Rep. Melvin Price, D-Ill., died April 22, 1988.*
[2] *Rep. Jim McCrery, R-La., was sworn in April 26, 1988, to succeed Buddy Roemer, D, who resigned March 14, 1988, to become governor of Louisiana.*
[3] *Rep. James J. Howard, D-N.J., died March 25, 1988.*
[4] *Rep. Mario Biaggi, D-N.Y., resigned Aug. 8, 1988.*
[5] *Rep. John J. Duncan, R-Tenn., died June 21, 1988.*
[6] *Rep. Dan Daniel, D-Va., died Jan. 23, 1988.*

## KEY

Y Voted for (yea).
# Paired for.
+ Announced for.
N Voted against (nay).
X Paired against.
- Announced against.
P Voted "present."
C Voted "present" to avoid possible conflict of interest.
? Did not vote or otherwise make a position known.

Democrats   *Republicans*

| | 1 | 2 | 3 | 4 | 5 | 6 | 7 | 8 |
|---|---|---|---|---|---|---|---|---|
| **ALABAMA** | | | | | | | | |
| 1 *Callahan* | Y | N | Y | Y | N | N | N | Y |
| 2 *Dickinson* | Y | N | Y | N | N | N | N | Y |
| 3 Nichols | Y | Y | Y | N | N | N | Y | ? |
| 4 Bevill | Y | Y | Y | N | ? | N | Y | Y |
| 5 Flippo | Y | Y | Y | N | N | Y | ? | Y |
| 6 Erdreich | Y | Y | Y | N | N | Y | Y | Y |
| 7 Harris | Y | Y | Y | Y | N | N | Y | Y |
| **ALASKA** | | | | | | | | |
| AL *Young* | Y | Y | Y | N | N | N | N | ? |
| **ARIZONA** | | | | | | | | |
| 1 *Rhodes* | Y | N | Y | Y | N | N | N | N |
| 2 Udall | N | Y | Y | N | Y | ? | Y | Y |
| 3 *Stump* | Y | N | N | Y | N | N | N | N |
| 4 *Kyl* | Y | N | N | Y | N | ? | N | N |
| 5 *Kolbe* | Y | Y | N | Y | N | N | N | N |
| **ARKANSAS** | | | | | | | | |
| 1 Alexander | N | Y | Y | N | Y | Y | Y | Y |
| 2 Robinson | Y | Y | N | N | N | N | Y | Y |
| 3 *Hammerschmidt* | Y | N | Y | N | N | N | N | Y |
| 4 Anthony | N | Y | Y | N | Y | Y | Y | Y |
| **CALIFORNIA** | | | | | | | | |
| 1 Bosco | N | Y | Y | N | Y | Y | Y | Y |
| 2 *Herger* | Y | N | N | Y | N | N | N | Y |
| 3 Matsui | N | Y | Y | N | Y | Y | Y | Y |
| 4 Fazio | N | Y | Y | N | Y | Y | Y | Y |
| 5 Pelosi | N | Y | Y | N | Y | Y | Y | Y |
| 6 Boxer | N | Y | Y | N | Y | Y | Y | Y |
| 7 Miller | N | Y | Y | N | Y | # | Y | Y |
| 8 Dellums | N | Y | Y | N | Y | Y | Y | Y |
| 9 Stark | N | Y | Y | N | Y | Y | Y | Y |
| 10 Edwards | N | Y | Y | N | Y | Y | Y | Y |
| 11 Lantos | N | Y | Y | N | Y | Y | Y | Y |
| 12 *Konnyu* | Y | N | N | Y | N | N | N | ? |
| 13 Mineta | N | Y | Y | N | Y | Y | Y | Y |
| 14 *Shumway* | Y | N | N | Y | N | N | N | N |
| 15 Coelho | N | Y | Y | N | Y | Y | Y | Y |
| 16 Panetta | N | Y | Y | N | Y | Y | Y | Y |
| 17 *Pashayan* | Y | Y | Y | N | N | N | Y | Y |
| 18 Lehman | N | Y | Y | N | Y | Y | Y | Y |
| 19 *Lagomarsino* | Y | N | Y | N | N | N | N | Y |
| 20 *Thomas* | Y | N | Y | Y | X | N | # | N |
| 21 *Gallegly* | Y | N | N | Y | N | N | N | N |
| 22 *Moorhead* | Y | N | N | Y | N | N | N | N |
| 23 Beilenson | N | Y | Y | N | Y | Y | Y | N |
| 24 Waxman | N | Y | Y | N | Y | Y | Y | Y |
| 25 Roybal | N | Y | Y | N | Y | Y | Y | Y |
| 26 Berman | N | Y | Y | N | Y | Y | Y | Y |
| 27 Levine | N | Y | Y | N | Y | Y | Y | Y |
| 28 Dixon | N | Y | Y | N | Y | Y | Y | Y |
| 29 Hawkins | N | Y | Y | N | Y | # | Y | Y |
| 30 Martinez | N | ? | Y | N | Y | Y | Y | Y |
| 31 Dymally | N | Y | Y | ? | Y | Y | Y | Y |
| 32 Anderson | N | Y | Y | N | Y | Y | Y | Y |
| 33 *Dreier* | Y | N | N | Y | N | N | N | N |
| 34 Torres | N | Y | Y | N | Y | Y | Y | Y |
| 35 *Lewis* | Y | N | Y | Y | ? | N | N | # |
| 36 Brown | N | Y | Y | N | Y | Y | Y | Y |
| 37 *McCandless* | Y | N | Y | N | N | N | N | N |
| 38 *Dornan* | Y | N | N | Y | N | N | N | N |
| 39 *Dannemeyer* | Y | N | N | Y | N | N | N | N |
| 40 *Badham* | Y | N | Y | X | X | N | - | ? |
| 41 *Lowery* | Y | N | N | Y | N | N | Y | Y |
| 42 *Lungren* | Y | Y | N | Y | ? | N | N | N |

| | 1 | 2 | 3 | 4 | 5 | 6 | 7 | 8 |
|---|---|---|---|---|---|---|---|---|
| 43 *Packard* | Y | N | Y | Y | N | N | N | Y |
| 44 Bates | N | Y | Y | N | Y | Y | Y | Y |
| 45 *Hunter* | Y | N | N | Y | N | N | N | N |
| **COLORADO** | | | | | | | | |
| 1 Schroeder | N | Y | Y | N | Y | Y | Y | Y |
| 2 Skaggs | N | Y | Y | N | Y | Y | Y | Y |
| 3 Campbell | N | Y | Y | N | Y | Y | Y | ? |
| 4 *Brown* | Y | Y | N | Y | N | N | N | N |
| 5 *Hefley* | Y | N | N | Y | N | N | N | N |
| 6 *Schaefer* | Y | N | N | N | N | N | N | Y |
| **CONNECTICUT** | | | | | | | | |
| 1 Kennelly | N | Y | Y | N | Y | Y | Y | Y |
| 2 Gejdenson | N | Y | Y | N | Y | Y | Y | Y |
| 3 Morrison | N | Y | Y | N | Y | Y | Y | Y |
| 4 *Shays* | N | N | Y | N | Y | Y | Y | Y |
| 5 *Rowland* | Y | Y | Y | N | N | N | N | N |
| 6 *Johnson* | Y | Y | Y | N | N | Y | N | Y |
| **DELAWARE** | | | | | | | | |
| AL Carper | N | Y | N | N | Y | Y | Y | N |
| **FLORIDA** | | | | | | | | |
| 1 Hutto | Y | N | Y | N | N | N | Y | Y |
| 2 Grant | Y | Y | Y | N | N | Y | Y | Y |
| 3 Bennett | Y | Y | Y | N | Y | Y | Y | Y |
| 4 Chappell | Y | Y | Y | Y | N | N | Y | Y |
| 5 *McCollum* | Y | N | Y | N | N | N | N | N |
| 6 MacKay | N | Y | Y | N | Y | Y | Y | Y |
| 7 Gibbons | Y | Y | Y | N | Y | N | Y | Y |
| 8 *Young* | Y | N | Y | N | N | N | N | N |
| 9 *Bilirakis* | Y | N | Y | N | N | N | N | Y |
| 10 *Ireland* | Y | N | N | Y | N | N | N | N |
| 11 Nelson | Y | Y | Y | N | N | N | Y | Y |
| 12 *Lewis* | Y | N | Y | N | N | N | N | N |
| 13 *Mack* | Y | N | Y | X | N | N | N | Y |
| 14 Mica | N | Y | Y | N | ? | ? | Y | Y |
| 15 *Shaw* | Y | N | # | Y | N | N | N | N |
| 16 Smith | Y | Y | Y | N | Y | Y | Y | Y |
| 17 Lehman | N | Y | Y | N | Y | Y | Y | Y |
| 18 Pepper | Y | Y | Y | N | Y | Y | Y | Y |
| 19 Fascell | Y | Y | Y | N | Y | Y | Y | Y |
| **GEORGIA** | | | | | | | | |
| 1 Thomas | Y | Y | Y | Y | N | N | Y | Y |
| 2 Hatcher | Y | Y | Y | N | N | N | Y | Y |
| 3 Ray | Y | N | Y | ? | ? | ? | Y | X |
| 4 *Swindall* | Y | N | N | Y | N | N | N | N |
| 5 Lewis | N | Y | Y | N | Y | Y | Y | Y |
| 6 *Gingrich* | Y | N | N | Y | N | N | N | N |
| 7 Darden | Y | Y | Y | N | N | N | Y | Y |
| 8 Rowland | N | N | Y | Y | N | Y | Y | Y |
| 9 Jenkins | Y | Y | Y | Y | N | Y | Y | Y |
| 10 Barnard | Y | N | Y | ? | N | N | Y | N |
| **HAWAII** | | | | | | | | |
| 1 *Saiki* | Y | Y | Y | Y | N | Y | Y | Y |
| 2 Akaka | N | Y | Y | N | Y | Y | Y | Y |
| **IDAHO** | | | | | | | | |
| 1 *Craig* | Y | N | N | Y | X | N | N | N |
| 2 Stallings | N | Y | Y | N | ? | Y | Y | Y |
| **ILLINOIS** | | | | | | | | |
| 1 Hayes | N | Y | Y | N | Y | Y | Y | Y |
| 2 Savage | N | Y | Y | N | Y | Y | Y | Y |
| 3 Russo | N | N | Y | N | Y | Y | Y | Y |
| 4 *Davis* | Y | N | X | N | N | N | N | N |
| 5 Lipinski | Y | Y | Y | N | N | N | Y | Y |
| 6 *Hyde* | Y | N | Y | N | N | N | N | Y |
| 7 Collins | N | Y | Y | N | Y | Y | Y | Y |
| 8 Rostenkowski | N | Y | Y | N | ? | Y | Y | Y |
| 9 Yates | N | Y | N | ? | ? | Y | Y | Y |
| 10 *Porter* | Y | Y | N | Y | N | N | Y | Y |
| 11 Annunzio | N | Y | Y | N | Y | Y | Y | Y |
| 12 *Crane* | Y | N | N | Y | N | N | N | N |
| 13 *Fawell* | Y | N | N | Y | N | N | N | N |
| 14 *Hastert* | Y | N | Y | N | N | N | N | N |
| 15 *Madigan* | Y | ? | ? | Y | N | N | N | Y |
| 16 *Martin* | Y | N | Y | N | N | N | N | Y |
| 17 Evans | N | Y | Y | N | Y | Y | Y | Y |
| 18 *Michel* | Y | N | Y | N | N | N | N | N |
| 19 Bruce | N | Y | Y | N | Y | Y | Y | Y |
| 20 Durbin | N | Y | Y | N | Y | Y | Y | Y |
| 21 Price [1] | N | ? | ? | ? | | | | |
| 22 Gray | N | ? | ? | N | Y | Y | Y | Y |
| **INDIANA** | | | | | | | | |
| 1 Visclosky | N | N | N | N | Y | Y | Y | Y |
| 2 Sharp | N | Y | Y | N | Y | Y | Y | Y |
| 3 *Hiler* | Y | N | Y | N | N | N | N | Y |
| 4 *Coats* | Y | N | N | N | N | N | N | N |
| 5 Jontz | N | Y | Y | N | Y | Y | Y | Y |

ND - Northern Democrats    SD - Southern Democrats

generally; registration and licensing of vessels; rules and international arrangements to prevent collisions at sea; international fishing agreements; Coast Guard and Merchant Marine academies and state maritime academies.

### D 25 - R 17

Walter B. Jones, N.C. (1981-89)
*Norman F. Lent, N.Y. (resigned post in July 1986)*
*Robert W. Davis, Mich. (through 100th Congress)*

**Coast Guard and Navigation** — Gerry E. Studds, Mass. (99th Congress); Earl Hutto, Fla. (100th Congress)
**Fisheries and Wildlife Conservation and the Environment** — John B. Breaux, La. (99th Congress); Gerry E. Studds, Mass. (100th Congress)
**Merchant Marine** — Mario Biaggi, N.Y. (99th Congress; indicted March 16, 1987, and required to step down from chairmanship); Glenn M. Anderson, Calif. (acting chairman, resigned post in 100th Congress); Walter B. Jones, N.C. (through 100th Congress)
**Oceanography** — Barbara A. Mikulski, Md. (99th Congress); Mike Lowry, Wash. (100th Congress)
**Oversight and Investigations** — Walter B. Jones, N.C. (resigned post in 100th Congress); Thomas M. Foglietta, Pa. (through 100th Congress)
**Panama Canal/Outer Continental Shelf** — Mike Lowry, Wash. (99th Congress); W. J. "Billy" Tauzin, La. (100th Congress)

## Post Office and Civil Service

Postal and federal civil services; census and the collection of statistics generally; Hatch Act; holidays and celebrations.

### D 13 - R 8

William D. Ford, Mich. (1981-89)
*Gene Taylor, Mo.*

**Census and Population** — Robert Garcia, N.Y. (99th Congress); Mervyn M. Dymally, Calif. (100th Congress)
**Civil Service** — Patricia Schroeder, Colo.
**Compensation and Employee Benefits** — Mary Rose Oakar, Ohio (99th Congress); Gary L. Ackerman, N.Y. (100th Congress)
**Human Resources** — Gary L. Ackerman, N.Y. (99th Congress); Gerry Sikorski, Minn. (100th Congress)
**Investigations** — Gerry Sikorski, Minn. (99th Congress); William D. Ford, Mich. (100th Congress)
**Postal Operations and Services** — Mickey Leland, Texas
**Postal Personnel and Modernization** — Frank McCloskey, Ind.

## Public Works and Transportation

Flood control and improvement of rivers and harbors; construction and maintenance of roads; oil and other pollution of navigable waters; public buildings and grounds; public works for the benefit of navigation including bridges and dams; water power; transportation, except railroads; Botanic Garden; Library of Congress; Smithsonian Institution.

### D 27 - R 19 *(99th Congress)*
### D 30 - R 20 *(100th Congress)*

James J. Howard, N.J. (1981-88; died March 25, 1988)
Glenn M. Anderson, Calif. (through 100th Congress)
*Gene Snyder, Ky. (99th Congress)*
*John Paul Hammerschmidt, Ark. (100th Congress)*

**Aviation** — Norman Y. Mineta, Calif.
**Economic Development** — Henry J. Nowak, N.Y. (99th Congress); Gus Savage, Ill. (100th Congress)
**Investigations and Oversight** — James L. Oberstar, Minn.
**Public Buildings and Grounds** — Robert A. Young, Mo. (99th Congress); Fofō I. F. Sunia, American Samoa (100th Congress)
**Surface Transportation** — Glenn M. Anderson, Calif.
**Water Resources** — Robert A. Roe, N.J. (99th Congress); Henry J. Nowak, N.Y. (100th Congress)

## Rules

Rules and order of business of the House; emergency waivers under the Congressional Budget Act of required reporting date for bills and resolutions authorizing new budget authority; recesses and final adjournments of Congress.

### D 9 - R 4

Claude Pepper, Fla. (1983-89)
*James H. Quillen, Tenn.*

**Legislative Process** — Butler Derrick, S.C.
**Rules of the House** — Joe Moakley, Mass.

## Science and Technology

*(Renamed Science, Space and Technology in the 100th Congress)*

Scientific and astronautical research and development, including resources, personnel, equipment and facilities; Bureau of Standards, standardization of weights and measures and the metric system; National Aeronautics and Space Administration; National Aeronautics and Space Council; National Science Foundation; outer space, including exploration and control; science scholarships; federally owned or operated non-military energy laboratories; civil aviation research and development; energy research, development and demonstration (except nuclear research and development); National Weather Service.

### D 24 - R 17 *(99th Congress)*
### D 27 - R 18 *(100th Congress)*

Don Fuqua, Fla. (1979-87)
Robert A. Roe, N.J. (1987-89)
*Manuel Lujan Jr., N.M.*

**Energy Development and Applications** (99th Congress) — Don Fuqua, Fla.

**Energy Research and Development** (100th Congress) — Marilyn Lloyd, Tenn.

**Energy Research and Production** (99th Congress) — Marilyn Lloyd, Tenn.

**International Scientific Cooperation** (100th Congress) — Ralph M. Hall, Texas

**Investigations and Oversight** — Harold L. Volkmer, Mo. (99th Congress); Robert A. Roe, N.J. (100th Congress)

**Natural Resources, Agriculture Research and Environment** — James H. Scheuer, N.Y.

**Science, Research and Technology** — Doug Walgren, Pa.

**Space Science and Applications** — Bill Nelson, Fla.

**Transportation, Aviation and Materials** — Dan Glickman, Kan. (resigned post in 99th Congress); George E. Brown Jr., Calif. (through 99th Congress); Dave McCurdy, Okla. (100th Congress)

## Select Aging

Problems of older Americans including income, housing, health, welfare, employment, education, recreation and participation in family and community life. Studies and reports findings to the House, but cannot report legislation.

**D 38 - R 26** *(99th Congress)*
**D 39 - R 25** *(100th Congress)*

Edward R. Roybal, Calif. (1983-89)
*Matthew J. Rinaldo, N.J.*

**Health and Long-Term Care** — Claude Pepper, Fla.

**Housing and Consumer Interests** — Don Bonker, Wash.

**Human Services** — Mario Biaggi, N.Y. (99th Congress; indicted March 16, 1987, and required to step down from chairmanship); Thomas J. Downey, N.Y. (acting chairman, 100th Congress)

**Retirement, Income and Employment** — Edward R. Roybal, Calif.

## Select Children, Youth and Families

Problems of children, youth and families including income maintenance, health, nutrition, education, welfare, employment and recreation. Studies and reports finding to the House, but cannot report legislation.

**D 15 - R 10** *(99th Congress)*
**D 18 - R 12** *(100th Congress)*

George Miller, Calif. (1983-89)
*Dan Coats, Ind.*

**Task Forces**

**Crisis Intervention** — Lindy (Mrs. Hale) Boggs, La.

**Economic Security** — Patricia Schroeder, Colo.

**Prevention Strategies** — William Lehman, Fla.

## Select Committee to Investigate Covert Arms Transactions With Iran

Conduct an investigation and study regarding direct or indirect sale or transfer of arms, technology or intelligence information to Iran or Iraq involving U.S. government officers, employees, consultants, agents or persons acting in concert with them, or occurring with their approval or knowledge; the relations of such sale or transfer to efforts to obtain the release of hostages and to U.S. policy regarding dealings with nations supporting terrorism; diversion or intended diversion of the funds realized in connection with such sale or transfer for financing assistance to anti-government forces in Nicaragua or any other disposition apart from deposit in the treasury; operational activities and the conduct of foreign and national security policy by the staff of the National Security Council or other White House personnel; authorization and supervision or lack thereof of these matters by the president and other entities outside the government, including foreign countries, entities and persons, in connection with these matters; inquiries regarding these matters, including actions based on those inquiries, by the attorney general, the Departments of Justice, State and Defense, the intelligence community, the White House and other governmental entities; actions of individuals in destroying, concealing or failing to provide any evidence or information of possible value to those inquiries.

**D 9 - R 6** *(100th Congress)*

Lee H. Hamilton, Ind. (1987-88)
*Dick Cheney, Wyo.*

No standing subcommittees.

## Select Hunger

Comprehensive study and review of hunger and malnutrition, including U.S. development and economic assistance programs; U.S. trade relations with less-developed nations; food production and distribution; agribusiness efforts to further international development; policies of development banks and international development institutions; and food assistance programs in the United States. Review of executive branch recommendations relating to programs affecting hunger and malnutrition, and to recommend legislation or other action with respect to such programs to the appropriate committees of the House.

**D 10 - R 7** *(99th Congress)*
**D 16 - R 10** *(100th Congress)*

Mickey Leland, Texas (1984-89)
*Marge Roukema, N.J.* (resigned post in August 1987)
*Bill Emerson, Mo.* (through 100th Congress)

**Task Forces**

Domestic — Leon E. Panetta, Calif.
International — Tony P. Hall, Ohio

## Select Intelligence

Legislative and budgetary authority over the Central Intelligence Agency, the Defense Intelligence Agency, the National Security Agency, intelligence activities of the Federal Bureau of Investigation and other components of the federal intelligence community.

**D 10 - R 6** *(99th Congress)*
**D 11 - R 6** *(100th Congress)*

Lee H. Hamilton, Ind. (1985-87)
Louis Stokes, Ohio (1987-89)
*Bob Stump, Ariz.* (99th Congress)
*Henry J. Hyde, Ill.* (100th Congress)

**Legislation** — Anthony C. Beilenson, Calif. (99th Congress); Matthew F. McHugh, N.Y. (100th Congress)
**Oversight and Evaluation** — Dave McCurdy, Okla. (99th Congress); Anthony C. Beilenson, Calif. (100th Congress)
**Program and Budget Authorization** — Louis Stokes, Ohio

## Select Narcotics Abuse and Control

Problems of narcotics, drug and polydrug abuse and control including opium and its derivatives, other narcotic drugs, psychotropics and other controlled substances; trafficking, manufacturing and distribution; treatment, prevention and rehabilitation; narcotics-related violations of tax laws; international treaties and agreements relating to narcotics and drug abuse; role of organized crime in narcotics and drug abuse; abuse and control in the armed forces and in industry; criminal justice system and narcotics and drug law violations and crimes related to drug abuse. Studies and reports findings to the House, but cannot report legislation.

**D 15 - R 10**

Charles B. Rangel, N.Y. (1983-89)
*Benjamin A. Gilman, N.Y.*

No standing subcommittees.

## Small Business

Assistance to and protection of small business including financial aid; participation of small business enterprises in federal procurement and government contracts.

**D 25 - R 17** *(99th Congress)*
**D 27 - R 17** *(100th Congress)*

Parren J. Mitchell, Md. (1981-87)

John J. LaFalce, N.Y. (1987-89)
*Joseph M. McDade, Pa.*

**Antitrust and Restraint of Trade Activities Affecting Small Business** (99th Congress) — Charles Hatcher, Ga.
**Antitrust, Impact of Deregulation and Privatization** (100th Congress) — Dennis E. Eckart, Ohio
**Energy and Agriculture** (100th Congress) — Charles Hatcher, Ga.
**Energy, Environment and Safety Issues Affecting Small Business** (99th Congress) — Charles W. Stenholm, Texas
**Export Opportunities and Special Small Business Problems** (99th Congress) — Ike Skelton, Mo.
**Exports, Tourism and Special Problems** (100th Congress) — Ike Skelton, Mo.
**General Oversight and the Economy** (99th Congress) — Nicholas Mavroules, Mass.
**Procurement, Innovation and Minority Enterprise Development** (100th Congress) — Nicholas Mavroules, Mass.
**Regulation and Business Opportunities** (100th Congress) — Ron Wyden, Ore.
**SBA and SBIC Authority, Minority Enterprise and General Small Business Problems** (99th Congress) — Parren J. Mitchell, Md.
**SBA and the General Economy** (100th Congress) — John J. LaFalce, N.Y.
**Tax, Access to Equity Capital and Business Opportunities** (99th Congress) — Thomas A. Luken, Ohio

## Standards of Official Conduct

Measures relating to the Code of Official Conduct; conduct of House members and employees; Ethics in Government Act.

**D 6 - R 6**

Julian C. Dixon, Calif. (1985-89)
*Floyd Spence, S.C.*

No standing subcommittees.

## Veterans' Affairs

Veterans' measures generally; compensation, vocational rehabilitation and education of veterans; armed forces life insurance; pensions; readjustment benefits; veterans' hospitals, medical care and treatment.

**D 20 - R 14** *(99th Congress)*
**D 21 - R 13** *(100th Congress)*

G. V. "Sonny" Montgomery, Miss. (1981-89)
*John Paul Hammerschmidt, Ark.* (99th Congress)
*Gerald B. H. Solomon, N.Y.* (100th Congress)

**Compensation, Pension and Insurance** — Douglas Applegate, Ohio
**Education, Training and Employment** — Thomas A. Daschle, S.D. (99th Congress); Wayne Dowdy,

Miss. (100th Congress)

**Hospitals and Health Care** — Bob Edgar, Pa. (99th Congress); G. V. "Sonny" Montgomery, Miss. (100th Congress)

**Housing and Memorial Affairs** — Richard C. Shelby, Ala. (99th Congress); Marcy Kaptur, Ohio (100th Congress)

**Oversight and Investigations** — G. V. "Sonny" Montgomery, Miss. (99th Congress); Lane Evans, Ill. (100th Congress)

## Ways and Means

Revenue measures generally; reciprocal trade agreements; customs, collection districts and ports of entry and delivery; bonded debt of the United States; deposit of public moneys; transportation of dutiable goods; tax exempt foundations and charitable trusts; Social Security.

### D 23 - R 13

Dan Rostenkowski, Ill. (1981-89)
*John J. Duncan, Tenn. (died June 21, 1988)*
*Bill Archer, Texas (through 100th Congress)*

**Health** — Fortney H. "Pete" Stark, Calif.
**Oversight** — J. J. Pickle, Texas
**Public Assistance and Unemployment Compensation** — Harold E. Ford, Tenn. (99th Congress; indicted April 24, 1987, and required to step down from chairmanship); Thomas J. Downey, N.Y. (acting chairman, 100th Congress)
**Select Revenue Measures** — Charles B. Rangel, N.Y.
**Social Security** — James R. Jones, Okla. (99th Congress); Andrew Jacobs Jr., Ind. (100th Congress)
**Trade** — Sam Gibbons, Fla.

## Political Committees

**Democratic Congressional Campaign Committee** (campaign support committee for Democratic House candidates) — Tony Coelho, Calif. (99th Congress); Beryl Anthony Jr., Ark. (100th Congress)
**Democratic Personnel Committee** (selects, appoints and supervises Democratic patronage positions) — Joe Moakley, Mass. (99th Congress); Jack Brooks, Texas (100th Congress)
**Democratic Steering and Policy Committee** (schedules legislation and makes Democratic committee assignments) — Thomas P. O'Neill Jr., Mass. (99th Congress); Jim Wright, Texas (100th Congress)
**National Republican Congressional Committee** (campaign support committee for Republican House candidates) — Guy Vander Jagt, Mich.
**Republican Committee on Committees** (makes Republican committee assignments) — Robert H. Michel, Ill.
**Republican Personnel Committee** (99th Congress; selects, appoints and supervises Republican patronage positions) — John T. Myers, Ind.
**Republican Policy Committee** (advises on party action and policy) — Dick Cheney, Wyo. (until June 4, 1987); Jerry Lewis, Calif. (through 100th Congress)

**Republican Research Committee** (at leadership's request, provides information and recommendations on specific policy issues likely to come before Congress) — Jerry Lewis, Calif. (until June 4, 1987); Mickey Edwards, Okla. (through 100th Congress)

# Joint Committees

Joint committees are set up to examine specific questions and are established by public law. Membership is drawn from both chambers and both parties. When a senator serves as chairman, the vice chairman usually is a representative, and vice versa. The chairmanship traditionally rotates from one chamber to the other at the beginning of each Congress.

## Economic

Studies and investigates all recommendations in the president's annual Economic Report to Congress. Reports findings and recommendations to the House and Senate.

Rep. David R. Obey, D-Wis., chairman (99th Congress)
Sen. Paul S. Sarbanes, D-Md., chairman (100th Congress)
*Sen. James Abdnor, R-S.D., vice chairman (99th Congress)*
*Rep. Lee H. Hamilton, D-Ind., vice chairman*
*(100th Congress)*

**Agriculture and Transportation** (99th Congress) — Sen. James Abdnor, R-S.D.
**Economic Goals and Intergovernmental Policy** — Rep. Lee H. Hamilton, D-Ind.
**Economic Growth, Trade and Taxes** (100th Congress) — Sen. Lloyd Bentsen, D-Texas
**Economic Resources and Competitiveness** (100th Congress) — Rep. David R. Obey, D-Wis.
**Economic Resources, Competitiveness and Security Economics** (99th Congress) - Rep. David R. Obey, D-Wis.
**Education and Health** (100th Congress) — Rep. James H. Scheuer, D-N.Y.
**Fiscal and Monetary Policy** (100th Congress) — Sen. Edward M. Kennedy, D-Mass.
**International Economic Policy** (100th Congress) — Sen. Paul S. Sarbanes, D-Md.
**Investment, Jobs and Prices** — Rep. Parren J. Mitchell, D-Md. (99th Congress); Rep. Augustus F. Hawkins, D-Calif. (100th Congress)
**Monetary and Fiscal Policy** (99th Congress) — Sen. Steven D. Symms, R-Idaho
**National Security Economics** (100th Congress) — Sen. William Proxmire, D-Wis.
**Trade, Productivity and Economic Growth** (99th Congress) — Sen. William V. Roth Jr., R-Del.

## Library

Management and expansion of the Library of Congress; receipt of gifts for the benefit of the library; development and maintenance of the Botanic Garden; placement of statues and other works of art in the Capitol.

Rep. Frank Annunzio, D-Ill., chairman (99th Congress)
Sen. Claiborne Pell, D-R.I., chairman (100th Congress)
*Sen. Charles McC. Mathias Jr., R-Md., vice chairman*
*(99th Congress)*
*Rep. Frank Annunzio, D-Ill., vice chairman*
*(100th Congress)*

No standing subcommittees.

# Printing

Probes inefficiency and waste in the printing, binding and distribution of federal government publications. Oversees the arrangement and style of the *Congressional Record.*

Sen. Charles McC. Mathias Jr., R-Md., chairman
(99th Congress)
Rep. Frank Annunzio, D-Ill., chairman (100th Congress)

*Rep. Frank Annunzio, D-Ill., vice chairman*
*(99th Congress)*
*Sen. Wendell H. Ford, D-Ky., vice chairman*
*(100th Congress)*

No standing subcommittees.

# Taxation

Operation, effects and administration of the federal system of internal revenue taxes; measures and methods for simplification of taxes.

Sen. Bob Packwood, R-Ore., chairman (99th Congress)
Sen. Lloyd Bentsen, D-Texas, chairman (100th Congress)
*Rep. Dan Rostenkowski, D-Ill., vice chairman*

No standing subcommittees.

# Post-Election Sessions

Congress has held seven post-election sessions since 1945.

**1948.** The 1948 post-election session of the 80th Congress lasted only two hours. Both chambers swore in new members, approved several minor resolutions and received last-minute reports from committees.

In addition to final floor action, several committees resumed work. The most active was the House Un-American Activities Committee, which continued its investigation of alleged communist espionage in the federal government.

**1950.** After the 1950 elections, President Harry S Truman sent a "must" agenda to the lame-duck session of the 81st Congress. The president's list included supplemental defense appropriations, an excess profits tax, aid to Yugoslavia, a three-month extension of federal rent controls and statehood for Hawaii and Alaska. During a marathon session that lasted until only a few hours before its successor took over, the 81st Congress acted on all of the president's legislative items except the statehood bills, which were blocked by a Senate filibuster.

**1954.** Only one chamber of the 83rd Congress convened after the 1954 elections. The Senate returned Nov. 8 to hold what has been called a "censure session," a continuing investigation into the conduct of Sen. Joseph R. McCarthy, R-Wis. (1947-57). By a 67-22 roll call the Senate Dec. 2 voted to "condemn" McCarthy for his behavior.

In other post-election floor action, the Senate passed a series of miscellaneous and administrative resolutions and swore in new members.

**1970.** President Richard Nixon criticized the lame-duck Congress as one that had "seemingly lost the capacity to decide and the will to act." Filibusters and intense controversy contributed to inaction on the president's request for trade legislation and welfare reform.

Congress nevertheless claimed some substantive results during the session, which ended Jan. 2, 1971. Several major appropriations bills were cleared for presidential signature. Congress also approved foreign aid to Cambodia, provided interim funding for the supersonic transport (SST) plane and repealed the Tonkin Gulf Resolution that had been used as a basis for American military involvement in Vietnam.

**1974.** In a session that ran from Nov. 18 to Dec. 20, 1974, the 93rd Congress cleared several important bills for presidential signature, including a mass transit bill, a Labor-Health, Education and Welfare appropriations bill and a foreign assistance package. A House-Senate conference committee reached agreement on a major strip-mining bill, but President Gerald R. Ford vetoed it.

Congress approved the nomination of Nelson A. Rockefeller as vice president. It also overrode presidential vetoes of two bills — one broadening the Freedom of

---

## Recent Lame-Duck Sessions

| Year | Congress | Dates |
|------|----------|-------|
| 1948 | 80th | Dec. 31, 1948 (2-hour session) |
| 1950 | 81st | Nov. 27, 1950 — Jan. 2, 1951 |
| 1954 | 83rd | Nov. 8, 1954 — Dec. 2, 1954 |
| 1970 | 91st | Nov. 16, 1970 — Jan. 2, 1971 (Senate) |
| 1974 | 93rd | Nov. 18, 1974 — Dec. 20, 1974 |
| 1980 | 96th | Nov. 12, 1980 — Dec. 16, 1980 |
| 1982 | 97th | Nov. 29, 1982 — Dec. 23, 1982 (Senate) Nov. 29, 1982 — Dec. 21, 1982 (House) |

---

Information Act, a second authorizing educational benefits for Korean War and Vietnam-era veterans.

**1980.** The lame-duck session of the 96th Congress was productive, at least until Dec. 5, the original adjournment date set by congressional leaders. By that date a budget had been approved, along with a budget reconciliation measure. Ten regular appropriations bills had cleared, though one subsequently was vetoed. Congress had approved two major environmental measures — an Alaskan lands bill and toxic waste "superfund" legislation — as well as a three-year extension of general revenue sharing.

After Dec. 5, however, the legislative pace slowed noticeably. Action on a continuing appropriations resolution for those departments and agencies whose regular funding had not been cleared was delayed, first by a filibuster on a fair housing bill and later by more than 100 "Christmas tree" amendments, including a $10,000-a-year pay raise for members. After the conference report failed in the Senate and twice was rewritten, the bill was shorn of virtually all its "ornaments" and finally cleared by both chambers on Dec. 16.

**1982.** Despite the reluctance of congressional leaders, President Reagan urged the convening of a post-election session at the end of the 97th Congress, principally to pass remaining appropriations bills.

Rising unemployment — and Democratic election

zen should tremble, nor the world shudder, if a child stands in a classroom and breathes a prayer. We ask you again — give children back a right they had for a century and a half or more in this country.

The question of abortion grips our Nation. Abortion is either the taking of a human life or it isn't; and if it is — and medical technology is increasingly showing it is — it must be stopped.

It is a terrible irony that while some turn to abortion, so many others who cannot become parents cry out for children to adopt. We have room for these children; we can fill the cradles of those who want a child to love. Tonight I ask you in the Congress to move this year on legislation to protect the unborn.

In the area of education, we are returning to excellence and again the heroes are our people, not government. We are stressing basics of discipline, rigorous testing, and homework, while helping children become computer smart as well. For 20 years Scholastic Aptitude Test scores of our high school students went down. But now they have gone up two of the last three years.

We must go forward in our commitment to the new basics, giving parents greater authority and making sure good teachers are rewarded for hard work and achievement through merit pay.

## Violence and Crime

Of all the changes in the past 20 years, none has more threatened our sense of national well-being than the explosion of violent crime. One does not have to be attacked to be a victim. The woman who must run to her car after shopping at night is a victim; the couple draping their door with locks and chains are victims; as is the tired, decent cleaning woman who can't ride a subway home without being afraid.

We do not seek to violate the rights of defendants. But shouldn't we feel more compassion for the victims of crime than for those who commit crime? For the first time in 20 years the crime index has fallen two years in a row; we have convicted over 7,400 drug offenders, and put them, as well as leaders of organized crime, behind bars in record numbers.

But we must do more. I urge the House to follow the Senate and enact proposals permitting use of all reliable evidence that police officers acquire in good faith. These proposals would also reform the habeus corpus laws and allow, in keeping with the will of the overwhelming majority of Americans, the use of the death penalty where necessary.

There can be no economic revival in ghettos when the most violent among us are allowed to roam free. It is time we restored domestic tranquility. And we mean to do just that.

## Working for Peace

Just as we are positioned as never before to secure justice in our economy, we are poised as never before to create a safer, freer, more peaceful world.

Our alliances are stronger than ever. Our economy is stronger than ever. We have resumed our historic role as a leader of the free world — and all of these together are a great force for peace.

Since 1981 we have been committed to seeking fair and verifiable arms agreements that would lower the risk of war and reduce the size of nuclear arsenals. Now our determination to maintain a strong defense has influenced the Soviet Union to return to the bargaining table. Our negotiators must be able to go to that table with the united support of the American people. All of us have no greater dream than to see the day when nuclear weapons are banned from this Earth forever.

Each Member of the Congress has a role to play in modernizing our defenses, thus supporting our chances for a meaningful arms agreement. Your vote this spring on the Peacekeeper missile will be a critical test of our resolve to maintain the strength we need and move toward mutual and verifiable arms reductions.

For the past 20 years we have believed that no war will be launched as long as each side knows it can retaliate with a deadly counterstrike. Well, I believe there is a better way of eliminating the threat of nuclear war.

It is a Strategic Defense Initiative aimed ultimately at finding a non-nuclear defense against ballistic missiles. It is the most hopeful possibility of the nuclear age. But it is not well understood.

Some say it will bring war to the heavens — but its purpose is to deter war, in the heavens and on Earth. Some say the research would be expensive. Perhaps, but it could save millions of lives, indeed humanity itself. Some say if we build such a system the Soviets will build a defense system of their own. Well, they already have strategic defenses that surpass ours; a civil defense system, where we have almost none; and a research program covering roughly the same areas of technology we are exploring. And finally, some say the research will take a long time. The answer to that is: "Let's get started."

## Aid and Trade

Harry Truman once said that ultimately our security and the world's hopes for peace and human progress, "lie not in measures of defense or in the control of weapons, but in the growth and expansion of freedom and self-government."

Tonight we declare anew to our fellow citizens of the world: Freedom is not the sole prerogative of a chosen few; it is the universal right of all God's children. Look to where peace and prosperity flourish today. It is in homes that freedom built. Victories against poverty are greatest and peace most secure where people live by laws that ensure free press, free speech, and freedom to worship, vote, and create wealth.

Our mission is to nourish and defend freedom and democracy and to communicate these ideals everywhere we can.

America's economic success is freedom's success; it can be repeated a hundred times in a hundred different nations. Many countries in East Asia and the Pacific have few resources other than the enterprise of their own people. But through low tax rates and free markets they have soared ahead of centralized economies. And now China is opening up its economy to meet its needs.

We need a stronger and simpler approach to the process of making and implementing trade policy and will be studying potential changes in that process in the next few weeks.

We have seen the benefits of free trade and lived through the disasters of protectionism. Tonight I ask all our trading partners, developed and developing alike, to join us in a new round of trade negotiations to expand trade and competition, and strengthen the global economy — and to begin it in this next year.

There are more than 3 billion human beings living in Third World Countries with an average per capita income of $650 a year. Many are victims of dictatorships that impoverish them with taxation and corruption. Let us ask our allies to join us in a practical program of trade and assistance that fosters economic development through personal incentives to help these people climb from poverty on their own. We cannot play innocents abroad in a world that is not innocent. Nor can we be passive when freedom is under siege. Without resources, diplomacy cannot succeed. Our security assistance programs help friendly governments defend themselves, and give them confidence to work for peace. And I hope that you in the Congress will understand that dollar for dollar security assistance contributes as much to global security as our own defense budget.

We must stand by all our democratic allies. And we must not break faith with those who are risking their lives on every continent, from Afghanistan to Nicaragua, to defy Soviet-supported aggression and secure rights which have been ours from birth.

The Sandinista dictatorship of Nicaragua, with full Cuban Soviet-bloc support, not only persecutes its people, the church, and denies a free press, but arms and provides bases for communist terrorists attacking neighboring states. Support for freedom fighters is self-defense, and totally consistent with the OAS [Organization of American States] and U.N. Charters. It is essential that the Congress continue all facets of our assistance to Central America. I want to work with you to support the democratic forces whose struggle is tied to our own security.

## Two American Heroes

Tonight I have spoken of great plans and great dreams. They are dreams we can make come true. Two hundred years of

American history should have taught us that nothing is impossible.

Ten years ago a young girl left Vietnam with her family, part of the exodus that followed the fall of Saigon. They came to the United States with no possessions and not knowing a word of English, 10 years ago. The young girl studied hard, learned English, and finished high school in the top of her class. And this May, May 22 to be exact, is a big date on her calendar. Just 10 years from the time she left Vietnam she will graduate from the United States Military Academy at West Point.

I thought you might like to meet an American hero named Jean Nguyen.

Now, there is someone else here tonight — born 79 years ago. She lives in the inner city where she cares for infants born of mothers who are heroin addicts. The children born in withdrawal are sometimes even dropped at her doorstep. She helps them with love.

Go to her house some night and maybe you will see her silhouette against the window as she walks the floor, talking softly, soothing a child in her arms. Mother Hale of Harlem, and she, too, is an American hero.

Jean, Mother Hale, your lives tell us that the oldest American saying is new again — anything is possible in America if we have the faith, the will, and the heart.

History is asking us once again to be a force for good in the world. Let us begin — in unity, with justice and love.

Thank you and God bless you.

[Applause, the Members rising.]

# Reagan's Statement on SALT II

*Following is the White House text of President Reagan's June 10, 1985, statement regarding U.S. compliance with the unratified SALT II (strategic arms limitation treaty) agreement.*

In 1982, on the eve of the Strategic Arms Reductions Talks [START], I decided that the United States would not undercut the expired SALT I agreement or the unratified SALT II agreement as long as the Soviet Union exercised equal restraint. Despite my serious reservations about the inequities of the SALT I agreement and the serious flaws of the SALT II agreement, I took this action in order to foster an atmosphere of mutual restraint conducive to serious negotiation as we entered START.

Since then, the United States has not taken any actions which would undercut existing arms control agreements. The United States has fully kept its part of the bargain. However, the Soviets have not. They have failed to comply with several provisions of SALT II, and we have serious concerns regarding their compliance with the provisions of other accords.

The pattern of Soviet violations, if left uncorrected, undercuts the integrity and viability of arms control as an instrument to assist in ensuring a secure and stable future world. The United States will continue to pursue vigorously with the Soviet Union the resolution of our concerns over Soviet noncompliance. We cannot impose upon ourselves a double standard that amounts to unilateral treaty compliance.

We remain determined to pursue a productive dialogue with the Soviet Union aimed at reducing the risk of war through the adoption of meaningful measures which improve security, stability and predictability. Therefore, I have reached the judgment that, despite the Soviet record over the last years, it remains in our interest to establish an interim framework of truly mutual restraint on strategic offensive arms as we pursue with renewed vigor our goal of real reductions in the size of existing nuclear arsenals in the ongoing negotiations in Geneva. Obtaining such reductions remains my highest priority.

The U.S. cannot establish such a framework alone. It will require the Soviet Union to take the positive, concrete steps to correct its noncompliance, resolve our other compliance concerns, and reverse its unparalleled and unwarranted military buildup. So far, the Soviet Union has not chosen to move in this direction. However, in the interest of ensuring that every opportunity to establish the secure, stable future we seek is fully explored, I am prepared to go the extra mile in seeking an interim framework of truly mutual restraint.

Therefore, to provide the Soviets the opportunity to join us in establishing such a framework which could support ongoing negotiations, I have decided that the United States will continue to refrain from undercutting existing strategic arms agreements to the extent that the Soviet Union exercises comparable restraint and provided that the Soviet Union actively pursues arms reduction agreements in the currently ongoing Nuclear and Space Talks in Geneva.

As an integral part of this policy, we will also take those steps required to assure the national security of the United States and our allies which were made necessary by Soviet noncompliance. Appropriate and proportionate responses to Soviet noncompliance are called for to ensure our security, to provide incentives to the Soviets to correct their noncompliance, and to make it clear to Moscow that violations of arms control obligations entail real costs.

Certain Soviet violations are, by their very nature, irreversible. Such is the case with respect to the Soviet Union's flight-testing and steps towards deployment of the SS-X-25 missile, a second new type of ICBM [intercontinental ballistic missile] prohibited by the unratified SALT II agreement. Since the noncompliance associated with the development of this missile cannot be corrected by the Soviet Union, the United States reserves the right to respond in a proportionate manner at the appropriate time. The MIDGETMAN small ICBM program is particularly relevant in this regard.

Other Soviet activities involving noncompliance may be reversible and can be corrected by Soviet action. In these instances, we will provide the Soviet Union additional time to take such required corrective action. As we monitor Soviet actions for evidence of the positive, concrete steps needed on their part to correct these activities, I have directed the Department of Defense to conduct a comprehensive assessment aimed at identifying specific actions which the United States could take to augment as necessary the U.S. strategic modernization program as a proportionate response to, and as a hedge against the military consequences of, those Soviet violations of existing arms agreements which the Soviets fail to correct.

To provide adequate time for the Soviets to demonstrate by their actions a commitment to join us in an interim framework of true mutual restraint, we will plan to deactivate and dismantle according to agreed procedures an existing POSEIDON SSBN as the seventh U.S. *Ohio*-class submarine puts to sea later this year. However, the United States will keep open all programmatic options for handling such milestones as they occur in the future. As these later milestones are reached, I will assess the overall situation in light of Soviet actions correcting their noncompliance and promoting progress in Geneva and make a final determination of the U.S. course of action on a case-by-case basis.

I firmly believe that if we are to put the arms reduction process on a firm and lasting foundation, and obtain real reductions, our focus must remain on making best use of the promise provided by the currently ongoing negotiations in Geneva.

Our policy, involving the establishment of an interim framework for truly mutual restraint and proportionate U.S. response to uncorrected Soviet noncompliance, is specifically designed to go the extra mile in giving the Soviet Union the opportunity to join us in this endeavor.

My hope is that if the Soviets will do so, we will be able jointly to make progress in framing equitable and verifiable agreements involving real reductions in the size of existing nuclear arsenals in the Geneva negotiations. Such an achievement would not only provide the best and most permanent constraint on the growth of nuclear arsenals, but it would take a major step towards reducing the size of these arsenals and creating a safer future for all nations.

---

# Reagan's Speech on U.S.-Soviet Summit in Geneva

*Following is the White House text of President Reagan's Nov. 21, 1985, remarks on the U.S.-Soviet summit meeting held in Geneva, Switzerland, as delivered to a joint session of Congress.*

Mr. Speaker, Mr. President, members of the Congress, distinguished guests, my fellow Americans:

It's great to be home, and Nancy and I thank you for this wonderful homecoming. And before I go on, I want to say a personal thank you to Nancy. She was an outstanding ambassador of good will for all of us. [Applause.] She didn't know I was going to say that.

Mr. Speaker, Senator [Robert] Dole [R-Kan.], I want you to know that your statements of support here were greatly appreciated. You can't imagine how much it means in dealing with the Soviets to have the Congress, the allies, and the American people firmly behind you. [Applause.]

I guess you know that I have just come from Geneva and talks with General Secretary [Mikhail S.] Gorbachev. In the past few days, we spent over 15 hours in various meetings with the General Secretary and the members of his official party. And approximately five of those hours were talks between Mr. Gorbachev and myself, just one on one. That was the best part — our fireside summit.

There will be, I know, a great deal of commentary and opinion as to what the meetings produced and what they were like. There were over 3,000 reporters in Geneva, so it's possible there will be 3,000 opinions on what happened, so — [applause] — maybe it's the old broadcaster in me but I decided to file my own report directly to you. [Applause.]

## 'A Constructive Meeting'

We met, as we had to meet. I had called for a fresh start — and we made that start. I can't claim we had a meeting of the minds on such fundamentals as ideology or national purpose — but we understand each other better, and that's the key to peace. I gained a better perspective; I feel he did, too.

It was a constructive meeting. So constructive, in fact, that I look forward to welcoming Mr. Gorbachev to the United States next year. [Applause.] And I have accepted his invitation to go to Moscow the following year. [Applause.] We arranged that out in the parking lot. [Applause.]

I found Mr. Gorbachev to be an energetic defender of Soviet policy. He was an eloquent speaker, and a good listener. Our subject matter was shaped by the facts of this century.

## Summit's Historic Background

These past 40 years have not been an easy time for the West or for the world. You know the facts; there is no need to recite the historical record. Suffice it to say that the United States cannot afford illusions about the nature of the USSR. We cannot assume that their ideology and purpose will change. This implies enduring competition. Our task is to assure that this competition remains peaceful. With all that divides us, we cannot afford to let confusion complicate things further. We must be clear with each other, and direct. We must pay each other the tribute of candor.

When I took the oath of office for the first time, we began dealing with the Soviet Union in a way that was more realistic than in, say, the recent past. And so, in a very real sense, preparations for the summit started not months ago but five years ago when, with the help of Congress, we began strengthening our economy, restoring our national will, and rebuilding our defenses and alliances. America is once again strong — and our strength has given us the ability to speak with confidence and see that no true opportunity to advance freedom and peace is lost. [Applause.] We must not now abandon policies that work. I need your continued support to keep America strong.

That is the history behind the Geneva summit, and that is the context in which it occurred. And may I add that we were especially eager that our meetings give a push to important talks already under way on reducing nuclear weapons. On this subject it would be foolish not to go the extra mile — or in this case the extra 4,000 miles.

We discussed the great issues of our time. I made clear that before the first meeting that no question would be swept aside, no issue buried, just because either side found it uncomfortable or inconvenient.

I brought these questions to the summit and put them before Mr. Gorbachev.

## Nuclear Arms Reduction - 1

We discussed nuclear arms and how to reduce them. I explained our proposals for equitable, verifiable, and deep reductions. I outlined my conviction that our proposals would make not just for a world that feels safer but one that really is safer.

I am pleased to report tonight that General Secretary Gorbachev and I did make a measure of progress here. [Applause.] While we still have a long way to go, we're still heading in the right direction. We moved arms control forward from where we were last January, when the Soviets returned to the table. We are both instructing our negotiators to hasten their vital work. The world is waiting for results.

Specifically, we agreed in Geneva that each side should move to cut offensive nuclear arms by 50 percent in appropriate categories. In our joint statement we called for early progress on this, turning the talks toward our chief goal, offensive reductions. We called for an interim accord on intermediate-range nuclear forces, leading, I hope, to the complete elimination of this class of missiles. And all this with tough verification. [Applause.]

We also made progress in combating together the spread of nuclear weapons, an arms control area in which we've cooperated effectively over the years. We are also opening a dialogue on combating the spread and use of chemical weapons, while moving to ban them altogether. [Applause.] Other arms control dialogues — in Vienna on conventional forces, and in Stockholm on lessening the chances for a surprise attack in Europe — also received a boost. And finally, we agreed to begin work on risk reduction centers, a decision that should give special satisfaction to Senators [Sam] Nunn [D-Ga.] and [John W.] Warner [R-Va.] who so ably promoted this idea. [Applause.]

## Strategic Defense Initiative - 1

I described our Strategic Defense Initiative [SDI] — our research effort that envisions the possibility of defensive systems which could ultimately protect all nation[s] against the danger of nuclear war. This discussion produced a very direct exchange of views.

Mr. Gorbachev insisted that we might use a strategic defense system to put offensive weapons into space and establish nuclear superiority.

I made it clear that SDI has nothing to do with offensive weapons; that, instead, we are investigating non-nuclear defensive systems that would only threaten offensive missiles, not people. If — [applause] — our research succeeds, it will bring much closer the safer, more stable world we seek. Nations could defend themselves against missile attack, and mankind, at long last, escape the prison of mutual terror. And this is my dream.

## Nuclear Arms Reduction - 2

So I welcomed the chance to tell Mr. Gorbachev that we are a nation that defends, rather than attacks, that our alliances are defensive, not offensive. We don't seek nuclear superiority. We do not seek a first strike advantage over the Soviet Union.

Indeed, one of my fundamental arms control objectives is to get rid of first-strike weapons altogether. And this is why — [applause] — this is why we've proposed a 50 percent reduction in the most threatening nuclear weapons, especially those that could carry out a first strike.

## Strategic Defense Initiative - 2

I went further in expressing our peaceful intentions. I described our proposal in the Geneva negotiations for a reciprocal program of open laboratories and strategic defense research. We're offering to permit Soviet experts to see first-hand that SDI does not involve offensive weapons. American scientists would be allowed to visit comparable facilities of the Soviet strategic defensive program, which, in fact, has involved much more than research for many years.

Finally, I reassured Mr. Gorbachev on another point. I promised that if our research reveals that a defense against nuclear missiles is possible, we would sit down with our allies and the Soviet Union to see how together we could replace all strategic ballistic missiles with such a defense, which threatens no one.

## Regional Peace Process

We discussed threats to the peace in several regions of the world. I explained my proposals for a peace process to stop the wars in Afghanistan, Nicaragua, Ethiopia, Angola, and Cambodia — [applause] — those places where insurgencies that speak for the people are pitted against regimes which obviously do not represent the will or the approval of the people. I tried to be very clear about where our sympathies lie; I believe I succeeded. [Applause.]

## Human Rights

We discussed human rights. We Americans believe that history teaches no clearer lesson than this: Those countries which respect the rights of their own people tend, inevitably, to respect the rights of their neighbors. [Applause.] Human rights, therefore, is not an abstract moral issue — it is a peace issue.

## Increased Cultural Exchanges

Finally, we discussed the barriers to communication between our societies, and I elaborated on my proposals for real people-to-people contacts on a wide scale.

Americans should know the people of the Soviet Union — their hopes and fears and the facts of their lives. And citizens of the Soviet Union need to know of America's deep desire for peace and our unwavering attachment to freedom.

As you can see, our talks were wide-ranging. And let me at this point tell you what we agreed upon and what we didn't.

We remain far apart on a number of issues, as had to be expected. However, we reached agreement on a number of matters, and, as I mentioned, we agreed to continue meeting and this is important and very good. [Applause.] There's always room for movement, action, and progress when people are talking to each other instead of talking about each other.

We've concluded a new agreement designed to bring the best of America's artists and academics to the Soviet Union. The exhibits that will be included in this exchange are one of the most effective ways for the average Soviet citizen to learn about our way of life. This agreement will also expand the opportunities for Americans to experience the Soviet people's rich cultural heritage — because their artists and academics will be coming here.

We've also decided to go forward with a number of people-to-people initiatives that will go beyond greater contact not only between the political leaders of our two countries, but our respective students, teachers and others as well. We have emphasized youth exchanges. And this will help break down stereotypes, build friendships and, frankly, provide an alternative to propaganda.

## Other Agreements

We've agreed to establish a new Soviet Consulate in New York and a new American Consulate in Kiev. This will bring a permanent U.S. presence to the Ukraine for the first time in decades. [Applause.]

And we have also, together with the government of Japan, concluded a Pacific Air Safety Agreement with the Soviet Union. This is designed to set up cooperative measures to improve civil air safety in that region of the Pacific. What happened before must never be allowed to happen there again. [Applause.]

And as a potential way of dealing with the energy needs of the world of the future, we have also advocated international cooperation to explore the feasibility of developing fusion energy.

All of these steps are part of a long-term effort to build a more stable relationship with the Soviet Union. No one ever said it could be easy. But we've come a long way.

## Soviet Expansionism

As for Soviet expansionism in a number of regions of the world — while there is little chance of immediate change, we will continue to support the heroic efforts of those who fight for freedom. But we have also agreed to continue — and to intensify — our meetings with the Soviets on this and other regional conflicts and to work toward political solutions.

## A Worthwhile Meeting

We know the limits as well as the promise of summit meetings. This is, after all, the 11th summit of the postwar era — and still the differences endure. But we believe continued meetings between the leaders of the United States and the Soviet Union can help bridge those differences.

The fact is, every new day begins with possibilities; it's up to us to fill it with the things that move us toward progress and peace. Hope, therefore, is a realistic attitude — and despair an uninteresting little vice.

And so: Was our journey worthwhile?

Well, thirty years ago, when Ike — President Eisenhower — had just returned from a summit in Geneva, he said, ". . . the wide gulf that separates so far East and West is wide and deep." Well, today, three decades later, that is still true.

But, yes, this meeting was worthwhile for both sides. [Applause.] A new realism spawned the summit, the summit itself was a good start; and now our byword must be: Steady as we go.

## Hopes for the Future

I am, as you are, impatient for results. But good will and good hopes do not always yield lasting results. And quick fixes don't fix big problems.

Just as we must avoid illusions on our side, so we must dispel them on the Soviet side. I have made it clear to Mr. Gorbachev that we must reduce the mistrust and suspicions between us if we are to do such things as reduce arms, and this will take deeds, not words alone. I believe he is in agreement.

Where do we go from here? Well, our desire for improved relations is strong. We're ready and eager for step-by-step progress. We know that peace is not just the absence of war. We don't want a phony peace or a frail peace; we didn't go in pursuit of some kind of illusory détente. We can't be satisfied with cosmetic improvements that won't stand the test of time. We want real peace.

As I flew back this evening, I had many thoughts. In just a few days families across America will gather to celebrate Thanksgiving. And again, as our forefathers who voyaged to America, we traveled to Geneva with peace as our goal and freedom as our guide. For there can be no greater good than the quest for peace and no finer purpose than the preservation of freedom. [Applause.]

It is 350 years since the first Thanksgiving, when Pilgrims and Indians huddled together on the edge of an unknown continent. And now here we are gathered together on the edge of an unknown future — but, like our forefathers, really not so much afraid, but full of hope, and trusting in God, as ever.

Thank you for allowing me to talk to you this evening and God bless you all. [Applause.]

# President Reagan's 1986 State of the Union Address

*Following is the White House text of President Reagan's State of the Union address to a joint session of Congress Feb. 4, 1986.*

Mr. Speaker, Mr. President, distinguished members of the Congress, honored guests and fellow citizens, thank you for allowing me to delay my address until this evening. We paused together to mourn and honor the valor of our seven *Challenger* heroes. And I hope that we are now ready to do what they would want us to do — go forward America and reach for the stars. [Applause.] We will never forget those brave seven, but we shall go forward.

## Salute to Speaker O'Neill

Mr. Speaker, before I begin my prepared remarks, may I point out that tonight marks the 10th and last State of the Union message that you've presided over. And on behalf of the American people, I want to salute you for your service to Congress and the country. [Applause.]

## On the Move

I have come to review with you the progress of our nation, to speak of unfinished work, and to set our sights on the future. I am pleased to report the state of our Union is stronger than a year ago, and growing stronger each day. [Applause.] Tonight, we look out on a rising America — firm of heart, united in spirit, powerful in pride and patriotism — America is on the move!

## 'The Great American Comeback'

But, it wasn't long ago that we looked out on a different land — locked factory gates, long gasoline lines, intolerable prices and interest rates turning the greatest country on Earth into a land of broken dreams. Government growing beyond our consent had become a lumbering giant, slamming shut the gates of opportunity, threatening to crush the very roots of our freedom.

What brought America back? The American people brought us back — with quiet courage and common sense; [applause] with undying faith that in this nation under God the future will be ours, for the future belongs to the free.

Tonight the American people deserve our thanks — for 37 straight months of economic growth; for sunrise firms and modernized industries creating 9 million new jobs in three years; interest rates cut in half, inflation falling over from 12 percent in 1980 to under 4 today; and a mighty river of good works, a record $74 billion in voluntary giving just last year alone.

And despite the pressures of our modern world, family and community remain the moral core of our society, guardians of our values and hopes for the future. Family and community are the costars of this Great American Comeback. They are why we say tonight: Private values must be at the heart of public policies.

What is true for families in America is true for America in the family of free nations. History is no captive of some inevitable force. History is made by men and women of vision and courage. Tonight, freedom is on the march. The United States is the economic miracle, the model to which the world once again turns. We stand for an idea whose time is now: Only by lifting the weights from the shoulders of all can people truly prosper and can peace among all nations be secure.

## An 'Agenda for the Future'

Teddy Roosevelt said that a nation that does great work lives forever. We have done well, but we cannot stop at the foothills when Everest beckons. It's time for America to be all that we can be.

We speak tonight of an "Agenda for the Future," an agenda for a safer, more secure world. And we speak about the necessities for actions to steel us for the challenges of growth, trade and security in the next decade and the year 2000. And we will do it — not by breaking faith with bedrock principles, but by breaking free from failed policies. [Applause.]

Let us begin where storm clouds loom darkest — right here in Washington, D.C. This week I will send you our detailed proposals; tonight, let us speak of our responsibility to redefine government's role: Not to control, not to demand or command, not to contain us; but to help in times of need, and above all, to create a ladder of opportunity to full employment so that all Americans can climb toward economic power and justice on their own.

## Broken Budget Process

But we cannot win the race to the future shackled to a system that can't even pass a federal budget. We cannot win that race held back by horse-and-buggy programs that waste tax dollars and squander human potential. We cannot win that race if we're swamped in a sea of red ink.

Now, Mr. Speaker, you know, I know, and the American people know the federal budget system is broken. It doesn't work. Before we leave this city, let's you and I work together to fix it. [Applause.] And then we can finally give the American people a balanced budget. [Applause.]

## Promise of Gramm-Rudman-Hollings

Members of Congress, passage of Gramm-Rudman-Hollings gives us an historic opportunity to achieve what has eluded our national leadership for decades, forcing federal government to live within its means.

Your schedule now requires that the budget resolution be passed by April 15th, the very day America's families have to foot the bill for the budgets that you produce.

How often we read of a husband and wife both working, struggling from paycheck to paycheck to raise a family, meet a mortgage, pay their taxes and bills. And yet, some in Congress say taxes must be raised. Well, I'm sorry — they're asking the wrong people to tighten their belts. [Applause.] It's time we reduce the federal budget and left the family budget alone. [Applause.] We do not face large deficits because American families are undertaxed; we face those deficits because the federal government overspends.

The detailed budget that we will submit will meet the Gramm-Rudman-Hollings target for deficit reductions, meet our commitment to ensure a strong national defense, meet our commitment to protect Social Security and the truly less fortunate, and, yes, meet our commitment to not raise taxes. [Applause.]

How should we accomplish this? Well, not by taking from those in need. As families take care of their own, government must provide shelter and nourishment for those who cannot provide for themselves. But we must revise or replace programs enacted in the name of compassion that degrade the moral worth of work, encourage family breakups, and drive entire communities into a bleak and heartless dependency.

## Call for Line-Item Veto

Gramm-Rudman-Hollings can mark a dramatic improvement. But experience shows that simply setting deficit targets does not assure they'll be met. We must proceed with Grace Commission reforms against waste. And tonight, I ask you to give me what 43 Governors have — give me a line-item veto this year. [Applause.] Give me the authority to veto waste, and I'll take the responsibility, I'll make the cuts, I'll take the heat.

This authority would not give me any monopoly power, but simply prevent spending measures from sneaking through that could not pass on their own merit. And you can sustain or override my veto — that's the way the system should work. Once we've made the hard choices, we should lock in our gains with a balanced budget amendment to the Constitution. [Applause.]

## Commitment to Defense

I mentioned that we will meet our commitment to national defense. We must meet it. Defense is not just another budget expense. Keeping America strong, free, and at peace is solely the responsibility of the Federal Government; it is Government's prime responsibility. We have devoted five years trying to narrow a dangerous gap born of illusion and neglect. And we've made important gains. Yet the threat from Soviet forces, conventional and strategic, from the Soviet drive for domination, from the increase in espionage and state terror remains great. This is reality. Closing our eyes will not make reality disappear.

We pledge together to hold real growth in defense spending to the bare minimum. My budget honors that pledge. And I'm now asking you, the Congress, to keep its end of the bargain. The Soviets must know that if America reduces her defenses, it will be because of a reduced threat, not a reduced resolve. [Applause.]

Keeping America strong is as vital to the national security as controlling Federal spending is to our economic security. But, as I have said before, the most powerful force we can enlist against the Federal defi-

cit is an ever-expanding American economy, unfettered and free.

## Push for Tax Overhaul

The magic of opportunity — unreserved, unfailing, unrestrained — isn't this the calling that unites us? I believe our tax rate cuts for the people have done more to spur a spirit of risk-taking and help America's economy break free than any program since John Kennedy's tax cut almost a quarter century ago.

Now history calls us to press on, to complete efforts for an historic tax reform providing new opportunity for all and ensuring that all pay their fair share — but no more. We've come this far. Will you join me now and we'll walk this last mile together? [Applause.]

You know my views on this. We cannot and we will not accept tax reform that is a tax increase in disguise. True reform must be an engine of productivity and growth, and that means a top personal rate no higher than 35 percent. True reform must be truly fair and that means raising personal exemptions to $2,000. True reform means a tax system that at long last is pro-family, pro-jobs, pro-future, and pro-America. [Applause.]

## Efforts for Freer Trade

As we knock down the barriers to growth, we must redouble our efforts for freer and fairer trade. We have already taken actions to counter unfair trading practices to pry open closed foreign markets. We will continue to do so. We will also oppose legislation touted as providing protection that in reality pits one American worker against another, one industry against another, one community against another, and that raises prices for us all. If the United States can trade with other nations on a level playing field, we can out-produce, out-compete, and out-sell anybody, anywhere in the world. [Applause.]

## International Currencies

The constant expansion of our economy and exports requires a sound and stable dollar at home and reliable exchange rates around the world. We must never again permit wild currency swings to cripple our farmers and other exporters. Farmers, in particular, have suffered from past unwise government policies. They must not be abandoned with problems they did not create and cannot control. We've begun coordinating economic and monetary policy among our major trading partners. But there's more to do, and tonight I am directing Treasury Secretary Jim Baker to determine if the nations of the world should convene to discuss the role and relationship of our currencies. [Applause.]

## Social Agenda

Confident in our future, and secure in our values, Americans are striving forward

to embrace the future. We see it not only in our recovery, but in three straight years of falling crime rates, as families and communities band together to fight pornography, drugs, and lawlessness, and to give back to their children the safe and, yes, innocent childhood they deserve.

We see it in the renaissance in education, the rising SAT scores for three years — last year's increase the greatest since 1963. It wasn't government and Washington lobbies that turned education around, it was the American people who, in reaching for excellence, knew to reach back to basics. We must continue the advance by supporting discipline in our schools; vouchers that give parents freedom of choice; and we must give back to our children their lost right to acknowledge God in their classrooms. [Applause.]

We are a nation of idealists, yet today there is a wound in our national conscience; America will never be whole as long as the right to life granted by our Creator is denied to the unborn. For the rest of my time, I shall do what I can to see that this wound is one day healed. [Applause.]

## Re-Evaluating Welfare Programs

As we work to make the American Dream real for all, we must also look to the condition of America's families. Struggling parents today worry how they will provide their children the advantages that their parents gave them. In the welfare culture, the breakdown of the family, the most basic support system, has reached crisis proportions — in female and child poverty, child abandonment, horrible crimes and deteriorating schools. After hundreds of billions of dollars in poverty programs, the plight of the poor grows more painful. But the waste in dollars and cents pales before the most tragic loss — the sinful waste of human spirit and potential.

We can ignore this terrible truth no longer. As Franklin Roosevelt warned 51 years ago, standing before this chamber, he said, "Welfare is a narcotic, a subtle destroyer of the human spirit." And we must now escape the spider's web of dependency. Tonight I am charging the White House Domestic Council to present me by December 1, 1986, an evaluation of programs and a strategy for immediate action to meet the financial, educational, social, and safety concerns of poor families. I am talking about real and lasting emancipation, because the success of welfare should be judged by how many of its recipients become independent of welfare. [Applause.]

## Affordable Health Insurance

Further, after seeing how devastating illness can destroy the financial security of the family, I am directing the Secretary of Health and Human Services, Dr. Otis Bowen, to report to me by year end with recommendations on how the private sector and government can work together to address the problems of affordable insurance for those whose life savings would otherwise be threatened when catastrophic illness strikes.

## Message to Young People

And tonight I want to speak directly to America's younger generation, because you hold the destiny of our nation in your hands. With all the temptations young people face it sometimes seems the allure of the permissive society requires superhuman feats of self-control. But the call of the future is too strong, the challenge too great to get lost in the blind alleyways of dissolution, drugs, and despair.

## Wonder and Achievement

Never has there been a more exciting time to be alive — a time of rousing wonder and heroic achievement. As they said in the film "Back to the Future": "Where we are going, we don't need roads." Well, today physicists peering into the infinitely small realms of subatomic particles find reaffirmations of religious faith. Astronomers build a space telescope that can see to the edge of the universe and possibly back to the moment of creation.

## Continuing the Space Program

So, yes, this nation remains fully committed to America's space program. We're going forward with our shuttle flights, we're going forward to build our space station, and we are going forward with research on a new Orient Express that could, by the end of the next decade, take off from Dulles Airport, accelerate up to 25 times the speed of sound, attaining low Earth orbit or flying to Tokyo within two hours. [Applause.]

## Anti-Missile Defense

And the same technology transforming our lives can solve the greatest problem of the 20th century. A security shield can one day render nuclear weapons obsolete and free mankind from the prison of nuclear terror. [Applause.] America met one historic challenge and went to the moon. Now America must meet another — to make our strategic defense real for all the citizens of planet Earth.

## U.S.-Soviet Relations

Let us speak of our deepest longing for the future — to leave our children a land that is free and just and a world at peace. It is my hope that our fireside summit in Geneva and Mr. [Mikhail S.] Gorbachev's upcoming visit to America can lead to a more stable relationship. Surely no people on Earth hate war more or love peace more than we Americans. [Applause.]

But we cannot stroll into the future with childlike faith. Our differences with a system that openly proclaims and practices an alleged right to command people's lives

and to export its ideology by force are deep and abiding.

Logic and history compel us to accept that our relationship be guided by realism — rock-hard, clear-eyed, steady, and sure. Our negotiators in Geneva have proposed a radical cut in offensive forces by each side, with no cheating. They have made clear that Soviet compliance with the letter and spirit of agreements is essential. If the Soviet government wants an agreement that truly reduces nuclear arms, there will be an agreement. [Applause.]

But arms control is no substitute for peace. We know that peace follows in freedom's path and conflicts erupt when the will of the people is denied. So we must prepare for peace not only by reducing weapons but by bolstering prosperity, liberty, and democracy however and wherever we can. [Applause.]

## Advancing Opportunity

We advance the promise of opportunity every time we speak out on behalf of lower tax rates, freer markets, sound currencies around the world. We strengthen the family of freedom every time we work with allies and come to the aid of friends under siege. And we can enlarge the family of free nations if we will defend the unalienable rights of all God's children to follow their dreams.

## Support for 'Freedom Fighters'

To those imprisoned in regimes held captive, to those beaten for daring to fight for freedom and democracy — for their right to worship, to speak, to live and to prosper in the family of free nations — we say to you tonight: You are not alone, Freedom Fighters. America will support you with moral and material assistance your right not just to fight and die for freedom, but to fight and win freedom — [applause] — to win freedom in Afghanistan; in Angola; in Cambodia; and in Nicaragua. [Applause.]

This is a great moral challenge for the entire world. Surely, no issue is more important for peace in our own hemisphere, for the security of our frontiers, for the protection of our vital interests — than to achieve democracy in Nicaragua and to protect Nicaragua's democratic neighbors.

This year I will be asking Congress for the means to do what must be done for the great and good cause. As [Sen. Henry M.] "Scoop" Jackson [D-Wash.], the inspiration for our Bipartisan Commission on Central America, once said, "In matters of national security, the best politics is no politics." [Applause.]

## The Race to the Future

What we accomplish this year, in each challenge we face, will set our course for the balance of the decade, indeed for the remainder of the century. After all we've done so far, let no one say that this nation cannot

reach the destiny of our dreams. America believes, America is ready, America can win the race to the future — and we shall.

The American Dream is a song of hope that rings through night winter air. Vivid, tender music that warms our hearts when the least among us aspire to the greatest things — to venture a daring enterprise; to unearth new beauty in music, literature, and art; to discover a new universe inside a tiny silicon chip or a single human cell.

## 'Heroes of Our Hearts'

We see the dream coming true in the spirit of discovery of Richard Cavoli — all his life he's been enthralled by the mysteries of medicine. And Richard, we know that the experiment that you began in high school was launched and lost last week, yet your dream lives. And as long as it's real, work of noble note will yet be done — work that could reduce the harmful effects of X-rays on patients and enable astronomers to view the golden gateways of the farthest stars.

We see the dream glow in the towering talent of a 12-year-old, Tyrone Ford — a child prodigy of gospel music, he has surmounted personal adversity to become an accomplished pianist and singer. He also directs the choirs of three churches and has performed at the Kennedy Center.

With God as your composer, Tyrone, your music will be the music of angels.

We see the dream being saved by the courage of the 13-year-old, Shelby Butler — honor student and member of her school's safety patrol. Seeing another girl freeze in terror before an out-of-control school bus, she risked her life and pulled her to safety.

With bravery like yours, Shelby, America need never fear for our future.

And we see the dream born again in the joyful compassion of a 13-year-old, Trevor Ferrell. Two years ago, age 11, watching men and women bedding down in abandoned doorways — on television he was watching — Trevor left his suburban Philadelphia home to bring blankets and food to the helpless and homeless. And now, 250 people help him fulfill his nightly vigil.

Trevor, yours is the living spirit of brotherly love. Would you four stand up for a moment? [Applause.]

Thank you, thank you. You are heroes of our hearts. We look at you and know it's true — in this land of dreams fulfilled, where greater dreams may be imagined, nothing is impossible, no victory is beyond our reach, no glory will ever be too great.

So now, it's up to us, all of us, to prepare America for that day when our work will pale before the greatness of America's champions in the 21st century. The world's hopes rest with America's future; America's hopes rest with us. So let us go forward to create our world of tomorrow in faith, in unity, and in love.

God bless you and God bless America. [Applause.]

# President Reagan's Fiscal 1987 Budget Message

*Following is the text of President Reagan's budget message sent to Congress Feb. 5, 1986.*

TO THE CONGRESS OF
THE UNITED STATES:

The economic expansion we are now enjoying is one of the most vigorous in 35 years. Family income is at an all-time high; production and productivity are increasing; employment gains have been extraordinary; and inflation, which raged at double-digit rates when I took office, has been reduced dramatically. Defense capabilities, which had been dangerously weakened during the 1970s, are being rebuilt, restoring an adequate level of national security and deterrence to war. Moreover, an insupportable growth in tax burdens and Federal regulations has been halted.

Let me give you a few highlights:

● Employment has grown by 9.2 million in the past three years, while the unemployment rate has fallen by 3.8 percentage points; during the three years preceding my administration, employment grew by only 5.5 million and the unemployment rate rose 0.8 percentage points.

● The highest proportion of our adult population [60%] is now at work, with more blacks and other minorities employed [14 million] than ever before.

● Inflation, which averaged 11.6% a year during the three years before I took office, has averaged only a third of that — 3.8% — during the last three years.

● Real GNP [gross national product] has grown at a 4.5% annual rate during the past three years, compared with only a 2.2% annual rate during the last three years of the previous administration.

● The prime rate of interest and other key interest rates are less than half what they were when I took office.

● Some 11,000 new business incorporations are generated every week, and since early 1983, investment in plant and equipment has risen 44% in real terms.

● During the past three years, industrial production has risen by 25%.

● During the same period, corporate profits increased 117% and stocks nearly doubled in value.

● Federal tax revenues have returned to historic levels of approximately 18½% of GNP, as tax rates have been cut across-the-board and indexed for inflation.

● As a result of all of the above, real after-tax personal income has risen 10.6% during the last three years — an average increase of $2,500 for each American household.

This dramatic improvement in the performance of our economy was no accident. We have put in place policies that reflect our commitment to reduce Federal Government intrusion in the private sector and have eliminated many barriers to the process of capital formation and growth.

We continue to maintain a steadfast adherence to the four fundamental principles of the economic program I presented in February 1981:

● Reducing the growth of Federal spending;

● Limiting tax burdens;

● Relieving the economy of excessive regulation; and

● Supporting a sound and stable monetary policy.

Conditions are now in place for a sustained era of national prosperity. But, there is a major threat looming on the horizon; the Federal deficit. If this deficit is not brought under control, we risk losing all we've achieved — and more.

We cannot let this happen. Therefore, the budget I am presenting has as its major objective setting the deficit on a downward path to a balanced budget by 1991. In so doing, my budget meets or exceeds the deficit reduction targets set out in the Balanced Budget and Emergency Deficit Control Act, commonly known for its principal sponsors as Gramm-Rudman-Hollings.

At the end of the last session of Congress there emerged a bipartisan consensus that something had to be done about the deficit. The result — Gramm-Rudman-Hollings — committed both the President and the Congress to a fixed schedule of progress. By submitting this budget, I am abiding by the law and keeping my part of the bargain.

This budget shows, moreover, that eliminating the deficit is possible *without* raising taxes, *without* sacrificing our defense preparedness, and *without* cutting into legitimate programs for the poor and the elderly. A tax increase would jeopardize our economic expansion and might well prove counterproductive in terms of its effect on the deficit. We can hardly back away from our defense build-up without creating confusion among friends and adversaries alike about our determination to maintain our commitments and without jeopardizing our prospects for meaningful arms control talks. And frankly we must not break faith with those poor and elderly who depend on Federal programs for their security.

## The Deficit and Economic Growth

Until the Second World War, the Federal budget was kept in balance or ran a surplus during peacetime as a matter of course. But in the early 1960s this traditional fiscal discipline and political rectitude began to break down. We have run deficits during 24 of the last 25 years. In the past ten years, they have averaged 2.5% of GNP. But last year the deficit was over 5% of GNP. This trend is clearly in the wrong direction and must be reversed. Last year's deficit amounted to nearly $1,000 for every man, woman, and child in

the United States. To eliminate the deficit solely by increasing taxes would mean imposing an extra $2,400 burden on each American household. But taxes are already higher relative to GNP than they were during the 1960s and early 1970s — before inflation pushed them to levels that proved insupportable. The American people have made it clear they will not tolerate a higher tax burden. Spending is the problem — not taxes — and spending must be cut.

The program of spending cuts and other reforms contained in my budget will lead to a balanced budget at the end of five years and will thus remove a serious impediment to the continuation of our economic expansion. As this budget shows, such reforms can be accomplished in an orderly manner, without resorting to desperate measures.

Inappropriate and outmoded programs, and activities that cannot be made cost effective, must be ended. Activities that are essential, but that need not be carried out by the Federal Government, can be placed in the private sector or, if they are properly public in nature, turned over to State and local governments. As explained in the Management Report I am also submitting today, efficiencies can be realized through improved management techniques, increased productivity, and program consolidations.

The need to cut unnecessary Federal spending and improve management of necessary programs must be made a compelling guide to our policy choices. The result will be a leaner, better integrated, more streamlined Federal Government — stripped of marginal, nonessential and inappropriate functions and activities, and focusing its energies and resources entirely on its proper tasks and constitutional responsibilities. That way, resources will be allocated more efficiently — those things best done by government will be done by government; those things best done by the private sector will be directed by the marketplace.

The Balanced Budget and Emergency Deficit Control Act [Gramm-Rudman-Hollings] requires that spending be reduced in accord with a prescribed formula if projected deficits exceed the predetermined targets. This mechanism will operate in a limited fashion during the current fiscal year. However, we should avoid such across-the-board cuts in the future, and they will not be necessary if Congress adopts this budget. Achieving budget savings by taking into account relative priorities among programs is a much better way than resorting to an arbitrary formula. The latter could dangerously weaken vital programs involving the national security or public health and safety, while leaving marginal programs substantially intact.

If the spending cuts and other reforms proposed in this budget are approved, the

Federal deficit will be reduced by $166 billion over the next three years. This represents about $700 for every individual American and about $1,900 for every household. I believe this is the appropriate way to deal with the deficit: cut excessive Federal spending rather than attack the family budget by increasing taxes, or risk a deterioration in our national security posture, or break faith with the dependent poor and elderly.

## Returning the Federal Government to Its Proper Role

The task of reducing the deficit must be pursued with an eye toward narrowing the current wide scope of Government activities to the provision of those, but only those, necessary and essential services toward which all taxpayers should be contributing — and providing them as efficiently as possible. This is the underlying philosophy that I have used in shaping this year's budget. Let me explain:

**High priority programs should be adequately funded.** Despite the very tight fiscal environment, this budget provides funds for maintaining — and in some cases expanding — high priority programs in crucial areas of national interest. Necessary services and income support for the dependent poor and the elderly receive significant funding in this budget. So do other programs of national interest, including drug enforcement, AIDS [acquired immune deficiency syndrome] research, the space program, nonmilitary research, and national security.

While national security programs continue to be one of my highest priorities, they have not been exempt from general budgetary stringency. Last summer I reluctantly agreed with Congress to scale back the planned growth of defense appropriations to a zero real increase for 1986 and only a 3% real increase each year thereafter. Congressional action on 1986 appropriations and the subsequent sequestration for 1986 under Gramm-Rudman-Hollings have cut defense budget authority well below last year's level. The budget I am submitting would return defense funding to a steady, well-managed growth pattern consistent with the program levels agreed to in last year's budget resolution and consistent with what the country needs in order to provide for our national security.

During the past five years, we have reversed the decline in defense spending and have made significant progress in restoring our military capabilities. The moderate increases that are now requested are necessary to maintain this progress and enable us to move forward with meaningful arms reduction negotiations with the Soviet Union.

**Unnecessary programs are no longer affordable.** Some government programs have become outmoded, have accomplished their original purpose, represent an inappropriate area for Federal involvement in the first place, or are marginal in the current tight budgetary environment. If it would not be appropriate or feasible for the private sector or for State or local governments to assume such functions, this budget proposes that programs of this variety be terminated immediately, phased out in an orderly manner, or eliminated when their legal authority expires. Examples include Small Business Administration credit programs, Amtrak grants, Urban Development Action Grants, the Appalachian Regional Commission, the Economic Development Administration, the Interstate Commerce Commission, Maritime Administration loan guarantees, education subsidies for health professionals, the work incentives program, and subsidies for air carriers.

**Many other programs should be reduced to a more appropriate scale.** Some Federal programs have become overextended, misdirected, or operate on too expansive a scale given the current tight budgetary environment. This budget proposes reforms to limit the costs and future growth of medicare and medicaid, subsidized housing, Civil Service pensions and health benefits, postal subsidies, interstate highway grants, the Forest Service, and many other programs.

**The Government should not compete with the private sector.** Traditionally, governments supply the type of needed services that would not be provided by the private marketplace. Over the years, however, the Federal Government has acquired many commercial-type operations. In most cases, it would be better for the Government to get out of the business and stop competing with the private sector, and in this budget I propose that we begin that process. Examples of such "privatization" initiatives in this budget include sale of the power marketing administrations and the naval petroleum reserves; and implementation of housing and education voucher programs. I am also proposing the sale of unneeded assets, such as loan portfolios and surplus real estate, and contracting out appropriate Federal services.

**Many services can be provided better by State and local governments.** Over the years, the Federal Government has preempted many functions that properly ought to be operated at the State or local level. This budget contemplates an end to unwarranted Federal intrusion into the State and local sphere and restoration of a more balanced, constitutionally appropriate, federalism with more clearly delineated roles for the various levels of government. Examples include new consolidations of restrictive small categorical grant programs into block grants for transportation and environmental protection, at reduced Federal costs. Continued funding is maintained for existing block grants for social services, health, education, job training, and community development.

Administration of the agricultural extension service should be turned over to State and local governments. Also, the Federal Government should get out of the business of paying for local sewage treatment systems, local airports, local law enforcement, subsidies to State maritime schools, and local coastal management.

**Remaining Federal activities should be better managed.** As we proceed with the deficit reduction process over the next several years, it is important that all remaining Federal operations be well managed and coordinated to avoid duplication, reduce costs, and minimize regulatory burdens imposed on the private sector. Management efficiencies must accompany the process of developing a leaner, more carefully focused Federal role. We can no longer afford unnecessary overhead and inefficiencies when we are scaling back the role and cost of the Federal Government.

Substantial savings in overhead costs have been achieved under provisions of the Deficit Reduction Act of 1984. As described in my Management Report, more savings are possible, and these effects are incorporated in this budget. Outmoded, inefficient systems of agency cash and credit management are being replaced; administrative policies and procedures, approaches to automatic data processing, and agency field structures will be streamlined and upgraded; and waste, fraud, and abuse will be further reduced. All these initiatives, part of our Reform '88 program, will take advantage of efficiencies made possible by modern management techniques, improved communications, and new information technology. We shall run the Federal Government on a business-like basis — improving service delivery and reducing taxpayer costs.

Administration of Federal agencies will be made more efficient through the adoption of staffing standards, automation of manual processes, consolidation of similar functions, and reduction of administrative overhead costs. A program to increase productivity by 20% by 1992 in all appropriate Government functions is being instituted, and a major effort is proposed to revamp our outmoded management of a $250 billion Federal credit portfolio. This effort will include establishing prescreening, origination fees, administration and penalty charges, use of collection agencies, charging appropriate interest rates, and the sale of loan portfolios.

Our management improvement program will result in a leaner and more efficient Federal structure and is described in greater detail in my separate Management Report. Improving the management of the Government must be accorded a crucial role and the priority it deserves.

We must also reduce unnecessary costs and burdens on the nonfederal sector and have already made considerable progress in reducing the costs imposed on businesses and State and local governments by Federal regulations. These savings are estimated to total $150 billion over a 10-year period. We have reduced the number of new regulations in every year I have been in office and have eliminated or reduced paperwork requirements by over 500 million hours. In addition, regulations are now more carefully crafted to achieve the greatest public protection for the least cost, and wherever possible to use market forces instead of working against them.

**Finally, user fees should be charged for services where appropriate.** Those who receive special benefits and services from the Federal Government should be the ones to bear the costs of those services, not the general taxpayer. Accordingly, this budget imposes fees and premiums for Federal guarantees of loans, and imposes user fees and charges for Federal cost recovery for meat and poultry inspection, National park and forest facilities, harbor and inland waterway use, Coast Guard and Customs inspections, and for many other services.

### Reform of the Budget Process

Over the years, Federal spending constituencies have become increasingly powerful. In part because of their strong and effective advocacy, Congress has become less and less able to face up to its budgetary responsibilities. The Congressional budget process is foundering; last year it fell apart time and time again. The budget resolution and appropriations bills were months late in passing, and few real deficit reductions were achieved.

Gramm-Rudman-Hollings offers a significant opportunity to avoid many of these problems in the future. That act not only sets deficit targets leading to a balanced budget by 1991, it provides a mechanism for automatic spending cuts and incorporates certain reforms in the budget process

itself. But Gramm-Rudman-Hollings does not go far enough in this regard. To meet the clear need for a greatly strengthened budget process, I propose a number of additional reform measures.

As before, I ask Congress to pass a balanced budget amendment to the Constitution. In addition, I continue to seek passage of a line-item veto — authority now possessed by 43 of the Nation's governors. I also urge, for 1988 and beyond, changing the budget resolution to a joint resolution subject to Presidential signature and establishing binding expenditure subcategories within the resolution budget totals. Moreover, I urge that serious study be given to proposals for multiyear appropriations and to the development of a capital budget.

As I have pointed out time and again, there's not a State in the Union that doesn't have a better budget process than the Federal Government. We can — and we must — do better.

### Conclusion

As I said in my address to Congress yesterday, the State of the Union is strong and growing stronger. We've had some extraordinarily good years, and our economy is performing well, with inflation coming under control. Economic growth and investment are up, while interest rates, tax rates, and unemployment have all come down substantially. Our national security is being restored. The proliferation of unnecessary and burdensome Federal regulations has been halted. A significant beginning has been made toward curbing the excessive and unsustainable growth of domestic

spending. Improving the management of the Government has been given priority and is achieving results. I think most Americans would agree that America is truly on the move!

The large and stubbornly persistent budget deficit remains as a dark and threatening cloud on the horizon. It threatens our prosperity and our hopes for continued healthy economic growth.

Congress has recognized this threat. It has mandated a gradual, orderly movement to a balanced budget over the next five years. The proposals in this budget are a blueprint for achieving those targets while preserving legitimate programs for the aged and needy, providing for our national security, and doing this without raising taxes.

I realize it will be difficult for elected officials to make the hard choices envisioned in this budget. But we must find the political will to face up to our responsibilities and resist the pleadings of special interests whose "era of power" in Washington must be brought to an end — for taxpayers as a whole can no longer be expected to carry them on their backs. All this will call for statesmanship of a high order. We must all realize that the deficit problem is also an opportunity — an opportunity to construct a new, leaner, better focused, and better managed Federal structure. Let's do it.

I look forward to working with Congress on meeting these formidable challenges. It is our job. Let's get on with it.

RONALD REAGAN

February 5, 1986

---

# Reagan's Statement on Arms Treaty Policy

*Following is the White House text of President Reagan's May 27, 1986, statement on U.S. compliance with the SALT I and II (strategic arms limitation treaty) agreements.*

On the eve of the Strategic Arms Reductions Talks [START] in 1982, I decided that the United States would not undercut the expired SALT I Interim Offensive Agreement or the unratified SALT II agreement as long as the Soviet Union exercised equal restraint. I took this action, despite my concerns about the flaws inherent in those agreements, to foster an atmosphere of mutual restraint conducive to serious negotiations on arms reductions. I made clear that our policy required reciprocity and that it must not adversely affect our national security interests in the

face of the continuing Soviet military buildup.

### U.S. Observance of Pacts

Last June, I reviewed the status of U.S. interim restraint policy. I found that the United States had fully kept its part of the bargain. As I have documented in three detailed reports to the Congress, most recently in December 1985, the Soviet Union, regrettably, has not. I noted last June that the pattern of Soviet noncompliance with their existing arms control commitments increasingly affected our national security. This pattern also raised fundamental concerns about the integrity of the arms control process itself. A country simply cannot be serious about effective arms control unless it is equally serious about compliance.

### Going the Extra Mile

In spite of the regrettable Soviet record, I concluded last June that it remained in the interest of the United States and its allies to try, once more, to establish an interim framework of truly mutual restraint on strategic offensive arms as we pursued, with renewed vigor, our objective of deep reductions in existing U.S. and Soviet nuclear arsenals through the Geneva negotiations. Therefore, I undertook to go the extra mile, dismantling a Poseidon submarine, *U.S.S. Sam Rayburn*, to give the Soviet Union adequate time to take the steps necessary to join us in establishing an interim framework of truly mutual restraint. However, I made it clear that, as subsequent U.S. deployment milestones were reached, I would assess the overall situation and determine future U.S. actions on a case-by-case basis in light of Soviet behavior in exercising restraint comparable to our own, correcting their non-compliance, reversing their unwarranted military buildup, and seriously pursuing equitable and verifiable arms reduction agreements.

Later this month, the 8th Trident submarine, *U.S.S. Nevada*, begins sea trials. In accordance with our announced policy, I have assessed our options with respect to that milestone. I have considered Soviet actions since my June 1985 decision, and U.S. and Allied security interests in light of both those actions and our programmatic options. The situation is not encouraging.

## Soviet Pattern Of Non-Compliance

While we have seen some modest indications of improvement in one or two areas, there has been no real progress toward meeting U.S. concerns with respect to the general pattern of Soviet non-compliance with major arms control commitments, particularly in those areas of most obvious and direct Soviet non-compliance with the SALT and ABM [anti-ballistic missile] agreements. The deployment of the SS-25, a forbidden second new Intercontinental Ballistic Missile [ICBM] type, continues apace. The Soviet Union continues to encrypt telemetry associated with its ballistic missile testing in a manner which impedes verification. The Krasnoyarsk radar remains a clear violation. We see no abatement of the Soviet strategic force buildup. Finally, since the November summit, we have yet to see the Soviets follow up constructively on the commitment made by General Secretary Gorbachev and myself to achieve early progress in the Geneva negotiations, in particular in areas where there is common ground, including the principle of 50 percent reductions in the strategic nuclear arms of both countries, appropriately applied, as well as an interim agreement on Intermediate-range Nuclear Forces [INF].

Based on Soviet conduct since my June 1985 decision, I can only conclude that the Soviet Union has not, as yet, taken those actions that would indicate its readiness to join us in an interim framework of truly mutual restraint. At the same time, I have also considered the programmatic options available to the U.S. in terms of their overall net impact on U.S. and Allied security.

When I issued guidance on U.S. policy on June 10, 1985, the military plans and programs for fiscal year 1986 were about to be implemented. The amount of flexibility that any nation has in the near term for altering its planning is modest at best. Our military planning will take more time to move out from under the shadow of previous assumptions, especially in the budgetary conditions which we now face. These budgetary conditions make it essential that we make the very best possible use of our resources.

The United States had long planned to retire and dismantle two of the oldest Poseidon submarines when their reactor cores were exhausted. Had I been persuaded that refueling and retaining these two Poseidon submarines would have contributed significantly and cost-effectively to the national security, I would have directed that these two Poseidon submarines not be dismantled, but be overhauled and retained. However, in view of present circumstances, including current military and economic realities, I have directed their retirement and dismantlement as planned.

As part of the same decision last June, I also announced that we would take appropriate and proportionate responses when needed to protect our own security in the face of continuing Soviet non-compliance. It is my view that certain steps are now required by continued Soviet disregard of their obligations.

Needless to say, the most essential near-term response to Soviet non-compliance remains the implementation of our full strategic modernization program, to underwrite deterrence today, and the continued pursuit of the Strategic Defense Initiative [SDI] research program, to see if it is possible to provide a safer and more stable basis for our future security and that of our Allies. The strategic modernization program, including the deployment of the second 50 Peacekeeper missiles, is the foundation for all future U.S. offensive force options. It provides a solid basis which can and will be adjusted over time to respond most efficiently to continued Soviet non-compliance. The SDI program represents our best hope for a future in which our security can rest on the increasing contribution of defensive systems that threaten no one.

It is absolutely essential that we maintain full support for these programs. To fail to do so would be the worst response to Soviet non-compliance. It would immediately and seriously undercut our negotiators in Geneva by removing the leverage that they must have to negotiate equitable reductions in both U.S. and Soviet forces. It would send precisely the wrong signal to the leadership of the Soviet Union about the seriousness of our resolve concerning their non-compliance. And, it would significantly increase the risk to our security for years to come. Therefore, our highest priority must remain the full implementation of these programs.

Secondly, the development by the Soviet Union of its massive ICBM forces continues to challenge seriously the essential balance which has deterred both conflict and coercion. Last June, I cited the Soviet Union's SS-25 missile, a second new type of ICBM prohibited under SALT II, as a clear and irreversible violation. With the number of deployed SS-25 mobile ICBMs growing, I now call upon the Congress to restore bipartisan support for a balanced, cost-effective, long-term program to restore both the survivability and effectiveness of the U.S. ICBM program. This program should include the full deployment of the 100 Peacekeeper ICBMs.

But it must also look beyond the Peacekeeper and toward additional U.S. ICBM requirements in the future, including the Small ICBM to complement Peacekeeper. Therefore, I have directed the Department of Defense to provide to me by November 1986 an assessment of the best options for carrying out such a comprehensive ICBM program. This assessment will address the basing of the second 50 Peacekeeper missiles and specific alternative configurations for the Small ICBM in terms of size, number of warheads, and production rates.

Finally, I have also directed that the Advanced Cruise Missile program be accelerated. This would not direct any increase in the total program procurement at this time, but rather would establish a more efficient program that both saves money and accelerates the availability of additional options for the future.

This brings us to the question of the SALT agreements. SALT II was a fundamentally flawed and unratified treaty. Even if ratified, it would have expired on December 31, 1985. When presented to the U.S. Senate in 1979, it was considered by a broad range of critics, including the Senate Armed Services Committee, to be unequal and unverifiable in important provisions. It was, therefore, judged by many to be inimical to genuine arms control, to the security interests of the United States and its allies, and to global stability. The proposed treaty was clearly headed for defeat before my predecessor asked the Senate not to act on it.

The most basic problem with SALT II was that it codified major arms buildups rather than reductions. For example, even though at the time the Treaty was signed in 1979, the U.S. had, and only planned for, 550 MIRVed ICBM launchers, and the Soviet Union possessed only about 600, SALT II permitted each side to increase the number of such launchers to 820. It also permitted a buildup to 1,200 MIRVed ballistic launchers [both ICBMs and Submarine Launched Ballistic Missiles, SLBMs] even though the U.S. had only about 1,050 and the Soviet Union had only about 750 when the treaty was signed. It permitted the Soviet Union to retain all of its heavy ballistic missiles. Finally, it limited ballistic missile launchers, not the missiles or the warheads carried by the ballistic missiles. Since the signing of SALT II, Soviet ballistic missile forces have grown to within a few launchers of each of the 820 and 1,200 MIRVed limits, and from about 7,000 to over 9,000 warheads today. What is worse, given the failure of SALT II to constrain ballistic missile warheads, the number of warheads on Soviet ballistic missiles will continue to grow very significantly, even under the Treaty's limits, in the continued absence of Soviet restraint.

## Call for 'Mutual Restraint'

In 1982, on the eve of the START negotiations, I undertook not to undercut existing arms control agreements to the extent that the Soviet Union demonstrated comparable restraint. Unfortunately, the Soviet Union did not exercise comparable restraint, and uncorrected Soviet violations have seriously undermined the SALT structure. Last June, I once again laid out our legitimate concerns but decided to go the extra mile, dismantling a Poseidon submarine, not to comply with or abide by a flawed and unratified treaty, but rather to give the Soviet Union one more chance and adequate time to take the steps necessary to join us in establishing an interim framework of truly mutual restraint. The Soviet Union has not used the past year for this purpose.

Given this situation, I have determined that, in the future, the United States must base decisions regarding its strategic force structure on the nature and magnitude of the threat posed by Soviet strategic forces, and not on standards contained in the SALT structure which has been undermined by Soviet non-compliance, and especially in a flawed SALT II treaty which was never ratified, would have expired if it had been ratified, and has been violated by the Soviet Union.

Since the United States will retire and dismantle two Poseidon submarines this summer, we will remain technically in observance of the terms of the SALT II

Treaty until the U.S. equips its 131st B-52 heavy bomber for cruise missile carriage near the end of this year. However, given the decision that I have been forced to make, I intend at that time to continue deployment of U.S. B-52 heavy bombers with cruise missiles beyond the 131st aircraft as an appropriate response without dismantling additional U.S. systems as compensation under the terms of the SALT II Treaty. Of course, since we will remain in technical compliance with the terms of the expired SALT II Treaty for some months, I continue to hope that the Soviet Union will use this time to take the constructive steps necessary to alter the current situation. Should they do so, we will certainly take this into account.

The United States seeks to meet its strategic needs, given the Soviet buildup, by means that minimize incentives for continuing Soviet offensive force growth. In the longer term, this is one of the major motives in our pursuit of the Strategic Defense Initiative. As we modernize, we will continue to retire older forces as our national security requirements permit. I do not anticipate any appreciable numerical growth in U.S. strategic offensive forces. Assuming no significant change in the threat we face, as we implement the strategic modernization program the United States will not deploy more strategic nu-

clear delivery vehicles than does the Soviet Union. Furthermore, the United States will not deploy more strategic ballistic missile warheads than does the Soviet Union.

In sum, we will continue to exercise the utmost restraint, while protecting strategic deterrence, in order to help foster the necessary atmosphere for significant reductions in the strategic arsenals of both sides. This is the urgent task which faces us. I call on the Soviet Union to seize the opportunity to join us now in establishing an interim framework of truly *mutual* restraint.

Finally, I want to emphasize that no policy of interim restraint is a substitute for an agreement on deep and equitable reductions in offensive nuclear arms, provided that we can be confident of Soviet compliance with it. Achieving such reductions has received, and continues to receive, my highest priority. I hope the Soviet Union will act to give substance to the agreement I reached with General Secretary [Mikhail S.] Gorbachev in Geneva to achieve early progress, in particular in areas where there is common ground, including the principle of 50 percent reductions in the strategic nuclear arms of both countries, appropriately applied, as well as an interim INF agreement. If the Soviet Union carries out this agreement, we can move now to achieve greater stability and a safer world.

---

# Reagan's Speech on U.S.-Soviet Summit in Iceland

*Following is the White House text of President Reagan's speech, as delivered Oct. 13, 1986, on his meetings in Reykjavik, Iceland, with Soviet leader Mikhail S. Gorbachev.*

Good evening. As most of you know, I have just returned from meetings in Iceland with the leader of the Soviet Union, General Secretary Gorbachev. As I did last year when I returned from the summit conference in Geneva, I want to take a few moments tonight to share with you what took place in these discussions.

The implications of these talks are enormous and only just beginning to be understood. We proposed the most sweeping and generous arms control proposal in history. We offered the complete elimination of all ballistic missiles — Soviet and American — from the face of the Earth by 1996. While we parted company with this American offer still on the table, we are closer than ever before to agreements that could lead to a safer world without nuclear weapons.

But first, let me tell you that, from the start of my meetings with Mr. Gorbachev, I

have always regarded you, the American people, as full participants. Believe me, without your support, none of these talks could have been held, nor could the ultimate aims of American foreign policy — world peace and freedom — be pursued. And it is for these aims I went the extra mile to Iceland.

## Definition of Terms

Before I report on our talks though, allow me to set the stage by explaining two things that were very much a part of our talks, one a treaty and the other a defense against nuclear missiles which we are trying to develop. Now you've heard their titles a thousand times — the ABM Treaty and SDI. Those letters stand for, ABM, anti-ballistic missile, SDI, strategic defense initiative.

## M.A.D. and Anti-Missile Defense

Some years ago, the United States and the Soviet Union agreed to limit any defense against nuclear missile attacks to the emplacement in one location in each country of a small number of missiles capable of

intercepting and shooting down incoming nuclear missiles, thus leaving our real defense — a policy called Mutual Assured Destruction [M.A.D.], meaning if one side launched a nuclear attack, the other side could retaliate. And this mutual threat of destruction was believed to be a deterrent against either side striking first.

So here we sit with thousands of nuclear warheads targeted on each other and capable of wiping out both our countries. The Soviets deployed the few anti-ballistic missiles around Moscow as the treaty permitted. Our country didn't bother deploying because the threat of nationwide annihilation made such a limited defense seem useless.

## Soviet ABM Treaty Violation

For some years now we have been aware that the Soviets may be developing a nationwide defense. They have installed a large modern radar at Krasnoyarsk which we believe is a critical part of a radar system designed to provide radar guidance for anti-ballistic missiles protecting the entire nation. Now this is a violation of the ABM Treaty.

## Strategic Defense Initiative - 1

Believing that a policy of mutual destruction and slaughter of their citizens and ours was uncivilized, I asked our military a few years ago to study and see if there was a practical way to destroy nuclear missiles after their launch but before they can reach their targets rather than to just destroy people. Well, this is the goal for what we call SDI and our scientists researching such a system are convinced it is practical and that several years down the road we can have such a system ready to deploy. Now, incidentally, we are not violating the ABM Treaty which permits such research. If and when we deploy, the treaty — also allows withdrawal from the treaty upon six months' notice. SDI, let me make it clear, is a non-nuclear defense.

## Iceland Summit Talks

So here we are at Iceland for our second such meeting. In the first and in the months in between, we have discussed ways to reduce and in fact eliminate nuclear weapons entirely. We and the Soviets have had teams of negotiators in Geneva trying to work out a mutual agreement on how we could reduce or eliminate nuclear weapons. And so far, no success.

On Saturday and Sunday, General Secretary Gorbachev and his Foreign Minister [Eduard A.] Shevardnadze and Secretary of State George Shultz and I met for nearly 10 hours. We didn't limit ourselves to just arms reductions. We discussed what we call violation of human rights on the part of the Soviets, refusal to let people emigrate from Russia so they can practice their religion without being persecuted, letting people go to rejoin their families, husbands and wives separated by national borders being allowed to reunite.

In much of this the Soviet Union is violating another agreement — the Helsinki Accords they had signed in 1975. Yuri Orlov, whose freedom we just obtained, was imprisoned for pointing out to his government its violations of that pact, its refusal to let citizens leave their country or return.

We also discussed regional matters such as Afghanistan, Angola, Nicaragua, and Cambodia. But by their choice the main subject was arms control.

We discussed the emplacement of intermediate-range missiles in Europe and Asia and seemed to be in agreement they could be drastically reduced. Both sides seemed willing to find a way to reduce even to zero the strategic ballistic missiles we have aimed at each other. This then brought up the subject of SDI.

## Strategic Defense Initiative - 2

I offered a proposal that we continue our present research and if and when we reached the stage of testing we would sign now a treaty that would permit Soviet observation of such tests. And if the program was practical we would both eliminate our offensive missiles, and then we would share the benefits of advanced defenses. I explained that even though we would have done away with our offensive ballistic missiles, having the defense would protect against cheating or the possibility of a madman sometime deciding to create nuclear missiles. After all, the world now knows how to make them. I likened it to our keeping our gas masks even though the nations of the world had outlawed poison gas after World War I.

We seemed to be making progress on reducing weaponry although the General Secretary was registering opposition to SDI and proposing a pledge to observe ABM for a number of years as the day was ending.

## Negotiations Through the Night

Secretary Shultz suggested we turn over the notes our note-takers had been making of everything we'd said to our respective teams and let them work through the night to put them together and find just where we were in agreement and what differences separated us. With respect and gratitude, I can inform you those teams worked through the night till 6:30 a.m.

Yesterday, Sunday morning, Mr. Gorbachev and I, with our foreign ministers, came together again and took up the report of our two teams. It was most promising. The Soviets had asked for a 10-year delay in the deployment of SDI programs.

## U.S. Arms Proposal

In an effort to see how we could satisfy their concerns while protecting our principles and security, we proposed a 10-year period in which we began with the reduction of all strategic nuclear arms, bombers, air-launched cruise missiles, intercontinental ballistic missiles, submarine launched ballistic missiles and the weapons they carry. They would be reduced 50 percent in the first five years. During the next five years, we would continue by eliminating all remaining offensive ballistic missiles, of all ranges. And during that time we would proceed with research, development, and testing of SDI — all done in conformity with ABM provisions. At the 10-year point, with all ballistic missiles eliminated, we could proceed to deploy advanced defenses, at the same time permitting the Soviets to do likewise.

## U.S.-Soviet Debate

And here the debate began. The General Secretary wanted wording that, in effect, would have kept us from developing the SDI for the entire 10 years. In effect, he was killing SDI. And unless I agreed, all that work toward eliminating nuclear weapons would go down the drain — canceled.

I told him I had pledged to the American people that I would not trade away SDI — there was no way I could tell our people their government would not protect them against nuclear destruction. I went to Reykjavik determined that everything was negotiable except two things: our freedom and our future.

I'm still optimistic that a way will be found. The door is open and the opportunity to begin eliminating the nuclear threat is within reach.

## Realistic Approach to Soviets

So you can see, we made progress in Iceland. And we will continue to make progress if we pursue a prudent, deliberate, and, above all, realistic approach with the Soviets. From the earliest days of our administration, this has been our policy. We made it clear we had no illusions about the Soviets or their ultimate intentions. We were publicly candid about the critical moral distinctions betweeen totalitarianism and democracy. We declared the principal objective of American foreign policy to be not just the prevention of war but the extension of freedom. And, we stressed our commitment to the growth of democratic government and democratic institutions around the world. And that's why we assisted freedom fighters who are resisting the imposition of totalitarian rule in Afghanistan, Nicaragua, Angola, Cambodia, and elsewhere. And, finally, we began work on what I believe most spurred the Soviets to negotiate seriously — rebuilding our military strength, reconstructing our strategic deterrence, and, above all, beginning work on the strategic defense initiative.

And yet, at the same time we set out these foreign policy goals and began working toward them, we pursued another of our major objectives: that of seeking means to lessen tensions with the Soviets, and ways to prevent war and keep the peace.

Now, this policy is now paying dividends — one sign of this in Iceland was the progress on the issue of arms control. For the first time in a long while, Soviet-American negotiations in the area of arms reductions are moving, and moving in the right direction — not just toward arms control, but toward arms reduction.

But for all the progress we made on arms reductions, we must remember there were other issues on the table in Iceland, issues that are fundamental.

## Human Rights in Soviet Union

As I mentioned, one such issue is human rights. As President Kennedy once said, "And, is not peace, in the last analysis, basically a matter of human rights?"

I made it plain that the United States would not seek to exploit improvement in these matters for purposes of propaganda. But I also made it plain, once again, that an improvement of the human condition within the Soviet Union is indispensable for an improvement in bilateral relations with the United States. For a government that will break faith with its own people cannot be trusted to keep faith with foreign powers. So, I told Mr. Gorbachev — again in Reykjavik as I had in Geneva — we Americans place far less weight upon the words that are spoken at meetings such as these, than upon the deeds that follow. When it comes to human rights and judging Soviet intentions, we're all from Missouri — you got to show us.

## Soviet Military Actions

Another subject area we took up in Iceland also lies at the heart of the differences between the Soviet Union and America. This is the issue of regional conflicts. Summit meetings cannot make the American people forget what Soviet actions have meant for the peoples of Afghanistan, Central America, Africa, and Southeast Asia. Until Soviet policies change, we will make sure that our friends in these areas — those who fight for freedom and independence — will have the support they need.

## Cultural Exchanges

Finally, there was a fourth item. And this area was that of bilateral relations, people-to-people contacts. In Geneva last year, we welcomed several cultural exchange accords; in Iceland, we saw indications of more movement in these areas. But let me say now the United States remains committed to people-to-people programs that could lead to exchanges between not just a few elite but thousands of everyday citizens from both our countries.

So I think, then, that you can see that we did make progress in Iceland on a broad range of topics. We reaffirmed our four-point agenda; we discovered major new grounds of agreement; we probed again some old areas of disagreement.

## Strategic Defense Initiative - 3

And let me return again to the SDI issue. I realize some Americans may be asking tonight: Why not accept Mr. Gorbachev's demand? Why not give up SDI for this agreement?

Well, the answer, my friends, is simple. SDI is America's insurance policy that the Soviet Union would keep the commitments made at Reykjavik. SDI is America's security guarantee — if the Soviets should — as they have done too often in the past — fail to comply with their solemn commitments. SDI is what brought the Soviets back to arms control talks at Geneva and Iceland. SDI is the key to a world without nuclear weapons.

The Soviets understand this. They have devoted far more resources for a lot longer time than we, to their own SDI. The world's only operational missile defense today surrounds Moscow, the capital of the

Soviet Union. What Mr. Gorbachev was demanding at Reykjavik was that the United States agree to a new version of a 14-year-old ABM Treaty that the Soviet Union has already violated. I told him we don't make those kinds of deals in the United States.

## Why Not Have Missile Defense?

And the American people should reflect on these critical questions.

How does a defense of the United States threaten the Soviet Union or anyone else? Why are the Soviets so adamant that America remain forever vulnerable to Soviet rocket attack? As of today, all free nations are utterly defenseless against Soviet missiles — fired either by accident or design. Why does the Soviet Union insist that we remain so — forever?

So, my fellow Americans, I cannot promise, nor can any President promise, that the talks in Iceland or any future discussions with Mr. Gorbachev will lead inevitably to great breakthroughs or momentous treaty signings.

We will not abandon the guiding principle we took to Reykjavik. We prefer no agreement than to bring home a bad agreement to the United States.

## Prospects for Another Summit

And on this point, I know you're also interested in the question of whether there will be another summit. There was no indication by Mr. Gorbachev as to when or whether he plans to travel to the United States, as we agreed he would last year in Geneva. I repeat tonight that our invitation stands and that we continue to believe additional meetings would be useful. But that's a decision the Soviets must make.

## Dealing From Strength

But whatever the immediate prospects, I can tell you that I'm ultimately hopeful about the prospects for progress at the summit and for world peace and freedom. You see, the current summit process is very different from that of previous decades; it's different because the world is different; and the world is different because of the hard work and sacrifice of the American people during the past five and a half years. Your energy has restored and expanded our economic might; your support has restored our military strength. Your courage and sense of national unity in times of crisis have given pause to our adversaries, heartened our friends, and inspired the world. The Western democracies and the NATO alliance are revitalized and all across the world nations are turning to

democratic ideas and the principles of the free market. So because the American people stood guard at the critical hour, freedom has gathered its forces, regained its strength, and is on the march.

So, if there's one impression I carry away with me from these October talks, it is that, unlike the past, we're dealing now from a position of strength, and for that reason we have it within our grasp to move speedily with the Soviets toward even more breakthroughs.

Our ideas are out there on the table. They won't go away. We're ready to pick up where we left off. Our negotiators are heading back to Geneva, and we're prepared to go forward whenever and wherever the Soviets are ready. So, there's reason — good reason for hope.

I saw evidence of this in the progress we made in the talks with Mr. Gorbachev. And I saw evidence of it when we left Iceland yesterday, and I spoke to our young men and women at our naval installation at Keflavik — a critically important base far closer to Soviet naval bases than to our own coastline.

## Committed to Freedom

As always, I was proud to spend a few moments with them and thank them for their sacrifices and devotion to country. They represent America at her finest: committed to defend not only our own freedom but the freedom of others who would be living in a far more frightening world — were it not for the strength and resolve of the United States.

"Whenever the standard of freedom and independence has been … unfurled, there will be America's heart, her benedictions, and her prayers," John Quincy Adams once said. He spoke well of our destiny as a nation. My fellow Americans, we're honored by history, entrusted by destiny with the oldest dream of humanity — the dream of lasting peace and human freedom.

Another President, Harry Truman, noted that our century had seen two of the most frightful wars in history. And that "the supreme need of our time is for man to learn to live together in peace and harmony."

## Pursuit of an Ideal

It's in pursuit of that ideal I went to Geneva a year ago and to Iceland last week. And it's in pursuit of that ideal that I thank you now for all the support you've given me, and I again ask for your help and your prayers as we continue our journey toward a world where peace reigns and freedom is enshrined.

Thank you and God bless you.

# Reagan's Address on Arms Shipments to Iran

*Following is the White House text of President Reagan's address, as delivered Nov. 13, 1986, on U.S. shipments of arms to Iran.*

Good evening. I know you have been reading, seeing, and hearing a lot of stories the past several days attributed to Danish sailors, unnamed observers at Italian ports and Spanish harbors, and especially unnamed government officials of my administration. Well, now you are going to hear the facts from a White House source, and you know my name.

## Secret Discussions With Iran - 1

I wanted this time to talk with you about an extremely sensitive and profoundly important matter of foreign policy. For 18 months now we have had under way a secret diplomatic initiative to Iran. That initiative was undertaken for the simplest and best of reasons — to renew a relationship with the nation of Iran, to bring an honorable end to the bloody six-year war between Iran and Iraq, to eliminate state-sponsored terrorism and subversion, and to effect the safe return of all hostages.

Without Iran's cooperation, we cannot bring an end to the Persian Gulf war; without Iran's concurrence, there can be no enduring peace in the Middle East.

## Getting to the Facts

For 10 days now, the American and world press have been full of reports and rumors about this initiative and these objectives.

Now, my fellow Americans, there is an old saying that nothing spreads so quickly as a rumor. So I thought it was time to speak with you directly — to tell you firsthand about our dealings with Iran. As Will Rogers once said, "Rumor travels faster, but it don't stay put as long as truth." So let's get to the facts.

## No Arms-for-Hostages Swap

The charge has been made that the United States has shipped weapons to Iran as ransom payment for the release of American hostages in Lebanon — that the United States undercut its allies and secretly violated American policy against trafficking with terrorists.

Those charges are utterly false.

The United States has not made concessions to those who hold our people captive in Lebanon. And we will not. The United States has not swapped boatloads or planeloads of American weapons for the return of American hostages. And we will not.

Other reports have surfaced alleging U.S. involvement. Reports of a sealift to Iran using Danish ships to carry American arms. Of vessels in Spanish ports being employed in secret U.S. arms shipments. Of Italian ports being used. Of the U.S. sending spare parts and weapons for combat aircraft. All these reports are quite exciting, but as far as we are concerned, not one of them is true.

## Arms Shipments to Iran

During the course of our secret discussions, I authorized the transfer of small amounts of defensive weapons and spare parts for defensive systems to Iran. My purpose was to convince Tehran that our negotiators were acting with my authority, to send a signal that the United States was prepared to replace the animosity between us with a new relationship. These modest deliveries, taken together, could easily fit into a single cargo plane. They could not, taken together, affect the outcome of the six-year war between Iran and Iraq — nor could they affect in any way the military balance between the two countries.

Those with whom we were in contact took considerable risks and needed a signal of our serious intent if they were to carry on and broaden the dialogue.

## Iran's Influence in Hostages' Release

At the same time we undertook this initiative, we made clear that Iran must oppose all forms of international terrorism as a condition of progress in our relationship. The most significant step which Iran could take, we indicated, would be to use its influence in Lebanon to secure the release of all hostages held there.

Some progress has already been made. Since U.S. government contact began with Iran, there's been no evidence of Iranian government complicity in acts of terrorism against the United States. Hostages have come home — and we welcome the efforts that the government of Iran has taken in the past and is currently undertaking.

## Strategic Importance of Iran

But why, you might ask, is any relationship with Iran important to the United States?

Iran encompasses some of the most critical geography in the world. It lies between the Soviet Union and access to the warm waters of the Indian Ocean. Geography explains why the Soviet Union has sent an army into Afghanistan to dominate that country and, if they could, Iran and Pakistan.

Iran's geography gives it a critical position from which adversaries could interfere with oil flows from the Arab states that border the Persian Gulf. Apart from geography, Iran's oil deposits are important to the long-term health of the world economy.

For these reasons, it is in our national interest to watch for changes within Iran that might offer hope for an improved relationship. Until last year, there was little to justify that hope.

## No Need for Permanent Conflict

Indeed, we have bitter and enduring disagreements that persist today. At the heart of our quarrel has been Iran's past sponsorship of international terrorism. Iranian policy has been devoted to expelling all Western influence from the Middle East. We cannot abide that, because our interests in the Middle East are vital. At the same time, we seek no territory or special position in Iran. The Iranian revolution is a fact of history, but between American and Iranian basic national interests there need be no permanent conflict.

Since 1983, various countries have made overtures to stimulate direct contact between the United States and Iran. European, Near East, and Far East countries have attempted to serve as intermediaries. Despite a U.S. willingness to proceed, none of these overtures bore fruit.

With this history in mind, we were receptive last year when we were alerted to the possibility of establishing a direct dialogue with Iranian officials.

## U.S. Interest in Dialogue - 1

Now, let me repeat. America's long-standing goals in the region have been to help preserve Iran's independence from Soviet domination; to bring an honorable end to the bloody Iran-Iraq war; to halt the export of subversion and terrorism in the region. A major impediment to those goals has been an absence of dialogue, a cutoff in communication between us.

It's because of Iran's strategic importance and its influence in the Islamic world that we chose to probe for a better relationship between our countries.

## Secret Discussions With Iran - 2

Our discussions continued into the spring of this year. Based upon the progress we felt we had made, we sought to raise the diplomatic level of contacts. A meeting was arranged in Tehran. I then asked my former national security adviser, Robert McFarlane, to undertake a secret mission and gave him explicit instructions. I asked him to go to Iran to open a dialogue, making stark and clear our basic objectives and disagreements.

The four days of talks were conducted in a civil fashion, and American personnel were not mistreated. Since then, the dialogue has continued and step-by-step progress continues to be made.

## U.S. Interest in Dialogue - 2

Let me repeat: Our interests are clearly served by opening a dialogue with Iran and thereby helping to end the Iran-Iraq war. That war has dragged on for more than six years, with no prospect of a negotiated settlement. The slaughter on both sides has been enormous; and the adverse economic and political consequences for that vital region of the world have been growing. We sought to establish communication with both sides in that senseless struggle, so that we could assist in bringing about a ceasefire and, eventually, a settlement. We have sought to be evenhanded by working with both sides and with other interested nations to prevent a widening of the war.

This sensitive undertaking has entailed great risk for those involved. There is no question but that we could never have begun or continued this dialogue had the initiative been disclosed earlier. Due to the publicity of the past week, the entire initiative is very much at risk today.

### Precedent for Secret Diplomacy

There is ample precedent in our history for this kind of secret diplomacy. In 1971, then-President Nixon sent his national security adviser on a secret mission to China. In that case, as today, there was a basic requirement for discretion and for a sensitivity to the situation in the nation we were attempting to engage.

### Danger of False Rumors

Since the welcome return of former hostage David Jacobsen, there has been unprecedented speculation and countless reports that have not only been wrong, but have been potentially dangerous to the hostages and destructive of the opportunity before us. The efforts of courageous people like Terry Waite have been jeopardized. So extensive have been the false rumors and erroneous reports that the risks of remaining silent now exceed the risks of speaking out. And that's why I decided to address you tonight.

It's been widely reported, for example, that the Congress, as well as top Executive Branch officials, were circumvented. Although the efforts we undertook were highly sensitive and involvement of government officials was limited to those with a strict need to know, all appropriate Cabinet Officers were fully consulted. The actions I authorized were and continue to be in full compliance with Federal law. And the relevant committees of Congress are being and will be fully informed.

### No Tilt Toward Iran

Another charge is that we have tilted toward Iran in the Gulf war. This, too, is unfounded. We have consistently condemned the violence on both sides. We have consistently sought a negotiated settlement that preserves the territorial integrity of both nations. The overtures we've made to the government of Iran have not been a shift to supporting one side over the other. Rather, it has been a diplomatic initiative to gain some degree of access and influence within Iran — as well as Iraq — and to bring about an honorable end to that bloody conflict. It is in the interests of all parties in the Gulf region to end that war as soon as possible.

### 'No Concessions' Policy Intact

To summarize, our government has a firm policy not to capitulate to terrorist demands. That "no concessions" policy remains in force — in spite of the wildly speculative and false stories about arms for hostages and alleged ransom payments. We did not — repeat — did not trade weapons or anything else for hostages — nor will we. Those who think that we have "gone soft" on terrorism should take up the question with [Libyan leader] Colonel Gadhafi.

We have not, nor will we, capitulate to terrorists.

We will, however, get on with advancing the vital interests of our great nation — in spite of terrorists and radicals who seek to sabotage our efforts and immobilize the United States.

Our goals have been, and remain:
- to restore a relationship with Iran,
- to bring an honorable end to the war in the Gulf,
- to bring a halt to state-supported terror in the Middle East,
- and finally, to effect the safe return of all hostages from Lebanon.

As President, I've always operated on the belief that, given the facts, the American people will make the right decision. I believe that to be true now.

I cannot guarantee the outcome. But, as in the past, I ask for your support because I believe you share the hope for peace in the Middle East, for freedom for all hostages, and for a world free of terrorism. Certainly there are risks in this pursuit but there are greater risks if we do not persevere.

It will take patience and understanding; it will take continued resistance to those who commit terrorist acts; and it will take cooperation with all who seek to rid the world of this scourge.

Thank you and God bless you.

---

# Reagan, Meese on Iran-Nicaragua Arms Deals

*Following is the White House text of the Nov. 25, 1986, statements by President Reagan and Attorney General Edwin Meese III regarding the U.S. role in arms shipments to Iran and the transfer of funds to the Nicaraguan contras. The statements were made before reporters.*

## President Reagan's Statement

PRESIDENT REAGAN: Last Friday, after becoming concerned whether my national security apparatus had provided me with a security, or a complete factual record with respect to the implementation of my policy toward Iran, I directed the Attorney General to undertake a review of this matter over the weekend and report to me on Monday. And yesterday, Secretary Meese provided me and the White House Chief of Staff with a report on his preliminary findings. And this report led me to conclude that I was not fully informed on the nature of one of the activities undertaken in connection with this initiative. This action raises serious questions of propriety.

I've just met with my National Security advisers and Congressional leaders to inform them of the actions that I'm taking today. Determination of the full details of this action will require further review and investigation by the Department of Justice.

Looking to the future, I will appoint a special review board to conduct a comprehensive review of the role and procedures of the National Security Council staff in the conduct of foreign and national security policy.

I anticipate receiving the reports from the Attorney General and the special review board at the earliest possible date. Upon the completion of these reports, I will share their findings and conclusions with the Congress and the American people.

Although not directly involved, Vice Admiral John Poindexter has asked to be relieved of his assignment as Assistant to the President for National Security Affairs and to return to another assignment in the Navy. Lieutenant Colonel Oliver North has been relieved of his duties on the National

Security Council staff.

I am deeply troubled that the implementation of a policy aimed at resolving a truly tragic situation in the Middle East has resulted in such controversy. As I've stated previously, I believe our policy goals toward Iran were well-founded. However, the information brought to my attention yesterday convinced me that in one aspect, implementation of that policy was seriously flawed.

While I cannot reverse what has happened, I'm initiating steps, including those I've announced today, to assure that the implementation of all future, foreign, and national security policy initiatives will proceed only in accordance with my authorization.

Over the past six years, we've realized many foreign policy goals. I believe we can yet achieve, and I intend to pursue, the objectives on which we all agree — a safer, more secure and stable world.

And now, I'm going to ask Attorney General Meese to brief you.

**Q:** What was the flaw?

**Q:** Do you still maintain you didn't make a mistake, Mr. President?

**P:** Hold it.

### No Mistake Was Made

**Q:** Did you make a mistake in sending arms to Tehran, sir?

**P:** No, and I'm not taking any more questions, and — just a second, I'm going to ask Attorney General Meese to brief you on what we presently know of what he has found out.

**Q:** Is anyone else going to be let go, sir?

**Q:** Can you tell us — did Secretary Shultz —

**Q:** Is anyone else going to be let go? There have been calls for —

**P:** No one was let go; they chose to go.

**Q:** What about Secretary Shultz, Mr. President?

**Q:** Is Shultz going to stay, sir?

**Q:** How about Secretary Shultz and Mr. Regan, sir?

**Q:** What about Secretary Shultz, sir?

**Q:** Can you tell us if Secretary Shultz is going to stay?

**Q:** Can you give Secretary Shultz a vote of confidence if you feel that way?

**P:** May I give you Attorney General Meese?

**Q:** And who is going to run National Security?

**Q:** What about Shultz, sir?

**Q:** Why won't you say what the flaw is?

ATTORNEY GENERAL MEESE: That's what I'm going to say — what it's all about.

**Q:** Why can't he?

MEESE: Why don't I tell you what is the situation and then I'll take your questions.

### Attorney General Meese's Statement

On Friday afternoon — or Friday at noon, the President asked me to look into and bring together the facts concerning the — particularly the implementation of the strategic initiative in Iran and more precisely, anything pertaining to the transfer of arms. Over the weekend this inquiry was conducted. Yesterday evening I reported to the President. We continued our inquiry and this morning the President directed that we make this information immediately available to the Congress and to the public through this medium this noon.

Let me say that all of the information is not yet in. We are still continuing our inquiry. But he did want me to make available immediately what we know at the present time.

What is involved is that in the course of the arms transfers, which involved the United States providing the arms to Israel and Israel in turn transferring the arms — in effect, selling the arms to representatives of Iran. Certain monies which were received in the transaction between representatives of Israel and representatives of Iran were taken and made available to the forces in Central America which are opposing the Sandinista government there.

In essence, the way in which the transactions occurred was that a certain amount of money was negotiated by representatives outside of the United States with Iran for arms. This amount of money was then transferred to representatives as best we know that can be described as representatives of Israel. They, in turn, transferred to the CIA, which was the agent for the United States government under a finding prepared by the President — signed by the President in January of 1986. And, incidentally, all of these transactions that I am referring to took place between January of 1986 and the present time. They transferred to the CIA the exact amount of the money that was owed to the United States government for the weapons that were involved plus any costs of transportation that might be involved. This money was then repaid by the CIA to the Department of Defense under the normal procedures and all governmental funds and all governmental property was accounted for and statements of that have been verified by us up to the present time.

The money — the difference between the money owed to the United States government and the money received from representatives of Iran was then deposited in bank accounts which were under the control of representatives of the forces in Central America.

---

# President Reagan's Fiscal 1988 Budget Message

*Following is the text of President Reagan's budget message sent to Congress Jan. 5, 1987.*

TO THE SPEAKER OF THE HOUSE OF REPRESENTATIVES AND THE PRESIDENT OF THE SENATE:

The current economic expansion, now in its 50th month, is already one of the longest of the postwar era and shows promise of continuing to record length. This has not been due simply to chance — it is the result of successful policies adopted during the past 6 years. Disposable personal income is at an all-time high and is still rising; total production and living standards are both increasing; employment gains have been excellent. Inflation, which raged at double-digit rates in 1980, has been reduced dramatically. Defense capabilities, which had been dangerously weakened during the 1970's, have been substantially rebuilt, restoring a more adequate level of national security. An insupportable growth in tax burdens and Federal regulations has been halted, an intolerably complex and inequitable income tax structure has been radically reformed, and the largest management improvement program ever attempted is in full swing in all major Federal agencies. It has been a good 6 years.

Now in its 5th year, the current expansion already has exceeded 5 of the 7 previous postwar expansions in duration, and leading economic indicators point to continued growth ahead. Our policies have worked. Let me mention a few highlights of the current economic expansion:

● In the past 4 years 12.4 million new jobs have been created, while the total unemployment rate has fallen by 3.7 percentage points. By comparison, jobs in other developed countries have not grown significantly, and unemployment rates have remained high.

● Inflation, which averaged 10.3 percent a year during the 4 years before I came to office, has averaged less than a third of that during the last 4 years — 3.0 percent; inflation in 1986, at about 1 percent, was at its lowest rate in over two decades.

• The prime rate of interest, and other key interest rates, are less than half what they were in 1981.

• Between 1981 and 1986, numerous change[s] in the tax code, including a complete overhaul last year, have simplified and made the tax law more equitable, and significantly lowered tax rates for individuals and corporations. Six million low-income taxpayers are being removed from the income tax rolls. The inhibitive effect of our tax code on individual initiative has been reduced dramatically. Real after-tax personal income has risen 15 percent during the last 4 years, increasing our overall standard of living.

• Our defense capabilities have been strengthened with modernized equipment and successful recruiting and retention of higher caliber personnel; the readiness, training, and morale of our troops has been improved.

• After years of unsustainably rapid growth, Federal spending for domestic programs other than entitlements has been held essentially flat over the last 4 years.

• Since 1981, the amount of time spent by the public filling out forms required by the Federal Government has been cut by over 600 million hours, and the number of pages published annually in the *Federal Register* has been reduced by over 45 percent.

• Our continuing fight against waste, fraud, and abuse in Government programs has paid off, as the President's Council on Integrity and Efficiency has saved $84 billion in funds that have been put to more efficient use.

• Finally, Federal agencies have instituted the largest management improvement program ever attempted to bring a more businesslike approach to Government.

The dramatic improvement in the performance of our economy stemmed from steadfast adherence to the four fundamental principles of the economic program I presented in February 1981:

• limiting the growth of Federal spending;

• reducing tax burdens;

• relieving the economy of excessive regulation and paperwork; and

• supporting a sound and stable monetary policy.

### Need for Deficit Reduction

The foundation has been laid for a sustained era of national prosperity. But a major threat to our future prosperity remains: the Federal deficit. If this deficit is not brought under control by limiting Government spending, we put in jeopardy all we have achieved. Deficits brought on by continued high spending threaten the lower tax rates incorporated in tax reform and inhibit progress in our balance of trade.

We cannot permit this to happen. Therefore, one of the major objectives of this budget is to assure a steady reduction in the deficit until a balanced budget is reached.

This budget meets the $108 billion deficit target for 1988 set out in the Balanced Budget and Emergency Deficit Control Act, commonly known for its principal sponsors as Gramm-Rudman-Hollings. Gramm-Rudman-Hollings committed both the President and Congress to a fixed schedule of progress toward reducing the deficit. In submitting this budget, I am keeping my part of the bargain — and on schedule. I ask Congress to do the same. If the deficit reduction goals were to be abandoned, we could see unparalleled spending growth that this Nation cannot afford.

This budget shows that eliminating the deficit over time is possible without raising taxes, without sacrificing our defense preparedness, and without cutting into legitimate programs for the poor and the elderly, while at the same time providing needed additional resources for other high-priority programs.

### Deficit Reduction in 1988

Although the deficit has equaled or exceeded 5 percent of the gross national product [GNP] in each of the past 4 years, each year I have proposed a path to lower deficits — involving primarily the curtailment of unnecessary domestic spending. Congress, however, has rejected most of these proposals; hence, our progress toward reducing the deficit has been much more modest than it could have been.

This year there appears to be a major turn for the better. The 1987 deficit is estimated to be about $48 billion less than in 1986 and should decline to less than 4 percent of GNP. As the economy expands, Federal receipts will rise faster than the increase in outlays Congress enacted for the year.

However, there is no firm guarantee that progress toward a steadily smaller deficit and eventual budget balance will continue. On a current-services basis the deficit will continue to decline over the next 5 years, but this decline is gradual and vulnerable to potential fiscally irresponsible congressional action on a multitude of spending programs. It is also threatened by the possibility of a less robust economic performance than is projected, for that projection is based on the assumption that the necessary spending cuts will be made.

This 1988 budget can deal the deficit a crucial blow. If the proposals in this budget are adopted and if the economy performs according to the budget assumptions for growth and inflation, then for the second consecutive year the deficit should shrink substantially, by $65 billion, and thus decline to less than 2 1/2 percent of GNP. Reducing the deficit this far would bring it within the range of our previous peacetime experience and bring our goal of a balanced budget much closer to realization.

Moreover, if Congress adopts the proposals contained in this budget, it will en-sure additional deficit reductions in future years, because in many cases the savings from a given action, although small in 1988, would mount in later years. Given the good start made in 1987, Congress has an opportunity this year — by enacting this budget — to put the worst of the deficit problem behind us.

Adopting the spending reductions and other reforms proposed in this budget would reduce the Federal deficit an average of $54 billion annually for the next 3 years. This represents $220 each year for every individual American and about $600 for every household. I believe this is the appropriate way to deal with the deficit: cutting excessive Federal spending rather than attacking the family budget by increasing taxes, weakening our national security, breaking faith with the poor and the elderly, or ignoring the requirements for additional resources for other high priority programs.

### A More Competitive, Productive America

The task of deficit reduction is a formidable one — but it can and should be achieved with serious attention to the effects on America's economy, businesses, State and local governments, social organizations, and individual citizens. Reducing the deficit will reduce the burden the Federal Government places on private credit markets. The specific deficit reduction measures proposed in this budget would also help make our economy more competitive — and more productive. These objectives have been major considerations in the formulation of this budget.

High priority programs must be funded adequately. Despite the very tight overall fiscal environment, this budget provides adequate funds for maintaining and, in selected cases, expanding high priority programs in key areas of national interest. For example:

• essential services and income support for the aged and needy are expanded;

• the prevention, treatment, and research efforts begun in my 1987 drug abuse initiative are continued, while resources devoted to drug law enforcement have tripled since my administration began;

• the budget allocates $85 million to more intensive health care for those with the highest incidence of infant mortality;

• over half a billion dollars is provided for AIDS [acquired immune deficiency syndrome] research and education in 1988 — a 28 percent increase above the 1987 level and more than double our 1986 effort [an additional $100 million is provided for AIDS treatment and blood screening by the Veterans Administration and the Department of Defense];

• building upon the Nation's pre-eminence in basic biomedical research, the budget seeks funding for the full multiyear costs of biomedical research grants made by the National Institutes of Health;

• a $200 million increase over the 1987 level is proposed for compensatory education for educationally disadvantaged children;

● current ineffective programs intended to assist dislocated workers are replaced by an expanded billion-dollar program carefully designed to help those displaced from their jobs move quickly into new careers;

● a 68 percent increase in funding is provided to permit the Federal Aviation Administration to modernize the Nation's air-traffic-control system; this includes the procurement of Doppler radars capable of detecting severe downdrafts that imperil landings and takeoffs at airports where this is a hazard;

● for 1988, $400 million is provided to carry out newly enacted immigration reform legislation;

● substantial increases in funding for clean-coal technology demonstrations, as well as research on acid-rain formation and environmental effects, are provided to address the acid-rain problem; and

● a new civil space technology initiative, together with previously planned increases to construct a space station, develop a national aerospace plane, and foster the commercial development of space, are provided in this budget.

Restoring our national security also has been one of my highest priorities over the past 6 years due to the serious weakness arising from severe underfunding during the middle and late 1970's. Nonetheless, defense and international programs have not escaped the effects of fiscal stringency. The defense budget actually has declined in real terms in each of the past 2 years. This trend cannot be allowed to continue. I am proposing in this budget a 3 percent real increase over last year's appropriated level. This request — some $8 billion less than last year's — is the minimum level consistent with maintaining an adequate defense of our Nation.

Likewise, my request for our international affairs programs is also crucial to our effort to maintain our national security. I urge Congress not to repeat last year's damaging cuts, but rather to fund these programs fully.

The incentive structure for other Federal programs should be changed to promote efficiency and competitiveness. One of the problems with many Federal programs is that they provide payments without encouraging performance or efficiency. They are perceived to be "free" and, therefore, there is potentially unlimited demand. This has to be changed — and this budget proposes creating needed incentives in critical areas.

Our farm price support programs, under the Food Security Act of 1985, are proving much too costly — half again as costly as estimated when the bill was enacted just one year ago. The $25 billion being spent on farm subsidies in 1987 is 14 percent of our total Federal deficit and equivalent to taking $415 of each non-farm family's taxes to support farmers' incomes — over and above the amount that price supports add to their grocery bills. Some of the provisions of the Act encourage farmers to overproduce just to receive Federal benefits. Other provisions give the greatest benefits to our largest and most efficient agricultural producers instead of to those family farmers most in need of help.

My administration will propose amendments to the Food Security Act to focus its benefits on the full-time family farmer by placing effective limitations on the amount paid to large producers and removing the incentive for farmers to overproduce solely to receive Federal payments.

Reform of the medicare physician payment system is also proposed. Under the proposals, medicare would pay for radiology, anesthesiology, and pathology [RAP] services based on average area costs instead of inflationary fee-for-service reimbursements. The current fee-for-service payment distorts incentives and induces inappropriate billing for unneeded services. This initiative would remove the distortions caused by medicare's current reimbursement rules, eliminating a key barrier preventing the restoration of traditional arrangements between RAP physicians and hospital staffs.

The budget proposes continued increases in federally supported basic research that will lead to longer term improvements in the Nation's productivity and global competitiveness. For example, the budget projects a doubling within 5 years of the National Science Foundation's support for academic research. I also propose to increase support for training future scientists and engineers, and to foster greater technology transfer from Government to industry.

Another way of attaching a "value" to Government-provided services — and an incentive to use them only as needed — is to charge user fees where appropriate. Those who receive special Federal services — not the general taxpayer — should bear a greater share of the costs of those services. Accordingly, this budget imposes fees for Federal lending activities, for meat and poultry inspection, for National park and forest facilities, for Coast Guard services, for Customs inspections, and for many other services.

The Government should stop competing with the private sector. The Federal Government interferes with the productivity of the private sector in many ways. One is through borrowing from the credit markets to finance programs that are no longer needed — as in the case of the rural housing insurance fund, direct student financial assistance, urban mass-transit discretionary grants, vocational education grants, the Federal Crop Insurance Corporation fund, sewage plant construction grants, justice assistance grants, the Legal Services Corporation, and rural electrification loans. I am proposing in this budget that we terminate these programs and rely instead on private or State and local government provision of these services.

The budget also proposes that a number of programs that have real utility be transferred back to the private sector, through public offerings or outright sales. Following our successful effort to authorize sale of Conrail, I am now proposing the sale of the Naval Petroleum Reserves, Amtrak, the Alaska Power Administration, the helium program, and excess real property. In addition, I am proposing legislation to authorize study of a possible divestiture of the Southeastern Power Administration. These "privatization" efforts continue to be a high priority of my administration and, I believe, will result in increased productivity and lower total costs of providing these services. The Federal Government needs to provide essential services that are truly public in nature and national in scope. It has no business providing services to individuals that private markets or their State or local governments can provide just as well or better.

The Federal Government should depend more on the private sector to provide ancillary and support services for activities that remain in Federal hands. The budget proposes that the work associated with over 40,000 Federal positions be contracted out to the private sector as yet another way to increase productivity, reduce costs, and improve services.

Federal credit programs should operate through the private markets and reveal their true costs. The Federal Government provides credit for housing, agriculture, small business, education, and many other purposes. Currently, over a trillion dollars of Federal or federally assisted loans are outstanding. Including lending of Government-sponsored enterprises, federally assisted lending amounted to 14 percent of all lending in U.S. credit markets in 1985.

Under current treatment, loan guarantees appear to be "free"; they do not affect the budget until and unless borrowers default. Direct loans are counted as outlays when they are made, but as "negative outlays" when they are repaid; thus, direct loans seem "free" too, inasmuch as it is presumed they will be repaid. But neither direct loans nor loan guarantees are free. Besides the better terms and conditions a borrower gets from the Government, there is the matter of default. When a borrower does not repay a direct loan, the negative outlay does not occur, and this is a subsidy implicit in the original loan transaction. When a borrower defaults on a guaranteed loan, the Government has to make good on repayment — also a program subsidy.

Since these effects are poorly understood and lead to grave inefficiencies in our credit programs, we will ask Congress to enact legislation whereby the true cost to the economy of Federal credit programs would be counted in the budget. By selling a substantial portion of newly made loans to the private sector and reinsuring some newly made guarantees, the implicit subsidy in the current practice will become explicit. This reform will revolutionize the way Federal credit activities are conducted.

The private sector will also be increasingly involved in the management of our huge portfolio of outstanding loans and loan guarantees. Delinquent Federal borrowers will be reported to private credit bureaus, and private loan collection agencies will be used to help in our collection efforts. The Internal Revenue Service [IRS] will expand its "offsetting" of refunds to pay off delinquent Federal debts, and Federal employees who have not paid back Federal loans will have their wages garnished.

Increased role for State and local governments. Over the past 6 years I have sought to return various Federal services to State and local governments — which are in a much better position to respond effectively to the needs of the recipients of these services. To me, this is a question of reorganizing responsibilities within our Federal system in a manner that will result in more productive delivery of the services that we all agree should be provided. Thus, this budget phases out inappropriate Federal Government involvement in local law enforcement, sewage treatment, public schools, and community and regional development. Transportation programs will be consolidated or States will be given greater flexibility in the use of Federal funds for highways, mass transit, and airports.

Federal regulations must be reduced even further to improve productivity. My administration will continue the deregulation and regulatory relief efforts that were begun in 1981. The Task Force on Regulatory Relief, headed by the Vice President, has been reinstated. In the past, excessive Federal regulations and related paperwork have stifled American productivity and individual freedom. We must continue our efforts to streamline the regulatory process and to strike the proper balance between necessary regulation and associated paperwork on the one hand, and the costs of these requirements on the other.

Federal activities should be better managed. The American people deserve the best managed Federal Government possible. Last year, I initiated the Federal Government Productivity Program, with the goal of improving productivity in selected areas by 20 percent by 1992. A substantial portion of total direct Federal employment falls within the program, including such activities as the Department of Agriculture meat and poultry inspection, Navy aircraft maintenance and repair, Social Security claims processing, National Park maintenance, operation of Federal prisons, and IRS processing of tax returns.

Credit reform, privatization, productivity improvement, and other proposals will be described in more detail in the Management Report to be issued this month. It will also identify further measures to reduce waste, fraud, and abuse; to improve management of the Government's $1.7 trillion cash flow; to institute compatible financial management systems across all Federal agencies; and other initiatives to improve the management of Government operations. These ambitious management reform undertakings, called "Reform '88," constitute the largest management reform effort ever attempted.

The budget also proposes a new approach to paying Federal employees who increase their productivity. I ask that Congress approve a new plan to transform the current system of virtually automatic "within grade" salary increases for the roughly 40 percent of employees eligible each year for these 3 percent hidden pay raises to one that is "performance-oriented." This will give Federal employees stronger incentives to improve service delivery.

I include with this budget my recommendations for increases in executive-level pay for the executive, legislative, and judicial branches of the Federal Government. The Quadrennial Commission report submitted to me on December 15, 1986, documented both the substantial erosion in the real level of Federal executive pay that has occurred since 1969 and the recruitment and retention problems that have resulted, especially for the Federal judiciary. The Commission is to be commended for its diligent and conscientious effort to address the complicated and complex problems associated with Federal pay levels.

Every one of the Quadrennial Commissions that have met over the past 18 years has recognized that a pay increase for key Federal officials was necessary. Each Commission concluded that pay for senior Government officials fell far behind that of their counterparts in the private sector. They also understood that we cannot afford a government composed primarily of those who are wealthy enough to serve. Unfortunately, the last major Quadrennial Commission pay adjustment was in 1977 — a decade ago.

However, I recognize that we are under mandated efforts to reduce the Federal deficit and hold down the costs of Government to the absolute minimum level. In this environment, I do not believe it would be appropriate to implement fully the Quadrennial Commission recommendations.

Accordingly, I have decided to propose a pay increase, but have cut substantially the recommendations made by the Quadrennial Commissioners in their report to me last month. Moreover, I have decided to establish a Career Manager Pay Commission to review and report to me by next August on appropriate pay scales for our elite corps of Government managers. The pay increases I am proposing to Congress, plus the results of this new Commission, should place Government compensation on a fairer and more comparable footing.

## Peace Through Strength

I have become convinced that the only way we can bring our adversaries to the bargaining table for arms reduction is to give them a reason to negotiate — while, at the same time, fulfilling our responsibility to our citizens and allies to provide an environment safe and secure from aggression.

We have built our defense capabilities back toward levels more in accord with today's requirements for security. Modest and sustained growth in defense funding will be required to consolidate the real gains we have made. Because of severe fiscal constraints, we are proceeding at a slower pace than I originally planned, and the budget I propose provides the minimum necessary to ensure an adequate defense.

I am also submitting, for the first time, a two-year budget for National Defense. This will permit greater stability in providing resources for our defense efforts and should lead to greater economy in using these resources.

## Budget Process Reform

The current budget process has failed to provide a disciplined and responsible mechanism for consideration of the Federal budget. Budget procedures are cumbersome, complex, and convoluted. They permit and encourage a process that results in evasion of our duty to the American people to budget their public resources responsibly. Last year Congress did not complete action on a budget for 8 months and 2 weeks — 2 weeks past the statutory deadline. Except for the initial report of the Senate Budget Committee, Congress missed every deadline it had set for itself just 9 months earlier. In the end, Congress passed a yearlong, 389-page omnibus appropriations bill full of excessive and wasteful spending. Because Congress had not completed action on the annual appropriations bills, at one point I was compelled by law to initiate a shutdown of Federal Government activities. Such abrogation of a responsible budget process not only discourages careful, prudent legislation — it encourages excessive spending and waste.

Furthermore, since I, as President, do not have a line-item veto, I had to ignore the many objectionable features of the omnibus appropriations legislation and sign it to avoid a Federal funding crisis. I am sure that many Members of Congress do not approve of this method of budgeting the Federal Government.

Last Fall's funding crisis and its slapdash resolution are only one of the most obvious manifestations of the flaws in the system. Congress passes budget resolutions [without the concurrence of the President] based on functions; it considers 13 separate, but related, appropriations bills based on agencies, not functions; it develops a reconciliation bill; it passes authorizing legislation, sometimes annually; and it enacts limits on the public debt. The words alone are obscure and confusing; the process behind it is chaotic. The process must be streamlined and made more accountable.

Shortly, I will outline specific reforms designed to make the process more efficient and increase accountability, so that we can give the American people what they deserve from us: a budget that is fiscally responsible and on time.

## Conclusion

Looking back over the past 6 years, we can feel a sense of pride and satisfaction in our accomplishments.

Inflation has been brought under control. Growth and investment are up, while interest rates, tax rates, and unemployment rates have all come down substantially. A foundation for sustained economic expansion is now in place. Our national security has been restored to more adequate levels. The proliferation of unnecessary and burdensome Federal regulations has been halted. A significant beginning has been made toward curbing the excessive growth of domestic spending. Management of the Government is being improved, with special emphasis on productivity.

Important tasks, however, still remain to be accomplished. The large and stubbornly persistent budget deficit has been a major source of frustration. It threatens our prosperity and our hopes for continued economic growth.

Last year, the legislative and executive branches of Government responded to this threat by mandating gradual, orderly progress toward a balanced budget over the next 4 years. The proposals outlined here achieve the 1988 target while preserving legitimate programs for the aged and needy, providing for adequate national security, devoting more resources to other high-priority activities, and doing this without raising taxes.

This budget presents hard choices which must be faced squarely. Congress must not abandon the statutory deficit targets of Gramm-Rudman-Hollings. Honoring the provisions and promises of this legislation offers the best opportunity for us to escape the chronic pattern of deficit spending that has plagued us for the past half century. We must realize that the deficit problem is also an opportunity of a different kind — an opportunity to construct a new, leaner, better focused, and better managed Federal structure supporting a more productive and more competitive America.

RONALD REAGAN

January 5, 1987

# President Reagan's 1987 State of the Union Address

*Following is the White House text of President Reagan's State of the Union address to a joint session of Congress Jan. 27, 1987.*

Thank you very much. Mr. Speaker, Mr. President, distinguished Members of Congress, honored guests and fellow citizens. May I congratulate all of you who are members of this historic 100th Congress of the United States of America. In this 200th anniversary year of our Constitution, you and I stand on the shoulders of giants — men whose words and deeds put wind in the sails of freedom.

## Constitution's Spirit and Promise

However, we must always remember that our Constitution is to be celebrated not for being old, but for being young — young with the same energy, spirit, and promise that filled each eventful day in Philadelphia's State House. We will be guided tonight by their acts; and we will be guided forever by their words.

Now, forgive me, but I can't resist sharing a story from those historic days. Philadelphia was bursting with civic pride in the spring of 1787, and its newspapers began embellishing the arrival of the Convention delegates with elaborate social classifications.

Governors of states were called "Excellency." Justices and Chancellors had reserved for them "Honorable" with a capital "H." For Congressmen, it was "honorable" with a small "h." And all others were referred to as "the following respectable characters." [Laughter.]

Well, for this 100th Congress, I invoke special Executive powers to declare that each of you must never be titled less than Honorable with a capital "H." [Applause.] Incidentally, I'm delighted you're celebrating the 100th birthday of the Congress. It's always a pleasure to congratulate someone with more birthdays than I've had. [Laughter.]

## New House Speaker

Now, there's a new face at this place of honor tonight. And please join me in warm congratulations to the Speaker of the House, Jim Wright [D-Texas]. [Applause.] Mr. Speaker, you might recall a similar situation in your very first session of Congress, 32 years ago. Then, as now, the Speakership had changed hands and another great son of Texas, Sam Rayburn — "Mr. Sam" — sat in your chair. I cannot find better words than those used by President Eisenhower that evening. He said, "We shall have much to do together; I am sure that we will get it done and that we shall do it in harmony and goodwill." [Applause.]

Tonight, I renew that pledge. To you, Mr. Speaker, and to Senate Majority Leader Robert Byrd [D-W.Va.], who brings 34 years of distinguished service to the Congress, may I say: though there are changes in the Congress, America's interests remain the same. And I am confident that, along with Republican leaders [Rep.] Bob Michel [R-Ill.] and [Sen.] Bob Dole [R-Kan.], this Congress can make history. [Applause.]

## Administration's Results

Six years ago, I was here to ask the Congress to join me in America's New Beginning. Well, the results are something of which we can all be proud. Our inflation rate is now the lowest in a quarter of a century. The prime interest rate has fallen from the 21 1/2 percent the month before we took office to 7 1/2 percent today, and those rates have triggered the most housing starts in eight years.

The unemployment rate — still too high — is the lowest in nearly seven years, and our people have created nearly 13 million new jobs. Over 61 percent of everyone over the age of 16, male and female, is employed — the highest percentage on record.

Let's roll up our sleeves and go to work, and put America's economic engine at full throttle. [Applause.]

We can also be heartened by our progress across the world. Most important, America is at peace tonight, and freedom is on the march. And we've done much these past years to restore our defenses, our alliances, and our leadership in the world. [Applause.] Our sons and daughters in the services once again wear their uniforms with pride.

## Iran-Contra Affair

But though we've made much progress, I have one major regret. I took a risk with regard to our action in Iran. It did not work, and for that I assume full responsibility.

The goals were worthy. I do not believe it was wrong to try to establish contacts with a country of strategic importance or to try to save lives. And certainly it was not wrong to try to secure freedom for our citizens held in barbaric captivity. [Applause.] But we did not achieve what we wished, and serious mistakes were made in trying to do so. We will get to the bottom of this, and I will take whatever action is called for.

But in debating the past — [applause] — in debating the past, we must not deny ourselves the successes of the future. Let it never be said of this generation of Americans that we became so obsessed with failure that we refused to take risks that could further the cause of peace and freedom in the world. [Applause.]

Much is at stake here, and the nation and the world are watching — to see if we go forward together in the national interest, or if we let partisanship weaken us.

## U.S. Policy on Terrorism

And let there be no mistake about American policy: we will not sit idly by if our interests or our friends in the Middle East are threatened, nor will we yield to terrorist blackmail.

And now, ladies and gentlemen of the Congress, why don't we get to work? [Applause.]

## Military/Foreign Aid Budget

I am pleased to report that, because of our efforts to rebuild the strength of America, the world is a safer place. Earlier this month, I submitted a budget to defend America and maintain our momentum to make up for neglect in the last decade. Well, I ask you to vote out a defense and foreign affairs budget that says "yes" to protecting our country.

While the world is safer, it is not safe.

## Soviet Expansionism

Since 1970, the Soviets have invested $500 billion more on their military forces than we have. Even today, though nearly one in three Soviet families is without running hot water, and the average family spends two hours a day shopping for the basic necessities of life, their government still found the resources to transfer $75 billion in weapons to client states in the past five years — clients like Syria, Vietnam, Cuba, Libya, Angola, Ethiopia, Afghanistan, and Nicaragua.

With 120,000 Soviet combat and military personnel and 15,000 military advisers in Asia, Africa, and Latin America, can anyone still doubt their single-minded determination to expand their power? Despite this, the Congress cut my request for critical U.S. security assistance to free nations by 21 percent this year, and cut defense requests by $85 billion in the last three years. [Applause.]

These assistance programs serve our national interests as well as mutual interests, and when the programs are devastated, American interests are harmed. My friends, it's my duty as President to say to you again tonight that there is no surer way to lose freedom than to lose our resolve. [Applause.]

## Afghan Rebels' Resolve

Today, the brave people of Afghanistan are showing that resolve. The Soviet Union says it wants a peaceful settlement in Afghanistan, yet it continues a brutal war and props up a regime whose days are clearly numbered. We are ready to support a political solution that guarantees the rapid withdrawal of all Soviet troops and genuine self-determination for the Afghan people.

## Commitment to Contras

In Central America, too, the cause of freedom is being tested. And our resolve is being tested there as well. Here, especially, the world is watching to see how this nation responds.

Today, over 90 percent of the people of Latin America live in democracy. Democracy is on the march in Central and South America. Communist Nicaragua is the odd man out — suppressing the Church, the press, and democratic dissent, and promoting subversion in the region. We support diplomatic efforts, but these efforts can never succeed if the Sandinistas win their war against the Nicaraguan people.

Our commitment to a Western Hemisphere safe from aggression did not occur by spontaneous generation on the day that we took office. It began with the Monroe Doctrine in 1823 and continues our historic bipartisan American policy. Franklin Roosevelt said we "are determined to do everything possible to maintain peace on this hemisphere." President Truman was very blunt: "International communism seeks to crush and undermine and destroy the independence of the Americans. We cannot let that happen."

And John F. Kennedy made clear that "communist domination in this hemisphere can never be negotiated." [Applause.]

Some in this Congress may choose to depart from this historic commitment, but I will not. [Applause.] This year we celebrate the second century of our Constitution. The Sandinistas just signed theirs two weeks ago — and then suspended it. We won't know how my words tonight will be reported there, for one simple reason: there is no free press in Nicaragua.

Nicaraguan freedom fighters have never asked us to wage their battle, but I will fight any effort to shut off their lifeblood and consign them to death, defeat, or a life without freedom. There must be no Soviet beachhead in Central America. [Applause.]

## Strategic Defense Initiative

You know, we Americans have always preferred dialogue to conflict, and so we always remain open to more constructive relations with the Soviet Union. But more responsible Soviet conduct around the world is a key element of the U.S.-Soviet agenda. Progress is also required on the other items of our agenda as well — real respect for human rights, and more open contacts between our societies, and, of course, arms reduction.

In Iceland last October, we had one moment of opportunity that the Soviets dashed because they sought to cripple our strategic defense initiative — SDI. I wouldn't let them do it then. I won't let them do it now or in the future. [Applause.] This is the most positive and promising defense program we have undertaken. It's the path — for both sides — to a safer future; a system that defends human life instead of threatening it. SDI will go forward.

The United States has made serious, fair, and far-reaching proposals to the Soviet Union, and this is a moment of rare opportunity for arms reduction. But I will need, and American negotiators in Geneva will need Congress' support. Enacting the Soviet negotiating position into American law would not be the way to win a good agreement. [Applause.] So I must tell you in this Congress I will veto any effort that undercuts our national security and our negotiating leverage. [Applause.]

## U.S. Trade Policy - 1

Now, today, we also find ourselves engaged in expanding peaceful commerce across the world. We will work to expand our opportunities in international markets through the Uruguay round of trade negotiations and to complete a historic free trade arrangement between the world's two largest trading partners — Canada and the United States.

Our basic trade policy remains the same: we remain opposed as ever to protectionism because America's growth and future depend on trade. But we would insist on trade that is fair and free. We are always willing to be trade partners but never trade patsies. [Applause.]

Now from foreign borders, let us return to our own because America in the world is only as strong as America at home.

## 100th Congress' Responsibilities

This 100th Congress has high responsibilities. I begin with a gentle reminder that many of these are simply the incomplete obligations of the past. The American people deserve to be impatient because we do not yet have the public house in order.

We've had great success in restoring our economic integrity, and we've rescued our nation from the worst economic mess since the Depression.

## Balanced Federal Budget - 1

But there's more to do. For starters, the federal deficit is outrageous. [Applause.]

For years I've asked that we stop pushing onto our children the excesses of our government. [Applause.] And what the Congress finally needs to do is pass a constitutional amendment that mandates a balanced budget — [applause] — and forces government to live within its means. States, cities, and the families of America balance their budgets. Why can't we? [Applause.]

## Sorry Budget Process

Next — the budget process is a sorry spectacle. [Applause.] The missing of deadlines and the nightmare of monstrous continuing resolutions packing hundreds of billions of dollars of spending into one bill must be stopped. [Applause.]

## Line-Item Veto

We ask the Congress, once again: Give us the same tool that 43 Governors have — a line-item veto so we can carve out the boondoggles and pork — [applause] — those items that would never survive on their own. I will send the Congress broad recommendations on the budget, but first I'd like to see yours. Let's go to work and get this done together. [Applause.]

## Balanced Federal Budget - 2

But now, let's talk about this year's budget. Even though I have submitted it within the Gramm-Rudman-Hollings deficit-reduction target, I have seen suggestions that we might postpone that timetable. Well, I think the American people are tired of hearing the same old excuses. [Applause.] Together, we made a commitment to balance the budget; now, let's keep it. [Applause.]

As for those suggestions that the answer is higher taxes, the American people have repeatedly rejected that shopworn advice.

They know that we don't have deficits because people are taxed too little; we have deficits because big government spends too much. [Applause.]

Now, next month, I'll place two additional reforms before the Congress.

## Welfare Reform

We've created a welfare monster that is a shocking indictment of our sense of priorities. Our national welfare system consists of some 59 major programs and over 6,000 pages of federal laws and regulations on which more than $132 billion was spent in 1985.

I will propose a new national welfare strategy — a program of welfare reform through state-sponsored, community-based demonstration projects. This is the time to reform this outmoded social dinosaur and finally break the poverty trap. Now, we will never abandon those who, through no fault of their own, must have our help. But let us work to see how many can be freed from the dependency of welfare and made self-supporting, which the great majority of welfare recipients want more than anything else. [Applause.]

## Catastrophic Health Care

Next, let us remove a financial specter facing our older Americans — the fear of an illness so expensive that it can result in having to make an intolerable choice between bankruptcy and death. I will submit legislation shortly to help free the elderly from the fear of catastrophic illness. [Applause.]

Now, let's turn to the future.

## U.S. Trade Policy - 2

It's widely said that America is losing her competitive edge. Well, that won't happen if we act now. How well prepared are we to enter the 21st century? In my lifetime, America set the standard for the world. It is now time to determine that we should enter the next century having achieved a level of excellence unsurpassed in history.

We will achieve this: first, by guaranteeing that government does everything possible to promote America's ability to compete. Second, we must act as individuals in a quest for excellence that will not be measured by new proposals or billions in new funding. Rather, it involves an expenditure of American spirit and just plain American grit.

The Congress will soon receive my comprehensive proposals to enhance our competitiveness — including new science and technology centers and strong new funding for basic research. [Applause.]

The bill will include legal and regulatory reforms and weapons to fight unfair trade practices. Competitiveness also means giving our farmers a shot at participating fairly and fully in a changing world market.

Preparing for the future must begin, as always, with our children.

## Goals in Education

We need to set for them new and more rigorous goals. We must demand more of ourselves and our children by raising literacy levels dramatically by the year 2000. Our children should master the basic concepts of math and science, and let's insist that students not leave high school until they have studied and understood the basic documents of our national heritage. [Applause.]

## War Against Drugs

There's one more thing we can't let up on. Let's redouble our personal efforts to provide for every child a safe and drug-free learning environment. [Applause.] If our crusade against drugs succeeds with our children, we will defeat that scourge all over the country.

## School Prayer

Finally, let's stop suppressing the spiritual core of our national being. Our nation could not have been conceived without divine help. Why is it that we can build a nation with our prayers but we can't use a schoolroom for voluntary prayer? [Applause.] The 100th Congress of the United States should be remembered as the one that ended the expulsion of God from America's classrooms. [Applause.]

## Modernizing the Work Place

The quest for excellence into the 21st century begins in the schoolroom but must go next to the work place. More than 20 million new jobs will be created before the new century unfolds, and, by then, our economy should be able to provide a job for everyone who wants to work.

We must also enable our workers to adapt to the rapidly changing nature of the work place, and I will propose substantial new federal commitments keyed to retraining and job mobility.

## Legislative Initiatives

Over the next few weeks, I will be sending the Congress a complete series of these special messages — on budget reform, welfare reform, competitiveness, including education, trade, worker training and assistance, agriculture, and other subjects.

The Congress can give us these tools, but to make these tools work, it really comes down to just being our best, and that is the core of American greatness.

The responsibility of freedom presses us towards higher knowledge and, I believe, moral and spiritual greatness. Through lower taxes and smaller government, government has its ways of freeing people's spirit. But only we, each of us, can let the spirit soar against our own individual standards. Excellence is what makes freedom ring. And isn't that what we do best?

We're entering our third century now, but it's wrong to judge our nation by its years. The calendar can't measure America because we were meant to be an endless experiment in freedom — with no limit to our reaches, no boundaries to what we can do, no end point to our hopes.

## Constitution: An Inspired Vehicle

The United States Constitution is the impassioned and inspired vehicle by which we travel through history. It grew out of the most fundamental inspiration of our existence: that we are here to serve Him by living free — that living free releases in us the noblest of impulses and the best of our abilities. That we would use these gifts for good and generous purposes and would secure them not just for ourselves, and for our children, but for all mankind. [Applause.]

Over the years — I won't count if you don't — nothing has been so heartwarming to me as speaking to America's young. And the little ones especially — so fresh-faced and so eager to know — well, from time to time I've been with them, they will ask about our Constitution, and I hope you Members of Congress will not deem this a breach of protocol if you'll permit me to share these thoughts again with the young people who might be listening or watching this evening.

### 'We the People'

I have read the constitutions of a number of countries — including the Soviet Union's. Some people are surprised to hear they have a constitution, and it even supposedly grants a number of freedoms to its people. Many countries have written into their constitution provisions for freedom of speech and freedom of assembly. Well, if this is true, why is the Constitution of the United States so exceptional?

Well, the difference is so small that it almost escapes you — but it's so great it tells you the whole story in just three words: We the people.

In those other constitutions, the government tells the people of those countries what they are allowed to do. In our Constitution, we the people tell the government what it can do and that it can do only those things listed in that document and no others.

Virtually every other revolution in history has just exchanged one set of rulers for another set of rulers. Our revolution is the first to say the people are the masters, and government is their servant. [Applause.]

And you young people out there, don't ever forget that. Some day, you could be in this room — but wherever you are, America is depending on you to reach your highest and be your best — because here, in America, we the people are in charge.

Just three words. We the people. Those are the kids on Christmas Day looking out from a frozen sentry post on the 38th Parallel in Korea, or aboard an aircraft carrier in the Mediterranean. A million miles from home. But doing their duty.

We the people. Those are the warm-hearted whose numbers we can't begin to count who'll begin the day with a little prayer for hostages they will never know and MIA families they will never meet. Why? Because that's the way we are, this unique breed we call Americans.

We the people. They're farmers on tough times, but who never stop feeding a hungry world. They're the volunteers at the hospital choking back their tears for the hundredth time, caring for a baby struggling for life because of a mother who used drugs. And you'll forgive me a special memory — it's a million mothers like Nelle Reagan who never knew a stranger or turned a hungry person away from her kitchen door.

We the people. They refute last week's television commentary downgrading our optimism and idealism. They are the entrepreneurs, the builders, the pioneers, and a lot of regular folks — the true heroes of our land who make up the most uncommon nation of doers in history. You know they're Americans because their spirit is as big as the universe and their hearts are bigger than their spirits.

We the people. Starting the third century of a dream and standing up to some cynic who's trying to tell us we're not going to get any better.

Are we at the end? Well, I can't tell it any better than the real thing — a story recorded by James Madison from the final moments of the Constitutional Convention — September 17, 1787. As the last few members signed the document, Benjamin Franklin — the oldest delegate at 81 years, and in frail health — looked over toward the chair where George Washington daily presided. At the back of the chair was painted the picture of a sun on the horizon. And turning to those sitting next to him, Franklin observed that artists found it difficult in their painting to distinguish between a rising and setting sun.

Well, I know if we were there, we could see those delegates sitting around Franklin — leaning in to listen more closely to him. And then Dr. Franklin began to share his deepest hopes and fears about the outcome of their efforts, and this is what he said: "I have often looked at that picture behind the President without being able to tell whether it was a rising or setting Sun: But now at length I have the happiness to know that it is a rising and not a setting Sun."

Well, you can bet it's rising, because, my fellow citizens, America isn't finished; her best days have just begun.

Thank you, God bless you and God bless America. [Applause.]

---

# Reagan's Address on Tower Board Investigation

*Following is the White House text of President Reagan's March 4, 1987, address in which he responded to the Tower commission report on the Iran-contra affair.*

My fellow Americans, I've spoken to you from this historic office on many occasions and about many things. The power of the Presidency is often thought to reside within this Oval Office. Yet it doesn't rest here; it rests in you, the American people, and in your trust.

### Powers of Leadership

Your trust is what gives a President his powers of leadership and his personal strength and it's what I want to talk to you about this evening.

For the past three months, I've been silent on the revelations about Iran. And you must have been thinking, "Well, why doesn't he tell us what's happening? Why doesn't he just speak to us as he has in the past when we've faced troubles or tragedies?" Others of you, I guess, were thinking, "What's he doing hiding out in the White House?"

Well, the reason I haven't spoken to you before now is this: You deserved the truth. And, as frustrating as the waiting has been, I felt it was improper to come to you with sketchy reports, or possibly even erroneous statements, which would then have to be corrected, creating even more doubt and confusion. There's been enough of that.

### The Price of Silence

I've paid a price for my silence in terms of your trust and confidence. But I've had to wait, as you have, for the complete story. That's why I appointed [former NATO] Ambassador David Abshire as my special counselor to help get out the thousands of documents to the various investigations. And I appointed a special review board, the Tower Board, which took on the chore of pulling the truth together for me and getting to the bottom of things. It has now issued its findings.

I'm often accused of being an optimist, and it's true I had to hunt pretty hard to find any good news in the Board's report. As you know, it's well-stocked with criticisms, which I'll discuss in a moment, but I was very relieved to read this sentence, ". . . the Board is convinced that the President does indeed want the full story to be told." And that will continue to be my pledge to you as the other investigations go forward.

I want to thank the members of the panel — former Senator John Tower [R-Texas], former Secretary of State Edmund Muskie, and former National Security Adviser Brent Scowcroft. They have done the nation, as well as me personally, a great service by submitting a report of such integrity and depth. They have my genuine and enduring gratitude.

I've studied the Board's report. Its findings are honest, convincing and highly critical, and I accept them. And tonight I want to share with you my thoughts on these findings and report to you on the actions I'm taking to implement the Board's recommendations.

First, let me say I take full responsibility for my own actions and for those of my administration. As angry as I may be about activities undertaken without my knowledge, I am still accountable for those activities. As disappointed as I may be in some who served me, I am still the one who must answer to the American people for this behavior. And as personally distasteful as I find secret bank accounts and diverted funds — well, as the Navy would say, this happened on my watch.

## Arms for Hostages

Let's start with the part that is the most controversial. A few months ago I told the American people I did not trade arms for hostages. My heart and my best intentions still tell me that is true, but the facts and the evidence tell me it is not. As the Tower Board reported, what began as a strategic opening to Iran deteriorated in its implementation into trading arms for hostages. This runs counter to my own beliefs, to administration policy, and to the original strategy we had in mind. There are reasons why it happened, but no excuses. It was a mistake.

I undertook the original Iran initiative in order to develop relations with those who might assume leadership in a post-Khomeini government. It's clear from the Board's report, however, that I let my personal concern for the hostages spill over into the geopolitical strategy of reaching out to Iran. I asked so many questions about the hostages' welfare that I didn't ask enough about the specifics of the total Iran plan.

Let me say to the hostage families, we have not given up. We never will. And I promise you we'll use every legitimate means to free your loved ones from captivity. But I must also caution that those Americans who freely remain in such dangerous areas must know that they're responsible for their own safety.

## Transfer of Funds

Now, another major aspect of the Board's findings regards the transfer of funds to the Nicaraguan Contras. The Tower Board wasn't able to find out what happened to this money, so the facts here will be left to the continuing investigations of the court-appointed Independent Counsel and the two Congressional investigating committees. I'm confident the truth will come out about this matter as well. As I told the Tower Board, I didn't know about any diversion of funds to the Contras. But as President, I cannot escape responsibility.

## Management Style

Much has been said about my management style, a style that's worked successfully for me during eight years as Governor of California and for most of my Presidency. The way I work is to identify the problem, find the right individuals to do the job, and then let them go to it. I have found this invariably brings out the best in people. They seem to rise to their full capability, and in the long run you get more done.

When it came to managing the NSC [National Security Council] staff, let's face it, my style didn't match its previous track record. I have already begun correcting this. As a start, yesterday I met with the entire professional staff of the National Security Council. I defined for them the values I want to guide the national security policies of this country. I told them that I wanted a policy that was as justifiable and understandable in public as it was in secret. I wanted a policy that reflected the will of the Congress as well as of the White House. And I told them that there'll be no more freelancing by individuals when it comes to our national security.

You have heard a lot about the staff of the National Security Council in recent months. I can tell you, they are good and dedicated government employees, who put in long hours for the nation's benefit. They are eager and anxious to serve their country.

One thing still upsetting me, however, is that no one kept proper records of meetings or decisions. This led to my failure to recollect whether I approved an arms shipment before or after the fact. I did approve it; I just can't say specifically when. Well, rest assured, there's plenty of record-keeping now going on at 1600 Pennsylvania Avenue.

For nearly a week now, I've been studying the Board's report. I want the American people to know that this wrenching ordeal of recent months has not been in vain. I endorse every one of the Tower Board's recommendations. In fact, I'm going beyond its recommendations, so as to put the house in even better order.

I'm taking action in three basic areas — personnel, national security policy, and the process for making sure that the system works.

## Personnel

First, personnel. I've brought in an accomplished and highly respected new team here at the White House. They bring new blood, new energy, and new credibility and experience.

Former Senator Howard Baker [R-Tenn.], my new Chief of Staff, possesses a breadth of legislative and foreign affairs skills that's impossible to match. I'm hopeful that his experience as Minority and Majority Leader of the Senate can help us forge a new partnership with the Congress, especially on foreign and national security policies. I'm genuinely honored that he's given up his own presidential aspirations to serve the country as my Chief of Staff.

Frank Carlucci, my new National Security Adviser, is respected for his experience in government and trusted for his judgment and counsel. Under him, the NSC staff is being rebuilt with proper management discipline. Already, almost half the NSC professional staff is comprised of new people.

Yesterday I nominated William Webster, a man of sterling reputation, to be Director of the Central Intelligence Agency. Mr. Webster has served as Director of the FBI and a U.S. District Court Judge. He understands the meaning of "rule of law."

So that his knowledge of national security matters can be available to me on a continuing basis, I will also appoint John Tower to serve as a member of my Foreign Intelligence Advisory Board.

I am considering other changes in personnel, and I'll move more furniture as I see fit in the weeks and months ahead.

## National Security Policy

Second, in the area of national security policy, I have ordered the NSC to begin a comprehensive review of all covert operations. I have also directed that any covert activity be in support of clear policy objectives and in compliance with American values. I expect a covert policy that if Americans saw it on the front page of their newspaper, they'd say, "That makes sense."

I have had issued a directive prohibiting the NSC staff itself from undertaking covert operations — no ifs, ands, or buts.

I have asked Vice President [George] Bush to reconvene his task force on terrorism to review our terrorist policy in light of the events that have occurred.

## Making the System Work

Third, in terms of the process of reaching national security decisions I am adopting in total the Tower Report's model of how the NSC process and staff should work. I am directing Mr. Carlucci to take the necessary steps to make that happen. He will report back to me on further reforms that might be needed. I've created the post of NSC Legal Adviser to assure a greater sensitivity to matters of law.

I am also determined to make the Congressional oversight process work. Proper procedures for consultation with the Congress will be followed, not only in letter but in spirit. Before the end of March I will report to the Congress on all the steps I've taken in line with the Tower Board's conclusions.

## Going Forward

Now, what should happen when you make a mistake is this: You take your knocks, you learn your lessons, and then you move on. That's the healthiest way to deal with a problem. This in no way diminishes the importance of the other continuing investigations, but the business of our country and our people must proceed. I've gotten this message from Republicans and

Democrats in Congress, from allies around the world — and if we're reading the signals right, even from the Soviets. And, of course, I've heard the message from you, the American people.

You know, by the time you reach my age, you've made plenty of mistakes. And if you've lived your life properly — so you learn.

You put things in perspective. You pull your energies together. You change. You go forward.

My fellow Americans, I have a great deal that I want to accomplish with you and for you over the next two years. And, the Lord willing, that's exactly what I intend to do.

Good night and God bless you.

# Reagan's Speech on the 'Iran-Contra Mess'

*Following is the White House text of President Reagan's Aug. 12, 1987, address to the nation on the Iran-contra affair.*

My fellow Americans, I've said on several occasions that I wouldn't comment about the recent Congressional hearings on the Iran-Contra matter until the hearings were over. Well, that time has come, so tonight I want to talk about some of the lessons we've learned.

But rest assured, that's not my sole subject this evening. I also want to talk about the future and getting on with things, because the people's business is waiting.

These past nine months have been confusing and painful ones for the country. I know you have doubts in your own minds about what happened in this whole episode. What I hope is not in doubt, however, is my commitment to the investigations themselves.

So far, we've had four investigations — by the Justice Department, the Tower Board [a special review board, appointed by the president and headed by former Sen. John G. Tower, R-Texas], the Independent Counsel, and the Congress. I requested three of those investigations, and I endorsed and cooperated fully with the fourth — the Congressional hearings — supplying over 250,000 pages of White House documents, including parts of my own private diaries. Once I realized I hadn't been fully informed, I sought to find the answers.

Some of the answers I don't like. As the Tower Board reported, and as I said last March, our original initiative rapidly got all tangled up in the sale of arms, and the sale of arms got tangled up with hostages. Secretary [of State George P.] Shultz and Secretary [of Defense Caspar W.] Weinberger both predicted that the American people would immediately assume this whole plan was an arms for hostages deal and nothing more. Well, unfortunately, their predictions were right.

As I said to you in March, I let my preoccupation with the hostages intrude into areas where it didn't belong. The image — the reality of Americans in chains, deprived of their freedom and families so far from home, burdened my thoughts. And this was a mistake.

My fellow Americans, I've thought long and often about how to explain to you what I intended to accomplish, but I respect you too much to make excuses. The fact of the matter is that there's nothing I can say that will make the situation right. I was stubborn in my pursuit of a policy that went astray.

## Diversion of Funds

The other major issue of the hearings, of course, was the diversion of funds to the Nicaraguan Contras.

Col. [Oliver L.] North and Adm. [John M.] Poindexter believed they were doing what I would've wanted done — keeping the democratic resistance alive in Nicaragua. I believed then and I believe now in preventing the Soviets from establishing a beachhead in Central America.

Since I have been so closely associated with the cause of the Contras, the big question during the hearings was whether I knew of the diversion. I was aware the resistance was receiving funds directly from third countries and from private efforts and I endorsed those endeavors wholeheartedly. But, let me put this in capital letters, I did not know about the diversion of funds. Indeed, I didn't know there were excess funds.

Yet the buck does not stop with Adm. Poindexter, as he stated in his testimony; it stops with me. I am the one who is ultimately accountable to the American people. The Admiral testified he wanted to protect me; yet no President should ever be protected from the truth. No operation is so secret that it must be kept from the Commander-in-Chief. I had the right, the obligation, to make my own decision.

I heard someone the other day ask why I wasn't outraged. Well, at times, I've been mad as a hornet. Anyone would be — just look at the damage that's been done and the time that's been lost. But I've always found that the best therapy for outrage and anger is action.

## Making Changes

I've tried to take steps so that what we've been through can't happen again, ei-

ther in this administration or future ones. But I remember very well what the Tower Board said last February when it issued this report. It said the failure was more in people than in process.

We can build in every precaution known to the world. We can design the best system ever devised by man. But in the end people are going to have to run it. And we will never be free of human hopes, weaknesses and enthusiasms.

Let me tell you what I've done to change both the system and the people who operate it.

First of all, I've brought in a new and knowledgeable team. I have a new National Security Adviser, a new Director of the CIA [Central Intelligence Agency], a new Chief of Staff here at the White House. And I've told them that I must be informed and informed fully.

In addition, I adopted the Tower Board's model of how the NSC [National Security Council] process and staff should work and I prohibited any operational role by the NSC staff in covert activities.

The report I ordered reviewing our nation's covert operations has been completed. There were no surprises. Some operations were continued and some were eliminated because they'd outlived their usefulness.

I am also adopting new, tighter procedures on consulting with and notifying the Congress on future covert action findings.

We will still pursue covert operations when appropriate, but each operation must be legal and it must meet a specific policy objective.

The problem goes deeper, however, than policies and personnel. Probably the biggest lesson we can draw from the hearings is that the executive and legislative branches of government need to regain trust in each other. We've seen the results of that mistrust in the form of lies, leaks, divisions, and mistakes. We need to find a way to cooperate while realizing foreign policy can't be run by committee. And I believe there's now the growing sense that we can accomplish more by cooperating.

And in the end, this may be the eventual blessing in disguise to come out of the Iran-Contra mess.

## Looking Ahead

But now let me turn to the other subject I promised to discuss this evening — the future. There are now 17 months left in this administration and I want them to be prosperous, productive ones for the American people.

When you first elected me to this office, you elected me to pursue a new, different direction for America. When you elected me the second time, you reaffirmed your desire to continue that course. My hopes for this country are as fervent today as they were in 1981. Up until the morning I leave this house, I intend to do what you sent me here to do — lead the nation toward the goals we agreed on when you elected me.

Let me tell you where I'm going to put my heart and my energies for the remainder of my term.

## Bork Nomination

For my entire political life, I've spoken about the need for the Supreme Court to interpret the law, not make it. During my presidency, I've proudly appointed two new justices who understand that important principle — Justice Sandra Day O'Connor and Justice Antonin Scalia.

I've now nominated a third — Judge Robert Bork. When I named him to the U.S. Court of Appeals, the American Bar Association gave Judge Bork, who is a brilliant scholar and jurist, its very highest rating. As a member of that court, Judge Bork has written more than 100 majority opinions and joined in another 300. The Supreme Court has never reversed a single one of these 400 opinions.

His nomination is being opposed by some because he practices judicial restraint. Now, that means he won't put their opinions ahead of the law; he won't put his own opinions ahead of the law. And that's the way it should be. Judge Bork would be an important intellectual addition to the Court, and I will fight for him because I believe in what he stands for.

As soon as the Senate returns from its recess next month, it should consider Judge Bork's qualifications and then vote yes or no, up or down. This nation and its citizens deserve a full bench with nine justices when the Court convenes in October.

## U.S.-Soviet Arms Agreement

In the months ahead, I also hope to reach an agreement, a comprehensive and verifiable agreement, with the Soviet Union on reducing nuclear arms. We're making real progress on the global elimination of an entire class of nuclear weapons — the U.S. and Soviet intermediate-range, or INF, missiles.

I first proposed this idea to the Soviets back in 1981. They weren't too keen on it and, in fact, walked out of the negotiations at one point. But we kept at it. Until recently, the Soviet Union had insisted on the right to retain some of its INF missiles.

But in mid-July, General Secretary [Mikhail S.] Gorbachev announced that he was prepared to drop this demand. That was welcome news, indeed.

We've come this far because, in 1980, you gave me a mandate to rebuild our military. I've done that. And today, we're seeing the results. The Soviets are now negotiating with us because we're negotiating from strength.

This would be an historic agreement. Previous arms control agreements merely put a ceiling on weapons and even allowed for increases; this agreement would reduce the number of nuclear weapons. I am optimistic that we'll soon witness a first in world history — the sight of two countries actually destroying nuclear weapons in their arsenals. And imagine where that might lead.

We're also ready to move ahead on a START [Strategic Arms Reduction Talks] agreement that would cut intercontinental nuclear forces by 50 percent, thereby eliminating thousands of nuclear missiles. I urge the Soviets to move ahead with us. And I say to General Secretary Gorbachev, both our nations could begin a new relationship by signing comprehensive agreements to reduce nuclear and conventional weapons.

What we seek in our relationship with the Soviet Union is peace and stability. That is also what we seek in the Persian Gulf and the Middle East more generally. And bringing stability to this troubled region remains one of the most important goals of my Presidency.

## Economic Bill of Rights

Over the next 17 months, I'll also be advocating an Economic Bill of Rights for our citizens. I believe the American people have a right to expect the nation's budget to be handled responsibly. Yet chaos reigns in the budgetary process. For the past several months, there's been much debate about getting our fiscal house in order, but the result once again has been inaction. The Congressional budget process is neither reliable nor credible — in short, it needs to be fixed.

We must face reality — the only force strong enough to stop this nation's massive runaway budget is the Constitution. Only the Constitution — the document from which all government power flows, the document that provides our moral authority as a nation — only the Constitution can compel responsibility.

We desperately need the power of a constitutional amendment to help us balance the budget. Over 70 percent of the American people want such an amendment. They want the federal government to have what 44 state governments already have — discipline.

To get things moving, I am proposing tonight — if Congress agrees to schedule an up-or-down vote this year on our balanced budget amendment, then I will agree to negotiate on every spending item in the budget.

If the Congress continues to oppose the wishes of the people by avoiding a vote on our balanced budget amendment, the call for a constitutional convention will grow louder. The prospect for a constitutional convention is only two states away from approval, and one way or another, the will of the people always prevails.

## Democratic Resistance In Nicaragua

And there's another area that will occupy my time and my heart — the cause of democracy. There are Americans still burning for freedom — Central Americans, the people of Nicaragua. Over the last 10 years, democrats have been emerging all over the world. In Central and South America alone, 10 countries have been added to the ranks. The question is, will Nicaragua ever be added to this honor roll?

As you know, I am totally committed to the democratic resistance — the freedom fighters and their pursuit of democracy in Nicaragua. Recently there's been important progress on the diplomatic front, both here in Washington and in the region itself.

## Central American Peace Plan

My administration and the leadership of Congress have put forth a bipartisan initiative proposing concrete steps that can bring an end to the conflict there. Our key point was that the communist regime in Nicaragua should do what it formally pledged to do in 1979 — respect the Nicaraguan people's basic rights of free speech, free press, free elections, and religious liberty. Instead, those who govern in Nicaragua chose to turn their country over to the Soviet Union to be a base for communist expansion on the American mainland.

The need for democracy in Nicaragua was also emphasized in the agreement signed by the five Central American presidents in Guatemala last Friday. We welcome this development and pledge our support to democracy and those fighting for freedom. We have always been willing to talk — we have never been willing to abandon those who are fighting for democracy and freedom.

I'm especially pleased that in the United States' diplomatic initiative we once again have the beginnings, however uncertain, of a bipartisan foreign policy. The recent hearings emphasized the need for such bipartisanship, and I hope this cautious start will grow and blossom.

These are among the goals for the remainder of my term as President. I believe they're the kinds of goals that will advance the security and prosperity and future of our people. I urge the Congress to be as thorough and energetic in pursuing these ends as it was in pursuing the recent investigation.

My fellow Americans, I have a year-and-a-half before I have to clean out this desk. I'm not about to let the dust and cobwebs settle on the furniture in this office, or on me. I have things I intend to do, and with your help, we can do them.

Good night and God bless you.

| | Vote Total | Per-cent |
|---|---|---|
| 13 Connie Mack (R)* | 187,794 | 75.0 |
| Addison S. Gilbert III (D) | 62,694 | 25.0 |
| 14 Daniel A. Mica (D)* | 171,961 | 73.8 |
| Rick Martin (R) | 61,185 | 26.2 |
| 15 E. Clay Shaw Jr. (R)* | X | X |
| (No Democratic candidate) | | |
| 16 Lawrence J. Smith (D)* | 121,213 | 69.7 |
| Mary Collins (R) | 52,807 | 30.3 |
| 17 William Lehman (D)* | X | X |
| (No Republican candidate) | | |
| 18 Claude Pepper (D)* | 80,047 | 73.5 |
| Tom Brodie (R) | 28,803 | 26.5 |
| 19 Dante B. Fascell (D)* | 99,203 | 69.1 |
| Bill Flanagan (R) | 44,455 | 30.9 |

## GEORGIA

**Governor**

| | | |
|---|---|---|
| Joe Frank Harris (D)* | 828,465 | 70.5 |
| Guy Hunt (R) | 346,512 | 29.5 |

**Senate**

| | | |
|---|---|---|
| Wyche Fowler Jr. (D) | 623,707 | 50.9 |
| Mack Mattingly (R)* | 601,241 | 49.1 |

**House**

| | | |
|---|---|---|
| 1 Robert Lindsay Thomas (D)* | 69,440 | 100.0 |
| (No Republican candidate) | | |
| 2 Charles Hatcher (D)* | 72,482 | 100.0 |
| (No Republican candidate) | | |
| 3 Richard Ray (D)* | 75,850 | 99.7 |
| (No Republican candidate) | | |
| 4 Pat Swindall (R)* | 86,366 | 53.2 |
| Ben Jones (D) | 75,892 | 46.8 |
| 5 John Lewis (D) | 93,229 | 75.3 |
| Portia A. Scott (R) | 30,562 | 24.7 |
| 6 Newt Gingrich (R)* | 75,583 | 59.5 |
| Crandle Bray (D) | 51,352 | 40.5 |
| 7 George "Buddy" Darden (D)* | 88,636 | 66.4 |
| Joe Morecraft (R) | 44,891 | 33.6 |
| 8 J. Roy Rowland (D)* | 82,254 | 86.4 |
| Eddie McDowell (R) | 12,952 | 13.6 |
| 9 Ed Jenkins (D)* | 84,303 | 100.0 |
| (No Republican candidate) | | |
| 10 Doug Barnard Jr. (D)* | 79,548 | 67.3 |
| Jim Hill (R) | 38,714 | 32.7 |

## HAWAII

**Governor**

| | | |
|---|---|---|
| John Waihee (D) | 173,655 | 52.0 |
| D. G. "Andy" Anderson (R) | 160,460 | 48.0 |

**Senate**

| | | |
|---|---|---|
| Daniel K. Inouye (D)* | 241,887 | 73.6 |
| Frank Hutchinson (R) | 86,910 | 26.4 |

**House**

| | | |
|---|---|---|
| 1 Patricia Saiki (R) | 99,683 | 59.2 |
| Mufi Hannemann (D) | 63,061 | 37.5 |
| Blase Harris (LIBERT) | 5,633 | 3.3 |
| 2 Daniel K. Akaka (D)* | 123,830 | 76.1 |
| Maria M. Hustace (R) | 35,371 | 21.7 |
| Ken Schoolland (LIBERT) | 3,618 | 2.2 |

## IDAHO

**Governor**

| | | |
|---|---|---|
| Cecil D. Andrus (D) | 193,429 | 49.9 |
| David H. Leroy (R) | 189,794 | 49.0 |
| James A. Miller (I) | 4,203 | 1.1 |

**Senate**

| | | |
|---|---|---|
| Steve Symms (R)* | 196,958 | 51.6 |
| John V. Evans (D) | 185,066 | 48.4 |

**House**

| | | |
|---|---|---|
| 1 Larry E. Craig (R)* | 120,553 | 65.1 |

| | Vote Total | Per-cent |
|---|---|---|
| Bill Currie (D) | 59,723 | 32.3 |
| David W. Shepherd (I) | 4,848 | 2.6 |
| 2 Richard H. Stallings (D)* | 103,035 | 54.4 |
| Mel Richardson (R) | 86,528 | 45.6 |

## ILLINOIS

**Governor**

| | | |
|---|---|---|
| James R. Thompson (R)* | 1,655,945 | 52.7 |
| Adlai E. Stevenson (IL SOL) | 1,256,725 | 40.0 |
| Democratic ticket — no candidate for governor | 208,841 | 6.6 |
| Gary L. Shilts (LIBERT) | 15,647 | 0.5 |
| Diane Roling (SOC WORK) | 6,843 | 0.2 |

**Senate**

| | | |
|---|---|---|
| Alan J. Dixon (D)* | 2,033,926 | 65.1 |
| Judy Koehler (R) | 1,053,793 | 33.7 |
| Einar V. Dyhrkopp (IL SOL) | 15,805 | 0.5 |
| Donald M. Parrish Jr. (LIBERT) | 13,892 | 0.5 |
| Omari Musa (SOC WORK) | 5,671 | 0.2 |

**House**

| | | |
|---|---|---|
| 1 Charles A. Hayes (D)* | 122,376 | 96.4 |
| Joseph C. Faulkner (R) | 4,572 | 3.6 |
| 2 Gus Savage (D)* | 99,268 | 83.8 |
| Ron Taylor (R) | 19,149 | 16.2 |
| 3 Marty Russo (D)* | 102,949 | 66.2 |
| James J. Tierney (R) | 52,618 | 33.8 |
| 4 Jack Davis (R) | 61,633 | 51.6 |
| Shawn Collins (D) | 57,925 | 48.4 |
| 5 William O. Lipinski (D)* | 82,466 | 70.4 |
| Daniel John Sobieski (R) | 34,738 | 29.6 |
| 6 Henry J. Hyde (R)* | 98,196 | 75.4 |
| Robert H. Renshaw (D) | 32,064 | 24.6 |
| 7 Cardiss Collins (D)* | 90,761 | 80.2 |
| Caroline K. Kallas (R) | 21,055 | 18.6 |
| Jerald Wilson (I) | 1,348 | 1.2 |
| 8 Dan Rostenkowski (D)* | 82,873 | 78.7 |
| Thomas J. DeFazio (R) | 22,383 | 21.3 |
| 9 Sidney R. Yates (D)* | 92,788 | 71.6 |
| Herbert Sohn (R) | 36,715 | 28.4 |
| 10 John Edward Porter (R)* | 87,530 | 75.1 |
| Robert A. Cleland (D) | 28,990 | 24.9 |
| 11 Frank Annunzio (D)* | 106,970 | 70.7 |
| George S. Gottlieb (R) | 44,341 | 29.3 |
| 12 Philip M. Crane (R)* | 89,044 | 77.7 |
| John A. Leonardi (D) | 25,536 | 22.3 |
| 13 Harris W. Fawell (R)* | 107,227 | 73.4 |
| Dominick J. Jeffrey (D) | 38,874 | 26.6 |
| 14 J. Dennis Hastert (R) | 77,288 | 52.4 |
| Mary Lou Kearns (D) | 70,293 | 47.6 |
| 15 Edward R. Madigan (R)* | 115,284 | 100.0 |
| (No Democratic candidate) | | |
| 16 Lynn Martin (R)* | 92,982 | 66.9 |
| Kenneth F. Bohnsack (D) | 46,087 | 33.1 |
| 17 Lane Evans (D)* | 85,442 | 55.6 |
| Sam McHard (R) | 68,101 | 44.4 |
| 18 Robert H. Michel (R)* | 94,308 | 62.6 |
| Jim Dawson (D) | 56,331 | 37.4 |
| 19 Terry L. Bruce (D)* | 111,105 | 66.4 |
| Al Salvi (R) | 56,186 | 33.6 |
| 20 Richard J. Durbin (D)* | 126,556 | 68.1 |
| Kevin B. McCarthy (R) | 59,291 | 31.9 |
| 21 Melvin Price (D)* | 65,722 | 50.4 |
| Robert H. Gaffner (R) | 64,779 | 49.6 |
| 22 Kenneth J. Gray (D)* | 97,585 | 53.2 |
| Randy Patchett (R) | 85,733 | 46.8 |

## INDIANA

**Senate**

| | | |
|---|---|---|
| Dan Quayle (R)* | 936,143 | 60.6 |
| Jill Lynette Long (D) | 595,192 | 38.5 |
| Bradford L. Warren (LIBERT) | 8,314 | 0.5 |
| Rockland R. Snyder (AM) | 5,914 | 0.4 |

| | Vote Total | Per-cent |
|---|---|---|
| **House** | | |
| 1 Peter J. Visclosky (D)* | 86,983 | 73.4 |
| William Costas (R) | 30,395 | 25.7 |
| James E. Willis (LIBERT) | 660 | 0.6 |
| Tracy E. Kyle (WL) | 403 | 0.3 |
| 2 Philip R. Sharp (D)* | 102,456 | 61.9 |
| Donald J. Lynch (R) | 62,013 | 37.4 |
| Richard Smith (LIBERT) | 1,156 | 0.7 |
| 3 John Hiler (R)* | 75,979 | 49.8 |
| Thomas W. Ward (D) | 75,932 | 49.8 |
| Kenneth K. Donnelly (LIBERT) | 596 | 0.4 |
| 4 Dan Coats (R)* | 99,865 | 69.6 |
| Gregory Alan Scher (D) | 43,105 | 30.0 |
| Stephen L. Dasbach (LIBERT) | 602 | 0.4 |
| 5 Jim Jontz (D) | 80,772 | 51.4 |
| James R. Butcher (R) | 75,507 | 48.1 |
| Brent Waibel (LIBERT) | 727 | 0.5 |
| 6 Dan Burton (R)* | 118,363 | 68.3 |
| Thomas F. McKenna (D) | 53,431 | 30.9 |
| Pamela Webe (LIBERT) | 1,371 | 0.8 |
| 7 John T. Myers (R)* | 104,965 | 66.8 |
| L. Eugene Smith (D) | 49,675 | 31.6 |
| Barbara J. Bourland (LIBERT) | 2,523 | 1.6 |
| 8 Frank McCloskey (D)* | 106,662 | 53.0 |
| Richard D. McIntyre (R) | 93,586 | 46.5 |
| Marilyn Stone (LIBERT) | 909 | 0.5 |
| 9 Lee H. Hamilton (D)* | 120,586 | 71.9 |
| Robert Walter Kilroy (R) | 46,398 | 27.7 |
| Douglas Boggs (LIBERT) | 719 | 0.4 |
| 10 Andrew Jacobs Jr. (D)* | 68,817 | 57.7 |
| Jim Eynon (R) | 49,064 | 41.2 |
| Frederick Peterson (LIBERT) | 1,285 | 1.1 |

## IOWA

**Governor**

| | | |
|---|---|---|
| Terry E. Branstad (R)* | 472,712 | 51.9 |
| Lowell L. Junkins (D) | 436,987 | 48.0 |

**Senate**

| | | |
|---|---|---|
| Charles E. Grassley (R)* | 588,880 | 66.0 |
| John P. Roehrick (D) | 299,406 | 33.6 |
| John Masters (I) | 3,370 | 0.4 |

**House**

| | | |
|---|---|---|
| 1 Jim Leach (R)* | 86,834 | 66.4 |
| John R. Whitaker (D) | 43,985 | 33.6 |
| 2 Tom Tauke (R)* | 88,708 | 61.3 |
| Eric Tabor (D) | 55,903 | 38.7 |
| 3 David R. Nagle (D)* | 83,504 | 54.6 |
| John McIntee (R) | 69,386 | 45.4 |
| 4 Neal Smith (D)* | 107,271 | 68.4 |
| Bob Lockard (R) | 49,641 | 31.6 |
| 5 Jim Lightfoot (R)* | 85,025 | 59.2 |
| Scott Hughes (D) | 58,552 | 40.8 |
| 6 Fred Grandy (R) | 81,861 | 50.9 |
| Clayton Hodgson (D) | 78,807 | 49.0 |

## KANSAS

**Governor**

| | | |
|---|---|---|
| Mike Hayden (R) | 436,267 | 51.9 |
| Tom Docking (D) | 404,338 | 48.1 |

**Senate**

| | | |
|---|---|---|
| Robert Dole (R)* | 576,902 | 70.0 |
| Guy MacDonald (D) | 246,664 | 30.0 |

**House**

| | | |
|---|---|---|
| 1 Pat Roberts (R)* | 141,297 | 76.5 |
| Dale Lyon (D) | 43,359 | 23.5 |
| 2 Jim Slattery (D)* | 110,737 | 70.6 |
| Phill Kline (R) | 46,029 | 29.4 |
| 3 Jan Meyers (R)* | 109,266 | 100.0 |
| (No Democratic candidate) | | |

| | Vote Total | Per-cent |
|---|---|---|
| 4 Dan Glickman (D)* | 111,164 | 64.5 |
| Bob Knight (R) | 61,178 | 35.5 |
| 5 Bob Whittaker (R)* | 116,800 | 71.1 |
| Kym E. Myers (D) | 47,540 | 28.9 |

## KENTUCKY

**Senate**

| | | |
|---|---|---|
| Wendell H. Ford (D)* | 503,775 | 74.4 |
| Jackson M. Andrews (R) | 173,330 | 25.6 |

**House**

| | | |
|---|---|---|
| 1 Carroll Hubbard Jr. (D)* | 64,315 | 100.0 |
| (No Republican candidate) | | |
| 2 William H. Natcher (D)* | 57,644 | 100.0 |
| (No Republican candidate) | | |
| 3 Romano L. Mazzoli (D)* | 81,943 | 73.0 |
| Lee Holmes (R) | 29,348 | 26.2 |
| Estelle DeBates (SOC WORK) | 899 | 0.8 |
| 4 Jim Bunning (R) | 67,626 | 55.1 |
| Terry L. Mann (D) | 53,906 | 43.9 |
| Walter T. Marksberry (I) | 735 | 0.6 |
| W. Ed Parker (AM) | 485 | 0.4 |
| 5 Harold Rogers (R)* | 56,760 | 100.0 |
| (No Democratic candidate) | | |
| 6 Larry J. Hopkins (R)* | 75,906 | 74.3 |
| Jerry W. Hammond (D) | 26,315 | 25.7 |
| 7 Carl C. Perkins (D)* | 90,619 | 79.6 |
| James T. Polley (R) | 23,209 | 20.4 |

## LOUISIANA

**Senate**

| | | |
|---|---|---|
| John B. Breaux (D) | 723,586 | 52.8 |
| W. Henson Moore (R) | 646,311 | 47.2 |

**House**

| | | |
|---|---|---|
| 1 Bob Livingston (R)* | X | X |
| 2 Lindy (Mrs. Hale) Boggs (D)* | X | X |
| 3 W. J. "Billy" Tauzin (D)* | X | X |
| 4 Buddy Roemer (D)* | X | X |
| 5 Jerry Huckaby (D)* | X | X |
| 6 Richard Baker (R) | X | X |
| 7 Jimmy Hayes (D) | 109,205 | 57.0 |
| Margaret Lowenthal (D) | 82,293 | 43.0 |
| 8 Clyde C. Holloway (R) | 102,276 | 51.4 |
| Faye Williams (D) | 96,864 | 48.6 |

## MAINE

**Governor**

| | | |
|---|---|---|
| John R. McKernan Jr. (R) | 170,312 | 39.9 |
| James Tierney (D) | 128,744 | 30.1 |
| Sherry E. Huber (I) | 64,317 | 15.1 |
| John E. Menario (I) | 63,474 | 14.9 |

**House**

| | | |
|---|---|---|
| 1 Joseph E. Brennan (D) | 121,848 | 53.2 |
| H. Rollin Ives (R) | 100,260 | 43.7 |
| Plato Truman (I) | 7,109 | 3.1 |
| 2 Olympia J. Snowe (R)* | 148,770 | 77.3 |
| Richard R. Charette (D) | 43,614 | 22.7 |

## MARYLAND

**Governor**

| | | |
|---|---|---|
| William Donald Schaefer (D) | 907,301 | 82.4 |
| Thomas J. Mooney (R) | 194,187 | 17.6 |

**Senate**

| | | |
|---|---|---|
| Barbara A. Mikulski (D) | 675,229 | 60.7 |
| Linda Chavez (R) | 437,419 | 39.3 |

**House**

| | | |
|---|---|---|
| 1 Roy Dyson (D)* | 88,113 | 66.8 |
| Harlan C. Williams (R) | 43,764 | 33.2 |
| 2 Helen Delich Bentley (R)* | 96,745 | 58.7 |

| | Vote Total | Per-cent |
|---|---|---|
| Kathleen Kennedy Townsend (D) | 68,200 | 41.3 |
| 3 Benjamin L. Cardin (D) | 100,161 | 79.1 |
| Ross Z. Pierpont (R) | 26,452 | 20.9 |
| 4 Tom McMillen (D) | 65,075 | 50.2 |
| Robert R. Neall (R) | 64,651 | 49.8 |
| 5 Steny H. Hoyer (D)* | 82,098 | 81.9 |
| John Eugene Sellner (R) | 18,102 | 18.1 |
| 6 Beverly B. Byron (D)* | 102,975 | 72.2 |
| John Vandenberge (R) | 39,600 | 27.8 |
| 7 Kweisi Mfume (D)* | 79,226 | 86.7 |
| Saint George I. B. Crosse III (R) | 12,170 | 13.3 |
| 8 Constance A. Morella (R) | 92,917 | 52.9 |
| Stewart Bainum Jr. (D) | 82,825 | 47.1 |

## MASSACHUSETTS

**Governor**

| | | |
|---|---|---|
| Michael S. Dukakis (D)* | 1,157,786 | 68.7 |
| George Kariotis (R) | 525,364 | 31.2 |

**House**

| | | |
|---|---|---|
| 1 Silvio O. Conte (R)* | 113,653 | 77.8 |
| Robert S. Weiner (D) | 32,396 | 22.2 |
| 2 Edward P. Boland (D)* | 91,033 | 65.9 |
| Brian P. Lees (R) | 47,022 | 34.1 |
| 3 Joseph D. Early (D)* | 120,222 | 100.0 |
| (No Republican candidate) | | |
| 4 Barney Frank (D)* | 134,387 | 88.8 |
| (No Republican candidate) | | |
| Thomas D. DeVisscher (AM) | 16,857 | 11.2 |
| 5 Chester G. Atkins (D)* | 113,690 | 99.9 |
| (No Republican candidate) | | |
| 6 Nicholas Mavroules (D)* | 131,051 | 99.9 |
| (No Republican candidate) | | |
| 7 Edward J. Markey (D)* | 124,183 | 100.0 |
| (No Republican candidate) | | |
| 8 Joseph P. Kennedy II (D) | 104,651 | 72.0 |
| Clark C. Abt (R) | 40,259 | 27.7 |
| 9 Joe Moakley (D)* | 110,026 | 83.8 |
| (No Republican candidate) | | |
| Robert W. Horan (I) | 21,292 | 16.2 |
| 10 Gerry E. Studds (D)* | 121,578 | 65.1 |
| Ricardo M. Barros (R) | 49,451 | 26.5 |
| Alexander Byron (I) | 15,687 | 8.4 |
| 11 Brian J. Donnelly (D)* | 114,926 | 100.0 |
| (No Republican candidate) | | |

## MICHIGAN

**Governor**

| | | |
|---|---|---|
| James J. Blanchard (D)* | 1,632,138 | 68.1 |
| William Lucas (R) | 753,647 | 31.4 |
| Martin McLaughlin (WL) | 9,477 | 0.4 |

**House**

| | | |
|---|---|---|
| 1 John Conyers Jr. (D)* | 94,307 | 89.2 |
| Bill Ashe (R) | 10,407 | 9.8 |
| Peter Banta Bowen (I) | 539 | 0.5 |
| Andrew Pulley (I) | 529 | 0.5 |
| 2 Carl D. Pursell (R)* | 79,567 | 59.0 |
| Dean Baker (D) | 55,204 | 41.0 |
| 3 Howard Wolpe (D)* | 78,720 | 60.4 |
| Jackie McGregor (R) | 51,678 | 39.6 |
| 4 Fred Upton (R) | 70,331 | 61.9 |
| Dan Roche (D) | 41,624 | 36.6 |
| Richard H. Gillmor (I) | 1,649 | 1.5 |
| 5 Paul B. Henry (R)* | 100,577 | 71.2 |
| Teresa S. Decker (D) | 40,608 | 28.8 |
| 6 Bob Carr (D)* | 74,927 | 56.7 |
| Jim Dunn (R) | 57,283 | 43.3 |
| 7 Dale E. Kildee (D)* | 101,225 | 79.6 |
| Trudie Callihan (R) | 24,848 | 19.5 |
| Gene Schenk (I) | 1,099 | 0.9 |
| 8 Bob Traxler (D)* | 97,406 | 72.6 |
| John A. Levi (R) | 36,695 | 27.4 |

| | Vote Total | Per-cent |
|---|---|---|
| 9 Guy Vander Jagt (R)* | 89,991 | 64.4 |
| Richard J. Anderson (D) | 49,702 | 35.6 |
| 10 Bill Schuette (R)* | 78,475 | 51.2 |
| Donald J. Albosta (D) | 74,941 | 48.8 |
| 11 Robert W. Davis (R)* | 91,575 | 63.0 |
| Robert C. Anderson (D) | 53,180 | 36.6 |
| Phil Belfly (I) | 648 | 0.4 |
| 12 David E. Bonior (D)* | 87,643 | 66.4 |
| Candice S. Miller (R) | 44,442 | 33.6 |
| 13 George W. Crockett Jr. (D)* | 76,435 | 85.2 |
| Mary Griffin (R) | 12,395 | 13.8 |
| Barbara L. Putnam (I) | 597 | 0.7 |
| Lucy Bell Randolph (I) | 318 | 0.3 |
| 14 Dennis M. Hertel (D)* | 92,328 | 72.9 |
| Stanley T. Grot (R) | 33,831 | 26.7 |
| William Osipoff (I) | 506 | 0.4 |
| 15 William D. Ford (D)* | 77,950 | 75.2 |
| Glen Kassel (R) | 25,078 | 24.2 |
| James H. Stamps (I) | 584 | 0.6 |
| 16 John D. Dingell (D)* | 101,659 | 77.8 |
| Frank W. Grzywacki (R) | 28,971 | 22.2 |
| 17 Sander M. Levin (D)* | 105,031 | 76.4 |
| Calvin Williams (R) | 30,879 | 22.5 |
| Charles E. Martell (I) | 1,477 | 1.1 |
| 18 William S. Broomfield (R)* | 110,099 | 73.8 |
| Gary L. Kohut (D) | 39,144 | 26.2 |

## MINNESOTA

**Governor**

| | | |
|---|---|---|
| Rudy Perpich (DFL)* | 790,138 | 55.8 |
| Cal R. Ludeman (I-R) | 606,755 | 42.9 |
| W. Z. "Bill" Brust (WL) | 4,208 | 0.3 |
| Joseph A. Rohner III (LIBERT) | 3,852 | 0.3 |
| Tom Jaax (SOC WORK) | 3,151 | 0.2 |

**House**

| | | |
|---|---|---|
| 1 Timothy J. Penny (DFL)* | 125,115 | 72.4 |
| Paul H. Grawe (I-R) | 47,750 | 27.6 |
| 2 Vin Weber (I-R)* | 100,249 | 51.6 |
| Dave Johnson (DFL) | 94,048 | 48.4 |
| 3 Bill Frenzel (I-R)* | 127,434 | 70.1 |
| Ray Stock (DFL) | 54,261 | 29.9 |
| 4 Bruce F. Vento (DFL)* | 112,662 | 72.9 |
| Harold Stassen (I-R) | 41,926 | 27.1 |
| 5 Martin Olav Sabo (DFL)* | 105,410 | 72.7 |
| Rick Serra (I-R) | 37,583 | 25.9 |
| Clifford Mark Greene (I) | 2,004 | 1.4 |
| 6 Gerry Sikorski (DFL)* | 110,598 | 65.8 |
| Barbara Zwach Sykora (I-R) | 57,460 | 34.2 |
| 7 Arlan Stangeland (I-R)* | 94,024 | 49.7 |
| Collin C. Peterson (DFL) | 93,903 | 49.6 |
| Jon Hall (CIT) | 1,326 | 0.7 |
| 8 James L. Oberstar (DFL)* | 135,718 | 72.6 |
| Dave Rued (I-R) | 51,315 | 27.4 |

## MISSISSIPPI

**House**

| | | |
|---|---|---|
| 1 Jamie L. Whitten (D)* | 59,870 | 66.4 |
| Larry Cobb (R) | 30,267 | 33.6 |
| 2 Mike Espy (D) | 73,119 | 51.7 |
| Webb Franklin (R)* | 68,292 | 48.3 |
| 3 G. V. "Sonny" Montgomery (D)* | 80,575 | 100.0 |
| (No Republican candidate) | | |
| 4 Wayne Dowdy (D)* | 85,819 | 71.5 |
| Gail Healy (R) | 34,190 | 28.5 |
| 5 Trent Lott (R)* | 75,288 | 82.3 |
| Larry L. Albritton (D) | 16,143 | 17.7 |

## MISSOURI

**Senate**

| | | |
|---|---|---|
| Christopher S. "Kit" Bond (R) | 777,612 | 52.6 |
| Harriett Woods (D) | 699,624 | 47.4 |

|  | Vote Total | Per- cent |
|---|---|---|

**House**

| 1 | William L. Clay (D)* | 91,044 | 66.1 |
|  | Robert J. Wittmann (R) | 46,599 | 33.9 |
| 2 | Jack Buechner (R) | 101,010 | 51.9 |
|  | Robert A. Young (D)* | 93,538 | 48.1 |
| 3 | Richard A. Gephardt (D)* | 116,403 | 69.0 |
|  | Roy Amelung (R) | 52,382 | 31.0 |
| 4 | Ike Skelton (D)* | 129,471 | 100.0 |
|  | (No Republican candidate) |  |  |
| 5 | Alan Wheat (D)* | 101,030 | 70.9 |
|  | Greg Fisher (R) | 39,340 | 27.6 |
|  | Jay Manifold (LIBERT) | 2,204 | 1.5 |
| 6 | E. Thomas Coleman (R)* | 95,865 | 56.7 |
|  | Doug R. Hughes (D) | 73,155 | 43.3 |
| 7 | Gene Taylor (R)* | 114,210 | 67.0 |
|  | Ken Young (D) | 56,291 | 33.0 |
| 8 | Bill Emerson (R)* | 79,142 | 52.5 |
|  | Wayne Cryts (D) | 71,532 | 47.5 |
| 9 | Harold L. Volkmer (D)* | 95,939 | 57.5 |
|  | Ralph Uthlaut Jr. (R) | 70,972 | 42.5 |

## MONTANA

**House**

| 1 | Pat Williams (D)* | 98,501 | 61.7 |
|  | Don Allen (R) | 61,230 | 38.3 |
| 2 | Ron Marlenee (R)* | 84,548 | 53.5 |
|  | Richard "Buck" O'Brien (D) | 73,583 | 46.5 |

## NEBRASKA

**Governor**

| Kay A. Orr (R) | 298,325 | 52.9 |
|---|---|---|
| Helen Boosalis (D) | 265,156 | 47.0 |

**House**

| 1 | Doug Bereuter (R)* | 121,772 | 64.4 |
|  | Steve Burns (D) | 67,137 | 35.5 |
| 2 | Hal Daub (R)* | 99,569 | 58.5 |
|  | Walter M. Calinger (D) | 70,372 | 41.3 |
| 3 | Virginia Smith (R)* | 136,985 | 69.8 |
|  | Scott E. Sidwell (D) | 59,182 | 30.2 |

## NEVADA

**Governor**

| Richard H. Bryan (D)* | 187,268 | 71.9 |
|---|---|---|
| Patty Cafferata (R) | 65,081 | 25.0 |
| "None of these candidates" | 5,471 | 2.1 |
| Louis R. Tomburello (LIBERT) | 2,555 | 1.0 |

**Senate**

| Harry Reid (D) | 130,955 | 50.0 |
|---|---|---|
| Jim Santini (R) | 116,606 | 44.5 |
| "None of these candidates" | 9,472 | 3.6 |
| Kent Cromwell (LIBERT) | 4,899 | 1.9 |

**House**

| 1 | James H. Bilbray (D) | 61,830 | 54.1 |
|  | Bob Ryan (R) | 50,342 | 44.0 |
|  | Gordon Michael Morris (LIBERT) | 2,145 | 1.9 |
| 2 | Barbara F. Vucanovich (R)* | 83,479 | 58.4 |
|  | Pete Sferrazza (D) | 59,433 | 41.6 |

## NEW HAMPSHIRE

**Governor**

| John H. Sununu (R)* | 134,824 | 53.7 |
|---|---|---|
| Paul McEachern (D) | 116,142 | 46.3 |

**Senate**

| Warren B. Rudman (R)* | 154,090 | 62.9 |
|---|---|---|
| Endicott Peabody (D) | 79,222 | 32.4 |
| Bruce Valley (I) | 11,423 | 4.7 |

**House**

| 1 | Robert C. Smith (R)* | 70,739 | 56.4 |
|  | James M. Demers (D) | 54,787 | 43.6 |
| 2 | Judd Gregg (R)* | 85,479 | 74.2 |
|  | Laurence Craig-Green (D) | 29,688 | 25.8 |

## NEW JERSEY

**House**

| 1 | James J. Florio (D)* | 93,497 | 75.6 |
|  | Fred A. Busch (R) | 29,175 | 23.6 |
|  | Jerry Zeldin (LIBERT) | 931 | 0.8 |
| 2 | William J. Hughes (D)* | 83,821 | 68.3 |
|  | Alfred J. Bennington Jr. (R) | 35,167 | 28.6 |
|  | Len Smith (I) | 3,812 | 3.1 |
| 3 | James J. Howard (D)* | 73,743 | 58.7 |
|  | Brian T. Kennedy (R) | 51,882 | 41.3 |
| 4 | Christopher H. Smith (R)* | 78,699 | 61.1 |
|  | Jeffrey Laurenti (D) | 49,290 | 38.3 |
|  | Earl G. Dickey (I) | 789 | 0.6 |
| 5 | Marge Roukema (R)* | 94,253 | 74.6 |
|  | H. Vernon Jolley (D) | 32,145 | 25.4 |
| 6 | Bernard J. Dwyer (D)* | 67,460 | 69.0 |
|  | John D. Scalamonti (R) | 28,286 | 28.9 |
|  | Rose (Zeidwerg) Monyek (I) | 2,023 | 2.1 |
| 7 | Matthew J. Rinaldo (R)* | 92,254 | 79.0 |
|  | June S. Fischer (D) | 24,462 | 21.0 |
| 8 | Robert A. Roe (D)* | 57,820 | 62.8 |
|  | Thomas P. Zampino (R) | 34,268 | 37.2 |
| 9 | Robert G. Torricelli (D)* | 89,634 | 69.0 |
|  | Arthur F. Jones (R) | 40,226 | 31.0 |
| 10 | Peter W. Rodino Jr. (D)* | 46,666 | 95.9 |
|  | (No Republican candidate) |  |  |
|  | Chris Brandlon (SOC WORK) | 1,977 | 4.1 |
| 11 | Dean A. Gallo (R)* | 75,037 | 68.0 |
|  | Frank Askin (D) | 35,280 | 32.0 |
| 12 | Jim Courter (R)* | 72,966 | 63.5 |
|  | David B. Crabiel (D) | 41,967 | 36.5 |
| 13 | H. James Saxton (R)* | 82,866 | 65.4 |
|  | John Wydra (D) | 43,920 | 34.6 |
| 14 | Frank J. Guarini (D)* | 63,057 | 70.7 |
|  | Albio Sires (R) | 23,822 | 26.7 |
|  | Herbert H. Shaw (I) | 1,825 | 2.0 |
|  | William Link (I) | 525 | 0.6 |

## NEW MEXICO

**Governor**

| Garrey E. Carruthers (R) | 209,455 | 53.0 |
|---|---|---|
| Ray B. Powell (D) | 185,378 | 47.0 |

**House**

| 1 | Manuel Lujan Jr. (R)* | 90,476 | 70.9 |
|  | Manny Garcia (D) | 37,138 | 29.1 |
| 2 | Joe Skeen (R)* | 77,787 | 62.9 |
|  | Mike Runnels (D) | 45,924 | 37.1 |
| 3 | Bill Richardson (D)* | 95,760 | 71.3 |
|  | David F. Cargo (R) | 38,552 | 28.7 |

## NEW YORK

**Governor**

| Mario M. Cuomo (D, L)* | 2,775,229 | 64.6 |
|---|---|---|
| Andrew P. O'Rourke (R, C) | 1,363,810 | 31.8 |
| Denis E. Dillon (RTL) | 130,802 | 3.0 |
| Lenora B. Fulani (NA) | 24,130 | 0.6 |

**Senate**

| Alfonse M. D'Amato (R, C, RTL)* | 2,378,197 | 56.9 |
|---|---|---|
| Mark Green (D) | 1,723,216 | 41.2 |
| John Dyson (L) | 60,099 | 1.4 |
| Frederick D. Newman (NA) | 10,559 | 0.3 |
| Michael Shur (SOC WORK) | 7,376 | 0.2 |

**House**

| 1 | George J. Hochbrueckner (D) | 67,139 | 51.2 |
|  | Gregory J. Blass (R) | 55,413 | 42.3 |
|  | Dominic J. Santoro (C) | 4,345 | 3.3 |
|  | William J. Doyle (RTL) | 4,134 | 3.2 |
| 2 | Thomas J. Downey (D)* | 69,771 | 64.3 |
|  | Jeffrey A. Butzke (R, C) | 35,132 | 32.4 |
|  | Veronica Windishman (RTL) | 3,651 | 3.3 |
| 3 | Robert J. Mrazek (D)* | 83,985 | 56.4 |
|  | Joseph A. Guarino (R, C) | 60,367 | 40.6 |
|  | Charles W. Welch (RTL) | 4,440 | 3.0 |
| 4 | Norman F. Lent (R, C)* | 92,214 | 64.8 |
|  | Patricia Sullivan (D, L) | 43,581 | 30.6 |
|  | George E. Patterson (RTL) | 6,493 | 4.6 |
| 5 | Raymond J. McGrath (R, C)* | 93,473 | 65.3 |
|  | Michael T. Sullivan (D, L, RTL) | 49,728 | 34.7 |
| 6 | Floyd H. Flake (D) | 58,317 | 67.7 |
|  | Richard Dietl (R, C) | 27,773 | 32.3 |
| 7 | Gary L. Ackerman (D)* | 62,836 | 77.4 |
|  | Edward Nelson Rodriguez (R, C) | 18,384 | 22.6 |
| 8 | James H. Scheuer (D, L)* | 70,605 | 90.2 |
|  | (No Republican candidate) |  |  |
|  | Gustave Reifenkugel (C) | 7,679 | 9.8 |
| 9 | Thomas J. Manton (D)* | 50,738 | 69.4 |
|  | Salvatore J. Calise (R) | 18,040 | 24.7 |
|  | Thomas V. Ognibene (C) | 4,348 | 5.9 |
| 10 | Charles E. Schumer (D, L)* | 76,318 | 93.3 |
|  | (No Republican candidate) |  |  |
|  | Alice Gaffney (C) | 5,472 | 6.7 |
| 11 | Edolphus Towns (D, L)* | 41,689 | 89.4 |
|  | Nathaniel Hendricks (R) | 4,053 | 8.7 |
|  | Alfred J. Hamel (C) | 874 | 1.9 |
| 12 | Major R. Owens (D, L)* | 42,138 | 91.5 |
|  | Owen Augustin (R) | 2,752 | 6.0 |
|  | Joseph N. O. Caesar (C, RTL) | 1,168 | 2.5 |
| 13 | Stephen J. Solarz (D, L)* | 61,089 | 82.4 |
|  | Leon Nadrowski (R) | 10,941 | 14.8 |
|  | Samuel Roth (C) | 2,106 | 2.8 |
| 14 | Guy V. Molinari (R, C)* | 64,647 | 68.8 |
|  | Barbara Walla (D) | 27,950 | 29.7 |
|  | Joseph F. Sulley (L) | 1,375 | 1.5 |
| 15 | Bill Green (R)* | 58,214 | 58.0 |
|  | George A. Hirsch (D, L) | 42,147 | 42.0 |
| 16 | Charles B. Rangel (D, R, L)* | 61,262 | 96.4 |
|  | Michael R. Berns (C) | 1,288 | 2.0 |
|  | William Seraile (NA) | 995 | 1.6 |
| 17 | Ted Weiss (D, L)* | 95,094 | 85.5 |
|  | Thomas A. Chorba (R, C) | 15,587 | 14.0 |
|  | James Mangia (NA) | 581 | 0.5 |
| 18 | Robert Garcia (D, L)* | 43,343 | 93.5 |
|  | Melanie Chase (R) | 2,479 | 5.4 |
|  | Lorraine Verhoff (C) | 531 | 1.1 |
| 19 | Mario Biaggi (D, R, L)* | 87,774 | 90.2 |
|  | Alice Farrell (C) | 6,906 | 7.1 |
|  | John J. Barry (RTL) | 2,669 | 2.7 |
| 20 | Joseph J. DioGuardi (R, C)* | 80,220 | 53.9 |
|  | Bella S. Abzug (D) | 66,359 | 44.5 |
|  | Florence T. O'Grady (RTL) | 2,341 | 1.6 |
| 21 | Hamilton Fish Jr. (R, C)* | 102,070 | 76.5 |
|  | Lawrence W. Grunberger (D) | 28,339 | 21.3 |
|  | Karen A. Gormley-Vitale (RTL) | 2,988 | 2.2 |
| 22 | Benjamin A. Gilman (R)* | 94,244 | 69.5 |
|  | Eleanor F. Burlingham (D) | 36,852 | 27.2 |
|  | Richard Bruno (RTL) | 4,560 | 3.3 |
| 23 | Samuel S. Stratton (D)* | 140,759 | 96.4 |
|  | (No Republican candidate) |  |  |
|  | James Joseph Callahan (SOC WORK) | 5,279 | 3.6 |
| 24 | Gerald B. H. Solomon (R, C, RTL)* | 117,285 | 70.4 |
|  | Ed Bloch (D) | 49,225 | 29.6 |
| 25 | Sherwood Boehlert (R)* | 104,216 | 69.0 |
|  | Kevin J. Conway (D) | 33,864 | 22.4 |
|  | Robert S. Barstow (C, RTL) | 12,999 | 8.6 |

|  | Vote Total | Per-cent |
|---|---|---|
| 26 David O'B. Martin (R, C)* | 94,840 | 100.0 |
| (No Democratic candidate) | | |
| 27 George C. Wortley (R, C)* | 83,430 | 49.7 |
| Rosemary S. Pooler (D) | 82,491 | 49.1 |
| Dennis R. Burns (RTL) | 2,105 | 1.2 |
| 28 Matthew F. McHugh (D)* | 103,908 | 68.3 |
| Mark R. Masterson (R, C, RTL) | 48,213 | 31.7 |
| 29 Frank Horton (R)* | 99,704 | 70.7 |
| James R. Vogel (D) | 34,194 | 24.2 |
| Robert C. Byrnes Jr. (C) | 4,762 | 3.4 |
| Donald M. Peters (RTL) | 2,348 | 1.7 |
| 30 Louise M. Slaughter (D) | 86,777 | 51.0 |
| Fred J. Eckert (R, C)* | 83,402 | 49.0 |
| 31 Jack F. Kemp (R, C, RTL)* | 92,508 | 57.4 |
| James P. Keane (D) | 67,574 | 42.0 |
| Gerald R. Morgan (L) | 913 | 0.6 |
| 32 John J. LaFalce (D, L)* | 99,745 | 91.0 |
| (No Republican candidate) | | |
| Dean L. Walker (C) | 6,234 | 5.7 |
| Anthony J. Murty (RTL) | 3,678 | 3.3 |
| 33 Henry J. Nowak (D, L)* | 109,256 | 85.1 |
| Charles A. Walker (R, C) | 19,147 | 14.9 |
| 34 Amo Houghton (R, C) | 85,856 | 60.1 |
| Larry M. Himelein (D) | 56,898 | 39.9 |

## NORTH CAROLINA

**Senate**

| | | |
|---|---|---|
| Terry Sanford (D) | 823,662 | 51.8 |
| James T. Broyhill (R)* | 767,668 | 48.2 |

**House**

| | | |
|---|---|---|
| 1 Walter B. Jones (D)* | 91,122 | 69.5 |
| Howard Moye (R) | 39,912 | 30.5 |
| 2 Tim Valentine (D)* | 95,320 | 74.6 |
| Bud McElhaney (R) | 32,515 | 25.4 |
| 3 Martin Lancaster (D) | 71,460 | 64.5 |
| Gerald B. Hurst (R) | 39,408 | 35.5 |
| 4 David E. Price (D) | 92,216 | 55.7 |
| Bill Cobey (R)* | 73,469 | 44.3 |
| 5 Stephen L. Neal (D)* | 86,410 | 54.1 |
| Stuart Epperson (R) | 73,261 | 45.9 |
| 6 Howard Coble (R)* | 72,329 | 50.0 |
| Robin Britt (D) | 72,250 | 50.0 |
| 7 Charlie Rose (D)* | 70,471 | 64.2 |
| Thomas J. Harrelson (R) | 39,289 | 35.8 |
| 8 W. G. "Bill" Hefner (D)* | 80,959 | 57.9 |
| William G. Hamby Jr. (R) | 58,941 | 42.1 |
| 9 J. Alex McMillan (R)* | 80,352 | 51.3 |
| D. G. Martin (D) | 76,240 | 48.7 |
| 10 Cass Ballenger (R) | 83,902 | 57.5 |
| Lester D. Roark (D) | 62,035 | 42.5 |
| 11 James McClure Clarke (D) | 91,575 | 50.7 |
| Bill Hendon (R)* | 89,069 | 49.3 |

## NORTH DAKOTA

**Senate**

| | | |
|---|---|---|
| Kent Conrad (D) | 143,932 | 43.8 |
| Mark Andrews (R)* | 141,797 | 49.1 |
| Anna Belle Bourgois (I) | 3,269 | 1.1 |

**House**

| | | |
|---|---|---|
| AL Byron L. Dorgan (D)* | 216,258 | 75.5 |
| Syver Vinje (R) | 66,989 | 23.4 |
| Gerald W. Kopp (I) | 3,114 | 1.1 |

## OHIO

**Governor**

| | | |
|---|---|---|
| Richard F. Celeste (D)* | 1,858,372 | 60.6 |
| James A. Rhodes (R) | 1,207,264 | 39.4 |

**Senate**

| | | |
|---|---|---|
| John Glenn (D)* | 1,949,208 | 62.5 |
| Thomas N. Kindness (R) | 1,171,893 | 37.5 |

**House**

|  | Vote Total | Per-cent |
|---|---|---|
| 1 Thomas A. Luken (D)* | 90,477 | 61.7 |
| Fred E. Morr (R) | 56,100 | 38.3 |
| 2 Bill Gradison (R)* | 105,061 | 70.7 |
| William F. Stineman (D) | 43,448 | 29.3 |
| 3 Tony P. Hall (D)* | 98,311 | 73.7 |
| Ron Crutcher (R) | 35,167 | 26.3 |
| 4 Michael G. Oxley (R)* | 115,751 | 75.1 |
| Clem T. Cratty (D) | 26,320 | 17.1 |
| Raven L. Workman (I) | 11,997 | 7.8 |
| 5 Delbert L. Latta (R)* | 102,016 | 65.0 |
| Tom Murray (D) | 54,864 | 35.0 |
| 6 Bob McEwen (R)* | 106,354 | 70.3 |
| Gordon Roberts (D) | 42,155 | 27.8 |
| Amos Seeley (I) | 2,829 | 1.9 |
| 7 Michael DeWine (R)* | 119,238 | 100.0 |
| (No Democratic candidate) | | |
| 8 Donald E. Lukens (R) | 98,475 | 68.1 |
| John W. Griffin (D) | 46,195 | 31.9 |
| 9 Marcy Kaptur (D)* | 105,646 | 77.5 |
| Mike Shufeldt (R) | 30,643 | 22.5 |
| 10 Clarence E. Miller (R)* | 106,870 | 70.4 |
| John M. Buchanan (D) | 44,847 | 29.6 |
| 11 Dennis E. Eckart (D)* | 104,740 | 72.4 |
| Margaret R. Mueller (R) | 35,944 | 24.9 |
| Werner J. Lange (I) | 3,884 | 2.7 |
| 12 John R. Kasich (R)* | 117,905 | 73.4 |
| Timothy C. Jochim (D) | 42,727 | 26.6 |
| 13 Don J. Pease (D)* | 88,612 | 62.8 |
| William D. Nielsen Jr. (R) | 52,452 | 37.2 |
| 14 Thomas C. Sawyer (D) | 83,257 | 53.7 |
| Lynn Slaby (R) | 71,713 | 46.3 |
| 15 Chalmers P. Wylie (R)* | 97,745 | 63.7 |
| David L. Jackson (D) | 55,750 | 36.3 |
| 16 Ralph Regula (R)* | 118,206 | 76.3 |
| William J. Kennick (D) | 36,639 | 23.7 |
| 17 James A. Traficant Jr. (D)* | 112,855 | 72.3 |
| James H. Fulks (R) | 43,334 | 27.7 |
| 18 Douglas Applegate (D)* | 126,526 | 100.0 |
| (No Republican candidate) | | |
| 19 Edward F. Feighan (D)* | 97,814 | 54.8 |
| Gary C. Suhadolnik (R) | 80,743 | 45.2 |
| 20 Mary Rose Oakar (D)* | 110,976 | 84.9 |
| Bill Smith (R) | 19,794 | 15.1 |
| 21 Louis Stokes (D)* | 99,878 | 81.6 |
| Franklin H. Roski (R) | 22,594 | 18.4 |

## OKLAHOMA

**Governor**

| | | |
|---|---|---|
| Henry Bellmon (R) | 431,762 | 47.5 |
| David Walters (D) | 405,295 | 44.5 |
| Jerry Brown (I) | 60,115 | 6.6 |
| Nelson Freckles Little (I) | 12,753 | 1.4 |

**Senate**

| | | |
|---|---|---|
| Don Nickles (R)* | 493,436 | 55.2 |
| James R. Jones (D) | 400,230 | 44.8 |

**House**

| | | |
|---|---|---|
| 1 James M. Inhofe (R) | 78,919 | 54.8 |
| Gary D. Allison (D) | 61,663 | 42.8 |
| Carl E. McCullough Jr. (I) | 3,455 | 2.4 |
| 2 Mike Synar (D)* | 114,543 | 73.3 |
| Gary K. Rice (R) | 41,795 | 26.7 |
| 3 Wes Watkins (D)* | 114,008 | 78.1 |
| Patrick K. Miller (R) | 31,913 | 21.9 |
| 4 Dave McCurdy (D)* | 94,984 | 76.2 |
| Larry Humphreys (R) | 29,697 | 23.8 |
| 5 Mickey Edwards (R)* | 108,774 | 70.6 |
| Donna Compton (D) | 45,256 | 29.4 |
| 6 Glenn English (D)* | X | X |
| (No Republican candidate) | | |

## OREGON

**Governor**

|  | Vote Total | Per-cent |
|---|---|---|
| Neil Goldschmidt (D) | 549,456 | 51.9 |
| Norma Paulus (R) | 506,986 | 47.8 |

**Senate**

| | | |
|---|---|---|
| Bob Packwood (R)* | 656,317 | 63.0 |
| Rick Bauman (D) | 375,735 | 36.0 |

**House**

| | | |
|---|---|---|
| 1 Les AuCoin (D)* | 141,585 | 61.7 |
| Anthony "Tony" Meeker (R) | 87,874 | 38.3 |
| 2 Robert F. Smith (R)* | 113,566 | 60.2 |
| Larry Tuttle (D) | 75,124 | 39.8 |
| 3 Ron Wyden (D)* | 180,067 | 85.9 |
| Thomas H. Phelan (R) | 29,321 | 14.0 |
| 4 Peter A. DeFazio (D) | 105,697 | 54.1 |
| Bruce Long (R) | 89,795 | 45.9 |
| 5 Denny Smith (R)* | 125,906 | 60.5 |
| Barbara Ross (D) | 82,290 | 39.5 |

## PENNSYLVANIA

**Governor**

| | | |
|---|---|---|
| Bob Casey (D) | 1,717,484 | 50.7 |
| William W. Scranton (R) | 1,638,268 | 48.3 |
| Heidi J. Hoover (CON) | 32,523 | 1.0 |

**Senate**

| | | |
|---|---|---|
| Arlen Specter (R)* | 1,906,537 | 56.4 |
| Bob Edgar (D) | 1,448,219 | 42.9 |
| Lance S. Haver (CON) | 23,470 | 0.7 |

**House**

| | | |
|---|---|---|
| 1 Thomas M. Foglietta (D)* | 88,224 | 74.7 |
| Anthony J. Mucciolo (R) | 29,811 | 25.3 |
| 2 William H. Gray III (D)* | 128,399 | 98.4 |
| (No Republican candidate) | | |
| Linda R. Ragin (NA) | 2,096 | 1.6 |
| 3 Robert A. Borski (D)* | 107,804 | 61.8 |
| Robert A. Rovner (R) | 66,693 | 38.2 |
| 4 Joe Kolter (D)* | 86,133 | 60.4 |
| Al Lindsay (R) | 55,165 | 38.7 |
| Emily C. Fair (POP) | 1,296 | 0.9 |
| 5 Richard T. Schulze (R)* | 87,593 | 65.7 |
| Tim Ringgold (D) | 45,648 | 34.3 |
| 6 Gus Yatron (D)* | 98,142 | 69.1 |
| Norm Bertasavage (R) | 43,858 | 30.9 |
| 7 Curt Weldon (R) | 110,118 | 61.3 |
| Bill Spingler (D) | 69,557 | 38.7 |
| 8 Peter H. Kostmayer (D)* | 85,731 | 55.0 |
| David A. Christian (R) | 70,047 | 45.0 |
| 9 Bud Shuster (R)* | 120,890 | 100.0 |
| (No Democratic candidate) | | |
| 10 Joseph M. McDade (R)* | 118,603 | 74.7 |
| Robert C. Bolus (D) | 40,248 | 25.3 |
| 11 Paul E. Kanjorski (D)* | 112,405 | 70.6 |
| Marc Holtzman (R) | 46,785 | 29.4 |
| 12 John P. Murtha (D)* | 97,135 | 67.4 |
| Kathy Holtzman (R) | 46,937 | 32.6 |
| 13 Lawrence Coughlin (R)* | 100,701 | 58.5 |
| Joseph M. Hoeffel (D) | 71,381 | 41.5 |
| 14 William J. Coyne (D)* | 104,726 | 89.6 |
| (No Republican candidate) | | |
| Richard Edward Caligiuri (LIBERT) | 6,058 | 5.2 |
| Mark Weddleton (SOC WORK) | 3,120 | 2.7 |
| Thomas R. McIntyre (POP) | 1,487 | 1.3 |
| Phyllis Gray (WL) | 1,468 | 1.2 |
| 15 Don Ritter (R)* | 74,829 | 56.8 |
| Joe Simonetta (D) | 56,972 | 43.2 |
| 16 Robert S. Walker (R)* | 100,784 | 74.6 |
| James D. Hagelgans (D) | 34,399 | 25.4 |

| | Vote Total | Per-cent |
|---|---|---|
| 17 George W. Gekas (R)* | 101,027 | 73.6 |
| Michael S. Ogden (D) | 36,157 | 26.4 |
| 18 Doug Walgren (D)* | 104,164 | 63.0 |
| Ernie Buckman (R) | 61,164 | 37.0 |
| 19 Bill Goodling (R)* | 100,055 | 72.9 |
| Richard F. Thornton (D) | 37,223 | 27.1 |
| 20 Joseph M. Gaydos (D)* | 136,638 | 98.5 |
| (No Republican candidate) | | |
| Alden W. Vedder (WL) | 2,114 | 1.5 |
| 21 Tom Ridge (R)* | 111,148 | 80.9 |
| Joylyn Blackwell (D) | 26,324 | 19.1 |
| 22 Austin J. Murphy (D)* | 131,650 | 100.0 |
| (No Republican candidate) | | |
| 23 William F. Clinger Jr. (R)* | 79,595 | 55.5 |
| Bill Wachob (D) | 63,875 | 44.5 |

## RHODE ISLAND

**Governor**

| | Vote Total | Per-cent |
|---|---|---|
| Edward DiPrete (R)* | 208,822 | 64.7 |
| Bruce G. Sundlun (D) | 104,508 | 32.4 |
| Robert J. Healey Jr. (I) | 5,913 | 1.8 |
| Anthony D. Affigne (CIT) | 3,481 | 1.1 |

**House**

| | Vote Total | Per-cent |
|---|---|---|
| 1 Fernand J. St Germain (D)* | 85,077 | 57.7 |
| John A. Holmes Jr. (R) | 62,397 | 42.3 |
| 2 Claudine Schneider (R)* | 113,603 | 71.8 |
| Donald J. Ferry (D) | 44,586 | 28.2 |

## SOUTH CAROLINA

**Governor**

| | Vote Total | Per-cent |
|---|---|---|
| Carroll A. Campbell Jr. (R) | 384,565 | 51.0 |
| Mike Daniel (D) | 361,325 | 47.9 |
| William Griffin (LIBERT) | 4,211 | 0.6 |
| Millard Smith (AM) | 3,309 | 0.4 |

**Senate**

| | Vote Total | Per-cent |
|---|---|---|
| Ernest F. Hollings (D)* | 465,500 | 63.1 |
| Henry D. McMaster (R) | 262,886 | 35.6 |
| Steve Vandervelde (LIBERT) | 4,789 | 0.7 |
| Ray Hillyard (AM) | 4,588 | 0.6 |

**House**

| | Vote Total | Per-cent |
|---|---|---|
| 1 Arthur Ravenel Jr. (R) | 59,969 | 52.0 |
| Jimmy Stuckey (D) | 55,262 | 48.0 |
| 2 Floyd Spence (R)* | 73,455 | 53.6 |
| Fred Zeigler (D) | 63,592 | 46.4 |
| 3 Butler Derrick (D)* | 79,109 | 68.4 |
| Richard Dickison (R) | 36,495 | 31.5 |
| 4 Liz J. Patterson (D) | 67,012 | 51.4 |
| Bill Workman (R) | 61,648 | 47.3 |
| Bob Wilson (AM) | 1,644 | 1.3 |
| 5 John M. Spratt Jr. (D)* | 95,859 | 99.7 |
| (No Republican candidate) | | |
| 6 Robin Tallon (D)* | 92,398 | 75.5 |
| Robbie Cunningham (R) | 29,922 | 24.5 |

## SOUTH DAKOTA

**Governor**

| | Vote Total | Per-cent |
|---|---|---|
| George S. Mickelson (R) | 152,543 | 51.8 |
| R. Lars Herseth (D) | 141,898 | 48.2 |

**Senate**

| | Vote Total | Per-cent |
|---|---|---|
| Thomas A. Daschle (D) | 152,657 | 51.6 |
| James Abdnor (R)* | 143,173 | 48.4 |

**House**

| | Vote Total | Per-cent |
|---|---|---|
| AL Tim Johnson (D) | 171,462 | 59.2 |
| Dale Bell (R) | 118,261 | 40.8 |

## TENNESSEE

**Governor**

| | Vote Total | Per-cent |
|---|---|---|
| Ned McWherter (D) | 656,602 | 54.3 |
| Winfield Dunn (R) | 553,449 | 45.7 |

**House**

| | Vote Total | Per-cent |
|---|---|---|
| 1 James H. Quillen (R)* | 80,289 | 68.9 |
| John B. Russell (D) | 36,278 | 31.1 |
| 2 John J. Duncan (R)* | 96,396 | 76.2 |
| John F. Bowen (D) | 30,088 | 23.8 |
| 3 Marilyn Lloyd (D)* | 75,034 | 53.9 |
| Jim Golden (R) | 64,084 | 46.1 |
| 4 Jim Cooper (D)* | 86,997 | 100.0 |
| (No Republican candidate) | | |
| 5 Bill Boner (D)* | 85,126 | 57.9 |
| Terry Holcomb (R) | 58,701 | 39.9 |
| Charlie Daniels (I) | 2,033 | 1.4 |
| Russell Hancock (I) | 658 | 0.4 |
| Kenneth Wayne Bloodworth (I) | 609 | 0.4 |
| 6 Bart Gordon (D)* | 102,180 | 76.8 |
| Fred Vail (R) | 30,823 | 23.2 |
| 7 Don Sundquist (R)* | 93,902 | 72.3 |
| M. Lloyd Hiler (D) | 35,966 | 27.7 |
| 8 Ed Jones (D)* | 101,699 | 80.4 |
| Dan H. Campbell (R) | 24,792 | 19.6 |
| 9 Harold E. Ford (D)* | 83,006 | 83.4 |
| (No Republican candidate) | | |
| Isaac Richmond (I) | 16,221 | 16.3 |

## TEXAS

**Governor**

| | Vote Total | Per-cent |
|---|---|---|
| William P. Clements Jr. (R) | 1,813,779 | 52.7 |
| Mark White (D)* | 1,584,515 | 46.1 |
| Theresa Doyle (LIBERT) | 42,496 | 1.2 |

**House**

| | Vote Total | Per-cent |
|---|---|---|
| 1 Jim Chapman (D)* | 84,445 | 100.0 |
| (No Republican candidate) | | |
| 2 Charles Wilson (D)* | 78,529 | 56.7 |
| Julian Gordon (R) | 55,986 | 40.5 |
| Sam I. Paradice (I) | 3,838 | 2.8 |
| 3 Steve Bartlett (R)* | 143,381 | 94.1 |
| (No Democratic candidate) | | |
| Brent Barnes (I) | 6,268 | 4.1 |
| Don Gough (LIBERT) | 2,736 | 1.8 |
| 4 Ralph M. Hall (D)* | 97,540 | 71.7 |
| Thomas Blow (R) | 38,578 | 28.3 |
| 5 John Bryant (D)* | 57,410 | 58.5 |
| Tom Carter (R) | 39,945 | 40.7 |
| Bob Brewer (LIBERT) | 749 | 0.8 |
| 6 Joe L. Barton (R)* | 86,190 | 55.8 |
| Pete Geren (D) | 68,270 | 44.2 |
| 7 Bill Archer (R)* | 129,673 | 87.4 |
| Harry Kniffen (D) | 17,635 | 11.9 |
| Roger Plail (LIBERT) | 1,087 | 0.7 |
| 8 Jack Fields (R)* | 66,280 | 68.4 |
| Blaine Mann (D) | 30,617 | 31.6 |
| 9 Jack Brooks (D)* | 73,285 | 61.5 |
| Lisa D. Duperier (R) | 45,834 | 38.5 |
| 10 J. J. Pickle (D)* | 135,863 | 72.3 |
| Carole Keeton Rylander (R) | 52,000 | 27.7 |
| 11 Marvin Leath (D)* | 84,201 | 100.0 |
| (No Republican candidate) | | |
| 12 Jim Wright (D)* | 84,831 | 68.7 |
| Don McNeil (R) | 38,620 | 31.3 |
| 13 Beau Boulter (R)* | 84,980 | 64.9 |
| Doug Seal (D) | 45,907 | 35.1 |
| 14 Mac Sweeney (R)* | 74,471 | 52.3 |
| Greg Laughlin (D) | 67,852 | 47.7 |
| 15 E. "Kika" de la Garza (D)* | 70,777 | 100.0 |
| (No Republican candidate) | | |
| 16 Ronald D. Coleman (D)* | 50,590 | 65.7 |
| Roy Gillia (R) | 26,421 | 34.3 |
| 17 Charles W. Stenholm (D)* | 97,791 | 100.0 |
| (No Republican candidate) | | |
| 18 Mickey Leland (D)* | 63,335 | 90.2 |
| (No Republican candidate) | | |
| Joanne Kuniansky (I) | 6,884 | 9.8 |

| | Vote Total | Per-cent |
|---|---|---|
| 19 Larry Combest (R)* | 68,695 | 62.0 |
| Gerald McCathern (D) | 42,129 | 38.0 |
| 20 Henry B. Gonzalez (D)* | 55,363 | 100.0 |
| (No Republican candidate) | | |
| 21 Lamar Smith (R) | 100,346 | 60.6 |
| Pete Snelson (D) | 63,779 | 38.5 |
| Jim Robinson (LIBERT) | 1,432 | 0.9 |
| 22 Thomas D. DeLay (R)* | 76,459 | 71.8 |
| Susan Director (D) | 30,079 | 28.2 |
| 23 Albert G. Bustamante (D)* | 68,131 | 90.7 |
| (No Republican candidate) | | |
| Ken Hendrix (LIBERT) | 7,001 | 9.3 |
| 24 Martin Frost (D)* | 69,368 | 67.2 |
| Bob Burk (R) | 33,819 | 32.8 |
| 25 Michael A. Andrews (D)* | 67,435 | 100.0 |
| (No Republican candidate) | | |
| 26 Dick Armey (R)* | 101,735 | 68.1 |
| George Richardson (D) | 47,651 | 31.9 |
| 27 Solomon P. Ortiz (D)* | 64,165 | 100.0 |
| (No Republican candidate) | | |

## UTAH

**Senate**

| | Vote Total | Per-cent |
|---|---|---|
| Jake Garn (R)* | 314,608 | 72.3 |
| Craig Oliver (D) | 115,523 | 26.6 |
| Hugh A. Butler (LIBERT) | 3,023 | 0.7 |
| Mary C. Zins (I) | 1,863 | 0.4 |

**House**

| | Vote Total | Per-cent |
|---|---|---|
| 1 James V. Hansen (R)* | 82,151 | 51.6 |
| Gunn McKay (D) | 77,180 | 48.4 |
| 2 Wayne Owens (D) | 76,921 | 55.2 |
| Tom Shimizu (R) | 60,967 | 43.7 |
| Stephen Carmichael Carr (LIBERT) | 1,302 | 0.9 |
| Scott Alan Breen (I) | 200 | 0.2 |
| 3 Howard C. Nielson (R)* | 86,599 | 66.6 |
| Dale F. Gardiner (D) | 42,582 | 32.7 |
| David P. Hurst (I) | 893 | 0.7 |

## VERMONT

**Governor**

| | Vote Total | Per-cent |
|---|---|---|
| Madeleine M. Kunin (D)* | 92,379 | 47.0 |
| Peter Smith (R) | 75,162 | 38.2 |
| Bernard Sanders (I) | 28,430 | 14.5 |
| Richard F. Gottlieb (LIBERT) | 662 | 0.3 |

**Senate**

| | Vote Total | Per-cent |
|---|---|---|
| Patrick J. Leahy (D)* | 124,123 | 63.2 |
| Richard A. Snelling (R) | 67,798 | 34.5 |
| Anthony N. Doria (C) | 2,963 | 1.5 |
| Jerry Levy (LIBERT) | 1,583 | 0.8 |

**House**

| | Vote Total | Per-cent |
|---|---|---|
| AL James M. Jeffords (R)* | 168,403 | 89.1 |
| (No Democratic candidate) | | |
| Peter Diamondstone (LIBERT) | 7,060 | 3.7 |
| John T. McNulty (I) | 7,404 | 3.9 |
| Morris Earle (I) | 5,850 | 3.1 |

## VIRGINIA

**House**

| | Vote Total | Per-cent |
|---|---|---|
| 1 Herbert H. Bateman (R)* | 80,713 | 56.0 |
| Robert C. Scott (D) | 63,364 | 44.0 |
| 2 Owen B. Pickett (D) | 54,491 | 49.5 |
| A. J. "Joe" Canada Jr. (R) | 46,137 | 41.9 |
| Stephen P. Shao (I) | 9,492 | 8.6 |
| 3 Thomas J. Bliley Jr. (R)* | 74,525 | 67.0 |
| Kenneth E. Powell (D) | 32,961 | 29.7 |
| J. Stephen Hodges (I) | 3,675 | 3.3 |
| 4 Norman Sisisky (D)* | 64,699 | 99.8 |
| (No Republican candidate) | | |
| 5 Dan Daniel (D)* | 73,085 | 81.5 |
| (No Republican candidate) | | |

|  | Vote Total | Per-cent |
|---|---|---|
| J. F. "Frank" Cole (I) | 16,551 | 18.5 |
| 6 Jim Olin (D)* | 88,230 | 69.9 |
| Flo Neher Traywick (R) | 38,051 | 30.1 |
| 7 D. French Slaughter Jr. (R)* | 58,927 | 98.3 |
| (No Democratic candidate) | | |
| 8 Stan Parris (R)* | 72,670 | 61.8 |
| James H. Boren (D) | 44,965 | 38.2 |
| 9 Rick Boucher (D)* | 59,864 | 99.0 |
| (No Republican candidate) | | |
| 10 Frank R. Wolf (R)* | 95,724 | 60.2 |
| John G. Milliken (D) | 63,292 | 39.8 |

## WASHINGTON

### Senate

|  | Vote Total | Per-cent |
|---|---|---|
| Brock Adams (D) | 677,471 | 50.6 |
| Slade Gorton (R)* | 650,931 | 48.7 |
| Jill Fein (SOC WORK) | 8,965 | 0.7 |

### House

|  | Vote Total | Per-cent |
|---|---|---|
| 1 John R. Miller (R)* | 97,969 | 51.4 |
| Reese Lindquist (D) | 92,697 | 48.6 |
| 2 Al Swift (D)* | 124,840 | 72.2 |
| Thomas S. Talman (R) | 48,077 | 27.8 |
| 3 Don Bonker (D)* | 114,775 | 73.6 |
| Joe Illing (R) | 41,275 | 26.4 |
| 4 Sid Morrison (R)* | 107,593 | 72.1 |
| Robert Goedecke (D) | 41,709 | 27.9 |
| 5 Thomas S. Foley (D)* | 121,732 | 74.7 |
| Floyd L. Wakefield (R) | 41,179 | 25.3 |
| 6 Norman D. Dicks (D)* | 90,063 | 71.2 |
| Kenneth W. Braaten (R) | 36,410 | 28.8 |
| 7 Mike Lowry (D)* | 124,317 | 72.6 |
| Don McDonald (R) | 46,831 | 27.4 |

|  | Vote Total | Per-cent |
|---|---|---|
| 8 Rod Chandler (R)* | 107,824 | 65.2 |
| David E. Giles (D) | 57,545 | 34.8 |

## WEST VIRGINIA

### House

|  | Vote Total | Per-cent |
|---|---|---|
| 1 Alan B. Mollohan (D)* | 90,715 | 100.0 |
| (No Republican candidate) | | |
| 2 Harley O. Staggers Jr. (D)* | 76,355 | 69.5 |
| Michele Golden (R) | 33,554 | 30.5 |
| 3 Bob Wise (D)* | 73,669 | 64.9 |
| Tim Sharp (R) | 39,820 | 35.1 |
| 4 Nick J. Rahall II (D)* | 58,217 | 71.3 |
| Martin Miller (R) | 23,490 | 28.7 |

## WISCONSIN

### Governor

|  | Vote Total | Per-cent |
|---|---|---|
| Tommy G. Thompson (R) | 805,090 | 52.7 |
| Anthony S. Earl (D)* | 705,578 | 46.2 |
| Kathryn A. Christensen (LAB F) | 10,323 | 0.7 |
| Darold E. Wall (I) | 3,913 | 0.3 |
| Sanford Knapp (I) | 1,668 | 0.1 |

### Senate

|  | Vote Total | Per-cent |
|---|---|---|
| Bob Kasten (R)* | 754,573 | 50.9 |
| Ed Garvey (D) | 702,963 | 47.4 |
| Peter Y. Taylor Sr. (I) | 19,266 | 1.3 |
| Margo Storsteen (SOC WORK) | 2,926 | 0.2 |
| Eugene A. Hem (I) | 2,234 | 0.2 |

### House

|  | Vote Total | Per-cent |
|---|---|---|
| 1 Les Aspin (D)* | 106,288 | 74.3 |
| Iris Peterson (R) | 34,495 | 24.1 |
| John Graf (LAB F) | 2,354 | 1.6 |
| 2 Robert W. Kastenmeier (D)* | 106,919 | 55.6 |
| Ann J. Haney (R) | 85,156 | 44.2 |
| Syed Ameen (I) | 443 | 0.2 |
| 3 Steve Gunderson (R)* | 104,393 | 64.1 |
| Leland E. Mulder (D) | 58,445 | 35.9 |
| 4 Gerald D. Kleczka (D)* | 120,354 | 99.6 |
| (No Republican candidate) | | |
| 5 Jim Moody (D)* | 109,506 | 99.0 |
| (No Republican candidate) | | |
| 6 Thomas E. Petri (R)* | 124,328 | 96.7 |
| (No Democratic candidate) | | |
| John Richard Daggett (I) | 4,268 | 3.3 |
| 7 David R. Obey (D)* | 106,700 | 62.2 |
| Kevin J. Hermening (R) | 63,408 | 36.9 |
| Joseph D. Damrell (LAB F) | 1,599 | 0.9 |
| 8 Toby Roth (R)* | 118,162 | 67.4 |
| Paul F. Willems (D) | 57,265 | 32.6 |
| 9 F. James Sensen-brenner Jr. (R)* | 138,766 | 78.2 |
| Thomas G. Popp (D) | 38,636 | 21.8 |

## WYOMING

### Governor

|  | Vote Total | Per-cent |
|---|---|---|
| Mike Sullivan (D) | 88,879 | 54.0 |
| Pete Simpson (R) | 75,841 | 46.0 |

### House

|  | Vote Total | Per-cent |
|---|---|---|
| AL Dick Cheney (R)* | 111,007 | 69.5 |
| Rick Gilmore (D) | 48,780 | 30.5 |